THE
FIRE CHIEF'S
HANDBOOK

FIFTH EDITION

THE
FIRE CHIEF'S
HANDBOOK

FIFTH EDITION

Edited by
Joseph R. Bachtler and Thomas F. Brennan

FIRE ENGINEERING® BOOKS AND VIDEOS
A DIVISION OF PENNWELL® PUBLISHING COMPANY

Disclaimer

The recommendations, advice, descriptions, and methods in this book are presented solely for educational purposes. The author and publisher assume no liability whatsoever for any loss or damage that results from the use of any of the material in this book. Use of the material in this book is solely at the risk of the user.

Published by Fire Engineering® Books & Videos
A Division of PennWell® Publishing Company
Park 80 West, Plaza 2
Saddle Brook, NJ 07663
United States of America

DIRECTOR OF BOOK PUBLISHING: Joanne Ezersky
EDITORS: Joseph R. Bachtler and Thomas F. Brennan
PROJECT EDITOR: Betsy W. Kaplan
DESIGN AND PRODUCTION: Bernard Schleifer
ORIGINAL CHARTS: Arlene S. Goldberg/Terry Guglielmino
COVER DESIGN: David Derr
INDEXER: Mary Jane Dittmar

Library of Congress Cataloging-in-Publication Data

The fire chief's handbook / edited by Joseph R. Bachtler and Thomas F. Brennan.
—5th ed. Includes bibliographical references and index. 1. Fire departments—Management.
I. Bachtler, J. R., 1928-   . II. Brennan, Thomas F.
TH9146.F54 1995 363.37'068—dc20 95-5748
ISBN 0-912212-40-3

1 2 3 4 5 6 7 8 9 10

Printed in the United States of America

Contents

II. HUMAN RESOURCES

III. EQUIPMENT

IV. OPERATIONS

V. FIRE PREVENTION AND LOSS REDUCTION

VI. THE FUTURE

About the Editors

JOSEPH R. BACHTLER, retired senior instructor Maryland Fire and Rescue Institute and Fire Chief, U. S. Steel, Gary, IN. His 52 years in the fire service have been spent in active duty as a fire officer in both municipal and industrial fire departments, and as an educator and author. He spent 23 years with the University of Maryland Fire Service Extension as senior instructor and director and also served as an E & T specialist and associate superintendent of the National Fire Academy. He is the author of *The Fire Instructor's Training Guide, Second Edition.*

THOMAS F. BRENNAN, Chief of Department, Waterbury, CT Fire Department. His more than 30 years experience in the fire service include 11 with the Fire Department, City of New York, and volunteer service in Long Island. He has served as Deputy Chief Instructor of the Suffolk County, NY Fire Academy, as an adjunct instructor at the National Fire Academy, and is active in a number of executive boards in Connecticut fire service organizations. He was the editor of Fire Engineering Magazine for eight years, and continues to contribute the monthly column, "Random Thoughts." He is the author and host of the video series, *Forcible Entry,* and serves as technical advisor for Fire Engineering.

Special acknowledgment to Fire Chief Charles H. Steele, retired, Annapolis, MD who assisted in proposing and outlining sections and chapters for this edition of *The Fire Chief's Handbook.*

About the Authors

JACK A. BENNETT, Retired Chief, Menlo Park CA Fire Protection District. His career began in 1955 with the L.A. City Fire Department where he was promoted to the rank of Assistant Chief. For the past 15 years he has been a fire service instructor and writer. He is a member of the IAFC, the NFPA Fire Service and Wildland Fire Management Sections, the Fire Districts Association of California and the California State Firefighters Association.

FRANK W. BORDEN, Assistant Chief, L.A. City Fire Department. In this position he commands the Bureau of Support Services and manages the operations of the Training Division, the Division of Supply and Maintenance, the Department Dispatch Center and Management Information Systems. Over his 35-year career he has held such special assignments as developer of the Disaster Preparedness Program and Exercise Coordinator, and Designer and Director of the City of L.A. Community Emergency Response Team program. He is involved in the Urban Search and Rescue System through a number of different organizations nationally and internationally and has had articles published in all the major national fire and rescue service magazines.

GENE CARLSON, Director of International Marketing, Fire Protection Publications. During his 16 years with FPP/IFSTA, Carlson has been active with the NFPA as Chair of NFPA 1001, Firefighter Professional Qualifications, and a member of the NFPA Fire Service Training and Hazardous Materials Response Personnel committee. He has written, edited, and lectured extensively for the North American fire service.

JOHN N. CARR. Retired, 24-year career veteran Fire Officer. Having graduated from the U.S.A.F. Firefighting School, he has held many varied positions, including Flight Engineer, Cargo Aircraft, USAF; advisor to the Airline Pilots Safety Committee; ARFF Committee Secretary, IFSTA; and Coordinator for ARFF/Airlines Personnel Recurrent Aircraft Emergency Egress Training. He has written for national fire publications and been a speaker and instructor for many state and national seminars. He currently is a consultant on aircraft rescue.

WILLIAM E. CLARK, Retired Battalion Chief, Fire Department, City of New York, NY. Continuing his contributions to the fire service, Clark lectures both nationally and internationally, writes for *Fire Engineering* and other national magazines, has published the second edition of *Firefighting Principles and Practices,* and contributed to a number of other programs, including the Open Learning Program at the NFA. In addition to spending 20 years with the FDNY, he has been the head of one of the largest county fire service in the U.S., and director of State Fire Service Training in both Wisconsin and Florida. He founded the ISFSI, has held top committee positions with the NFPA and IAFC, and is a life member of the IAFF.

RAND-SCOTT COGGAN, served as Chief of the City of Redmond, WA Fire Department, Chief of Naples, FL and Ventura County, CA Chief. His fire service career began 17 years ago in Prince George's County, MD. He serves on the NFPA Protective Clothing and Equipment Technical Committee, is the 1994 Vice President of the King County Fire Chiefs Association, and speaks and writes extensively in the areas of incident command and fire department safety.

RONNY J. COLEMAN, California State Fire Marshal. Prior to 1992, when he was appointed CSFM, Coleman served as Fire Chief for the City of Fullerton, CA, and San Clemente, CA, Operations Chief for Costa Mesa, CA, Fire Department and worked for the U.S. Park Service in fire protection. As 1994 Chair of the National Fire Service Accreditation Committee, Vice President of the International Technical Committee for the Prevention and Extinction of Fire, and a past president of the IAFC, he has more than 25 years of experience in the fire service. He holds a number of awards, has written nine fire service textbooks, and contributes to fire service publications.

GLENN P. CORBETT, fire science faculty member, John Jay College, NYC, technical editor *Fire Engineering* magazine, and firefighter, Waldwick, NJ Fire, Department. He previously held the position of Administrator of Engineering Services, San Antonio Fire Department, and was a fire protection engineer in the Austin, TX Fire Department. He holds a Master of Engineering degree in Fire Protection Engineering and has received a professional engineer's license from the state of Texas. His fire service career began in 1978 when he joined the Waldwick, NJ, Fire Department.

PAUL J. DE SILVA, Senior Associate, Schaardt and Fullan Architects, PC of Bellmore, NY. De Silva is a licensed architect in the states of New York since 1975 and, most recently, in New Jersey. He is certified by the National Council of Architectural Review Boards, a member of the National Trust for Historic Preservation and the NFPA. He has been involved since 1971 in the design and construction of over 250 firestations.

STEPHEN N. FOLEY, Senior Fire Service Safety Specialist, National Fire Protection Association and staff liaison for the Technical Committee on Fire Service Occupational Safety and Health Programs. Previously Chief of Department in Longmeadow and Ashburnham, MA, he has been active in the fire service for more than 16 years, of which 10 have been spent on the NFPA 1500 Technical Committee. He is a contract instructor and course developer for the National Fire Academy and one of the co-authors of the NFPA's 1500 handbook.

GEORGE GOLDBACH, MA, BS, AAS, Chief of Department, West Metro Fire/Rescue, Colorado, a 250 member urban/suburban department along the foot hills of the Rocky Mtns. He previously served as Director of South Metro Fire Academy helping to train over 500 career firefighters. Prior to that he was the Chairman of the Public Service Department at Red Rocks Community College responsible for the Criminal Justice and Fire Science programs. The first 20 of more than 35 years in the fire service were spent with the busiest fire companies in the New York City Fire Department. He has taught Leadership and Management classes around the country, received numerous awards and citations, and continues his career in the third largest department in Colorado.

JOHN A. GRANITO, Professor and Vice President for Public Service and External Affairs of the State University of New York, (ret.) He joined his first fire department in 1949, and spent 21 years as an active fire-fighter and officer. He was Supervisor of Fire Training for New York State, Director of the International Fire Administration Institute for the IAFC, and an elected Fire Commissioner. He continues to lecture and write on fire service administration and operations and is the coordina-tor of the NFPA's Urban Fire Forum.

JOHN R. HAWKINS, Division Chief, California Department of Forestry and Fire Protection, Paradise, CA. More than 30 years ago he began his career in the fire service as a seasonal firefighter. He earned degrees in Fire Science and Forest Management and is a certified California Chief Fire Officer, NFA Executive Fire Officer, and swiftwater rescue tech-nician. His experience includes performing on both CDF and national Incident Command Teams. He is an instructor of ICS, command and firefighter survival classes, rescue systems, and led the development of the ICS Operations Section Chief training course.

WILLIAM S. JOHNSON, Chief, West Haven, CT, Fire Department, First Fire District. With almost 40 years' experience in the fire service, he began as a volunteer in 1956 and became a career firefighter in 1966. Having worked his way through the ranks, he became Chief of depart-ment in 1981. His involvement in the fire service extends to member-ship in the IAFC Program Planning Committee, Connecticut Fire Chiefs Association—Fire Marshals Association and Fire Department Instructors Association. He has also served as the chiefs association's representative to the Commission on Fire Prevention and Control and is a contract instructor for the National Fire Academy.

CHARLES G. KING, Supervising Fire Marshal, New York City Fire Department and Special Investigator for the New Jersey State Commission of Investigation on Organized Crime and Corruption, (ret.) He currently lectures on arson investigation and has a fire analysis consulting firm in New York City. He has written a book and numerous articles for major fire service publications and has contributed to the *New Jersey Arson Investigation and Prosecution Manual.* He also has taught fire investigation for the Office of the Attorney General, State of New Jersey.

WILLIAM M. KRAMER, Ph.D., Director of Fire Science, University of Cincinnati, Chairman, Open Learning Fire Service Education Consortium, National Fire Academy; and Administrative Chief, Cincinnati Fire Department. His almost 30 years in the fire service have been spent in career and volunteer departments and as a fire service educator. He is the educational commentator for "American Heat" videos, has written course guides for the NFA, and is co-author of the *Fire Officer's Guide to Disaster Control.* He also has been active in both the International Association of Fire Chiefs and the ISFSI.

BENJAMIN F. LOPES, III, Deputy Chief, Santa Clara County, CA, Central Fire Protection District. He began his career in the fire service in 1972. A college graduate, he holds a master's degree in Human Resources and Organization Development from the University of San Francisco. His more than 23 years of experience in the fire service contribute to his success as a adjunct faculty member at both the National Fire Academy and the California Fire Academy.

RICHARD A. MARINUCCI, Chief, Farmington Hills, MI, Fire Department and former adjunct professor, Fire Science program, Madonna University and Oakland Community College. He is also a team member/course co-author for the NFA Open Learning Fire Service Program, and fire chief representative on the Oakland County SARA Title III LEPC. He has been on the faculty of numerous IAFC, state and collegiate programs and seminars and works with the Michigan Municipal League on fire service subjects.

JAMES L. MCFADDEN, Chief, California Department of Forestry and Fire Protection/San Luis Obisbo County, Fire Department. Beginning more than 35 years ago, he has served 25 years as chief officer and more than 15 years in firefighter training. He is a consultant for NFA courses, contributed to IFSTA/FPP texts, co-authored *Wildland Firefighting,* and directed the development of the ICS training courses. He continues to provide instruction for the California Chief Officer curriculum and other programs.

MARY NACHBAR, Supervisor, Public Education and Fire Data Analysis, Deputy State Fire Marshal, Minnesota. She has served 14 years as a firefighter with the City of Minnetonka, MN, Fire Department and has been with the State Fire Marshal's Division since 1989. She is also a Fire Safety Education Representative for the NFPA-LNTB Curriculum and works with schools and fire service personnel in a six-state area providing in-service training to school systems initiating fire safety curriculums.

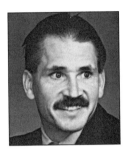

GREGORY G. NOLL, CSP, Senior Partner, Hildebrand and Noll Associates, Inc., member Lancaster Township Fire Department, and President of the Pennsylvania Association of Hazardous Materials Technicians. He served as Hazardous Materials Coordinator for the Prince George's County (MD), Fire Department. He has over 23 years' experience in fire protection and occupational safety and health, is a Certified Safety Professional, content expert and contract instructor for the NFA, author of textbooks and journal articles, and member of the IAFC Hazardous Materials Committee and the NFPA 471 and 472 Technical Committee.

LESLIE P. OMANS, San Jose, CA, Fire Department. His 20 years in the fire service include experience as Airport ARFF Commander; Reserve Instructor, U.S. Naval Firefighting School, Treasure Island, CA; Director, Aircraft Rescue and Firefighting Working Group; State of California Master Fire Instructor, Chief Officer, and Hazardous Material Technician certifications. He is a member of the NFPA 1405 Committee, has written for national fire publications and has lectured and been an instructor for many state and national seminars.

WILLIAM C. PETERS, Battalion Chief and Apparatus Supervisor, Jersey City, NJ, Fire Department. A 20-year veteran of the Jersey City Fire Department, Peters' previous experience includes service as a suburban firefighter, county training academy instructor, and civilian truck mechanic. He is a member of the IAFC Apparatus Maintenance Section, served two years on the board of directors of the National Association of Emergency Vehicle Technicians, and is on the editorial advisory board of *Fire Engineering* magazine. He wrote the text, *Fire Apparatus Purchasing Handbook,* and lectures extensively around the country on the subject.

JOHN RUKAVINA, Chief, Asheville, NC, Fire Department. Prior to 1986, he served as both Fire Chief and Acting City Manager in St. Joseph, MO. He began his fire service career 23 years ago in Minnesota and worked at the University of Minnesota's Fire Information, Research and (Fire) Education Center, the Roseville FD and the St. Paul FD. A contract instructor in the National Fire Academy's Field Delivery Program since 1981, he also serves on the Board of Directors of the NC Association of Fire Chiefs. In 1991 he was selected as one of six recipients of the FEMA/NFA Fellowship for the Harvard Program for Senior Officials in State and Local Government.

GORDON M. SACHS, emergency services educator, writer, and consultant. With more than 17 years of fire service and EMS experience, he has been a firefighter, EMT, and command officer in both career and volunteer departments, including having served as Safety Officer on the Fairfax County, Virginia Fie and Rescue Department and Deputy Chief of the Fairfield, Pennsylvania Fie Company. He was a program manager with the USFA, directing major projects that dealt with fire and EMS management and operations, responder health and safety, incident command, and EMS public education. He is now an adjunct instructor at several colleges, universities, fire/EMS academies and the National Fire Academy.

ED SPAHN, P.E., President and Owner, Fire Protection Engineering Co. Prior to establishing his own company, he was Orange County Fire Official and Deputy Chief, Orange County, FL, Fire and Rescue Services Division. He has been involved in fire protection engineering and design and fire department management for almost 30 years, is a member of the Society of Fire Protection Engineers, and is a licensed Professional Engineer in Fire Protection. He holds a degree in electrical engineering from Purdue University.

RUSSELL J. STRICKLAND, faculty member at the Maryland Fire and Rescue Institute, University of Maryland at College Park. During his more than 14 years with the Institute, he served in a number of supervisory positions, and is currently the assistant director for the Field Programs Division, responsible for development and delivery of the Institute's field programs. Active in Maryland fire, rescue, and EMS for 20 years, he has served with a number of fire departments and is also involved with the Maryland Fire Service Personnel Qualifications Board, the Chesapeake Society of Fire and Rescue Instructors and the Maryland Council of the Fire and Rescue Academies.

BRUCE H. VARNER, Chief and Emergency Management Director, Carrollton, TX, Fire Department. Prior to 1992 he held a number of different positions in the Phoenix, AZ, Fire Department, advancing to Deputy Chief. He serves on the NFPA Technical Committee on Firefighter Protective Clothing and Equipment and is currently the Chair of NFPA 1976, Task Group on Proximity Protective Clothing. He is also a member of the IAFC Safety and Health Committee and has been a board member and vice president of SAFER.

MICHAEL T. WREN, independent information systems consultant and developer, specializing in fire service strategic information systems planning and microcomputer-based multiuser systems. Before establishing his consultintg business, he was Chief of Lee's Summit, MO, Fire Department, co-founder of the Kansas City Area Metro Fire Chiefs Council and its first president. With more than 30 years' experience in the fire service, he is making his contribution to the fire service through developing programs and instructing at the National Fire Academy and Emergency Management Institute.

Foreword

*T*HE world is running fast, and no group in any business is running faster—for progress and for survival—than chief fire executives.

In just a decade—a dot on the American fire service continuum—the business of providing emergency response has been transformed with unprecedented speed by unprecedented proportions. Never has fire service tradition been so thoroughly scrutinized, exploded, and rewritten. Never have fire departments experienced the magnitude of "organizational culture" change, nor has successful fire department management heretofore depended on a level of such managerial sophistication and complex decision making. Never has there been such a redefinition of the fire service at its very roots.

While the ultimate objective of the fire chief—to deliver the highest level of emergency response with the greatest margin of safety for firefighters in the most fiscally responsible way—is immutable, the modern playing field is altogether revised. This has occurred through dramatic changes in four major areas of concern: economics; legislation, codes, and standards; legal accountability and liability; and information exchange technology. The well-familiar "do more with less" directive is now the law of the land, providing no room for comfort for the fire department manager who out of necessity wears the hats of ubiqitous leader, creative accountant, social thinker, personnel relations specialist, chief safety officer, lawyer-in-training, public speaker, and computer hack, among many others (not to mention incident commander!). Indeed, the modern fire manager in many cases is asked not only to maintain expected service quality, administer to a well-trained and well-equipped corps of members, stay educated in industry developments and management practices, and toe the bottom line, but to make a profit for the city, too! This level of responsibility transcends fire department type, whether it be career, volunteer, combination, or private.

To be effective, the modern chief fire executive must function more like a captain of industry than a salty fireline manager with a management style forged exclusively by hard years in the trenches. The chief has discovered that competing in this "brave new world" demands a continuing education in and a global perspective encompassing worlds both in and outside the fire service. The proactive chief is a proficient user of resources and has expanded his or her arsenal of management tools. And so we come to the purpose of *The Fire Chief's Handbook,* Fifth Edition.

The Fire Chief's Handbook, like the fire service itself, has grown and changed. The First Edition, published in late 1932 and at that time the first and only complete textbook ever produced for the fire service, was created to fill a great void in information available on basic firefighting techniques and technologies. The Second Edition, which followed 28 years later, preserved and updated the first's "how-to" focus. The Third Edition, published in 1967, jumped the gap to more closely align the work's focus with the needs of the fire chief, including information on community risk analysis, preplanning, and practical and theoretical management concepts. Editor James. F. Casey, in the Foreword of that edition, wrote, "How things have changed, and particularly for the fire chief! Today's chief is basically a manager, and not just the highly skilled technician of yesteryear. He must know everything about his department and everything his department may be called upon to do. He must know these things in the broad sense, but in sufficient depth to properly direct the men who will actually do the job. . . ."

Surely, that understanding guided Casey in editing the Fourth Edition in 1978. It also is the spirit with which Fire Engineering, Fifth Edition editors Tom Brennan and Joe Bachtler, and 29 distinguished authors approached the most recent undertaking of this landmark text. *The Fire Chief's Handbook,* Fifth Edition, is a *fire service manager's* guide. It was designed and created with one specific purpose: to make the fire service manager better prepared for the challenges ahead.

The commitment to that purpose is evident in this weighty volume. No text is a panacea for solving all problems, but with the on-the-job experience distilled into each chapter and mix of practical and theoretical elements therein, the Fifth Edition will undoubtedly serve as a useful guide for seasoned chiefs and aspiring officers alike.

The challenges confronting you are enormous, but the fruits of your efforts will be that much sweeter. Use this information well, and best of luck as you lead the fire service of the future.

BILL MANNING
Editor, *Fire Engineering*
1995

I. MANAGEMENT

1

Management in the Fire Service

RONNY J. COLEMAN

CHAPTER HIGHLIGHTS

- Management versus leadership.
- Managerial activities.
- The cycle of management.
- The leadership role of the fire chief.

WHEN A PERSON enters the fire service as a probationary firefighter the furthest thing from their mind is how to manage the fire department. The emphasis at the entry level of the fire service is on developing the knowledge, skills, and abilities to react to emergency incidents. The job tends to be oriented around physical tasks, primarily conducted under the direction of others. Developing competency in the various critical tasks associated with entry-level responsibilities encompasses the fundamentals of firefighting tools and equipment, emergency medical services, and hazardous materials. These skills are essential for an individual's survival under the high-stress conditions of emergencies.

As soon as the same firefighter begins to move up the promotional ladder he will be given more and more responsibility to manage the time and efforts of other individuals in the fire company, the platoon, or division. Eventually a person may be asked to fill the shoes of the role of fire chief with total responsibility for the department. The knowledge, skills, and abilities that are required to use these financial and human resources effectively differ completely from those that were developed to handle emergencies. On the surface this may not be readily apparent.

For example, the skills of problem-solving and decisionmaking may be somewhat interchangeable from emergency to nonemergency conditions. However, the similarity ends quickly when you begin to compare the tools used to operate in an emergency with the tools of managing a fire organization. The fireground demands skill in fire stream placement whereas management requires skill in placing personnel in appropriate roles. Emergency operations require tactics and strategy, management requires short- and long-range planning efforts. The tools of emergency operations personnel are axes, hoses, and apparatus; the tools of those in the hierarchy of management are more likely to be laws and regulations, budgets, SOPs, and spreadsheets.

The word management is often used as a synonym for other words in fire department jargon. It is not uncommon to find the word linked with the supervision of subordinates. In other cases, the term management is used to describe leadership activities. To more fully understand what management is we must draw a distinction between it and other processes.

Management is not supervision. Supervision has to do with overseeing the operations of subordinates. Granted, it takes a great deal of interpersonal dynamics to achieve that objective, but a person is not managing people if he is just supervising them.

Management consists of the processes used to provide an orderly structure to all of the events in the life cycle of an organization. It is a skill that can be acquired. It is an ability that people can refine over the years. The competencies required to become an effective fire service manager are not easily acquired in the context of the normal officer development process in most fire agencies. Yet when a person is promoted to a top-level fire executive job, he is expected to display these competencies immediately upon receiving the responsibility. A person's success or failure in the role of manager may depend on how quickly he can bring these abilities to bear. Furthermore, the person's ability to retain the job of chief officer, without experiencing job stress and conflict, may depend on how much he can grow after he has been promoted. Many a fire officer has been promoted through the ranks of the fire service without changing from using the methodology of fireground command to a broader based organizational management model. Frankly, there has been little to motivate fire officers in the past to learn about a more generic management model.

It has often been stated that the fire service is 200 hundred years of tradition unhampered by progress. That is not true. The fire service is 200 years of change marked by dramatic shifts in the technology and the methodology of fire protection services.

For example, in the last 20 years or so, we have seen a marked increase in both emergency and nonemergency activities. To the dismay of many fire officers the fireground has become even more complicated as a result of the demands of hazardous materials and emergency medical services incidents. On a day-to-day basis, the actual time that a fire officer spends handling emergencies is very small. The majority of the time is spent in the administration of budgets, personnel policies and procedures, and compliance with an ever increasing number of state and federal mandates.

So, it follows that a contemporary fire officer must have a broad-based knowledge of both incident and resource management methods. Simultaneously, the fire officer must realize that these two environments are not the same and be prepared to use different methods and techniques in order to remain in command of both scenarios.

DEFINITION OF TERMS

The purpose of this chapter is to lay down a foundation for the reader to review before learning about the specifics of dealing with day-to-day fire agency operations. It might be helpful to establish this foundation by reviewing a few terms that are often used, even as synonyms, to describe the activities of chief officers. They are:

- management;
- manager;
- leadership; and
- leader.

Management is the term that is used to imply that an organization is financed, structured, staffed, directed, and evaluated in such a way that it accomplishes its mission in an effective manner. Management means that everything in the organization is being done the way that it is supposed to be done.

A manager is the person who makes sure that things are done right. A manager knows all of the rules, the guidelines, the policies, and practices that have been adopted by the organization to control the processes internal to the organization. A manager is someone who knows how to make the system function in a standardized, uniform manner. He is focused on the organization's behavior of being consistent, with form and function working to support the workforce in achieving the organization's mission and its goals and objectives.

Leadership is not the same as management, but is often used in the same context. It is not a synonym. Leadership is taking an organization from where it is now to where it has to be sometime in the future. This often involves vision and influence, but leaders are not always responsible for getting a job done, only for motivating others to want to do a job. Leadership is providing a direction, or a focus that drives the organization to move in a specific direction. Leadership is often in conflict with management, in that when leadership is being exercised it may force rules to be ignored or changed. Leadership behavior is most often outside of the accepted norms for a stable management environment. Leadership is almost always based on challenging the status quo.

A leader is a person who takes it upon himself to motivate members of the organization to seek new ways of accomplishing old tasks. Leaders are people who challenge traditional solutions, or who redefine what is the right thing to do. They are people who maintain a strong sense of commitment to change instead of consistency. A leader is very often a person who is not afraid of criticism or who has little fear of challenge.

Leadership and leaders then are what cause organizations to move from one place to another, ideally in the direction of improving the organization's ability to perform its mission.

Using these two definitions we can observe that emergency incidents and nonemergency scenarios both require some management skill, and leadership. However, we must quickly distinguish between the fact that scene management uses different timeframes and standardized policies and practices than nonemergency environments.

A good example is the application of the Incident Command System. An incident command system is designed to provide an orderly structure to emergency scene management. In that environment it is useful. In day-to-day operations we do not have the option of directing the behaviors of elected officials, controlling the actions of state and federal agencies that impose requirements on our environment, or limiting the impact of legal or financial departments on the organization. We have to use different management tools.

Management then is the operation of an agency in a manner that is consistent with the accepted ways of doing business, both internally and externally. Management used in the context of the fire service is a process of structuring the activities of the organization in such a way that it achieves efficiency and effectiveness in the use of human and physical resources to protect life and property. Managers are held responsible for making sure that things are done right, at the right time.

THE BASIC FUNCTIONS OF MANAGEMENT

There are numerous textbooks that describe the recognized functional activities of management. For years there was a popular acronym—POSDCORB—which stood for planning, organizing, staffing, directing, coordinating, overseeing, recruiting, and budgeting. Contemporary management literature offers many such acronyms in order to try and remind people of the various functions of management. The fire service does not need to invent a management theory to support its activities. Instead we need to understand the basic principles of management theory and then skillfully apply them to the operation of fire service agencies.

For our purpose, fire service basic management techniques, we're going to use an even simpler series of activities: planning, structuring, establishing direction, coordinating, conducting programs (program activity), staffing, and evaluating.

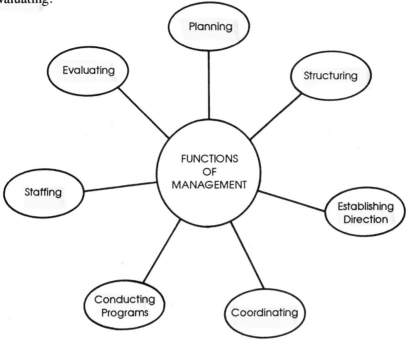

Figure 1-1.

Planning

The process of planning involves looking to the future. The planning process used in the fire service has essentially three cycles. The first of these is a year-to-year plan, often reflected in the form of a budget. The second level of planning is a three-to-five-year phase which is commonly classified as a capital improvement or capital outlay plan. The third is a long-range plan which is called either a master plan or a strategic plan.

The planning process involves identifying what needs to be done to achieve the overall mission of the organization. Planning has two distinctly separate levels: formal planning processes, which are reflected in documents, and informal planning processes that we use on a daily, weekly, or monthly basis to predict, or at least anticipate, events as they begin to emerge from activities.

Fire chiefs must recognize that "to plan" is a verb, meaning that action must be taken to achieve information to give a direction to the organization. A "Plan" is a noun which implies that when you take action to develop a future scenario it needs to be documented and placed into some context in order for it to make sense. In its most simplistic form, a plan is nothing more than a vision of the future. No plan becomes a reality by itself. If a plan is not followed adequately by the individuals who conduct the rest of the management processes, the plan will never become reality. In short, a plan is only a road map and planning is the process used to make the trip.

Two of the skills and abilities that a person must be able to bring to bear in the area of planning are the ability to create both short- and long-term goals and objectives for the organization, and to bring a broad sense of perspective to the job in order to keep the organization's plans in context with the overall needs of the jurisdiction. Some people call that vision or insight. To be successful at planning, a person must think about the future at the same time that he has a plan for the present.

Structuring

Structuring is essentially organizing the resources of an organization so that the work plan makes sense. There are some basic terms used in structuring an organization: chain of command; unity of command; span of control; division of labor; and the use of the exception principle.

Structuring requires the use of the techniques required to supervise the work of others. For example, chain of command is the hierarchial relationship between levels of authority within an organization, i.e., the relationship between supervisors and subordinates. Span of control is the number of people that one supervisor can handle effectively under specific circumstances. Unity of command is the definition of who works for whom, for a person should only be accountable to one boss in a system. Division of labor is the term for the system that divides up tasks according to some similarities or logic.

Finally, the exception principle is a concept of delegating authority so that decisions will be handled as quickly as possible from the lower levels of the organization, with the ability to ask for help on the "exceptions" from superior officers. Problems or exceptions can be passed upward until they arrive on the desk of someone who has the authority to solve them. Managers must use these techniques, but using the techniques alone is not managing.

The fire service has used the aforementioned principles extensively because they lend themselves to the creation of a "scalar" organization, or an organization that is paramilitary in its structure. While that concept was useful for many years it has not been effective in dealing with the increased complexity of fire service operations in the last few decades. So, while the management process implies that an organization must have some degree of structure to it if its plans are ever to be achieved, the hierarchial relationship with or without other relationships is equally appropriate.

Contemporary management theory includes the use of a lot of techniques that are not part of the "scalar" organizational structure. These include "task force" or "matrix" management techniques. These concepts employ methods whereby individuals work across conventional lines of authority. There is no legitimate reason why fire service organizations cannot use processes that preserve traditional hierarchial relationships for day-to-day emergency operations, but also use nontraditional "teaming" concepts to pursue program goals and objectives. The real test of managerial skill is the ability to accomplish complicated tasks while at the same time maintaining the fire service's desire for organizational discipline and need for expediency under emergency conditions.

However, the fire chief has a responsibility to structure an organization to achieve its plan and not necessarily conform to any artificial tradition that is counterproductive to the plan. Structure implies a table of organization. That is one of the reasons for creating a table of organization, to show that relationships can be outlined, job descriptions can be defined, and roles and relationships can be laid out in advance of activity.

The two primary skills used to structure an organization are problem analysis and the ability to prioritize. The two dimensions allow a successful manager to use the existing resources in the most effective manner.

The management responsibility to provide structure to an organization also implies that if plans change, the organization's structure may need to change. There is a dynamic relationship between the vision of the future and the day-to-day activities of an organization in achieving that vision.

Establishing direction

This management process is linked to the plan and is a function of the organizational structure. It is the process whereby the organization defines its goals and objectives and starts marching in a specific direction to achieve them. It also is linked to the concept of the mission of the organization.

The best comparison of this concept is to relate it to a trip that a person might wish to take. To plan the trip a person must have a destination. If the location is just next door he doesn't spend much time thinking about the trip. However, if the destination is miles away, or across the country, he must have some way of getting there. He can choose to drive, fly, or walk. Each will take him in a slightly different way; seldom are any of them direct. There are zigs and zags to the trip. What is important is the fact that he has a compass bearing for the destination.

One of the best compass bearings or ways of establishing direction in an organization is the mission statement. The mission statement is the basic reason for the organization's activities. In order for the mission to be accomplished the organization must accomplish goals which take the organization in a specific direction. The mission statement of an organization, coupled with goals and objectives, is like a flight plan for an aircraft. You might have to deviate for bad weather, but you always end up at the right airport after a period of time.

Establishing direction involves the process of training and counseling sub-ordinates to create policies, practices, and procedures, even day-to-day prac-tices, to take the organization in a specific direction. It cannot be inferred that because an organization has a plan and it has organized its resources that it will achieve anything. This particular management function involves making incre-mental decisions on a day-to-day basis. The management function we see here is one of the proverbial crossing of t's and dotting of i's. Establishing a direc-tion for an organization is not a one-time effort. It is a constant, ongoing strug-gle on a daily basis. In the same way that an automobile requires that you constantly monitor the steering wheel as you navigate it down the highway, an organization must be steered.

This management function uses a host of specific techniques to make sure that direction is there. These may include, but are not limited to, creating and modifying such documents as goals and objectives, priorities, and work per-formance plans, and even preparing training and education plans for the per-sonnel in the organization. If the organization is not adjusted periodically it can find itself in difficulty. Not unlike the automobile analogy used before, an organization can slow down when it really needs to be speeded up. The man-ager's job is to provide the necessary changes in direction based on both inter-nal and external influences.

Coordinating

Coordinating activities consists of maintaining the day-to-day working relationships of both the inner workings of the agency and the relationships with organizations that interface with the fire department. These other entities may include, but are not limited to, water departments, building departments, police departments, dispatch communication systems, other municipal depart-ments, neighboring fire departments, county government, state government, federal government, and community organizations. Typical management coor-dination activities consist of navigating both the organization's internal activ-ities and monitoring the status of the organization's external relationships.

This particular management activity cannot be overestimated when there is a possibility of contradiction or conflict between one organization's activities and those of another. For example, a fire agency must manage its relationship with both water and building departments to assure that the fire agency has an effective code enforcement program. Failure to do this can result in conflict that compromises the ability of a fire agency to manage the community's fire problem. Failure to maintain an effective relationship with law enforcement can result in reduced effectiveness in dealing with emergency problems in the community.

Liaison also implies being skilled in developing cooperation and consensus building and having both oral and written communication skills. A key factor in maintaining balance among organizations is having an understanding of the other organizations' plans, structures, and directions as they affect the organization being managed. Unfortunately, many individuals do not understand that coordination is a management function, but feel instead that everyone must conform to their wishes. Nothing could be more counterproductive in terms of operation and efficiencies. The coordinating function also includes an analysis of redundancy, underlap, or both, between an organization and companion or peer groups.

Program activity

The vast majority of a fire chief's time is devoted to program management. While an organization may have an overall plan, have an organizational structure in place, and have direction, and at the same time be coordinating with others, the fact is that it is what is done on a day-to-day basis to address the mission statement that makes the organization effective, efficient, or both. Therefore, program management consists of a number of essential sub-management techniques.

The first among these is the manager's responsibility to define acceptable standards of performance. The second component is to define workload. The third is the manager's role in measuring whether or not the organization has the ability to achieve the workload.

One of the management functions is classified as defining acceptable standards in the community. Another way of saying this is that a manager's job is to set the minimum standards. What is the community standard for response time? How often should buildings be inspected for fire safety? How many hours of training should an individual receive in a given year? Defining minimum standards in the management context is not entirely devoid of the impact of individual value systems. Not uncommonly, people engage in program activity that is driven by the individual values of the person in charge of a program. Effective managers are individuals who define standards that are appropriate for the community and are not biased by their personal values.

Once the minimum acceptable standard has been established for a particular program, the next management function is to define the total workload that this standard imposes on an organization. Let's say, for example, that an organization determines that all occupancies in its area should be inspected once a year. The first step is to count the number of occupancies in the community to get a first cut at the workload. It's possible that 3,000 or 4,000 buildings need to be inspected.

The second step in the management of the problem is to define how long it would take to conduct an average "activity." One figure multiplied by another begins to define the workload for the community.

If this type of activity is conducted for each type of program conducted by a department, it can very shortly lead to the definition of the staffing requirements to achieve that workload. It follows that if a community has a certain expectation and there is a certain amount of this work that must be accomplished and only so many personnel to accomplish it, one of three things will occur in the context of the organization. First, if you achieve everything that the community expects, you probably have an adequate staff to deal with the task. The second is that you may not achieve everything the community expects. You are doing the right things, but there is too much to be done because you are understaffed. Finally, you may not achieve something that the community expects because the resources are being used to work in another area. This is a problem of prioritization, not workload.

Staffing

If there is any one arena that is controversial in the fire service it is the issue of staffing. Yet staffing emerges from a management task of clearly identifying what needs to be done and how well it needs to be done. As we said earlier, if we were in the private sector, the ground rules would be different. If you have to produce an automobile, and certain tasks have to be accomplished before that automobile is finished, you have two choices. One is to put a sufficient number of personnel on the assembly line so that tasks are done in a certain number of hours; the other is to use fewer people and take longer to produce the same vehicle. The problem with this theory in the fire service is that in the past much of the fire service's workload has not been defined clearly.

Evaluating

Evaluating is a management task that focuses on determining whether the plan is being executed. All too often this management task is treated superficially because it does not have a great deal of immediate response. However, that does not remove it from the inventory of what makes for an effective management operation. Almost all contemporary management literature implies that evaluation is as important to the planning process as the other management functions. The late W. Edwards Deming, a founder of the quality movement, often made a major point about the fact that we should not be inspecting for defects. The reason he says this is that if we continue to inspect for defects we will continue to find defects.

Instead, he says, we should focus our evaluation on the process. Try to determine what it takes to *eliminate* defects. Total quality management and the impact of such programs as quality circles are dependent on the use of skills in evaluating processes, not in evaluating failures.

Evaluation also is linked to accountability. The phrase, "What gets measured gets done," means that if we are looking at activities of programs and individuals and evaluating whether they have been achieved or not and everyone knows that, there is a tendency to continue to achieve. If we don't evaluate programs and activities, it is conceivable that resources will be used inappropriately for nonproductive activities.

MANAGEMENT AS A CYCLE

Now that we have defined these events as being processes, we need to reinforce the fact that they are not one-time events. In his book, *Timing is Everything,* author Dennis Waitley implies that the management cycle is probably illustrated best by looking at how a farmer operates. A farmer must plan his crop for the following year, he must plant seeds, he must cultivate, water, and otherwise nourish his crop, and then he must harvest it in order to achieve his reward and determine whether the yield was high enough. Waitley says this same kind of process is an important part of management of all organizations. Fire agencies do not just live for the moment. They exist to provide a service over the life cycle of a community. So, it follows that fire service agencies should have a portion of their time spent on planning for the future, a period of time devoted to creating and implementing programs, and a proper amount of time devoted to nourishing growth and development of personnel if they expect to celebrate accomplishment as part of their annual activities.

The management horizon in the fire service is not limited to one year. If you contemplate the fact that a chief officer may go through decades of repeating this process, then we can readily see that the cycle can begin to be taken for granted. There are two aspects of this cycle that bear some consideration by students of fire service management.

First, it is easy to be seduced by the fact that this year's budget needs to look a lot like last year's budget. A few years ago there was a popular concept called zero-based budgeting. It was based on the notion that each and every year an agency has to rejustify its programs and activities anew. The concept created a lot of anxiety among individuals who were unsure of their true purpose. On the other hand, others used it to elevate their understanding of the organization's mission, goals, and objectives to a higher state of visibility. Zero-based budgeting, in this author's opinion, was just a fad that eventually ran out of supporters. Nonetheless, those who learned from the exercise, making sure they were confident in the basic underpinnings of the organization's reason for existence, came out of the exercise even stronger.

As the cycle renews itself you should take a very close look at past decisions. Failing to do this can allow an organization to build up a layer of insulation between reality and organizational activity. While it is not necessary to throw out the baby with the bath water, it is important that every year the budget cycle be given a fresh look. Programs should be evaluated to see if they are accomplishing what they were supposed to accomplish. A manager should be assessing the expenditures in the budget cycle as if they were investments, not expenses. Think, "What should I be investing in for the next year in order to accomplish the organization's mission."

The second dimension of this cycle from a management point of view is the realization that if the community changes, the organization must change with it. Any time that the plan, the structure, the direction, and the program activity remain almost identical for more than five to seven years, an organization may be working its way toward inefficiency and ineffectiveness.

The last dimension of the cycle that requires our attention is the fact that all of the cycles are moving targets. In other words, five annual budgets make up one five-year plan. The minute you have completed one calendar year and it falls off the end of the cycle, there is often a need to re-evaluate and establish a new five-year plan. A series of five-year plans may make up the 20-year master plan. Yet when you are five or ten years through that cycle, the master plan should be revisited and extended into the future to assure that it remains realistic. The management task here can best be referred to as linkage, or keeping a perspective on what you are doing in terms of where you are trying to take the organization.

We also must draw another distinction. Management as used in the context of the private sector is different from management in the public sector. There have been people who have tried to state that fire departments should be run more like a business, but the fact is that it is not the same.

There are many ideas from contemporary management theory offered by the likes of Drucker, Deming, Naisbitt, Covey, and others that lead fire departments to become more effective and efficient. However, there is one key distinction between the management of a fire department and private sector management environments. A fire department is a monopoly. It does not have the ability to alter the price of its services or enter into a competitive field in which users have options to accept or reject its services for a competitor's firm.

Having drawn that distinction, we also must add one other dimension to management in the public sector. When we are given resources by a community in order to serve a broad interest of ensuring fire safety and life safety in that community, management implies a tremendous amount of accountability and responsibility. Those fire officers who do not employ management processes can be accused of wasting the community's resources. If the fire service does not produce a quality service the consequences will be felt in losses to the community.

Comparing these two issues, it then follows that managing public sector resources means we can use a lot of the same techniques used to manage private sector resources, but our work is performed in an environment where good management results in cost containment and an increased level of service rather than a profit.

LEADERSHIP AS A ROLE

Now to the tricky part. An effective fire officer must, at the same time, possess the knowledge, skills, and abilities to be a manager and a **leader.** Two quick interpretations of this phenomenon are appropriate. The first is that anyone who chooses to fulfill one of these roles to the total exclusion of the other is headed for an organizational disaster unless he understands that he needs help from others. The second point is that a person who fails to recognize which role to play in any specific situation is headed for a personal conflict with the organization.

What is important for the fire officer to recognize is that the behaviors needed to display competency in both of these areas are different. If a person exhibits a tendency to use the same behaviors to solve all of the organization's problems or prefers one type of behavior over another, there is a very good possibility that the response will be unsatisfactory.

The best analogy that comes to mind here is describing how a person handles a canoe. If you are in a canoe and paddle from one side only, you will travel in a circle. If you don't paddle at all you will go only as fast as the current will carry you. If there are two people in a canoe and each paddles on his own side, the canoe will move along quickly, but the person who has the strongest stroke will dominate the canoe's direction. Experienced canoeists know that you should alternate the sides on which you paddle and that the person in the back is responsible to both paddle and steer. In the context of the fire officer's role you need to be able to exercise administrative and management skills to propel the organization, and leadership skills to provide it with a direction. To do anything else makes an organization falter. Balance is what we are talking about. A fire officer must balance the need for doing things right, doing the right things, and doing them the right way.

Earlier we mentioned that sometimes these terms are used as synonyms. In a positive sense, the reason that this often may occur is that people who are really good at fulfilling all roles simultaneously may be given a label that fits one of these areas, when in fact they are good at both. In a negative sense a person may be given one label and the other languishes, unused. I know I have heard of fire officers who were called "great leaders," when I knew that these same people were effective managers too. I also have heard of a person labeled as "a good manager, but . . ." The key distinction to be drawn from this chapter is the fact that effective fire officers have developed the knowledge, skills, and abilities to fulfill both of these roles when needed.

For example, good managers are well grounded in organizational theory. They understand the function that structure brings to an organization. They are well aware of the need to bring a sense of order to the way business is done. They know budgets, and understand the need for goals and objectives. They have the ability to see the overall system and each of the components at the same time.

They are also well informed in the area of motivational theory and have a sense of the future. They are unafraid of experimentation and risk taking. They understand their people and the various ways to get them to perform at their best. They have a sense of the organization's culture, employee morale, and the need for providing subordinates the opportunity to grow and change over time.

You might ask how one person can fulfill both roles at one time. The answer is simple, but the application is not. The answer is that hardly anyone is good at both roles all of the time. This leads to the implication that an effective executive (fire officer-chief officer) is someone who understands the need for all appropriate behaviors, consciously works to develop the knowledge, skills, and abilities required to succeed in both roles, and at the same time recognizes his own weaknesses. Effective officers develop themselves and their team of subordinates. They create a set of conditions that maximizes their own strengths, and eliminates their weaknesses and vulnerabilities by finding others who can provide those competencies. To the degree that a person really sees himself clearly, and to the degree that he has developed a strategy to function realistically, he can become more successful.

Almost everyone has strengths and weaknesses. It is human nature to have a personal preference for certain behaviors. Most of us have a strong desire to operate using our strengths and ignoring our weaknesses. The more successful individuals are those who are very accurate in assessing the input from their bosses and from their subordinates.

As a fire officer accumulates responsibility through promotion, assignment or both, he must keep these factors in perspective. Balancing out his role as leader, manager, and administrator, and keeping an eye on the results of specific situations can make an average person into an above-average performer. Notably, however, a person with above-average skills in one area who understands this phenomenon can become an outstanding performer.

SUMMARY

Managers in fire departments are not people who spend one day managing and one day being a leader. Like a gourmet cook, they know all the ingredients and use each of these skills as appropriate in the context of the organization. The most important thing a fire department officer should constantly remind himself of is perspective. As an executive within an organization, you are 100 percent responsible for its accomplishments *and* its failures. Therefore, the more you pay attention to taking care of the basics, the more likely the organization will be to continue its success. If you begin to focus on leading the organization and fail to manage it correctly, it may become highly visible and then crash in flames. If a leader of an organization focuses entirely on giving orders and directing others to perform, the organization will lack the backbone to be able to survive once that individual has gone on, to retire or to leave for other reasons.

It is important to distinguish between leading an organization and managing it. If you are leading the organization it is going somewhere. If you also are managing the organization, then when it gets there it will have its act together. Some of the most effective leaders are people who recognize that their management skills are weak and who surround themselves with people who are good at accomplishing the tasks we have just mentioned.

Some of the successful managers who lack charisma and the visibility to achieve strong leadership roles have empowered people in their organizations to perform that task. A strong manager is rarely threatened by a strong individual in the organization.

Good managers tend to be people who are constantly alert to improving their management skills through education and training. They recognize that there is such a thing as managerial obsolescence, which is different than technological obsolescence. Effective managers endeavor to acquire new techniques to implement the management tasks that they have already practiced.

Management is a function that can and must be learned. It is within the realm of possibility for almost everyone to acquire the skills to become an effective manager. But becoming a successful manager means placing a continuous emphasis on learning how to get things done the right way.

2

Office Management and Work Flow

BENJAMIN F. LOPES III

C H A P T E R H I G H L I G H T S

• Fire department elements, including the office and the local community, are interrelated parts of a "system."

• Office functions are determined by the complexity, standardization, and level of decisionmaking authority in an organization.

• Records management requires a planned and integrated system.

• Information technologies are "tools" for empowering the organization.

*T*HIS CHAPTER EXPLORES strategies for office management, including how a plan for office layout and work flow, records management, and information technology can improve fire department personnel functions. The information presented here applies equally to small or large, rural or metropolitan, career or volunteer fire departments.

Fire department offices come in all shapes and sizes. Offices range from public reception areas in fire stations to headquarters centered in high-rise buildings. While the office is generally regarded as the administrative place of business, it is much more. Organizations are more complicated than the location of their offices. Organizations are composed of structures, technologies, and processes. A change to any element is a change to the entire organization.

Another way to view this relationship is through a model. Many organizational theorists use the "open systems" model to view organizations, and, in this way the components and their relationships may be studied. An open system is a biological metaphor referring to an organism transforming inputs to outputs for survival. The change of inputs to goods and services for organizations takes place in a specific environment. In the case of the fire department that environment is the local community.

In the private sector, organizations must compete for limited resources by making the cycle of inputs and outputs profitable. The public sector domain may be monopolistic, but the relationship between inputs, outputs, and the environment remains the same. As part of an organization, office functions must contribute to the mission and goals of the organization. Whether supporting various divisions of the organization or providing direct service to customers, the role of the office is critical to the success of the fire department.

STAFFING

Local needs and available space will determine whether the fire department offices are located in a fire station, city offices, or stand-alone administrative facilities. The office provides both nonemergency direct services to citizens of the community and support services internally for the department as part of an "open system." Examples of nonemergency direct services include fire and life safety plans review, public education, and incident record-keeping. In an internal support role the office serves as a conduit to other fire department facilities, providing policy, coordination, and distribution necessary for fire department operations. This clouds the traditional distinction between line and staff positions, which considered line positions to provide the service, while staff supported the line functions.

The expectation of the modern fire department, like most government agencies, is to do more with less. Budgets, and subsequently the number of personnel, have not grown at a rate equal to local growth and demand for services. In fact, most recent budgets face limited growth or cuts. Personnel costs comprise 80 to 90% of career fire department budgets. In volunteer organizations, where personnel costs are minimal, the budget still directly affects the resources available. While no agency can staff at levels to handle all potential risks or demands, fire departments are measured by their ability to provide service in a timely manner. Without improvements in set tools and techniques used, staffing levels required for routine emergencies would become inadequate to manage current levels of risk.

Determining assignments, Delegating responsibilities and performing followup

Assignments and delegation of responsibility should take place at the lowest level in the organization where individuals possess the skills and knowledge to complete them. This may fly in the face of what many emergency responders see as their primary mission. In a climate of public sector competitiveness, however, downsizing and streamlining organizations will require more of employees. On the positive side, many human resources experts believe that job enrichment is achieved through more diverse assignments and autonomy.

Organizational development experts predict that the manager of the 21st century will accomplish work by using teams of employees. After human resources, the most valuable resource will be information. The traditional hierarchical organization is not representative of staffing needs for the future because assignments will become increasingly information based. Clerical duties will become the responsibility of the information user. Computer word processing and the next generation of interactive technical devices will make it possible for much of the documentation and records storage to be decentralized.

The need to work as a member of a number of teams also will result in personnel who are "cross-functional," that is, one person or group will no longer be responsible for file collection, typing, and records storage. Organizations will need to use their resources more fully. All personnel will take more responsibility for information input and completed staff work.

Staffing levels

Organizational staffing must fit the environment. The office secretary once held the pivotal position with access to key information and records, but

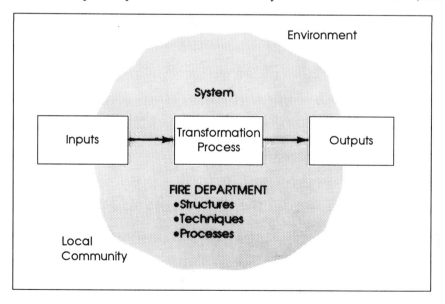

Figure 2-1.

the information explosion is changing that. Information can be available in "real time" at a computer terminal or over a network. Fire chiefs and firefighters are producing and storing their own documents. In many cases the computer has allowed the fire chief the freedom to draft documents while making effective use of support staff time with previously unrelated tasks. Without a plan, however, an organization can simply speed up duplication of effort or production of useless paper.

In many fire departments it has become necessary to establish a dedicated position for the management of information and technology. The position can have many titles: information manager, data administrator, systems administrator, etc. The distinguishing characteristics of this position are to provide technical support and training to fire department personnel. Technical support can include selecting and purchasing hardware and software, ensuring the compatibility of components and programs, updating system-wide data, recommending and monitoring information systems policy, and troubleshooting system problems. Training can involve implementing new programs and providing on-line help for users.

A basic premise in staffing is to make assignments that enable the department to accomplish its mission and reach its goals. In other words, the personnel strategy should support the organizational strategy. Staffing may be determined by analyzing the *complexity, standardization,* and *decisionmaking* requirements in an organization.

Complexity includes the number of tasks required, span of control, and geographic layout of the department. Complexity issues generally relate to size. Larger organizations typically specialize more in assignments. Are individuals assigned solely to training, supply, or other specialized tasks? Does the department have a single station or multiple battalions? What are the travel distances necessary to support the operation? What are the impacts of having support personnel perform multiple functions (reception, phones, payroll, clerical)? How do teams come together?

While bureaucracies favor specialization, complexity generally works against excellence. Increased size and specialization slow an organization's ability to react to environmental changes. Single-purpose positions make it difficult for individuals to grasp the "big picture." Recommendation: Keep single-purpose support staff to a minimum. Large organizations should have proportionally fewer support staff positions based on economies of scale.

A second factor in determining organizational structure is the amount of **standardization** required. Are goals, rules, policies, procedures, job specifications, and training formalized? The more routine the work, the more it can be structured. With a high degree of standardization emergency personnel can complete many clerical functions. Recommendation: The organization should have an infrastructure or conceptual framework for operations that includes mission statement, goals and objectives, policy manual, job specifications, and a training manual. Standardization should stimulate open opportunities by creating a framework for initiative and participation. Standardization should guide norms, rather than simply regulating them.

The last factor in determining office staffing within the organization is the question of centralization, that is, where does the **decisionmaking** take place? Do procedures and staff reports come from several points in the organization or a single individual? How do support personnel serve multiple masters? Team leaders may possess the knowledge, but not necessarily the position power. Recommendation: Make decisions at the lowest level at which individuals possess the knowledge, abilities, and resources to complete the assignment. Empower employees to contribute and make a difference.

Office staffing is an obvious part of the organizational structure, but it also is part of the "system." The office serves as the point of contact for employees and citizens in nonemergency service delivery, between the fire department and its environment—the community. Ultimately, how an organization is staffed tells a lot about its values, mission, and goals.

OFFICE DESIGN CONSIDERATIONS

It may not fit the heroic image, but the simple fact is that much of the service provided by a fire department takes place in the office setting. Countless hours often go into the design of fire apparatus. Significant effort is invested in training and equipping emergency responders. While these endeavors generally comply with national guidelines, requirements and layouts for fire department offices vary from community to community. While some facilities are the focal point for community pride and symbolism, others are merely utilitarian. In either case office layout should be examined from the perspective of these questions:

- How much access to reports and records is required during an hour or a day?
- How much short- or long-term storage is needed?
- How much time is spent working at a computer terminal, talking on the telephone, working with plans at the counter, etc.?
- Is there the correct contrast between the light in the office, the color of the walls, and the computer?
- Is there a way for personnel to keep valuables protected, or important documents secured?

If you have trouble answering these questions, help is available! There are several professional organizations that promote standards for office design. Two of these organizations are listed (with addresses and telephone numbers) in the Technical Resources for Chapter 2, located at the end of the Handbook.

These organizations can provide written and professional references to help you design and equip an office.

Office layout

Written guidelines or goals will assist managers in assessing and designing office and meeting area needs. The guidelines should address the organization's *image, work flow, space requirements, and safety.*

IMAGE

The image of the fire department is defined not only by the level of service provided, but also by the appearance of personnel, equipment, and facilities. Department and public office areas should present a productive, efficient, and professional image to visitors and employees. How employees view themselves is also influenced, in large measure, by how they feel about their work environment. How an organization is viewed by employees and the public is determined largely by perceptions.

Well-designed, functional, safe, professional, and attractive stations, offices, and meeting spaces contribute greatly to high morale, productivity, and efficiency and should be consistent with community image and the value an organization places on its employees. While the resources and facilities available within each jurisdiction may vary considerably, office management and layout should receive the same consideration and planning as other service elements.

WORK FLOW

A survey of work flow is the first step in determining office layout. Figure 2-2, a work flow and space requirements survey, is a tool to help you consider the relationship between work flow, space needs, and assigned functions. With a systematic approach to identifying the various elements of the office environment, office traffic patterns, information management, equipment, and personnel can become more efficient.

SPACE REQUIREMENTS

Work areas should provide adequate space to conduct business. A minimum square footage guideline is one approach to sizing work areas. Guidelines may be determined based on position or functional requirements. In either case space should be determined by the nature of the work conducted. If work areas do not meet minimum established guidelines, the department should be committed to improving the work environment and look for opportunities to enhance space requirements.

Figure 2-2. Work Flow & Space Requirements Survey

Name:_____**Title:**_____**Date:**_____

Job Description (briefly describe your job function and responsibilities):

_____

_____

_____

_____

_____

OFFICE EQUIPMENT
• Equipment: Identify the office equipment used in your work area. Include systems equipment (CRT terminals, printers, recorders, typewriters, etc.). Include dimensions, manufacturer name, model number (if available), amperage and voltage requirements of the units.

Equipment Dimensions Manufacturer Model # Electrical Requirement Shared

_____

_____

_____

_____

_____

_____

Telecommunications: Do you have your own phone or do you share a phone?

        Own   Shared

If shared, with whom? _____

• What is the percentage of time that you spend on the phone daily?

5%   20%   More than 20%

• Are conversations confidential?   Yes   No

Computer: Do you have your own computer or do you share?

        Own   Shared

If shared, with whom? _____

• What is the percentage of time that you spend on the computer daily?
5%   20%   More than 20%

• Are data confidential?   Yes   No

Personal Materials: Identify all the materials that must be stored in your work
space, i.e., books, binders, files, etc. Include the size of the material (letter size:
8½ × 11, etc.) and the inches of space necessary for each type. Linear inches
are determined by measuring the total length of each material now stored. Note
materials that require security.

Material   *Size (length × width)   Linear Inches*

_____

_____

_____

_____

Reference Materials: Identify all the reference materials used frequently used in
your work area such as catalogs, phone books, mailing lists, etc. Include the size
of the material and the linear inches of space required for each type.

Material   *Size (length × width)   Linear Inches*

_____

_____

_____

_____

Furniture: Identify any specialized furnishings, such as drawing boards, files,
cabinets, tables, maps, charts, etc. Include dimensions.

Quantity   *Description*   *Dimensions*

_____

_____

_____

_____

_____

Special Design Considerations:

• Are You: right-handed   left-handed

• Special needs (disability, wheelchair, lighting, etc.):

INTERACTION AND WORK FLOW

• Prioritize the individuals with whom you work most closely inside your department. Give the reason for the interaction, such as work flow, shared files, shared equipment or common projects.

Name   *Reason*

_____

_____

_____

_____

_____

• Is work completed, then filed?   Yes   No
  If so, where?

_____

• Is work sent to another individual or department for completion and/or storage?   Yes   No

_____

_____

Special Areas and Requirements: Identify and describe any special areas, e.g., reception area, storage, etc., necessary to accommodate functional requirements.

Special Area   Description

_____

_____

_____

Conferences: Does the job require conferences in the assigned work space?

               Yes   No

• On the average, how often are conferences held per week?
  1–10   10–15   15 or more

• On the average, how many individuals attend these conferences?
  1–5   5–10   10 or more

• How long do the conferences usually last?
  10–30 min   30–60 min   More than 2 hours

- Are these conferences confidential?

              Yes   No

- Who is responsible for scheduling conference areas?

       Name: _____

- List any requirements, including materials, audio/visual, writing, display surface, etc., used during the conferences.

  _____

  _____

  _____

Sketch each work area: How do the work areas relate to information flow? Interaction? Storage? Privacy?

Figure 2-3 gives sample space guidelines for offices furnished with traditional freestanding or modular work-station furniture by position. Modular furnishings generally make better use of available space and simplify reconfiguration of space to accommodate changing requirements. Ranges in square footage allow flexibility to tailor spaces to specific requirements.

Support Areas. Square footage for file rooms, copy rooms, break rooms, libraries, restrooms, and telecommunication rooms should be determined on a case-by-case basis.

Circulation Areas. Hallways, corridors, and aisles should comprise no more than 35% of usable office square footage.

Growth Factors. In evaluating space needs, be sure to project organizational growth for a five-year period. Apply the expected percentage of growth to the gross total of current space needs.

Too much open space also can be a problem. Vast open spaces can be disorienting. Architects know that proportion (the space and scale of a room) has a lot to do with the occupants' sense of security and sense of being somewhere. Space also contributes greatly to how productive people are. The elements of the building, the furnishings, and the nature of the work must be balanced.

SAFETY

Fire department facilities should be designed to provide the highest degree of operational safety and security. Facilities should meet essential services standards and, at a minimum, reflect local fire and building code require-

Figure 2-3.

Personnel Categories	Square Footage	
	Freestanding	*Modular*
SENIOR MANAGER (Chief, Assistant)	280–320	200–220
EXECUTIVE MANAGER (Deputy, Division)	200–220	160–180
PROGRAM MGR. (Admin. Asst.)	140–160	100–120
Secretary to Exec. Mgr.	120	80
TECHNICAL (Plan Checker)	100–120	80–120
SUPERVISOR	100	80–100
OFFICE SUPPORT (Clerk Typist, Secretary, Account Clerk)	60–80	35–65

PUBLIC/MEETING ROOMS—Conference rooms, reception areas, auditoriums.

Capacity	*Net Square Footage*
4	95
6	125
8	154
12	225
20*	300*

*Add 15 square feet for each additional person after a total of 20.

ments. Public agencies lose credibility when they enforce standards not evident in their own facilities. Two safety areas that cannot be overlooked in office layout are *disaster safety* and *ergonomics.*

With respect to disaster safety, many areas are at risk for moderate to severe earthquakes, tornadoes, hurricanes, or similar violent catastrophic events. Offices located in risk areas must incorporate life safety features to protect employees and the public. High-rise offices may require more stringent safeguards and should be evaluated carefully. Examples of earthquake guidelines include

Overhead Work Area Storage Components:
- Bookshelves must have a raised outer lip or other type of restraining device.
- Storage units must be enclosed using doors or self-locking latches.
- Storage should not be allowed on top of units.

Suspended/Hanging Files:
- Units should not exceed four feet in height.
- Return panels must be installed according to the manufacturer's guidelines.
- Sliding file drawers must have locks and/or an interlock that prevents more than one drawer from opening at a time.

Freestanding File Cabinets and Bookcases:
- Lateral file cabinets are limited to four sliding drawers with self-latching and locking mechanisms.
- Cabinets and bookcases should be fastened back to back for stability. The larger the footprint, the more stable the units in an earthquake.
- Units should not be fastened end to end forming long rows unless they are counterbalanced with similar components and fastened back to back.
- Use of unsecured cabinets and bookcases should be avoided. If no alternatives are possible, unsecured units must not exceed four feet in height and must not be located where they could fall into a work station area or exit corridors.
- Minimum aisle widths should be measured with file drawers in the open position.
- File cabinets should not be located in primary exit corridors with drawers opening in the corridor area.

Office Equipment:
- Equipment (video monitors, printers, sound covers, copy machines, computer components, etc.) should be fastened to carts and stands.
- Carts and stands should be large enough to accommodate the equipment placed on them.
- Valuable or heavy desktop equipment, such as computers and printers, should be anchored with Velcro or rubber friction pads.

Wall Hangings and Plants:
- Heavy framed artwork should not be anchored to partitions.
- Framed materials should be nonbreakable glass or plastic.
- Hanging plants should not be located over desks or seating areas.
- Hanging signs should be constructed of lightweight material and should be hung with metal rather than plastic hangers.

Ergonomic considerations should be an integral part of the design process, promoting efficiency and preventing work-related injuries. Ergonomics is the study of the relationship between people and the tools of their occupation. In particular, ergonomics focuses on the physical relationship of people and the way they use their equipment. A tool, for example, a computer work station, is said to have good ergonomic design when it can easily be adjusted to fit the user.

Office tasks often require rigid or unnatural body postures, repetitive motions, and intense concentration. With good ergonomics, users do not have to contort their bodies in ways that could cause discomfort, strain, or even injury while using the tools required on the job.

Good ergonomic design can help reduce tension, stress, and injury in the workplace, and have a positive effect on productivity, quality of work, and morale. Absenteeism and job turnover can be controlled through awareness and ergonomic design. Conversely, poor ergonomics can lead to Cumulative Trauma disorder, which is defined as:

Cumulative Trauma Disorder (CTD). Physical disorders may develop from, or be aggravated by the cumulative application of biomechanical stress to tissues and joints. Acute trauma, or injury caused by a single event, does not fall within this definition. Examples of CTD include bursitis, ligament strains, muscle strains (e.g., neck-tension syndrome), nerve entrapment (e.g., carpal tunnel syndrome), stenosing tenosynovitis (e.g., trigger finger), etc. Symptoms may include pain from exertion or pressure, change in skin color, numbness or tingling, decreased range of motion, decreased grip strength, or swelling of a joint or part of a limb.

CTD risk is composed of the following factors:
- *Frequency*—the rate at which specific physical motions or exertions are repeated;
- *Force*—physical exertion by or pressure applied to any part of the body;
- *Duration*—the length of any period of work activity which poses a CTD risk;
- *Posture*—the position of a body part during work activity;
- *Vibration*—localized or body exposure;
- *Exposure* of hands and feet to extreme temperatures which cause discomfort; and
- *Recovery time*—the amount of time separating repetitive motions or exertions, or separating periods of any work activity posing a CTD risk, which is needed to prevent fatigue of the body parts performing the activity.

Perform periodic inspections of work sites to reduce or eliminate the risk of office CTD hazards. Inspections should include the following:

- Evaluate clerical work areas for processes, procedures, equipment, or work activities which may increase the risk of repetitive stress injuries and symptoms. Evaluate injury records for evidence of CTD. Provide a written description of measures to control the problem.
- Implement administrative and engineering control measures. Administrative controls include providing "job-specific" training for awareness of symptoms and remedies, the use of rest periods, and redesign of work activities which pose a risk to employees. Engineering control measures include modifications to work stations, equipment, chairs and processes.

Work station design and layout play the most critical role in eliminating sources of injury and postural problems in the office environment. Musculoskeletal effects and visual fatigue are the primary concerns; these usually can be controlled through proper design and use of the work station. An important point to remember is that **office equipment should adjust to the user, not the other way around.** More active participation in the design, installation, and development of office work areas is likely to encourage stronger support for any changes made. Involving the users **and** management is a fundamental prerequisite to success.

A first step in the ergonomic evaluation of a computer work station is to establish the optimal posture of the operator, that is, making sure that heights and angles of the equipment (e.g., chair, table, copyholder, keyboard, monitor, etc.) fit the individual; this in turn helps increase comfort and productivity.

Described below are some of the physical factors that affect a computer operator's performance and health. The factors are keyed to the numbered diagram to help visualize these factors.

Figure 2-4.

1. The chair should be easily adjustable to provide good support for the lower back and allow for the proper height interface with the keyboard. The seat pan should be height-adjustable to fit the operator comfortably above the floor and should be able to tilt forward or backward. The chair should be fitted with casters if the task requires the operator to get up or move around the work station frequently. Be sure that the casters selected are appropriate for the type of office floor (i.e., carpet versus vinyl).

2. Body posture should be as shown, with right angles at the elbow, hip, and knee. The head should be held in a neutral position facing straight ahead with the eyes gazing forward or slightly down.

3. A footrest may be needed when the operator's feet do not comfortably reach the floor, although this should not be necessary if both the table and the chair are height-adjustable. The feet should reach and touch the floor in a flat, relaxed manner. Foot and leg circulation will be affected if overextension of the feet occurs.

4. The keyboard support table can be adjustable to allow proper upper body posture, or the chair height can be adjusted to achieve the same result. The keyboard should be detachable to permit flexible positioning. A wrist rest should be available for those who desire it. Keeping the wrist level straight and in a relaxed position offers the worker maximum comfort for extended hours of work.

5. A document holder should be provided and should be adjustable in height and angle of tilt, to the same height and plane the operator views the majority of the time. This position typically will be at or just below screen level, allowing the operator to hold his head in the neutral position shown in the diagram.

6. If eye fatigue, vision problems, or both are experienced by video display terminal users, they should see an ophthalmologist to rule out any need for prescription glasses. The display monitor should be positioned so that the distance from the eye to the screen can be adjusted, allowing the center of the screen to be positioned so that the viewing angle is 15 to 25 degrees below eye level. Display monitors placed too low will increase musculoskeletal tension and fatigue to the back and neck; display monitors placed too high will increase visual fatigue. The screen should be detached from the keyboard so that each can be positioned in an optimal manner.

7. General lighting for the office and display monitor varies among oper-

ators. Light above and in front of the display monitor will glare onto the screen. Reduce glare onto the screen by placing the display screen appropriately in the room. The display monitor should be oriented so that the operator does not face an unshielded window or a bright light source. Ideally, the screen should tilt to help eliminate screen reflections. Reduce mirror-like reflections on the screen by using an etched screen surface, a thin film coating, or a hood. Other types of reflections on the screen can be reduced by using a neutral density, micro-mesh, or glare-resistant filter.

8. Given the work demands on computer operators, it is important to monitor environmental factors, such as temperature (68° to 78°F), and humidity (30 to 70%). Noise should be kept within comfortable limits, (less than 75db or as low as possible). Noise from printers and nearby equipment may be reduced with sound screens or well-placed absorbent materials such as acoustical ceiling tile, carpets, curtains, and upholstery.

Computer users have raised the issue of the various types of radiation (e.g., X-ray and ELF) produced by computer equipment. Exposure levels to radiation during computer use are very low (not significantly above background) and there currently is no accepted scientific evidence to suggest that radiation exposure from computer use is harmful. Adhering to the philosophy of "prudent avoidance" (if radiation is an issue of concern) would dictate staying about arms length from the monitor to eliminate almost all exposure.

Office of the chief

In addition to its other functions, the fire chief's office serves as the point of origin for much of the organization's business, planning, and meetings. It is significant not only to the individual who occupies it but also to the organization and to the community the organization represents. It is a reflection of the individual and the values of the organization. Is the chief a "visionary" who requires information for the "big picture?" Does the chief value people-oriented interaction? Are storage and privacy needed for an efficient operation? In addition to considering image, work flow, space requirements, and safety, as previously mentioned, the following issues deserve special attention.

PRIVACY

Many of the issues handled at the fire chief's level require privacy. Strategic planning, personnel actions, and labor relations are just a few of the sensitive issues discussed in the chief's office. Privacy is more than simply meeting behind closed doors. It also means an area where confidential topics can remain confidential by controlling access, visibility, and sound transmission.

COMMUNICATIONS

The chief should have access to the organization's common communications. Telephones, voice mail, computer networks, electronic mail, and emergency radio communications are all examples of information media. The fire chief needs the tools to keep in touch with the department and the community, including the ability to monitor local radio or television.

CONFERENCE AREA

The office should have seating for a small group, typically four to six. The nature of business conducted in the fire chief's office will determine whether a conference table is a requirement.

REFERENCES

Reference requirements vary with management styles. The more technical or information driven the chief is, the greater the need for reference materials. Library materials can range from personal notes and documents, catalogs, rules and regulations, to state and federal administrative codes. The reference materials in the chief's office should be for personal use only. Access to and removal of materials should be allowed only with the express permission of the chief.

RECORDS MANAGEMENT

At some time every fire chief probably wonders if the fire in fire department is fueled by the sheer volumes of paperwork required. There are federal, state, and local reporting requirements, financial records, budget documents, payroll and personnel records, codes and ordinances, apparatus records, and on and on. Sometimes it seems that for every ten minutes of service provided it takes ten hours of paperwork to keep the department running. The saying, "The job isn't done until the paperwork is finished," unfortunately appears to be true.

Even the best administrator can be intimidated when the volumes of required paperwork are analyzed. How can a 21st century fire chief keep ahead of this tidal wave of paper? A records management system lays the groundwork for a more comprehensive Information Management System. Consider the strategies to attack the problem:

Identify the problem. Ask how other fire chiefs handle reports and records. Network! Network! Network! The idea is simple, but powerful. Network with peers and experts. Lawyers, accountants, personnel specialists, certified mechanics, etc., all are familiar with the requirements for special documentation in their respective fields of expertise. Read the city charter, national standards, state administrative codes governing the formation and activities of the fire department, and the publications of professional organizations. Acquiring knowledge is like a treasure hunt—you must keep digging to find it.

Plan. "No one plans to fail. They just fail to plan." A records management plan is part of the fire department's infrastructure. Without a plan, records management, like fireground activities, becomes a happening. Everyone works hard but the results are unpredictable.

A systems approach formalizes procedures for records and reports. This does not mean that organizations require a bureaucracy or the paperwork implied. It does mean, however, that with some centralized planning even the most decentralized, empowered organization can be more efficient. A systems approach replaces uncertainty with structure. It provides a standard set of operating procedures. To plan you need a strategic fire department plan, information management system plan, and an analysis of the department. This allows you to determine elements of the system.

Systems should not be viewed as obstructions to initiative, upward delegation, or an endorsement of decisionmaking centralization. Following rules

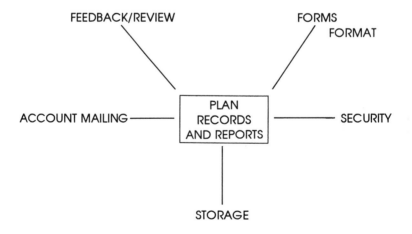

Figure 2-5.

should not become more important than getting the job done. A systems approach to reports and records produces standard meaningful information that can be used efficiently. The process should contribute to the speed and clarity with which information will flow. Standard information should assist the planning and decisionmaking process. What elements constitute a reports and records plan? The following key areas apply to both paper and electronic records:

- *Accountability*—Someone must be responsible to write, process, complete, act on, and store each report or record. While reference may be by individual, title, or position, remember, **groups are not accountable, individuals are.** Without accountability paperwork can fall into a "black hole." A requirement for a signature or initials identifies the originator, reviewer, authorization, etc.
- *Routing*—A rule of effective office management is to handle each piece of paper or communication only once. Two of the most common elements in any communication are TO: and FROM:. If routing takes place in between, it is either wasted motion or the document is inaccurately addressed.
- *Storage*—Determine whether a record is active or archived, and whether it requires short- or long-term storage. If the record is active it must be accessible to the person or persons using the information. If the information is archived, consideration must be given to storage space required and retrieval. Each type of archived information should have its own location.
- *Security*—Is the record sensitive and in need of secure storage? Is it for general publication or should access be strictly on a need-to-know basis? Is there a legal requirement for security?
- *Format*—At a minimum, fire department reports should have: letterhead or logo, form title and/or stock number, and revision date. Official documents should be in this format.

Ask if the record or report is really necessary. It can be tempting to create a new form for every new situation. That's what bureaucracies do best. Every possible action is formalized and recorded. *Do not* require special records, reports, or forms unless they will be used frequently, something useful will be done with them once they are completed, or they are required by law.

Finally, communicate the plan. Employees should know the who, what, where, when, why, and how of communications handling in the organization. The plan should clearly state the need for records security and authorized access. An action guide or procedures manual is an excellent way to standardize and streamline paperwork. One of the advantages of written communications is that it provides consistency over time.

Reports needed

Federal, state, and local requirements should provide the primary guidelines for the need to produce and retain records. The five broad categories of reports and records generated and maintained by fire departments—financial records, personnel administration records, incident reports, code enforcement records, and internal documentation—are outlined below. These examples are not all-inclusive but give some insight into the paperwork generated by the average fire department. Analyzing reports and records by category helps to simplify the records and reports planning process for the fire chief.

FINANCIAL RECORDS

(Retention varies with statutory requirements.)

- Journals/Ledgers

Accounts receivable	Accounts payable	Disbursements
Payroll journal	Taxes receivable	Warrant register

- Source Documents

Bank Statements	Bills	Checks
Claims	Invoices	Purchase Orders
Reimbursement requests	Requisitions	Time slips
Vouchers	Warrants	

- Statements

Balance Sheet	Cash receipts/ disbursements	
Fixed assets	Fund balance	Revenues

- Other

Audits	Budgets	Capital asset records
Inventory records	Lease-purchase records	Long-term debt
Schedule of investments		

PERSONNEL ADMINISTRATION RECORDS

(*Rather than following statutory minimums, it is recommended that personnel records be retained indefinitely. Issues may arise long after separation.)

- Administrative Files

Job specifications	Labor Agreement	Rules, regulations, policies

- Confidential Personnel File (Not available to employee and/or immediate supervisor.)

Communicable exposure reports		Credit reports
EEO status record	Employment tests	Employment references
Pictures	Interviewer comments	Medical exams
	Police reports	Records checklist
	Separation report	Worker's comp. documentation

- Employee Action File (Available for review by employee and supervisor (based on need).)

Insurance sign-up	School records	Payroll deductions
Application	Attendance reports	Certifications
Current job description	Current disciplinary actions	
Tax records	Equipment issued	Grade changes
Employment agreements	Performance appraisals	Records checklist
Payroll records	Training records	Transfers

INCIDENT REPORTS

(*Incident reports are usually retained indefinitely. Documentation may be used for personnel issues or exposure.)

Incident action plans	Incident run records	Investigation reports
Patient field records	Public education reports	Tactical worksheets

CODE ENFORCEMENT RECORDS

(Code enforcement records are generally retained for the lifetime of the property or occupancy.)

Annual inspections	Building inspection records	
Certificates of occupancy	Hazardous materials storage plan	
Hydrant acceptance tests	Material Safety Data Sheets	
Permits	Plan check record	Site plan and conditions

INTERNAL DOCUMENTATION

(Documentation retention varies. Some records are needed for the life cycle of the facility or equipment. Other records facilitate operations on a short-term basis and should be discarded on a routine basis.)

- Apparatus and Equipment Records

Annual pump tests	Daily operator's checklist
Fuel records	Preventive maintenance
Specifications	Vehicle accident reports

- Facility Records

ADA compliance	Maintenance requests	Safety inspections

- Supply Records

Inventory	Order forms

- Other

Contracts	Disaster preplans	Minutes of meetings
SOPs	Station log books	Training manual

Office communications

Many of the day-to-day communications that take place in a fire department are in a written form, including personnel assignments, hydrant or street information, upcoming events logged for subsequent shifts, apparatus repairs needed, etc. Written communications have the advantage of relaying a message and lasting over an indefinite period of time.

Modern management principles emphasize the importance of good communications among all levels in an organization. Sender rank may not be the determining factor in a written communication's importance. In many departments firefighters may have key roles in budgeting and project management, and the necessary authority to facilitate communications. At some point, however, it becomes necessary to determine which communications are official and must be retained and which are not. Intra-office communications also should be addressed in the reports and records plan.

Depending on the size of department it may be advantageous to formalize how intra-office communications are defined, authorized, distributed, and retained. The following example covers key elements for such communications:

XYZ FD POLICY:
Written Intra-Office Communications

XYZ Fire Department (FD) written communications include informal and formal messages. Only approved information shall be distributed and posted in FD facilities.

INFORMAL: Informal communications include typed or handwritten messages and electronic mail to an individual or small group. Messages may be generated and routed by all FD personnel for approved FD business. Messages are not retained or logged in the Notice & Memo Binder.

FORMAL: A Notice & Memo Binder is required for retention of formal fire department communications. The binder provides a system for the distribution and storage of written communications to all personnel, all stations, and/or special groups. It also provides hard copy portability for reference at station meetings.

Company officers shall read, initial, and date new Notices and Memos during morning briefings. Vacationing, sick, and injured personnel shall read, initial and date appropriate communications upon return to duty.

- **NOTICES**—A Notice is a formal written FD communication of a specific nature distributed to all personnel. Notices require approval for distribution by the Fire Chief. They shall be maintained in the Notice and Memo binder for sixty (60) days. They shall be disposed of after sixty (60) days or as indicated on the Notice.
- A permanent record shall be maintained by (a designated individual) for future FD reference.

- **MEMORANDUM** (Memo)—A Memo is a formal written FD record or reminder and is distributed to assigned personnel or small groups. Memos require approval for distribution by a Program Manager/Chief Officer. They shall be maintained in the Notice and Memo binder for sixty (60) days. They shall be disposed of after sixty (60) days or as indicated on the Memo.

- **ANNOUNCEMENTS**—An Announcement is a communication of an informative nature. Announcements require approval for distribution by a chief officer. They require posting on the station bulletin board for sixty (60) days. They shall be disposed of after sixty (60) days or as indicated on the Announcement.

FORMAT: All FD Messages, Notices, and Memos shall contain
- **FD** heading
- Type of communication—**MESSAGE, NOTICE, MEMO**
- **DATE:** The date the communication is written.
- **TO:** The person or group to which the communication is directed.
- **FROM:** The originator of the communication.
- **SUBJECT:** The topic of the communication.
- **APPROVED FOR DISTRIBUTION:** (Notices & Memos) Chief Officer name and title authorizing distribution.

INFORMATION TECHNOLOGIES

This is the information age. At no time in history has so much information, covering virtually every facet of life, been available. Acquiring information is not difficult. The problem is determining how it can be used. The term "office" implies a place where information is available. The fire department office serves as the "central nervous system" for information. A station, maintenance facility, or fire inspector may be the end user of information, but generally the office helps facilitate information processing.

A conceptual approach to information management makes it obvious that information defines the service. Firefighting requires a particular knowledge, or area of information. EMS requires knowledge of local protocols. Code enforcement requires knowledge of local and state codes and ordinances. Virtually every service provided by the modern fire department has a qualified body of knowledge, an information base. The very nature of the service is matching the correct information to the given circumstances. Information technologies include the information, equipment, techniques, and processes that are converted to outputs for the organization.

Technology—A scientific method for achieving a practical purpose. Technology includes tools and techniques (or scientific methods) to gain power or leverage, making a task easier (practical purpose.) In physics Power = Work/Time. More work in less time gives more power. Leverage produces an output force greater than the input force.

Technology does not mean that you need the latest or most powerful gee-whiz gizmo, but instead is a philosophy that advocates the use of tools, together with **ideas** to achieve a purpose. The "systems model" also promotes the idea that technology can have a significant influence on the organizational structure of the fire department. Tools designed for speed and efficiency can have significant cascading effects on the organization's social system. With the power of technology it's not who you know but how you know.

Organizations should be organized around processes instead of tasks. Processes cover a range of activities when compared to "compartmentalized" tasks. This means people must cross traditional barriers or "turf" to deliver service. Technology can help overcome three facts of organizational life: "people are busy; people are in different places; and information is not always where it is needed."

Benefits

Automated systems assist with repetitive tasks, report compilation, record updates, and report generation. For the fire chief, the significant benefits of an automated system are *leveraging time, communicating, information access, and shaping the department's culture.*

- *Leveraging time*—Computers do not decrease workloads, they merely increase the capability to deal with information. As previously stated, with more information than ever available to process, a computer's speed of retrieving, sorting, and selecting allows more information to be "crunched."
- *Communicating*—In the past the "grapevine" was the fastest method to "get the word out." "Telephone, tell a friend, tell a fireman," has been an axiom for the speed of informal communication. With communication technologies information can be distributed over distances in real time. The person who generates a record can create, distribute, and store information in a few keystrokes, or with a fax, or conference call. Electronic communication is not a substitute for face-to-face communication. It does, however, allow a fire department, particularly one with multiple facilities, to link ideas and expertise regardless of location.
- *Information access*—The real strengths of computing are speedy information storage, retrieval, and manipulation. Days and weeks of searching and calculation have been compressed to seconds. People who are held accountable must have access to plans, procedures, and other people. Computer technologies, particularly networking, allow more opportunities for all personnel to participate. Networking allows employees to "cross barriers of space, time, and social category to share expertise, opinions, and ideas."
- *Shaping the department's culture*—Information is power. To draw an analogy, some economists focus on the distribution of wealth and note that the trend appears to be a shrinking middle class. Conversely, with information technologies, more people have access to information; therefore, more people can make informed decisions.

Limitations

Technology can be seductive. Speeding up existing processes may only result in marginal improvements in effectiveness. Traditional organizational structures are built around efficiency and control, whereas the new paradigm is service and quality. The information age requires an organization that is built around outcomes, not tasks.

There is a difference between automating and informating. "Automating tends to concentrate on the smart machine and to cut out or reduce people. Informating organizations also use smart machines but in interaction with smart people." Smart machines need smart people to work with them. The smart people who work with these machines need to consider

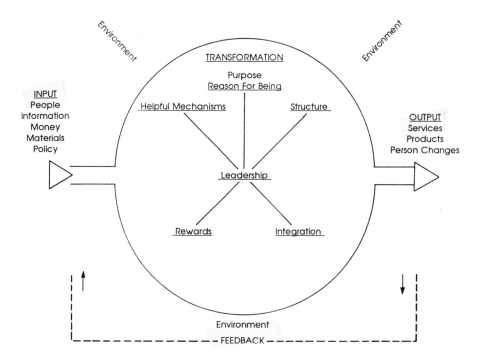

Figure 2-6. Basic Systems Theory Model
  (With Weisbord Model For Transformation)

- ***It's a tool for the job, not THE job***—Information technology, like a fire service command system, is a strategy, or approach, to processing information. How we use tools can sometimes seem to appear more important than getting the job done. If the technology becomes the focus of our labor it can obstruct what it was intended to do, that is, assist us in our tasks. Flexibility and initiative should always be valued in the fire service, on the emergency scene, and in the office. Empowerment implies a degree of "looseness." Technology is not the end product, service is. Technology should be transparent. It is merely a tool.

- ***Garbage in/Garbage out***—Since the inception of computerized systems the rule remains the same, "garbage in equals garbage out." Outputs (data) are only as good as inputs (the information entered). A seemingly small error in data entry can distort the "reality" of the information. Users have to understand the use, or audience, and implications of the data stored.

- ***Information technology's impersonality***—People have more trouble sensing what others are feeling when communicating electronically compared to face-to-face communications. "Flaming" (rude and impulsive behavior) is more common in electronic communications. Tendencies to be outspoken in electronic communication may lead to increased group conflict.

- ***Information Overload***—More and more information moves faster and faster. Electronic group decisionmaking can take more time. Answering electronic mail inquiries is time-consuming. Learning about software and systems takes time. Manipulating more data requires time.

- ***Control***—"Not surprisingly, people often resist changes in information control that diminish their position." The access to information can be a great equalizer in the workforce. "Often, information overload is really an argument about control." "Typically the problem is not too much information, literally, but lack of control over information exchange." Sharing information and employee empowerment do not fit everyone's leadership style, fortunately only the unenlightened few.

Plan your information system to address users, needs, and processes. If information is stored in the "wrong" format, or is not accessible by the end user, the system becomes inefficient. Policies should encourage information exchange and define parameters clearly. A written policy may help to establish a degree of standardization for the system.

XYZ FD Policy: Computer Use

PURPOSE: The XYZ Fire Department operates computers and stores data on behalf of the citizens served. The system is continuously evaluated for security, access, and applications by designated personnel. There will be unforeseen circumstances as system use develops, requiring further refinement of operating procedures. As such, certain restrictions for protection from accidental or intentional destruction, unauthorized modification, and/or disclosure of information must apply.

CODE OF ETHICS: All data, files, and software stored, maintained, or placed on any FD computer equipment or computer media, including transferable media such as diskettes, are FD property, without exception. The fact that individual items or collections of data or software are public in nature, or actually are public records, does not diminish the "proprietary" aspects of FD ownership.

- Use of an assigned computer requires permission from the responsible owner.
- Only authorized software is allowed. At no time shall software be added or removed from the network without the express permission of the System Manager.
- Unauthorized pirating of software may result in severe fines and disciplinary actions against the responsible employee. Some data security violations can carry criminal punishment; some misuse can be deemed a misdemeanor.
- Do not knowingly omit data, falsify records, make misleading entries, or destroy official records.
- Do not interfere with or snoop around in other people's computer work.

Public interest must always precede self-interest. Individual actions must uphold and safeguard the FD's ability to operate efficiently, confidentially, and accurately.

Essentials for success

A study of managing information technologies was completed by the Syracuse University School of Information Studies. The study examined how county governments used technology to collect, organize, manipulate, and disseminate information. The Syracuse Study highlights several factors as essential to the successful use of information technologies. To extract the maximum value from information technologies, an organization must have:

LEADERSHIP

Top officials must establish a supportive environment, through formal policies, visible support, and their own use of information technologies. Not only must they be interested in and conversant with information technologies, they also must champion a commitment to technology at all levels.

PRACTICAL VISION

There must be a vision of the organization's future complete with an understanding of the role technology can play in realizing it and a clear information technology plan to guide the organization toward that vision.

VALUED TOOLS

Information technologies must be integrated into government as tools that enable it to carry out administrative functions, deliver services, comply with mandates, and respond quickly to new demands. Efficiency is measured, and effectiveness is valued.

ONGOING TRAINING

Training of end-users at all levels is critical to realize the maximum return on an investment in information technologies, to ensure productivity, and to encourage creative solutions.

ADEQUATE RESOURCES

The organization must allocate people, facilities, and money to information technologies; verbal support is not enough. Know what you have and ask for what you need.

TEAMWORK

A project team, including technical experts, managers, and end-users is vital. All players should be involved, informed and heard.

And, in addition, officials should remember to:

- Be creative. Encourage innovation.
- Focus on doing it better; improvement is always possible.
- Make the technologies "invisible" to the end-users; they should concern themselves with their productivity, not how the technologies work.
- Look outside your own territory; benchmark your practices against the best.
- Focus on useful information: technology is an enabling tool. Treat it that way.

Records storage alternatives

HARD COPY

Requires no special knowledge to create, update, store, or retrieve.
No special equipment is needed.
Authenticity is readily determined.

MICROFICHE

Stores 60 to 98 pages per film.
Readers capable of hard copy prints.
May be used for active and archived files.
Capable of computer interface for automated search.

ROLL MICROFILM

Stores 2,000 to 3,000 pages per film.
Limited copy capabilities.
Primarily used for archived files.
Capable of computer interface for automated search.

COMPUTERIZED DATA

(Performance capabilities improve routinely)
Disk, Hard disk, Flash chip, Digital analog tape, Optical drive, Personal
    digital assistant, Scanners, Software
Electronic Mail (E-mail)—Lets groups of computer users, connected by
    a network, send messages and share information.

Information Transmission

The telephone probably remains the predominate electronic communication device in use today. Its versatility increases in step with emerging electronic communications technologies. The simple telephone has expanded its role to include service as an intercom, and an answering machine. It can be used to facilitate conference calls, page announcements, and forward calls through simple one-button speed dial. Telephones are available as part of business systems, and can be cordless, or mobile. Figure 2-7 (from *Connections*) compares the benefits of various communications technologies. Asynchrony means senders and receivers do not need to attend to the same communication at the same time. They can send and receive at their convenience.

It appears that the communications industry is positioned for the information revolution of the 21st century. Communications companies are consolidating their resources to provide telephone, television, computer, and related electronic communications. This unprecedented variety promises accelerated changes for the future of office technology. Fax, video, computer, telephone, digital assistants, etc., will become linked as electronic communications become integrated. Mechanisms for transmission and storage of information will be limited only by imagination. Networking through new computing devices will become a daily necessity. The public and private sector are working to resolve the logistical and legal problems of an "information highway."

Expanding the envelope of information technology will be:

- "Smart" forms that travel from location to location in real-time automat-

Figure 2-7. Comparing communication on a computer network with other communication technologies

			Technology Attributes			
	Asynchrony	Fast	Text content only	Multiple address-ability	Externally recorded memory	Computer-processable memory
Meeting	no	yes[a]	no	yes	no[b]	no
Telephone	no	yes[a]	no	no[b]	no[b]	no
Letter	yes	no	no	no[b]	yes	no[c]
Telex	yes	yes	yes	no	yes	no[c]
Facsimile	yes	yes	no	no[b]	yes	no[c]
Voice mail	yes	yes	no	yes	no[b]	no
Electronic mail	yes	yes	yes	yes	yes	yes

a. Although conversation is instantaneous, meetings are fast only if people do not have to travel to the meeting place. Telephone conversations are fast only when both parties are simultaneously available to talk and don't have to play telephone tag.

b. Special actions can be taken to approximate the attribute in question. For example, memory can be provided by recording or transcribing meetings or telephone conversations. Voice messages can be stored. Multiple addressability is achieved with conference calls, certain facsimile machines that can be programmed to dial multiple telephone numbers, and letters that are copied and mailed to several people.

c. Special actions can be taken to improve retrieval properties of paper-based technologies. Vertical filing systems improve the retrievability of paper documents. Imaging systems that "annotate" facsimile images make the resulting documents easier to search. When facsimile or other image-handling technologies are integrated with computers, their retrievability capabilities approach those of electronic communication.

SOURCE: Sproull, L., and S. Kiesler, *Connections,* MIT Press, Cambridge, MA: 1993

ically. At each stop new information is added or deleted. The forms can be programmed to self-check entries for errors.

- Groupware that expands the environments for group activities such as meetings. Groupware allows activity: "(1) same time and same place (a face-to-face meeting); (2) same time, different places (a telephonic or video conference); (3) different times, same place (group recording); different times, different places (dispersed projects and committees)." Teams of people can work together with better access to information and one another. Electronic brainstorming can become a forum for ideas.
- Computing devices that recognize handwriting and voice, making it possible to integrate existing human skills with technology.

As the technology expands so too does our view of information itself. Traditionally information in the fire service meant data collected as historical records, a past-tense view of what has already taken place. Forms and records were stored in cabinets and retrieved as "static" documents for analysis.

Office-related information increasingly will become available as emergency operations information. A current generation of information technology already allows weather prediction for planners on large wildfire incidents. Digital information allows storage and manipulation of preplans and mapping. Incident commanders access databases via radio and cellular modems. Incident commanders track resources with mobile data terminals (MDTs) and laptop computers. Dispatchers are taking an increasing role in incident management.

The next generation of information will make us more action oriented and help us in incident decisionmaking. The information management support function may be provided remotely, possibly out of the fire department's offices. On-board video monitors and sensors can feed information back on existing conditions. Computerized occupancy files integrated in geographic information systems (GIS) increasingly will be accessed for plot plans, hazardous storage, and relationships with surrounding neighborhoods. Support (office) personnel miles away will take an active role in suppression and enforcement efforts.

SUMMARY

Fire chiefs must hear the alarm. Government is reinventing itself. Whether we call it downsizing, right-sizing, or just plain change, the service delivery is expected to improve and be customer based. Many of the functions necessary to provide that service are delivered through or supported by the "office." The office is an integral part of the fire department, an "open system." The relationship of the parts is synergistic.

As we move into the 21st century, fire departments must function as part of "the information society." "The essential requirement, therefore, of all its workers is that they are able to read, interpret, and fit together the elements of this currency, irrespective, almost, of what the data actually relate to. That is a skill of the brain." Fire department personnel, including the fire chief, must become "cross-functional," increasingly filling more of an "office" role. Staffing roles will be determined by the complexity, standardization, and decisionmaking styles of the organization. Individuals will take more responsibility for information input and completed staff work.

Records management must be planned thoroughly. Without a plan, electronic communications and automated processes can actually increase inefficiency. More "horsepower" does not necessarily lead to improvements in service. With thoughtful planning by fire personnel, a records system can streamline input, use, manipulation, storage, and recall of documents.

Information technologies are empowering tools, allowing more of the organization to communicate issues, ideas, problems, and solutions. Caution is also in order—technology can be seductive. It is not an end result; it is a means to provide better results and better service. Information technology will change the way we live and work. The fire department of the future will be measured by its ability to deal with information.

NOTES

Sproul, L. and Kiesler, S. *Connections*, (Cambridge, MA: MIT Press, 1993) p. 19.

——Ibid

Handy, p.149.

Sproul, L. and Kiesler, S. *Connections*, (Cambridge, MA: MIT Press, 1993) p. 105.

Fletcher, Bretschneider, Marchand, Rosenbaum, Bertot, and Richter. Managing Information Technology: Transforming County Governments in the 1990's, *Governing*, August 1992.

Sproul, L. and Kiesler, S. *Connections*, (Cambridge, MA: MIT Press, 1993) p. 70.

3

Financial Management

MICHAEL T. WREN

C H A P T E R   H I G H L I G H T S

- Define agency strategic direction(s) for the future.
- Link, through the budgeting process, agency impact in the community, agency outputs, and jurisdiction inputs of policy and funding.
- Change the focus of budgeting from one of cost and purchasing decisions to one of risk and service level setting.
- Develop properly justified budget proposals.
- Develop and evaluate revenue sources.

Financial Management: the Art or Skill of directing the Aquisition and Judicious Use of Money to Accomplish An End.

WHILE NOT ONE of the most glamorous aspects of operating the modern fire department, few would argue that financial management isn't a critical management function. At the same time, many overlook the strategic implications of financial management. Most would agree it is an ever increasing challenge. Among the issues that complicate the job are:

- increasing service demands with declining revenues;
- mandated, but unfunded programs and requirements (SARA III, ADA, FLSA, NFPA 1500, etc.); and
- demand for more accountability from elected officials and the public.

Every organization is challenged to take care of its financial affairs. In the private sector, this is essential for survival. But in private enterprise everything is quantifiable: profit, loss, market share, cost of production, even customer satisfaction.

Many fire service managers argue that such business practices are not always possible in the public sector, especially under emergency or crisis conditions. This is true, but it is not a valid reason to dismiss such business practices as not applicable at all to the fire service. To the degree that a fire service agency can quantify those aspects of the business that can be foreseen and measured, the more visible the needs of the department can become, including those in direct support of potential emergencies.

One complaint often heard from fire service managers is that those in political and policy positions outside of the fire service don't understand this business. Many of those same people are business and professional men and women who are right at home with market analyses, sales forecasts, production schedules, and profit statements. How can fire service managers in a non-profit business, with no marketing budget and no sales forecasts, apply business practices from private enterprise, especially quantitative performance and budget analysis techniques? This is one of the key questions addressed in this chapter, that, when answered, should help fire service managers to make better decisions, contribute to making politicians more informed (and favorably influenced) and—consistent with your mission—help you to create a safer community.

Some of the other questions examined in this chapter include:

- Where should emergency managers look for measurable indicators of their business condition or success?
- How can a budget process serve the needs of department program managers and still meet "city hall's" submission format demands?
- How can a fire department develop sound, defendable budget proposal justifications?
- What are the traditional—and some potentially new—revenue sources for funding a fire department? How can or should new revenue sources be evaluated for inclusion in proposals?
- How do strategic planning and long-range goals and objectives relate to budgeting?

BACKGROUND

Another relevant question is, "Just what are the rules of the game?" This is a valid question, because while there are generally accepted accounting practices (GAAP, see page 127) and standard principles of governmental accounting, financial management is more than the mechanics of budget submission and accounting. The "rules" of local jurisdictions vary greatly. The universal feature is that the game is political! The fire service would-be-manager who has not realized this is in for a rude awakening. Some of the rules may be written: the required forms (or format) and schedule of submission, spending and transfer authority, are examples. Other rules often are unwritten: Who may lobby whom, when, and under what circumstances? What forms may "lobbying" take?

A little background is in order to understand not only who the players are, but "from where they come."

There was a day when the "holy mission" of the department was all that was required as justification, both in volunteer and paid department environments. Of course, those also were the days of political patronage, longer hours, low wages, and barely adequate (for those days) equipment.

Early in the century, as an attempt to bring the patronage machines under control, governmental fiscal accountability became the order of the day. It was in those days that the line-item budget was born. (The line-item budget was adopted in 1921 by the federal government; it is still the most widely used form of budgeting in governmental departments. Its features and deficiencies, and other forms of budgeting, are covered in the section starting on page 82.)

By the late 1940s it was recognized that while the line-item budget met fiscal control needs, it did little or nothing to support policymaking and program management. The search was on for other methods of budgeting. A number of other budget formats emerged, but a return to line-item occurred more times than not. There are several reasons for this: it is the easiest to develop (just add [or subtract] x% to [from] last year's figures); and, more significant to our current question, it offers the most control to fiscal bureaucrats. That's their job, their responsibility. It doesn't make them all bad, but they often have more influence on CEOs and policymakers than the fire chief or department program managers.

PERSPECTIVES: PLAYERS IN THE GAME

Obviously, some of the important players in the budget game have a control orientation. There are actually several other, seemingly opposing perspectives in the game. These form what could be described as a dual dichotomy, illustrated in Figure 3-1.

Some additional discussion of each perspective or term in Figure 3-1 may be helpful to understand the agendas that may develop in the game. We also must recognize that there are exceptions and that overgeneralizing may be unfair and dangerous to your mission.

The first term in Figure 3-1 is control. As mentioned, this is the typical perspective of the fiscal bureaucrat. Some official titles often given to this position are Finance Officer, Director of Finance, Budget Officer, Budget Analyst, and Finance Clerk. They often are accused of not caring about the needs of the fire department. In the words of one frustrated fire executive, "Those people know the cost of everything . . . and the value of nothing!" Sometimes it may seem that these individuals are more concerned that budget forms are filled out properly than whether you have the resources necessary for effective programs. Occasionally this may even be true.

The fiscal bureaucrat could also easily turn this discussion around and point out that fire officers typically do not understand the fiscal officer's job and its pressures. One of their primary responsibilities is to keep everyone—yes, even you—out of trouble. They must be able to assure elected officials, CEOs, and other concerned parties that the jurisdiction's financial and other

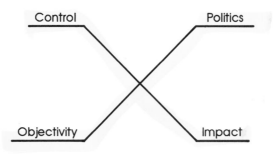

Figure 3-1. Dual Dichotomy

resources are protected and accounted for, where income and expenses stand relative to expectations (budget), that the cash flow is being optimally managed, that idle funds are earning the highest returns with acceptable risks and will be available when needed, and that legal and contractual requirements in the fiscal affairs of each agency are up to date. Perhaps by showing a greater interest in and understanding of, these responsibilities, the fire executive can further the department's mission with these individuals.

The bottom line objective of "control" is to ensure that what we are doing is being done efficiently, and that legal, contractual, policy, and procedural requirements are being followed.

The second term, impact, has to do with the bottom line, with effectiveness, or are we doing the right thing? Having a positive impact in the community, consistent with the department's mission, is the dominant perspective of the progressive program manager. Rules, regulations, line-item accounting, purchasing policies, forms, and paperwork often seem to be obstacles to delivering an effective program. As much as the fire executive may desire it, it rarely occurs that a lump sum is allocated to the department or program with instructions to spend it, without restriction, for maximum benefit to the community.

In terms of politics, the most obvious key political players are, of course, the elected officials. Their bottom line often seems obvious, i.e., to get re-elected. In fact, most take their role as policymakers very seriously. They often are frustrated by a lack of adequate information, which would allow them to do their job of setting acceptable risk and service levels (consistent with resources at their disposal) through budgeting and policy. In the absence of risk and service level analysis information, elected officials are left only with line-item budget proposals to scrutinize, something they know the public expects of them.

On whom are elected officials dependent for accurate, objective risk and service level analysis? The fire chief and his staff, that's who! Contrary to the impression they give some fire officers, elected officials are not bestowed, through the ballot box, with expert knowledge about every jurisdictional service. With this knowledge, the fire chief must use discretion and finesse in educating elected officials.

Sometimes the chief's efforts at "education" will be blocked by other political players, such as nonelected, nonfire-service folk, like city or county managers and staff, and other department heads, all of whom have their own agendas. These individuals often serve as official (or self-appointed) filters or screens for the elected officials, insulating them from the potentially overwhelming volume of pressure from various interests, or from interests contrary to their personal agenda. City and county staff sometimes perceive or impose more screening when they deal with department staff than with the public or community (special interest) groups. Again, the chief must use finesse, tact, and diplomacy in getting the department's message across to elected officials. (A more thorough discussion of message packaging is included later in this chapter.)

The perspective of community (special interest) groups also can be described as political. Many public information and public relations presentations are actually subtle attempts by the chief to gain their support for upcoming budget battles.

One of the most valuable skills for the chief officer in his dealings in the political arena is the ability to identify and mesh with the WIIFM ("What's in it for me?," pronounced wif'em) of the individual or group at hand. Whether elected, nonelected, or community group, the chief needs to step out of the department perspective and sell the program as good for the community from that group's perspective.

Not to be overlooked in the political arena is the department's members—the rank and file. The chief must remember that from the members' perspective, their chief is the agent of the city or county. The members often are not privy to the "big picture" insight that the chief may have about resource limits and other constraints. They also have a WIIFM that needs to be identified and understood. One thing the chief can do is to Make Thinking Visible, that is, as much as possible, share the vision of the future, and the changes it will bring with department members.

The last term referred to in Figure 3-1 is objectivity. Everything the department does, everything it consumes, and produces, even the effect it has on the community, is quantifiable. All programs, old and new, have measurable costs, measurable production, and measurable impact. In the purely objective world, programs can be analyzed in terms of their cost-benefit, and prioritized for funding with available resources.

While it is recognized that objective data and analysis are the best foundation for budget justification, there are some pitfalls. First, the cost in time, effort, expertise, and other resources to do thorough cost-benefit analysis may be more expensive than the difference in the benefit of implementing a less analyzed and somewhat less effective program. Second, and probably most significant, is that even if the effort of thorough cost-benefit analysis is undertaken, there is no guarantee that the best (or any) program will be selected and funded in the political arena. Third, cost-benefit analysis isn't an exact science; when undertaken by executives unpracticed in its execution, overly optimistic benefits and underestimated costs are common.

This should not be construed as an argument against doing cost-benefit analysis. Rather, it underscores again the conflicting views that will need to be evaluated and balanced in the local environment. The time and expertise available, the local political and economic situation, the size and scope of the problem, and the cost of the proposed solution(s) must be examined to determine if a full cost-benefit analysis is justified. Often, less intense professional staff estimates are adequate. (Professional, in this case, means relevant knowledge, research, and experience applied to the evaluation, not necessarily "paid").

A balancing act

To whom does the challenging job of keeping this dual dichotomy (control/impact, politics/objectivity) in balance belong? The fire chief, of course! At times, the progressive chief functions in any one of these four perspectives, although there are appropriate times for each. Most of the time progressive chiefs exert their time and effort at the fulcrum, ensuring balance. Consider this analogy: if an overload of politics is tilting the system one way, what does the chief need to do? Focusing more effort on the objectivity arm is one way to regain balance. Another is to resist the political weight, by pushing up on that arm. Often it is easier to focus more effort on objectivity.

One inappropriate perspective that hasn't been mentioned is that the fire department often makes its self-interests the **mission,** as if the department existed in a vacuum, or was someone's private empire. While these views sound extreme, they are not untypical of bureaucracies. The agency—its growth, rules, regulations, policies, forms, procedures, chain of command, rank perks, and yes, even its tradition—becomes a part of the mission. How often have you dealt with a bureaucracy of some type and been left with the impression that the prevailing attitude was, "This would be a really good place to work, if it wasn't for all these pesky customers!"? A fire service manifestation of the same attitude is evident when you walk into a fire station as an out-of-town visitor, in civilian clothes, and are greeted with, "What'a you want? (you're bothering our TV program and we would just as soon have you go away!)"? Thankfully, most departments aren't like that.

The fire service, while remembering and cherishing its tradition, must never forget that it exists to serve its customers (the community), and that the community and its needs are changing. The fire service also must change. It will change. The question is, who will influence and control its change? Will it be external influences that view the department as an ineffective, inefficient, reactive, **expense** to the community, or will it be the department's leadership (formal and otherwise) who recognize not only the need to be proactive in changing the department, but, to the degree possible, active in changing the community in a way that reduces the need for response resources?

The most noble efforts of the fire service are those in which it strives to put itself out of business, at least in terms of its traditional combat role. While to do this entirely is impossible, it may be feasible to effect changes in the community that will reduce the demand for combat resources.

The department that resists changing its role and responsibilities to include anything other than traditional combat is probably in trouble already. (In this context, traditional combat refers to on-scene fire suppression, heavy rescue, and hazardous materials release control operations.) Such a department should not try to justify its entire budget based on emergency operations alone. In a study of three departments: large (500+ members), medium (150), both fully paid, and one small combination paid (30)/volunteer (45), the **maximum** average percentage of time spent in traditional combat was only 1.8 percent. While it is true that individual companies, primarily in inner city areas, often record higher percentages, their averages still remain in the single digits.

Success in budgeting depends to a considerable degree on the community's perception of the fire department's value to the community. While this public opinion extends to the public's elected officials, it must begin within the department itself. That is, the department and its membership must project their value to the community.

It was mentioned earlier that line-item budgeting causes critical focus on the department as an expense; on the money and community resources it consumes. It was also mentioned that the real job of elected officials is to set acceptable risk and service levels in the community, consistent with available resources. Is there a way to change the fundamental focus of budgeting, the way the elected officials, the public, and the fire department look at the department and its role and value in the community?

THE FIRE DEPARTMENT AS AN OPEN SYSTEM

Perhaps a model will help to illustrate the department, community, and focus of various budgeting systems. An open system is one that receives input (in our case, policy, money, and other resources), transforms the raw materials (procedures, processes, production), and outputs to the environment finished products and services. Besides the inputs, the system also is affected by environmental pressures (service demands, hazards, special interest groups). These pressures can cause changes in the transformation process (new training, response plans, modified interpretations of regulations). Like most open systems, the fire department also has an impact, through its outputs, on the environment, the community. In the model these impacts are called outcomes, the effect of the department's outputs interacting with the environment.

It is in the analysis and projection of community outcomes that the fire department can change the perception it has of itself, the perception the public has, the focus of the budgeting process, and provide elected officials a more obvious connection between risk, service levels, and budget.

At the beginning of the chapter, the definition of financial management

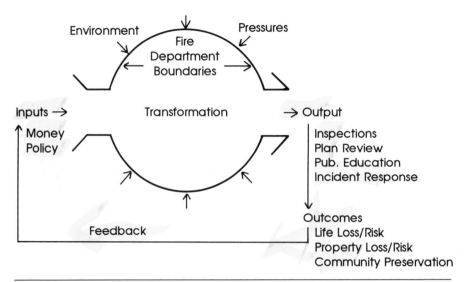

Figure 3-2. Fire Department as an Open System

concluded with the phrase ". . . **to Accomplish An End.**" The **End** in question should be the outcomes, not the outputs, of our financial management efforts. That is, the budgeting of resources should be done with the objective of affecting community life, property, and environmental safety, or other community-based outcomes, rather than to build stations and hire personnel. Even responding to alarms or performing inspections is *output* oriented; emergency response represents a failure, while inspections sometimes are considered an unwelcome intrusion.

Fire and rescue as a system of systems

Before we tear into the meat of a budgeting system, it may be useful for us to step back. The department and its leadership need to recognize that maximum positive change toward a safer community (and successful emergency operations) is dependent on many other organizations (systems) working together toward that end.

Figure 3-3 indicates that some of the department's outputs serve as inputs, or, in some cases, external pressures to other systems. Other departments in turn, further transform the fire department's contribution and their own resources to produce outputs that have an impact on the outcomes the fire department also wishes to effect. In some cases, others produce an impact in the community that is indirectly related to fire department outcomes; for example, public works strives for good streets and traffic patterns among other things. That supports good response times and creates less wear and tear on apparatus. This type of support may be viewed as a positive environmental pressure or input depending on how directly it contributes to the outcomes of the fire department.

In isolation, when looking only at its own perspective as a response agency, the fire department is often quick to propose new stations, apparatus, and additional personnel for every fire-related problem. Consider the following story.

The outcry was severe after losses involving 2 isolated fires in seasonal housing, 12 miles up a mountain pass from the district's population center. While the community proper had 16,000 residents, with appropriate protection from 1 station, the entire mountain pass had fewer than 400 seasonal residents. Together the two fires resulted in seven fatalities, tragedies for sure. The department had proposed, and actually had begun raising funds for a modest station, that, with apparatus and equipment, was to cost $350,000. That cost, of course, was not to include staffing; volunteer personnel were to be recruited from among the 400 residents. Finally, someone said, "Wait, what is it we wish to accomplish?"

The initial response was, "Build a new station!"

"No," the person said, "I mean, why? A station right up the road, even a manned station, wouldn't have saved any of those people!"

Working with the Jaycees, the district raised $10,000 and bought smoke detectors, not only for every dwelling up the mountain valley, but

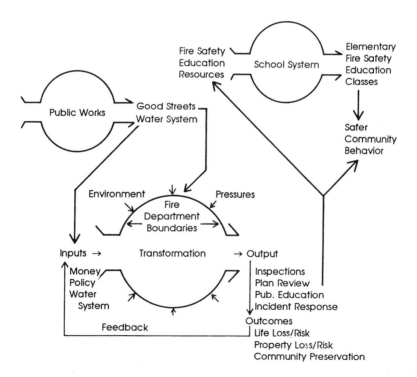

Figure 3-3. A System of Systems

for anyone else in the community who requested one. A total of 500 hours was devoted to installation, voluntary home inspections, and instruction on detector care, maintenance, and other safety concerns. During the voluntary inspections, four defective heating appliances and/or flue installations were discovered (the cause in at least one of the fatal fires) and corrected, in addition to other hazards. An annual battery replacement program was funded by members of the Chamber of Commerce.

The only substantial occupancy up the mountain valley, a small ski resort, agreed to install a complete sprinkler system and provide housing and initial manpower for a four-wheel-drive first response vehicle to be provided by the district. It was shown that the combination of sprinklers and local fire apparatus would result in insurance savings that would pay for the sprinkler system in just over five years.

This points out the need to look beyond solutions that involve only new apparatus or stations, or more personnel. In the table below, several key organizations are listed, along with their primary responsibilities in, and contributions to, the fire and rescue system:

Table 3-1.
Key Organizations and Their Responsibilities

Police Department	Traffic/crowd control; police authority in arson investigations.
Public Works	Fire protection water system; streets; heavy equipment.
Building Insp. Dept.	Ensure safe building construction.
Schools	Safety education.
Hospitals	Emergency room services; Training & medical director to FD EMS program; field response in mass casualty incidents.

A worthwhile exercise for fire department staff and other principals is to modify and expand this list as appropriate for the local environment.

STRATEGIC PLANNING IN FINANCIAL MANAGEMENT

After first realizing that the department does not exist in a vacuum and, second, that it is not alone in its effort to have a positive impact on the community, it is worthwhile to **define** what that impact will be in the future and to make it **visible** for all to strive toward.

Traditional long-range planning consists of projecting future needs based on historic data. In the fire service this involves analyzing the run history, apparatus maintenance logs, records of employee age and turnover rates, and projected population growth to determine new station and other capital expansion, apparatus replacement, and personnel projections. These items all have obvious financial implications and are worthwhile components of agency fiscal planning.

Strategic planning differs somewhat. While long-range planning is based on an assumption of maintaining at least a semblance of the status quo, strategic planning assumes a future full of change. Again the question is asked, "Whose vision of the future?" "Whose change?" In strategic planning the guiding members of the organization envision the future and design the incremental steps to make it a reality. The strategic plan doesn't become real, and is no more than a nice exercise in "what if's," until a budget reflects and supports the implementation of those first incremental steps. Strategic planning is the glue that holds year-to-year budgets together.

Although the complete strategic planning process is beyond the scope of this chapter, there are many excellent texts and other training opportunities available that offer thorough coverage. This section focuses on the fire service's application of strategic planning versus the type typically found in the private sector (business enterprise). A few general comments are in order, however, because they are so crucial to the success of not only strategic planning, but the future health of the department:

- There is great trepidation about the amount of time strategic planning takes. The truth is, you can't afford not to plan, and you must plan at several levels: strategic, tactical, and operational. The time you save in the long run (by not floundering) more than offsets the initial investment. Also, a strategic plan doesn't need to be the monumental undertaking (in time and effort) that many fear. It should not go into every operational detail. As the name implies, it identifies big picture issues and direction. Defining every detail tends to put blinders on otherwise creative people. Precise operational planning is best left for those responsible for the operation—the managers and doers of the programs in question.
- The strategic plan should be a dynamic, living document. Using it as a framework for decisionmaking and reflecting it in budgeting can help make it so.
- While it is the "glue that holds multiyear budgets together," a strategic plan is not set in concrete. Rather, it should be reviewed and modified appropriately on a periodic basis; doing this annually, prior to budget planning, would be a reasonable schedule.

- Any planning effort must be undertaken with appropriate levels of involvement. As a general guideline, three constituency groups should be represented:
  1. Those in charge of money and policy. For strategic planning this typically would be the chief of department. Support and authorization from the mayor or city manager would be great. CEOs must show commitment.
  2. Those responsible for managing implementation, including any experts (from inside or outside the department) in the subject area.
  3. Those affected by the implementation in significant ways; this group actually consists of many constituencies and would include, at a minimum, the rank and file, and, if possible, in the case of strategic planning, citizen advisors. Each group has its own "WIIFM" and must be identified and included for its members' own talents and special needs.

Together, this team can develop and define a picture of the community of the future as it relates to fire and life safety (and other issues the group wishes to include), and the role of the fire department as the focus agency in the community system for achieving that future. If the chief develops the strategic plan without this team involvement, it will be his vision only. The opportunity for synergism is lost, and, just as importantly, there is no opportunity for others to "buy in." It always will be the chief's plan, not "everyone's plan."

Although personal vision is important to formulate this picture of the department's future, the guiding members must do more than simply polish the crystal ball. With all data available, the team must weigh the probability of all possibilities. This study should include a thorough review of:

- National and international fire service trends and available technology: emerging sprinkler and detection technology, compressed air foam pumpers, automatic defibrillators, etc.;
- Political and cultural growth in the community: its current and potential future readiness for more comprehensive codes;
- Community hazards, age and condition of the structures protected, trends in population and demographics;
- Economic and tax trends: continuing pressure to do more with less, especially fewer personnel;
- Current productivity, both actual and what is perceived by the public and elected officials;
- Current and future organizational Strengths, Weaknesses, Opportunities and Threats (SWOTs). SWs are internal; OTs are external. Some examples are depth of personnel talent and training (S or W), scandals in the building inspection department (maybe O, unless the fire depart-

ment has similar skeletons, then a T), public dissatisfaction with the private EMS provider (maybe an O); and

* Organizational culture and readiness for change (S or W from SWOT).

Defining desirable outcomes

The strategic planning process will produce a number of tangible products. Even if your agency chooses not to approach strategic planning as a formal process, the following items are crucial in our continuing discussion of fire service financial management, and, potentially, to your own agency's success.

Mission statement

A mission statement defines why your agency exists. If your mission seems obvious, and you don't feel it needs to be articulated and formally put in writing, try this exercise: ask *x* members of your department to put in writing why they think your department exists. You will get x different answers. Extend the exercise to other elected and appointed officials, and perhaps some citizens. You'll have quite a collection of what is hoped are similar statements of purpose; at the same time you'll also see many stereotypical views and outright misconceptions.

It's a good idea to keep the mission statement short, to make it easy to recall at least its essence if not its exact wording. It should define, in broad strokes: *what* primary *outcomes* the agency hopes to achieve, *who* are its customers, and *how* outcomes will be achieved (primary outputs). Here's a generic example:

> Our mission is to protect life and property [primary outcomes] from fire and other emergencies within the community [who] through public education, code management, and incident response [how].

The exact wording should be defined in local terms, using input from the three constituency groups as outlined above. (Remember, a mission statement written by the chief in isolation, without input from others, will always be just the chief's mission.)

The following phrases should be avoided, if possible. They create clutter and can be a source of pitfalls. However, it sometimes is necessary to include them to get political buy-in by some constituencies:

> ". . . state-of-the-art . . ." or ". . . best available . . ." or ". . . highest quality . . ." are subjective (in whose judgment?) and sound expensive.

". . . with the resources provided . . ." and ". . . in the most economical manner . . ." generally may be considered to be assumed.

Saying, "for the citizens," "taxpayers" "property owners," "visitors,"
etc., can potentially sound exclusionary unless you list them all; then it
gets rather long. "Community" is inclusive and has a warm sound.

Some alternate outcome phrases that can work well include:

". . . minimize life loss, suffering, and damage" and . . . "due to
fire, medical, and environmental emergencies . . ." The latter phrase
attempts to identify the agency's "distinctive competence" as it differs
from the police department, for example. Including "environmental" not
only encompasses disasters of all kinds, but also reflects the growing role
of many departments in community "safe environment" management.
Such relevant programs as household hazardous waste disposal, hazardous
materials use permits, weed and refuse abatement, abandoned property
abatement, and assumption of all building inspection responsibility would
be consistent with the inclusion of "environmental" in the mission
statement.

A subtle message about priority can be achieved by listing items in a certain order: ". . . through public education, code management, and incident
response."

Notice also, that the "how" does NOT say ". . . with a Class A pumper
every 1.5 miles, staffed with a minimum of 4 trained personnel . . ."
Everything in the mission statement should be broad and unconstrained. It
should give basic direction, but allow for creativity and flexibility.

Goal statements and impact objectives

Developing goals and impact objectives that define and articulate the system's desired outcomes for the community forms the foundation of budget justification. See page 60 for the open system diagram and the location of
outcomes in that model.

For the purpose of this chapter, goals and impact objectives both articulate
desired community outcomes; the difference is in the precision of the
specification.

Goals tend to be broader, but more focused than the mission statement.
They generally are open-ended (the implication being long in term). Goals may
serve to provide direction to specific divisions or functional areas, or to the
entire department.

Objectives (any kind) are specific statements of desired, measurable outcome over a period of time.

Compare the following statements:

"Reduce life loss and injuries from fire in our community."

"By 1999, reduce the 3-year average life loss and injury rates from fire in our community by 30 to 35 percent, based on the 3-year average as of 1994. Approximately 18 lives are projected to be saved over the 5-year period."

The first is a goal. The second in an impact objective. Both refer to a desired outcome in the community. We'll look back at these examples shortly and discuss the purpose of each in budget development and justification. But first, think back to the introduction of this chapter where it was argued that financial management is easier, and more straightforward, in private enterprise, because everything boils down to **profit.**

Let's answer the question, "Where should emergency managers look for measurable indicators of their business condition or success (their profit)?" Compare some typical strategic impact areas from private enterprise with equally valid "profit" areas for our fire/rescue system.

Just as in private enterprise, the value of defining goals is limited to the use that can be derived from having more direction of purpose. This can be valuable as you turn staff creativity loose on developing proposals for programs to address the goals. Goals that address the above impact areas are weak (but better than internal perspective verbiage) in terms of justifying the department budget because they use words like "improve" or "reduce"; in each case "how much" is left unanswered and is subject to interpretation and by whom? See the examples on pages 68 to 71 and 114 and 115.

In the ideal application of these concepts, the guiding members of the department would first define the mission, then develop more focused goals that would address the impact areas listed above. The members and functional division managers then would analyze potential programs' prob-

Table 3-2.
Desirable Outcome Indicators

Private Enterprise	Fire/Rescue System
Profit	Life loss (Saved) or at risk.
Return on investment	Property loss (Saved) or at
Market share	risk.
Name recognition	Community preservation.
Reduce cost of production	Quality of Life.
	Reduce the total cost of system

able impact(s) in measurable terms (impact objectives) based on various output productivity levels (process objectives). Costs are determined by creating enabling objectives and carrying out task analysis. The various programs then can be compared based on expected impact, output levels, and cost, which allows proposals to be prioritized for inclusion in the budget document.

Impact objectives are both fundamental to sound, solid budget justification, and a crucial product of strategic planning. They are how the fire service can show and measure its success, and how, through skilled definition, you can change the focus of your budget proposal document.

Life-loss impact objectives seem obvious enough. Life loss at the national statistical level was reduced nearly 50 percent in 10 years (1980 to 1990) as specified by the National Fire Prevention and Control Act of 1974 [it created the United States Fire Administration (USFA) and the National Fire Academy (NFA)]. Many of these gains have been attributed to better data collection and to widespread use of smoke detectors, both of which were USFA initiatives. At the local level, life-loss impact objectives tend to be more challenging, especially in smaller jurisdictions. The challenge is in the small data/annual experience sample. Many small jurisdictions go years without a fatality and with only a few injuries; a single incident can blow that record completely out of the water. In the example on the previous page, a periodic average was used to minimize the small data sample effect.

While lives **saved** because of direct fire department combat operations is a valid (though at least as unpredictable as life loss) annual statistic, it is seldom as readily available as loss data. Does your data system collect this data element? It requires more effort to establish, train, and evaluate standards with respect to what is a "save" (there is no slight case of death, although some "fire deaths" are actually from other causes).

Injury rates also fall within this impact category. Don't forget that life loss and injury impact objectives also pertain to, and in fact can be specifically written for, firefighter death and injury rates. We will look at this more closely later.

Using **Life Risk** impact objectives is another way to overcome small data samples. In the case of prevention programs, **at-risk** objectives are much more predictable than lives **lost** or **saved.** The use of "at-risk" objectives often requires some background statements (remember that those who review budget proposal documents sometimes lack insight into risk analysis) as shown below.

- **Background:**
  National statistics indicate that sleeping occupants are 50 percent less likely to die in a dwelling fire when smoke detectors are properly installed and operational.

- **Impact Objective:**

  Increase from 45 percent to 80 percent the percentage of residential occupancies that have properly installed, functioning smoke detectors by the end of fiscal year 199___.

Property loss impact objectives also are rather straightforward, although many of the same caveats pertaining to life loss and small data samples apply to them as well. Published standards should be reviewed and training provided to all officers who perform loss estimates. Tracking "Property Saved" adds a positive spin, but, once again, these estimates are subjective. The operative question must be, "How much property was reasonably at risk?" Did a fire in a processing machine or compactor result in saving the $8,000,000 manufacturing plant?

Again, "At Risk" is another angle of the property loss outcome area. Statistics show that the greatest factor relating to predicting property loss is age, or more specifically, currency with modern codes. An example impact objective that would be consistent with the information above would be:

Reduce from 30 to 20 percent the number of substandard building units by the end of 199___.

Other property and building construction features have been documented as having an impact on property risk: wood shake shingles, encroachment of brush and other fuels, use of fireworks, property spacing, and external finish are a few. Specific impact objectives that follow appropriate background statements could be written at the program level.

"Community Preservation" pertains to those elements, besides lives and property that make up the community. Jobs, tax base, historic and cultural value, and infrastructure (roads, bridges, other transportation facilities, utilities, etc.) are more important to the community than their monetary replacement value alone represents. Protecting and preserving these community assets may be quantified as shown below:

Reduce by 10 to 15 percent the number of jobs lost because of fire by the end of 199___ based on a 3-year average.

Stimulate a potential increase of 10 to 20 percent to the tax base [assessed valuation] in the inner city district in 199___ by improving building code compliance, and eliminating hazards and blight, thus encouraging additional investment and growth in the area.

In the first example, background on job loss history would be useful. This example is broad and could be addressed by any number of programs, most of them prevention related. The second is an example of both how focused an impact objective can be and how the fire department can provide and enjoy mutually beneficial efforts in the community with other departments and agencies, in this case, community development and renewal.

Quality of life is much more subjective in nature, and can change rapidly with one incident, or political issue. It pertains specifically to citizens' sense of well-being about their community and their lives in it, including how they feel about the job your department is doing.

Quality of life is a value-laden judgment. Take off your badge for a moment and consider your view of the fire department inspection services in each of the following situations:

You're an over-the-road truck driver who must leave your family in a large apartment building for days or weeks. You've seen fire department inspectors supervising trash removal from stairwells, maintaining sprinkler and warning systems, and upgrading emergency exits. They've even left brochures on renters' fire safety issues and offered to do an inspection of your unit.

You operate a rag goods salvage business. There is no way to predict the scheduling and volume of your inventory. The inspectors have written you up several times for overcrowding. Now they're telling you that you need to do more about enforcing a "no smoking" policy in the warehouse area. They found more evidence of smoking today, right under one of the "No Smoking" signs they made you put up several months ago.

Another drawback of "quality of life" as a performance indicator is that it is volatile—a single bad fire or other disaster, or a scandal, can cause the quality of life issue relative to the fire department to plummet. Ask anyone who lives around the Three Mile Island nuclear facility how their perception of quality of life changed in a single day.

This impact area is more difficult to quantify, but with some effort it can be done and may be well worth it. There are several valid approaches; in fact, the more ways you measure it the better. A simple accounting of cold-prickly versus warm-fuzzy letters (complaints and thank-you letters), a formal community survey, and an "after-the-fire" postpaid feedback questionnaire left with all customers can prove valuable in assessing quality of life. To be valid, such questionnaires must be left with, or sent to, all customers (or else to a truly random sample), not just the happy customers. (As an aside, many departments give residents and businesses a complete "After-the-Fire" information packet that outlines everything from how to document losses, and handle foodstuffs, smoke stains, and odors, to lists of resource contractors and public assistance agencies. The USFA has sample packets you can customize and have printed for your community.)

Some examples of "Quality of Life" impact objectives:

- Improve the compliment/complaint letter ratio from five to one to 10 to one in the calendar year 1995.
- Improve the percentage of "Approve/Satisfied" ratings the fire department receives in the city services community survey from 70 to 90 percent in 1996.
- Increase from 80 to 90 percent by the end of 1997, the percentage of survey respondents who feel at least reasonably safe from fire, knowledgeable about accessing emergency services, and informed on fire and safety practices.

Another measurable quality of life issue is the public's impression of timely response. In an interview with a witness to a gang assault, a local news reporter asked the shadowed figure, "Why did you FIRST call the fire department with a report of a fire at that address when you knew it was an assault?" The reply, "Because I knew the fire department would provide the fastest, nosiest, most aggressive response! . . . and when they got here they would give good care to the victim."

It is worth mentioning, as it was with the volatility issue, that because quality of life is so subjective a department can "gain points" or hurt itself, as the case may be, purely through image. A department that works at keeping its resources—human, apparatus, and facilities—fit and looking good without looking extravagant can contribute more to public approval than a department full of slouch bellies sitting on a bench out front.

Even the best intentions can have an adverse effect on image packaging. For example, one department that was promoting personnel fitness set aside exercise time at shift change and at the end of the "productive" workday (5:00 p.m.). Operationally, it made sense: departing members could shower after they were relieved by incoming personnel. At 5:00 p.m., personnel could change from dress uniform to sweats, work out, shower as necessary, and then change to evening uniform. However, what did the public see? During their morning and afternoon commutes to and from work every day, they saw fire personnel engaged in recreational activities. They saw fire apparatus parked at city parks with their personnel jogging or using physical fitness trails, and they saw basketball or volleyball games in progress behind (or in some cases on the front drive or front yard of) fire stations. Quality of life looked pretty good for the firefighters, but not for the citizens! This type of image could hurt later in the political/budget justification arena. Don't construe this as an argument against physical fitness programs; instead, think about public perception, and schedule wisely or inform the public as appropriate. Many departments have large signs and banners for apparatus that proclaim, "Your tax dollars at work: personnel conducting fire prevention inspections. Available for emergencies via two-way radio."

Quantifying quality of life and using it as the only indicator of system success would be dangerous at best. But taken in context with other, more objective measures it can be very valuable, not for justifying the budget, but to gain an understanding of, and insight into, the community's sense of well-being and the environment in which the budget justification will occur. It can also serve as an indicator of community readiness for particular types of programs and other change.

Total system cost is the other side of the ledger. The four indicators of "profit" above, must be balanced with the cost of the entire system. Many detailed indicators of efficiency are there if you seek them out.

By including total system cost, reductions also can be considered as "profit." Total cost refers to all expenses incurred to provide fire protection, not just the public fire department budget. These include insurance rates, the fire protection portion of the water supply system, and private protection facilities.

Many communities are finding it both economically and politically appropriate and beneficial for the community to shift the allocation of fire protection costs from public to private funding, especially for special or extraordinary hazards. Such an atmosphere makes hazard impact fees, benefit assessment charges, and service cost recovery charges approachable subjects. These topics will be covered more extensively in the Revenues section.

Cost-reduction and cost-avoidance impact objectives are often the best justification for programs in nonload-bearing functions, that is, support functions that don't directly deliver products and services to the community, such as administration and planning, and fiscal resource management.

Examples for a new computerization program:

- Reduce by 60 percent in 1995 the staff time and expense of searching for and compiling decisionmaking information.
- Avoid the cost of an additional full-time clerk position that would be required to meet new state incident reporting requirements effective 1996.
- Increase collections for EMS billings from 48 percent to 75 to 80 percent in fiscal year 1997. This will result in an additional $00,000 in revenue generation.

Programs within other support functions, such as human and physical resource management, can often be justified best by using very focused impact objectives:

- Reduce to zero deaths, injuries, and damage that occur because of on-scene fire department equipment failure, attributable to insufficient maintenance.
- Eliminate firefighter injuries and potential department liability attributable to the use of substandard protective equipment.

Additional examples will be included in the Justification section.

Process objectives

Another product of strategic planning is high-level process objectives. These are measurable targets of our system's outputs. Remember: process objectives are used in **conjunction** with impact objectives, not in **lieu** of them. Together they define, to the policymakers and the funding authority, in measurable terms, **what** (impact objectives) we want to accomplish in the community and **how** (process objectives) we expect to achieve the impacts.

Process and Activity Accounting is one area public sector agencies traditionally have quantified, sometimes to the point of counting for the sake of counting. If a nonfire-service person could reasonably ask, "Why do that?" (the answer isn't obvious by looking at the item counted), you need to look deeper for the desired impact objective. For example:

"Our agency conducted 187 inspections in the first quarter of 1995."

Why?

"To eliminate hazards in those businesses."

Why and how many?

"We found 236 hazards and violations and abated 194 of them. Those hazards represented 55 percent of the causal factors in 20 commercial and industrial fires last year. We are tracking the remaining violations through followups and long-term corrective plans for expensive corrections."

What is your bottom line?

"To reduce our commercial and industrial fire losses by 10 to 20 percent and to protect our tax base and jobs in the community through similar reductions in fires."

Beyond better justifications there is reason to pursue these correlations. Process and activity accounting is an important indicator of productivity in the fire department, but not by itself. When it is related to desired and actual program impacts and costs, it becomes an important quantifiable indicator of agency efficiency and effectiveness. In it we often find level-of-effort measures that help to determine the best alternative between competing approaches to a desired impact objective.

Functional planning, organizational design, and budgeting

Many departments discover, through the strategic planning process or for other reasons, that the traditional organization chart sometimes hinders mission accomplishment.

Picture for a moment a paid department, that, like most, has 90 percent or more of its budget in personnel costs and most of those personnel are in the organization chart branch labeled "Operations." Even though less than 2 percent of personnel time is spent in combat operations, there is tremendous pressure to maintain response company staffing levels in lieu of personnel assigned to "nonemergency" branches of the chart. Going a step further, picture in this same department the recognized strategic need to prevent fires through occupancy inspections. Involving the companies in the inspections sounds right, and it sounds easy. However, statements like, "That's not my job! Look at the organization chart . . . it says 'Operations'!" are not uncommon.

An alternative view of the organization, one that focuses on what gets accomplished, not who does it, may be helpful. In a functional model, everyone in every rank, regardless of the organizational box in which they are placed on the chart, has responsibilities in every functional area. Yes, the percentage of time spent will vary according to rank and assignment.

Before we look at a generic fire department functional model, consider this definition:

> A function is a collection of closely related processes, products, and services, that directly support a major area of the endeavor. Load-bearing functions are those whose primary products and services are deliverables to the customers. All others are support functions.

All businesses will have functions in three broad categories: load-bearing (produces and delivers products/services to customers); resource management; and administration and planning. As we look briefly at a generic fire department model, keep in mind that while it could be valid for just about any department, it won't be for yours unless you involve the right people in creating the definition. If this material provides ideas and a basis for discussion to your team, great, but ensure that your team has the chance to be just that. The same observations that pertain to group development of a mission statement are relevant here.

A typical business will have six to nine functional areas under the three broad categories (umbrellas). The fire service is no different:

In Table 3-4 the model actually shows a flat structure with each function contributing to mission accomplishment. The broad categories typically are discarded after the functional model gains consensus. With more than ten functions, the category titles could be retained to keep span-of-control concepts intact.

Table 3-3.

Load Bearing	Resource Management	Admin. & Planning
Safety Education	Human Resource Mgmt	Admin. Function
Code Management	Physical Resource Mgmt	Business Affairs
Incident Readiness & Response	Fiscal Management	Planning

Table 3-4.

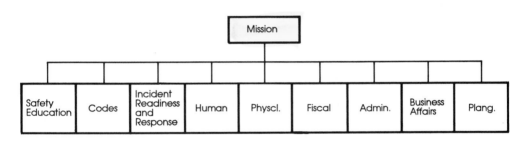

Each function would be defined and further subdivided into programs and services (those for internal consumption are usually called "processes").

The functional model integrates with the organization chart only to the degree that each function would have a high-level manager assigned responsibility for functional coordination. Each program (service, process) would have a program manager. A given manager might have responsibility for more than one function or program, and program managers often are not officers in the traditional sense.

The functional model serves a number of potential roles in budgeting:

- It provides logical groupings of programs presented in a program budget or in derivative formats.
- It provides high-level focus for programs and activities because each belongs to a function and contributes directly to the department's mission.
- It can provide a more realistic picture of personnel cost allocation, according to what the department actually does. A simple tally kept for

30 to 90 days for each rank can provide a good estimate of actual effort spent in each functional area (or at the program level, if desired).

• It can give elected officials and department members alike a new appreciation of the diversity of functions and programs the department provides to the community.

As part of the strategic planning process, a set of primary goals (the function's mission), impact, and process objectives should be developed for each functional area. Each function should be consistent with, and contribute to, the future as it is envisioned in the strategic plan; the incremental steps to that future are actually budgeted and implemented through functional activities.

Contingency planning

No planning process would be complete without considering contingencies. Each possibility should be analyzed both for probability of occurrence and fiscal implication. For each contingency circumstance, a set of "trip-wire" indicators should be identified in advance, so the agency is not caught off guard and managers know when to implement the contingency plan features. Having a good set of contingency plans helps the organization to be proactive and results in better decisions, because the framework has been laid in a pressure-free environment.

Some contingencies are so likely to occur that resources should be budgeted: for example, blizzards and ice storms in the Midwest. Not all contingency plans are purely operational in nature; don't overlook labor unrest, jurisdictional fiscal crises, proposed annexations and consolidations.

Managers often think of contingencies only in terms of negative circumstances. Picture a strategic plan that aims for maximum safety in the community through education, code enforcement, and built-in protection. The most likely code enforcement scenario would be increasingly stricter measures being adopted every few years and applied to new construction. But, an incident, change in political body, or breakthrough in technology causes a retroactive sprinkler ordinance to be passed and applied to all occupied structures. It's probably a good idea to have some contingency plans ready for positive, though not entirely likely, occurrences. The organization's image suffers if it flounders for months developing an implementation plan for something it had asked for for years.

A summary of strategic planning

Much has been covered in this section. It would be good to recap strategic planning and its role in budgeting before going on. Even if your agency doesn't adopt strategic planning as a formal process, the more of these principles you can put into practice, the more success you're likely to have.

Strategic planning gives the guiding members of the organization an opportunity to envision the future and design the incremental steps to make that future a reality.

Like any planning, strategic planning should involve three constituency groups:

- Those in charge of money and policy;
- Those responsible for managing implementation; and
- Those affected in significant ways by the implementation.

Make Thinking (and Plans) **Visible!**

The strategic plan should take a community perspective.

Thoroughly scan the department's environment—internal and external—city, county, state, and federal for issues affecting the community's future and the department's role in it.

The department's mission should be defined and communicated to all.

The agency's "profit," (its desired outcomes for the community) should be identified and expressed as impact objectives:

- Life loss (saved) or at risk,
- Property loss (saved) or at risk,
- Community preservation,
- Quality of life, and
- Total system cost.

CAN IT MAKE A DIFFERENCE?

How much of a difference can these principles make? In testimonials from departments that have developed and repackaged their budgets, implementing most or all of these concepts, it has made a big difference! When their packages included mission, desired outcome goals, a functional model organization of programs with defined impact and process objectives, and cost figures (in broad summary form if possible) in the prescribed format. That difference was often described as profound. In more than one case the bottom line was that they received, for the first time in their history, everything they asked for. In one case, the city council approved more funds than were requested, directing the department to implement one program city-wide that the department had proposed pilot testing in one district. (The program was to establish a "paramedic engine" in the hope of solving, from the department's perspective, the problem of medic unit personnel burnout. After the hearing, one council member, who was trying to help the chief understand what had happened, said, "How could we fund that program in only one district, when your chart clearly showed we were talking about lives saved or not! Statistically, in my district alone, we could be talking about two to four lives a year; I did the math!" The mayor, who had been listening to the conversation, started to walk away, then turned, slapped the chief on the shoulder, took his hand and said, "You guys finally got your act together, didn't you!" In the end, the paramedic engines did, as in other departments, significantly improve the burnout problem.)

Of course, your own success is not guaranteed; your own political and economic environment, and your department's fiscal credibility will play a role. Follow these concepts, and even if you're not as successful as you hope to be, you'll be on your way to improving the credibility issue, if you have one.

DETERMINING COSTS

Using Figure 3-2, the Open System Model, we are working our way backward from outcomes (impact objectives) to outputs (process objectives). We now are ready to back right into the transformation area. Here, the raw materials (resources and policy) are converted into output production capability. At this point we can determine, or at least estimate, the costs of producing the outputs.

Enabling objectives

In our effort to keep thinking visible and quantified, we can use a third type of objective—the enabling objective. An enabling objective is the measurable result of some activity, that, taken by itself, does not produce a complete program or deliverable service. Its role in budgeting is one of cost determination. All steps (enabling objectives) are identified as measurable milestones toward producing output (a process objective) intended to result in a particular outcome (impact objective).

For each enabling objective, costs are determined based on planned resource allocation. These costs should include not only new capital items, expansion personnel, and operating expenses, but also the cost of existing personnel. Only by tallying all expenses (and levels of effort) can competing programs be evaluated against each other and projected impact objectives for the best bang for the buck. When considering new programs, some may argue that existing personnel costs aren't real (try telling that to the finance officer, city council person, or the taxpayer at large) and shouldn't be included. Their thinking, of course, is that existing personnel costs already are included in the budget under some line item or existing program (like suppression) and that the new program will have a better chance of being adopted if those costs are not included. This thinking perpetuates the view of suppression forces as high-cost, evil necessities, while showing the cost of other programs as artificially low. The trick is to show honest level-of-effort costs without risking the loss of existing personnel if programs aren't funded. Keep track of them separately, label them as "opportunity costs" or "personnel cost reallocation," define the term as "those personnel costs budgeted under other programs, functions, categories and unavailable for deletion if this program is not funded." If the program is adopted, existing personnel will be denied the opportunity to do other activities (hence the term "opportunity costs"), even if those other activities are "nonproductive" stand-down time. The latter case is appealing to elected officials in that nonproductive, but costly time is converted to productive.

A table of enabling objectives with associated costs represents what is called a task analysis. (See the example in Table 3-5. Such information typically is not included with the budget document, but is referenced as "available details" in cases where there are questions about level of effort or cost estimates.

A brief discussion of where enabling objectives should NOT be used is in order. In dealings with fire service managers this is probably the most common type of objective seen, because, with minimal training, it's easiest to write an objective from one's own perspective. Given a blank box labeled "Program Objective(s)," on a program budget submittal form, task-oriented managers (as the fire service typically produces) will, more often than not, write task-based enabling objectives. A BAD example for the revitalized inspection program objectives: *Form code committee by October 15; hire 2 new inspectors by November 1, and study and recommend code changes/updates by November 1; pass new code by December 1, complete new inspector training by December 31; purchase new code books by January 1; provide 8 hours training times 60 personnel by February 1; identify target occupancies for inspection by February 1; develop new inspection form by February 1, and assign and inspect all target businesses by October 1; assign reinspections and extraordinary hazards to full-time inspectors.*

Put yourself in the role of an elected official who is presented with this form, among many similar others. Do you suppose you would even read it? If you did, would you like businesses in the community referred to as "targets?"

Would you wonder what constituted a target business? Would you wonder if your own was a target? Would you question the number of training hours? Would you fund this program? See page 115 for (what is hoped is) a better example for the same program.

The enabling objectives detailed above are appropriately used in a task analysis for planning program implementation and estimating program costs:

Table 3-5.

Task	Date	Resource	Effort	Cost
Form code committee	Oct. 15	F. Marshal & Chief	1 hr.	$50*
Study and recommend code changes/updates	Nov. 1	Committee	12 hrs	$240*
Hire 2 Inspectors	Nov. 1	F. Marshal & Persnl.	8 hrs	$400* $72,000
Pass new code	Dec. 1	Chief & Council	2 hrs	$80*
Train new inspectors	Dec. 31	F. Marshal Trng, Off. New insps.	40 hr 40 hr 160 hr	$1,200* $1,000* Above*
Purchase new code books	Jan. 1	F. Marshal Purchase	1 hr. 24	$35* $240
Provide 8 hours training times 60 personnel	Feb. 1	F. Marshal Trng. Offr. Shft. Prsnl.	30 hr 30 hr 480 hr	$900* $750* $9,600*
Identify target occupancies for inspection	Feb. 1	F. Marshal	8 hr.	$280*
Develop and print new inspection form	Feb. 1	F. Marshal Printer	8 hr.	$280* $80
Assign & inspect all target occupancies	Oct. 1	Shift Personnel	2500 hrs	$50,000*
Total Costs for program				$135,035*
*Opportunity Costs				$62,715*
New Funding startup:				$72,320

*Opportunity costs = those costs budgeted under other programs and unavailable for deletion if this program is not funded.

This is an example of the type of detail that, while useful in budget development, should **not** be included with the council's package. You run the risk of inviting micromanagement and nitpicking; instead, keep it available for reference.

All task analysis and costs on all programs are collected and prioritized within the department with appropriate references to identified impact objectives. At this point costs can be packaged and transferred into the prescribed budget format.

TYPES OF BUDGETS

We have referred in passing only to several of the budget formats that exist. What has been presented to this point is, in essence, "Program Budgeting." What if, in your jurisdiction, budgets must be submitted in another form. You may ask, "Can any of this work for me?" YES! YES! YES! Consider that:

- Every budget format is able to tolerate a cover letter that includes your mission statement and desired community outcome goals.
- Presenting the identified impact objectives by functional area is a good way to provide "budget highlights," a typical element expected in a cover letter or introduction.
- Depending on the dictated budget format, what should follow (arranged functionally if possible) is a page for each program, marked appropriately as new, expansion, maintenance, or reduced funding level. Include a brief informational background segment and identify, in separate sections, its impact and process objectives. Costs should be summarized only, into categories if required: personnel, operating expenses, and capital asset items (replacement and expansion). Show personnel costs with new and opportunity costs listed separately. It is desirable in all cost categories to break out startup and recurring costs separately.

Notice what the above approach accomplishes, regardless of dictated budget format. It promotes, almost forces, a high-level focus on community impact and service-level issues. By providing this "introduction," there is less of a tendency to nitpick line-item cost details.

In this section, the principal types of budget systems are introduced, with typical features, benefits, and deficiencies discussed. For each type of budget, a discussion of the steps necessary to apply the concepts presented in this chapter is provided.

In several cases, departments have reported that jurisdictions rigidly committed to a particular budget style have changed to program budgeting city-wide after the fire department "prefaced" the required format with program impact and allocated budget summaries as described above. In at least one case, the change was "ordered" by the city council.

There are derivative forms of budgeting, many adopted locally, that attempt to retain the positive features of the original and overcome the deficiencies. Modern computerization has made this approach possible. While these forms vary by nature, we will cover typical features below under the title of "Integrative Budgeting."

Line-item budget

The form of budgeting most commonly used by governmental departments is the line-item budget, which was adopted by the federal government
in 1921. After a few experiments with other forms—the most notable and
widespread of which was Zero-Based Budgeting (ZBB) during the Carter
administration—a return was made to line-item. It allows the most fiscal control of the types examined.

In the line-item budget, expense types are identified and grouped in
general categories, most often, personnel salaries and benefits, operating
expenses, maintenance, raw materials (private enterprise), and capital facilities (often broken out in a separate "fund") and equipment. Within the
categories, specific line items are as detailed as deemed necessary by the
local jurisdiction or department. Operating expenses, for instance, can
include line-item accounts for office supplies, printed forms, heating fuel,
electric, water, phone, motor fuel, station supplies, ambulance supplies,
cleaning/laundry, etc.

The line-item budget is simple to develop. Once the line-item titles are
identified, projected expenses of that type are determined for the period of the
budget, usually by fiscal year. In practice, once a line-item budget is in place,
each line-item is increased or decreased one year to the next, based on the previous year's experience. If the concepts from the previous sections are used,
the yearly adjustments would be more related to future need rather than past
experience.

No money is spent unless it is available in the specified line account. The
line-item budget is tied directly to the accounting system. Expenditures must
be accounted for by voucher, identifying line item, date of the transaction,
amount (to the penny), to whom the funds are to be distributed, and who
authorized the expenditures.

The high degree of accounting control provided by the line-item budget is
also one of its deficiencies. Managerial creativity, initiative, and flexibility can
be stifled. The line-item identification and accounting of expenses get more
attention than program effectiveness. There is little incentive to seek innovative alternate approaches to community service delivery. Managers are reluctant to take advantage of opportunities that may arise midstream because the
expense isn't in the correct line-item account and the mechanics of line-item
transfers are so much trouble, if they are allowed at all. Applying the concepts
of this chapter to a line-item budget, a tie between the proposed transfer and
identified impact objectives, is possible. Marketing such transfers is easier
and, in turn, line-item transfers become a useful tool in applying community
impact concepts.

The focus of the pure line-item budget (one without programmatic impact
justification) is on input. There is no indication of what will be accomplished,

either output or outcome. There is no obvious connection between risk, service level, and budget. Elected officials and others have only line-item expenses to subject to critical review. Once adopted, the line-item budget application focuses on procurement.

The program manager is often handicapped, especially if line-item reductions have been made to proposed items. Program managers ask, "Does the reduction affect my program or others? Do we all share the reduction?" Occasionally program managers find that accounts into which they budgeted particular expenses have been raided by other managers whose expenses also qualify for assignment to the line account. This places the chief of department, or the delegated budget assistant, in the role of account cop. Sometimes it's the chief who did the raiding. Such an atmosphere, if condoned, also places program managers in the position of needing to justify their expenses again or spend from their accounts as soon as possible.

Another phenomenon common to line-item budgets is the arbitrary reduction or cutting of an item from one account, while leaving other items from the same program untouched. The cuts often are made to achieve some target reduction, but too many times what was cut was crucial to program implementation or delivery, leaving the manager with some allocated resources but no way to transform them into the intended program for lack of the crucial item(s). Some examples are: equipment is approved but proposed personnel or overtime are cut; a new inspector is approved but his vehicle was cut; equipment and personnel are approved but you can't train them because that account was gutted.

The ultimate example of this is when a new station is built and apparatus is purchased, but there is no funding for staffing. Many chiefs allow this, even promote it (i.e., budget for the station and apparatus, with no mention of staffing); their thinking is that once the concrete and steel are in place, the city fathers will have to provide money for staffing. After all, wouldn't it be embarrassing to the city to have a new, unstaffed station? The problem is elected officials sometimes don't have much choice—resources just aren't available. Also, they often see through this ruse. Either way, the result may be that the chief is ordered to open the station with existing personnel, by cutting other programs, or reducing staffing at other stations.

Given a mandated line-item budget, to apply the program impact concepts presented earlier, the full "Introductory package" would need to precede the required line-item format.

THE SECRET

If your jurisdiction uses a computer-based line-item budget, there is an additional approach worth investigating. You may have a full integrative-budget-capable system in place, but not know it. To see, check the identifying numbers on your printout. You may see something like:

```
Fund:____                      These two are often in the report header
Department: _ _ _ _ _          (toward the top).

Object Code           Line-item description              Last Year . . .

__ ____ __-____       Xxxxxxx xxxxxxx xxxxx        $#,###,###.##
```

Sometimes you may see this form, again in the header:

```
          Fund: 02 General      Program: 0400 Fire Department
```

Ideally, you may see:

```
     Fund: 02 General     Dept: 040 Fire Department     Program: _ _ _ _
```

Either way, you have an integrative-budget-capable system. All you need to do is assign function and program numbers using the available undesignated digits from the department number or the program number field, if available. Below is an example that uses just the department number field: 0 4 0 0

City assigned Department Number 04. The trailing 00s mean all functions, all programs totaled.

Department assigned Function Number, 10 might be for Incident Readiness and Response. The trailing 0 would mean all programs totaled.

Program number assigned within function: 11 might be Personnel Readiness, including most shift O.T.

____ When all 4 digits are put together we might have:

0412 Fire Department, Incident Readiness and Response, Apparatus and Equipment Readiness: included might be periodic performance/standards compliance tests. Actual maintenance would be under a function called "Physical Resource Management" (0452).

0413 Fire Department, Incident Readiness and Response, Mapping, Preincident and Response Planning Program.

0414 Fire Department, Incident Readiness, Hydrant Testing, Water Availability Survey Program.

0415 Fire Department, Incident Readiness and Response, Communication/Dispatch.

Of course, in this type of system, with 4 digits, the first 2 used by the city for department number would limit the department to 9 functions with 9 programs each. It probably would be better if three or four digits were available for function/program identification. Perhaps a request to the city computer services could get the system expanded, if needed.

Once the function/program numbering system is established, a line-item budget is developed for each program or function as appropriate. The object codes (line-item accounts) are the same for any and all programs, that is, if 0411 10-0010 is the salary account for incident-ready personnel activity, then 0413 10-0010 is the salary account for Mapping and Preplanning, 0414 10-0010 is the salary account for Hydrant Testing, and 0415 10-0010 is the salary account for Communication/Dispatch.

Using the common object codes, the computer can consolidate the program budgets into functional area budgets (all resources allocated to Public Education, for instance), and, of course, the entire department budget. From the city's perspective the fire department is a program, hence you may see "Fund: 02 General—Program: 0400 Fire Department" on the city budget summary and printouts.

There are many benefits of program-level development of a line-item budget. It places budget planning in the hands of the program managers who should have a more intimate understanding of the programs' needs. It also assists in allocating expenses to department activities in the form of programs, changing the perception of the department as a nonproductive, reactive expense.

MICROCOMPUTER BUDGET WORKSHEETS

If the city's line-item budget is not computer based or the numbering approaches shown above cannot be accommodated, modern microcomputer spreadsheets can be invaluable.

The first step is to create a blank worksheet template with all object code line-item accounts defined. The cell into which the dollar amount for each account will be entered can be named for easy reference from external summary worksheets (rather than remembering the exact cell address, look under "named ranges" in your spreadsheet software documentation). A copy of this blank worksheet is made for each department program, given an appropriate name, and copied into a subdirectory or folder representing this year's budget work area.

On a master worksheet (one whose purpose is to consolidate and total details), formulae or macros can be created that will link all program-detailed budgets, by line item, into any summarization that is required. (Look under "Linking Spreadsheets" or "3-D Spreadsheets" in your software documentation.) Each functional area may have a master spreadsheet totaling all programs within the function. Also, a department master would total all functions.

One of the beauties of automating such budget development process is the ease with which subsequent years can be put together. This is especially true if actual expenses are tallied, not only by line object code, but charged to specific program budgets as well. Thus the worksheets can include a "Last Year" column (copied, with values only, from the "Final" column of that year's sheet), an "Actual" column (derived from expense accounting), and a "Proposed" column. When automated spreadsheet software is used, additional features can be exploited by adding +/− adjustment opportunities to categories and line-item objects.

Performance budgeting

Introduced in the 1950s and 1960s, performance budgeting focuses on system output. Taken to the extreme, measurement is also made within the "Transformation" process (See the Open System model). Performance budgeting uses quantitative data and process objectives to show the relationships of system input and outputs of services (not outcomes). Unit costs are developed based on level of effort and units produced.

The strength of performance budgeting is in the analysis of operating efficiency: how much work is performed. Tallies and projections of how many inspections were or are to be conducted, number of hydrants tested, fires fought, hoselines stretched, and ladders raised are established with a unit cost associated with each. Methods of reducing unit costs then can be examined and established.

The weaknesses of performance budgeting include the lack of focus on outcomes; we may be doing the wrong things very efficiently. The emphasis on unit cost and production also can be carried too far—the number of forms processed, windows washed, pencils sharpened—can become the focus of management activity. When the primary objectives involve unit cost reduction, managers may overlook or avoid creative ways to achieve a more effective outcome or reduce the number of units produced because that would actually increase unit cost. As an extreme example, preventing fires increases the unit cost (not losses) per fire given the same resources. Of course, the astute manager would reallocate some of those resource expenses (using the concepts presented earlier) to prevent fires, thus not only lowering the unit cost per fire response, but creating more production units (inspections or public education contacts) to count.

Today, performance budgeting is rarely used formally, that is, in its pure form, in government service agencies, but if it is your jurisdiction's dictated budget type, you will want to work into each performance program an impact objective that shifts the focus to outcomes rather than outputs.

The techniques that were developed when performance budgeting was used widely have evolved into the time-motion and performance audit disciplines. Some of these techniques can be used appropriately without formally adopting this budget style for such things as operational analysis for effectiveness and efficiency.

For instance, numerous emergency service agencies have applied these techniques to analyze call receipt, dispatch, and response procedures down to the second. Many have shaved 20 to 45 seconds from the effective response times by providing a pre-assignment announcement of incidents, i.e., with the caller still on line, as soon as basic incident recognition data are received, the dispatcher sounds a tone followed by an announcement such as, "Structure fire, 211 North Main Street." Contrary to the fears some dispatch personnel had that such a procedure would increase the pressure to formulate a response assignment in a timely fashion, experience has shown that the pressure is actually reduced; the caller is reassured that help is already en route and often is able to calm down and provide more information. The dispatcher is able to take the few extra seconds to double-check assignment and information accuracy. Response companies generally know their districts well enough that they already are gearing up, or in worst-case scenarios, checking their maps as the actual assignment is announced. In a few cases companies may even start their engine and pull onto the pad, only to shut down if they are not assigned, and no harm has been done. If such a procedure is used, one policy must be enforced rigidly: no companies should call dispatch on the phone or radio to advise, "That's our call," or ask, "Is that ours?" Likewise, company reports of "En route" should be held until the formal assignment dispatch has been made; that is the signal that the alarm has been logged properly and units can be associated properly with the incident, especially important when dispatch is computer aided.

Zero-based budgeting

Introduced to the federal government by President Carter, Zero-Based Budgeting (ZBB) survived only four years of use at the national level. In ZBB, each program budget is developed into "decision packages" at various levels, usually at annually determined $-x\%$ decrease, level funding, and $+y\%$ increase. Proposed expense levels are summarized into personnel, operating expenses, and capital asset item (replacement and expansion) categories. In all cost categories, a breakout of startup and recurring costs generally is made. Impact (outcome) and process (output) objectives are developed for each funding level. Further, an impact statement that results from program elimination also is required (thus the name "Zero-Based").

Each program is rated on a priority basis (1, 2, 3, etc.) at various levels of review: program/division manager, chief of department, city/county manager, and elected funding officials. The overall concept is that each progressively higher level of review will consider the priorities of the lower levels as it compares programs, their impacts, costs, and available resources. The resulting budget should provide full or expanded funding for the highest priority programs (presumably those with the highest impact per cost), level or reduced funding for moderate priority programs, and reduced funding for or elimination of, lowest priority programs.

ZBB's primary benefit was the obvious policy connection between various funding levels and impacts in the community. It also had a tremendous public relations value given that government had to rejustify every dollar it received annually.

Its obvious weakness was the significant management overhead and effort necessary to develop three budgets and corresponding projected impacts for each program alternative funding level.

Program budgeting

Program budgeting packages department activities into deliverable products and services (both external and internal) with specific impacts (outcomes) identified for each program. For each program the overall cost is identified, often summarized into personnel, operating expenses, and capital asset items (replacement and expansion) categories. In all cost categories, a breakout of startup and recurring costs generally is made.

Program budgeting focuses on policy questions of community service levels, linking input (funding), output, and results (risk level) at the elected official level.

While this chapter has promoted the concepts of program budgeting, this method is not without its deficiencies. One is the misconception that program budgets produce technically rational decisions in the political environment of government. There is no guarantee that the most accurate, honest, professional, and thorough cost-benefit analysis will result in program adoption.

To be used properly, program budgeting requires both program managers who have analytical skills and appropriate data to analyze. These conditions are important because if program budgeting is left in the hands of an analytically unskilled, subjective program manager, he could produce questionable impact projections. Standards for analytical and defendable approaches must be identified and articulated, and appropriate training provided to all managers before the budget is sent to the funding body. Submitting hollow benefit projections could cause your agency or one of its managers to lose credibility. As an example, let's say that initial studies suggest that Compressed Air Foam (CAF) systems increase the extinguishing efficiency of water by close to 1,000%. An analytically unskilled, subjective program manager, anxious for CAF, might translate that 10:1 performance ratio into a 90 percent reduction in fire losses. OK, let's be more conservative: a 50 percent reduction. Still sounds great; council will go for it! If the council approves CAF and you come back showing less than a 2 percent reduction in losses, you may have just hurt your credibility, even though the 2 percent reduction paid for the system several times over. What we may have forgotten in our excitement is that 90 percent or more of the dollar losses occurred before we arrived and that the only actual 90 percent reduction would be in water damage WHEN CAF was used. But that implies that we determine and collect data on water damage. . . . This could get complicated!

A departure from the traditional organizational chart can cause a conflict between functional responsibility and organizational and financial control by the line program manager. Again, organizational training and precise definitions of responsibilities may minimize the potential problem. For example, the fire marshal—whose budget was just gutted so that no layoffs of shift personnel would occur—has assigned 120 inspections to your station this month. You, on the other hand, are under "Operations" and you have just received a memo from the operations chief advising personnel at all stations to minimize fuel consumption and hours on the apparatus. Who's in charge here anyway?

It is essential, as this example shows, that there be effective, two-way communication between budget-builders and decisionmakers.

Planning-Programming-Budgeting (PPB)

Introduced to the U.S. Department of Defense in 1961 by Robert MacNamara, PPB incorporated (in fact, introduced) many of the concepts of program budgeting. It emphasized the use of data analysis and computers to evaluate the long-term impact of alternative strategies. The key characteristic of PPB is its extended time horizon; there is a recognition that it takes many years for some programs to show measurable impact, thus, they should be authorized and funded for an extended period.

PPB's benefits are the same as those of program budgeting—the importance of relating impact objectives to budget, and the value of program structure as the basis for budget decisionmaking. Under PPB it also was recognized that budget decisions have long-range impact.

The formal structure of PPB was abandoned quickly because of its deficiencies: the system's complexity, management overhead and extensive staff support required for analysis, and the belief that a rational decision would be made based on impartial data rather than on political considerations.

The greatest pitfall, especially at the local level, was the reluctance or inability of elected bodies to commit to multiyear programs. Many elected officials don't like the idea of a future legislative body voting to withdraw support for a multiyear program they installed (they fear being seen in later years as having been fiscally reckless).

Integrative budgeting

Integrative budgeting is an attempt to keep the best features of the budget types already described while discarding many of their deficiencies. Simply stated it is program budgeting that results in a line-item budget format when one is required.

The process begins at the program level with an identification of impact and process objectives. Separate line-item budgets are developed for each program area by using computer software that consolidates individual program budgets into functional or department line-item format.

The focus of integrative budgeting is at the policy/funding level on system outcomes (impact objectives).

Because it is computer based, it can provide the ideal in fiscal control at the program level. Managers can be kept apprised of the line-item expenditures and balances for their program(s). In the ultimate system, security features prevent other managers (except the chief) from raiding unauthorized program accounts, because expenditures (purchase orders) are allowed only by program IDs and line-item account codes which are tied to user IDs, passwords, and appropriate security levels.

Integrative budgeting has two deficiencies.

The first is a dependence on computer hardware, software, and personnel. This is not a significant problem in agencies that have recognized the strategic importance of information resources and have developed their information management system to one that is organization-wide with a high level of commitment.

Second, even with adequate computer facilities and appropriate software, a great deal of effort is still needed to gather data, and analyze and correlate (often with external sources) the information necessary to establish realistic impact objectives. (Or, put another way, defining the outcomes, that will result from the outputs, that will result from the transformation of the resources within the line-item budget for the program.)

Many agencies have the technical capability to use integrative budgeting and don't know it.

PREPARING THE BUDGET DOCUMENT

Regardless of the budget style your agency uses, keep in mind these general development considerations:

- Remember the three-constituency rule: Involve those with funding and policy control; those responsible for managing implementation; and those who are affected.

- Make thinking visible!
- Push to have actual needs definition, implementation planning, and cost calculations made as close to actual delivery responsibility as possible.
- Develop standards for proposal writing and train all personnel in their application. Consider a two-stage internal proposal process, especially for major programs or significant strategic and tactical delivery changes.

  In the feasibility stage, outline the concept, identify impact areas, and make initial estimates of outputs, level of effort, costs, etc. Then, on approval to proceed to the second stage (based on approval for the activities in the feasibility stage), complete proposal staff work, including justification based on sound impact objectives (outcomes from the community perspective), defensibly linked through appropriate research to the proposed program process objectives (outputs), and present it in standard form (computer based if possible).

- Establish reasonable deadlines for submission, publish them well in advance, and adhere to them.
- Require that all submissions, even small needs ideas, be submitted in writing. It's easy for people to say, "We need," but if they care about the idea, they will put it in writing!
- Use the department's mission and strategic plan as an initial "test" for appropriate consideration.
- Encourage and train proposal writers to develop impact objectives that are community outcome based, and avoid the use of undefined fire service acronyms and jargon.
- Be concise; try to illustrate by using charts and graphs.
- Develop an atmosphere that both supports ideas yet allows personnel to feel comfortable enough to play "critic" for each other. Test proposals on nonfire-service trial audiences (spouses, secretaries, and friends may serve this purpose); watch out for fire service acronyms and jargon.
- When proposals are not included in the final budget document to the jurisdiction authority, give feedback to the author. The author may want to know that:
  - given the fiscal constraints and agency priorities, the proposal didn't survive the internal cut;
  - it was an excellent proposal, but in the current political environment, it wasn't the right time, but, if politics change, it's ready to go. (And we all know that sometimes that change is brought about by a disaster . . . ours, a neighbor's, or the nation's.); or
  - the concept needs to be more fully developed, i.e., better impact objectives, more research to tie outcomes to process, better needs analysis, etc.

Whatever the reason the proposal was rejected, the author showed initiative and positive risk taking in its development; reward and recognize that, don't punish it.

The finished proposal should be clear, concise, and look and sound professional. It must stand on its own; you cannot assume that you'll have an opportunity to explain and verbally support your proposal. At the same time, don't overload it with too many details; if you want to include additional information, provide a details and reference section. See page 81 for a summary of basic packaging.

IDENTIFYING FUNDING SOURCES

No discussion of financial management would be complete without information on funding sources. While this has always been a concern for volunteer and fire protection district organizations, historically it was not a pressing concern for city and county departments. In those areas funding was a problem for the jurisdiction's finance department, mayor or county executive, and the elected body. This is changing.

Informal polls of students attending the National Fire Academy's *Financial Management* course, finds that more and more jurisdictions are imposing a budget policy, official or not, that states: make no budget spending proposal without identifying an offsetting source of income.

Starting on page 94, most of the available funding sources are listed. There currently are shifting trends in terms of primary source percentages. No observation will be made, beyond the fact that property tax, while often the highest percentage of local governmental income, continues its slide in popularity. As (potential) revenue sources are examined, the purpose of the tax or fee must be recognized. This goes beyond the obvious reason of simply raising money. The purposes (often more than one applies) are to pay for public facilities, infrastructure, and services; to exert control; to modify behavior; and to redistribute wealth. Each is described in detail.

PAY FOR PUBLIC FACILITIES, INFRASTRUCTURE, AND SERVICES.

The beneficiaries of the facilities or services should be identified to further determine the degree of public subsidy and which type of tax or fee is most appropriate. The good (benefit) received can be categorized as:

- **Private Good:** The benefit is obviously for the primary good of the specific user. Examples include public golf courses, community swimming pools, and other recreation facilities. Also included would be improvements that affect specific properties, like curbs and sidewalks. Some would argue that such facilities contribute to the overall quality of life in the community, and are a benefit to all, even those who don't use the facility, by attracting investment or keeping juveniles off the street. It then becomes a degree of subsidy based on the next category.

- **Merit Good:** The benefit is not only for the specific user, but the community as a whole. Programs to provide prenatal care to low-income mothers are an example; while the mother and child are beneficiaries, society avoids the greater costs of providing health care for infants born with preventable deficiencies.
- **Public Good:** The benefit is primarily for the community as a whole, for example, its infrastructure—streets, interstate highway system, bridges, etc.

Into which categories does the fire department fall? All of them. The availability of services to prevent conflagration, and manage mass casualty and community-wide disaster incidents is generally considered to be for the public good. Public education programs are consistent with the concept of the public good. Merit good activities would include some inspection services that not only benefit the specific occupancy, but also help protect jobs and the tax base. Some response activities also qualify as merit good services to the degree that they protect the environment and community neighborhoods from damage. Private good services include most responses to private business and personal properties, and individual EMS calls.

Clearly the lines between the categories are very fuzzy. While most would agree that plans review primarily benefits the developer and property owner (private good), most also would agree that the community benefits from having structures that conform to building, fire, and life safety codes (merit good). Where does fire suppression stop benefiting the private property owner and begin to benefit the community?

Answering these questions locally is fundamental in adopting service fees. It may seem radical, even unacceptable, to charge a fee for fire suppression or other traditionally "free" services provided by the fire department. But in these times of shrinking revenues it more often is a choice between charging actual users a fee for the service and removing or cutting back the service for all. See "Setting User Fees" on page 102 for additional information.

EXERT CONTROL

One reason societies establish governments is to exert control over certain activities and service providers. Professional licenses and the enforcement of certain standards are considered essential to protect the public. Sprinkler and alarm system contractors, electricians, and mechanical contractors are service providers who would be of concern to the fire service. Some permit fees fall under this purpose.

MODIFY BEHAVIOR

Another reason governments collect taxes or, in some cases, fees (in the words of the Missouri Supreme Court, "A tax by any other name, is still a tax.") is to modify behavior. To discourage certain types of behavior or activities, cigarette smoking for instance, many government entities impose so-called "sin" taxes. Taxes on liquor, tobacco, and gasoline, and tariffs on certain import items are examples.

Some taxes and fees are intended to modify behavior, provide control, **and** recover the costs of providing services from creators of extraordinary hazards. Many fees for such items as fireworks displays and sales, hazardous materials handling, blasting, and other hazardous processes serve a combination of these purposes.

Recognizing and determining these joint-purpose fee collections is important; it is undesirable to apply a "behavior-modifying" fee to a desirable activity. Installations of sprinkler and other private protection systems should be encouraged, not discouraged through unreasonably high fees. Some cost-of-service recovery may be warranted, as is control accounting of systems (a permit with a small fee helps the agency keep track of what properties are sprinklered), but don't overlook the merit good the community will receive when it sets new system permit fees. On the other hand, fees (fines) for negligent false alarms may appropriately be used to encourage better maintenance and management of the system.

REDISTRIBUTE WEALTH

Finally, governments collect funds to redistribute wealth. This is why income taxes are based on ever higher percentages of earnings. The redistribution takes the form of free or reduced cost services or grants to lower income families and individuals. At first glance this may not seem relevant to fire departments, but if sliding-fee scales, based on the ability to pay, are used for department services such as EMS, or bills are routinely written off for those unable to pay, this principle is being applied. Giving smoke detectors to poor families is another example of redistributing wealth.

Evaluate Revenue Sources

Once the purpose of revenue collection is established, the source may be evaluated against these criteria:

- **Equity:** How fair is the tax or fee based on the ability to pay as a percentage of total income? Sometimes it depends on whether or not the tax or fee is discretionary on the part of the payer. Taxes on basic neces-

Table 3-6.

| Revenue Source | Equity | Efficiency | | | Elastic |
		Easy to Collect	Obvious Link	Behavior Control	
Property Tax	Low	High	High	Low	High/L
Personal Prop. Tax	Low	Low	Low	Low	Low
Sales Tax	Low/H	High	Low	High	High
Income Tax	High/L	High	Low	Low	High
Franchise Tax	Low/H	High	Low	Low	High
Consumption Tax	High/L	High	Low/H	High	High
Insurance Tax	High	High	High/L	Low	High
Fire Tax	Low/H	High	High	Low/H	High/L
Use Tax	Low/H	Low/H	High	Low/H	High
Licenses/Permits	High	Low	High	High	High/L
Service Fees	High/L	Low	High	High	High/L
Subscription Fees	High/L	Low	High	High	High/L
Fines & Penalties	Low	Low	Low/H	High	Low
Contributions	High	Low	High	N/A	High

sities such as food or medicine tend to be inequitable because they take a higher percentage of total income from low-income families. This is why many jurisdictions don't tax food, medicine, and some other basic necessities; at a basic level they are not discretionary. On the other hand, a golf course green fee would be discretionary on the part of the payer because no one **has** to play golf (although an avid golfer might disagree!).

- **Efficiency:** This criterion can actually be evaluated on three planes: Can the tax or fee be collected efficiently? Does the tax or fee obviously connect to the services or facilities being supported? If the purpose is to modify behavior or gain control, how well is that objective met? All three subcriteria will be shown in the tables below.
- **Elasticity:** Does the revenue source expand (and contract) with the economy or with inflation? A service fee that is not adjusted for inflation occasionally is inelastic beyond the effect of increased usage when the economy grows. This may be sufficient if the service is able to enjoy some economy of scale (unit costs go down as output goes up).

Below we will examine briefly the most common forms of revenue collected and evaluate them using the above criteria. It is important to remember that actual evaluation must occur locally; the conditions of the specific application may be "special case" in the local environment. Some revenue types receive a "high/low" or "low/high" rating in one or more categories. In those cases the most typical rating is listed first, but local conditions, provisions, or details of the implementation can create the other rating.

PROPERTY TAX

Ad valorem (in proportion to the value) taxes are often the largest source of local government revenue. The tax is on real property (land or anything fixed to it), based on a percentage (or millage) of actual or assessed valuation. It rates low on the equity scale because it doesn't go down based on an individual's income or ability to pay. Its elasticity may be either high or low depending on local conditions, for example, if the jurisdiction is "landlocked," with no open property available for new construction, the tax base does not expand with the economy. This is a major problem where urban flight has resulted in inner city decline. Properties are abandoned or devalued, resulting in declining revenues at the same time service demands are increasing. Many taxpayer revolts have led to the passage of legislation to constrain tax rates.

PERSONAL PROPERTY

Annual taxes on boats, cars, airplanes, major appliances, furniture, jewelry, etc., are harder to assess because the items are movable, and other than vehicles, usually not matters of public record. Even millionaires generally declare the minimum allowed beyond registered vehicles.

SALES TAX

Imposed by states and many cities, sales taxes normally are determined based on the percentage of goods purchased. Certain necessities often are not taxed to lessen the low equity effect. The amount of revenue generated by sales taxes fluctuates with the economy and seasonal business cycles.

INCOME TAX

Imposed by the majority of states and some cities on income earned in the jurisdiction, income taxes are calculated like federal income tax, usually on a progressive scale. If a flat rate is imposed, there is usually a provision for forgiving taxes for low-income families; otherwise, the high equity effect is lost.

FRANCHISE TAX

This type of tax includes right-to-operate fees, taxes for using city facilities, right-of-way taxes, and alleys usage taxes; examples include cable television company fees, telephone company pole fees, and utility taxes. A franchise tax has the effect of an operating expense passed on to the consumer. It achieves high equity only when the consumer has discretion over his participation, for example, electrical service generally is considered a necessity, cable television is not.

CONSUMPTION TAX

So-called "sin taxes" include liquor, tobacco, and hotel and motel occupancy taxes. The purpose of sin taxes often is to modify behavior, or, in the case of an occupancy tax, to draw revenue from transient populations (that do increase service demand). While generally viewed as equitable by society, in reality sin taxes often draw higher percentages from low-income individuals. When they are adopted for specific purposes, and publicized as such, they can achieve high "obvious" efficiency. Tobacco taxes earmarked for fire protection, and liquor taxes earmarked for EMS and rescue services both make sense as service demand causal factors.

INSURANCE TAX

An insurance tax is based on the dollar amount of premiums paid to insurance companies. Some states earmark at least a portion of property insurance premium taxes for fire training, local department equipment, or operating expenses, thereby achieving a high obvious connection between property protected and fire services. Without earmarked funds, the connection is lost.

FIRE TAX

A tax imposed by a fire protection district, by its nature obviously connects property to the service provided. Generally administered by a district's board or commissioners, fire taxes are subject to special state laws. This tax suffers from the same low-equity effect as a property tax on retirees and others on low or fixed incomes unless provisions are made for "ability to pay" adjustments. A fire tax is low in behavior modification unless incentives are established for built-in protection, and it potentially suffers from the same low elasticity as a property tax if the jurisdiction is land-locked and already substantially developed.

USE TAX

Taxes on auto license plates, and those for vehicle inspection stickers, etc, are examples of use taxes. They often are based on weight (low equity) or value (high equity). Usually earmarked for transportation systems, some are used for EMS. Some states effect behavior modification by imposing higher fees for low-gas-mileage vehicles.

LICENSE/PERMIT FEES

Issuing licenses for dogs, and services like plumbers, electricians, exterminators, taxis, etc., generates license fees. Issuing permits for guns, buildings, hazardous materials use or storage, signs, massage parlors, liquor licenses, etc., generates permit fees. Their primary use is to control and modify behavior. Not usually a major contributor of revenue, they can help offset the costs of delivering some related services. Specific to the fire department, most building and fire codes provide for the establishment of reasonable fees for such items as materials storage, transportation, and use (explosives, gaseous and liquefied fuels, and other hazardous materials), process control (refinishing, welding, construction, and demolition), and standby operation services (fire watch, blaster, fire safety director).

FEES FOR SERVICE

Often called "cost recovery" fees, these are intended to offset some or all of the costs of delivering a service. The level of equity depends on whether the use of the service is discretionary on the part of the customer, or whether there are provisions for ability-to-pay adjustments. From a public safety and public relations standpoint you don't want low-income families to be reluctant to use emergency services because of high fees (even the perception of high fees). (See "Setting User Fees" on page 102 for additional information.)

SUBSCRIPTION FEES

Subscription fees or dues for annual service have been used by some volunteer organizations for years. The concept has spread to other types of organizations for a variety of services. Property owners pay [or make a donation] annually for the right to use the services in case of an emergency. Over the years there have been several incidents, widely publicized, where departments have responded to calls for a structure fire, but watched the building burn (after verifying that no lives were involved) once it was learned that the owner had not paid the subscription fee. The department is faced with an obvious dilemma: if word spreads that members will fight the fire even if the fee has not been paid, many residents will not pay. Some choose to roll the dice, especially if the department has a provision, as some do, that allows nonsubscribers to pay a higher fee, for example $500 (even that is a bargain), at the time of service.

The level of equity depends on whether provisions are made based on ability to pay. Behavior gets a "high" rating because of the high control that tracking these subscriptions gives the district; the district tracks its members through fee accounting. Higher fees scaled to the hazard also can potentially modify behavior by giving a discount for private protection systems.

The subscription concept also has been applied to EMS. One common difference is that Medicare, Medicaid, and private insurance are billed at a standard rate. The district forgives the percentage of the bill that insurance doesn't cover, and forgives the entire bill for the uninsured. This has not been without

Table 3-7.

Plan A pays $500 Plan B pays $1,000	No. of	Dues & Fees	Dues pool	Ins. Paid	Income fund
Members with co-insurance (A)	100	$25	$2,500		
Members w/out co-insurance (B)	100	$50	$5,000		
Co-insured Calls	2	$2,000	−$1,000	$1,000	$2,000
Non-Co-insured Calls	2	$2,000	−$2,000		$2,000
End of Year			$4,500		$8,500

its problems; some insurance companies have refused to pay their regular benefit percentage, saying that the bills aren't real because the uninsured are forgiven, or that the whole subscription plan represents co-insurance. One possible way around these problems is to make the program official, i.e., a co-op co-insurance plan. Subscription rates would need to be higher for those without private insurance. The unpaid portions then would be paid "on the books" with monies from the dues pool. See Table 3-5.

Perhaps fire departments need a lesson in insurance billing. Many homeowner policies have a provision to pay (usually up to $500) for fire suppression services. This provision is often valid only where there is no tax-supported fire department, just the type of environment in which the volunteer or subscription service department operates.

FINES AND PENALTIES

Not a major source of income, fines and penalties are assessed for traffic, health, building, fire, life safety, false alarm etc, violations of the law. Typically the funds are not earmarked, but can be accounted for, and add to justification arguments when significant.

CONTRIBUTIONS

The lifeblood of most volunteer organizations, contributions are a minor source of income for most paid departments. In paid departments, contributions most often are used for special projects. Recent examples of special projects include public fire safety education trailers, smoke detector giveaways, and purchases of special rescue equipment.

There are a few other sources of income that don't lend themselves to the above evaluation criteria, but nonetheless are worth exploration:

- **Intergovernmental Revenue:** Often called "revenue sharing," intergovernmental revenue was one way to redistribute federal tax dollars to communities based on need. Common in the 1970s and early 1980s, the money was restricted to specific uses, for example, low-income housing, transportation, urban development, job training, etc. These funds are much less available in the 1990s because of the many lessons learned about the use of (and dependence on) revenue sharing, i.e., the record-keeping was arduous and many jurisdictions and departments used "job training" programs to provide personnel expansions, only to be faced with absorbing salaries or laying personnel off as funds dried up.

- **Grants:** Available from the federal government (most notable and consistent availability is from the Farmers Home Administration), some states, and private foundations. Two publications that list sources of grants are the *Federal Domestic Assistance Program* and *Foundation Register.* (Both publications are available from the Government Printing Office.) While the economic downturn of the early 1990s has diminished the availability of grants, the application forms can be complicated, and many restrictions apply, if you have a unique idea that has potential for bettering your community, it may be worth applying. Some jurisdictions and larger departments have specialists in grantsmanship; also, numerous consultants will work on a contingency basis, taking only a percentage of the funds if your department secures a grant.

- **Debt:** There are several forms of indebtedness into which jurisdictions may enter:

SHORT-TERM OPERATING LOANS from financial institutions are usually available against expected income from other sources. As with other forms of borrowing, laws may limit a jurisdiction's debt ceiling, and the bond rating may be affected by excessive short-term borrowing, making long-term bonds more expensive.

BONDS are a very common source of revenue for capital improvements and major equipment purchases. The advantages include the ability for the jurisdiction to borrow from sources outside the city and secure large sums of money. With a good bond rating, a jurisdiction can secure a percentage rate below that available in the commercial market (The interest paid the bond holders is often tax free, a benefit to investors, allowing bonds to pay a lower rate and still be attractive). There are disadvantages. Issuing bonds can be expensive—up to 20 percent of the original issue. Costs include bond counsel, underwriter, rating agency, printing, legal, and accounting fees. There are also intangible costs, including the time and energy spent on passing the bond issue in a public election (required in most states), and in various delays. A poor bond rating and changes in tax laws also can drive up costs. Bonds should be used judiciously; financing equipment which has a life expectancy shorter than the life of the bond will leave the jurisdiction paying for an asset after it has been retired.

LEASE-PURCHASE AGREEMENTS are a method of acquiring assets without affecting the debt structure or bond rating. An investor purchases a contract into which the municipality enters; the interest is often tax exempt. Apparatus, communication and computer equipment, buildings, and other major purchases are all candidates for lease-purchase agreements. At the end of the lease period, the equipment either belongs to the jurisdiction, may be purchased at some prearranged prices, or may be walked away from, depending on the original contract.

LEASE-BACK AGREEMENTS are a variation of lease-purchase, with some unique and interesting features for a jurisdiction. In this arrangement the jurisdiction sells a current asset—land, building, or apparatus—to an investor, who in turn leases it back to the jurisdiction at an agreed-upon rate. This offers several potential advantages to all: the jurisdiction receives a major infusion of cash, with no restriction on its use, and usually with no adverse effect on its bond rating; and, if the investor is a profitable corporation, it may be able to use the purchase to provide a tax shelter for excess retained earnings. In any case, the investor is able to declare depreciation on the property for tax purposes, something the jurisdiction has no need to do, potentially sufficient to render the lease payments tax free or better (show a loss on paper that can reduce other tax liabilities).

- **Investment Income:** Government jurisdictions, like any other legal entity, are able to earn money from investments, either short-term investments of tax revenues received before they are needed for expenditure, or actual investments designed to generate revenue. In many cases, especially when the jurisdiction's bond rating is very good (AAA or better), revenue resulting from bond sales can be invested at a higher return than the bond interest paid. In any case, sound financial management expertise from qualified, honest managers is required.

- **Rental Income:** Usually not a major source of income, jurisdictions often rent out, on a short- or long-term basis, city-owned facilities. In some cases, the number of properties and volume of income may justify establishing an enterprise fund to manage the properties and account for the expenses and income.

- **Marketing Income:** Revenues from marketing usually are not a major source of income, but occasionally jurisdictions find themselves in an enterprise involving the sale of products or services that private enterprise isn't providing adequately. (Before embarking on such an enterprise a government jurisdiction should examine closely the issue of competition with private enterprise and its own mission.) Various fire departments have, at one time or another, been involved in fire extinguisher sales and service, smoke alarm sales, dive bottle filling, etc. Potential liability has caused many of those same departments to drop such sales activities.

On the other hand, many jurisdictions also have missed potential income from the sale of intangible assets created in the course of business. This might include patents on processes and inventions, and copyrights on training materials and software. Contrary to common belief, such items are not automatically in the public domain, nor are they the jurisdiction's property—unless you are the federal government. Without an agreement assigning rights, copyrights and patents legally "belong" to the individual(s) who provided "creative supervision" to the project. It may be a good idea to have employees assign rights as a condition of employment. Universities went through that phase with research professors; the quality of research went down and many of the best professors left. Now rights-sharing agreements are the norm and research universities once again derive a significant portion of their revenue from patents and copyrights. Be sure to consult your own legal authorities for the latest provisions applicable to your area and situation.

Whatever the marketing income project, if it is significant in dollars or level of effort, it may warrant setting up an enterprise fund. This is a special fund that encapsulates all expenses and income on a specific program for administration like a business—an enterprise.

SETTING USER AND IMPACT FEES

While usually thought of as different approaches to the idea of cost recovery, user fees, impact fees, and benefit assessments are related enough in issues of analysis and implementation that one discussion will serve all three.

User fees are charges made only to the actual recipient of some service. The most common in the fire service has been ambulance or EMS run charges. Others include inspection (or reinspection) fees, plans review fees, hazardous materials incident "cost-recovery" fees, event standby fees, dispatch fees (other agencies private ambulance, alarm monitoring, and special services) confined space operations for industry, and fire suppression charges.

Impact fees are generally one-time charges to the developer or owner of new properties. Sometimes these fees are applied across the board—by some formula—to all new properties. In other jurisdictions, the fees are applied only to "extraordinary" hazards (defined by size, occupancy type, process, or some combination thereof), or to properties built outside of primary response zones. One example of an impact fee formula would be the use of the standard fire flow formula, but instead of calculating gpms you would calculate dollars or dollars/x. The formula takes into account size and type of construction. The inclusion of a factor for fixed use hazard is good in concept; in practice though, uses do change, and unless the impact fee is reapplied with each change of use it may not be adequate. The formula also applies penalties for exterior combustible finish and gives credit for automatic sprinkler systems; both potentially behavior-modifying features.

Benefit assessments are fees usually charged annually, for a specified number of years, to all properties based on a formula designed to calculate the relative benefits and costs of providing public fire protection to the property. Such fees are in essence special taxes to make up for a shortfall of revenue from traditional tax sources.

In each of the approaches above, one of the goals is to more closely match benefit received to financial responsibility. With user fees, the cost to general taxpayers is kept at a minimum by shifting costs to those who actually use the service. In the latter two, the costs of making resources available to all are distributed based on the relative shared costs of resources needed for the particular property (type, size, etc.).

Setting user or impact fees for heretofore "free" (totally tax subsidized) services is at once an economic, political, and public relations decision. Each area must be examined, but not in any particular order. In some cases it may be wise to test the political waters before anything else; in fact, for some jurisdictions the push toward fees comes from the political arena—or from the public—in order to keep general tax rates from going up. Similarly, it is beneficial to determine actual costs of service delivery before pursuing the concept of fees in the political arena. Program budgeting makes cost determination much easier. In any case, if fees are adopted, they should be based substantially on actual costs; in fact, many states require this of political subdivisions that wish to charge a fee for services. More on the mechanics of fee determination shortly.

Another concern with respect to service fees is organization morale. It will change many people's perceptions; there will be fears, most unfounded or exaggerated. Some personnel may feel that imposing fees will tarnish the department in the public's eye. Some readers may feel that the concept is nearly immoral, or at least politically unthinkable in their jurisdiction. Many will fear losing the public's respect, or, in the case of inspection fees, increasing adversarial relations with the business community. All of these concerns must be discussed and worked through. Experience has shown that in many jurisdictions—some of which had the same fears mentioned above—when inspection fees were adopted, there was a year or two of minor grumbling from the business community, usually the same occupancies that grumble when they see the inspectors now. By the third year, the fees generally are accepted as just another cost of doing business. Above all, "make thinking visible!"

What follows are the general steps in establishing service fees. (Items 3, 4, and 6 ideally would include the participation of the elected body.)

1. Identify resources used or needed and determine the actual direct costs of delivering the service.
2. Determine the statutory authority and requirements for adopting fees for service.
3. Determine the beneficiary distribution of the service, i.e., private good, merit good, public good (see page 92).
4. Determine the goal of the fee program. Is it for cost recovery, and to what degree? Will it modify behavior, control uses and processes, or redistribute wealth? (See page 94).
5. Given the information gained in steps one to four above, select an appropriate cost model (see below) and calculate proposed fees. Determine or design the information system required to collect, track, follow up, renew, etc.; include in costs as appropriate.
6. Seek approval from your legislative body. Inform all employees.
7. Market the proposal. A basic recommended approach is to highlight the mission, primary impact goals, and objectives, and use a primary selling line. One example is, "In order to keep tax rates as low as possible to the general public (and businesses) without reducing services, actual users will be charged a fee for service (a one-time impact fee will be charged to those who create extraordinary hazards)."
8. Hold public hearings, pass ordinances, and hold elections as required by law (see step 2).
9. Implement and test the information system as appropriate.
10. Train personnel.
11. Implement the fee(s).

DESIGNING A COST MODEL

A cost model is a conceptual "black box" into which you place variables, "turn the crank," and spit out the cost of providing some product or service. The answer depends, of course, on the variables, but, more importantly, on what was desired (step 4), and the assumption made about the variables.

A microcomputer spreadsheet program is an excellent model-building tool. One benefit is that once built, the model is easily used in subsequent years to adjust costs on fees according to new variables, for instance, an increase in personnel salaries.

The simplest model would take the monetary amount of the entire budget and divide it by the number of responses. The problem is that the result would be an average cost per call as if all calls were the same and the department delivered no other programs. Neither assumption is fair or accurate.

The same concept applied to each program will produce the average cost of each program output. Again, this is made easier by program budgeting; the program's budget is divided by the number of units of output, resulting in an average cost per unit for inspections, EMS calls, structure fires, plan reviews, etc.

So far, only direct costs have been included. If the goal is total cost recovery, support programs and other overhead for facilities, equipment, and utilities must be folded in. One approach is to allocate to each load-bearing program (programs delivered to customers) a proportion of overhead expenses based on the level of effort of the program relative to total department productivity.

One assumption that is often appropriate (as politically determined) is that general taxes should support (and prepay) the availability of services to all, but that actual users should assume the cost of that use. This is consistent with the merit good concepts discussed on page 93. In this modification of the model, hourly personnel expenses (whether they produce output or not) and amortization of overhead are determined for each type of unit (pumper, aerial, EMS unit, inspector's car, etc), and used to produce an hourly rate for each type of unit that can be charged to actual users. This application of the model offers some appropriate advantages. Consider this example: an inspection judged to take two and a half inspector hours could be charged two and a half inspector hour units, even if the actual inspection was performed by an in-service engine company in one hour (one hour of engine resource most likely would be higher than two and a half inspector units because of the greater number of personnel and the higher overhead and apparatus costs of the pumper versus the inspector's car. However, it wouldn't be fair to charge the business for the pumper when the service was an inspection). This model can produce the most reasonable hourly rates for various services.

This model can be refined further based on political or economic desires. On the premise that taxpayers underwrite the availability of response resources, and that when those resources are on a response they are no longer available, it may be justifiable to have the model use overtime rates for personnel that are on actual calls. This provision theoretically would fund the recall of off-duty personnel at an overtime rate to staff reserve and other available apparatus. In this way the availability of response resources for simultaneous calls is only minimally diminished during responses.

Even if fees for all services are not adopted in the political arena, it may be worthwhile to apply cost models to all the services your department performs. This will help your department managers and your elected officials to evaluate unit costs of program output with the projected impact objectives. It also paves the way for more fee adoption—if politically directed—because costs already have been determined.

CASE STUDY

The political directive was for two EMS fee schedules: one for residents that recognized taxpayers pay for availability, but actual users should assume costs of use; the other for nonresidents or nontaxpayers in which they should assume the entire cost of service. Taking the council's directive one step further (primarily because with the computer spreadsheet it was easy to do so) both models (a: program budget with appropriate overhead, divided by actual response unit-hours produced; and b: total hourly unit availability costs) were used to set costs for all types of service for taxpayers/residents and nonresidents. The figures for resident/nonresident EMS fees were adopted by the council through an ordinance.

Each year the new figures for personnel salaries, units produced, unit hours available, and adjusted overhead were plugged into the computer spreadsheet and new EMS rates were set by council.

One evening a nontaxpaying petroleum company dumped a tractor-trailer load of gasoline in the median strip of the interstate. The fire department and other local agencies were on the scene for days. The morning after the incident was terminated, and after consultation with the city administrator and mayor, a bill was in the mail to the petroleum company for $37,557 in fire department service fees. Ten days later a check for that amount arrived. The council directed the police and public works departments to prepare invoices for the incident; it took them weeks.

As budget reductions, personnel costs, increased maintenance, deteriorating facilities and equipment, and demand for service seem to be on a collision course, don't dismiss service and impact fees, and benefit assessments simply because "we've never done that!" Remember that such decisions must be made in the political arena; once again, the elected officials are dependent on the professional staff work of department managers to provide various options and sufficient information to make informed decisions.

BUDGET JUSTIFICATION

In this section we will examine year-round activities and specific budget presentation approaches that can further enhance the department's ability to sell itself and its budget.

Marketing and public relations

In earlier sections, we discussed impact objectives as the foundation of budget justification. Marketing and public relations (PR) serve as the mortar that holds the foundation together. Marketing and public relations are also year-round activities that can make or break your budget justification efforts.

Marketing and PR begin with your everyday image. Presenting facilities, equipment, and personnel as neat, organized, and well maintained goes a long way toward ensuring that your budget proposals will be taken seriously. Your personnel need to know this; if you don't explain the public relations issue, the rules and regulations that deal with appearance and cleanliness may seem arbitrary, and housekeeping duties may seem like "make work." The bench in front of the engine house, cat-calls and whistles, and unbuttoned uniform shirts have done more harm to budget levels than anyone would like to hear.

Consider the following general ideas. Many departments (paid and volunteer) have found them worthwhile in presenting a professional image.

- Does the public know the diversity of services offered by your agency? Distributing a brochure with phone stickers is a good way to make your community aware of safety education, inspection services, household hazardous waste disposal, and other mission-related services you may provide.
- Would everyone in the organization recognize the elected officials if they walked into a station unannounced? While everyone should be greeted in a professional way, think of the impression that would be made if station personnel could greet council members by name. Several departments publish as internal documents biographic summaries with photos of all elected officials and other officials after every election, and require that department personnel read them.
- What image is communicated to citizens when they see fire apparatus parked at shopping centers, in the business district, or in front of bars and places of entertainment? Many departments have placed removable signs that say something like, "Fire company available for call by radio: conducting in-service . . . ," on apparatus.
- How many times have the news media misquoted or misinterpreted department officials or activities? Formalize your media relations. Conduct media hospitality events and orientations, invite media representatives to training burns, offer protective gear and invite them inside to gain the perspective they never get from the sidewalk. Give them operational background material that explains the most often misunder-

stood procedures like ventilation, salvage, and interior attack. Watch for reporter turnover; start over with new reporters. When issuing incident press releases, suggest headlines (your relationship should guide you in how subtle to be). Which conveys a better image? "Six families burned out of apartment building!" or "Fire department rescues four from burning apartment building!" Ask reporters if you may review their stories for technical accuracy.

- Work with local media to produce public service announcements (PSAs). Many movie theaters show 35 mm slides with local advertising before show time; they usually welcome PSA inserts about smoke detectors, home escape planning, etc. Make sure your department name and logo are displayed prominently on all PSAs.

- Keep your mission statement visible. Put it on the cover page of the budget and annual report, at the bottom of stationery and business cards (or on the back, if it's too long), put it on a plaque in each station lobby, on all literature distributed, and at the bottom of inspection and other department forms typically given to your customers.

- Involve everyone in developing ideas and delivering a positive image.

- Create an atmosphere in which everything the department does is executed with a commitment to excellence using the resources provided.

- Don't pass up an opportunity to assume or improve mission-related, high-visibility services such as EMS. If the resources aren't there, work hard at the concepts presented earlier on community impact and new revenue sources to try to make it happen. There are many departments whose history was always "too few personnel, inadequate equipment, poor public image . . ." who have seen complete turnarounds after taking on EMS responsibilities. EMS has such high visibility it often can carry bond issues for new stations and equipment, or public hearings on the department's general operating budget.

- The department should be involved and represented at many public gatherings, for example, city council meetings (even when you're not on the agenda). Planning commission, zoning hearings and arbitration board meetings are "must attends." Many times, issues that to the lay person aren't related to fire and life safety will come up and the department should have some say in them, or be available to answer a question about them. Even if nothing of concern comes up, the presence of a department representative says much about the department's interest in the community. Given that these meetings are held and attended by the movers and shakers, they are a good environment for the department's community interest to be noticed. These meetings also are an opportunity to gain trust, understanding, and insight into the various agendas and personalities.

Local politics

As mentioned in the introduction, financial management and budgeting are played out on a political field. This section will focus on the specifics of budget justification in the political environment. Actually, this political playing field has many levels.

Internal politics

The first place to look for political intrigue is in the team's own dugout. There may well be many agendas and priorities among various program managers, officers, shifts, stations, the union, management, clerical, alarm office, and various other influences. Even knowing that everyone is on the same team won't eliminate politics. Involving appropriate levels in the development of a mission, strategic plan, functional model, goals, objectives, and the entire budget can help use the internal politics to achieve a positive result. So, too, can standards of proposal submission, a code of conduct for group process, and employee interaction.

Many departments have found it worthwhile to develop statements of organization philosophy and values, and a code of conduct, in addition to mission, goals, and objectives. As a partial list of subjects typically covered, consider safety, respect for the community and private resources, respect for diverse opinions, honesty, cooperation, accuracy, willingness to work at process and fulfill commitments, and community and organizational good ahead of personal advantage. Articulating and publishing these goals and attributes is one more way to "Make Thinking Visible!"

It is important for employees to be informed about and feel a sense of involvement in their own future within the department. By the same token, they also must understand the decision process; in many cases, it is NOT democratic. Voting typically is polling for consensus. While compromise has a place, consensus is often the better group decisionmaking process. Compromise often dilutes two or more proposals, making them ineffective, when any one of the originals might have been very effective. Remember, there is often more than one right answer. Consensus, on the other hand, seeks a decision that all can support, even if it's not the one they personally would have selected. A good indication of whether consensus was truly reached is in the manager's or representative's report back to his own constituency—how often do you hear, "They decided . . ." versus "We decided . . ."?

Table 3-8.

Programs	Departments
Communications/dispatch	FD, PD, EMS, PW, IN, AC
Fleet Maintenance	All
Fire Investigation	FD, PD, Prosecutor
Photo Lab	FD, PD, CH*
Video/AV Production	FD, PD, CH*
Training Facilities	FD, PD, [Regional]
Print Shop	CH*

LEGEND: FD = Fire Department, PD = Police Department, EMS = Emergency Medical Service, PW = Public Works (Streets, water, sewer, and other city utilities), IN = Inspections (Building, health), AC = Animal Control, CH = City Hall (* and other departments through CH).

Interdepartmental politics

The next political plateau is interdepartmental. Traditionally, many jurisdictions have experienced much competition among various departments for pieces of the budget pie. Here again, putting your budget into programs with community-based objectives is much harder for people to criticize than one based solely on input of resources, or is presented in a way that conveys "empire" building with fancy chrome, bells, and whistles.

The chief not only needs to know the fire department programs and budget well, but needs to be familiar with other departments' major objectives and proposals, not so much to fend off competing budget proposals, but to look for complementary community-based initiatives.

As with program managers, department heads should strive to enter into joint programs and share resources where it is in the community's best interest to do so. Much local debate should focus on the appropriateness of joint programs. Table 3-8 lists some that have proved successful in at least some jurisdictions.

A word of caution about joint programs: some progressive departments have seen an attitude develop that, "If there's a need, and you want it done right, have the fire department do it!" Further, many departments, in seeking to gain political points or maintain high visibility (or build personal empires), agree to accept primary responsibility for all such joint programs. There is a real danger here of spreading department resources too thin, or working in areas outside the department's areas of expertise.

Primary mission functions can suffer as a result of trying to be all things to all people and needs.

Before you take on primary responsibility for joint programs, evaluate resource capability, and level of effort, and identify the benefit to the primary mission. If you consider taking on responsibility for joint communication and dispatch or training facilities, you probably can argue for control and relevance to your mission. In any case the chief must ensure that adequate resources are available to deliver the joint program's objectives without diminishing primary mission capabilities.

Funding Body Politics

In other situations, where city councils or other city officials view the department as nonproductive, tasks are assigned to the department that are clearly not mission related. Washing streets, changing street lights, etc., may use equipment and personnel skills, even gain a few points at budget time, but everyone involved must be honest and up-front about the underlying reasons for such assignments. Again, it is the chief's job to ensure that primary mission capabilities are not diminished.

How far afield can such assignments go when the department is viewed as nonproductive? One paid department was directed to detail a firefighter to remain in station, from 7:00 a.m. to 11:00 p.m. on the third Tuesday of every month, even when the company was on an alarm. The reason? So citizens could pick up their trash collection bags at a convenient location. When the chief pointed out that the directive would mean every company in town would be running short staffed during those hours, the response was that no vacation or sick leave should be granted on those days.

This is just one example of politics at the jurisdiction or funding policy level.

The type of jurisdiction can make a big difference in terms of political perspective and level of fire department involvement, both politically and economically. A city department usually interacts with either a strong mayor/council or a city administer/manager. A county (or parish) department generally answers to a county executive and county council, or to elected commissioners. In either case the fire department is one of many programs funded from the same budget pool. A fire protection district (FPD), on the other hand, is an autonomous political entity or taxing district, with an elected board, some of whom might be active or former members. With respect to volunteer organizations, some are state-chartered private corporations, most with non-profit status; some are county chartered or operated as FPDs; while some legally belong to incorporated cities, but are left to raise funds using their own creative means.

DO YOUR HOMEWORK

Regardless of the type of legal entity, or source of funding, keep the following points in mind—they can make or break your budget justification efforts:

- Know your community, its population, and its hazards;
- Know your customers' special needs;
- Know your programs, objectives, and budget;
- Know your current performance;
- Know your jurisdiction's budgeting system;
- Know your political system; and
- Know your audience.

Let's discuss each in turn:

- **Know your community, its population, and its hazards.**

There isn't much a chief can do that would be more embarrassing, or potentially damaging to his department's budget sales effort, than misstating some community detail that is held as common knowledge or would give the chief the appearance of being out of touch. Examples of this might include drastically under- or overstating some statistic like total population, or land area in the city limits, or making an offhand comment about ethnic populations. Have a general working knowledge of your community's demographics, and, more importantly, know how fire and life safety are affected by those conditions. General economic condition, age and upkeep of structures, unemployment rate, literacy levels, age, incidence of drug abuse, and blight all have a major impact on emergency service demands and fire problems. Be realistic about the local economic condition; presenting a grossly expansionary budget when the economy is in the pits and tax revenue is down may hurt credibility, unless those programs can help (as well defined and analyzed within the presented impact objectives) the community recover from the economic downturn.

Don't overlook major incident or disaster potentials, even if your history hasn't included such events. Every part of the country has the potential to suffer natural disasters; being unprepared for the inevitable could end your career, and be catastrophic for the community. A major fire, not even a conflagration, in an area where the chief and department have done nothing in terms of preparedness, may have a long-lasting negative impact on the department's credibility and budget.

• **Know your customers' special needs.**

Every community has special-needs populations, such as the elderly, or large numbers of non-English-speaking residents. Remember, these are your customers. Design programs to meet their needs and concerns. It might be safety education for the elderly or a daily phone check for shut-ins. Some may say phoning shut-ins is "not our business." But if the department provides EMS, has dispatchers that are not busy 100 percent of the time, and a computer to track the shut-ins, it may be a good fit, provide familiarity both ways, and score some points at budget time. One of the best examples of customer needs identification, special programs, and the effect on fundraising comes from the dairy state of Wisconsin:

> The department was significantly dependent on donations and sub-scription fees from the dairy farmers in the district. In analyzing the special needs of this type of customer, the department realized that a barn fire that put a milking operation down would be a significant problem because cows can't wait. The department members designed an entire system of apparatus, equipment, and special tactics to handle dairy barn fires. Taking the proposed program on the fundraising trail, the department guaranteed milking operations would be down no more than four hours. Here's how it works:

>> A used mobile construction crane was acquired, equipped with a hay clamshell bucket, painted red, and fitted with lights and a siren. When a barn fire was reported, this crane, along with more conventional pumpers and rural water supply tankers, would respond. Hose crews would enter the lowest (milking) level of the barn. Their task was to prevent as much dropdown fire and damage as possible. The heavy timber construction of the barn aided in this. Meanwhile the crane would be set up and, using the hay clamshell bucket, remove the roof. Then, under the cover of appropriate hose streams, the burning hay bales would be removed with the clamshell to an area where they could be spread out and doused. The loft areas would be cleaned to bare floor if needed. If the milkers lost electrical power, a trailered 220-volt generator was brought in, which department electricians would wire into the milkers. Sure enough, milking could be underway less than four hours after the fire. Dairy farmers and customers were happy, the cows were happy, and the department fundraising committee was happy. That's what "WIIFM" is about and how to use it!

• **Know your programs, objectives, and budget.**

Mission, impact objectives, and program initiatives are the basis of budget justification. It is much easier to play on the political field when you can use these items to provide focus. The more community based the justifications, the more palatable the expense. Consider the following example program objectives:

A. Perform preventive maintenance on all motorized apparatus and equipment every 25 to 30 hours of operation by hiring two additional full-time mechanics, upgrading tools and diagnostic equipment, and expanding spare parts inventory.

B. Ensure that no deaths, injuries, or property damage will result from on-scene equipment failures attributable to insufficient maintenance.

Another set . . .

C. Replace all breathing apparatus with positive pressure equipment that meets OSHA standards and NFPA 1500.

D. Reduce firefighter smoke inhalation injuries (and resulting Workmen's Compensation and insurance expenses) by 30 percent and avoid potential liability created by not providing breathing apparatus which meets current standards.

Both A and C are objectives written from an internal perspective; as fire service personnel we understand the desirability of each. In the justification arena though, it's the perception of the nonfire-service reviewer that is important. From an external perspective, A could easily sound expensive and downright unnecessary; after all, no one does preventive maintenance on his automobile every 25 hours of operation. C most likely would defy understanding; aren't those "oxygen" bottles already pressurized?

B and D are significant for the community in the same ways that A and C are, but they are understood by nonfire-service people. Preventing deaths, injuries, and property damage are words right from the mission statement, and, in an elected official's mind, they are fundamental to why a fire department is funded in the first place. Even the most calloused council person can understand wanting to prevent firefighter smoke inhalation injuries, even if it's only to prevent city liability. B and D are examples of how focused impact objectives can be.

Earlier, an example of a task analysis for a proposed company inspection program was used. Let's look at a similar program, pulling together a number of pieces from previous discussions:

Table 3-9.

Department: Fire	Function: Code Management	Program: Occupancy Inspections

- **Relevant Goals:** Reduce the effects of fire on the community and the economy. Assist businesses in providing a safe environment for customers and employees, avoid business interruptions, and reduce insurance costs and potential liability. Protect tax base and jobs.

- **Background:** Over the last three years the businesses in our community have experienced 36 fires resulting in 1 death, 9 injuries, and $827,000 in direct property damage. The job base has (as of this date) not recovered 78 positions. The tax base was permanently reduced by $3,642,000 in assessed valuation. (See attached graphs.)
  Based on the investigations of the causal factors of these fires, it is believed that an aggressive fire prevention program would prevent about 10 percent of these types of occurrences and reduce the damage in 15 percent of the others.

- **Impact Objective(s):** Reduce over a three-year period 10 percent of business fire injuries and losses to property, tax base, and jobs in the community.

- **Process Objective(s):** Provide at least one fire/life safety inspection to every business in the community within a three-year cycle, one per year on moderate- to high-hazard and high-occupancy facilities.
  Average 4,500 inspections per year.
  Clear 90 percent of the violations found by the second inspection. Approximately 5,000 hazards and violations will be found and cleared per year.

Table 3-10.

Budget	Startup	Recurring	Total
Personnel:			
2 new FTE	15,000*	60,000	75,000
Exist'g. shift prsnl	20,000*	140,000*	160,000
Expenses:	5,000	2,000	7,000
Capital Asset items:			
2 Inspectors' cars	30,000	6,000**	37,000
2 PC LAN Nodes	6,000	1,200**	7,200
Total Program Costs:	76,000	209,200	285,200
Opportunity costs*	35,000	141,000	176,000
	Startup	*Recurring*	*Ttl 1st yr*
New funding request	41,000	68,200	109,200

*Opportunity costs are personnel expenses funded under other programs within the budget that will be reallocated to this program if adopted. Not funding the program will not eliminate these expenses.
** Replacement sinking fund.

• Know your department's current performance.

Do you know specifically what progress is being made toward meeting your department's major goals and impact objectives (as defined in the strategic plan)? Take this little open-book quiz. Don't worry, you'll grade it yourself and you don't have to show it to anyone else! Seriously, do this. You might find it quite enlightening. Use a separate piece of paper. As you work, also include the time it took, or would take, to research the answers you can't give from personal memory.

1. What is your approximate budget?
2. What is the population protected? Is it growing or shrinking?
3. How many total responses were made last year? Fire? EMS?
4. What were the fire losses in dollars last year?
5. What was the motor fuel budget for the last budget year?
6. How many civilian fire fatalities did the jurisdiction suffer last year? The last three years? Is the per capita trend up or down from five years ago? Same questions for fire injuries.
7. If you charge for EMS, what was your collection rate last year? If you didn't charge for EMS, did the department produce any income? How much?
8. What were the top three structure fire causal factors, in descending order, last year?

Yes, these might be getting harder, but it is open book! Here's an easier one again . . .

9. Question number 6, but for fire personnel?
10. How many firefighter injuries caused lost time?
11. How many firefighter injuries occurred during nonemergency activities?
12. What were the three leading causal factors in fires where there was an injury or death?
13. What was the code blue (clinically dead at some point) save rate in your jurisdiction last year?
14. How many civilians were rescued from structure fires by department personnel last year?
15. How many prevention inspections did your agency conduct last year? How many violations were discovered?
16. How many violations were cleared by the first re-inspection? How many went to court?
17. What were the three most common violations?
18. How do the causal factors from questions 8 and 12 compare with violations found during inspections? How much training has the department conducted in hazard recognition?
19. How many total public education contacts did the department make last year? How many of those contacts focused on the causal factors identified in questions 8 and 12?
20. What was the total cost of your fire prevention efforts, including opportunity costs?

If you were able to answer all these questions accurately, immediately, and without referring to your annual report (or other sources of information), you are rare indeed. Or, your department has no alarms and no programs. If you were able to answer all questions by devoting just five minutes to each, or you found questions 8 and on just as easy to answer as questions 1 through 4, you are also in a rare department. If you found the questions getting progressively harder to answer, you're not alone. If you had questions you couldn't answer at all, you're also not alone. Maybe it's time to go get another cup of coffee, come back, close your door, and ponder just how serious your department wants to be in terms of prevention and any changes in emphasis, budget, or both, you may wish to make.

If you don't run an ambulance or have a formal EMS program, is that a valid reason for not knowing the answer to question 13? Maybe you don't have a definition for a "code blue save," but given the significance in impact of that outcome performance measure, maybe it's time to sit down with your medical director and some of the paramedics and have them develop one.

Maybe there are other holes in your information system that need to be filled. Every year, as impact objectives are identified, make sure the information system provides for data collection that will measure achievement. Also, if possible, gather baseline data about current performance. (Information management, planning, and financial management are very closely related. The National Fire Academy offers a two-course sequence, one on the first two, one the latter).

If you knew all the answers to all the questions, or at least knew where to look to quickly get the answers, wouldn't you feel much better prepared to enter the budget justification arena?

- **Know your jurisdiction's budgeting system.**
It is imperative that you know what budgeting system your jurisdiction

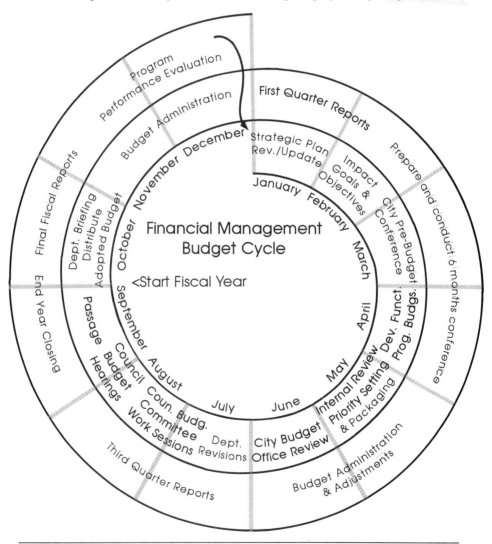

Figure 3-4.

uses. Understand the required format and how to work in programmatic impact statements.

Know the cycle and timing of budget activity. Figure 3-4 shows a typical cycle. It also points out that at any given time, a department may be dealing with two or more yearly budgets. The one that has just ended is closed out, final data are processed and correlated, and objectives, both impact and process, are checked for achievement. The budget most recently adopted is in the administration phase, with all of the requisite accounting activity, and planning is underway for the coming year's budget. That generally begins with a revision of the strategic plan, including a check on the continuing validity of the department's mission, community impact goals and objectives, and the functional business model.

Know the levels and timing of administrative reviews before the budget goes to the council. As we said early in this chapter, understand the personal agendas of those who can affect what *gets* to the council and the light in which it is presented. Especially in larger jurisdictions, these levels of bureaucratic review can be extensive; budget analysts, assistant finance directors, budget directors, assistant city managers, legislative aides, and the city manager may all review budget proposals before the council budget committee gets to see (what's left of) the proposal.

Have a working understanding of the major thrusts of other departments' budgets. Be prepared to give insight into interdepartmental dependencies and complementary programs.

- **Know your political system.**
Know the local rules of the political game. Know whom to lobby, who you can lobby, and when. Some of the rules may be unwritten. The word "lobby" may be taboo. Department members, even the chief, may be prohibited from initiating contact with elected officials. Understand the latitude of your response if a council person initiates the contact with a question or concern.

Make sure department personnel know the boundaries, and inform them about major department program features, goals, and objectives; it is unrealistic to think that no elected official will ever ask a firefighter what the rank and file think about some budget issue. A firefighter could be an elected official's long-time friend or neighbor.

Know where the community power centers are. Sometimes they are civic organizations; in other communities it may be a local restaurant where the movers and shakers meet for breakfast.

Know the personal agendas of the elected officials—what are their "hot buttons?" One council person was always concerned about the upkeep and appearance of the city's cemetery. The fire department proposed that a "Cleanup, Fix-up Week," designed to remove fire hazards from in and around buildings city-wide, be launched with a ceremony at the city cemetery, where new landscaping and fencing could be shown off. Always look for the WIIFM!

 • **Know Your Audience.**

When you give presentations on budget proposals or department activities, know your audience. Know their general education levels and political leanings. It may not be very effective to give a folksy, good-ol'-boy presentation to a group of engineers and business managers, just as a technical discussion of fire flow analysis and sprinkler head loading would not go over very well with a neighborhood group of homeowners. Always seek the group's WIIFM.

When you speak to Chamber of Commerce business owners, highlight how your programs will enhance **their** marketability, insurance rates, liability management, and business in general. Point out that fire department programs and services which they must use (plan review, permit management, inspections) are designed to maximize their access, will be completed in a timely fashion, and will minimize business interruptions. Then, make sure you can deliver on your promises. Explain how, if they experience a loss or fire, you can help them get up to speed with as little business interruption as possible. These assurances will interest business people more, and do more for your budget, than pictures of chrome and expensive equipment and stations.

Homeowners will appreciate knowing that your operations and training are aimed at, first and foremost, protecting their loved ones, and, second, protecting their property, (especially the irreplaceables—pictures, momentos, and valuable papers), not at breaking windows, cutting holes, squirting water, and getting back to the station ASAP. Think about the media coverage of residential fires and you can understand the public's concern. They see piles of burned rubble and personal belongings being shoveled out of broken windows. Have you ever seen a television or newspaper picture of furniture neatly protected by salvage covers? Or a stack of photos and family papers being handed to the fire victim? The most common interior news footage is of firefighters pulling lath and plaster and making a bigger mess. Sure it's a messy job, but try to understand the public's ignorance of the technical aspects, and their sensitivities about the destruction or rough handling of personal belongings.

Knowing your audience takes us to the next major focus of our justification efforts—the formal budget presentation before the funding body.

The formal budget presentation

Experience has shown that the real work in budget justification and sales, and in a budget's ultimate passage, typically has been done before it goes before the entire council or funding body in a formal presentation. Even so, the following points are also valid at preparatory review and work session meetings of budget subcommittees.

Be prepared. Have your staff work complete. It is up to you and your staff to do the research necessary to support the conclusion that the impact objectives you've predicted will result from the output levels you have proposed.

Don't overload the document or your presentation with too much detail. Keep the focus on impact objectives, risk, and service levels. Have the details available for reference. When it comes to key data supporting your objectives, it would be almost inexcusable to say, "I'll hav'ta get back to you on that; I don't have those data here." Of course, you can't anticipate everything. Some managers pride themselves on their ability to dazzle a council with "smoke and mirrors." It's better to be honest, and admit that you don't now have the answer—smoke eventually clears and mirrors can break. Don't risk hurting your future credibility.

Realize that the council is also on a stage. Its members will ask questions for which they already know the answers. In fact that type of question is one of their favorites. If they know the answer, there are no embarrassing surprises. Be careful how you answer, especially when your first impulse is to say, "If you had read the materials provided . . ." or, "As I already explained in your work session . . ." Council members often ask such questions for the public's benefit, or to get answers officially in the record, or to show other officials, the media, or the public that they are doing their job of critical review.

Have an articulate program manager make the presentation for a major new program. This must be coordinated with the city or county administrator, but the chief of department should not feel that he personally must present every program or detail. If it is compatible with local protocol, put together a team presentation; let the chief set the tone and introduce other staff and program managers, who often can provide better answers to detailed questions.

Be concise. The council's time is important so get to the point. Respect the council's agenda, even if others have not. If you run long, make sure it was their doing.

There is no better way to be concise than to use graphics. A good graphic will convey its primary message in seven seconds or less, and that's without an oral explanation. Remember, you won't always be there, so your charts and graphs must stand on their own. Most of the good microcomputer charting programs offer primers on selecting and designing good graphics for data display, so we'll just cover a few major or specialized points here.

Use one primary message per chart.

The message should be obvious/understood in seven seconds.

If multiple related messages are needed to show correlations, display ideas separately first, then combine them on one chart.

Use color, but use it judiciously and always for a reason. Use hot colors for negative issues, and cooler colors for positive aspects.

Choose the right type of graph:
—Pie charts to show proportional pieces of a whole.
—Bar or column graphs to make comparisons.
—Line graphs for a running value over a timeframe.

Mix graph types if your data allow it (three or more charts with the same general format will begin to run together in the audience's mind.)

Don't let the flashiness of graphs and charts, videos, slide dissolves, and special effects detract from your message or steal the show. A little bit of flash can add interest; use too much and the audience may begin to wonder how much your presentation cost.

If possible, and here again good microcomputer charting programs can help, show community data on a graphic with the community map as the background, and the data columns displayed on the tract, or council district to which they pertain. Elected officials will immediately focus on their districts and compare their data to others.

Use valid comparative data. Make comparisons to communities that are similar in size, demographics, and geography. Refer to national statistics, but be careful to refer to communities of similar size and within your area of the country.

Be aware of local identity sensitivities. Especially in smaller communities on the fringes of a major city, it may not be wise to say, "This is the way City Z does it." You may quickly be reminded, "We're not City Z and that's the way we like it!"

Be aware of body language. Build into your presentation several opportunities to jump to a summary. Have some alternate tacks in mind if you read negative reaction.

Know when to shut up! If you've got them sold, don't feel obliged to give your full presentation or you may just talk them out of it! If you read negative body language or sense a negative tone in their questioning, don't get argumentative. If the vote goes against you, take a deep breath, bite your tongue if you have to, and sit down and ponder any lessons learned. DON'T ARGUE! You will have other chances. Don't take it personally. If you presented a solid, community impact, objective-based program budget, you did your job.

BUDGET ADMINISTRATION

Regardless of how tattered or intact your budget is after final adoption, there are a number of details to attend to so that it is possible to administer what has just been passed.

- First, redistribute to the program budgets the actual amounts funded. Few things are more frustrating to a program manager than to have $X removed from a line-item budget without specifics as to what program(s) the reduction is supposed to affect. Ideally the funding authority, but if not, the chief must make those distributions.

- Develop a spending plan if one is not already in the budget submittal. This is more than taking each line-item amount funded and dividing by 12 months, although for some object codes that may be the case. Procurement timing and fluctuations in cash flow need to be projected by month. While these should be viewed only as estimates, they will help the fiscal officer invest idle funds for maximum return, yet have them available when projected. The fiscal officer will also have an estimate of income timing. If income is expected to fall behind the spending plan, program managers may have to delay spending, or justify the added expense of short-term borrowing.

- Review for possible needed changes, then train personnel, especially program managers and others involved in direct money handling, spending, or requisitions, in the policies and procedures that involve spending authority. Who is authorized to initiate procurement, for up to what amount, and under what circumstances? Someone needs to have emergency spending authority. In some departments that might be the chief only. In most departments the on-duty individual who has shift command responsibility is appropriate.

Transfer authority. From time to time, object code line item account balances may need to be adjusted, moving excess funds from one account to make up for shortages in another. This authority typically includes some restrictions on personnel salary account adjustments limiting FTE (full-time-employee) changes (minor adjustments to/from overtime and part-time accounts are usually allowed). Depending on the budgeting system used, this transfer authority typically rests in the hands of the program manager for transfer within the program, the division or functional area manager for transfers between the programs of the division, and the chief of department for transfers between divisions. The procedure for petitioning restricted transfers should be made clear.

Handling cash, both petty cash and money received in the course of business, must be managed carefully. In general, if a transaction involves cash, two people should have joint responsibility for it.

In the case of petty cash, only two people (at any one time) should have access. Periodically (weekly or monthly, or any time one person is going on leave and the key is passed to the other), they should do an audit together. They don't both need to be present to make a draw, but in every case a petty cash voucher should be placed in the box that identifies who made the draw, the date, purpose, and program and line-item object codes as appropriate.

Cash is received occasionally, even in offices where there typically are no public purchases or bill paying. Prenumbered receipts should be used to document all money received when it is received. A sign should be displayed that states that a numbered receipt must be issued for all cash received. Each receipt should be signed by the individual who accepts the funds, and include the date, the payer, and purpose. There should be a log to record each prenumbered receipt. If a receipt is voided, the log must be signed by a second individual (preferably an employee; if not, address and phone number also should be recorded) who has seen the voided receipt while the intended payer is still present. Periodically, two responsible employees should audit the receipts together and prepare a transaction to deposit the funds or transfer them to other control as appropriate.

These procedures may seem tedious, but employees must realize that they owe it to each other, to themselves, and to the organization to help protect not only the money, but more importantly, individual and organizational integrity. If the above procedures are followed, there should never be any question of integrity. Certainly a few mistakes will be made, but the individual who makes the mistake can be identified. If there are numerous mistakes, training, accountability, or reassignment of responsibility can be initiated before the problem becomes severe. If you are worried about conspiracy consider periodic round-robining or reassigning responsibility to minimize the danger.

Budget administration also includes periodic reporting (at least monthly) on the condition of program and line-item accounts. Managers should be trained to read these reports, which should show total funds budgeted for the year, what has been budgeted, spent, and committed by requisition (encumberance for the year to date), and variance (percentage high/low according to spending plan). In this age of computer networks it is possible to get account status on-line, in real time, and get up-to-the-minute account information. On-line entry of purchase requisitions and vouchers keeps the accounts up to date.

GOVERNMENTAL ACCOUNTING

It was mentioned earlier that the type of organization or legal jurisdiction can make a big difference in the department's level of involvement in fiscal affairs. Government accounting, beyond the extent of the basics discussed above, is one such area of differing involvement. In the case of city and county fire departments that are fiscally attached to the jurisdiction, the following items generally are under the purview of the jurisdiction's fiscal department. Fire protection districts and most volunteer organizations, on the other hand, must accept responsibility for the complete accounting function. In any case, the following is awareness-level information only, and should not be considered inclusive of all the legal and fiscal nuances of government accounting. Many excellent texts and college courses are available for those who have primary responsibilities in these areas.

Accounting is the recording, classifying, and summarizing of transactions and the interpretation of the results of those transactions. The purpose is to communicate to others (managers, taxpayers, owners, creditors, etc.) the fiscal and other resource conditions of the organization.

This communication is primarily through four documents, three of which are the basic types of accounting statements: balance sheet, income statement, and statement of changes in financial position. The fourth type of document is the "notes to financial statements." Each will be covered briefly.

A balance sheet provides a picture of the financial condition of the entity. The picture, like a snapshot, is only asserted to be accurate at a given point in time, i.e., the date (time) printed on the report heading. The next minute, literally, the condition may change as a result of ongoing business activities.

The name—balance sheet—is descriptive of the basic accounting formula that generally is presented in one of two ways, both equal (in balance):

$$\text{assets} = \text{liabilities} + \text{equity}$$
$$\text{assets} - \text{liabilities} = \text{equity}$$

Given the formula, the balance sheet is presented in three sections:

- **Assets:** Things of value that belong to the entity are grouped in categories:

CURRENT:
+ Cash or can be converted to cash within a year.
+ Prepaid expenses are goods or services that you have paid for but have not yet received.
+ Marketable securities (stocks and bonds).
+ Receivables are monies you are owed.
+ Inventory (consumable supplies and parts).

FIXED ASSETS
+ Property (land).
+ Buildings.
+ Equipment.
- Costs of placing these items in service.
- Accumulated depreciation (loss of capacity to yield value or service) may be shown as a reduction in value of the fixed asset, based on acquisition cost. (Depreciation is used in private enterprise as a deductible business expense for tax purposes. Government entities pay no taxes, so depreciation is not recorded as an expense).

OTHER ASSETS: Including patents, copyrights, trademarks.

- **Liabilities:** Claims against the assets are categorized as:

CURRENT: obligations due within a year:
+ Accounts payable for goods and services received.

+ Taxes payable (for government entities this would include the trust funds for taxes withheld from employee salaries and taxes collected for other government entities).
+ Current portion of debt.

LONG-TERM: claims that are due more than a year after the balance sheet date:

+ Bonds.
+ Notes payable.
+ Mortgages.

• **Equity:** The owners' claims on the assets—capital. In government entities this is shown as fund balances:

+ Outstanding stock.
+ Additional paid-in capital.
+ Retained earnings. In sole proprietorships and partnerships list owners share separately. Government entities may use retained earnings for enterprise funds; otherwise this is shown as a fund balance.

The Income Statement provides a summary of revenue and expenditures over a period of time shown as an "Ended" date in the report heading. The report usually covers the fiscal year, the last such statement produced generally will close out the budget year. Revenue is listed first, then expenditures are subtracted as operating and general expenses. The term "bottom line" originates from (is the result of) this statement. In some accounting texts you may see revenues referred to as "sales" and expenditures as "cost of sales," another example of the private enterprise focus of most accounting courses.

A Statement of Changes in Financial Position shows the financing sources, uses of working capital (those monies available for procurement of goods and services) and the difference in fund balance between the beginning and end of the year.

Sources include:

• current operations (fees and sales – expenses);
• sale of noncurrent (fixed) assets;
• borrowing from long-term lenders;
• sale of capital stock (a corporation's method of raising money for business expansion without borrowing money from a lending institution. This means selling shares of the corporation); and
• taxes collected in the case of government entities.

Uses include:

• purchase of noncurrent assets;
• prepayment of long-term debt;
• repurchase of capital stock (buying back shares of the business); and

• declaration of cash dividends (distribution of earnings to those holding shares in the company). (The state of Alaska is the only government entity in the U.S. to routinely do this in the form of a resident's share of the oil depletion fund).

The Notes to the Financial Statements are an integral part of the financial statement. They show relevant details not available on the face of the statements, including:

Significant accounting policies:
• Method of depreciation (not used as an expense in governmental organizations);
• Method of valuing inventory (The value of inventory will depend on how it is calculated as items are removed and replacements are added—first-in-first-out (FIFO), last-in-first-out (LIFO), or cost averaging);
• Recognition of revenue (time billed or received); and
• Recognition of encumbrances (time ordered, billed, or received).
Other information that may affect future conditions:
• Pending litigation (is the agency suing or being sued?);
• Fixed asset changes;
• Changes in, or features of, long-term debt (included here would be such significant features as scheduled balloon payments, prepayment and demand payment clauses); and
• Significant events: liens (contractor claims), judgments (the result of concluded litigation), pending applications for grants, patents, etc.

While many managers like to say it's the accountant's fault when a problem arises, it is important to remember that financial statements and notes are representations by the entity's management of its financial condition, even though they may be prepared by an accountant.

ACCOUNTING STANDARDS AND PRACTICES

Accountants are licensed by the states as CPAs only after they complete appropriate training, perform a proper internship, and take a two-and-a-half-day exam. CPAs are sworn to follow standards and a code of ethics set by the American Institute of Certified Public Accountants (AICPA). To keep a proper set of books an accountant needs to follow what are commonly called GAAPs (Generally Accepted Accounting Practices).

Among those standards is a methodology based on the *double-entry principle.* This principle is based on the assumption that every transaction that involves money or items of value has two sides. Described simply, double-entry bookkeeping records where value comes from and where it goes.

Another important related principle is the *debits equals credits rule*. This rule implies that as money changes hands (or accounts) none of it slips through the fingers. "Debits" and "credits" have been misunderstood terms since they were introduced. We will define them shortly.

Self-balancing system of accounts

To maintain the principles discussed above, accountants developed a system of account classes, and defined debits and credits for each account class. When transactions are recorded properly, the accounts automatically balance themselves. If the accounts do not balance, it is obvious that transactions were not recorded properly. It does not follow, however, that if the accounts are in balance, the transaction was entered properly; it is possible to get debits and credits backwards (see below) or to post to the wrong account.

The definition of a debit is an increase in an asset or expense account, or a decrease in a liability, equity, or revenue account.

The definition of a credit is a decrease in an asset or expense account, or an increase in a liability, equity, or revenue account.

There are those who are convinced that accountants devised this system of debits and credits as insurance for job security. Debit and credit are just words; they are not inherently positive or negative, or good or bad. If you look at the same definitions in table form you can see that they depend on the account class, or location, in the two-sided formula that determines the $-$ / $+$ of the entry:

$$\text{Assets}^{(A)} \quad = \quad \text{Liabilities}^{(L)} \quad + \text{Equity}^{(E)} \quad \text{(fund balance)}$$

Asset	Debit	=	Increase	Credit	=	Decrease
Liability	Debit	=	Decrease	Credit	=	Increase
Equity	Debit	=	Decrease	Credit	=	Increase
Revenue[E]	Debit	=	Decrease	Credit	=	Increase
Expense[A*]	Debit	=	Increase	Credit	=	Decrease

*The fact that an expense account is on the same side of the formula as assets may be another source of confusion. This makes sense if we consider that cash (an asset) can be converted (a decrease) to goods or services (an increase to something also having value, an asset), hence, an asset account. Notice that when we stay on the same side of the formula with both the debit and credit, one is an increase while the other is a decrease. If we are affecting accounts on both sides of the formula, we still have a debit and a credit for each transaction, but they are both either an increase or a decrease. This can be illustrated by the fact that revenue accounts are on the other side with equity. When tax bills go out, the tax revenue account is credited (increased) and accounts receivable (an asset) is debited (increased).

To illustrate these principles further, let's assume that our cash account (asset) has increased (debit) by some amount. At least one of the following had to have occurred:

- Some other asset account decreased (credit), which happens when someone pays an ambulance or hazardous materials service bill, or there is a tax-due account (receivable).
- A liability account increased (credit), which would happen if we borrowed the cash.
- An equity account increased (credit). In government entities, this only occurs with enterprise funds, that is, the city (owner) contributes the cash (seed money) to the fund balance (equity account) of the enterprise (airport, hazardous materials unit, if so set up).
- A revenue account increased (credit), which would happen if someone paid cash for copies of a report, prepaid taxes before they were due, or made a donation.
- An expense account decreased (credit), which could happen if we received a cash refund from a utility bill adjustment.

Remember the significance of that equal sign (=)—anything we do must balance.

Government accounting standards

Given the principles discussed above, government accounting goes a little farther in the effort to provide maximum protection of public funds through additional standards. The Municipal Finance Officers Association's National Committee on Governmental Accounting (NCGA) defined the standard, *Governmental Accounting, Auditing, and Financial Reporting (GAAFR)*, and, in 1974, AICPA issued *Audits of State and Local Governmental Units*.

NCGA cites 12 basic accounting principles (summarized below) which underlie the accounting and reporting for government operations:

1. Government systems must make it possible to present fairly in full conformity with GAAP, and determine and demonstrate compliance with finance-related legal and contractual provisions.
2. A fund basis is to be used. A fund is a fiscal and accounting entity with a self-balancing set of accounts that records the cash and other financial resources together with all related liabilities and residual equities or balances, and changes therein which are segregated for the purpose of carrying on specific activities.
3. The following eight types of funds in three categories are to be used by state and local governments:

Governmental

GENERAL FUND. All financial resources except those required to be accounted for in another fund. Most jurisdictions fund day-to-day fire department operations from the general fund.

SPECIAL REVENUE FUND. Special revenue sources that are legally restricted to specified purposes. Revenue sharing, grants, insurance premiums, taxes earmarked by some states to fund fire training, and the portion of the cigarette tax in Kansas City, Missouri earmarked for hazardous materials management are examples.

CAPITAL PROJECTS FUNDS. Financial resources to be used for the acquisition or construction of major facilities, such as new fire stations or water system expansions. This fund may be set aside from general or special revenue funds or seeded (funded) from the sale of bonds.

DEBT SERVICE FUNDS. To account for the accumulation of resources for, and the payment of, long-term capital debt principal and interest. It is through this fund type that bonds are repaid.

SPECIAL ASSESSMENT FUNDS. To account for the financing of public improvements or services deemed to benefit the properties (private good principle) against which the special assessments are levied. Sidewalks, sewage facilities, and fire protection impact and assessment fees are examples.

Proprietary

ENTERPRISE FUNDS. Operations financed and operated similar to private enterprise. Costs of providing the goods or services are recovered through user charges. Revenues and expenditures are encapsulated within the fund for capital maintenance, public policy, management control, or accountability. Typical historic uses include airports, convention facilities, public golf courses, and government-owned public utilities. Also being applied by some to EMS services, Hazardous Materials team operations, public safety photo labs (sale of accident, fire scene photos), and contract provision of fire services to neighboring jurisdictions.

INTERNAL SERVICE FUND. Financing goods and services provided by one department to another on a cost-reimbursement basis. Called "funny money" by some because all funds ultimately come from the general fund or other revenue pools, this really should be taken seriously. It is only through this aspect of accounting that actual costs of delivering various services from departments and programs can be identified.

Fiduciary

TRUST AND AGENCY FUNDS. To account for assets held by the government unit in a trustee capacity for individuals, private organizations, or other government units. Deferred compensation and pension trust funds are examples.

Returning to the 12 principles:

4. Government units should establish and maintain those funds required by law and sound financial administration. Only the minimum number of funds necessary should be established, however, because unnecessary funds result in a lack of flexibility, undue complexity, and inefficient financial administration.

5. A clear distinction should be made between fund fixed assets and general fixed assets, and fund long-term debt and general long-term debt. Fixed assets related to specific proprietary or trust funds should be accounted for through those funds. All others should be accounted for through the General Fund Fixed Assets Account Group.

   Long-term liabilities of specific proprietary, special assessment funds, and trust funds should be accounted for through those funds. All others should be accounted for through the General Fund Long-Term Debt Account Group.

6. Fixed assets should be accounted for at cost, or, if cost cannot be determined, at estimated value. Donated fixed assets should be recorded at their estimated fair market value.

7. Depreciation should not be recorded as an expense. It may be calculated for cost-finding analyses and recorded in the Fixed Assets Account Group of the pertinent fund in an account called Accumulated Depreciation.

In private enterprise this account would be in the Expense Account Group to be offset by income generated, and because depreciation is a tax-deductible business expense. The purpose of government entities is not to generate income and they have no need for tax deductions. However, assets do wear out and depreciate; for this reason depreciation should be calculated within the reporting period and credited (decreased) to the Asset Account Group so the cost of using the asset can be determined. Further, knowing the asset will wear out eventually, the jurisdiction may decide to set aside an amount equal to the cost of using the asset (amortization) in a "Reserve for Apparatus Replacement Fund." Because interest can be earned on that fund while it is idle, and because interest can be avoided on monies that would otherwise need to be borrowed in order to replace the apparatus, significant money can be saved.

8. The modified accrual or accrual basis of accounting should be used as defined below. ("Basis of accounting" refers to *when* revenue, expenditures, expenses, and transfers are recognized in accounts and reported in financial statements).

   —Government fund revenues and expenditures should be recognized on the modified accrual basis. That is, revenues should be recognized in the accounting period in which they become available and expenditures in the period in which the fund liability is incurred.

—Proprietary fund revenues and expenditures should be recognized on the basis of accrual. That is, revenues should be recognized in the accounting period in which they are earned and expenditures in the period incurred.

—Fiduciary funds are handled in a way consistent with the measurement objectives of the fund. Pension and Nonexistent Trust Funds are on the accrual basis, Expendable Trust Funds and Agency Funds are on the modified accrual basis.

9. An annual budget must be adopted. Further, the accounting system should provide the basis for appropriate budget control, and budgetary comparisons must be included in financial statements for each account group. The budget must be approved by the legislative body in conformance with applicable state law. This means that the vote must occur in an open public meeting in most states, also known as "sunshine" laws). Appropriations of the expenditures may be by line item, category, or in total by department or program.

Earlier we discussed the maximum control of the line-item versus the flexibility of resource allocation provided the manager by the program budget. Both approaches, and everything in between, are consistent with the above principles of government accounting.

10. Interfund transfers and proceeds of general long-term debt should be classified separately from fund revenues and expenditures. Government fund revenues should be classified by fund and source. Expenditures are classified by fund, function (or program), organization unit, activity, character, and principal classes of objects. Proprietary fund revenues and expenditures are classified in the same manner as similar business enterprises.

11. The same terminology is to be used throughout the system. Following are some terms not already defined above:
Appropriation—Legal authority to make expenditures for specific purposes.
Encumbrance—Commitment to purchase goods or services.

Once a purchase order has been issued, this commitment to pay is entered into the accounting system. The line-item appropriations account is credited (decreased) and the reserve for encumbrances debited (increased). This prevents obligating the jurisdiction to spend more than the appropriated amount and is another benefit associated with a computer-based system which can provide real-time account information to multiple users (PC-LAN or multiuser mini or mainframe).

Voucher Payable—Liabilities for goods or services which have been approved for payment, but have not been paid.

When goods or services are actually received several things happen in the accounting system. The asset or expense account (as appropriate for the purchased item or service) is debited (increased) and the encumbrances account is credited (decreased). When the voucher is approved for payment the encumbrances account is debited (increased), the reserve for encumbrances credited (decreased), followed immediately by a credit (increase) to the accounts payable and a debit (increase) to the accumulated budget spent account.

When the amount is paid automatically, accounts payable is debited (decreased) and cash is credited (decreased).

12. Periodic reports are produced on an interim and comprehensive annual schedule. These include the Balance Sheet, Combined Income and Revenue Statements, and Notes to the Financial Statements described in the previous section.

Creating a positive fiscal management atmosphere

Many values, rules of conduct, and standard practices should be identified and articulated within the department. Make it clear that all employees are responsible for protecting department and community resources. You can communicate this through policies, training, and the examples set by managers, both in the department and jurisdiction. If personnel see management ignoring or minimizing these concerns, they won't be very motivated to conserve resources either.

Certain practices (rules of the game) handicap this atmosphere. One is the "legal spender concept." It says, "Spend all of your budget! If you don't, we'll not only lose the amount you didn't spend this year, we'll lose it next year as well. City Hall will say, 'You didn't need it last year, so we won't give it to you this year!'"

Some jurisdictions try to short-circuit the rash of spending at the end of the year by freezing procurement during the last quarter of the fiscal year. This only works once! In subsequent years managers simply spend more sooner. The danger of this approach is that the resources won't be available if last quarter expenses are higher than the manager anticipated.

Another solution that hasn't worked well was exemplified by a fire protection board that gave the chief a bonus each year, based substantially on the amount of the department budget that was unspent. Things finally came to a head, and the chief "resigned," when the board discovered the firefighters were sharing rubber turnout coats among shifts.

There are several ways to minimize the effects of the "legal spender" attitude. The simplest is for the jurisdiction to allow unspent funds to carry over, either in place in the same programs/accounts, or within the budget at the chief's discretion. There still may be a perception that the jurisdiction will diminish the subsequent budget by a similar amount, but at least managers won't feel the need to argue for money they already have. Another approach is to have unspent monies routinely rolled into the department's apparatus replacement fund.

Another rule of the game that doesn't encourage a positive attitude is having to pad the budget with X percent fat in order to get what you really need. Using program budgeting, with well-written and researched impact objectives, can help minimize this. Breaking the budget down into programs in which outcomes, outputs and inputs (budget) are closely tied has two effects: it becomes harder for the department to pad, department-wide, X percent for the city hall's or council's ritual cutting, and, because reductions in program input can be tied to an impact, the council is less likely to wield its knife so brutally.

Auditing

There is a misconception that audits are intended to find fraud or inappropriate handling of funds, and that when one is conducted it is because something was believed to have been done wrong. The latter is just not so! While mishandling of funds or theft (or evidence of them) sometimes *is* uncovered during the course of an audit, this is not the primary purpose of an audit. Audits are routinely conducted to assure the users of an entity's financial statement of their accuracy. These users include elected and other officials and managers within the jurisdiction, citizens, creditors, financial institutions, bond underwriters, investors (bond purchasers), and other interested parties. If you are conducting your fiscal and resource management affairs in an honest manner, you have nothing to fear from an audit; in fact, it can help the chief to protect the community's resources and enhance the image of the organization and its managers.

There are many types of audits:

Operational audits are a review of the operating procedures and methods, and an evaluation of efficiency and effectiveness. Among the items examined would be the organizational structure, computer operations and information handling, training, production methods, relevance of activities to mission, and whether sufficient and accurate information is used in decisionmaking.

Compliance audits are used to determine whether the organization or individual (auditee) is following the rules set down by some higher authority. Compliance audits are used to check whether:

- accounting personnel are following prescribed procedures;
- wage rates are in compliance with minimum wage laws,

- compliance exists with requirements imposed by other government entities (there must be an annual audit, for instance); and
- taxpayers are in compliance with federal tax laws (IRS audit).

Audits of financial statements provide overall assurance that the information is accurate and is stated in accordance with generally accepted accounting principles (GAAPs). All four document types are reviewed (and required):

- statement of financial position (balance sheet);
- income statement (statement of revenue and expenditures);
- statement of changes in financial position (these last two often are combined and will be labeled as such); and
- the notes to the financial statements.

Audits are just another tool used in protecting the public's resources, the organization, and the officials and managers.

DEVELOPING A PURCHASING PROGRAM

Once again, the fire department's level of involvement in purchasing depends, to a large degree, on the type of entity. City and county governments typically have a centralized purchasing department; the fire department's role is usually limited to providing specifications, filling out requisitions and purchase order forms, and providing names of suppliers for specialized items. On the other hand, fire protection districts and many volunteer organizations, as independent entities, have to assume all purchasing responsibilities. Either way, purchasing bureaucracies can be a source of frustration for fire officers.

Purchasing functions and responsibilities

Understanding the following functions and responsibilities of a purchasing program may be helpful.

- Understand the needs of the various departments. This is easier in an independent fire district operation. The purchasing agent only needs to know about hose, nozzles, SCBA, personal protective equipment and clothing, pumps and apparatus performance standards, hydraulic equipment, hazardous materials control supplies, EMS equipment and consumables, radios, telephone switching equipment . . . well, you get the idea. Add to all the fire service vernacular the equally extensive special needs of other city/county agencies and it can be almost overwhelming.

- Be familiar with supply sources. For each product category several suppliers must be identified to make procurements competitive.
- Understand the nuances of the job, i.e., pricing (quantity breaks, units, packaging/handling, FPO), accepted practices (formal and informal quotes, provision of reference material, referrals, respect for proprietary information, etc.), market conditions, return policies, etc.
- Check the open market, even if items are on state or General Services Administration (GSA) contract price lists (many jurisdictions avoid the costs of getting bids by purchasing from vendors on these government procurement lists at preset government prices). Certain items, e.g., personal computer hardware and software, have such volatile pricing that you can often find better deals on the open market, especially in metropolitan areas.
- Know the legal requirements of public disclosure, bidding, bidder qualifications, purchasing authority policies of the jurisdiction and any specialized policies of the various departments. Most jurisdictions require multiple bids for each procurement; depending on the amount of purchase, these bids may be made by phone, informally in writing, or through a formalized sealed bid procedure. For certain services and supplies, standing, open purchase orders are allowed, but only after suitable bids and negotiations have secured reasonable cost structures.
- Deal with vendors effectively. Vendors are a resource and they must be treated respectfully, fairly, and with no hint of partiality. Orders placed are their reward for professional service to your needs. Vendors will catch on very quickly to jurisdictions that don't treat them fairly, don't pay their bills on time, attempt to return mistreated goods, and that use them only as a source of information and specifications before going out of the area for a slightly lower price, or to a preferred vendor.
- Assist in developing specifications. Without guidance and training those unfamiliar with performance purchasing may develop specifications around specific brand names or components. The danger is that the jurisdiction will either pay more for equipment than its needs require, or that the components specified will not work together. Specifications should be based on performance criteria, not brand names. Capacities, mean-time-between-failures, abrasion test performance, maintenance requirements and costs, weight-to-performance ratios, and performance test requirements are all valid specification criteria.
- Provide a system to take discounts for timely payment of accounts, and quantity discounts (when volume of usage, the cost of storage and spoilage warrant the quantity purchase), verify delivery and quality, conduct acceptance testing, record receipts, add to inventory, manage asset control, provide distribution, and manage defect returns and refunds.

Procurement decisions must include quantity, group, or individual purchase considerations. Would it be more economical to replace items all at once, individually, as they wear out, or when maintenance costs get too high on a particular item? This decision requires information on the life expectancy of the item, standards of performance, quantity price breaks, maintenance costs, downtime, capital investment, etc.

Whether a procurement system is operated directly by the fire department or is provided by a city or county department, you can avoid a lot of frustration by:

- Making purchasing personnel part of your operation. Invite them to the stations, and institute a ride-along program if there is interest. The purchasing clerk will understand your procurement needs better if he has seen the operation. Breathing apparatus, turnout coats, gloves, boots, etc., become much more real once you've worn them, held them in your hands, and seen the effects of normal fire service use.
- Avoiding fire service jargon and acronyms, unless they are defined in each document in which they are used.
- Attaching pictures to purchase requests; defibrillator batteries take on an entirely different meaning when a picture of the defib unit and batteries are provided (or when the agent has seen and held them in his hands).
- Showing purchasing personnel professional courtesy. Thank them now and then. When there is a mistake or something isn't clear, assume the fault may be just on your end; seek ways to improve your communication and their understanding.

TOTAL COST PURCHASING

Some jurisdictions have adopted what is known as total cost purchasing as part of their budgeting process. The budgeted amount includes all costs associated with a given item and its ongoing use and performance. Item cost, maintenance costs, replacement cost (into a replacement sinking fund based on life expectancy), warehouse expenses, purchasing costs, and overhead are all included. With such a system policymakers are kept informed about the long-term cost of acquisition (and providing the supported service), and program managers are more confident that vital resources will be maintained and replaced as necessary.

Cooperative purchasing programs

Cooperative purchasing by departments for both common commodities and specialized fire service equipment has resulted in substantial savings over individual agency procurement. Lower costs, more purchasing power, and standardized equipment in the mutual aid district are some advantages of joint purchasing.

Joint purchasing does have some disadvantages. It may require additional time to gather all needed information from all agencies, process the order, and receive delivery of the larger quantities. It requires additional effort on someone's part. There may be a lack of control, and agencies undoubtedly will have to make some compromises.

Other considerations include the level of service individual agencies will receive, and who will provide needed control, delivery point, warehousing, security, and distribution. Commonalities and differences must be identified; sometimes vendors can accommodate minor differences without adversely affecting pricing. There should be a written agreement that specifies each agency's rights and responsibilities, the length of the agreement, rights and conditions of termination, and cost allocation for administering the program.

SUMMARY

Financial management doesn't end when the budget is passed. Remember the illustration of the financial management cycle? The last activity for any given budget year is an evaluation of performance. Notice that in the illustration the timing is perfect to start a strategic planning review for the next year's budget.

Many agencies also have a formal review of program performance at the six-month point in a budget year. That period is long enough to get most new programs up and running, and if they're not producing measurable impacts at that point, they will at least be producing process output. Are these things on track? If not, the six remaining months are time enough to adjust major programs and possibly to see results by the end-of-year review.

Program and function managers, and the chief of department and staff, should be watching continually for tangible impact and process results or indications of problems.

Following these principles in a dedicated, professional way (and again, professional does not necessarily mean paid), will build on each past effort. All of the following will increase with each cycle through the ensuing budget years: credibility, the accuracy and completeness of impact performance measures and process output productivity databases, analysis skills, ease of strategic plan revision and application of these procedures. Problems will arise, of course, but the information and skills gathered by applying these principles consistently will help in earlier problem recognition and in better solutions.

In the long-term management of the department—achieving its mission, creating its future, and ensuring the fire, life, and environmental safety future of the community itself—not many things are more important than giving professional attention to the concepts presented in this chapter, and integrating this knowledge with the other information in this handbook.

ACKNOWLEDGMENTS

Tom Admire, Diane Breedlove, Alan Brunacini, Larry Damrell, Richard (Smokey) Dyer, Anne Fabyan, Michael Fay, Charles Fisher, John Granito, Phil Harris, Dave House, Richard Lehmann, Jim Nacy, Ron Poble, Vic Rasmussen, Bruce Roemelt, Randolf (Doc) Ryan, Joe Sieta, Dick Small, Gary Turner, Tim Turner, Bill Westhoff, and Kenneth Wright.

4

Management and the Law

JOHN RUKAVINA, J.D.

CHAPTER HIGHLIGHTS

- The American legal system.
- Federal statutes and cases, and how they affect fire departments.
- How state laws affect fire departments.
- The basis of negligence law and negligence defenses.
- The lawsuit process.

*T*HE CONCEPT OF LAW has been around as long as people (and fire) have existed. It is not far from the imposition of rules of conduct and behavior that governed a family, to the development of rules that governed a tribe or a society. Over time, those rules—written and unwritten—provided the means by which acts that would hurt a community ("an eye for an eye," for example) were controlled by that community.

In some societies, elected or appointed bodies of elders or other highly regarded members of the community wrote down those rules in the form of laws. In others, those rules were developed on a case-by-case basis by judges as they dealt with problems. In Great Britain, the principal parent of the American legal system, both written law—*statutory* law—and judge-made law—*common* law—governed the conduct of British citizens.

The Anglo-Saxon approach to law also distinguished between a legal wrong that affected one individual, and a legal wrong that injured a society as a whole. If one person suffered an injury, the Anglo-Saxon legal system provided a *civil* legal system the injured person could use to recover damages. If an act or injury hurt society as well as an individual, a murder, for example, the society would act on behalf of the individual through the *criminal* legal system. The goal of the criminal legal system was often to protect society from further criminal acts by punishing the criminal, rather than to help a victim recover.

FOUNDATIONS OF AMERICAN LAW

While the American legal system was built primarily from the British legal system,* the Americans added a unique feature of their own—a constitution.

Although the Americans won the Revolutionary War, their first efforts at organizing a new country were not successful. Since each state was unwilling to grant meaningful power to the Continental Congress, the states collectively could do very little. So each state sent representatives to a "Constitutional Convention" to try again to develop a system that would allow the states to work as a unit, but at the same time preserve the fundamental rights of each state to govern its own affairs.

This time, the states were more successful. Their representatives agreed on a basic formula: the states would create a federal government and give that federal government certain powers; all other powers would be in the hands of each state. The details of this formula were embodied in the United States Constitution, which was adopted by all the states in 1787.

The adoption of the Constitution marked the true end of the American Revolution. While the United States' legal system was based in large part on Great Britain's legal system, Great Britain has no constitution. Over the succeeding two centuries, the Constitution itself—and the struggle between and among the states and the federal government about what the Constitution says and means—have shaped the American legal system.

THE AMERICAN LEGAL SYSTEM

Law in the United States depends on two sources for development and explanation: legislative bodies (Congress and state legislatures) and courts, both state and federal.

Legislatures and Statutes

Legislatures create what lawyers call *statutory* law. A statutory law is adopted by a legislative body, written in the form of a statute and then signed

---

*In states that had been territories under France or Spain, state legal systems still reflect their French or Spanish roots. In Louisiana, traces of the French "Napoleonic Code" are still very much in evidence, and California land law had its roots in the Spanish legal system.

by the President or a state's Governor (or passed again over the President's or a Governor's veto). The intent of statutory law is to describe as clearly as possible conduct or behavior that is acceptable or unacceptable, and the consequences of violating those standards. In cases where the statute is not clear, lawyers will look at the legislative history of a statute (as chronicled in the *Congressional Record,* for example) for clarification and guidance.

Within constitutional limits, legislative bodies also can bestow some of their powers on other bodies. A state legislature can, for example, delegate to a state agency the power to create, enforce, and amend a state fire code. Such a code would not necessarily itself be a statute, but because it has the power of statutory law behind it, this state fire code would have the power of statutory law. Congress often passes broad statutes, and then grants federal agencies the power to adopt the specific rules necessary for enforcement of those statutes.

Since most counties, cities, towns, and other local governments were created by state statutes, the powers held by those local governments are also delegated powers.

Courts and Common Law

Courts create *common* (or case) law though decisions made in connection with a particular legal controversy; the decision applies to any future case involving the same (or similar) facts.

Not all courts have the power to create or change common law. Generally, state and federal trial courts cannot issue statements of law that are binding on other courts. Courts that have the power to create or change common law are called *appellate courts,* or *courts of record.* The decisions of these courts are published in the form of "opinions," which contain a statement of the facts of a case, a discussion of how those facts relate to existing common or statutory law, and a legal conclusion—a "finding."

Appellate courts have a great deal of respect for *precedent*—law set forth in earlier court decisions. Because common law is such an important part of the American legal system, judges are very reluctant to destabilize the legal system by frequent changes in common law. It may take a decade of discussion at the appellate level before an earlier case is overruled.

Jurisdiction

Statutory law and common law are not always distinct. A legislative body may, by statute, overrule common law. An appellate court may declare a statute unconstitutional (a power attributed to the federal courts as early as 1803 in the case of *Marbury* v *Madison*).

Other aspects of jurisdiction* are regulated by statutory law or rule. A decision by the North Carolina Supreme Court does not establish new law in California. A decision by the Federal District Court in Dallas does not bind a Federal District judge in Boston. (In matters involving fire departments and firefighters, only the U.S. Supreme Court has truly national jurisdiction.) And, a resident of Florida cannot sue his local fire department in a Louisiana court. Here are some general rules of jurisdiction in the United States:

- State laws apply only in each respective state.
- State appellate court statements of common law apply only in the state of origin.
- Federal courts have jurisdiction when federal laws or constitutional rights have been violated, or when there is "diversity of jurisdiction" (a case that involves people and laws of two or more states).
- Federal courts generally respect state common law in "diversity of jurisdiction" cases.

THE LAW AND THE FIRE SERVICE

The year 1964 marked a fundamental change in the relationship between the American fire service and the law. Before, a fire chief's encounter with the American legal system likely was associated with a fire code enforcement matter, or, occasionally, a grievance. But in 1964, Congress passed the first civil rights act since Civil War times. The Civil Rights Act of 1964 stimulated enormous interest in individual rights, including the right to obtain (and retain) a job as a firefighter.

Also by 1964, erosion of the concept of "sovereign immunity"—the absolute immunity from negligence lawsuits customarily enjoyed by local governments—was well underway, spreading from west to east, state by state. The decline of sovereign immunity was more than matched by a marked increase in litigation, and by expansion of the damage awards juries were likely to grant a plaintiff who had suffered some kind of injury.

The convergence of the Civil Rights Act of 1964 and the "negligence revolution" meant that fire chiefs would find themselves suddenly thrust into legal controversies that had little to do with fire codes or grievances. This trend continued through the 1970s, 1980s, and 1990s as complex environmental and safety laws were passed, and as Congress and legislatures began including local governments (and thus fire departments) in coverage of statutes like the Fair Labor Standards Act (FLSA).

---

*A note to the reader: The concept of jurisdiction is considerably more complex than this summary suggests. This summary is intended as a brief explanation of why a court decision or trial verdict in one state doesn't automatically apply in another.

DUE PROCESS

Fire chiefs sometimes run afoul of the Constitution in connection with disciplinary actions, particularly those that involve loss of pay, rank, or job. For employment law purposes, this simple checklist of the basic elements of due process will help the fire chief to maintain organizational discipline without violating rights.

- Provide clear notice of specific charges or allegations.
- Provide enough notice to allow the accused employee to defend himself.
- Provide a hearing where the employee can present his side of the story.
- Make sure the employee knows that he can bring legal help (the employer is not bound to pay for such help).
- Give the employee (or representative) the opportunity to question witnesses.
- Make sure that some kind of record of the hearing is maintained.
- Make a decision based on the evidence, not on circumstances not directly related to the charge or accusation.
- Impose disciplinary action that is proportionate to the offense.

Fire chiefs should remember that "due process" does not require disciplinary hearings to be conducted with the same formality as a criminal trial (courts consider disciplinary hearings to be civil, not criminal, even if the result of a hearing is loss of a job), but "due process" does assume fair treatment.

FEDERAL STATUTES AND CASES

Literally hundreds of federal laws affect fire chiefs throughout the U.S. Since these laws are implemented by federal agencies, they're accompanied by thousands of pages of federal regulations.

Of all those laws and rules, a relative handful are critical to fire department managers. Following are summaries of the most influential of the federal laws.

Civil Rights Acts

Congress has passed four civil rights acts since the end of the Civil War. The *Civil Rights Act of 1866* (42 U.S. Code, Section 1981) provides that "all persons . . . shall have the same right . . . to make and enforce contracts . . . as enjoyed by white citizens." The word "contracts" has been interpreted by courts to include the "contract" implied in hiring someone, so Section 1981 has been applied to governmental discrimination in hiring (the Civil Rights Act of 1991 broadens the concept of "contract" to include discrimination on the job after hiring). The *Civil Rights Act of 1871* (42 U.S. Code, Section 1983) prohibits ". . . the deprivation of any rights, privileges, or immunities secured by the Constitution and laws . . ." The application of Section 1983 is limited by other language to local governments, but Section 1983 is only a means by which "deprivation" of a specific Constitutional right at the local level can be punished by lawsuits.

The *Civil Rights Act of 1964* (42 U.S. Code, Section 2000) has probably done more to affect the public workplace than any other law. This Act in effect codified the Supreme Court's finding in *Brown* v *Board of Education* (1954) that segregation on the basis of race is inherently discriminatory, and thus a violation of the Constitution. Title VII of the Act prohibits employer use of race, color, religion, sex, or national origin in connection with any hiring, promotion, dismissal, or other employment decision, unless the employer can demonstrate that use of race, color, religion, sex, or national origin in such decisions is connected to a "bona fide occupational qualification" (BFOQ). Very few employers have ever been able to establish a BFOQ exemption under Title VII.

Starting in the second half of the 1980s, the U.S. Supreme Court handed down a series of rulings that provided for a more restrictive interpretation of the Civil Rights Acts of 1866 and 1964. After two years—and a Presidential veto—the *Civil Rights Act of 1991* was passed. The Civil Rights Act of 1991 is summarized in the following "before-and-after" table.

The Civil Rights Law of 1991 also affects discrimination in multinational U.S. corporations, expert-witness fee recovery, Americans with Disability Act "good-faith" defenses, and the availability of jury trials for intentional-discrimination cases.

Finally, the 1991 Act allows plaintiff recovery of compensatory damages as well as out-of-pocket expenses from the employer, including local government employers. Compensatory damages are "capped" at from $50,000 to $300,000, according to the size of the employer.

Figure 4-1. Civil Rights Act of 1991

BEFORE

AFTER

Section 1981 (the Civil Rights Act of 1866) covered discrimination in hiring and, in some cases, promotion, but did *not* cover harassment, discrimination in firing, etc. [*Patterson* v *McLean Credit Union,* 491 U.S. 164 (1989]

Section 1981 covers *all* forms of racial discrimination in employment.

A discriminatory seniority rule can only be challenged when the rule is adopted. [*Lorance* v *ATUT Technologies,* 490 U.S. 900 (1989)]

A discriminatory seniority system can be challenged when it is adopted *and* when it affects employees in the future.

White firefighters could challenge an affirmative-action consent decree (an agreement between parties approved by the court) several years after that decree was approved by the court. [*Martin v Wilks,* 490 U.S. 755 (1989)]

Consent-decree challenges are prohibited if the challenger had a "reasonable opportunity to object" at the time of the decree, or if the challenger's interests were "adequately represented by another party," a union, for example.

An employer would not be liable for discrimination in connection with an employment action if the employer could demonstrate that the action would have been taken without a discriminatory motive. [*Price Waterhouse* v *Hopkins,* 490 U.S. 228 (1989)]

Intentional discrimination is unlawful, even if the same action would have been taken without evidence of discrimination.

An employer did not have to prove "business *necessity*" to defend against employment practices that had a "disparate impact" on a protected group—the employer only had to provide a business *justification* for those practices. [*Wards Cove Packing* v *Atonio,* 490 U.S. 642 (1989)]

Employment practices that have a disparate impact on a protected group *require* "... demonstrat[ion] that the challenged practice is job-related for the position in question and consistent with business necessity," but plaintiffs are expected to specify the particular employment practices they are challenging.

Age Discrimination in Employment Act (ADEA)

ADEA (29 U.S. Code, Section 621) was passed in 1967. It prohibits discrimination on the basis of age against all persons 40 years of age or older, and covers private employers of 20 or more persons. There is still disagreement in different lower-court jurisdictions over whether ADEA applies to local governments that employ fewer than 20 employees, but a local government with 20 or more employees is covered.

In 1986, Congress amended ADEA. The amendments included a provision allowing state and local governments to retain mandatory retirement age requirements for firefighters, police, and correction officers, but that exemption was authorized only through 1993. In the 1993–94 Congress, an attempt to extend that exemption did not succeed. Debate on age versus physical disability as the best criterion for establishing readiness for retirement is likely to continue.

Fair Labor Standards Act (FLSA)

First enacted in 1938, FLSA (29 U.S. Code, Section 201) did not apply to government employees. The U.S. Supreme Court rebuffed suits brought by public employees to obtain FLSA coverage until *Garcia* v *San Antonio Metropolitan Transit Authority* (469 U.S. 528 (1985)). In the wake of *Garcia*, Congress amended FLSA to include public employees, and charged the U.S. Department of Labor with the development of rules on how FLSA was to be applied in local government workplaces.

FLSA governs work schedules; specifically, it establishes the right of employees to time-and-one-half compensation after a minimum number of hours worked in a defined work period. "Defined work period" in the fire service ranges from 7 to 28 days, while hours-worked thresholds vary according to a particular fire department's work schedule.

Equal Pay Act of 1963

The Equal Pay Act (29 U.S. Code, Section 206) is an amendment to FLSA that, in a phrase, requires "equal pay for equal work." The Act includes limited exceptions and a prohibition against reducing the salary of any employee to meet the "equal-pay" requirements of the Act.

Americans with Disabilities Act (ADA)

Although the ADA (42 U.S. Code, Section 1201) became law in 1990, many of its requirements had first been applied to many local governments as part of the Rehabilitation Act of 1973. The difference between ADA and the "Rehab Act" is that the 1973 Act applied to federal fund recipients; ADA applies to *all* local governments, regardless of the number of employees.

ADA protects "qualified individuals with disabilities" from discrimination in public service or employment. A "qualified individual" is defined as a person who can perform the "essential functions" of a job "with or without reasonable accommodation."

Employers generally (and fire chiefs in particular) have not had a great deal of difficulty in defining "essential functions," but are concerned about just how far employers must go to provide "reasonable accommodations." According to a national survey, however, most of the "reasonable accommodations" identified in implementation of ADA cost little or nothing.

For example, a "reasonable accommodation" in a fire department could be provision of eyeglass *frames* installed inside SCBA masks (ADA would not require the fire department to provide the lenses for those frames).

According to some fire chiefs, the most challenging aspect of implementing ADA is the fact that most departments currently employ firefighters with disabilities that, in most fire departments, would disqualify new applicants.

Firefighters who have suffered heart attacks, or have recovered from serious back injuries, for example, often return to regular firefighting duties; however, a firefighter *candidate* with the same medical history would be assumed by many chiefs to be unfit for employment as a firefighter.

Family Medical Leave Act (FMLA)

FMLA (January, 1993) established a right to unpaid medical leave for employers with 50 or more employees, including local governments. FMLA's provisions include the following:

- Up to 12 weeks of unpaid leave in any 12-month period for childbirth, adoption, the care of a child, spouse, or parent with a serious health problem, or for an employee's own serious health condition when that employee has exhausted sick leave or other benefits.
- An employee on FMLA leave is guaranteed health care benefits and his or her own job (or an equivalent job) on return from leave. Seniority does not automatically accrue unless the employer so chooses.
- The employee must have worked for the employer for at least one year

and cannot collect unemployment or other government benefits during the leave period.

- The employer can ask for medical opinions and other verification of the need for FMLA leave and can require that the employee who does not return to work after the leave repay the employer the cost of the health care benefits that are guaranteed during the leave.
- An employer can deny leave to any of the highest-paid 10 percent of its employees if allowing the leave would cause "substantial and grievous injury" to the employer's operations. In a typical city, this means that the fire chief, police chief and similarly compensated staff could be denied family leave under FMLA.

Note that in the case of fire departments that are part of a town, city, or county government, "employer" is that town, city, or county, not the fire department. This means that FMLA applies to a 35-member career fire department if the department's parent government has 50 or more total employees. The ten percent rule applies to the highest-paid ten percent of the employees of the town, city or county. A fire district that is not a part of another government unit would be covered by FMLA only if it had 50 or more employees.

Occupational Safety and Health Act (OSHA)

OSHA was enacted by Congress in 1973. Under the Act, the Occupational Safety and Health Administration (also known as OSHA) was created and empowered to develop workplace safety standards. OSHA also created a research office (National Institute of Occupational Safety and Health, or NIOSH).

OSHA coverage of local government employees generally (and firefighters in particular) varies according to whether a given state conducts no occupational health and safety actions of its own (and leaves such actions to federal OSHA), or operates its own occupational health and safety program, with standards at least as stringent as federal OSHA standards ("state plan" states). Federal OSHA usually does not cover local government employees; local government regulation is imposed by states.

Even though federal OSHA standards may not apply in a given jurisdiction, they can be introduced as evidence of a "community standard" in a civil lawsuit.

Of particular interest to fire chiefs are OSHA standards that deal with industrial fire brigades, hazardous materials scene workers, workers whose duties bring them into contact with bloodborne pathogens, and workers who must enter confined spaces.

Hazardous Materials

Although federal laws intended to protect the environment from hazardous wastes and materials were first passed nearly 20 years ago, only recently have federal laws included provisions dealing with firefighter exposure to the risks of hazardous materials incidents.

The Federal Water Pollution Control Act (1974) established the National Response Center and development of a "National Oil and Hazardous Substances Pollution Contingency Plan," but the focus of this Act was environmental protection, not hazardous materials emergency response. Therefore, after the "Love Canal" scandal of the late 1970s, Congress passed the *Comprehensive Emergency Response, Compensation and Liability Act of 1980* (also known as "CERCLA" and "Superfund"). The focus of CERCLA was on hazardous materials site cleanup; Congress estimated 400 such sites, but, at last count, some 10,000 sites had been identified.

When more than 2,500 people near a chemical plant in Bhopal, India were killed by a methyl isocyanate release, Americans became more concerned about the potential for a major release in the U.S. When the same substance was released in Institute, West Virginia (with no injuries, however), Congress responded in 1986 with the *Superfund Amendments and Reauthorization Act (SARA)*. SARA specifically addressed training for hazardous materials responders; Title III of SARA (the "Emergency Planning and Community Right-to-Know Act") provided for local and regional planning for chemical emergencies and reporting of chemical releases.

The latest addition to the SARA family of hazardous materials statutes is the *Hazardous Materials Transportation Uniform Safety Act of 1990*. This Act provides a funding mechanism—financed by registration fees from hazardous materials shippers and carriers—for state and local hazardous materials response training.

FEDERAL CASE LAW

In several areas, the federal government has spoken to fire-related issues through case law, or a combination of case law and statutes. Below are some major examples.

Arson investigation

Arson is a crime. As such, arson investigation is treated by the courts as is investigation of any crime; therefore, the rights of arson suspects are protected in the same manner as the rights of any other criminal suspects.

In the case of *Michigan* v *Tyler,* 436 U.S. 499 (1978), the U.S. Supreme

Court held that, absent an owner's or occupant's consent, the Fourth Amendment of the Constitution required a criminal search warrant for a fire investigation. In *Tyler,* the court held in favor of the investigators, who'd left the fire scene and then returned and entered the property shortly after the fire was extinguished, but restricted the virtually unlimited access to a fire scene that investigators previously had enjoyed.

Six years later, in *Michigan* v *Clifford,* 464 U.S. 287 (1984), the Supreme Court elaborated on the "Tyler Rules." In *Clifford,* the Court made clear that fire and arson investigators were required to obtain a search warrant before entering fire-damaged property. The Court gave recognition to investigations that occur while firefighters are still involved in fire control activities, but held that a warrantless search six hours after firefighters had left the scene violated the Fourth Amendment.

Inspections

Until 1967, the Supreme Court had consistently ruled that a fire inspection did not require a warrant. But the Court changed course that year in the cases of *Camara* v *San Francisco,* 387 U.S. 523 (1967) and *See* v *Seattle,* 387 U.S. 541 (1967). *Camara* and *See* held that fire, building, and similar "safety" inspections did not require a warrant as long as the owner or occupant consents. But absent an emergency, *Camara* and *See* stated, an "administrative" search warrant was required. Neither case imposed the criminal warrant "probable cause" standard on inspection warrants; an administrative warrant can be issued if the judicial officer issuing the warrant deems the inspection "reasonable."

Free speech

Courts are continuously confronted with the issue of when free speech goes beyond Constitutional limits. This contrast is particularly sharp in fire departments, where the right of firefighters to complain is limited by a court-recognized need for "esprit-de-corps" and efficient and safe operation. When a union officer was demoted from captain to lieutenant during a reorganization, even though a vacant captain position existed, a federal court held in *Williams* v *Valdosta,* 689 F. 2d 964 (1982) that the plaintiff had been wrongly demoted because he was ". . . somewhat of a 'thorn' in their side through the years . . ."

But when the fire chief in Kansas City attempted a reorganization of the department, a captain wrote the chief, observing that "With your hand at the controls, the Kansas City Fire Department could not possibly be more completely obstructed by anyone else on the face of the earth." *Germann* v *Kansas*

City, 776 F. 2d 761 (1985). When Germann was not promoted to Battalion Chief, he sued, alleging retaliation for, among other acts, his "completely obstructed" letter. The federal court held in favor of Kansas City, observing that "The . . . letter expressed a degree of personal animosity and distrust beyond the sharp conflict which could be expected as a consequence of opposing interests. It would be folly [to expect] that Germann as battalion chief would respect [the chief] and work diligently to implement and promote his policies."

Drug testing

The Constitution's Fourth Amendment prohibits unreasonable searches and seizures, and courts have agreed that drug testing by a public employer is a search within the meaning of the Fourth Amendment. But the Fourth Amendment is not absolute. In the case of public employee drug testing, courts continually work to balance an individual's interest in protection of his or her rights with the government's interests, particularly workplace and public safety interests.

The U.S. Supreme Court established the framework for balancing individual and governmental interests in two cases—*Skinner* v *Railway Labor Executives Association,* 489 U.S. 602 (1989) and *National Treasury Employees Union* v *Von Rabb,* 489 U.S 656 (1989). *Skinner* challenged Federal Railroad Administration regulations requiring drug testing after rail accidents and in cases of violations of certain safety rules. In *Skinner,* the Court balanced the compelling government interest in rail safety against the "limited" intrusion of a blood or urine test, and held in favor of the Federal Railroad Administration.

Von Rabb was handed down the same day as *Skinner,* and relied on the same "balancing act"; the personal rights of U.S. Treasury agents were held to be less compelling than those of the Treasury in maintaining confidence in agents who carried guns and had access to classified materials.

At the local level, challenges to "random" drug testing, or drug testing without reasonable suspicion, have resulted in state and federal court decisions on both sides of the issue. Generally, testing of law enforcement officers tends to be upheld, while testing of non-sworn personnel is more likely to be struck down.

Meanwhile, however, federal drug testing mandates have moved beyond federal law enforcement agents and railroads. The U.S. Department of Transportation is now required to enforce a broad mandatory drug testing program involving pilots, truck drivers, bus drivers, and others. Future court decisions will reveal whether the concept of mandatory drug testing of truck drivers will extend to fire apparatus operators.

STATE LEGAL SYSTEMS

Although each state has its own legal system, all 50 state systems share many common elements. Generally, state civil law is based on a combination of case law and statutory law, and state criminal law is based largely on statutory law. Here are typical areas of state legal control that affect fire chiefs on a daily basis.

Workmen's Compensation

All 50 states have adopted workers' compensation laws. The principle behind workers' compensation is simple—a "no-fault" insurance system in which the injured employee trades the right to sue the employer for guaranteed benefits. But the state-by-state reality is more complex. A growing number of states allow employees to collect workers' compensation benefits and sue the employer, if the employee can prove the employer to have been grossly negligent, or to have known of a dangerous condition in the workplace.

A few states have their own unique variations on the workers' compensation pattern. In South Carolina, for example, an injured employee can choose between suing the employer or collecting workers' compensation benefits. In some jurisdictions in New York, the local government employer can be sued if that employer failed to provide safety training in an area of known risk.

Since firefighting is an inherently dangerous occupation, firefighters often use the workers' compensation system. When disputes arise, they usually involve questions of whether a condition such as a chronic back problem is the result of one or more workplace injuries, or the extent of temporary total disability.

Personnel Relations

Many states have established government employee rights by statute. These include rights to a hearing before disciplinary actions are taken, and bargaining rights (and rights to arbitration) in states that authorize recognition of employee bargaining units as well as antidiscrimination laws. It is important for fire chiefs to know that these state civil rights laws are sometimes more stringent than federal laws.

Codes and Code Enforcement

State law approaches fire inspections in one of two ways. The state can adopt a code and require statewide enforcement, or the state can authorize local governments to adopt their own codes and enforce them. There is a wide range of variation in between. Some states establish a minimum fire code, but allow local governments to adopt more stringent amendments. Others give counties the choice of adopting a county-wide fire code, but limit a county to adopting only one specific model code if that county chooses to adopt a code.

Fire inspections tend to be maintenance inspections of buildings that already exist. States also regulate construction of new buildings through codes. In some states, the fire code can be a construction code as well as a maintenance code by including provisions for installation of sprinkler systems in new and existing construction. In others, a separate building code is adopted. As in the case of fire codes, some states allow local amendments to building codes, while others require use of a single code statewide. These statewide codes are known as "mini-maxi codes," because they establish minimum and maximum standards in the same code document.

The legal authority for code enforcement at the state and local level is the Constitutionally recognized concept of "police power," that is, the power of a government to regulate in the interests of the health and safety of its citizens. A government's police power is given great respect by courts when a government's right to regulate is called into question. But because police power is so broad, courts have imposed limits on police power. One limitation on fire inspection power is the requirement of either permission of an occupant to enter an occupancy for an inspection or an administrative search warrant. The legal theory behind this requirement (established in the *Camara* v *San Francisco* and *See* v *Seattle* cases in the U.S. Supreme Court) is that an inspection is an administrative "search" within the meaning of the Fourth Amendment of the Constitution. In the wake of the *Camara* and *See* cases, the states adopted statutory systems for procurement of administrative search warrants.

Firefighter Training and Certification

Although few states have developed statutory minimum training requirements for firefighters, most states have provided for voluntary firefighter training standards, either by statute or administrative rule. Knowledge of these standards is important for fire chiefs, because such standards would probably be admissible as evidence of a standard that local firefighters would be expected to meet in a negligence suit (see the "Standards and the Law" sidebar in the "Negligence" section of this chapter).

Criminal Laws

Every state has adopted misdemeanor laws that regulate the behavior of the public at fire or emergency scenes (accident scene traffic regulations, fire station and hydrant parking regulations, etc.) Most states have adopted laws that provide for greater criminal penalties for someone who assaults a police officer. Many states how have added firefighters and rescue workers to these peace officer assault statutes. There is a wide range of state criminal laws that deal with the crime of arson and related crimes. But no states (as of this writing) have developed criminal laws that apply specifically to firefighters.

Limitations on Liability

In response to case law that limited or eliminated "sovereign immunity" (see the "State Case Law" section below), many states adopted statutes that defined and limited local government (and firefighter) immunity from negligence suits. While each such statute is different, there are common elements:

- *"Scope of employment"*—liability-limitation law coverage is generally restricted to employees "acting within the scope of their employment," in other words, doing what they're authorized to do. A firefighter who decides to perform field surgery at an auto accident scene is probably acting beyond the scope of his employment.
- *Level of negligence*—liability-limitation laws usually do not cover reckless behavior or negligence that borders on intentional behavior. Some statutes exclude "willful or wanton negligence," "gross negligence," or "malicious and corrupt behavior" from protection.
- *Type of act or action*—some liability-limitation laws restrict their protection to actions that require judgment ("discretionary" acts), as opposed to acts that do not ("ministerial" acts). In one recent state case (*Invest-Cast* v *City of Blaine,* 471 NW 2d 368 (1991)), the Minnesota Supreme Court showed its reluctance to let a discretionary-act defense bar a lawsuit, and decided that whether a fire-attack decision was "discretionary" within the meaning of the law was a jury question. (Note that when the case was retried, the jury ruled in favor of the fire department and firefighters.)

Occupational Health and Safety

All states have laws that deal with occupational health and safety. Some states deal with health and safety in connection with workers' compensation.

Others rely totally on federal Occupational Health and Safety Act (OSHA) standards or inspectors.

Since the federal OSHA applies in all 50 states, its standards represent the minimum standards for most employees. Because of a historical (and Constitutional) reluctance on the part of the federal government to impose regulations on state and local employees, it is presently up to individual states to determine whether OSHA regulations apply to local government employees like firefighters, or to volunteer as well as to career firefighters. However, Congress has expressed interest in amending the 1973 OSHA to include coverage of all government employees in all 50 states.

States that have chosen to include firefighters in OSHA coverage either have their own enforcement system and state safety rules that are at least as strict as federal OSHA rules (so-called "state plan states"), or have no enforcement mechanism, and leave OSHA enforcement up to the U.S. Department of Labor's OSHA inspection and enforcement staff.

"Good Samaritan" Laws

As malpractice lawsuits became more frequent (more costly) in the '60s and '70s, health care professionals began calling for limitations on their liability when they acted as "Good Samaritans" at accident scenes. Many states responded by adopting "Good Samaritan" statutes that limited health care professional liability at accident scenes. Some states included firefighters and rescue workers in "Good Samaritan" coverage, but in other states, those "Good Samaritan" laws do not cover firefighters, or protect only volunteer firefighters.

Several states also have adopted "Good Samaritan" laws for those who help at hazardous materials incidents. In general, these laws provide that if a hazardous materials incident "Good Samaritan" was not responsible for the release, and does not act in a grossly negligent manner, such "Good Samaritans" have liability protection (the level of protection varies from state to state).

There are many other state statutes that regulate fire department activities ranging from emergency vehicle operation to property tax status of volunteers, to the color of fire truck warning lights.

STATE CASE LAW

Case law at the state level is developed by courts of record—appellate courts. In some states, only the state supreme court can establish precedent through case law. In others, an intermediate court—often called a court of appeals—can also establish or clarify state law in its decisions.

Case law can serve to clarify or define statutory law, or it can address legal issues not addressed in statutes. In some states, limitations on local government liability are set forth in statutes; in others, the only limitations on local liability will be found in state supreme court cases.

Outlined below are some significant areas of law that are most often established (or changed) by case law.

Firemen's Rule

When someone is injured by another person's action (or by a failure to act), that injured person can sue the other for negligence. But in many states, if a property owner violates the fire code, and a firefighter is injured fighting a fire in that occupancy, the injured firefighter cannot sue the negligent owner. That is because of a longstanding statement of case law called the Firemen's Rule. The theory behind the Firemen's Rule is simply that when someone becomes a firefighter, that person assumes the risks of the job. Those risks include exposure to the results of someone else's carelessness. In some states, the Firemen's Rule is not applied when the conduct that brought about the firefighter's injury was not "reasonably foreseeable," that is, no firefighter could have anticipated it.

In a number of states, the Firemen's Rule no longer exists. Many courts see it as an artificial rule of law that, in this world of hazardous materials, civil disorders, and infectious diseases, is no longer valid. Minnesota's legislature passed a law that simply abolished the Firemen's Rule.

Personal and Governmental Liability

While many states deal with a fire chief's personal liability and a local government's general liability with statutes, other states set standards for liability protection in case law. In North Carolina, for example, there are statutes that authorize a local government to reimburse an employee who loses a lawsuit, but the rules of when an employee can be sued are found in case law, not statutory law.

The standards courts use to limit local government and employee liability are the same, or similar to, those used in statutes; as long as employees are acting "within the scope of employment" and not acting in a "grossly negligent," "willfully and wantonly negligent," or "malicious and corrupt" manner, the employee avoids personal liability. If the act or decision is ministerial (as opposed to discretionary) or governmental (as opposed to proprietary), case law can protect local governments from liability as effectively as can statutory law.

"Duty" and Inspections

In order to prove negligence, an injured person must demonstrate that the person who caused the injury owed a "duty of care" to that injured person. In most cases, that duty of care is assumed. But some state courts have created a special rule to deal with fire inspector liability.

With fire codes running hundreds of pages, few courts would expect a fire inspector to do a perfect job. If fire inspectors were held strictly liable for perfect inspections, many courts argue, no community would ever have an inspection program. In these jurisdictions, the duty to enforce the fire code is a duty to the community at large; in legal terms, this means that the fire inspector owes no duty to any individuals in the building. This "duty doctrine" is not absolute—a fire inspector can, for example, create a duty to an occupant by assuring that occupant that the building is safe—but in states where it is followed, the duty doctrine can be a powerful defense.

LOCAL ORDINANCES AND RULES

Local government organizations and special districts each have their own rules and regulations, usually in the form of ordinances, a charter, or both. In some states, any local government action must be based on authority from the state government. In others, the local government may exercise any power that is not limited by the state. Sometimes, local governments operate under a combination of both authorities—state law and a local charter.

For fire chiefs, the most important ordinance or charter provision is that which establishes the fire department and describes its mission. This is because the success of a governmental immunity defense in a lawsuit often depends on whether firefighters or fire officers were "acting within the scope of their employment," that is, doing what they were authorized to do by law. Such ordinances also help define "scope of duty" for workers' compensation purposes.

Other local ordinances regulate subjects as diverse as salary plans, personnel procedures, fire station parking, use of fire hydrants for emergency and nonemergency purposes, and presentation of annual reports by the fire chief.

KEY LEGAL QUESTIONS FOR THE FIRE CHIEF

The time for a fire chief to make the acquaintance of the department's, town's, or city's attorney is *not* just after a lawsuit has been filed. Every fire chief should meet with the attorney who will represent him, and ask the following questions:

- What's the status of sovereign or governmental immunity in our state? (In other words, how much liability protection do I and my department have?)

- What are the major governmental immunity cases in our state? Do any of them deal with fire departments? (Ask for copies. Most legal decisions are not that difficult to read and understand.)

- Could you get me copies of any governmental immunity statutes that apply in our state?" (Ask for "annotated statutes," which include brief summaries of cases that interpret those statutes.)

- What is the status of the "duty doctrine" for fire inspections in our state? (The "duty doctrine" is a complex legal argument that says, in effect, that fire code enforcement is for the good of the public at large, rather than individuals; unless an individual can establish a duty, no negligence case will stand.)

- What other case law or statutory defenses do we have in our state against a negligence claim? (Assumption of risk? Discretionary versus ministerial? Governmental versus proprietary activities?)

- What do our courts or laws say about indemnifying an employee who loses a lawsuit arising out of that employee's work? What do they say about the town, city, county or district furnishing legal support or legal fees?

- Is there a Good Samaritan law in our state for rescuers, or for helpers at hazardous materials incidents? Does it cover firefighters? (Many Good Samaritan laws cover passers-by, but *not* firefighters.)

- Is the Firemen's Rule in effect in our state? What are the exceptions? (The Firemen's Rule limits the ability of firefighters to recover damages for line-of-duty injuries from a negligent property owner.)

- What right do public employees in our state have to sue for work-related injuries beyond workers' compensation benefits? When would I be liable as a supervisor or manager? (In some states, workers' compensation benefits are the only benefits an injured employee can get from an employer; in other states, under certain circumstances, an injured employee can sue the employer.)

NEGLIGENCE

Over the past several hundred years, English and American courts developed the concept of *tort,* injury to a person or that person's property. Today, tort law falls into two general classes. The first is an *intentional tort,* which includes defamation (libel and slander), malicious prosecution, and civil battery. The second, and by far the most common tort, is negligence.

The basic assumption behind negligence law is that each person owes a duty to others to act reasonably. An injury to a person or property is assumed to be the result of a failure to act reasonably, and unless the injured person was the negligent party, that injured person is entitled to "be made whole," that is, to be fairly compensated by the party responsible for the injury.

In order to prove negligence, an injured person must be able to demonstrate that:

- the responsible person owed a duty of care to the injured person;
- that duty was breached through an action, or failure to act;
- the act (or failure) was the proximate cause of the injury (the injury could reasonably have been foreseen); and
- the injured party must be able to prove actual injury (negligence law does not apply to a hypothetical situation, or to someone who fears a future injury).

Governmental Negligence Liability and Immunity

During the centuries of tort law evolution, governments were held immune from tort liability. This immunity was called sovereign immunity, from the early days when kings or queens made the laws. Since the sovereign created courts and judges, the theory went, the sovereign could not be sued in his or her own courts unless the sovereign agreed to allow such lawsuits. Although history records some unusual kings and queens, none was ever recorded as agreeing to be sued. When kings and queens disappeared from the scene, sovereign immunity became governmental immunity.

Through the first half of the 20th century, absolute governmental immunity remained the rule of law. As long as government employees acted within the scope of their employment, that is, did what they were authorized to do, those employees were protected by the same doctrine. But in the early 1960s, state supreme courts began to take a closer look at the governmental immunity doctrine.

One reason for this was a sense that justice was not serving people injured by governmental action, or failure to act. An injured plaintiff who could prove a very good negligence case could never win if the government was negligent.

A second reason was that the federal government already had defined limited situations where it would accept liability in negligence cases. So, in state after state, courts either abandoned the governmental immunity doctrine altogether, or put severe limits on its application.

This trend brought immediate reaction from state and local governments. The principal arena for debate over the decline of governmental immunity was in state legislatures. Since governmental immunity was a *case law* rule, legislatures could act independently of the courts to write *statutes* reinstating governmental immunity. Most state legislatures opted for *limited* governmental immunity, which means that state and local governments could be sued, but only under certain circumstances. Those circumstances were based primarily on two concepts.

The first involves *ministerial acts versus discretionary acts.* If the act that led to injury required *discretionary judgment,* a government was held to be immune from liability. Legislatures and courts reasoned that government employees needed to be unafraid to make judgments in difficult situations, and so provided immunity in those cases. But for acts that did not require special judgment— *ministerial* acts—immunity was withheld. One state court held that failure on the part of a housing inspector to correctly count electrical outlets to see if a house met a two-outlet-per-room requirement meant liability for that inspector's employer. Counting electrical outlets, the court reasoned, was ministerial, since counting required no discretionary judgment.

Most states hold fire apparatus drivers to the same standard of care, and liability, as drivers of any vehicles. This holding is a variation on the ministerial-versus-discretionary theory. Since anyone with a driver's license can legally operate a vehicle, no single class of vehicle operators receives any more legal protection than any other.

The second is *governmental versus proprietary,* a liability limitation concept based on government functions. According to this theory, governments should have liability protection for functions that are unique to governments. Otherwise, if governments are held liable, and decide to abandon those "governmental" functions, there is no one else that will act in a government's place. Examples of governmental functions in different jurisdictions include fire protection, law enforcement, and public assistance.

But governments also compete with the private sector, and, in those areas, should receive no immunity. The idea is that if government abandons one of these "proprietary" functions in the face of negligence lawsuit losses, the private sector could step in. Examples of proprietary functions in different jurisdictions include providing bus service, airports, hospitals, and water service.

The extent of governmental immunity varies from state to state; in general, within those immunity areas courts will dismiss negligence lawsuits. But if a court rules that a local government is *not* immune, that lack of immunity does not mean that the plaintiff has won, only that the plaintiff will have his day in court.

Local governments have all the defenses that any individual would have in a negligence suit, and at least one not generally available to defendants other than local governments. These defenses include:

- **Contributory (or comparative) negligence.** Courts have long held that an injured plaintiff should not recover damages for his own negligence. The modern-day legal translation in most states is that a damage award will be reduced to the extent that the plaintiff is responsible for injury. In some of those states that allocation is based on a jury determination of percent of responsibility. If, for example, a jury holds a plaintiff to be 35 percent responsible for his own injuries, any award of damages against the defendant will be reduced by 35 percent. But in a handful of states, *any* liability on the part of a plaintiff will bar recovery of damages. In North Carolina, for example, a plaintiff who is only 5 percent responsible for his injuries will lose the case.
- **Assumption of risk.** If an office building tenant is put on notice that his occupancy is in violation of the fire code, and that tenant is subsequently injured by a fire caused (or supported) by that violation, then it can be argued that the tenant "assumed the risk" of that injury by staying in the building or not eliminating the violation. More common is the bystander at an emergency scene who moves inside the barricade tape and is injured by an action connected with the emergency. The fact that the bystander has made his way to the wrong side of the barricade tape is evidence of assumption of risk.
- **Duty.** The question of whether a defendant owed a duty of care to the plaintiff is at the heart of negligence law. In some states, courts of record have established a "duty doctrine" that is applied in code enforcement situations.

    This "duty doctrine" presumes that fire and other safety codes were enacted for the good of the community, not for the benefit of any particular person. Therefore, a fire inspector who fails to notice a fire code violation during an inspection owes no duty on account of that failure to *any particular person* who is injured as a result. As one court stated that doctrine, "a duty to all is a duty to no one," so no individual can establish the duty relationship that a negligence action requires.

    However, an inspector can create a duty to an individual. If an inspector tells an occupant that the building is safe, for example, and that occupant is injured later as a result of the inspector's failure to detect a violation, that injured occupant can argue that he relied on the inspector's representation of safety. That inspector's representation would establish a "duty relationship" with the occupant; the duty doctrine defense would be lost.

    A fire code requirement that protects particular classes of persons, (for example, occupants of day care centers) creates a duty relationship with those occupants. Courts have ruled that the duty-doctrine defense does not apply in these cases.

Personal negligence liability and immunity

The same state laws (or court cases) that define or limit governmental liability and immunity generally deal with the liability of individual government employees. Those laws and cases approach personal liability in a variety of ways.

In some states, an employee can be found negligent, and so will share the cost of negligence with the governmental employer (unless that employer is otherwise immune). Those same states generally authorize employer provision of legal counsel to an employee who has been sued, and employer reimbursement of an employee who loses a suit in some circumstances.

In other states, employee liability is limited as long as that employee's act was within the scope of employment, that is, the employee was doing what he was authorized to do. Using this approach, a firefighter who is negligent in rescuing someone from a hazardous materials emergency may be protected, but a firefighter who grabs a gun to shoot a fleeing felon is doing something firefighters typically are not authorized to do, and may be personally liable.

A third approach centers on just how negligent the act was. This approach draws a distinction between "ordinary" negligence and "willful or wanton," "gross," or "malicious" negligence. Ordinary negligence can merit legal protection; gross negligence can leave the employee unprotected. What is the difference between these levels of negligence? Foreseeability is one way that courts draw the line. If an injury resulting from an act was virtually certain, and a "reasonable person under the same or similar circumstances" would have thus avoided the act, that act can be characterized as "willful." Another distinction is based on the concept of "recklessness"; if the circumstances surrounding the act indicate that only someone acting in a reckless manner could have brought about the injury, the negligence meter needle moves into the red zone.

Aside from statutory or case law protection, local government employees can invoke customary negligence defenses (comparative/contributory negligence, assumption of risk, etc.).

It is essential to note that legal rules governing personal negligence of public employees are different in every state. Fire chiefs should talk with their department's, city's, town's, county's or district's attorneys for information on where fire chiefs in their community stand with regard to personal negligence exposure.

LEGAL TROUBLE SPOTS

When fire departments (or fire chiefs) are sued, the lawsuit usually occurs as a result of one or more of the following actions:

- *Doing something unauthorized.* If a fire department is not authorized by ordinance, charter, or other official statement to deal with hazardous materials incidents, for example, this issue will be raised in the wake of a legally "messy" hazardous materials incident. Lawyers do not read fire service books or periodicals to keep up with trends in the fire service. They always start their research with dustier sources, like city ordinances. That's a good reason for fire chiefs to review the ordinances or charters that empower the fire department to do what it does, and to ask for changes to cover things which they *are* doing but are not empowered to do.
- *Ignoring legally mandated procedures.* There are some things that laws require a fire chief to do, whether he wants to do them or not. Signing documents that require the fire chief's signature is one example. Fire chiefs should not delegate legally mandated procedures if the law does not allow it.
- *Departing from rules, regulations, and standard operating procedures.* If someone is injured as a result of something a firefighter does (or does not do), the first place a plaintiff's lawyer will look for a "standard of care" is in the department's own rules, regulations, or standard operating procedures. If a fire chief issues an order, establishes a rule, or authorizes an SOP, the fire chief needs to know that, like it or not, a standard is being set, and department members will be held to that standard.
- *Violating civil rights.* By now, every fire chief ought to know the dangers of discrimination, but there are enough civil rights complaints and lawsuits on file to show that not every chief has learned this lesson. The astute fire chief knows the difference between "legal" discrimination (in some jurisdictions, refusal to hire a smoker is perfectly legal) and illegal discrimination, which involves Constitutionally protected classes like race and gender.

- *Denying due process.* Even in "right-to-work" states, local government employees like firefighters are still entitled to a hearing before dismissal, even for cause. The American sense of fair play has been translated into a legal expectation that before a public employee loses something—a job, pay (through disciplinary action) or promotional opportunity—that employee is entitled to a hearing.
- *Failure to document.* As long as two years after a fire, most states allow someone who alleges injury as a result to file a lawsuit. How good is the typical fire chief's memory of an incident after two years? If that incident involved death, serious injury, or major property loss, will a copy of the incident report be enough when that chief is on the witness stand? Lawyers are great believers in "diaper documentation," or covering one's backside with paper.

THE LAWSUIT PROCESS

Each state (and the federal government) has its own specific rules of civil procedure, the rules that govern how a lawsuit is handled. There are variations from state to state, but the fundamental structure of lawsuit procedure is consistent.

A lawsuit starts with a *complaint.* The complaint, filed by the *plaintiff* (the injured person), is essentially a story of the incident that caused the alleged injury, allegations of the defendant's negligent behavior, and a request for *damages* (*compensatory* damages, which cover the actual loss suffered by the plaintiff, and, in some cases, *punitive* damages, which are intended to punish the defendant's negligent behavior to deter others).

Once the complaint is filed in court and served on the *defendant*—the person accused of negligence—the defendant responds with an *answer.* This answer reviews the story of the case presented in the complaint, and includes denials when the defendant's story differs from the plaintiff's version.

While plaintiffs and defendants can serve as their own attorneys, most hire an attorney to represent their interests and lead them through the legal system. It is very important to note that, in the American legal system, the primary responsibility of an attorney is to represent the interests of the client. So, the plaintiff's attorney will work very hard to question (and in the process cast doubt upon) any statement, evidence, or testimony that the defendant offers. The defense attorney will do the same on behalf of the defendant. The

American legal system relies on the judge and jury to sort out the evidence, apply case law or statutory law to that evidence, and arrive at the right decision.

Once the complaint and answer preliminaries are over, the process of collecting evidence begins. This process is called *discovery.*

Contrary to what goes on in television courtrooms, the American legal system does not encourage "surprise" witnesses or evidence. Because our legal system actually encourages settlements in civil cases, it also encourages the revelation of all evidence before trial, during the discovery process, in the hope that the plaintiff and defendant will be able to settle their dispute without a trial.

The discovery process includes *depositions* (statements taken outside court, under oath), *written interrogatories* (questionnaires completed by witnesses or others with an interest in the case), and *requests for production of documents* (lists of reports, memos, and other documents that relate to the lawsuit). When the discovery process is complete and there is no sign of a settlement, the suit proceeds to trial. A civil lawsuit may be heard by a judge and jury, or (most often at the plaintiff's option) a judge alone, who also acts as the jury.

The respective roles of the judge and jury are at the heart of the American legal system. The judge is the trier of law, that is, he applies the rules of civil procedure in court, and tells the jury what the law is as the jury hears testimony and examines evidence. The jury is the trier of fact; the jury decides what the facts are in a case, based on testimony and evidence, and then applies the law (as defined by the judge) to those facts in coming to a verdict. With few exceptions, a jury's decision on the facts is the final decision. Courts of appeal (appellate courts) regularly review judicial decisions and statements on what the law is, but are reluctant to interfere with a jury's findings of fact.

During the trial, the plaintiff's and defendant's attorneys continue in their roles as advocates for their clients. They present their cases through testimony by *witnesses* who have some direct knowledge of the events that brought about the lawsuit (including the defendant and plaintiff), and by *expert witnesses,* who are authorized by the judge to testify about matters not generally known or understood by the public. The attorneys may introduce documentary or physical evidence to demonstrate facts about the case. They also may compare testimony at the trial with what they learned during the discovery process, pointing out inconsistencies to the jury.

In their roles as advocates, attorneys will seek to call into doubt, or discredit, testimony offered by witnesses for "the other side." This process is called *impeachment of witnesses.* But attorneys will not call witnesses to tell a jury what the law says about a case. Again, declarations of law come only from the judge.

Trials are governed by complex rules of procedure. Many of those rules deal with what can be offered to a jury as *evidence.*

A fundamental aspect of the American legal system is that jurors should always see and hear the best, most reliable, evidence. Direct testimony by a

STANDARDS AND THE LAW

In negligence lawsuit situations, a critical question for judges and juries is whether a "standard of care" was met.

In the eyes of the law, each of us owes the other a duty to behave as a "reasonable person," to exercise "reasonable care." How is "reasonable care" defined when it comes to firefighting, fire safety, hazardous materials incident management, or training? Generally, courts look to what a "reasonable fire officer" or a "reasonable fire chief" would have done under the same or similar circumstances.

If a fire department has its own rules, regulations, or standard operating procedures, they are what a court would examine to find evidence of a standard of behavior or care. If the legal issue goes beyond a local fire department's practices, courts will look to other standards.

National Fire Protection Association standards are examples of such standards. So too are student manuals for National Fire Academy courses [(and International Fire Service Training Association (IFSTA) manuals)]. These organizations are national in scope. and fire departments across the U.S. often use NFPA, National Fire Academy, IFSTA and other nationally recognized organizations' materials as benchmarks for rules, regulations, and standard operating procedures.

NFPA 1500, *Standard on Fire Department Occupational Safety and Health Program,* is an example of a standard that has legal implications. By its very nature, NFPA 1500 probably would be used as an example of a standard of care or behavior, assuming that a lawsuit relied on a part of NFPA 1500 as its foundation.

When such standards exist, the best strategy a fire chief can undertake is to read and understand the standard and develop a plan on how each part of a standard is to be addressed (*not* necessarily adopted) in that chief's department. A decision on how a standard is to be addressed implies that the standard was studied carefully, and the fire chief's response takes into account not only the standard, but local conditions. **The worst strategy is to ignore such standards.**

TIPS FOR WITNESSES

Chief officers can expect to be called on to testify in court at least once in their careers. Because they have knowledge about fires, firefighting, and fire prevention that the general public does not have, fire chiefs generally will be qualified to testify as experts (whether they feel like experts or not, and whether they are chiefs of career or volunteer departments).

Here are a few important tips for fire chiefs to remember about being a witness:

- *Keep your résumé up to date.* The "friendly" lawyer (assuming you are not testifying as a hostile witness) will need it to make sure he is familiar with your qualifications, and the jury will want to know about your background.
- *Wear your uniform.* The American fire service is an honorable institution, and its members are entitled to the respect that a fire service uniform commands.
- *Do not be late.* Although the justice system is often slow, individual judges have little patience for anyone who thinks that anything is more important than their courtrooms and cases.
- *When asked a question, listen to the whole question.* Don't try to answer the question before the lawyer finishes asking it. Also, think before you begin to answer it.
- *Answer only what you are asked.* Once the first round of questioning (direct examination) is out of the way, witnesses are fair game for leading questions. Don't try to speed up the process. One wise old lawyer once said, "There are only four good answers to any question a witness is asked. They are 'Yes'; 'No'; 'I don't know'; and 'Would you repeat the question?'"
- *Don't joust with the lawyers.* A good lawyer for the opposing side will do as much as the rules of procedure allow to poke and prod witnesses into losing their tempers or arguing. After all, angry witnesses have been known to self-destruct. Be patient with lawyers, and do not get into arguments or debates.

Don't forget that you are as sophisticated on their turf—the courtroom—as you would expect one of them to be on yours.

> • *Never lie.* As bad as the truth may sound, it is never as bad as
> untruth. Lawyers are trained in law school and by experience to
> pounce on inconsistencies that indicate the truth is not being
> told. A witness caught lying is destroyed as a witness and may
> be guilty of the crime of perjury.

witness about statements that witness made will be admitted into evidence;
generally, what a third person reports someone to have said *(hearsay)* will not
be admitted as evidence. Other rules are designed to keep a trial on track. If
testimony seems to have nothing to do with the issues at trial, the judge may
exclude that evidence because it is irrelevant.

The goal of each attorney is to demonstrate by a greater weight (or *preponderance*) of the evidence that his client is right. Preponderance of the evidence
can be a tricky concept. One way to think of preponderance is a tilt of the
scales of justice in favor of the client. Another is to visualize a football game
where the client scores as soon as he crosses the 50-yard line. Preponderance
of the evidence is *not* the same as the criminal standard of "beyond a reasonable doubt" (which, using the football analogy, requires a trip all the way to
the end zone).

At the close of the trial, the judge tells the jury the law that the jury must
apply to the facts it has heard. A jury's deliberations on the law and the facts
lead to a verdict. If the verdict is in favor of the defendant, the plaintiff can
appeal; the defendant can appeal a verdict in favor of the plaintiff.

FUTURE LEGAL ISSUES FOR THE FIRE SERVICE

As law and legal processes continue to evolve, new legal issues will arise
for fire chiefs, and some old issues will take new directions.

Standards and volunteer fire departments

Although it is clear that some laws (the Family Medical Leave Act, for
example) do not yet apply to volunteer fire departments, other laws do. In the
face of more difficulty in recruiting and retaining volunteer members, volunteer chiefs and firefighters will have to devise new strategies for meeting state
and federal mandates.

The strongest mandate challenge will be in department safety standards.
Federal OSHA rules do not yet apply to all fire departments in the U.S. One
state has attempted to exempt fire departments in communities of fewer than

5,000 people, but trends indicate that fire departments can expect stronger (rather than weaker) safety regulations.

Because EMS involves handling injured people on a regular basis, volunteers already are confronting a proliferation of basic and continuing education requirements that are driven by liability concerns on the part of medical control facilities. This area of regulation will not peak as long as new technology and techniques (automated defibrillators, for example) are added to a volunteer fire department's EMS jump kit.

Evolving definitions of firefighter fitness

What physical attributes must a person have to become—and remain—a firefighter? The Americans with Disabilities Act already is forcing fire chiefs to take a very careful and specific look at essential physical requirements, and the continuing debate over expiration of the Age Discrimination in Employment "exception" for firefighters will bring about a much closer look at how a firefighter's physical ability to do the job will be measured.

Controlled substances

Court decisions seem to indicate a general trend toward authorizing "random" drug testing for firefighters (or, at the least, fire apparatus operators). Very few fire chiefs understand how a legal, organized, and truly random drug testing program should be initiated and maintained. Fire departments will have to look to the trucking and railroad industries for guidance on proper design of drug testing programs.

Free speech

Paramilitary organizations like fire departments can regulate firefighter speech to a greater extent than "civilian" agencies can regulate employee speech. But that regulation is very limited. Fire chiefs faced with budget cuts, layoffs, company shutdowns, or fire chiefs implementing controversial programs, can anticipate firefighters will respond more vocally and publicly than in the past.

Courts generally have never approved of a firefighter taking an internal grievance into the public spotlight, but courts uphold the rights of employees to publicly discuss (critically or otherwise) departmental matters of public interest. Of public interest, according to a review of firefighter free speech cases, includes public challenges of company staffing practices, station locations, and department reorganizations. But courts also draw a line where "public interest" comment tends to interfere with the ability of a fire department to deliver its services and to maintain public confidence.

Sexual harassment

Over the past several years, the federal court system has begun edging away from a philosophy that "women must take the workplace as they find it" to defining activities of a sexual harassment nature from the point of view of what a woman would find to be offensive.

Over the next several years, the U.S. Supreme Court will be asked to rule more specifically on what constitutes sexual harassment. Given the provisions of the Civil Rights Act of 1991, fire chiefs may find their personal liability exposure greatly increased if they fail to deal promptly and fairly with sexual harassment complaints.

SUMMARY

A fire chief's authority to make personnel decisions, to assume command at an emergency incident, or to order withdrawal of firefighters in the face of a major hazardous materials incident is based on the law. The recent evolution of American common and statutory law has resulted in the imposition of new legal *responsibilities* on the fire chief, alongside the chief's traditional authority.

This evolution does not mean that fire chiefs need law degrees.

In the 1960s many fire chiefs could not have foreseen the proliferation of hazardous materials in their communities, and were not equipped by training or experience to deal with LPG explosions or major anhydrous ammonia leaks. But once those chiefs understood the potential harm of hazardous materials, they learned. Today, the fire chief who *has not* learned the basics of dealing with hazardous materials is rare indeed.

By applying the same familiarization process to legal issues, today's fire chief can prepare to deal more effectively with the challenges raised by new legal responsibilities. As in the case of hazardous materials, there are a few basic concepts to master—concepts discussed in this chapter—and there are more and more frequent training opportunities. And, finally, there is "mutual aid," in the form of fire chiefs who have had legal experience (good and bad) and who are willing to share that experience with other chiefs through organizations like the International Association of Fire Chiefs, and through fire service books and periodicals.

Fire chiefs can not immunize themselves against lawsuits and other outcomes of these legal responsibilities. But by treating the legal aspects of fire protection as a new feature of the fire service environment to be studied and "preplanned," fire chiefs can successfully meet the challenges of the fire service and the law.

A fire chief who understands the broad concepts of the American legal system (federal, state, and local), who has a working knowledge of negligence law, and who understands in general terms the path that a civil lawsuit takes is prepared to deal effectively with the continuing legal challenges confronting the American fire service.

5

Insurance Grading of Fire Departments

RAND-SCOTT COGGAN

CHAPTER HIGHLIGHTS

- A historical perspective of the development of current insurance rating surveys.
- An overview of the 1980 Fire Suppression Rating Schedule and how it differs from the 1974 Municipal Grading Schedule.
- An in-depth understanding of the Fire Suppression Rating Schedule, including what is reviewed and how each element is evaluated.
- How the survey process operates, from initial request through actual survey, to the final report and grading.

*B*ECAUSE YOU'LL PROBABLY HAVE AT LEAST ONE ENCOUNTER with an insurance rating survey during your fire service career, it is important to have a basic knowledge of what a survey is, how it works, and how to prepare for one. This chapter will introduce you to:

- what insurance surveys are and how they have changed over the years;
- how the current 1980 schedule operates;
- the factors considered in the 1980 schedule, including fire department operations, water supply, and receipt of fire alarms; and
- how the survey process actually proceeds from initial request to final report.

Understanding these basic principles and concepts should make your first encounter with insurance surveys less intimidating.

What is the ISO?

The ISO is a nationwide nonprofit service organization that provides services to the property and casualty insurance industries and was formed over the course of many years by the consolidation of various regional and state insurance rating organizations.

The ISO is actually much broader in scope than just that part we in the fire service normally see and interact with. Located in New York, the ISO was formed when more than 20 different insurance-related organizations merged; it now employs more than 2,500 people.

ISO provides various services to the following lines of insurance: Boiler and Machinery; Commercial Automobile; Commercial Inland Marine; Commercial Multiple Line; Crime; Dwelling Fire and Allied Lines; Farm and Farm Owners; General Liability; Glass; Homeowners; Nuclear Energy Liability; Personal Inland Marine; Personal Insurance Coverage; Private Passenger Automobile, and Professional Liability and Flood, in conjunction with the National Flood Insurance Program of the Federal Insurance Administration.

The ISO has as a non-profit subsidiary corporation the Commercial Risk Services (CRS). It performs the functions of specific property surveys and public protection surveys that previously were conducted by the ISO and its predecessors. CRS provides full services in 44 states and limited services in other states. CRS does not grade municipalities in Washington, Idaho, Hawaii, Mississippi, Texas, Louisiana or the District of Columbia, because these states have their own rating organizations, for example, the Washington Surveying and Rating Bureau in Washington state. Most of these state bureaus do, however, apply schedules that are the same as or similar to the schedules currently used by CRS (only two states, Mississippi and Washington, do not use the current CRS grading schedule).

CRS's own statistics show that its representatives visit more than 3.5 million buildings in the U.S. and make information on those buildings available to more than 1,300 affiliated insurance companies. In addition, CRS surveys more than 2,400 communities in the 44 states in which it operates. Buildings are inspected every 10 years or every 15 years, depending on the survey schedule, unless a special request is made.

The history of fire department surveys

The original Municipal Fire Protection Surveys were initiated in 1889 as a way to assist cities with their fire protection problems.

At that time, the National Board of Fire Underwriters (NBFU) hired a representative, a former fire department officer, to examine the conditions and to evaluate the needs of fire departments and fire facilities throughout the country. At first, the degree of public fire protection available was evaluated subjectively, based on the representative's judgment. Later, to standardize public fire protection evaluation, a committee of the National Fire Protection Association was formed to develop a public fire protection "rating" schedule. This schedule provided for five classes of protection. For each class, a few specifications were given for the water system and the fire department.

Keep in mind that at the beginning of the 20th century the urban centers of most of America's large cities consisted mostly of wood frame or wood joist masonry multiple-story buildings. With little space between them there were significant exposure problems. The lack of good transportation systems at this time made it economically expedient to concentrate diverse mixtures of business in small quadrants. Complicating this early urban scenario were relatively new water supply systems. These systems were expensive to construct and, to hold costs down, they frequently were undersized, unstable, and unreliable, no match for the potential suppression demands that these dense and potentially catastrophic urban centers posed. Early firefighting forces sometimes had to rely only on hydrant pressure, occasionally augmented by hand or steam-operated pumps, to produce fire streams that were too weak to reach and penetrate the significant fire loads they often encountered.

It was only a matter of time before a number of severe conflagrations occurred, demonstrating the need for sweeping changes in how fire protection was assessed and provided. The Baltimore conflagration in 1904 focused national attention on the vulnerability of many of America's cities to widespread, devastating conflagrations. This conflagration also alerted the nation's insurers to the significant financial exposure to their industry as a whole of uncontrolled and apparently unchecked fire risk, for the Baltimore conflagration caused more than $50 million in damage (the equivalent of $688 million in today's dollars). Cities were growing rapidly, most with little or no advance planning and seldom with building or zoning laws. For insurance companies, the message was clear: they needed advance information on fire loss characteristics of cities to conduct their business prudently and efficiently.

After the Baltimore conflagration the NBFU assembled an engineering staff whose sole purpose was to survey the fire conditions and fire susceptibility of metropolitan U.S. cities. The reports they generated were designed to include a wide variety of information, including the fire department, alarm systems, water supply, fire loss, fire-prevention-related codes and their enforcement, streets, buildings, and conflagration hazard areas (their probability and potential). In these early reports, even the city's police department was surveyed.

After these reports were compiled, recommendations were made to the city regarding improvements that could be made in each of the areas reviewed, and underwriting information was furnished to the insurance companies about the fire risks inherent in each locality. The intention was that these teams would revisit the areas periodically to see whether their advice was being heeded and improvements made.

It is interesting to note that many of these early reports pointed out significant failure rates in both fire apparatus and equipment, as well as inadequacies in water systems which could have or did contribute to fires that outpaced local resources.

In 1905 the NBFU developed a model building code that could be adopted by those cities which wanted to begin controlling hazards which had, for a long period of time, gone relatively unchecked. In October 1905, the NBFU released a report on San Francisco that said, in part:

> Not only is the hazard extreme within the congested value district, but it is augmented by the presence of a compact surrounding great-height, large-area frame residential district, itself unmanageable from a firefighting standpoint by reason of adverse conditions introduced by topography. In fact, San Francisco has violated all underwriting traditions and precedent by not burning up. That is has not done so is largely due to the vigilance of the fire department, which cannot be relied upon indefinitely to stave off the inevitable.

While perhaps not seen as prophetic when it was written, the NBFU's prophecy was in fact fulfilled on April 18, 1906, when the Great San Francisco earthquake caused fires that resulted in an estimated $350 million worth of damage (the equivalent of close to $5 billion worth of damage today!)

In 1909, contrary to the program's original intent—making the surveys "one-time shots" with followup inspections to detail progress—it was decided to make the program permanent.

In 1916 the first grading schedule was released. It included seven features to be reviewed and the corresponding points that could be assigned to each.

Features	Deficiency Points / % of Total
Water Supply	1,700/34%
Fire Department	1,500/30%
Fire Alarm	550/11%
Police	50/1%
Building Laws	200/4%
Hazards	300/6%
Structural Conditions	− 700/14%−
Total	5,000/100%

The format of the 1916 grading schedule was used for the next 64 years. The 1916 schedule established criteria that identified which communities were well protected. Deficiency points were assigned whenever a community was unable to meet a portion(s) of a given criterion. Deficiency points also could be assigned for significant effects of an area's climate, as well as for what would become known as "divergence," that is, the difference between a fire department's capabilities and the usability of the water supply. Perhaps the most significant difference between the 1916 schedule and later versions was the apparent intent of the 1916 schedule to look at fire protection as it applied to the "central business core." The 1916 schedule evaluated a whopping total of 236 items and sub-items; (today's schedule reviews only 119 items).

Changes in the grading schedule after 1916 were linked primarily to changes in society and technology, and to how cities were developing. Changes in the 1920s and 1930s mirrored the changes in the fire service, which progressed from horse-drawn apparatus to motorized apparatus. Changes in the 1940s emphasized protection beyond the central core as businesses moved to the outskirts of cities, whereas the 1950s and 60s continued the emphasis on protecting cities as a whole. During this period significant improvements also were made to municipal water systems.

It was in 1971 that the ISO was formed. The organization's main interest in public protection was to recognize the impact that effective public protection had on individual property fire rates, given that public fire protection could affect the percentage of loss (value) that could be expected in a fire situation.

The 1974 schedule, referred to as the "Grading Schedule for Municipal Fire Protection," contained modifications that continued to recognize changes in society and technology and in the fire service. The point value assigned to water supply reliability was reduced by giving equal weight to the water supply and the fire department; the point value of fire alarm box systems was reduced and the structural conditions element was eliminated. The central business district was de-emphasized; instead, it was evaluated like any other part of a city. Rather than concentrating on the central business district, attention was given to the built-up areas of the city. The focus of the schedule changed, commencing with the 1974 revision from conflagration-type fires and the level of protection needed to contain them, to concern for fires in individual buildings. In order to emphasize the new focus on individual building ratings, this schedule included a caveat in the introduction that stated that the schedule was to be used as a fire insurance rating tool, not to analyze all aspects of a public fire protection program, and that it should not be used for purposes other than insurance rating. In other words, the new system was not intended to be used to rate public fire protection needs, city programs, or both, and should not be used for such!

It was in 1980 that the sweeping changes were made to the schedule that would result in the system still in use today.

Modern insurance grading—the Fire Suppression Rating Schedule

In 1980, the Fire Suppression Rating Schedule (FSRS) was released. It lists ten different protection classifications of which Class 1 areas receive the lowest insurance rates and Class 10 areas the highest (or no recognition). The Fire Suppression Rating Schedule (FSRS) simply identifies varying levels of fire suppression capabilities that are applied to the individual property fire insurance rate relativities.

In developing a modified insurance classification system for cities, the emphasis had been on the objective analysis of evaluating suppression features, of measuring major differences among cities, and of recognizing the potential for interface between the ISO's individual building survey and rate-making function and its city-wide classification function. *The current classification system is not intended to present a complete analysis of the public fire protection needs of a city and should not be used for such an evaluation.*

The ISO reduced the strong emphasis which had been placed on reliability by redundancy, and, instead, measures existing performance. The ISO no longer evaluates street box alarm systems because these systems have been abused extensively in recent years by persons reporting false alarms, and because only a small percentage of alarms are received from street alarm boxes versus telephone alarms.

Because of the direct interface with another of its functions, individual building surveys and rate-making, the ISO no longer considers it necessary to evaluate building, electrical, and fire prevention laws. Enforcing these laws has its greatest impact on conditions in individual buildings which are surveyed and rated separately. Insurance rates for those buildings are evaluated using a commercial rating schedule after a field survey has been conducted by an ISO Field Rating Representative. Individual rates consider many of the same factors controlled by these municipal laws and also reflect the level of enforcement if unsatisfactory conditions are permitted to exist. The impact of laws and enforcement on residential property is measured by the influence on losses for that general class of property.

The new classification system for cities is a credit-type schedule, as opposed to a deficiency-type schedule like its predecessor, although the new schedule can "take points away" in circumstances where actions or activities deemed improper occur. The system is objective in that each item can be evaluated mathematically and a corresponding amount of credit calculated. This system attempts to evaluate a city's ability to suppress fires in buildings of "average" size once they are actually burning, and avoids penalizing cities for the effects of fire in large buildings by creating a separate section that establishes individual classifications for buildings that require large fire flows to suppress much larger fires.

Overview of the Fire Suppression Rating Schedule (FSRS)

The Fire Suppression Rating Schedule (FSRS) is divided into two sections. Section I is a Public Protection Classification (PPC) which is an indication of an entity's ability to handle fires in small- to moderate-size buildings. These are defined as buildings which have a Needed Fire Flow (NFF) of 3,500 gpm or less. Section II of the Fire Suppression Rating Schedule (FSRS) consists of individual public protection classification numbers for larger properties that have Needed Fire Flows (NFF) greater than 3,500 gpm.

Because most communities design their fire protection based on normally expected fires, this design is recognized in the different concepts of these two sections. The Public Protection Classification (PPC) number or class determined in Section I applies to average-size buildings with a Needed Fire Flow (NFF) less than 3,500 gpm, while the aspect of the fire protection demands for larger buildings (those that need fire flows of more than 3,500 gpm) has been removed from that evaluation. Section II is applied individually to each building with a Needed Fire Flow (NFF) greater than 3,500 gpm in order to develop an individual classification number that reflects the available protection for that specific property.

The Fire Suppression Rating Schedule (FSRS) establishes a Needed Fire Flow (NFF) in gallons per minute for suppression of a fire in a building. Representative building locations are selected throughout a city, and a Basic (mean) Fire Flow is determined. All properties that exceed a Needed Fire Flow (NFF) of 3,500 gpm are reviewed separately because fire protection control for these larger buildings is considered to be more the responsibility of the individual property owner. Sprinkler systems, smoke detectors, construction upgrades, and other fire protection improvements therefore become more of an incentive to these property owners.

The Fire Suppression Rating Schedule (FSRS) has three major features: Fire Alarm; Fire Department; and Water System, all of which directly affect the measurement of fire suppression insofar as their city-wide effect is concerned.

The Fire Alarm section examines how the public reports a fire and how the fire department receives that report. In a typical alarm received by telephone, the call taker will receive the call and alert firefighters, advising them of the location of the emergency. Because different cities receive fire alarms in different ways, the Fire Suppression Rating Schedule (FSRS) attempts to review all possible variations and assigns points to indicate equivalencies.

The Fire Department section considers apparatus, equipment, staffing, automatic and mutual aid, prefire planning, and training. The interrelationships of engines, truck companies, minor equipment, paid and volunteer fire-fighters, and department training are all evaluated using a point system to relate equivalencies.

The Water System section considers the supply works, main capacity to deliver fire flow, distribution of hydrants, hydrant size, type and installation, hydrant inspection and condition, and alternative water supplies.

The following chart describes and details the changes made over the years in the grading schedules which have been used to rate cities.

	1916 Schedule	1974 Schedule	1980 Schedule
Water Supply	34%	39%	40%
Fire Department	30%	39%	50%
Fire Alarm	11%	.9%	10%
Police	1%	N/A	N/A
Building Laws	4%	1.7%	N/A[1]
Hazards	6%	N/A	N/A
Structural Conditions	14%	N/A	N/A
Electricity Laws	N/A	.8%	N/A[1]
Fire Prevention Laws	N/A	10.5%	N/A[1]
Climate Conditions	Variable	Variable	N/A[1]

1. The elimination of building and electrical laws, fire prevention, and climatic conditions apparently was based on the following rationale:

- As most cities have adopted model codes, it is no longer necessary to measure differences;
- Evaluation of enforcement of codes and the effects of climatic conditions are too subjective; and
- Laws and their enforcement are observable as actual conditions when individual properties are surveyed and do not need to factor separately.

Differences between the 1980 Fire Suppression Rating Schedule (FSRS) and the 1974 grading schedule for municipal fire protection

A more in-depth analysis compares the actual changes in the individual elements that were analyzed by the 1974 schedule under each category to the 1980 Fire Suppression Rating Schedule (FSRS). The underlying rationale for eliminating elements reviewed appears to fall into two separate categories:

- the elimination of elements whose review is subjective; and
- the elimination of elements which have become relatively "dependable" or "reliable" over the years, so as to cause little deviation in their ratings

between cities reviewed (i.e., certain water elements of the water system, etc.).

Figure 5-1. Comparison of Review of Water Supply

1974 Schedule	Total Relative Weight	1980 FSR Schedule	Relative Weight
(within water supply area)			
• Adequacy of Supply Works	6%	• Supply Works	
• Reliability of Source of Supply	6%	• Fire Flow Delivery	
• Reliability of Pumping Capacity	3%	• Distribution of Hydrants	_____
• Reliability of Power Supply	4%		35%
• Condition, Arrangement, Operation and Reliability of System Components	4%	• Hydrants: Size, Type and Installation	2%
• Adequacy of Mains	16%	• Hydrants: Inspection and Conditions	3%
• Reliability of Mains	2%		40%
• Installation of Mains	2%		
• Arrangement of Distribution System	2%		
• Additional Factors and Conditions Relating to Supply and Distribution	4%		
• Distribution of Hydrants	5%		
• Hydrants: Size, Type and Installation	2%		
• Hydrants: Inspection and Condition	2%		
• Miscellaneous Factors and Conditions	6%		
	64%[1]		
(adjusted percentage =	39%)[2]		

1. If a water supply was "100% deficient" there would be 3,200 deficiency points assigned which equals 64% of the 5,000 total deficiency points in the 1974 schedule.

2. Because water supply is limited to 1,950 points, or 39% of the 5,000 total points in the schedule, points in excess of the 1,950 are simply not assigned, keeping the maximum deficiency to 1,950 points or 39% of the total.

Figure 5-2. *Comparison of Review of Fire Department*

1974 Schedule	Total Relative Weight	1980 FSR Schedule	Relative Weight
(within fire department area)			
• Pumpers	4.8%	• Engine Companies	11%
• Ladder Trucks	3.4%	• Ladder/Service Companies	6%
• Distribution of Companies and Types of Apparatus	4.0%	• Distribution of Companies	4%
• Pumper Capacity	4.4%	• Pumper Capacity	5%
• Design, Maintenance, and Condition of Apparatus	3.0%	• Department Staffing	15%
• Number of Officers	2.0%	• Training	9%
• Department Manning	8.0%		50%
• Engine and Ladder Company Unit Manning	6.4%		
• Master and Special Stream Devices	1.0%		
• Equipment for Pumpers and Ladders	2.0%		
• Hose	2.8%		
• Condition of Hose	1.6%		
• Training	6.0%		
• Response to Alarms	2.0%		
• Fire Operations	8.0%		
• Special Protection	6.0%		
• Miscellaneous Factors and Conditions	6.0%		
• ─────			
	71.4%[1]		
(adjusted percentage =	39%)[2]		

1. If the fire department was "100% deficient" there would be 3,570 deficiency points assigned which equals 71.4% of the 5,000 total deficiency points in the 1974 schedule.

2. Because the fire department is limited to 1,950 points, or 39% of the 5,000 total points in the schedule, points in excess of the 1,950 are simply not assigned, keeping the maximum deficiency to 1,950 points or 39% of the total.

Figure 5-3. Comparison of Review of Fire Alarm/Dispatch

1974 Schedule	Total Relative Weight (within fire alarm area)	1980 FSR Schedule	Relative Weight
• Communication Center	0.8%	• Receipt of Fire Alarms	2%
• Communication Center Equipment and Current Supply	2.8%	• Operators	3%
• Boxes	1.2%	• Alarm Dispatch Circuit Facilities	5%
			10%
• Alarm Circuits and Alarm Facilities, Including Current Supply at Fire Stations	2.0%		
• Material, Construction, Condition and Protection of Circuit	1.0%		
• Radio	0.8%		
• Fire Department Telephone Service	1.7%		
• Fire Alarm Operators	0.8%		
• Conditions Adversely Affecting Use	1.3%		
• Credit for Boxes Installed in Residential Districts	−1.4%		
• ―――	12.4%[1]		
(adjusted percentage =	9%)[2]		

1. If fire alarm/dispatch was "100% deficient" there would be 620 deficiency points assigned which equals 12.4% of the 5,000 total deficiency points in the 1974 schedule.

2. Because fire alarm/dispatch is limited to 450 points or 9% of the 5,000 total points in the schedule, points in excess of the 450 are simply not assigned, keeping the maximum deficiency to 450 points or 9% of the total.

(NOTE: The total maximum percentages shown under the 1974 schedule total only 87%. This is because of the 13% that was attributable to building laws, electrical laws, and fire prevention laws addressed under the 1974 schedule, was not addressed under the 1980 Fire Suppression Rating Schedule and therefore not shown here for comparison.)

The major differences in the Fire Suppression Rating Schedule (FSRS) versus the 1974 Grading Schedule for Municipal Fire Protection, as shown in the previous charts, can be summarized into several broad conceptual changes. First, the FSRS attempts to take a view of fire protection that is macroscopic as opposed to microscopic. The Fire Suppression Rating Schedule (FSRS) attempts, on a relative scale of 1 to 10, to quantify or assess the capability of a community to control and suppress fires when they occur and thereby limit fire loss. Remember that limiting fire loss is what is most important to CRS; fire protection and suppression are merely mechanisms to limit that loss. Therefore, the only items reviewed are those which directly affect and assist (or hinder) the suppression of a fire.

Second, the Fire Suppression Rating Schedule (FSRS) operates on a credit basis rather than on a deficiency basis (as did its predecessor(s)). The 1974 schedule was based on a theoretically perfect community with hypothetically perfect scores in each area being graded. Every community evaluated was compared to the "perfect" score and was given "deficiencies" for each area in which it did not match up. Taking points away for not doing certain things implied that communities were penalized for not having excellent fire protection and tended to imply that the ISO was "grading" fire protection, a notion, as previously stated, that the ISO has tried to dispel.

The Fire Suppression Rating Schedule (FSRS) has inverted this process by setting minimum criteria; the conditions found in a certain community are "credited" from that minimum. The ISO philosophy is that such an approach helps to offset the misrepresentation that it is setting standards for fire protection.

In addition, the Fire Suppression Rating Schedule (FSRS) has had all "subjective" criteria removed (it is hoped that this has resulted in an objective survey), and has concentrated on significant differences among communities and de-emphasized the time spent on those items that seem to be fairly uniform among communities. It is a "performance schedule" as compared to the "specification" type schedule which preceded it. Rather than setting out specific criteria as to how each area reviewed is to be structured, the Fire Suppression Rating Schedule (FSRS) looks more at *whether* the criteria are met than at *how* they are met. For example, where previous schedules required that a city have a water system to receive anything other than a Class 9 rating, the Fire Suppression Rating Schedule (FSRS) allows alternative methods of water delivery, such as tanker shuttles and large diameter hose to be used, as long as the appropriate quantity of water can be delivered. Finally, with the exception of the 1974 schedule, which allowed the needed fire flow in a sprinklered building to be reduced by as much as half, predecessors to the Fire Suppression Rating Schedule (FSRS) did not recognize the importance of fire sprinkler systems. The Fire Suppression Rating Schedule (FSRS) recognizes the importance of sprinklers by excluding properties that are fully sprinklered, and are "graded" as sprinklered, from the development of needed fire flows. It is important that a building be graded as "sprinklered," because buildings that are not so graded, i.e., buildings that are only "partially" sprinklered, are not exempted from the flow requirements.

THE CONTENTS OF THE FIRE SUPPRESSION RATING SCHEDULE

Contained within the grading survey are numerous areas that are reviewed and scored, and then used cumulatively, along with the other areas reviewed, to determine a city's rating. What follows is an overview of the contents of the survey, with particular attention given to the areas reviewed and *how* they are reviewed.

Introduction (items 100–106)

The introduction contains the background material necessary to properly apply the schedule. It defines "city" as including everything from cities to districts and it explains how numbers are rounded and decimal points dropped for the purposes of computing calculations. Several portions warrant a closer look. Section 101, titled "Scope," states that the schedule measures the major elements of a city's fire suppression system and contains the following disclaimer:

> "The schedule is a fire insurance rating tool, and is not intended to analyze all aspects of a comprehensive public fire protection program. It should not be used for purposes other than insurance rating."

Item 106 addresses the minimum facilities and conditions that are required to get any rating other than a 10 (municipality with less than recognized protection). These requirements include:

- A permanently organized entity under state or local law.
- Person in charge (fire chief).
- The fire department serves an area with definite boundaries, and is either legally or contractually obligated to protect same.
- Membership shall ensure the response of at least four people to structure fires.
- Training must be conducted two hours every two months for each member.
- There shall be no delay in receipt of alarms and dispatch of equipment.
- There shall be at least one piece of apparatus meeting NFPA 1901, *Standard for Pumper Fire Apparatus*, and all apparatus shall be protected from the weather.

(Note: this is a partial list only)

Application of particular section to types at minimum facilities (items 200–201)

Classes 1–8: This section tells under what circumstances different portions of the schedule shall be applied. For instance, if a city has both a piece of apparatus with a pump that has a rated capacity of 250 gpm or more at 150 psi *and* a water system (alternatives will be discussed later) capable of delivering 250 gpm or more for a period of two hours plus consumption at the maximum daily rate, then Sections 300–301 are applied (i.e., the city can obtain between a Class 1 and Class 8).

Class 9: If the city lacks the water system but has a piece of apparatus with a pump that has a capacity of 50 gpm or more at 150 psi and at least a 300-gallon water tank, then the city can obtain a Class 9 (Items 800–802).

Class 10: If the city lacks all the above, then the schedule doesn't apply to them. They automatically get a Class 10 (i.e., less than minimum recognized protection).

Needed fire flow (NFF) (items 310–340)

This section discusses how Needed Fire Flow (NFF) is determined and specifies what kinds of buildings should *not* be used in determining Needed Fire Flow.

The factors used to determine Needed Fire Flow are: 1) construction class; 2) occupancy class; and 3) exposure factor. Normally, a specified number of buildings that are suspected to have a large needed fire flow (based on findings by ISO representatives) are selected to determine Needed Fire Flow. It is important to note that buildings which are graded sprinklered are not subject to being included in the group of buildings used to determine Needed Fire Flow. Therefore, it is to a community's advantage to fully sprinkler as many buildings as possible (and assure that they are graded sprinklered). The fewer buildings that require a larger Needed Fire Flow (and are used in calculating a city's Needed Fire Flow), the lower the Needed Fire Flow; this results in a potentially better classification. *It is important for a city to carefully review any buildings used for Needed Fire Flow (NFF) calculations; there have been instances of fully sprinklered buildings used for Needed Fire Flow (NFF) because the ISO had not graded them as sprinklered, because it lacked this information or lacked sprinkler tests for the buildings in question.* Needed Fire Flow also is used for various other calculations in the schedule.

Receiving and handling fire alarms (items 400–433)

The first area of review is Receiving and Handling Fire Alarms; it represents ten percent of the total grade. Included under this section are areas concerning telephone service, operators (call takers) and dispatch circuitry involved in the receipt and dispatch of emergency calls.

Telephone service is reviewed to ascertain general accordance with NFPA 1221, *Standard for the Installation, Maintenance and Use of Public Fire Service Communication Systems*. The number of telephone lines needed (both emergency and business) is based on the size of the population served, and range from one fire line and one business line for a population up to 40,000, to four fire lines and three business lines for populations of 300,000 or more. Be aware that certain phone service situations can create a substantial loss of credit. For example, if nonfire emergency calls are received on fire emergency lines, then the number of lines needed has to be doubled. Automatic telephone dialing equipment used to report alarms requires separate lines. If only one phone number is listed in the telephone directory for both fire and business purposes, no credit is given for the fire line(s). Finally, even though the 1980 schedule is a "credit system," points are actually deducted if information concerning a fire is received by one call taker who then must pass the information on to another communications center. If the original call taker transfers the actual caller (patches the call) to another communications center which takes the information, then no points are deducted.

The telephone directory also is reviewed for the following areas of compliance: 1) that the fire emergency number is printed on the inside front cover of the white pages (blank lines for the customer to fill in the fire emergency number do not comply); 2) that both the emergency number and the business number are listed under "Fire Department" in the white pages; and 3) that both the emergency number and business number are listed under the name of the city in the white pages. (NOTE: If the individual fire station phone numbers are listed, additional points are deducted from the overall points credited).

The last telephone-service-related requirement is that there must be a device that permits immediate playback of calls received.

The next area covers operators. The number of operators needed, and defined by NFPA 1221, is determined by the number of "calls received," i.e., all calls required to be handled by the operator. According to the current edition of NFPA 1221, for a jurisdiction that receives fewer than 600 calls annually the schedule allows the following variations in operator requirements. If the jurisdiction receives from 600 to 2,500 alarms per year, at least one specially trained operator shall be on duty at all times. If more than 2,500 calls per year are received, then at least two fully trained operators shall be on duty at all times, with more as required by actual traffic. If a jurisdiction receives more than 10,000 calls per year, then three on-duty operators are required with two backup operators, for a total of five, although the two backups may be doing other work or resting. To assess whether a municipality complies with this section, the most current edition of NFPA 1221 should be reviewed for up-to-date requirements.

The final communications area reviewed is dispatch circuits, which includes a requirement for: two separate dispatch circuits (i.e., radio and telephone, radio and microwave, etc.) of which one circuit must be:

- a supervised wire circuit;
- a radio channel with duplicate base transmitters, receivers, mikes and antenna (if the primary transmitter fails, switchover to the backup must be automatic with visual and audible indication to the operator, unless the controls are located where someone is always on duty; then manual switchover is permitted if it can be accomplished within 30 seconds of failure);
- a microwave-supervised carrier channel;
- a polling of self-interrogating redundant radio or microwave radio system;
- a properly arranged, supervised phone circuit.

The second dispatch circuit does not have to be supervised and can be either a wired circuit or radio channel; if the second circuit is a radio channel, it does not require duplication as would be required for the primary circuit.

When two dispatch circuits are required, all alarms for fires in buildings must be transmitted from the communications center to the fire stations by two means (i.e., radio and printer, telephone and radio, etc.)

If fewer than 600 calls are received annually, then only one circuit is required.

The following types of dispatch circuits are credited under the schedules:

- Radio, voice-amplification, facsimile or teletype; visually recorded (facsimile and teletype) devices shall be accompanied by an audible alerting device to alert personnel.
- Radio receivers carried by firefighters, and a transmitter at the communications center.
- Outside sounding devices.
- Voice receivers at firefighters' homes or businesses and a transmitter at the communications center.
- Group alerting telephone circuits.

Circuits and other system components are required to be monitored so that defects and faults which would affect system performance can be detected rapidly. Circuits also are required to be recorded, either taped or hard-copied, depending on the type of dispatch circuits being used (i.e., radio, teletype, etc).

Supervision of the primary power supply is not required. An emergency power supply is not required, but may receive credit if provided at the site of transmitters (communications center) and receivers (fire stations). Acceptable emergency power supplies are batteries that last for four hours, automatically started generator, manually started generators, wet cell batteries or dry cell for radio receivers of the voice-amplification type.

Total credit for receiving and handling fire alarms includes the sum of "credit for telephone service" plus "credit for operators" plus "credit for dispatch circuits."

Fire department (items 500–590)

The fire department, the next major area to be reviewed, represents 50% of the total grade. The review begins with "needed" engine companies, based on maximum number needed for basic fire flow, distribution and/or operations.

Basic Fire Flow (BFF) is the fifth largest Needed Fire Flow (NFF) of all the Needed Fire Flows (NFF) which are calculated in Items 310–340, with the maximum Basic Fire Flow being 3,500 gpm (i.e., if the Needed Fire Flows (NFF) calculated were 600, 700, 1,000, 1,500, 2,000, 2,300, 2,700, 3,000, 3,150, 3,200 and 3,400 gpm, then the Basic Fire Flow (BFF) would be 2,700 gpm). The number of needed engine companies for Basic Fire Flow (BFF) is one engine for 500 to 1,000 gpm Basic Fire Flow (BFF), two engines for 1,250 to 2,500 gpm Basic Fire Flow (BFF), and three engines for 3,000 to 3,500 gpm Basic Fire Flow (BFF).

By distribution, an additional engine company is needed for each area where a company that is required by Basic Fire Flow (BFF) will not meet the first due response distance to 50 percent of the built-upon, i.e., hydranted area that is within the satisfactory response travel distance. Travel distance is defined as one and a-half miles as measured on "all-weather" roads for engine companies. In addition, if responses outside the city deplete resources available to the city, then additional engine companies may be required. The total number of engine companies needed by distribution is the number of needed existing engine companies plus the number of additional needed engine company locations. For operations, the standard response is two engine companies, except when only one engine is required by Basic Fire Flow. The number of needed engine companies is the greatest number of engines needed based on either Basic Fire Flow (BFF), distribution, or operations, plus any additionally required companies.

In contrast to needed engine companies is the credit given for existing engine companies. Engines that are staffed on first alarms are given credit as existing engine companies, if, based on a certification test or three-hour acceptance test, the pump meets all these requirements:

- 100 percent of rated pressure at 150 psi net pump pressure;
- 70 percent of rated pressure at 200 psi net pump pressure; and
- 50 percent of rated pressure at 250 psi net pump pressure.

A pump must be permanently mounted and must have a minimum rating of 250 gpm at 150 psi in order to qualify an apparatus for credit. There are two additional ways to receive engine company credit. The first is that apparatus which carry engine and ladder/service company equipment will be credited as existing engine companies, if needed. Second, automatic aid engine companies that are within five miles of a city, and that respond according to a plan, are credited if they replace the need for engine companies.

While the formula is somewhat complex, if a staffed engine company responds on a first alarm and is considered "extra," it can be counted either as a ladder/service company when it carries the appropriate equipment, or it may be credited as part of a two-piece engine company; in this case the credit for the equipment it carries can be combined with the equipment credited on another engine in order to gain the maximum credit available under engine equipment.

For each apparatus that meets the criteria for an existing engine company, the following additional items are reviewed:

(1) pump capacity up to 500 gpm;
(2) hose 2½ inches up to 400 feet, plus an additional 800 feet of 2½-inch or longer;
(3) pumper equipment and hose:
- 300-gallon booster tank
- 200 feet booster hose at 1½ inch
- 400 feet 1½-inch hose
- 200 feet 1½-inch hose spare (or carried)
  (NOTE: 1¾-inch hose is acceptable in lieu of 1½ inch-hose)
- one master stream device (1,000 gpm)
  (NOTE: not needed for BFF of less than 1,500 gpm)
- one distributing nozzle
- one foam nozzle
- ten gallons foam carried
- fifteen gallons foam spare or carried
- two 2½-inch play pipes with shutoff
- two 2½-inch straight stream and spray shutoffs
- two 1½-inch straight stream and spray shutoffs
- four SCBAs (30-minute minimum)
- four additional SCBA spare cylinders (carried)
- two 12 × 18 foot-salvage covers
- two handlights
- one each: hose clamp, 2½-inch hydrant hose gate, 2½-inch booster

hose jacket, 2½ × 1½ × 1½ inch-gated wye, portable and mobile radio, roof ladder and 24-foot extension.

Equipment credit is then prorated depending on quantity possessed versus quantity required.

In addition, each engine must be pump tested annually (similar to the NFPA 1901 certification test) with decreasing credit for less frequent tests down to once every five years. Hose also must be tested annually as described in NFPA 1962, *Standard for the Care, Use and Maintenance of Fire Hose, Including Connections and Nozzles* with credit decreasing at lower psi achieved (250, 200 or 150 psi) and for less frequent tests down to once every five years. If no records of pump tests are maintained, then the credit is reduced by 20 percent. If the equipment is carried on an automatic aid engine, then based upon such variables as common communications, interdepartmental training, etc., the maximum credit than can be derived for that equipment is 90 percent of the total credit awarded.

One reserve engine is required for every eight engine companies needed. Pump, hose, and equipment on reserves are credited just as they are on existing engines.

Pump capacity also is reviewed with the requirement that the available pump capacity of all existing engines be sufficient to meet Basic Fire Flow.

Ladder/service companies are reviewed next. The number needed is the higher of the number needed for "distribution" or "operations." From a distribution perspective, every protected area must have a ladder or service company response, and if any protected area is beyond 2½ miles of an existing ladder/service company, then additional ladder/service companies may be needed. In these cases, the need may be met by ladder/service companies at existing or needed "engine" company locations obviously to prevent requiring locations just for ladder/service companies.

From the operational perspective, any standard response on first alarms for building fires should have a ladder/service company. If a ladder/service company does not respond, an engine company responding with any ladder/service company equipment should be considered as an engine/ladder or engine/service company.

Whether a ladder or service company is needed depends on the type of area protected. Response areas with five or more buildings that are 3 stories or 35 feet or more in height, or with 5 buildings that have a Needed Fire Flow exceeding 3,500 gpm, or any combination of the 2, should have a ladder company. In considerations of building height, all buildings, including those with sprinklers, are used. If no "individual" response area needs a ladder company, but the buildings in the city as a whole meet the above requirements, then at least one ladder company is needed. Response areas that do not need a ladder company should have a service company.

Companies that respond to first alarms carrying any of the equipment required for ladder companies will be considered existing ladder companies when ladder companies are needed. While the rules are quite complex, generally an existing engine company that carries any ladder company equipment is considered an engine/ladder company and gets credited as one half of an existing ladder company. If it is not credited as an engine company, but it carries ladder company equipment, an engine company will be credited as one ladder company. The same general rules apply to engine/service companies.

The following equipment is required on a service company:

- one large spray nozzle (500 gpm minimum);
- six SCBA (30-minute minimum);
- six spare cylinders;
- ten 12×18-foot salvage covers;
- one electric generator;
- three 500-watt floodlights;
- one smoke ejector;
- one oxyacetylene cutting unit;
- one power saw;
- four handlights;
- one hose roller;
- six pike poles (6-foot, 8-foot, 2-foot);
- two radios (1 mounted, 1 portable); and
- two ladders (10-foot attic, 14-foot extension).

In addition to the service company equipment, the following equipment is required for ladder companies:

- one 16-foot roof ladder;
- one 20-foot roof ladder;
- one 28-foot extension ladder;
- one 35-foot extension ladder;
- one 40-foot extension ladder; and
- one elevated stream device (able to reach the lesser of 100 feet or the height of any building protected).

An annual test of the aerial ladder/elevating platform also is required; variable credit is given depending on the frequency of tests—from a high of 100 percent credit for annual tests to a low of zero credit for a test frequency of five years and over. In addition to the annual test, a nondestructive test (NDT), as defined in NFPA 1904, is needed every five years.

If there are no records of the tests which an agency claims to have conducted, then the points awarded are reduced by 20 percent, emphasizing the importance of proper recordkeeping.

For every eight ladder or service companies needed, one reserve ladder or service company is needed. If one of the eight needed companies is a ladder, then the reserve should be a ladder as well, as opposed to just a service company. The equipment on the reserve ladder/service companies shall be credited according to previous equipment schedules for ladder and service companies.

Part of the formula for fire department credit includes a review of company distribution, which requires an engine company within 1½ miles of every built-up area of the city and a ladder/service company within 2½ miles of every built-up area of the city.

The next area examined under the fire department is "existing company personnel," which is the average number of firefighters and company officers on duty for existing companies as determined by certain criteria. The total number of members on duty shall be the yearly average of on-duty personnel, including all time off. Chief officers and nonsuppression personnel are not included in computing on-duty strength, except when more than one chief officer responds; then, those who perform company duties may be credited as firefighters. While the ISO does not discuss "minimum staffing," this is the one area of the survey where a city can receive unlimited points, i.e., the more on-duty personnel that respond, the more points credited.

Personnel on apparatus not credited as existing engine, ladder, or service companies but who regularly respond to first alarms to aid existing companies are included for the purpose of increasing total company strength, while personnel on units such as ambulances may be credited if they are involved in firefighting operations, depending on the extent to which they are available and used for first-alarm response.

On-call, volunteer and off-duty paid members responding to first alarms are credited based on the average number staffing apparatus on first alarms. Call and volunteer shall be credited the same as on-duty paid personnel proportionately for the time they spend sleeping at stations; otherwise every *three* volunteers or call personnel credited as responding count for *one* on-duty person. The importance of good records comes into play here again, for if good records are not kept to document response, the credit ratio of volunteers to on-duty increases from 3:1 to 6:1, i.e., six volunteers equal one paid person.

The last area reviewed under the fire department is "training." Facilities, aids, and actual training provided are examined. Facility and aids credit is given for drill towers, fire buildings, including smoke rooms, flammable liquid pits, library and training manuals, slide and movie projectors, pump and hydrant cutaways, and training areas, which may include streets and open areas when no other training facility is provided. Videos on fighting combustible/flammable liquid fires could replace the need for flammable liquid pits. The points credited for facilities and aids are then prorated for "use" with credit being given for the following:

(a)   eight half-day company drills (3 hours) per year.
(b)   four half-day multi-company drills (3 hours) per year.

(c)   two night drills (3 hours) per year.

The fewer of the above drills held, the less credit is given for facility and aids. Some drills may qualify for multiple credit (i.e., a single-company drill held for three hours at night can credit as (a) and (c); a multi-company drill held for 3 hours at night can get credits as (a), (b) and (c).

The following additional training also is examined and credited:

- up to 20 hours per member per month of company training at the station;
- up to 2 days per year for all officers;
- up to 4 half-day sessions for driver/operators;
- up to a 40-hour class for all new driver/operators;
- one-half day per member per year on radioactivity (hazardous materials training could replace the need for separate training on radioactivity); and
- up to 240 hours per new recruit.

In addition, "prefire" planning inspections, including updated notes and sketches of all commercial, industrial, institutional and similar buildings should be made twice a year.

The total points given for training are reduced 10% for incomplete records and 20% for no records.

Credit for fire department is the sum of the total credits given for "engine companies" plus "reserve pumpers" plus "pumper capacity" plus "ladder service" plus "reserve ladder service" plus "distribution" plus "company personnel" plus "training."

Water supply (items 600–640)

The third and final major area to be reviewed is the water supply, which counts for the remaining 40% of the grade. This item reviews the water supply that is available for the city's fire suppression. If it is determined that more than 85 percent of the community being graded is not within 1,000 feet of a recognized water system, the area devoid of fire hydrants may get no better than a Class 9 rating.

Several elements go into determining the "supply works capacity" which is one of the four factors used in calculating the credible rate of flow at each test location. Maximum daily consumption is the average rate of consumption on the maximum day. The maximum day is that 24-hour period with the highest consumption in the last three-year period, excluding highs caused by unusual operations (i.e., major fires) or that won't occur again due to system changes. A water system is reviewed at a residual pressure of 20 psi. The fire flow duration should be two hours for NFFs up to 2,500 gpm and three hours for those of 3,000 to 3,500 gpm. The ability of the water supply system to deliver the NFF is measured at representative locations throughout the city and at each location. The supply works capacity, main and hydrant distribution are reviewed separately.

The supply works capacity is determined by subtracting the maximum daily consumption from the sum of the average maximum water storage plus the effective pumping capacity of pumps (expressed in gpms) when delivering at normal operating pressures and the delivery capabilities of filters plus emergency supplies (i.e., supplies not normally used). To this amount is then added: 1) suction supply (static supplies from which a fire department can draft to supply water); and 2) fire department supply (water delivered by fire department vehicles). This last area, fire department supply, is perhaps the most significant change in the grading schedule and represents a major philosophical shift from the method of water delivery to how much water can be delivered with little emphasis on its delivery method. This change has had a major beneficial effect on those communities that are not connected to large municipal water systems, for it has allowed them, through tanker shuttles and other alternatives, to establish deliverable flows that meet or exceed the 250 gpm required for two hours under Item 201; this enables a city to obtain a rating better than a Class 9. Many communities formerly rated a "9" have improved two to three classes under this new alternative. This alternative requires a CRS field representative to witness each tanker's fill time, dump time and set-up time. This information then is converted into a gpm flow for each tanker by dividing the amount of water carried (less 10% for spillage) by the dump and fill time and travel time. Also recorded is the pump capacity, travel and set-up time at the fire and supply point, as well as folding tank and fire site pumper tank capacities. All this is then processed through computer software which computes the theoretical flow available. Considering that 40% of a city's total grade is water related, this alternative was not only long overdue, but a welcome relief to much of the nation's fire service.

Main capacity also is reviewed at the same test locations considered under supply works capacity. The results of actual flow tests at these locations indicate the ability of mains to carry water to those locations.

The final element used in determining the creditable flow rate at each test location is hydrant distribution. Each hydrant within 1,000 feet of a test location (measured as hose can be laid) is reviewed to determine if it can satisfy the NFF at that location. Gallons-per-minute credit for hydrants is as follows:

> For each hydrant within 300 feet of test site, measured to the nearest corner of the test site/building credit, 1,000 gpm; if within 301 feet to 600 feet, credit 670 gpm; and if within 601 feet to 1,000 feet of the test site, credit 250 gpm. If, for instance, there were two hydrants within 300 feet and one hydrant within 600 feet, the total maximum flow by distribution would be 2,670 gpm (1,000 gpm + 1,000 gpm + 670 gpm).

Hydrant credit can be further limited according to size and number of ports as follows:

(a) at least one pumper outlet	1,000 gpm max
(b) two or more house outlets, no pumper outlet	750 gpm max
(c) one house outlet only	500 gpm max

Hydrants which are in another city but within measurable distances of the test site are credited as any other hydrant. If a fire department can demonstrate; by the use of large diameter hose, that it can flow greater quantities than allowed above, then the actual flow shall be used for calculating flow by distribution. This is based on whether the department's standard operating procedure requires a pumper at the hydrant and the large-diameter hose between the pumper and the fire.

The capability of the water system at the test site will be calculated using the *lesser* of the Needed Fire Flow (NFF) at that site, what the building requires, the supply works capacity at the site, i.e., how much water is available, the main capacity at the site, i.e., how much water can actually be flowed, and hydrant distribution at the site, i.e., number and distance of hydrants.

Credit for the supply system is determined by factoring the capability of the water system (at the test locations) and the Needed Fire Flow (NFF) (at the test locations).

Credit for hydrants is given based on points assigned to various types of hydrants, with maximum points being given to hydrants with a six-inch or larger branch and a pumper outlet with or without 2½-outlets, and the fewest points being given to hydrants with: a) only one 2½-outlet; and b) less than a six-inch branch, as well as to hydrants that are flush types, as well as cisterns and suction points. Points are prorated according to the number of hydrants of each type compared with the total number of hydrants.

Inspection and condition of hydrants is the last area reviewed under water supply. Inspection and condition of hydrants should be in accordance with American Water Works Association (AWWA) Manual M-17. The credit given for this area is based on frequency of inspection and condition of the hydrants. The frequency of inspection is the average time interval between the three most recent inspections, with maximum credit given for half-year cycles and minimum credit for cycles of five years or more. Points are deducted for incomplete or no records, if hydrants are not subject to full system pressure during tests and if inspection of cisterns and suction points does not include actual pumper drafting. Condition is reviewed by giving credit for three categories: a) standard (no leaks, well located, operates easily); b) usable; and c) not usable.

Credit for water supply is determined by the total of the "credit for supply system" plus the "credit for hydrants" plus the "credit for inspection and condition."

The public protection classification

The Public Protection Classification (PPC) is determined by adding the points credited to "Handling and Receiving Fire Alarms, up to 10 points, plus those credited to the fire department, up to 50 points, plus those credited to water supply, up to 40 points. From this total is deducted what's called "divergence," which is 50% of the difference between 80% of the fire department credit and 100% of the water supply credit. The divergence represents the disparity, if any, between the fire department's capabilities and the ability to supply water.

Divergence = 50% (100% water supply credit − 80% of fire department credit)

Percentage to Class correlations are as follows:

Class	Percentage
1	90.00 or more
2	80.00 to 89.99
3	70.00 to 79.99
4	60.00 to 69.99
5	50.00 to 59.99
6	40.00 to 49.99
7	30.00 to 39.99
8	20.00 to 29.99
9	10.00 to 19.99
10	0.00 to 9.99

As an example, if a city received the following credits:

a)	Receiving & Handling Fire Alarms	9 points (out of 10 possible)
b)	Fire Department	35 points (out of 50 possible)
c)	Water Supply	31 points (out of 40 possible)

its divergence would be "-1.5" (i.e., $.5[(31) - .8(35)]$) and its PPC would be a Class 3; $(9 + 35 + 31 = 75 - .5[(31) - .8(35)] = 73.5$; 70.00 to 79.99 = Class 3).

Cities which cannot meet the requirements in Item 201 (previously discussed) to obtain at least a Class 8 may obtain a Class 9 if under Items 800–802 they can meet the following minimum criteria:

(1) one piece of apparatus, which is NFPA 1901 compliant, with a permanently mounted pump capable of delivering 50 gpm or more at 150 psi and a 300-gallon tank;

(2) records which indicate date, time, and location of fires, the number of responding members, meetings, training, maintenance of equipment and apparatus, and an up-to-date member roster; and

(3) at a minimum the following equipment:
- at least two 150-foot lengths of ¾ or 1-inch booster, 1½-inch preconnect or equivalent, each with a nozzle that can discharge both a straight and a spray stream;
- two portable extinguishers for use on Class A, B, or C fires and with a minimum rating of 20-BC in dry chemical, 10-BC in CO_2 and 2-A in water;
- one 12-foot ladder with hooks;
- one 24-foot extension ladder;
- one pick head ax;
- two handlights; and
- one each—pike pole, bolt cutter, claw tool, crow bar.

Out of 80 possible points for 1, 2, and 3 above, a city must get at least 70 in order to get a Class 9; otherwise it will receive a Class 10.

Individual properties

Section II of the Fire Suppression Rating Schedule (FSRS) deals with public protection classifications for specifically rated properties that have a Needed Fire Flow (NFF) of more than 3,500 gpm. While specific details of how those classifications are arrived at will not be reviewed in this chapter, suffice it to say that the protection class of an individual property is the lower of either of two protection factors—fire department companies or water supply. The protection class of a subject building will be the same as that for the city unless the individual Public Protection Classification (PPC) indicates a poorer class, in which case the poorer class, but not less than Class 9 when the city is a Class 9 or better, will apply to the subject building.

The survey process

There are several methods by which a survey can be initiated. First a community, because of what it perceives to have been significant changes or improvements to its water system or fire department, may request a regrading. This request, which details the changes or improvements, is normally made in writing from the chief executive officer of the city to the ISO. The ISO will do an office review to determine if the changes to the fire protection would alter the community classification. If it is determined that it is probable, ISO will schedule an appointment with the community for a regrading. This will largely depend on how "backed up" the particular ISO office is and could run anywhere from three months to a year or longer, unless the ISO already plans to be in the area.

Another way that a regrading may occur is if a major annexation occurs which significantly changes the boundaries of the city, or a new city incorporates with its own fire department, and either one of these is brought to the attention of the ISO, in which case it will probably initiate a regrading.

Finally, the ISO has a generally established resurvey cycle of its own which attempts to regrade communities with a population less than 25,000 every 15 years and those with populations over 25,000 every 10 years.

In the case of a field survey, the ISO field office will notify the city several weeks prior to the survey. At that time it also will request certain information from the city. This information may either be requested in advance or the city may be advised to have it ready for the field representative upon its arrival. Materials requested may include, but not be limited to, a listing of all the significant representatives of the city (i.e., city manager, fire chief, public works director, mayor, etc.); a map of the city showing all fire station locations; a map showing the location of all hydrants in the city; pertinent information concerning the city's water system (i.e., maximum daily consumption, pump capacity, etc.); and pertinent information regarding the city itself (i.e., population, etc.). In addition, an information sheet for each piece of fire apparatus which the fire department operates will be required to be completed listing information about areas such as pump, tank, and all equipment carried on board.

In addition to the above material, it would be extremely helpful to have ready the following information in a "user-friendly" form for the field representative:

(1) staffing records for the last year, including minimum and maximum levels if applicable;

(2) records of all time off during the last year, including vacation, sick leave, Kelly days, etc.;

(3) a training record for each member of the department, broken down by category of training;

(4) a list of all training facilities and aids;

(5) information regarding the communications center, including number of calls received, number of operators on duty, and type and numbers of dispatch circuits;

(6) copies of all preplans completed, including sketches showing frequency and dates completed;

(7) a complete set of water system maps, including schematics of all plants and distribution sites;

(8) copies of all formal written automatic aid agreements;

(9) a complete record of all hours spent in stations and all responses made if volunteers are part of the system; and

(10) a record of all structural responses for the last year, including the number of personnel responding to each.

Once the field representative arrives, he will familiarize himself with the material that has been presented to him and then proceed to set out a schedule of activities to be accomplished during his stay. This will include station visits to spot check facilities, equipment, and apparatus listed on the information sheets discussed above, inspecting the communications center, and identifying the buildings which will constitute the test locations. The department will need to have the necessary personnel available to assist the field representative with the flow tests which will be done at each test location. It also would be wise to review the batch list compiled of properties in the city and make sure that all buildings that are sprinklered are so identified so that sprinklered complexes do not enter into the computation of BFF, which may help reduce the number of needed engine companies.

After the field representative has completed all tasks necessary on site, he will return to the field office where all the final computations will be done. Once the grading is completed, it will be forwarded for review. After review, the final survey results will be released during the next reporting cycle.

While the ISO normally will only inform the city of its classification, if the city so requests, the ISO will furnish a copy of the classification details showing the number of points awarded in each of the subcategories under the three main categories as compared to the maximum number of points available. This is very helpful in determining areas which can be improved.

If a city's classification improves, the implementation will be immediate. If, however, the city regresses, i.e., the classification becomes worse, then implementation normally will be delayed and the city will be given an opportunity to make any necessary improvements or changes to avoid the regression. This normally will require city personnel to communicate a plan of action in writing to the ISO, along with a timetable for implementation.

Located in the appendix are two different classification details for surveys that were conducted. One is for a 1990 survey conducted by the ISO/CRS using the 1980 Fire Suppression Rating Schedule (FSRS); the other is a 1991 survey by the Washington Surveying and Rating Bureau which still uses the 1974 Municipal Grading Schedule. While both communities received a Class 3, note the different approaches taken in the two surveys to reach the same conclusion.

SUMMARY

While it is true that a reduction in the classification of a city can reduce the amount of insurance premiums paid by its residents and businesses, it is equally true that the cost of making the improvements necessary to obtain that reduction (which translates into higher taxes paid by those same residents and businesses) can exceed the insurance savings realized. All too often a fire chief, tempted to want the "bragging rights" which go along with lower classifications, seeks to make improvements, citing a better rating as the reason, without comparing the cost of improvements to the benefit to the taxpayer.

Very often a property owner can realize just as much in savings to his own particular property by making fire safety improvements therein (i.e., fire alarm or extinguishing systems) which will result in a reduction in his own premium, as could be realized by a reduction in classification. This is particularly true for homeowners, for in many states, once a community reaches a certain classification, Class 4 for instance, the homeowner's premium does not change, even if there is further improvement in the city's rating. This is precisely the reason that the ISO stresses the fact, as previously mentioned, that the Fire Suppression Rating Schedule (FSRS) is an insurance rating tool and not intended to be used as a means of evaluating the quality of fire protection provided by a community. The truth is, however, that until something else comes along which allows a fire department to evaluate how good a job it is doing compared to like fire departments providing fire protection to like communities, the ISO classification is the only means available to do so.

While it is quite possible that the accreditation project currently being examined by the International Association of Fire Chiefs and the International City/County Management Association may prove to be that needed evaluation tool, only time will tell for sure. Until then the ISO classification scheme will continue to fill a gap that it is really not designed to fill.

APPENDIX I

1990 ISO/CRS Classification Details for Survey
Utilizing the 1980 Fire Suppression Rating Schedule

ISO COMMERCIAL RISK SERVICES, INC.
4070 BOULEVARD CENTER DRIVE JACKSONVILLE, FL 32207
(904) 396-3901 FAX: (904) 396-0262

December 10, 1990

Mr. John Jones
City Manager
100 Main Street
Anytown, Florida

Dear Mr. Jones:

We are enclosing a copy of the Classification Details in response to your recent request. These details cover the items which are reviewed in our Fire Suppression Rating Schedule, and which are of importance in determining your fire insurance classification.

These Classification Details were developed using the information obtained during our 1990 survey, and considers that the other conditions in your city have remained the same.
They refer only to the fire insurance rating classification of your city which may be used in the calculation of property insurance premiums and are not for property loss prevention or life safety purposes.

The city classification applies to properties with a needed fire flow of 3500 gpm or less. The private and public protection at properties with larger needed fire flows are individually evaluated, and may vary from the city classification.

Please contact us if you have any questions concerning the enclosed material.

Very truly yours,

Robert Smith
Public Protection Department

rrr:dgf
Enclosure

A SUBSIDIARY OF INSURANCE SERVICES OFFICE, INC.

ISO COMMERCIAL RISK SERVICES, INC.

4070 BOULEVARD CENTER DRIVE   JACKSONVILLE, FL 32207

(904) 396-3901   FAX: (904) 396-0262

CLASSIFICATION DETAILS

Municipality Anytown   State Florida   Population 20,831

Date Surveyed August 8, 1990   Total Credit 72.27   Class 3

SUMMARY OF CREDIT

Feature	Assigned	Maximum Credit
Receiving and Handling Fire Alarms	10.00%	10.00%
Fire Department	33.19	50.00
Water Supply	31.61	40.00
*Divergence	−2.53%	_____
	72.27	

The Public Protection Class is based on the total percentage credit as follows:

Class	%
1	90.00 or more
2	80.00 to 89.99
3	70.00 to 79.99
4	60.00 to 69.99
5	50.00 to 59.99
6	40.00 to 49.99
7	30.00 to 39.99
8	20.00 to 29.99
9	10.00 to 19.99
10	0 to 9.99

The above classification has been developed for use in property insurance premium calculations only.

*Divergence is a reduction in credit to reflect a difference in the relative credits for Fire Department and Water Supply.

RECEIVING AND HANDLING FIRE ALARMS

This section of the Fire Suppression Rating Schedule reviews the facilities provided for the general public to report fires, and for the operator on duty at the communication center to dispatch fire department companies to the fires.

		Actual	Maximum
		Credit	
1.	**(Item 414)** Credit for Telephone Service This item reviews the facilities provided for the public to report fires, including the listing of fire and business numbers in the telephone directory.	2.00	2.00
2.	**(Item 422)** Credit for Operators This item reviews the number of operators *on-duty* at the communication center to handle fire calls.	3.00	3.00
3.	**(Item 432)** Credit for Dispatch Circuits This item reviews the dispatch circuit facilities use to transmit alarms to fire department members.	5.00	5.00
4.	**(Item 440)** Total Credit for Receiving and Handling Fire Alarms	10.00	10.00

FIRE DEPARTMENT

This section of the Fire Suppression Rating Schedule reviews the engine and ladder-service companies, equipment carried, response to fires, training and available fire fighters.

		Actual	Maximum
		Credit	
1.	**(Item 513)** Credit for Engine Companies This item reviews the number of engine companies and the hose and equipment carried	6.04	10.00
2.	**(Item 523)** Credit for Reserve Pumpers This item reviews the number of reserve pumpers their pump capacity and the hose and equipment carried on each	.55	1.00
3.	**(Item 532)** Credit for Pump Capacity This item reviews the total available pump capacity	5.00	5.00
4.	**(Item 549)** Credit for Ladder Service This item reviews the number of ladder and service companies and the equipment carried	4.88	5.00
5.	**(Item 553)** Credit for Reserve Ladder Service This item reviews the number of reserve ladder and service trucks, and the equipment carried	.17	1.00
6.	**(Item 561)** Credit for Distribution This item reviews the percent of the built-upon area of the city which has an adequately-equipped, responding first-due engine company within 1½ miles and an adequately-equipped, responding ladder-service company within 2½ miles.	2.05	4.00
7.	**(Item 571)** Credit for Company Personnel This item reviews the average number of equivalent fire fighters and company officers on duty with existing companies.	8.83	15.00*

8.	**(Item 581)** Credit for Training		
	This item reviews the training facilities and their use.	5.67	9.00
9.	**(Item 590)** Total Credit for Fire Department	33.19	50.00*

*This indicates that credit for manning is open-ended, with no maximum credit for this item.

WATER SUPPLY

This section of the Fire Suppression Rating Schedule reviews the water supply system that is available for fire suppression in the city.

		Credit	
		Actual	*Maximum*
1.	**(Item 616)** Credit for the Water System		
	This item reviews the supply works, the main capacity and hydrant distribution	27.35	35.00
2.	**(Item 621)** Credit for Hydrants		
	This item reviews the type of hydrants, and method of installation	1.86	2.00
3.	**(Item 631)** Credit for Inspection and Condition of Hydrants		
	This item reviews the frequency of inspections of hydrants and their condition	2.40	3.00
4.	**(Item 640)** Total Credit for Water Supply	31.61	40.00

APPENDIX II

1991 Washington Surveying and Rating Bureau Classification Details for Surveys Utilizing the 1974 Municipal Grading Schedule

WASHINGTON SURVEYING AND RATING BUREAU

FIRE INSURANCE AND APPURTENANT COVERAGES
300 MARKET PLACE ONE • 2001 WESTERN AVENUE
SEATTLE, WASHINGTON 98121-2190
(206) 441-6676

REX W. CLARK
GENERAL MANAGER

June 21,1991

Honorable James Doe
City of Yourville
1001 North Avenue
Yourville, Washington

Dear Mayor Doe:

It is my pleasure to inform you that the fire protection classification of your City has improved from Class 4 to Class 3 effective August 1, 1991.

This change reflects the improvements made in recent years to your fire communications, fire department, and water system.

This survey was not conducted for property loss prevention or for life safety purposes. The purpose was to gather information needed to determine a fire insurance classification which may be used to develop fire insurance rates. The new class will reduce fire insurance rates on most commercial and institutional property that meet our minimum requirements for water supplies and fire hydrants but will have little effect on residential property and commercial property equipped with automatic sprinkler systems.

I with to thank the Chief and Water Superintendent for their cooperation during the inspection.

Please find enclosed the new Grading Summary, flow test results, and a detailed grading breakdown.

If you have any questions concerning your new classification, please let me know.

Very truly yours,

William White
Field Representative
Public Protection

JZ/dl
Enc.

WASHINGTON SURVEYING AND RATING BUREAU

FIRE INSURANCE AND APPURTENANT COVERAGES
300 MARKET PLACE ONE • 2001 WESTERN AVENUE
SEATTLE, WASHINGTON 98121-2190
(206) 441-6676

REX W. CLARK
GENERAL MANAGER

YOURVILLE

POPULATION: 35,781 _____   INSPECTED: April, 1991 _____

	Water Supply	Fire Department	Fire Service Communications	Fire Safety Control	Climatic Conditions	Divergence	Total Points	CLASS
Point of Deficiency	335	524	49	316	52	0	1,276	3

The class of a community is based on a total maximum of 5,000 points of deficiency as follows:

1st Class	0 to	500 points
2nd Class	501 to	1,000 points
3rd Class	1,001 to	1,500 points
4th Class	1,501 to	2,000 points
5th Class	2,001 to	2,500 points
6th Class	2,501 to	3,000 points
7th Class	3,001 to	3,500 points
8th Class	3,501 to	4,000 points
9th Class	4,001 to	4,500 points
10th Class	more than	4,500 points

RELATIVE VALUES

	Points
Water Supply	1,950
Fire Department	1,950
Fire Service Communications	450
Fire Safety Control	650
	5,000

DETAILED GRADING

Grading Schedule for Municipal Fire Protection

Date Graded: June, 1991   Municipality: Yourville

Total Deficiency: 1,276   Protection Class: 3   Graded by: William White

WATER SUPPLY

	Item		*Assigned Points*
1.	Adequacy of Supply Works		5
2.	Reliability of Source Supply		84
3.	Reliability of Pumping Capacity		0
	a. with one pump out		
	b. with two pump out		
4.	Reliability of Power Supply		0
	a. one electric device out		
	b. overhead lines		
	c. other		
5.	Condition, Arrangement, Operation, and Reliability of System Components		32
6.	Adequacy of Mains		20
	a. commercial districts.	15	
	b. residential districts.	5	
7.	Reliability of Mains		11
8.	Installation of Mains		15
9.	Arrangement of Distribution System		16
10.	Additional Factors and Conditions Relating to Supply and Distribution		25
11.	Distribution of Hydrants		72
	a. Commercial districts.	53	
	b. Residential districts	19	
12.	Hydrants—Size, Type and Installation		0
13.	Hydrants—Inspection and Condition		18
14.	Miscellaneous factors and Conditions		37
	a. Plans and Records	3	
	b. Emergency Provisions	11	
	c. Valve Spacing	5	
	d. Bldg. Const.	0	
	e. Other Factors	18	
		TOTAL	335

FIRE DEPARTMENT

			Assigned Points
Item			
1.	Pumpers		0
	a. Required pumpers	___	
	b. Reserve pumpers	___	
2.	Ladder Trucks		18
	a. Required ladder trucks	0	
	b. Reserve ladder trucks	18	
	c. Ladder service where truck not required	0	
3.	Distribution of Companies and Type of apparatus		18
4.	Pumper Capacity		0
	a. Capacity available	___	
	b. Reserve pumper capacity available	___	
5.	Design, Maintenance, and Conditions of Apparatus		19
6.	Number of Officers		17
	a. Chief	0	
	b. Company	17	
7.	Department Manning		120
	a. Day shift	60	
	b. Night shift	60	
8.	Engine and Ladder Company Unit Manning		60
9.	Master and Stream Devices		2
10.	Equipment for Pumpers and Ladder Trucks		5
11.	Hose		0
	a. 2½-inch	___	
	b. 1½-inch	___	
	c. Booster	___	
12.	Condition of Hose		4
13.	Training		118
14.	Response to Alarms		3
15.	Fire Operation		95
	a. First alarm fires	9	
	b. Large fires	86	
16.	Special Protection		0
17.	Miscellaneous Factors and Conditions		45
	a. Records	1	
	b. Fire stations	5	
	c. Fuel	4	
	d. Possible delays in response	18	
	e. Other	17	
		TOTAL	524

FIRE SERVICE COMMUNICATIONS

Item		Assigned Points
1.	Communication Center	5
2.	Communication Center Equipment and Current Supply	5
3.	Boxes	0
4.	Alarm Circuits and Alarm Facilities Including Current Supply at Fire Stations	11
5.	Material, Construction, Condition, and Protection of Circuits	3
6.	Radio	1
7.	Fire Department Telephone Services	8
8.	Fire Alarm Operators	4
9.	Miscellaneous	12
	TOTAL	49

FIRE SAFETY CONTROL

Item		Assigned Points
1.	Flammable or Compressed Gasses	14
2.	Flammable or Compressed Liquids	68
3.	Special Hazards	64
4.	Miscellaneous Hazards	63
5.	Supplemental Fire Prevention Activities	45
6.	Building Laws	29
7.	Electricity	33
8.	Heating and Ventilating Installations	
	TOTAL	316

ADDITIONAL DEFICIENCIES

Item		Assigned Points
1.	Adverse Climatic Conditions	22
2.	Earthquake	30
3.	Divergence Between Water Supply and Fire Department	0
	TOTAL	52

SUMMARY OF DEFICIENCY POINTS

Water Supply	335
Fire Departments	524
Fire Service Communications	49
Fire Safety	316
Additional Deficiencies	52
TOTAL	1,276

6

Leadership for Today and Tomorrow

GEORGE GOLDBACH

C H A P T E R   H I G H L I G H T S

• Definitions of management and leadership, and the differences and the relationship between the two.

• The major goals of a fire department.

• What is meant by the "comfort work zone."

• What a commitment to excellence means and what it can do for you.

• The two motivation theories.

• The theories of Abraham Maslow, Fredrick Herzberg, and Victor Vroom, and how they relate to effective leadership.

• Situational, contingency and path-goal approaches to leadership.

• Five functions of management.

• Explanations of Unity of Command, Span of Control, Specialization of Labor, Line/Staff Relationships, Delegation of Responsibility, and Authority.

• Definitions of logical assignment, communications, motivation, evaluation and appraisal, and team building.

IT HAS BEEN SAID that an effective leader does not have to be an effective manager, and conversely, an effective manager does not have to be an effective leader. This is analogous to the old fog nozzle of yesteryear versus the solid stream nozzle, or the 1½″ hose versus the 2½″ hose arguments in that they make for a lot of heated kitchen discussion but, in the end, the situation and the people involved determine the correct answer.

LEADERSHIP VERSUS MANAGEMENT

"You may be whatever you resolve to be. Determine to be something in the world, and you will be something. 'I cannot' never accomplished anything; 'I will try' has wrought wonders."

—JOEL HAWES

Ron Coleman states in Chapter 1 that "management is a process of structuring the activities of an organization in such a way that it achieves the maximum efficiency and effectiveness in the use of human and physical resources." This is true. However, once the "structuring" is completed, someone, a leader, must lead, someone whom people will follow willingly. This chapter is about leadership: how to distinguish between leadership and management and how they relate to each other.

In the organized fire service we can observe leaders whom firefighters would follow into hell, but when it comes to managing their resources, these leaders are totally at a loss. On the other hand, there are leaders in the fire service who would put Andrew Carnegie to shame when it comes to managing resources, but their leadership skills are practically nil. The key to success in the fire service, as a line officer, staff member, or chief, is to combine both managerial and leadership skills into a total package.

Good management skills should be based on good leadership skills. Really effective managers know how to manage their most important resource—people. People can make or break a department's ability to deliver the services that it is intended to deliver.

Leaders must remember that their subordinates observe and imitate them, and, if they like what they see, often become mirror images of their leaders.

Goals of a fire department

- To protect life and property.
- To prevent fires from occurring.
- To confine fires to their area of origin.
- To extinguish fires.
- To provide emergency medical services.
- To provide assistance to the public in times of emergencies.

Case in point

Let us consider the chief of a medium-size department of 225 uniformed members who kept his department operating in the black with no indebtedness. This is practically unheard of in the fire service today. Almost every department must go into debt at some time or other. Through creative management of resources, this chief was able to keep the department furnished with the latest in firefighting and EMS equipment, and provide a high level of protection to the community.

What the chief did not consider was the morale of the members of his department and how that would affect the efficiency of the department. His leadership style was totally "autocratic." He would not tolerate questions or suggestions from the people who worked for him. Sick leave and absenteeism began to climb. People began to request monetary reimbursement for time spent on projects and committees that would otherwise have been volunteer work.

The chief was not a "people person" and before long the complaints and rumblings of the membership about his crass and rough handling of the people in the department reached the district board. The members of the department rallied and asked the board to recall the chief and not renew his contract. The chief, although an excellent manager, could not add people skills to his excellent management skills.

How could the chief have prevented his own failure and the failure of his department? To begin with, he could have treated those who worked for him with respect and dignity, as he himself wished to be treated. The CEO of every fire department, paid or volunteer, large or small, must realize that without the full cooperation of the personnel, the department will never reach its full potential. When they are not treated with respect and dignity, people will do just enough to get along. This is called "operating in the comfort work zone."

Comfort work zone

People have minimum and maximum levels of performance. They feel comfortable working within this zone. Working above or below this "comfort work zone" for extended periods of time can lead to serious physical and emotional problems. People who are not responsive to the leadership style of their managers will operate in the lower levels of their comfort work zone. They will do just enough to get by. In order to realize their full potential and maximum effectiveness, people should be inspired to work at the upper levels of their comfort work zone.

According to Abraham Maslow, people who work at their maximum potential become "self-actualized." People have a need to become what they are capable of becoming, i.e., to maximize their potential and to accomplish something that is meaningful to them. Simply stated, self-actualization is the realization of a person's hopes and expectations.

Effective leadership skills and proven managerial practices

Chief officers and officers at every level must use effective leadership skills in conjunction with proven managerial practices. This should stimulate people to perform at their optimal level of effectiveness. It follows then that people who are happy with the work they produce are happy with themselves. It was von Goeth who said, "It is not doing the thing we like, but liking the thing we have to do that makes life happy." A happy, self-motivated employee should be a department's greatest and most sought-after asset.

> *"Self-actualization—when it is difficult to tell the difference between work and play."*
>
> —KEN BLANCHARD

TOOLS FOR EFFECTIVE LEADERS

> *"We have moved from a sense of obligation—of duty—to a sense of entitlement . . . Everybody appears to deserve a break today except the General Interest . . . We must learn to moderate our claims to entitlement. We must begin to make the kind of investment of personal time and commitment which will assure that those who come after us will live as well."*
>
> —CHARLES W. BRAY III

Effective leadership characteristics

The following characteristics of effective leadership are not all-inclusive, but they should be considered the most important characteristics a leader can possess.

A COMMITMENT TO EXCELLENCE

Effective leadership starts on the inside of a person and moves out. If you are not feeling truly good about yourself, it is very difficult for you to help other people feel good about themselves. The way to feel good about oneself is to develop self-esteem. Developing self-esteem could be the simple act of developing a commitment to excellence. A commitment to excellence is a commitment to be the best, to be the standard, the benchmark by which the rest of the fire service is measured. Having made this commitment there can be no second best for you. That commitment could, and should, lead to feeling good now and in the future.

Develop a commitment to excellence in both your personal life and your professional life. Always strive to make or do things better. Look for new ideas and new methods and do not be afraid to try them. Remember that excellence is not a destination, it is a journey. Excellence is a never-ending, minute-by-minute, day-by-day search for the best way to serve your department, your firefighters, the people you are sworn to protect and, most importantly, yourself.

A VISION

From your commitment to excellence a vision will emerge. Your vision is what you are all about; it is your purpose. Your vision will tell you where you are heading and where you want to be in the future. A vision is like a dream, and in the words of the old song, "You gotta have a dream . . .'cause if you don't have a dream . . . how you 'gonna make a dream come true."

An example of someone with a vision is seen in the story about the man who encountered a group of people breaking granite on the side of a mountain. He asked one man, "What are you doing? The man replied, "I am trying to break this _____ rock." He asked another man what he was doing and the man responded, "I am part of a team that is building a cathedral." The second man had a vision.

Another example of someone with a vision is in the story about the fire chief who was making a visit to one of his fire stations. He asked the junior firefighter what her job was. She responded, "Oh, I am just the "hydrant hookup." The chief, who had his own vision, said, "No you are not. You are an important member of a team that is responsible for saving lives and extinguishing fires."

MISSION STATEMENT

Your vision will lead to a mission statement. The three most important features of a mission statement are:

- The statement must be based on facts;
- The statement must be understandable by all of the personnel in your department; and
- Everyone in the department must buy into the mission statement and be totally committed to it.

A common error made in mission statement development is becoming too involved with vague things like God, mother, flag, and country. The mission statement should be broad and not too specific, but not so broad as to be incomprehensible. The mission statement should be something that can form the basis for decisions and goal setting.

Specific tasks and objectives enter the picture when your personnel are developing their goal statements which support your mission statement.

An example of an effective and valid mission statement is:

> We the Officers, Firefighters, Paramedics, and EMTs of the Grandview Fire Department commit ourselves to be the best in our field, to be the benchmark by which the rest of the fire service is measured, and to provide the people whom we are sworn to protect with the finest possible fire protection and medical care available anywhere.

This is a statement that everyone in the department can "buy into." What firefighter, paramedic, or fire officer does not want to be the best, and to be considered the best by the rest of the people in his field? This is also a statement around which decisions and plans can be made and goals can be set.

RESULTS ORIENTED

To be effective, a leader must be results oriented. Results-oriented leaders have a positive attitude toward results. They get things done. Effective leaders set up strategies and systems that get the results and outcomes that they want. The results-oriented leader is a facilitator. He delegates a task and then provides the "wherewithal" for the employee to complete the task and clears away any obstacles that might prevent the completion of the task.

GOAL SETTING

Part of being results oriented is the process of goal setting. Every employee, from the raw recruit up to the chief of department, should have a set of goals that:

- Support the mission statement; and
- Enable the department to attain its goals.

Goal setting tells each employee what will be expected of him in the future. It also provides a basis for the employee evaluation and rewards systems.

Unit and Individual Goals

An example of a fire department unit goal would be:

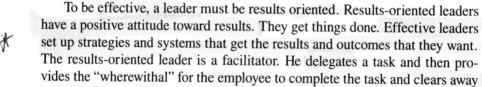

NAME: *Firefighter I and II Certification*

"To have all assigned firefighters certified FF I within the next 12 months and Firefighter II in the following 12 months."

Supporting objectives for the above goal would be:

• Schedule in-service Essentials of Firefighting classes for all shifts.
• Schedule make-up classes for those members on vacation.
• Schedule state certification examinations for all members.

An example of an individual goal would be:

NAME: *Driver/Operator Certification*

"To become Driver/Operator certified by the end of the next fiscal year."

Supporting objectives for the above goal would be:

• Attend a Hydraulics class at the community college.
• Attend the next Driver/Operator class at the department.
• Drive the apparatus back from alarms.

Some confusion exists as to what a goal is and what an objective is. Some authors use the words interchangeably. It is easier to understand the concepts if we keep in mind that each has a separate and distinct meaning.

An analogy can be made comparing goals and objectives to using a portable ladder to gain entry into an upper floor window. The window into which we wish to gain entry is our goal. In order to achieve this goal we must accomplish certain objectives: placing our feet, one at a time, on the rungs of the ladder until we reach our goal, the window. Hence, the supporting objectives are the rungs of the ladder.

Units and individuals should have only three to five goals. If more than five goals are attempted the usual result is that efforts become too diffused and unfocused. Setting three to five goals allows the employees to "focus in," to concentrate their efforts. By concentrating their efforts they will be more likely to turn out a better product.

Goals, in order to be effective, must be:

Attainable. Each individual will be able to complete the goal.
Measurable. The supervisor and the individual will be able to see how much of the goal is completed while they are working on the goal.
Quantifiable. Individuals and supervisors understand the "how much" of the goal, the unit by which progress is measured.

The goal statement should be brief and to the point and contain the following information:

- Name of the goal;
- How the goal will be measured;
- When the goal is due; and
- The priority of the goal.

An example of a fire prevention goal statement is:

NAME: *Preplanning of Target Hazards*

"I will preplan at least one "target hazard" per shift, completing 100 percent of the unit's "target hazards" within 6 months."

INNOVATIVE

An effective leader should be innovative. To be innovative a leader does not have to be a great genius. Innovation is a commitment to continuous improvement. An innovative leader is future oriented, always challenging the status quo. The leader should not gather people or staff who are afraid or reluctant to tell the truth. How can leaders be innovative if they do not know what is really happening? The leader must promote truthful and honest communications.

This holds true for all the levels of supervision in the fire service. The supervisor must establish an atmosphere where subordinates will be willing to be honest, without fear of reprisal. In other words, the supervisor "will not kill the bearer of bad tidings."

The innovative leader is always open to new ideas and is willing to be exposed to new ideas. One way of exposing oneself to new ideas is to read as many trade publications, research papers, and texts as possible. You do not have to reinvent the wheel. Take other people's ideas and modify them to fit your own particular needs.

Learning is a continuous process; you can never be too old to learn. Harold Geneen, CEO of ITT, read one to two management books per week while he was managing the largest and most successful corporation in the world.

COURAGE

Courage is the state or quality of mind or spirit that enables one to face danger with self-possession, confidence, and resolution, a definition that says nothing about fear.

Courage is not the absence of fear or the opposite of fear. It is the ability to act in spite of our fears. Courage means sticking to what you believe in and making the hard interventions. Courage is standing out and maybe exposing yourself as not always being as correct as you would like to be.

Effective Leadership is

READY?	Prepare
FIRE!	Act
AIM.	Courage to review, refine, learn

Four kinds of courage absolutely necessary for an effective leader to possess are the

- Courage to make hard "people decisions."
- Courage to stand fast, show "courageous patience," and stay the course in the face of adversity.
- Courage to deal with conflict via confrontation, that is, not to run away from or avoid conflict, but to be straightforward in difficult people situations.
- Courage to admit that you are wrong.

INTEGRITY—HONESTY

"There is no pillow as soft as a clear conscience"
—COACH WOODEN, UCLA

Integrity is the capacity to walk your talk, to deal with issues straight out and to do what you say in your mission statement. Employees become very upset when their supervisors imply or suggest that they will do something and then don't. You must assure that there is justice in the workplace or people will not follow. People do not have to agree with you, but if you are clear about where you stand, and your behavior reflects it, your subordinates will respect and follow you.

An important aspect of both integrity and honesty is consistency. Consistency is a double-edged sword in that it has to be applied equally to all employees as well as to the supervisor. The leader's behavior must be consistent with the behavior expected of subordinates.

Consistency means that the rules and regulations apply equally to everyone in the department. The saying that "rank has its privileges" does not hold true when it comes to the regulations.

"To thine own self be true, and it must follow, as the night follows the day, thou canst not then be false to any man."
—WILLIAM SHAKESPEARE

LEAD BY EXAMPLE

Your people will tend to follow your lead and take on your attitudes, your behavior, your values, and your opinions. They will do what you do. Your people are watching you. You are in a fishbowl.

All of the above statements are true. The effective leader must take these statements into account and act accordingly.

In the past the leader's job was just to direct, control, and supervise people's behavior, and to set goals, sit back and evaluate, judge and criticize. Today, firefighters are much more educated, informed, and sophisticated. They will not buy into the idea of a leader sitting "on his high horse."

Today's fire service leaders must be willing to work hard and commit much more of their personal time to the task of leading. Today's fire service leaders must be willing to be cheerleaders, to encourage, support, facilitate and, most importantly, listen and be a role model.

Motivation theory

"I have yet to find a man, however exalted his station, who did not do better work and put forth greater effort under a spirit of approval, than under a spirit of criticism."

—CHARLES SCHWAB

A discussion of leadership would not be complete without at least a cursory examination of motivation theory. Motivation theory can be broken into two categories: content theory and process theory.

CONTENT THEORY OF MOTIVATION

The content theory of motivation assumes that the answer to motivation problems lies within the complete understanding of the people involved. Once the solution is identified it can be implemented and, through motivation of individuals, will change to the desired situation. In other words, it is the people involved in a situation that affect the degree of motivation, not the situation.

ABRAHAM MASLOW AND FREDRICK HERZBERG

Two proponents of content theory are Abraham H. Maslow and Fredrick Herzberg. Maslow identified a hierarchy of needs in human beings. Those needs and possible satisfiers are:

- **Physiological**—food, shelter, clothing

  SATISFIERS: Adequate salary
  Reasonably comfortable personal life
- **Security or safety**—physical danger and fear of the loss of job, property

  SATISFIERS: Modern, state-of-the-art equipment
  Personal protective clothing and equipment that meet current NFPA standards
  Adequate pension and insurance plans
  Job security
  Quality supervision
  State-of-the-art training
- **Affiliation or Acceptance**—belonging and acceptance by others

  SATISFIERS: Quality supervision
  Interpersonal relations
  Department policies
  Unit affiliation
  (Rescue, Hazardous Materials, Engine, Truck)
- **Esteem, power**—prestige, status, and self-confidence

  SATISFIERS: Advancement
  Recognition
  Status
- **Self-actualization**—maximization of one's potential

  SATISFIERS: Challenging work
  Achievement
  Growth in the position
  Responsibility

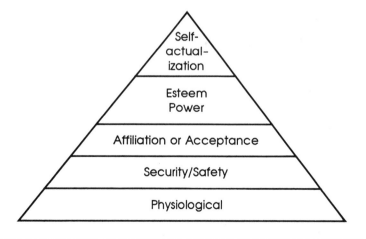

Figure 6-1.

A satisfied need is not a motivator and a need that is not satisfied is a motivator. A leader's responsibility, therefore, must be to, first, identify the needs of each subordinate, and, second, to approach the motivation of that person from that point of view.

Herzberg proposed a two-factor theory of maintenance needs and motivational needs. His maintenance needs correspond to Maslow's physiological, security, and social needs. Herzberg's motivational needs correspond to Maslow's identified needs for esteem and self-actualization. According to Herzberg, the maintenance factors of physiological, security, and affiliation needs must be fulfilled before a worker can even begin to be motivated. Herzberg further states that the true motivators are the need for esteem and self-actualization. This being true, supervisors in the fire service must give considerable attention to upgrading and maintaining job content and creating meaningful and challenging situations.

This "job enrichment" can be accomplished by first training and educating subordinates in the skills necessary to perform their tasks. Once a subordinate is properly trained in a task, then the supervisor must delegate both authority and responsibility to the subordinate.

PROCESS THEORY OF MOTIVATION

On the other hand, proponents of the process theory view motivation as externally induced. As Robert M. Fulmer puts it, the proponents of content theory might say, "If you want to move a body of water, you don't analyze the water or talk to it, you change the channel and the water follows right along." It is the situation and the leadership climate that effect change in people.

EXPECTANCY THEORY

Victor Vroom describes the manner in which two variables, preference and expectation, interact on each other to determine the degree of motivation. Preference refers to the possible outcomes of an act and the outcome the worker would prefer. Expectation has to do with the worker's expectation that a desired outcome can actually happen. Hence, according to Vroom, a worker will be motivated if that worker expects that his action will lead to the preferred outcome.

In other words, Vroom's theory is that people's motivation toward doing anything will be determined by the value they place on the outcome of their effort, multiplied by the confidence they have that their efforts will materially aid in achieving a goal. In addition, Vroom's theory recognizes that people's perceptions differ from reality and differ at various times.

The effective leader must know:

• The needs of the people he supervises;

- The values of the people he supervises; and
- The relationship between those needs and values.

SITUATIONAL APPROACH TO LEADERSHIP

The situational approach to leadership contrasts to theories that rely solely on what the leader brings to the situation. The situational approach to leadership theorizes that leaders are products of a situation. The leader's leadership style emerges as a result of the situation, and people follow because they perceive that following will be a means of obtaining their own personal goals.

An example of the situational approach to leadership is depicted time and time again in the movies. The scene is a shipwreck or a plane crash that has put a lot of people in jeopardy. The situation calls for a strong leader who emerges from among the passengers.

This approach to leadership is important because it recognizes that there is an interaction between a group and the leader. The leader who knows the group will be better able to adopt a leadership style that is effective for a particular situation and person. This approach does not lend itself to the fire service as easily as it does to other organizations, but there are a few situations where leaders should acquiesce or relinquish their leadership of the group to the expertise of a subordinate. An example of this is the hazardous materials incident or technical rescue. The officer is technically in charge, yet the members of the different teams have the expertise to lead and accomplish the task.

CONTINGENCY APPROACH TO LEADERSHIP

The contingency approach to leadership theory, as proposed by Fred E. Fiedler, states that a leader's ability to lead is based on the task situation and the degree to which the leader's style, approach, and personality fit the group. This theory also recognizes that there is interaction between the group and the leader. Fiedler claims that, "If we wish to increase organizational and group effectiveness we must not only train leaders more effectively but also teach them how to build an organizational environment in which the leader can perform well."

It is the chief's responsibility to establish a department environment that encourages the personal growth of all its people. One approach to determining an organizational environment that is conducive to personal growth is to determine:

- What the predominant personality traits are of the members of the department; and
- What traits the members of the department desire in their leaders.

Once these traits have been determined, a training program can be established which teaches these leader traits.

PATH-GOAL APPROACH TO LEADERSHIP

"If a man does not keep pace with his companions, perhaps it is because he hears a different drummer. Let him step to the music that he hears, however measured or far away."

—HENRY DAVID THOREAU

Robert House developed the path-goal approach to leadership. He reasons that the most effective leaders are those who assist their subordinates to achieve both their personal goals and the goals of the organization. This theory lends itself readily to the fire service organization. Firefighters and their officers spend long periods of time together in the relative intimacy of the fire station. The leader can become acutely aware of the needs and desires of his people. Once he knows the needs and desires of the members, an effective leader can formulate and develop plans that will assist these people in reaching their goals.

CONCLUSION

In summary, it may be useful to cite research conducted by Chester A. Scheisheim, James M. Toliver, and Orlando C. Behling into studies that have been done on effective leaders. They claim that 3,000 leadership studies have been done in the past 70 years. They traced attempts to identify effective leadership traits from before the time of Christ to the present.

They also claim that three distinct phases or schools of thought have existed in the study of leadership:

- **The Trait Phase** began before Christ and lasted into the 1940s. The theorists tried to determine a universal set of effective leadership characteristics. This approach has obvious defects, the most glaring of which was the assumption that leaders are born and not made ("Great Man" Theory).
- **The Behavioral Phase** began in the 1940s and lasted in popularity until the 1960s. This phase attempted to determine a universal leadership style or universally best combination of leadership behaviors. The defect in this approach and the trait approach is that they did not take into account personal and situational variables.
- **The Situational Phase** began in the 1960s and is still enjoying popularity with students of leadership behavior and characteristics. This approach attempts to determine a combination of leader, subordinate, and situational characteristics which interact to produce effectiveness.

This approach takes into consideration the variables that affect good leadership.

A leader who attempts to use the situational approach to leadership must have knowledge about the personnel and the situation in which the leader and the subordinate are interacting. Information about the situation is obtained through job knowledge and training. Information about the personnel is obtained through personal contact.

In the face of the enormous amount of conflicting information on effective leadership styles and characteristics, this writer feels that the reader should attempt to sort the "wheat from the chaff" and use the style of leadership that suits the situation, the subordinate, and the leader. Leadership is both a science and an art. Leadership is a science because it is a learnable, teachable body of knowledge. Leadership is an art because this body of knowledge has to be applied to "real life" with skill and deftness.

This can be accomplished only through diligent study and application by trial and error, until the leader develops a style that fits the situation, the subordinate, and, most importantly, himself.

TOOLS FOR MANAGERS

"Before you begin a thing, remind yourself that difficulties and delays quite impossible to foresee are ahead. If you could see them clearly, naturally you could do a great deal to get rid of them, but you can't. You can only see one thing clearly and that is your goal. Form a mental vision of that and cling to it through thick and thin.

—Kathleen Norris

What techniques do successful managers use to attain their goals? How can managers properly use their money, apparatus, equipment, methods, and people to maximize their chances of success in their endeavors?

The basic components of successful management are summarized in these five management functions:

- planning
- organizing
- directing
- coordinating
- controlling

These management functions are a useful framework with which to organize knowledge about management. There are no new ideas or techniques that cannot be placed in one of these classifications. For this reason this chapter will cover these five management functions only.

Planning

Looking ahead and creating a scheme or method to attain a particular goal or objective is called planning. Before any endeavor can be launched, a plan of action must be developed. In the management arena, planning precedes the other four management functions since it is an integral part of each function.

Planning as a function of management affects every level of the organization, from first-line supervisors to top-level commanders. Properly prepared plans assure us of the most successful outcome of any activity, whether it be the daily duties of a firefighting unit or the long-range plans of an entire department.

For planning to be effective, it must neither be done in a vacuum nor be rigid. Planning in a vacuum is planning without taking into consideration the needs of the community, its citizens, the members of the department, and the department itself. The flexibility of a plan lies in having alternatives or fall-back solutions to problems that may arise after the fact.

The best way to begin planning is to start with a goal statement and then list the steps necessary to accomplish the goal. Plans can be long-intermediate- or short-range. Short-range plans are the most specific. Short-range plans should contain the following information:

- list of tasks to be accomplished;
- the people and/or units, and their alternatives, who will accomplish the tasks;
- the resources that will be required, such as materials and equipment;
- timeframes and deadlines; and
- control and reporting systems.

Intermediate plans of two to three years should be a little more vague than short-range plans. Intermediate plans must allow for changes in personnel, shortfalls in the budget, or a change in department philosophy. Long-range plans of more than three years might be only a broad goal statement. As the time to begin implementing the long-range plan nears, development of the plan becomes more and more specific.

Planning should include a variety of different solutions so that, if necessary, the manager will have alternatives from which to choose. To develop alternative solutions the leader should encourage as much creativity as possible among the subordinates involved. Effective leadership practices will help to bring out the creative capabilities in most people.

A form of short-range plan is the Standard Operating Procedure or SOP.

SOPs are developed to be a guide for the department's routine, day-to-day operations. They can be used for everything from fires and emergencies to routine station duties. Emergency SOPs should allow for deviation (for just cause) at the discretion of the officer in charge of the situation.

To assure that an SOP is effective, it should:

- State clearly the action expected of each person involved.
- Indicate specific methods of performing where applicable.
- Be instituted only after it has been shown by a test to be "the one best way."
- Have controls built into it so that management can verify that it is being followed.

SOPs have both advantages and disadvantages. On the positive side, SOPs:

- facilitate delegation;
- allow for consistency;
- enable leaders to manage more efficiently;
- make the training of new employees easier; and
- are based on the "one best way."

The disadvantages of SOPs are that they:

- lack flexibility;
- tend to become obsolete;
- tend to stifle initiative; and
- take time and money to develop.

Another planning tool is the budget. Formulating the budget is planning how you will allocate your funds for a given period of time. The most effective way to prepare a budget is to call on the various units within the department to submit budgets. The chief or a staff member can coordinate the process. This member should advise the unit heads as to the limits of their budgets and act as a mediator to resolve conflicts among the units. It is the responsibility of the chief or the designated staff member to ensure that all interests within the department are served. When preparing a budget, the person responsible for it should keep in mind that the people closest to the operation are most able to furnish realistic information for determining budget requests.

ORGANIZING

"Executive ability consists of getting the right people in the right places and keep-ing them willingly at the top notch."
—Herbert G. Stockwell

The organizing phase of management occurs when the manager takes all the aspects of the plan, brings them together, and organizes them into a smooth working unit. In the organizing phase, responsibilities of the partici-pants and lines of communication must be established and clearly understood. In addition, the participants must be aware of the department's entire organi-zational structure. Therefore, the department must have a current organiza-tional chart in place and available to all members of the department.

UNITY OF COMMAND

To ensure that a unit or an organization will function efficiently there must be no confusion as to who is in charge and who is responsible for getting the job done. This concept is called unity of command. Simply stated, unity of command means an individual should be responsible to only one supervisor. Every member knows to whom he reports, and who reports to him.

SPAN OF CONTROL

Span of control is another concept that must be considered in the organiz-ing phase. Span of control establishes how many subordinates a supervisor can manage effectively. If a supervisor must manage too many or too few subor-dinates, it weakens the organizational structure. Span of control is determined by four factors:

- the ability of the supervisor;
- the ability and degree of cooperativeness of the subordinate;
- the nature of the task to be accomplished; and
- geography or the dispersal of those being supervised.

When all four of these factors are considered, then the effective span of control for a supervisor can be determined.

SPECIALIZATION OF LABOR

Still another concept to be considered in the organizing phase is special-ization of labor. In most fire departments work is divided by units, bureaus, or divisions. For instance, the fire prevention unit does building inspections and public education, and the investigation unit conducts fire investigations. Briefly stated, functional responsibility is assigned by the nature of the work.

LINE AND STAFF RELATIONSHIPS

Line functions usually relate directly to the accomplishing of the department's goals, and staff functions usually refer to those functions that support the line functions. In industry, functions that deal directly with the customer or client are referred to as line functions. In the fire service, however, a function such as fire prevention is referred to as a staff function, but because fire prevention and various other staff positions deal directly with the public there is a tendency to reclassify them.

There is often conflict between line and staff personnel in an organization. Sometimes this conflict is very subtle; at other times it can be flagrantly hostile. In either case the supervisors in both line and staff must put an end to this conflict because it wastes time, it is costly, and it is detrimental to the accomplishment of the department's goals. One way to accomplish this is to stress teamwork rather than competition between the two groups. Also, clarify the basic relationships between line and staff and train all concerned carefully as to what their responsibilities and powers are.

DELEGATION OF RESPONSIBILITIES AND AUTHORITY

"Never tell people how to do things. Tell them what to do and they will surprise you with their ingenuity."

—George S. Patton

In order for subordinates to carry out the responsibilities delegated to them, they must be given the authority to take whatever action is needed to complete the task. There should be certain parameters established beyond which the subordinate cannot go, but for the most part the task should be arranged so that it can be completed without first checking back with the "chief."

In order for supervisors to delegate effectively:

- They must feel secure about their own position in the department and understand the need for, and the benefits of, delegating.
- Management must establish an environment that is conducive to delegating.
- The person who accepts the assignment must accept it as a forward step in his own progress.
- The delegator must be available to give the subordinate whatever assistance is needed.

- The person to whom the delegation is made has the ability and the time to do the job.
- The delegator must be prepared to accept and to deal with the consequences of the subordinate's actions.

THE INFORMAL ORGANIZATION

An informal organization exists within all formal organizations, but nowhere does it have a greater impact than in the fire service. The informal organization is usually composed of a group of employees who share the same general goals, likes and dislikes, and interests. This informal group must be identified by the supervisor, understood, and considered, if it is to be channeled properly to meet the department's goals and objectives.

Identifying this group and its leaders is essential so that the supervisor can understand how the informal group operates and what its relationships are to the rest of the organization. Understanding this, the supervisor can more readily spot disagreement so that it can be brought out into the open. The supervisor must see that the objectors have a chance to voice their opinions and then reach consensus.

Directing

> "The best executive is the one who has sense enough to pick good people to do what he wants done, and self-restraint enough to keep from meddling with them while they do it."
>
> —THEODORE ROOSEVELT

To direct a department, division, bureau or unit, and to do it well, the supervisor must select men and women who are able to carry out the duties, functions, and responsibilities that are assigned to them. The efficiency of the organization depends on these people.

LOGICAL ASSIGNMENT

The "right" person for the job demands that a careful analysis of the job be made to determine what factors are needed to succeed in that specific job or function. This should be followed by recruitment, either from within the department or from outside. When the selection is made, training should begin, followed by a constant and consistent program of directing and motivating to keep these "right" people operating at peak performance.

COMMUNICATIONS

"Every man . . . should periodically be compelled to listen to opinions which are infuriating to him. To hear nothing but what is pleasing to one is to make a pillow of the mind."

ST. JOHN ERVINE

A major aspect of directing is effective communications. A leader or manager must be able to convey ideas, attitudes, and objectives. These ideas, attitudes, and objectives have to be received, accepted, and understood by subordinates. Effective communication also includes being in touch with the subordinates' feelings, hopes, fears, and dislikes. Being a good communicator means being a good listener; a leader or manager who is in close contact with his subordinates will be that.

There are several different types of communication within an organization. Vertical communication occurs when a member of the organization communicates either upward or downward in the chain of command. Communication among peers on the same level of the organization is termed horizontal communication.

Informal communication, also known as the "grapevine," consists of communication among members of the informal organization. Inaccurate informal communication can be extremely detrimental to the department's morale. When a supervisor learns of inaccuracies in informal communication, the supervisor should assure that the information is made accurate.

MOTIVATION

"When someone does something good, applaud! You will make two people happy."

—SAMUEL GOLDWYN

The behavioral sciences have taught us a lot about motivation. Managers in the fire service must recognize the principles involved and apply them at work. As discussed earlier in this chapter, according to Fredrick Herzberg, the true motivators of people are achievement, recognition for achievement, the work itself, responsibility, and advancement.

In order to provide these "true motivators" for personnel, the following strategies might be applied:

- Participative decisionmaking. Each person who will be involved in implementing a decision is asked to help make the decision.
- Decentralization. People are allowed to make decisions at their level, freeing them from close control and giving them some freedom to direct their own activities.

- Job enlargement. People are allowed to do more than one aspect of a task or project.
- Quality of work life programs. People meet to discuss and develop a means of making the work environment more satisfying.

EVALUATION AND APPRAISAL

"I have never seen a man who could do real work except under the stimulus of encouragement and enthusiasm and the approval of the people for whom he is working."

—Charles Schwab

People like to know how they are doing. Supervisors have an obligation to keep their people informed about their progress or lack of progress. The old adage, "If I don't criticize you, then you know that you are doing OK" just does not make it in the modern work scene.

Besides letting employees know how they are doing, an evaluation program can:

- provide a regular period of time to review work-related performance;
- provide informative data and information for promotions;
- be a basis for salary and wage adjustments; and
- provide a basis for the design and implementation of training.

Everyone who will be involved in the evaluation must understand the process: what will be expected, when it will be discussed, how the ratings work, and what criteria will be used. Each item should be clear to both the employee and the supervisor.

TEAM BUILDING

To be effective, a fire service manager must develop a team spirit among the members. A lot is said about having "team spirit." But what is team spirit, how is it created and how is it sustained? Motivation is central to creating and sustaining team spirit. Team spirit goes beyond motivation, however. Team spirit is the drive that keeps the team bubbling with enthusiasm, cohesive, and producing good results.

According to Charles Mallory in *Team Building*, team building is a complex and rewarding job. As you build your team and manage it, you must keep in mind the following key points:

- Understand how and why people work together.
- Set goals, objectives, and checkpoints.
- Select the right people.

- Demand the most from yourself and your skills as the team leader.
- Delegate with tact and thoroughness.
- Motivate your team members by meeting their needs and wants, and by rewarding them.
- Eliminate problems quickly when they arise.
- Give rewards to the whole team rather than to individuals.
- Instill team spirit. Monitor team morale and togetherness, and keep the team running at an optimal pace.

Team spirit occurs when a leader gives a clear-cut assignment, works with the team to supply necessary resources, bolsters the team with encouragement, makes all team members feel valuable, and rewards a job well done. Remember, teamwork is like excellence, i.e., it is not a destination, it is a journey.

Coordination

Coordination has been defined as the orderly synchronization of the efforts of a group to assure that its efforts are properly timed and are correct as to quantity and quality of work expected. Coordination involves directing the execution of these efforts so that they are unified and result in the effective accomplishment of a goal or a set of goals.

Supervisors must ensure cohesiveness in three separate areas:

- Coordination within a group, among individuals;
- Coordination among divisions, bureaus, and units within the department; and
- Coordination among various outside agencies.

Effective coordination eliminates overlapping of tasks and duplication of efforts. Optimal coordination occurs when all individuals see how their position contributes to the goals of the unit, division, bureau, or department.

VERTICAL COORDINATION

Vertical coordination is coordination of the various levels within the department. This is illustrated by the department's organizational chart. This type of coordination usually starts at the top of the chart and works its way down through the different levels of the department.

HORIZONTAL COORDINATION

This type of coordination deals with activities that occur within a level of the organization. In theory, this type of coordination is the responsibility of the supervisor of the units at that particular level of the department. However, the effectiveness of horizontal coordination depends on the relationship among the supervisors at that level. Good communications and provisions for bypassing regular channels where necessary will go a long way toward helping these supervisors achieve a close working relationship.

COMMITTEES

A committee, sometimes called a task force, is an effective method of facilitating coordination. The committee should be comprised of representatives of the various groups that will be affected by the task at hand. At committee meetings, different and varied ideas can be aired, unified, and integrated into the common plan.

Committees may encourage participative management, but remember, a committee is only as good as the people who serve on it. Guidelines for committee work are:

- A prescribed course of action must be outlined by the chair of the committee.
- Everyone must understand the goals that they are trying to meet.
- The degree of coordination and cooperation to be maintained must be established.
- All participants must abide by the decisions that are made.
- All participants must put aside their own personal agendas.

Unless everyone on the committee is competent, and works together, the meetings will be a waste of time and will work against coordination.

Control

"Give to every other human being every right that you claim for yourself."
—ROBERT G. INGERSOLL

Control is a process established by leaders or managers that ensures that a task is being carried out, completed, or both. A control process also determines whether the quality of the project being carried out meets established standards.

The leader or manager should not wait until a project is finished to see if everything went according to plan. Control points must be established so that trouble can be identified and corrected before it can do real damage.

How do you know how much a project should be controlled and when to use control points? You can decode based on these three criteria:

1. the magnitude of the results;
2. the competency of the personnel; and
3. the complexity of the project.

If there will be no serious losses, then control can be minimal. However, if the consequences of a failed project will be greatly detrimental to the department, then a high degree of control should be placed on the project. If the personnel working on the project are experienced and competent, then controls can be lax; however, if they are inexperienced and lack competence, then they require close controls. If the project is long or complex, it requires close surveillance. Conversely, if it is a short or simple project it requires less stringent control.

Control can run the gamut of the occasional phone call to daily written or verbal reports. Personnel have a tendency to resist control, mainly because it has been overdone or an inappropriate focus has been placed on it. Another reason personnel resist control is their fear of accountability.

To overcome this resistance to control, the leader or manager should assure that the established controls are reasonable and do not place an undue burden on the subordinates. The leader or manager also should encourage employees to participate in planning and implementing the control system.

CONCLUSION

For those of you who are in a leadership position such as chief of department, and who are able to have an impact on the departmental management environment, we recommend the following:

- Sit down with the people in your department and write a mission statement based on the pursuit of excellence.
- Make sure that everyone in the department can buy into the mission statement.
- With the help of your own people develop and implement an evaluation system for the members of your department.
- Ensure that everyone is trained in, and understands, your evaluation system.
- Develop an environment where the people who work for you will not be afraid to be honest and to tell you the truth.

- Start a training program wherein every member of the department will receive the necessary training and education to carry out their tasks.
- Institute participative management.

Those of you who read this chapter and report to a higher level of management might say to yourselves, "Sure this sounds great, but my chief will never go for this." You may not be the policy maker in your department. You may not be responsible for establishing the management environment. You do, however, have an effect on everyone with whom you come in contact. Remember, the longest journey begins with one small step.

It is up to you to persuade your superior officers of the value of having a vision and defining a mission statement. It is up to you to begin devoting yourself to excellence, to sell your ideas and, perhaps, to effect changes in the chief's views on the job. Begin now to practice participative management and give the people you work with a chance to show you what they have.

In the words of the English poet, John Donne, "Ask not for whom the bell tolls, it tolls for thee."

One small chapter could not possibly cover all that is necessary to know about leadership and management. So, in the spirit of exposing you, the reader, to as much information about leadership and management as possible, a reading list of published work on the subject is included. Please do not think of this list as all-inclusive. Volumes and volumes have been published on the subject. Go out and get it!

NOTES

Maslow, Abraham H. The Theory of Human Motivation. *Psychology Review*, July 1943. pp. 370–396.

Blanchard, Ken and Brian Tracy, "Blanchard and Tracy on Leadership." Audio tapes. (California: Blanchard Training and Development, Inc., and Brian Tracy learning Systems, 1989).

Fulmer, Robert M. *The New Management*. (New York: Macmillan Publishing Co., Inc., 1978).

Maslow, Abraham H. *Psychology Review*, July 1943. Herzberg, Fredrick. *Work and the Nature of Man*. (New York: World Publishing Company, 1966), pp. 370–396.

Vroom, Victor. *Work and Motivation*. (New York: John Wiley and Sons, 1964.)

Koontz, Harold, Cyril O'Donnell, and Heinz Weihrich. *Essentials of Management*. (New York: McGraw-Hill Book Co., 1982.)

Fiedler, Fred E. *The Theory of Leadership Effectiveness*. (New York: McGraw-Hill Book Co., 1967.)

House, Robert. A Path Goal Theory of Leadership Effectiveness. *Administrative Science Quarterly*, Vol. 16, (September 1971), pp. 321–338.

Schriesheim, Chester A., James M. Tolliver, and Orlando C. Behling. In P. Hersey and J. Stimson (Eds.), *Perspective in Leadership Effectiveness.* (Chapt. 1) (Ohio State University: Center for Leadership Studies, 1980.)

Dale Carnegie & Associates. *Managing Through People.* (Garden City, NY: Dale Carnegie & Associates, Inc., 1987.)

Mallory, Charles. *Team Building, How to Build a Winning Team.* (Shawnee Mission, KS: National Press Publications, 1991.)

II. HUMAN
RESOURCES

7

Personnel Administration

WILLIAM S. JOHNSON

- The modern fire chief.
- AAPs, E.E.O., OSHA, and EAPs.
- Pensions.
- Labor relations.

*T*HIS CHAPTER DEALS WITH personnel administration, touching on the important facets of the subject and presenting a reference guide of information with which you must be familiar.

Generally speaking, the traditional four objectives of fire protection are:

- to prevent fires from starting;
- to prevent loss of life and property from fire;
- to confine the fire to its original point of origin; and
- to extinguish the fire.

The goal of this chapter is to assist you in accomplishing the above four objectives by properly selecting, training, and promoting personnel to accomplish these objectives, all within the guidelines of applicable federal and state laws and regulations. We also will cover established benefit plans which provide security, enabling the firefighter to be a better, more well-rounded employee with high morale. Finally, we will present suggestions and facts helpful in negotiating and administering the labor instrument.

Personnel administration is an important factor in fire departments of all sizes: large, small, urban, suburban, rural and combination. This function cannot be neglected. A department with an efficient, cost-effective personnel administration program will have higher morale, and provide better service to the taxpayer.

If a dedicated fire chief of years gone by were to descend upon us from that "Great Firehouse in the Sky" and happen to overhear today's fire chiefs discussing ADA, affirmative action, discrimination, sexual harassment, health care benefits, COBRA, communicable disease, bloodborne pathogens, SARA, EAPs, pensions, ERISA, FLSA, NLRA, OSHA, paramedics, etc., he might be tempted to ask, "Do they still take the knob and get to the seat of the fire?" And today's well-trained fire chief should answer in the affirmative. Adding, however, that "getting the wet stuff on the red stuff" today involves a much more difficult, winding, and we might add, safer road to travel. It is imperative that today's fire chief be attuned to the requirements imposed on fire departments by federal, state, and local legislation.

Throughout our nation, there are many fire protection delivery systems. Municipal, career, and combination, volunteer, independent fire districts, and private fire departments are funded in myriad ways, the most common of which is a fire department funded by the municipality through taxation. The common denominators in all of these fire departments are the infantry (firefighters) and the general (fire chief). Today's fire chief, in any type of organization, career, volunteer, or otherwise, has a very difficult job. First and foremost, the chief must provide leadership. Most fire protection in this country is provided by small- to medium-sized departments. Therefore, the chief should be known, respected, and involved in the community. This enhances the department. In many departments, the chief is expected to be in command of major incidents; therefore, he must be well versed in the principles of fire science and the Incident Command System. In addition, the chief must be a manager, able to administer all of the regulations, directives and, in the case of a department represented by a labor organization, the labor instrument. In these areas, many fail because of a lack of knowledge and understanding. However, in personnel administration, failure can have a devastating effect on the morale of all firefighters. Improper handling of an employee's health claims, payroll, worker's compensation claims, or a failure to adhere to required OSHA, SARA or other mandatory state or federal regulations can result in fines against the community, bad publicity, poor morale and, in general, a deterioration of the department. In many fire departments, the major portion of personnel administration is carried out by the community's personnel or human resources department. This practice does not, however, relieve the fire chief of the responsibility to be knowledgeable of all required personnel procedures. If any administrative policy or procedure goes awry and is not adjudicated properly, you, as fire chief, can be guaranteed that the problem will end up in your office. Whether the problem was caused by your lack of knowledge or the personnel manager's lack of knowledge, if you, as fire chief, know the correct procedure for processing the problem, it is incumbent on you to so advise the personnel manager, thereby avoiding a problem or grievance.

PRERECRUITING SELECTION AND TESTING

Aggressive recruitment through various sources is a must. The most effective recruitment sources for the fire service are newspaper ads, employee referrals, colleges and universities, advertising in trade magazines, and contacting fire service professional societies. In the recruitment process, your efforts to recruit cultural minorities and women should be with the assistance of minority leaders in your community, religious leaders and by setting up recruitment stations in predominantly minority neighborhoods. High schools and colleges are excellent sources for female candidates. Keep in mind that in the recruitment and testing process, a community does not have to vary its standards. The key is to have all candidates "play the same game on the same playing field," provided that the rules of the game meet all applicable laws and regulations.

SELECTION AND TESTING

Few things are as critical to an organization as the selection of new employees. Many employers rely solely on interviews and resumes, but these subjective criteria can lead to unpleasant surprises. As a result, many employers have turned to tests for objective, cost-effective ways of identifying the best candidates. Properly validated tests are a useful supplement to other selection devices, such as interviews and reference checks. It is imperative that your department have a comprehensive job description that is issued to all applicants when they begin the job application process. This job description should cover:

- starting salary;
- last date for filing the application;
- general statement of duties;
- supervision received;
- minimum qualifications, including "knowledge, skills and abilities";
- character requirements;
- special requirements;
- physical requirements, citizenship;

and general information such as:

- composition of the exam,
- written test;
- who is conducting the exam; and
- how tie scores will be resolved.

In addition the candidates should be advised whether the agility test is graded on performance or is strictly a pass-or fail-type exam; that is, fail one of the agility stations and the candidate automatically fails the agility portion.

Needs Assessment

Before using tests, first determine what it is you are trying to find out about applicants; this will determine the appropriate tests.

Types of Tests

There are many kinds of tests, each of which provides different information. Some are designed for employers to administer and score themselves; others require a skilled professional to ensure proper use. It is important to know how the publisher expects the test to be used; otherwise it may not be valid.

- **Intelligence** testing is really a test of learning ability, particularly the ability to learn through the use of printed material.
- **Aptitude** testing attempts to determine what an applicant may be able to do; it may evaluate physical dexterity, or test for mechanical, clerical, or similar forms of comprehension.
- **Achievement** testing determines the degree of knowledge in specific fields such as electrical or mechanical theory, bookkeeping know-how, and other skill areas.
- **Personality** tests attempt to assess applicants in terms of "traits," such as introversion versus extroversion, drive, decisionmaking style, and temperament. They can be useful in predicting whether an applicant has the traits that are usually associated with success in particular jobs, such as sales or supervision.
- **Honesty** tests, sometimes called "integrity tests," are designed to determine the integrity of people who take them by measuring attitudes toward dishonesty and propensity for theft-type behavior. Some employers say they can reduce theft and related problem behaviors by using the results of honesty tests.

Under the Civil Rights Act of 1964, employers may use "any professionally developed ability test," provided that the results are not used as a basis for discrimination. Tests that have an "adverse impact" on minorities and are not justified by business necessity are discriminatory, according to Equal Employment Opportunity Commission (EEOC) guidelines that have been upheld by the U.S. Supreme Court.

One typical procedure is described as follows. After all the legal notices and advertisements have been published, the recruitment process is over, and the Call of Exam has been made available to eligible candidates, the candidate fills out his application form (Appendix I). Some departments charge a fee ($10.00 to $25.00) when the application is submitted. This helps defray the cost of administering the exam. The firm or agency conducting the exam mails the entry-level exams to an impartial moderator. The moderator then brings the unopened exams to the examination site, where they are opened in front of proctors and a chief officer of the department. If many candidates are taking the exam, they are processed and assigned exam rooms. When multiple rooms are used, the moderator gives instructions to all candidates via closed circuit television. Each exam room has a proctor. The clock for timed portions of the exam is displayed at the moderator's console. The examination booklet number and corresponding candidate's name are recorded by the proctor and turned over to the moderator only. Once he completes the exam, each candidate's answer sheet is turned in and copied. The original is mailed back to the testing authority by the moderator. The other copy is given to the candidate so that at a later date there can be no complaints of tampering with the answer sheet. Once the exams are corrected, the examiner mails the results, by exam number, to the moderator and to the department. However, the moderator is the only person who can match the number to a name. At this point, the department and the moderator meet and record the scores by name. The department then immediately notifies those who failed. The required number of top scorers then are instructed to take the pass-fail agility exam (Appendix II, agility exam). Once this is completed, the top candidates are ranked and notified. Then all other candidates who passed, but were not in the top group, are notified of their written score. The eligibility list then is certified by the Authority Having Jurisdiction, and the hiring process begins. This is a fair and foolproof method of conducting an entry-level examination.

EEOC GUIDELINES ON TESTING

The federal *Uniform Guidelines on Employee Selection Procedures* have been adopted by the U.S. Departments of Labor and Justice, the EEOC, and the Office of Personnel Management (civil service). They apply to all employers covered by Title VII of the Civil Rights Act. Originally developed as technical standards for validating formal tests, the guidelines have gradually been expanded to cover all aspects of employee selection. This includes application blanks, oral interviews, experience and skill requirements, plus any other factor used by employers in selecting applicants. The main principles underlying the guidelines are described here.

Adverse Impact

Employer policies and practices that have an unfavorable impact on any race, gender, or ethnic group are illegal unless justified by business necessity. "Business necessity" means that there must be a clear relationship between what is evaluated by the selection procedure and the performance required by the job.

Do not start a testing program without professional advice. Procure tests from established sources well versed in the management process. Keep a complete record of all tests given both to employees and rejected applicants.

Probation

The candidate, once hired, is generally on "probation." This probation period is usually one year and must be covered in the labor instrument.

The purpose of having a special review program for newly hired employees is to force supervisors to make corrections in work habits and to reach a decision about whether or not to keep the employee. It is unlikely that a new employee who sloughs off work, arrives late, or just doesn't seem to care will somehow get better over time. If a new broom won't sweep clean, it never will.

The purpose of the probationary period is to provide guidance to new employees and to have company officers work with them to make them into efficient firefighters. For a probation program to be effective, the worker's immediate supervisor should be required to approve, in writing, the retention or termination of the employee before the probationary period ends. If the employee is to be retained, policy also may provide for an increase in wages based on satisfactory completion of the probationary period. An ongoing review process should be used periodically during the probationary period and should include periodic appraisals and counseling.

If possible, do not refer to employees who complete probation as **permanent employees.** That expression implies that the worker has a right to lifetime employment with your organization, and it can be used against you in a wrongful discharge case.

Using the term **probationary** also may be a mistake. A sharp attorney representing a former employee in a wrongful discharge suit can make a big deal of the fact that the worker was "no longer probationary," and therefore should be entitled to due process and terminated only for cause. One suggested phrase to replace the term probationary is "a special review program for newly hired employees."

Most departments use the probationary period as a tool for introducing the employee to the organization, and for getting the new worker's full attention turned to performing the duties of the job well; this gives the firefighter a greater sense of belonging to the organization.

One important point to remember is that all new employees should go through an initial review period and be evaluated to determine if they should be retained, whether or not they serve out a formal probationary period. Another is that generally any form of employee review after the probationary period passes is considered a condition of employment and, as such, may have to be negotiated if the department falls under the purview of a labor instrument. (Appendix III, probationary review form.)

PROMOTIONAL TESTING AND TRAINING

Promotions within a department are one of the most important functions the fire chief must administer. On one hand, they can raise morale; on the other, if there are no promotions, or if they are tainted, they can cause morale to plummet.

Departments conduct promotional exams in a variety of ways. They may be conducted within the fire department by department personnel or by the municipal personnel department. The general scope of advancement is usually from firefighter to company officer, lieutenant or captain, then on to the various grades of chief officer. In most cases, a certain time in grade must be served before an individual can advance to a higher position or rank.

Once a need for a promotional exam arises within a department, for example, because of a vacancy or vacancies within the officer ranks, a notice is promulgated informing those eligible of the pending examination. This should be done well in advance of the anticipated vacancy, to give those eligible as much time as possible to prepare for the exam. At this time the department should provide a list of study materials from which the examination will be drawn.

A job description and an appropriate application form should be provided before a predetermined deadline. Exam procedures can be written, written and oral, oral only, written and an assessment center, or an assessment center only. In any event, the various components of the exam generally are weighted, for example, 50 percent written and 50 percent oral. In most cases, the written portion of the exam is given first and the candidate must receive a passing grade on it before proceeding to the next phase.

If an outside contractor is used, the conductor of the written portion of the exam should ensure that the exam is validated, that is, that the exam will stand up in a court of law and that the firm will support the exam in any litigation process. Oral boards are usually composed of officers of ranks higher than the position being tested, and often are chosen from other departments; they frequently are "drafted" from professional organizations within the fire service.

Many departments now are using the assessment center as part of the examination process, sometimes in conjunction with a written exam. The rationale is that this type of exam is more thorough and demonstrates a candidate's ability to "think on his feet" more so than the traditional oral-type examination. The assessment center exam may consist of demonstrating the ability to establish priorities via an "in-basket" process, providing concise written reports, and participating in real-world situations via the role-playing process.

It is imperative that when a department conducts this type of exam that it selects an experienced firm or in-house group to conduct the process. The examination administrator is responsible for briefing the candidates; procuring, training and briefing the assessors; becoming familiar with the job description and various Standard Operating Procedures (SOPs); and for being an efficient facilitator of the entire process.

Once the candidates are ranked (again, the selection process varies according to the department, the labor instrument, and the promotional policies of the community or department), the administrator charged with selecting the candidates (it is hoped this will be the fire chief) may, by regulation, have to select the top candidate, one of the top three candidates, or use some other selection process. In addition, there may be an interview process that involves the department's top administration, depending on the size of the department and the promotional rank involved.

One example of how a promotional examination process might be conducted is described here.

The examination process is negotiable. Union and management must agree on the person who will conduct the written exam. Once the need arises for a promotional examination, a copy of the job description is sent to the examiner and a bibliography is promulgated. The exams are sent to the moderator who brings the unopened box of exams to the exam site and opens them in front of the candidates. The exam booklet number, along with the candidate's name, is given to the moderator. The moderator conducts the exam. Upon completion of the exam, a copy is made of the exam answer sheet and is given to the candidate, thereby eliminating the possibility of any exam tampering. The moderator then mails the exams back to the examiner for correction. When the exams are corrected, the candidate's mark and his number are sent to the moderator and to the department. The department then must meet with the moderator to match the mark and number to a name. Seventy percent is a passing grade and accounts for 50 percent of the total score. Only those candidates who pass the written portion of the exam are eligible to move on to the oral phase. If the second portion of the exam is strictly an oral exam, a three-member oral panel is selected from other departments. However, no member of this panel should be from a contiguous community.

If an assessment center type exam is conducted, it must be used consistently to avoid having one captain selected by an assessment center and another later candidate selected by a traditional oral panel. In both types of exam, a moderator should be present to resolve any problems that may arise. After the oral portion, the assessors turn their marks in to the moderator and the written and oral marks are added to establish the final mark. Candidates are notified by mail of their marks, the list is certified by the Authority Having

Jurisdiction, and the appointment is made. The appointment should be made within a few weeks after the oral portion to avoid any demoralizing time lapses.

AFFIRMATIVE ACTION

What is Affirmative Action?

Affirmative action means taking positive steps to recruit, hire, train, and promote individuals from groups which have been subject to discrimination on the basis of race, gender, and other characteristics. Affirmative action goes beyond "equal employment opportunity," which requires employers only to eliminate discriminatory conditions and to treat all employees equally in the workplace.

Affirmative action requirements may be imposed by state or federal regulations for government contractors, subcontractors, and loan recipients as part of conciliation agreements by state and federal agencies, by court order, and under employers' voluntary affirmative action programs (AAPs). Basically such programs are required to provide the following:

- An analysis of all major job categories together with statistical information on the minority and female population of the surrounding labor area for comparison with the total work force in the facility.
- Goals, timetables, and commitments designed to correct identifiable deficiencies.
- Support data for the above analysis compiled and kept up to date, together with seniority rosters and applicant flow data.
- Special attention to the upper categories, from craftsworkers to officials and managers, as defined in the EEO-1. Analyses must be made for all job categories for which there are availability statistics, and employers must declare any underuse, even for a figure as low as one percent. In some cases, separate AAPs also are required for disabled individuals and veterans.

Is Reverse Discrimination a real problem?

On one hand each employer is required to hire, promote, develop, and train its work force in a nondiscriminatory fashion. Yet if imbalances develop in the representation of minorities, then cities that are required to have affirmative action plans must try to eliminate the underrepresentation. Similarly, cities that do not fall under affirmative action requirements may want to correct the underrepresentation to avoid discrimination charges from minorities. Be advised that denying job opportunities to any class of worker, including majority workers, simply because the management of an organization "thinks" it should hire or train more minorities is an invitation to be sued for reverse discrimination.

Nevertheless, in more than one case an employer has survived challenges to voluntary AAPs when its plan included four basic elements:

1. The employer made a detailed and thoroughly documented self-analysis to determine whether minorities were underrepresented.
2. Finding that there were fewer minority members in the work force than would normally be expected, the employer took reasonable action, relative to the degree of underrepresentation, to correct it. This included establishing specific but reasonable written goals and time tables for correcting the underrepresentation. In one case, the employer set a 50 percent hiring ratio and implemented it by selecting applicants alternately from two applicant lists: one for minorities and one for nonminorities; this way, no group was totally excluded from opportunities.
3. The affirmative action plan was for a limited period of time (12 months) and was suspended when goals were met.
4. It did not result in displacement of nonminority employees, nor did it unduly restrict opportunities for nonminorities.

It is clear, based on Supreme Court decisions, that the courts are going to uphold any reasonable AAP, at least for the time being, based on widespread support for affirmative action. Keep the following caveats in mind:

- Organizations should not enter into voluntary AAPs unless there is a real and verifiable imbalance in the employer's work force compared to the percentage of women and minorities in the labor market.
- No AAP should be used completely to deny opportunity to a class of worker; rather, it is expected that goals will be flexible, not rigid quotas, and that the AAP will move slowly but deliberately toward achieving its objectives.
- Factors such as gender and race may be considered in making hiring and promotion decisions, for example, to place more women in positions where they are underrepresented, providing that those are not the only criteria used. This could mean, for example, that an organization can select a slightly less qualified female or minority worker based on a lower but passing test score within a pool of qualified workers, without fear of losing a reverse-discrimination suit if the selection meets 1 and 2 above.

It should be noted that the affirmative action policies outlined above are administered by the town or city of which the fire department is an integral part of government.

EQUAL EMPLOYMENT OPPORTUNITY

Equal employment opportunity gives employees rights under a number of laws:

- The **Civil Rights Act of 1964** (Title II) prohibits discrimination in employment because of "race, color, religion, sex or national origin." It covers all employers with 15 or more employees, including state and local governments. Title VII is administered by the federal Equal Employment Opportunity Commission (EEOC). It can investigate and act in cooperation with state and other federal agencies and can bring suit for enforcement of its decisions. Where there is an approved state or local agency, complaints must be filed with that agency, which then has 60 days before the EEOC assumes jurisdiction.
- The **Age Discrimination in Employment Act** (ADEA) prohibits discrimination against persons over the age of 40. It covers all private employers of 20 or more employees, members of labor unions with 25 or more members, local and state governments, and employment agencies that serve covered organizations. The ADA is administered by the Equal Employment Opportunity Commission.
- The **Equal Pay Act of 1963** is an amendment to the Fair Labor Standards Act (FLSA) and therefore covers all employees engaged in interstate commerce. State and local government employees (except elected and policy-making officials) also are covered. This law forbids employers from discriminating by paying lower wage rates or providing a diminished benefit package to employees of one sex versus the other when the work they do is equal and is performed under similar working conditions. The EEOC is responsible for enforcement and can conduct investigations and bring suit for enforcement of its decisions. The act is enforced by the federal government without the assistance of state and local agencies.
- The **Rehabilitation Act of 1973** deals with government contractors and employees who receive federal assistance.
- The **Americans with Disabilities Act of 1990** (ADA) affects all employers covered by the Civil Rights Act. It applies to employers of 25 or more workers beginning on July 26, 1992 and was effective for employers of 15 to 24 employees as of July 26, 1994. The major provisions of this act are discussed under "Definitions," "Reasonable Accommodation," and "Physical Examinations" below. Although there are several acts that deal with the protection of handicapped persons,

following the guidelines for the ADA meets most of the requirements for the other acts as well. Exceptions are noted below. **Definition of Disabled:** A disabled person is one who:

- has a physical or mental impairment that substantially limits one or more major life activities;
- has a record of such impairment, e.g., a former drug addict or a recovered heart attack victim; or
- is regarded as having such an impairment.

This includes any physiological disorders such as retardation, emotional illness, and specific learning disabilities. The words "substantially" and "major" were inserted to eliminate minor, irrelevant claims of discrimination; however, courts have found a variety of characteristics, including bad backs, shortness of stature, and obesity to be disabilities under certain circumstances. Therefore, a disability is, in reality, any factor that is a potential impairment to performing a job, including a factor that an employer perceives to be a disability.

- **Disease:** Employers who receive federal funds cannot discriminate against employees disabled by contagious diseases unless they currently pose a real risk of infection to others or cannot perform their jobs. Although temporary illnesses do not qualify as disabilities, Supreme Court decisions indicate that anyone with a continuing medical problem may be covered.
- **Drug and Alcohol Abuse:** Individuals who have serious debilitating addictions to drugs or alcohol are protected under the law, provided they are able to perform the job safely and effectively. Practically speaking, the law would probably protect most recovered alcoholics and former drug addicts—including those currently undergoing treatment—but few (if any) current users of illegal substances.

REASONABLE ACCOMMODATION

These acts protect individuals who, with "reasonable accommodation," can perform the "essential functions" of the job. If they cannot perform these essential functions—even with reasonable accommodation—then they legally may be rejected. Accommodation may include altering facilities, restructuring jobs, and revising schedules. It is not necessary to start remodeling the work area or making other "prospective" accommodative changes to your facility. None of this must be done until you must actually accommodate an individual, and then only if the accommodation is reasonable.

Disabled individuals may be rejected only if, with reasonable accommodation, they still are unable to perform the job's essential functions. They cannot be rejected because they are unable to perform occasional or marginal assignments. Therefore, a person who, with reasonable accommodation, cannot operate a typewriter need not be hired as a clerk-typist. But to reject an applicant for a typist's position because he can't drive to the bank one a week would likely be a mistake. This means that it is necessary to be able to distinguish between the essential and nonessential functions of each job. *The best way to do this is with job descriptions.*

While the law does not require job descriptions, they are valuable for many reasons. They can give essential guidance to interviewers, supervisors, and physicians. If you already have job descriptions, make sure they are current. Consider adding an "essential functions" section to the descriptions, or otherwise identifying those aspects of the jobs that are truly essential to their performance.

PHYSICAL EXAMINATIONS AND RECORDS

The ADA permits physicals to be administered after an offer of employment has been made, but before the individual actually starts work. The offer may be conditional on passing the exam if (1) the employer requires all entering employees in the same classification to take an exam, (2) the results are confidential, and (3) the exam is job-related. The act also permits drug testing. It does not protect individuals currently using illegal drugs or alcoholics who are unable to do their jobs.

Employee medical information must be kept in confidential files separate from the general personnel folder; access to medical files should be severely restricted. The act does not specify what should be held in the file, but it certainly should include any physical examination results, information related to worker's compensation claims, and any details of an employee's nonjob-related illnesses or injuries.

Be certain that all interviewers, first-line supervisors, and members of management are familiar with the requirements of these laws.

Employers are required to screen applicants in a nondiscriminatory manner, which means that inquiries that disproportionately screen out women and minorities are prohibited. The EEOC considers inquiries about an applicant's race, color, religion, or national origin to be totally irrelevant in terms of job ability; such inquiries, whether direct or indirect, may be regarded as evidence of discrimination.

There are exceptions. Pre-employment inquiries made pursuant to the requirements of a local, state, or federal fair employment practices law are permissible. Also excepted are those infrequent instances where religion and national origin are "bona fide occupational qualifications," or where the employer can prove that the inquiry is justified by business necessity that is job-related.

Before choosing a new employee from a pool of applicants, decide whether you can reasonably accommodate any disabilities that have come to your attention. Assess the reasonableness of the needed accommodation; if you can't provide it, ask the applicant whether he can. Before you reject a disabled applicant, evaluate whether you have considered all possible accommodations. Make sure the rejection is based on the applicant's inability to perform an essential job function. Document the accommodations you've considered and the reasons for their rejection.

The law requires affirmative action only for applicants or employees who are qualified to perform the job with reasonable accommodation to their disability, and not those who might interfere with productivity or create dangers in the workplace. However, an employer can no longer make broad assumptions about a disabled individual's ability to perform. If an employment decision is made on the basis of a disability, the employer should be able to prove that even after reasonable accommodation the individual cannot satisfactorily accomplish the duties of the job.

A department does not have to change or alter its examination process to conform to the requirements of ADA.

SEXUAL HARASSMENT

Sexual harassment of any employee or job applicant is prohibited. Such harassment is defined as any unwelcome sexual advances or requests for sexual favors or any conduct of a sexual nature when (1) submission is made explicitly or implicitly a term or condition of employment, (2) submission or rejection is used as the basis for employment decisions, or (3) such conduct has the purpose or effect of substantially interfering with an individual's work, or creates an intimidating, hostile, or offensive working environment.

Posting

All employers of three or more workers must post a notice informing employees that sexual harassment is illegal.

Training

All employers of 50 or more workers must provide their supervisory employees 2 hours of education and training on the federal and state sexual harassment regulations and the remedies that are available to victims of sexual harassment. Any training these employees have received after October 1, 1991 may be counted toward the two-hour requirement which should have been completed by October 1, 1993.

New supervisors must receive the training within six months of becoming supervisors. Supervisors who have completed their training must be given an update on legal interpretations and other developments related to sexual harassment once every three years. Supervisory personnel who are to be trained include supervisors, work leaders, administrators, managers, executives, executive officers and directors. Training must be carried out in a classroom-like setting; simply passing around periodical articles on the subject will not meet the requirements of the proposed regulations.

Records

Employers that conduct supervisory training must keep records of the names and titles of those trained, when they were trained, by whom, and the content of the training. Records must be kept for two years, or longer if any related complaints have been filed.

Federal Guidelines

Employers are liable for acts of sexual harassment by their employees, and may be held liable for such acts of nonemployees where the employer knows of the conduct or should have known about it, unless the employer can show it took immediate and appropriate corrective action. The employer may be accused of sex discrimination if a person who qualified for an employment opportunity was denied that opportunity because it was given to one who submitted to an employer's sexual advances.

Establish a policy on sexual harassment stating departmental disapproval and intent to take appropriate disciplinary action against violators. Cover the following points:

- **Definition.** Specify what types of acts constitute sexual harassment.
- **Complaint procedures.** State to whom the individual should report alleged harassment; this typically is the supervisor, fire chief, or the personnel department (include women in the list of those to whom complaints can be reported).
- **Supervisor's responsibilities.** State to whom supervisors should report complaints, and what actions they should take.
- **Investigation.** List who will conduct the investigation of the alleged harassment.
- **Disciplinary action.** Describe what types of action may be taken depending on the severity of the harassment and other factors.
- **Prevention.** Spell out management's responsibility to notify workers of the sexual harassment policy and its enforcement procedures.

    Communicate the policy to all employees, informing them of their right to bring complaints to management and to appropriate agencies. Immediately investigate and take action on all claims of sexual harassment. Finally, maintain thorough records of all actions taken under this guideline.

SEXUAL ORIENTATION

You cannot discriminate against individuals on the basis of their sexual orientation. This includes having a past or current preference for heterosexuality, homosexuality, or bisexuality, or being identified with such preference, and applies to all public and private employers, except religious entities, where the work is connected to the purpose of the entity.

Employers cannot discipline or discharge, discriminate in wages and conditions of employment, or refuse to hire on the basis of sexual orientation. Professional associations cannot refuse membership, employment agencies cannot fail to refer individuals for employment, and labor unions cannot exclude persons from full membership.

Some employers have expressed fear that individuals may now be more open about their sexual preferences. But employers still have the right to set standards of conduct. You can prohibit any activities that disrupt the workplace, you can require everyone to wear standard attire for the work being performed, and you can control any form of harassment, sexual or otherwise. This has been true for years and has not changed as a result of the new law.

PENSIONS

A firefighter's pension plan or any employee's pension plan is a major benefit. In the fire service, most provisions of the pension plan are covered under a union contract and the provisions thereof are negotiable. Generally, the fire chief is on the pension board, or in some way administers the pension. Therefore, it is important that the chief understands not only the department's pension, but laws and regulations that apply to pensions.

All pension plans fall under the jurisdiction of the *Employee Retirement Income Security Act of 1974 (ERISA)*. ERISA provides mandatory rules on all pension, profit-sharing, and stock bonus plans, as well as some welfare plans.

The basic purpose of the act is to protect the rights of employees in terms of participation and vesting under pension plans, to set standards for management of the funds involved, and to require reports to be filed with the government and given to each participant in summary form.

The U.S. Departments of Labor and Treasury jointly administer ERISA. All pension, profit-sharing, and welfare plans involve the IRS code.

Vesting

Vesting refers to the percentage of the employees' benefit accounts that they are entitled to retain after leaving their employer. For plan years beginning after 1988 (or for collectively bargained plans up until 1991), these alternatives are available for vesting pensions, deferred profit-sharing, or any other type of retirement income plan:

There are essentially two types of pension plans:

Defined-Benefit Plans

The employer agrees to pay retirement benefits based on a formula that is typically some percentage of salary for each year of service.

Defined-Contribution Plans

The employer agrees to contribute to the employee's account a specific amount of money, typically a percentage of pay.

In addition, for reporting purposes, ERISA treats as pension plans any form of deferred compensation such as deferred profit-sharing, stock purchases, or savings and thrift plans, as well as pension plans. A bonus plan under which payments are systematically deferred and paid out over several years is also considered a pension plan for reporting purposes.

A cash bonus plan, a cash profit-sharing plan pertinent to the fire service, and severance pay of less than two years are considered forms of compensation and are not regulated by ERISA.

The contributions made by the employer and the rights obtained under such plans by employees involve substantial sums; therefore, no plan should be set up or amended without the advice of an attorney, accountant, or benefits specialist who is experienced in this field.

SUBSIDIZED EDUCATIONAL PROGRAMS

Many fire departments provide subsidies for educational advancement, most notably in the field of fire science or administration. Stipends may be paid for obtaining an associate, bachelor's or master's degree in fire science or fire administration. Stipends may be paid for a certain number of credits obtained toward the above degrees. Some departments pay for all or for a portion of the cost of this education, provided the firefighter receives a passing grade. In addition, monies may be paid for additional technical knowledge and skills such as paramedic or Emergency Medical Technician (EMT) certification, fire investigator certification and other advanced technical skills that may be acquired.

Some departments that are fortunate to have an educational institution within their jurisdiction may have a cooperative agreement in place that allows firefighters to attend a university, college, or community college at a reduced rate.

For example, the University of New Haven, located in West Haven, Connecticut, has a policy under which police and firefighters within the city may enroll in the fire science program or criminal justice program at one-half the tuition rate. This is certainly beneficial for those who want to take advantage of the educational opportunity.

In addition, the West Haven Fire Department has a live-in program under which fire science students are selected to live in the local fire stations. They must have some prior experience, but are trained accordingly and perform the same firefighting functions as members of the department.

The subsidizing of educational programs and pay incentives for educational achievement described above should lead to a better trained, more highly motivated department, provided the leadership of the department encourages the program and provides guidelines to firefighters in their quest for educational advancement.

OSHA

The Occupational Safety and Health Act of 1970 (OSHA) governs safety and health in the private sector. Many states, in addition to meeting federal OSHA requirements, must adhere to their own state's occupational safety and health plan. The federal law is enforced by the Occupational Safety and Health Administration, U.S. Department of Labor.

The major provisions of the Occupational Safety and Health Act are:

- Inspection without advance notice. Investigations may be made on either a routine basis or because of a specific complaint. The courts have sustained arguments that inspection without notice is unconstitutional, but, as a practical matter, the government can obtain a warrant without proof of any violation. Under these circumstances, there isn't much point to refusing access to an OSHA representative.
- Representative employees must accompany inspectors during a visit. In a nonunion facility, the investigator may select the employees. The U.S. Department of Labor amended regulations in 1977 to require that employers must compensate employees for time spent in "walk-around" inspections and for any conferences arising from the inspections. Since then, however, OSHA has withdrawn this regulation because the major-

ity of employees on walk-arounds already are compensated by their employers or unions.
* Employees are entitled to file a complaint confidentially.
* Protection is afforded for employees who exercise their rights under the law; retaliation is forbidden.

General Duty Clause

The law includes an extremely broad "general duty clause" that requires employees to comply with safety rules.

SPECIFIC OSHA STANDARDS

OSHA regulations cover specific areas, including:
–Hazard communication (the "right-to-know" laws).
–Walking and working surfaces, i.e., guarding openings, ladders, scaffolds, power lifts, and housekeeping.
–Exits—emergency exits, emergency plans, and fire prevention plans.
–Environmental control—ventilation, noise exposure, radiation, hazard signs, and tags.
–Hazardous materials—gases, flammable liquids, explosives, hazardous waste, emergency response.
–Personal protective equipment—protection of eyes, face, head, and feet, and respiratory protection.
–Fire protection—extinguishers and sprinkler systems, detection and alarm systems.
–Materials handling and storage.
–Guarding and operating machinery.
–Training in, and operation of, welding, cutting, and glazing.
–Electrical wiring and electrical equipment.
–Operating hand-held equipment.

Reports and Posters

All employers covered by OSHA must display a government poster in each place of employment. Employers of ten or more also must maintain the following records for any injury or illness beyond first aid, for each of their establishments.

The *OSHA-101 Supplementary Record* is substantially the same as the accident report required under the Connecticut Workers' Compensation Act. Most insurance forms can be used for both of these reports.

The OSHA-200 Log and Summary of Occupational Injuries and Illnesses requires a chronological listing that gives the employee's name, department, occupation, nature of injury or illness, and extent of lost time or other outcome. All log entries must be posted within six work days of the event. The OSHA log is not the same as the company first-aid log. For worker's compensation purposes, companies are wise to insist that a record be kept of every injury or potential work-related illness, but not every first-aid case belongs on the OSHA-200 log.

Minor injuries that require only first-aid treatment need not be recorded. Examples of what OSHA defines as first-aid treatment include any "one-time" treatment of minor cuts, scratches, burns, or splinters. Injuries that must be recorded include those requiring medical treatment, those involving loss of consciousness, injuries that result in restriction of work or motion, and injuries that require transfer to another job.

OSHA defines illness as a work-related medical condition that results from anything other than an "instantaneous event." Included are acute and chronic illnesses or diseases that may be caused by inhalation, absorption, ingestion, or direct contact. These must be recorded.

The summary section of OSHA-200 or a copy of the totals must be posted by February 1 and remain in place until March 1 each year at each establishment where employee notices are usually posted. The summary is to be held on file for five years. Access to the log (OSHA-200) must be permitted to employees, former employees, and their representatives.

In addition, a special report must be made by employers, regardless of size of company, to the U.S. Secretary of Labor within 48 hours of any accident or health hazard that results in a fatality or in the hospitalization of 5 or more employees.

Noise Exposure

Whenever employee noise level exposure exceeds 85 db as an average over an 8-hour day, the employer is required to take the following steps:

- Monitor noise levels in the plant and keep records of that monitoring for two years.
- Establish an audiometric testing program for all employees exposed to 85 db or more, including initial testing by a competent audiology technician with followup tests at least annually, at no cost to employees; records of audiometric tests are to be kept as long as the employee is employed by the firm.
- Watch for shifts in audiogram results and notify employees of such changes within 21 days of the test.

- Make a variety of hearing protection devices available at no cost to exposed employees.
- Train exposed employees in the use of hearing protection, the effects of noise, and in how to understand audio tests results.
- Allow access to noise-level and audiometric test results to employees and former employees or their designated representatives, and to OSHA officials.

It is imperative that all fire chiefs, career and volunteer, be fully aware of all federal and state OSHA requirements. A lack of knowledge can result in monetary losses to the community, not to mention the serious health and safety problems that can affect all employees.

PHYSICAL FITNESS IN THE FIRE SERVICE

It should be evident that the requirement for all firefighters to be physically fit is justified. Firefighting is one of the few professions that requires employees to work in a very hostile environment. Many departments, both career and volunteer, maintain some type of voluntary physical fitness program. Others have requirements or provisions in the labor instrument for maintaining a certain type of physical fitness program. In many departments, the firefighters and the administration work hand-in-hand to provide physical fitness equipment.

An efficient method of maintaining physical fitness throughout a firefighter's career is to institute or negotiate a lean body fat program. Firefighters must conform to the provisions listed on a chart for body fat content.

AGE	MEN	WOMEN
24 and <	20%	26%
25–29	21%	26%
30–34	22%	26%
35–39	22%	26%
40–44	24%	27%
45–49	24%	27%
50–54	25%	29%
55 and >	25%	29%

The general procedure is to have entry-level candidates take the lean body fat test after passing the written and medical portions of their entry exams. Once hired, testing is done on an annual basis by an outside testing firm. Tests may be conducted by weighing the firefighter in water or by using calipers. If the employee fails to meet the prescribed weight, then he shall submit to successive weigh-ins. Repeated failures could eventually lead to termination. Fire chiefs should keep in mind that the purpose of the process is not to discipline, but rather to counsel and assist employees who have a tendency to exceed body fat requirements.

The main thrust of this type of physical fitness program is that the requirement to maintain one's fitness rests with the employee. In this situation, it is incumbent upon the fire chief to work with and provide time and equipment for firefighters to work out while on duty.

EMPLOYEE BENEFITS

Background

The term "benefit" or "fringe benefit" has historically been used to cover all paid time not worked, and all additions to pay for the benefit of employees. Benefits accounted for only about four percent of payroll costs prior to World War II. At that time, the federal government instituted wage controls that froze the pay of many workers. One way these "frozen" workers could get a raise was to quit and be hired by another employer; this led to employers developing enhanced benefit programs as a means of keeping employees from leaving. This, combined with collective bargaining, recognition of employees' needs for security, and the desire to provide some form of tax-free reward to employees, has led to major expansions of benefit programs. Today, benefits have become so important, and so costly, that referring to them as "fringes" has become passé.

Employee Health Care

The Chamber of Commerce of the U.S., in its annual *Employee Benefits Report,* places benefit costs at 40.2% of payroll, equivalent to an average of $6.58 per hour, and $13,686.40 per year, per employee.

This expensive and much-needed benefit is most important to the firefighter and his family. The fire chief must be familiar with the benefits provided and the process of handling such claims. Problems with health care benefits, even though they may be administered by a personnel director, will eventually end up on the fire chief's desk for assistance in adjudicating the problem. Poor handling of employee health benefits can lead to lowered morale in the department.

There are many types of health care plans currently available and in use.

Cafeteria/Flexible Benefits Plans

The terms "flexible benefits," "flex plan," and "cafeteria plan" are, in practice, used interchangeably. Strictly speaking, however, flexible benefit plans (or flex plans) are any type of plan that provides employees a choice of benefits; cafeteria plans offer employees a choice of both the type of benefits and the extent of coverage. Cafeteria plans can be established as tax-qualified under Section 125 of the IRS code, allowing employees to reduce their taxable income by using pretax dollars to pay for benefits. Many IRS and ERISA regulations affect cafeteria plans, so an employer that wishes to establish such a plan should do so only under the guidance of an experienced CPA or benefits consultant. Among the types of plans are:

- **Premium-Only Plans (POP).** Also known as premium-conversion accounts, POPs are the least complex type of flex plan. Employees pay for their health, life, and disability insurance coverage with pretax dollars by reducing their salaries (via payroll deduction) by the exact amount of their insurance premiums. Since this reduces taxable income, employees then save on federal and state income taxes, while both employees and employers save on Social Security taxes.
- **Flexible Spending Accounts (FSA).** Also referred to as reimbursement accounts or salary reduction plans, FSAs permit employees to use pretax dollars to pay for health care costs not covered by the employer's insurance plan. Employees must estimate these expenses in advance for the year; this amount is deducted from their pay. Employees then pay out of pocket as expenses are incurred, and are later reimbursed by the employer. Flexible spending accounts also can be used to finance up to $5,000 annually in dependent care (or elder care) expenses. Although FSAs can be used independently, they typically are set up in conjunction with POPs.
- **Full Flex/Cafeteria Plans.** Employees are given a set dollar amount to spend on a "cafeteria menu" of benefits: life, health, dental, vision, disability, 401K, and even vacation time; expenses beyond the allotted dollar amount are covered through a POP or FSA. Employees make their own choices for types of coverage and deductible amounts. Full cafeteria plans, the most complex type of flexible benefit plan, normally are feasible only for employers of 100 or more, and typically must be managed either in-house using computer software packages, or by an outside firm that specializes in flexible benefit administration. Some health care benefits are paid entirely by the municipality, although the trend today is to institute some form of co-pay to offset the rising costs of health care benefits.

Other types of group health insurance plans that are available include:

- **Commercial policies** that insure on an indemnity basis, paying a specific amount toward each covered expense. Commercial policies are post-paid plans, i.e., they pay a specified amount of money toward covered expenses after the medical care has been given.
- **Blue Cross and Blue Shield,** for the most part, insure on a service basis, paying the full cost of specific services, regardless of the amount. Blue Cross and Blue Shield are post-paid plans.
- **Health Maintenance Organizations** (HMOs) provide service directly, either through their own staffs of medical professionals or by contracting with groups of professionals who spend most of their time caring for HMO patients. HMO plans are prepaid, that is, the cost of all services is covered by the premiums (sometimes with a small copayment) and no bill is issued to the person receiving care.
- **Self-insurance** is practical for large employers who pay claims directly through their own insurance plans. Some small firms self-insure, but limit their exposure through insured major medical coverage. Self-insured plans, for the most part, are regulated by the federal government under ERISA.
- **Major Medical Insurance** supplements the basic hospital/surgical/medical coverage so that when the basic coverage has been exhausted, the major medical takes over. Major medical coverage initially was developed as a separate policy; more recently, however, we have seen the development of "comprehensive" medical plans that combine the features of both the basic hospital/surgical/medical and major medical policies into one package.

    Because of the rapid increase in medical expenses, employers have been seeking ways to reduce costs, including shifting some of the expense to the employees. To do this, both supplemental plans and comprehensive plans often make use of four features: employee contributions to premiums, deductibles, co-insurance, and maximum benefits.
- *Employee Contributions.* Surveys show that a slight majority of employers pay 100 percent of the insurance premium for employees, but only about one-third pay the full premium for dependents.
- *Deductibles.* With a deductible feature, the insured employee will pay a set amount of expense before the plan takes over; this might be $100.000 to $200.00 per individual, and $200.00 to $400.00 or more for an entire family. The deductible may be paid on a per-year or per-cause basis.
- *Co-Insurance.* The plan pays some set percentage of the medical expense, say 80 percent, while the worker pays the balance.
- *Maximum limits on benefits.* Where they are imposed, maximum limits

are usually very high, for example, $1,000,000 for a lifetime of coverage.

The purpose of these limitations, of course, is not only to reduce costs directly, but also to give employees some incentive to control medical expenses by having the insured employee bear part of the cost.

Need for Major Medical

As discussed above, major medical insurance originally was developed to cover medical catastrophes. With the ever-increasing cost of hospitalization and allied medical services, this type of coverage has become a typical benefit in some states. The welfare services and the various health associations make contributions to families confronted with medical disasters, but these agencies typically require the individual family to use its own resources to the maximum extent before they help. This means that even a middle-income family can be financially devastated by a medical emergency or extended hospital stay. A supplemental major medical or comprehensive insurance plan can help an employee to literally avoid bankruptcy in certain situations.

Major Medical Insurance—A Recommendation

A supplemental major medical or comprehensive plan is a fringe benefit that should be instituted provided the employer can afford the cost. Of course, employees can contribute to the cost of the premiums, thereby reducing the cost to some degree.

Because health insurance is a necessity, it is important that there be a clear and definite understanding with new employees as to the date on which their coverage begins and, similarly, will terminate, if and when employees leave the department.

EMPLOYMENT SEPARATION—"COBRA" CONSOLIDATED OMNIBUS BUDGET RECONCILIATION ACT OF 1985

Public Law *(PL) 99-272 (COBRA)* requires that individuals who lose coverage under group plans (e.g., because of termination) must be given the opportunity to continue the coverage. Employers of fewer than 20 workers need only to comply with applicable state laws. However, COBRA clearly applies to 20 or more workers. Federal COBRA covers hospital, medical, surgical, dental, prescription drugs, hearing and vision, and group insurance plans.

Upon termination of employment, said plans are in effect for a maximum of 18 months, unless termination was for gross misconduct. In layoffs, the coverage is for 18 months. In the case of divorce or legal separation, the covered spouse and dependents may continue coverage for 36 months. Qualified individuals must elect to continue coverage within 60 days of notification of the qualifying event. The covered employee or dependent must make the first premium payment to the employer within 45 days of their election to take the COBRA benefits.

In addition, the fire chief should be well aware of applicable state laws that apply to COBRA.

EMPLOYEE ASSISTANCE PROGRAMS (EAPs)

EAPs are confidential counseling programs designed to help workers, and sometimes their families, with personal problems. Employers establish EAPs to provide employees with affordable access to treatment; in turn, they reap savings by reducing the costs associated with poor productivity, on-the-job injuries, excessive absenteeism, and turnover.

Originally established to handle the problems associated with alcohol and substance abuse, EAPs now also deal with emotional, mental health, financial, and family/marital problems. They sometimes are operated through the organization's own medical or health department, or they may be provided by an outside firm on a contract basis, either in house or at the outside firm's facility. Employees often are permitted to use the services of the EAP voluntarily, and without the employer's knowledge of the nature of the problems being handled. On the other hand, employees may be required to make use of the EAP as part of a rehabilitation program, after having shown up to work in an unfit condition, for example.

THE "GRAPEVINE"

"Rumor Central" is a viable organization within the fire service. During periods of negotiations, impending changes, or promotional exams, the "grapevine" flourishes.

The fire chief must take steps to reduce the problem. The best methods for accomplishing this are to be honest and upfront. If a chief deals with the union executive board in an honest and forthright manner, has an interdepartmental communication system in place, and talks with firefighters and officers, then the "rumor mill" will become almost defunct. If the chief gets word of a rumor, then he should inform the parties concerned that what they have heard is, in fact, a rumor. Many times, the fire chief or the administration fosters the rumor problem by "shooting from the hip" or by divulging information before it should be disseminated. The old World War II saying, "loose lips sink ships," holds true in the fire service. The adage, "We have met the enemy and he is us," is, in many cases, one of the problems that leads to rumors being bantered about the department.

In a volunteer department, the same problems exist and the "grapevine" flourishes just as readily. To reduce the problem, the same principles hold true. Deal with the leadership of the department, be honest and upfront and, in some cases, since the chief is a member of the volunteer company, the floor of a company meeting may be the arena to dispel any rumors that are in play.

LABOR RELATIONS

Fire chiefs who manage a unionized fire department face a challenge that, in many cases, can be very rewarding, provided the fire chief is aware of relevant labor laws, maintains integrity in dealing with firefighters and, above all, takes part in labor-management negotiations. Any administrator who negotiates a contract or settles a grievance without the fire chief being present and taking part in the process is courting disaster. If a fire chief has well-trained employees, has established SOPs, practices unity of command, treats all personnel in a fair and equitable manner (including issuing disciplinary action), and has compassionate personnel, then, generally, the labor relations problems are greatly reduced. There will always be some problems, conflicts, and differences in the interpretation of the contract. The key to settling the differences is the willingness of both sides to sit down and discuss the problem. Don't be afraid to express your views. There will be times when agreement cannot be reached. In these cases, the key is for both sides to *disagree* in an *agreeable* manner and let the grievance procedure established in the contract take its course.

However, at times when the problem reaches this stage, conflicts may result in some form of retaliation. As the conflict escalates, innocent firefighters often are "hit with shrapnel" and the problem escalates further. The key here is for the fire chief to maintain his personal integrity, not retaliate for the sake of "getting even," issue discipline fairly if there are violations of rules and regulations, stand firm and, above all, be willing to discuss the issue further if necessary. Conflict management benefits no one, not the union, the department, and above all, those whom we serve: the citizens and taxpayers.

If the fire chief leads the department (keeping in mind that we lead firefighters and manage things), and is honest in all dealings with both firefighters and those who are the Authority Having Jurisdiction, then conflict management will be reduced greatly and the citizens and firefighters will have a department that benefits from community involvement, a department where all concerned can be proud of their association with it.

APPENDIX I: APPLICATION FOR EMPLOYMENT

U. S. MILITARY SERVICE

Branch of Service: _____From: _____ To: _____

Rank & Type of Service: _____

Training/Experience Received: _____

REFERENCES   (Do not include relatives)

	Name	Occupation	Years Known	Address
1:				
2:				
3:				

A P P L I C A N T ' S   S T A T E M E N T

I understand that the employer follows an "employment at will" policy, in that I or the employer may terminate my employment at any time, or for any reason consistent with applicable state or federal law; this "employment at will" policy cannot be changed verbally or in writing, unless the change is specifically authorized in writing by the chief operating officer of this organization. I understand that this application is not a contract of employment. I understand that federal law prohibits the employment of unauthorized aliens; all persons hired must submit satisfactory proof of employment authorization and identity; failure to submit such proof will result in denial of employment.

I understand the agree that any claim I may wish to file against the employer or any of its employees or agents regarding my employment or termination of employment (including but not limited to any claim for any tort, discrimination, breach of contract, violation of public policy, or statutory claim for wrongful termination) must be submitted for binding and final arbitration before an Alternative Dispute Resolution forum within six months of either the occurrence of which I am complaining or the termination of my employment, whichever occurs first. I specifically agree not to commence any such claim more than six months after the date of termination of my employment and waive any statute of limitations to the contrary.

I understand this application will be active for a period of 60 days; after that time, if I wish to be considered for employment, I must submit a new application.

I understand that the employer will thoroughly investigate my work and personal history and verify all data given on this application, on related papers, and in interviews. I authorize all individuals, schools, and firms named therein, except my current employer if so noted, to provide any information requested about me, and I release them from all liability for damage in providing this information.

I certify that all the statements herein are true and understand that any falsification or willful omission shall be sufficient cause for dismissal or refusal of employment.

Your Signature: _____Date: _____

APPLICANTS—PLEASE DO NOT WRITE BELOW THIS LINE

INTERVIEWED BY (1) _____(2) _____DATE: _____
STARTING DATE: _____RATE: _____ CLASSIFICATION: _____
RELOCATION INFORMATION: _____
AGENCY FEE ARRANGEMENTS: _____
OTHER COMMITMENTS: _____
APPROVED BY (1) _____(2) _____(3): _____

APPENDIX II: VALIDATED AGILITY TEST—
WEST HAVEN, CT. FIRE DEPT.

Events

1. MILE RUN You will run in groups of ten (10) or fewer. You will be given a running time at the end of each lap. As the first group of runners starts, a second group will be called on deck. The on-deck group will have 8 to 10 minutes before it begins. All warm-ups shall take place off the track surface. Do not interfere with runners or timers. The run must be completed in ten (10) minutes.

   Job Relatedness: Cardiovascular endurance is important to a fire-fighter because of the stress of firefighting. Wearing heavy equipment and performing physical work under extreme heat impacts very seriously on the ability to breathe while wearing Self-Contained Breathing Apparatus.

2. POWER AGILITY You will take the power agility individually. You will be called on deck which will give you a 2 to 3 minute warning. The time will start with your movement. If you miss an obstacle, you must stop, return, and clear the obstacle before you proceed. All candidates will wait in the bleachers until they are called on deck. Bring warm clothing; the Power Agility will be conducted outside. The Power Agility must be completed in twenty-three (23) seconds.

   Job Relatedness: Firefighting requires the ability to overcome obstacles through quickness and being able to get over, under or around various things to accomplish rescue and/or extinguishment.

3. DRAG AND LIFT You will take the drag and lift test individually. As above, the on-deck call will give you a 2 to 3 minute warning. This test consists of dragging a dummy weighing approximately 150 pounds fifty feet and lifting a 50 pound object four feet off the floor onto a table.

   Job Relatedness: This event demonstrates the person's ability to effectively remove a victim from a fire or help to lift a person onto a stretcher.

4. SIT AND REACH You will take this test in groups of 4 or 5. You will be held by the ankles for support. You will be given 45 seconds to reach the floor 2″ beyond your heels. The timers will command "READY," (pause) "BEGIN," and, at the end of 45 seconds, the timer will say

"STOP." If you touch while the clock is running, your tester will tell you "TARGET," you may cease and relax until "STOP." Do not leave the area until after the "STOP" command.

Job Relatedness: This test is designed to evaluate normal joint range of motion. Lack of flexibility can impact on a firefighter's ability to conduct numerous fire control operations.

5. SIT-UPS You will take this test in groups of 3 or 4. You will lock your feet into the monkey bars. Your knees will remain locked. Your tester will count the number of sit-ups. The tester will inform you of "TARGET" upon completion of 29 sit-ups. The timer will give the command "READY," (pause) "BEGIN," and, at the end of one minute, "STOP." A sit-up will only be counted if:

  A. Knees are locked.
  B. Hands touch a point below the knee.
  C. Shoulder blades return to the mat.

If informed of "TARGET," you may relax until the "STOP" command.

Job Relatedness: Sit-ups test abdominal strength and are sometimes used as indicators of lower back problems.

6. WATER-RELATED EVENT You will jump into the pool (approximately 4 feet deep), walk to a submerged object, retrieve object from the bottom and carry it to opposite end of pool.

Job Relatedness: The West Haven Fire department routinely performs water rescue in Long Island Sound and Lake Phipps and it is imperative that firefighters not have a fear of water which would keep them from performing this duty.

Power Agility

This consists of running a prescribed course in at least 23 seconds. A 50-foot by 90-foot area is needed for this course. The subject runs 10 feet, climbs over a 6-foot high chain link fence, turns left and runs 30 feet, turns right and runs 30 feet, turns right and runs around three cones spaced 10 feet apart, runs 20 feet and jumps over a 5-foot long prescribed area, runs 15 feet, turns right, runs 15 feet and goes under a 1½ foot bar, runs 15 feet and turns right, runs 40 feet to the finish line.

OBSTACLE COURSE—23 seconds for completion time.

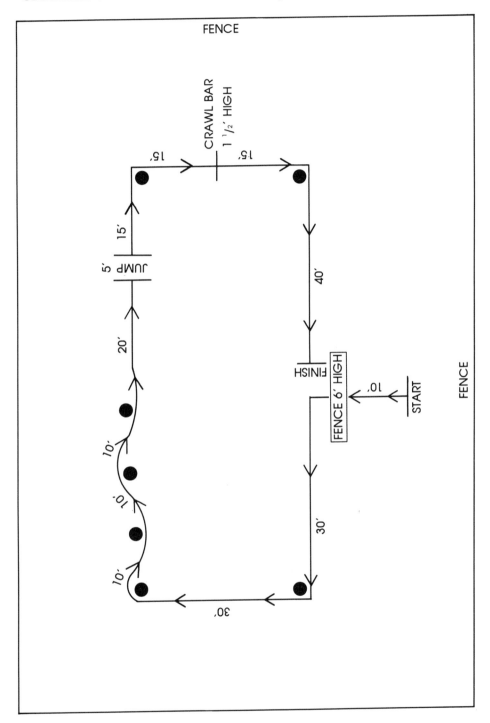

APPENDIX III: WEST HAVEN CONNECTICUT FIRE DEPARTMENT, PERFORMANCE EVALUATION

Name: _____

Date: _____

Introduction:

Personnel evaluation is a means of regularly determining the manner in which, and the degree to which, an employee is fulfilling his/her duty as a professional in the field of Fire and EMS Safety during their probationary period and, also, the degree to which the employee aids the Department in meeting its goals.

To be effective, evaluation must be an ongoing process based on observations of the employee's behavior, and it should serve as the means to analyze behavior and professional growth of the ratee. The evaluating process should provide the ratee and the Department with a knowledge of his/her strengths and weaknesses. Subsequent training and discussion should be designed to enable the ratee to eliminate or correct the weaknesses and to develop the strengths.

In completing the evaluation, the rater must always bear in mind that personnel performance evaluation is a serious procedure, which may have an impact on the future career of the ratee. Consequently, every effort must be made to be fair and objective in preparing a firefighter's evaluation. The rater's personal prejudices, likes and dislikes which may influence the ratee's strengths and weaknesses must not cloud the rating of the evaluation attributes. The evaluator must studiously avoid his/her own personal need for acceptance, peer pressure or friendships from influencing either negatively or positively the ratings given an employee. Evaluations should be based on direct observations by the evaluator, personnel records, and accurate facts, rather than upon speculation.

1. LAST NAME FIRST NAME MI	2. RANK
3. PRESENT WORK ASSIGNMENT	4. PERIOD OF EVALUATION
5. EVALUATOR	6. EVALUATOR RANK

TO EVALUATOR: Thoroughly review instructions on preceding page prior to beginning evaluation. For each attribute, *circle only the one statement* that most adequately describes the ratee.

1. JOB KNOWLEDGE: Awareness of standard operational procedures, concepts, techniques and policies related to the individual's specific job function and appropriate application of that knowledge.

HIGH		AVERAGE		LOW	
Consistently uses knowledge of Dept. policies and procedures as a guide to effective performance.	Applies a knowledge of up-to-date techniques to his/her job.	Performs in accordance with policies and procedures of assigned unit.	Knowledge of Dept. policies and procedures is adequate generally.	Does not exhibit basic knowledge of his/her job function.	Knowledge of Dept. policies & procedures is inadequate for effective performance.

RATING:

| 5 | 4 | 3 | 2 | 1 | 0 |

EXPLAIN RATING:

2. ATTITUDE: The manner of acting, thinking or feeling which indicates one's disposition towards the Fire Service profession, the Department itself, and the performance of one's job.

HIGH		AVERAGE		LOW	
Exhibits an interest in his/her job assignment and continually seeks to improve job performance.	Accepts constructive criticism as integral to job performance and improves following criticism.	Exhibits objective work disposition and willingness to complete work assignments.	Reasonably cooperative in accepting work assignments and reasonably supportive of Dept. policies.	Consistently complains about Dept. policies and exhibits no interest in self improvement.	Exhibits a negative approach to work assignments and often acts without purpose.

RATING:

| 5 | 4 | 3 | 2 | 1 | 0 |

EXPLAIN RATING:

3. INITIATIVE: The ability to actively influence events rather than to passively accept them; the ability to conduct individual performance without direct supervision.

HIGH		AVERAGE		LOW	
Imaginative; often makes suggestions for positive change within the Dept.	Interested in his/her work with the ability to handle or begin work with little supervision.	Completes work assignments satisfactorily but may often require supervision to complete tasks.	Completes work assignments, but often relies on others to make decisions for him/her.	Rarely takes the lead in work assignments and refuses to accept responsibility for decision making.	Never initiates a task on his/her own and consistently relies upon supervision for work assignments.

RATING:
   5   4   3   2   1   0

EXPLAIN RATING:

4. DEMEANOR: Personal and professional bearing, including physical condition, neatness and grooming.

HIGH		AVERAGE		LOW	
Consistently presents a calm and professional image and is neat, confident, well groomed and physically fit.	Takes pride in Fire Service profession and him/herself is self-assured about ability to perform job assignment.	Maintains adequate bearing and physical condition and is reasonably self-assured.	Personal grooming standards are in conformance with Dept. standards.	Frequently unkempt when reporting for work assignments and presents poor image to public.	Sloppy in dress, personal hygiene and professional bearing and exhibits no pride in his/her profession.

RATING:
   5   4   3   2   1   0

EXPLAIN RATING:

5. INTERPERSONAL RELATIONS: The ability to interact professionally and amicably with individuals with whom the employee comes into contact in the performance of his/her assigned duties, including co-workers and the public in general.

HIGH		AVERAGE		LOW	
Inspires confidence and respect with all individuals and exerts extra effort to be friendly as well as fair and impartial in his/her judgment.	Works effectively within the group and is able to exercise self-control, patience and discretion when dealing with people.	Effective at his/her job assignment and maintains cordial relations with co-workers and the public.	Generally cheerful, personable and easy to work with.	Displays an abrasive attitude when dealing with people.	Insensitive to the needs of people.

RATING:

5	4	3	2	1	0

EXPLAIN RATING:

6. DEPENDABILITY: Predictable job performance and behavior, including attendance, promptness, acceptance of job responsibility, and reaction to stress, boredom and criticism.

HIGH		AVERAGE		LOW	
Self-reliant with excellent work habits and a responsible person who puts effort into his/her work and reacts well under pressure.	Reports to work regularly and on time and reacts well to stress and constructive criticism.	Attends work regularly and punctually, but does only the specific work assigned.	Maintains adequate work habits but is not too enthusiastic about his/her work assignments.	Unable to successfully handle more than one job assignment at a time, and often requires assistance from others.	Not reliable and consistently fails to properly follow instructions.

RATING:

5	4	3	2	1	0

EXPLAIN RATING:

7. ADAPTABILITY: Ability to alter one's behavior in order to adjust to varying situations or circumstances.

	HIGH		AVERAGE		LOW
Reacts extraordinarily well in stressful situations and able to control his/her own emotions.	Professional and versatile in handling work assignments.	Competently handles most stressful situations, but occasionally allows personal feelings to interfere.	Reasonably controlled and responsible under pressure.	Immature and allows personal affairs to interfere with response to work assignments.	Lacks self-control and unable to react well in stressful situations.

RATING:

5	4	3	2	1	0

EXPLAIN RATING:

8. COMMUNICATIONS: Firefighter is able to communicate through the use of written and verbal skills and ability to follow and understand written and verbal instructions.

	HIGH		AVERAGE		LOW
Articulates well both written and orally. Follows instructions extremely well.	Good ability to comprehend and relay info oral/written.	Presents facts generally in a logical manner as well as understanding said facts.	Weak on both facets written and oral (may come with experience).	Lacks ability communicating. Does not follow instructions well.	Totally unable to communicate or follow instructions.

RATING:

5	4	3	2	1	0

EXPLAIN RATING:

EVALUATION SUMMARY

—————

EVALUATOR

TOTAL SCORE (Sum of all ratings): _____

The completed evaluation must be presented and explained to the individual being evaluated.

———————————
SIGNATURE OF INDIVIDUAL BEING EVALUATED

8

Occupational Safety and Health

STEPHEN N. FOLEY

CHAPTER HIGHLIGHTS

- An overview of NFPA 1500, *Standard on Fire Department Occupational Safety and Health Program* (1992 Edition).
- The fire department occupational safety and health program as part of a jurisdiction's risk management plan.
- The roles and responsibilities within the fire department, and within the health and safety committee.
- Examples of implementing components of a safety and health program.

*T*HE ROLE OF THE fire service has changed dramatically in the last ten years. Some changes were influenced by external forces, while the impetus for others was the organization itself. All of the changes have increased the risks of the profession. The fire service now responds to hazardous material incidents, advanced emergency medical situations, high-angle rescue and confined-space rescue incidents, trench and collapse operations, underwater rescue, and more. It has been said that "When the experts panic, they call the fire department!" How true!

As the risks of the profession have increased, it has become appropriate to ask what level of risk is acceptable to you and to your department. This chapter explains the fundamentals of putting together a risk management program, including a health and safety program. As a necessary step, you, as a chief officer, need to identify what risks there are to your jurisdiction, and how you and your department can or should respond to them.

OVERVIEW OF NFPA 1500

Based on 15 years of data compilation and analysis by the National Fire Protection Association (NFPA), fire service personnel have averaged 115 to 120 fatalities a year, and approximately 100,000 occupationally related injuries. These statistics have been tracked by the United States Fire Administration (USFA), the International Association of Fire Fighters (IAFF), and other organizations. Their data parallel those of the NFPA (See Appendix).

While these statistics have been used by some to "glamorize" the dangers of the fire service, the process of trying to reduce deaths and injuries has begun. Statistically the fire service has associated insurance costs of more than $300 million dollars a year in worker's compensation claims, a sum the private sector would find intolerable.

In 1983 the NFPA began the process of forming a technical committee to consider a standard on fire department occupational health and safety programs. This committee included firefighters, both career and volunteer, fire chiefs, and equipment manufacturers. It also included attorneys, physicians, risk management professionals, and representatives from other associated fields. Among the organizations represented were the International Association of Fire Chiefs (IAFC), IAFF, National Volunteer Fire Council (NVFC), International Society of Fire Service Instructors (ISFSI), the Fire Marshals Association of North America (FMANA), and associated NFPA Sections. This committee has the largest fire service representation of any NFPA committee.

The committee began work on developing a document to address the health and safety concerns of municipal fire departments. There was no differentiation among career, volunteer, or combination departments. Initially, the only document available for the fire service was the Occupational Safety and Health Administration's (OSHA) Regulation CFR 1910.156 *Fire Brigades* which originally was designed for industrial fire brigades. At the time, the standard was being used for enforcement purposes, in some states for municipal fire departments, yet did not address some of the important issues of firefighter health and safety.

Over a four-year period, the committee worked with other NFPA technical committee: protective clothing and equipment, fire apparatus and equipment, training, and the professional qualifications committees. All addressed areas in other standards that affected firefighter health and safety. Standard 1500 was first issued by the NFPA in the summer of 1987.

Since then the committee has revised the standard periodically, through the standards-making process, a process that accepts input from any interested party, NFPA member or not, that submits either a proposal or comment. The five-year revision cycle ended in 1992, when the revised 1500 Standard was accepted and issued by NFPA's Standards Council in August 1992. It is known as NFPA 1500, *Standard on Fire Department Occupational Safety and Health Programs* (1992).

The original concept was for 1500 to be an umbrella document, that is, its chapters ultimately would become specific stand-alone documents. This process has grown to the point where these additional documents have specific standard numbers, and are overseen by their own task groups. These task groups in turn report to the full technical committee. The task groups include fire department incident management, infectious disease control for the fire service, medical requirements for firefighters, and fire department safety officer.

How does NFPA 1500 fit into a fire department's or jurisdiction's risk management plan?

Risk Management

An assessment of risk, or risk analysis, needs to be a comprehensive risk–versus–benefit process. When it has been completed, all parties involved (firefighters, supervisors, chief officers, and the community) need to know what is an acceptable risk at every level of the organization. Among the parameters to consider in the risk management process or model are identified community risks, i.e., a significant life safety problem, built-in protection systems, large commercial or industrial complexes, or the potential for transportation hazardous material accidents. Also considered are the services the fire department provides and staffing levels. Is the department career, volunteer, or combination?

Included in the analysis is task initiation time. Rather than simply looking at the department's overall response time; ask how long it takes for the personnel on scene to begin a task safely and efficiently. If one firefighter arrives in four minutes, and four arrive in six minutes, how is that figured into the analysis? The area of total risk management is a critical part of the equation when we speak of occupational safety and health for the fire service.

Putting this process together requires a commitment of time and personnel. One formula to put some reality into this process is to look at the components in this fashion:

- **Risk Identification.**
- **Resource Numbers.** Personnel and equipment, including mutual aid, automatic response.
- **Task Identification and Evaluation [tactical evolutions].** Number of people, and how long it takes to complete the task. For example, an engine company deploying a 1¾-inch handline, a truck company deploying a 35-foot ground ladder, or intubating a patient in respiratory arrest).

- **Identify Training Levels and Objectives.**
- **Consensus Risk Planning,** including other towns' departments, insurance carriers, outside agencies, and financial implications!

In some communities part or all of the community Comprehensive Emergency Management Plan (CEMP) can be used to identify risks in the community. Part of the CEMP is specific resource management identification for all agencies that may be needed. Agencies that may help you put your CEMP together could include your insurance carrier, the Federal Emergency Management Agency (FEMA) and its Emergency Management Institute (EMI), your state emergency management agency, the International Association of Fire Chiefs, and other professional risk management associations.

ORGANIZATIONAL STRUCTURE

The first step in developing an overall health and safety program is to create opportunities for all relevant parties to participate, including fire service personnel, insurance carriers, community officials, physicians, and risk management personnel. In fact, specific language in Chapter 2-4.3.1 states, **"It shall be the right of each member to be protected . . . and to participate or be represented in the research, development, implementation, and evaluation of the occupational health and safety program."** Involve all interested and expert groups in the overall program.

A planned program approach should identify specific goals and timelines to assure compliance with NFPA 1500. Built into the planning process should be timeframes for periodic reviews and updates, based on:

- when the standard is revised;
- changes in departmental policies, or procedures;
- new equipment;
- training requirements;
- municipal practices; and
- contractual requirements.

A budgetary process should be established that can be built into a department's fiscal and capital planning program. This commitment to the process will help to ensure its viability.

This working safety and health program document should be made available to all parties involved, and allow a process for all those affected to give their input. This can be accomplished in a number of ways. Some of the more successful programs use "quality circles" or a "total quality management program." Everyone, including all ranks, both career and volunteer personnel, and any organizational representation, such as firefighters' associations, union affiliation, or officers' association, has a right to representation on the committee.

This is also the time to identify the Authority Having Jurisdiction (AHJ). This is critical, especially for OSHA-regulated states, because OSHA is identified as the AHJ and it uses that enforcement authority. There are also states that have adopted parts of this document as enforceable legislation. This has given many departments cost-prohibitive guidelines that create problems for departmental and local planning processes. Experience shows that successful programs use the planned program approach to implement a health and safety plan.

Safety Program Manager/Safety Officer

Once the health and safety committee is established it must create a structure for the committee, and identify an organizational structure within the department. The structure of the committee should include a Safety Program Manager. This person may be a department Safety Officer, or someone with an appropriate health and safety background. Today there are qualified individuals who can fill this important role. NFPA 1521, *Standard for Fire Department Safety Officer,* recently was revised and reissued. This document identifies areas of competency, and assists in identifying the appropriate requisite background for Incident Safety Officer. The National Fire Academy has developed two courses that address the roles and responsibilities of safety officer/manager: *Incident Safety Officer* and *Health Safety Officer. Incident Safety Officer* deals with those responsibilities under the command staff of incident management and what the role entails at the incident scene. *Health Safety Officer* looks at the roles of the health and safety program manager. It introduces the application of risk management and how it is a key component of the health and safety program. These two courses cover the performance objectives of NPFA 1521.

The Fire Department Safety Officers Association (FDSOA) is another group that is working toward the common goals of safety officers. This organization provides another avenue to assist with the networking process; it offers training programs for safety officers, and training programs in how to implement NFPA 1500.

Once the committee has been established and starts to work, it should look into the community to see if there are any companion programs already operating. In some cases, there may be significant cost savings by dove-tailing into existing programs. In some communities there is an overall community health and safety committee that has representation from each municipal or county department. There will obviously be areas that are pertinent only to the fire service or law enforcement, but there are many areas that are important to all departments. It is important to note that the integral parts of the health and safety program can, and usually do, become intertwined.

Training

The backbone of any health and safety program begins with training and education. The 1500 committee included an equivalency statement in the 1992 edition that says **"the AHJ shall be permitted to approve an equivalent level of qualifications for the requirements specified in the training chapter sections, provided that the fire department has technical documentation to demonstrate equivalency."** These levels shall secure as nearly equivalent training, education, competency, and safety as possible and shall require that training, education and competency be commensurate with those functions the members are expected to perform as specified in your organization statement and the training statement, which are both required. This training is to be documented, and in no case shall the equivalency afford less competency of members or less safety of members. This became an issue for the committee in 1987, when users confused the issues of training and certification. Training is an ongoing process that is based on standards required by the AHJ. Certification is documented completion and testing to a nationally recognized standard. The two are not synonymous, and this was an effort by the committee to recognize those training programs that met the professional qualification standards, yet did not require certification.

The need for training is self-evident in our profession and it is with respect to training that safety is logically discussed. The training environment should be made as safe as possible. The training program needs to address all levels within the department. These typically are identified through the various professional qualification standards, and spell out various training and education levels within each standard.

The professional qualification standards recently have been revised to include performance objectives applicable to today's profession. These include, but are not limited to, Firefighter Levels I and II, which include Hazardous Materials Awareness training at Level I, and Hazardous Materials Operational Training at Level II. The medical requirements previously contained in NFPA 1001, *Standard on Fire Fighter Professional Qualifications,* now are included in a new standard, NFPA 1582, *Standard on Medical Requirements for Fire Fighters,* which will be discussed under the medical requirements of a health and safety program.

Fire Instructor

Also included under the training requirements of the standard is a section on instructors, which states that they shall be trained to the minimum of Fire Instructor I as outlined in NFPA 1041. It also says that training and education shall be conducted by qualified individuals. This allows the department to use trainers who may specialize in certain areas, yet are not fire department instructors, such as outside EMS personnel, building trade individuals, railroad safety personnel, and anyone who can assist a department to be better trained, with safer firefighters.

Structural Firefighting Training

Given past and recent injury and fatality statistics, we can see the importance of firefighter training. This includes a minimum of 24 hours of structural firefighting training annually, or 10 monthly structural firefighting training sessions. It is ironic that the more we stress and promote public education and prevention, the more training we need for structural firefighting! In many areas the "experience" side of the firefighting equation is diminishing. Live fire training is one vehicle available to departments to assist in filling this gap. These training evolutions shall comply with NFPA 1403, *Standard on Live Fire Training Evolutions in Structures.* The need for realistic live fire training is important, and past accidents involving firefighter injuries and fatalities highlight the need for the strict application of this standard. Associated with issues of live fire training is the application of, and training for, your Incident Command System (ICS). This opportunity allows you to "practice" your system, including accountability procedures, communication models, and supervisory training for company-level supervisors and incident commanders.

Fire Officer Training

Training needs in other areas also must be stressed. The fire service has, in the past, promoted personnel and then sometimes provided additional training in the necessary skills. The recently revised NFPA 1021, *Standard for Fire Officer Professional Qualifications,* offers a menu approach that outlines performance objectives for fire officers. This approach allows jurisdictions to decide to which level of the Standard they want their personnel trained. These performance objectives may be used as a career ladder by both paid and volunteer officers. The areas outlined in the standard address performance objectives from first-line supervisor to administrator. While the officer in a smaller department frequently may function as a front-line supervisor, he also must have an appropriate level of knowledge of the administration and management of the department. A department or individual may use the standard to establish each level, one through four, for promotion or to equate each level of 1021 to a specific rank or responsibility.

Today we stress the need for training before promotion. Supervisory positions require many skills, none of which is more important than dealing with human resource management. The "First-Line Supervisor Training Program," developed by the City of New York Fire Department, is an excellent example of this type of training. The National Fire Academy offers a number of supervisory-level courses that have a direct impact on the training of present and future officers. The one program that has gained the most attention is the "Executive Fire Officer Program." This four-part program is an in-depth curriculum that includes case studies, research papers, group dynamics training, and projects. The program has received graduate-level credit recommendations from the American Council on Education.

In looking at the training requirements for any fire department, it is essential to look at the roles that fire service personnel fill in the community. This identification process of training levels and requirements will be a part of your risk management assessment. This increases personnel safety, in that personnel are not put in situations for which they have not been trained. In kind, it also tells the jurisdiction, "this is the level to which the department is trained," as identified, through analysis of risk, time, money, and personnel. Personnel must be trained to address perceived needs, and members who perform in any special operations must be trained at the appropriate level. These roles could be:

- hazardous material technician or specialist;
- specialized rescue (water, high-angle rescue, confined space);
- emergency medical services (BLS & ALS);
- code enforcement/plan review/fire prevention; and
- public educator.

Continuing Education and Training

Training programs need to be updated and kept current. The continuing education requirements within a jurisdiction may vary; what doesn't vary is the need for the most advanced training to keep up with the rigors of the profession. A competently trained and competently supervised firefighter is a safer firefighter. State and local training academies should have implemented a continuing education program that is directed not only toward basic skills training, but also ongoing training programs to increase professionalism.

Vehicles and Equipment

The advances in apparatus and firefighter equipment have been enormous over the last few years. The safety needs of the members of a fire department who are responding to, operating at, and returning from an incident, in addition to training, are affected by the apparatus on which they respond and the equipment they use.

Today's fire apparatus are safer in a number of aspects, but these technological advances were made, unfortunately, as a result of firefighter fatalities and injuries. The apparatus manufacturers and NFPA committees worked to study the nature of these incidents.

Their primary goal was to make a safer vehicle for firefighters. Where specific safety improvements were identified, it was incumbent on the technical committee to include them in the standard. The 1500 Standard and 1900 series of apparatus standards are identical when it comes to the specifics of safety for fire apparatus. Among the specifics included are:

- a belted and seated position for all who are riding on the apparatus;
- totally enclosed cabs; and
- proper and secure storage for all tools and equipment.

When specifying new apparatus you must state how many people will ride on the apparatus; there must be an enclosed seated and belted position for each person. This does not exclude commercial cab apparatus. If you have only two or three personnel responding, they can ride in a commercial cab without any alterations or additions.

The driver/operator or engineer shall be licensed for the type of vehicle driven. NFPA 1002, *Standard for Fire Apparatus Driver/Operator Professional Qualifications,* which at this time is being updated, is an excellent tool for establishing training qualifications. Volunteer Firemen's Insurance Services (VFIS) of York, Pennsylvania, offers an excellent Emergency Vehicle Operator's Course, as does Liberty Mutual Insurance. Other major insurance companies and regional safety councils (under the National Safety Council) also offer vehicle training programs. The Federal Emergency Management Agency offers a training program titled **"Emergency Vehicle Driver Training."** One of the benefits of this training could be a reduction in department insurance rates. These savings could be used for purchases of equipment, protective clothing, or training materials and the savings also could be a selling point for administrators, boards of engineers, or commissioners. This promotes your proactive posture as a chief.

The driver shall know all the applicable emergency response procedures and how to apply them in driving situations. Are your personnel licensed to drive the sizes of apparatus that your department has? Are their licenses up to date. Are any under suspension or revocation? These are questions that will be asked during an accident investigation. It is far better to have the answers and documentation beforehand. Remember, if your apparatus does not arrive, your mission is doomed to failure!

Some of the causes of apparatus accidents are:

* speed;
* improper training;
* improperly maintained apparatus; and
* failure to follow applicable laws

Incorporated into the current version of NFPA 1500 are the recent National Transportation Safety Board (NTSB) recommendations relating to railroad crossings, engine retarders, and brake-limiting devices. (See USFA Report #FA-104 dated September 1991, and NTSB report #5453 NTSB/SIR-91/01 dated March 19, 1991). The driver and the officer in the right front seat are equally responsible for the personnel on the apparatus, for getting to the scene, and for returning safely.

In discussions of apparatus purchase and design, decisions must be made on where people can ride, and where and how they can ride to nonemergency department functions. Specific attention must be paid to:

* travel in EMS vehicles;
* hose loading;
* details of parades and funerals; and
* wildland firefighting.

The committee stated **"That members actively performing emergency medical care, in an ambulance or rescue unit, while the vehicle is in motion shall be secured to the vehicle by a seatbelt or a safety harness designed for occupant restraint . . . to the extent consistent with the effective provision of emergency medical care."** This section also addresses wildland firefighting. It strictly prohibits members from riding on the outside of a brush rig, in some type of pump and roll configuration.

Inspection and Maintenance

Inspection and maintenance of the apparatus, tools, and equipment are safety items that are included as part of a routine preventive maintenance program. Equipment shall not be placed back in service until all noted safety items are checked and made operational. Specific NFPA and American National Standards Institute (ANSI) standards are referenced for the inspection and testing of air, hose, ladders (ground and aerial), and pumps. Most departments are performing these functions in an annual program, but they need to make sure that inspections and tests are documented. All significant maintenance and repairs must be done by personnel who are trained and qualified. The person who inspects or repairs your aerial or pumper has the lives of your personnel in his hands. There is no room today for the backyard mechanic to be maintaining a piece of emergency apparatus. As mentioned earlier in this chapter, this is an area your insurance company or carrier would consider to be effective risk management. The money spent on preventive maintenance is well spent compared to the liabilities which might be incurred as a result of an improperly maintained vehicle involved in an accident.

New Apparatus and Equipment

Included in this chapter of 1500 is language that says that any new equipment purchased shall meet applicable NFPA standards. Your insurance carrier or apparatus manufacturer can assist in outlining a documented program for you to follow. There also may be specific bidding laws in your jurisdiction that need to be followed. The purchasing agent, town accountant, procurement officer, or other jurisdiction officials should be able to assist in this process.

Protective Clothing and Equipment

What could be yellow, red, black, brown, or white? One answer is protective clothing. The work and testing done by manufacturers and fire service personnel have focused on providing the safest, lightest, and most comfortable firefighter protective clothing. This protective ensemble includes a coat, protective trousers, gloves, boots, helmet, protective hood, PASS alarm, and SCBA. Each of the components that make up the ensemble has separate and applicable standards. These individual standards are referenced in 1500, and are listed as part of the health and safety document. This ensemble shall be NFPA compliant; therefore, if you had compliant clothing when it was purchased, it meets the requirements of 1500. The standard requires that when you replace your protective clothing, you must upgrade to the current level of the applicable standard. The way clothing and equipment interface is also important; this is addressed in the standard and was an important concept of the PROJECT FIRES report issued by the IAFF and the U.S. Fire Administration. The past practice of using hand-me-down protective clothing, and noncompliant clothing is no longer acceptable.

Specifying and Purchasing Protective Clothing and Equipment

In purchasing new protective clothing there are many considerations to review and to evaluate. The changes and improvements to protective clothing are taking place quickly. The end user of the products—the **firefighter**—should be involved in establishing type, design, and wear-testing process. This process involves forming a committee of firefighters, officers, the safety officer, and the chief or his designee. The wear-testing process allows for firefighter input into what works well and, more importantly, what does not! The committee then can look at costs, type, style, manufacturers, and any other important factors in developing specifications. The protective clothing and equipment standards now require third-party certification. No longer can you rely on the manufacturer's word that the clothing you specified meets the standard. Labeling is included that states that a third party, i.e., Underwriters Laboratories, Factory Mutual, or another designated testing agency certifies that in fact the product meets the standard.

The heat levels that build up between the human body and the protective clothing are an important consideration. Studies currently are being done to look at the increases in body core temperatures, heart rate, blood pressure, and other physiological effects on the body. These factors become increasingly important as we study the amount of work firefighters are performing, the conditions under which they are performing them, and their level of physical condition. The climatic conditions in which firefighters operate vary across the world, an important consideration in specifying protective clothing.

Station Uniforms

Another area that has generated a great deal of discussion is what is worn under protective clothing. Documentation has shown that certain clothing may actually fail and melt onto the firefighter's body, with no damage to his protective clothing. Some synthetic and polyester materials will degrade to the point that they will melt. The clothing worn shall not contribute to the thermal instability of the protective clothing garments. If a fire department requires that station work uniforms be worn, they shall meet the requirements of NFPA 1975, *Standard on Station/Work Uniforms for Fire Fighters*. This standard also provides protection for personnel operating in the fire station environment. What do you do with volunteer personnel, people who sleep at the station, and personnel who respond off duty from home or work? Institute an educational program to advise members of the potential problems associated with wearing certain clothing under their protective garments. An educated firefighter is an informed firefighter, better able to make appropriate choices.

The standard also has addressed firefighter safety as it relates to other clothing we may be required to wear. These include:

- NFPA 1976, *Standard on Protective Clothing for Proximity Fire Fighting;* NFPA 1977, *Standard on Protective Clothing—Wildland fire Fighting;* and
- NFPA 1999, *Standard on Protective Clothing for Emergency Medical Operations.*

It also addresses chemical protective clothing, including vapor-protective clothing, liquid splash protective suits, and support functions protective garments. These referenced standards are included because we have taken on these additional roles and personnel need to be protected. No areas have received more attention than hazardous materials, and emergency medical services. Fire departments that respond to EMS-related calls, either first responder, BLS, or ALS, find that these calls account for anywhere from 50 to 75 percent of their responses. Obviously we need to care for our people in all the potential situations to which they respond.

There should be an ongoing inspection and maintenance program for protective clothing. The life of the clothing will vary depending on the amount of wear and tear in donning and doffing, and in what environment it is worn. The 1500 standard references other NFPA standards, as well as the manufacturers' recommendations for proper care and maintenance. The technical committee has started to work with manufacturers of garments, and manufacturers of materials to develop a new document that addresses the care, inspection, maintenance, and removal from service of protective clothing. Health and safety considerations for departments to review include the transporting of protective clothing in a personal vehicle, and taking it to a firefighter's home. If it is not clean, what potential contaminants is the firefighter taking home, and subjecting family and friends to? Departments today have a number of options for cleaning their protective clothing and equipment, including in-house systems that use commercial washing and drying equipment, contracting with a commercial laundry firm, or using a national firm that also does repair and cleaning. A number of these companies also will set up a protective clothing loaner program with 24-hour service, so that while your gear is being cleaned and repaired, clothing is available for personnel to use.

In the area of equipment, we must look at SCBA, ropes and harnesses, hardware, and PASS alarms. These areas also are covered by NFPA standards. SCBA today must meet NFPA 1981, *Standard on Open-Circuit Self-Contained Breathing Apparatus for Fire Fighters,* and be NIOSH/MSHA certified. This standard also is referenced in NFPA 1404, *Standard for a Fire Department Self-Contained Breathing Apparatus Program,* another area that promotes the need to use training as a safety factor. We also must consider quality control of breathing air. Air shall be tested quarterly and shall meet applicable ANSI/

CGA G7.1, *Commodity Specification for Air.* This applies in all cases, whether the fire department compresses its own air, or purchases it from a service facility.

The issue of facial hair also is discussed in the standard as it pertains to the issue of interference with the ability to get a proper facepiece seal. No facial hair that interferes is allowed. This is stressed in both the manufacturer's warranty, and in the OSHA regulations. There also must be ongoing maintenance, inspection, and testing programs as part of the respiratory inspection program. The advances made in SCBA are for the protection of firefighters. Past high incident rates of firefighter lung cancer can be directly attributed to the lack of use of SCBA. Fire departments should have mandatory mask rules, not mandatory bottle rules, and enforce them. Firefighters who may operate in a hazardous environment should be wearing their masks, not just carrying bottles on their backs. An excellent SOP is "anywhere a firefighter may come in contact with a hazardous environment, he shall wear and use SCBA." Unfortunately, we still see pictures in all of the trade journals of firefighters who are not wearing their protective clothing and equipment.

The need for hearing protection and eye protection is also part of a safety program. The long-term effects of open cab apparatus, air horns, and loud sirens exact a toll on firefighter hearing. Hearing protection is included for individuals who are riding on apparatus, and who work around loud equipment. A hearing protection program should be a component of the fire department health and safety program. An excellent document, published by the U.S. Fire Administration in conjunction with the International Association of Fire Fighters, is *Hearing Conservation Program Manual.* It discusses the hearing process, occupational hearing loss, standards for noise exposure, noise control practices, and other areas. It outlines a step-by-step approach to reducing excessive noise exposure to fire and EMS personnel. The publication is free and available from the USFA. In many communities the local school system provides hearing testing for school children. As a cost savings to your department, contact local school authorities and ask to have firefighters tested.

Eye protection shall be provided, both at the station and at the incident scene. The eyeshields attached to helmets may or may not provide adequate protection based on what type they are. Helmet eye protection may protect only portions of the eye and face. The user should receive training that addresses the limitations of that protection, and must use primary eye protection for the specific hazard. In the ANSI Z 88.5 *Practices for Respiratory Protection for the Fire Service*, primary eye and face protection requirements are spelled out. These include the full facepiece of SCBA, but may need to be more specific for a particular hazard.

The use of protective clothing and equipment is essential to our ability to do our job safely and efficiently. The mind set of previous generations needs to be banished to the past. The protective clothing and equipment available today are state-of-the-art in safety. The requirements to wear it are for your safety and the safety of your personnel.

EMERGENCY OPERATIONS

In looking at the 1993 NFPA statistics for firefighter fatalities, 54.5 percent of career firefighter deaths, and 40.0 percent of volunteer firefighter deaths occurred on the fireground. Operations in dwellings and apartments are particularly hazardous. Statistics also show us that 58.3 percent of career, and 27.3 percent of volunteer fireground deaths occurred in those occupancies in 1993. We need to do a better job of protecting our personnel at the types of responses we handle routinely. Your safety program needs to address the types of incidents to which you respond, and the hazards associated with them. This risk assessment is a function of your department risk management process. A safety program should incorporate factors that will make the emergency scene a safer environment in which to operate. What follows are a number of different areas that may or may not already be addressed in your department.

The need for adequate personnel resources to perform safe and effective operations is a hotly debated topic. In the original 1987 version of the 1500 Standard it was stated that "the fire department shall provide an adequate number of personnel to safely conduct emergency scene operations." This same language is included in the 1992 revision of the standard. The need to perform only those operations that we can do safely, with the number of personnel on scene, is the reason for that language. The standard outlines this further in the areas of risk versus benefit in the risk management section. Many studies have shown the correlation of firefighter injuries and fatalities to the number of on-scene personnel. These studies include those conducted by the IAFF and other fire service organizations.

Other factors that have a direct impact on firefighter safety at incident scene operations include incident management, accountability, rapid intervention crews, use of a safety officer, risk management, management of civil disturbances, firefighter rehabilitation, and post-incident analysis.

Incident scene management (ISM) is the overall key to scene safety. There has been a strong push to train fire service personnel in hazardous material incident scene management. These requirements have been outlined in the OSHA hazardous materials regulations, and are being enforced by OSHA. It is obviously important to use a management system at hazardous materials incidents, but it is equally important to use incident scene management for every incident to which we respond. In 1987 a task force of the NFPA 1500 committee developed NFPA 1561, *Standard for Fire Department Incident Management System.* Issued in 1990, and currently in the revision process, it is a generic version of incident management which identifies the key elements of a system. Proper incident scene management is a key factor in firefighter

NFPA 1500

Fire Department Occupational Safety and Health

1992 Edition

Reference: 1-5, 6-4.1.1*, and A-6-4.1.1
TIA 92-1 (NFPA 1500)

Pursuant to Section 15 of the NFPA Regulations Governing Committee Projects, the National Fire Protection Association has issued the following Tentative Interim Amendment to NFPA 1500, *Standard on Fire Department Occupational Safety and Health Program*, 1992 edition. The TIA was processed by the Fire Service Occupational Safety and Health Committee and was issued by the Standards Council on July 23, 1993, with an effective date of August 20, 1993.

A Tentative Interim Amendment is tentative because it has not been processed through the entire standards-making procedures. It is interim because it is effective only between editions of the standard. A TIA automatically becomes a proposal of the proponent for the next edition of the standard; as such, it then is subject to all of the procedures of the standards-making process.

1. Add the following new definition to Section 1-5:

Working Structural Fire. Any fire that requires the use of a 1½-inch or larger fire attack hose line and that also requires the use of self-contained breathing apparatus for members entering the hazardous area.

2. Add the following new 6-4.1.1 and A-6-4.1.1 to read as follows:*

6-4.1.1* At least four members shall be assembled before initiating interior fire fighting operations at a working structural fire. All fire fighting operations shall be conducted in accordance with 6-4.3 and 6-4.4.

Exception: If, upon arrival at the scene, members find an imminent life-threatening situation where immediate action may prevent the loss of life or serious injury, such action shall be permitted with less than four persons on the scene, when conducted in accordance with the provisions of Section 6-2.

A-6-4.1.1 The assembling of four members for the initial fire attack can be accomplished in many ways. The fire department should determine the manner in which it plans to assemble members in its response plan. The four members assembled for initial fire fighting operations can include any combination of members arriving separately at the incident.

Members who arrive on the scene of a working structural fire prior to the assembling of four persons may initiate exterior actions in preparation for an interior attack. These may include, but are not limited to, actions such as the establishment of a water supply, the shutting off of utilities, the placement of ladders, the laying of the attack line to the entrance of the structure, or exposure protection. If members are going to initiate actions that would involve entering of a structure because of an imminent life-threatening situation where immediate action may prevent the loss of life or serious injury, and four members are not yet on the scene, the members should carefully evaluate the level of risk that they would be exposed to by taking such actions. If it is determined that the situation warrants such action, incoming companies should be notified so that they will be prepared to provide necessary support and backup upon their arrival.

Such action is intended to apply only to those rare and extraordinary circumstances when, in the member's professional judgment, the specific instance requires immediate action to prevent the loss of life or serious injury and four persons have not yet arrived on the fireground.

health and safety. Statistics have shown how many firefighters are injured or killed at incident scenes and raise such questions as whether there was someone in command. Were there sufficient resources? Was there an accountability system in place? These are all critical factors in our ability to survive at an incident scene. The system is predicated on each person doing his assigned function. This has to begin with the Incident Commander providing the functions of command. In most of the fire service, this task initially falls on the first-arriving firefighter or company officer. The person who fills that function must assure that a strategy is developed, tactical objectives assigned to support the strategy, and sufficient resources are available for the tasks. "The first five minutes is worth the next five hours," is a well-known truth. If you look at incident scene management and how successful or unsuccessful the outcome was, it is often because of the initial decisions!

Risk management was mentioned briefly at the beginning of this chapter. Risk management is a function that should be performed at every incident scene, and should be an integral component of a department's incident management system. This is a priority as it relates to the Incident Commander's strategy development, and also needs to be part of the company officer's plan for accomplishing his specific tactical objective. His ability to evaluate the limits of acceptable and unacceptable risks for members who are accountable to him is an important safety consideration. This process of risk analysis is ongoing, as the supervisor evaluates how he and his crew are performing each tactical objective assigned. Do they have the training to do the task? Do they have sufficient resources? Can it be done safely? Is it part of a coordinated operation? The successful supervisor understands and supports the overall strategy of the operation, and how the tactics assigned affect that strategy.

Another key component of any well-run incident management system is a personnel accountability system. This system should have the capability of tracking personnel, both by location and by function. The system does not have to be expensive or elaborate. There are "passport systems" which include Velcro tags attached to passports where crews are kept intact and use the passport to get from one place to another. The actual passport is a hardened piece of plastic that uses Velcro to attach the nametag to it. These can be carried on apparatus, or by the Incident Commander, to form crews or companies to perform a tactical objective. A system can be as simple as a brass or plastic tag assigned to each fire department member. These are then attached to a board or clip to account for each individual at the incident scene. The system should be used in conjunction with some type of tactical worksheet. Remember, "the palest ink is better than the clearest memory." When you are assigning tactical objectives to crews and mutual aid companies, and you are rotating crews through rehabilitation, you must have an effective system to record the information. The Incident Commander is responsible for overall personnel accountability at the incident. This reflects back to training, because personnel must understand how to operate within the management system. Vince Lombardi once said, "practice like you are going to play." Use your system at every incident, include it in training, and it will become second nature, part of the routine.

There are incidents to which we respond that have the potential to escalate into something beyond our normal scope, incidents that are not routine. These incidents require different operating criteria, including the need for adequate numbers of personnel who are properly trained and supervised. The span of control is normally 5 personnel to 1 supervisor. However, in high-hazard operations, this number should be reduced to 3 or 2 to 1. Members who are operating in a hazardous area must operate in teams of two. There must be at least one team member outside the hazardous area but in close proximity, who maintains contact via radio, lifeline, or visual contact. That standby member may be doing other tasks, but maintains constant communication with the team in the hazardous area. This is required for the initial stages of the operation. The purpose of this individual's role is to initiate rescue of the team members if required. If additional teams have been assigned, then the incident moves beyond the "initial stage" of operation, necessitating "rapid intervention crews" or 'RICs'." Included also in well-managed emergency operations is the highest level of emergency medical care available. These requirements are included in NFPA 473, *Standard for Competencies for EMS Personnel Responding to Hazardous Materials Incidents.* At other types of incidents the IC can evaluate which level of EMS is appropriate, but nothing less than basic level life support, with transport capabilities available, should be provided.

Rapid Intervention Crews

In the past, one of the primary responsibilities of a rescue company has been to rescue fire department members. For departments which operate rescue companies, that is still true but, unfortunately, not all departments have a separate rescue company. From a health and safety standpoint, we can assess all the risks, gather all the information possible, take all the precautions, but, as we know, Murphy's Law can still come into play. For an Incident Commander, one of the worst nightmares is for a crew to call on the radio or sound an emergency signal indicating that it is trapped, or has a member missing. For incidents which expand beyond those initial stages, we need to have rapid intervention crews available for member rescue. RICs must be fully equipped with the appropriate protective clothing, SCBA, protective equipment, and any specialized rescue equipment based on the specifics of the ongoing operation. Every incident scene will present different requirements for RICs, and the Incident Commander needs to have flexibility given the assigned personnel; in all cases, however, they must be ready to redeploy as a RIC. In any high-hazard or special operation, a minimum of one RIC should be standing by.

Incident Scene Rehabilitation

The term rehabilitation or "rehab" is another area addressed under incident scene management. Physical abilities can be overtaxed, and fire and rescue personnel operate under all kinds of different conditions. Our physical capabilities, weather conditions, and the tasks we are performing all have a cumulative effect on how long we can operate. Even with state-of-the-art SCBA, and protective clothing, personnel still need to rehydrate and cool down or warm up. Included as part of rehab should be medical monitoring, at least at the basic life support level. The difference between heat exhaustion and heat stroke may be very small. As an IC you must plan for adequate personnel to rotate crews in and out of the hazardous environment. This is another integral part of the incident management plan. A tired firefighter is much more likely to get hurt. Take the steps beforehand to minimize those possibilities.

For many years there have been concerns about the roles and responsibilities of the fire service in civil disturbances. The fire service must develop SOPs for assuring member safety during responses to civil disturbances, hostage activities, violent crimes, drug situations, and other law-enforcement-type calls. The need for interagency training, and cooperation is imperative in these situations. It is the responsibility of the Incident Commander to judge the risk, and not jeopardize his personnel. There are fire departments that routinely respond with law enforcement SWAT Teams, or other specialized units. Those members need specialized training in their roles and responsibilities. These problems are not limited to big-city operations; civil disturbances and violent crime can occur in communities of any size.

Emergency operations have always been used as opportunities for learning, but these learning environments, and the lessons they teach, can be very expensive. One of the best features in the magazine *WNYF (With New York Fire)* is the "Lessons Learned" articles. Backstep analysis and critiques, and more formalized ones at the company, battalion, or departmental level, can provide any department with local lessons learned. There should be a comprehensive review of what was done right, what went wrong, and how overall operations can be improved through training, standard operating procedures, and other factors which affect personnel health and safety. There should be a standard format for investigating those incidents where there are injuries or fatalities. The IAFC Health and Safety Committee has developed a set of guidelines for use in investigating firefighter injuries and fatalities. This document has incorporated ideas and concepts from FDNY, Phoenix, L.A. City, and other departments. Another task force of the NFPA 1500 technical committee is considering developing a standard along the same format as the IAFC's, using the IAFC document as a foundation.

Facility Safety

Fire stations must comply with all the applicable building, health, safety, and fire codes. It is hypocritical for us to inspect facilities in the community for fire and safety compliance, and yet not enforce these regulations in our facilities. Among the basics required in each fire station are smoke detectors, required fire ratings, smoke-free environments, exhaust ventilation systems, and facilities for disinfecting equipment and supplies. Sprinklers should be installed.

Your safety program should outline areas to protect firefighters from infectious disease. There must be designated areas and equipment for cleaning emergency medical equipment, protective clothing, and other protective equipment. This designated cleaning area shall be physically separated from areas used for cooking, sleeping, and personal hygiene, and separate from the EMS cleaning area. Personal hygiene guidelines cover hand washing, clean restroom facilities, and grooming recommendations. An excellent guideline to use to address these safety concerns is NFPA 1581, *Standard on Fire Department Infection Control Program,* and the U.S. Fire Administration's *Guide to Developing and Managing an Emergency Service Infection Control Program* (FA-112) March 1992.

Looking ahead, it would be proactive to require that all new facilities be sprinklered and to add sprinklers when more than 50 percent of the current structure is remodeled. This is not currently required, but the fire service must set the example for others by installing sprinklers in its buildings. This is another area of possible insurance savings, and a great example of risk management. When a fire station and equipment are destroyed in a fire, which does in fact happen, it has a negative effect on the entire community. What better way to send a positive message than by installing sprinklers in all new fire stations and considering retrofitting sprinkler protection in existing facilities.

Medical and Physical

The medical requirements for firefighting previously were included as part of NFPA 1001, *Standard for Fire Fighter Professional Qualifications.* These requirements originally were taken from the military, but never updated. In 1987 the 1500 committee formed a subcommittee with fire department occupational doctors and personnel from the 1001 committee to establish medical requirements for firefighters. This committee produced a new document, NFPA 1582, *Standard on Medical Requirements for Fire Fighters,* issued in August 1992. The 1582 document developed by this group broke the requirements down into A and B categories. The A requirements were items that would cause immediate medical concern, e.g., not hiring or providing for medical dismissal, or non-structural firefighting assignment while the B category provided specifics for looking at the medical problem, with the AHJ deciding if another opinion or a second medical evaluation would be required. This document is considered both for entry-level and ongoing medical maintenance. Written with input from fire department doctors, it includes a set of guidelines and explanatory material for the general practitioner who may conduct your physical exams. When this document was being written, the Americans with Disabilities Act (ADA) was being promulgated, and the requirements of this law were taken into consideration. It is not yet known to what extent the ADA will be used in hiring for our profession although many disabled persons are already employed as dispatchers and in other positions. The standard calls for an entry-level physical exam and ongoing medical evaluation at no cost to the firefighter.

In implementing this part of a safety program, some avenues of assistance to pursue include an ongoing community medical program (county medical association), physicians or medical facilities, and your insurance carrier.

Given that heart attacks are the number one cause of firefighter fatalities, there is a continuing need to promote a healthful lifestyle that includes medical evaluations, proper nutrition, and exercise. Members who engage in emergency operations shall be evaluated and certified annually as meeting the physical requirements. If a member is unable to meet these requirements, there should be a rehabilitation component built into the program.

Physical fitness programs should be designed based on firefighting functions. This structured program shall require the participation of all members. There are a number of local colleges that may be able to assist the fire department in designing a program. Some departments use the local health club, or even the local YMCA or YWCA to assist with program development. The program should include aerobic and cardiovascular workouts, monitored weight reduction programs, and nutritional information for a proper diet. It also should include an ongoing strength training regimen that tones and strengthens the most commonly used muscle areas. The focus should be on helping the firefighter to maintain a healthy lifestyle, both on and off duty, and to live longer.

This program should include the services of a fire department physician. Preferably the physician should have a background in occupational health and safety, or in emergency medicine. This person should be a key member of the department's occupational health and safety committee. The department physician also should oversee the confidential health database, which includes information on medical evaluations, physical performance testing, any exposure forms, and any inoculations or vaccinations against contagious diseases.

The program should assist in rehabilitation after injuries or illnesses. The bottom line is to get the firefighter physically able, if at all possible, to return to full active duty. In all aspects the primary focus is to maintain a healthy, comfortable, and productive life during and after service with the fire department. An excellent reference book for all these areas is *Worker Fitness and Risk Evaluations* edited by Jay S. Himmelstein, M.D., M.P.H. and Glenn S. Pransky, M.D., M.P.H.

Member Assistance Program

The stressful lifestyles of today can affect members of the fire department family. These stresses occur not only on the job, but during off-duty hours as well. Firefighters have always looked out for one another. That kind of concern is part of a member assistance program. This may be part of a community-wide Employee Assistance Program (EAP) carried through the medical insurance carrier, county mental health association, or visiting nurses association. There is no requirement in your safety program to have an exclusive EAP, but you must provide your members access to a program. In order for this program to be successful, members must be assured of confidentiality. This program should be outlined for an employee when hired.

Alcohol or substance abuse, stress, and family problems have a direct effect on a firefighter, and on his ability to work safely. If a firefighter cannot perform safely, it affects him individually, and the entire crew as well.

A members' assistance program can be monitored by a county mental health group, the local chapter of Alcoholics Anonymous, or other appropriate organizations that provide human resource counseling. The program is designed to assist members and their families in dealing with any type of crisis that affects their ability to perform as firefighters. There must be a simple and confidential way for members and their immediate families to access the program. The primary focus should be on assisting people in getting their lives back to normal. There must be written policies and procedures to identify appropriate and effective ways to assist members.

Critical Incident Stress

Another process that fire departments and other emergency services have used is the post-incident stress debriefing. In some cases it is identified as a Critical Incident Stress Debriefing (CISD) for incidents that involve mass casualties, fatalities that involve children or fire department members, and other situations that affect firefighter physical or psychological well-being. There are many departmental or regional CISD teams available. It is critical to recognize the symptoms of critical incident stress and to get help promptly for the people affected. Careers have been destroyed or lost because members could not cope with a stressful situation. The ability to react in future situations may depend on the type of stress reduction and assistance they receive.

Finally, there should be a smoking cessation program. In addition to smoke-free stations, diesel exhaust systems, and the mandatory use of SCBA, there should be assistance for members who want to quit smoking. Many jurisdictions today require new members to sign a statement that they will not use tobacco products on or off duty. In the Commonwealth of Massachusetts it is directly tied to the Presumptive Cancer Law, and the Pension Reform Act. This covers career and volunteer personnel alike.

My good friend and mentor Chief Alan Brunacini of the Phoenix Fire Department has said, "the fire service has suffered the most severe occupational discrimination as it relates to health and safety." Our job as fire chiefs is to lead the fight, support the cause, and inform the people who run the cities and towns that the safety and health of our personnel is our number one priority. "Let's keep safe out there!"

APPENDIX

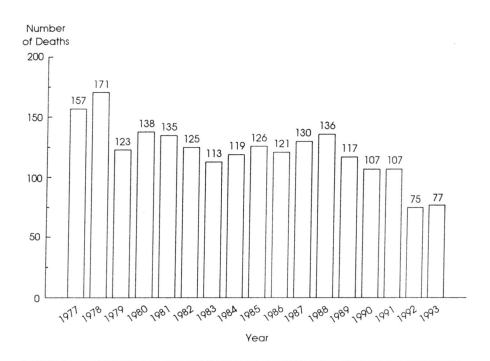

Figure 8-1. On-Duty Firefighter Deaths 1977-1993

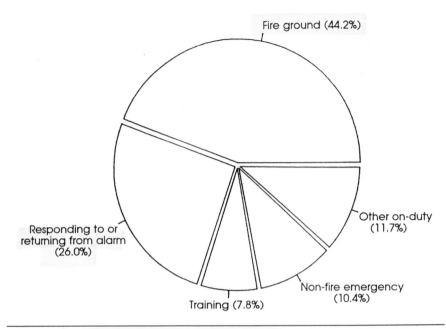

Figure 8-2. Firefighter Deaths by Type of Duty 1993

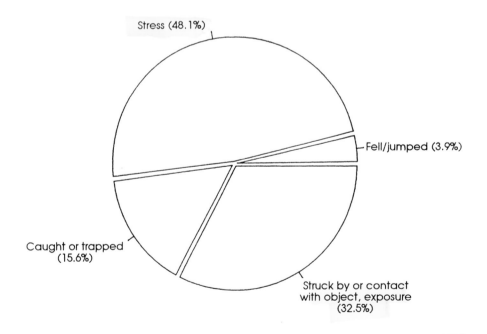

Figure 8-3. Firefighter Deaths by Cause of Injury 1993

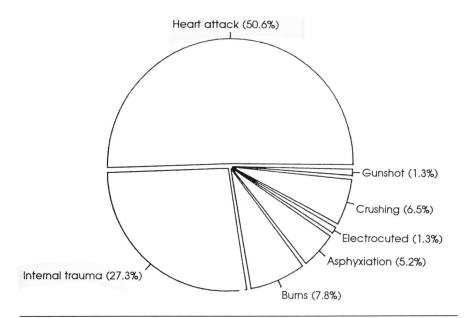

Figure 8-4. Firefighter Deaths by Nature of Injury 1993

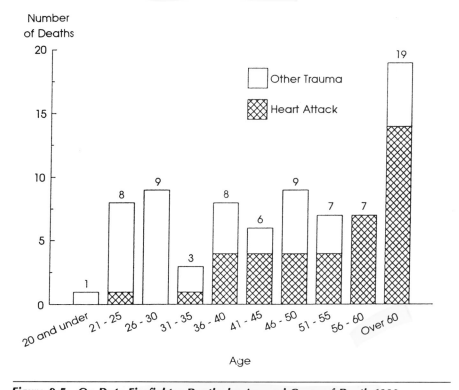

Figure 8-5. On-Duty Firefighter Deaths by Age and Cause of Death 1993

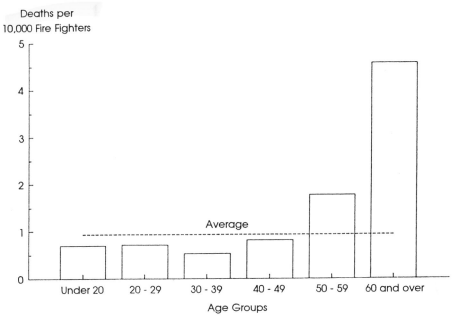

Note: These figures combine career and volunteer fire fighters. The two groups may have very different age distributions, which are not reflected here.

Figure 8-6. On-Duty Death Rates per 10,000 Firefighters 1989-1993

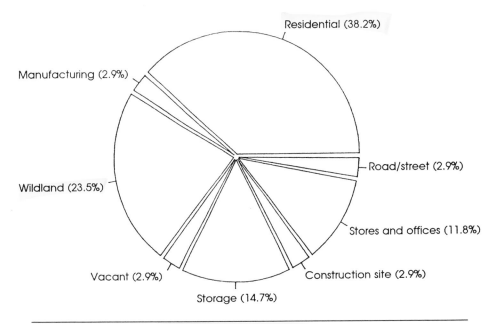

Figure 8-7. Fireground Deaths by Fixed Property Use 1993

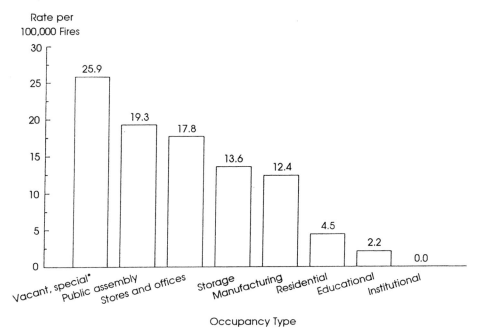

*Includes idle buildings under construction and demolition, etc.

Figure 8-8. On-Duty Fireground Deaths per 100,000 Structure Fires 1988-1992

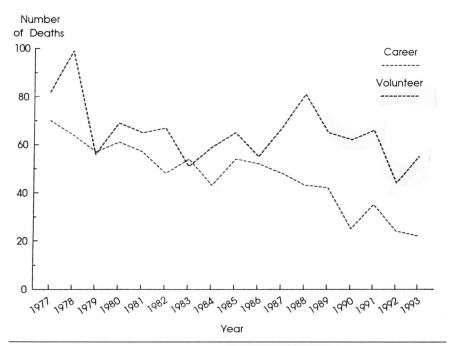

Figure 8-9. Firefighter Deaths 1977-1993 Local Career vs. Local Volunteer

9

The National Professional Qualifications System

RUSSELL J. STRICKLAND

CHAPTER HIGHLIGHTS

• The importance of fire service professional qualification certification and its impact on the fire service.

• The benefits of national certification, both professional and personal, to fire service personnel.

• The national professional qualifications standards (NFPA).

• The three principal national certification systems.

• The accreditation process available through the National Board on Fire Service Professional Qualifications for local, state, and provincial certification systems.·

THE KEY WORD in the title of this chapter is "professional." The fire service has evolved from an organization whose single responsibility was fire suppression to an emergency services organization that provides fire suppression, fire prevention, fire code enforcement, fire investigation, fire inspection, emergency medical services (basic and advanced life support), hazardous materials mitigation, and specialized rescue operations (urban search and rescue, wilderness search and rescue, high-angle rescue, confined space rescue, and trench collapse rescue). With these increased responsibilities come some of the greatest response challenges in our history. Professionalism is the key to our present and to our future.

Webster's dictionary defines the word professional as "of, engaged in, or worthy of the high standards of a profession"; it defines a profession as "a vocation or occupation requiring advanced education and training, and involving intellectual skills, as medicine, law, theology, engineering, teaching, etc."

According to this definition, education and training are key elements in becoming a professional. Training is "the process of or experience of being trained . . . ," "to prepare or make fit . . . , and to instruct so as to make **proficient** or **qualified**." The most important words here are **proficient** and **qualified.**

Thus, for a fire chief to be considered a "professional," he would be educated, trained, and experienced in the field of emergency services. Demographics, economics, and geography are not factors in whether the fire service is a profession and fire service personnel are professionals. Are the chief and members of the department proficient in performing their functions and are they qualified?

Ultimately the question is whether a fire chief should permit uncertified, unlicensed firefighters, fire officers, or emergency medical responders to serve. Given that the public expects and deserves the same degree of professionalism from the fire service as it does from any profession, the answer to the question is a resounding no!

PROFESSIONAL QUALIFICATIONS SYSTEMS

If the public expects and deserves qualified, competent, and professional emergency services personnel, then it is obvious that professional qualifications are needed in the emergency services field. The fire chief must both assure that the highest degree of professionalism exists, and that professionals are certified.

Certification systems must be realistic, credible, and valid. Once established, these systems offer the professional a readily identifiable sense of credibility and validity by establishing the measures by which the professional will be judged and so certified to perform. Generally, these systems are peer evaluations of measurements of minimum standards.

CERTIFICATION

One challenging question fire chiefs ask is why certify? According to Fire Chief M.H. "Jim" Estepp of the Prince George's County (Maryland) Fire Department, and chair of the National Board on Fire Service Professional Qualifications, "In its most simple form, certification means that an individual has been tested by an accredited examining agency on a body of clearly delineated materials and found to meet or exceed the minimum standards. In this instance, certification provides the fire service individual with the opportunity to test skills and knowledge against peers from every type of fire department configuration: career, volunteer or combination." Another reason to certify is the increasingly litigious nature of our society. Still other reasons for certification, particularly national certification, include:

- *Recognition.* Emergency services personnel receive national, state, local, departmental, and peer recognition for demonstrating proficiency in the requirements of a national professional qualifications standard.
- *Credibility.* Certification to a national professional qualification standard establishes a nationally recognized base for measuring the abilities of fire service personnel. By achieving certification, they gain credibility legally, functionally, and socially within the fire service community.
- *Professionalism.* Certification provides the badge or symbol that identifies a professional. Regardless of whether the individual is a member of a career or volunteer, small or large department, certification identifies that person as a professional. Certification is a statement of accomplishment.
- *Budget justification.* Certification provides a nationally recognized basis for justifying our profession and rewards our achievements.
- *Transferability.* National certification gives fire service personnel improved mobility. A certified fire service professional can quickly and easily transfer from one department to another.

STANDARDIZATION

A collateral benefit of certification systems is that they standardize our education and training programs. The standards we recognize today are performance standards, many of which have become the core of our education and training programs. The intent of performance standards is to evaluate an individual regardless of his education, training, and experience. Over time, these standards have become the instrument we use to evaluate an individual upon completion of an education and training program.

In the summer of 1993, the NFPA released the first professional qualifications standard that was revised using a new format. This format states the performance objective, followed by subsections that state the prerequisite skills, knowledge, or both. The standard in this format addresses the education and training necessary (prerequisites) to meet the performance objective. Education and training programs can be developed to encompass the requirements of the standard by simply covering the prerequisites.

These objectives are established by the following government regulatory agencies or consensus organizations:

- National Fire Protection Association (NFPA)
- American National Standards Institute, Inc. (ANSI)
- Occupational Safety and Health Administration (OSHA)
- National Institute for Occupational Safety and Health (NIOSH)
- World Safety Organization (WSO)
- United States Department of Transportation (USDOT)
- Commission on Accreditation of Ambulance Services (CAAS)

- Commission on Accreditation of Air Medical Services (CAAMS)
- Emergency Management Accreditation and Certification System (EMACS), a wholly owned subsidiary of the International Society of Fire Service Instructors (ISFSI)
- National Coordinating Council on Emergency Management (NCCEM)
- National Environmental Training Association

Conferences known as the Wingspread conferences, held in 1966 and 1976, called for professionalism of the fire service. The first conference was held in February 1966 when a group of fire service individuals gathered at the Wingspread conference center of the Johnson Foundation in Racine, Wisconsin. The Johnson Foundation funded the conference and the publications produced as a result of the conferences. The fire service people who attended felt that further study was needed because they viewed the service as thousands of individual fire department organizations attempting to cope with their vast number of responsibilities. At the conferences, fire service representatives discussed fire service administration, education, and research, and examined avenues to enhance and develop all aspects of the fire service. One of these was certification.

In 1970, as a result of the first Wingspread conference, a meeting was held in Williamsburg, Virginia. Called by then-NFPA President Charles S. Morgan, he assembled chief executives of the principal fire service organizations to discuss issues of interest. The result was the creation of the Joint Council of National Fire Service Organizations (JCNFSO). In 1971 the JCNFSO appointed a committee to develop a national firefighter certification system, and, in 1972, this committee created the National Professional Qualification Board (NPQB or "Pro-board") and the first technical committees for each type and level of fire service professional qualifications. Later came the National Professional Qualifications System (NPQS) and the first state certification systems accredited by the NPQB: Iowa, Oregon, and Oklahoma.

Certification systems

A survey conducted in 1992 by the University of Illinois, and additional information compiled in 1993 by the University of Maryland, revealed that some type of certification system exists in each of the 50 states. Since certification systems can be created at the local, county, regional, and state level as well as nationally, credible systems based on acceptable standards can be used and recognized in different formats. States can develop their own sets of standards and criteria or states can adopt any or all of the nationally recognized standards published by the National Fire Protection Association (NFPA) or the American National Standards Institute (ANSI). Today certification system administration ranges from bureaucratic boards with mandatory standards to volunteer boards with voluntary standards. What is important is that all participants agree on the type of system and what they reasonably expect from it.

Professional Qualifications Standards

NFPA 1000, *Standard on Fire Service Professional Qualifications Accreditation and Certification Systems,* provides to the certification systems a guideline for their operation. The minimum criteria for certification bodies as well as for the assessment and validation of the process to certify individuals are established in this standard. Any organization interested in national accreditation for its certification system should adhere to NFPA 1000 and operate according to its guidelines.

NFPA 1001, *Standard for Fire Fighter Professional Qualifications,* one of the four original professional qualification system standards, is perhaps the most widely used and definitive standard in the fire service. In a sense it is the starting point for all standards in the professional series. At the entry level, the firefighter must be able to define and describe a range of topics relating to all aspects of suppression activity, including the basics of fire behavior, firefighting strategies and equipment, fundamentals of emergency rescue, and methods of identifying a hazardous materials incident, and demonstrate proficiency in all areas. As a firefighter progresses through this standard, each of these topics is investigated in greater depth, with the expectation being that mature firefighters have a better understanding of all aspects of the firefighting mission. At every level of this standard, firefighters are expected to ably demonstrate a thorough knowledge of safety equipment, including, but not limited to, self-contained breathing apparatus.

NFPA 1002, *Standard for Fire Apparatus Driver/Operator Professional Qualifications,* applies to all legally licensed fire department apparatus drivers/operators, whether they are designated apparatus drivers, or all firefighters who drive fire department vehicles under emergency response conditions. All firefighters must meet the requirements of Fire Fighter I in NFPA 1001, *Standard for Fire Fighter Professional Qualifications,* before they can be certified as a Fire Apparatus Driver/Operator. While the driver/operator standard requires candidates to perform simulated operations and responses on apparatus equipped with a fire pump, apparatus equipped with an aerial device, apparatus equipped with a tiller, apparatus designed for wildland fire suppression, and apparatus used for airport crash and rescue operations, emphasis and order of priority are determined locally. Candidates also are responsible for knowing preventive maintenance and emergency response safety. In addition, all tests and routines necessary to maintain the safety and integrity of fire department vehicles are examined.

NFPA 1003 *Standard for Airport Fire Fighter Professional Qualifications,* is a single-level standard, and achieving it is, indeed, a commitment to professional growth. Airport firefighters are multifaceted public safety employees who are responsible for protecting apparatus and people from fire and other hazards on airport property. Standard 1003 stipulates that they be proficient in airport procedures and layout, the details of both military and civilian aircraft, fire prevention, and emergency rescue and emergency medical care techniques. Airport firefighters also must have the same knowledge of general fire suppression techniques, preplanning and recordkeeping that nonairport firefighters have.

NFPA 1021, *Standard for Fire Officer Professional Qualifications,* prepares firefighters to qualify for leadership positions within the service. It recognizes four levels of progressive achievement, from the junior officer level to chief fire officer. It is a comprehensive standard that requires candidates to perform to the highest levels of both fireground command and fire department administration and management. As officers move through the fire officer series, they are expected to augment their fire training with knowledge gained from other disciplines, including psychology, public administration, local, state, and national government, and legal issues, and to demonstrate the ability to communicate within and outside the service. Today's fire officers, at all levels, must command culturally diverse suppression forces as well as be prepared to assume leadership roles within the community.

NFPA 1031, *Standard for Professional Qualifications for Fire Inspector,* requires that fire inspectors at all levels be skilled communicators. The scope of an inspector's job is enormous considering that fire inspectors have the power to declare a building reasonably free of all predictable fire hazards. In this capacity, the fire inspector works closely with community members and other professionals outside the fire department, including engineers, architects, and builders. With a knowledge of locally mandated codes and regulations, the fire inspector must be able to apply them to monitor building practices and materials. To be certified as a fire inspector, candidates are asked to describe aspects of fire behavior, to detail specific hazards and risks, to identify all types of fire suppression systems, and to approve emergency evacuation plans.

NFPA 1033, *Standard for Professional Qualifications for Fire Investigator,* governs fire investigators who are responsible primarily for investigating fires, explosions, and other property-destroying events of suspicious or accidental origin. The standard requires professional growth in both fire and legal disciplines; in fact, many jurisdictions mandate that fire investigators be trained to meet the requirements of law enforcement officers. In this sense, fire investigators must be trained in both worlds, and must be able to move easily between investigatory and scientific modes, collecting evidence and helping to prepare documents for courtroom presentations. Their area of expertise is vast, ranging from salvage, overhaul, and rescue procedures, to specific knowledge of hazardous materials, to the storage, handling, and use of flammable and combustible materials. To achieve certification as a fire investigator signifies the mastery of at least two challenging professions.

NFPA 1035, *Standard for Professional Qualifications for Public Educator,* describes the three progressive levels of competence required for the public fire educator—that person (or persons) within a fire department or public safety agency who interacts regularly with schools, civic groups, and members of communities to dispense fire safety educational information and materials. Standard 1035 mandates that the public fire educator understand how the fire department serves the community, although the public fire educator may be a civilian member of the fire service. To be certified as a fire educator, individuals must have knowledge of techniques of building construction, general fire hazards, and suppression systems, and be familiar with all applicable community codes and standards. In addition, the public fire educator, at all levels, must be able to demonstrate excellent written and oral communication skills, as well as methods of classroom and informal group instruction.

NFPA 1041, *Standard for Professional Qualifications for Fire Service Instructor,* establishes the minimum professional levels of competence required of fire service instructors. Four levels of instructorship are examined, each representing a particular phase in professional development. For instance, a Fire Service Instructor I is asked to define terms and concepts relating to elementary levels of educational theory and to demonstrate several components of instructional techniques; at the highest level, Fire Service Instructor IV candidates are tested on their ability to administer and manage a fire service training program. At all levels candidates are asked to demonstrate a range of skills, including goal-setting, recordkeeping, and budget preparation. All candidates seeking certification as Fire Service Instructors should expect to have their communication skills assessed.

NFPA 472, *Standard for Professional Competence of Responding to Hazardous Materials Incidents,* was created to recognize the increasing role of emergency responders in hazardous materials incidents. The standard provides professional guidelines for those who encounter hazardous materials situations in the course of their normal duties, and for those for whom hazardous materials mitigation is their sole responsibility. At the awareness level, a candidate is expected to recognize a hazardous materials emergency, be able to identify visible hazards, and to initiate the notification process. At the responder level, candidates must be able to describe and demonstrate all methods of hazardous materials data collection and analysis, estimate potential risk, begin a response, and initiate the incident management system, among many other skills. At the incident commander level, candidates are asked to meet all the competencies of both the awareness and operations responder levels, as well as all other training mandated by state and federal agencies. Their responsibilities include involvement in community-wide master planning for hazardous materials incidents that encompasses risk assessment and plans for the safety of citizens and their property during a hazardous materials incident.

Major Systems

NATIONAL BOARD ON FIRE SERVICE PROFESSIONAL QUALIFICATIONS

The National Board on Fire Service Professional Qualifications (NBFSPQ) was created after the dissolution of the Joint Council of National Fire Service Organizations in 1990. With the dissolution of the Joint Council, the former National Professional Qualifications Board had no "home" or sponsoring body for the National Professional Qualifications System (NPQS). The NBFSPQ was established to preserve the activities of the qualifications system. The International Association of Fire Chiefs (IAFC), International Association of Arson Investigators (IAAI), National Association of State Directors of Fire Training and Education (NASDFTE), and the National Fire Protection Association (NFPA) make up the NBFSPQ's membership. When the NBFSPQ was formed originally in 1990, the International Association of Fire Fighters (IAFF) and the International Society of Fire Service Instructors (now The Alliance for Fire and Emergency Management) were members. They have since left the NBFSPQ.

The NBFSPQ has a Committee on Accreditation (COA), which serves the functions of the former NPQB. This committee continues the accreditation of state and local certification systems. As of September 1993, there were 16 accredited certification systems, either states or Canadian provinces. These individual systems issue voluntary national certificates with their certifications in one or more levels of the appropriate standards. The NBFSPQ, with its predecessor, has issued more than 15,000 national certificates.

INTERNATIONAL FIRE SERVICE ACCREDITATION CONGRESS

The International Fire Service Accreditation Congress (IFSAC) was established through the efforts of the Oklahoma State University in 1991, and was the product of a national meeting sponsored by the National Association of State Directors of Fire Training and Education. This meeting focused on the review and discussion of fire service certification and accreditation issues. Meeting participants were exploring an avenue of accreditation to meet the

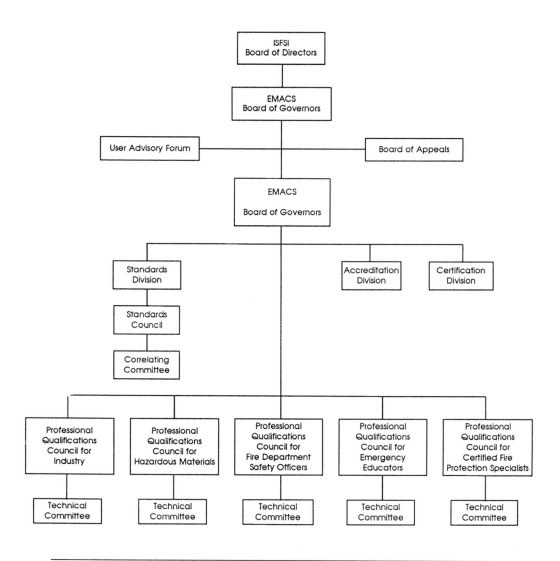

Figure 9-1.

needs of their particular certification systems. At the time, the future of the NPQB was uncertain because of the dissolution of the Joint Council.

The Congress's members are representatives of all certification systems interested in participating in the system. Any jurisdiction, state, or provincial that has a certification system may participate in the Congress. Approximately 15 state, local, or provincial certification systems have been accredited by the Congress since its inception. IFSAC has issued more than 15,000 certifications through its accredited entities.

EMERGENCY MANAGEMENT ACCREDITATION CERTIFICATION SYSTEM

In 1991 the International Society of Fire Service Instructors, (now The Alliance for Fire and Emergency Management) sponsored a meeting in Greenbelt, Maryland, the purpose of which was to "explore and review certification, and to eliminate the confusion associated with certification within the fire service and other areas of emergency response." Based on the meeting, it was concluded that certain areas of emergency services response or training lacked certification. This void was filled with the creation of the Emergency Management Accreditation and Certification System (EMACS) by the Emergency Management Accreditation and Certification System Board which is responsible for maintaining EMACS. The Board currently is addressing the following four major areas of professional certification:

- safety, through the Professional Qualifications Council for Fire Department Safety Officers;
- hazardous materials, through the Hazardous Materials Certification Board;
- industry-related issues, through the Industrial Emergency Management Accreditation and Certification Board; and
- instructor-related issues, through the Instructor Emergency Management Accreditation and Certification Board.

The four boards mentioned above are all suborganizations of the EMACS Board of Governors for the purposes of administering the program. This accreditation system is supported by the Board of Directors of The Alliance for Fire and Emergency Management.

APPLICATION

Application to one of the major certification systems must be through a local, county, state, or provincial certification system or training agency, whereas individuals interested in national certification must apply for it through a body that has been accredited by the national certification body. The major certification systems simply accredit existing local, county, state or provincial certification systems or programs. National Fire Protection Association 1000, *Standard for Fire Service Professional Qualifications Accreditation and Certifications Systems,* is used as the core guidance document.

The application process is consistent across all the major accreditation systems, and consists of the following steps:

First, the local certification system files an application seeking accreditation with the accreditation system.

Second, the local certification system completes a self-study type of document for the accreditation system.

Third, representatives of the accreditation system schedule a date to conduct a site visit of the certification system. During the site visit, a team reviews the certification system's operations. The team is interested primarily in how and to what degree the certification system has adequately evaluated a performance standard. The team reviews the testing and examination elements of the system, asking:

- Is it fair?
- Is the test valid and reliable?
- Is the test a realistic measure of the standard?
- Are those who participate in the certification system satisfied with the system?

The visitation team consists of members from the national certification body. They use the criteria established by their certification body to assess and evaluate the site. The members have extensive experience in local, state, or provincial certification systems, are well versed in the standards applied, and have attended "on-the-job" training programs for visitations.

Finally, once the site visit has been conducted, the visitation team develops a report for, and makes recommendations to, the parent body, which, in turn, renders a decision and notifies the certification system. The decision rendered can be anywhere on a continuum from pass to fail, but, generally, if the visitation team identified any areas that needed clarification or enhancement, applicants are asked to produce the necessary materials and the body then renders another decision. The request for additional documentation may coincide with a provisional accreditation that is maintained for a specified period of time while the body awaits the information.

The accreditation of a certification system is valid for a specified period of time and in accordance with the rules and regulations of the accreditation system. An accredited certification system is reaccredited on a periodic basis.

THE ADVANTAGES OF ACCREDITED CERTIFICATION SYSTEMS

The major advantage of having an accredited certification system is national recognition. Another advantage is that it standardizes a defined performance level(s) within the emergency services. Accredited certification systems identify individuals who are competent within a standard; as such these individuals can be nationally mobile. These individuals have proved successfully, to defined performance/competency standards, their abilities for a particular level of fire service activity, and, as such, will be recognized by all participants of the national system through which certification is issued. Certified individuals can move freely within the fire service community and not request unnecessary and time-consuming training and education. They need only familiarization with local protocols.

National certification also offers to fire chiefs opportunities for increased public awareness, exposure, and good community relations. The fact that department personnel have achieved national certification should be advertised and promoted. Progressive fire chiefs and executives, aware of public apathy, can use this opportunity to the fire service's advantage. Like physicians, attorneys, or school teachers, fire service personnel have demonstrated professional competencies in accordance with nationally accepted standards. Unfortunately, the peer-driven national certification system has been slow to develop within the fire service.

THE DISADVANTAGES OF ACCREDITED CERTIFICATION SYSTEMS

The only real disadvantage is cost. Obviously, maintaining any nationally accepted and easily accessible system costs money. To be cost effective, it must be run like a business; the fees charged must be sufficient to maintain the integrity of the accreditation system.

Another disadvantage of the accreditation system is local parochialism. While all modern fire chiefs and executives agree that their personnel must be trained and certified to a defined level, local levels are based on nationally recognized professional qualifications standards as published by the National Fire Protection Association. Unfortunately, some fire chiefs and executives see only local benefits, not necessarily the national benefits and recognition.

TYPES OF SYSTEMS

All 50 states have some form of certification system in place. These systems vary in operation from state to state, but the most prevalent is a standard-based, recognized test system. Individuals are permitted to sit for the examination after presenting themselves either with or without a defined level of education and training. This is the concept of a performance-based standard. The National Board for Fire Service Professional Qualifications requires that those agencies it accredits offer a challenge examination "regardless" of the individual's education and training. The test simply evaluates the applicant's performance. The tests generally consist of two parts: written and practical. Candidates must successfully pass both parts. The state of Delaware, for example, offers this type of examination process. Some systems include a third oral interview component during which a candidate is quizzed on his knowledge as outlined in the standard. The three-part examination process is used in Georgia.

Another type of system is a program-based certification. This type of system requires that individuals complete a defined program (curriculum) which has been evaluated and found to meet the performance standard. This evaluation is conducted as part of the education and training program, and consists of written and practical examinations as well as evaluator sign-offs. In essence, individuals complete a sound educational training program and, upon successful completion, can be certified. An example of this type of system is used in Maryland. Similar is California's program-based certification where the state fire marshal's office accredits the program, certifies the instructors, and then issues the certification.

Some states offer a variety of methods for certification with national accreditation that include:

- Successful completion of a program based on a defined standard, and a clearly defined education and training program that addresses the standard and evaluates the candidate's performance to the standard.
- Any combination of training programs as identified and found to address and evaluate the defined standard; this requires the applicant to clearly identify all the education and training programs he has completed and how they correlate to the standard. This correlation is presented to a board that evaluates the applicant's performance in terms of the standard.
- Successful completion of a challenge exam or examination process based on a defined standard.

California, Florida, and New York, which are not accredited by any national body, have their own systems. They have either developed their own standards, use similar standards, or adopt parts of the national standards. They issue certifications through state government agencies. Their evaluation methods are similar to those listed above, i.e., accredited program completion and challenge examinations.

SUMMARY

Today several options exist for the accreditation of certification systems. A local, county, state, or provincial certification system must exist in order for a national system to offer accreditation. There are three major accreditation systems:

National Board on Fire Service Personnel Qualifications
Office of the Secretary-Treasurer
P.O. Box 492
Quincy, MA 02269
(617) 984-7468

International Fire Service Accreditation Congress
Oklahoma State University
Fire Publications Building
Stillwater, OK 74078-0118
(405) 744-8303

Emergency Management Accreditation Certification System
30 Main Street
Ashland, MA 01721
(508) 881-5800

Local, county, state or provincial certification must apply and be successfully evaluated by one of these accreditation systems.

CONCLUSION

National accreditation of certification is a reality. As with other professions in today's society it is a must. As the fire service strives for professionalism, it must establish, through accreditation, the credibility and validity that only certification can offer. Through certification the fire service establishes peer recognition of peer performance, based on acceptable and realistic performance criteria, also developed by peers.

10

Training and Education

WILLIAM M. KRAMER

- Types of information available through training programs at the local level, and state training academies.
- Federal initiatives in training.
- Interrelationship of the three components of the "Learning Triad": Education, Training, and Experience.
- The differences and similarities between training and education.
- Associate and bachelor's degrees and the types of institutions capable of delivering all levels of education.
- Overlaps between education and certification.
- How experiential learning can be used in the fire service and converted to collegiate-level credit.
- The link between higher education and direct promotional opportunities.
- Alternative paths toward higher education in the fire service.
- Fire department training components.
- Five types of training methods.
- The role and mission of the National Fire Academy in Emmitsburg, Maryland.
- Safety concerns relative to fire service training.
- Procedures to use for recordkeeping and documentation of training.

WE HAVE WITNESSED dramatic growth and change in the fire service over the past several decades. The fire chief was once characterized as a rather static and reactionary leader, usually considered brave, capable of handling all emergencies, and beyond scrutiny. Today's chief is more of an administrative leader, who now must also manage an organization which is quite complex in terms of its mission and duties, regardless of size. While the fire service has always enjoyed the respect of the citizens it serves, the fire service of today has emerged as the leading emergency organization, expected to react to all incidents, regardless of their size or nature.

Both career and volunteer fire chiefs, regardless of the size of their organization, must manage and direct not only fire suppression forces, but also fire prevention bureaus, hazardous materials mitigation teams, and complex prehospital emergency service organizations, in short, organizations far more complex than those they inherited from their predecessors.

As the fire service's scope and mission have broadened, the need for enhancements in both training and education have grown proportionately. There are greater demands to keep today's firefighter current in handling the increased array of equipment from hypodermic needles and defibrillators to static kernmantle rope, rigging equipment, and various product-specific foams, and the internal fire protection systems in structures of increasing complexity.

As the fire service has increased in complexity so too has fire service management. Fire service leaders need a new dimension of managerial expertise to balance risks and benefits across this multidimensional organization.

In the past, fire chiefs may have felt that the best training was done strictly within the fire service. That attitude is changing as specialists and specialty organizations, including community colleges, government training agencies, private sector technical specialists, and others offer their services to modern fire departments.

As fire service organizations have become more sophisticated, the need for higher levels of education among its leaders has become greater. No longer can the fire chief or fire officer consider himself merely the "lead firefighter." More than anything else, the fire chief of today is a manager who must understand personnel management, budgets, organizational structures, and a host of similar subjects that have long been included in the domain of private sector businesses and are now recognized as key functions in the fire service. Also, education is needed simply to have the vision to recognize the complex problems appearing on the horizon and to devise techniques and find paths necessary to seek and implement solutions and alternatives.

To be successful in this expanded mission, fire service leaders of today must be educated. The education can be formal or informal, since some of the most knowledgeable fire service professionals are often those who have excelled without a great deal of formal education. They are the exception, however, and those who are self-educated lack the documentation or credentials to help them secure the more prestigious chief officer positions available throughout the United States and Canada. Hence, there is a growing need for formal education. Fortunately, there are many flexible resources and opportunities for bringing higher education well within the reach of all fire service personnel.

A combination of good training of firefighters, and good education for command staff officers, led to a successful game plan to contain this high-rise fire at the First Interstate Bank Building in Los Angeles on May 4, 1988.

PHOTO COURTESY OF AL KIRSCHNER

THE LEARNING TRIAD

Education and training in the fire service are complemented by an equally important third factor: experience. The three component parts—education, training, and experience—make up what has been described as a "learning triad." A healthy mix of all three is required for an effective fire officer, but as he moves through a career, the mix and the proportion of each tend to vary, with education becoming more and more important. Figure 10-1 gives a capsulized description of each of these three and shows their changing proportional relationship over time.

THE OVERLAP BETWEEN TRAINING AND EDUCATION

While both training and education are necessary in the fire service, they are not the same. While there is some overlap, they differ essentially in that training is designed to show practitioners how to get a job done, and education shows why the job is necessary. Education provides a broader base that not only allows a fire officer to perform the job more skillfully but allows broader interaction with the world and the environment. Figure 10-2 provides a brief comparison of education and training.

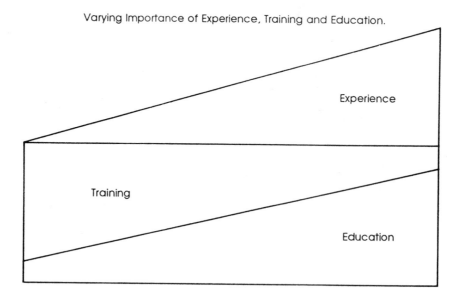

Varying Importance of Experience, Training and Education.

Experience

Training

Education

Figure 10-1. The Learning Triad

Figure 10-2. Training versus Education.

Training	Education
Task Oriented	Theory based
Memorization	Reasoning
Skills	Knowledge
Practice	Judgment
• "How"	• "How" and "Why"
Learning is	Learning is
• more predictable	• less predictable
• more easily measured	• less easily measured
"Hands-on"	Cerebral

While training is concerned essentially with *skills,* it is not limited to the "practice environment" or drill ground. Much of the foundation for skills training—purpose, functions, common nomenclature, safety, etc.—is laid in the classroom.

As firefighters began to achieve the education and training necessary in their careers, organizations outside of the fire service began to assist with this mission, and to produce evaluation tools to measure the proficiency of their

"Arched Truss Roofs," as shown on this repair shop, are found in cities and villages large and small. Education is of more value than experience in identifying dangerous roofs prior to the positioning of ventilation crews.

PHOTO COURTESY OF THE UNIVERSITY OF CINCINNATI

achievement. After World War II, many colleges and universities began offering certificate programs identifying a series of fire-related courses successfully achieved, and later, associate and baccalaureate degrees in fire-related disciplines.

While there are many variations in fire-related college degree programs and variations in the certification requirements from state to state, they are all intended to serve similar purposes. They are intended to identify in measurable ways the knowledge or skills to be achieved by individuals in the fire service field. It is often difficult to simultaneously earn a college education and state certification simply because the missions of the organizations are quite different. In addition to the differences between training and education, many fire service organizations have missions which often are narrowly defined. Therefore, it may be possible for a firefighter in a given state to earn an associate or bachelor's degree in a fire service discipline, yet still not qualify for various certification levels. Conversely, a fully certified firefighter or fire officer in most states may have acquired few, if any, college credits for his efforts to achieve that certification.

Training and education do have the common denominator of "knowledge" and, where possible, are finding common ground. Movement in both directions has meant that firefighters now are able to receive college credits for the education components of certification and, in turn, may receive certification for certain college courses in community colleges or universities. For example, in June 1992, at a meeting of participants from Texas community colleges and the Texas Fire Commission, which handles certifications for the state, it was decided that the Collin County Community College would award 18 semester hours of credits to students who completed a certificate program (firefighter and officer certifications I through VI). Other Texas universities, and Western Illinois University, which serves the state of Texas through the National Fire Academy's Open Learning Fire Service Program, are providing similar opportunities.

Texas is not alone. Similar initiatives have been started in Georgia, Ohio, and elsewhere. One international example is a cooperative venture between the University of Cincinnati and the Alberta Fire Training School in Canada. The university accepts graduates of the Alberta Fire Training Academy in its degree program, recognizing the curriculum of the Alberta Fire Training School as a substitute for the first 26 credit hours of the fire science curriculum. Each student is evaluated on a case-by-case basis for entry into the baccalaureate or associate degree program.

In August 1993 the National Fire Academy hosted the National Academic Fire Programs Workshop. Attending were representatives of two- and four-year fire-related degree programs, and state fire training directors. Workshop participants discussed how to collaborate to create a unified higher education network, how to share resources, curricula, and ideas for mutual benefit, and how to jointly help achieve National Fire Academy goals.

EXPERIENTIAL LEARNING

Since it is universally agreed that the "school of hard knocks" is one of the best teachers, it was inevitable that colleges and universities would recognize experiential learning and make provisions for accepting it into higher education curricula. Firefighters, who by nature of their work experience, or personal or professional endeavors, have achieved a body of knowledge outside of the classroom which is equivalent to that taught in various college courses, now may receive collegiate credit for this informal learning. This generally is referred to as an "experiential learning" or "portfolio" process. The latter name is derived from the formal documentation required to substantiate such learning. By this mechanism, personally obtained knowledge can be converted to college credit. Examples would include authorship of fire department master plans, or disaster plans, documentation of leadership used in innovative community safety programs, and the attainment of various state levels of certification, including EMT and paramedic certification.

Thus, while it is true that the missions of universities and the state certifying agencies are certainly different, and can essentially be divided along the lines of training versus education, it also is true that where significant overlaps in these missions do exist, it is now possible to have the knowledge gained in one arena transferred to the other. Many fire service professionals who have obtained a measure of professional achievement in their fields have no doubt already completed a portion of a college degree without even realizing it. Certain other options which shorten the time and effort needed to earn a college degree, without weakening or diminishing its strength or knowledge base, include CLEP (College Level Entrance Preparation) tests which allow students to test out of some of the basic college courses in the educational process; accelerated courses offered in various locations; and college education that makes use of personal computers, satellites, and the medium of video.

Figure 10-3 shows the steps to a formal education for the fire service professional, the positions for which these steps qualify a fire service professional, and the various paths that can be used either separately or in combination to achieve these educational levels. Note that in Figure 10-3 a minimum education requirement of four years of high school is assumed. This usually is sufficient for individuals who wish to remain in entry-level positions in all fire departments, regardless of size or status as career or volunteer. While it is true that some fire departments now require two years of college or an associate degree for even entry-level positions, it also is true that many of these same departments also allow the substitution of various forms of experience for the college credentials.

Throughout the United States, there is an emerging trend toward linking higher education directly to promotions. In Iowa, all of the major career fire departments have adopted a standard requiring a college certificate for the first

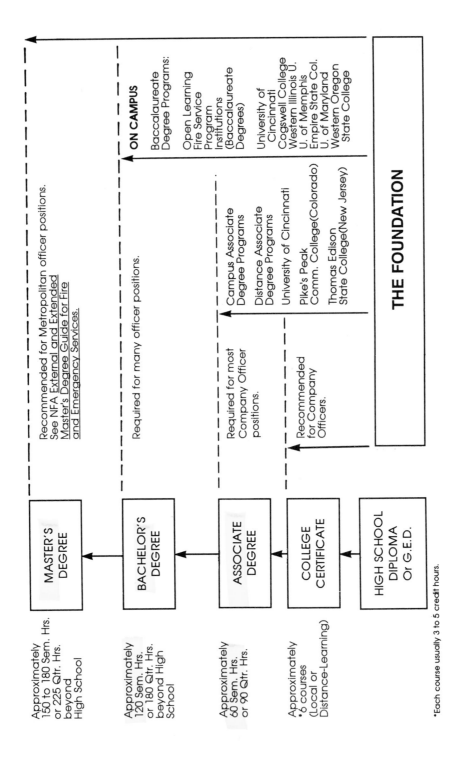

Figure 10-3. Fire Service Education

promotion, and one year of college for each additional promotion. This has spurred new interest and bolstered enrollments in Iowa's fire science institutions, especially Kirkwood Community College, one of the driving forces in the Iowa educational initiative.

NEW PATHS TO HIGHER EDUCATION

As firefighters aspire to higher positions, and seek promotions, the need for education becomes increasingly important. An associate degree is required for many positions as fire chief and is recommended for all. It is not uncommon to find volunteer fire departments commanded by chief officers with academic credentials, although not necessarily in a fire service discipline. For intermediate to large cities, a bachelor's degree often is required, and always recommended. For departments in very large cities, a master's degree is recommended and soon may be required, at least in some parts of the nation.

Because fire personnel generally tend to have irregular work schedules, it is difficult for them to attend traditional college courses which meet at the same place and time each week. This does not, however, preclude attendance at conventional courses. Many options make conventional classroom instruction quite possible for career fire officers. Consider these examples.

- Many instructors have a flexible attendance policy and will allow firefighters to substitute home assignments for every third class. Captain Roy Woodruff of the New Orleans Fire Department pointed out that he was able to earn associate, bachelor's and master's degrees the traditional way and only one time in his career did he encounter a professor who would not bend the attendance requirements.
- Fire chiefs often permit, and should encourage, firefighters to trade small blocks of time with one another to facilitate their attendance at conventional college courses.
- Many colleges and universities offer multiple sections of various college courses on different nights, allowing firefighters to attend either of two sections which are kept synchronized.

Firefighters no longer must attend classes to earn fully certified academic credentials. A well-known fire science degree program in the United States is the "Open Learning Fire Service Program" offered by the University of Cincinnati. The University of Cincinnati serves students throughout the continental United States and from numerous foreign countries by offering a combination of distance-learning courses, accelerated "residency weeks" throughout the North American continent, and video instruction that uses the

American Heat video series and the satellite-based Fire Education Training Network (FETN). Six other universities also are members of the National Open Learning Fire Service Education Consortium, chaired by the University of Cincinnati, which delivers accredited "Open Learning" baccalaureate degree programs in conjunction with the National Fire Academy. The other universities are Cogswell College in California, Western Oregon State College, University of Memphis, the University of Maryland, Western Illinois University, and Empire State College in New York.

A fire-related master's degree program at this time seems unnecessary, and, perhaps, ill-advised. The rationale is that once students have achieved an associate degree in a fire discipline, followed by a bachelor's degree, and are seeking a master's-level education, they no longer will be fire practitioners. Rather, they are going to be managers and will not need additional fire knowledge, but will need additional business and administrative skills such as those taught in MBA (Master of Business Administration) or MPA (Master of Public Administration) programs. The National Fire Academy has published a catalog of existing externally based, distance-learning master's degree programs which could be of value to the fire service.

If we accept the premise that higher education makes fire service managers more capable fire service leaders, then we should provide incentives to train the fire service's present and future leaders. Some incentives include:

- State education incentives. The state of Florida regularly provides $50 per month in additional salary to any state firefighter with an associate degree, and $110 in additional salary to any firefighter who holds a bachelor's degree.
- Local education incentives. The City of Waterbury, Connecticut, provides direct monetary incentives to its firefighters for completing higher education courses.
- Direct promotional incentives. Although resisted in more traditional civil service establishments, the awarding of bonus points for the achievement of various levels of higher education tends to make sense. This is especially true where education is seen as an alternative to experience. For example, a requirement for promotion to captain might be ten years as a lieutenant or five years as a lieutenant plus an associate fire science degree.
- Indirect promotional incentives. Where the posted reference material and textbooks needed for promotional exams can be aligned with those used in local or regional fire science programs at community colleges and universities, a method is in place for firefighters and fire officers to be assisted through the material needed to be completed to compete successfully on a promotional exam.

Departmental training

Training in all its forms is the single most important ingredient in the readiness of firefighters and emergency responders to fulfill their assigned missions. We will look first at local or departmental training. Training often spells the difference between success and failure in an emergency, when action must be swift and decisive.

Fire Engineering reported that within a three-year period two U.S. Air flights crashed on New York's La Guardia Airport Runway #1331. Many successful rescues were performed for both U.S. Air flight #5050 on September 20, 1989, and for the crash of U.S. Air flight #405 on March 22, 1992. In the first incident, 55 passengers and six crew members were rescued and there were only two fatalities. In the second incident 27 people died, but 24 were rescued.

The rescues at New York's La Guardia Airport succeeded mostly because of intense training and preparation. *Fire Engineering* documented how the Port Authority and the Fire Department of New York insisted on many types of training to prepare personnel for aircraft rescues:

- Contingency plans designed exclusively for aircraft emergencies at both of New York's major airports.

Members of the Milwaukee, Wisconsin Hazardous Materials team undergo realistic "hands-on" hazardous materials training. Note the support staff necessary for the donning of protective suits, similar to that needed in actual conditions.

PHOTO COURTESY OF SCOTT FRANKEN

- Annual interagency disaster drills held on airport grounds.
- Frequent full-scale operational response exercises that simulated aircraft crashes, both on land and in the water.
- Regular airport familiarization drills (including water relay, escort procedures, and airplane rescue procedures).
- Tabletop exercises during which various agencies participated in an aircrash disaster problem.

Over the years fire service work has become less physically demanding and more mentally challenging. Lighter weight hose, ladders, and breathing apparatus, combined with incident management procedures that require team actions, have reduced the need for individual firefighters to depend solely on strenuous physical labor. A properly functioning incident management system emphasizes that companies work as teams, reducing the frequency of one-on-one labor-intensive rescues. Meanwhile, as more firefighters have had to become trained as both firefighting technicians and emergency medical technicians, the job has become more mentally challenging. Likewise, truly proficient firefighters must learn about hazardous materials, modern building construction techniques, and a host of technical subjects in greater detail than ever before.

Over time, as the mental requirements have caught up with the physical, training needs have necessitated both the use of physical training grounds and classroom space, as shown in Figure 10-4.

Figure 10-4. Dual Training Needs

Training Grounds	Classroom
Hazardous Materials—Practice	Hazardous Materials—Knowledge
Driving	EMS
SCBA	Fire Tactics
Hose Evolutions	Small Tools and Equipment
Ladder Evolutions	Administrative Regulations
Rescue Operations	Fire Prevention and Codes

The local fire department is charged with training its members in routine operational procedures, not only because it is desirable to field a capable and qualified emergency service, but also because many federal and state laws and regulations now specify minimum hours of training in such areas as:

- Hazardous materials—required under the Superfund Amendments and Reauthorization Act;
- Emergency medical certification—minimum hours mandated by state law; and

- Basic firefighter certification—mandated by state law.

As the demands for knowledge have accelerated among members of the fire service, and as legislated training mandates have increased, many new fire training staffs have not kept pace. In 1993, the following guidelines were applicable in terms of the number of full-time training personnel needed to handle the fire service training mission adequately:

- One full-time training officer, at a minimum, for fire departments with up to approximately 50 members. In very small departments this function could be shared with other duties.
- Approximately one full-time training person per 50 members up to 400; in larger departments, one training officer per 75 members. In Figure 10-5 actual figures are shown from cities which have met these minimum guidelines.

Figure 10-5. Full-Time Training Staffs In Selected Cities

City	Number of Uniformed Personnel	Number Assigned to Training
Memphis, TN	1500	20
Prince William County, VA	1050	12
Cincinnati, OH	750	10
Pasadena, CA	200	4
Shaker Heights, OH	50	1

Fire department training academies vary in terms of size and number of staff in direct proportion to the number of personnel they serve. There are common activities, however. In the following profile of the Memphis, Tennessee, Fire Department Training Academy, you will find elements that should be common to all local fire training academies.

PROFILE OF THE MEMPHIS, TENNESSEE FIRE DEPARTMENT TRAINING ACADEMY

Staff

1 Chief of Training
1 Battalion Commander of Training
1 Battalion Commander of Research and Planning
1 Secretary
1 Lieutenant—Research and Analysis
13 Lieutenants—Instructors
1 Course Development Specialist
1 Personnel Analyst

Organization and programs

— Education Programs
  — Resident Programs
    — Courses offered on site at the academy
    — Offered in 4-hour to 40-hour formats

— Field Programs
  — Recruit training (480 Hours) + 240 Hr. E.M.T.
  — Certification coordination
  — Skills maintenance training

— Research and Planning
  — Coordination/Revision of disaster planning
  — Coordination of new equipment testing
  — Equipment specification writing
  — Coordination of monthly/annual award program

— Research and Analysis
  — Coordination/Compilation of monthly/annual records
  — Analysis of department and NFIRS data
  — Specialized research projects
  — Analysis of response time data
  — Strategic fire station location planning

— Course Development, Revision, and Methods
  — Design of courses to NFA standards
  — Revision/Updating of courses
  — Instructor certification/staffing continuing education
  — Media production

Local/regional education coordination

— The Memphis Fire Academy, in cooperation with local two- and four-year academic fire degree programs, promotes college-level credit for fire department training completed by its personnel.

A word of caution is in order for fire chiefs and fire training officials. As fire training academies have grown more complex and sophisticated, there can be a tendency for fire company officers to abdicate their responsibility for daily drills and training to the training academy. If this happens, it is a tremendous disservice to individual firefighters who deserve daily instruction and drills, and to the public which may receive service that is substandard. Likewise, at the battalion and division levels, multi-unit drills, often used in conjunction with preincident planning at the various sites, can extend this individual company training in the field across battalion or district lines.

TRAINING FACILITIES

In planning for training, the fire department must arrange for classroom space that is comfortable, sufficiently large, and flexible in terms of seating configurations. Classroom facilities must be capable of accommodating training classes in basic firefighting, emergency medical techniques, hazardous materials, preincident planning, video training, familiarization with SCBA (self-contained breathing apparatus), and training in the use of smaller tools and equipment.

A modern fire training academy should include state-of-the-art classroom facilities as well as structural fire training buildings, SCBA training facilities, autos, tank trucks, aircraft, electrical vaults, structures, oil pits, and other simulated occupancies found in the jurisdiction where the training is to take place. Care must be taken, however, to avoid acquiring outdated equipment such as tank trucks which have obsolete valving but which an oil company may be happy to discard. It is far wiser to invest in the types of tank trucks firefighters are likely to encounter, or at least to supplement obsolete mock-ups with slides, overheads, or other visuals which show the differences, and explain operational changes. The same concept applies to all training ground props.

If a fire training academy is designed to conduct training beyond routine daily operations, to include disaster planning, the requirements for the facility grow considerably. In the book, *Fire Officer's Guide to Disaster Control,* recommended features are listed for advanced academies. Among the recommendations are fire and rescue problems that can be simulated with built-in gas lines, tape-recorded cries for help from loudspeakers on upper floors of buildings, mechanical ejection of dummy "jumpers," shut-off valves to interfere with water supplies, etc. Also suggested are driver training courses with narrow winding roads, dead-end streets, steep hills, and obstacles. Where academies are located in coastal areas or in river cities, ponds with sunken vehicles might be advisable.

New technology has enhanced fire training facilities. In 1994, firefighters in Bergen County, New Jersey, were using a state-of-the-art police and fire academy. Participating in the design of this new academy were fire instructors, fire chiefs, fire advisors, and fire academies in several states. The final product was a realistic "city" that includes a restaurant, tenement, body shop, service station, grocery, warehouse, townhouse, dwelling, retail store, hotel, high-rise office, and beauty shop. It includes a computerized propane fire simulator that can create a wide variety of fire scenarios. In seven minutes the complex's smoke system can fill an entire building with nontoxic smoke, forcing firefighters to use a common kneeling search technique. This smoke can be ventilated completely from three floors within one minute. Additional amenities include an auditorium, movie theater, and basement space designed for additional rescue scenarios.

If this training facility sounds complex, and appears out of reach of most budgets, consider the fact that many jurisdictions are now pooling their resources to jointly construct and operate training facilities. One example is

Tactical scenarios can be devised that require quick sound decisions by fire officers. For example, in this Farmington Hills incident an officer in charge of a second arriving engine would be asked to list options when faced with multiple burning residential structures.   PHOTO COURTESY OF CHIEF RICHARD MARINUCCI

the training center that serves Inglewood, Redondo Beach, Manhattan Beach, Hermosa Beach and El Segundo, California. This was constructed in 1972 using $800,000 in bonds under a cooperative venture among the five participating communities and has been serving all five ever since.

TRAINING METHODS

Training can be divided into five essential types:

* Routine operations training;
* Tabletop training;
* Simulation;
* Dry runs; and
* Actual incidents.

Routine operations training

Routine operations training includes the hose, ladder, and practice evolutions that are necessary in day-to-day fire department operations. It includes practice with both new and standard equipment. Along with hose, ladders, and in-line foam eductors, automatic telemetry equipment and environmental measuring meters often are used. Firefighters who have mastered the basic equipment carried today are not only proficient in the routine daily emergencies they face but can also extrapolate this knowledge readily and better handle large-scale or disaster-like incidents.

Tabletop training

In one form of tabletop training, multiple company operations are provided a measure of realism with three-dimensional structures and an audio system to simulate transmission of radio messages. Miniature buildings, streets, and roadways are physically positioned on a large table and participants watch a miniature event unfold successfully or unsuccessfully, depending on the tactics used.

While this system has been used in Great Britain for years with varying degrees of success, its use is less common but often quite helpful in the United States. Simpler forms of tabletop exercises essentially involve printed materials on which actions are documented and recorded using radios and time logs.

Simulation

While most of us are familiar with flight simulators used to create realism for airline pilots undergoing training, we may not be as familiar with the same technology which has been used successfully by the fire service. One example is a 28-foot van trailer used at the Elgin Air Force Base in Florida. It permits firefighters to handle multi-alarm fires that could arise anywhere within the Air Force base, including docks, runways, tank farms, and structures. Using a 35mm slide projector, tape recorders, intercom, and overhead projectors, scenes are projected from the back of the van to a screen in the front. Deployed apparatus is shown on the screen, along with hose layouts and other tactical configurations controlled by the student. Projected simulations are fairly common and have been used since the mid-1960s in many state and county training programs. They have been displayed in a variety of trade shows over the years.

For simulations of a less technical nature the fire service often has substituted dummies for victims, training towers for high-rise buildings, colored water for hazardous liquids, and so forth. The fire service has shown remarkable creativity in this area of training.

Dry runs

A dry run, or disaster drill, is designed to handle larger scale scenarios such as disasters. While similar to simulation or tabletop exercises, people are actually deployed in dry run drills and decisions are made as if an actual disaster were unfolding. While expensive, this type of training has such side benefits as increasing community awareness and allowing firefighting forces the opportunity to make mistakes in practice before an actual event.

Actual incidents

Many fire departments miss a chance to receive some of the most valuable training of all if they fail to learn from operations at actual events. A postincident critique, conducted in a nonthreatening educational manner, very often can pinpoint areas where improvement is needed, as well as identify situations where training has paid quality dividends, thus providing positive reinforcement.

VIDEO TECHNOLOGY

We have already discussed the use of videos in fire service education. The *American Heat* video series and training films from *Fire Engineering* are two examples of excellent programs designed to supplement the education and training needs of the fire service. There also is the Fire Education Training Network (FETN), a live daily broadcast sent via satellite into fire stations coast to coast. FETN provides informative news coverage as well as technology updates. Officials involved in fire service training should also consider the internal use of videos for fire service training. If fire companies involved in training in a typical drill yard setting are videotaped during their evolutions, and shown the results toward the end of the training session, they can learn from both what they did well and any errors or mistakes they made.

In some departments, members of the training division are dispatched to multiple-alarm fires and other unusual incidents to videotape operations for study and for use in training.

FIRE ACADEMIES

The term academy connotes a higher level of learning, that is, a physical place where the leaders of a chosen profession go to gain the latest available information. Just as the FBI Academy provided a national focal point for the police service and served as a clearinghouse for the latest technological and tactical information available for the nation's police departments, so too has the National Fire Academy (NFA) in Emmitsburg, Maryland, become a center of learning and research for the fire service in the United States. The National Fire Academy has lived up to its legislative mandate to enhance the professional development of the nation's fire service. Although the 1974 report, *America Burning*, criticized the United States for leading all major industrialized countries in per capita deaths and property loss from fire, this country's record is improving. Advances are attributable in large measure to a new professionalism in the fire service, much of which is based on information developed and disseminated by the National Fire Academy.

The National Fire Academy offers resident programs to fire service and allied professionals from throughout the United States.

At the Emmitsburg campus, the academy conducts two-week specialized training courses and advanced management programs of national impact. These courses are offered in a concentrated, campus-based setting that is most conducive to intensive learning. On-campus resident programs are targeted to middle- and top-level officers, fire service instructors, technical professionals, and representatives from allied professions. Any person with substantial involvement in fire prevention and control, rescue, or fire-related emergency management activities is eligible to apply for academy courses. A catalog of all programs, updated yearly, is available by writing to the National Fire Academy, National Emergency Training Center: 16825 South Seton Avenue, Emmitsburg, MD 21727, or by calling 1-800-238-3358.

The National Fire Academy also has an extensive network of field programs delivered to all parts of the United States. One of the NFAs creative ventures is the Train-the-Trainer program which has a multiplier effect— instructors are taught not only the course but also how to teach it to the other members of their fire service organizations and regions.

Because many volunteer and career fire service personnel do not have the time to attend on-campus resident programs, these two-day, off-campus training opportunities are proving to be quite valuable in local communities of all sizes.

Each year the Academy trains approximately 4,000 participants at the Emmitsburg site. Off-campus courses are delivered directly to 15,000 participants. By 1994, more than 125,000 participants were being reached annually through academy hand-off courses available through the National Audiovisual Center.

The Open Learning Fire Service Program, an NFA initiative discussed earlier, expands the academic outreach through a network of seven colleges and universities, making baccalaureate programs in fire technology and management available to fire service personnel who, because of their work hours and locations, would not otherwise have those opportunities.

STATE AND PROVINCIAL TRAINING

The majority of the 50 states and many Canadian provinces have their own fire training academies which predate the National Fire Academy and which have long been hallmarks of professional education and training for members of their own states and provinces. Also, many universities have conducted fire schools, supplementing their educational mission with the training mission.

State training programs vary widely from one location to another and in terms of organization. In some states, for example, Iowa and Illinois, they are tied directly to the community college system, as state training feeds quite naturally into an associate degree program. In other states, such as Ohio, they are organized under the office of the state fire marshal. While the political make-up may vary, the mission is rather consistent. Most academies include physical facilities, either at a separate independent campus or at a community college or at state university locations.

Texas A & M

An example of a state fire academy is the famous Texas Agricultural and Mechanical (Texas A & M) Institute, which for years has been considered a hallmark among fire training institutions. What follows is an historical perspective on the Texas A & M Institute.

In 1948, the Texas Engineering Extension Service (TEEX) became a state agency with the mandate to provide vocational and technical training programs on an extension basis to the citizens of Texas. In the spirit of this mandate, the Texas Engineering Extension Service provides technical services in a number of vocational areas and offers training programs and related services regionally, nationally, and internationally to public, private, and industrial clients. TEEX is headquartered in College Station and is part of the Texas A & M University System.

The Fire Protection Training Division of the Texas Engineering Extension Service was established in 1930 to train municipal firefighters in Texas. Since then the division has expanded to include a 60-acre training field in College Station designed to accommodate public and industrial clients. The division also has staff members based at regional training centers across the state. Some of the programs offered are an annual municipal firefighters' training school, annual hazardous materials control school, annual Spanish "bomberos" training school, annual international aircraft rescue and firefighting school, schools for marine fire protection, and many industrial fire protection schools.

Illinois Fire Service Institute

A different example is the Illinois Fire Service Institute. It is operated as a continuing education and public service activity by the University of Illinois and is administered through the university's Office of Corporate and Public Services. The institute has become a model program, imitated in many other states.

The institute is financed by a tax on fire insurance and related premiums. One-eighth of this one-percent tax is designated for Illinois Fire Service Institute use. This allows the institute to offer most courses and services free of charge.

The Illinois Fire Service Institute uses several types of instructional staff to conduct its programs. Full-time faculty coordinate and teach the several types of specialized courses offered both on and off campus. They also are responsible for most of the institute's consultation, evaluation, and research activities.

To supplement the full-time faculty, the institute uses part-time instructors. They teach most of the institute's own field training programs, such as confined space rescue. They also are used to teach classes in their areas of specialization. When courses require additional expertise, guest instructors are used. They may be fire service personnel or university faculty, and frequently are used in the fire officer and hazardous materials curricula.

Tennessee State Fire School

Another model of a state training facility that would be considered similar to those found in many parts of the United States is located in Murfreesboro, Tennessee. Here the Tennessee State Fire School is a part of the Area Vocational-Technical School system, which is governed by the Board of Regents of the State of Tennessee. The Board of Regents also oversees all two-year and four-year state colleges and universities with the exception of the University of Tennessee system.

The Tennessee State Fire School employs a director, a coordinator, one secretary, four full-time instructors, and approximately 25 part-time instructors to deliver training to career and volunteer personnel across the state. Training is conducted on campus, in the fire departments and regionally. Industrial fire training is conducted on campus and at industrial sites.

Training is offered in basic firefighting, industrial firefighting, "smoke diving," pump operations, officer and instructor training, and apparatus maintenance. National Fire Academy courses also are taught by fire school personnel and NFA adjunct instructors.

TRADE

TRADE (Training Resources and Data Exchange) is a regional network designed to foster the exchange of fire-related training information and resources among the federal, state, and local levels of government.

TRADE was initiated in 1984 by the National Fire Academy to address the difficulties that state and local fire training systems were having in disseminating quality training programs effectively. The essential components of the TRADE system are the ten regional networks which correspond to the existing federal regions. These networks provide a mechanism for the exchange of resources and materials within and among regions. Regional TRADE co-chairs, one selected by the state training directors and the other by the metropolitan fire services in each region, serve as the points of contact for both intra- and interregional networking activities.

The heart of TRADE is the participation of its members and their efforts to promote the vital exchange of fire training information and knowledge among the 50 state fire training agencies and 130 member departments.

SAFETY CONCERNS

The role of safety officer has become increasingly important both in training sessions and at actual incidents. Too often, however, the job of safety officer is simply listed on the organization chart, or this function is tacked on to the job responsibilities of another already-busy person involved in the training process. Fire departments must take steps to make safety, and the functions of the safety officer, priorities rather than pay them mere lip service. Also, the safety officer should have absolute power to stop or alter training processes to ensure the safety of those involved.

While training is an essential ingredient in a modern fire department, it is also a source of many firefighter injuries and even fatalities. For example, a multiple-fatality training fire in Milford, Michigan, on October 25, 1987, resulted in three firefighter fatalities. Accelerants used in the live burn produced an explosion that engulfed the three firefighters, trapping them on an upper floor. Prior to this fire the National Fire Protection Association (NFPA) identified 53 training-related firefighter line-of-duty deaths from 1977 to 1986. Fortunately, the record since 1986 has improved, mostly because of an improved emphasis on safety. Training also can help to reduce injuries on the fireground. As seen in Chapter 8, when we think of safety in the fire service today we think of NFPA's Standard 1500.

In Chapter 3 of the standard, Training and Education, NFPA professional qualification standards are referenced as minimum training requirements for the various job assignments in a typical fire department. In addition, because of the deaths and injuries that have occurred during live fire drills, NFPA 1403, *Standard on Live Fire Training Evolutions in Structures,* was written.

LIVE BURNS

NFPA 1403 makes an important distinction between acquired structures and training center burn buildings. The standard recognizes that a burn building is much safer to use and is easier to manage safely than are acquired structures. Quite simply, at the training center burn building it is easier to control the work site. The contents of formerly occupied buildings present a considerable hazard during live fire training, and often must be removed. There also are problems with exposure buildings, water supply, parking, and security when using acquired structures. These typically are not problems at a properly designed training center burn building.

Some of the requirements of NFPA 1403 for acquired structures or training center burn buildings are

FUELS

- Class "A" materials only may be used, and they must be known materials (straw, wooden skids, etc.). Flammable liquids are allowed to start the fire, but not for use as a continuing fuel source.

SAFETY OFFICER

- The position of safety officer must be filled.
- Assistance must be provided for extensive operations.

FIRE LINES AND BACKUP LINES

- There must be sufficient fire flow for the planned fire problem and backup lines of sufficient size.
- Minimum line is 95 gpm.

INSTRUCTORS

- There must be an instructor on a backup line.
- An instructor must accompany each crew entering the building (crew size should not exceed five trainees).
- Additional instructors must be stationed inside building to handle unexpected events.

EMERGENCY MEDICAL SERVICE

- On-site medical assistance is necessary.

COMMUNICATIONS

- Communications must be in place to off-site resources (fire department, EMS, etc.).

PLANNING

- The training exercise must be planned in advance, and an emergency building evacuation plan must be developed.

PROTECTIVE CLOTHING

- Protective clothing shall be donned prior to entering the live fire structure and during any part of the live fire training exercise.
- Protective clothing shall be inspected by the safety officer.

- Protective clothing shall meet applicable NFPA standards.
- Self-contained breathing apparatus (SCBA) must be used by personnel operating in atmospheres that are or could become toxic.

PERSONNEL TRACKING

- A head count must be taken before and after each evolution.

CRITIQUE

- A critique of the exercise must be conducted and documented.

NFPA 1403 explains in detail the specific requirements listed above. This standard should be studied and used by every fire department training bureau.

Also included in NFPA 1403 is a checklist that should be used before any live burn in an acquired structure or dedicated burn building.

RECORDKEEPING AND DOCUMENTATION

Proper recordkeeping in the training section of a modern fire department is not only essential for internal documentation, but also is mandated by law in many instances. SARA, Title III, mandates that front-line firefighters and

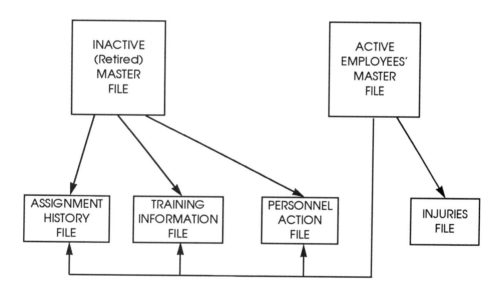

Figure 10-6. Personnel Information System Preliminary DataBase Design

- Unlimited Number of User-Specified Topics
- Schedule up to 20 Topics Per Day
- Plan Training Schedule for up to a Year
- Keeps Attendance in 1/2 hour increments
- Can Also Track Absences
- Ability to Keep Grades of Attendees
- Summary of Hours by Attendee and Topic
- Select Dates to be Included in Summaries
- Complete Record of Training History

```
                     Training Plan For 01/06/88

          Topic        ---Time---   Loc
          Code    P/C  Start Stop   Code  Instructor   Comments

  1.      10       C    093   110    8    Duty Shift   Search & Rescue
                                                         SCBA - Air Packs
  2.      10       C    193   210    8    Duty Shift   Smoke Drill in garage
                                                         SCBA - Air Packs
  3.      03       C    110   120    8    Duty Shift   Liquid fire demo
                                                         Extinguishers
  4.      03       C    210   220    8    Duty Shift   Liquid fire demo
                                                         Extinguishers
  5.


  Select Line No. _   (0 - Select next date)
```

```
Blenside Fire Protection District                        06-02-1988
Training Detail For Ronald Havelka                  From 010188-033188

           Tr      Status                              -- TIME --
  Date    Code     Code    ------- Topic --------    Start   Stop   Hours

01/02/88   P        A      1   Orientation           1930 - 2200    2.5
01/09/88   P        A      2   Fire Behavior         1930 - 2200    2.5
01/16/88   P        A     10   SCBA - Air Packs      1930 - 2100    1.5
01/16/88   P        A      3   Extinguishers         2100 - 2200    1.0
01/23/88   W        A      6   Ropes & Knots         1930 - 2200      0
01/30/88   P        A     66   Squad Operations      1930 - 2200    2.5
02/06/88   P        A     66   Squad Operations      1930 - 2200    2.5
02/13/88   P        A     40   Installed Systems     1930 - 2200    2.5
02/20/88   P        A     43   Pumps                 1930 - 2200    2.5
02/27/88   P        A     60   Apparatus Drive/Oper  1930 - 2200    2.5
03/01/88   P        A     61   Engine Operation      1930 - 2200    2.5
03/13/88   P        A     62   Aerial Operations     1930 - 2200    2.5
03/20/88   P        A     20   Hose                  1930 - 2200    2.5
03/27/88   P        A     55   Fire Prevention       1930 - 2200    2.5
                                          Total Hours               30.0
```

Figure 10-7. Training System

hazardous materials responders receive a minimum level of direct training, and that the records documenting such training be maintained by the fire department.

While recordkeeping can be done manually, this approach makes little sense in this modern era of computers and electronic data processing. If your fire department is one of the few still to be computerized, training records might be a logical place to start. The types of documentation that need to be maintained include:

- Participants' names;
- Training subjects;
- Number of hours of training;
- Certification dates; and
- Certifications, and other official records of training completion plateaus.

We have seen that injuries can result from training; they also must be documented and recorded. Figure 10-6 shows a series of interactive files that can be used to create a preliminary database design for a personnel information system, including the training function.

Many computer software companies such as *FireSoft,* ™ and *FiSerWare,* ™ and others that serve the fire service sell prepackaged database programs, including recordkeeping, for training purposes. While there may be an occasional need to customize such programs for specific training needs, they often are far superior to inventing or developing software from scratch.

Figure 10-7 shows a typical computerized training record for an individual. A computerized database permits the rapid assembling and printing of records by subject area, by individual, by hours, or by any combination of desired criteria.

SUMMARY

The modern fire department, regardless of size or configuration, is essentially incomplete and virtually nonfunctional without adequate education and training. If the leaders of the organization have attained an educational level that allows them to supervise and manage the organization effectively, its ability to achieve its complex mission is enhanced. Today's chief is forced to be both a manager of people and a leader of the organization. While the fire service leaders of today are faced with many complex problems, current needs also must be balanced against future needs and a sense of direction. The difference between *good* fire departments and *great* fire departments, and the difference between *capable* leaders and *great* leaders, is a matter of knowledge—knowledge gained through training and education.

III. EQUIPMENT

11

Fire Department Apparatus

WILLIAM C. PETERS

CHAPTER HIGHLIGHTS

- Major types of fire apparatus, the functions or purposes of each, and which apparatus are appropriate for departmental and community needs.
- The various types of ancillary equipment permanently mounted or carried on fire apparatus, and which are appropriate for departmental and community needs.
- How to devise and implement a preventive maintenance program appropriate for departmental needs.

S PECIFYING, ACQUIRING, AND maintaining fire apparatus are among a fire chief's most challenging administrative duties. Modern fire apparatus is a major investment for the community; therefore, it must fill not only the needs of today, but carry the department into the next decade and beyond. Because apparatus is replaced infrequently, this involved process might present itself only once in a chief's career. For that reason, a thorough understanding of the types of apparatus that are available, the applicable standards, and the local procurement process is essential. In many cases the vehicles parked in the fire station will actually cost more than the building that houses them!

These "chariots of fire" were not merely a means of transporting firefighters and equipment to a fire, but rather an object of pride and respect. They provided firefighters with the needed tools and capabilities to carry out their tradition of service—saving lives and protecting property.

The history of fire apparatus in this country dates to the late 1600s when hand pumpers were imported from England. The late 1700s brought ladder companies whose duties were to rescue victims from the upper floors of the then taller buildings. Major improvements were made in the 1800s with the addition of hose companies, the use of steam to pump water, and horses to pull the apparatus. Mounted aerial ladders started appearing late in the century. The beginning of the 1900s was the end of the horse-drawn era and the introduction of motorized fire apparatus as we know it today.

NFPA STANDARDS

For many years, NFPA 1901, *Standard on Automotive Fire Apparatus,* served as the guide for specifying and purchasing all motorized fire apparatus. Just as the previous paragraph described the progression of fire apparatus through this country's history, the NFPA Technical Committee on Fire Department Equipment realized that modern fire apparatus was growing in complexity and new technical innovations needed to be addressed. It was the committee's opinion that one standard to cover all of the variations to the basic unit of apparatus would not suffice, so the committee organized the apparatus standards into the following categories:

NFPA 1901—*Standard for Pumper Fire Apparatus*
NFPA 1902—*Standard for Initial Attack Fire Apparatus*
NFPA 1903—*Standard for Mobile Water Supplies; and*
NFPA 1904—*Standard for Aerial Ladder and Elevating Platform Fire Apparatus.*

The 1991 editions of 1901, 1902, 1903, and 1904 are referenced in this chapter, As this text goes to press, the committee is in the process of combining all apparatus, including special-purpose, into one standard again. (The anticipated completion date is in 1996.)

SAFETY CONCERNS

In addition to separating apparatus by function, the standards incorporate many new safety features which were adopted to enhance and improve the health and safety of the personnel who would use the apparatus. The requirements include:

- total enclosure of all crew seating areas with requirements for seats and seat belts for all members;
- safety door latches;
- maximum stepping heights;
- access handrails;
- intake pressure relief system for pumpers;
- a minimum 250-pound aerial ladder tip load;
- various interlocks;
- additional warning lights;

- reductions in cab noise levels; and
- addition of reflective striping for increased visibility.

Each standard clearly defines the basic requirements and performance criteria of the apparatus, and contains an Appendix "C", a multipage checklist that outlines each item that should be considered in apparatus purchasing. It is the purchaser's responsibility to provide bidders with information sufficient for them to prepare a bid proposal (or sample specification); completing the checklist ensures that most areas of concern will be addressed.

The process of using the Appendix C checklist will help make the task of preparing specifications easier, and should reduce the probability of omitting important features of the specification.

The NFPA apparatus standards use the terms pumper, mobile water supply apparatus, aerial ladder and elevating platform apparatus, initial attack vehicle, and special purpose vehicles. The Incident Command Systems, adopted in many parts of the country, use different designations for these units and for other fire service vehicles. This chapter, since it draws so heavily on the NFPA apparatus standards, uses the NFPA designations to facilitate cross referencing and use of the standards.

General apparatus requirements of the NFPA standards

VEHICLE AND AXLE WEIGHTS

Recently there has been much concern about fire apparatus exceeding Gross Vehicle Weight Ratings (GVWR) and Gross Axle Weight Ratings

The 1991 edition of the NFPA apparatus standards contained many new safety-related requirements. Some of them shown here include the total enclosure of the crew seating area, reflective striping to enhance night visibility and the mounting of audible warning devices low and to the front of the apparatus. PHOTO COURTESY OF R. JEFFERS

(GAWR) recommended by the manufacturers. Legislation has been adopted in several states to restrict the axle weights of all vehicles, including fire apparatus, on roads and highways.

When you purchase new apparatus, the GVWR and GAWR must be sufficient to carry the fully equipped apparatus, including tank and water, hose load, and ground ladders, as well as provide an allowance for miscellaneous equipment (2,000 pounds for pumpers) or more if specified by the purchaser. In addition, personnel, calculated at 200 pounds each, shall be added for the maximum number of persons that will ride on the apparatus. In some cases this will require the use of tandem rear axles to carry the load and provide added braking capacity.

Specifying the proper GVWR is an important safety aspect because overloading a vehicle can result in poor brake performance, reduced vehicle control, and possible failures of driveline, axles, springs, tires, and related components.

ROAD PERFORMANCE REQUIREMENTS

It is critical in apparatus purchasing that the engine, transmission, and driveline combination be completely compatible with each other and be of sufficient size to deliver the expected performance from the apparatus. In addition to the engine having the necessary horsepower and torque to drive the fire pump adequately, it must be able to provide enough power and performance to operate safely on the roads and terrain on which it will be driven. The following road test criteria, established by the NFPA, will provide the minimum requirements for apparatus performance.

The fully loaded apparatus must be capable of passing the following road performance test on dry, level, paved roads in good condition:

- From a standing start, the vehicle shall attain a speed of 35 mph within 25 seconds; 30 seconds for aerial apparatus.
- From a steady speed of 15 mph the vehicle shall accelerate to a speed of 35 mph within 30 seconds, in the same gear.
- The vehicle shall attain a minimum top speed of 50 mph. and
- The apparatus shall be able to maintain a speed of at least 20 mph on any grade up to and including 6 percent.

The braking performance of the apparatus also is specified. The service brakes shall be capable of bringing the fully loaded vehicle to a complete stop from a speed of 20 mph, in a distance not exceeding 35 feet, on a level hard surface road and shall hold the fully loaded apparatus parked on at least a 20 percent grade.

DRIVING AND CREW COMPARTMENT

A fully enclosed driving compartment with seating for a minimum of two persons is required. The maximum number of personnel who will ride on the apparatus must be specified, and seats with approved seat belts must be provided in a *fully enclosed area.*

In an effort to reduce firefighter hearing, loss the maximum noise level at any seat location shall not exceed 90 dB at a speed of 45 mph, without warning devices in operation. To meet this requirement, manufacturers have added insulation to the engine compartment, used larger mufflers, and, in some cases, actually moved the engine out of the cab to the rear or midship area of the apparatus.

In conjunction with reducing cab noise, a new requirement stipulates that all sound-producing warning devices, such as sirens and air horns, must now be mounted as low and as far forward as practical. The apparatus standard now prohibits their being located on the cab roof where they are only inches away from firefighters' ears.

Another important safety improvement is the requirement that door handles be either protected against or designed to prevent accidental opening. Many accidents have been attributed to instances of clothing or other equipment catching on protruding door handles, causing firefighters to have been either ejected or dragged by the moving apparatus.

PUMPERS

The basic unit of fire apparatus is the fire department pumper.

A pumper, according to NFPA 1901, is an automotive fire apparatus with a permanently mounted fire pump, water tank, and hose body, hence the name "triple-combination pumper." The unit must be designed for sustained pumping operations during structural firefighting and be capable of supporting associated fire department operations. The vehicle also may be equipped with an optional water tower to provide an elevated master stream for fire suppression.

Fire Pump

The minimum rated capacity of a mounted fire pump is not less than 750 gallons per minute (gpm). Pumps of higher capacity are rated in 250-gpm increments, considered to be a standard hoseline stream. Pumps that deliver 1,000, 1,250, or 1,500 gpm are popular in the municipal fire service. The pump must be of centrifugal design with stainless steel shaft and bronze impellors.

The pump and related equipment must be able to deliver the following percentage of rated capacity at the net pump pressure indicated: 100 percent at 150 psi, 70 percent at 200 psi, and 50 percent at 250 psi, at draft.

An additional requirement of being able to deliver 100 percent of rated capacity at 165 psi net pump pressure is intended to test the ability of the apparatus engine to provide additional power when needed.

There are individuals who believe that the apparatus' fire pump does not need to be specified as larger than what the local water system can supply adequately. However, this theory needs to be evaluated carefully because of the pump's rated capacity characteristics. A fire pump's capacity is rated at 150 psi. As you increase discharge pressure above this figure, available volume decreases.

If a maximum 1,000-gpm flow is available from the water system and a 1,000-gpm pump were in service, you could expect to pump maximum capacity at 150 psi. If a long relay were involved, using standard 2½-inch or 3-inch fire hose, and requiring a 250-psi pump pressure, theoretically you could expect only 50 percent, or 500 gpm, from the pumper.

If a larger 1,500-gpm pump were in service, the unit could deliver at least 750 gpm at 250 psi or 1,050 (70 percent) at 200 psi.

So, before you select a pump size, consider the maximum pressure requirements as well as gallons per minute of capacity available at the higher pressures.

The basic unit of fire apparatus is the "triple-combination pumper," containing a permanently mounted fire pump, water tank, and hose body. PHOTO COURTESY OF R. JEFFERS

Single or two stage?

Most modern fire pumps in use today are either single- or two-stage centrifugal units; single-stage units are used more often. A two-stage pump is constructed of two impellers mounted in the pump housing and driven by a common shaft. It is actually two pumps contained in one housing. When operated in the parallel (volume or capacity) position, an equal amount of water enters each stage and is discharged at the same pump pressure. When pumping in series (pressure) position, all water that enters the first stage is pumped from the discharge of the first stage into the intake of the second stage where the pressure is increased. This changeover is accomplished by the use of the transfer valve. An important characteristic of the centrifugal pump is the ability to take advantage of incoming pressure.

Improved engine designs and the development of single-stage pumps that will easily deliver the range of volume and pressure required in the standards have led to an increase in single-stage pumps on new fire apparatus. One advantage of this design is that single-stage pumps have fewer internal parts; this results in reduced maintenance and repair costs. Other benefits include lower initial cost, and ease of training. With a single-stage pump the operator need not be concerned with properly selecting either the pressure or volume mode to pump in, or at what point the changeover must occur.

From an efficiency point of view, less engine horsepower is needed to cover the two-stage pump's range of operation. In the higher-pressure, low-flow conditions that often are encountered in structural firefighting (less than half the capacity of the pump being used), the two-stage pump in the pressure (series) mode, will provide the needed flows at lower engine rpms than the single stage. This results in less wear and tear on the engine, drive train and pump, and conserves fuel, an added benefit.

In making the decision to specify a single- versus two-stage pump, survey the fire department's needs. If supplying high-rise buildings or if long relays are regular occurrences, a two-stage pump would probably best suit your needs.

Related pump requirements

Regardless of the size of the pump or the number of stages, certain other equipment and controls are required to provide a safe and efficient operation.

DISCHARGES

A sufficient number of discharge outlets must be provided to move water out of the pump efficiently. A minimum of two 2½-inch outlets must be provided and the remaining capacity of the pump can be discharged through additional 2½-inch or larger outlets. The following are pump outlet sizes and their rated flow:

- 2½-inch/250 gpm
- 3-inch/375 gpm
- 3½-inch/500 gpm
- 4-inch/625 gpm
- 4½-inch/750 gpm
- 5-inch/1,000 gpm.

All discharges not in a preconnected hose storage area must be equipped with a suitable cap and a 30-degree downward sweep elbow fitting.

Two 1½-inch or larger outlets with 2-inch plumbing shall be provided in the specified hose storage areas to be valved and piped for use as preconnected attack lines.

All valves that are 3 inches or larger must be equipped with a "slow-acting" mechanism that will not allow the valve to be operated from full close to full open or vice versa in less than three seconds. This requirement is an

In addition to color coding the intakes and discharges, the center of this pump panel shows a top view of the apparatus, with a line directing the operator to the location of the function that the gauge and electronic valve control. PHOTO COURTESY OF AUTHOR

attempt to avoid a dangerous water hammer condition. The delay can be accomplished by adding a slow-acting device to a standard valve or by using regulated air or hydraulic valve controls.

Additionally, no discharge valve larger than 2½ inches can be located at the pump operator's position. This important safety feature was intended to keep the high-volume, large diameter hose (LDH) lines away from the pump operator, to prevent injury in case of a burst length or disconnected coupling. By the same token, LDH intake relief valves should be installed away from the operator's position for the same obvious safety reasons.

Many fire departments find it advantageous to color code various pump discharges, valves, and gauges. In order to avoid confusion in color coding, a standardized list of functions and colors was developed and is included in Appendix A of NFPA 1901.

On the subject of discharges, many fire departments have eliminated the traditional low-flow booster line and replaced it with preconnected "trash" lines. This allows a quick, powerful knockdown of nuisance fires in the immediate area of the apparatus and eliminates the temptation to stretch a booster line that is inadequate in gpm flow into a structure.

PRESSURE REGULATION

Standard 1901 requires a pressure-regulating device that is connected to the pump's discharge and must limit the pressure rise to a maximum of 30 psi in the range of 90 psi up to 300 psi. This control is possible by using either a pressure relief valve or a pressure governor unit.

RELIEF VALVES

The function of the relief valve is to bypass excess water from the discharge side of the pump back to the intake side, thus preventing dangerous pressure buildup. In most systems this is accomplished by using a pilot valve, mounted on the pump panel, to control the internal relief valve inside the pump. When set by the pump operator, excess discharge pressure acting against the spring tension of the pilot valve causes the relief valve in the pump to open. This action then directs the water under excess pressure from the discharge to the suction side of the pump. When the pressure subsides, the relief valve closes and the steady discharge pressure is maintained. To help the operator properly set the valve, a yellow indicator light is required to illuminate on the pump panel when the valve is open and dumping.

PRESSURE GOVERNOR

The pump pressure governor has been in service in various forms for many years. The difference between this system and the relief valve is that a pressure governor controls the engine speed in order to maintain a constant pump pressure, rather than dealing directly with the water. Many of the old systems became unreliable because of sloppy mechanical linkage connections and the distinct possibility of being knocked out of adjustment from work being done on the engine.

Modern diesel engines with electronically controlled fuel injection have renewed interest in this system for pressure control because they can be interfaced well with the pressure governor's pump controller.

When the pump operator sets the desired discharge pressure, engine rpms increase automatically to reach the selected pressure. Discharge pressure is monitored continuously by a pressure sensor, which supplies the information to a microprocessor in the pump governor. The engine's rpms are adjusted automatically, as needed, to maintain a steady pump pressure. Because the pressure governor system adjusts the engine's rpms, it could help prolong engine and pump life, as well as reduce fuel consumption, a critical factor during a long-duration operation.

INTAKE RELIEF VALVE

Another pressure-regulating device now required is the Intake Pressure Relief system. The purpose of this system is to relieve excess pressure that develops in the supply side of the pump. This rapid increase would most likely occur when water is received in relay and a shutdown of supplied streams or devices occurs. A properly set suction relief valve would dump excess water to the ground, thus reducing any dangerously high intake pressure, and avoiding overpressurization of the pump and hoselines. Standard 1901 calls for it to cover a range of 75 to 250 psi and it may be operator adjustable. The valve's discharge should be away from the pump operator and terminate in a male hose thread fitting. Some departments choose to attach a length of hose to this fitting to carry the water away from the area of the apparatus. This procedure could be dangerous unless the open butt is secured properly. If the intake relief valve opens and discharges water under high pressure into the hose, the loose, open butt end of the hose, if not secured, will whip around, possibly injuring firefighters or bystanders.

Water tanks

Apparatus water tanks are to be constructed of noncorrosive material or other materials that are protected against corrosion and deterioration. Modern plastics, fiberglass composite materials, and rust-inhibited steel are being used extensively to eliminate the old, leaky booster tank that has plagued the fire service for many years. Many of the tank manufacturers offer warranties that cover their tank construction for the life of the apparatus.

The rated water capacity of the tank must be not less than 500 gallons, with a tank-to-pump piping and valve arrangement that will be able to deliver water to the pump at a minimum rate of 500 gpm. This is to allow the use of two 1¾-inch preconnected lines, one 2½-inch preconnect or a prepiped deck gun. A check valve to prevent back pressure from entering the tank must be installed in the line as well.

An overflow outlet that will discharge any overflow water behind the rear wheels is to be provided, as well as ample tank venting to prevent unwanted pressure when the tank is being filled.

Another construction feature that is extremely important to the safe operation of the vehicle is the installation of swash partitions in the design of the tank interior. These baffles prevent the momentum of the moving water in the tank from exerting force in any one direction caused by the motion of the vehicle. Without this compartmentation the vehicle would be dangerously unstable to drive on curves and turns.

A tank's durability is dependent largely on proper installation. To prevent cracking, the tank must be attached securely to the apparatus yet allow for the flexing that occurs as the vehicle is driven over uneven roads or terrain.

Compartmentation

Pumpers obviously must carry a vast array of equipment to allow fire personnel to cope with the many tasks and details they must perform. To keep this equipment protected from the elements, yet quickly accessible, compartments are specified. NFPA 1901 indicates that a pumper should have a minimum of 30 cubic feet of enclosed, weather-resistant compartmentation, and that the compartments must be vented, lighted and have provisions for drainage of moisture.

Specifying adequate compartmentation to carry all of your equipment is extremely important. Large, bulky items such as LDH manifolds and positive pressure ventilation fans require compartments of substantial size with full-sized openings.

Several manufacturers have found creative ways to make the best use of the compartment space available, including roll-out shelves, roll-out, tilt-down drawers, and vertical boards on roll-outs.

The requirement to provide an SCBA unit *and spare cylinder* for each seat installed in the apparatus could consume a large amount of available compartmentation. One place to store spare SCBA cylinders that has worked successfully for some departments, is in individual wheel well compartments. These compact storage compartments hold one cylinder with an access door to the outside and are an efficient way to use the dead space at the top of the wheel wells. Another way to deal with this storage problem is to use air pack seat-

Efficiently utilizing available space can enhance the equipment-carrying capacity of the apparatus. This rescue unit is equipped with shelves that roll out and drop down, to allow firefighters to easily reach the equipment that they hold. Five-gallon cans of foam are hoisted to a rooftop storage area that would normally be considered "dead space." PHOTO COURTESY OF R. MILNES

Roll-up compartment doors have been used successfully in Europe for many years and are now gaining wide acceptance in this country. PHOTO COURTESY OF R. JEFFERS

backs for the SCBA units and to specify high side compartments on one side of the apparatus for storage of spare cylinders only.

Compartment doors are of two types. Doors of box pan construction with slam latches tend to be standard. A type used in Europe for many years and one recently gaining in popularity is the roll-up or shutter type door. Some benefits of the roll-up door are that its opening will not be obstructed by objects next to the apparatus, such as parked cars, and that it does not protrude past the side of the apparatus when open, which eliminates the "forcible removal" of the door when the apparatus leaves quarters. It lends itself nicely to use on compartmentation that is inside the cab or rescue body because there is no door swing area with which to contend. One disadvantage of the shutter type door is the possibility that equipment could become dislodged and jam the door in the closed position.

Be sure to tell the manufacturer about any equipment of special size or shape that is to be carried on the apparatus so that proper design accommodations can be made.

Hose Storage

A minimum area of 55 cubic feet of space is required for stowing hose on new pumper apparatus. With the extensive use of 4-inch and 5-inch large diameter hose for water supply, and large capacity pumps for fire attack lines, an increased hose bed area should be considered.

One adjustable hose bed divider must be provided to accommodate split loads, but of course you may specify as many dividers as needed to customize the hose bed for your particular operations. The minimum allowable length of the hose bed is 60 inches. The floor of the hose bed is to be constructed of non-corrosive material with provisions for ventilation and must be removable.

At least two areas, each to accommodate a minimum of 200 feet of 1¾-inch hose, shall be provided. These usually are used for the required preconnects.

Specifications for hose compartments should include a cover to keep the hose clean, free from damage, and dry in inclement weather. Any cover that is specified should be easy to remove for hose packing operations.

FOAM SYSTEMS

Several types of foam systems, both Class A and Class B, can be added to the pumper to enhance its firefighting capabilities. The requirements for the proper configuration and installation of these systems are specified in NFPA 1901.

In-line eductor

In-line foam eductors can be used either on the outside of the discharge or mounted in the pump outlet plumbing of selected discharges. When the foam concentrate valve is opened and the proper percentage of solution is selected, water passing through the eductor creates a *venturi* effect and the concentrate is mixed in the stream. It is essential to properly match the nozzle with the flow range of the eductor; there are limitations on the amount of hose that can be used from the discharge.

Although in-line eductors are easy to operate and maintain, there are several important limitations you must keep in mind. One is the pressure drop that occurs when the water passes through the venturi, thus limiting the reach of the stream; the other is that if the eductor is mounted externally, several personnel must be committed to handling a supply of bulky, five-gallon pails of foam concentrate if a continuous, long-term supply of foam is required. At the 6 percent setting, 6 gallons of concentrate is combined with 94 gallons of water to produce 100 gallons of mixed foam before expansion. For a large flammable liquid fire, you will need numerous cans of foam to maintain the attack until extinguishment.

Around-the-pump proportioning system

An around-the-pump proportioning system consists of an eductor mounted between the pump's discharge and intake. Water from the pump's discharge passes through the eductor and causes foam concentrate to be introduced into the suction side of the pump. The proportioner can be controlled with either a manual metering valve or by installing an automatic system that uses a flow meter to monitor discharge and adjust the concentrate flow accordingly.

One disadvantage of this system is that once it is activated, foam is produced from all discharges and water cannot be discharged simultaneously. Another is that pump intake pressure is critical to foam discharge performance and must be monitored closely by the pump operator.

Premixed systems

There are two types of premixed systems, both of which use a tank in which the foam and water have been premixed in the proper proportion.

The first, the pressure type system, is usually found on quick-attack vehicles and uses premixed foam in a pressure vessel. The tank is pressurized by compressed gas and the mixture is propelled from the discharge device, usually a hose reel.

The second type uses a tank at atmospheric pressure that is connected to the water pump's intake. The premixed concentrate is introduced into the pump from the tank and discharged as required.

This type of system can be created by adding the correct amount of foam concentrate to the water tank of a fire apparatus (batch mixing). However, adding foam directly to the water tank on a piece of apparatus that was not designed for premix usage could cause damage to the tank, pump, and plumbing. Consult the manufacturer before you attempt this operation.

Balanced pressure systems

One type of balanced pressure system uses a pressure vessel with an internal bladder that contains foam concentrate. When operated, water pressure enters the container and exerts pressure on the bladder, expelling the foam concentrate at pressure equal to the ratio controller (proportioner) for discharge.

The second type uses a separate foam concentrate pump which pumps concentrate at a pressure equal to the pump pressure to a metering valve which then directs it to a ratio controller (proportioner) connected to the discharge.

Direct injection and compressed air foam

The direct injection method uses a separate positive-pressure pump to inject the foam concentrate into the water pump's discharge. The correct rate of concentrate is controlled by a microprocessor which receives an electrical signal from a flow meter attached to the discharge and adjusts the injection rate as needed.

Compressed air foam systems (CAFS) are a derivation of the direct injection system. The system uses a foam agent pump and air compressor in conjunction with the fire pump. As with direct injection, foam concentrate is injected into the discharge from the concentrate pump that is regulated by use of a flow meter in the discharge. Foam agent and compressed air then are mixed by a mixer unit installed in the water pump discharge. The result is a light, fluffy foam.

EQUIPMENT CARRIED ON PUMPERS

The equipment that is to be carried on pumpers is listed in three categories in NFPA 1901. First is equipment supplied by the contractor, second is equipment required by the standard to be carried; last is additional equipment that is recommended for inclusion.

The objective of these recommendations is to ensure that a pumper that arrives at the scene of a fire or emergency will have the proper equipment available to immediately begin emergency operations. The variations in services provided in each community, as well as the availability of other specialized units responding, will cause the list to vary, but the equipment generally is considered to be the minimum.

Supplied by contractor

The following equipment should be supplied and mounted by the apparatus manufacturer: one 14-foot (minimum) straight ladder with roof hooks; one 24-foot extension ladder (minimum) and one 10-foot folding ladder. Where no ladder trucks are in service or their anticipated arrival will be delayed, a 35-foot extension ladder in place of the 24-foot ladder may be a desirable alternative.

A minimum of 15 feet of hard or soft suction hose to supply the pump shall be provided. The selection of the type of suction hose is dependent on its intended use. The buyer might want to include both types, if both hydrant and drafting operations are anticipated. If hard suction is provided, a strainer and double female swivel also must be furnished.

Hydraulic and electrically powered racks that keep ground ladders and hard suction hoses stored over the hose bed and out of the way have become popular in recent years. Activating the power unit lowers this heavy and bulky equipment to a comfortable level for safe removal and use. An added benefit of this configuration is that it allows the side body space, normally used for ladder storage, to become available for extra storage compartments.

A list of equipment that is required on a pumper is contained in the Technical Resources section of this book.

VARIATIONS ON THE STANDARD PUMPER

Elevated water tower

Some fire departments find it desirable to equip their pumpers with a telescoping or articulating elevated water tower. These versatile compact units range in height from 30 to 75 feet. The ability to place an elevated master stream in service quickly can be a valuable asset on the fireground for fast knockdown of fires on upper floors. "Squrts" as they are commonly called,

Racks that store ladders and other equipment over the hose bed increase the amount of usable compartment space available. On this apparatus, it allowed the fire department to store Self-Contained Breathing Apparatus in the upper compartments on both sides of the apparatus. Some of these racks are power operated and can hold other bulky equipment such as hard suction hoses or folding tanks. PHOTO COURTESY OF R. MILNES

Some departments equip their pumpers with an elevated water tower. This allows them to place an elevated master stream in service quickly and if equipped with a ladder, the apparatus can double as an aerial device when an urgent rescue must be performed. PHOTO COURTESY OF R. JEFFERS

have proved extremely effective in urban areas where interior firefighting in dilapidated vacant buildings poses a great risk to firefighters.

The addition of a ladder to the boom device allows the pumper to double as an aerial apparatus when an urgent rescue must be made from upper stories before a truck company arrives.

If the water tower is furnished with a ladder attached to the booms, it must meet all of the requirements for a standard aerial device, including 18-inch minimum width, rungs that are 14 inches on center, and 12-inch side handrails.

The rated tip load of the water tower shall be 250 pounds carried at the tip, in the horizontal position and maximum extension. The unit must be able to operate in any position while carrying this load, without water flowing.

With 1,000 gpm of water flowing, the tower shall have a 250-pound capacity at 45 degrees of elevation and full extension.

Design and performance requirements for this apparatus are contain in NFPA 1901 and call for the water tower to be constructed of two or more booms designed to telescope, articulate, or both. The waterway system must be designed to supply a minimum capacity of 1,000 gpm at 100 psi from the tower's elevated nozzle.

One of the disadvantages of this combination unit is that the additional height and weight added to the pumper must be considered in light of station design. Also, because the tower usually is mounted directly at the rear of the apparatus, its base passes through the center of the hose bed. Hose must be packed along the side or forward of the base, which might alter your normal hose stretch procedures.

High-pressure units

Some fire departments include high-pressure fog streams in their daily operations for brush as well as structural fires. Low flows of water at high pressure (400 to 750 psi) are pumped through high-pressure-rated booster lines to a high-pressure nozzle which atomizes the stream to a very fine mist of water fog from 18 to 30 gpm. For interior firefighting, the low volume of this type of stream severely limits its effectiveness and could possibly expose firefighters to greater personal hazard than conventional higher volume handlines.

A common way to provide high-pressure output is to add a third stage to the two-stage fire pump. When it is activated, water discharging from the second stage enters the third stage where the pressure is increased accordingly.

Four-stage, high-pressure, low-volume pumps also have been used for high-pressure booster use with pressures up to 1,000 psi.

High-pressure, high-volume pumps

Some city fire departments operate special three-stage high-pressure units, that can supply several standard hose streams at 700 psi to overcome the head pressure in high-rise building standpipe systems.

High-volume units

Triple-combination pumpers with pump capacities of 2,000 gpm or greater generally are considered high-volume units. Their configuration basically matches that of other pumpers, except that they require a larger than normally specified engine to supply the needed horsepower to drive the pump, and an additional number of discharges to accommodate the increased pump capacity. Many high-volume units will have two or more LDH discharges and carry greater than normal quantities of LDH to make it easier to move their high-volume capacity to the scene.

Some also feature a large-capacity deck gun permanently mounted and piped to the pump. When fed by two pumpers, some of these guns are capable of discharging 3,000 gpm, making them formidable weapons against conflagrations.

High-volume pumpers, especially when using large diameter hose, and large capacity deck-gun, can provide a formidable weapon when needed. PHOTO COURTESY OF R. JEFFERS

COMBINATION PUMPER UNITS

In an effort to get maximum efficiency from each vehicle, and to address the requirements for added capabilities, the basic pumper can be modified and adapted to complete additional tasks. These combination vehicles can be cost effective because they offer expanded capabilities; this reduces the number of vehicles in the fleet that require fuel, maintenance, and repairs.

One obvious disadvantage of this concept is that when they are being used for their special function, they are removed from service as a basic pumper and when committed as a pumper the special service is temporarily suspended. Another is that when a combination unit is unavailable because of maintenance or mechanical failure, you lose two capabilities rather than one.

Paramedic pumper

Across much of America, fire departments are charged with providing advanced life support services to citizens. With their geographical locations and quick response times, pumpers often are dispatched as the first responder to medical emergencies. Pumpers used for medical responses have secure storage areas for the additional equipment needed.

Some fire departments have specified command cab type pumpers with special secure storage compartments inside the cab. This way, the sensitive medical supplies and equipment are stored safely and kept accessible, without the loss of compartmentation needed for basic firefighting equipment.

Rescue pumpers

Rescue pumpers usually have additional compartmentation to carry such needed items as extrication equipment, cribbing, air bags, generators, high-angle rope rescue equipment, wood, metal, and concrete cutting tools and a wide assortment of other special rescue tools.

Combining the pumper and rescue functions into one vehicle has the added benefit of providing the necessary charged hoseline at the scene of an auto extrication or other transportation-related incident.

Hazardous materials pumper

Some combination hazardous materials pumpers contain foam systems, special extinguishing agents such as Class D extinguishers, and polar solvent foams, as well as spill and leak abatement equipment, protective entry suits, and necessary hazardous monitoring meter equipment. Additional specialized compartments may be necessary to carry this equipment properly.

Command cab pumper

Command cab pumpers use the spacious open cab created by the modern technology of mid or rear engine design. With the raised roof design, added headroom and visibility make it possible to install a command center that is on scene and protected from the elements. Including such equipment as a desk, radio console, computer equipment, reference materials, and cellular telephone turns the command center into a mini operations center.

This type of apparatus can transport more firefighters and be used as an air-conditioned rehabilitation area as well.

A command cab's increased weight and size could necessitate using a greater capacity front axle as well as a longer wheel base; these add to the cost of the apparatus.

The modern technology of mid or rear engine configuration makes it possible to add a small command center to the cab of the pumper. This haz-mat command pumper contains a writing desk with reference material, several radios and cellular telephone and fax machine. PHOTO COURTESY OF AUTHOR

INITIAL ATTACK FIRE APPARATUS

Initial attack units are designed for initial fire suppression attack on structural, vehicular, or vegetation fires, and consist of an attack pump, water tank, limited hose, and equipment.

All of the previously described safety improvements and vehicle performance requirements contained in NFPA 1901 also apply to initial attack fire apparatus.

VEHICLE AND AXLE WEIGHT

The requirements for the Gross Axle Weight Rating (GAWR) and the Gross Vehicle Weight Rating (GVWR) for initial attack apparatus vary according to the vehicle's components, number of personnel, and the amount of miscellaneous equipment to be carried.

The chassis GVWR shall be adequate to carry the fully equipped apparatus, including hose load, full water tank, ladders, miscellaneous equipment, and personnel calculated at 200 pounds each.

Initial Attack Units are designed for initial fire suppression operations on structural, vehicular or vegetation fires. Their small size and fast response can often provide a quick "knock down" before larger apparatus arrive. PHOTO COURTESY OF R. MILNES

Miscellaneous equipment allowances are:

Chassis GVWR	Equipment
10,000 to 15,000 pounds	900 pounds
15,001 to 20,000 pounds	1,500 pounds
>20,001 pounds	2,000 pounds

PUMP

A minimum 250-gpm capacity attack pump shall be mounted on the apparatus. Larger pumps of higher capacity (up to 700 gpm) may be used if desired.

The rated pump capacity for the attack pump is the same as that for a standard fire pump. It shall deliver 100 percent at 150 psi, 70 percent at 200 psi, and 50 percent at 250 psi. In addition, if the apparatus is capable of pump and roll operations, the pump must deliver a minimum of 10 gpm at 100 psi at 5 miles per hour.

An attack pumper is required to have a minimum of one 2½-inch discharge. In addition two 1½-inch outlets are to be provided in the hose storage area to be used as preconnects. Additional discharges should be specified to provide adequate outlets for the rated capacity of the pump.

WATER TANK

For initial attack apparatus a minimum 200-gallon water tank is to be provided and constructed of noncorrosive material, or material protected against deterioration, and be equipped with swash partitions. Suitable venting and overflow provisions must be available.

The required flow rate, from the tank to the pump, for tanks up to 500 gallons, is at a rate of 250 gpm. Tanks larger than 500 gallons shall be capable of a 400-gpm flow.

COMPARTMENTS AND HOSE BEDS

A minimum of 18 cubic feet of ventilated, lighted, weather-resistant compartmentation for storage of equipment shall be provided.

A hose bed or reels capable of holding 300 feet of 2½-inch or larger hose and two areas to accommodate a minimum of 200 feet of 1¾-inch hose each is to be provided.

If hose beds are used, a 50-inch minimum length is required in addition to all of the design and construction features outlined for pumpers.

LADDERS

The standard calls for an extension ground ladder to be carried on the attack vehicle. The minimum length is in accordance with the vehicle weight rating:

- 10,000 to 15,000 GVWR—12 feet
- 15,001 to 20,000—14 feet
- 20,001 and up—16 feet

A list of equipment that is to be carried on the attack vehicle is located in the Technical Resources Section at the back of this book.

MOBILE WATER SUPPLY FIRE APPARATUS

Mobile Water Supply Apparatus are designed to transport water to the scene of fires or emergency incidents.

All of the previously described safety improvements and vehicle performance requirements contained in NFPA 1901 also apply.

VEHICLE AND AXLE WEIGHT

The chassis Gross Vehicle Weight Rating (GVWR) must be adequate to carry the fully equipped apparatus, including full water tank, hose load, ladders, and personnel calculated at 200 pounds each. An additional 1,000 pounds is to be allowed for miscellaneous equipment.

WATER TANK CONSTRUCTION

A minimum 1,000-gallon capacity water tank is to be provided and constructed of noncorrosive material suitably protected against deterioration and corrosion. Tanks of several configurations are available. Their size, center of gravity, and the vehicle's handling characteristics will vary with each design. The tank may extend the full width of the apparatus over the wheels, thus lowering the load for greater stability.

Swash partitions or baffles must be provided and are most important with respect to safe driving. The standard calls for a sufficient number of swash partitions so that the maximum horizontal dimension of any space in the tank does not exceed 48 inches. Without these partitions, the inertia that would build from the water traveling inside the tank and changing direction could cause the vehicle to suddenly go out of control.

Suitable venting and overflow provisions must be made to prevent the tank from being damaged from overpressurization during filling. The overflow must direct the water behind the rear axle so that it will not interfere with traction.

Using commercial petroleum tank trucks converted for fire service use could present a serious danger if they are not modified properly. The demands placed on fire apparatus vary considerably from those of commercial vehicles. An oil truck might lack the power and performance for a swift response as well as the braking capabilities needed for use as fire apparatus. Such modifications as sufficient tank venting and baffling are absolutely essential during the conversion. Protection from rust and corrosion inside the tank also must be addressed.

OFF LOADING

The tank must have provisions to discharge its water to the left, right, and rear of the apparatus. Using either individual valves on each side of the tank or a single valve mounted in the center of the rear and a chute or piping to direct the water to either side meets this requirement.

Off loading of water must be done at a minimum average rate of 1,000 gpm for 90 percent of the capacity of the tank. Increased rate of discharge can be accomplished, over the normal gravity dump, by installing either a jet-assist system or pneumatic pump.

The water tank on a Mobile Water Supply Apparatus must be able to discharge its water to the left, right, and rear of the apparatus. This is sometimes accomplished with a chute or piping to direct the water. PHOTO COURTESY OF W. CIRONE

The jet assist is accomplished by installing a single jet nozzle that directs its discharge at the gravity dump from inside the tank. The nozzle is supplied by a pump that forces the water out of the dump.

A second type of jet-assist system has two or more jets installed in the discharge piping outside the dump. When supplied by the pump they cause the tank water to be drawn through the dump at an increased rate of efficiency.

The pneumatic system uses a pump to pressurize the tank, expelling the water at an increased rate.

TANK FILLING

The apparatus must have a direct tank fill connection that is capable of a minimum tank fill rate of 1,000 gpm. The valved intake must be equipped with a strainer, 30-degree elbow, and suitable cap.

FIRE PUMP

If the mobile water supply apparatus is equipped with an attack pump (250 gpm to 700 gpm), or a fire pump (over 750 gpm), all provisions of NFPA 1901's pump requirements for capacity, discharges, and pressure controls are repeated.

TRANSFER PUMP

A transfer pump is a centrifugal water pump that is mounted on the apparatus and is used primarily for water transfer from its tank. The pump can be driven either by a separate engine or by power take-off from the apparatus transmission. The minimum rated capacity of the transfer pump shall be 250 gpm at 50 psi. It also should be capable of pumping a minimum of 100 gpm at 115 psi.

The tank-to-pump intake line must be capable of supplying water to the pump to satisfy the pump's rated capacity at 50 psi discharge pressure. Sufficient discharge outlets must be provided to discharge the pump's rated capacity.

COMPARTMENTS AND HOSE BEDS

A minimum of 18 cubic feet of ventilated, lighted, weather-resistant compartmentation for storage of equipment shall be provided on the mobile water supply unit.

A hose bed area, compartment, or reel capable of accommodating 200 feet of 2½-inch or larger hose is to be provided. If the apparatus is equipped with an attack or fire pump, hose storage for 200 feet of 1¾-inch hose must be provided. Normally a mobile water supply unit does not include fire attack capabilities. However, if a suitable pump is installed, this line might prove valuable in protecting the apparatus from a fast-spreading fire.

A list of equipment that is to be carried on a mobile water supply unit is contained in the Technical Resources section of this book.

FIRE DEPARTMENT AERIAL UNITS

While pumping apparatus can be traced back to the late 1600s, aerial apparatus is a relative newcomer to the fire service, appearing almost 200 years later. The original truck companies carried only ground ladders on a wagon; the longest reached 75 feet and required 9 people to raise it! Early attempts at an apparatus-mounted, self-supporting aerial failed. The first successful aerial truck was built and patented by Daniel D. Hayes, a machinist with the San Francisco Fire Department. The unit's 85-foot aerial was raised by a horizontal worm gear operated by 4 to 6 personnel. It could be rotated to any position.

In 1935 the Pirsch Company built the first completely powered 100-foot aluminum alloy aerial ladder, ushering in the age of the metal aerial ladder as we know it today.

The first attempt at an aerial platform was in Chicago around 1870 when a cage was mounted on an 84-foot "Skinner" aerial ladder. The cage did not work and the idea was abandoned.

Chicago was once again the site of another attempt to devise an aerial platform. In 1958 Fire Commissioner Robert J. Quinn had the fire department shops outfit a commercial elevating platform with a $3\frac{1}{2}$-inch hose and basket-mounted monitor. This successful concept led to the telescoping and articulating platform apparatus so common in the fire service today.

Aerial ladder apparatus designs

Among the several designs of aerial apparatus in service today, the tractor-drawn aerial trucks so popular in the past are purchased now in much smaller numbers. Although their increased maneuverability, made possible by using the steerable rear axle, makes this type of apparatus extremely valuable on narrow city streets, operating a tractor-drawn aerial truck requires a great deal of coordination between the driver and the tillerman. Training and ongoing practice are important for safe operations. In addition to the extra training needed, reduced manpower, the units' increased overall length and higher cost, and reduced staffing to operate them have made these units less desirable than in the past.

There are several variations of the single chassis aerial. One is the aerial turntable's mounting location. In the past, midship-mounted 75', 85' and

TOP: *The popularity of the tractor drawn aerial apparatus has diminished over the years. This is mainly due to the general reduction of manpower that the fire service has experienced and the extensive coordination and training that are required to operate the unit safely.* MIDDLE: *The single-chassis, mid-mount aerial was quite common in the past. The location of the turntable often caused the aerial ladder to extend past the rear of the apparatus.* BOTTOM: *Gaining in popularity is the rear-mount aerial apparatus. By mounting the turntable at the rear of the apparatus, and bedding the ladder over the cab roof, the entire apparatus chassis can be manufactured shorter than the bed section of the ladder. The advantage of this configuration allows better maneuverability of the truck.* PHOTOS COURTESY OF R. JEFFERS, R. MILNES, AND AUTHOR

100-foot aerials were common; the aerial tip extended past the rear of the apparatus. Recently the rear-mount design has become widely accepted in the fire service. By mounting the turntable at the extreme rear of the apparatus and projecting the tip over the cab, the entire chassis can be manufactured to be shorter than the aerial ladder's bed section. The value of this feature becomes evident when the aerial is 100 feet or longer, which correspondingly increases the length of the bed section.

With longer and stronger aerial devices the vehicle's weight also has increased considerably. These units often need tandem rear axles to carry the weight safely as well as to provide the necessary stability and braking power to stop the apparatus. Tandem rear axles reduce the maneuverability of the apparatus somewhat but also enhance the vehicle's operational safety.

Aerial apparatus comparisons

Comparisons between aerial ladders and elevating platforms should be considered in light of each type's distinct and different characteristics and abilities.

It is up to fire department personnel to consider all of these, and make informed decisions about which design will best serve the community's needs. The fact that both aerial ladders and elevating platforms are available certainly enhances the fire department's rescue and elevated stream capabilities.

Platform apparatus

Platform apparatus are manufactured in several configurations for the fire service.

An aerial platform is basically a heavy-duty aerial ladder with a platform mounted at the tip.

A telescoping boom apparatus has several sections that telescope inside one another with the platform attached to the end. This type of apparatus may be equipped with an escape ladder on top of the boom.

The articulating boom apparatus has a hinged elbow that connects two boom sections with a platform attached.

A relative newcomer to the platform scene in this country is the telescoping/articulating boom apparatus. This combination unit basically is a telescoping aerial platform with a short articulating arm that is capable of reaching over obstacles such as roof parapets. Its versatility and vertical reach of more than 200 feet make this type of unit quite attractive to some aerial purchasers.

PLATFORM ADVANTAGES

Each platform type has its own unique advantages and disadvantages in terms of style and design. Some of the basic advantages of all platform apparatus versus standard aerial ladders are described here.

- Greater minimum load-carrying capacity—a 750-pound (minimum) versus a 250-pound minimum for aerial ladders. Keep in mind that many aerial manufacturers produce "heavy duty" versions of this ladder; this allows them to increase the tip load in 250-pound increments.
- A platform gives firefighters a safe and more comfortable place to carry out rescue, ventilation, exterior overhaul and aerial stream application duties.
- Victims especially the young, elderly, and infirm, feel safer stepping onto a platform than climbing down an aerial ladder.
- The platform can be used as a work station at an elevated location, supplying hose outlet, electrical power source, mounted hand tools and miscellaneous equipment, as well as face masks with remote air lines from the platform's breathing air system.
- The articulated boom, which can reach over obstacles, adds an element of versatility to the platform concept.

Telescoping-articulating apparatus combine the features of a telescoping aerial platform and have the added ability to reach over obstacles with the end of the articulating arm. PHOTO COURTESY OF AUTHOR

- Rescue and removal of incapacitated victims on litters or in baskets are accomplished more easily with a platform versus an aerial ladder.
- The platform can be moved quickly between different points, within its range, to effect rescue.
- Generally, a platform has greater elevated stream capacities.

DISADVANTAGES

Compared to standard aerial ladder apparatus, platforms tend to be more expensive, larger in size and weight, and might require a wider stabilizer (jack) spread. Some of the individual disadvantages of each type of platform are described below.

Telescoping

To remove multiple victims or elevate several firefighters to upper floors, the telescoping boom apparatus must cycle through raising and lowering evolutions. Likewise, if during an operation of long duration a change in platform personnel is required, the stream normally must be shut down and the tower lowered to the ground for exchange.

These disadvantages can be eliminated by including a boom-mounted ladder. The standard requires that this ladder meet all requirements of a standard aerial, including side rails, to provide a safe path between the platform and the turntable.

Articulating

When articulating apparatus is being used, the operator must, at all times, be aware of the position of both the platform and the "elbow." Such obstructions as trees, poles, and overhead wires, as well as narrow streets, pose operational and safety problems. As is the case with some boom apparatus, numerous trips to the ground might be necessary to remove multiple victims.

Because of design considerations, most articulating boom apparatus cannot be equipped with an escape ladder. Therefore, removing personnel from an elevated but malfunctioning unit could be problematic.

The horizontal reach from the centerline of the truck of an articulating boom apparatus is somewhat less than that of an aerial or telescoping boom platform. This can be critical if the fire building is set back from the roadway and out of reach.

Telescoping/Articulating

Telescoping/articulating platform apparatus address many of the short-comings of each of the other types of platforms, however, because of their more complex capabilities, personnel need extensive training to be able to use them.

Quads and quints

When quads and quints are discussed, some people feel that these combination apparatus are pumpers with extra ladder capabilities, while others feel that they are ladder trucks with pumper capabilities.

A "quad" (quadruple) apparatus is equipped with a fire pump, water tank, hose bed storage, and the addition of a full complement of ground ladders. This type of apparatus is most useful in areas where a ladder company's services are either nonexistent or expected to be severely delayed.

A "quint" (quintuple) apparatus is equipped with a fire pump, water tank, hose bed storage, a full complement of ground ladders, and an aerial device. A popular configuration is a 75-foot rear-mount aerial ladder with a 1,500-gpm fire pump. A true quint complies with all of the requirements of

A disadvantage of a combination "quint" type unit is that sometimes the aerial device will be out of position if the unit is operating as a pumper. The elevating tower in this photo could not be used because the apparatus was committed to a hydrant that was too far from the fire building. PHOTO COURTESY OF AUTHOR

a pumper, including tank, hose bed, discharges, and equipment. This should not be confused with an aerial truck that is equipped with a pump but does not have the required tank and hose bed.

These combination units, if staffed adequately, are extremely versatile, offering the company officer the capability to immediately operate as a truck company for aerial or ground ladder rescue situations or as an engine company to confine and extinguish the fire. The obvious problem is that it is difficult to "serve two masters." When the aerial is needed for an elevated master stream, the apparatus might be at a hydrant a block away or the unit might have the aerial set up in front of the building without an adequate water supply.

Combination units such as these have been operating successfully in many cities. With the continued goal of getting the maximum efficiency from each unit, it appears that this trend will continue.

AERIAL APPARATUS REQUIREMENTS

Minimum requirements for new aerial apparatus apply to all vehicles designed for elevated firefighting and rescue capability. Such a vehicle has a power-operated, self-supporting aerial device, permanently mounted on a suitable chassis with associated equipment and storage provisions.

All of the previously described safety improvements and vehicle performance requirements contained in NFPA 1901 also apply to aerial apparatus.

Vehicle and axle weights

Due to the expanded array of equipment carried on an aerial apparatus, the chassis gross vehicle weight and gross axle weight ratings must allow for 2,500 pounds of miscellaneous equipment for truck work in addition to full water tank, ground ladders, and hose load, as well as 200 pounds per person for the maximum number of personnel who will ride on the apparatus.

Driving and crew compartments

All of the 1901 requirements for fully enclosed driving and riding compartments apply for aerial apparatus as well. Where a tractor-drawn vehicle is provided, several additional requirements must be met.

Tiller compartment requirements

A fully enclosed compartment with an adjustable seat, rearview mirrors on both sides, and seat belt must be provided. A heater, defroster, windshield wiper and washer must be installed in the tiller compartment. This is a vast improvement over the old open tiller seat with folddown windshield!

A communications system between the drivers, either voice intercom or signal buzzer, as well as turn signal indicator lights shall be provided. As an added safety measure, a control to prevent the vehicle from starting without the tillerman in place, must be installed.

The aerial device

Several standard requirements for all aerial devices are outlined in this NFPA standard. The aerial device shall be a minimum of 50 feet in vertical height and consist of two or more ladder sections with skid-resistant rungs that are 14 inches on center. Minimum 12-inch side rails must be provided as well as two folding steps for ladder pipe operation. A minimum width of 18 inches inside the narrowest aerial siderails is specified. Both the aerial ladder and the elevating platform apparatus are required to have a weather-resistant voice intercom between the turntable and the upper operating position. The tip or platform communications station must be a hands-free operation.

Aerial rated capacity

A very important safety feature that was added to this standard is the 250-pound rated tip load. Before this requirement was added, many of the "light-duty" aerial ladders were not designed to operate at low angles of elevation, even without personnel on the ladder. Some of these devices had to be retracted before the elevation could be raised. This obviously increased the risk to personnel operating on the ladder if fire broke out below their position. In addition, overloading these devices at low angles actually caused some of the ladders to fail, resulting in firefighter injuries and deaths.

This NFPA standard now indicates that the rated capacity of the aerial shall be a minimum of 250 pounds at the tip with the aerial at maximum extension in the horizontal position. The aerial must be capable of operating in any position while carrying its rated load. If a permanent waterway is attached, this requirement is without water in the system.

When the system is discharging water, the rated tip load shall be 250 pounds at or above 45 degrees of elevation. Additional capacity ratings shall be at 250-pound increments. (The weight of an equipped firefighter.)

When a mix of the old style "light duty" and the new generation ladders are in service in the same department, it is important that the members who operate the equipment understand the difference in the capacity of each, and observe all safety indicators as well as the manufacturer's safe operating instructions.

Aerial waterway

When a permanently mounted waterway is provided, the system must be capable of flowing 1,000 gpm at 100 psi nozzle pressure with no more than 100 psi friction loss in the system. A preset relief valve, flow meter and 1½-inch drain valve also must be provided.

If a permanent waterway is not installed, a ladder pipe with tips and sufficient 3-inch hose is to be provided for elevated master stream application.

Elevating platforms

The minimum load rating of an elevating platform is 750 pounds and the device must be able to carry this load safely in any operating position. This rated load is in addition to any firefighting equipment installed on the platform by the manufacturer.

The minimum platform load is reduced to 500 pounds when discharging 1,000 gpm in any configuration allowed by the manufacturer.

Platform breathing air system

A breathing air system that consists of a minimum 400-cubic-foot breathing air supply cylinder, valve, regulator, and piping designed to supply breathing air for two personnel on the platform is to be installed. When air volume is at or below 20 percent, a low air warning system shall alert the personnel at both the platform and the turntable operator's position. Some units provide air hoselines that are long enough to allow the firefighter to leave the platform. A disadvantage of platform-supplied air lines or hoselines, is that both tie the aerial to a single position and make it impossible to move quickly, in an emergency, to any other place on the facade of the building.

Platform water system

The platform water system must be capable of discharging 1,000 gpm from one or more permanently installed monitors on the platform controlled by a screw-type shutoff valve connected to each monitor. A 75-gpm water curtain system with quick-acting valve must be installed to provide a cooling spray under the platform. Other water system requirements include a 2½-inch gated discharge at the platform, flow meter at the operator's position, preset relief valve, and system drain valve.

Compartmentation

A minimum of 30 cubic feet of ventilated, lighted, weather-resistant compartmentation for equipment storage must be provided.

Specifications for special compartment configurations or mounting requirements should be detailed in the purchase specifications.

Hose storage

If hose is to be carried it is the buyer's responsibility to specify both size and amount as well as special requirements, e.g., preconnect beds. All hose beds must conform to the construction requirements described for pumpers.

Ground ladders

The length and number of portable ground ladders that are to be carried on a ladder truck have slowly been reduced over the past several years. The original requirement for 208 feet was reduced to 163 feet in the last edition; it currently requires 115 feet. The change came about partly because of the lack of staffing available to raise ground ladders, as well as the need to provide compartment space on the apparatus for additional tools and equipment.

Standard 1904 indicates that the following minimum complement of ground ladders shall be carried:

- One 10-foot folding attic ladder
- Two 16-foot roof ladders with folding roof hooks
- One 14-foot combination ladder
- One 24-foot extension ladder
- One 35-foot extension ladder

Remember—this is the *minimum* required complement. If your community has several tall buildings, you might want to specify additional ladders or longer lengths.

A list of equipment that is to be carried on a ladder truck is contained in the Technical Resources section of this book.

Pump and Tank Requirements

If the aerial apparatus is equipped with a fire pump or smaller (250-gpm) attack pump, all provisions of NFPA 1901 pump requirements for capacity and pressure controls are repeated.

The minimum size water tank allowed is 150 gallons which would permit operation of a single, low-volume hose stream. For tanks of 300 gallons or greater capacity, a 250-gpm flow rate is required. This differs from the 500-gpm requirement of a pumper.

[handwritten margin notes: "? conflict", "(flow rate)?", "359", "750 gpm"]

SPECIAL-PURPOSE APPARATUS

While standard fire apparatus (pumpers and trucks) usually have their duties and capabilities clearly defined, special-purpose units (hazardous material, rescue, and air supply) all can be designed and purchased in varying sizes and configurations to suit all needs.

The first step in drafting specifications for this type of apparatus is to define clearly the mission and capabilities expected of the unit. Based on this information you can determine the type and amount of equipment needed to accomplish your tasks. Special features that you want the apparatus to have also should be considered.

All of these factors can then be evaluated to determine the configuration and size of the vehicle needed.

HAZARDOUS MATERIALS

Hazardous materials vehicles can range from light-duty vans, to beverage-type trucks, to enclosed heavy-duty apparatus similar to larger rescue trucks.

In many cases the hazardous materials unit needs to transport only the necessary protective clothing, monitoring and hazard determination equipment, and spill control supplies to the scene of the incident. The more elaborate units feature a climate-controlled command center with communications, reference materials, fax machine, and computer. A vehicle-mounted breathing air system to replenish SCBA cylinders as well as a generator to power lights and electrical equipment also are desirable features.

The level of training and expertise of the crew as well as the community's need for such a unit may help dictate the type of apparatus in use.

AIR SUPPLY UNITS

Given the dangerous products of combustion present at the fires we fight, the use of self-contained breathing apparatus (SCBA) is a necessity. Gone are the days of "smoke eaters" who prided themselves on the amount of smoke they could breathe. Each apparatus now is required to supply one SCBA for each seating position and one spare cylinder for each unit. At incidents of any magnitude, this basic supply will be consumed quickly. At high-rise fires, deep-penetration assignments, or extended hazardous materials incidents, it will be necessary to replenish or replace air cylinders rapidly.

Air supply units, like hazardous materials and rescue units, are manufactured in several styles and sizes to meet the needs of the community.

CYLINDER TRANSPORT

One of the simplest units (without filling capabilities) transports quantities of spare, ready-to-use cylinders to the scene of the fire or emergency for distribution to the companies. Empties are picked up and taken to a compressor site for refilling, and a shuttle is established.

An important feature and one that must be included in a cylinder transport unit is a secure method of holding cylinders in place during transport. Placing them in the rear of a vehicle to roll around is an invitation to disaster if a valve breaks. A simple solution is to fashion a honeycomb of PVC pipe, cut, glued and banded together with hold-down straps across the top. These homemade honeycombs can be installed in a surplus fire department van, giving you a very functional and inexpensive air supply unit.

CASCADE AND BOOSTERS

The next type of unit for on-scene filling is the mobile cascade unit, which can be installed easily on rescue, hazardous materials, or other existing apparatus.

The basic unit contains several large cylinders of breathing air, a cascade-control panel, and fragmentation shields for cylinder filling. This configuration works quite well, especially with low-pressure (2,216-psi) SCBA cylinders. Air is cascaded, starting with the lowest-pressure storage cylinder in the system, and slowly builds up until the full cylinders on the cascade "top off" the SCBA cylinders. This system is somewhat less effective when used with high-pressure (4,500-psi) SCBA cylinders because the cascade bottles used for topping off are depleted quickly, causing a less-than-full condition in the SCBA cylinders that are being replenished.

What is needed is to add a "booster pump" to the system to pump the SCBA bottles to 4,500 psi. These small, closed-circuit compressors take air from the cascade banks and boost it to the preset pressure. Some booster pumps are driven by an electric motor; this means you will need an on-board generator. With the high current draw needed to start the booster, a 10-kW generator might be needed to handle the load. With an adequate generator and the right equipment, the air supply unit also could serve as a lighting truck.

Both the mobile cascade unit and the booster systems must have their air storage banks refilled when the apparatus returns to quarters.

MOBILE CASCADE/COMPRESSOR SYSTEMS

Mobile compressor units maintain their storage banks by compressing ambient air rather than using the storage cylinder air that the closed-circuit systems transport to the scene. The benefit of this configuration is that the amount of air available is limited only by the compressor's rated output for a given period of time. For safety reasons, the unit's air intake must be directed away from both the truck's exhaust and smoke and combustion products of the fire that is being fought. Several filtering and safety alarm systems can be incorporated to prevent breathing air contamination.

This cascade-booster unit transports spare cylinders and has the ability to fill from its cascade storage. The booster pump allows the operator to fill all cylinders to capacity when the cascade pressure is diminished. PHOTO COURTESY OF AUTHOR

OPTIONAL EQUIPMENT

As an optional accessory to the air supply unit, a lightweight hand truck with drop-down lip, pneumatic tires, and a binder strap has been used successfully to transport cylinders from the truck to the scene.

If you plan to use the apparatus as a lighting unit, install several wire reels and portable floodlights.

Also equip the apparatus with fire extinguishers suitable for Class A, B, and C fires.

Regardless of the type of air supply unit that you specify, the Gross Vehicle Weight Rating (GVWR) must be sufficient to carry the heavy load of storage bank cylinders, machinery, equipment, and spare cylinders. Weight distribution also is a factor in vehicle stability.

RESCUE UNITS

As is the case with the hazardous materials unit, the degree of training and capability of the crew, and the amount of storage space needed for the equipment to perform these capabilities should dictate the size of the rescue truck needed.

In some parts of the country an ambulance with a hydraulic rescue tool and basic forcible entry tools is considered a rescue unit yet in others the EMS component is only a minor rescue crew duty, since victims are treated and transported by ambulance. Fireground search, rescue, and release from entrapment are the normal duties of a fire-rescue unit.

What you expect your rescue company to do helps you decide the types and amount of equipment to carry. Rescue company operations include forcible entry, ventilation, vehicular extrication, heavy-lifting capabilities, high-angle rope rescue, confined-space rescue, water rescue, metal cutting, and advanced masonry breaching capabilities.

The new apparatus should include room for future expansion. As the crew acquires new skills and talents, additional equipment will be needed. A unit that is "just right" to hold your equipment when purchased may become overcrowded quickly.

Do not fail to consider the number of personnel who are going to respond with the apparatus and where they are going to be seated. In the past, rescue crew members traditionally mounted the rear of the box and stood up, getting dressed on the way to a call. In the event of a sharp turn, quick stop, or vehicle accident, the firefighters, along with their SCBAs and hand tools, sometimes were thrown around the body of the unit. This very dangerous practice can be eliminated by either specifying a cab with enough seats for the entire crew, or by requiring the members in the rear to be seated and belted during travel.

TRAILERS AND PLATFORMS ON DEMAND (PODS)

To save money and increase efficiency some departments are using multiple-function trailers or platforms on demand (PODs) to fill their special apparatus needs.

A hazardous materials unit can be equipped with two trailers: one for carrying entry suits, SCBA, and leak abatement equipment, and the other outfitted as a decontamination unit. If a sizable incident were in progress, the first trailer could be left at the scene to begin operations, while the tractor retrieves the decontamination unit. Other dual-trailer possibilities include large diameter hose wagon, air compressor unit, command post, or foam tender.

PODs are an option for accomplishing several special tasks while using and maintaining only one base vehicle. A POD is a container-like box that is loaded onto a transport vehicle and is rolled off at the scene of an emergency. These units also can be used to store equipment for multiple functions—command center, building collapse, or trench rescue—at a central location, and called to the scene as needed.

As with other combination units, the only drawback is that if the transport vehicle is involved in an accident or suffers a mechanical malfunction, you

Some fire departments have made use of trailer type units that can be disconnected at the scene, freeing the tractor to return for other differently equipped trailers.
PHOTO COURTESY OF R. JEFFERS

then lose the capabilities of all of your individual functions. However, they can be a potential cost saver, providing many services with only one prime mover.

FIREBOATS

Some jurisdictions with waterfront areas to protect find it valuable to have a fireboat. The duties of the marine firefighting unit can include fire suppression and protection for piers, docks, and wharves as well as for pleasure boat marinas and waterfront structures. Marine firefighting crews also fight fires on board vessels that are docked or in the vicinity of their response area.

Waterfront flammable liquid storage facilities are not uncommon; they make it convenient for ships and barges to load and unload their cargoes of petroleum products and chemicals. In addition, most marinas, which represent an exposure problem (pleasure boats and luxury yachts are docked side by side) contain boat refueling facilities. If your area has this type of hazard the fireboat should be equipped with provisions for an on-board foam system. Some boats also function as a marine hazardous materials unit, carrying booms to contain spills and leaks until they can be removed and disposed of properly.

Fireboats also have been used in water rescue and recovery operations, especially smaller, swifter fireboats that can usually arrive on scene quickly.

In the past, powerful fireboats used extensively as water-borne pumping stations have demonstrated their worth during major fires and natural disasters. Large diameter hose connections from the boat's manifold can be used to supply several engine companies on land.

Unfortunately, the big boats, those with pumping capacities of 10,000 to 20,000 gpm, are slowly beginning to vanish from the scene. Because of their limited capabilities (compared to land companies) and infrequent use, many cities are finding it difficult to justify the salaries of the required marine pilot, engineer, and full-time crew, and associated high costs of maintenance and storage. Many are being replaced with smaller, shallow-draft craft that flow up to 3,000 gpm from their deck guns and are staffed by cross-trained crews from land-based companies. In this case, secure docking facilities or provisions to transport by trailer are necessary because these boats tend to lack regular staffs. Some jurisdictions have addressed this concern by constructing fire stations at waterfront locations.

A relative newcomer to the fireboat scene is the Surface Effect Ship (SES). These units are capable of responding quickly (at a speed of 30 knots) and can pump up to 7,000 gpm. The SES has hollow cavities under the hull, from the bow to the stern, with the ends sealed by rubber curtains. When the unit responds, fans inflate this area and the ship rises up approximately 30 inches on a cushion of air, dramatically reducing the resistance of the hull in the water; this accounts for its swift response.

When the SES begins operations, the pilot must deflate the cushion to place the pump intakes back in the water, and to add resistance to counter the reaction of the monitors.

These high-tech units are relatively expensive and still require docking facilities.

Amphibious fireboats that can traverse land and be launched near a marine incident eliminate the need for docking facilities, trailer, and permanent crew. This type of unit is stored in a fire station when not in use and is staffed by a cross-trained crew. This unit can function as a large mobile pumping station on land (operating from a hydrant water supply) or draft from a body of water.

Other than having your own fireboats or relying on mutual aid for fireboat protection, there are United States Coast Guard vessels that have limited fire-fighting capabilities but may respond to assist when available. The Coast Guard's response varies depending on location, workload, and local commitment.

The size of the boat and equipment carried must be based on an evaluation of local waterfront hazards, the capabilities expected of the craft, and available funding.

Use of small, high-speed boats with pumping capacities of 750 to 1,250 gpm addresses the considerations of rapid response and budget limitations. On the other hand, the lack of adequate fire flows to control large fires, protect exposures, and extinguish flammable liquid fires in a timely manner could pose a problem.

A combination of a smaller boat for quick rescue and a holding action, followed by a larger craft for extinguishment, could be a very effective combination.

AIRPORT CRASH TRUCKS

Many cities purchase and staff airport crash-fire rescue apparatus as part of their municipal fire protection. These large, special-purpose vehicles provide firefighting and rescue services for aircraft, airport buildings, and hangars.

Their design and performance requirements are listed in NFPA 414, *Standard for Aircraft Rescue and Fire Fighting Vehicles*. Designed for rapid acceleration and high top speeds to reach all areas of an airport quickly, they must operate in a "self-contained" manner, i.e., carry large quantities of water and foam concentrate and possibly other extinguishing agents, such as dry chemical and Halon.

Off-highway performance on soft ground and snow is required since crash trucks frequently must leave paved access roads and runways to approach an aircraft emergency. This makes individual all-wheel drive mandatory.

NFPA 414 categorizes aircraft firefighting vehicles as major firefighting vehicles, rapid-intervention vehicles (RIV) and combined-agent vehicles.

The size, number, and type of aircraft firefighting apparatus needed is determined according to Federal Aviation Administration (FAA) regulations. Each airport receives a rating (or index) that is based on a combination of length of passenger aircraft and number of daily departures of the aircraft. Airports that do not provide the minimum amount of fire protection that corresponds to their rated index cannot operate.

In some cases, additional apparatus—nurse tanker for replenishing water and foam concentrate, rescue unit, and incident command vehicle—can be very helpful to have.

APPARATUS NEEDS ANALYSIS

While determining the number, type, and capacity of fire apparatus is an important component of a fire department's ongoing evaluation, how do you know what you'll need in the future? The first step is to ascertain whether the apparatus you have is suitable for current demands, if it is meeting the needs of the community, or whether additional capabilities are needed.

The progressive fire chief who realizes that any new apparatus must serve the municipality for an extended period of time, considers upgrading not only to the levels needed now, but to anticipated levels as well. Look to your city's master plan and building codes to help define changes in the community and

Airport Crash-Fire-Rescue (CFR) units carry large quantities of water and foam concentrate as well as possibly other extinguishing agents. PHOTO COURTESY OF A. KNOBLOCH

areas of potential concern. For example, if new housing developments are inevitable, additional apparatus or stations located in the subdivisions could be necessary to serve the increased population. Plans that allow taller buildings might dictate the need for an aerial ladder or platform apparatus. Additional highways will increase the duties of rescue companies that perform vehicle extrication and, depending on the industrial zoning regulations, a hazardous materials unit could easily be justified.

The fire chief should keep abreast of these changes and ensure that the community's requirements for adequate fire protection can be fulfilled.

Apparatus life expectancy

Apparatus replacement is not dependent solely on age. A unit's routine workload, its physical condition, and the amount of preventive maintenance it has received during its lifetime tend to be better indicators of whether the apparatus is still reliable for first-line duty.

Apparatus life expectancy varies greatly from one location to another. A 10- to 15-year life expectancy is considered normal for pumpers that are used daily in moderate- to heavy-response areas. First-line pumpers must respond to many routine auto, brush, and rubbish fires as well as perform long-duration pumping operations; these activities take their toll on the chassis, body, engine, driveline, and pump.

Aerial apparatus should last somewhat longer, in the range of 15 to 20 years, if their response criteria and vehicle workload are considerably less than those of pumpers.

Apparatus used in light-duty situations, such as rural and suburban settings, can remain dependable for longer periods of time if operated and maintained properly. In most cases, apparatus over 25 years old should not be used in first-line service.

Replacement considerations

What justifies and magnifies the need for apparatus replacement are escalating maintenance costs, increased downtime, and noncompliance with new standards. The need to address these concerns, and the desire to increase efficiency are good reasons to replace outdated equipment.

Maintenance costs

As we discover with our personal automobiles, maintaining older vehicles tends to be more costly than maintaining modern units. Undersized engines and drive trains often are taxed to their maximum ability. Wear and metal fatigue from years of cold engine starts, maximum output responses, and torsional stresses on the chassis, frame, and body take their toll on the internal components of the engine, and transmission, and on other major components.

Historically, parts for older apparatus have been difficult to acquire, if available at all, and cost considerably more to purchase. Several major apparatus manufacturers have gone out of business, placing an additional burden on the customers who own that particular brand of apparatus.

While some of the more common replacement parts are available from commercial truck sources, many components are manufactured for a specific model of fire apparatus. A lack of spare parts is certain to increase apparatus downtime.

One of the most time-consuming maintenance chores is the upkeep for apparatus electrical systems. Fire departments continuously add equipment that taxes the charging system. Accessories such as additional warning lights, air conditioning, power invertors, hand lights, and portable radio chargers all burden the system. The larger alternators and related equipment on modern apparatus provide several hundred amps of current to power these accessories as well as to maintain the batteries; older units might be able to provide only 100 amps.

As new equipment and procedures are developed for fire service use, we always find a way to mount, tie, or hang the needed equipment on the apparatus. This can cause the vehicle's suspension to become overloaded and seriously affect the unit's stability. Overloaded, under-braked apparatus pose a severe threat, not only to the firefighters who respond with the unit, but to the public in general.

Aside from transporting firefighters safely to an emergency scene, the central function of the apparatus is its fire pump or aerial device. The annual pump test or aerial load test and inspection are essential in determining whether the apparatus can still perform its mission capably. In some cases, worn pump components or reduced available horsepower from the engine will render the apparatus unable to draft or pump at rated capacity. The five-year requirement for a nondestructive aerial device test is a way to uncover damage that might dictate extensive repairs or even replacement to enhance firefighter safety.

SAFETY COMPLIANCE WITH NEW STANDARDS

The current NFPA apparatus standards have increased requirements for firefighter safety considerably. Fully enclosed cabs, seating and belts for all members, noise reduction, and higher visibility are only some of the safety features that have been included. Although older apparatus are not required to meet current standards, continuing to allow firefighters to ride on a portion of the apparatus that is prohibited, such as the tailboard, should be recognized as an unsafe act.

Attempts to bring older apparatus into compliance can be expensive to start and might be impossible or impractical to finish. Adding lights, reflective striping, and seat belts should not pose a problem, but complying with the 250-pound rated tip load of an aerial ladder most likely will be impossible. New, fully compliant apparatus is the way to enhance the operating safety of your fleet.

Efficiency

The final, easily understandable justification criterion is increased overall efficiency. Modern trends in apparatus and equipment, such as large diameter hose discharges, Class A foam systems, preconnected attack lines, larger water tanks, and combination units can increase a fire company's output significantly. True efficiency is performing the mission of the department at the lowest possible cost. Using modern techniques and equipment increases the efficiency of the fire attack and reduces life loss and property damage.

Response capabilities

The fire department should be prepared to provide the necessary response of apparatus, equipment, and staffing to control the anticipated routine fire load for its community.

The NFPA *Fire Protection Handbook* (17th Ed.) cites the following apparatus response for each designated condition:

High Hazard (Schools, hospitals, nursing homes, explosives plants, refineries, high-rise buildings, and other high life hazard or large fire potential occupancies).

At least four pumpers, two ladder trucks (or combination apparatus with equivalent capabilities), two chief officers, and other specialized apparatus as needed to cope with the combustibles involved.

Medium Occupancies (Apartments, offices, mercantile, and industrial occupancies not normally requiring extensive rescue or firefighting forces).

At least three pumpers, one ladder truck (or combination apparatus with equivalent capabilities), one chief officer, and other specialized apparatus as needed or available.

Low-hazard Occupancies (One-, two- or three-family dwellings and scattered small business and industrial occupancies).

At least two pumpers, one ladder truck (or combination apparatus with equivalent capabilities), one chief officer, and other specialized apparatus as needed or available.

Rural Operations (Scattered dwellings, small businesses, and farm buildings).

At least one pumper with a large water tank (500 gallons or more), one mobile water supply apparatus (1,000 gallons or larger) and such other specialized apparatus as may be necessary to perform effective initial firefighting operations.

Additional Alarms At least the equivalent of that required for first alarms for rural operations plus equipment as needed based on the type of emergency and the fire department's capabilities. This may involve the immediate use of mutual aid companies until local forces can be supplemented with additional off-duty or volunteer personnel. In some communities, single units are "special called" when needed, without always resorting to a multiple alarm. Additional units also may be needed to "move up" to fill at least some empty fire stations.

The figures you have just seen show that rural areas, with their normally small scattered buildings, don't require a response as large as that needed in densely populated cities. Rural departments tend to be more concerned with obtaining a continuous (and mostly conservative) water supply from a remote location, whereas the urban chief relies on large volumes of water and the appliances to use it properly, in order to confine the fire, protect exposures, and prevent a conflagration.

The vast difference in water availability may dictate that the apparatus used in rural operations include larger tanks to supply initial attack, portable tanks and water supply apparatus shuttles, long lays of large diameter hose for supply from a static water source, and possibly the use of agents such as Class A foam to increase the efficiency and extend the available water supply.

Urban fire departments tend to rely more on relatively short, high-flow attack lines. In this case, large diameter hose is a definite asset for relays between pumpers and to feed master stream devices. Aerial ladders and platforms must be available for rescue, ventilation, and quick access to upper floors of buildings.

In high-hazard areas, there is also a greater need to have additional apparatus available to respond to multiple-alarm fires and to be positioned for simultaneous fires. This additional apparatus might be extra companies not committed on the first alarm, ready reserve apparatus staffed by recall personnel, or possibly mutual aid companies called to stand by in vacant quarters.

Cities and metropolitan counties also are more likely to need such specialized apparatus as hazardous materials, heavy rescue, building collapse units, breathing air supply, or salvage companies. These services are used less frequently in sparsely populated areas.

Even the general performance requirements of the apparatus are usually different. In some cases the overall size and weight of rural units are not of great concern. However, in urban centers with traffic congestion and narrow streets a highly maneuverable vehicle with a short wheelbase and tight-turning radius is desirable.

FINANCING THE PURCHASE

The last item in analyzing the apparatus needs of a particular jurisdiction is the jurisdiction's financial resources. It certainly makes no sense to study designs and prepare specifications for a piece of apparatus that exceeds what the fire department can spend.

Some of the fiscal methods available to finance a purchase include municipal taxation, capital improvement bonds that are sold by the municipality, grant monies from other governmental agencies, or possibly, the imposition of "impact fees." Developers who intend to construct buildings that create an added hazard are required to address the problem by supplying funding (impact fees) for additional fire protection. Volunteer fire departments in areas which lack or have only partial tax funding usually will rely on funds accumulated from ongoing fundraising activities, special fund drives, grants, and donations.

A fairly new concept in financing is the lease/purchase program, which can be arranged either privately or in conjunction with most of the major apparatus manufacturers. A community or independent fire company saving for a new apparatus may find that its savings are shrinking because of both inflation and the routine periodic price increases set by apparatus manufacturers. The lease/purchase program is a viable alternative for meeting community needs immediately with a modern, compliant unit while the lease is paid off over a period of years.

This process might be the only alternative available if a piece of apparatus must be replaced quickly because a major component fails, or the unit is destroyed in an accident, fire, or building collapse.

APPARATUS PREVENTIVE MAINTENANCE

There are several important reasons to establish a proper Preventive Maintenance (PM) program:

- First, because of the critical nature of the service, fire apparatus must always be in top condition and ready to perform at a moment's notice.
- Second, during emergency responses the safety of the crew and the general public depends heavily on a vehicle that has brakes, tires, steering,

and mechanical equipment maintained to factory specifications at all times.

- Third, the astronomical cost of modern fire apparatus requires that it be maintained in the best possible condition in order to extend its working life and to protect a major capital investment.
- Finally, an improperly maintained vehicle can be a source of legal liability problems.

In 1991, the National Transportation Safety Board issued a report and safety recommendations to the nation's fire departments which said, in part:

> The National Transportation Safety Board (NTSB) has recommended several actions the nation's fire departments should take to improve the safety of getting to and from emergencies. They include the enhancement of vehicle maintenance programs, the establishment of periodic inspection programs, mandatory and enforced use of occupant restraints, and procedural changes in the use of some mechanical equipment.
>
> The recommendations are contained in the Board's Special Investigation Report on Emergency Fire Apparatus, based on its investigations of eight traffic accidents involving fire department vehicles in 1989 and 1990.
>
> Data from the National Fire Protection Association indicate that during the 1980s, 179 firefighter deaths (15 percent) occurred as a result of accidents involving fire equipment en route to alarms.
>
> Among the problems noted during the Board's investigations was the lack of maintenance and inspection programs for these vehicles.

In a news release that accompanied the NTSB report, the board stated, "Because fire apparatus are frequently operated at higher speeds than conventional vehicles, with more frequent need to stop quickly, and are operated under hazardous conditions, it is essential that they be properly maintained."

Operator preventive maintenance

Every PM program, from the one used for the family automobile to the largest fire department fleet, begins with the vehicle operator. Routine maintenance, such as checking the fuel, oil, and coolant levels, lights, wipers, and warning devices, is an absolute must. Even the act of checking the gauges when the vehicle is in operation and detecting problems by sight and sound are considered operator maintenance.

The extent of this first-echelon maintenance program should be established on a local level and be based on frequency of use, personnel qualifications, and manufacturers' recommendations.

A daily or weekly apparatus maintenance checklist should be available to guide the operator through his responsibilities and provide a record of the results.

In most career and part-paid fire departments, the apparatus chauffeur is responsible for the operator's maintenance and inspection. In some locations this duty is rotated by tour, thereby giving each member the opportunity to participate in, and gain experience from, the maintenance function.

Many volunteer departments designate a group of individuals to perform these first-level responsibilities based on their experience or training.

Any comprehensive maintenance program **must** include the proper procedures for documenting, reporting, and correcting serious deficiencies that require immediate attention, as well as routine items not considered urgent.

Shop preventive maintenance

Apparatus must be taken to the shop for periodic, scheduled servicing. Whether the work is performed by an outside contractor or fire department mechanics, it is important that a specific list of required procedures be followed to ensure that the apparatus is maintained properly. Most apparatus manufacturers can help you to establish an acceptable program, which is especially important if the unit is still under warranty.

A scheduled visit to the maintenance shop should include, at a *minimum*, the following:

- **Complete chassis lubrication.** This should include greasing all lubrication points per the manufacturer's recommendations as well as applying the specified lubricant to door and compartment hinges, valve mechanisms, turntables, outrigger jacks, and any other moving parts that require lubrication.
- **Oil change.** During oil changing it is essential to follow the engine manufacturer's recommendations for grade and viscosity.
- **Oil filters.** The oil filter(s) should always be changed when motor oil is changed. Considering the relatively low price of new filters, it is foolish to pass clean oil through contaminated filters and leave several quarts of dirty oil in the system when motor oil is changed.
- **Fuel filters.** Fuel filters are absolutely critical to the reliable operation of a modern diesel engine. Contamination and condensation in the fuel can easily restrict fuel filters, causing reduced power or complete failure.
- **Automatic transmission.** The fluid and filter(s) for the automatic transmission should be serviced as recommended by the manufacturer. If a change is not scheduled, the mechanic should at least examine the

dipstick reading to check for proper level, discoloration, or a "burned smell," which might indicate the presence of a problem.

- **Brake examination.** One of the most critical safety checks that must be performed during PM is of the apparatus brake system. Before starting a brake examination, the wheels should be chocked, both front and back, to avoid accidents during the inspection.

  The mechanic should first visually inspect all working parts for signs of excessive wear, misalignment, or broken components. In most cases inspection ports are provided in the backing plates of drum-type brakes to evaluate the amount of residual brake lining. This is also an opportune time to detect wheel seal leakage into the drum.

  It is essential to check the brake adjustment of each wheel by measuring the stroke travel of the brake chamber pushrod. This simple procedure is done by marking the pushrod at the face of the chamber with the brakes released. After the brakes are applied (with 100 psi system air pressure), measure from the chamber to the previous mark to determine the travel. The maximum allowable travel distance can be found in the axle manufacturer's literature that is supplied with the apparatus.

  Another necessary brake check is of the air system pressure drop. NFPA 1901 indicates that exceeding the following air pressure drops indicates a need for immediate service:

  —More than two psi in one minute for single vehicles or three psi in one minute for vehicle combinations, with the engine stopped and service brakes released.

  —More than three psi for single vehicles and four psi for combinations, with the engine stopped and service brakes fully applied.

- **Tires.** The wear patterns of the apparatus tires can give the mechanic a good indication of problems that require attention. Incorrect inflation pressure is the leading factor in premature tire wear. Properly inflated tires should wear evenly across the tread. Overinflation causes the middle of the tread to wear more rapidly, while underinflation is indicated by excessive wear of the outside edges.

  Other unusual wear conditions should warrant further investigation for axle or front-end problems.

  Tires should be inspected for physical damage, e.g., sidewall cuts or tread damage. Lugs should be examined for evidence of movement and lug nuts should be retorqued to the manufacturer's specs.

- **Front end.** During front-end lubrication, conduct a thorough inspection of all components. Signs of excessive wear or looseness should be investigated and corrected.

- **Driveline.** The drive shafts, universal joints, hangers, and related components should be inspected for wear, misalignment, or unusual conditions. Fluid level checks and lubrication procedures for the differential and pump gear case, if so equipped, should be performed at this time.

- **Lights.** All vehicle driving and warning lights should be checked for proper operation. While the malfunction of an external light is obvious, do not overlook compartment or dashboard lights.
- **Belts and hoses.** During the check of the engine compartment, all belts and hoses should be inspected. Leaking or chaffing of hoses requires immediate attention.

  Belts should be examined for cracking, wear, and proper tension according to the manufacturer's recommendations.
- **Fluid levels.** All fluid levels should be checked, including power steering, prime oil, windshield washer fluid, and brake fluid, if the vehicle is equipped with hydraulic brakes.
- **Cooling system.** Checks of the cooling system should be performed when the apparatus is cool. Exercise caution when removing the radiator cap since the system could be under pressure.

  The coolant should be examined for signs of contamination as well as tested for sufficient low-temperature protection. The proper coolant level, allowing for expansion, is one to two inches below the bottom of the radiator neck. If the system has a filter, it should be changed at the proper service interval. The front surface of the radiator should be observed for excessive dirt or obstruction, and cleaned if necessary.
- **Batteries.** Maintaining electrolyte levels, and cleaning cables and terminals are important to maintain reliable starting. If starting difficulty is reported the batteries should be load tested to analyze their reliability.

  Some progressive departments automatically change the batteries after a preset number of months of service. The batteries then are recycled into less critical municipal vehicles, such as public works or sanitation trucks, where a battery failure would not be considered critical.
- **Air filter.** The air filter should be opened only when the restriction gauge indicates a less-than-full air flow. The routine practice of removing the filter for inspection or "blowing it out" with compressed air should be avoided as it dislodges dirt that can then enter the engine and cause damage.
- **General inspection.** A final general inspection for leaks, worn components, or necessary adjustments should be conducted, and the necessary repairs made.

Other special maintenance items such as pump components, generator, and aerial device servicing should be included in the program in accordance with individual manufacturers' recommendations.

This is also an excellent opportunity for the mechanic to review the operator's daily reports to detect such items as excessive oil or coolant consumption which could be an indication that a more serious problem is developing.

Determining the PM interval

Setting a proper PM interval is dependent on the amount and type of work that the vehicle performs in a given period of time. This work can be measured in miles or engine hours, or averaged based on calendar days.

Unless the apparatus is used in a rural setting where long responses are normal, mileage is a poor indicator of the apparatus' workload during the maintenance cycle. For example, in an urban environment the apparatus might travel only six or eight blocks, but pump at capacity for several hours.

The engine hour system may be a better method of establishing a proper PM cycle, but it too has some drawbacks. First, all apparatus must have the same type of hour meter to consider the readings valid in establishing a fleet service program. Electrical units that actually measure the time that the engine is running are one kind. Their main disadvantage is that the readings fail to indicate whether the unit was idling, driving, or pumping at full power during the indicated hours. Adding another hour meter, one that reads the hours that the pump or aerial PTO was engaged, would be helpful in obtaining a uniform evaluation.

Apparatus PM can be scheduled based on calendar days. Depending on the size of the fleet and its use, each unit can be scheduled on a quarterly or semi-annual basis. This gives the shop mechanics a regular schedule for PM, allowing them to schedule other needed work.

It is important that the PM cycle you select is compatible with the vehicle manufacturer's recommendations.

Staff vehicle preventive maintenance

Given the different nature of their use, staff vehicles should be scheduled into the shop based on 3,000 miles of use or the manufacturer's recommendations. Without the excessive idling or pumping that affects apparatus, mileage is a fairly accurate measurement of their work output.

Preventive maintenance for staff vehicles should include lubrication, oil and filter change, and inspections of belts, hoses, fluid levels, wiper blades, and lights. Uneven tire wear could indicate that the front end might have worn components or require alignment.

Maintaining the PM schedule

Maintaining the PM schedule for a smaller fleet could consist of a manual accounting system as simple as marking the calendar. For larger fleets, a personal computer makes this task much more manageable. A simple database program that lists the vehicle with a description, monthly or hourly reading when maintenance is due, and the unit's previous two service dates works nicely. The system's flexibility allows you, at a glance, to see whether the apparatus is approaching its PM date, or it can give you a look at the entire fleet's preventive maintenance schedule. Several commercial computer software programs for fire department fleet management are advertised regularly in fire service publications.

Engine oil analysis

Proper oil analysis can be used to save or extend the life of your engine by early detection of problems that fail to exhibit symptoms or obvious signs. Conditions such as diesel fuel dilution or antifreeze contamination in the oil result in costly repairs and downtime. If you discover them and take corrective action quickly, you can short circuit a minor condition before it becomes a major engine overhaul.

Oil analysis, performed by a laboratory, uses a spectrometer to detect the presence of wear metals, additives, and other contaminants, such as silicone (dirt). A laboratory device burns a small quantity of the oil using an electrical arc, identifies the composition of the sample, and relays the information to a computer terminal for evaluation.

Other physical and chemical testing techniques are used to identify such contaminants as fuel, water, and antifreeze. Viscosity and lubricity, measured using crankcase deposits and depletion of detergents in the sample, also are determined and recorded.

All test data are entered on the computer and read by a technician who adds comments as to the possible source of any abnormal readings, as well as noting corrective actions that might be taken. This comprehensive report is then sent to the fleet manager.

A fire department that is interested in using the services of an oil analysis laboratory should ask truck and transportation companies in the immediate area to recommend a facility that can perform the required tests.

Reading the report

Once the oil analysis report has been received, the maintenance supervisor should evaluate it carefully. Compare the results of previous samplings, if on file, to the current readout to assess whether a previous abnormal condition has improved, remained unchanged, or deteriorated.

If oil is analyzed before the PM date, the laboratory reports will have been returned for evaluation before the apparatus reports to the shop for PM service. This way mechanics can investigate the cause of any abnormal readings indicated in the report. Additionally, if contamination is found in a sample that is taken during PM, the oil and filters that were just changed may have to be drained and changed again after corrective measures are taken.

In addition to motor oil, transmission fluid, gear lubricant, and hydraulic oils used in aerial devices can be similarly analyzed for contamination. Early detection of contamination could be a critical factor in avoiding scored hydraulic pistons and pump failures.

Pump service test

Another important component of an ongoing maintenance program is the pump service test. This service test should be conducted after any major pump repair or annually at a minimum. The pump service test was developed to ensure that the unit's fire pump can perform to the level for which it was designed. The details of this test are specified in NFPA 1911, *Standard on Service Tests of Pumps on Fire Department Apparatus.*

Briefly, the standard specifies:

1. Checking and comparing the no-load governed engine speed to the readings when the unit was new. This is to ensure that the engine is capable of producing the necessary rpms.
2. Operating the primer pump until 22 in. Hg of vacuum is developed with all intakes capped and discharges closed and uncapped. The vacuum will not drop more than 10 in. Hg in 5 minutes.
3. Operating the pump at 100 percent of capacity at 150 psi for 20 minutes, 70 percent of capacity at 200 psi for 10 minutes, and 50 percent of capacity at 250 psi for 10 minutes.
4. Conducting a test of the pump's pressure control. While pumping capacity at 150 psi the pressure control device shall be set. All discharges shall be closed in less than 10 seconds but not more rapidly than 3 seconds, and the pump pressure shall not rise more than 30 psi.

   While pumping at capacity, the pressure then should be reduced to 90 psig and the same test duplicated. The pump pressure shall not rise more than 30 psi.

   The third part of the test shall be conducted at 250 psig and 50 percent capacity. When the discharges are closed the pump pressure shall not rise more than 30 psi.
5. Calibrating and verifying for accuracy each gauge or flow meter.

Aerial ladder testing

Aerial devices, like fire pumps, need to be tested and inspected annually to ensure safe, reliable, continuous operation. The requirements for this test, as well as for nondestructive testing, are outlined in NFPA 1914, *Standard for Testing Fire Department Aerial Devices.* It is important to note that 1914's requirements are *in addition to the manufacturer's recommendations for inspection.*

Inspections

The annual inspection process can be completed by fire department personnel or properly qualified mechanics. A full inspection of the aerial device, outriggers, and mountings in accordance with the manufacturer's recommendations should be conducted before the operational and load tests. This should include a visual inspection for defective structural welds, worn hydraulic lines, fluid leaks, etc. If qualified personnel are unavailable, several outside testing agencies with mobile equipment can perform a proper inspection.

What follows is a brief overview of these basic aerial device tests. *Before*

Aerial devices require annual inspection and testing to ensure safe, reliable continuous operation. If qualified personnel are not available in the fire department, a third-party testing agency should be retained to perform the inspections. PHOTO COURTESY OF P. GIUNCHINI

you attempt them you must review and make sure that you understand the complete recommendations of the current edition of NFPA 1914 and the manufacturer's detailed instructions.

Operating test

After the apparatus is stabilized, the ladder shall be fully elevated, rotated 90 degrees, and fully extended. The unit should complete this evolution in 60 seconds or less. If a permanent waterway is installed, 105 seconds is allowed.

Horizontal load test

After the apparatus is stabilized, the ladder is extended to the maximum horizontal extension over the rear and parallel to the vehicle's centerline. The amount of beam twist is not to exceed the manufacturer's tolerances.

A weight equal to the rated live load shall be added gradually to the top rung of the ladder by using a test weight container. After five minutes the weight should be removed and a visual inspection of all load-supporting elements should be made. Any sign of deformity or damage shall constitute noncompliance.

Maximum elevation load test

After vehicle stabilization the ladder shall be rotated over the rear of the apparatus, extended to maximum elevation and fully extended. A weight equal to the manufacturer's specified rated live load shall be applied gradually to the top rung using a test container suspended by a cable. After five minutes the weight will be removed and all load-supporting elements inspected for any sign of damage or noncompliance.

It is important to note that at no time during these tests should the ladder be moved with the test weight applied.

Water system test

A permanently piped waterway should be fully inspected and pressure tested. A valve on the discharge end of the waterway should be closed after filling the system with water and removing all air. With the ladder at full extension, 200 psi should be applied for 2 minutes without leaks.

Elevating platforms

Elevating platforms are subject to similar inspection, operational, and load tests in accordance with their manufacturers' recommendations. In addition to operational tests, platform controls, and leveling capabilities, as well as platform control deactivation from the lower controls, shall be demonstrated.

Nondestructive testing

The nondestructive testing procedures specified in NFPA 1914 shall be performed at least every five years, whenever the aerial device is damaged, or when visual inspections or load tests indicate a potential problem.

The personnel who perform this testing must be certified as Level II technicians in the test methods used as specified by the American Society for Nondestructive Testing, a professional organization devoted to promoting knowledge of nondestructive testing. In most cases, this means using the apparatus manufacturer or a third-party testing agency. Many of these testing agencies advertise their services regularly in fire service publications.

Nondestructive testing allows a thorough inspection of all exposed metal components of the aerial, outriggers, and supporting members without disassembly or causing stress damage. Among the methods used are ultrasonic high-frequency vibrations, magnetic particle tests for steel components, conductivity tests on aluminum devices, and penetrant inspections in which dye bleeds into the surface and flaws are revealed under ultraviolet light.

Any minor deficiencies found by the inspector must be corrected before a ladder inspection certificate can be issued. Major structural defects will be cause to remove the unit from service.

If at any time the aerial device is subjected to structural damage, the manufacturer should be notified immediately in writing. The device then must be repaired to the manufacturer's standards, and be nondestructively tested before it is placed back in service.

SUMMARY

Future trends in apparatus manufacturing are moving in the direction of electronics, automation, and reducing staffing for physical tasks. Beginning with the automatic transmission and power steering and continuing with pump pressure governors, flow meters, electrically controlled valves and hydraulic ladder racks, technology is replacing the need for brute strength and time-consuming repetition. Many of these innovations allow firefighters to concentrate more on safety while driving to and operating at fire scenes.

Microprocessors are being used more now than ever before. Anti-lock brakes, traction control, diesel fuel injection, automatic transmission control, and pressure governors are only some of the apparatus systems that are being controlled by computers.

Along with this high-tech equipment comes the need for qualified technicians and sophisticated diagnostic equipment to maintain and repair the units. It is almost certain that in the near future requirements to certify emergency vehicle technicians to perform these tasks will be promulgated.

Informed, intelligent procurement practices, coupled with an ongoing maintenance program, will provide the community with safe, efficient and reliable fire apparatus that can perform many years of service.

12

Apparatus Specification and Purchasing

WILLIAM C. PETERS

CHAPTER HIGHLIGHTS

- Apparatus purchasing, committee selection, timeframe and research.
- Organizing specifications.
- How to produce a functional purchasing document.
- The bidding, inspection, acceptance, and training phases of fire apparatus purchasing.

SPECIFYING AND PURCHASING fire apparatus can be a very difficult exercise for the fire chief who is unfamiliar with the procedures involved. Because this process takes place infrequently, most chiefs never have the opportunity to become thoroughly familiar with the intricacies of apparatus purchasing. The method used most often is to rely solely on the advice and guidance of an apparatus salesperson, an approach that increases the anxiety and apprehension of the chief who wants to buy suitable apparatus at a reasonable price.

This chapter will help guide the chief through the purchasing maze in an orderly fashion by explaining how to properly research, evaluate, and justify the purchase.

THE PROCESS

The purchasing process is dependent on such variables as time, money, and the physical and tactical requirements of the apparatus. The following outline covers the steps that may be necessary to turn the initial proposal step into the end product—a functioning piece of fire apparatus.

THE PURCHASING OUTLINE

1. Determine who will research and formulate the specifications.
   a. Fire chief
   b. Staff member(s)
   c. A committee
2. Establish and define the amount of time that is available from the beginning of the project through the delivery of the apparatus.
3. Consider the financial implications and replacement options available.
   a. Purchase
   b. Lease
   c. Refurbish
4. Conduct research.
   a. Basic types of apparatus
   b. Features and options available
   c. Manufacturer's reputation
5. Secure funding needed for the purchase.
6. Outline preliminary requirements using NFPA standards (Appendix C).
7. Compile a list of acceptable manufacturers and request sample specifications and representative drawings.
8. Using information provided, assemble a preliminary specification.
9. Hold a prebid conference if required or desired.
10. Distribute the final specifications for a public bid.
11. Evaluate the bids and make a recommendation of award of contract based on the best value (not necessarily the low bid).
12. Attend a preconstruction conference with the manufacturer to discuss each detail of construction.
13. Conduct other inspections as specified, for example:
    a. Completed chassis or prepaint inspection
    b. Final inspection
14. Take delivery and perform acceptance testing.
15. Schedule manufacturer's training classes, if included in the specifications.
16. When all members have been trained in the use of the apparatus, place it in service.

Who should formulate the specifications?

In large metropolitan fire departments apparatus specifications and purchasing usually are addressed by an apparatus or maintenance officer, planning department or support services staff, with final specifications approved by the fire chief.

In smaller career departments without extensive staff personnel the duties usually will be handled directly by the chief of department. In this case, the chief should consider holding information-gathering discussions with deputies or possibly the company officers who ultimately will use the apparatus. Some chiefs seek the counsel of personnel from larger departments who are more familiar with the process or ask for assistance from fire protection consultants. Considering the financial implications of the purchase, using outside help is usually a wise decision.

Volunteer fire companies typically form a committee to deal with the purchase. The make-up of this committee can be critical to the successful outcome of the project. While all members of the company should be able to voice their opinions, a select group of knowledgeable individuals should be charged with researching and evaluating the features and options that ultimately will be part of the finished apparatus.

Regardless of the size or type of department, the following personnel should be considered for their input and expertise:

- *Company Officers* can make suggestions relative to the tactical and operational objectives that they expect from the apparatus.
- *Drivers/Operators/Engineers* should provide input regarding the performance expected of the vehicle, including driving and operational controls, and pump panel layouts.
- *Maintenance Personnel* can focus on the mechanical and maintenance portions of the vehicle, e.g., concerns such as the electrical system, component size and performance expectations, and ease of operator preventive maintenance.
- *Training Officers* tend to be well-versed in current practices and procedures that can be applied to enhance the operational efficiency of the apparatus. Innovations such as Class A foam, high-output, preconnected attack lines, and large diameter hose (LDH) evolutions should be researched and considered for inclusion in the specifications.
- *Safety Officers* are concerned with overall apparatus safety. Especially important are ensuring a sufficient number of seats for responding personnel, providing adequate visual and audio warning devices, and evaluating steps and handrails.

Committee members coordinate their efforts and interact with each other to facilitate the purchase. For instance, the safety officer might consider a siren or lighting configuration that would place an undue strain on the electrical system. The maintenance person evaluates the condition and works with the safety officer to find a compromise arrangement that is both adequate and practical.

Before the committee begins its work, ground rules must be laid that determine how final decisions will be made. Will the decisionmaking process be a democratic vote by the entire fire company or the apparatus committee, or will the chief make the ultimate decision after considering input from other members? While this is a local decision, it is one best made *before* embarking on the project and before clashing or dominant personalities burden the entire process.

Time frame

How much time is available until the new apparatus you need is delivered? Product research, sales presentations, preparing specifications, holding a public bid, evaluating the results, and awarding a contract typically take from 6 to 12 months.

The period of time from the signing of the contract to delivery varies according to the manufacturer's backlog and the intricacies of the specifications. Taking from 6 to 12 additional months to complete the unit is about average. Often, additional time is required to get aerial units, special customization, or a fire apparatus chassis that is not manufactured by the apparatus builder.

The premature replacement of apparatus due to accident, fire, or building collapse may significantly reduce the purchasing timeframe. PHOTO COURTESY OF RICHARD SIKORA

Realistically speaking, allow 18 to 24 months to complete the purchasing process.

If the apparatus that is being replaced is out of service because of a mechanical failure or accident, the timeframe requirement may have to be reduced significantly. In this case, you might want to ask several manufacturers if stock or demonstrator units are available. Most manufacturers have demonstrator units, sometimes at reduced prices, that have been driven around the country to apparatus shows and shown to potential customers. These units usually are equipped with the latest features and could be a viable option if you are pressed for time.

Before rushing to purchase one of these units, be certain that it has the proper design and performance features to satisfy your department's requirements. Remember that this apparatus probably will last 20 years and it should be fully capable of fulfilling the present mission of the department as well as carrying it into the future. If special requirements cannot be met, perhaps the community should ask to borrow a unit from a neighboring department or purchase a used piece of equipment to fill the void until the new unit can be properly specified and built.

Purchase, lease, or refurbish?

Just as the time frame will have a direct impact on the replacement of apparatus, so too will financial arrangements. In most cases where the municipal government is responsible for maintaining fire protection, outright purchasing using the capital improvements budget is normal. Funds for these major projects are borrowed and paid back over a period of time by selling municipal bonds. Bond purchasers receive a favorable return on their investment, and, because in many cases it is tax free, the municipality enjoys a lower interest rate than the business community.

In many locations, the amount of bond indebtedness that a municipality can carry at any one time is limited, so if the city can borrow only a certain amount, the fire department will be competing with other city agencies for its piece of the "capital budget pie." Besides providing fire protection, the governing body must consider road resurfacing, and schools, libraries, parks, recreational facilities and public buildings that need improvements. Obviously, each agency considers its projects to be top priority. This is why considering the needs analysis and justification for replacement, discussed in Chapter 11, is critically important.

When capital funding is unavailable, another viable alternative might be a lease/purchase plan. Most manufacturers either provide leasing themselves or can make the necessary arrangements for the purchaser. Similar to financing for a family automobile, the apparatus is delivered and annual payments, for a duration of from seven to ten years, are made. When the last payment is made, the title to the apparatus is turned over to the municipality. Obviously, interest charges raise the total cost of the apparatus, but when funding is not available, this is one way to maintain proper fire protection at an affordable rate.

Many independent volunteer fire companies have found that while they attempt to save the necessary funds for a purchase, inflation and routine price increases keep moving the project further into the future. With proper documentation, they too can qualify for a lease plan and enjoy the benefits of a reliable replacement while making annual payments.

Insurance and maintenance during the lease period usually are the purchaser's responsibility.

When discussing the funding for replacement apparatus, inevitably the question of refurbishing the existing unit will be raised. No fire department can answer that question without thoroughly understanding the refurbishment process and the costs involved.

Refurbishment is considerably more involved than just surface body work and a coat of new paint. With the proper research, there might be more reasons why refurbishment is *not* a viable alternative than why it is. Consider the following points before considering refurbishment:

- In what condition are the vehicle's engine, transmission, driveline and differential? Do they need to be replaced, rebuilt, upgraded or converted from gas to diesel or standard transmission to automatic?
- What is the condition of the functional units of the apparatus? Is the pump adequate to meet your present and future operational objectives? Will it easily pass the annual pump test? Can the aerial device meet the extensive requirements of the annual inspection and load test as well as the five-year nondestructive test?
- Is the unit's manufacturer still in business? Can repair parts be obtained easily now and will they still be available in the future?
- In addition to obvious body work and painting, what unseen conditions might be encountered in the substructure or chassis that would require additional work?
- Is the apparatus able to conform to modern, more efficient firefighting procedures, such as preconnected attack lines, large diameter hose equipment, larger water tanks, prepiped deck gun, or class A and B foam systems?
- Is the aerial device long enough and strong enough to accomplish the tasks that it encounters? Are taller buildings beyond its reach or are housing "setbacks" causing older light-duty aerials to be used at dangerously low angles?
- The final and most important question that must be asked: "Is the fire department willing to delay the extensive safety upgrades of the current standards for another five to seven years?"

Evaluate all of these questions seriously before you decide to refurbish. Too many negative answers are a signal to replace rather than refurbish.

Whether a decision to purchase or lease is made, the chief or committee should plan to conduct extensive research into the basic types of apparatus, the features and options available, and the many manufacturers' reputations for quality, service, and warranty. Outlined below are several ways to carry out this research.

Advertisements

The first research method used by manufacturers of all products is advertising. There are several national and many local fire service publications that rely on advertising for their revenue. In most cases, apparatus manufacturers use periodicals to showcase new products, innovations, and special promotions. Use the reader service card that usually accompanies the magazine; it should bring you a rapid response from the advertisers you select.

These same publications often contain informative articles about the latest apparatus and equipment trends, maintenance procedures and problem-solving ideas. Use them as a resource.

Apparatus and equipment shows provide the best opportunity to inspect, evaluate, and ask questions about the units on display. PHOTO COURTESY OF WM. PETERS

Trade shows

Another excellent way to gather information is to attend the many trade shows presented around the country. The International Association of Fire Chiefs and The Alliance for Fire and Emergency Management are among the national organizations that have shows in conjunction with their conferences, held in different parts of the country. Literally acres of fire apparatus and equipment are on display for the perusal of conference-goers. Many regional conferences also are held by local chiefs' organizations, apparatus maintenance groups, and instructor associations.

Apparatus manufacturers are well represented at these events and display their latest designs, innovations, and features. Your committee gets convenient access to knowledgeable factory personnel from many manufacturers, all in one location. These representatives can answer most questions about their products. You also get a chance to examine closely the workmanship and quality of the apparatus you are contemplating for purchase.

With the vast array of vehicles on hand, it is advisable to take notes, photograph or videotape the units, and collect manufacturers' brochures and business cards. With so much information available, it is foolish to attempt to commit it to memory.

Apparatus associations

Joining and participating in the activities of the many apparatus associations are other ways to gather valuable information. Many of these groups offer training programs on apparatus maintenance, as well as information on the latest NFPA standards and on specifications preparation. In addition to viewing presentations from experts in the apparatus field, participants get the all-important opportunity to network with others who share a common interest in apparatus. Often, valuable information can be swapped during friendly conversations with counterparts from other parts of the country.

Among the national apparatus associations and organizations are the International Association of Fire Chiefs (IAFC) Apparatus Maintenance Section, the National Association of Emergency Vehicle Technicians (NAEVT) and the Fire Department Safety Officers Association (FDSOA). There also are numerous well-organized regional apparatus associations. An additional benefit of membership in these organizations is the newsletter that most publish on a regular basis. It too provides for an exchange of information on current apparatus trends, problems, solutions, and maintenance tips.

In most cases you need not be an apparatus mechanic or technician to join these organizations; you need only a desire to advance your knowledge of apparatus technology.

Visit manufacturing facilities

To see how a particular piece of fire apparatus is built, visit the manufacturer's facility. Many routinely offer guided tours and most welcome inspections of their facility. Examining apparatus in various stages of the building process is a very enlightening experience; you actually get to see the important subassemblies that make up the apparatus before they are hidden under sheet metal and numerous coats of shiny paint.

Oftentimes, inspecting apparatus that are finished and awaiting delivery can stimulate new ideas or highlight different methods of accomplishing certain goals. As with the apparatus shows, record items of interest for future reference.

Visit other fire departments

Visiting neighboring departments that have acquired a certain piece of apparatus is another way to network visually. Most manufacturers will happily supply the names of the customers who have placed their apparatus in service.

Visiting an apparatus manufacturer's facility provides the opportunity to examine apparatus in various stages of the building process. PHOTO COURTESY OF SAULSBURY FIRE EQUIP.

You can call for an appointment yourself or ask the apparatus dealer to set up the visit. Each method has its advantages and disadvantages. In some cases the customer might be more "candid" if the dealer's representative is not present. On the other hand, having the representative present gives you a chance to ask questions about variations to the basic apparatus that the customer might not be able to answer accurately. A compromise that uses both methods might be the best way to get the complete picture. When you make the appointment for the visit, request that the apparatus salesperson join you an hour or more after you arrive to discuss options and variations to the apparatus that is being displayed.

On this type of visit, it also is wise to talk to both the officials who were responsible for the purchase, to gain information about the manufacturer's reliability, conformance to specifications, and general disposition, and to the members who drive and operate the unit. This should give you a well-rounded opinion of the product and the manufacturer.

When you call for the appointment, ask if a copy of the bidding specifications and, possibly, a shop drawing are available for you to have. They will be valuable when you research products and make comparisons.

Decisions

Before you move on to the final research phase—sales presentations—several decisions have to be made about the unit's basic requirements. If you develop an outline you can provide the manufacturer with the necessary information about the department's wishes. This helps to expedite the presentation and estimated pricing.

This outline also serves as a foundation on which to build and develop a complete set of bidding specifications.

Some items to include in your basic requirements are:

- Basic type of unit—pumper, aerial, platform, rescue, mobile water supply, initial attack or combination vehicle;
- Chassis—custom or commercial; maximum number of firefighters to be seated; diesel or gasoline engine; standard or automatic transmission; cab construction material (if there is a preference); cab type (split tilt, full tilt, fixed); special chassis requirements such as tight-turning radius or short wheelbase;
- Body—standard or extra-large compartmentation; high side compartments; type of compartment doors (hinged or roll-up), body material (if there is a preference), hose load;
- Aerial Device—aerial ladder, platform, telescoping, or articulating boom, length, waterway output, outrigger spread, tip load requirements if they exceed the standard;

- Pump—rated GPM output, single or multistage, pressure control by relief valve or pressure governor, gauges or flow meters, special requirements for suctions or discharges;
- Tank—size, construction material (if known), special requirements such as tank-to-pump flow rate, direct filling capabilities, tank dump systems, or foam capabilities; and
- Special options and features—scene lighting, generator, booster reel, trash line, ladder rack, or prepiped deckgun.

Sales presentations

Based on your previous research, several "acceptable" manufacturers should be contacted for a sales presentation. Give them a copy of your basic outline in advance and request "ballpark" pricing. Most dealers are happy to provide brochures, sales information and even recent shop drawings for your consideration. This material is a good starting point for developing your own specifications.

Keep in mind that the estimated price of the apparatus might not include all of your requirements such as bonding, inspection trips, delivery expense, training, and equipment. These will all have to be addressed before you arrive at a specific dollar amount of funding to request.

It's also important to designate one member of the committee to record the details of the meeting and to assemble the material provided in a neat, orderly fashion for future reference.

Funding commitment

After approximate prices and delivery times have been established, the committee should report back to the governing body to have the necessary funding approved. When seeking funding, provide an honest estimate but be careful not to cut yourself short. In the apparatus industry there are frequent price fluctuations and other variables that have to be considered when the final bid is prepared. Also, ideas that were not addressed originally might be included in the final specifications. Given the amount of work that is required and the life expectancy of the apparatus, it is better to err on the high side rather than having to settle for less than you want or having to go back to the city officials to ask for more money, which could seriously jeopardize funding for the entire procurement.

Approaching city officials

Approaching city officials to request a large sum of money for the purchase of a piece of apparatus can be intimidating to say the least! This is especially true when the spokesperson does not have a background in public speaking. Consider the following items before entering this arena:

- Be Prepared! All areas of justification must be fully explored and documented. Anticipate all possible questions and have answers prepared that are rehearsed and flow naturally. This is the type of preparation that the President undergoes before a debate or news conference. Being properly prepared also helps to reduce the jitters that you might experience. Never "wing it"!
- Stress escalating maintenance costs and inefficiency. Elected officials must be convinced that in the long run this is a wise economic decision. Be prepared to explain why refurbishment is not economically feasible, if this is the case.
- Explore the issue of public safety. Are the citizens at risk because of an unreliable piece of apparatus? Don't make statements that can't be proved. Produce maintenance records that highlight the number of times the apparatus was out of service at the shop.
- Don't get emotional. Stay calm. Remember that ultimately this is a business transaction and it is always easier to do business in a rational manner.
- Don't threaten. No one likes to be "put in a corner." Threats in the form of recall elections or adverse publicity are counterproductive.
- Subtly point out the liability factor involved if the apparatus fails to respond or if members are still riding without seats or proper restraints. The price of one lawsuit would easily cover the cost of the replacement apparatus.
- Don't count on major public support. Most taxpayers are more interested in how the purchase will affect their tax rate rather than in how much more reliable their fire protection will be. No one ever visualizes a fire in his own home.
- Emphasize your complete commitment to work with the administration by expressing an understanding of budget limitations. Keep the specifications basically "frills-free," and consider offering to take on extra duties such as EMS or hazmat response if a combination vehicle will help to save money.
- Stress the time frame involved (18 to 24 months) and the anticipated price increases associated with delaying the order.
- ALWAYS BE DIPLOMATIC!

A recent magazine article by the chief of a volunteer department indicated that he very successfully educated his public officials by inviting them to tour the firehouse one evening. Before their visit a basic outline of the fire department's history, apparatus, training subjects and number of staff hours committed, as well the type and number of calls to which the department responded during the previous year was delivered to each member of the city council.

During the visit, the officials were shown how well the apparatus and equipment were being maintained. Rescue techniques were demonstrated and problems (e.g., the need for a diesel exhaust system) were pointed out.

At the conclusion of the visit, refreshments were served and the officials were treated to a video and slide presentation on recent local fires.

After this enlightening experience the governing body gained a much better understanding of fire department operations, and its members' sincerity, and their needs.

Apparatus requirements

Once funding is committed, the fire department must begin the process of developing the bidding specifications. The first step in this process is determining which NFPA standard applies to the purchase. This determination is based on the primary function of the apparatus. For instance, a 1,250-gpm pumper equipped with a water tower should comply with the provisions of NFPA 1901, *Standard for Pumper Fire Apparatus.* An aerial apparatus, equipped with the same 1,250-gpm pump, should be constructed in accordance with the recommendations in NFPA 1904, *Standard for Aerial Ladder and Elevating Platform Fire Apparatus.*

The general requirements section of each apparatus standard contains the following statement:

> Responsibility of Purchaser: It shall be the responsibility of the purchaser to specify the details of the apparatus, its required performance, the maximum number of fire fighters to ride on the apparatus, and any hose, ground ladders or equipment it will be required to carry that exceed the minimum requirements of this standard.

This effectively places the burden of specifying everything that is needed to perform the defined duties on the purchaser. To assist specifiers in this awesome task, the 1991 editions of the apparatus standards contain a section entitled "Appendix C." While using the appendix is not a requirement of the standard, it is included for informational purposes. Appendix C is divided into subject headings that follow the order of the standard. Written in a question-and-answer-type format, it has an easy, "fill-in-the-blanks" style. The section of the standard that deals with each question is listed in a column to the right of the page, making research of the requirements easier for the specifier.

Making proper use of Appendix C helps to reduce apprehension over missing critical specification requirements of the apparatus.

The completed Appendix C, along with all options and features that are required, then should be given to several "qualified" apparatus manufacturers, requesting "sample" specifications that comply with your requirements.

Qualifying manufacturers

What procedure should the fire department use to determine the qualifications of a manufacturer? From the previous research, the committee should evaluate each interested manufacturer on the following points:

- A commitment to fulfilling the requirements of the fire department with the least number of exceptions. Many times, if a particular feature or option is unavailable or difficult to provide, apparatus sales representatives might attempt to talk you out of it, rather than trying to comply with the requirement.
- The manufacturer's reputation based on past performance and input about customer satisfaction obtained from other departments that you should have contacted as part of your research.
- Design and reliability factors. Is the apparatus designed well?
- Ease of service and maintenance. Preventive maintenance is the key to maintaining apparatus in a state of readiness. If these routine chores are difficult, there is a greater likelihood that they will be overlooked. Ease of maintenance correlates directly to the amount of downtime that will be required to repair and replace parts.
- Manufacturer's delivery schedule. This is particularly important if the current apparatus is out of service. In some cases, it could be a major concern for the fire department.
- The availability of a local dealership or private affiliated service facility which is qualified to properly maintain the apparatus and provide reliable warranty service. This requirement should be evaluated carefully by the purchaser.
- Parts availability. The fact that replacement parts are readily available also correlates directly to the amount of downtime the unit will experience. If the manufacturer has parts either available at a local dealership or a good network express shipping supply, out-of-service time will be reduced considerably. This requirement is difficult to measure, and is based mostly on information from present owners.
- Estimated price. While price is not necessarily your most important consideration in a critical purchase that might have a 20-year life span,

we all live in the real world of budget constraints. The best apparatus could conceivably be priced considerably beyond your budget.

After considering all of the points above, certain manufacturers will be able to meet your requirements and should be deemed qualified to provide information for the development of *your* specifications.

Using sample specifications

It is safe to say that most apparatus specifiers are not automotive engineers nor do they have the qualifications to tell a manufacturer what dimensions the frame rails must be, or how many crossmembers are needed to provide the strength and stability necessary for the apparatus. This is why specifications should be written by people who are qualified. By using an established specification as a guide, we have quantitative values to use to compare to other bidders. For instance, if the specifications indicate that the front bumper should be a certain size and thickness, it is easy to determine if the other bidders meet or exceed the requirements. If the specifications state only that a bumper be

The requirement of a local facility to provide service and warranty work for the apparatus is extremely important. PHOTO COURTESY OF WM. PETERS

provided, and no minimum standards are set, essentially *any* bumper that is installed will meet the specifications.

It is extremely important that you provide a method of taking exceptions or explaining clarifications because it allows other bidders a fair way to present their version of compliance with the *intent* of the specifications. Often a bidder's exception will exceed the minimum requirements of the specifications.

Use the information contained in a manufacturer's specifications as a sample for your specs, but do not use it as the bid document.

Certain "proprietary" items undoubtedly will be contained in the language that other bidders will find difficult or impossible to meet. A manufacturer that provides specifications would include only items he could meet!

Because computers typically generate specifications, confusing or conflicting requirements often result. For instance, in one specification this author examined, the cab portion of the specifications was described with all of the standard features explained (i.e., fixed side windows). If you prefer side windows that slide open, the manufacturer would not alter the original wording of the specification but list them as an option, and the language would read "the fixed side windows will be replaced by sliders." This could be confusing for other bidders who are not familiar with the format of the specifications. It is better to describe the features correctly the first time in your own language.

Most manufacturers' specifications contain large amounts of text, from several paragraphs to several pages, that describe sections of the apparatus. This makes bid evaluation extremely difficult because the other bidders could take exception to an entire section and address the components of their assembly in the same manner. If the spec writer takes the information provided in the sample and converts it into smaller, more manageable units, the specification is more easily understood; bidders who take exception then must address each element individually.

Another good reason for rewriting specifications is that items you thought were included might inadvertently have been left out, or features that are considered standard for one manufacturer might be optional with other bidders. For instance, if the supplier of the "sample" specs routinely provides a certain style of padding in the cab, it might not be sufficiently explained in the specifications for the other bidders to match.

Finally, it could raise ethical questions on the part of other bidders. While there is nothing wrong with using manufacturers' specifications as a sample or guide to the way you expect the apparatus to be constructed, imagine the embarrassment at a bid hearing if you had to admit that the successful bidder actually *provided the bid document!*

Remember that the NFPA standards place the burden of specifying all of the details of the apparatus and its performance on the purchaser. Take the information provided by reputable builders and modify it to meet the needs of your department.

TYPES OF SPECIFICATIONS

Specifications generally can be put into three categories: design, performance, and a combination of the two, design-performance.

Design specifications contain a preconceived arrangement of detail and form, with all of the details of construction spelled out. Most specifications obtained from the manufacturers could be categorized as being heavily design oriented. Often the design features of components are described down to the last nut and bolt.

Each type of specification has certain advantages and disadvantages. The advantages of a design type specification include the following:

- Everything is clearly defined and identifiable.
- Fleet uniformity benefits the maintenance, parts, and training functions.
- It is easy to evaluate bids. Other manufacturers will have to compare every item in their bids to the design features specified.
- More accurate estimations of the cost of the apparatus are possible.

Design specifications have the following disadvantages:

- They are restrictive. Depending on how narrow the design criteria are, the specification could be overly restrictive to other responsible bidders.
- They limit innovation, which could result in reduced effectiveness. By identifying every component, progressive new ideas sometimes are overlooked.
- They encourage favoritism. As noted earlier, most specification writers are not automotive engineers and therefore are incapable of designing a vehicle from the ground up. For that reason, many of the design features of the apparatus are taken from a manufacturer's specification. Realistically, incorporating an overabundance of nonessential design features from one manufacturer, without liberally interpreting exceptions from the other bidders, could be construed as favoritism.
- They can drive up costs. If you use a tight design specification from one manufacturer, it is possible that the cost of the apparatus will increase because there is less competition. Other manufacturers' bids will rise as they try to meet the design criteria specified if they differ from their normal method of construction.

Performance specifications are written to the required functional criteria of the apparatus. In this type of specification, all of the details of performance are outlined as well as the associated testing necessary to quantify the results.

This specification tells the bidder what the apparatus must do, but not necessarily **how to** accomplish it.

Advantages of performance-oriented specifications:

- Allow manufacturers to build in their own styles in order to meet your performance criteria; this results in competitive pricing.
- Encourage innovation. All new innovations in fire apparatus were ideas to meet certain performance objectives. Without restricting the design, better use can be made of innovative features.
- Allow manufacturers to use innovative ideas that could result in a more effective apparatus.

On the other hand, disadvantages of performance specifications may be to:

- Reduce the number of design definitions. This can cause interpretations to be flawed.
- Make it difficult to measure performance. This could become a problem unless testing criteria are defined clearly in the specifications.
- Do not promote fleet uniformity. Maintaining uniformity for training, maintenance, and parts stock can be beneficial to the fire department. If a performance specification is used, it is unlikely that the fleet will remain uniform.

The third type is a combination design-performance specification. This type couples both the necessary conceptual details (design features) with the preconceived functional criteria (performance) to arrive at a specification that will provide an apparatus that is designed to fit your needs as well as perform as desired. The design elements of this type of specification should detail the important features while allowing the manufacturer to meet the nonessential requirements in his own manner. For instance, some specifications are so descriptive about the components that make up the cab that they actually specify the diameter of the steering wheel and the number of spokes that it will have! This unnecessarily causes other bidders to take an exception and explain their steering wheel. If the steering wheel has a specific performance requirement, such as the ability to adjust (tilt), that should be included, but the rest of its design should not be unnecessarily restrictive.

The combination design-performance specification has many advantages and because it is adaptable, actually has no disadvantages. The pluses are outlined below.

- If you combine the correct number of important design features with the necessary performance, a **practical** specification is developed.
- This type of specification allows for more **competition** among bidders.

- Increased competition helps to **reduce the cost** of the apparatus.
- Key components that are *design* in nature are **identifiable** and comparable for bid evaluation.
- Uniformity of certain components is ensured. For example, the fire pump can be maintained by outlining its components as design rather than performance features.
- This type of spec adds **credibility.** Rather than using a manufacturer's specification word for word, the combination specification is really *your* specification.

Each type of specification can be modified in terms of the degree of difficulty necessary to meet it. The term "tight" often is applied to a highly restrictive design type specification and "loose" to one that is more relaxed. Often the degree of this variable is controlled by the purchasing department or the community's administration. Some have very specific rules that must be followed about how restrictive a specification can be.

"Open" specifications are relatively free of specific components or manufacturing styles and do not restrict properly documented exceptions or clarifications. This type of specification is more competitive and typically results in more bidders and sometimes a better price. Unfortunately, it also can attract bidders of lesser quality apparatus who can meet the relaxed specifications.

"Tight" bidding specifications are highly restrictive in nature and provide a detailed description of all components and construction designs. Often there is less tolerance for exceptions and deviations and no exceptions allowed for certain requirements. A tight spec usually limits the number of bidders, which in turn increases costs because of reduced competition. However, this type of specification sometimes is necessary to ensure delivery of a specific piece of apparatus.

GENERAL REQUIREMENTS

One of the biggest pitfalls in specification writing is a weak or poorly written set of general requirements. Sometimes referred to as a "boilerplate," this section outlines the bidding instructions and defines the "ground rules" that apply to using the specifications. The general requirements sometimes are more important than the construction specifications in relation to determining the validity and evaluation of a manufacturer's bid.

Outlined below are some of the important issues that should be explained completely in the general portion of the specifications. Remember, a manufacturer's sample specifications might not contain all of the items that the fire department considers important and certainly will not contain anything that would be difficult or impossible to meet.

- *Statement of intent*—A general statement that describes the apparatus and the requirement to comply with the appropriate NFPA standard as well as federal, state, and local motor vehicle laws.
- *Bid Submission Requirements*—The method and form of submitting a bid, including how deviations and exceptions may be outlined (in bid order) and whether contractor specifications and drawings are required. This section should include, in very direct language, a statement that the fire department's specifications will prevail over any proposal submitted, unless a properly defined exception is granted. This helps to avoid a problem that sometimes surfaces when a bidder doesn't take exception but proposes to build according to his own standards, regardless of the specification.
- *Performance Requirements*—Performance requirements, including road and operational functions, should be included. Simply indicate the appropriate NFPA paragraphs or consider outlining your own special requirements.
- *Delivery and Payment Terms*—The locations of acceptance and delivery, whether at the factory or in your community, should be established. Payment terms also should be defined clearly. Some manufacturers offer a discount for prepayment of components or for progressive payments as the apparatus is being built. As a word of caution, require that the component being paid for, such as the chassis, be invoiced and a certificate of ownership issued. Some fire departments have lost chassis that were prepaid when manufacturers suddenly declared bankruptcy.
- *Special Construction Requirements*—Items such as whether a custom or commercial chassis is acceptable, the type of material to be used in the construction of the cab and body, and whether one manufacturer is to build the entire apparatus. The latter is a very restrictive requirement that sometimes is used to help prevent the possibility of divided responsibility for warrantied items. This does, however, restrict the number of bidders on a project.
- *Approval Drawings*—If approval drawings are required, deadlines for them should be established, as well as whether the matter of the approval drawings or the written specifications take precedence. Consider adding that the fire department will make every effort to correct the approval drawings, but the written specifications, along with any corrections, will prevail.
- *Manufacturer's Experience and Reliability*—Requirements that outline the criteria establishing a manufacturer's reliability and reputation should be included. Such items could include the number of years in business, previous customers who can provide references and, possibly, a financial statement from a nationally recognized financial rating service. Consider stating if you are not willing to accept a "prototype" or first-of-a-kind-apparatus built by the manufacturer. This helps to iden-

tify whether the manufacturer has built apparatus similar to the one described in your specifications.

- *Bonding and Insurance*—Bonds are a form of insurance that bidders will comply with certain requirements of the bid. A bid bond ensures that bidders are responsible and will execute a contract if awarded the bid. You then have recourse if, for instance, a bidder submits an inaccurate price or later decides not to proceed with the contract. A performance bond is issued after the contract is awarded and indicates that the bidder will perform according to the provisions of the contract. If the contractor does not meet the requirements, the bonding company is responsible only to provide a suitable replacement apparatus at the bid price. This does not mean that the department will receive a free vehicle, only that the bonding company will pay any difference between the bid price and the actual cost of the apparatus provided. Bonding provides an element of protection, but also increases the price of the apparatus.

  Liability insurance is another item often required. Multimillion-dollar policies are maintained by larger manufacturers, but such a policy might be difficult for smaller ones. Some departments include only a phrase stating that the manufacturer is responsible for defending any and all lawsuits resulting from the use of the apparatus.

- *Factory Inspection Trips*—Factory trips are an essential part of the apparatus construction and inspection process. The number of trips, number of participants, and which associated costs will be borne by the bidder all should be included. Some departments require a set dollar amount for the trips to be included by all bidders; others pay for the trips themselves in order to eliminate any unfair advantage that a bidder who is geographically closer to the department might have.

- *Warranty and Followup Service*—A requirement that a factory-authorized service center be within easy travel distance of the purchaser is sometimes specified. Requiring bidders to supply the size of the facility, number of employees, number of mobile units, and capabilities of the facility helps you to determine whether the service center meets your requirements. The location where warranty service will be performed, i.e., at the fire station or at the repair facility, also can be specified.

- *Time to Build*—This is especially important if time is of the essence. The specifications should require the number of calendar days from the signing of the contract until delivery. Warn bidders that stating a time from the receipt of the chassis or other major component until delivery is unacceptable. Some purchasers include a penalty clause or liquidated damages for late delivery. This helps to get a fair appraisal of the actual anticipated delivery date. The penalty clause should include apparatus that are delivered incomplete or do not meet specifications.

- *Special Requirements*—Include special requirements, e.g., specific size, weight, or turning radius should be outlined.
- *Training*—If you wish to have a representative of the manufacturer provide training, outline this expectation clearly in the specifications; include the number of days or special hours and do not overlook evenings and weekends for volunteer departments. Some departments require that a program curriculum be submitted in advance for approval by the training officer to avoid conflicts that might occur if the manufacturer's training program is not consistent with fire department standard operating procedures. Videotapes or handouts also should be included if desired. Some departments include a training program for the mechanics who will maintain the apparatus. This could be particularly important especially if it is the department's first piece of apparatus produced by a particular manufacturer.
- *Warranty Requirements*—The requirements as to the length of warranty and method of requesting warranty service on the apparatus should be outlined. Individual components such as the engine, transmission, and pump will be covered by their respective manufacturers' warranties. Some purchasers' specifications require that the dealer act as the warranty agent, coordinating claims with the component builders. When the purchaser has specific warranty requirements, it is advisable to warn bidders that any difference between the warranty requirements stated in the specifications, and the warranty offered by the bidder will be taken as an exception. Many times a bid will contain a phrase that the bidder's "stated" warranty applies. It is important that the bidder cite the differences as exceptions.

Controlling "frills"

Because apparatus is so expensive, and cities and towns struggle with limited tax bases, specs should limit the number of nonessential options that might be considered "frills." Nothing halts a purchasing proposal faster than governing officials believing that the fire department is oblivious to their serious budget concerns. Unnecessary options—chrome wheels, a bell, fancy murals and logos painted on the rig, or an excessive number of inspection trips—all give the appearance of extravagance. (One specification outlined five inspection trips each for five department members! Apparently the whole fire company was going to the factory to supervise the building at one time or another!)

Do not confuse these unnecessary items with legitimate options and features. Accessories such as anti-lock brakes, a pressure governor, or an auxiliary braking device can be justified completely in the name of safety or efficiency. By comparing the cost of the feature to the cost of a liability claim if a preventable accident occurred, the accessory usually can be justified. Reducing brake maintenance costs by using a retarder is a way to demonstrate the efficiency of the investment in the option.

Spreading the cost of the option over the life of the apparatus shows that the feature adds little to the overall annual cost of the apparatus. It is much more difficult to justify the cost of options that do not enhance efficiency or operational safety in the same manner. The cost of expensive gold leaf cannot be justified when reflective lettering that enhances night visibility not only identifies the fire company but does it more safely.

THE BID PROCESS

When your committee is satisfied that its specifications have been refined and are complete, it is time to advertise for public bid. Some jurisdictions require an intermediate step known as a prebid conference. Announce the conference when you make preliminary bidding specifications available. Some purchasing departments require that manufacturers which intend to bid attend the prebid meeting to avoid contradictions or misunderstandings that might surface later.

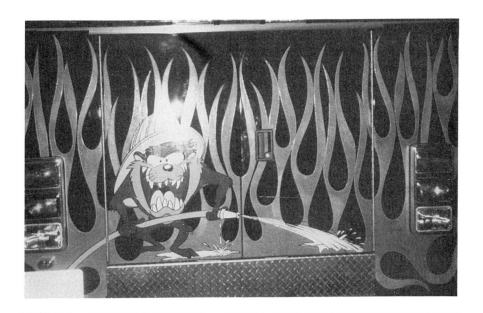

Including unnecessary options in the specifications, such as fancy decorations, give the appearance of extravagance and can jeopardize the funding for the project.
PHOTO COURTESY OF WM. PETERS

At the meeting, each item of the specification is read and discussed by the participants. Minor changes and adjustments might be made at the conference; however, if a major change is proposed, the bid might have to be delayed while the fire department investigates the viability of allowing a change or substitution. Any amendments containing changes, clarifications and corrections must be sent to all vendors that received the bid specifications.

While some consider this step an unnecessary inconvenience, it could help to expedite the bid process by uncovering errors, inconsistencies or misunderstandings.

When the final bidding specifications have been distributed, the date, time, and location of the bid opening, as well as the method of submitting a bid must be stated clearly. In most cases the community's purchasing authority or governing body handles the bid opening process.

It is likely that the fire department will participate in the bid evaluation and recommendation phase of the procedure. The sheer volume of information can make bid evaluation a difficult task. Thorough evaluations of proposals determine the lowest *responsible* bidder, not to be confused with a low bidder who does not meet the specifications, or who proposes a substandard product, hoping to get the contract award based on price alone.

First check that the bid contains the required documentation: bonding, insurance, financial report, customer list, construction specifications, sample drawings; then make sure the general form of the bid proposal is appropriate. The omission of such items as a bid bond or insurance coverage should immediately disqualify the bid.

When you evaluate apparatus bids, compare each item in the bidder's proposal to your specifications to check for compliance. Bids submitted with exceptions and corrections as instructed (in bid order) make the process go more smoothly. Prepare a bid evaluation report for each submission and list each exception or deviation. In some cases, a bidder's exception might equal or actually exceed your requirements. If so, note that the exception is granted. Watch for bids that include exceptions to whole areas of the specification (e.g., the body) and contain blanket statements such as "The body will be constructed in accordance with our standard manufacturing methods." Competing bidders know how their products differ from the specifications; it is their responsibility to outline the deviations if they want to be considered for the award.

Use the customer list provided by the bidder! Take the time to make some random telephone calls and network with other fire departments that are using the same apparatus. If they are not pleased, you usually will find out quickly.

When all of the information has been evaluated, the committee should prepare a written recommendation for the award of the contract. It should be based on the bidder who best meets the intent of the specifications, with the least number of exceptions and deviations. The price should be a secondary consideration. It is interesting to note that in some jurisdictions prices are submitted separately in a sealed envelope where they remain until after the bids have been evaluated. The proposals are evaluated strictly on their quality and on the manufacturers' ability to meet the specifications, and only after the selection is made is the price of the manufacturer who won the bid revealed; the others are returned unopened.

Some jurisdictions conduct a postbid hearing. Bidders are allowed to comment on the evaluation procedure and ask questions of the committee. If you elect to hold a bid hearing, it is essential to prepare and justify the reasons for your decisions. If the committee did its "homework" it is unlikely that its decisions will be questioned.

If the governing body agrees with the fire department's recommendation, a contract is awarded to the successful bidder and the apparatus construction process begins.

Unfortunately, at times a difference of opinion will develop, usually based on a low bid that does not meet the specs. If this occurs, it is incumbent on the apparatus committee to detail each and every discrepancy between the requirements of the specifications and the manufacturer's bid. If the purchasing authority decides that it wants to accept less than was specified, the specifications should be rewritten and a new bid held.

Factory inspections

One or more trips to a manufacturer's facility for the purpose of inspecting the apparatus that is being built is an integral and necessary part of the purchasing process. Sometimes justifying these trips to the city's governing body is harder than doing the inspections! When you discuss the trips with your officials, explain that they are not a new or unusual idea. NFPA standards indicate that interim trips to the manufacturer's facility might be necessary to ensure compliance with the specifications; the Appendix C questionnaire provides an area to indicate the number of trips and participants. Also, manufacturers require an inspection of the finished apparatus before it is shipped so that corrections or adjustments can be made easily. Given the large investment in the apparatus, and the enormous number of variables involved, it is foolish not to comply with this requirement.

The first trip is often the preconstruction or prebuilding conference, the purpose of which is to meet with the product specialist or engineer to discuss variations, and to determine your needs. Since there can be several ways to meet the intent of the specifications, these suggestions often yield a better overall finished product.

Any fire department personnel who travel to the manufacturing facility should understand the purchasing rules and regulations regarding change orders. Change orders are official changes or clarifications to the specifications, some of which could require an adjustment in price. Extensive changes that have a major impact on the bid price might not be allowed by law because this could be construed as tainting the bid process. It is equally important to document all clarifications and changes, whether they have a financial impact or not, and make them an addendum to the specifications. Have one member of the committee be responsible for maintaining accurate notes about any agreed-upon changes so that a change letter can be composed after the meeting.

Many decisions have to be made at the prebuild conference, from where certain equipment will be mounted, to the shape and design of the lettering. If a committee is handling the purchase and inspections, members should determine in advance how these decisions will be made. Some rely on the ranking officer's opinion while others use the democratic method of majority rule, but in either case, it should be understood clearly *before* the trip to the manufacturer's facility. Internal conflicts also should be resolved before departing. It is unprofessional to argue and bicker at the meeting or to try to have company officials side with one opinion or another. Approach the meeting as *one* customer purchasing *one* piece of apparatus.

If an adjustment or clarification is requested after the meeting, don't rely

A preconstruction conference affords the fire department personnel the opportunity to discuss the various methods to meet the intent of the specifications with the manufacturer's representative. PHOTO COURTESY OF ROBERT MILNES

on verbal communications to accomplish the change. Follow up any telephone discussions with a letter or fax and make them part of the specifications addendum.

Two other inspection trips often are specified: a chassis or prepaint inspection, and the final inspection. Depending on the fire department's preference, the intermediate inspection can be held either when the chassis is complete and before the body is installed, or after the body is installed but before the apparatus is painted. Each has its own advantages. For example, if you specify the chassis inspection, it is easier to examine the components of the chassis such as the pump, transmission, driveline, hoses and wiring before they are covered by the body. The biggest advantage of the prepaint inspection is the flexibility to making any necessary corrections to the body.

The final inspection is the most important trip of the three. While every manufacturer has quality control procedures, it is *your* inspection that determines the condition of the apparatus when it is delivered. It is extremely important that you systematically check every item in the specifications for compliance, operation, and finish.

Rather than trying to follow the order of the specifications as you check and jumping from one location to another, prepare a checklist that groups each item in the specifications by its physical location on the apparatus. For

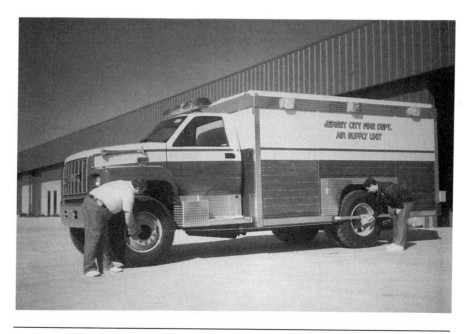

At the final inspection, every item of the specification should be systematically checked for compliance, operation, and finish. PHOTO COURTESY OF ROBERT MILNES

instance, the dashboard, cab controls, seats, interior finish, etc., are grouped in the "cab" section. The inspecting party then checks all items pertaining to the cab before it moves on to another part of the apparatus. Using this system saves a great deal of time, and ensures that important items in the specifications are not overlooked.

The last items are road and operational tests. When the apparatus is driven on the road, listen for any unusual noises and try to sense whether there are vibrations. Do not confuse this with the road test for acceptance, as outlined in the NFPA standards. That test is conducted after delivery, with a full tank of water and all equipment installed. Operating the aerial device or observing pump operations also should be part of the final inspection.

Delivery

The method of delivery and location of acceptance of the completed apparatus must be specified. Delivery by road, "under its own power," is the preferred method because it allows a break-in period for the vehicle. Many purchasers specify a predelivery service similar to a new car's "dealer prep" (oil is changed, chassis lubricated, all systems checked and the unit is cleaned) for the new apparatus. Any difficulties that the transport driver had are addressed at this time.

Some buyers opt to take delivery at the factory and drive the apparatus to their community. If this is your choice, make arrangements for payment, licensing, and proper insurance documentation ahead of time.

Most buyers specify delivery at their location. This method adds somewhat to the cost of the apparatus, but has its advantages.

When you take delivery at your location, the manufacturer is responsible for the apparatus until it arrives there safely, so accidents, mechanical malfunctions, or unforeseen occurrences such as tire damage or broken glass, are not your concern.

Most manufacturers use the services of a "drive-away" company. These companies employ properly licensed drivers and maintain insurance on the vehicle until it is delivered. While most states have waived the requirement for a commercial driver's license (CDL) for firefighters performing duties within their own state, there had been considerable debate about whether transporting a piece of apparatus across state lines is considered part of a firefighter's duties. So it is unknown whether the waiver applies to drivers from outside the state. This is a local decision. It would be unfortunate for a piece of apparatus being transported from the factory to be involved in an accident and not have been driven by someone properly licensed to operate that class of vehicle in the state.

Acceptance

Acceptance means that the purchasing authority agrees with the contractor that the terms and conditions of the contract have been met. "Acceptance tests" are those tests performed at the time of delivery to determine compliance with the specifications. In most cases, the apparatus is conditionally accepted at the factory pending the results of the acceptance tests at the purchaser's location.

The criteria for acceptance testing are decided by the purchaser and must be included in the specifications. At a minimum they should include the road performance tests outlined in the NFPA standards and the operational and capacity testing of the various apparatus systems. Road tests should be performed with a full water tank and full complement of equipment and personnel.

Acceptance tests vary according to the purchaser's specifications. Often an abbreviated version of the annual pump test is required to be performed upon delivery. Other times, extensive testing that goes far beyond normal operations is required. The City of New York conducts a pumper acceptance test on its 1,000-gpm units that requires pumping 800 gpm at 200 psi for 15 minutes, 500 gpm at 320 psi for 15 minutes, and 250 gpm at 600 psi for 6 hours! When a purchaser lacks drafting facilities to test a pumper, third-party certification tests performed at the factory to ensure compliance are used. Again, the number and conditions of acceptance testing are determined by the purchaser and must be part of the specifications.

Training

All users of the new apparatus must be thoroughly trained. If the bidder is expected to provide this training, include this in the specifications. Outline scheduling, number of days, and course content.

Scheduling and numbers of days tend to differ between career and volunteer departments. Career departments typically need to schedule the instruction to cover each shift. The number of days the delivery engineer would have to spend with the department varies depending on the work schedule. Volunteer departments might prefer to have the training given in the evening or on weekends when most of their members are available. Determining the number of days depends on the class size and on how much instruction is necessary to make users proficient.

It typically takes more training to use aerial apparatus because much of the instruction will be hands-on; individual operators must master the techniques of the operation. It usually is easier to learn pumper operations because most of the functions of the operating controls are similar from

Acceptance tests are performed at the time of delivery to determine that the apparatus meets the performance criteria outlined in the specifications. PHOTO COURTESY OF GREG CARIDDI

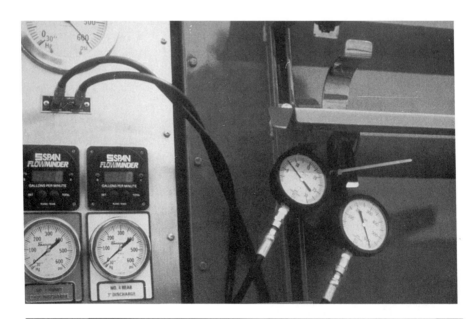

Tests for acceptance will vary according to the purchaser's requirements. The pumpers shown here are required to pump 600 psi for 6 hours. That is more than twice the pressure required by the standard. PHOTO COURTESY OF GREG CARIDDI

unit to unit. Previously trained pump operators can usually grasp the differences easily.

Sometimes driver training is included in the specifications. This is an expensive, time-consuming process, especially when a fire company has many members. As a suggestion, two or three members could participate in a "train the trainer" type of course and then go on to practice with and qualify the other members of the fire company.

The course outline should be submitted to the fire chief or training officer before training begins. Review the outline for potential conflicts with your department's Standard Operating Procedures (SOPs) and to confirm that all aspects of the training are covered. If the outline is followed all members should receive the same training, with nothing inadvertently overlooked.

Consider including operator preventive maintenance in the course outline. All members need to understand how to maintain the apparatus properly. Some departments also include a block of training in shop preventive maintenance for their municipal or fire mechanics. This too could be a worthwhile investment, especially if the apparatus is different from any in the department's current inventory.

Specify whether the contractor is to provide course materials, for example,

The degree of training to be provided by the apparatus manufacturer after delivery is dependent upon the terms of the specifications and the complexity of the apparatus.
PHOTO COURTESY OF WM. PETERS

a commercially produced videotape of apparatus operations or student hand-outs. Some departments like to videotape the delivery engineer's presentation for future reference. If this is your intention, state it in the specifications. That way the contractor can select an instructor who is comfortable being recorded.

Once the initial instructional period is over, encourage members to prac-tice and drill with the apparatus continuously to hone their driving and oper-ating skills. Training in apparatus operations must be an ongoing process.

SUMMARY

Preparing specifications and purchasing fire apparatus are major respon-sibilities that represent a sizable 20-year investment of a community's funds.

To approach a project this complex in an orderly fashion, an outline of tasks, arranged in sequential order, should be established and followed. Allowing enough time to complete all phases thoroughly is another important consideration.

Intelligent decisions based on investigation, research, and evaluation of available products should result in the needed purchasing justification. In undertaking this serious work, fire chiefs must decide whether they are con-tent to be followers, specifying a minimally compliant unit, or innovators, tak-ing advantage of the latest options and features.

13

Protective Clothing and Equipment

BRUCE VARNER

CHAPTER HIGHLIGHTS

- Information fire chiefs need to make informed choices about which protective clothing and equipment are appropriate for use within their own department.
- The applicability of NFPA standards and the requirements of those standards.
- Management information on the specification, purchase, distribution, and use of a wide range of these vital resources.

PROTECTIVE CLOTHING AND equipment are items that have been used by members of the fire service since the service began. The firefighter's helmet is as much a symbol of our service as the Maltese cross or the fire chief's crossed bugles. The type and complexity of this clothing and equipment have changed dramatically over the past three decades and the pace of the change has not slowed.

This chapter will provide fire chiefs with the information needed to make informed choices on which protective clothing and equipment are appropriate for use within their own department. The chapter will explain the applicability of National Fire Protection Association (NFPA) standards and the requirements of those standards, and provide other management information on the specification, purchase, distribution, and use of a wide range of these vital resources.

The original function of protective clothing was to shed water and to provide the firefighter with some minimal protection from falling debris. Today, protective equipment protects firefighters from the extremes of heat and cold, supplies them with clean breathing air to use as they work, protects them from the hazards of falling debris and liquids, and from hazardous materials, and prevents the transmission of disease.

NFPA STANDARDS

One of the most comprehensive and exhaustive bases of information about firefighter protective clothing and equipment is contained in NFPA standards. NFPA 1500, *Standard on Fire Department Occupational Safety and Health Program,* provides requirements for the use and maintenance of protective clothing and equipment and other NFPA standards provide performance requirements for all types of protective clothing and equipment. What follows is an overview of the NFPA standards process and the requirements of specific NFPA protective clothing and equipment standards.

Chiefs and other readers should be aware that requirements contained in any NFPA standard may be modified between editions by TIAs (Tentative Interim Amendments) issued by the NFPA and by the release of subsequent editions. Before you stake your career on a requirement of any NFPA standard, it is best to make sure that the requirement has not been modified by a TIA and to make sure that you have the most current edition of the standard.

NFPA standards are developed by committees consisting of users such as members of fire departments, manufacturers of protective clothing and equipment, outside organizations such as testing laboratories, and other interested parties. NFPA regulations prevent any one interest group from holding a majority on any committee. As a standard is created or revised, there are many ways that a member of the fire service can have an impact on its contents.

Before a standard is developed or revised, a call for proposals is made. Proposals can be submitted to the NFPA at any time and must be considered by the appropriate committee in the next revision cycle after the submission of the proposal. A proposal form is included with every NFPA standard or can be obtained by calling the NFPA. The proposal process allows members of the fire service to provide direct input into the standards-making system.

After a committee has completed a draft of a new or revised NFPA standard, the document is published as a Report on Proposals (ROP). All of the standards to be voted on by NFPA members at a fall or annual meeting are published together. For example, all standards to be considered at the NFPA's 1995 Annual Meeting are contained in one book, all those to be considered at the Fall 1995 meeting are contained in another, and so on. Copies of ROPs are sent to many NFPA members and to anyone who requests them from the NFPA. Anyone may comment on any requirement contained in the ROP. This is your second opportunity to have direct input into the standards-making process at no cost other than your time and the cost of a postage stamp. A form and time deadline are contained in every ROP to allow individuals or organizations that want to change, add to, or delete from a proposed standard or revised standard to do so. The committee responsible for the standard must respond to every public comment submitted before the deadline.

Once the deadline for comments on the ROP has expired, committees meet to review and consider all public comments. If the comment is accepted in full or in part, the standard must be modified to reflect that action. If the comment is rejected in full or in part, the committee must give a reason for its rejection. A comment may also be held for further study if the committee needs more time to consider or research the information contained in the comment. Any comment held for further study automatically becomes a public proposal for the next edition of the standard. The result of all committee consideration of public comments is then published as a Report on Comments (ROC). The ROC is sent to many NFPA members and to anyone who requests it from the NFPA.

After the ROC has been published, members of the NFPA who attend the annual or fall meeting vote on the standard as proposed in the ROC and modified by the ROC. Discussion of specific requirements can occur and changes are often made on the floor of the meeting. After the standard is approved by the membership at a meeting, the standard goes through several other steps at the NFPA prior to being printed and issued to the public. Participation in the NFPA process is important for members of the fire service. These standards affect every facet of our operations and we should have a hand in their development and processing.

The term "NFPA Approved" is heard often. The NFPA does not approve any process, design, installation, or procedure. Some NFPA standards, such as some protective clothing standards, require third party certification of a piece of clothing or a clothing design. The third party organization must not be affiliated with the manufacturer and must be an independent organization such as the Underwriters Laboratories (UL). This certification is intended to confirm that a piece of clothing will provide the level of protection required by a standard. Items of clothing or equipment that have received third party certification are referred to as "NFPA compliant" (they have been tested and found to comply with an NFPA standard). This is similar to a pump test for a new pumper performed by an organization such as Underwriters Laboratories.

NFPA 1500

It is hard to imagine any fire chief in North America who has not heard and read volumes of information about NFPA 1500. This safety standard has perhaps the greatest impact on the operation of a fire department of any standard issued recently. The standard provides basic requirements for the provision of a safe working environment for firefighters. NFPA 1500 requires that an implementation plan be developed by any fire department which adopts the standard. In some cases the standard has been statutorily mandated by the state and the decision to adopt it is not an option for the local fire department. Court cases have been influenced by the requirements of NFPA 1500 as a nationally recognized standard. If you go to court, the requirements of NFPA 1500 will be the subject of discussion, **whether or not it is adopted as law in your state or province.**

There has been a great deal of apprehension and misunderstanding about NFPA 1500. Many requirements attributed to the standard, and many misunderstandings of the standard, can be overcome by taking the basic step of carefully and thoughtfully reading the standard.

As this book went to press, the most current edition of NFPA 1500 was the 1992 edition. Chapter five of the 1992 edition of NFPA 1500 covers requirements dealing with protective clothing and protective equipment. The following is a summary of the requirements of that edition that relate to protective clothing and equipment.

> The fire department is responsible for providing each member with protective clothing and protective equipment which will provide protection from the hazards to which the firefighter is likely to be exposed. (Firefighters who fight wildland fires should have wildland protective clothing and equipment, inner city structural firefighters should have structural protective clothing and equipment, and firefighters who fight both types of fires should have both types of equipment.)

> The use of protective clothing is required when the member is exposed or could be exposed to the hazards for which the clothing is provided.

> Members must be trained in the care, use, inspection, maintenance, and limitations of their protective clothing and equipment. The clothing and equipment must be properly maintained and a program to oversee maintenance, with responsibilities identified, must be established.

> Structural protective clothing must be cleaned at least every six months as outlined in NFPA 1581, *Standard on Fire Department Infection Control Program.*

> When station/work uniforms are worn, they must comply with NFPA 1975, *Standard on Station/Work Uniforms for Fire Fighters.* Firefighters must avoid wearing any clothing that may injure them if they are exposed to high levels of heat. (Clothing made of fibers such as polyester or polypropylene may melt when exposed to heat, injuring firefighters more than they would have been injured by exposure to the heat without the polyester or polypropylene clothing. This applies to uniform items as well as underwear, socks, tee shirts, and any other clothing items.)

> The fire department must provide for the cleaning of protective clothing and station/work uniforms. Cleaning can be done by an outside agency or company or by the fire department at a central facility or with equipment provided in each fire station. If fire stations are equipped with washers, they must be used for washing protective and work clothing only.

(Washing will remove hazardous substances such as dirt, soot, products of combustion, and bloodborne pathogens from the clothing. The use of washing machines for protective and work clothing **only** will prevent cross contamination of such other items as bedding, towels, and firefighters' personal clothing. Cross contamination could lead to the exposure of other fire department members or it could lead to the exposure of a firefighter's family.)

Firefighters who engage in or are exposed to the hazards of structural firefighting must be provided with structural firefighting protective clothing. This clothing must include protective coats and trousers or a protective coverall which complies with NFPA 1971, *Standard on Protective Clothing for Structural Fire Fighting,* helmets which meet the requirements of NFPA 1972, *Standard on Helmets for Structural Fire Fighting,* gloves which meet the requirements of NFPA 1973, *Standard on Gloves for Structural Fire Fighting,* footwear that meets the requirements of NFPA 1974, *Standard on Protective Footwear for Structural Fire Fighting* and hoods that meet the requirements of NFPA 1971. If protective coats and trousers are used rather than a protective coverall, a two-inch overlap between the two must be present. If protective coats are provided with extended wristlets which cover the hand, gloves may be provided which do not have extended wristlets. (Coats with extended wristlets have proved to dramatically reduce the incidence of burns to the hands and wrists. It is very difficult to don gloves with knit extended wristlets when you are wearing a coat with an extended wristlet; this is why the allowance is given for gauntlet-type gloves.)

SCBA must be provided for and used by members working in areas where the atmosphere is hazardous, suspected of being hazardous, or may rapidly become hazardous.

Open-circuit SCBA must be positive pressure and must meet the requirements of NFPA 1981 *Standard on Open-Circuit Self-Contained Breathing Apparatus for Fire Fighters.* Closed-circuit SCBA must be National Institute for Occupational Safety and Health/Mine Safety and Health Administration (NIOSH/MSHA) certified with a minimum service life of 30 minutes and must be capable of operating only in the positive-pressure mode. Open-circuit SCBA exhaust exhaled air to the outside atmosphere. Closed-circuit SCBA retain exhaled air, remove some components such as carbon monoxide, add oxygen, and return the air to the user to be rebreathed.

Although not specifically protective clothing or equipment requirements, this chapter of NFPA 1500 also requires that members who are using SCBA must work in teams of two, and the atmosphere of confined spaces must be monitored or firefighters operating in a confined space must be provided with and use SCBA. Members are prohibited from removing the SCBA in a hazardous atmosphere such as in a rescue situation. (The thinking here is that firefighters will be safer working in teams, that many confined spaces contain hazardous atmospheres which could injure or kill a firefighter, and that a firefighter can serve a fire victim best by the expedient removal of the victim from the hazardous atmosphere and not by sharing his breathing air with the victim.)

The fire department must develop and implement a respiratory protection program which includes selection, use, inspection, maintenance, training, and air quality testing. Firefighters who use SCBA are required to be certified in its safe and proper use at least once a year.

Compressed air used in SCBAs must meet an American National Standards Institute/Compressed Gas Association (ANSI/CGA) specification. If the fire department makes its own air, the air must be tested at least every three months by an accredited laboratory. If the fire department purchases air from a vendor, the vendor must provide certification that the air has been tested by an accredited laboratory and that it meets the requirements of the ANSI/CGA specification. According to the ANSI/CGA G7.1 *Commodity Specification for Air,* air used by firefighters must be minimum Grade D. NFPA 1500 also requires a dew point level of –65° F or dryer (224 ppm v/v or less), and a maximum particulate level of 5 mg/m3 of air. The water vapor level (dew point) is particularly important in colder climates. Water may condense in the regulator when air with high levels of water vapor is used. This condensed water may freeze and lead to a malfunction of the regulator.

SCBA cylinders are required to be hydrostatically tested at intervals specified by the manufacturer of the cylinder or by governmental agencies. (Generally, steel air cylinders are required to be tested every five years and composite cylinders are required to be tested every three years. The best source of information on testing frequency is the SCBA or cylinder manufacturer.)

Qualitative facepiece fit testing is required for all new firefighters and on an annual basis for all firefighters. This fit testing also must be performed if a new type of SCBA or facepiece is used during the year. Firefighters must have a properly fitted facepiece to operate in a hazardous atmosphere. (Qualitative fit testing is often performed by having the firefighter don a facepiece fitted with a filter that restricts air flow into the facepiece. The firefighter can still breathe but the restriction provided by the filter creates a negative pressure in the facepiece as the firefighter breathes. The filter is also designed to remove the smell of the pungent substance being used to perform the test. The firefighter is placed into a tent or enclosed space where a pungent substance such as banana oil is introduced. If the firefighter cannot smell the pungent substance after it is introduced into the area, the fit is considered acceptable.)

Nothing is allowed to interfere with the face-to-face-piece seal. (This includes facial hair such as beards, temple straps from sport-type eye-

glasses, or anything else.) This requirement is effective in all situations, even if the firefighter can get a seal that passes qualitative fit testing with facial hair or other seal penetrations in place. Soft contact lenses and eyeglasses mounted inside of the facepiece are permitted for firefighters who need them to see. Hard contact lenses are not allowed.

Hoods are to be donned after the facepiece is in place. (Donning the facepiece over the hood makes it almost impossible to produce and maintain an effective seal. In addition, the SCBA facepiece straps will be provided with thermal protection from the hood for an added measure of safety.)

Firefighters who participate in firefighting activities that present high radiant heat exposure must be provided with protective clothing and equipment that is designed for those types of exposures. Aircraft Rescue Fire-Fighting (ARFF) and flammable liquids firefighting are examples of situations where high radiant heat levels are present. Protective coats, protective trousers, and protective coveralls must meet the requirements of NFPA 1976, *Standard on Protective Clothing for Proximity Fire Fighting (1992).* Other protective clothing items such as helmets, footwear, SCBA, and gloves, must meet the applicable NFPA standard as well as provide additional radiant reflective protection sufficient to protect the firefighter from radiant heat exposure. (Protective covers, most often with an aluminized outer layer, may be placed over helmets or SCBA to provide additional radiant heat protection.)

Firefighters or other fire department members who perform emergency medical activities must be provided with protective equipment that meets the requirements of NFPA 1999, *Standard on Protective Clothing for Emergency Medical Operations (1992).* (These clothing items range from gloves to overalls and are designed to protect the caregiver from exposure to diseases such as hepatitis and other biological hazards.)

Firefighters who engage in activities which may place them in contact with hazardous materials are required to have proper protective clothing. The type of clothing depends on the hazard presented by the chemical or chemicals, the form of the chemical or chemicals (solid, liquid, or gas) and the degree to which the firefighter will be exposed. Vapor-protective suits must meet the requirements of NFPA 1991, *Standard on Vapor-Protective Suits for Hazardous Chemical Emergencies,* liquid splash-protective suits must meet the requirements of NFPA 1992, *Standard on Liquid Splash Protective Suits for Hazardous Chemical Emergencies,* and support function protective garments must meet the requirements of NFPA 1993, *Standard on Support Function Protective Garments for Hazardous Chemical Operations.* The specific suit selected must be chosen based on the suit manufacturer's penetration information, the chemicals known or suspected to be present, and several reference publications.

SCBA use is required when called for by the chemical and suit type.

Outside sources of air are permitted if they provide positive pressure, and are NIOSH/MSHA certified.

These suits generally are not permitted for use for protection from atmospheres which are flammable, or from cryogenic, radiological, or biological agents. (Firefighters have been severely injured from fires that have occurred during hazardous materials operations. These suits are generally flammable although flash covers may provide some level of thermal protection.)

Chemical protective clothing is required to be inspected and maintained according to the technical data provided by the manufacturer. If decontamination cannot restore the chemical protective clothing to full use, it must be disposed of properly. (Because these suits are extremely expensive, chief officers may want to consider cost recovery from the owner or operator of the facility where the suit was used.)

Personal Alert Safety System (PASS) devices are required to be worn and used by firefighters involved in fire suppression and other hazardous duties. The PASS device itself must meet the requirements of NFPA 1982, *Standard on Personal Alert Safety Systems (PASS) for Fire Fighters.* The PASS device must be tested weekly and prior to each use. PASS devices are recommended for installation on the firefighter's protective clothing rather than on the SCBA. A firefighter death in the Midwest at a wildland fire might have been averted if the firefighter had worn a PASS device. The firefighter became separated from his crew, became incapacitated, and died before his disappearance was discovered.

It may be difficult to isolate a location for the PASS device that is suitable for use in all hazardous situations. For example, placing the PASS device on the structural protective clothing does not guarantee that it will be worn at wildland fires. (In the case of the Midwestern firefighter, placing the PASS device on the firefighter's structural fire protective coat probably would not have helped.) This is another validation of the need to work in teams and for firefighters to look out for one another.

Eye and face protection must be provided when stipulated. The helmet face shield provides limited protection for the eyes and face. When engaging in operations such as automobile extrication where particulates and other flying objects may come up under the face shield, goggles must be worn or the facepiece of an SCBA (with regulator in place for SCBAs equipped with face-piece-mounted regulators) may be used for eye and face protection.

Hearing protection must be provided for members riding or operating fire apparatus, operating tools and equipment, or in other situations where noise levels exceed 90 dB. The fire department is required to engage in a hearing conservation program in which harmful sources of noise are identified and controlled and audiometric testing of members is conducted. (Hearing conservation is not just a protective equipment issue. It is an

operational issue which deserves the attention of chief officers. Fire service job-related hearing loss has been a problem for years and has just
begun to receive the attention it deserves.)

All life safety rope, harnesses, and hardware used by firefighters for
supporting the weight of a human must meet the requirements of NFPA
1983, *Standard on Fire Service Life Safety Rope, Harness, and Hardware.*
Life safety rope used to support the weight of fire department members
or other persons during rescue may not be used for any other purpose. The
type of device used depends on the type of rope operation. Rope may be
reused if it is inspected before and after each use in accordance with the
manufacturer's instructions, and if the rope has not been damaged by heat,
abrasion, or chemical exposure, has not been subjected to an impact load,
and has not been exposed to anything known to deteriorate rope. (In the
past the standard required that all life safety rope be destroyed after one
use.) The required inspection must be performed by a qualified person, be
governed by a local procedure, and records must be kept.

THE PROTECTIVE CLOTHING STANDARDS

> *Existing protective clothing (that clothing already owned
> by the fire department) and equipment that met the applicable
> NFPA standard at the time it was manufactured may continue
> to be used. All new clothing must meet the current edition of
> the applicable standard.* (Protective clothing and equipment
> that are in use or in the possession of the fire department that met
> the edition of the appropriate NFPA standard when manufac-
> tured may continue to be used. All new clothing purchased by
> the fire department must meet the newest edition of the
> standard.)

As discussed earlier in this chapter, the original intent of firefighter protective clothing was to keep the firefighter dry and to provide some limited
form of protection from falling debris. At the time rubberized coats, pull-up
boots, and leather helmets were the fashion and provided reasonable protection
for firefighters engaged in the fire fight from the exterior of a building.

As members of the fire service we honor our traditions. Sometimes this
honor is at the expense of firefighter safety. There are still fire departments
today whose members fight interior structural fires dressed in rubberized
coats, pull-up boots, and leather helmets, none of which meet NFPA standards.
A more prudent approach to firefighter safety is to combine the best of new
technology and tradition by providing firefighters with equipment that meets

NFPA standards and allows them to perform their duties while benefiting from the extra margin of protection provided by their protective clothing.

NFPA 1500 requires that firefighters engaged in structural firefighting be provided with and wear a protective ensemble which consists of a protective coat, protective trousers (or a protective coverall), protective hood, helmet, SCBA, gloves, and footwear. The standard requires that the equipment be provided and that the firefighter use the equipment. The responsibility for firefighter safety rests with both the fire department and with each individual member.

Protective coats, protective trousers, and protective coveralls have a lot in common. The purpose of each garment is to provide the firefighter with protection from the environmental hazards encountered while fighting a structural fire. These hazards include hot liquids, steam, embers, convective, conductive and radiant heat, and other hazards. The clothing protects the firefighter from heat by providing an outer shell that is highly resistant to ignition from flame contact or radiant heat and by providing insulation through the use of multiple layers of nonflammable insulation material and air between the outer shell and the firefighter's skin.

 All structural protective clothing consists of an outer shell, a vapor barrier (previously referred to as a moisture barrier), and a thermal liner. The outer shell is designed to provide resistance to abrasion and resistance to ignition from high levels of heat or exposure to flame. The vapor barrier provides the firefighter with protection from hot water and other liquids and helps to keep the firefighter dry. Some vapor barriers allow sweat to be transmitted from the firefighter to the outside of the clothing while still shedding water. The thermal liner consists of fire-resistant material which is designed to insulate the firefighter from exposure to the heat of the fire. Many fire departments add extra layers of protective fabric to areas that may be compressed during firefighting, e.g., knees and shoulders. Compression (such as from kneeling and SCBA straps) may reduce the protective qualities of protective clothing since air is squeezed from between the layers. Air is one of the best insulators known and when it is squeezed out, heat can pass through more freely.

Many configurations of protective coats, trousers, and coveralls are available. Some use short coats and high pants; others use pants with near normal fit and coats which overlap to provide additional coverage. A minimum overlap between the coat and the trousers must be two inches. This coverage must be an overlap of all layers, not just the outer shell. One-piece protective coveralls are available which provide no gap between the coat and trouser. All of these configurations are aimed at providing the firefighter with the lightest weight, most effective garment possible. While the standard provides a minimum level of thermal protection, in general, the lighter the weight of the garment, the less physical stress will be placed on the firefighter.

Protective clothing for structural firefighting (NFPA 1971)

The primary NFPA standard for firefighter protective clothing is NFPA 1971. As this handbook went to press, NFPA 1971's most current edition is the 1991 version.

Like all of the NFPA protective clothing standards, NFPA 1971 is a performance document, not a technical specification. Fire departments should base their protective clothing purchasing specifications on the NFPA standard and add information on items such as garment design that best suit local conditions.

NFPA 1971 requires that structural firefighting protective coats, trousers, and coveralls be constructed of at least three layers. The outer shell is highly resistive to flame and heat, the vapor barrier provides protection from hot water and other fluids, and the thermal barrier provides additional insulation and protection from heat. The standard provides thermal protection for firefighters who wear the clothing by requiring a minimum Thermal Protective Performance (TPP). This value is derived by exposing a composite of the outer shell, the vapor barrier, and the thermal liner to a test that is outlined in NFPA 1971. The test and TPP values in general are explained in more detail later in this chapter. The standard does not specify what materials are to be used in each layer; it only requires that the three layers be present and that they provide the stated minimum level of protection.

The standard provides that materials used to make up the composite have some minimum flame resistance, regardless of their location in the garment. A test is used which exposes a preconditioned sample of every material to flame. The flame is held in place for a specified period of time. The char length is measured after the flame is removed and the amount of time is measured from the point of flame removal until the material has stopped burning or glowing. This time is called afterflame and it is measured in seconds. The procedure for conducting the test and the apparatus used to perform the test are specified in NFPA 1971.

The following is an outline of the requirements of the 1991 edition of NFPA 1971.

NFPA 1971 is not intended to specify protective clothing for any operation other than structural firefighting. The standard does not specify requirements for proximity or approach firefighting, or protection from other hazards such as chemical, radiological, or biological agents. Any jurisdiction may, at its option, exceed the requirements of the standard.

Protective garments and their interface components, such as protective hoods, are required to be certified as being in compliance with the standard by an approved certification organization. Labeling that indicates the certification is required. In addition, requirements for a certification program are outlined.

Additional labeling is required which provides use, maintenance, and cleaning advice to the user as well as providing identification of the materials used and information on the manufacturer.

Garments are required to be made up of a composite of an outer shell, a vapor barrier, and a thermal barrier. The composite may be a single layer or multiple layers.

For fire departments that use station/work uniforms, the standard allows the protection afforded by these uniforms to be considered as a part of the thermal barrier. In other words, fire departments that use fire-resistive uniforms may use protective coats, trousers, or coveralls that provide somewhat lower levels of protection since additional protection for the firefighter is provided by the uniform.

Requirements for the visibility of retroflective and fluorescent trim material also are specified. Three hundred twenty-five square inches of trim are required on the coat and 80 square inches are required on the trousers. Trim is required to be retroreflective (it reflects light so firefighters can be seen at night) and fluorescent (brightly colored for day and night visibility).

Requirements for closure of the garment are outlined. Hardware is not permitted to penetrate from the outer shell through to the firefighter's body. Heat could be conducted by hardware items such as rivets, zippers, and tacks. The standard does allow hardware to touch the firefighter's body if it is covered on its external surface. There can be no continuous path of hardware from the outer shell to the firefighter's skin. For example, a rivet that goes from the exterior of the garment to the firefighter's skin would not be allowed.

A minimum four-inch collar is required. The collar also must have an outer shell, moisture barrier, and a thermal barrier.

A minimum TPP of 35 is required. TPP is measured by exposing all layers of a protective garment to a standard test. The test uses radiant heat and direct flame contact to simulate a flashover. TPP roughly equates to time of protection from a flashover. TPP divided by two equals seconds of protection from second-degree burns. It should be stressed that the TPP test does not guarantee a firefighter any fixed amount of time that he would be protected from a burn. TPP is a lab test designed to be performed to a standard—fires are not standard. A firefighter exposed to flashover conditions should not stay in the flashover any longer than necessary!

Seam-breaking strength is specified.

The materials used for the outer shell, moisture barrier, thermal barrier, collar liners, trim, and winter liner (if used) must be individually tested for flame resistance. Average char length and afterflame characteristics are specified as well as a requirement that no material melts or drips when tested according to procedures defined in the standard.

Shrinkage resistance of materials used in the garment is specified and thermal resistance of all materials in the garment, not limited to the composite materials, is specified.

The tear resistance, char resistance, and water absorption properties of the outer shell and collar lining materials are specified. Additional requirements for moisture barriers, thermal barriers, winter liners, thread, trim, and hardware are also specified.

Performance requirements for protective hoods are specified. The protective hood must provide a TPP of at least 20.

Performance requirements for protective wristlets are specified. The protective wristlet must provide a TPP of at least 20.

Helmets for structural firefighting (NFPA 1972)

The firefighter's helmet is, perhaps, the piece of equipment most valued by firefighters. Helmets are used to protect the wearer from falling debris and water. The helmet provides limited face protection through the use of a face shield, and many fire departments use markings on the helmet or a special helmet front to identify the company assignment and fire department name of the wearer.

In the past helmets were made of a leather or aluminum shell with no internal parts to protect the wearer's head. Today's helmets may have shells made of leather, fiberglass, kevlar, or plastic, among other materials. Internal linings provide the wearer with additional protection from penetration and impact, a retention system (usually a chin strap) is provided, ear covers or earflaps are provided, a face shield is provided, and retroreflective markings to aid in visibility are attached.

There are many helmets that comply with NFPA 1972, *Standard on Helmets for Structural Fire Fighting*. The choice of which helmet to use is based on comfort, cost, fit, weight, support from the manufacturer, and appearance. A chief officer seeking to make a choice about which helmet to purchase should assess all available helmets, provided that they meet the NFPA standard, and choose the one that best suits his department. At this time the most current edition of this standard is the 1992 edition.

The following is an outline of the requirements of the 1992 edition of NFPA 1972.

Helmets are required to be certified as being in compliance with the standard by an approved certification organization. Labeling that indicates the certification is required. In addition, requirements for a certification program are outlined.

Additional labeling on the helmet or on a card provided with each helmet is required. The labeling must provide use and maintenance advice to the user and identify the manufacturer.

The helmet is required to consist of a shell, an energy-absorbing system, a retention system, retroreflective markings, ear covers, and a face shield.

The field of vision allowed by the helmet when worn is specified. Four square inches of retroreflective material are required to be visible when the helmet is viewed from any angle.

"4 square"

The protection provided by the helmet from impacts coming from all sides and the top is specified. The helmet's resistance to penetration, heat, and flame is specified, as is the electrical insulation provided. Performance of the retention system, ear covers, face shield, labels, and retroreflective markings is specified. Test methods to assess performance of each are specified in the standard.

Gloves for structural firefighting (NFPA 1973)

Protecting firefighters' hands from hazards on the fireground makes sense. Gloves that meet NFPA 1973 protect the wearer from cutting hazards, abrasion, heat, and materials that can melt or drop when exposed to heat. There are many different types of gloves on the market. Gloves that do not comply with NFPA 1973 can be found, often at a much lower cost than gloves that do meet the standard. Chiefs are cautioned to avoid the temptation to save money in the short run. Hand injuries are among the most expensive injuries to rehabilitate. Even a minor hand injury can prevent a firefighter from performing his job for an extended period of time.

Firefighting gloves most often are made of leather outer shells with flame-resistant linings. Other materials used for the outer shell include pigskin, elk skin, and other animal skins. Some gloves incorporate fire-resistant materials such as kevlar into outer shells.

The two most difficult problems associated with firefighter gloves are fit and liner retention (the liners pull out when the hand is removed). Firefighters come in all sizes and the standard recognizes this by requiring gloves to be provided in five sizes, ranging from extra small to extra large. Each fire department should review the range of sizes offered by each manufacturer to determine if sizes are available which meet the needs of its members.

The second most common problem is that of the propensity of the linings of wet gloves to turn inside out as the firefighter removes his hand from the glove. Every firefighter has a story from sometime in his career when he removed his glove at a fire and was unable to put it back on because the liner had become tangled.

The standard requires that a glove be constructed in a manner that provides secure and complete thermal protection. Chief officers and others responsible for purchasing are encouraged to look at samples of gloves *in each size,* get the samples wet, and assure that the lining will stay in the glove when the wearer's hand is removed.

The most recent edition of NFPA 1973 is the 1993 edition. This standard is a good example of how a Tentative Interim Amendment (TIA) can modify the requirements of a standard. The published 1988 version of NFPA 1973 required that gloves resist water penetration. This requirement was removed from the standard by a TIA and then restored to the 1993 edition by the committee. The requirement for water penetration resistance is based on the idea that steam burns can be avoided if the firefighter's hands are kept dry. Water penetration resistance in a firefighter's glove is nonetheless very important and was reintroduced in the requirements of the 1993 edition of the standard. In addition, an important side benefit of water penetration resistance is the ability of the glove to protect the wearer from contact with body fluids such as blood. Firefighters' gloves worn by members as they perform such functions as removing fire victims or automobile extrication often result in contact with blood and body fluids.

The following is an outline of the requirements of the 1993 edition of NFAA 1973.

> The standard is intended to apply to gloves used for structural firefighting. Gloves for specialized functions such as wildland firefighting must be designed for such use.
>
> Gloves must be designed to provide secure thermal protection, minimal interference with the use of firefighting tools, wrist protection, and to avoid having irritating surfaces come into contact with the wearer's skin.
>
> The glove must extend at least one inch above the wearer's wrist crease and fit snugly to prevent the entry of embers and other debris. This minimal distance is specified to allow fire departments that use protective coats with extended wristlets to purchase gloves without extended wristlets. Fire departments that do not use protective coats with extended wristlets are encouraged to do so and to use gloves with extended wristlets in the meantime.
>
> Gloves must be available in sizes XS, S, M, L, and XL.
>
> Gloves must be labeled according to instructions in the standard. Labels include information on compliance with the standard, manufacturer name, country of manufacture, and other information. Serviceability information such as maintenance and cleaning instructions also must be provided with each pair of gloves.
>
> The standard specifies heat resistance, flame resistance, conductive heat resistance, cut resistance, puncture resistance, a dexterity test, and a

grip test. Testing methods are specified in the standard. The glove also must have a TPP of 35.

Protective footwear for structural firefighting (NFPA 1974)

Firefighter footwear is available in rubber, leather, and combination rubber/fabric materials. In the past, most firefighters' boots were made of rubber and a variety of rubber compounds. Many of us remember when these boots came in two sizes: "too small" and "too large." Better construction methods and sizing requirements in the standard have resulted in considerable improvements. More recently, boots have been manufactured in leather in the traditional configuration as well as in lace-up configurations. Leather boots may provide a better fit and better ankle support than rubber boots, but often are more expensive. The expense of leather boots may be offset to an extent by the longer service life they offer. There has not been enough experience with leather boots to make a definitive cost/benefit statement. The type of service for which boots are used may have a major impact on their service life. For example, brush firefighting most often is performed while standing, whereas structural firefighting tends to be performed while firefighters are crawling or kneeling. These two situations present two entirely different wear conditions for boots. Brush firefighting is harder on the soles than the toe cap while structural firefighting may be harder on the toe caps than the sole. Testing in your fire department will provide better information on wear in your situation.

The following is an outline of the requirements of the 1992 edition of NFPA 1974.

Footwear is required to be certified as being in compliance with the standard by an approved certification organization. Labeling that indicates the certification is required. In addition, requirements for a certification program are outlined.

Additional labeling within the footwear or on a card provided with the footwear is required. The labeling provides use and maintenance advice to the user and identifies the manufacturer.

The standard requires the footwear to consist of a sole with heel, upper with lining, and an insole with puncture resistance and a crush-resistant toe cap (often known as a steel toe).

The footwear must be at least eight inches in height and available in sizes 5 to 13 in men's and 5 to 10 in women's, including at least two widths for each size and half sizes.

Metal parts are prohibited from penetrating from the outside to the inside of the boot and no metal parts such as tacks may be used to attach the sole to the boot.

The standard requires tests for heat resistance, corrosion resistance of metal parts, puncture resistance, electrical resistance, toe compression resistance, cut resistance, abrasion resistance, conductive heat resistance, water penetration resistance, bend resistance, and label permanency. Test methods for each test are specified in the standard.

Station/work uniforms for firefighters (NFPA 1975)

NFPA 1975 is not a standard on uniform design. It specifies minimum properties for materials used to make firefighter station/work uniforms. The style and cut of the final uniform are not even discussed in the standard.

As chief officers evaluate the uniforms that have been worn by their members (before compliance with NFPA 1975), they may find that the noncompliant uniforms do not even meet the minimum flame-resistance requirements for children's sleepwear. If you look at the work normally performed by on-duty firefighters, e.g., fueling and maintaining power equipment, using shop equipment such as grinders and saws, and activities performed at fire scenes by members not wearing protective clothing, such as bringing tools to members working near a fire building, some form of fire-resistive clothing should be worn at all times. All of us can vividly recall the pictures of the firefighter in the northwestern United States descending the ladder with his uniform on fire. While protective clothing should have been used in that case, we are all aware of situations in which our members could benefit from the protection afforded by fire-resistive uniforms when protective clothing is not in use.

Uniforms should be provided that will not contribute to a firefighter injury or cause any reduction in the protection afforded by a firefighter's structural protective clothing. These uniforms are designed to be worn while performing normal station duties and to be worn under protective clothing when fighting fire. In the past, many fire departments chose uniforms made of untreated polyester because of the easy care and good appearance characteristics of that fabric. An unintended consequence of the use of untreated polyester was that the polyester material, when exposed to heat, could melt into a burn injuring firefighters more severely than they would have been if they had not worn anything under their protective clothing.

The purpose of NFPA 1975 is to provide the fire service with a means to specify a fabric for uniforms that *will not contribute to the severity of any injury* received by a firefighter.

Not all firefighters wear uniforms. Volunteer and paid-call firefighters, for example, respond in whatever clothing they are wearing when they are called to an emergency. Civilian clothing does not need to have the flame resistance that should be present in firefighter uniforms but is often exposed to the same hazards. Firefighters who respond to emergencies in other than uniforms that comply with NFPA 1975 should be strongly encouraged to choose clothing that does not contain fabrics that can melt and cause more severe injuries if exposed to heat. The use of natural fibers, such as cotton or clothing of high cotton content should be encouraged. Chief officers also might consider providing some sort of jumpsuit for members to don at night when they respond from home or to be donned on arrival at the station to provide an additional layer of protection. The downside to this additional layer is that it will add weight, increase heat retention, and possibly cause additional stress.

The following is an outline of the requirements of the 1994 edition of NFPA 1975.

Station/work uniforms are required to be certified as being in compliance with the standard by an approved certification organization. Labeling that indicates the certification is required. In addition, requirements for a certification program are outlined.

Additional labeling on or with the station/work uniform is required which provides use and maintenance advice to the user and identifies the manufacturer.

Fabrics, inner linings, and thread are required to be tested for flame resistance and heat resistance. The materials cannot melt or drip as a result of the testing. Labels must undergo testing to assure their readability. Testing methods are specified in the standard.

Protection for hazardous chemical emergencies (NFPA 1991, 1992, and 1993)

These three NFPA standards provide performance requirements for protective clothing for firefighters engaged in activities that bring them into contact with hazardous chemicals. NFPA 1991, *Standard on Vapor-Protective Suits for Hazardous Chemical Emergencies,* describes suits that offer protection from chemicals in gas and liquid forms; NFPA 1992, *Standard on Liquid Splash-Protective Suits for Hazardous Chemical Emergencies,* describes suits that provide protection from chemicals in liquid form; and NFPA 1993, *Standard on Support Function Protective Garments for Hazardous Chemical Operations,* addresses clothing that provides protection from chemicals for personnel who are outside the "hot" zone while they perform support functions during hazardous chemical emergencies. All three standards were first issued in 1990 and revised in 1994.

The requirements of these three standards are summarized below.

Each standard requires the compliance of the suit or garment to be certified by an independent certification agency. Labeling that indicates the certification is required. In addition, requirements for a certification program are outlined.

Additional labeling on the suit or garment is required. The labeling details the types of chemicals for which the suit or garment has been designed and certified for use. The standard requires that each suit or garment be capable of withstanding exposure to a specific list of chemicals, depending on the garment. Additional chemical resistance may be listed by the suit or garment manufacturer in the technical data package.

A technical data package must be provided by the manufacturer for each suit or garment. The data package must include information on the suit or garment components, including type and material, chemical penetration resistance documentation, suit or garment component documentation, and physical property documentation, depending on the suit or garment type.

Each standard also details design and performance requirements as well as methods to test or verify the performance requirements.

Protective clothing for emergency medical operations (NFPA 1999)

Emergency medical operations have become an important part of fire department services. It is imperative that firefighters be protected from hazards posed by contact with liquid-borne pathogens. Liquid-borne pathogens are defined as infectious bacteria or viruses carried in human, animal, or clinical body fluids, organs, or tissues. The most commonly known liquid-borne pathogens are hepatitis and HIV, the virus that causes AIDS.

There have been cases of caregivers infected after contact with a person who has an infectious disease. The caregiver can contract the disease if an open wound or cut, or any other mucous membrane such as the eyes or mouth come into contact with infected fluids. Extreme care should be taken to avoid contact with body fluids. Since firefighters cannot know if any particular patient is infected, they must be cautious in all cases of patient contact.

The first edition of NFPA 1999 was released in 1992. Its requirements are outlined below.

The standard covers requirements for emergency medical garments, gloves, and face protection devices.

Emergency medical protective clothing is required to be certified as being in compliance with the standard by an approved certification organization. Labeling that indicates the certification is required. In addition, requirements for a certification program are outlined.

Additional labeling on or with the emergency medical protective clothing is required which provides use and maintenance advice to the user and identifies the manufacturer.

Upon request of the user or the purchaser, the manufacturer of the emergency medical protective clothing must provide a documentation package. The package must contain information on the materials used to make the item, construction methods, flame-resistance characteristics, and penetration resistance to liquid-borne pathogens (both after abrasion and after flexing), among other information.

Each piece of emergency medical protective clothing must be watertight, and resist the penetration of a specific biological agent for one hour. Test methods are specified in the standard.

Emergency medical garments and gloves must be tested for tensile strength, and puncture resistance, among other specific tests, such as a dexterity test for the gloves. Test methods are specified in the standard.

Protective clothing for proximity firefighting (NFPA 1976)

Proximity firefighting presents firefighters with situations where high levels of radiant heat are present. These heat levels are present in bulk flammable liquid and flammable gas fires as well as in Aircraft Rescue Fire Fighting (ARFF) emergencies. In order to attack the fire effectively, firefighters often must approach the fire at a distance that exposes them and their protective clothing to levels of radiant heat that are beyond the protective capability of regular structural firefighting protective clothing.

NFPA 1976 is intended to provide equivalent levels of protection to protective coats, trousers, and coveralls that meet the requirements of NFPA 1971 with added protection from radiant heat exposure.

The following is an outline of the requirements of the 1992 edition of NFPA 1976.

Proximity protective clothing is required to be certified as being in compliance with the standard by an approved certification organization. Labeling that indicates the certification is required. In addition, requirements for a certification program are outlined.

Additional labeling on or with the proximity protective clothing is required which provides use and maintenance advice to the user and identifies the manufacturer.

Many of the requirements of this standard echo requirements of NFPA 1971.

Nonradiant-reflective trim, leather wear pads, or lettering are specifically prohibited by the standard. These items, if present, could limit the ability of the garment to reflect heat. In fact, these items could absorb heat and increase the chances of burning the firefighter.

The outer shell material must have a radiant reflective capability as specified in the standard.

PROTECTIVE CLOTHING AND EQUIPMENT FOR WILDLAND FIREFIGHTING (NFPA 1977)

NFPA 1977, *Standard on Protective Clothing and Equipment for Wildland Fire Fighting* (1993), was adopted by the membership of the NFPA and issued as a standard in 1993. The standard includes requirements for protective clothing, helmets, gloves, footwear, and fire shelters to protect firefighters from the hazards of wildland fire fighting.

The proposed requirements of the standard are summarized below.

Wildland protective clothing, helmets, gloves, footwear, and fire shelters are required to be certified as being in compliance with the standard by an approved certification organization. Labeling that indicates the certification is required. In addition, requirements for a certification program are outlined.

Requirements for wildland protective clothing include closure systems for pockets and fronts, detailed sizing requirements, labeling requirements, and performance requirements such as fabric radiant heat protection, flame resistance, thermal shrinkage, tear resistance, seam strength, and other requirements. Testing procedures for each performance requirement are specified.

Protective shelters are required to meet a U.S. Forest Service specification and labeling must be provided.

Wildland protective footwear requirements are similar to the requirements of NFPA 1974. Protective toe caps, however, are not required by NFPA 1977.

Wildland protective glove requirements are similar to the requirements of NFPA 1973.

Wildland protective helmet requirements include a weight limit, two design types, a requirement for a sweatband, and a requirement for a chin strap. Face and neck shrouds, winter liners, and lamp brackets are specifically permitted, as well as other accessories. Performance requirements for wildland helmets include electrical resistance, penetration resistance, impact resistance, heat resistance, and requirements for separation of the suspension system from the helmet on impact. The performance requirements are similar, but not exactly the same as the requirements of NFPA 1972. Testing procedures for each requirement are included in the standard.

OPEN-CIRCUIT SELF-CONTAINED BREATHING APPARATUS (SCBA) FOR FIREFIGHTERS (NFPA 1981)

Perhaps the single most important piece of protective equipment provided to firefighters is SCBA. Fire departments with enforced mandatory SCBA use regulations, combined with effective search and operational tactics, seldom experience another respiratory injury. The hazards of breathing any smoke are well known and SCBA units are designed to prevent this needless exposure.

Open circuit SCBAs used by the fire service are most often rated for a 30-minute or 60-minute service time. As anyone who has ever worn one can tell, the rating time almost never equals the actual service time experienced by a firefighter. Eleven to 17 minutes is the real-life average duration of use on a 30-minute cylinder. Programs such as smoke diver schools and general physical fitness development for firefighters can extend this time, but 30 minutes of working time is rarely, if ever, achieved under fireground operational conditions.

The requirements of the 1992 edition of NFPA 1981 are summarized below.

SCBAs are required to be certified as being in compliance with the standard by an approved certification organization. Labeling that indicates the certification is required. In addition, requirements for a certification program are outlined. Additional labeling on or with the SCBA is required which provides use and maintenance advice to the user and identifies the manufacturer.

NFPA 1981 requires that all new SCBA units maintain a positive pressure in the facepiece during a specified test routine which simulates breathing under various physiological loads. The purpose of this test is to assure that firefighters working at an incident cannot overcome the ability of the SCBA to provide air and draw contaminated air into the facepiece from the outside environment.

The standard also requires that the SCBA withstand and operate in hot and cold environments, resist damage caused by vibration, flame contact and heat exposure, resist corrosion, resist malfunction caused by exposure to particulates, that the lens resists abrasion, and that communications through the facepiece meet a minimum standard.

The most significant test performed on the SCBA is a full flame immersion of the SCBA mounted to a test mannequin for twenty seconds.

PERSONAL ALERT SAFETY SYSTEMS (PASS) FOR FIREFIGHTERS (NFPA 1982)

PASS devices were created in the late 1970s and early 1980s in response to a series of firefighter deaths that occurred in situations where other firefighters could have rescued the downed firefighter if they had known the person's location. California, through the California Occupational Safety and Health Administration (CALOSHA), led the nation in developing the first standard for PASS devices. Shortly thereafter, in 1983, the NFPA issued NFPA 1982. A new edition of the standard was approved and released in 1993.

PASS devices are designed to sound an alarm if the wearer becomes motionless for a specified period of time or if the wearer activates the alarm manually. The first PASS devices developed for the fire service were saddled with sensitivity problems, cases and electronics that failed to withstand firefighting exposure, and alarm sounds that resembled too closely the sound of a smoke detector and other fire alarm annunciators. Many of these problems have been eliminated in the new generation of PASS devices.

NFPA 1500 recommends that PASS devices be worn on protective clothing rather than attached to the SCBA harness so that the PASS device will be available for use in firefighting situations where the SCBA is not worn, such as wildland firefighting. Many fire departments, however, use PASS devices mounted to the SCBA harness. The thinking is that the SCBA will be worn in the vast majority of cases where the PASS device may be needed.

The requirements of the 1988 edition of NFPA 1982 are summarized below.

The PASS device must be tested by the manufacturer and certified to be in compliance with the standard. The PASS device must be labeled as compliant with the NFPA 1982 standard if testing proves it to be so. The manufacturer's use and maintenance instructions also must be provided with each unit.

The PASS actuation switch must be operable by a gloved hand. Two separate actions must be taken to change the PASS device from automatic mode to off in order to prevent accidental deactivation. A visual and audible indication must be present to indicate that the PASS is operational.

The PASS device must sound a prealert signal if its wearer remains motionless for 20 seconds, plus or minus 5 seconds. The alarm signal must be activated after the device has been motionless for 30 seconds plus or minus 5 seconds. The alarm may be pre-empted if the unit is moved while in pre-alert.

The alarm signal tone must conform to frequency specifications and must produce a sound level of 95 dB measured at a distance of 9.9 feet.

The signal must be capable of continuous operation for at least one hour. A low-battery signal is required.

The PASS device must be equipped with a retention system which allows it to be attached to the wearer. It cannot weigh more than 16 ounces, it must be intrinsically safe for use in hazardous atmospheres, it must have provisions for water drainage, and it must resist corrosion. Test methods to evaluate the PASS device's compliance with the standard are detailed in the standard.

FIRE SERVICE LIFE SAFETY ROPE, HARNESSES, AND HARDWARE (NFPA 1983)

NFPA 1983 was developed partially in response to the deaths of two firefighters during an attempted rope rescue when a rope parted under the weight of a firefighter who was picking up the weight of a trapped firefighter at a sixth floor window. Until the development of NFPA 1983, there were no standards for the design, performance, or testing of fire service rope, harnesses, or hardware.

The current edition of NFPA 1983 was issued in 1990. The requirements of the standard are summarized below.

Life safety equipment must conform to accepted standards to provide the widest margin of safety for the rescuer and the victim.   PHOTO COURTESY OF BOB PRESSLER

Life safety rope, harnesses, and hardware are required to be certified as being in compliance with the standard by an approved certification organization. Labeling that indicates the certification is required. In addition, requirements for a certification program are outlined.

The standard specifies the load capacity, classification, fiber source, and construction type for life safety rope. Labeling is required within the rope and on a tag attached to the rope. The information on the labels includes the manufacturer's name, lot number, and the name of the certification organization. The tag must contain warnings about the use of the rope and the rope's working characteristics.

The standard specifies strength characteristics for the rope, a method of classification, and test methods to assure the compliance of the rope.

Life safety harnesses are classified into three groups. The sizing, labeling, and performance requirements for harnesses are included in the standard. Hardware design, construction, labeling, and performance requirements also are detailed. Testing methods to assure compliance are presented.

SPECIFICATION AND PURCHASE OF PROTECTIVE CLOTHING ITEMS

One of the most technical and fast-changing areas of our service is that of protective clothing. The multitude of standards are largely unfamiliar to most fire service members. It is hoped that the summaries provided in this chapter will add to the understanding of these important standards. To add to the confusion, the technology of the fabrics, construction methods, and hardware that goes into this equipment is in a constant state of change.

While chief officers often are not directly responsible for the development of protective clothing specifications, they do have a responsibility to their firefighters and to those who ultimately pay for the equipment to make sure that proper levels of protection are provided. Chief officers also are responsible for making sure that funds used to purchase protective clothing and equipment are spent wisely. The following guide to the specification and purchase of protective equipment is offered.

A guide to the specification and purchase of protective clothing

WALK BEFORE YOU RUN.

Specifying and purchasing protective clothing and equipment is an extremely complicated process. Start out with an item of clothing that is easier to specify. Gloves and helmets are good first tries since the options associated with both of these items are limited and the number of manufacturers is relatively small. Don't try and replace your entire SCBA inventory the first time you sit down to write a spec.

GET SOME HELP, BUT NOT TOO MUCH.

Other members of your department will be interested in participating in the process; form a small team to help. Ask that a member of your department's occupational safety and health committee be appointed to help you. If your department has a member organization such as a labor union, ask one of the union officers to be involved. If you are a civilian or a uniformed member of the department assigned to staff, ask a member of your department who is more directly involved in service delivery to help. Get representation from all interested areas of your department but resist the temptation to form a large committee. Try and keep your working team to no more than six members. Different teams can work on different pieces of protective clothing and equipment; membership may vary.

TALK TO SOME DISTRIBUTORS.

All of the major manufacturers of protective clothing and equipment operate a dealer or distributor network. Look in the Yellow Pages under fire or safety equipment and see what you find. Each year the NFPA publishes the *Buyer's Guide—Fire Protection and Fire Service Reference Directory* through the *NFPA Journal*. The guide lists the manufacturers of all types of fire equipment and provides names, addresses, and phone numbers for each. *Fire Engineering* magazine also publishes a very useful buyer's guide edition each January. Write or call distributors and manufacturers, tell them you are in the process of writing a specification, and ask them to send you information on their products. Local distributors may be willing to visit your department, explain their products, and offer assistance in specification development. Advertisements in fire service publications, such as *Fire Engineering*, coupled with reader service return cards, can be excellent sources of information.

READ THE NFPA STANDARD.

Many of the misunderstandings of the requirements of any NFPA standard can be resolved by simply reading the document. Explanatory material for sections that have an asterisk (*) next to the paragraph number are contained in the back of the standard. NFPA standards are available from the NFPA. Most fire prevention divisions maintain copies of all NFPA standards. If you do not have copies, your county or state training organization may have a complete set. Other sources of NFPA documents are fire protection contractors, architects, consultants, county or city building departments, and other professional organizations.

TALK TO OTHER DEPARTMENTS.

Ask friends in other departments in your area about their experience. Ask them for copies of their specifications. There is no sense in reinventing the wheel. If a neighboring department has an established specification that incorporates all of the features that you want in your protective clothing, copy it. In cases where more than one department buys clothing and equipment using the same specification, cost savings may be realized by pooling your orders.

BEWARE OF PATENTS.

As might be expected, protective clothing and equipment manufacturers are in business to make money. In order to protect themselves and assure that the money they spend on research and development is recovered, they may patent their processes or features. If you decide that a feature is something you want, specify it. Be aware that other manufacturers may not be able to provide the feature and that they may choose not to bid on your specification. You may find as you do your research that there are features that you do not want to do without. There is nothing wrong with specifying a feature that can only be provided by one manufacturer as long as you are aware of what you are doing.

DON'T FLY BLIND.

Ask manufacturers and dealers to send you samples of their equipment or ask that they come to your department and demonstrate their clothing or equipment. For accounting reasons they may ask you to send a letter requesting the loan or may issue an invoice with the loan that allows you to return the item at no cost within a specified time period, such as 60 days. If you plan on using the borrowed clothing or equipment in a way that may soil or destroy it, let the person loaning it to you know that. In most cases you or your department are responsible for anything that happens to borrowed equipment when it is in your possession.

ATTEND SEMINARS AND SHOWS.

Each of the major fire service organizations holds meetings and shows around the country throughout the year. Many offer low-cost, one-day passes. Trade shows provide an excellent opportunity to view products, interact with the manufacturers, and get answers to your questions. All of the major fire service manufacturers attend these shows. They are very willing to speak with you and provide information about their product lines. These conferences also provide a tremendous opportunity to establish additional networking contacts with your peers. If a show is in your area or within driving distance, attending it is time well spent. If funding is available, your department also may be able to send you to a show.

JOIN LOCAL SAFETY GROUPS.

In many parts of the country, safety officers and others interested in firefighter safety meet on a regular basis to discuss safety issues. Many times these discussions include protective clothing and equipment. Since Southern Area Fire Equipment Research (SAFER) was founded in Southern California in 1976, three other sister organizations have been established. Northern Area and Central Area (NAFER and CAFER) exist in the California and a group called FIERO exists in the southeastern part of the country. These organizations are an excellent example of information sharing, networking support, and vendor/user interaction. Many manufacturers, suppliers, and vendors are members and active participants in these organizations. Even if you are not able to attend the meetings in person, all four groups publish newsletters that carry the details of items discussed in their meetings.

REPLACEMENT SCHEDULING.

Be cautious of replacing critical safety items such as SCBAs and PASS devices in a piecemeal fashion. In times of extreme stress, firefighters will fall back on their training. A department that operates with more than one SCBA model, and thus more than one mode of operation, may be placing firefighters at risk. In a time of extreme stress, such as when a firefighter is lost, will the firefighter have time or the presence of mind to remember that he is wearing SCBA model A or SCBA model B?

ASK FOR COMMENTS ON YOUR DRAFT SPECIFICATION.

Send copies of your draft specifications to different vendors or manufacturers and ask for their comments. Ask them to suggest improvements and estimate costs. It is a sales representative's job to sell his product. Many times suggestions from vendors for specification modifications may, if adopted, give one vendor an advantage over the other. Be aware of this possibility and evaluate suggestions thoroughly.

GO OUT TO BID.

If you are purchasing a medium to large quantity of clothing or equipment, it may be to your advantage to advertise for and accept bids for the order. In many jurisdictions, bidding for any purchase over a certain dollar amount is required. Small or single-item orders may not be worth the trouble and expense of a bid unless you are buying a stock item. In some cases, a local vendor may have exclusive distribution rights for a product. In cases like these, working directly with the vendor is encouraged.

SUMMARY

Protective clothing and equipment are the first line of protection for firefighters. Along with proper training and support from other firefighters, this vital clothing and equipment can allow the firefighter to perform his job safely and effectively.

14

Fire Station and Facility Design

PAUL de SILVA

C H A P T E R   H I G H L I G H T S

- Functions of a fire station.
- Basic concepts.
- Design concepts.
- Construction system and equipment selection.
- The construction process.

FUNCTIONS OF A FIRE STATION

IN ITS STANDARD 1201, the NFPA establishes the primary functions of a fire station as:

fire prevention and risk reduction;
fire suppression;
rescue and emergency medical services;
hazardous materials response; and
disaster planning.

Beyond these primary functions are other, less official, but still important functions:

- **Civic.** A fire station is a part of the basic commitment between a municipality and its citizens. It represents government at its best and, ideally, the structure should reflect that fact as an asset to the community. Additionally, fire stations often provide space for specific civic functions such as polling places for elections and temporary shelter in time of disaster.

- **Social.** Club facilities and meeting rooms for department members, other community groups, and the general public are an important part of most volunteer and some paid departments' responsibilities. In many of the 3,000 communities that support firefighting services, the fire station is the principal social hall.

While the critical functions of emergency response in fire and rescue situations shape the basic fire station, all of the functions noted above must be housed and provided for in a fire station's physical plant.

BASIC CONCEPTS

There are four basic considerations which should be kept in mind at all times during the fire facility design process:

Multipurpose. The facility must serve each of the functions listed herein and all of their associated requirements.

Multi-user. The facility will serve many different department members during its life; individual members and shifts have their own needs and abilities. It should not be tailormade to serve one particular group, at one particular point in time.

Response. The facility must function safely, consistently, and efficiently to enhance department mission and response. No other function should be permitted to interfere with this most basic responsibility.

Long life. The facility will represent a major investment of time and money. It should be planned to last 50 years or more. Its design must be flexible and allow for modifications over its lifetime.

DESIGN CONCEPTS

Site planning and selection

LOCATION

The first consideration is station location and response time is the most critical item in site selection. Generally a target for response distance should be set in accordance with practical department experience and accepted standards:

- Commercial areas: one mile.

- Residential areas: two miles.
- Low-density areas: three miles.

These standards must be adjusted for local traffic conditions, levels of fire hazard, and budget constraints. It may be helpful to prepare a map that relates the following factors:

- street layout;
- traffic density;
- response hazards: railroad grade crossings, drawbridges, narrow streets, low clearances, areas subject to flooding, overhead wires, etc.;
- special needs: schools, hospitals, nursing homes, chemical plants, places of public assembly;
- response history: alarm response record;
- anticipated changes: areas of future growth, planed street widenings or reroutings, major new construction, overall city plan; and
- volunteers' residences: members anticipated to respond for volunteer departments.

These items all can be put on one map or on several overlays. The potential sites then can be plotted and response times evaluated. Responses must be plotted along the street grid, of course, not a "straight-as-the-crow-flies" pattern.

SITE CHARACTERISTICS

After considering optimal location for response time, assess the fire station site in terms of the following criteria designed to enhance facility efficiency:

- **Topography.** The site should be generally level. Apparatus response up or down slopes of more than 1:20 (1 foot of rise for every 20 feet of run) adds difficulty and delay. Drainage of rainwater and potential icing conditions must be considered. Apparatus tilting on a steeply sloped ramp will require additional headroom as it enters or exits the building. The apparatus bays are best located slightly above the adjacent street levels. The site itself is best located on high ground to avoid flooding and so that most response travel will be in a downhill direction.
- **Traffic.** The site should be located on a secondary street of sufficient width to allow easy maneuverability of the apparatus. Main streets should be avoided because heavy traffic may block or delay responding apparatus. Avoid locations with unusual traffic patterns such as diagonal streets or five-way intersections which may confuse the public as the apparatus exits the site.

- **Environmental Hazards.** Areas subject to locally high winds or flooding should be avoided. Utilities such as main power company lines, gas, or water mains which might be damaged during a natural disaster should likewise be considered potential problems. Hazards of the political environment such as protected wetlands, forests, or historic districts will delay the construction process and hinder future expansion because of the need for approvals from outside agencies.
- **Soil Condition.** Compacted soils that have a bearing capacity of two tons per square foot or more are best suited for construction. Weaker soils can be used but require special foundation work that slows construction and increases costs. Rocky sites may require blasting. Those with a high water table require pumping to place foundations and may preclude a cellar. Soil-bearing capacity is determined by test borings and, if soil quality is questionable, it would be wise to have test borings analyzed before the property is acquired.
- **Size.** The site must be selected for present and future needs. The building size must be estimated and the following minimums added (See Figure 14-1):
  - **Street Aprons:** Fifteen feet *longer* than the longest anticipated apparatus. Check for planned street widenings.
  - **Apparatus Maneuvering Space:** Add 10 percent to the manufacturer's stated turning radius of the least maneuverable vehicle to assure ease of operation by all personnel.
  - **Parking.** Allow 350 sq. ft. per car and a minimum width of 65 feet for a double-sided aisle and 45 feet for a single-sided aisle.
  - **Landscaping:** Zoning ordinances may have specific requirements for planting buffers, which should be followed even if not mandatory. If no requirements exist it is good practice to plant a five-foot-wide buffer from any adjacent residential property. A well-designed site should anticipate that 10 percent of the property will be lawn and planting areas.

The above guidelines are definitely *minimums*. Add more space whenever possible. Future needs are very difficult to predict and somehow always grow rather than shrink.

Station planning

FUNCTION CONCEPTS

The fire department's organization should have an impact on the design of its stations. Look at the type of department and each station's assignment.

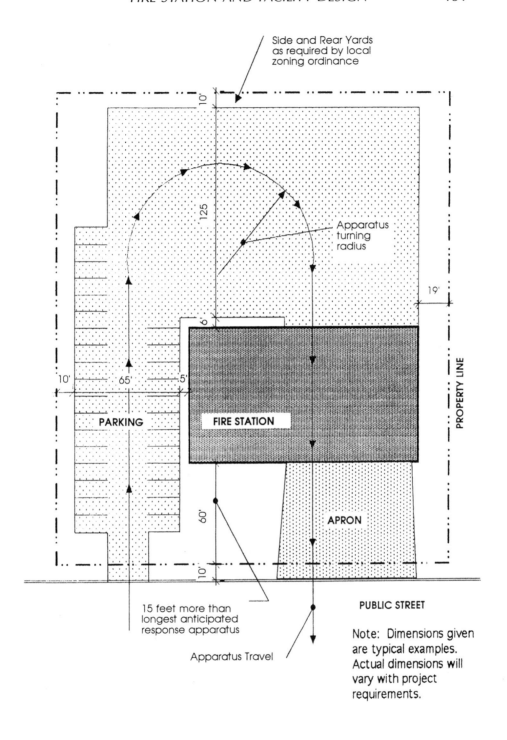

Side and Rear Yards
as required by local
zoning ordinance

Apparatus
turning
radius

PROPERTY LINE

PARKING

FIRE STATION

APRON

15 feet more than
longest anticipated
response apparatus

Apparatus Travel

PUBLIC STREET

Note: Dimensions given
are typical examples.
Actual dimensions will
vary with project
requirements.

Figure 14-1. Site Layout Concepts Typical Drive Through Layout

TYPE OF DEPARTMENT

- **Paid Departments.** Layouts for fire stations for paid departments tend to be based on the assumption that the firefighters will be responding from the dayroom, offices, or sleeping quarters to the apparatus. It would seem, therefore, that the offices and dayroom, where two-thirds of the day are spent, should be most accessible to the apparatus bays, with the sleeping quarters made the next most accessible. While access must be made as immediate as possible, care must be taken to isolate these spaces, particularly sleeping quarters, from the noise and fumes of the apparatus. Living in a fire station on call for days at a time is an intense experience and firefighters should be able to wind down after a fire in pleasant, relaxed surroundings wherever possible. The status of a paid department as a municipal agency serving the public should be reflected in its buildings.
- **Volunteer Departments.** On the other hand, a fire station for a volunteer department serves a community organization that requires a more cooperative, less formal, group atmosphere. More social functions are hosted there; in fact, the social activities of the fire department are a major attraction for volunteers. Money spent on amenities that increase the number of volunteers is money well spent. Sleeping quarters often are not required or may have limited use. While some personnel response will be from the recreation facilities, most routine response will, in fact, be from outside the building. Parking and access to the apparatus from outside must be designed to provide safe and effective response while maintaining building security.
- **Combination Departments.** Departments that have both paid and volunteer firefighters require a very flexible building. Obviously the need to provide each segment of the department with the facilities it needs must be balanced against minimizing the potential for conflict. The proportion of paid to volunteer members will vary as the department grows and changes. Suitable modifications of the fire station must be simple to accomplish.

FUNCTIONAL ASSIGNMENT

Different fire stations serve different organizational functions. While combinations and variations are common, these functions can be defined as headquarters, and staffed and unstaffed substations.

Headquarters is a large facility that houses the central offices, training, and dispatch facilities, as well as response apparatus. Apparatus maintenance may be located here, as well as the major meeting and social

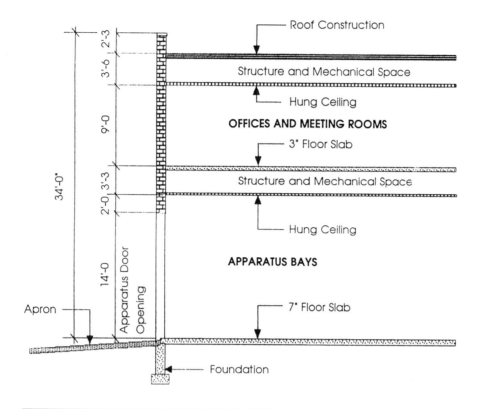

Figure 14-2. Vertical Layout of a 2 Story Fire Station

facilities of a volunteer department. These are complex, multi-use buildings.

A **staffed substation** may in fact be as large as a headquarters facility, but it does not serve the additional functions mentioned above and is more focused on response. Most stations of paid departments fall into this category. Volunteer stations where members are anticipated to be present for most of the day also qualify.

An **unstaffed substation** is as close to a "garage" as a fire station gets. It usually is a small volunteer facility with, at most, two double bays, minimal support facilities, and, possibly, a small dayroom.

BASIC LAYOUT CONCEPTS

The layout of the fire station plan, i.e., how the rooms and spaces are arranged, has a major impact on the efficiency and day-to-day livability of the building. There is no one right way; each layout is, invariably, a compromise among different functional conflicts. But beware, there are many wrong ways to lay out a fire station and it takes only a few months of occupancy to reveal just how bad one can be.

The defining concept in a fire station is the relationship of the support areas to the apparatus bays. There are only five basic layouts (Figure 14-3):

- *Central.* In this layout, the support areas wrap around three sides of the apparatus bays. This yields the most compact and efficient plan because the maximum number of spaces can be in direct contact with the apparatus bays. It is very restrictive, however, in that it makes any future expansion of the apparatus area difficult and it precludes the use of drive-through bays. It works only for relatively small stations with few support spaces. It is probably the best layout for a tight site where expansion and drive-through facilities are not possible anyway.

- *Single-sided.* Here all support spaces are located to one side of the apparatus bays. This is the most flexible layout since it provides for ease of expansion in all directions and allows for all bays to be the drive-through type. It also is an economical layout because the support and bay areas each can be designed as independent systems, allowing more efficient use of building materials. For volunteer departments it also gives the easiest access to the apparatus from outside the building. It does not work for very large stations, however, since the response distances from one end of the building to the other become too large.

- *Double-sided.* In this layout the support spaces are placed in two groups, one on each side of the apparatus bays. Expansion of the apparatus bays is difficult but it does permit them to be drive-through. It is a good layout for larger one- and two-story stations where the single-sided layout will not work and there already are so many apparatus bays that expansion is unlikely.

- *L-Wrap.* This is a compromise between the single-sided and central layouts. Support spaces are located to one side and the rear of the apparatus bays. It permits expansion but not drive-through bays. It is a good layout in certain situations, but the support spaces at the rear of the apparatus bays often are awkward to build and to use.

- *Split.* This is the reverse of the double-sided layout. Here the support spaces are in the middle with apparatus bays on both sides. It has all the advantages of the single-sided scheme (it is, after all, two single-sided stations back to back) but will not work if the support area is too large. It is a good layout for a two-story station where most support spaces are on the second floor over the apparatus bays. There are operational problems to work out with two separate apparatus rooms but solutions are possible.

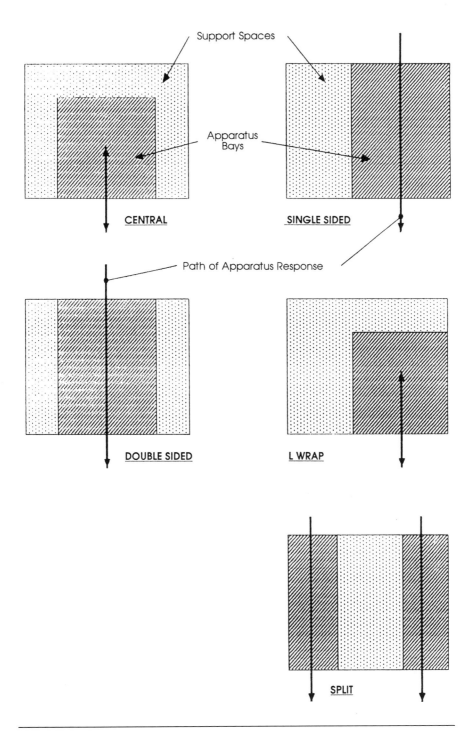

Figure 14-3. Basic Fire Station Layouts

APPEARANCE CONSIDERATIONS

The exterior appearance of the fire station should be considered in light of the following factors:

- its appropriateness to the importance of its mission;
- whether it enhances its surroundings, either by complementing them, or by establishing a new, higher standard, where appropriate;
- whether it is visually pleasing to the public it serves and the firefighters who occupy it; and
- whether it can accomplish all of these things throughout the changes in public taste that will occur during its lifetime.

Meeting all these criteria is not easy. The tools for the job are described below.

Style

Current architectural thinking has arrived at three broad categories of "style":

- **Traditional** is any style that evokes a former era, usually one that is fondly remembered. Colonial, Federal, and Pueblo are examples. While this style is usually the safest tack to take to obtain public approval, a contemporary fire station is not functionally a traditional building by any means. Oversized apparatus bays must be proportioned carefully to avoid looking grotesque. Excessive ornamentation increases building maintenance. Will a Colonial firehouse function 30 years from now when apparatus is transported on laser-powered Hovercraft™?
- **Modern** is a style that originated in the 1920s to define a new, sleek, efficient style for the machine age. "Form follows function" is the basic concept. Philosophically it is a very appropriate style for a fire station, a building for machines, but many people find it cold and unappealing. Many bad buildings have been called "modern" but well-designed modern buildings can be breathtaking.
- **Postmodern**, a style born in the 1980s, attempts to blend the efficiency and boldness of the best in modern architecture with the satisfying richness of detail found in more traditional styles. It is characterized by bold colors, unusual proportions, and reinterpretations of traditional forms. To some it is garish, to others, lyrical.

Massing

Within each style, the massing of the building—the way its shapes are arranged—strongly affects how the building is perceived. A fire station is shaped by its apparatus, which consist of relatively large vehicles. In architectural terms it lacks human scale. This can be compensated for by breaking the large volume into a number of smaller, more personal shapes. This is particularly important in a residential neighborhood where the objective is to fit in with an inviting appearance, not to introduce a threatening one. In a downtown urban or industrial setting of large buildings, however, the opposite might be true. The bulk of the building might be emphasized to establish its importance.

SPECIAL DESIGN CONSIDERATIONS

The special nature of a fire station and special local conditions, along with recent and ongoing changes in construction codes, require consideration in the early stages of the design process to avoid backtracking and corrective work.

- **Seismic and hurricane design.** Recent natural disasters in the U.S. have made people more cognizant of the need to consider the risk of earthquakes, hurricanes and tornadoes. As an emergency response facility, a fire station is expected to continue to function during these types of disasters. Many codes assign earthquake risk factors based on both location and functional importance. Therefore, there are many areas where a fire station would be designed to resist an earthquake, whereas a retail store might not be. Hurricane-resistant design also must be considered in areas subject to high wind velocities. Specially reinforced walls and structural connections are required in both cases and add significantly to the cost of construction.
- **Floodproofing.** The Federal Emergency Management Agency (FEMA) has designated certain areas as flood plains where special floodproofing requirements must be met. This can consist simply of raising the floor level above the anticipated flood level, where possible. If this is not possible, special (and expensive) floodproof construction must be undertaken.
- **Fume hazards.** The fumes from petroleum-fueled vehicles are hazardous in two ways. First, there is the health hazard to personnel from exhaust fumes. OSHA and other regulatory agencies are increasing the ventilation requirements for apparatus bays. Special exhaust systems have been designed, including those that connect directly to apparatus tailpipes with a quick disconnect coupling. Another type of system provides oversized exhaust fans which pull fumes directly from both the floor and ceiling levels. Second is the explosion hazard. The *National*

Electrical Code addresses explosion hazards in Article 511, which defines various levels of hazards and lists special building electrical system design requirements to reduce these hazards.

- **Energy conservation.** Energy-efficient building designs continue to develop as a result of both code requirement changes and new technology. Insulation requirements have grown stricter and requirements for energy-saving lighting are undergoing major changes. As a side effect, concern is growing regarding "sick building syndrome," a condition of poor ventilation caused by weather-tight buildings which can lead to outbreaks of disease among occupants. Active solar energy systems which collect solar energy for use in heating currently are considered economically infeasible. On the other hand, Passive Solar Design, where a building is oriented and shaded to best use available energy, is becoming more and more prevalent.

- **Handicapped accessibility.** With the implementation of the federal Americans with Disabilities Act (ADA), the question of handicapped accessibility is no longer a sometimes-enforced sideline of the building code, but is now a question of compliance with the law. The idea that there are no handicapped firefighters doesn't account for other fire department employees or the general public who may need access to the building. While there are some exceptions, all buildings, *new and existing,* must now be completely handicapped accessible unless it can be proved to be impractical for a very specific reason. It also must be remembered that handicapped accessibility does not mean simply wheelchair accessible; the seeing and hearing impaired, for instance, also must be considered.

- **Fuel storage.** In areas of the country where fuel storage is perceived as a hazard to the drinking water supply, new state and federal regulations that address fuel storage tanks for apparatus fuel or building heating system fuel have gone into effect. Double-walled tanks and piping, liners, test wells, dikes for aboveground tanks, and monitoring systems have all substantially increased the costs of fuel storage.

- **Fire safety and security.** As the leaders in the call for safer buildings, the fire service is expected to set an example. State-of-the-art fire detection, alarm, and fire sprinkler systems should be included in fire station construction whether required by code or not. Unstaffed stations in particular are at risk from arson and other malicious acts and should be protected by appropriate fire and intrusion alarm systems.

- **Technological advancements.** As mentioned above, construction technology changes continually. The most obvious area currently undergoing change is that of highly sophisticated electrical and mechanical systems, including computerized energy monitoring and controls; other areas, including the expanding use of plastics, also are changing rapidly. Judgments must be made as to the appropriateness of the new technologies. Are they safe? Will they stand up over time? Will we be able to maintain them with our current staff? Asbestos and lead were once considered wonder materials, but now are hazardous waste.

SPACE REQUIREMENTS

Overall station size can be estimated by adding up all the anticipated spaces with a factor for circulation (corridors, stairs, etc.) and construction (walls, partitions). The following guidelines can be used for most stations. If a facility has some unusual or special characteristics (unusual apparatus, climate, or manning, for instance) modifications must be made.

- **Number of floors.** It has always been a general axiom in construction that a two-story building is less expensive per sq. ft. than a one-story building, because it is more compact and requires less foundation work. In the case of a fire station, however, this equation is reversed: *two stories cost more than one story for the same usable floor area!* Why? The height of the apparatus bays makes a two-story station closer to three stories in height and a resulting larger volume of space is enclosed than is used, particularly over any first floor support spaces. Additionally, new laws, such as the ADA, require elevators in two-story buildings. This adds about $80,000 (1994 dollars) to the cost of the project with no gain in functional space. The problem of vertical response by firefighters also must be considered. Neither the traditional fire pole nor stairs are particularly safe when firefighters are rushing to respond. On the other hand, a two-story building *is* more compact and energy efficient than a one-story building. In many cases two-story buildings are required because of building size, site restrictions, or both, but one-story facilities are preferred wherever possible.

    A cellar is one way to gain less expensive space, depending, of course, on site and soil conditions. The elevator will still be a requirement. Many types of spaces simply are not practical when located in a cellar. One rule is to **avoid cellars below apparatus rooms.** This was a common practice in the 1920s and '30s, but the weight of modern apparatus makes the cost of constructing such a facility prohibitive. Most older buildings of this type have serious structural problems. While a floor can be designed to support current apparatus, no one can predict what future weight increases might be.

- **Apparatus bays.** Bays can be laid out as single-ended, where the apparatus must be backed in upon returning, or drive-through, where front and rear apparatus doors allow apparatus to be driven in a forward direction at all times. Drive-through bays have obvious safety advantages, but there is a trade-off in terms of additional building maintenance and reduced energy efficiency. The advantages generally outweigh the disadvantages, and drive-through bays are now the preferred layout. Of course, site clearances must be large enough to permit this.

Fire apparatus has grown in both size and weight over the years, a trend that can be expected to continue. Currently, a bay width of 15 feet appears ample. This is usually achieved with 12-foot-wide doors, with 3-foot piers between them. Bays as narrow as 12 feet are possible, but not recommended; they may not provide enough space to freely open side compartment doors. Bay length is usually 40 feet for a pumper or heavy rescue truck with a double bay of 80 feet to accommodate two engines or one aerial ladder. Chiefs' cars, brush trucks, ambulances, etc., require only one 25-foot bay length. A door height of 12 feet is common. The recent trend for aerial and heavy rescue apparatus to exceed 12 feet in height might make a 14-foot door more practical, however. The operating mechanism of the door usually requires 20 to 24 inches of clearance above the door, giving a 16-foot ceiling height if 14-foot doors are used.

In a two-story building, ceiling and floor construction will require 2 to 3 feet, resulting in a floor-to-floor height of 18 to 19 feet, and a total building height in the neighborhood of 35 feet.

Airport crash rescue apparatus generally are oversized, requiring 14-foot by 14-foot doors, with 2 feet between doors as a minimum. The United States Air Force (USAF) P-2, for instance, requires a 20-foot-high door. The turning radius on these vehicles is also much wider than normal.

- **Apparatus support.** Equipment associated with the apparatus bays can be housed between bays, in a widened end bay, in alcoves, or in separate rooms. These requirements for associated equipment include:

  Hose dryers: 5 ft. × 10 ft.
  Hose tower: 12 ft. × 12 ft.
  Hose storage: 5 ft. × (length of racks required)
  Hose washer: 5 ft. × 10 ft.
  Turnout gear: 3 ft. × 3 ft. per firefighter
  Gear wash sink: 9 ft. × 5 ft.
  Hazardous Materials shower: 4 ft. × 8 ft.
  SCBA fill: 50 to 150 sq. ft.

- **Dispatch.** The space required for dispatch varies greatly depending on operations. A simple radio and writing desk for an unstaffed station requires only a space 4 × 4 feet towards the front of the apparatus bays. At the other extreme, a 24-hour staffed dispatch center, including console, radio and computer equipment, toilet and kitchenette, would require an area of 16 × 30 feet or larger.

- **Apparatus maintenance.** The amount of maintenance performed on apparatus within a fire station can range from a few tasks to total maintenance. Active apparatus bays should not be used for anything other than very basic, routine maintenance chores since a lot of activity interferes with response. Full facilities will require a separate maintenance bay (15 ft. × 80 ft.) able to handle the largest apparatus. It should be equipped to lift the apparatus five feet off the ground. The alternative—maintenance pits—is hazardous and the pits are subject to stringent OSHA regulations. An overhead hoist for removing engines, tanks, and pumps also is required. This will result in a bay height of 25 feet for 12-foot-high apparatus. The shop support areas (tools, parts storage, office, records, washroom, showers, etc.) should be anticipated to be the size of another full bay (15 ft. × 80 ft.).
- **Training.** Classroom and conference room space should be planned at 16 sq. ft. per person, designed to accommodate 15 to 25 people (240 to 400 sq. ft.). Space for practical, hands-on training varies with the type of equipment used. Physical training (weights, universal gym, etc.) requires a minimum size of 12 × 16 feet; twice that amount would be more appropriate in a larger station.
- **Dayroom, Lounge, and Recreation.** Paid departments usually require a room about 12 × 20 feet; volunteer substations the same or less; and volunteer headquarters 25 × 30 feet or more.
- **Bunk rooms.** An open dormitory style requires 6 × 10 feet for each firefighter. Individual cubicles will take 8 × 11 feet (7-foot × 7-foot cubicles plus aisles). In stations where bunks are seldom used, folddown bunks can be installed in a space normally used as a classroom.
- **Offices.** Offices should have 100 sq. ft. per person. Offices can be individual or combined for more than one person. Headquarters requires substantially more offices than substations. Volunteer districts may require a commissioner's office which serves as a hearing room as well; this usually is 20 × 25 feet or larger.
- **Storage.** Response equipment and supplies, apparatus maintenance tools and parts, office supplies, training materials, building maintenance and custodial supplies, tables and chairs, and records and files all must be stored. Separate rooms for each function are recommended. If more than one company is housed in the station, each may require its own storeroom. A minimum size for each room would be 6 × 10 feet or 10 × 10 feet if possible. Department and district records and legal documents should be stored in a fireproof vault.
- **Large meeting rooms.** A volunteer headquarters building often requires meeting rooms for 200 to 400 people. These should be estimated at 15 sq. ft. per person (table seating). Rooms generally should be square or as close to square as possible.
- **Kitchens:** The food preparation area for a small station should be about

10 × 12 feet with a dining area of 20 sq. ft. per person. Large meeting rooms will require a full commercial kitchen as large as 16 × 32 feet. Each company in a multicompany station may require its own cabinets and refrigerator.

- **Toilet facilities.** The number of fixtures required is governed by building codes. The following dimensions are approximate:

  Water closets: 1 per 15 people (27 sq. ft. each)
  Urinals: substitute for water closets (15 sq. ft. each)
  Lavatories: 1 per 20 people (15 sq. ft. each)
  Showers: 1 per 10 people (20 sq. ft. each)
  Drinking Fountains: 1 per floor (6 sq. ft. each)
  Mop sinks: 1 per floor (16 sq. ft. each)
  Separate facilities for men and women must be provided. Handicapped accessible facilities require about 15 percent more circulation space.

- **Mechanical spaces.** Space for the machinery that operates the building must be provided. Often, the various systems can be combined in one space. Average requirements are:

  Boiler room: 9 × 12 feet for a small building, 10 × 20 feet for an average size building, 12 × 20 feet for a large building;
  Electric switch gear: 6 × 12 feet;
  Water service: 2 × 8 feet; and
  Emergency generator: 10 × 20 feet for a 75-kW generator.

- **Vertical movement:** A two-story fire station will require at least two stairs (8 × 20 feet each) and, to comply with handicapped accessibility requirements, an elevator (7 × 9 feet) and elevator machine room (6 × 8 feet).

ESTIMATING TOTAL AREA REQUIREMENTS

A program should be prepared which lists all of the required spaces and assigns them an estimated size in line with the information above. When these spaces have been totaled, you have the **net area** of the building. Adding a factor of 15 percent for walls, corridors, and miscellaneous spaces will give you the anticipated **gross area** of the building. This gross area should fall within the following ranges:

Unstaffed substation (2 double bays): 4,000 to 5,000 sq. ft.
Staffed substation (5 double bays): 9,000 to 10,000 sq. ft.
Headquarters (6 double bays): 25,000 to 35,000 sq. ft.

Design budgets

Once the anticipated gross area has been calculated, it then is possible to establish a project budget by multiplying the gross area by the anticipated cost per square foot, adding in nonconstruction costs, and allowing for a probable inflation factor.

- **Square foot costs.** The cost to construct any building varies based on the standard of quality you set. The standards for a permanent municipal structure such as a fire station must be set high if the functional requirements are to be met over the life of the facility. There are sophisticated and complex systems in almost every fire station today. Additionally, a fire station is taller than the average one-story building. Twice as much is actually built on each square foot of a 20-foot-high fire station as opposed to a 10-foot-high retail store, for instance. Therefore, the cost to build a fire station will be higher than the average cost of commercial construction in a given area. In 1994 dollars, a reasonable national average is $105 per square foot. This must be modified for each geographic region by multiplying by a local cost index which is expressed as a percentage of the national average. The range of these variations is shown in the following sampling:

Mobile, Alabama	85%
Anchorage, Alaska	125%
Los Angeles, California	113%
Orlando, Florida	84%
Wichita, Kansas	85%
Boston, Massachusetts	118%
Lincoln, Nebraska	81%
Reno, Nevada	102%
New York City, New York	131%
Toledo, Ohio	99%
Portland, Oregon	100%
Dallas, Texas	96%
Norfolk, Virginia	82%

In other words, a design budget should assume a cost of $89.25 per square foot in Mobile, Alabama ($105 × 85 percent) but $137.50 in New York City ($105 × 131 percent). A 10,000-square-foot fire station would then be budgeted at \$892,500 in Mobile (\$89.25 × 10,000), but \$1,375,000 in New York (\$137.5 × 10,000).

- **Inflation.** It must be assumed that it will take some time to get a complex construction project like a fire station underway. Four years is a reasonable timeframe to get from the first rough ideas to the actual start of construction. Currently (1994) the inflation factor for construction in most parts of the country is low. Historically, however, national construction costs have risen to two and a quarter times what they were in 1975, an average of just under five percent per year. Therefore a prudent design budget should include an inflation factor of about five percent annually. This means that our 10,000-square-foot fire station in Mobile should anticipate a cost when construction begins in 1998 of \$1,085,000 (\$892,500 × 1.05 × 4 years).
- **Nonconstruction costs.** The following additional items should be anticipated in the overall project budget:

    Financing: Interest on bonds or mortgage as well as fees from banks, brokers, etc.

    Legal fees: Attorneys' fees to draw up and/or review contracts, or resolve disputes with contractors.

    Architectural fees: Fees for architects, engineers, and special consultants when needed.

    Surveys and permits: Building department and other municipal agency review fees, utility hookup fees, test borings, topographic surveys.

    Insurance: Fire, theft, and liability insurance.

    Furnishings: Desks, tables, chairs, bunks, shelving, file cabinets, draperies.

    Equipment: Telephone and communication systems, SCBA fill system, tools, any response- or apparatus-related equipment.

    Moving and setup: Cost of relocating from present location.

- **Contingency.** A prudent budget allows for the unexpected by providing a contingency fund. This should start out at the early planning stages of the project at 15 percent and be reduced gradually as progress is made and the risk of unhappy surprises diminishes. A contingency of five percent should remain at the start of construction, as a minimum.

CONSTRUCTION SYSTEM AND EQUIPMENT SELECTION

Selection criteria

Concurrently with space planning, design, and layout, the systems used to construct the fire station and the special equipment to be housed must be selected. During the selection process keep in mind the following:

- **Durability:** Will the selected system serve satisfactorily for 50 years or more?
- **Maintainability:** Can the system be maintained by the staff available? Will it require little maintenance or constant attention?
- **Fire safety:** Is the system combustible? What is its contribution to the fire hazard of the building?
- **First cost:** Is the cost to buy and install the system appropriate to the overall budget? Will it use funds better spent elsewhere?
- **Life cycle cost:** What is the total cost of the system over the life of the building? Will a high first cost actually save money by reducing maintenance and replacement costs?

Pre-engineered buildings

Commonly referred to as prefab buildings, these are metal building systems which are designed and prepackaged by a manufacturer to provide a simple structure at a reduced cost and in a shorter construction time. Originally used for warehouse and factory buildings, they now are used for all types of one- or two-story buildings, including fire stations. It must be remembered that the structural system and enclosing walls represent a smaller-than-usual portion of the cost of a complex facility such as a fire station. The cost savings, therefore, on the total project may be less than anticipated. Maintenance costs over the life of these buildings are generally higher than for more traditional structures. Any changes made to lessen the utilitarian appearance of the basic structure will, of course, add to the cost as well. They do provide a way to build a minimal fire station when the budget or time constraints are tight. Conversely, in rural areas where contractors capable of building a complex structure may be rare or nonexistent, a pre-engineered building may in fact provide the best readily available structure.

Foundations

The foundations of a building are usually poured concrete or masonry. The most common and economical type is a spread footing system where 12-inch or thicker pads of concrete support piers and walls, spreading the concentrated weight of the building to the bearing soil below. Where soil conditions are poor, a number of expensive options are available, including:

- **Controlled fill.** The poor soil is removed completely and replaced by good fill compacted carefully to obtain the required bearing capacity. Spread footings are placed on top of the controlled fill. Care must be taken to assure that the bearing capacity of the soil below the entire apparatus bay floor is proper as well.
- **Grade beams.** Point supports are designed to carry the entire load of the building by going down below the level of poor soil until good bearing is reached. This can be done by constructing deep piers or by driving wood, steel, or concrete piles. Then the foundation walls are designed as beams spanning between these point supports.

Floor slabs

The first floor directly on grade is invariably a poured, reinforced concrete slab, usually five inches thick in the support areas and seven inches or more with double reinforcing in the apparatus bays. The apparatus floor must be pitched for drainage, usually to point drains or trench drains at the doors. In some jurisdictions the run-off from apparatus is considered hazardous waste since it potentially contains petrochemicals from the apparatus plus whatever may have been picked up at the fire scene. If it is collected into drains it would require a holding tank, which would have to be pumped out on a regular basis and disposed of at some cost. This issue can sometimes be sidestepped by pitching the floor out the doors and not collecting the run-off at all, but the feasibility of this system must be verified on the local level.

Structural system

The structural system will usually be either a frame system where a steel, concrete, or wood skeleton supports the building, or a bearing wall system where the walls of the building, usually masonry, support the roof and second floor framing. Often a combination of the two systems is used. The choice tends to be based on the sequence of construction, since a bearing wall system is economical only if all the walls can be run up before the framing is placed.

The larger the building, the more likely it is that a frame system should be used. Steel, poured concrete, precast concrete, or heavy wood timbers can be used for the frame. The choice is based on local economics and availability of materials. Different materials are preferred in different parts of the country.

Whenever possible, the frame should be designed to eliminate columns from the apparatus bays. They are a hazard both to apparatus and to personnel responding to the apparatus. Columns can be eliminated by increasing the size of the framing members; this increases the cost of the building but it is a worthwhile investment in terms of safety and future adaptability.

The supported floors and roofs can be precast concrete plank, poured concrete slabs on steel joists, metal decks, or plywood-on-wood joists. Again, local conditions will dictate which is most economical, but concrete floors and metal roof decks are most common. Light-plate-connected wood trusses represent a very economical way to build a pitched roof; however, concerns have been raised about collapse potential during fire conditions. To date all national codes recognize them as an acceptable system, and there is no conclusive evidence that they are any more unsafe than other systems.

Walls

Walls can be either bearing or non-bearing. Bearing walls usually are limited to masonry construction—brick, concrete block, or both. Nonbearing walls can be masonry, precast concrete, metal panels, or any number of proprietary systems.

Generally masonry, or precast concrete represent the most durable, cost-effective, low-maintenance wall systems, but they must be designed and constructed carefully for proper performance. Both brick and block are available in a large variety of colors and textures. Both can be set in decorative patterns. Precast concrete can be fabricated to almost any shape, texture, and color. Its cost effectiveness varies from region to region depending on transportation costs. Natural stone veneers are durable but expensive.

Metal panels can be inexpensive or very expensive depending on the design and material selected. The joints have a tendency to leak, however, and the less expensive systems deteriorate rapidly.

Exterior Finish and Insulation Systems (EFIS) represent one of the fastest growing new technologies in construction. They consist of a thin coating of synthetic acrylic or epoxy-modified stucco applied over fiberglass mesh and foam insulation board. The board can be applied to metal studs or a masonry back-up. EFIS offer ease of construction combined with good insulation and highly decorative surfaces at very little cost. They are not very durable, however, and are easily damaged. They should be avoided in areas subject to abuse or vandalism.

Roofs

Roofs can be flat or pitched. Flat roofs should not really be flat. They should be pitched for drainage about ⅛ to ½ inch per foot. Pitched roofs are generally pitched at slopes of 4 on 12 (4 inches of rise for each 12 inches of run) or steeper.

Flat roofs are economical in that they do not require excessive structure to create their shape. They have a bad reputation as being prone to leaks. The flat geometry, of course, does increase the possibility that water will remain on the roof and find a hole or imperfection to penetrate. If properly constructed, however, a flat roof will perform as well or better than a pitched roof. Built-up roofing consisting of multiple layers of felts with asphalt or coal tar binder is the traditional way to build a flat roof. During the 1970s and 1980s, however, problems began to develop with builtup roofs because of changes in the quality of the materials being furnished and the lack of skilled installers. Recently the industry has improved, but the performance record in many parts of the country is still not good.

Into this void stepped a new technology, the single-ply roof. This consists of one layer of a synthetic waterproof membrane installed over insulation and held in place by adhesives, mechanical fasteners, or stone ballast. EPDM is the most common type; others include modified bitumen and PVC. The performance record of these systems has been quite good when responsible manufacturers and installers were involved.

Pitched roofs can be covered with asphalt shingles, slate, tile, wood shakes, or metal systems. Asphalt shingles are the least expensive and are available in multiple textures and colors which can be expected to last 25 years or more. Slate and tile are more durable but more expensive and harder to maintain. Metal systems require careful design and construction; in fact, the less expensive types should be avoided. Wood shakes should not be used in areas of high humidity and their inherent combustibility makes their selection questionable for any fire station. Sometimes local appearance codes mandate their use, however.

Whenever possible the selected roofing system should have a UL class A fire rating and, where high winds are a concern, a UL class 90 wind uplift rating.

Windows

Windows are available in wood, steel, aluminum, or vinyl. They can be custom made or standard sizes. Vinyl is least expensive, followed by wood, aluminum, and steel in that order.

Vinyl windows are relatively new and their performance over time is unknown. Wood windows, particularly the vinyl or aluminum-clad types, perform very well. Wood provides a strong, lightweight, energy-efficient frame, while the cladding reduces maintenance. Originally available only in stock sizes for residences, their use has expanded and their performance has improved. Aluminum and steel windows in the HC or heavy commercial grades are sturdy products intended for hard usage. In the cheaper grades, however, they are poor performers. They require special thermal break construction to obtain the same energy efficiency inherent in wood.

The glazing selected in all climates except the mildest should be high-performance, low-E insulated units with an R factor of 2.5 or better. The slight increase in cost is easily justified in energy savings and comfort. In high-vandalism areas, polycarbonate, an impact-resistant plastic, should be considered. Where fire-rated glazing is required, wire glass is most commonly used, but it breaks easily and can cause injuries. New high-tech fire-rated glass, gel, and ceramic composites which outperform wire glass recently have become available but they are much more expensive.

Operationally, windows can be double or single hung, sliding, projected, casement, or fixed. All work well and the choice is usually based on the building style. Fixed windows are the cheapest, of course, but at least some of the windows in each room should be operational for ventilation. Sliders are the cheapest operating type. Double hungs are prone to operating problems in the larger sizes. Projected and casement provide the maximum opening for a given size.

Glass block has undergone a revival and is often substituted for fixed glass. It is available in many styles and is energy efficient. It requires a first-class mason for proper installation, however.

Doors

Exterior doors are usually steel "hollow metal," or aluminum and glass. Wood doors can be used but require additional maintenance. Proper weather stripping is important in cold climates. Hardware should be rust resistant, handicapped accessible, and suitable for heavy usage. Hollow metal doors should be galvanized.

Apparatus bay doors can be roll-up or sectional types. Roll-up doors are more expensive and generally slower. Sectional doors are most common. Wood doors are acceptable in milder climates and they are easily repaired if damaged. In colder climates, however, doors must be insulated and insulated wood doors often develop warping and delamination problems. Insulated and weather-stripped steel or aluminum doors are best for these situations.

These doors must be dependable. Install a first-quality door. Heavy-duty geared motor operators and high-cycle six-inch torsion springs should be used.

The tracks must be properly anchored and supported. If the assembly sways or racks, the door can fail or jam. There are special low headroom and restricted sideroom types available but the standard doors are faster and most reliable. Safety door edges, both electric and pneumatic, that stop the door if it comes down on a vehicle or person are available. Controls can be local and remote, including radio controlled from the apparatus.

Interior partitions

Masonry should be used in areas subject to rough usage such as the apparatus bays. Gypsum board on metal studs is common for other spaces. Partitions must be properly designed and constructed for their required fire ratings. Finishes should include a spray glaze or high-gloss paint in rough usage areas, ceramic tile in washrooms, semigloss paint or vinyl wall covering in other areas. Flat paint is usually not appropriate, except possibly in office areas. Wood paneling can be used but it must have the proper flame spread rating, particularly in areas of public assembly.

Ceilings

Costs can be cut by omitting hung ceilings wherever they are not required for a fire rating. Both appearance and acoustics will suffer, however. Acoustic ceilings come in a wide variety of styles, particularly the 2×2 lay-in type. The 2×4 lay-in is least expensive. Concealed spline types and gypsum board ceilings interfere with maintenance of electrical and mechanical systems. Care must be taken to obtain the proper installation in areas where a fire rating is required.

Floor finishes

Vinyl composition tile, carpet, wood, and ceramic tile all can be used as appropriate. In each material heavy-duty grades should be selected. High-gloss finishes can cause slipping and falling injuries and should be avoided.

Apparatus bay floors can be left as concrete with a sealer or paint, but this will not stand up over time. Terrazzo is a very durable but expensive option. Seamless floors, usually epoxy with a sand aggregate, provide a durable floor. Applied in multiple layers to a thickness of about one-eighth inch, they are wear resistant, easily cleaned, and slip resistant. They can be laid out with inlaid colored guidelines to aid drivers in aligning apparatus. If improperly installed, however, they may peel up.

HVAC systems

Heating, Ventilating, and Air Conditioning (HVAC) systems make up a sizable portion of the construction, operating, and maintenance budget of fire stations. They should be selected carefully.

The choice of heating fuel will be dictated by local economics. Electricity, fuel oil, natural gas, or propane all can be used. The availability of the fuel selected must be dependable. The fire hazards and potential leaks from storage of fuel oil or propane must be anticipated. Many codes now require the installation of costly containment and leak detection systems.

Heating can be a hydronic system consisting of a boiler with steam or hot water distribution, a direct-fired hot-air ducted system, or local direct-fired radiant heaters. Hydronic systems provide a high-quality, comfortable, controllable, efficient and even heat for each type of use within the building. They are expensive to design and install, however. Hot air systems are economical to install, especially when combined with the air conditioning ductwork, but they can be drafty and subject to wide variations in temperature. They usually will not serve the apparatus bays well and must be supplemented. Radiant heaters are well suited to high spaces such as the apparatus bays, but inappropriate for the rest of the building. In colder climates the apparatus bay system must be capable of heating up returning frozen apparatus as quickly as possible.

Ventilation of the apparatus bays requires removal of both exhaust fumes and combustible vapors as quickly as possible. This requires heavy-duty fans and adds to the requirements for the heating system when the heated air is sucked out of the building. Systems which have been used successfully include central fans with intakes at both floor and ceiling levels, and direct coupled systems which connect to the apparatus exhaust pipes through a quick-disconnect coupling. In maintenance bays a simple through-the-wall sleeve and tube system will suffice, although more sophisticated overhead piped systems are available.

Ventilation of commercial grade kitchens requires special hoods with grease filters, fire suppression systems, and make-up air systems where called for by energy conservation requirements.

Air conditioning by through-the-wall units is only practical in very small stations. Central systems generally are more efficient and easier to control. Environmental concerns over the use of freon currently are causing a change-over in the types of refrigerant available. Some disruption in supply should be anticipated. In areas of high electric rates, gas adsorption units which burn gas to create cooling are being reintroduced with some success.

Controls for HVAC systems are now quite sophisticated, particularly in areas where energy codes dictate high efficiencies. Care must be taken to avoid installing overly complex systems which department personnel do not understand and cannot maintain.

Response systems

Systems that directly serve to enable fire and rescue response sometimes are treated as equipment or furnishings and purchased separately from the building. Their operation is basic to the fire station's purpose, however, and they must be integrated into the building as it is built (Figure 14-4).

- **Booster fill.** A system is needed to fill the water tanks on the apparatus. Such a system usually consists of overhead lines in the apparatus bays. They can be simple hose drops at each apparatus position or mounted on centralized electrically powered reels. One and a half-inch hose with a trigger nozzle similar to a gasoline pump works well. If reels are used they must be specially equipped with hose guides and clutches to feed from a vertical position. A 40-foot hose mounted on a reel between two double bays can serve four apparatus positions.
- **Battery Chargers.** To ensure that apparatus will start immediately when needed, battery chargers often are installed. The chargers can be located in the apparatus room ceiling or a storage room with low-voltage distribution to the apparatus, or the chargers can be on the apparatus with the building providing a 110-volt current. Electric reel drops at each apparatus position are common. Care must be taken to locate the drops at the proper side of the apparatus. The drops must have automatic disconnect couplings or they must be flagged to warn the driver to disconnect before moving the apparatus.
- **Turnout gear.** Racks to hold firefighter turnout gear must be sturdy. They should provide a separate compartment or area for each firefighter's helmet, boots, turnout coat, and pants. They can be located on the apparatus bay floor or in a separate alcove. Gear must be washed off when personnel return from a fire. A large stainless-steel or cast terrazzo sink with separate spray hoses works well.
- **Hose.** Space must be provided for storage of replacement and extra hose. Storage is usually on sturdy three-tier racks that consist of a pipe frame, steel brackets, and wood hose supports. The racks must be adequately braced and supported. There are special hose-washing machines which usually can be stored out of the way and rolled into position for use.

    Not all types of hose require drying, but for the ones that do it is essential. Gas or electric hose-drying machines are available, convenient, and relatively inexpensive. A hose tower where hose is hung to dry is the more traditional method (Figure 14-5). The tower must be tall enough to hang hose doubled over a support bracket, usually about 30 feet above the floor. A hoist (powered or chain type) is needed to lift the hose, as is a spiral stair or enclosed ladder for access to the hoist and

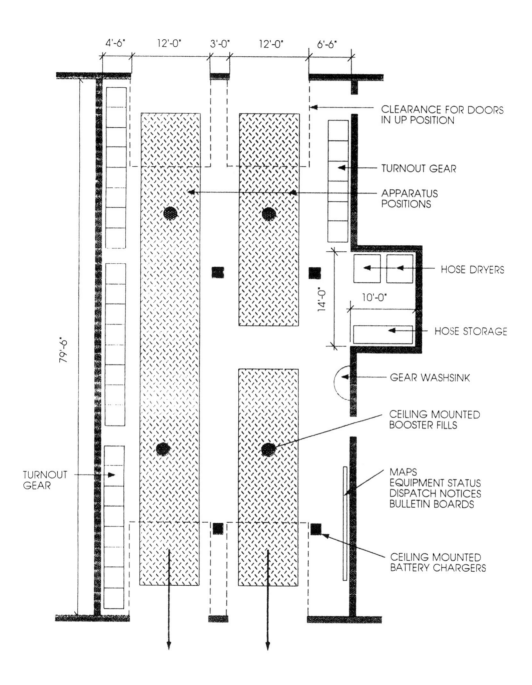

Figure 14-4. Apparatus Bay Layout

brackets. Proper guards and safety rails must be installed to protect personnel working at the top of the tower.

• **Sirens.** Both sirens and air horns have been used to summon volunteers to the fire station. In recent years, some communities have opposed them because of the noise and disturbance they cause. Systems such as pagers and radio alert can be more efficient than the traditional siren, without causing ill will. If sirens or horns must be used they should be mounted on sturdy bases accessible for maintenance. They should not be located near areas frequented by personnel since their noise levels can cause hearing loss.

• **Dispatch.** Dispatch includes receiving an alarm, notifying and directing responding firefighters, and logging and recording the event. Not all stations handle all of the dispatch functions since dispatch often is centralized at department headquarters or at municipal or county-wide central alarm bureaus.

A full dispatch center requires 24-hour staffing, so it must include space for a lavatory and a food preparation area (Figure 14-6). The dispatch console itself can be custom-built cabinetry or a purchased modular unit. It can contain radios, telephones, paging systems, apparatus door controls, security monitors, alarm systems, traffic controls, recording systems, computerized maps, and databases. Often this equipment becomes quite sophisticated and, in addition to the console itself, a separate equipment room is necessary. The amount of electrical wiring fed into a console requires special wireways and numerous conduits. The conduits must be sized to handle prewired connectors as well as the actual wire. Separate conduits must be provided for power and communication circuits to avoid interference. Spare conduits should be provided for future expansion or change.

• **Apparatus Maintenance.** Where apparatus maintenance is performed in a fire station, a separate dedicated maintenance shop should be provided (Figure 14-7). This facility can include any or all of the following:

- Vehicle lift: adjustable 2- or 3-post fixed lift or portable axle lifts with a vehicle capacity of more than 45,000 pounds.
- Overhead trolley hoist: motorized or manual five-ton capacity for engines, pumps, and tanks.
- Compressed air system: for pneumatic tools and lube system.
- Central lubrication system: to distribute oil, transmission fluid, etc., from central drums to each shop position by overhead reels.
- Special electric circuits: 60 amp or more for welding machines.
- Parts storage: 15 × 40 feet or larger
- Shop office
- Showers and locker room
- Paint spray booth and/or wash rack (these require their own dedicated bay).

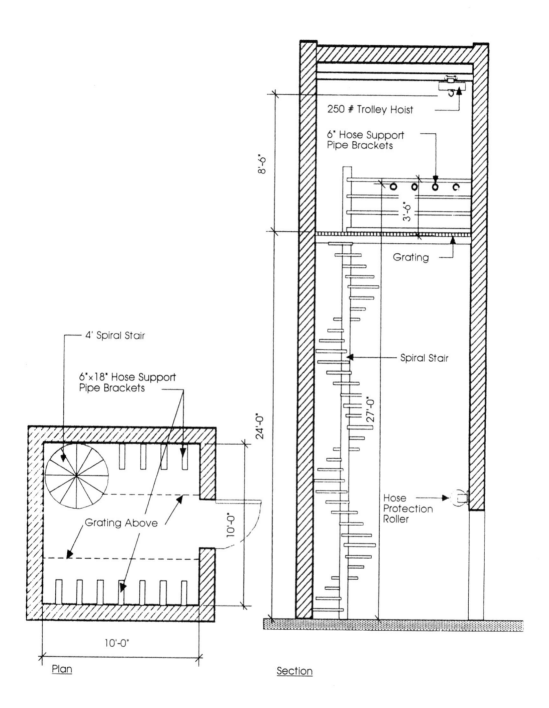

Figure 14-5. Hose Tower Layout

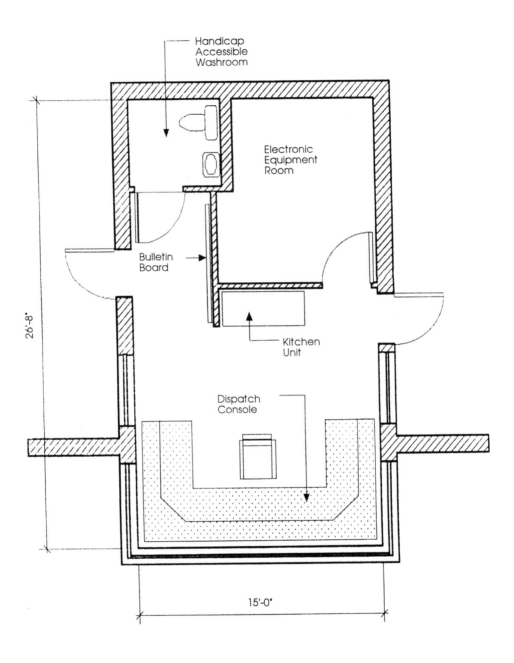

Figure 14-6. Typical Dispatch Area Layout

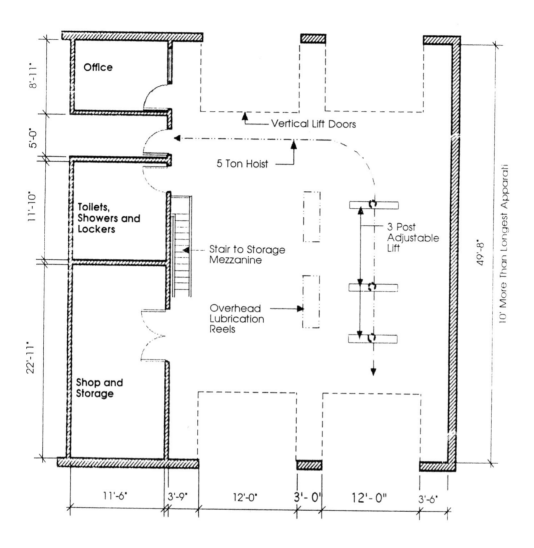

Note: Compressed Air and Heavy Duty Electric
Circuits Should be Provided.

Figure 14-7. *Apparatus Maintenance Area Layout*

- **Emergency Generator.** If a fire station is to function during a power outage an emergency source of power will be required for all except the most basic functions. Generators can be gasoline, diesel, natural gas, fuel oil, or propane fired. Special exhaust systems and silencers, along with sizable fresh air intake and exhaust louvers, are required. The generator will require a transfer switch to disconnect from the utility source and connect the generator on line. This can be manual or automatic. The generator must be tested or exercised on a daily or weekly basis to ensure that it will start when required. The generator must be sized to the electric load it will carry; it need not carry the entire building, only emergency functions. For most fire stations a generator of 75 kW will suffice.

THE CONSTRUCTION PROCESS

Project timetable

The entire project time, from first concept to occupancy, can be quite lengthy. It will vary with the complexity of the project, unexpected difficulties, and, most importantly, the priorities established by the participants. The order of events also can vary and events will probably overlap, but a typical sequence after site selection and a decision is made to proceed would be as follows:

Appointment of Building Committee	1 month
Selection of Architect	4 months
Preliminary Design	3 months
Commitment of Funding	3 months
Construction Documents	6 months
Building Department Review	3 months
Bidding	1 month
Award of Contracts	1 month
Contractor Mobilization	1 month
Construction	12 months
Move in and Occupancy	1 month
Contract Close-out	3 months
TOTAL TIME TABLE	39 MONTHS

Participants

The construction of a complex fire facility requires careful planning and a logical progression of steps. It requires a team of experts from both within and outside the department.

THE DEPARTMENT

As soon as the need for a new or renovated facility is seriously considered, responsibility for its study should be assigned to a building committee. A good size is three to five members. This will be a long-term project that will require the committee's focused attention. The members should be selected for their ability to get things done, their level of fire service expertise, knowledge of department operations, and diplomacy.

While these members will have primary responsibility, they should not assume total ownership of the project. Input should be taken throughout the process from all department members. For one thing, no one can know all the needs of the department. For another, the users of the facility must feel that they are participating or they may well resent an imposed facility. In a volunteer department, in particular, opposition from the firefighters will disrupt and probably doom the attempt to construct a fire station, no matter how necessary it is.

THE COMMUNITY

In a municipal department, of course, the elected officials will have the final say on funding the project. Beyond this, however, in any department community support must be encouraged if the community is to be served properly. Both during site selection and design of the building's exterior appearance, the community leaders, whether individuals or groups, should be consulted and decisions explained to them.

THE EXPERTS

You will require the services of an attorney familiar with construction law, a financial adviser to organize the funding, and an architect to design and oversee the construction. Most departments already have an attorney and a financial adviser for their other contracts and procurements. In most cases these individuals will be able to provide the necessary expertise. There are, however, specialists in both these fields who can be very helpful when needed.

Some departments also have an ongoing relationship with an architect. However, in many cases, an architect will be retained solely for this project. An architect is an individual licensed by the state to design structures that will safely and properly serve their occupants and conform to all codes and regulations. While all licensed architects can adequately discharge this duty, the architect selected to design a fire station should have two other qualifications. First, he should be familiar with municipal construction law. In most states the use of public funds is safeguarded by special rules and regulations to which private construction projects are not subject. Knowledge of these will save time and avoid mistakes which might require redoing the construction documents or halting construction entirely. Second, the architect should be familiar with fire department operations. There are many aspects of firefighting with which the lay person is unfamiliar, but that firefighters take for granted and would not even mention until something was amiss. At that point it would probably be too late to correct the problem except at great expense.

Architects provide a service—the design—not a product. The building itself is built by a team of contractors who undertake to construct it according to the architect's design. Finding an architect who can provide the service you need requires some research. It's helpful to contact the local American Institute of Architects (AIA) for a list of local architects suitable for your project; however, not all architects belong to the AIA, which is a voluntary trade association for architects. Look at other fire stations, both for ideas you like and to locate architects whose work appeals to you. Ask other departments in your area for recommendations. Try to come up with a list of three to four architects and interview them all. During the interview look for appropriate experience and for the firm with which you feel the department can best work. Make sure that all firms are talking about the same level of service. Architectural services can run from a very basic set of building department plans through an extensive range of services that include:

- conducting program development;
- performing schematic design;
- producing cost estimates;
- participating in public meetings;
- preparing preliminary plans and specifications;
- selecting finishes and colors;
- obtaining agency approvals;
- obtaining contractors' bids;
- analyzing contractors' bids;
- writing construction contracts;
- holding weekly job inspections;
- holding monthly job meetings;
- reviewing contractors' shop drawings;
- approving subcontractors;
- reviewing contractors' requisitions for payment;
- reviewing contractors' progress schedule;
- resolving disputes;

- preparing punch lists of corrective work;
- preparing as-built drawings;
- obtaining project close-out documents; and
- performing final inspection.

All of these services will be required during the fire station construction. If the architect does not provide them, someone else must. Architects who have previous municipal construction experience will be familiar with this list; architects who have strictly commercial or residential experience may not.

After you have selected the firm you feel is best qualified, ask about the fee. It is a mistake to purchase any professional service (medical, legal, architectural, etc.) based solely on how much it costs. The costs in a professional practice are pretty constant and so are the fees. If the fee is lower, expect a lower level of service. Ask other departments what they paid. If the fee does seem excessive you can ask the next firm what its fee would be, but give your first choice the benefit of the doubt; if you like that firm best, it probably is best for you and will be well worth a slightly higher fee.

Architects are paid on a fixed fee, cost plus, or percentage basis.

Fixed fee presumably gives you a set price to plan on, but not necessarily. A fixed fee is based on a fixed scope of work. If your project changes in size or complexity along the way, your architect will have to charge you for those changes or reduce his services. Scope changes often become a source of disagreement and conflict, resulting in harsh feelings and a restricted and unsatisfactory building.

Cost plus is used in projects where time is important and money is no object; very few fire departments have that kind of budget. The architect is paid for all his costs (salaries, fees, etc.) plus a multiplier in the range of two and a half to three and a half times cost for overhead and profit.

Percentage of construction cost allows your architect to pursue the best design for your project since he knows he will be compensated adequately according to the complexity of the final project. There is the risk that the architect will build up the project to increase his fee, but in reality that means increased costs for him as well, not necessarily increased profits. Additionally, most fire department budgets just won't permit such increases. The project will go over budget and the architect will be forced to redesign or the project won't be built. The architect's increased costs will far outweigh any increased fee he might have anticipated.

Percentage fees for full services on a fire station project should range from 7 percent to 10 percent of the construction cost for a new building, or up to 12 percent for a renovation based on the size of the project. The smaller the project, the higher the percentage. A fixed fee should be roughly equivalent. Therefore, for a $1,000,000 fire station you should anticipate fees of $80,000 to $90,000. Payments are incremental, e.g., $3,000 to $5,000 for preliminary design, 75 percent of the fee at completion of plans and specifications, and monthly fees during construction until 100 percent of the fee is reached might be a typical arrangement.

CONTRACTORS

The actual construction of the facility will be undertaken by a business or group of businesses that undertake or contract to construct the facility in accordance with the plans prepared by the architect. The owners (fire district, fire company, or municipality) will enter into direct contracts with one or more principal or prime contractors (general construction, site, plumbing, HVAC, electrical) to construct the building. The prime contractors will in turn enter into separate contracts with subcontractors to furnish to the contractor certain special portions of the project. The subcontractors then may enter into further subcontracts or will in fact furnish the actual labor and materials used to build the building. This chain of responsibility is governed by contract, union agreements, and, where applicable, laws governing municipal procurements.

Obviously there is no direct relationship between the actual workers on the job and the actual user of the building, a situation that can be frustrating for an owner who wants to obtain a quality job but has no legal right to give direction to the workers. He must direct his comments to the prime contractor who must pass them down the line until, it is hoped, they reach the responsible party. The amount of subcontracting on a job can vary, but in our age of specialization it is becoming more prevalent.

It is important, therefore, that every effort is made to obtain first quality contractors who can, in turn, be depended on to hire quality subcontractors and to control them properly. Unfortunately, many "general contractors" today are little more than brokers who take no part in the construction, except to collect checks and make excuses for the poor quality of their low-priced subcontractors. On the other hand, the widely held opinion that all contractors are dishonest is just not true. Contracting to construct buildings is a business that carries a high financial risk. The contractor enters into an agreement to construct a building for a fixed price even though there is little control over what the costs will be over the term of construction. A reputable low bidder will in fact be working on a relatively low profit margin which can disappear with one or two mistakes or a change in the economy. The failure rate among contractors is quite high.

The usual procedure for hiring contractors is to offer the job out for interested and qualified contractors to bid on the contracts. This can be a closed bid where the owners select a small group of bidders (3 to 10) based on the quality of their previous work on similar projects. The alternative is an open bid where the job is publicly advertised and anyone can bid. The open bid in one form or another is usually required by the laws governing municipal construction. Under this system the owner usually has little choice but to select the lowest bid. Still, every effort should be made to check the qualifications of the lowest bidders and disqualify any that cannot demonstrate the proper experience, quality of work, or financial resources to undertake the project. Ask for references and check them by phone or by actually visiting the projects. Keep in mind, however, that even if a contractor performed adequately on a previous contract he may not use the same subcontractors on your project, so there are no guarantees.

Construction sequence

There are certain basic steps that all construction projects follow in one form or another. The "ins and outs" of each step are beyond the scope of this discussion, but this is one area where you must be able to rely on your experts—lawyers and architects—to guide you.

BIDDING

During the bidding process certain concepts must be understood and used to obtain the best possible contractors for the best possible price. First off, the bid documents must include all items required by the laws governing construction contracts in your state. Construction in the United States is usually done under some form of the standard contracts which have been drawn up by the American Institute of Architects or other national organizations. These contracts attempt to foresee all possible problems, assign specific areas of responsibility, and outline the resolution of any conflicts. In addition, when the owner is a government entity that derives its funds from tax dollars, most states impose additional requirements intended to ensure that tax money is spent properly.

To avoid bid rigging, some type of noncollusion certification may be required by law and the contract may be required to be divided into four or more prime contracts. To protect workers, a minimum wage rate, as established by the state, may be required to be paid. **Bid bonds** that ensure the bidder will honor his bid or forfeit a substantial sum of money protect against frivolous bids. Likewise, **performance bonds** ensure that if the successful bidder is unable to complete the project, another party, his bonding company, will complete it. Insurance requirements and protection against liens must be clearly spelled out.

Bidders are usually given about one month to prepare their bids and a specific time and place for actual submission of the bids. If, during this period, any questions arise it is usually the responsibility of the architect to answer the questions and furnish these answers to all bidders in the form of an addendum to the contract.

CONTRACT AWARD

When the bids are opened they must be checked to verify that all bidders submitted all required information. Incomplete or nonresponsive bids should be rejected. The bids are then usually reviewed by the architect, references are checked, and a recommendation is made to the owner as to which bid should be accepted. Contracts then are drawn up and signed by both the owner and the contractor.

CONSTRUCTION

It is typical for the contract to specify how soon the contractor must start work after signing as well as the time period allowed to complete the project. The contractor should be required to submit a project time schedule and a schedule of values (itemized values of individual portions of the project) to the architect for approval at this point. These allow all parties to track the actual progress of the job and payments made against the proposed schedule so that any problems can be anticipated and adjustments made. Payments are made to the contractor on the basis of a monthly requisition he submits which the architect reviews and certifies for payment, reduction or rejection. A portion of the payment due, the retainage, is usually withheld by contract to ensure that the contractor is never paid for more work than he has actually completed. This is often set by law or custom at somewhere between 5 and 10 percent.

The architect usually will inspect the project on a weekly or monthly basis to verify that the intent of the contract documents is being followed. In addition, on larger projects, the owner may retain a **clerk of the works** to record on a daily basis what occurs at the job site and to contact the architect when a problem arises.

The contractors will submit shop drawings and manufacturers' literature to the architect for review to verify that the materials they propose to use comply with the contract specifications. These must be revised and resubmitted if rejected by the architect.

During the course of construction it is very common for changes to the contract to occur. These can arise if the owner changes what is wanted, if there is an oversight in the contract documents or an unexpected field condition, or if a suggestion by one party or another seems to improve the project. These changes are handled by **change orders,** supplemental agreements as to a change in the scope of work and an associated change in contract price.

Job meetings often are scheduled on a monthly basis so that all parties can meet and iron out problems as they develop. The scheduling of each piece of a construction project can become quite complex and, invariably, conflicts arise. It is at the job meetings that the appropriate compromises must be worked out.

When serious problems arise the owners should make sure they understand what has happened and what their options are. Since substantial sums of money can be involved, strong disagreements will arise as to responsibility for the problem and the best solution. It would seem obvious that any problems should be corrected so that the work conforms to the intent of the contract documents. Often, however, this is extremely difficult and a total correction would cause unacceptable delays or disruptions. Compromises often are reached that satisfy no one, but get the building built.

As the project nears completion, the architect will prepare a **punch list.** This is a list of all the remaining work and work which has been performed improperly and must be corrected. Often these lists center on questions of workmanship, a subjective judgment of acceptable quality, and further disagreements arise. Completion of punch list work often drags out since the contractor considers himself finished and has already moved on to the next project. Patience and persistence on the part of the owner and architect are absolutely necessary at this point.

PROJECT CLOSE-OUT

At some point the architect will certify that the project is "substantially complete." This is a specific legal term that indicates that the building, while not 100 percent finished, is ready to be used for its intended purpose and the owners can begin to move in. Specific provisions of the contract kick in at substantial completion that pass responsibility for the building from the contractor to the owner. Items such as maintaining the building's heating system, paying utility bills, building security, watering the lawn, and general maintenance now become the responsibility of the owner. The contractors' guarantee period (usually one year) begins at this time.

There are requirements the contractors must meet at completion as well. The owners should be instructed in the operation and maintenance of all installed systems such as heating, air conditioning, elevators, etc. All equipment manuals, manufacturers' literature and guarantees should be turned over to the owners. Small quantities of maintenance materials, such as replacement floor tiles, matching paint, and filters, often are required to be turned over to the owners as well. A set of as-built construction documents (drawings and specifications that have been modified to indicate any changes made during construction) usually are required. These should be kept in a safe place for future reference.

There are legal close-out requirements as well. A release of liens, certifications from all subcontractors and material suppliers that have been paid, consent of the bonding company to final payment, and the contractors' own written guarantees are items usually required.

After moving in, any problems the owners discover should be brought to the attention of the contractor immediately so that they can be corrected as soon as possible. Conversely, a contractor who has performed properly deserves some recognition of his accomplishment. A letter of recommendation is appreciated.

SUMMARY

The completion of construction is not the end of the process, of course. Every fire station, just like the apparatus it houses, must be maintained if it is to function properly. Each system in a building has its own special needs. Small problems become big ones if not corrected promptly. Firefighter morale does not benefit from working in a facility that is dirty, leaks, and malfunctions.

The exterior walls and roof should be inspected on an annual basis for cracks, leaks, clogged drains, and peeling paint. Mechanical systems should be inspected at the start of each season. Filters should be replaced on a regular basis. Interior floors must be cleaned regularly or the abrasives in the dirt will destroy the finish. Lighting fixtures should have their lenses cleaned annually because the dirt that accumulates seriously lowers the light output. The manufacturers of every device and material have recommended maintenance procedures. Get this information from the contractor, keep in a central file, and follow it closely. A maintained facility will serve its department well for many years.

Such a facility is not a monument, but an active, efficient means of providing fire protection services. It must change and evolve in order to house an active, efficient, and always changing fire service.

APPENDIX I
DESIGN PORTFOLIO

The following is a collection of 11 fire stations that serve a wide range of departments and functions. They are intended as explanatory examples of the concepts presented in this chapter. They are presented in size order, from small substations to a large volunteer headquarters.

Design A: Ocean Beach, NY (3,000 sq. ft.)

This small wood frame volunteer facility serves a summer beach colony located on an island with limited access. The apparatus is limited to brush trucks and jeeps.

Design B: Coram, NY (3,900 sq. ft.)

This substation for a then semi-rural volunteer department provides minimum facilities. The structure is a simple flat roof masonry building broken visually into distinct functional masses.

Design C: Sayville, NY (5,100 sq. ft.)

A somewhat larger volunteer substation located in a residential area for a suburban department. Traditional styling was used and the building was arranged so that the apparatus areas are concealed at the rear of the building.

Design D: Oakhurst, NJ (5,500 sq. ft.)

A substation for a volunteer company. The difficult and restricted site generated a complex shape.

Design E: Glens Falls, NY (12,000 sq. ft.)

Located in northern New York, this station includes a separate bay for washing apparatus inside in cold weather. This is the headquarters for a private volunteer company. The building is located in a commercial district and is designed to complement the surrounding structures.

Design F: Hicksville, NY (14,000 sq. ft.)

This is a substation for a large, active suburban volunteer company. The building is located between residential and retail areas. The pitched roof houses a mechanical equipment mezzanine.

Design G: Harrisburg, PA (14,000 sq. ft.)

This substation for a paid department is located in an urban area. It was designed with excess apparatus capacity to house apparatus that could be displaced by flood conditions at other stations in low-lying areas of the city. The roof of the hose tower was designed to support a solar domestic hot water system.

Design H: Port Washington, NY (14,200 sq. ft.)

This is the headquarters for a private volunteer company in a suburban district. The site is very tight, located in a residential neighborhood. There is a partial cellar.

Design I: Spring Lake, NJ (14,500)

This is a combined fire and police facility. There is a complete security separation of the two functions within the building. The exterior was designed to complement the existing buildings within the municipal complex.

Design J: North Amityville, NY (23,000 sq. ft.)

This is an expansion of an older facility for a suburban volunteer company. The original building was converted to office functions and new apparatus areas and meeting hall were constructed. The station is located on a major roadway which was realigned so that it now angles past the front of the original building. This created the tapered shape of the addition.

Design K: Central Islip, NY (29,200 sq. ft.)

This is the headquarters for a large suburban volunteer district. Included are 10 apparatus bays, 2 maintenance bays, 24-hour manned dispatch, district offices, and complex meeting facilities for over 500 people. The exterior uses two different types of brick along with precast concrete trim.

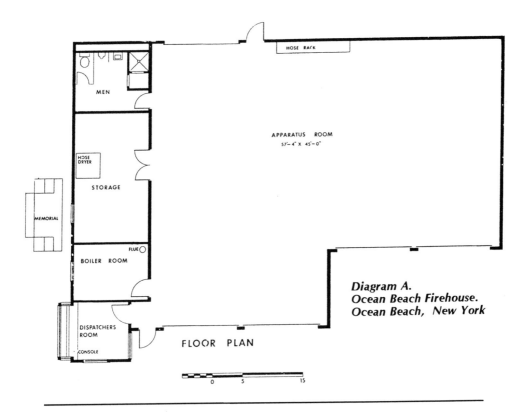

HOSE RACK

MEN

APPARATUS ROOM
57'-4" X 45'-0"

HOSE DRYER

STORAGE

MEMORIAL

FLUE

BOILER ROOM

DISPATCHERS ROOM

CONSOLE

**Diagram A.
Ocean Beach Firehouse.
Ocean Beach, New York**

FLOOR PLAN

0   5   15

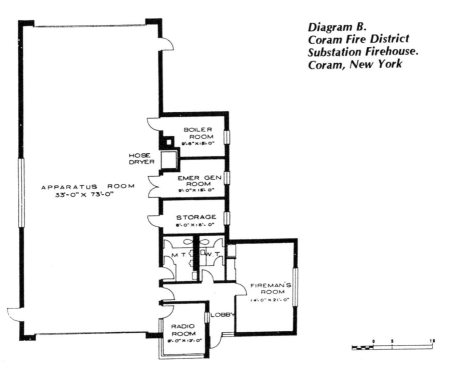

**Diagram B.
Coram Fire District
Substation Firehouse.
Coram, New York**

BOILER ROOM
9'-6" X 15'-0"

HOSE DRYER

APPARATUS ROOM
33'-0" X 73'-0"

EMER GEN ROOM
9'-0" X 15'-0"

STORAGE
8'-0" X 15'-0"

M T   W.T

FIREMAN'S ROOM
14'-0" X 21'-0"

LOBBY

RADIO ROOM
9'-0" X 12'-0"

0   5   15

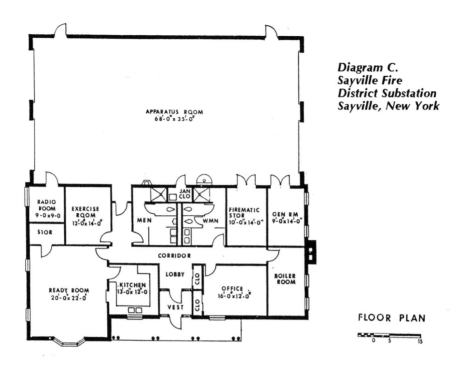

Diagram C.
Sayville Fire
District Substation
Sayville, New York

APPARATUS ROOM
68'-0" x 35'-0"

RADIO ROOM 9-0 x 9-0

STOR

EXERCISE ROOM 12'-0 x 14'-0"

MEN

JAN CLO

WMN

FIREMATIC STOR 10'-0" x 14'-0"

GEN RM 9'-0 x 14'-0"

CORRIDOR

READY ROOM 20'-0 x 22'-0"

KITCHEN 13'-0 x 12'-0

LOBBY

CLO

VEST

CLO

OFFICE 16'-0 x 12'-0"

BOILER ROOM

FLOOR PLAN

0   5   15

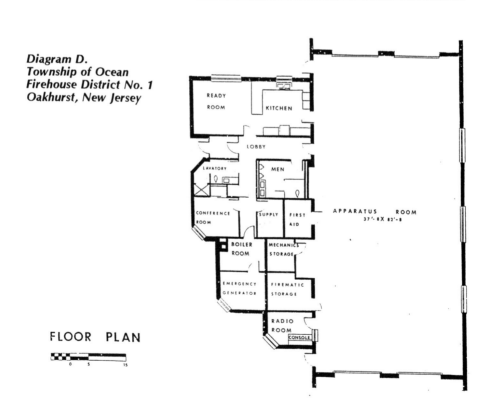

Diagram D.
Township of Ocean
Firehouse District No. 1
Oakhurst, New Jersey

READY ROOM

KITCHEN

LOBBY

LAVATORY

MEN

CONFERENCE ROOM

SUPPLY

FIRST AID

APPARATUS ROOM
37'-8 X 82'-8

BOILER ROOM

MECHANICS STORAGE

EMERGENCY GENERATOR

FIREMATIC STORAGE

RADIO ROOM

CONSOLE

FLOOR PLAN

0   5   15

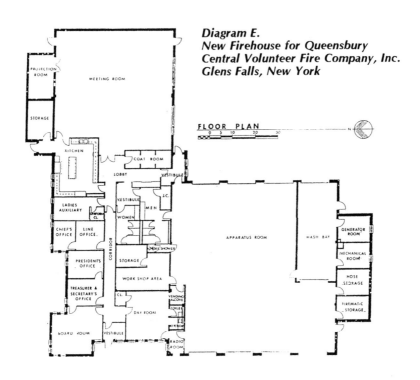

Diagram E.
New Firehouse for Queensbury
Central Volunteer Fire Company, Inc.
Glens Falls, New York

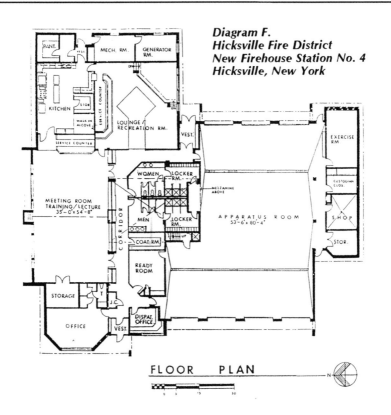

Diagram F.
Hicksville Fire District
New Firehouse Station No. 4
Hicksville, New York

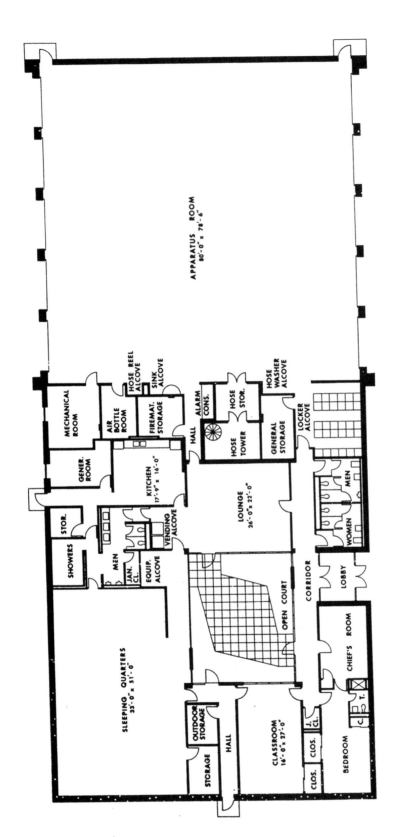

FLOOR PLAN

0 5 15

Diagram G.
Fire Stations No. 1 and No. 2
City of Harrisburg
Harrisburg, Pennsylvania

APPARATUS ROOM
80'-0" x 78'-6"

MECHANICAL ROOM

HOSE REEL ALCOVE

AIR BOTTLE ROOM

SINK ALCOVE

FIREMAT. STORAGE

HALL

ALARM CONS.

HOSE STOR.

HOSE WASHER ALCOVE

GENER. ROOM

KITCHEN
17'-9" x 16'-0"

HOSE TOWER

GENERAL STORAGE

LOCKER ALCOVE

STOR.

MEN

JAN. CL.

VENDING ALCOVE

EQUIP. ALCOVE

SHOWERS

LOUNGE
26'-0" x 22'-0"

MEN

WOMEN

SLEEPING QUARTERS
33'-0" x 51'-0"

OPEN COURT

CORRIDOR

LOBBY

OUTDOOR STORAGE

HALL

STORAGE

CLASSROOM
16'-0" x 27'-0"

CLOS.

CLOS.

J. CL.

CHIEF'S ROOM

BEDROOM

C.

T.

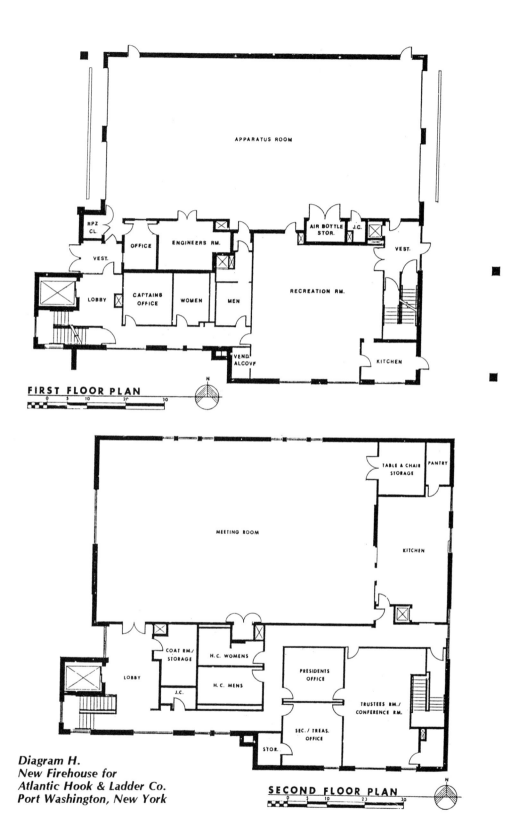

APPARATUS ROOM

RPZ CL.

OFFICE

ENGINEERS RM.

VEST.

AIR BOTTLE STOR.

J.C.

VEST.

LOBBY

CAPTAINS OFFICE

WOMEN

MEN

RECREATION RM.

VEND ALCOVE

KITCHEN

FIRST FLOOR PLAN

0 5 10 20 30

N

TABLE & CHAIR STORAGE

PANTRY

MEETING ROOM

KITCHEN

LOBBY

COAT RM./ STORAGE

H.C. WOMENS

J.C.

H.C. MENS

PRESIDENTS OFFICE

TRUSTEES RM./ CONFERENCE RM.

SEC./ TREAS. OFFICE

STOR.

Diagram H.
New Firehouse for
Atlantic Hook & Ladder Co.
Port Washington, New York

SECOND FLOOR PLAN

0 5 10 20 30

N

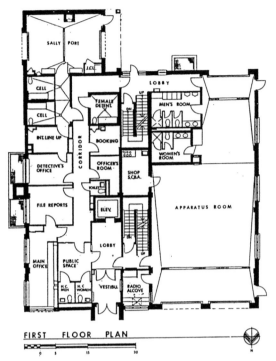

FIRST FLOOR PLAN

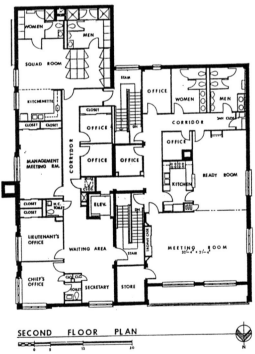

SECOND FLOOR PLAN

Diagram I.
Combined Fire/Police Facility
Borough of Spring Lake, New Jersey

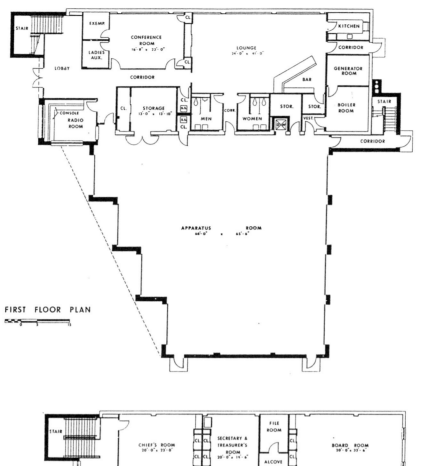

FIRST FLOOR PLAN

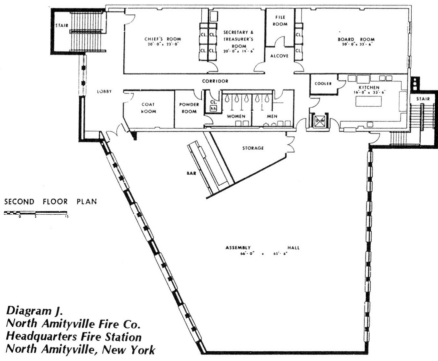

SECOND FLOOR PLAN

Diagram J.
North Amityville Fire Co.
Headquarters Fire Station
North Amityville, New York

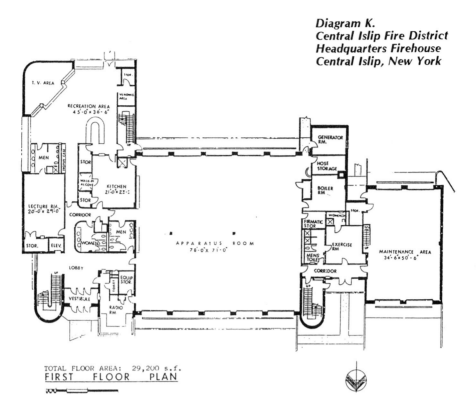

TOTAL FLOOR AREA: 29,200 s.f.
FIRST FLOOR PLAN

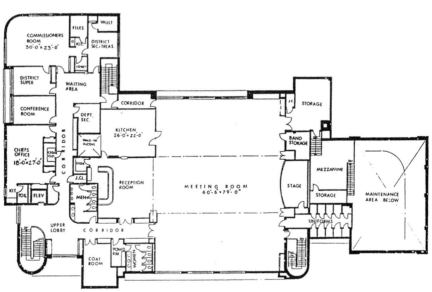

SECOND FLOOR PLAN

IV. OPERATIONS

15

Fire Department Communications

EDWIN J. SPAHN

CHAPTER HIGHLIGHTS

* General tasks common in communication centers.
* Management, staffing, and characteristics of communications personnel.
* Organizing and managing a center (funding).
* Physical plant considerations (emergency operations).
* Telecommunications (911 operations).
* Dispatch methods (computer-aided dispatch, manual records).
* Radio communications equipment and systems.
* Licensing, coordination, and specifications.

*F*IRE DEPARTMENT OPERATIONS depend on the team concept and team concept depends on the ability of one team member to let the other team members know what has been done, what needs to be done, and what might need to be done in the future. Effective communication systems allow managers and fireground commanders to be everywhere at once. Geographical areas covering thousands of square miles are reduced to the size of an office or Command Post workstation. Modern electronic technology and modern management techniques coalesce to make fire department administration and management more efficient and safe. This chapter intends to introduce readers to, or reinforce, the major areas of concern in communications. From management to hardware, from written SOPs to structured verbal communications, this chapter intends to provide insight into the broad spectrum of topics relevant to the subject.

Without regard to whether a fire service agency is rural, suburban, urban, or metropolitan, or even a state-wide agency, this chapter sets forth fundamentals applicable to all agencies. Communications challenges in Los Angeles; Chicago; Sanford, Florida; and Hastings, Nebraska have common threads. In fact, the inability of the smaller community to address problems without help may be greater because of resources, in terms of both personnel and finances.

HISTORY OF FIRE SERVICE COMMUNICATIONS

Communications technology, like almost everything else in the fire service, wasn't the result of planned development. Communications techniques evolved. Watchmen stationed in the towers of ancient Eastern and European towns and villages most certainly were the predecessors of today's fire and rescue dispatcher. The town crier who walked the streets of England and the colonies of the Northeastern United States carrying a lighted lamp, a bell, or mechanical rattle represented the best early warning and alerting of the local fire brigade available at the time.

Communications by voice or by means of some kind of noisemaker remained the only medium to transmit information from one person to another, and one place to another, until the discovery of the tremendous potential of electricity. The mere discovery of electricity was not enough. Application and harnessing of this marvel took additional years.

The telegraph key, Morse Code, batteries, and wires strung between remote locations represented advances in technology exceeding what had been experienced during the preceding several centuries.

Laboratory adventures into the wonders of the electronic vacuum tube and the intense curiosity of amateur radio technicians and operators brought the rewards of communications over long distances to public safety agencies. History says law enforcement first used radio communications. Later, other public safety organizations recognized its value.

While some radio communications equipment found applications in the late 1930s in the fire service, it did not become commonplace until after World War II. Technology, quickly developed for the war effort, soon found its way into the fire service. By the late 1950s, and definitely in the 1960s, radio became widely used.

Today's technology far exceeds the wildest imagination of the user in the 1950s. Nevertheless, by the year 2000, the rate of technological change will exceed that experienced during the last 20 years.

With that in mind, a fire service leader must prepare to review the operating procedures and policies now in effect in his present communications operation. Why are operating procedures as they are? Is it principally because they were that way last year . . . and the year before?

MISSION OF A COMMUNICATIONS CENTER

From time to time there is considerable discussion about whether a communications center should be associated with the operations section of a fire agency or be relegated to the support section. There is often the implication that the support functions are not as important as the operations functions. On the other hand, why should communications not stand alone as a department?

Definition of terms is very important in almost every endeavor. What is the real meaning of the terms *operating department* and *support department?* Most commonly the operating department or function is that department or function that provides services to, or interfaces directly with, the client of the organization. In the case of a fire agency the client is usually the citizen. A support department or function is that department or function that provides services to, or interfaces directly with, operating agencies within an organization. Using this common definition, it is most appropriate to classify a communications section as both an operating and support organization. Figure 15-1.

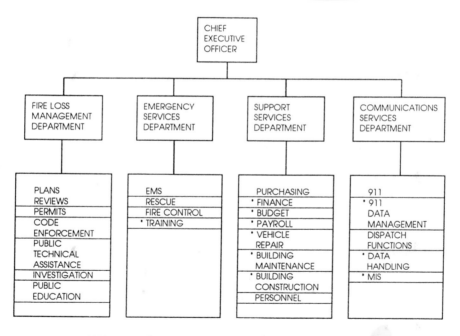

* Indicates the Function provides services directly to the public or the client rather than services to persons within organization only.

Figure 15-1. *Management must understand the difference in missions between Operating Departments and Support Departments. Service to the citizen client is the ultimate objective of the total organization.*

While it is commonplace to visualize the fire department communications section, or communications center, as part of the fire department, it is not always necessary to organize it that way. Without doubt, it is important that the local fire service agency maintain a strong control over how fire department affairs are administered by a communications center. At the same time there is no absolute reason a fire communications center must be under the direct command or supervision of a fire department. Most communications providers to the fire service are under the direct supervision of the fire department because they evolved that way, not because it is necessary or because it works better that way. In every fire service agency, volunteer or career, the assigned field operations duty officer must be aware of what the communications center is doing. This means that the field operations supervisor must have an awareness of what is going on in the jurisdiction at all times he is on duty. The majority of fire service agencies that do not directly supervise communications operations cannot afford to place a full-time fire officer in the communications center. Good disaster planning calls for assignment of a high-ranking officer to the communications center during times of major emergency operations to direct how resources are allocated and called up.

What is the mission of a communications center? While the following list includes certain functions that might be placed elsewhere in an organization, it suggests tasks that can be carried out in a communications center:

- Establish and maintain a center the public client can contact (place a call) for emergency assistance with the expectation that some corrective action or emergency service will result from that call.
- Establish and maintain a system to which emergency calls for service result in prompt dispatch of proper agencies, personnel, and equipment to effectively address the emergency.
- Establish and maintain a system wherein properly trained and dedicated personnel closely monitor the progress of the agencies, personnel, and equipment en route to the scene of the emergency and assist in prompt arrival of the services.
- Establish and maintain a system wherein resources remaining available to an emergency service agency are redistributed throughout the service area to minimize extended service response times because of "holes" in the coverage.
- Provide, in a timely manner, and upon request from the field emergency units, additional resources which match the field request as closely as possible.
- Generate accurate and precise records as required by the emergency response system. The emergency response system includes the communications center.
- Monitor the emergency situation to its conclusion, exchanging with field units any record-related or administrative information required by

standing orders. Upon stabilizing or abating the emergency, properly close the records on the incident, file the records, and move on to the next incident.

- Establish and maintain a properly designed radio communications system able to provide reliable dispatch of emergency units in stations or the field and provide reliable information flow between the communications center and the field units, and the field units one with another at any time, including nonemergency periods.

- Establish and maintain a properly designed radio, information, and telecommunications system able to provide reliable information flow between the agency that addresses an incident and other agencies or jurisdictions that may be drawn into the incident.

- Develop and maintain a database and records that allow the communications center to identify the location of the call for service so the proper operational agency can respond. The records should contain information allowing the communications center to determine how to refer the call if it is not in the communications geographic or functional area of responsibility. Only in the smallest communication center is the database likely to be entirely manual. *Manual,* in this case, means that the data are kept on loose or index cards, sheets of paper, or similar kinds of access assistance. The advent of 911, Enhanced-911, additional dispatch center workloading because of increased population, broader scope of services, and higher service levels by fire and EMS departments, essentially have forced dispatch centers to embrace electronic data processing and information retrieval. However, dispatch center managers must keep in mind that if and when a failure occurs in the electronic information retrieval system, an organized manual retrieval system must be available immediately to insert into the dispatching system until the electronic system is restored. The time period over which the manual system might be used can be as short as minutes, or as long as days. Anticipation of an electronic system failure is one of the primary duties of a communications center manager.

The preceding list has a very generic flavor. The intent is to start with the fundamentals and proceed from there.

When considering the global aspect of providing communications services it becomes apparent that information and data flow into the communications center, then flow out. Between the in-and-out times, the data are processed, selectively stored or discarded. There are many sources providing the input. There are many sources receiving the output. The service scope of the communications center needs definition.

Certainly we all can agree that law enforcement, fire, rescue, emergency medical services (EMS), civil emergency management (formerly Civil Defense), public works, public utilities, and animal control, as examples, can be identified as emergency service providers. It is up to management to determine which of these agencies shall be served by the central, or principal, communications center. Alternatively, multiple communications centers are established. Someone, somewhere, must decide what the communications work flow and load should be, and how dispatch center configurations best expedite intercommunications among agencies. These are policy decisions.

INFORMATION FLOW IN COMMUNICATIONS CENTERS

Information in communications centers is categorized into two major categories: nonemergency communications, and emergency communications.

Nonemergency and emergency policies and procedures

The routine, day-to-day exchange of messages, phone calls, memos, Standard Operating Procedures (SOPs), etc., is an example of nonemergency communications. These messages originate both inside and outside the organization. It is possible to break the topic of nonemergency communications down by one more layer into the following categories: policies and procedures.

Policies

Policies determine *what must be done given a set of circumstances that allows for several paths of action.* Policies are determined by management decisionmaking procedures. This process involves management personnel carefully considering several paths of action that might be taken toward providing a solution to a problem. Instead of permitting the employee to implement any solution to the problem, the group decides that the prescribed path is the best one to follow. Communications center management establishes communications center policies. The communications center, likewise, influences policy in other agencies.

Internal policies

- Maximum time allowed to process an alarm.
- Performance standards.
- Codes of conduct.
- Television, radio, and newspaper media contact personnel.
- Minimum staffing during vacations.

Communications center top management personnel make policy.

External policies

Since the communications center interfaces so closely with other field operations agencies, it is apparent that the center becomes the vehicle for administering, or cooperating in, policies established by other managers. The team concept becomes very clear in these cases. The communications manager has the responsibility to reach agreement, or cause to reach agreement, on a mutual understanding between the field operating agency and the communications center manager. The communications manager takes on the burden of making certain that the ultimate policies are uniformly administered within the communications center. Obviously, all field agencies served by the communications center must understand that policy administration must be uniform.

For instance, assume that a communications center serves three different fire departments. The policy on calls for service handling must be uniform across the three departments insofar as the communications center is concerned. This task is perhaps one of the most difficult management tasks of the communications center manager.

Examples of external policies are

* Definition of apparatus to be dispatched to various types of emergency incidents.
* Identification of fire department management personnel who are to be notified regarding certain types of emergency incidents.
* Limitations on degree of decisionmaking placed in the hands of communications center supervisors regarding "fill-ins," "move-ups," or other prescribed covering assignments during an emergency.

Managers of served agencies and the communications center management arrive at agreements on policy. Supervisors and dispatchers carry out policies.

Procedures

Procedures explain to the supervisory and dispatch floor personnel **how** to carry out policy. While it is indeed difficult at times to formulate policy, it is an even greater challenge to put procedures into a form easily understood by employees. Remember, the manager has the advantage of knowing what he is thinking. Therefore, when the manager reviews his policy statement and asks subordinates to prepare procedures to carry out the policy, his original intent frequently is lost.

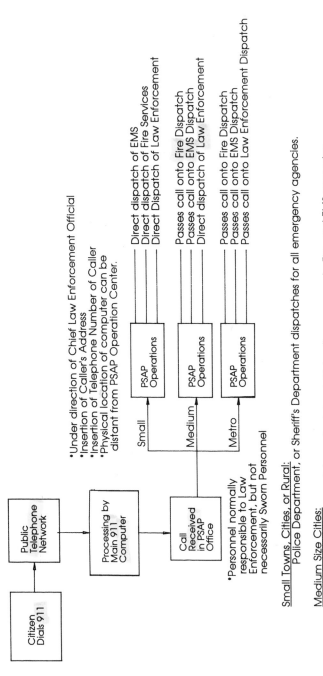

Figure 15-2. *Not all 911 Emergency Reporting Systems are configured in the same way. Most often how the management task is approached depends on the size of the community.*

Internal procedures

One of the most common products of procedure preparation is the *Standard Operating Procedure (SOP)*.

It is helpful to display procedures in a graphic manner. Because most employees are visual learners, flow charts and outlines get the point across better than instructions presented in text.

Examples of internal procedures are:

- The route through which information flows as a call for service proceeds from the 911 call taker to the main frequency dispatcher.
- The step-by-step procedure a dispatcher takes to perform first-echelon maintenance on a tape-recording machine.
- The step-by-step procedure a dispatch supervisor uses to proceed through a call-out list to ensure dispatchers are given proper opportunity for overtime.
- The method dispatchers use to select vacation and other times away from the job.

External procedures

Procedures also originate from the field operations agencies served by the communications center. The communications center manager must be prepared to work closely with outside agencies to make certain that procedures are clear, concise, and in a form the communications center employees can understand.

The communications center manager must assume the posture of a true diplomat when working with outside agencies in developing understandable procedures. The communications manager must be sensitive to "turf" issues when dealing with outside agencies. At the same time, the efficiency of the communications center employee and minimum confusion in service delivery must prevail.

Examples of external procedures are:

- Sequence in which certain apparatus and equipment are dispatched over dispatch frequencies by the dispatcher for a given agency.
- Step-by-step procedure used by a dispatch supervisor to proceed through an operations department overtime call-out list to ensure that overtime opportunities are offered to employees in accordance with an employee collective bargaining agreement.

Processing calls for service

Communications centers process two types of calls: emergency and nonemergency, or administrative calls. The communications center must process administrative calls in a businesslike fashion. Prompt, courteous handling goes a long way toward convincing the client—the citizen—that the communications center is a competently run operation. While it seems obvious to suggest a businesslike setting, just how is that accomplished?

Plan the administrative telephone system carefully. Place yourself in the position of the calling party. As a caller, what irritates you more—a ringing phone that is not answered, or a busy signal? Based on interviews with telephone receptionists in large office centers, or in large administrative offices, it seems that while neither condition is well received, the ringing phone with no answer is the most irritating. You can control this condition by limiting the number of "roll-over" numbers available on the main calling line. If too many roll-over numbers are available, the answering clerical or receptionist personnel may be forced to let the phones ring during peak traffic periods. On the other hand, if the number of incoming roll-over numbers is limited, callers will get a busy signal. Ask your local telephone company to help you identify an optimal configuration.

The receptionist or clerical person designated to answer the phones sets the stage for the caller's first impression of the organization. A pleasant voice and a cooperative attitude are necessities. Scheduling special training in how to deal with people under the many stressful conditions that face dispatch personnel is a very worthwhile program for dispatch center management to arrange. Many community colleges offer courses such as "Dealing with Difficult People." This training is invaluable for dispatchers, especially telephone operators, supervisory personnel, and management personnel.

COMMUNICATIONS CENTER ORGANIZATION

The ultimate responsibility for making certain that the communications center provides proper service can fall to any of a number of agencies. The management organizational chart often depends on the depth and breadth of the communications services offered. If a communications center serves the fire agency only, the management table usually reflects fire officers. But upon inspection, the corollary of this proposition is that the fire communications center is simply one of several communications centers. This scenario represents the situation where there is no real central communications system. Usually this represents a rather provincial, narrow view of what modern communications and modern communications centers are all about.

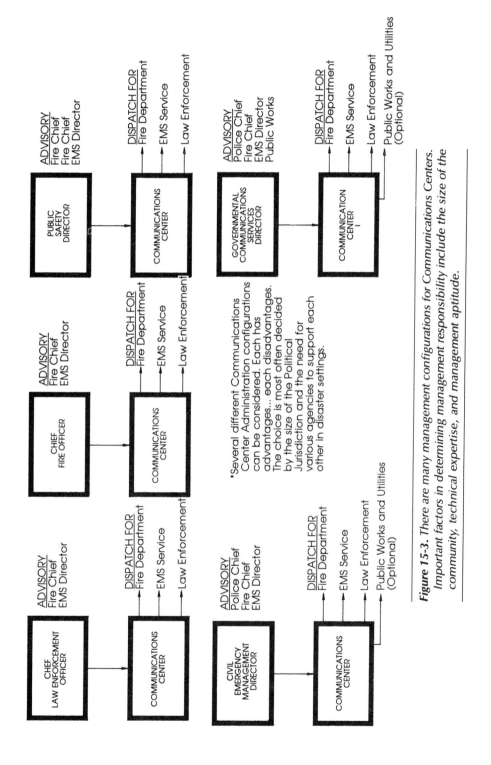

Figure 15-3. *There are many management configurations for Communications Centers. Important factors in determining management responsibility include the size of the community, technical expertise, and management aptitude.*

Let's take a look at communications practices. The following agencies manage communications centers:

- fire service organizations, specifically fire departments;
- separate county or city communications departments;
- other fire or police agencies in other jurisdictions;
- civil emergency management agencies; and
- private sector companies or corporations.

FIRE SERVICE ORGANIZATIONS

In certain cases, fire service agencies operate communications centers that provide services to law enforcement, or to other city or county departments. But the examples are few. Most fire department communications sections fall under the supervision of either the fire chief or an assistant chief. Often, the communications section is a spin-off of the supply or support section of a fire department. The size of a fire department usually dictates how the communications center is organized and staffed.

Small fire departments are found in areas up to 30,000 population. In small fire departments the manager is usually the fire chief, but the dispatch function itself very often is given to a nonuniformed person. Consider that many volunteer departments, which make up the vast majority of small organized fire departments, still use part-time dispatchers or dispatchers who are given free living accommodations at the fire station in return for dispatch services. In very small career departments, budgetary constraints usually dictate that a paid firefighter spend part of the duty day performing phone and radio watch in a communications room where the local citizen calls for assistance. At the same time, in many high-population areas where small volunteer departments serve bedroom and service communities, dispatch is often provided from a central dispatch communications center by nonuniformed, or civilian dispatchers.

Medium-sized fire departments are identified as those serving population groups of 50,000 to 200,000. These departments typically are career departments. Career firefighters traditionally serve as dispatchers in fire communications systems located in these communities. Most of these cities are steeped in tradition. That is, communications in these departments evolved from the first radios purchased decades ago and each system evolved independently. There was no emphasis on disaster control or interagency cooperation at the outset. Therefore, like many features and functions in medium-sized cities, services are provided this year the same way they were last year. The police department, fire department, sanitation, public works department, and utilities department, all went separate ways, and many continue to do so today. Mutual distrust and "turf" considerations often hold back communications centralization.

On the other hand, the general trend in larger cities and counties is to use civilian dispatchers in a communications center that serves at least all the public safety interests. The perceived communications bond of public safety agencies allows each to gravitate to a central dispatch configuration. There is often a general lack of desire to integrate public works, utilities, animal control, building department, and similar agencies into the communications center because some believe that their missions are too far removed from that of public safety. Nevertheless, the adoption of an Incident Command System and the implementation of hazardous materials handling programs have reinforced the concept that these other departments are interrelated in terms of the potential services they can provide during fire service operations. This awareness contributes to including limited interconnect and dispatch features for nonpublic-safety agencies in public safety dispatch centers.

INDEPENDENT CITY OR COUNTY COMMUNICATIONS AGENCIES

Operational convenience and budgetary crunches frequently force local government to consider the practicality of merging all or most of the government's communications services into a single communications agency. The construction of new radio communications systems, such as trunking systems, also increases the pressure to centralize communications centers for technical reasons.

One of the most effective gains realized is greater efficiency in interdepartmental radio communications services. Two factors promote this higher efficiency.

First, the communications center's management and dispatch operational personnel are familiar with the operations of all or most of the local government departments.

Second, the technical planning, procurement, and implementation of the communications system tend toward one common goal. Policy regarding the communications system is set by the communications agency management and the various departments simply become "subscribers."

OTHER INDEPENDENT AGENCIES OR JURISDICTIONS

Often, small-to-medium-sized city or village governments elect to contract with a nearby community to provide communications services. These services are provided under contract. Or another department within or outside the local government jurisdiction provides dispatch services for the fire department. For example, the police department provides dispatch services for the fire department, or a fire department in a nearby jurisdiction provides dispatch services for another jurisdiction's fire department.

PRIVATE SECTOR AGENCIES

In some jurisdictions the private sector delivers communications services. For example, a private corporation is authorized by the local jurisdiction, or jurisdictions, to set up a privately owned communications facility. An example of privatization, this service and the way it fits into emergency service provision is no different than the way private EMS ambulance service fits into a local government's EMS delivery system.

Center management configuration—A comparison

Fire service organizations

Advantages: Under direct control of the fire service manager; full attention of personnel directed to fire, EMS, and rescue activities; procedures not modified by other procedures in other governmental agencies; change comes easily.

Disadvantages: Tends to develop "tunnel vision" regarding how other government agencies fit into an emergency incident; usually technical capability to communicate electronically with other agencies is deficient; operating personnel not familiar with other agency procedures; inefficient application of community communications financial resources.

Commonly Found in Following Settings: Volunteer departments; rural departments; small municipalities; older established municipalities of any size; political jurisdictions without 911 services.

Independent city or county communications centers

Advantages: Operation tends to have more a "global" approach to communications services; more opportunity to implement modern communications techniques such as trunking systems; better control during widespread emergency; contributes integrated preplanning for emergencies by agencies; workload on center personnel more even and efficient; more efficient application of community communications financial resources.

Disadvantages: Loss of tight control by all agencies involved in procedures and tasks performed by center personnel; expertise and specific knowledge of personnel regarding fire service topics diluted; personnel busy with communications activities and not available for fire department file and database management and updating.

Commonly Found in Following Settings: Large counties; growing medium to large cities; new jurisdictions of any size.

Other independent agencies or jurisdictions

Advantages: Allows small cities to assign dispatch and 911 duties to another agency to release to street duty firefighters and police officers normally assigned to dispatch duty; promotes better communications among different agencies served by the common communications center; More efficient application of community communications financial resources.

Disadvantages: Loss of tight control by all agencies involved in procedures and tasks performed by center personnel; expertise and specific knowledge of personnel regarding fire service topics diluted; personnel busy with communications activities and not available for fire department file and database management and updating; knowledge of dispatchers not as detailed regarding specific fire department operations needs and procedures; dispatcher knowledge of the service area not as detailed as desired due to more global nature of service.

Commonly Found in Following Settings: Very small cities; rural fire Departments.

Private sector agencies

An honest and comprehensive analysis of this method of dispatch is not available. However, this method is listed here because it exists as an option. When turning the communications function over to private agencies was proposed in the past, the traditional fire service had viewed the idea with distrust, principally because of the fear of losing control. From a technical and management point of view, the probability of success for this kind of service depends on the quality and experience of the management-level personnel provided by the private sector agency. Theoretically, the service could work as it does when the private sector provides correctional facility operations, data processing, or motor vehicle repair and maintenance. Certainly many fire service leaders will shudder at this proposition, reciting a litany of reasons why it won't work. At the same time, until it is demonstrated repeatedly that the service can't work, the proposition remains an unknown quantity, waiting for some enterprising municipality or county to explore. The commitment to, and investment in, communications equipment and systems already in place and owned by governmental agencies are additional reasons why fire departments are reluctant to explore this option. The 911 and E-911 systems are examples of the private sector providing critical hardware and software to public safety agencies. 911 systems, while enabled by public sector legislation, depend on a relatively small investment in personnel and hardware by the public sector to operate. The reliability of the electronic system is dependent entirely on private sector resources.

MUTUAL AID, JOINT RESPONSE, CONTRACTUAL RELATIONSHIPS

It is imperative that the communications center be alerted to existing or impending changes in interlocal or contractual agreements. These two words, *interlocal* and *contractual,* are used because every agreement into which a jurisdiction enters is not necessarily an interlocal mutual aid agreement.

Mutual aid contracts tend to be very vague in their written form. The details are usually worked out between the fire chiefs or their designees. In these side agreements are the details of who and what goes where and when. The communications center's management must be aware of the resources provided by other jurisdictions. At the same time the communications center's management must know what the jurisdiction it serves will provide to others and under what conditions this aid will be provided. It is impractical to waste time obtaining routine response approvals from supervisory personnel when it is more prudent to state these policies in Standing or Standard Operating Procedures (SOPs).

Joint response agreements stipulate that the closest apparatus appropriate for the emergency responds to the site of the emergency, without regard for political boundaries. This type of agreement is fast gaining favor in metropolitan areas where, for the most part, jurisdictional political boundaries reflect the collection of revenue by a political entity rather than quality emergency service to the general public. There is no room for delay in dispatches related to these agreements. If the proper response is not made, then no one responds. This is in contrast to a mutual aid agreement that stipulates that at least the primary responsible agency is already on the scene of the emergency when a request for assistance is made.

Contractual agreements, in the context of this discussion, differ from mutual aid contracts and joint response contracts in that jurisdictions often pay a certain amount to other jurisdictions to take full and complete responsibility for emergency services. The communications center's management must understand the responsibility of the providing agency in managing the call for service. Usually this responsibility extends to autonomous incident communications and recordkeeping.

FUNDING

Funding for communications systems comes from various sources. When the communications center is operated by a municipality or county, the funding most often comes from *ad valorem* taxes (property taxes). On the other hand, some states have statutory provisions which allow assessment of certain fees for services provided by the communications center. Whether these fees are sufficient to provide a significant revenue source depends on the size of both the communications center and the community. Managers must identify these revenue sources and assess the magnitude of the probable funds. Then managers must detail the precise personnel services costs, operating costs, and capital costs associated with the center to determine whether implementation of fee revenues represents a sufficient sum to warrant the administration costs usually associated with most legislated fees. In almost every case, managers cannot expect the actual realized fee funds to cover the center's total annual cost completely.

Examples of these fees are the costs to reproduce audio tapes of events in the center, provide copies of records generated in the center, and provide copies of databases or maps accumulated in the center.

COMMUNICATIONS CENTER ORGANIZATION AND PERSONNEL

Insofar as public safety agencies are concerned, communications centers represent the start and finish of all emergency calls for service. The center bridges the gap between the client—the citizen—and the provider—the public safety agencies.

Public safety agencies have a language all their own. It is a language, in fact, full of jargon. On the other hand, the citizen uses a more common language approach to describing a problem. It therefore falls to the communications center to translate the citizen's version of the problem into the language and jargon of the proper public safety agency.

Functional relationship to public safety agencies

Fire service

The traditional fire service is principally a loose, quasi-military organization. Despite its military orientation, the communications center must be prepared to take calls for service requests from citizens who lack a military orientation. Communications center managers need to be aware that dispatchers and call takers must be capable of making this transition in their interpersonal relations. If they cannot, inefficiencies and confusion may disturb the dispatch process.

Emergency medical services

While emergency medical service personnel do not view themselves as "military" (as the fire service views itself), their rigid medical procedures and standing orders tend to produce a very technical and structured view of an emergency incident. Their jargon and their approach become very important and uncompromising because all players must speak the same language. Communications center managers train and increase the awareness of the dispatch personnel to the unique view of the EMS personnel, as contrasted with the fire and rescue-oriented personnel and field supervisors.

Civil emergency management

The communications center also provides services to this sector of public safety. In a properly organized county or municipality, all public service and safety agencies need at least limited communications capability with one other during normal operations. However, the issue becomes nonnegotiable during a natural or technological disaster. At this point the probability is high that Civil Emergency Management (CEM) will begin to function in the role of resource manager for any one, or all, of the local government agencies. Floods, storms, explosions, and hazardous materials incidents all often outstrip the normally available resources of the individual local government service organizations. Interdepartmental communication becomes a mandatory function during a CEM emergency.

Communications agency manager

The level of service and progressive nature of any organization can never exceed the dedication and competency of the leader of that organization. An inspection of any major communications center will verify the proposition.

Many texts and commentaries have been written about the distinguishing characteristics of a manager. Applying these management theories is absolutely important in this setting. What are some of the major distinguishing characteristics of the communications manager?

1. *The manager must establish credibility with his communications staff* by identifying relevant tasks that need to be addressed and then identifying paths to take toward a solution. The communications center manager must moderate many interests. The communications center is where all local government public safety and service agencies interface. The manager is faced with the prospect of meeting the communications needs, policies, and operational needs of all these departments, without compromising the order of the entire communications network and the needs of communications center staff.

2. *The manager must be a leader.* Leadership in a communications center requires more than leading the staff through one exotic program after another. Choosing a certain project or service and then convincing the

staff and the managers of all departments served that the pet program or perceived special service a certain department demands is in the best interest of the total system does not exhibit leadership.

3. *Technical knowledge is a must for the communications manager.* It is not necessary that the manager be a communications engineer. The ability to recognize potential technical problems is essential. A competent manager must be able to receive and comprehend descriptions of technical concepts from engineering personnel from both within and outside the communications organization.

The levels of technical competency required depend, of course, on the complexity of the communications system under the manager's direction. Nevertheless, each manager, to the degree that his communications center applies the following technologies, must have a grasp of the following areas:

- Radio communications technology.
- Computer operations and applications.
- Database management, both manual and electronic.
- Electrical power systems as applied to communications centers. Particular emphasis should be placed on redundant power sources.
- Telephone service and switching technology. When a communications center is served by 911 technology, the manager must have a grasp of the services available from telephone service providers.
- The manager must be able to write, or cause to be written, appropriate technical specifications for electronic apparatus and systems.
- The manager must understand the responsibility of the fire agency director or chief to decide certain procedural policies within the communications center. If the communications center is under the direct supervision of the fire department, then the manager must be prepared to accept the fire chief as the ultimate supervisor of the dispatch personnel.

THE SUPERVISOR

In all settings, the supervisor represents the "personnel-controlling arm" of the communications center manager. Most supervisors perceive their interests to be more closely aligned with the employees with whom they work daily than they do with the goals and objectives of the manager, with whom they have less contact. Nevertheless, the manager must select supervisors carefully to maintain as much continuity in management philosophy as possible. Since most communications centers are around-the-clock operations, the manager is faced with concern about whether the supervisor will represent his interests when he is absent. Some of the distinguishing characteristics of a good communications supervisor are described below.

The supervisor needs *a self-assured attitude,* with enough confidence to provide leadership during peak periods of communications or crises. The supervisor must be prepared to work harder and longer than any of the personnel being supervised.

His *understanding of the technical operation* of the communications system must be broad enough so that he can identify and isolate malfunctions to major components.

The supervisor needs *technical knowledge* and a level of articulation that permits him to describe to maintenance and repair personnel, or the agency, malfunctions that occur during the tour of duty.

He must be able to *handle employee disagreements,* grievances, and training effectively and in an efficient manner.

The supervisor must be able to *interact in an efficient manner with peers and managers* in other departments and divisions in matters relating to communications procedures and service delivery. This ability is of particular importance during service hours outside the normal 8:00 a.m. to 5:00 p.m. workday.

THE DISPATCHER

The dispatcher and the call taker are the two positions through which the communications center fulfills the proposition that it is an *operational* organization. That means the system interfaces directly with the public. The face of the fire department is the communications center dispatcher or call taker.

Depending on the center's workload, and usually the size of the center, an employee may be assigned to perform as a *call taker.* The call takers devote their energies entirely to the task of talking with the citizen who is lodging the complaint or describing the emergency. This task assignment does not involve sending emergency apparatus to a certain location.

In most instances, the employee called the *dispatcher* makes certain that the proper apparatus is sent to the scene in a timely fashion. While the equipment is en route the dispatcher is charged with the responsibility of ensuring that pertinent information that becomes available after the equipment leaves the station is provided in an orderly fashion.

On the surface, the call taker or the dispatcher position might seem to be very similar, or even equal, to that of a clerk typist. In fact, many personnel departments place classified advertisements for professional dispatcher or call taker vacancies in the clerical part of the want ads. Unfortunately, this is a poor personnel management practice. These positions require a very high degree of self-discipline. Perhaps this is the first and foremost requirement. Certainly the abilities to type, to speak, and to communicate are important. Nevertheless, without self-discipline, skills in the other areas are meaningless and useless.

The call taker's ability to remain composed and in control of his mental faculties under high-stress situations is imperative. The employee must be able to address several stress-filled, highly demanding incidents at once. This is a highly critical characteristic, one that must be considered during recruitment and the hiring process.

Because the dispatcher interrelates with other operational agencies within the jurisdiction, he must think globally. It is common knowledge that each agency uses jargon peculiar to its business, so the dispatcher must recognize this and be accommodating when an emergency arises that calls for interaction with other agencies.

CLERICAL AND RECORDKEEPING PERSONNEL

Recordkeeping is a task that is directly associated with dispatching and communications center activities. Depending on the size of the communications center, the records clerk also may function as a secretary or assistant to the center manager. Other duties such as telephone receptionist also may be thrust on this employee.

The records clerk needs many office and business-related talents and must be pleasant and patient. If the jurisdiction classifies the position as a clerical position, the communications manager must brief the jurisdiction's personnel department on the unique demands of the position. A communications center records clerk has a separate set of pressures and needs to have different people skills than the clerk in the personnel section.

CONSIDERATIONS FOR HANDICAPPED EMPLOYEES

Communications centers offer ideal working conditions for certain types of handicapped people. Individuals who are confined to wheelchairs are particularly suited to dispatch and call taker assignments. Administrative telephone receptionist positions offer other opportunities.

Whether the communications center facility is a private sector or public sector facility, the owner is obliged to provide workplace and access assistance to the handicapped. Ramps, elevators, restroom facilities, eating facilities, entry and hallway dimensions, to name a few, must be configured to assist the handicapped to fulfill their duties in the workplace.

The Americans with Disabilities Act (ADA) of 1992 is very specific about required building features and functions. Local building officials are a good source of information on these requirements and should be consulted if construction of a new facility is projected.

ADMINISTRATIVE SERVICES

This topic relates to the planning, organization, and preplanning the communications center management must address outside the actual call taking and dispatching services normally associated with a communications center.

Alarm ordinances

Some communities have considered and adopted *alarm ordinances*. The function of their relative advantages or disadvantages will not be discussed here.

Alarm ordinances are based most often on the proposition that an occupancy is required by some law, local or state, to have a *fire protection system* connected to either a central station or the fire department dispatch center. Note the use of the term *fire protection system*. When a call for *alarm* service is received by electronic annunciation, it is presumed that there is an emergency at the protected location and the communications center orders the response of the necessary equipment. In some jurisdictions, fire chiefs and municipal administrators determine that responding to these calls for service costs money and institute a schedule of charges for all calls that exceed a predetermined number of calls within a certain time period. The calls in question must be identified as *false alarms* or *system failures,* or some other category designated by the fire chief or other authority. If an alarm ordinance is under consideration, think through the process carefully. Give special attention to the identification of the cause of the alarm as defined by the attending apparatus officer. Give special training to fire company officers so they can identify the precise nature of the alarms to which they respond.

From time to time communications center personnel are designated to administer the false alarm fee program. Typically some kind of fee schedule is established. The fee takes effect after the calls for service to an occupancy reach a certain number within a specified period of time. If a fee process is used, then arrangements must be made to administer the fee collection process. This requires establishing some form of arbitration, or mediation, to reconcile whether the alarm was caused by a malfunction or not. This involves an investment in equipment and personal services. Certainly it is improper and shortsighted to embark on a program of this type without measuring the projected revenues against the expenditures required to support the program. Consider fee accounts for which no fee recovery is made. Finally, consider carefully the public relations aspect of a program such as this. Examine why so many false alarms are being experienced. Attack the problem at the root. Often, the cause of the problem is inexperience or incompetent installation and maintenance of alarm systems. Therefore, the problem really requires efficient regulation of installers. Unfortunately, fire departments themselves often are the cause of excessive false alarms because plan reviewers and field inspectors of fire alarm systems do not recognize inferior or improper installations.

First responder

Fire protection systems include all kinds of fire suppression systems and all kinds of fire detection/initiation and annunciation systems (also called fire alarm systems). Most of the calls for service associated with activation of these systems require a response from the public fire department. These responses are performed by either fire department or private sector personnel.

Fire department personnel

Fire department personnel must know precisely what actions they are expected to take when called to automatic fire system activations. In almost every case, field personnel request some kind of assistance from the communications center when the call is not the result of an obvious fire-related problem, highlighting the need for preplanning in two areas. First, the fire department personnel must be trained in fire alarm system operation. Second, communications center employees need structured classes on fire alarm system operations.

Fire companies in the field and fire dispatchers must communicate effectively on fire alarm systems conditions. This is necessary especially when the dispatchers must relay the alarm status back and forth between a fire alarm central station operator and the fire company in the field. *Central station* in this context should not be confused with a central fire dispatch service. A fire alarm central station is an alarm monitoring facility most often operated by private sector interests. This service monitors fire, security, and industrial process alarms. These facilities must meet rigid construction, employee training, and recordkeeping standards to maintain their Underwriters Laboratory certification. Private sector central stations are most common in those parts of the country where model building codes make monitoring of automatic built-in fire control systems mandatory. If the communications center is the monitoring point for community-installed fire alarm systems, it is even more imperative that the dispatcher know how to communicate system signaling and system condition to field companies. However, as a practical matter, many fire dispatch centers have determined that the workload presented by full-time monitoring of a "central station" equivalent is not practical from a liability, personal services cost, and capital investment point of view. This business decision places this function in the private sector where the huge number of alarm systems monitored require sophisticated, expensive electronic systems. Some central stations serve not only a metropolitan area, but also several states.

Private sector personnel

Central stations may or may not provide *first responders*. First responders are private sector technicians who come to the scene of an activated fire alarm system and take control of the building from the responding fire company. Further responsibilities include securing the structure if fire companies forced entry to provide service. Finally, the first responder restores the fire alarm system to service and talks with the communications center personnel in the process.

NFPA 72, *National Fire Alarm Code* Section 4.3, identifies the actions central stations should take upon receipt of an alarm. (*Note:* NFPA 71 was consolidated into NFPA 72 in 1993–1994). Whether the response patterns and obligations are enforced or not is determined by the Authority Having Jurisdiction (AHJ). Keep in mind that the provisions of NFPA 72 must be enforced only if that engineering standard has been adopted at the local or state level.

The communications center must assemble a database which provides, at a minimum, the following instant information regarding the central stations:

- Names of central stations;
- Addresses of central stations;
- Phone numbers of the monitoring points;
- Phone numbers of the supervisor, or duty supervisor of the monitoring point; and
- Phone number of the central station manager.

To facilitate communications between the communications center dispatchers and any central station services, a specially designated telephone line is recommended. Depending on the amount of traffic between the communications center and the central stations, more than one line might be indicated. Nevertheless, the number, or numbers, should be known and used only by central station interests.

Funding

Communications center operations are expensive. Regardless of the size of the agency it serves, it takes a significant part of the agency's resources to operate. This is true principally because the communications center must be in a state of readiness 24 hours per day to receive calls for service.

In most cases, the communications center function is funded with tax dollars, except in those cases where the service is provided by the private sector. Even in those cases the funds ultimately come from tax dollars in almost every case.

In some states there may, from time to time, be grant funds available that can be used for certain operational and technical needs. If you are planning to seek grant funds, make sure that the conditions of the grants do not interfere with local operational procedures, goals, and objectives.

As a general rule, communications center managers should maneuver to avoid depending on grants or similar sources of funds to apply toward personal services. This kind of money, grant money, is called *soft money.* Soft money depends on funds which are not assured from year to year. While such funds are acceptable to a point for capital purchases, managers should avoid soft money for other applications, particularly personal services. While applying soft money to capital expenses or consumable expenses is a common and sound practice, using this money for personal services, such as dispatchers or support personnel, relies on uncertain and unpredictable revenue sources to pay continuing salaries, a problem when the grant expires. This places the manager in the position of addressing layoffs of personnel now performing routine work the alarm center has come to depend on.

COMMUNICATIONS SYSTEMS

Communications center managers must avoid the tendency to zero in on radio communications equipment alone as the center of *a communications system.* A more global approach to this topic is required, even in rural operations.

ELEMENTS OF COMMUNICATIONS SYSTEMS

A global view or analysis of communications systems finds that, indeed, the entire effort is an interlocking systems effort. The electronics, electrical systems, brick and mortar, support, construction levels, infrastructure, and other considerations constitute the features and functions of a communications system.

PHYSICAL PLANT

The integrity of the physical plant is the cornerstone of the communications system. Where it is, and how it is built, protected, and supported, all have a direct effect on the communications system's reliability.

Site selection

Security is necessary for the communications center site. Security means more than simply making the site impervious to human assault. It extends to making the site secure against natural or technological emergencies or disasters.

The communications center's operating environment is very important. If the center is an existing facility, an assessment must be performed to determine the site's vulnerability to wind, water, fire, and lightning.

The site supports what is called the communications center's *infrastructure*. This is development and planning jargon for the basic facilities, equipment, services, and installations that all work together for the growth and functioning of a system, in this case, the communications center. The reliability and consistency of the communications system operations are only as good as the system's weakest link. Take steps to make certain the communications center is not that weak link.

Determine whether the site is in, or near, a flood plain. Planning departments and municipal engineering departments usually have maps that depict areas that would be affected by a "100-year" storm. Use these documents with some degree of caution. With all the development and construction that have taken place during the last 15 years, it is not clear exactly how precise and accurate these maps are.

Lightning protection is a high-profile site consideration. Most often, lightning protection is considered from a building or structure protection point of view. In a communications center setting, it is most important that the complex's or site's protection be addressed. Use caution when drawing up specifications for new construction. Few architects and few general engineering firms are qualified to address complex lightning protection topics. Seek qualified specialists if the lightning threat is significant in the geographic area.

Building construction

A discussion of building construction includes any structure associated with the communications system function. Not only is the integrity of the communications center main building of concern, but equally important are transmitter buildings, auxiliary power enclosures, vehicle protection facilities, and all other facilities. From time to time, the term *radio shack* enters conversations between technicians. The term "radio shack" is jargon for a radio communications equipment shelter.

The structural design of the building determines its resistance to failure brought on by manmade or natural catastrophes. There is a tendency to design structures to the model building codes. In the case of communications centers, the model building codes may not provide adequate design criteria, because they represent **minimum** design practices. Depending on the geographic locations, the buildings' resistance to wind and storm damage or earthquake movement becomes very important. Finally, be aware that most model building codes call for higher quality construction in communications facilities than they do for structures that have similar occupancy classifications.

The geometric shape of the building determines its resistance to wind. Communications centers typically are classified as *commercial buildings* by designers and users. Unfortunately, throughout most of the United States commercial buildings are outfitted with flat roofs. Flat roofs are among the most wind-vulnerable roof configurations, but initially are economical to construct on a new structure.

New and existing buildings are required by law to comply with requirements for handicapped-accessible features and functions. If the building has more than one floor, elevator facilities are needed. Before undertaking a remodeling of an existing structure or building a new structure, it is important that the communications center manager make certain that designers confer with local building department officials to determine exactly what handicapped-accessible features are applied in that locale, and how they are interpreted. This meeting is called a *preconstruction conference.*

Site and building features that provide security from hostile human elements are more or less important, depending on the nature of the community. As a general rule, the more people the facility serves, the more attention should be paid to this feature. There are many ways of looking at this kind of security. Placement of fences, motor vehicle entry and exiting, parking, shift change capacity, and vulnerability of the building to siege are important.

Evaluate existing or potential structures with respect to the following environmental terms.

- *Wind.* Is the construction sturdy enough to withstand peak wind expectations with little or no damage? Are the structures in the complex situated so they are not exposed to falling trees?
- *Water.* Is the structure so situated as to be safe from rising waters that could threaten the actual operations in the structure?
- *Lightning.* While there is some advantage to placing the communications building on a hill, does this make it more vulnerable to lightning strikes?

Infrastructure integrity

Public or private electric utility companies most often provide day-to-day power to communications centers and outlying communications system buildings. There are guidelines that dictate how this power is supplied and the routes it should follow. The public utilities should supply power from two directions. If this is not practical, then emergency power systems must be installed on site.

Emergency power usually is provided by diesel- or gasoline-powered engine generator sets. It also is a common practice to use natural or liquefied petroleum gas (LPG). In fact, as environmental considerations and regulations regarding underground petroleum product storage tanks contribute to operating costs, natural and LPG are becoming attractive primary fuel sources.

The engine generator sets consist of an internal combustion engine mechanically connected to an electrical generator, more commonly called an *alternator*. The engine driving speed is carefully controlled by a speed governor to make certain the output voltage and current of the generator half of the assembly are very close to 60 Hertz, or in other terminology, 60 cycles per second.

The engine generator set must be selected carefully. Some of the considerations are:

- How much of the communications center does the management want on emergency power, the entire center or selected circuits?
- Does the engine generator set have enough reserve power to supply high-starting-demand appliances, like air conditioners, heating/ventilating and air conditioning air movers (fans)?
- Is the engine generator set certified for continuous commercial duty service?
- Is the published frequency stability of the engine generator set compatible with other communications equipment? This stability becomes more important when electronic data processing or computer-aided dispatch systems take power directly from the voltage generated by the engine generator. Often, computer-related equipment relies on the power line frequency for some timing operations. This dependence disappears when the computer electronic system derives its power from what is called *Uninterruptable Power Supply (UPS)*. It is not practical to state a hard and fast rule for the engine generator frequency stability in this kind of handbook. However, it is important for a communication system manager to inspect the particular system at hand and use professional assistance during planning stages.

When planning an expansion of a communication center or facility powered by an engine generator, it is wise to request the assistance of a qualified generator supplier or an engineer in determining generator sizing. Any facility that has an electric-motor-driven fire pump must ensure that the engine generator can provide current to the pump motor during what is called a *locked-rotor* operating condition. This demands a particularly sturdy generator.

Where the engine generator is located is another consideration. Place it at an elevation high enough that even extraordinary rainfall or flooding conditions will not jeopardize reliable operation. If there is any question about the security of the generator from flooding, place a dike around the generator assembly. If flooding does occur, a high-capacity pump can be placed inside the dike area and used as necessary, or in conjunction with a high-water-level detection device, to pump water out of the dike enclosure. However, the best approach to generator reliability is to locate the generator where water intrusion is unlikely.

Select a fuel supply that has a low likelihood of becoming difficult to obtain or transport during an emergency. Do not use a fuel supplied by public utility companies if the fuel is not stored entirely on site. Put another way, do not use natural gas or an equivalent if the fuel is provided from pipes in the public right-of-way. In a disaster situation there is no control over the reliability of service. There is no control over the certainty of repair of piping from the central serving point. Use diesel, gasoline, or liquid petroleum gases (LPG). Store a quantity of fuel sufficient to support full load operating conditions for a minimum of 72 hours.

Potable water

During an emergency, potable water is necessary to support the maximum number of communications center personnel required to keep the site operating for at least 72 hours without outside deliveries. While drinking water is certainly a concern, water for showers, normal hand washing, and food preparation is included in this calculation. Whether toilet water is included in the potable water supply depends on whether the emergency operations toilet facilities are the normal toilets or chemical toilets.

In any case, it is obvious that this water must be stored on site. Local building officials or the plumbing industry in the region can provide information on how many gallons are needed per person per day. The cache of water needs a safe storage site and frequent changing so the water supply is not a threat to the users when the emergency occurs. Careful consideration is needed regarding the reliability of the routinely provided waste disposal systems. Septic tanks and drain fields are sensitive to flooding conditions. Public waste systems that are highly dependent on lift stations in the vicinity of the communications center need reliable electrical power to operate. The manager must be knowledgeable about the reliability of the public waste system.

Fire control and other damage control features

A communications center is not exactly a facility that can be evacuated easily without adverse, even disasterous, results. A fire in a busy communications center becomes not only a threat to the emergency communications operation itself, but also a grave threat to the community it serves. Therefore, including appropriate and reasonable automatic fire protection systems becomes a mandatory feature, without regard to whether it is required by the local building code or not. The design goal is for the internal suppression system to control or suppress the fire completely until the public fire department arrives.

The fundamentals of fire control are to *protect* or to *separate*. To *protect* implies the installation of automatic suppression systems. To *separate* means to place physical barriers between one part of the building and the others so fire and products of combustion cannot spread to critical parts of the building. Portable fire extinguishers must be selected carefully and placed to suppress a fire quickly. The number of fire extinguishers also must be adequate. And the presence of portable fire extinguishing devices is meaningless unless employees are trained to use them competently.

Damage control is a concept that applies broadly to the need to anticipate possible infrastructure, structure, and system failure. The need for fire protection and damage control is very evident in the case of ships because of limited opportunities for occupants to escape safely or move to areas of refuge. Upon reflecting on the nature of a communications center, the same holds true.

Roof assemblies must be designed to withstand wind, water, snow, and other extreme weather conditions. It is not appropriate to allow the design criteria of the model building codes to determine the quality of construction. Remember, these codes set minimum design criteria.

Antenna tower system

Antenna and tower systems are considered later in this chapter from a signal radiating viewpoint. However, in this section they are considered as a part of the complex physical plant.

In almost every case, the antenna tower is a critical part of the communications system path. It performs no actual electrical function; rather, it lifts the radiating antenna elements to the height for adequate radio signal coverage of the service area. Where these towers are placed relative to the communications center is important for several reasons.

- The tower must be close enough to the transmitting and receiving equipment to prevent excessive signal losses in the coaxial cable that extends between the transmitting and receiving equipment on the ground and the antenna high in the air.
- Since the tower is connected to the communications center by electrical conductors, a tower remote from the communications center consoles or transmitters and receivers presents a difficult lightning protection design problem. The closer the tower is to the communications center building, the easier the lightning protection problem becomes. Given that this is a very complicated topic, a qualified lightning protection

specialist should be consulted if the communications center manager wants to pursue the matter. Lightning protection service companies and technicians should not be confused with electrical contractors. Local or state building officials can usually supply a list of contractors licensed as lightning control specialists. If this source of information is not available, check the local or regional telephone directory listings under "lightning protection." Interview several potential contractors. Finally, above all else, ask for references and talk with these individuals to determine their level of satisfaction.

The antenna tower design approach determines how much real estate is necessary to support the tower. While guyed towers have a larger footprint than self-supporting towers, self-supporting towers cost more per 100 feet of height.

Since antenna support is a critical link in system reliability, it is important to consider radio system security as it relates to the vulnerability of the tower to sabotage. The self-supporting tower is much less susceptible to intentional damage since it is easier to place all supporting elements inside a safe compound. The wide-ranging supporting guy wires of the guyed antenna offer more opportunity for undetected cutting of the wire guys.

Selecting an appropriate antenna, or antenna system, is one of the most important tasks associated with radio communications systems. Each antenna system installation is unique, with its own radiation pattern. The overall radio communications system antenna design merits a high attention to detail. It likewise is important to place adequate emphasis on mobile radio antenna installation practices and the selection of hand-held radio antennas.

Emergency supplies

While a communications center may project an office-like atmosphere, it requires more logistical support than an office. In most cases, the business office does not operate 24 hours a day; it can shut down during weather emergencies when the occupants cannot get to work. This is not true of a communications center.

Regardless of whether a communications center is existing or planned, the following logistical needs must be met:

- Food. The manager must estimate the length of time the center might be inaccessible. Adequate provisions to support the building population for 72 hours is a starting point.
- Water. In addition to required drinking water, water for washing, cooking, and toilet facilities also is required!
- Sanitation. While the need to address sanitation problems is obvious,

the solutions are not always easy to accomplish. Flooding conditions present perhaps one of the most frustrating challenges to efficient handling of sewage. Access to chemical toilets during these periods is a quick and efficient solution. Keep in mind, however, that these appliances need a source of clean water to keep them working.

- Consumables. This topic covers a broad spectrum of commodities. Napkins, towels, toilet paper, personal hygiene products, paper plates, and plastic knives, forks, and spoons (to conserve dishwater) are just a few of the items the communications center must stock. These items are mentioned here to encourage the communications center management to consider specifically what consumables typically are used, and what might be placed in service to reduce the loading on other emergency storage requirements.
- Personal comfort features. Assuming a typical stay of 72 hours, the communications center worker needs, indeed, expects, some level of rehabilitation. Personal comfort extends to sleeping facilities, eating facilities, some minimal level of entertainment, and an assortment of games, televisions, radios, or other items to divert the attention of the resting worker. Television, or entertainment radio, for that matter, might not be available. Do not rely on these features exclusively to help pass the resting worker's time.

When planning rehabilitation and personal comfort features, have the plan reflect that the communications center site might be inaccessible. Heavy snow, flood waters, and roads obstructed by downed trees and power poles could isolate the center for several days. Frequently, public officials and administrators attempt to turn communication centers into showpieces. They often are placed in high-visibility locations, in structures that have more symbolic value than substance. Consider taking a page from military strategy principles—communication centers should be designed to be a "combat-hardened site."

It is not always prudent to locate a communications center in the middle of the business section of a metropolitan city. Give top priority to convenient access to the center during times of civil disorder or natural disaster. Evaluate carefully where in a building the center is located. Avoid basements that can flood, and avoid upper levels of high-rise buildings where natural disasters or building fires can expose and interrupt communications center operations.

TELECOMMUNICATIONS

General

Another element of a communications system, and a communications center, is the telephone communications element. For the most part, the first

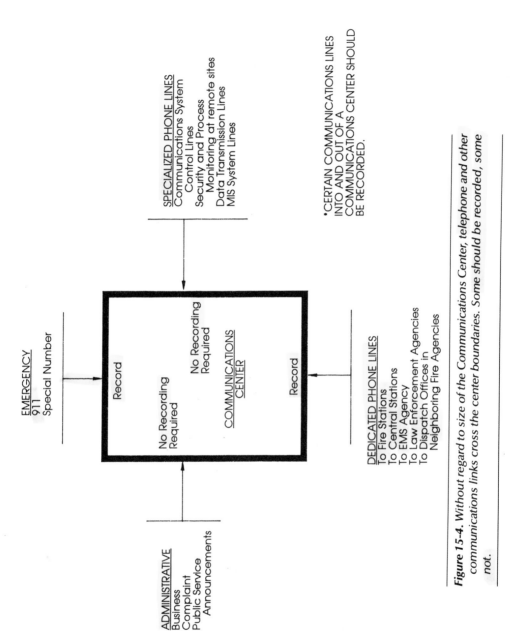

Figure 15-4. *Without regard to size of the Communications Center, telephone and other communications links cross the center boundaries. Some should be recorded, some not.*

impression of the emergency organization as a whole is conveyed by telephone. Certainly in the case of calls for emergency service, the orderliness and precision with which the dispatch office addresses the needs of the caller establishes the disposition of the caller toward the total organization. If an engine company makes an error during firefighting, it is unlikely that anyone outside the fire service will notice. However, a stumble in call-taking interpersonal relations often causes a media event. It is more orderly to evaluate an existing center or plan for a proposed center if the telecommunications plan is broken down into categories, after which reliability requirements and failure priorities are assigned.

There are two fundamental types of telephone circuits in a communications center: *administrative* lines, and *operations* lines. The operations telephone lines can be further broken down into *emergency* and *nonemergency* lines.

Administrative telecommunications

Regardless of the size of the organization, nonemergency calls take place in a communications center.

The technical arrangement of the telephone lines that serve an administrative section of a communications center often does not receive enough thought. First, a policy decision is necessary. As the manager of the center, determine (with respect to the administrative lines) whether you want your client to receive a circuit *busy signal* or whether you want your client to receive a telephone *ringing signal*. Each has a psychological effect on the calling party. Depending on the number of telephone *answering personnel* available in the center, it is conceivable the answering employees might become overloaded because of too many incoming calls. Now comes the policy decision. Do you want your client to listen to an unanswered ring signal, or a busy signal? Most clients appear to interpret an unanswered ring signal as an inattention to telephones. A busy signal on the other hand, while irritating, seems to imply a busy staff.

To determine the telephone traffic loading, create a telephone traffic log. Look for peak loading, that is, how many peak telephone call hits occur within a 30-second to 60-second time period. The window time element is arbitrary. Determine how long it takes a telephone call taker to either handle a call or hand it off. Ask for assistance from the local telephone company to decide how many *roll-over* lines the center needs. Explain to the telephone company how many simultaneous administrative calls the communications center can accommodate. When that number is reached, explain that a busy signal is desired. In a similar vein, identify the peak number of phone calls likely to be placed inside the facility at the same time. Pass that information on to the telephone analyst. There is more to determining how many incoming and outgoing administrative lines are necessary than a simple educated guess. The local telephone company is equipped to provide competent assistance in analyzing communication center needs.

The *public lines* are those lines randomly accessed by the general clients. *Dedicated lines* are those which might be necessary between the communications center and other fire agency facilities, FAX lines, and administrative data lines. Identify these telephone lines, their application, and the frequency with which they are used. If the lines are not in use constantly, perhaps a single unpublished phone line could serve multiple activities, such as FAX and administrative computer modem lines.

Many fire departments have installed *intercoms* in each fire station. The intercom feature allows station personnel to talk with one another, with headquarters, and with the communications center without using a dial telephone line. By simply pressing a certain number or button, one station can talk back and forth with another station or other facility. Some fire departments make the initial alarm dispatch over an intercommunications circuit rather than a radio circuit. The choice can be simply a procedural decision or one based on the relative reliability of the radio or telecommunications system.

The ability to "get the word out to the troops" is very important in fire department management. The very nature of fire departments implies facilities spread out over wide geographic areas. Training and information dissemination often is accomplished by using *teleconferencing systems.* Some departments, large and small, use video transmission systems. These systems lend themselves well to training opportunities as well as information dissemination.

The modern fire department is equipped with data handling and processing equipment of various types. For the most part, the communication among computer equipment in fire stations, repair shops, headquarters, and the communications center is accomplished using telecommunications wire lines. *Modems* are used to connect the computing equipment to the wire lines. A modem is needed at each end of the wire line circuit.

Many fire departments take advantage of a fire-service-related *bulletin board* called ICHIEFS, offered by International Association of Fire Chiefs. Bulletin boards allow users to talk to one another by computer, and leave messages for other users with what is called a *mailbox* feature. Or, one user can leave a message for the entire membership of a bulletin board. Fire-protection-related databases are available on these bulletin boards.

Wire lines provide the transmission path for FAX machines. This technology has changed the way many fire departments do business. FAX machines speed up the transmission of department recordkeeping by allowing instant transmission of policies and procedures and training, and attendance records.

Emergency telephone circuits

The emergency telephone circuits are the most important. They are the heart of the communications center. Close inspection of the emergency telephone circuits identifies the following types: *fire alarm signaling circuits* and *critical communications signaling and control circuits.*

Fire Alarm Circuits

This class of telephone circuits is made up of several similar, yet different, categories. *Central station, proprietary station,* and *street box* telephone lines fall under the category of fire alarm circuits.

Central stations monitor the condition of *fire protection systems* in distant structures, occupancies, or complexes. These monitoring facilities are normally private sector companies operating in specially designed facilities. In some cases, usually in smaller departments, the fire department performs central station monitoring. In other cases, fire departments are relieving themselves of this function.

Central stations, according to national standards, provide certain services to the fire department. There are detailed standards for the actions the central station takes when signals of various types are received from the protected premises. Communications centers define the procedures and policies regarding interface with the central stations in accordance with these national standards.

Proprietary stations monitor the condition of *fire protection systems* in structures, occupancies, or complexes that belong to the corporation which is performing the monitoring. Other than that specific difference, the proprietary station facilities and functions are very similar to those of the central station. The communications center establishes procedures and policies which identify the actions to be taken on the part of the proprietary station and the communications center. These policies are established in national standards.

Street box fire alarm circuits exist principally in older communities. They originally were installed because of the lack of telephone service and instruments in neighborhoods and business areas. The proliferation of telephone service, even in the most financially disadvantaged neighborhoods, has diminished the need for the street box. In many cases fire departments themselves supported line maintenance crews to keep the circuits operating. Subsequently these responsibilities were turned over to the commercial telephone companies. Now, radio transmitters in street boxes eliminate entirely the need for telephone lines.

In any case, if these services and responsibilities are present in the communications center it is appropriate to identify a special telephone number, or set of numbers, to service the central stations and proprietary stations. In all cases, the level of reliability assigned to these telephone circuits must be higher than that of communications administrative lines. It is very convenient and efficient for central stations and proprietary stations to have special circuits identified and set aside for communications between the monitoring services and the communications center. This is accomplished by establishing an unpublished telephone number for them to use when they notify the fire department of an alarm.

Critical Signaling and Control Circuits

Often, the less visible telecommunications circuits are overlooked. In very many cases the radio system transmitters and receivers are remote from the communications centers. In those cases where repeater transmitters and *satellite* or *voting* receivers are part of the radio system, telecommunications wire lines are a vital part of system reliability. The priority of these telecommunications circuits is higher than that of the general administration circuits.

Not only do wire line telecommunications circuits carry the voice and data transmission and receptions, but in many cases, separate wire circuits carry the control commands for the radio communications equipment. The command to turn a transmitter on or off is performed by digital command. The operating conditions of transmitters and receivers are in many cases reported to communications operation centers by means of digital signals on wire lines.

It is not true that the entire path of voice, data, and control functions is via wire lines. But it is true that a significant amount of the path is made up of wire circuits. The reliability of these circuits is critical to the communications center management.

Communications center managers take measures to be aware of the circuit conditions. Information on circuit numbers and routing also must be carefully recorded and kept handy in the communications center operations section.

DISPATCH ELEMENTS

The total process of responding to a fire or medical incident is a relatively complicated one. A look at the *time-temperature curve* of a model fire shows that burning activity occurs before either automatic fire protection systems signal for assistance or the burning becomes obvious on the exterior of a building. Modern building construction methods can assist in or deter early detection. Even energy-saving features in building construction delay visual, external detection of a fire event.

Calls for service processing

Fire Incident
A fire incident does not start with notification to the fire department. It

is more complicated than that. The elements of fire progress appear to be the following:

1. Ignition occurs.
2. Process of burning expands in all directions, fire and smoke plume propagates upward and outward when horizontal barrier reached.
3. If automatic detection devices are present, signal sent.
   - Signal sent to a monitoring station where operator determines nature of signal and calls public fire department. This same process occurs in private residences when occupant hears the automatic signaling device.
   - Public fire department verifies the central station call for service and subsequently determines proper response pattern in terms of apparatus and manpower.
4. If automatic detection devices are not present,
   - Fire burn continues until smoke or visible flame shows on the exterior of the structure.
   - Random passerby observes the condition, assesses the actual meaning of the signs.

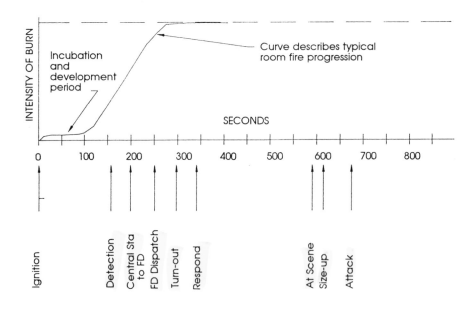

Figure 15-5. *Rapid handling of calls for emergency service is a must for Communications Centers. Fire expands in an exponential manner. The process of responding to a fire incident is more than traveling over the road.*

- Passerby locates some kind of signaling device such as a street box or, more likely, a telephone and calls the fire department.
- Call taker/dispatcher at fire department interviews the caller to determine all information necessary to determine proper response of fire and other emergency equipment.

  5. Notification made to proper responders by what is typically called a *fire alarm dispatch.*
  6. Responders in remote fire stations react to dispatch. Proper protective equipment is donned, and fire apparatus is mounted and driven from station. This is commonly called the turn-out period.
  7. Over-the-road response. This time element depends on the time of day, environmental conditions, and distance of fire incident from station. Fire dispatchers assist the responders while on the road, making certain they arrive at the scene in a safe and timely fashion.
  8. Arrival at scene, assessment of situation, deployment of suppression agent equipment and supply lines, entry and location of the fire incident, and application of suppression agent to the seat of the fire. Fire dispatchers monitor fire scene activities to assist with additional resources. Provide monitoring of elapsed time during the event. Listen for radio transmissions that might be missed by scene supervision.
  9. Fire growth and spread brought under control.
  10. Fire declared out, equipment leaves scene, check with communications center for proper incident numbers, times, or other information required by fire department policy and procedures.

A review of the 10 steps listed above shows heavy activity by the communications center. The timeliness of the incident handling depends on efficient and quick actions on the part of the communications center. To assess the efficiency of the fire suppression response system, the communications manager outlines the timing involved in each of the steps above. The manager modifies the model above to include other steps in local policies and procedures. Then the manager makes an attempt to shorten, by whatever means, the time required to perform the tasks. The goal is to shorten the time between receipt of a call for service and dispatch of resources. At the point of dispatch receipt, the time required to arrive on the scene is, for the most part, in the hands of fire department operations.

Medical (EMS) Calls for Service

The medical assistance response system configuration is determined in a manner very similar to the fire incident analysis. An after-event arrival on the scene of four to six minutes is a practical design criterion. Obviously it cannot always be met. Use the same time analysis charting (10 steps) shown above to determine where significant reductions in medical responses are necessary in the response system.

After all, it is not effective to cut a 5-second process in half, claiming a 50 percent reduction in a response task, if another part of the dispatch task takes 3 minutes. Go for the lengthy process first and cut it as much as possible.

Computer-Aided Dispatch

Often referred to as CAD, there are other technical meanings for CAD. Even in the fire protection industry, CAD also can be an acronym for Computer-Aided Design used in fire apparatus design, cartography, and other engineering applications.

There are many computer-aided dispatch packages on the market. Managers, fire chiefs, and design personnel all hold numerous seminars, meetings, and symposia on the topic. Yet for all practical purposes CAD exists principally in the mind of the person speaking.

CAD can perform a large number of tasks. What makes it a topic to discuss is defining the spectrum of tasks the purchaser wishes to perform.

There are two approaches to CAD. A prospective user must determine whether the system should be principally a computer dispatch system, or a computer-aided dispatch system. Technology is available today, and will become commonplace in the future, to fulfill both approaches.

The *computer dispatch system* depends principally on the computer to perform the following tasks:

- Identify the calling location.
- Identify the type of call.
- Identify the response pattern.
- Locate the nearest available equipment to the address and prepare a dispatch order.
- Present the dispatch order to a communications center operator for approval.
- Upon receipt of approval, proceed with the dispatch order.
- Await confirmation from the apparatus that the dispatch order was received.
- Perform all appropriate time-stampings to this point.
- Receive information from arriving units regarding the nature and severity of the incident.
- Receive requests for additional equipment or special apparatus from field units.
- Prepare a dispatch for approval by the communications center operator.
- Upon receipt of approval, proceed with the dispatch order.
- If the incident is severe enough, proceed with *move-ups,* otherwise known as *fill-ins* or *relocations.*
- Bring the incident to conclusion by communicating with field appara-

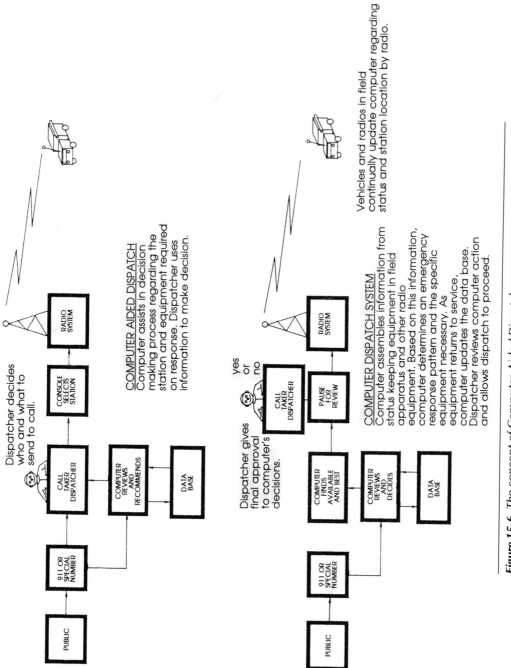

Figure 15-6. *The concept of Computer-Aided Dispatch encompasses more than simple systems that recommend actions to dispatchers.*

tus. This involves releasing move-ups as regular equipment returns to service.

All of these activities take place based on previously programmed response patterns and time/distance criteria. Most of the communication takes place using digital messages. Field apparatus make free use of mobile data terminals.

A more commonly used approach to computer application in dispatch is called *computer-aided dispatch*. Dispatchers are the principal decisionmakers. Their decisions are based on a series of quickly displayed resource information messages provided by computers. The computer-aided dispatch system has the following distinguishing characteristics:

- The computer identifies the calling location.
- The type of call is received by the call taker or dispatcher who *inputs* the information into the computer. Upon reviewing the dispatcher's analysis of call type, and the location of the call, which is automatically fed to the computer's central processing unit (CPU), the computer recommends a response pattern.
- The dispatcher reviews the recommendations, makes changes to the dispatch patterns and the recommended units as required, then moves on to the radio or intercom dispatch process.
- The dispatcher makes the announcement to the selected response units. This announcement is made either by voice or by digital transmission.
- As the units respond from the fire station or from their locations in the field, the apparatus report their status by voice or digital transmission. If the status is reported by voice transmission, the dispatcher feeds this information to the computer. The computer then updates the visual displays to the dispatch personnel. If the response from the field units is by digital transmission, then the computer might be updated automatically by the radio system. In other cases, the digital response is displayed visually to the dispatchers who, in turn, manually feed the information to the computer.

There are many possible variations of this dispatch process description. The intent here is to give an example of the difference in approach. There are many variations and combinations in between.

Expanded Use of Computer-Aided Dispatch
The extended or expanded applications of the CAD system are almost endless because of the extreme flexibility of computer software.

As the apparatus is responding to any type of call, it is a great help to receive from the communications center additional information that may be either extended or expanded applications of the CAD system.

Additional information may be received in the dispatch office because of additional phone calls from the scene. Reports from central stations or proprietary stations may report additional internal fire protection system activations. This gives a clue to an expanding emergency. Dispatchers may look at ancillary files and provide information on structure features or hazardous materials stored in the occupancy.

Ancillary Files

There is an almost endless list of ancillary or supporting files a communications center can access to enhance field operations. Consider the following examples:

- **Prefire Planning Information**

    Virtually every fire department engages in some level of prefire planning. The most significant difficulty experienced by field operations is orderly access to the information. Keeping information timely is another planning and logistics problem. Many fire department operations sections decided that keeping prefire information in orderly, quickly updated computer files is operationally practical. Experienced commanders concede that asking a dispatcher for assistance is often more advantageous than paging through voluminous three-ring binders in adverse weather and lighting conditions.

- **Hazardous Materials Information**

    Hazardous materials constitute one of the most talked-about operational problems facing field operations and one of the most difficult to manage. If the fire department insists on keeping information on occupancy hazardous materials in the operations section, where the data shall be kept, and how these data will be kept up to date become serious data management problems. A properly designed database, maintained by field operations, and accessible to the communications center, is a good compromise. Of course, the obvious flaw is the timeliness and accuracy of the information given the quick turnover of hazardous materials in most occupancies. However, the point here is to establish the fact that this database can be set up, can be maintained by field operations, and the database accessed by the communications center for distribution to the field by voice or digital communications.

- **Building Ownership Contacts**

    Activations of fire protection systems in buildings frequently require field operations companies to force entry. When it is time to secure the structure, building contacts are needed. This information is most conveniently kept in the communications center where frequent database maintenance is performed by either the communications center personnel or field operations personnel.

These are simply examples of the information and data that a computer-aided dispatch system can include. Other examples of databases are central station telephone and first-responder telephone lists, resources relative to emergency medical services, and SARA Title III information. Only need and imagination limit the number of databases a computer-aided dispatch system might access.

911 SYSTEMS

The 911 system provides the public with a quick, convenient method of summoning emergency services. Based on a common model used throughout much of the nation, 911 systems often are managed by agencies other than the fire department organization. In fact, law enforcement agencies usually have more influence over 911 system direction and management than do fire agencies.

In public information, education, and relations activities, do not underestimate the need to emphasize to the public that the number to be dialed is "nine-one-one." Repeated references to "nine-eleven" in public relations programs and media exposure have resulted in recorded examples of frustrated members of the public attempting to locate the number "11" on the telephone keypad.

SYSTEM CONFIGURATIONS

There are two configurations of 911 systems. The 911 system is strictly an emergency telephone call-receiving system. Calls for service are received and processed by operators in a *Public Safety Answering Point* (PSAP).

One type is the simple 911 system. In this configuration, any call from any telephone within a 911 coverage area accesses a central PSAP, or PSAPs, when the numbers 9, then 1, then 1, are pressed on a telephone keypad. While the calling party may have no idea which political jurisdiction provides emergency service, the 911 call is automatically routed to the proper PSAP. The call-taking and dispatch personnel at the PSAP make certain the proper jurisdiction then responds. The dispatch personnel send the emergency equipment to the addressed provided by the calling party.

A second configuration is called E-911, or *Enhanced 911*. In this configuration all the actions described above occur. In addition, the telephone number of the telephone line used during the call, and the address of the telephone line are displayed on a small television-like screen in front of the operator. Typical operating procedures call for the receiving telephone operator to ask for the name, address, and phone number of the calling party. The operator compares the verbal responses of the calling party against the display on the screen in front of him to verify the call.

MANAGEMENT AND OPERATIONS

It is common to find more than one PSAP in a medium to large-size 911 system. For example, if there are several medium to large municipalities within a county or region, each of the police departments in the municipalities could be expected to have a PSAP. A PSAP commonly exists when a political jurisdiction determines that phone calls for citizens in that jurisdiction should terminate at a law enforcement agency serving that jurisdiction alone. Fire department communication centers commonly receive calls for service from that jurisdiction through PSAPs set up for law enforcement.

ELEMENTS OF A 911 SYSTEM

Management

Local government is the principal supplier and supervisor of personnel for 911 general management and call taking. Normally a 911 manager oversees the business relationship between the jurisdiction and the private sector telecommunications company. The manager also supervises a section of one or more employees who keep the 911 system street and development database up to date. Every time a street is added to the jurisdiction's inventory, the 911 system database must reflect that change. Most 911 systems include a built-in method by which the 911 manager can access the 911 computer and make adjustments. This function is extremely vital to the credibility and reliability of the entire 911 system. Therefore, appropriate resources, working area, and assignment of dedicated responsible personnel are absolutely necessary.

Operations

Depending on the size of the jurisdiction 911 call takers may or may not, be dedicated strictly to that function. In other words, the 911 call takers do not perform law enforcement or fire and EMS services dispatching. On the other hand, in relatively small jurisdictions where the call-taking workload does not warrant such specific duties, the dispatch personnel also may function as 911 call takers.

Hardware

The enhanced 911 system provides the call taker or dispatcher with a cathode ray tube (CRT), or television-type screen, typed readout of the calling telephone number and the address of the telephone location. These features become invaluable in cases where the caller is not certain of his location, becomes incapable of carrying on a conversation because of physical or mental distress, or where the telephone system fails during the early stages of the telephone conversation. These are simply some of the reasons why what is called an *E-911* system is superior to a regular 911 system. In law enforcement settings many implied messages can be transmitted in hostage settings. However, that is not the point of this discussion.

Hardware can be provided by local telecommunications system providers. 911 hardware systems are best characterized as part of a commercial telecommunications system. On the other hand, the public sector can purchase hardware systems which are subsequently integrated into the commercial telecommunications system. Management of this process is achieved under agreements between the 911 system's management and the local telecommunications provider. Certainly, all the communications media, such as wire lines, microwave, and other carriers of 911 communications, are under the control of the private telecommunications agency.

Signaling circuits and maintenance

The 911 system's integrity is critically important. Therefore, definite responsibility for the condition and repair of the signaling circuits falls to the private sector telecommunications company. The public sector 911 manager and the private sector telecommunications company must communicate continuously and with care regarding the physical condition and capacity of the system.

The feature of E-911, that of local display of the calling telephone number and address of the telephone, can be used in computer-aided dispatch systems. The digital signal at the communications center 911 hardware can be *patched* over to the CAD system. This information can, if desired, become part of a newly assigned incident number. This eliminates the time lost when dispatchers must type onto the incident screen. This information often is inserted into another database, from which all hard copy incident reports are generated. This reduces the amount of clerical time required to generate this public record. It also reduces the probability of error brought on by typing the information incorrectly.

FUNDING

As with virtually every other service function in the communications industry, there must be a source of revenue to carry out these services. There are a number of different sources possible for the funding of a 911 department. *Ad valorem* taxes or telephone user fees serve as typical revenue sources.

Many 911 departments use a combination of tax and fee revenues to fund operations.

The tax method is relatively straightforward.

A fee-revenue-gathering approach might be charges added to every telephone instrument, or some similar plan. This revenue-gathering method is indeed a fee and not a tax. It provides for a nominal monthly surcharge on telephone lines or on telephone instruments to support 911 operations. Other uses for this fee might be to provide a sinking fund to permit orderly replacement or addition of equipment as the jurisdiction grows.

An innovative fee revenue source proposed by some jurisdictions is an automatic charge attached to each conviction of a moving traffic violation. This fee is predicated on the fact that the moving traffic law violator has a tendency to cause motor vehicle accidents. Motor vehicle accidents and the injuries they cause are a great part of 911 traffic.

Legislative action to establish a nuisance fire and burglary alarm fee schedule represents another way to generate funds. This process consists of identifying a schedule of charges for owners of fire alarm and burglar alarm systems that generate an excessive number of calls for service from the installed systems. This process must be carefully thought out from a public relations point of view. Also, the costs to support the "fine" accounts-receivable section must be factored into any determination of significant net financial recovery.

COMMUNICATIONS SYSTEMS CONFIGURATIONS

At one time in the past there were no real choices available in radio communication system configurations. Now there are two generic communications radio communications system configurations: one is known as the conventional radio system configuration; the other is called the trunking radio system configuration.

Conventional radio system

The conventional radio system is the fire service radio system that was provided to users in the 1960s and 1970s. For all practical considerations there was no other choice.

The major distinguishing characteristic of a conventional radio system is the assignment of a specific radio frequency to a specific user. Put another way, when the using agency makes a radio transmission, the frequency on which the transmission is made is predictable from one time to the next unless the dispatcher takes some action to change to another assigned frequency. The following illustration presents an example of a simple conventional radio sys-

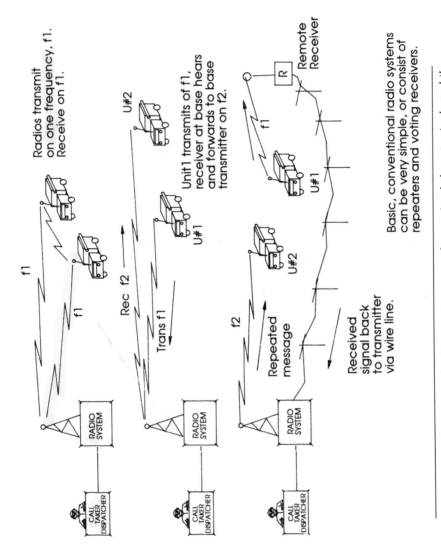

Figure 15-7. Radio communications systems range from a simple base to single mobile unit to complicated transmitter repeaters and voting, or satellite, receivers.

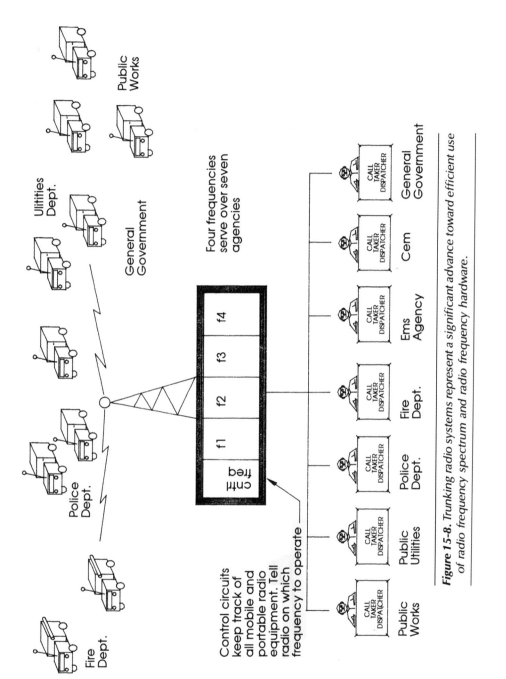

Figure 15-8. *Trunking radio systems represent a significant advance toward efficient use of radio frequency spectrum and radio frequency hardware.*

tem. Note that in this case the transmitters and receivers serve only one branch of public service agency.

There are many ways to expand and vary the conventional radio system configuration. In one variation, the addition of repeating transmitters increases the coverage of hand-held and mobile radio transmitters. Another variation adds *voting receivers,* also called *satellite receivers,* to the conventional radio system. Regardless of the variations, the system transmission frequency is predictable and dedicated to one service.

Trunking radio communications systems

The application of trunking technology in communications systems is not new. The telephone industry long ago employed this technology. Most of the currently available radio spectrum is overloaded and unable to accept more radio traffic.

Recently, radio communications channels have become available in the 800-MHz and 900-MHz region. Since there is an insufficient radio spectrum to permit each user to have exclusive use of an assigned radio frequency, trunking principles, such as those used in the telephone industry, were applied to the radio communications process.

Some of the most important distinguishing characteristics of a radio trunking system are:

* There are more users than there are radio frequency channels in the radio system.
* The frequency or channel on which a given transmission takes place is determined by the trunking system controller. As the communications system call loading changes, the conversations are moved from channel to channel as the system controller deems necessary. In the normal course of events dispatchers do not decide which frequency is used; the trunking system controller changes the frequency quietly and smoothly in the background.
* Priorities are assigned to the system users in the event the system suffers a peak demand for communication time. Depending on the assigned priority, a user may or may not have absolute access to system air time. For instance, during a period of high demand for air time, such as a widespread wind, snow, and ice emergency, public safety agencies are guaranteed access and air time, while lower-priority agencies, such as building departments or certain administrative agencies may experience system busy signals for some period of time. The principle is the same in telephone service. When one subscriber calls another subscriber, and the second subscriber is using the phone, a busy signal results. A second kind of busy signal occurs when one subscriber decides to call another

and all the paths in the *trunk lines* between the two subscribers are in use. In this case, a busy signal is experienced by the calling party. This kind of busy signal, trunk busy, typically occurs at a faster rate than a subscriber busy signal. This condition is almost always rectified by hanging up and immediately dialing again. Likewise, the trunking radio system provides a busy signal to the calling radio. When a circuit clears, some radio systems provide notifications to the calling party that a circuit is now clear.

Radio Communications System Elements

Radio communications systems consist of the following building blocks:

- fixed radio, or base units;
- mobile radio units;
- portable, or personal units; and
- specialized equipment such as paging units or medical communications units.

These building blocks are configured by designers of radio systems to meet some kind of system performance specifications. After the system performance specifications have been determined, the subcomponents of the system are defined. Before exploring specifications, it is important to identify the different kinds of building blocks.

Fixed radio or base units

This category of radio equipment includes base transmitters, control consoles, fixed receivers, and satellite equipment. In most cases the base radio transmitters and receivers are located in isolated compartments, attics, small rooms, or even in small buildings distant from the radio room in the fire station or dispatch office. *Control consoles* located in dispatch offices or radio rooms send commands to the remote transmitters and receivers by means of wire cables.

Control consoles contain meters, lights, audio speakers, and various kinds of controls which adjust the volume coming from loudspeakers on the console. Other controls, either push buttons or twist knobs, provide a means for the operator to control the functions of the communications system.

Mobile radio units

Mobile radio units include those pieces of radio equipment installed in a motor vehicle or equivalent. Another distinguishing characteristic of a mobile radio unit is that it is used while the vehicle in which it is installed moves around the service area.

The difference between a mobile radio unit and a fixed radio unit is found principally in the mechanical construction of the unit. Certainly mobile units are subjected to significantly more vibration, mechanical shock, and severe moisture conditions than fixed units. The ability of the electronic units to survive these conditions is one of the most important considerations in mobile unit purchasing.

An important factor in mobile equipment installation is careful consideration of location. The electronics enclosure must be mounted where moisture, heat, cold, or other environmental attacks on the mobile equipment will not cause periodic failure or shorten the life of the equipment.

Virtually all mobile equipment commercially available in today's marketplace is what is called *solid state equipment*. This means *semiconductor* technology is used in the circuit designs. This technology does have its limits with respect to high and low temperatures. The higher the quality and price of the radio equipment the less susceptible it is to temperature variations. Careful attention must be given to the published environmental specifications for the equipment when it is considered for purchase.

Portable or personal radio equipment

Portable radio equipment is characterized mainly by the exclusive use of battery power supplies. In fact, the development of portable equipment was held back for many years because of lagging battery technology. The first portable radio equipment used small vacuum tubes. Vacuum tubes contain elements called *filaments*. Filaments consumed large quantities of energy from the battery supplies. This made portable equipment not only inefficient, but also expensive, because of the need to replace batteries frequently.

Modern semiconductor technology eliminated energy waste in filament power since semiconductors used all power toward useful electronic applications. Heat development in the package allowed higher electronic densities in the design, therefore smaller radio equipment packages.

Portable hand-held radios represent perhaps the most impressive application of semiconductor technology. Portable equipment evolved from units the size of a small bread box to today's palm-sized radio transceivers.

Carefully consider the features of any portable radio equipment purchased. The ideal portable radio unit has only one control, the on-off control.

Understandably, that is not practical. Some radio equipment has what are called *keypads* located on the side of the radio. This keypad permits the user to program the portable unit for many applications. Keypads are frequently found on portable units used in trunking radio systems.

Evaluate the portable radio equipment carefully in light of who will be using it and where it will be used. Portable equipment with many features may not be the best choice. Communications must be reliable and simple in emergency, stress-filled settings such as the fireground. Limited visibility because of smoke conditions, self-contained breathing apparatus, firefighters' gloves and other features of turn-out equipment often make operation of portable equipment difficult. Purchase specifications should address the need for simple controls and careful selection of options on portable radios. Any options selected should be chosen with the ultimate user in mind. In most cases the command officer's portable radio needs more features than the company officer's portable radio. Do not load radios with unnecessarily complicated features.

Specialized radio communications units

Paging systems play a major role in fire service communications. Paging system applications had their beginnings in the volunteer fire service home monitoring radio. When radio replaced telephone "pyramid" calling systems, only technology prevented this communications method from growing. The entrance of semiconductor circuitry into the fire service radio environment speeded the natural progression from home monitor radios to belt pagers.

While the application of belt pagers to volunteer fire departments is evident, there are further applications in career fire departments. Not all career fire departments can afford the luxury of adequate staff on duty. Paid personnel can be called back from off-duty jobs to fire department duty when the emergency workload overruns the on-duty staffing. Historically the American fire service has featured fire department facilities spread out over the response area. This distribution causes key department officers to be on the road for considerable periods of time. These same officers often are required to be in business meetings where it is impractical for fire department radios to be left on. Pagers offer a way to contact these individuals immediately.

Medical communications equipment

While not always identified by the user as radio communications equipment, medical equipment that transmits voice or data signals to medical facilities is indeed part of a radio communications system. It is subject to all the planning and specification details of the more commonly used fire service voice communications circuits. These units often are able to send data transmissions to hospital facilities.

The data transmission contains information about the patient's condition and vital signs. These data are transmitted principally to allow medical personnel at the hospital to diagnose the patient's condition based on the information received. The hospital personnel then are able to give direction to fire department medical personnel in the field. Nevertheless, it is practical to point out that the practice of sending data and waiting for advice is not necessarily increasing in frequency. Many fire departments no longer use this method of patient treatment. As paramedic skills increase, and as confidence in standing medical orders for paramedics is bolstered, paramedics are given the latitude to provide patient care based broadly on patient signs and symptoms. This is mentioned here to provide any manager contemplating the purchase of these medical units appropriate options in patient care delivery.

In conventional radio systems, medical communications almost always are assigned special medical radio frequencies. In trunking radio systems, medical communications are treated the same as any other radio communications. Care and planning are necessary when transmission of data is implemented. High data transmission rates are not always compatible with many existing communications systems. Older FM systems have characteristics that limit data transmission "speeds." Therefore, the manager should consult with the manufacturer of the data transmission equipment and the radio communications equipment to make certain the two systems are compatible. If the radio communications equipment is not compatible, then replacing the radio equipment is usually the only solution for transmitting at higher rates.

Special attention must be paid to the environmental operating conditions under which these medical units must operate. Water, shock, vibration, and other forms of abuse must be identified and considered. Only after these matters have been taken into account can meaningful specifications be written.

Personal or Mobile Communications Systems

It is appropriate to mention that there is a subtle difference between *personal* and *mobile* communications systems. The difference lies in the system performance specifications. Radio communications systems specify predictability and reliability of communications in the following terms.

The communications shall be X percent reliable over Y percent of the service area. Typical numbers for the quantity X range between 90 and 95 percent. Any number can be inserted. The quantity Y number is determined by the need to communicate with high reliability over the entire service area. Typically this number for "Y" ranges between 85 and 95 percent. The most accurate statement regarding the identification of this number is that the user must work with the radio communication system designers to establish a meaningful number. This is a very important economic consideration. As reliability and coverage numbers approach 100 percent, the cost of the system rises astronomically.

With this as background, consider the difference between the communications approaches, specifically personal and mobile communications systems.

A personal communications system contains base transmitters and receivers carefully placed throughout the service area to provide communications to and from hand-held radio communications equipment. The reliability and area coverage are called for in the specifications.

A mobile communications system contains base transmitters and receivers carefully placed throughout the service area to provide communications to and from mobile radio communications equipment. The reliability and area coverage are called for in the specifications.

It is immediately evident that hand-held radio units typically operate at power levels lower than mobile units. Further, the antenna systems are less efficient than mobile units. Therefore, it follows that the cost and difficulty of providing a personal communications system over a mobile system design increase exponentially.

Licensing and coordination

In the United States, radio system licenses are issued by the Federal Communications Commission (FCC). But there are many tasks that must be performed before a license is issued. The process preceding license approval is called *coordination*.

The steps required for coordination today are different than in years past. Years ago frequencies were assigned to individual organizations. The frequency spectrum in which the organization operated depended on the service provided. Coordination consisted of a check of other agencies operating on or near the frequency. This check principally was an attempt to determine whether the geographic separation between the agencies' transmitting antennas would produce minimum interference.

Presently there are very few frequencies available in the VHF region in most regions of the United States. Almost all new radio systems are forced to move to the 800-MHz or 900-MHz spectrum. New radio applications in urban areas are, for the most part, forced to join what might be classified as area trunking radio systems. Coordination and licensing procedures in these cases concentrate on the number of frequencies that an agency or set of agencies might request. The number of radio communications units is reviewed. When and if an agency provides adequate proof of need and adequate proof of a sufficient quantity of radio units, a license is issued.

One of the most delicate and difficult conditions of licensing is the limitation imposed on radiation of transmitted signals outside the assigned radio trunking system geographic area. For instance, the license may stipulate a significantly lowered signal strength three miles outside the assigned system service area. This quantity is measurable on sensitive instruments.

Coordination advice and guidance are available through equipment manufacturers, the International Association of Fire Chiefs (IAFC), and the Association of Police Communications Officers (APCO). Regional fire chiefs associations or police chiefs associations can provide more detail on access.

Specifications

No new system can be purchased and placed in service without some kind of specifications from the owner or user. This principle holds true for upgrades or changes to existing systems. The task of generating specifications for a radio system is tricky. Carefully think the problem through. The perception that it is time for a new radio system because the existing system "is clearly inadequate" is not a good position from which to start.

There are several general principles to keep in mind if a new system is contemplated, or an existing system seems to be deficient. It is necessary to carefully define what is desired, or define the operational problem. Two basic approaches may be taken in the development of specifications: *equipment specifications* and *performance specifications.*

Equipment Specifications

Equipment specifications define the characteristics of the hardware the user wishes to buy. The key word here is *hardware,* not *system.* This kind of specification is used when the user is very certain that inserting the hardware into the system will result in some expected performance.

For example, the fire chief may want to outfit a new sedan or apparatus with a new radio. This vehicle operates in a radio communications system that consists of one or two radio frequencies. This is a relatively simple addition to the radio fleet. He may choose, for his own reasons, to specify the same exact radio found in other apparatus in the fire department fleet. Simply ordering or specifying new equipment identical to other radio equipment used in similar organization applications and making the purchase is an example of equipment specifications.

What are the hazards of this approach? In most cases there are few hazards when the radio system is simple. However, if the existing equipment is older, and radio equipment has not been purchased for awhile, then the existing equipment may be obsolete, no longer manufactured, or otherwise unsuitable for use with newly purchased equipment.

If only one or two pieces of radio apparatus are required, a good, simple approach is to invite field sales representative from several respected manufacturers to visit and provide advice and pricing.

Performance Specifications

When contemplating major modifications to existing systems, or deciding to construct completely new systems, it is always safe to turn to performance specifications. Performance specifications identify what the user *wants the system to do,* that is, *how the system should operate.* Note the use of the word *system,* not *hardware.*

Performance specifications identify the number of field units, hand-held and mobile, the size of the radio service area, and the desired reliability of system communications. Performance specifications describe who will have radios, what each user expects the radio to do, where the radios will be carried or mounted, where the radios will be used, inside or outside, what the user will be wearing, and other considerations. These are only a few of the topics defined in performance specifications.

Summary

Performance specifications represent the safe route for those not knowledgeable in the field of radio communications. The most significant risk in performance specifications is the possibility of overlooking a critical performance criterion in the specification. This often results in quotes or bids from manufacturers of equipment that are not suited for the application. System incompatibility can be the result if the system performance specifications do not state specifically that any newly acquired equipment must work "hand-in-glove" with existing equipment. Because of the high cost of a modern radio system of just about any size, it is prudent to procure outside assistance in making certain the specifications are complete.

There is no absolutely safe way to write and publish specifications. The safest way is to become knowledgeable about radio communications topics. Then it is up to the user to recognize the limits of his knowledge. There is a point at which professional advice and assistance are prudent and reasonable.

Communications system maintenance

Any radio system requires periodic maintenance. Communications systems managers decide how to maintain the system using either in-house or outside radio maintenance.

The efficiency of any radio maintenance service is measured based on:

- response time;
- turnaround time for radio unit repair;
- sensitivity to user needs;
- knowledge of the manager and staff; and
- overall cost to provide the service.

The exact nature of the word *maintenance* can be defined as

- routine scheduled adjustments and service that minimize unforeseen breakdowns in radio equipment.
- installation of radio equipment in motor vehicles or in structures; and
- repair service for mobile, hand-held, and base stations.

As radio frequencies continue to increase into the 800-MHz and 900-MHz region, radio repair becomes as much an art as a science. When radios in these frequencies are subject to repair and component replacement, the repair shop's skill in making certain the components are placed in the radio carefully and "tuned" carefully becomes very important.

In-house Radio Maintenance (Public Sector)

In-house radio maintenance is popular in larger fire departments. Often the fire department has a radio shop. Even more often, the public safety agencies share radio repair services. The common need of public safety agencies for 24-hour service is the basis for this bond.

However, large municipalities and counties often put together a radio service shop to serve the needs of all the divisions and departments in the municipality or county. The determination of how this service is provided and how it is funded usually falls outside the purview of the police and fire departments. The public safety agencies are "charged" some kind of "user's fee" or other method of transferring funds from the public safety agency over to the radio service agency. This is often invisible to the police or fire agency and is performed by what is called a *journal transfer* by fiscal management personnel in still another agency of the municipality or county. Of particular concern are fire agencies which are not part of a municipality or county general fund. There are selected agencies which, through special governing boards, receive revenues through special tax levies. Managers in these agencies must take special care to identify the rationale used in management offices to determine these service costs levied by county or municipality general funds. While most fire departments do not fall into this category, those that are subject to this method of paying *service costs* should be aware of the process. In any case, the quality of management in the *radio shop* determines the cost effectiveness of the public-sector-owned radio repair service.

The effectiveness of the public sector radio service needs continuous review. Many public sector radio service agencies exist today simply because they existed yesterday. Obviously, lack of service level monitoring does not contribute to continued high service levels.

Private Sector Radio Maintenance Service

Private sector radio maintenance shops usually operate as either a local direct representative of major communications equipment manufacturers or as a franchise organization. Operating a radio communications shop requires a considerable amount of capital investment. Test equipment, radio frequency screening rooms, the building itself, and mobile test centers, not to mention the costly inventory of replacement parts, preclude poorly funded, or fly-by-night operations from surviving. Qualified radio technicians also are very difficult to find. They demand reasonably high wages, and often move back and forth between competing companies in a region depending on the wages offered and the skills of the technician. What is the point? The point is that the private sector must fund these costs. The result is high hourly charges to the customer.

If a public sector agency intends to procure services from a private sector maintenance organization, the best approach is to write a contract for services.

Combination In-house and Private Sector Maintenance

Finally, one possible solution to the maintenance problem is a combination service—part from the private sector, part from the public sector.

Sirens, public address systems, and mobile equipment intercoms present maintenance needs in the audio spectrum. This spectrum is not as critical as the radio frequency (RF) spectrum with regard to maintenance skills. Fire departments can safely assume these maintenance responsibilities. If a fire department or municipality or county decides it wishes to end its relationship with a private sector repair agency and set up its own repair shop, it is recommended that the process be staged. Start with installation and audio equipment repair before embarking on radio frequency equipment repair. If, for whatever reason, an efficient service cannot be brought about in installation and audio equipment repair, there is no further reason to consider moving into RF maintenance.

Mobile radio equipment installation is a task often taken on by fire departments of all sizes. This task calls more for care in mounting and care in routing cables than technical knowledge. Perhaps it can best be characterized as pride in workmanship. Antenna placement requires careful consideration. The installer must understand antenna ground plane requirements and radiation patterns.

As the manager begins to consider providing basic, in-house RF equipment maintenance, the questions of test equipment, maintenance facilities, and spare parts stock begin to affect the decision. But perhaps the most imposing question has to do with the personal services budget for a qualified technician. Certainly there is an adequate number of licensed technicians in the labor force. However, technology has left many technicians behind. Typically, municipal and county personnel services agencies are not skilled in screening the candidates who respond to an advertisement. Complicating this recruiting program is the matter of salary. Because of the limitations in discretion allowed public sector personnel departments, and a lack of understanding of a profession not common in the public sector, salaries often are neither competitive nor properly determined.

SUMMARY

The nature of public safety communications has progressed as much in the last 10 years as it did in the previous 35 years. As technology from advanced military and space technology filters down to commercial uses, the fire and EMS services are beginning to reap the benefits of research.

Modern fire service communications managers and fire service administrators are faced with a wide range of highly technical communications topics. Depending on the nature and size of the communications system improvement, the manager must consider carefully whether he should attempt to specify equipment or performance. When specifying either, the manager must honestly assess whether in-house expertise is adequate to carry the task from an idea to reality. Once the equipment and system are in place, the task of ongoing maintenance must be administered. Avoid moving in the wrong direction regarding in-house maintenance; make sure there is firm commitment from elected officials in the case of political jurisdictions, and boards of directors in the case of the private sector to adequately fund the capital equipment and facilities needed to support this kind of operation. Test equipment quickly becomes obsolete and capital facilities require constant maintenance. Perhaps most critical is the realization on the part of municipal and county personnel departments of the competitive market in competent electronic technical personnel.

In large organizations the fire service director is seldom skilled in the technical aspects of communication center management, necessitating careful selection and continued education of a communications center manager. All personnel involved in the communications chain require screening for acceptable mental discipline characteristics.

Finally, the fire service director or fire chief (or whatever title describes the person holding the position) must recognize that the fire service is not an island of service or an influence unto itself. It depends on constant interaction and communications with other public safety agencies, not only in the community it serves, but in nearby communities as well. Communications is a term with widespread implications.

16

Fire Department
Water Supply

GENE P. CARLSON

C H A P T E R   H I G H L I G H T S

- Formulae for Required Fire Flow (Theoretical and/or Fireground)
- Definitions of Needed Fire Flow and Basic Fire Flow.
- Five Duties of a Water Supply Officer.
- Two Solutions to water supply problems in the rural/urban interface.

WATER REMAINS THE most-used fire suppression agent in structural and wildland firefighting. Most fire apparatus are designed with the primary purpose of supplying water to a fire. Firefighting tactics center on exposure protection, confinement and extinguishment with water. Whether in a large city, a rural farm, or a forest, water is the extinguishing agent the fire service uses most often. This chapter will focus on fire suppression water supply, and examine the chief officer's responsibilities for assuring adequate water supply in municipal and rural areas.

FIRE FLOW REQUIREMENTS

Generally, fire flow requirements (the amount of water necessary to control a fire incident) are determined for specific buildings—especially large buildings, structural complexes, or target hazards. Fire flow requirements can be set for areas that contain similar construction features and occupancies. An example would be an apartment complex or residential neighborhood. Necessary fire flows also should be determined for buildings and complexes in areas not served by municipal water systems so that adequate alternative means of supplying water can be developed. In setting fire flow requirements you must consider building height and area, type of construction, contents or fire loading, and the proximity of adjacent buildings.

The most basic question with respect to water for firefighting is how much is needed. Among the many approaches for determining fire flows is the much-respected Insurance Services Office's (ISO) formula for Needed Fire Flow, which was published in 1980. Two other methods are the 1974 ISO *Guide for Determination of Required Fire Flow*, and the formula developed by the Illinois Institute of Technology Research Institute. Several other methods that have more direct application to fireground use are those from Iowa State University, the National Fire Academy, and NFPA 1231, *Water Supplies for Suburban and Rural Fire Fighting*.

Needed fire flow

The ISO Needed Fire Flow (NFF) is defined as the rate of flow expressed in gallons per minute at 20 psi residual pressure necessary to control a fire incident within a specific structure. Needed Fire Flow is used to determine the adequacy of a water distribution system during the classification of a city using the *Fire Suppression Rating Schedule*. NFF is determined based on the construction, occupancy (building use), exposures, and the protection provided openings in party walls or passageways. NFF cannot be greater than 12,000 gallons per minute (8,000 for frame and ordinary construction), nor less than 500 gpm. It is rounded to the nearest 250 gpm up to 2,500 gpm and the nearest 500 gpm for flows that exceed 2,500 gpm. The NFF for residential property that does not exceed two stories in height depends on the distance between structures.

Distance	NFF
> 100 feet	500 gpm
31 to 100 feet	750 gpm
11 to 30 feet	1,000 gpm
< 10 feet	1,500 gpm

Basic fire flow

Another fire flow term used in municipal classification is Basic Fire Flow (BFF). The BFF is used to determine the number of needed engine companies.

The fifth highest Needed Fire Flow in the city is selected as the Basic Fire Flow and is considered a representative flow for the community. The maximum BFF is 3,500 gpm.

Fire flow duration can vary from 2 to 10 hours depending on the quantity required. The duration for the maximum Basic Fire Flow requirement of 3,500 gpm is 3 hours. For requirements of 2,500 gpm or less the time is 2 hours and increases by 1 hour for each 1,000 gpm required.

Gallons per Minute Required	Duration in Hours
<2,000	2
3,000	3
4,000	4
5,000	5
6,000	6
7,000	7
8,000	8
9,000	9
>10,000	10

ISO required fire flow (1974)

This system uses the formula: $F = 18\ C\ (A)^{0.5}$
where
F is the required fire flow in gallons per minute,
C is the coefficient related to the construction type, and
A is the total floor area of all floors except the basement in the building.

A is modified for fire-resistive construction. The fire flow is increased or decreased by 25 percent depending on the occupancy. The figure then can be reduced for automatic sprinkler protection. Finally, a percentage ranging from 5 to 25 percent is added for exposed structures within 150 feet. Anyone who wishes to use this guide should get a copy and become familiar with the details of its application.

IIT formulae

Illinois Institute's formulae are based on research of actual fires. This was done by regression analysis and considerations for construction, occupancy, and exposures are necessary in their use.

For residential buildings: $9 \times 10^{-5} A^2 + 50 \times 10^{-2} A$,
which can be simplified as: $(.00009) A^2 + \frac{1}{2}A$
where A is the area of the fire in square feet.
For a room in a home 20 feet by 20 feet the formula would be:
$(.00009)(400)(400) + \frac{1}{2}(400) =$
14.4 + 200 or 214.4 gallons per minute

For other buildings: $-1.3 \times 10^{-5} A^2 + 42 \times 10^{-2} A$
which can be simplified as: $(-.000013)A^2 + .42A$
where A is the area of the fire in square feet.
For a fire in an area of 50 feet by 50 feet in a nonresidential occupancy
the formula would compute as:
$(-.000013)(2500)(2500) + .42(2500) =$
-81.25 + 1050 or 968.75 gallons per minute

FIRE FLOW TESTING

Once a theoretical fire flow requirement has been determined for a building or an area, the fire department should test the water supply provided from the available source(s) [water system, static source, or fire department operations (relays or shuttles)] to determine if it can meet the need adequately.

There are two fallacies associated with the testing of water distribution systems. First, a high pressure reading on a hydrant (static pressure) does not automatically equate to a large, let alone adequate, amount of available water for firefighting. Second, the water measured flowing from a single hydrant is not necessarily the total amount of water available in the area for fire or emergency operations. Proper fire flow tests have to be conducted according to standardized procedures to determine the amount of water *actually available* in an area. Some of the texts that outline the procedures for conducting fire flow tests include *Fire Service Hydraulics,* edited by James Casey, the IFSTA-validated *Water Supplies For Fire Protection,* and *Fire Protection Hydraulics and Water Supply Analysis* by Pat Brock. Water system testing should be coordinated with the director or supervisor of the water department and it is the fire chief's responsibility to seek the cooperation of the water department. For information on rural water supplies (static and flowing water, hose relays, and apparatus shuttles) consult *The Fire Department Water Supply Handbook* by William Eckman.

FIREGROUND FORMULAE

IOWA FORMULA

The "Iowa Formula," developed by the Iowa State University, is based on the quantity of water in gallons per minute that when changed to steam will displace the oxygen in an enclosed space. This is basically a field method that can be applied on the fireground. The formula is:

$$\text{Required Flow in gpm} = \frac{L \times W \times H}{100}$$

where
L = Length,
W = Width, and
H = height of the enclosed area measured in feet.
An example of this in a one-story taxpayer 30W by 80L by 10H would be:

$$\text{Required Fire Flow} = \frac{(30)(80)(10)}{100}$$

Required Fire Flow = 240 gallons per minute

Essentially, the formula requires one gallon per 100 *cubic* feet of space. Since this formula considers only the size of the building and not the occupancy or fire loading, the dimensions of the entire building generally are used. It is recommended the amount of water required be applied in 30 seconds for the most effective fire control. Some texts recommend that the quantity determined using this formula be multiplied by a factor of 2, 3, or 4 to compensate for inefficient water application and occupancy hazards.

NATIONAL FIRE ACADEMY FORMULA

The fireground formula developed by the National Fire Academy for Required Fire Flow is:

$$\text{Required Flow in gpm} = \frac{L \times W}{3} \times \text{Number of Floors Involved}$$

where
L = Length, and
W = width of the structure in feet.
The Required Fire Flow is for a fully involved structure. If only a portion of the building is involved, the amount should be reduced proportionally, generally to 50 or 25 percent of the calculated required flow. In multistory buildings, floors below and those not involved in the fire are not considered in the

calculation. Add one-fourth of the Required Fire Flow for each exposed building or exposed floor in a multistoried building.

Using this formula for a 100-by-100 five-story building with exposures on two sides and fire on the third floor extending upward, the following Required Fire Flow would be obtained:

$$\frac{(100)(100)}{3} \times 1 + \frac{1}{4} \text{ RFF for floor above} + \frac{1}{2} \text{ RFF for exposures}$$

3,333 + 833 + 1666

5,832 or 5,800 gallons per minute

PLANNING TO MEET DETERMINED FIRE FLOWS

Once the tests have been run and the results computed, the amount of water available can be compared to the Needed Fire Flow determined earlier. This will quickly show the adequacy or inadequacy of the system, static source, or fire department operations. If adequate water is not available, the fire department must develop two action plans.

First, the staff must devise operations to immediately provide additional water to the site. This could involve relay operations, the use of large diameter hose, water shuttles, auxiliary equipment, or by initiating automatic/mutual aid.

Second, the fire chief should work with the water department and municipal officials to plan infrastructure improvements that will increase the available water supply for the area. In rural areas this could mean working with township supervisors or county commissioners to develop water supply points. Often, simple suggestions by the fire department can make substantial improvements in water delivery. For example, pointing out where water mains can be cross-connected to form a grid or looped with large feeder mains can be very helpful. This is an opportunity for the fire department to state its case for direct involvement in future water system planning and overall long-range planning of the entire infrastructure.

Fire department needs

The fire department should be directly involved in community planning, especially in the area of water supply for proposed important new housing tracts, shopping or apartment complexes, or industrial parks. Plans should be reviewed before construction begins. Close cooperation with water department officials ensures that they will understand fire protection needs, which will exceed those for domestic consumption. Plan for adequate protection during the building construction phases of new developments. Water demands will include domestic consumption, fixed fire protection systems, and additional water for fire department's suppression activities. The municipal system must

Plan for future growth. LEFT:
Underground valves.

be planned for a significant number of years into the future and consider potential growth in adjacent areas and how it will affect water supply requirements. Areas of concern include storage capacity, main sizes, establishing grids with numerous cross connections so there are parallel mains to provide water flow from several directions (reducing friction loss), and large feeder mains looping the grid. Additional items are valves, hydrant branch sizes and valves, and an adequate number of hydrants suitably located with proper spacing. Where large fire flows are required, several hydrants are needed close to the building. Hydrants generally are limited to a maximum flow of approximately 3,000 gallons per minute. Plan review of new buildings is important in water supply analysis because hydrant and placement accessibility for fire department operations are vital. Do not overlook hydrant location with respect to automatic sprinkler or standpipe connections—hydrants should not be more than 100 feet from these fire department connections.

WATER SYSTEM MAPS

Another aspect of developing a good relationship with the water department is to obtain maps of the water system. Maps of the water system are invaluable in preincident planning and for the incident command staff during emergencies. Adequate water maps are needed in the command post at major fires as well. All operational chief officers' vehicles should have water maps, at least for the sections of the city to which they regularly respond. With today's technology, you can scan water maps into a computer and bring them up on the apparatus terminal while a unit is responding. Include information on hydrant locations, main sizes, and available fire flow. Make sure that dispatchers have access to water maps on their computer. Institute procedures for continuously updating the computer-based maps.

In your work with the water department, suggest system updates to improve firefighting capability, including recommendations to connect dead-end mains and create loops. Replace older, undersized mains and/or improve primary feeder mains. Replace, relocate or add fire hydrants. Seek the installation of new mains where necessary as replacements or for expansion. Also seek regular examinations of the condition and actual diameter of mains affected by encrustation or tuburculation.

ADEQUACY AND RELIABILITY

Officials of the water utility, government administrators, and elected boards or councils often do not understand the fire-protection-related concerns of water systems. It then becomes the fire chief's responsibility to explain to those in authority what these requirements are and why they are necessary. Although water department personnel understand sources, storage, and distribution, at least for domestic consumption, they often do not realize the fire service needs for immediate large water flows to quickly control a spreading fire, nor the concepts of adequacy and reliability.

Adequacy is defined as the water system's ability to deliver maximum daily domestic consumption plus the Needed Fire Flow at a given location. This includes having an adequate number of fire hydrants within a reasonable distance to deliver the required flow. In most street situations the maximum the fire department can deliver from a single hydrant is 2,000 gallons per minute.

Reliability is defined as the ability to continuously supply water even if a part of the system is out of service. In other words the system is redundant; there is more than one way to provide an ample water supply to meet fire flow requirements.

Sources

Water systems obtain water from a variety of sources, including reservoirs that collect runoff, rivers, lakes, underground aquifers, and wells. Most static sources are adequate unless there are extended periods of drought. Wells can go dry or the water table can drop, but most problems are associated with insufficient capacity or the number of sources. The major difficulties with sources are the adequacy of the transmission lines bringing water to the system, and their reliability. In simple terms, do they carry enough water, or, if a transmission line fails, is there a second line or alternative method of using the source of water. At prolonged fires during the peak domestic consumption phase, this can cause severe problems for the fire department.

Storage

Most water systems maintain several hours of treated water storage to allow for peaks in consumption, breakdowns in the system, a treatment facility that cannot keep up, and, in many areas, to provide pressure to the system. Water can be stored in underground reservoirs, and in ground storage tanks (usually placed on high ground), and in elevated storage tanks. In some cases it is necessary to pump from the storage into the system; in others, gravity flow is sufficient. The reliability of gravity systems is good, but if reliability is not built in, a pump malfunction or power outage can nullify the storage capacity of a pump-reliant system. The adequacy of the storage is usually the greater problem; it is not sufficient for maximum daily consumption and the duration required for Needed Fire Flow.

Distribution

Distribution systems are reliable if there is a good cross-connected grid that provides water from several different directions. Reliability also is enhanced if the system has adequate valving so that only short sections of pipe must be closed for repairs. Of course, adequacy depends on pipes sized to meet both the domestic consumption and fire protection requirements. Small mains in older sections of a city or in rural water districts, long dead ends, the lack of a grided system, or buildup in the mains can decrease distribution system adequacy. Comparing current fire flow test results with past tests will indicate changes in adequacy. The minimum main size recommended for fire protection is six inches; six-inch mains should be used only in residential neighborhoods and be cross-connected frequently. The American Water Works Association has developed standards for the pipes and hydrants used in distribution systems.

Hydrant use

Fire departments often underuse the capacity of the system and adjacent hydrants, especially at large fires and where hydrants are spaced relatively far apart. Departments have a tendency to lay 500 feet or more of 4-inch hose in the street, bypassing a closer hydrant when there is a six-inch or larger main beneath the ground.

Hydrants on large mains with good pressure generally will supply two pumpers. A large-volume, low-pressure system also will support two pumpers with the pumps developing the necessary fire stream pressures. In sections of a distribution system where large mains are cross-connected at relatively short intervals, a single hydrant may even supply three pumpers. A guide for hooking up additional pumpers is the residual pressure as read on the pump's intake gauge as each pumper is connected to the hydrant and discharges its streams. A figure of 10 to 20 psi is considered a safe minimum to maintain. No additional pumpers should be placed at the hydrant once this figure is reached, and once it is, should be reported to the water supply officer.

Placing two (or three) pumpers on a single hydrant offers the following operational advantages:

- The speed with which the second or third engine company can stretch handlines to supply heavy stream appliances.
- The reduction in the amount of hose used at large fires. The same

Three engines connected to a large flow hydrant. PHOTO COURTESY OF EDWARD PRENDERGAST

amount of water can be directed on the fire with fewer lengths of hose. Remaining hose can be used for additional lines to increase water delivery on the fire. When less hose is used, the time to place companies back in service can be reduced, a plus when staffing is low and/or rehabilitation required.

- Grouping apparatus close together improves the efficiency of the operation. Fewer blocked streets and less stopped traffic mean less private and public transportation is inconvenienced.
- There is more effective use of pump pressure that is normally wasted in friction loss when hose stretches are long.
- Shorter hoselines means that water from deck guns, portable monitors, or elevated master streams reaches the fire faster and increases the potential discharge capacity since pump pressures can be used more efficiently. This can be the difference between an offensive attack with early extinguishment and retreating to a defensive operation.

WATER SYSTEM MAINTENANCE

Water system maintenance with respect to available fire flow is a concern for the fire chief. If annual flow tests show progressive reductions in flow, the chief needs to communicate this information to water department officials, ask whether they can explain the lower flow, and cooperate with them to remedy the problem. The fire chief may have to take the added step of helping the water department administration to have improvements or major renovations made to clean and line older water mains.

Hydrant maintenance

In some cities the fire department is responsible for hydrant maintenance. It is up to the chief to see that this maintenance is done properly and on schedule, that repairs are completed quickly, and that adequate records are being maintained. Hydrant inspections should be conducted at least twice yearly: in the fall so that repairs can be completed before winter, and in the spring to repair damage caused by freezing weather. For dry barrel hydrants always be sure they drain or are pumped out. A good maintenance inspection includes:

- Checking visually for hydrant damage
    Struck and out of line
    Cracks in barrel, bonnet, or caps
    Damaged operating nut
    Missing caps or chains
    Objects in barrel
    Obstructions that have been added

A pitot reading is being taken as part of routine maintenance check.

- Performing a pressure test
    Checking for leaks in bonnet, stem packing, and nozzle caulkings
    Checking for a defective drain valve
    Checking for underground leaks
- Flushing the hydrant
    checking its operation and stem stiffness
    Flowing until discharge is reasonably clear
- Checking the drain operation
- Checking the condition of outlet threads with a female coupling
- Ensuring free movement of hydrant cap chains, remove excess paint
- Checking cap gaskets
- Lubricating cap and outlet threads
- Lubricating hydrant if required
- Painting if necessary

Hydrants located in areas of cold climates must be checked frequently. If necessary, thaw with steam, pump on a regular schedule, or treat against freezing.

Newspaper vending machines have created an obstruction to this hydrant.

Here hydrant has been bagged to show it is unusable.

Some common hydrant installation problems are:

- Hydrant facing the wrong direction
- Outlets located too high
- Outlets located too low, especially the pumper connection
- Obstructions to outlets or hydrant wrench use
- Inaccessible locations
- Hidden locations

Any hydrant found to be unusable for firefighting must be noticeably marked so that a responding fire company does not attempt to use it in an emergency. Any companies that respond to the area should be notified that the hydrant is out of service.

Hydrant branch valves also may need to be operated and maintained. If individual hydrant flows drop, the water department should be asked to check valves on the lines to make sure that all are fully open.

Records should be kept of hydrant inspections, maintenance, and repairs; individual hydrant flows and area fire flow availability; and recommendations for water system improvements. These records should be stored in a computerized database where they can be easily accessed and updated.

HYDRANTS

The fire chief or the department's appointed water supply officer should further assist the water department in selecting locations for new or replacement hydrants. In addition to choosing appropriate locations, selecting the type of hydrant also is important. Hydrants vary from one to six outlets of various sizes. The most common type is a three-way hydrant with two 2½-inch outlets and one pumper (usually 4½-inch) connection. However, the department may prefer a hydrant that has two pumper connections installed on large mains at target hazards. These hydrants need a large branch main (8-inch minimum) and barrel size to accommodate large flows. Hydrant barrels range in size up to 16 inches. Be sure to make suitable arrangements for protecting operating nuts, caps, and valves on hydrants from unauthorized use. If special wrenches or tools are required, be sure responding units have them.

The department may elect to use a hydrant color coding or marking system. Hydrants can be marked for individual flows by painting the bonnet and caps according to NFPA 291, *Recommended Practice for Fire Flow Testing and Marking of Hydrants*. An alternative is to code the water system by main size—paint with a color code or stencil the main size on hydrants. Fire flow results also can be stenciled on a hydrant for the use of pump operators. Some departments have a specific paint scheme to indicate the limitations of hydrants on dead-end mains. Improve hydrant visibility by using a paint for the barrel that reflects headlights of responding units. This type of paint usually has a reflective glass bead in it to improve visibility. Other departments increase hydrant visibility by using distinctive reflective markers, usually blue, in the center of the street. Reflective paint can be used on the street, to paint an arrow, for example, to show hydrant locations. However, in areas where snow or ice would cover the street, consider marking hydrants with a red metal flag or post visible above drifts. A good public relations program is to have local residents adopt a hydrant and keep it visible and accessible during the winter.

WATER SUPPLY OFFICER

Every department, no matter what size, should have a Water Supply Officer (WSO) who supports the incident commander by monitoring water for fire suppression use and fireground operations on a day-to-day basis. Since the WSO's primary objective is to ensure an adequate water supply during emergencies there must be close liaison with water department officials. The WSO's responsibilities include acquiring and keeping up-to-date water system maps; developing procedures for notification of out-of-service hydrants; scheduling and/or monitoring inspections, ensuring that hydrants are maintained and repaired; recommending system improvements; and planning fire suppression needs for water system expansion.

The WSO needs to work with the fire prevention bureau's plan review division to plan the number, location, and size for new hydrants. Another function is to assist operational officers to develop Standard Operating Procedures (SOPs), especially those necessary for adequate water supply. In some cases special alternate operations will be needed to produce the required fire flow.

The WSO needs to be included in writing specifications for new fire apparatus. The WSO will ensure versatility in design for water delivery; adequate hose, fittings, adapters, and outlets; and provide input on pump and water tank capacities.

On the fireground, the Water Supply Officer must determine the amount of water being delivered and if additional water will be needed. Then calculate how much more water is available, or whether special water supply operations need to be initiated. Pump operators should be taught to record static pressures before pumping. The WSO can collect the static pressures, check the residual pressures, and determine the amount of additional water available. The WSO should always respond to multiple-alarm fires or if not available, a temporary WSO should be appointed. Sometimes the water department may need to respond to the scene or change normal operating procedures to increase the flow. The WSO may have to see that additional pumpers are dispatched as water supply units or that special pumping operations are established.

Standard operating procedures

A recommended procedure is to have each pumper operator record, by mechanical or electronic means, the location of the pumper and hydrant, type and size of hydrant connection, static pressure, number and size of discharge lines for estimating flow, (using flow meters to obtain total flow is more accurate, especially if automatic nozzles are used), and residual pressure. Then the additional capacity of the water system can be calculated. Assign a Water Supply Company on an extra alarm to provide additional pumping capacity, hose for water supply use, and staff. To limit radio traffic, assign firefighters to collect the water supply information from the pumping companies and bring it to the WSO. Then they can assist in analysis, and be used to correct or improve water supply operations. Some solutions are as simple as adding another intake line between the hydrant and the pumper. Review department SOPs to make sure they provide adequate water supplies. Depending upon the water system's capabilities, forward or reverse lays are required in areas where hydrants are widely spaced, reverse or split lays are needed. SOPs also should be written to maximize pumper capability. For example, a 1,500-gpm pumper with two 1¾-inch lines operating at a major working fire is NOT being used to its capability. Departments that use 2½- and 3-inch hose must be trained in the use of parallel and siamesed lines to increase fireground water supply. Other pumping operations that increase fireground flow include relays; tandem, dual, and supplemental pumping; and the use of large diameter hose.

Placement of pumpers at hydrants

There are several ways to connect more than one pumper to the same hydrant, but varying street widths, the number of outlets on the hydrant and their direction (street or building), and other factors all affect the choice of method.

Two pumpers can take their water from a single hydrant if the first pumper is connected to the 4½-inch connection and the second pumper to the other connection or connections. A hydrant gate valve(s) or gated wye should be placed on the other connection(s) by the first pumper. An alternative is to connect the first pumper to the 4½-inch connection of the hydrant and the second pumper to the unused intake connection of the first pumper. Having a large valve on the intake of either or both pumpers expedites this operation. This is known as dual pumping.

Combining the two methods will place three pumpers on one hydrant. The first pumper connects to the pumper outlet of the hydrant, the second pumper attaches to the unused intake of the first pumper (dual), and the third pumper to the other outlet(s). The third pumper can be connected by dual lines from the gated outlets or a gated wye, or by using an increaser from a 2½-inch outlet to a larger threaded hoseline.

If the large hydrant connection is not used when hooking up a pumper, much of the capacity of the system is wasted as the pressure to move a high volume is expended overcoming the friction loss in the small diameter supply lines. Reduce this friction loss by using short, large diameter intake lines or soft sleeves.

OTHER PUMPING OPERATIONS

Relay pumping uses large diameter or multiple hose lines to pump water from a source pumper to an attack pumper located more than 800 feet away. Depending on distance, hose size, and required flow, additional intermediate pumpers may be needed. In the Northeast, relays that use large diameter hose for distances of one and a half miles are not uncommon. **Tandem** pumping is a short relay between two pumpers, often referred to as a wagon and a pumper. The attack pumper (wagon) makes a straight lay and the pumper connects to the source and pumps through the line. An alternative is to have a second pumper lay hose from the discharge of a unit already connected to a source (preferably with large diameter hose) and connect the line to its intake. In this operation, the advantage is that the wagon or second pumper receives water under pressure and can use it to build its own discharge pressure. To remember tandem, think of one pumper behind the other as with the wheels of a *tandem* axle. **Dual** pumping is two pumpers connected to the same hydrant. Although they can connect to different outlets, normally this is done by connecting the intake side of the two pumps together. The objective is to get full use of the hydrant with minimum hose lays. Think of dual pumping as one pumper next to the other, like *dual* wheels.

Supplemental pumping is a pumper at a secondary source supplying additional water to one or more pumpers at the scene that already are working from a water supply, but in need of more water to provide effective streams. Of the several ways to accomplish this, the most common is to have Water Supply Company connect to a large main on an adjacent street and then discharge into the unused intake of the pumper(s) at the fire scene.

Supplying fire systems

The fire department often will find it necessary to provide support to private fire protection systems such as automatic sprinklers or standpipes. Private yard hydrants on the lines supplying these systems should not be used by the fire department, because they generally are inadequate and can rob the system

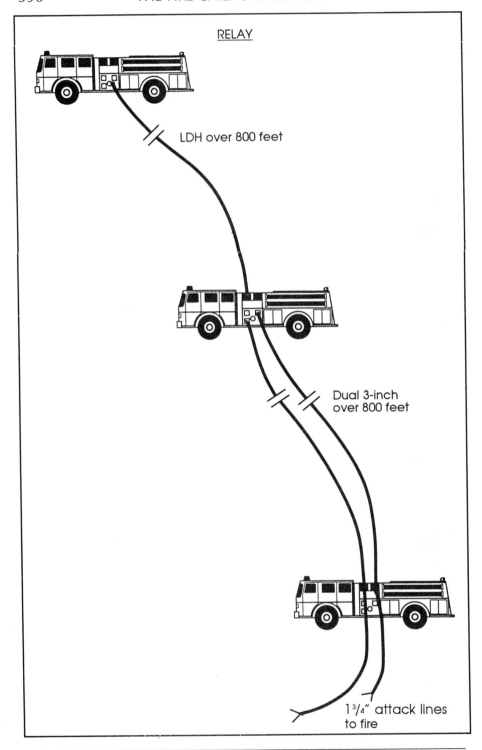

Figure 16-1.

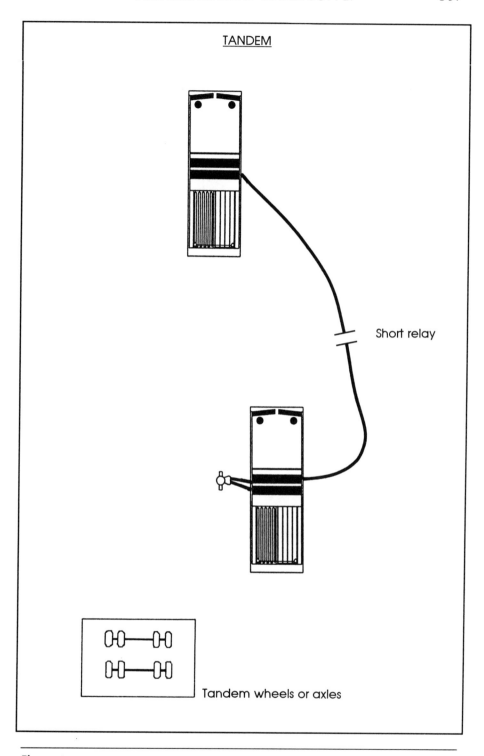

Figure 16-2.

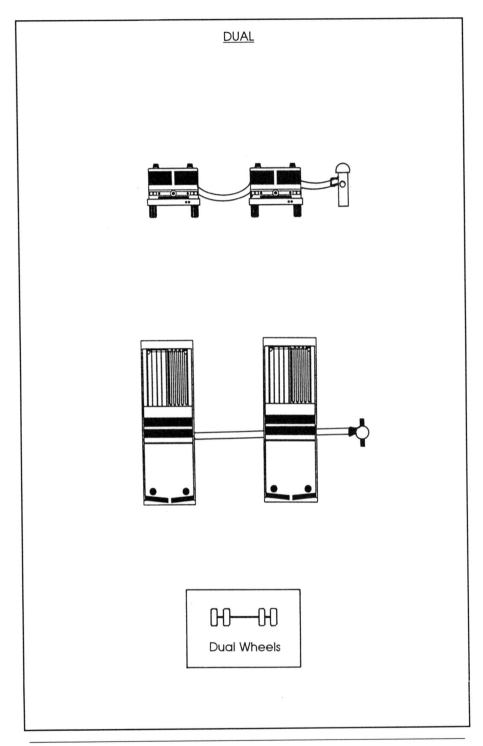

Figure 16-3.

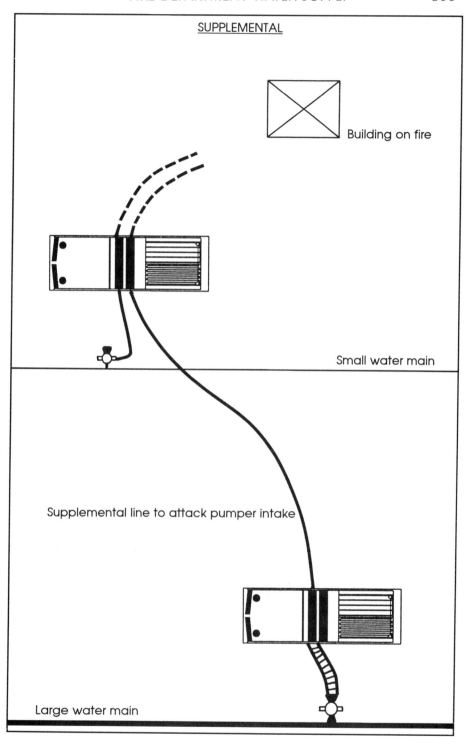

SUPPLEMENTAL

Building on fire

Small water main

Supplemental line to attack pumper intake

Large water main

Figure 16-4.

of needed supply. Similarly, hydrants on the public water supply to these systems may be incapable of supplying the fire protection system and additional handlines for the fire department. These hydrants should be tested before an incident and the results recorded in the prefire plan.

Buildings equipped with standpipe systems must be supported by the first hoseline from the first-arriving engine company. This is essential for a dry standpipe if it is to be used. Special supply operations are required for standpipe systems equipped with pressure-reducing valves. Apparatus operators must be properly trained where these situations are possible.

In sprinklered buildings, one of the first lines from the first-due pumper must be hooked into the sprinkler fire department connection. Large diameter hose is recommended for supporting both types of systems. Consideration must be given to how standpipe and sprinkler systems can be supported if the fire department connection has been damaged.

SUBURBAN AND RURAL WATER SUPPLY

Water supply requirements for fire suppression in rural-urban interface (suburban) areas and in rural areas actually do not differ from those in urban areas served by a municipal water system. In terms of water supply, the differences are where the supply is found and how it is delivered from the source to the fireground. Essentially, determining fire flow requirements, prefire planning with emphasis on water supply, SOPs for delivering water in rural districts, assigning a water supply officer, apparatus considerations, and developing rural water sources are very similar in scope to the operations necessary where a water system is in place.

Minimum water supply formula

The methods for estimating required fire flow described earlier also can be used in rural situations. Another method often used in areas that are beyond a water system is described in NFPA 1231, *Standard on Water Supplies for Suburban and Rural Fire Fighting*. This system bases the Minimum Water Supply (MWS) on the total amount of water that should be necessary for a fire in the structure, given in gallons, on the size on the structure, an occupancy classification which relates to the fire load, and a construction class. When there are exposures the MWS is multiplied by a factor of 1.5

The formula is:

$$\frac{\text{Volume of the Structure}}{\text{Occupancy Hazard}} \times \text{Construction Classification}$$

For a one-story frame dwelling of 40 × 50 the volume is the length × the width × the height. For the area below a peaked roof use one half of the height of that section. For a dwelling with a peaked roof the figures would be 40 × 50 × (10 + ½ × 8) = 28,000 cubic feet. The Occupancy Hazard figure ranges from 3 for severe hazards to 7 for light hazards. This dwelling would be a light hazard with an OH of 7. The Construction Classifications range from 0.5 for fire resistive to 1.5 for wood frame; however, frame dwellings have the classification of 1.0. Thus, the MWS in this example would be:

$$\frac{28,000}{7} \times 1 = 4,000 \text{ gallons}$$

The fire department should have the capability of using the water at rates from 250 to 1,000 gallons per minute, depending on the total water supply required. Of particular interest in rural areas are target hazards such as schools, day care centers, halfway houses, and homes with multiple elderly, or physically or mentally challenged occupants. Large potential loss structures, including manufacturing, processing, and entertainment facilities, frequently have water for domestic use only.

Once the required fire flow or MWS is determined, chief officers must establish a strategy. They must develop preincident plans that will determine both necessary resources and how these resources will be brought together on the fireground. A vital portion of the plan is to identify water sources available for the rural structure and how to move the water from the source to the fire in quantities adequate to meet the determined fire flow requirement. Calculations should be worked out to determine the size and amount of hose and the number of pumpers, or the number of mobile water supply apparatus required. It may be possible to control fires in smaller buildings with the water carried on responding units. Prefire plans should include the location, distance, and amount of flow available at the water source and its reliability and accessibility. If special operations might be needed, for example, making a hole with an augur or other device through the ice at a drafting site, this too should be indicated on preincident plans.

ISO requirements

The Insurance Services Office will credit the water supply provided by fire departments through relay or shuttle operations within 5 miles of the fire station if 250 gpm can be established in 5 minutes after arrival and sustained for 2 hours. Alternatives are 2,500 gallons every 10 minutes, 7,500 gallons every 30 minutes, or 15,000 gallons every hour. ISO will credit the amount (gpms) that can be developed within 15 minutes and then sustained. Mutual aid can be used to achieve the maximum flow. The relay or shuttle must be demonstrated to receive the credit and a lower insurance classification.

Departments that elect to meet these requirements will need to do ample planning before attempting the demonstration. Develop fill sites or sources that offer a minimum of 500 gpm. Determine an adequate first and second alarm response. Include a Strike Team on the second alarm that consists of five MWSA and a fill site unit for shuttles, or five pumpers with adequate hose for relay operations. If a shuttle is used, there must be large storage capacity at the unloading site.

Water Sources

Fire departments often overlook the numerous water sources in rural areas, some of which can be developed with minimal expenditures and work. Others, especially around target hazards, may have to be constructed. Survey the static sources in your district: lakes, ponds, rivers, streams, irrigation canals, swimming pools (above and in-ground, inside and out), and gravel pits, and record the sources on water supply maps. Give the maps wide distribution. Many departments mark static sources with signs for easy recognition. Calculate the capacities of these sources and record them, with any seasonal changes that may occur noted. Formulae for calculating the water in streams, swimming

Fill site marked as static water source.

pools, and ponds can be found in *Planning For Water Supply And Distribution in The Wildland/Urban Interface.* This text also provides superb information on how to install dry or drafting hydrants and construct cisterns.

CONSIDERATIONS AT STATIC SOURCES

Are the sources accessible to a pumper or initial attack unit, or will hoselines have to be stretched from multiple portable pumps? Has the owner given permission to use the source in emergency situations? What preparatory work is necessary, e.g., putting a gate in a fence, dumping gravel or stones for access, or installing a dry hydrant? Can stream sites be improved by installing a manhole in the bridge pavement for inserting the hard suction, alleviating the need to place the hose over the bridge rail, building a weir to enhance the volume available, or sinking barrels in the stream bed to provide ample depth for drafting? Are there problems of silt and debris that must be overcome to avoid pump damage?

Do not overlook the issue of seasonal accessibility. Is the static source reliable during all seasons of the year? Consider heavy human or vehicle traffic that could cause time delays and safety problems: soft ground in the spring; thin ice; thick ice that can be driven on, but must be pierced; and lower water levels during the summer that require long horizontal or vertical lays of suction hose. Information on static sources is available in IFSTA's *Water Supplies For Fire Protection* and in NFPA 1231, which also details constructing water sources such as cisterns.

SOPs for nonhydrant areas

Standard Operating Procedures are important for nonhydrant areas, where an adequate response on the first alarm usually means bringing additional water supply units. For large structures, target hazards, and where distances are great, it may be necessary to establish mobile water supply strike teams of five mobile water supply apparatus plus a fill site pumper for loading operations. Where communications are available, use an automatic aid system. If the water supply must be provided through a relay operation, ample pumpers with adequate hose to transport the fire flow must respond. Large diameter hose greatly enhances relay operations; however, the hose resources may not be available locally for a lengthy relay. Relays of multiple 2½ and/or 3-inch hoselines usually are limited to 2,500 feet. Large diameter hose relays of 1½ miles and more have been used. An important part of your SOP may be to have an engine company respond to the nearest water source on the first alarm to set up a mobile water supply unit filling station or act as the source pumper for a relay. Use the largest capacity pumper available for this evaluation and equip the Water Supply Company with all the necessary fittings and adapters to accommodate local apparatus and hose.

SUBURBAN/RURAL WATER SUPPLY OFFICER

Water supply officers in suburban and rural areas have to perform a variety of duties, both fireground and nonfire. During an incident the WSO should confer with the first-arriving units immediately to be sure they are aware of the available water sources and the SOPs to use them, and to initiate operations if they are needed. The WSO then assumes responsibility for overall water control by knowing how much is being used, maintaining an adequate supply, and planning for additional needs. Meeting additional needs means initiating shuttles or pumper relays, requesting apparatus as needed for these operations, and assigning personnel to loading and unloading sites for shuttles. The WSO maintains apparatus in reserve, at least one pumper and mobile water supply unit, for breakdowns or additional supplies. The water supply officer must coordinate and communicate water supply orders and brief the fireground commander on water supply conditions.

Before an incident the rural water supply officer needs to:

- Determine water supply needs (initial attack, fire flow, total Minimum Water Supply, duration of need).
- Determine deficient areas and make recommendations to improve supply.
- Maintain maps of water supply sources.
- Survey and test water supply sources.
- Maintain records of inspections and tests of the sources.
- Determine locations for constructing static sources and dry hydrants.
- Ask property owners for permission to use their water supplies as static sources.
- Help to write rural water supply SOPs based on available resources.
- Train officers and firefighters in rural water supply operations.
- Research new equipment and methods to improve water supply operations.
- Communicate with adjacent WSOs, share resource data and operational improvements, and conduct joint training exercises.

Apparatus

Two types of apparatus used in rural water supply operations: those used for attacking the fire, relaying water or mobile water supply filling operations,

Dry hydrant installation.

and those used for transporting water. The first type can be standard structural pumpers or pumper-tankers with water tanks larger than 1,000 gallons. These apparatus must meet the design and performance specifications of NFPA 1901, *Standard for Pumper Fire Apparatus.* Their designs should be versatile, with sufficient hose loads and equipment to meet the needs of rural firefighting. Apparatus used primarily to transport water must meet the design and performance specifications of NFPA 1903, *Standard for Mobile Water Supplies,* and may have pumps of any capacity; however, a pump is not a requirement.

Mobile water supply apparatus must be constructed for safety and efficiency. They should have tank capacities that will not overload the chassis, or cause weight to be poorly distributed. Often a small, fast unit with a low center of gravity has better transport capability than a larger vehicle. Loading and unloading rates must be at least 1,000 gallons per minute. Many properly designed units far exceed this minimum. An adequate chassis, power, and brakes; proper tank baffling; and proper tank security will ensure good road handling. Units should be capable of unloading to either side or the rear of the vehicle (this can be accomplished simply with a flexible hose). Gravity unloading can be enhanced by water-jet-assisted dumps which create a venturi action. If unloading is accomplished by pumping there must be adequate tank-

MWSA capable of unloading to rear or either side.

Concrete mixer used as auxiliary water supply unit.

to-pump plumbing for the required flows. No matter how the tank is unloaded there must be adequate venting and air movement across the top of the tank. NFPA 1231, 1903, and *The Fire Department Water Supply Handbook* all provide details on mobile water supply apparatus construction.

Auxiliary tank vehicles for major fires or natural disasters can include bulk milk trucks, commercial tank vehicles, street flushers, and concrete mixers. Establish procedures for their response, loading, unloading, and subsequent cleaning, when required. They can be extremely useful if plans have been made in advance and SOPs developed.

APPARATUS FLOW CAPABILITY

The flow capability of fire department mobile water supply apparatus can be estimated by the formula:

$$Q = \frac{V}{A + B + C}$$

where
Q = gpms delivered,
V = Vehicle tank capacity,
A = Unloading time,
B = Roundtrip travel time, and
C = Loading time.

If a mobile water supply unit with a 2,000-gallon tank is in a shuttle that has a loading and unloading time of 2 minutes, and a travel time of 6 minutes, the flow capability can be calculated as:

$$Q = \frac{2,000}{2 + 6 + 2}$$

Q = 200 gallons per minute

The Insurance Services Office calculates the travel time for apparatus with the formula: T = 0.65 + 1.7 D
where
T = Time in minutes, and
D = Distance in miles

Shuttle operations

The key to shuttle operations is to *keep all units moving!* Anytime a MWSA is stopped, it is **not** transporting the needed water supply. The best way to minimize downtime is to improve loading and unloading times, and then to make sure that units are not obstructed after they are loaded or unloaded. Numerous items of assistance in this area include quick couplings on hose and tank inlets; sufficient large fill openings; filling stations and apparatus; properly placed large vents; stream shapers for pumping directly from outlets into portable tanks; large unloading valves; jet dumps, sufficient air movements across the top of the tank (baffle openings); and remotely controlled unloading valves and vents.

An important component of water movement is operational organization. Plan for water movement in advance for both relays and shuttles. For relays, this includes determining whether the constant pressure method will be used, selecting source pumper, and maintaining the relay by using a dump line when attack lines are temporarily shut down. The constant pressure relay is designed so that all units discharge at the same pressure and maintain a constant flow volume. The distance and hoselines between units are matched. If more water is needed, additional hoselines are laid between units. The relay is maintained by a dump line that is opened to discharge water when firefighting lines are shut down. That way the other pumpers in the relay do not have to constantly decrease and increase pump pressure to maintain the relay. For a relay operation a pumper should be dispatched immediately to the source and set up. As stated earlier, this should be the largest capacity pumper available.

The two major concerns in shuttle operations are the distance from the source to the fire and the number and carrying capacity of the Mobile Water Supply Apparatus. To keep the MWSA transporting water, consider the number and placement of portable tanks for unloading, assignment of officers and personnel to the loading and unloading site(s), supplying attack pumpers with a short relay from water supply pumpers at the unloading site where fireground space is limited, and how units are going to load and unload most effectively. To maintain flow rates on the fireground of 500 gallons per minute or more, three or more portable tanks are required. The attack pumper should have a corner of the center tank placed at its intake, with additional tanks placed adjacent to it for easy access by shuttle units. Water then is transferred from the side tanks into the middle one for use.

Both loading and unloading sites need to be managed; someone must organize the site and maintain communications, aided by staff to direct traffic, make and break connections, open vents, and perform loading or unloading operations. Sometimes it is necessary to unload the MWSA some distance from the fireground. In those cases a pumper is needed to draft from the portable tanks or nurse tanker and relay the water to the attack pumper. Units can unload through a gravity dump, a jet-assisted dump, by pumping the water off, or with a combination of dumping and pumping. Vehicles should be checked for the quickest method and this used when space limitations of the unloading site permit. The most efficient methods of filling are to use multiple 2½-inch direct inlets, large diameter hose inlets, and large flow top-filling devices. Familiarity with the units in the shuttle allows loading site personnel to be prepared to fill them quickly.

Whenever possible use a circular traffic flow pattern so that vehicles in the

Dump line for constant pressure relay. PHOTO COURTESY OF WILLIAM ECKMAN

Multiple portable tanks for unloading site.

shuttle do not have to slow down to pass each other on narrow roads. In other words have all of them move in the same circular direction when both full and empty. This may increase travel distance, but the increased safety and reduced time make up for it.

Coordinating operations into an organized strategy can be enhanced with SOPs for nonhydrant areas. SOPs for positioning and operations of attack pumpers, water supply pumpers, and mobile water supply apparatus should be included. With good operations, either large delivery handline or master stream attacks can be achieved, resulting in quick knockdown and early extinguishment. Train all members in the evolutions and drill everyone in the SOPs for relays, large diameter hose, and apparatus shuttles.

SUMMARY

This chapter has discussed water supply concerns for chief officers in urban, suburban, and rural areas. We have looked at how to determine needed water and several methods for approaching water supply problems. In essence, using water supply officers, planning water supply needs, and working with water department officials at all levels leads to better water availability for fire protection. Then it is up to the chief officer to see that good water supply operating procedures are developed and used in the department, and to provide the leadership and encouragement to help your department overcome any water supply problems.

17

Fire Company Operations

WILLIAM E. CLARK

- Improving fireground operations through better use of companies.
- Reducing injury frequency and severity.
- Systematic analysis and planning.
- Factors that influence progress and change in the fire service.

The fire chief's responsibility in firefighting strategy and tactics is three-fold. It involves: (1) Establishing standard operating procedures. (2) Planning and evaluating operations training. (3) Directing and evaluating fireground operations.

Inasmuch as the delivery of operational services is accomplished through the use of companies, this chapter will provide chief officers with a brief review to help them in dealing with these topics, but it is also intended to assist the many company officers who will read this text by giving them an understanding of how their duties and responsibilities contribute to the total effort.

FIREFIGHTING IS NOT AN ART. It is not a science. It is a craft. Artistic ability is more inherited than learned. As for science, although firefighting is based on scientific principles, it lacks the certainty and predictability of true science. The bouncing of a football also follows scientific principles, but is difficult to predict or repeat exactly. The few letters of the alphabet can be combined to make thousands of different words. So it is with the elements of a fire.

Firefighting is a craft because its principles can be learned, and the necessary skills can be developed through training. Success in firefighting requires the application of that knowledge and those skills.

Firefighting is also the application of muscle, bone, and brain. And the fire company must supply all of the muscle, all of the bone, and part of the brain. It is true that equipment is important, too; just as baseball bats are essential to a ball game. However, ball games are not won by the bats but by the skills of the players using them. So it is with firefighting.

The company is a group of firefighters trained to act as a team to control hostile fires and certain other emergencies. The company may work alone or in harmony with other companies to accomplish the same goal. The overall strategy may be well conceived, but its implementation by the companies determines how the job gets done, for better or worse.

DEVELOPMENT

A knowledge of the past helps to understand the present, and form the future; so let us review the development of the fire company and the factors that have influenced it. The major elements are equipment, tactics, and staffing. The equipment influences the tactics and the tactics set the staffing requirements. A significant advance in equipment technology precipitates changes in tactics and staffing. There have been four distinct eras of firefighting in North America, with the change from each to the next brought about by a technological breakthrough.

First there was a period of about 100-years with leather buckets to carry and throw water.

Then came 150 years when pumps were pulled by hand and pumped by hand.

The third period began with the adoption of a horse-drawn, steam-operated pump in Cincinnati in 1853.

The fourth era began about fifty years later when gasoline-operated, self-propelled pumpers were introduced. The diesel engine is a subphase of this period, which still prevails.

Engine Companies

The introduction of hand-operated pumpers led to the formation of companies. The company had three functions: to pull the apparatus to the fire, to pump and apply water, and to maintain the equipment.

Truck Companies

During the period when hand pumpers were in vogue the need for tactics beyond the application of water was discovered and was met by the creation of what were then called hook and ladder—now commonly called truck—

companies. As firefighting grew more sophisticated, additional duties were given to the truck companies as discussed in the "dry tactics" part of this chapter. In the late eighteen hundreds the theory of ventilation was advanced and became an important duty of the truck company.

Rescue Companies

In the early part of the twentieth century the "rescue company" was introduced to handle special situations at train wrecks, industrial accidents, and other incidents, as well as special problem fires. These companies are discussed in another chapter.

Squads

At about the same time some cities formed companies called "manpower squads" to provide more firefighters quickly at major fires. But today several departments have them respond to structural fires on the first alarm to work as the incident commander decides. Some cities use the rescue squad for the same purpose.

E.M.S.

The adoption of emergency medical service by fire departments in the nineteen sixties has had a tremendous impact on the fire service, and in many departments it is the busiest component by far. It is handled in a variety of ways. This service is the subject of another chapter in this book.

EQUIPMENT AND TECHNOLOGY

Equipment and its application (technology) influence tactics which, in turn, set the staffing requirements. There is need for a technical history of the fire service. It would be a worthy project for a graduate student and would be valuable to fire chiefs in two ways. It would help them to evaluate the basis of our technology, and it would save them the cost and disappointment of repeating forgotten failures.

Apparatus

Since the days of the hand pumpers there have been two major break-throughs. The first was the introduction of the steam operated pump; the second was the adoption of self-propelled, gasoline driven pumpers and trucks. The first began in 1853; the second, about 50 years later.

Horse-drawn steam engines—when compared to the hand-drawn and operated—could travel faster and farther, and pump better and longer with fewer firefighters needed.

The replacement of steam by gasoline engines allowed not only faster and longer responses, and pumping power equal to steam, but did away with the bothersome horses which had to be trained, fed and cared for, and which were prone to disease. But some significant tactical changes followed the adoption of gasoline power. The pumper could carry hose, and separate hose wagons were no longer needed. This was called the double-combination pumper. It also could carry a water tank (triple-combination).

TACTICAL CHANGES

The standard tactic of laying hose from hydrant to fire with the hose wagon was replaced by that of laying from fire to hydrant with the pumper, although some companies retained mechanized hose wagons as well.

Horse-drawn ladder trucks and water towers were converted by use of gasoline tractors. The aerial equipment and raising mechanisms remained unchanged. In fact some formerly horse-drawn trucks served an additional thirty years. Motor operated raising mechanisms came much later.

The next change of significance also involved power: the switchover from gasoline to diesel engines. This was much more subtle than dramatic, but has had considerable impact. More power allows heavier loads and thus bigger water tanks; and these permit tactical changes.

For years 250-gallon tanks were the common size and they were used to supply small lines at small fires, but when tanks of much larger capacity became feasible, engine companies could handle more than 90 percent of their fires with the tank water, applied with preconnected hose lines up to 2½'' diameter. Two firefighters could quickly stretch and operate a preconnected line with enough water available instantly to suppress a fire involving four rooms in a dwelling—at least. Although most will stretch one, some companies do not charge a supply line unless it is needed.

This change to large tank, quick attack tactics led to a reduction of personnel in many jurisdictions. In the case of paid departments it became an economical solution. In volunteer departments it helped when personnel shortages existed.

The advent of large diameter hose allowed this tactic to be applied to fires of greater size because if the tank water ran out, the supply line could usually give the pump close to its rated capacity.

Synthetic hose

What could—in this context—be considered a side effect, is that synthetic fiber hose is not only lighter in weight but doesn't require the drying out after use that cotton did, thus eliminating drying racks or towers and a lot of labor.

The use of lightweight synthetic materials helped large diameter hose to become accepted. Hose up to 4'' diameter was available almost 100 years ago, but was not very popular. During World War II the British used hose up to 6'' diameter, but 3½'' was the largest used in North America. The new synthetic lightweight hose with sexless couplings was imported from Europe in the sixties but took a long while to catch on, not becoming very popular until the eighties. Now it is considered an emblem of modernization to use large diameter hose.

Aerials

Until the end of World War II, metal ladders were rarely seen, but in a short time metal aerial and ground ladders replaced the wooden. The metal aerials couldn't do any more and they took longer to raise, but were stronger than the spring hoist wood aerials. They are also heavier, but again the diesels will transport aerial platforms with gross vehicle weights exceeding 50,000 lbs.; however precautions should be taken to compensate for the weight when traveling and positioning.

S.C.B.A.

Another advance which has had great impact is the widespread use of self-contained breathing apparatus. In some departments it replaced the popular but dangerous filter masks. Others that adopted it had never used any respiratory protection. S.C.B.A. had been available for years but was not widely used until the filter mask was withdrawn in the early seventies (largely because of product liability lawsuits over deaths and injuries).

The improved S.C.B.A., combined with heavily insulated clothing, allowed more aggressive firefighting and required less frequent relief.

Other improvements include the reduction of the weight of hose and couplings. The present all synthetic hose is about half the weight of the cotton jacket, rubber lined hose prevalent until the sixties. This advantage is offset somewhat by the increase in weight of protective clothing and S.C.B.A., but reductions are becoming available.

Attack Hose

A standardization of hose took place in the eighteen hundreds, when section length was established at 50 feet; couplings and hose diameters at 2½ inches. Hose of 1½ inch diameter became available by 1920 but was first accepted for use only at trash fires and for washing down after overhaul. Gradually it became the choice for initial attack lines because it was easier to use than 2½ inch. It also required less personnel for stretching and operating. The seventies saw many fire departments adopting 1¾'' and 2'' hose; increasing flow without requiring more personnel than needed for the 1½'' size.

Foam

Firefighting foams have been around for over a hundred years. The post World War II years have seen improvements but none that affect tactics to any degree except high expansion foam, which arrived in the sixties and is one of the few new concepts. It was widely adopted in the sixties and seventies but is not nearly as popular now.

OTHER TECHNOLOGICAL INNOVATIONS SINCE 1937

Fire chiefs should know what has been tried before and how it fared. Some of the most prominent introductions since 1937 are discussed briefly below.

Additives

The nineteen fifties saw the fire service eagerly accepting "wet water" (surfactants) as the new cure-all. Great claims were made that a small percentage added to water would greatly increase the extinguishing power. But like other cure-alls, it soon wore out its welcome. In the nineties there had been a push for a similar additive, but with a different method of generating the foam, which is called compressed air foam or Class A foam.

Other additives to improve the effectiveness of water did not gain much acceptance. There were gels and slurries to make water adhere to the surface of the burning material, but they were costly and difficult to apply.

"Rapid water" was the name given to a polymer additive that reduced friction loss in hose. The rationale is you can use smaller hose. Smaller hose allows fewer firefighters, so you save money. It was introduced in New York City and picked up by a few others, but didn't last long at any of them.

Portable Fans

Electric fans for smoke removal were available in the thirties but did not get much acceptance until the fifties. Then water motor fans and gasoline motor fans became available. Neither proved very popular. A problem with gasoline motors was that when they were pulling smoke out of a room it would get into the carburetor, and stall the motor. Somebody got the bright idea of using the fan to push instead of pull the smoke, and so prevent the stalling. Thus was born positive pressure ventilation back in the sixties. For years the concept languished although some California fire departments kept using it. About twenty years after it was first demonstrated, the concept was enthusiastically rediscovered by the rest of the fire service and appears to be the latest cure-all.

Platforms

The articulating boom (snorkel) platform was adapted from industry in the early sixties but only Chicago and a few other cities bought any for ten years, then the bandwagon started to roll. However, the most recent indications are that the telescopic platform (tower ladder) is becoming much more popular.

A platform suspended from a helicopter for high rise rescues was introduced in the seventies but got no acceptance.

Mini-Pumpers

In the seventies there was great enthusiasm for the mini-pumper, a comparatively small vehicle with the ability to respond rapidly and supply the initial attack, to be supplemented by a larger pumper, if needed. Enthusiasm for this concept has waned, and now we see 1500 gpm pumpers doing the same thing: supplying one or two handlines.

Salvage

A great change with adverse impact took place in the seventies. Up until then insurance underwriters placed such emphasis on salvage that they provided that service in most major cities. It was done by fire companies known as the "fire patrol" or "salvage corps," which were operated and financed by the insurance industry.

These companies had their own stations, apparatus and equipment. They responded to fires on the first alarm to protect against water damage below the fire and also performed other tasks to safeguard buildings and contents.

They were effective, especially at industrial fires, but today they exist only in New York City—and there on reduced scale. Fire departments hard pressed to meet other fireground needs are not able to perform salvage as fully, and in many places it is now a lost art.

Radio

The most remarkable advances of benefit to the fire service since 1937 have been in wireless communication. Portable radios, especially, provide increased safety as well as better command and control. It is hard for today's firefighters to visualize the days when we had no radio of any kind. Fireground communication was by shouting and sending runners to and from sectors. It was not until the fifties that radio began to spread in the fire service and even then progress was not rapid. This important subject is covered in another chapter.

High-pressure Fog

An outstanding example of the revival of a discarded idea is the concept of high-pressure fog. It was introduced to American fire departments at the end of WW II, and enjoyed considerable acceptance during the 1950s.

The theory behind high-pressure fog is that water applied at very high pressures will break into a fine spray and increase extinguishing power because the many tiny drops offer a larger surface area. Many fire departments, especially in rural areas, but also in some of the larger cities, went for the concept but in due time became disillusioned.

Now, to the surprise of many who remember this history, high-pressure fog is being revived in Sweden and England. It will be interesting to see how long this revival lasts.

The concept is theoretically sound, and works well on small gas and liquid fires, but has serious deficiencies in other applications. The high pressure needed limits hose size and pump capacity. These, in turn, limit flow. The most popular was 30 gpm at 600 psi, through ¾-inch high-pressure hose. This limited the effectiveness only to fires that could be extinguished by that flow.

High-pressure fog had another undesirable characteristic: the violent movement of air caused by the high nozzle pressures. Fires were driven through buildings, and firefighters driven out, or, in some cases, burned when these high-air velocity, low-water volume streams were used.

STAFFING

The functions of pulling the hand pumper to a fire and then pumping it were labor intensive; and a lot of people were needed to fulfill them. Pumping manually was one of the most arduous forms of exercise ever invented; frequent relief was necessary.

The spirited rivalry among the volunteer companies frequently became violent much to the dismay of city officials, but they regarded the problem as one they must reluctantly endure. A paid force that could be controlled was preferable, but the cost of paying that many people was too great.

Paid department

The advent of steam pumpers made a smaller force feasible and a paid department affordable. Cincinnati started to replace the volunteers with paid firefighters. Soon, other cities followed suit. One engineer could make the steam pump deliver more water than dozens of men pumping by hand, and three horses could pull the apparatus faster than the men could.

In New York City when Jackson Engine No. 24 of the volunteer department was replaced by Engine No. 3 of the new Metropolitan fire department, the roster changed from 2 officers and thirty-eight firemen to two officers, an engineer, a driver and 8 firemen. Although they worked a continuous duty system of 24 hours a day and only one day off a month, there were members off on meal leave (three hours a day) or street patrol. Therefore, the on-duty strength was six firefighters plus the officers, engineer, and driver.

Staffing changes

What does all this mean today? It means that the staffing pattern set in our major cities at that time became the prevailing standard for the next fifty years. The advent of gasoline operated pumpers allowed the positions of engineer and driver to be consolidated; and the reduction to an 84 hour work week forced some cities to drop shift personnel levels to an officer, driver and five firefighters. This standard remained popular until quite recently, although some cities deviated from it.

When the once very influential grading schedule of the fire underwriters (insurance services) was designed, it specified that same standard and maintained it for many years.

So, with some variations, the standard of six or seven people (including the officer) survived until a trend to smaller companies began in the nineteen sixties. The reduction has become widespread and is the most controversial fire service issue of the past fifty years (except for hair length and apparatus color, neither of which have much impact on fire losses). For that reason, and also because the people are the most important ingredient of the company, we are dwelling on that subject here.

Engine staffing

By 1982, according to a nationwide study, engine companies in cities of 100,000 or greater population were staffed with an average of 3.8 persons, including the officer and driver. Another survey of the same population group in 1991 showed an even lower average.

In order to discover the situation in smaller cities in 1992, I checked forty randomly selected cities of less than 100,000 population with completely career departments and found that engine companies had an average complement of 2.92. Averages are not always meaningful, so by taking a deeper look we find that only 5 of the forty departments are using engine crews of four; eight are riding with two; the rest with three.

Truck staffing

The truck companies are even smaller, with an average of 1.52 firefighters. Only 15 of the forty are responding with more than two. Nine respond with one.

Some of these departments are responding with a total of two vehicles with two people on each. Yet they are buying 1500 gpm pumpers with six-seat cabs, and have instituted elaborate incident command and personnel accountability systems. We now have two separate worlds in the fire service; the world of theory, and the world of reality. The gap between them is widening.

We also have another dynamic driving the staffing of companies: economics.

It is reasonable to assume that most of these departments did not arrive at their staffing schedules as a result of a thorough systems analysis. Research by the International Association of Fire Fighters has focused on the relationship of staffing to injuries with considerable evidence that the reduction from four members to three results in a significant increase in injuries. There is evidence in one study that fire damage increased also.

Staffing tests

There have been a few time and motion studies published. Starting with the first tests published (which we conducted in Wisconsin in 1960), and followed with general agreement by others later, we find the not-so-startling conclusion that the more firefighters performing a prescribed job, the less time it will take. The important questions are when does the reduction in crew size become critical and what factors are causative? The I.A.F.F. decided that the difference between four and three is critical and the principal cause is the increased injury rate. But it should be remembered that four is a reluctantly conceded minimum, not a recommended standard.

Determining needs

What then, is adequate company strength? It depends upon need. The need in a district of well-spaced, one-story homes is not the same as an area covered with six-story combustible tenements, each occupied by more than 100 people. In some cities needs will vary from one part of town to another. Station location and additional aid availability from within or without are other factors. There are more, all of which can be included in a rational needs analysis, which is a much better navigation system than dead reckoning; and less expensive than trial and error.

Initial response tasks should be divided—for analytic purposes—into simultaneous and sequential, which will be discussed elsewhere in this chapter. Some can be performed in sequence; others must be done simultaneously, especially in early operations.

In addition to the safety factor there is also the consideration of efficiency. The three member engine company has one third of the crew supervising, one third operating the pump, and one third doing everything else. A four member crew would have one fourth supervising; one fourth pump operating, and one *half* doing the rest, thus doubling the strength of the hose team.

True example: A city with three-member engine companies had twelve engines at a high rise fire because of manpower needs. Only one pumper was needed to supply the standpipe system; the drivers of the others each took a hydrant and dutifully stayed there listening to the radio for the duration of the fire. Therefore, almost one third of the manpower summoned wasn't used; and 12 officers were directing 12 privates. The same total personnel deployed in nine companies with four members each, would give the interior attack teams a substantial increase of 50 percent more privates.

Truck company staffing should be based on the number of initial attack tasks that must be performed simultaneously (discussed in the "dry tactics" section of this chapter). Furthermore, if the nature of the district may require

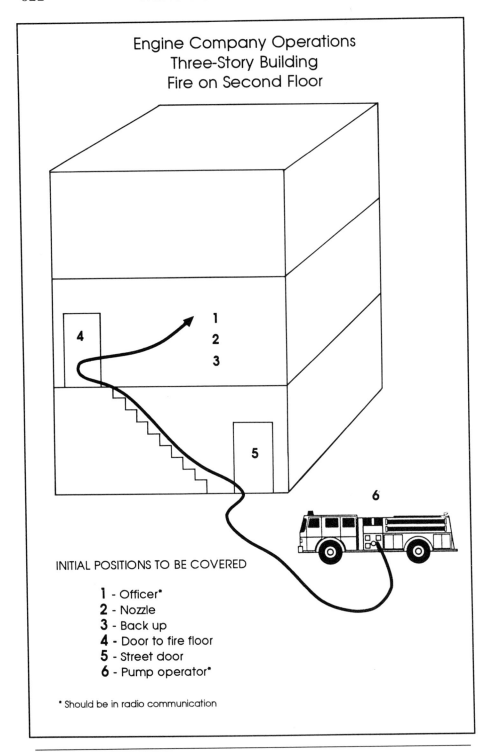

Engine Company Operations
Three-Story Building
Fire on Second Floor

INITIAL POSITIONS TO BE COVERED

1 - Officer*
2 - Nozzle
3 - Back up
4 - Door to fire floor
5 - Street door
6 - Pump operator*

* Should be in radio communication

Figure 17-1.

rescue by ground ladders from second or third floors, the crew should have the capability of raising them quickly.

Squads

Using the "Squad" as a method for bringing additional personnel to the scene, is a worthy solution if the squad arrives in a reasonable time. After arrival the members of the squad can function as a team or can be dispersed among other units. Some chiefs feel that the proper staffing at the fireground is a matter of total personnel present rather than how many are in each company; and the squad helps to meet the established minimum.

Initial response

The reasoning that it is the group total that really matters raises the question of what that total should be. Recommended minimums for initial response range from 12 to 16; but in actual practice vary from 4 to 35. Here again the correct number depends upon the character of the area to be protected.

TACTICS

Let us state some fundamentals of tactics and then relate them to company operations. Firefighting should follow the commonly accepted outline for systems analysis as used in business, industry, and education:

- Analysis;
- Design;
- Application;
- Evaluation; and
- Revision.

Analysis

In firefighting the analysis is usually called "size-up". The design is the "action plan". The other elements remain as named above. The size-up gathers and analyzes important information about the fire and the structure it is threatening. Knowing the building the fire is in is as important as knowing the fire in the building.

Design

The action plan should be based on the selection of objectives, the methods of achieving them, and the timing. The plan should be flexible because objectives and priorities can change. For example, the top priority of removing an endangered occupant is resolved as soon as he is safely on a ladder.

There are immediate objectives, those that require immediate attention such as confining the fire, and secondary objectives, such as secondary search and salvage. And there are remaining objectives like overhaul and restoration. A new objective must be considered when the need for it is discovered, such as when a first floor fire has traveled between walls and entered the attic.

Application

The objectives are assigned to companies to carry out. The chief should only have to tell what he wants done. In a well-trained department he should

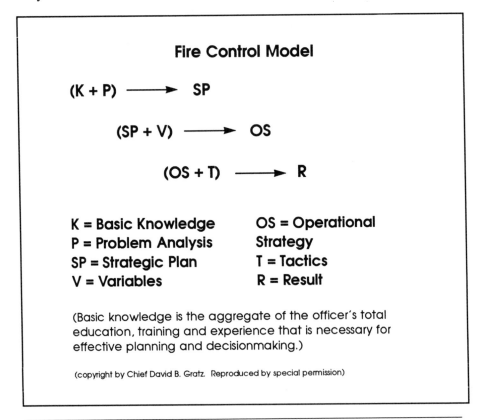

Fire Control Model

$$(K + P) \longrightarrow SP$$

$$(SP + V) \longrightarrow OS$$

$$(OS + T) \longrightarrow R$$

K = Basic Knowledge   OS = Operational
P = Problem Analysis   Strategy
SP = Strategic Plan   T = Tactics
V = Variables   R = Result

(Basic knowledge is the aggregate of the officer's total education, training and experience that is necessary for effective planning and decisionmaking.)

(copyright by Chief David B. Gratz. Reproduced by special permission)

Figure 17-2.

not have to tell how to do it, but if there is any doubt about an order, it is proper to explain it rather than risk a mistake.

Evaluation and revision

If tactics are going according to plan, but the desired results aren't, you should consider making some changes. General Patton said something to the effect that if the plan isn't working, it is better to change the plan to meet the situation than to try to change the situation to meet the plan.

Four basic rules

We shall divide tactics into two distinct types: "dry tactics" and "wet tactics" but first, some basic rules for both dry and wet tactics. They are offered here because chiefs have final responsibility for tactics and training, and should ascertain that company officers know and observe fundamentals, because that is where errors can be costly. Incident and sector commanders should be constantly alert to these rules:

Rule 1. Don't allow hose streams to oppose each other.
Rule 2. Don't aim outside streams into the same floor where firefighters have entered or are trying to enter.
Rule 3. Make a chimney for smoke and heat to escape.
Rule 4. Don't put water into the top of the chimney you just created.

Reasons

These rules are based on the following reasoning.
Rule 1. Many fire departments require that if the first line is in the front, the second hose should be taken to the rear. This is an open invitation for opposing streams which drive heat and smoke at each other, and nobody can advance. Fog streams, especially, but solid streams, too, move a great amount of air. Also, in many cases the second line isn't necessary or could be better used elsewhere.
Rule 2. Firefighters have been burned or driven out of advantageous interior positions by outside streams directed through windows or roof openings. Streams push heat, smoke and air with considerable force. In some cases they accccelerate the fire by forcing air into portions of the combustion area that the water is not reaching.
Rule 3. Heat, smoke, and gases will rise until they meet an obstruction and will then spread horizontally or bank down. Making an opening at the top

of stairs or other vertical shafts will create a "chimney effect," by which these products escape quickly and are replaced by fresh air coming in doors and windows.

Rule 4. This rule is frequently violated. *True example*: (seen on T.V. news). The scene shows firefighters cutting a hole in the roof of a townhouse. When the roof opening is made, a column of thick smoke shoots up like a geyser, and the windows become air intakes. But then a hose stream is aimed into the hole forcing the smoke, heat, and gases back down, thus endangering the lives of occupants and firefighters in the building.

DRY TACTICS

Many fire chiefs—even in some fair sized cities—do not understand the functions of the truck (ladder) company. Some think that because these companies travel to fires with an aerial apparatus equipped with ladders that they are limited to functions involving that equipment, such as applying water from heights and raising ladders. In fact some departments don't send truck companies to fires in one or two story buildings; some dispatch aerial trucks with only a driver, and some don't even send the truck except when the incident commander decides one is needed and calls for it.

On the other hand, some of America's busiest truck companies work effectively at most of their fires without raising even one ladder. They perform their duties with the use of tools. Those duties are listed in *Firefighting Principles and Practices* under the acronym "Rovers" for easy remembering:

R—rescue
O—overhaul
V—ventilation
E—entry
R—reconnaissance
S—search

Pre-assigned duties

These are the "dry" tactics, meaning they don't use water. These functions should not be neglected, but they may be, if not assigned *before* the fire. Major departments not only assign these duties specifically to truck companies, but also pre-assign the duties within the company so that each member carries certain tools, and performs specified duties upon arrival at the fire scene, without the need for further orders. This practice assures that vital tasks will not be overlooked and will be done promptly. Of course, when conditions at the scene require it, changes can be made.

An example of pre-assigned duties for first due truck company members at a multiple dwelling fire:

1. (Officer) Direct and supervise.
2. Forcible entry, search and ventilate fire floor
3. Forcible entry, search and ventilate fire floor
4. Outside ventilation, enter, search
5. Outside ventilation, enter, search
6. Vertical ventilation, search assist
7. Vertical ventilation, search assist

Ideally this would call for six firefighters and an officer. In the good old days that's what we had, and today a good volunteer truck company would have them. But today's fire chief must be a realist. The following is an example of how flexibility may have to be incorporated into policy for the application of these necessary duties. When truck company personnel are fewer in number, theory must concede to reality and we must consolidate tasks to some extent:

Five members

1. (Officer) Direct and supervise—(forcible entry, search and ventilate fire floor.)
2. Forcible entry, search and ventilate fire floor
3. Outside ventilation, entry, and search as indicated
4. Vertical ventilation
5. Assist either 3 or 4—assure team concept and safety

To consolidate further, when necessary:

Four members

1. (Officer) Direct and supervise—(forcible entry, search and ventilate fire floor.)
2. Forcible entry, search and ventilate fire floor
3. Outside team—account for vertical ventilation and outside ventilation, entry and search
4. Outside team—account for vertical ventilation and outside ventilation, entry and search

Priority sequence

When the first due truck company doesn't have enough members to meet immediate objectives by performing required tasks simultaneously, priorities

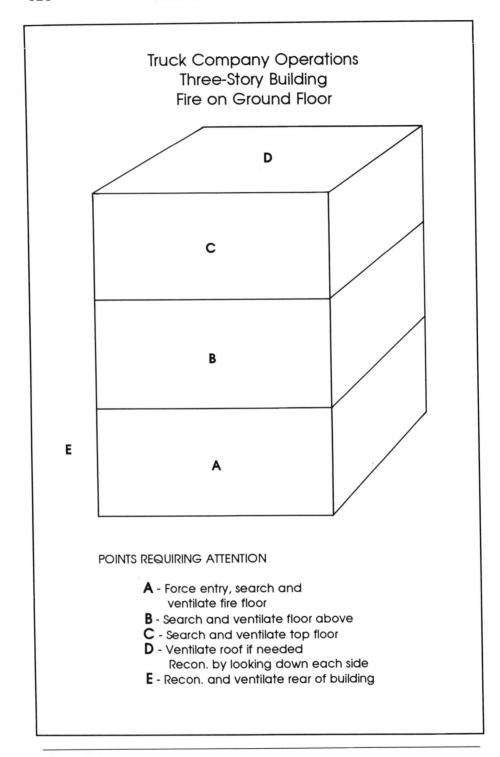

Truck Company Operations
Three-Story Building
Fire on Ground Floor

POINTS REQUIRING ATTENTION

A - Force entry, search and
        ventilate fire floor
B - Search and ventilate floor above
C - Search and ventilate top floor
D - Ventilate roof if needed
        Recon. by looking down each side
E - Recon. and ventilate rear of building

Figure 17-3.

will have to be established for performing them in sequence according to the situation encountered.

Any adjustments to the plan have to be made by the truck officer, who should be free to observe, evaluate the situation, direct the company's operations and order changes, as well as look for safety hazards and prevent unsafe acts. All this would be difficult to do if that officer is performing any of the manual tasks.

Some paid departments have the members of the EMS unit assist the truck company to make up for personnel shortages. Some departments—especially volunteer—will have the second or third due engine company do the truck work, either by preassignment or by orders upon arrival (or enroute).

It may be desirable for truck company members to work in pairs, but it isn't always possible. In the world's busiest truck company members worked alone part of the time at most "workers," even when an officer and six firefighters were present. Take a four or five story multiple dwelling with two apartments per story. It was one member to the roof, and two to force entry and search the fire floor. That left three to search and ventilate up to eight apartments. We never had a casualty caused by this procedure and this was before we had breathing apparatus.

Search and removal

The volume of smoke is usually the best indicator of life hazard, and the need for a thorough search. Most occupant fatalities are smoke incurred. My experience was that with a quick response and prompt search there was a fifty percent chance of finding victims alive. It should never be assumed that everybody is safe or anybody is dead until a thorough search has been made.

Rescue

Although seldom required, rescue of entrapped occupants is the foremost consideration. Rescue in this context means safe removal from serious danger. It does not mean escorting or guiding someone out of a building because there is a fire in it. The need for real rescue is sometimes obvious; sometimes not. The obvious case would be someone in a window calling for help. An opposite case is when the fire gases have rendered a person unable to escape or call for help. For this person to be discovered, a thorough, systematic search is usually essential.

One of the toughest problems is that of multiple rescues. On rare occasions there may be several people in need of assistance at once, and the limited resources of the first alarm units may not be able to rescue them simultaneously. It is better to take a very short time to analyze the situation and establish priorities and an action plan, rather than plunge into action helter-skelter. Quickly answer the questions of where, when, who (does it) and how. Coolness and discipline must be maintained.

Sometimes it might be better to get the fire out rather than the people. It is a tough decision when resources are limited, but there have been cases where the decision to put all hands into the rescue effort intensified the life hazard by neglecting the fire.

Types of search

Primary search is an integral part of rescue, but it should also be used to discover fire extension and perform ventilation. The theory of *secondary* search was advanced about 1970. It simply means that when the fire is knocked down and visibility is almost normal, vulnerable areas should be searched again. Secondary search gains considerable importance when an occupant is reported missing.

True examples:

(1) When the fire was over, fire investigators combed the scene and decided that it was a case of arson. Three days later, the owner, cleaning out the debris, found a body.

(2) A man walking his dog found a body in a pile of debris outside a building that burned months before. The fire happened in midwinter, and the cold prevented decomposition until spring.

Thorough secondary search will prevent such unfavorable reflections, but more importantly, may save a life.

Search inventory

The following is a search "inventory" for company officers to help them direct and supervise a search successfully.

1. Search should be systematic to prevent omission and duplication.
2. In hazardous, large, or complex areas use a tag line or keep in contact with a member at an exit.
3. Search for extension of fire as well as victims.
4. Ventilate while searching.
5. When searching near the fire stay low, not just for better visibility, but in case the fire intensifies suddenly.
6. When conditions permit, secondary search should be carried out.

Reconnaissance

1. Reconnaissance is necessary to gather information of importance to the incident commander:
   a. fire location;
   b. fire extension: actual and probable;
   c. structural conditions;
   d. exposure hazards (what and where);
   e. effectiveness of operations; and
   f. search status.
2. Reconnaissance can be conducted both outside and inside a building.
3. Reconnaissance can be combined with search and ventilation.
4. Sometimes action can be taken during reconnaissance. For instance, closing a door between the fire area and an uninvolved area.
5. Reconnaissance findings are of little value unless promptly and correctly reported to the sector or incident commander. It is the responsibility of the incident commander to evaluate the information and plan accordingly.

Overhaul

1. Overhaul should be systematic so that no place where fire may remain is overlooked.
2. There are two kinds: overhaul of contents and overhaul of the building.
3. It is usually safer to move charred contents to the outside in case they may rekindle.
4. It should be understood that thorough overhaul may require the opening of ceilings, floors, walls, door and window frames. Officers need to know where to expect that fire may have extended.
5. Officers should be aware that overhaul is more than just wetting down the fire area.
6. A thorough search for fire extension should be made above the fire area.
7. Members performing overhaul should be alert to discover and preserve evidence of fire cause.
8. In some severe cases, a "watch line" connected to a hydrant is left in place in case of rekindle. This requires that some members be left also, to discover rekindle and operate the line; the line will not go into action by itself.

Ventilation at fires

Ventilation of structural fires is an essential, but often neglected strategy. And as a tactic it is sometimes performed incorrectly and even dangerously.

One of the important tasks of chief officers is that of making sure that the scope and timing of ventilation are coordinated with other activities both for safety and effective operations.

Objectives and precautions

The objectives of fire ventilation are to save lives, improve operational efficiency, and control fire spread by the removal of heat smoke and gases generated by a fire in a structure or vessel. Certain precautions must be considered:

1. Ventilation can accelerate a fire quickly. Charged hose lines should be in position before ventilation begins, although some departments make an exception to this rule in cases where rapid ventilation may save life.
2. Fires often move toward openings, so don't ventilate where openings might cause unwanted fire spread.
3. Flames may leap out a window that has been opened and endanger persons above on ladders or fire escapes, or at windows. Also, when windows are to be opened on more than one story it is safer to start at the top and work down. For similar reasons when windows are being opened from a fire escape or ladder, the nearest should be opened last.
4. Power fans can intensify and spread the fire. If employed, they should be used carefully.
5. Although true backdrafts rarely occur, the results can be quite harmful. Officers should be quick to identify such potential and act to prevent the occurrence or lower the risk of injury. Judicious rise of ventilation can sometimes do either or both.

Entry

The incident commander at a structural fire often has to consider where and how to make entry. In some sections of the country forcible entry means the forced opening of doors and windows. In other regions it means opening up walls, floors, or ceilings to get at concealed fire (also called "opening up").

Locked doors

The complexity of the task of forcing doors can vary considerably, and has increased in recent years. There was a time when only the big cities had very many "burglar proof" locks. But as the fear of crime has spread, so have more sophisticated locks, and so has the need for more sophisticated means of forcing them.

New methods include those which use special tools to effect entry without the brute force which was always used in the past. These implements can save time and damage, but add to the tool inventory and pose the problem of selecting the right tool for the occasion, since it is not feasible to carry all of them into every fire building. Life was simpler when all forcible entry could be done with a flathead ax and a Halligan tool (and this is still the favorite way in most cases).

Some departments rely heavily on what could be called "alternate entry" by way of a window. This method should be used with caution because of the problem of safety if quick retreat becomes necessary.

In some cases, such as a one-family home, the entry is a one-door job. But in some occupancies several doors may have to be forced.

In some action plans it is customary to have the forcible entry team remain with the engine company to open ceilings or walls for the application of water.

Task inventory

The task inventory for the company officer will include:

1. Size-up the problem, including safety hazards.
2. Order methods and procedures
3. Decide what forcible entry tools should be brought to the work site.
4. Supervise with minimum interference and maximum safety.

WET TACTICS

Wet tactics are those in which water (or other extinguishing agents) are applied. They can be of two types: offensive streams or defensive streams, each of which can be subdivided into two other categories: interior streams (where the nozzle team is inside the building), and outside streams.

Interior streams

Interior streams can range from 30 gpm to 350 gpm but mostly are from 95 to 200 gpm Today, most fires are fought with hose lines of 1½'', 1¾'' or 2'' diameter, and only rarely is the nozzle flowing more than 200 gpm

Most inside streams are probably in the range of 100 to 180 gpm. Dave Fornell in his text *Fire Stream Management Handbook* states that one firefighter of average size can safely and effectively operate for at least ten minutes with a nozzle reaction (kickback) of 66 pounds. He points out that this would be the reaction from a [fog] nozzle flowing 125 gpm at 100 psi, or a ¹⁵⁄₁₆-inch tip flowing 185 gpm at 50 psi

When water has been applied for more than a half minute and the fire continues to burn, it can be for either of two reasons: (1) the water is not reaching the burning material; or (2) the volume (gpm) is below the critical rate.

Critical rate

The critical rate of flow is the amount needed to lower the temperature of burning material to the point where it ceases to give off the combustible gases which are the fuel. Or, in other words, stops burning.

A few gallons over the critical rate will extinguish the fire, a few gallons below it will let the fire continue to burn. Going well over the critical rate will extinguish the fire quicker and may actually require less total water for a lasting knockdown.

Flow rate formula

There is a formula for quickly estimating the amount of gallons per minute needed, called the "ideal rate of flow" by its authors, Keith Royer of Iowa State University, and his associate, the late Floyd W. Nelson.

This formula is amazingly simple and reasonably accurate. Stated in words, the volume of the room in cubic feet divided by 100 equals the discharge of water needed in gpm So just multiply length times the width, times the height and divide by 100. The quantity derived is usually somewhat higher than the critical rate, and if it reaches the fire will prove effective in thirty seconds. If it doesn't, the nozzle should be moved elsewhere, or tactics changed.

There have been some attempts to alter this formula, mostly by those who don't understand the reasoning behind it. It should be left alone. I have seen it tried on fires in a variety of structures and in rooms up to 80,000 cubic feet, heavily loaded and it worked well. The formula should be calculated for the entire undivided fire area, whether it is a room, a store, or a church.

Reaching the fuel source

However, most fires that continue after the engine company has applied water do so not because of insufficient water, but because the water is not hitting the burning material. This is common at large fires where (in my belief) only about twenty percent of the total application does any good. In other words, one stream out of five.

But this problem can happen at small fires, too, and is often why some of them become large fires. Flame may come out a window remote from the burning material. Sometimes the actual combustion is in another room but the gases don't ignite until they reach the air at a window. For water to extinguish the fire it must strike the burning material. Aiming it at flame will not always accomplish that result.

Defensive wet tactics

Some hose lines may be used just to prevent the spread of fire. In some cases nozzles are opened and streams are used to keep fire from passing a selected point, but many times the line is placed into position as a precaution and not used unless absolutely necessary. This requires discipline to prevent opposing streams or pushing the fire into uninvolved areas.

One defensive tactic is to use the hose line to protect occupants by keeping the fire from cutting off escape routes such as halls, stairs or fire escapes. More common needs, however, are preventing a basement fire from extending up the stairs to the first floor or keeping a stairway fire from entering the top floor of a multistory building.

Protecting exposures

Defensive wet tactics can be used to protect exposures by wetting the combustible exterior of an exposed structure, or by taking a hose line inside the building to prevent fire from entering it.

The effective way to protect the surface of an exposure from heat radiation is to keep it wet, rather than setting up a water curtain. Radiant heat is electromagnetic energy which can penetrate any transparent material including a water curtain. It becomes thermal energy upon striking a solid surface, which then heats up. Wetting the surface removes the heat from it to prevent ignition.

Limited access

There will be some situations where the failure to extinguish is due to another factor: insufficient access. This is particularly true at some fires in high rise buildings.

A prison guard told about being on duty in the dining hall when 400 prisoners rioted. He said, "As soon as I got my back into a corner, it didn't matter whether there were 400 or 4,000. Only two of them could hit me at a time." This is comparable to some large area high rise fires. Usually there are only two stairways and the only access to the fire is through the two doorways. There may be 400 firefighters available but only two access points; and in some cases only one of them will give effective access to the fire.

Heat can get around obstructions that water streams can't. This can make conditions inside the doorways almost intolerable. And the large fire area may require a critical flow rate that is hard to apply because of limited access. To be honest about it, most of the large high rise fires are extinguished by removal of the fuel. The fuel is removed by the fire consuming it until it has diminished to the point at which engine companies can move in and arrest the process. There is nothing new about this technique. It is what we did years ago on sub-cellar fires three stories below street level. Personnel requirements were determined then by the need for relieving the smoke casualties. Now, with respiratory protection, it is heat that sets the relief requirements at limited access fires.

Heat exposure limits

Short exposure should result in short recovery time, and another turn on the line without harm. Too long an exposure may put the firefighter in such a condition that suitable recovery will require a lengthy period. Some departments try to place a five minute limit on extreme heat conditions.

Fog and solid streams

The controversy over fog versus solid stream has increased in pitch and volume in the eighties and nineties. The first fog nozzle was introduced in 1863, and some think it was the best ever made. Yet it gained limited acceptance and the use of fog disappeared before 1900. It remained virtually forgotten until World War II when the U.S. Navy adopted a combination fog and solid stream nozzle. (A German fog nozzle had been introduced in North America just before the war but was little known.)

After the war the fog wave inundated the country. It became the miracle quick-fix we had been waiting for. It became the only way, and those of us who were skeptical were derided. Ridiculous claims were made for it, but worse, they were accepted without question, except by a few of us who believed what we saw rather than what we were told. But just as it fell out of favor once, it is losing again. Respected authors such as Richman and Fornell have been rational and convincing on the value of solid streams. Wider field experience has helped the younger generation of firefighters to appreciate solid streams. This revision of fire stream tactics is the strongest trend of the nineties.

CONTROL, COORDINATION, AND COMMUNICATION

Incident command

Ever since the days when the command post was marked by a kerosene lantern, major fire departments have followed a system of fireground command and control with duties and responsibilities specified. But in California the system became more formal and documented because of the large brush fires occuring there. By the sixties the California Division of Forestry and some of the larger fire departments, including both Los Angeles County and City, had extensive plans for "campaign" fires, i.e., those brush fires or forest fires which require hundreds of firefighters and many days to control.

This plan was very well presented by Chief Klinger and Battalion Chief Manchester of L.A. County at national staff and command schools in 1961, 1962 and 1964, where it was offered as a pattern for any large scale disaster operation. In more recent years the National Fire Academy developed a version adaptable to various extensive operations including structural fires; it is named the "Incident Command System."

This system has been widely disseminated and enthusiastically received, so there is no need to expound it again here. But since this system involves fire companies and company officers, and because sometimes the company officer may be the incident commander for awhile, let us look at some of the pertinent features.

For a small incident, the individual in charge of the ICS may perform many tasks of the ICS. There may not be any need to delegate them. This has been misunderstood.

True example: A small fire department responded to a fire in a store. Shortly after arrival the IC (the captain first to arrive) called for mutual aid. The reason was that after all of the ICS tasks had been delegated, there was no one left to fight the fire.

The system is meant to be adapted, not adopted. Fire chiefs should train their company officers to interpret the plan as well as learn the tasks recommended. It is not as inflexible as the rules for a football game. It allows for expansion or contraction to fit the circumstances. To attempt to apply the system rigidly on all occasions may do more harm than good.

A good system will help the incident commander, but will not solve problems automatically. The incident commander must still orchestrate the actions of the companies by deciding which one should advance or which one should retreat, and when each move should be made. A well-conducted attack is a pleasure to behold, but without good coordination the operation may resemble high school kids holding a Saturday car-wash.

Coordination and Communication

Close control of companies is essential to their safety as well as the efficiency of incident command. Coordination is necessary to obtain objectives cooperatively, and you can't control or coordinate if you can't communicate. The span of control should be broken down into reasonable numbers, and there should be a constantly available line of communication from and to each company. If it is not direct to the incident commander it should at least be to a sector chief who has access to the IC.

Every company should have at least one radio. Ideally, each firefighter should get a radio. Right now every cop has a hi-tech portable radio which will let him call everybody from his corporal to his congressman.

If for some reason nothing else will work, you can fall back on direct oral communication or oral communication relayed by messenger, which was the only way in the old days. Whether carried out by radio or any other means, communication is a two-way street. Orders flow down; information flows up. Each depends on the other.

Accountability

The 1912 edition rules of the New York fire department stated that officers shall be held accountable for the whereabouts of their subordinates, thus setting into motion the concept that recently has become known as "accountability."

The renewed emphasis on this old concept has led to some new ideas. The old New York system was for the company officer to carry on his person a list of the firefighters in the company. Now we can use transponders and computers to locate firefighters. Each department—paid or volunteer—should adopt some method to track the whereabouts of personnel. But more than that, each officer should know not only where his subordinates are, but what they are doing, how they are doing and what condition they are in.

When a company officer is queried by radio, his answer should be explicit. But in order to get a good answer, the question must be definite. "How are you doing?" is vague and invites a vague response such as "O.K." which in one case might mean we have advanced twenty feet, and in another case might mean we are still alive.

TACTICAL PRIMER FOR COMPANY OFFICERS

The company officer has a limited responsibility but it is also a heavy one, often involving life safety as well as an opportunity to cause or prevent a great amount of damage.

Company size-up

The size-up at the company level is important but does not have to be as complete as that of the incident commander unless the company officer is the first to arrive and thereby becomes the incident commander until the arrival of someone higher in rank. (The New York City rules promulgated in 1738 established that procedure and it has been followed by the fire service of North America ever since.)

Initial command

Sizeup for the company officer arriving first and assuming command.
The first considerations are life hazard, fire hazard, and extension hazard. Let us re-state these as questions:
(1) What is the life hazard to occupants, the firefighters, and others (spectators and neighbors)?
(2) What is the location, intensity, extent, and type of fire?
(3) What is the probability and likely direction of extension; and what will be the consequences?

Action plan

Stated most simply the action plan is: locate, confine, extinguish.
That is the way it has been expressed for more than a century in Latin English. But for those who prefer the lengthier but more descriptive Saxon English, we would say: Find the fire. Keep it from spreading. Put it out.
Usually all three steps are taken simultaneously and there is no need for other activity. Textbooks emphasize rescue and exposure protection, and each should be considered if necessary. But in the real world the average firefighter

has never seen a true rescue, and will go for years without ever seeing an exposure problem.

The company officer should anticipate how long he may be in charge and decide whether or not help should be called and should have the authority to call it.

Application

The tactics should follow department policy, but in order for that to happen, there should be clearly defined operational guidelines, and they should be understood by all officers. In the early days of implementing the first fire research and safety act, a representative group of second level chiefs was brought to a conference on tactics. Many of them complained that when they arrived at a fire their big job was to undo what the company officer had done wrong already. A clear policy for apparatus placement, hose size and placement, ventilation, and other practices should be spelled out, but should be flexible.

An example: "The first hoseline stretched at a structural fire shall be taken inside through the front entrance, unless it is obvious that it should be taken elsewhere."

When the first arriving officer is relieved by someone of higher rank, he should tell that officer what has taken place, including any change in the fire, and also transmit any other information of importance, especially problems not yet resolved.

When the higher ranking officer is satisfied with the briefing, he may order the company officer to return to his unit, or to undertake some other responsibility.

Sizeup for Company Officers Other than First to Arrive

Regardless of when they arrive, company officers should make a "mini size-up" to acquire the knowledge important to executing the company mission effectively and safely.

Some of it will be given—or should be—by the incident commander, but while reporting in or awaiting orders the company officer should attempt to note the following:

- Location, type and intensity of the fire.
- Direction of fire travel.
- Positions of hoselines, ladders, apparatus.
- Points of access, egress and ventilation.

Structure type and stability; Hazards to personnel

It is important for all officers to understand that knowing the building the fire is in is as important as knowing the fire that is in the building. They should have knowledge of building types and what to expect of them in certain situations. In addition to structural collapse probability, they should consider fire travel, especially in concealed spaces behind walls, above ceilings and through vertical shafts. In most areas they can become familiar with specific buildings by prefire inspections and memorize features that would be important during a fire. This information should be recorded to be used when needed, in planning and training, as well as on the fireground.

SUMMARY

The company is the keystone of the operational effort. The goal of firefighting operations is to keep injuries and property damage to a minimum. Strategy is the plan to achieve the goal, which must be attained through tactics. Tactical objectives are accomplished by the proper use of companies.

In attempting to present a concise and simple exposition of the principal considerations involved, I am reminded of a remark made by a firefighter many years ago. He said, "Some officers like to say firefighting is complicated, but it is really very simple."

Von Clausewitz, the German military genius, wrote, "In war, everything is very simple, but in war, the simple can be difficult."

So it may be with firefighting.

18

Rescue Operations

FRANK W. BORDEN

CHAPTER HIGHLIGHTS

- Overview of rescue operations.
- Information on the complexities involved in urban search and rescue and structural collapse.
- Overview of the Incident Command System and how it might be used to organize and manage rescue operations.

RESCUE MAY BE DEFINED as locating and removing trapped victims from confinement or danger and doing so rapidly and safely.

Fire departments have been rescuing people in life-threatening situations since their inception centuries ago.

Rescue operations have been multiplying and becoming more complex because of the growing population, increasing exposure to events that create a need for rescue, and rapid changes in technology and hazards associated with modes of transportation, equipment, chemicals, and structural designs.

Natural disasters such as earthquakes, hurricanes, tornadoes, and floods, and technological events such as vehicular and transportation accidents, explosions, hazardous material releases, fires, structural failure and collapse result in the multitude of conditions that require victim rescue. This chapter will focus on rescue operations, the use of the Incident Command System, and coordination.

Our challenge is to reduce the problems associated with rescue by developing and using effective incident management and coordination systems, and efficient rescue tools, and by providing the training necessary for safe rescue operations.

URBAN SEARCH AND RESCUE INITIAL RESPONSE STRATEGIES FOR RESCUE OPERATIONS

Most of the time the difference between an emergency and a disaster is the amount of preparation that goes on before the emergency. This preparation includes researching anticipated problems and developing scenarios from past events, identifying both the expertise and resources **needed** as well as what are **presently available,** and addressing the shortfalls in resources and training.

The causes of structural collapse, and its magnitude and complexity may vary widely. At one end of the spectrum would be a single or partial building or other structure collapse where sufficient resources are available. At the extreme other end of the spectrum is a serious earthquake, now considered a highly probable event in many areas across the country where many large or heavily occupied buildings may collapse. There may be hundreds or thousands of trapped victims there, and rescue efforts often have to be mounted with limited equipment and personnel.

What is common to these types of incidents is that a building, structure, tunnel, or enclosure has collapsed, trapping victims who may be seriously injured and who must be located quickly and removed to safety and medical care without unreasonable risk to the rescuers. The vast majority of live victims (more than 80 percent) are rescued during the first 24 hours of entrapment. The chances for survival diminish rapidly after what is called the "golden day."

Urban Search and Rescue (US&R), as defined by the Los Angeles City fire Department, is "the process of mobilizing and managing the resources necessary to safely and quickly locate and remove trapped and often injured victims from partially or totally collapsed structures or environments, and provide for rapid emergency medical care." This involves an integrated response system of highly specialized equipment, well-trained personnel from different disciplines, effective communications, and an established method of command, control, and logistical support. The complexities of the search and rescue function after a structural collapse require a coordination and incident management system that is commonly understood, constantly used, and effective. This system should be used in daily operations and expanded or easily applied to a variety of emergency incidents. It also requires that Standard Operating Procedures (SOPs) be developed for the strategic and tactical functions of the incident.

Depending on the size and complexity of a single- or multiple-structure collapse, the response may vary from only a few rescuers to a national (or even international) response of teams with the high levels of expertise needed for the incident. Operations at the rescue site may take only minutes, or weeks, depending on resource requirements and the difficulty of the extrication. It may involve everyone from highly skilled rescue specialists to volunteer bystanders.

National Urban Search and Rescue (US&R) Response System

Within the last few years, the Federal Emergency Management Agency (FEMA), the Department of Defense, and representatives from organizations across the country established a national US&R response system. Made up of 25 civilian task forces, each with 56 highly skilled and well-equipped members, it responds to difficult collapse rescue incidents anywhere in the country. One of the goals of this project is to develop multidisciplinary response teams from various parts of the country that will function under the Incident Command System. This National US&R Task Force Model is shown in Figure 18-1 where the search, rescue, medical, and technical team functions are directed by the Task Force Leader.

Basic Functions and Safety

The basic functions of urban search and rescue may be organized as follows:

- **Command and Coordination**—the management function of the overall operation, including strategic decisions, planning, and logistical and administrative support.
- **Search**—locating trapped victims using canine, electronic, and physical search strategies, tactics and techniques.
- **Rescue**—evaluating compromised areas, structural stabilization, breaching and site exploration, and victim extrication.
- **Medical**—emergency and possibly extended prehospital medical care, including helping to minimize health risks to rescue team members.
- **Technical**—technical advice and support to the overall operation, including the evaluation of hazardous or compromised areas, structural assessment, stabilization, hazardous materials monitoring, use of heavy equipment, and other specialized functions.

Hazards can present an enormous problem in rescue operations and safety considerations must be a high priority in the development and execution of strategies and tactics. Rescuers may face secondary collapse, extreme heat or cold, hazardous materials, toxic atmospheres, electrocution, exposure to communicable diseases, confined space, and rapid onset of fatigue and stress. Hazardous conditions can be mitigated by using:

- safe operating procedures based on experience and supported by training;
- good communications at all levels;

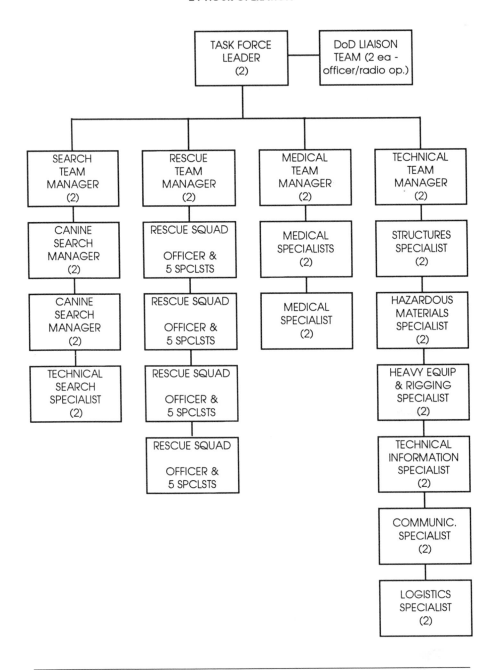

FEMA US&R TASK FORCE
56 CIVILIAN/4 DoD POSITIONS
24-HOUR OPERATION

Figure 18-1.

- protective equipment needed for the hazard;
- continuous monitoring procedures and tests of the rescue environment; and
- a training program that emphasizes both skills and safe operations.

The tools and equipment suitable for these special operations must be efficient, reliable, and used properly. Tools must be matched with the job and the environment in which they will be used.

Rescue Capability Levels

To better understand the overall management of rescue operations and structural collapse rescue scenarios, operational capability levels may be described according to the following four categories:

Injured, Not Trapped

- Injuries are usually caused by falling debris hitting the victim or the victim falling and hitting the ground. Persons injured in either way are known as "surface victims."
- Rescue efforts involve removing the victim to a safe location and treating his injuries.
- This category usually accounts for 50 percent of victims.

Basic level capability is a minimum requirement for rescue operations. At this level, rescuers should be **competent** in surface rescue which involves minimal movement of debris and building contents to safely and effectively extricate easily accessible victims. Rescue operations would include removing victims from under furniture, appliances, and the surface of a debris pile.

Rescues normally would be made by convergent volunteers and emergency service first responders.

Nonstructural entrapment

- The building may appear to be undamaged or may have had only some damage to the light-frame construction. (Rescues in these circumstances also are known as "light rescue."
- Victims are trapped by building contents like file drawers, book shelves, refrigerators, small pieces of debris, and internal building finishings, and furnishings.
- Rescue efforts involve locating and gaining access to the victim(s) by

lifting contents or debris with simple hand tools and removing to a remote location by hand with minimum shoring. This usually accounts for about 30 percent of victims.

The *light rescue* level represents the minimum capability to operate safely and effectively at a structural collapse incident involving the collapse or failure of light-frame construction.

Rescue personnel should be able to perform search operations intended to locate victims who are not readily visible but are trapped beneath debris or structural components. These rescue personnel should be able to recognize the unique hazards associated with the collapse of light-frame ordinary construction, i.e., collapse patterns, unstable areas, etc.

Rescuers also should be able to safely and efficiently extricate victims from under debris associated with light-frame ordinary construction., i.e., basic breaching, shoring, lifting, and patient stabilization and removal. A key point at this level of operations is the beginning of command discipline, coordination and control.

Rescues normally would be performed by trained volunteer community or business US&R teams, military teams, or emergency responders with basic search and team management skills, and basic knowledge of tools, utility control, collapse hazards, and first aid.

Void Space and Nonstructural Entrapment

- Buildings in this category appear to be damaged. A partial or complete collapse has occurred, presenting a very hazardous and dangerous situation.
- The victims are still trapped by building contents, such as file drawers, book shelves, appliances, and debris, but are trapped inside void spaces created by the collapsed structure. The rescue priorities are to secure the structure, locate victims, free victims from the building contents or debris, move victims to a safe location, and treat injuries.
- Rescuing a victim in this category is a slow and dangerous process, typically taking about four hours on average, and usually accounting for about 15 percent of all collapse victims.

At the *medium level* of capability, personnel should have the ability to operate safely and effectively at a structural collapse incident involving the collapse or failure of cinderblock, and reinforced and unreinforced masonry. Rescuers need to be skilled in technical search operations, hazard recognition, use of power tools, extrication techniques, breaching, cutting, shoring, lifting, victim packaging, removal, minimum basic life support, emergency medical care, and incident management.

Building's 1st floor in possible collapse—upper floors are light rescue level. Collapsed floor is medium level. Rescuers stabilize on search voids for victims.

Rescues in this category normally would be made by professional or well-trained teams, such as firefighters, specialized law enforcement, and medical teams, and specialized industrial and volunteer US&R teams.

Entombed

- The collapsed building no longer looks like the original structure. A partial or complete interior and/or exterior collapse has occurred. This is as hazardous and dangerous for the rescuer as it is for the trapped victim.
- Victims may be trapped by medium to heavy structural components like walls, floors and roofs.

These photos depict structure where victims are entombed. The highest level of skill, coordination, and control is mandatory.

- Rescue operations require securing the structure, locating the victim, breaching, shoring, tunneling, removing, or lifting the structural components away from them, moving victims to a safe location, and treating injuries.
- Rescuing entombed victims usually takes longer than four hours. The average time is about 8 to 12 hours, but operations could last for several days. This usually accounts for approximately five percent of all collapse victims.

At the *heavy level* of rescue capability, personnel should have the ability to operate safely and effectively at a structural collapse incident involving the collapse or failure of reinforced or unreinforced concrete and steel-frame construction.

Rescuers in this category need the highest level of skills to operate in these complex and often dangerous situations. They need all the skills mentioned in the medium category, plus additional rescue capabilities, equipment, and advanced life support medical capability.

US&R teams with extensive training and equipment and which have a multidisciplinary capability, i.e., medical responders, structural engineers, equipment operators, etc., are necessary for this level of response. Such teams would include the FEMA US&R Task Forces and specialized US&R teams from some fire departments and professional emergency services personnel.

Rescue Operation Phases

One of the critical responsibilities of the rescue team leader is to evaluate and prioritize rescue extrication operations. There are generally five phases of rescue operations at collapse incidents. The phases, described below, must be known and used innovatively by the Incident Commander based on continuous size-up.

Phase 1 Survey and Reconnaissance of the Entire Area for Trapped Victims.

Because collapse debris is extremely unstable, rescuers must choose their actions carefully. Many of their decisions will be based on where victims are located and how the attempt to rescue one may affect others. It is important to concentrate initial efforts where there are visible or witnessed victims and where possible victims are most likely to be found. The area is searched for possible victims (surface or buried) and evaluated for stability and danger to rescuers. Victim survey is an ongoing process throughout the five phases.

Phase 2   Immediate Rescue of Victims Who Are on the Surface of the Rubble

Although any kind of vibration threatens the stability of the rubble, the benefits of getting on top or to the edges of the pile to help anyone who is only partially buried at the surface level outweigh the risks. Experience has shown that at least half the victims rescued from a collapse are likely to be at the surface. This stage takes only a few rescuers so movement on the rubble can be minimized. It should be done as quickly and safely as possible.

Phase 3   Exploration of Void Spaces and Removal of Victims

Most of the collapse configurations—lean-to, V-shape, pancake, and tent—create spaces in which people may be trapped, yet still have a high chance of survival. These voids are the next rescue priority, and experience indicates they will yield another one-third of the victims. Only specially trained and equipped personnel should operate in voids and confined spaces.

Phase 4   Selected Debris Removal

To reach the victims who remain after phases two and three—and sometimes to reach those at the surface or in voids—rescuers must tunnel through the rubble or dig an open trench above the victim. Either procedure requires shoring. Any information about a victim's location before the collapse can be helpful during this operation.

Phase 5   General Debris Removal

After all victims whose locations are known have been located, the rest of the rubble pile must be removed. At this point, however, the objective in removing rubble is not to reach a specific point in the pile, but to discover the locations of any remaining victims. There might be unexpected victims, such as messengers or passersby, since building occupants giving information might not have been aware of their presence. Heavy equipment such as a crane might be needed, but the work must proceed carefully and systematically to prevent further injury to victims. Each load of rubble removed should be checked.

Rescue Operational Plan

The Rescue Group or Team or Task Force Leader must develop a rescue operational plan that includes the command structure, appropriate priorities, objectives, and resource requirements. The plan should be based on the following factors:

- **Time**
  The time of day or night provides information on the occupancy load and location of people in the structure.
- **Location**
  Access is important to an effective operation.
- **Construction**
  This is a major factor in planning rescue strategies and tactics. Each has probable collapse patterns, additional hazard definition, and risk increase in reduction to emergency personnel.
- **Occupancy** (hazards, type, multiple occupancies)
  Knowledge of the occupancy yields information on hazards, occupant use, and types and numbers of businesses and employees to account for.
- **Height and Area** (six sides)
  Consider all six sides and the area involved.
- **Size of Collapse Area and Structural Hazards**
  This assessment dictates resource requirements and indicates methods and personnel needed for successful and safe operation.
- **Fire Problem/Hazardous Materials**
  A collapsed structure rescue may be affected by a fire, hazardous materials problem, or both, that must be controlled simultaneously.
- **Exposures**
  Interior and exterior exposures should be considered to prevent additional damage or injury. Consider all six sides.
- **Utilities** (gas, water, electric)
  Utility control is a major safety factor for both rescuer and victim safety alike.
- **Weather**
  Temperature variations affect rescuers and victims; wind, rain, and snow certainly create additional problems inside and outside the structure.
- **Victims** (confirmed and others/witnesses and information)
  Victim location is a priority in the initial and ongoing rescue plan and may be determined by a variety of methods.
- **Traffic**
  Speed of response and access to the collapsed site are critical. Alternate routes and traffic control should be planned and coordinated in advance.

- **Rail**
Surface and underground rail systems may be part of the collapse problem; the vibration created by the systems can contribute to collapse problems.
- **Personnel**
Rescue operations require a multidisciplined response from fire, EMS, police, public works, building department, transportation department, volunteers, and many others.
- **Incident Command**
The complexities of rescue require an effective Incident Command System to manage and coordinate operations, planning, and support.
- **Communications**
Intra- and interagency communication capability are essential to effective and safe operations.
- **Medical**
Rescue medical operations need to provide for the victim as well as personnel, i.e., injury, rehab.
- **Safety**
Safety is a top priority in rescue planning and operations and must be considered throughout the incident.
- **Special Equipment**
Collapsed structure rescue operations may require the use of specialized search equipment, such as electronic listening devices, fiber-optic cameras, and portable cutting, breaking and breaching equipment.
- **Construction Equipment**
Large mechanized construction equipment may be needed to remove debris so that rescue operations can be expedited.
- **Shoring Materials**
Large quantities of shoring materials may be needed to gain access to the victim and to stabilize the structure. Preplanning to locate supply sources is important.
- **Information Updates**
Continuous information updates and recordkeeping are needed during every stage of the rescue operation.
- **Staging Areas**
Staging areas should be established for incoming resources so that the response into the rescue site can be managed effectively.
- **Rest, Recovery, and Relief of Members**
Long-term rescue operations necessitate periodic rest periods and rehabilitation for rescue workers; include provisions that allow operations to continue while some workers rest.
- **Secondary Collapse**
The potential for secondary collapse from an earthquake aftershock or already weakened structural support failure should be considered.

• **Golden Day** (24-hour survival)
  The first 24 hours of the rescue operation yield the most survivors. The term "Golden Day" is used for US&R as the "Golden Hour" is used in EMS.

A heavy capability rescue team may arrive at the scene of a collapsed structure incident some time after initial actions have been taken by volunteers or first-responder resources. The Rescue Team Leader commands a specialized resource that should assume those priority tasks that the team is trained and equipped to perform.

Before engaging in search and rescue operations, the Rescue Team Leader should meet with the Incident Commander or an appropriate member of the command staff to provide a briefing on the team's capabilities, determine the on-site command and communication system, and identify resources useful to the team's operation, such as equipment, technical advisors, and medical capability.

Information about past and current conditions and operations is needed, including the structural collapse situation, known hazards, and locations of trapped victims. A pre-engagement damage assessment survey should be made so that the team leader can develop an accurate strategic and tactical operational plan.

Medical Considerations

Time has proved to be a critical factor in the survivability of injured victims. Once the victim is injured, the clock starts ticking against declining body functions. Experienced rescuers believe that a maximum of 12 to 24 hours is available for the most effective lifesaving operations.

This theory is supported by the correlation between survival rates and rescue times from the 1976 Tangshan China Earthquake. Many deaths related to structural collapse were not instantaneous and the injured died hours after the event. Survival rates were high for victims rescued within one day of the earthquake, but fell dramatically after the first 24 hours. They ranged from 81 percent on the first day to 34 percent on the second to a low of 7 percent on the fifth day.

Victims die from trauma in one of three phases:

• First Phase
  In this phase, victims die within minutes, usually from multiple organ system failure caused by overwhelming trauma or asphyxiation.
• Second Phase
  In this phase, victims live for hours after an injury. Instead of dying from overwhelming trauma, they typically suffer uncontrolled hemor-

rhaging. Often, these victims might have been saved through proper extrication and emergency medical treatment techniques.

- Third Phase

  In this phase, victims do not necessarily die from immediate injury, but rather from a later complication such as an infection. Therefore, death occurs weeks or even months following the injury.

Studies have shown that rescuers can have the biggest impact on survivability in the second and third phases. In the second phase death may certainly be prevented, and in the third phase life-threatening complications can be reduced. It is essential that effective strategies and tactics be developed so that rescuers have the best possible chance to achieve the ultimate goal of saving lives.

Size-up

Proper medical care of trapped victims is dependent on a total size-up or assessment of the situation that includes such additional factors as:

- Single site versus multiple sites;
- Number and location of survivors;
- Condition of survivors;
- Short-term versus long-term survival potential;
- Medical capabilities
  —Hospitals
  —EMS personnel
- Time of disaster
  —Time of day or night
  —Day of the week
- Building construction;
- Population activities;
- Degree of extrication difficulty; and
- Weather and exposure of victims.

This size-up information allows responders to rescue the greatest number of victims in the least amount of time and to deploy available resources efficiently and effectively for the appropriate situation.

Stages of Medical Care

The stages of the rescue during which victims can receive medical care are determined during the situation size-up. Decisions about treatment are based on:

- injury severity;
- site stabilization;
- the environment;
- extrication difficulties;
- available personnel;
- time; and
- risk.

It is important to remember that of these factors, the most limiting is often extrication difficulties, not the lack of medical resources, in delivering definitive medical care to the victim.

The trapped victim should receive medical care when responders gain initial access and during secondary access.

Initial Access. When responders gain initial access to the victim, they should, as they would with any victim, attend to the ABCs (Airway, Bleeding, Circulation) first. Rescuers should be aware that dust inhalation can cause shortness of breath in victims, which can be aggravated by the rescue efforts that involve drilling, sawing, and rubble movement which cause additional dust to become airborne. Administering oxygen helps to decrease hypoxia and acidosis and should routinely be used as soon as possible. **The next critical task** is to control any open bleeding. Perhaps just as important as supporting the airway and controlling bleeding is providing psychological support for the victim. Several reports of suicide by trapped victims have been reported in the earthquakes of Mexico City and Armenia. Ongoing verbal contact with the victim can ease their anxiety and despair.

Secondary Access. Once rescuers gain greater access to the victim, they can make a better assessment. At this point, rescuers should concentrate on immobilizing the victim, including his cervical spine and any fractures. This is also the time to take precautions against environmentally related problems such as hypothermia and hyperthermia. Greater access allows rescuers to initiate advanced medical care, such as intravenous (IV) medication delivery. This advanced medical treatment becomes very important in the care of structural collapse victims because they tend to be patients for hours rather than minutes, and their long-term survival depends on the care they receive prior to extrication.

RESCUE INCIDENTS

The fire service today is involved in response to every conceivable type of rescue incident. Responders need a variety of rescue training techniques and specialized equipment. Many of the same rescue principles apply from one incident type to another, especially rescuer safety. The next part of this chapter will cover those types of rescue incidents that are both common and complex.

Transportation Accident Rescue

Many of the thousands of automobile accidents that occur each year result in hundreds of injuries and deaths. As the number of incidents increases so too must the skills and capabilities of rescuers. A comprehensive training program, efficient tools, and standardized safety procedures are needed to handle these emergencies.

Vehicular incidents that involve victim extrication require creative tactics and timely action. Safety is of paramount importance and the first-arriving fire company or ambulance must control operations and maintain safety for rescue personnel and victims at all times.

The following guidelines must be part of the strategy and tactics for vehicular extrication incidents:

- Establish a working area or zone to provide for the safety of rescuers and bystanders.
- Stabilize the vehicle(s) to prevent further injury and control hazards in the area such as fuel spills and electrical wires.
- Make locating and stabilizing victim(s) your first priorities. There may be victims and additional vehicles that are not readily visible to rescuers. It is critical to account for all possible victims.
- Gaining access to the victims could be as easy as opening a door or difficult enough to require the use of power tools. Initial access is intended for the first medical responder; secondary access may be made for additional rescuers, equipment, and a path for removal.
- Removing a victim normally requires immobilization and packaging to prevent further injury.

Multi-vehicular accidents or those that involve a vehicle and a building require a triage or sorting system to prioritize rescue operations; this is especially important as the initial response is limited.

The weight and speed involved in rail accidents introduce special problems that become much more complicated when the accident occurs in a tunnel. The Incident Commander's size-up should include:

- Incident location.
- Number of cars and passengers.
- Condition of cars.
- Hazardous conditions, i.e., fuel leaks, electricity, fire, smoke, reduced visibility, etc.
- A determination of resource requirements to handle the incident; including specialized equipment for search, extrication, victim removal, and medical care.

- Plans for establishing a rescue and escape corridor to provide safe access to and from the accident site.
- Establishing a system to monitor hazardous conditions such as rail car stabilization and atmosphere.

Because rail accident response involves many different agencies and requires close coordination and cooperation, it is essential to plan and train for this type of incident.

Water Rescue

Water rescue, which must be performed at the scene of rivers, lakes, oceans, and in flooded areas, is a unique operation that involves special skills. The appropriate training and equipment for the specific type of rescue operation could range from water safety awareness training and personal flotation devices to a fully equipped dive team capable of swift water and underwater rescue.

Fire departments across the country face various levels of risk with respect to the need for a water rescue capability. An important issue is whether other agencies have the water rescue capability that the fire department lacks. If the answer is none do, or assistance is too far away, the fire department should consider developing a water rescue capability that addresses the risks in its community.

Safety in water rescue operations is based on the buddy system. Working in an alien environment such as water is very dangerous. Rescuers who enter an underwater environment should be well trained and equipped and have a fellow rescuer close enough to assist if help is needed. No rescue attempt should compromise the lives of rescuers.

Confined Space Operations

Confined spaces are areas to which emergency response personnel may be summoned to perform rescue operations. Confined spaces present such dangers to responders as atmospheres that may be oxygen deficient, toxic, flammable or explosive, and that may expose rescuers to engulfing and mechanical hazards. These spaces are "confined" because they are configured in such a way that they inhibit a person's ability to enter, work in, and exit the space.

These potential hazards, coupled with recorded employee deaths and injuries, prompted the Occupational Safety and Health Administration (OSHA) to establish standards to protect workers who operate in confined spaces. On April 15, 1993, OSHA enacted Standard 29 CFR 1910.146, which lists regulations relating to safety and health for operations in and around **"Permit-required Confined Spaces."** The standard mandates requirements for practices, procedures, and training that must be in place to protect employees in general industries from the hazards of entry and emergency operations within confined spaces. This standard affects any emergency operation in a "confined space" that requires fire department assistance. The standard has a direct bearing on those fire departments in any state that has adopted OSHA regulations for its public employees through state legislation. These rules and regulations specifically outline standards for employers (fire department managers) who require employees (firefighters) to enter confined spaces for rescue purposes.

For those fire departments not covered by the OSHA regulations there is a compelling reason to follow them, that is, **personnel safety**. The regulations were promulgated as a result of occupational injury and death statistics. The standard cites a study by the Safety Sciences Division of WSA Inc., of San Diego, California, titled "Search of Fatality and Injury Records for Cases Related to Confined Spaces." The study reviewed 20,000 reports of industrial accidents nationwide for the period 1974 to 1977. Even in this limited sample there were 276 confined-space accidents which resulted in 234 deaths and 193 injuries. More recently OSHA examined its record of accident investigations for fatal confined-space incidents and found that "rescuers" accounted for more than 60 percent of confined space fatalities. OSHA determined from these data that untrained or poorly trained rescuers constitute an especially important "group at risk" and protected this group under the terms of the OSHA standard. Responsible fire service management needs to ensure that all appropriate policies, procedures, and practices are in place to protect personnel. The OSHA confined-space standard is an excellent reference document for this purpose.

If fire department administrators wish to comply with the law, and to provide a safe working environment for department members who work in confined spaces, they must be able to answer the following questions affirmatively.

Are department members trained to recognize a confined space and do they understand what constitutes an entry?

Many deaths and injuries in confined spaces can be attributed to workers' and rescuers' ignorance about what confined space is and what its potential hazards are. The ability to quickly identify a confined space helps to ensure that responders can size up an emergency successfully, identify that the operation is, indeed, in a "confined space" and, in turn, use the proper procedures. OSHA defines a confined space as one that:

- is large enough and so configured that a member can bodily enter the space and perform assigned work;
- has limited means for entry or exit; and
- is not designed for continuous occupancy.

Confined space entry is the action by which a member passes through an opening into a confined space. *Entry* includes ensuing work activities, considered to have occurred as soon as any part of the member's body breaks the plane of the opening to the space.

OSHA further divides confined spaces into permit-required and non-permit-required spaces. A permit-required space is one that contains or has the potential to contain a hazardous atmosphere, an engulfing hazard, an internal configuration that may pose a hazard to members, or any other recognized serious safety or health hazard. A non-permit-required space does not contain or have the potential to contain any of these hazards.

When department members respond to confined space emergencies they should treat all spaces as if they present the hazards of a permit-required space. This ensures that members operate safely and meet the requirements of the law.

Does the department have adequate air monitoring equipment to test confined space atmospheres?

OSHA's review of confined-space accident data indicates that most confined-space deaths and injuries are caused by atmospheric hazards. The standard requires that the internal atmosphere of the space be tested *prior* to allowing an employee, in this case the firefighter, to enter the space. A department that provides confined space rescue service tests the atmosphere first for oxygen content, then for flammable gases and vapors, and then for potential toxic air contaminants before allowing rescuers to enter. These tests must be performed in the order specified and with a calibrated direct reading instrument. This requirement dictates that the department have the proper equipment, that the equipment be maintained properly, and that personnel be trained in its use. OSHA specifically defines atmospheric levels that are considered hazardous as atmospheres that may expose employees to the risk of death, incapacitation, impairment of the ability to self-rescue, injury, or acute illness. Present in such an atmosphere would be:

- Flammable gas or vapor in excess of 10 percent of its lower flammable limit.
- Airborne combustible dust at a concentration that meets or exceeds its lower flammable limit.
- Atmospheric oxygen concentration below 19.5 percent or above 23.5 percent.
- Atmospheric concentration of any substance for which a dose or a permissible exposure limit is published.
- Any other atmospheric condition that is immediately dangerous to life and health.

Can the department change the atmosphere within the confined space if air monitoring instruments indicate hazardous levels?

The standard requires that the atmosphere within the space be free of hazards whenever an employee is inside the space. This necessitates the use of a forced air ventilation system that draws its air from a clean source and that does not increase the hazards in the space.

Are rescuers equipped with appropriate lighting equipment?

The standard requires that lighting equipment be provided to enable employees to see well enough to work safely and to exit the space quickly in an emergency. During rescue operations, consideration should be given to using portable, hands-free lighting that does not encumber the rescuer. Helmet-mounted lighting works well in this application. Consideration also should be given to providing lighting that does not itself pose an ignition source hazard. Such lighting is certified as safe for the potential environments in which it may be used.

Do personnel recognize the hazards of the confined space as well as understand information on the mode of exposure to potential contaminants and signs and symptoms of exposure?

Confined spaces present a multitude of potential exposures for personnel. All rescue members who enter the space must be aware of the potential exposures and the effects of those exposures, even if they are wearing respiratory protection and appropriate protective clothing. Poorly fitting facepieces and rips in clothing are just two examples of problems that could develop in the space. If rescuers are aware of the signs and symptoms of exposures they will be able to exit the space in a timely manner.

Confined spaces present hazards other than atmospheric hazards. The materials stored in the space may create an engulfing hazard. Engulfment refers to situations where a confined space occupant is trapped or enveloped by product. The worker then is in danger of asphyxiation, either by inhaling engulfing material or by having his torso compressed by the engulfing material. Effective rescue operations dictate that all rescuers be aware of the potential dangers of the space.

Do personnel understand the importance of ensuring that all processes, energy sources, or both are controlled appropriately before entry and are policies in place to ensure that these activities are carried out before entry?

Confined spaces in industry are classified as tanks, machinery, sump areas, pump pits, and different vessels which normally contain product(s) or processes that would pose a danger to personnel if they were allowed to enter the space and the machinery started to run during entry operations. For this reason it is important to take steps to ensure that this does not occur. Lock out/ tag out is the process of using padlocks or tags to lock out (secure in off position) the main source of power or energy. This includes machinery driven by electricity, pneumatics, hydraulics, or thermal energy. Blanking or blinding are steps taken to ensure the absolute closure of a pipe, line, or duct by fastening plates onto the conduits that completely cover the bores and that are capable of withstanding the maximum pressure of the pipe, line, or duct with no leakage beyond the plate. Rescuers should be familiar with all methods available to isolate the space from danger. Procedures should be in place to ensure that these steps are taken before an entry.

Does the department have the capability to communicate with rescuers entering the space?

The standard requires that the entry team be able to communicate with a member or attendant who is positioned at the entrance to the space. This attendant must remain at the opening to the space during the entry and must monitor the status of the entrants constantly. Entrants must be able to communicate with the attendant. Since some spaces may require that the entrants move out of voice contact range, suitable equipment must be available for communication.

Does the department have established procedures that define when a rescue team must exit the space?

Emergency responders are aggressive, "get-the-job-done" type of people who often are reluctant to leave a job even when conditions deteriorate. This attitude is evident often at structural fires when companies are told by the Incident Commander to leave the building. They often answer, "just a few more minutes and we've got it," a response made without benefit of the same information available to the Incident Commander. This attitude endangers personnel who delay evacuating the building as ordered and can be deadly if it carries over into confined space rescue operations. Rescuers must be disciplined and trained to follow all instructions from the officer positioned at the entrance to the space. The law requires that all operational personnel within the confined space exit from such space whenever:

- An order is given from the attendant;
- The entrant recognizes warning signs or symptoms of exposure to contaminants;
- The entrant detects a hazardous condition; or
- An evacuation alarm is activated.

Are rescue members trained in first aid and cardiopulmonary resuscitation?

The law specifically requires that rescuers who conduct confined space rescue be trained to this level and that such training be documented.

Is the department equipped with the appropriate harnesses, ropes, and retrieval equipment to conduct a rescue?

The law specifically requires that each entrant use a chest or full body harness attached to a retrieval line that is anchored to a mechanical device or a fixed point outside the space. A mechanical retrieval device must be available for any vertical operation that requires personnel to operate in a space deeper than five feet. This requires that members be proficient in deploying rigging systems, a skill that can be developed and maintained only through formal training programs.

Are personnel given the opportunity to practice simulated rescue operations?

The standard requires that rescue team members practice making rescues and removals from confined spaces that are *representative* of the spaces in which they will normally be required to operate. This training must be given at least *once every 12 months and be documented*. It requires that rescue personnel visit potential rescue sites and conduct drills to ensure proper and safe operations.

Are there written policies in place that guide personnel activities at confined space rescue sites?

If the fire department administration plans to send its personnel into confined spaces for rescue operations it must develop written procedures that comply with the law and include evaluation as well as documentation criteria. A fire department administrator who is unable to answer yes to any of the questions listed above is probably not in compliance with the law and may not be providing an appropriate level of safety for operating personnel.

All departments that provide confined space rescue services should read the standard in its entirety and develop appropriate policies, procedures, and practices. The standard was written and promulgated because of life losses in confined space operations and is designed to limit any future injury or loss of life.

Trench Rescue

Emergency responders often are called to accident scenes where victims are buried partially or completely as a result of cave-ins, trench or excavation collapses, and landslides. Most cave-ins that involve buried victims are caused by a failure to follow proper safety rules and the failure to provide adequate shoring and sheeting support.

Rescuers sometimes bypass safety procedures in their haste to free a buried victim, only to become victims themselves. It is essential to maintain discipline and take the time to establish safety measures. This greatly reduces the risk to both rescuers and victims.

In 70 percent of all trench collapses a secondary collapse occurs, often after rescuers have arrived. Some secondary collapses are caused by rescue efforts. One of the most important initial actions the Incident Commander can assume is to take charge and control the situation, moving people at risk out of the danger area.

Displaced soil in a cave-in or collapsed trench can cause severe trauma to the victim and is difficult to remove under rescue conditions without jeopardizing the safety of the victim and rescuer. The weight of the soil—100 to 125 pounds per cubic foot—poses the greatest problem. The cause of death of most collapsed trench victims is traumatic asphyxiation. As the soil surrounds the victim's chest area it presses on the rib cage and counteracts the efforts of the chest to expand. The inability to exchange air results in hypoxia and, finally, death.

The rescue operations plan for cave-in or trench collapses should include the following considerations:

Arrival

Upon arrival, apparatus should be placed well away from the site to prevent vibrations from disturbing the site. A command post should be set up and the person in charge of the excavation directed to that location.

Control

All persons should be removed from the collapse area. They generally add to the confusion and their movements around the trench could cause additional collapse.

Persons who are attempting rescue inside the trench should be removed. Ladders and assistance should be provided by rescuers.

All equipment in the area should be shut off to reduce vibration and to prevent anyone from using it in a rescue effort. Power equipment should not be used to dig out trapped persons.

Use yellow tape to set up a perimeter around the immediate area. Keep nonessential persons out of the area, including firefighters not directly involved in the rescue.

Request traffic control to keep all nonessential traffic out of the general area.

Size-Up

The person in charge of the trench project or a responsible party should be located and asked to answer at least the following questions:

- Who was working in or around the trench? This person may have victim and collapse information.
- Where was the trapped person working? If a general collapse occurred and the person is buried completely, rescuers will need to know where to establish "safe zones."
- What was the person doing at the time of the collapse? The person may have been standing, sitting, kneeling, etc.
- How many people were working in the trench? Additional victims may be buried.

Victim conditions should be assessed whenever possible so that a risk-benefit decision can be made at this time.

A "walk-around" inspection of the trench should be made. Check soil category, type, and condition. If the soil is stress cracked the possibility of a secondary collapse exists.

Determine what additional assistance is needed in the way of staffing and equipment. Rescue work is very tiring. Rescuers should be rotated every 15 to 20 minutes. Sometimes the rescue effort may begin from two different directions, requiring twice the personnel. A minimum of one company is necessary for shoring. Additional personnel should be requested early in the incident if needed.

Professional shoring and trench rescue equipment may be requested if it is not readily available at the site. If the collapse is at a general construction site, chances are good that adequate supplies of lumber for shoring can be obtained immediately. It may be necessary to request assistance from a local lumberyard. Payment for materials used could be arranged at a later time.

You will need to determine whether the trench is related to a utility problem or repair. The involvement of a gas or water leak in the rescue effort could have negative consequences. In all cases the involved utility company should be notified and a supervisor requested to respond to the Command Post. If appropriate, have the utility shut down the power or water.

Scene Management and Trench Stabilizing

A Safety Officer whose responsibility relates directly to the rescue operation is needed. It may be necessary to establish more than one Safety Officer depending on the needs of the rescue. An ideal location for the Safety Officer is where he can observe both sides of the trench and monitor all rescue operations directly. Safety zones should be established immediately prior to the start of the digging and shoring operation.

Patient Treatment

Patient treatment should begin as soon as possible from the top. An airway must be established and oxygen provided as the dirt is cleaned away from the chest area. A patient assessment also should be made as soon as it is possible and safe to do so to determine patient condition and additional emergency medical intervention.

All soil must be removed before any attempt is made to remove the victim. Trying to pull the patient out of the soil can cause further injury. At a minimum, cervical spine precautions shall be followed when extricating all victims.

Victim removal must be planned carefully. A patient may have to be extracted using a rope rescue system. This will depend on the depth of the trench, the victim's location, and rescue access. If the patient is to be removed by hand, all rescuers must be placed strategically and the patient removed "hand over hand." This is a team effort; rescuers should not attempt to remove the patient by themselves because this could lead to injury.

Unfortunately, fatalities do occur at trench collapses. If you learn that the rescue has become a body recovery, every precaution should be taken to provide for rescuer safety.

Terminating the Emergency

OSHA or local building and safety inspectors often arrive on the scene by the time a rescue has been completed. Inspectors should be permitted to view the emergency shoring in the trench prior to its removal. Pictures of the shoring should be taken for department records, if possible.

Temporary shoring installed by fire department rescuers should be removed and replaced with professional equipment provided by the contractor. Rescue shoring for minimum safety should never be left in the trench for continued use. The process of disassembling rescue shoring by reversing the installation process must be supervised.

At times, rescuers bypass safety procedures in their haste to free a victim. Discipline, taking the proper safety measures, realizing the dangers to both themselves and the victim, and operating with caution all can help rescuers prevent secondary collapse. Rescuers who operate under these guidelines can help keep themselves from becoming collapse victims.

Remember, most confined space rescues are time-consuming operations. When you put the action plan into motion, use all available resources, ensure the safety of all rescuers, and have a contingency plan.

INCIDENT COMMAND AND COORDINATION

The complexities of the search and rescue function require the use of a coordination and incident management system that is commonly understood, constantly used, and effective.

Coordination Systems

Many fire departments now use a Multi-Agency Coordination System and Incident Command System (ICS) that are field tested and proven. These systems can be applied to meet the challenge of urban search and rescue at a local or regional level.

The State of California's Multi-Agency Coordination System (MACS) is an adjunct to the Fire and Rescue Mutual Aid System. It provides a regional network for the coordination of information and resource allocation through the state level Office of Emergency Services. This MACS provides the following:

Regional Situation Status Information

Information from a local jurisdiction on the statewide status of incident type, size, complexity, and resources assigned.

Incident Priority Determination

Several incidents competing for the same resources will need to be prioritized; potential life loss is the most important consideration.

Resource Acquisition and Allocation

Once resource needs have been established, a system to acquire resources through mutual aid agreements must be implemented and they must be dispatched or allocated to each incident by priority.

Local-State-Federal Disaster Coordination

Coordinating large numbers of resources from various entities must be handled at a regional level or, if the disaster(s) is large enough, at the state level.

Local jurisdictions need an effective system to rapidly mobilize all available resources in a community for response and recovery operations. The City of Los Angeles has an emergency operations organization, emergency operations plan, and an emergency operations center, which together provide for the overall management and coordination of emergency activities in time of disaster.

Mutual aid agreements exist for statewide fire and medical resources, law enforcement, structural engineers, public works, and agreements with private contractors.

Earthquakes and other natural disasters often occur across jurisdictional boundaries and, in some cases, across state lines. When this happens, problems of multi-jurisdictational authority and responsibility can become issues.

Depending on the type and scope of the disaster, a large number of emergency response or disaster agencies may be involved in mitigation and recovery efforts. For example, fire service, law enforcement, medical, military, and other local, state, and federal disaster agencies may all be represented during incidents of this type. Generally, the greater the number of agencies involved, the more complex the problem can become in terms of who is in charge and who is responsible for the specific functions required to deal with the situation (Figure 18-2).

In most cases, the authority for overall command of natural disasters is well defined in statutes or laws governing specific jurisdictional areas. Authority and responsibility for overall command should be defined clearly and formal disaster plans understood by all involved agencies prior to any event.

Incident Command System

As important as the coordination of a major urban search and rescue response is, so too is an incident management system for field operations. The natural and technical complexities, danger, and massive resource requirements from various disciplines all require a command system that can be used effectively in all situations.

The impetus for the Incident Command System was a series of major wildland fires in Southern California in the 1970s and an analysis of the response to those fires. The system now is used throughout the country.

On-Site Management Structure

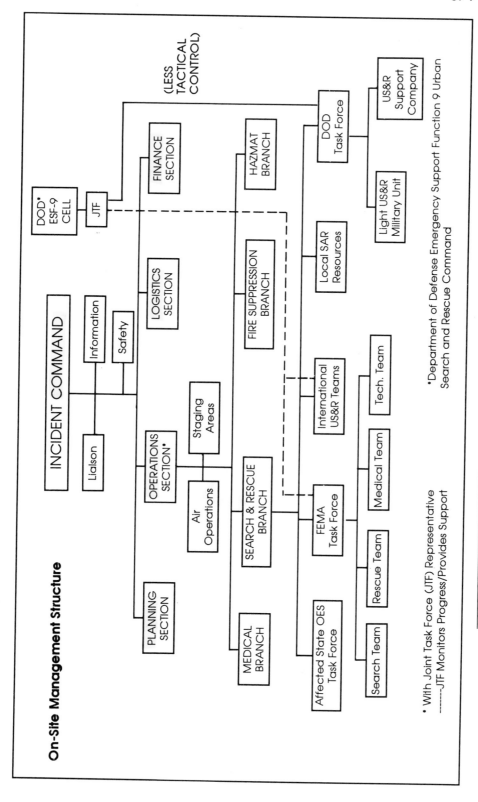

Figure 18-2.

System Design

The ICS is an emergency management organizational structure designed to provide common and effective procedures for diverse agencies working together under crisis conditions. The system consists of procedures for controlling personnel, facilities, equipment, and communications.

It is designed to begin developing from the time an incident occurs until the requirement for management and operations no longer exists. Incident Commander is a title that can be used equally by an engine company lieutenant or captain, or the chief of a department, depending on the situation. The structure of the ICS can be established and expanded depending on the changing conditions of the incident. It is intended to be staffed and operated by qualified personnel from any emergency service agency and may involve personnel from a variety of agencies.

The system can be used for any type or size of emergency, ranging from a minor incident that involves a single unit, to a major emergency that involves several agencies. The ICS allows agencies to communicate using common terminology and operating procedures. It also allows for the timely pooling of resources during an emergency.

The ICS is designed for an emergency response to natural or technological

incidents. The Los Angeles Fire Department has adopted the ICS as an all-risk management system. The following components provide the basis for an effective ICS operation:

- Common terminology improves multiagency operations.
- Modular organization provides a method to systematically build the system.
- An integrated communications systems is used to provide a means for each agency to rapidly communicate with another.
- Unified command structure may be established when an incident involves two or more jurisdictions or requires management by cooperating agencies, e.g., fire and police.
- Consolidated action planning brings multi-agency representation into the process to produce a single plan.
- Manageable span of control is the key to effective incident management. When the subordinate-to-supervisor ratio gets too high, more than 5 to 7, it is time to "delegate" responsibility.
- Predesignated incident facilities provide for the establishment of a command post, staging area, base, helibase, etc.
- Comprehensive resource management covers the entire range of the responsibilities of the command structure from command and planning to emergency operations and logistical and administrative support.

Command

The management of an emergency incident can be organized using five basic command functions: Command, Operations, Planning, Logistics, and Administration/Finance (Figure 18-3).

When an incident grows, the problems or specific needs that are identified may increase to a point where the Incident Commander (IC) cannot manage

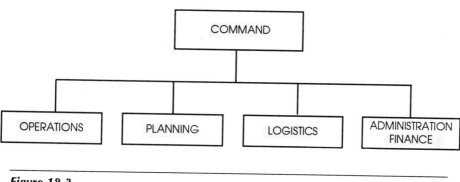

Figure 18-3.

all of them effectively. The solution is to delegate the responsibility for specific functions, other than command, to qualified personnel.

Oftentimes, the IC becomes overloaded if he waits until the need to delegate functional responsibilities becomes necessary. This happens when personnel are not available to assume those positions. When it is first apparent that the incident may escalate, the IC should anticipate the need for staff support and request qualified personnel to assume functional command positions promptly.

If specific functional command responsibilities are not delegated, it must be assumed that the IC will retain those responsibilities and be accountable for them, a likely situation in an earthquake with widespread damage and few available resources. The company officer is responsible for assessing the problems, prioritizing the response activities, and managing the available resources. For example, the IC may use trained emergency personnel, untrained volunteers from the community, private contractors with heavy equipment, medical personnel, or military personnel.

The IC's primary responsibilities are to identify the scope of the incident and the problems associated with it, and then determine an overall strategy, order and deploy necessary resources, and develop an organizational structure that is commensurate with the needs of the incident.

Additionally, the IC is responsible for ensuring the safety of emergency response personnel, using resources available from outside agencies effectively, and providing appropriate incident information to the news media and other concerned agencies. Activating the ICS Command Staff positions (Information, Liaison, and Safety) allows these functions to be delegated in a smooth and efficient manner.

Operations

The function of Operations is to deploy, direct, and coordinate tactical resources to meet the strategic goals established by the Incident Commander. Operations also is responsible for establishing and supervising staging areas used for controlling resource deployment.

The tactical activities required during an earthquake, hurricane, tornado, or flood often are multi-faceted. Although search and rescue, and medical treatment are major issues, fires and hazardous material releases may occur as well. The number and diverse nature of the individual emergency situations encountered during an earthquake and the proportionately large amounts of resources required to deal with them must be considered by the person responsible for the Operations function.

In order to maintain a manageable span of control when covering a large geographic area, additional elements of the ICS may be activated: Branches, Divisions, or Groups, and Task Forces or Strike Teams. (Figure 18-4.)

The branch organization may consist of Groups (functional) or Divisions

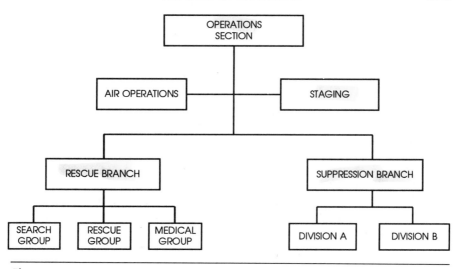

Figure 18-4.

(geographic). Operational units of groups or Divisions may be individual units or Companies, Task Forces, or Strike Teams.

Planning

Activating a formal Planning Section within the Incident Command System is necessary based on the complexities of natural disaster incidents, and the requirement to sustain emergency operators over a prolonged period of time.

The primary mission of the persons assigned to the Planning Section is to assist the Incident Commander in managing the emergency. This includes gathering, analyzing, and recording information that will be used in the Incident Commander's decisionmaking. Planning also is responsible for determining the effectiveness of current strategies or developing alternative strategies. A Victim Locator Unit also is part of the Planning Section. This unit's primary responsibility is to determine victim locations and to document all pertinent information to assure that rescue operations are timely and effective. The Victim Locator Unit is part of the intelligence gathering and thus can be assigned directly to the Search Group, if necessary.

Planning maintains situation and resource status records, documents any information relative to the incident, recommends the orderly release of resources, and provides required technical expertise.

An urban search and rescue incident requires the use of technical specialists whose area of expertise may include:

- search and rescue;
- building construction;

- heavy equipment operation; and
- structural engineering.

Logistics

The effort required to sustain operations during the various phases of an earthquake, hurricane, or tornado can be enormous. The larger the incident and the longer its duration, the more complex and demanding the logistics needs can become.

The potential complexity of logistical functions and the details that must be addressed during incidents of this type require timely activation of a Logistics Section. US&R teams that respond into devastated areas rely on an effective logistical support system. This support system may have to be set up for a predetermined operational period (e.g., three to seven days).

The organization of the Logistics Section consists of individual units responsible for specific functions, which report directly to the person in charge of Logistics. In large-scale incidents, however, maintaining a manageable span of control may dictate the creation of branches within that organization. For example, a Service Branch and a Support Branch can be created, with the Branch Directors responsible for operations within their command.

Administration and Finance

In many cases, natural disaster incidents incur considerable monetary costs associated with mitigation and recovery efforts. The ongoing financial impact of dealing with the emergency can be a source of great concern to local government officials responsible for the expenditure of funds.

Since most large disasters are not short-term situations, the costs for personnel, supplies, and equipment may be very large indeed.

If there is a severe economic impact on the local area where an incident occurs, it may be designated a disaster area by the federal government. When a disaster declaration is made, funds become available through the Federal Disaster Relief Fund. In many cases reimbursement for the costs of emergency operations associated with the disaster also are available. However, this reimbursement requires that detailed records of actual costs be submitted. Trying to develop financial records at the conclusion of an emergency may be difficult and the figures may be inaccurate. Financial recordkeeping must take place while the emergency is in progress.

The delegation of the Administration and Finance Section function by the Incident Commander will help to ensure that all financial aspects and risk analysis of the emergency will be addressed properly.

STRUCTURING AN INCIDENT COMMAND SYSTEM ORGANIZATION

The flexibility and modular expansion capabilities of the Incident Command System allow it to be used in an almost infinite number of ways. Figure 18-5 depicts an example of how the Incident Command System might be structured to deal with a large-scale earthquake incident. The example shown is not meant to be restrictive, nor to imply that this is the only way it could be used.

The organization of the Operations Section in this figure indicates the use of functional groups under the Operations Chief. However, during a large incident, the Operations Section can be broken down into specific branch functions, i.e., search and rescue and suppression, geographic areas (divisions), and various functional groups such as search, rescue, and medical.

It is important to remember that the Incident Command System organization expands from the top down. If the Incident Commander can deal effectively with all the major functional considerations the incident presents, there is no need to delegate. If, however, the size or complexity of the incident indicates that delegation of specific command functions should occur, it should be done selectively.

Any expansion of the Incident Command system should be based on the actual needs of a particular incident. The Incident Command system should be thought of as a tool box that can help the Incident Commander do a better job. **Use only the tools required for the job; leave all the others in the box.**

The 1994 Northridge Earthquake caused widespread damage and hundreds of incidents of all types, including rescues from buildings, structures, and vehicles.

The ICS organization used by the Los Angeles City Fire Department, and based on an area command concept (Figures 18-12, 18-13 and 18-14), provided for command, coordination, operations and logistical support covering the 464 square miles of the city. The Operations Section was organized using existing geographic division and battalion boundaries, with the addition of functional elements for urban search and rescue, emergency medical operations, and water resources.

The following series of organizational charts (Figures 18-6 through 18-11) show how a US&R Incident Command System can expand and yet remain flexible, based on the size, complexity, and needs of the incident. These examples depict one of several ways to organize a response to a hypothetical collapsed-structure incident where there is no fire or hazardous materials problem. The organization depicted in Figures 18-6 through 18-11 was developed for the US&R function of search, rescue, medical and support, beginning with the initial response of a single engine through the initial assignment, then

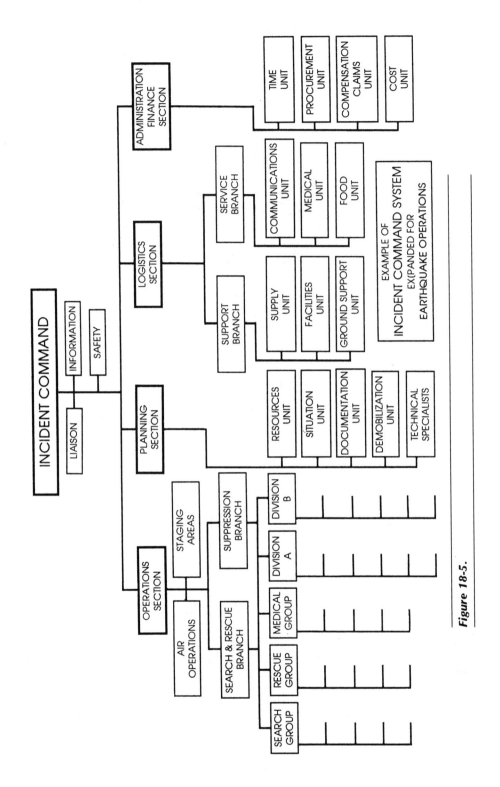

Figure 18-5.

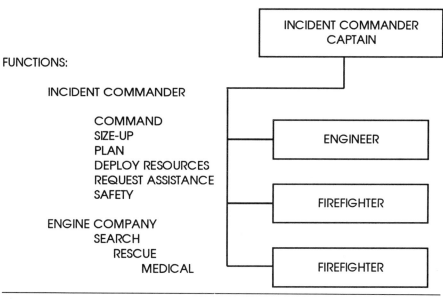

Figure 18-6.

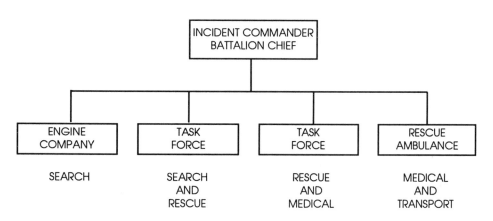

Figure 18-7.

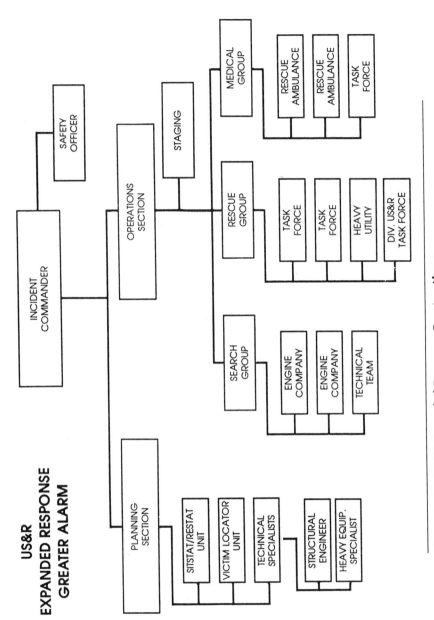

**US&R
EXPANDED RESPONSE
GREATER ALARM**

INCIDENT COMMANDER

SAFETY OFFICER

PLANNING SECTION

OPERATIONS SECTION

SITSTAT/RESTAT UNIT

VICTIM LOCATOR UNIT

TECHNICAL SPECIALISTS

STRUCTURAL ENGINEER

HEAVY EQUIP. SPECIALIST

STAGING

SEARCH GROUP

RESCUE GROUP

MEDICAL GROUP

ENGINE COMPANY

ENGINE COMPANY

TECHNICAL TEAM

TASK FORCE

TASK FORCE

HEAVY UTILITY

DIV. US&R TASK FORCE

RESCUE AMBULANCE

RESCUE AMBULANCE

TASK FORCE

Figure 18-8. US&R Expanded Response Greater Alarm

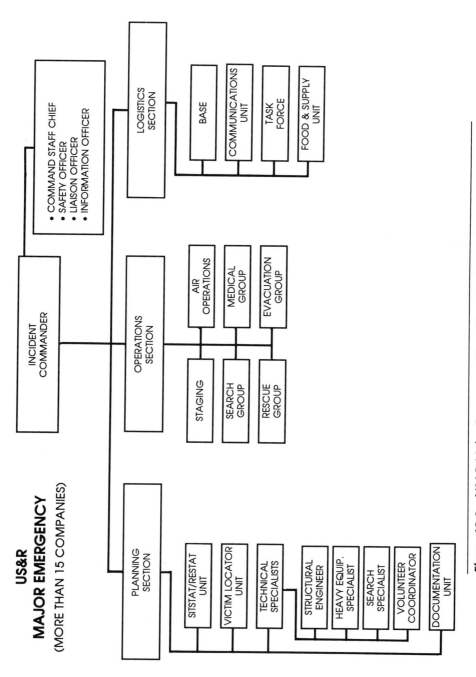

Figure 18-9. US&R Major Emergency (More Than 15 Companies)

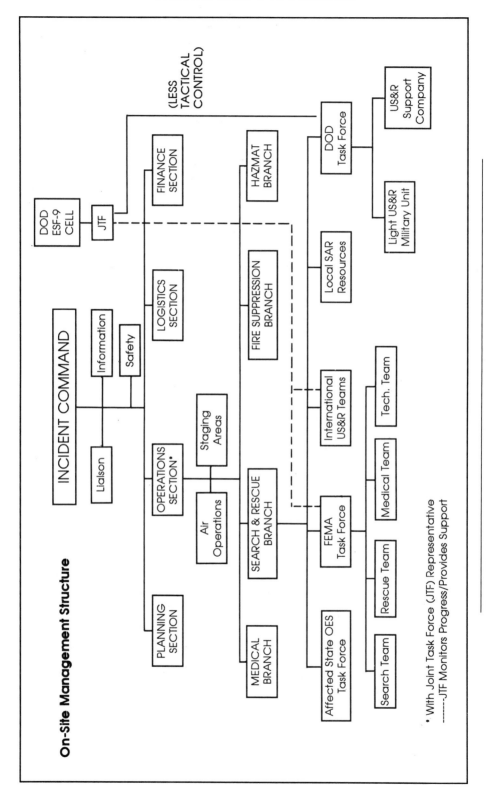

On-Site Management Structure

Figure 18-10.

* With Joint Task Force (JTF) Representative

----- JTF Monitors Progress/Provides Support

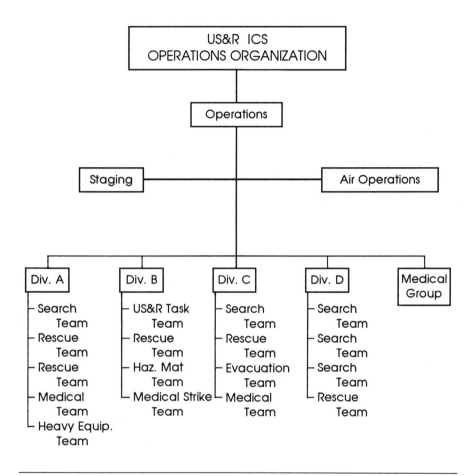

Figure 18-11.

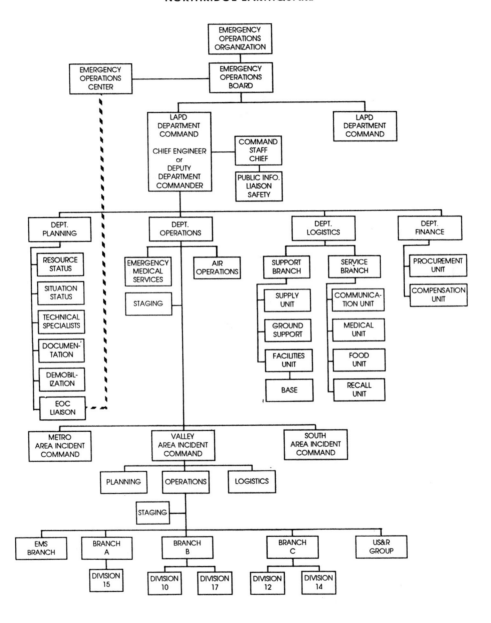

Figure 18-12.

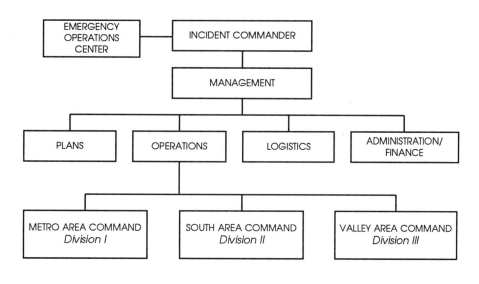

Figure 18-13.

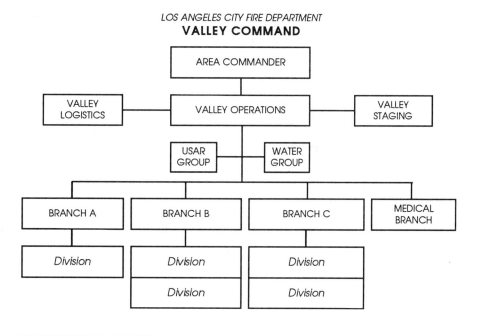

Figure 18-14.

a greater alarm, to a major emergency. It is based on resource designations and ICS methodology used by the Los Angeles City Fire Department.

Disaster Rescue Operations

The preceding diagrams illustrate how the US&R Incident Command System can expand, based on the size and complexity of the event. However, before they expand the Incident Command System and subsequent search and rescue operations, Incident Commanders must establish operational priorities based on problem assessment and available resources, while at the same time considering that the overall objective during a major disaster such as an earthquake or hurricane is to accomplish the following:

- **Save Lives.** The immediate life-saving problem should be evaluated on the basis of the complexity of the situation, availability of resources, and the criterion, "what actions will save the most lives." For example, Incident Commanders should ask whether scarce resources should be deployed to a long-term rescue operation that involves five victims versus working on a rescue operation that requires minimal time and saves 50 victims.
- **Save Property.** In a mass fire situation, the primary firefighting mission is to control those fires that have conflagration potential or loss-of-life potential. Involved structures or areas may have to be bypassed in order to accomplish this mission. For example, a wildland/urban interface fire that involves many structures and where the fire is being pushed by a strong wind may require a decision to get ahead of the fire in a location where forward progress can be stopped.

One of an Incident Commander's primary responsibilities is to establish realistic plans and priorities based on an objective appraisal of the known situation. The strategy and tactics used to accomplish the objectives will vary according to existing conditions. If individual Commanders are ever unable to receive direction or assistance, their activities should be guided by initiative and judgment in trying to accomplish the overall objective.

Reconnaissance activities normally should be conducted rapidly along a pre-established map route of "special considerations"—major roadways and bridges, hospitals, hazardous occupancies, schools, etc.—within each fire company district. This route may vary depending on the time of day or existing conditions.

Resource allocation requires a decisionmaking system that is based on accurate and timely information, an effective resource tracking system, and a command and communication system that manages emergency personnel and equipment and deploys people and equipment to the locations that require the most help.

The City of Los Angeles has emphasized the interdisciplinary requirements associated with this complex situation: preventive mitigation, planning and training or response from trained community volunteers. Additionally, fire, medical, public works, law enforcement, structural engineers, and equipment from other governmental agencies and the private sector are included. The solution to the problems associated with disaster search and rescue operations will only be realized through a well-managed and fully integrated response system.

SUMMARY

Developing an effective search and rescue capability from the local level to international response is clearly a challenge we face as more structures and people are exposed to the risk of collapse or accident. The complexities and hazards involved in rescue require a multi-disciplined approach and regional coordination, a research effort to provide us with the best methods and specialized equipment for the job, and an Incident Command System coupled with standard operating procedures that ultimately will be used to safely locate, extricate, and treat those victims trapped by structural collapse.

Our ultimate challenge is to improve our effectiveness so that more lives may be saved.

ACKNOWLEDGMENT

Special thanks to Robert E. Massicotte, Jr., Director of Training, Waterbury, CT Fire Department.

19

Hazardous Materials Operations

GREGORY G. NOLL, CSP

C H A P T E R   H I G H L I G H T S

• Key legislative, regulatory, and voluntary consensus standards that affect fire service hazardous materials planning and emergency response operations.

• An overview of the hazardous materials management system for managing the community hazardous materials problem.

• An eight-step methodology for the on-scene management of a hazardous materials emergency.

*T*HE DECADE OF the 1980s saw the emergence, growth, and acceptance of hazardous materials and environmental-related issues within the fire service. These issues have affected many aspects of our business, including training, community planning, fire code development and enforcement, live fire training, personal protective clothing and equipment (PPE), and the selection of fire extinguishing agents. In many respects, hazardous materials were to the 1980s what emergency medical services (EMS) were to the 1970s. As we move into the mid-1990s, the fire service will see hazardous materials and environmental responsibilities mature, and become fully established as one of the primary public safety responsibilities, along with fire, rescue and EMS.

Regardless of the "level" of hazardous materials response to be provided within a community, fire service executives must recognize that hazardous materials and environmental planning, prevention, training, and response issues are inherent elements of a comprehensive public safety program. The absence of a hazardous materials response team does not alter the basic premise that there is still a wide range of hazardous materials operational and regulatory issues that must be monitored and managed continuously by fire service executives.

Traditionally the fire service has been the primary local government agency responsible for hazardous materials emergency planning and response, although in some jurisdictions this responsibility has been delegated to other agencies, including the health department, police department, and emergency medical services. In addition, there are a number of other regional, state and federal agencies which also have hazardous materials and environmental responsibilities, including state and federal environmental agencies (e.g., EPA, DER), the United States Coast Guard (USCG), state and federal emergency management agencies (e.g., FEMA), and state and federal law enforcement agencies (e.g., State Police Environmental Crimes Unit, FBI, ATF). In essence, the growth of the fire service's involvement in the hazardous materials field also has been accompanied by the growth of the hazardous materials bureaucracy at other levels of government; intergovernmental communication and coordination are critical if the hazardous materials problem is to be managed effectively at the local level.

This chapter has been written to give chief fire officers and fire service executives an overview of the fire service's role in managing the hazardous materials problem. It is not meant to be a treatise on the subject, merely an overview with thoughts and ideas on where additional information and assistance can be obtained. It should be noted that a key resource in managing a fire service hazardous materials program is the fire department's Hazardous Materials Officer/Coordinator, or a senior fire officer charged with responsibilities in this area. In many respects, this individual serves as the fire department's "in-house environmental consultant."

HAZARDOUS MATERIALS LAWS, REGULATIONS, AND STANDARDS

Hazardous materials manufacturers, transporters, users, and fire service personnel are affected by a large body of laws, regulations, and voluntary consensus standards. These rules touch on virtually every facet of the hazardous materials business. Because of their importance to emergency planning and response operations, the chief fire officer must have a working knowledge of how the regulatory system functions. First, what is the difference between a law, regulation, and standard? These three terms are sometimes used interchangeably but they do have distinctly different meanings.

Laws are created primarily through an act of the U.S. Congress or by individual state legislatures. Laws typically provide broad goals and objectives, mandatory dates for compliance, and established penalties for noncompliance. Federal and state laws enacted by legislative bodies usually delegate the details for implementation to a specific federal or state agency. For example, the U.S. Occupational Safety and Health Act enacted by Congress delegates rulemaking and enforcement authority on worker health and safety issues to the Occupational Safety and Health Administration (OSHA).

Regulations, sometimes called *rules,* are created by federal or state agencies as a method of providing guidelines for complying with a law which was enacted through legislative action. A regulation permits individual governmental agencies to enforce the law through inspections which may be conducted by federal and state officials. Sometimes agencies such as EPA and OSHA adopt standards which have the effect of regulations.

Voluntary consensus standards normally are developed through professional organizations or trade associations as a method of improving the individual quality of a product or system. Within the fire service, the National Fire Protection Association (NFPA) is recognized for its role in developing consensus standards and recommended practices which have an impact on fire safety and fire department operations. In the United States, standards are developed primarily through a democratic process whereby a committee of subject specialists representing varied interests writes the first draft of the standard. The document then is submitted to either a larger body of specialists or the general public who then may amend, vote on, and approve the standard for publication. This procedure is known as the consensus standards process.

When a consensus standard is completed, it may be voluntarily adopted by government agencies, individual corporations, or organizations. Many hazardous materials consensus standards also are adopted as a reference in a regulation. In effect, when a federal, state, or municipal government adopts a consensus standard by reference the document becomes a regulation. An example of this process is the adoption of NFPA 30—*Flammable and Combustible Liquids Code,* and NFPA 58—*Standard for the Storage and Handling of Liquefied Gases*, as law in approximately 30 different states.

Federal hazardous materials laws

Hazardous materials laws have been enacted by Congress to regulate everything from finished products to toxic waste. Because of their lengthy official titles, most people simply use abbreviations or acronyms when referring to these laws. The following summaries will help you understand some of the most important laws affecting the fire service.

- **CERCLA**—The Comprehensive Environmental Response Compensation and Liability Act. Known as "Superfund," this law addresses hazardous substance releases into the environment and cleanup of inactive hazardous waste disposal sites. It also requires those companies responsible for the release of hazardous materials above a specified "reportable quantity" to notify the National Response Center.

- **RCRA**—The Resource Conservation and Recovery Act. This law establishes a framework for the proper management and disposal of all hazardous wastes, including treatment, storage, and disposal facilities. It also establishes installation and notification requirements for underground storage tanks.

- **CAA**—The Clean Air Act. This law establishes requirements for airborne emissions and the protection of the environment. The Clean Air Act Amendments of 1990 addressed emergency response and planning issues at certain facilities with processes using highly hazardous chemicals. This included the establishment of a national Chemical Safety and Hazard Investigation Board, the requirement for Risk Management and Prevention Plans (RMPPs) at these facilities, and OSHA's promulgation of 29 CFR 1910.119, Process Safety Management of Highly Hazardous Chemicals. In addition, certain facilities will be required to make information available to the general public regarding the manner in which chemical risks are handled within a facility.

- **SARA-Title III**—Superfund Amendments and Reauthorization Act of 1986. Also known as the Emergency Planning and Community Right-to-Know Act, this law requires chemical manufacturers to notify the Local Emergency Planning Committee (LEPC) and the State Emergency Response Commission (SERC) of hazardous substance inventories that exceed the "threshold planning quantity (TPQ)." Also, certain chemical manufacturing facilities are required to notify the Environmental Protection Agency of normal toxic chemical releases annually.

Of these four laws, SARA, Title III has had the greatest impact on fire service operations. As the name implies, SARA acted to both amend and reauthorize the Comprehensive Environmental Response, Compensation, and Liability Act of 1980 (CERCLA or Superfund). While many of the amendments pertained to hazardous waste site cleanup, SARA added a number of new requirements that established a national baseline with regard to planning, response, management, and training for hazardous materials emergencies.

Title III of SARA mandated the establishment of both state and local planning groups to review or develop hazardous materials response plans. The state planning groups are referred to as the State Emergency Response Commission (SERC). The SERC is responsible for developing and maintaining the state's emergency response plan, including ensuring that planning and training are taking place throughout the state, as well as providing assistance to local governments, as appropriate. States generally provide an important source of technical specialists, information, and coordination. However, they typically provide only limited operational support to local government and the fire service in the form of equipment, materials, and personnel.

The coordinating point for both planning and training activities at the local level is the Local Emergency Planning Committee (LEPC). LEPC membership includes representatives from the following groups:

Elected state and local officials
Fire department
Law enforcement
Emergency management
Public health officials
Hospital
Industry personnel, including facilities and carriers
Media
Community organizations

The LEPC is specifically responsible for developing, coordinating, or performing both functions for the local emergency response system and capabilities. A primary concern is the identification, coordination, and effective management of local resources. Among the primary responsibilities of the LEPC are:

- developing, regularly testing, and exercising the hazardous materials Emergency Response Plan;
- compiling information on hazardous materials facilities within the community. This includes chemical inventories, Material Safety Data Sheets (MSDS) or chemical lists, and points of contact; and
- coordinating the Community Right-to-Know aspects of SARA, Title III.

Hazardous materials regulations

As previously noted, laws delegate certain details of implementation and enforcement to federal or state agencies which then are responsible for writing the actual regulations which enforce the legislative intent of the law. Regulations are more detailed and either define the broad performance required to meet the letter of the law or provide very specific guidance.

FEDERAL REGULATIONS

The following summary includes some of the more significant federal regulations which affect the fire service.

Hazardous Waste Operations and Emergency Response (29 CFR

1910.120). Also known as HAZWOPER, this federal regulation was issued under the authority of SARA, Title I. The regulation was written and is enforced by the Occupational Safety and Health Administration in those 23 states with their own OSHA-approved occupational safety and health plans. In the remaining 27 states and the District of Columbia, fire service personnel are covered by a similar regulation enacted by the Environmental Protection Agency (40 CFR Section 311). See the Technical Resources Section for a listing of the states.

The regulation establishes important requirements for both industry and public safety organizations which respond to hazardous materials or hazardous waste emergencies. This includes firefighters, EMS personnel, and hazardous materials response team (HMRT) members. Requirements cover the following areas:

- Hazardous Materials Emergency Response Plan.
- Emergency Response Procedures, including the establishment of an Incident Command System, the use of a buddy system with backup personnel, and the establishment of a Safety Officer.
- Specific training requirements covering instructors and both initial and refresher training (see below).
- Medical Surveillance Programs.
- Post-emergency termination procedures.

Of particular interest to the chief fire officer are the specific levels of competency and associated training requirements identified within OSHA 1910.120(q)(6) and outlined below.

First Responder at the Awareness Level. These are individuals who are likely to witness or discover a hazardous substance release and who have been trained to initiate an emergency response notification process. The primary focus of their hazardous materials responsibilities is to secure the incident site, recognize and identify the materials involved, and make the appropriate notifications. These individuals would take no further action to control or mitigate the release. First Responder Awareness personnel shall have sufficient training or experience to objectively demonstrate the following competencies:

1. An understanding of what hazardous materials are, and the risks associated with them in an incident.
2. An understanding of the potential outcomes associated with a hazardous materials emergency.
3. The ability to recognize the presence of hazardous materials in an emergency and, if possible, identify the materials involved.
4. An understanding of the role of the First Responder Awareness individual within the local Emergency Operations Plan. This would include

site safety, security and control, and the use of the DOT *Emergency Response Guidebook.*
5. The ability to realize the need for additional resources and to make the appropriate notifications to the communication center.

The most common examples of First Responder Awareness personnel include law enforcement and plant security personnel, as well as some public works employees. There is no minimum hourly training requirement for this level; the employee would have to have sufficient training to objectively demonstrate the required competencies.

First Responder at the Operations Level. Most fire department suppression personnel fall into this category. These are individuals who respond to releases or potential releases of hazardous substances as part of the initial response for the purpose of protecting nearby persons, property, or the environment from the effects of the release. They are trained to respond in a defensive fashion without actually trying to stop the release. Their primary function is to contain the release from a safe distance, keep it from spreading, and protect exposures.

FIRST RESPONDER Operations personnel shall have sufficient training or experience to objectively demonstrate the following competencies:

1. Knowledge of basic hazard and risk assessment techniques.
2. Knowledge of how to select and use proper personal protective clothing and equipment available to the operations-level responder.
3. An understanding of basic hazardous materials terms.
4. Know how to perform basic control, containment and/or confinement operations within the capabilities of the resources and personal protective equipment available.
5. Know how to implement basic decontamination measures.
6. Possess an understanding of the relevant standard operating procedures and termination procedures.

First Responders Operations level shall have received at least eight hours of training or have had sufficient experience to objectively demonstrate competency in the previously mentioned areas, as well as the established skill and knowledge levels for the First Responder Awareness level.

Hazardous Materials Technician. These are individuals who respond to releases or potential releases for the purposes of stopping the release. Unlike the operations level, they generally assume a more aggressive role in that they often are able to approach the point of a release in order to plug, patch, or otherwise stop the release of a hazardous substance.

Hazardous materials technicians are required to have received at least 24 hours of training equal to the First Responder Operations level and have competency in the established skill and knowledge levels outlined below:

1. Implementing the community Emergency Operations Plan.
2. Classifying, identifying, and verifying known and unknown materials by using field survey instruments and equipment (direct reading instruments).
3. Functioning within an assigned role in the Incident Command System.
4. Selecting and using the proper specialized chemical personal protective clothing and equipment provided to the Hazardous Materials Technician.
5. Understanding hazard and risk assessment techniques.
6. Performing advanced control, containment, or confinement operations within the capabilities of the resources and equipment available to the Hazardous Materials Technician.
7. Understanding and implementing decontamination procedures.
8. Understanding basic chemical and toxicological terminology and behavior.

There are many communities which have personnel trained as Emergency Medical Technicians (EMT), yet do not have the primary responsibility for providing basic or advanced life support medical care. Similarly, Hazardous Materials Technicians may not necessarily be part of a hazardous materials response team. However, if they are part of a designated team as defined by OSHA, they also must meet the medical surveillance requirements under OSHA 1910.120.

Hazardous Materials Specialists. These are individuals who respond with and provide support to Hazardous Materials Technicians. While their duties parallel those of the Technician, they require a more detailed or specific knowledge of the various substances they may be called on to contain. This individual also would act as the site liaison with federal, state, local and other governmental authorities in regards to site activities.

Similar to the Technician level, Hazardous Materials Specialists shall have received at least 24 hours of training equal to the technician level and have competency in the following established skill and knowledge levels:

1 Implementing the community Emergency Operations Plan.
2. Classifying, identifying, and verifying known and unknown materials by using advanced field survey instruments and equipment (direct reading instruments).
3. Knowing the state emergency response plan.
4. Selecting and using the proper specialized chemical personal protective

clothing and equipment provided to the Hazardous Materials Specialist.

5. Understanding in-depth hazard and risk assessment techniques.
6. Performing advanced control, containment, or confinement operations within the capabilities of the resources and equipment available to the Hazardous Materials Specialist.
7. Determining and implementing decontamination procedures.
8. Developing a site safety and control plan.
9. Understanding basic chemical, radiological, and toxicological terminology and behavior.

Where the Hazardous Materials Technician possesses an intermediate level of expertise and is often viewed as a "utility person" within the hazardous materials response community, the Hazardous Materials Specialist possesses an advanced level of expertise. Within the fire service, the Specialist often will assume the role of the Safety Officer or Hazardous Materials Sector Officer, while an industrial Hazardous Materials Specialist may be "product specific." Finally, the Specialist must meet the medical surveillance requirements outlined under OSHA 1910.120.

On-Scene Incident Commander. Incident Commanders, who will assume control of the incident scene beyond the First Responder Awareness level, shall receive at least 24 hours of training equal to the First Responder Operations level. In addition, the employer must certify that the incident commander has competency in the following areas:

1. Knowing and being able to implement the community's incident command system.
2. Knowing how to implement the local emergency Operations Plan.
3. Understanding the hazards and risks associated with working in chemical protective clothing.
4. Know of the state emergency response plan and the Federal Regional Response Team.
5. Knowing and understanding the importance of decontamination procedures.

Hazard Communication Regulation (29 CFR 1910.1200). HAZCOM is a federal regulation which requires hazardous materials manufacturers and handlers to develop written Material Safety Data Sheets (MSDS) on specific types of dangerous chemicals. These MSDSs must be made available, upon request, to employees who want information about a chemical in the workplace. Examples of information on the MSDS include known health hazards, the physical and chemical properties of the material, first aid and firefighting and spill control recommendations, protective clothing and equipment requirements, and emergency telephone contact numbers.

The chief fire officer should recognize that fire service personnel also are covered by state and federal hazard communication and "Right-to-Know" laws. Depending on the jurisdiction, MSDSs must be on file for fire department supplies and materials that have hazardous ingredients, including cleaning supplies, and fire extinguishing agents.

Hazardous Materials Transportation Regulations (49 CFR). This is a series of regulations issued and enforced by the U.S. Department of Transportation. The regulations govern container design, chemical compatibility, packaging and labeling requirements, shipping papers, transportation routes and restrictions, and so forth. The regulations are comprehensive and strictly govern how all hazardous materials are transported by highway, railroad, pipeline, aircraft, and by water.

STATE REGULATIONS

Each of the 50 states and the U.S. territories maintains an enforcement agency responsible for hazardous materials. The three key players in each state usually consist of the state fire marshal, the state occupational safety and health administration, and the state department of the environment (sometimes known as natural resources or environmental quality). While there are many variations, the fire marshal typically is responsible for the regulation of flammable liquids and gases because of the close relationship between the flammability hazard and the fire prevention code, while the state environmental agency would be responsible for the development and enforcement of environmental safety regulations.

While known by various titles, most states have a government equivalent of the federal OSHA. Approximately 23 states have adopted the federal OSHA regulations as state law. This method of adoption has increased the level of enforcement of hazardous materials regulations such as the *Hazardous Waste and Emergency Response* regulation described above. State governments also maintain an environmental enforcement agency and environmental crimes unit which usually enforces the federal RCRA, CERCLA, and CAA laws at the local level. Increased state involvement in hazardous waste regulatory enforcement has significantly increased the number of hazardous materials incidents reported. This increase is expected to continue in the future and will continue to generate more fire service activity at the local level.

Voluntary consensus standards

Standards developed through the voluntary consensus process play an important role in making the workplace and the public safe from both fire and hazardous materials releases. Historically, a voluntary standard improves over time as each revision reflects field experience and adds more detailed requirements. As users of the standard adopt it as a way of doing business, the level of safety gradually improves over time.

Consensus standards also are updated more regularly than governmental regulations. For example, since the OSHA 1910.120 regulation was initially released in December, 1986, NFPA 472, *Standard for Professional Competence of Responders to Hazardous Material Incidents* (described below), has been revised twice.

In many respects, a voluntary consensus standard provides a way for individual organizations and corporations to self-regulate their business or profession. Interestingly, all of the national fire codes in the United States are developed through the voluntary consensus standards process. The two key players are the NFPA and Western Fire Chiefs Association. Many of the standards developed by these two organizations address hazardous materials storage and handling, personal protective clothing and equipment, and hazardous materials professional competencies.

Three important hazardous materials consensus standards used within the fire service are described here.

NFPA 471, Recommended Practice for Responding to Hazardous Material Incidents, covers planning procedures, policies, and application of procedures for incident levels, personal protective clothing and equipment, decontamination, safety, and communications. The purpose of NFPA 471 is to outline the minimum requirements that should be considered when dealing with responses to hazardous materials incidents, and to specify operating guidelines.

NFPA 472, Standard for Professional Competence of Responders to Hazardous Material Incidents, specifies minimum competencies for those who will respond to hazardous material incidents. Its overall objective is to reduce the number of accidents, injuries, and illnesses during response to hazardous materials incidents, and to prevent exposure to hazardous materials to reduce the possibility of fatalities, illnesses, and disabilities affecting emergency responders.

It is important to recognize that NFPA 472 is not limited to fire service personnel, but covers all hazardous materials emergency responders from both the public and private sector.

NFPA 472 provides competencies for the following levels of hazardous materials responders. These levels parallel those listed in OSHA 1910.120, with the exception that the Hazardous Materials Specialist has been deleted and the Off-Site Specialist Employee position has been expanded.

First Responder at the Awareness Level. These are individuals who, in the course of their normal duties, may respond first to the scene of an emergency involving hazardous materials. They are expected to recognize the presence of hazardous materials, protect themselves, call for trained personnel, and secure the area.

First Responder at the Operations Level. These are individuals who respond to releases or potential releases of hazardous materials as part of the initial response to the incident for the purpose of protecting nearby persons, the environment, or property from the effects of the release. They shall be trained to respond in a defensive fashion to control the release from a safe distance and keep it from spreading.

Hazardous Materials Technician. These are individuals who respond to releases or potential releases of hazardous materials for the purpose of controlling the release. Hazardous materials technicians are expected to use specialized chemical protective clothing and specialized control equipment.

Incident Commander. The person who is responsible for directing and coordinating all aspects of a hazardous materials incident.

Off-Site Specialist Employee. These are individuals who, in the course of their regular job duties, work with or are trained in the hazards of specific materials, containers, or both. In response to incidents involving chemicals, they may be called upon to provide technical advice or assistance to the incident commander relative to their area of specialization. There are three levels of off-site specialist employee:

- Level C are those persons who may respond to incidents involving chemicals, containers or both, within their organization's area of specialization. They may be called upon to gather and record information, provide or arrange for technical advice or technical assistance consistent with their organization's emergency response plan and standard operating procedures. These individuals are not expected to enter the hot/warm zone at an incident.

- Level B are those persons who, in the course of their regular job duties, work with or are trained in the hazards of specific chemicals or containers within their organization's area of specialization. Because of their education, training, or work experience, they may be called upon to respond to incidents involving chemicals. The Level B employee may be used to gather and record information, provide technical advice, and provide technical assistance (including working within the hot zone) at the incident consistent with his organization's emergency response plan and standard operating procedures, and the local emergency response plan.

- Level A are those persons who are trained specifically to handle incidents involving specific chemicals, containers for chemicals, or both used in their organization's area of specialization. Consistent with his organization's emergency response plan and standard operating procedures, the Level A employee shall be able to analyze an incident involving chemicals within his organization's area of specialization, plan a response to that incident, implement the planned response within the capabilities of the resources available, and evaluate the progress of the planned response.

NFPA 473, Standard for Professional Competence of Responders to Hazardous Material Incidents, specifies minimum requirements of competence to enhance the safety and protection of response personnel and all components of the emergency medical services system. The overall objective is to reduce the number of EMS personnel accidents, exposures, and injuries and illnesses resulting from hazardous materials incidents. There are two levels of EMS/HM responders:

EMS/HM
I

- *EMS/HM Level I.* Persons who, in the course of their normal duties, may be called on to perform patient care activities in the cold zone at a hazardous materials incident. EMS/HM Level I responders provide care only to those individuals who no longer pose a significant risk of secondary contamination. Level I includes varying competency requirements for Basic (BLS) and Advanced Life Support (ALS) personnel.
- *EMS/HM Level II.* Persons who, in the course of their normal duties, may be called on to perform patient care activities in the warm zone at a hazardous materials incident. EMS/HM Level II responders may provide care to those individuals who still pose a significant risk of secondary contamination. In addition, personnel at this level shall be able to coordinate EMS activities at a hazardous materials incident and provide medical support for hazardous materials response personnel. Level II includes varying competency requirements for Basic (BLS) and Advanced Life Support (ALS) personnel.

II

There are many other important standards-writing bodies, including the American National Standards Institute (ANSI), the American Society for Testing and Materials (ASTM), and the American Petroleum Institute (API). Each of these organizations approves or creates standards ranging from hazardous materials container design to personal protective clothing and equipment.

Hazardous materials liability issues

Since the passage of SARA, Title III, there has been a tremendous increase in interest in the subject of liability within the hazardous materials field. Communications between senior fire executives and their legal representatives are critical in this area.

The concept of **Standard of Care** has frustrated many fire service managers and emergency planners. Standard of Care is not static, but is constantly evolving as a result of new laws, regulations, standards, and court decisions. Within the hazardous materials field, the Standard of Care is defined by laws and regulations such as SARA, Title III, OSHA 1910.120, and EPA Section 311, and consensus standards such as NFPA 472 and 473. Unless fire department policies and procedures are updated on a regular basis to reflect the current Standard of Care, liability could be incurred.

There are four key elements that must exist in order to prove that negligence and liability exist:

1. **A duty or standard to act or perform.** The existence of a duty to perform establishes a standard of conduct. The duty to perform may be statutory or part of common law. An example of a duty to perform would be a fire marshal who has the responsibility to enforce the building code. Duties may be established by statutory law, common law, or by consensus standards organizations and bodies (e.g., NFPA).

2. **A breach of that duty,** which can be either an action or an omission. There must be a breach of duty to prove negligence. This violation may be either intentional or, as in most cases, unintentional.

3. **A connection between the failure and the resulting harm.** A cause and effect relationship must be established. It must be demonstrated that the failure actually resulted in the harm that is alleged. The harm may be direct, such as injury, or indirect, such as business disruption.

4. **An actual loss or harm to the parties involved.** There must be a measurable harm, which can be in the form of injuries, damage to properties, or mental anguish.

Liability in the hazardous materials field may arise in a variety of areas, the most common of which are:

Planning. Poor or incomplete emergency response plans and the necessary implementing of Standard Operating Procedures (SOPs) or guidelines are potential sources of liability. Remember, planning is an ongoing process and plans must be continuously improved and updated. Response plans and SOPs which are out of date, or which reflect obsolete capabilities or unrealistic planning assumptions are liability hazards. Hazardous materials Emergency Response Plans must be based on the hazards present and represent the realistic capabilities that are possessed by the community and the fire department.

Training programs and exercises. Failure to comply with the OSHA 1910.120 or EPA Section 311 hazardous materials training requirements may result in liability for the fire department from both the employee and the general public, if they are harmed. Training programs must be well documented, and personnel and organizational capabilities tested in safe and regular exercises.

Failure to identify chemical hazards or prioritize chemical hazards from a planning perspective. The hazards analysis and emergency planning processes are the foundations of an effective hazardous materials emergency response plan. Not only must a community and the fire service have an effective risk analysis process, but it must be based on accepted standards and practices, such as those outlined in NRT-1, *Hazardous Materials Emergency Planning Guide* and EPA's *Technical Guidance for Hazards Analysis* (see the References Section).

Failure to warn the public of impending hazards and threats. In the event of a hazardous materials release, the proper warnings and directions must be given (e.g., evacuate or shelter in place). If a warning message results in civilians moving toward or into a hazard rather than away from it, the liability potential is clear. In addition, some communities have suffered liability problems because they failed to activate outdoor warning systems at night, in order not to disturb the public. The fire service should ensure that its present community warning system meets the requirements for today's Standard of Care.

Negligent construction or operation of emergency response systems. The fire department must ensure that both the hazardous materials equipment and services they are providing are safe, well maintained, and operated properly. The use of old or outdated practices and equipment can be a major liability concern. An example of negligent operations would be a fire department hazardous materials response team which is not trained, staffed, equipped, or operated on scene to the Standard of Care established by both federal and state government regulations and voluntary consensus standards.

THE HAZARDOUS MATERIALS MANAGEMENT SYSTEM

The fire problem in the United States traditionally has been managed by fire suppression operations at the expense of prevention activities. Fortunately, since the release of *America Burning* in 1973, there has been an increasing emphasis on managing the fire problem from a systems perspective. Community master planning, public education, residential sprinklers, improved fire code enforcement, and fire protection engineering are some examples of this change.

A similar situation exists with respect to the hazardous materials problem in the community. The hazardous materials issue must be approached from a larger, coordinated perspective if it is to be managed and controlled effectively. There are four key elements in a hazardous materials management system: planning and preparedness, prevention, response, and cleanup and recovery. If the community is performing its responsibilities within the planning and prevention functions, it is hoped that communities will see a reduction in the number and severity of response and cleanup activities.

Planning and preparedness

Planning is the first and most critical element of the system. A community's ability to develop and implement an effective hazardous materials management plan depends on two elements: hazards analysis, and the development of a hazardous materials emergency operations plan. The fire service plays a major role in both.

Hazards Analysis is the analysis of the hazardous materials present in the community, including their location, quantity, specific physical and chemical hazards, previous history, and risk of release. Hazards analysis normally is performed by either the fire department or the local emergency management agency as part of the LEPC's development of the overall emergency response plan.

Emergency Planning is a comprehensive and coordinated response to the community hazardous materials problem. This response builds on the hazards analysis and recognizes that no single public or private sector agency is capable of managing the hazardous materials problem by itself. The emergency planning process and the development of the actual hazardous materials emergency response plan normally is coordinated through the LEPC. However, the fire department must be a major player during this planning process, as the data and information generated by these activities will allow both the LEPC and the fire service manager to assess the potential risk to the community, the level of hazardous materials response to be provided, and the allocation of resources as necessary.

HAZARDS ANALYSIS

Hazards analysis is the foundation of the planning process, and can be viewed as a "refined" preincident planning process. Community hazards analysis normally is the responsibility of either the fire department or the local emergency management agency, with the information then channeled through the LEPC for inclusion in the local emergency response plan and procedures. Fire service preincident plans often serve as the starting point for the hazards analysis process. The process should be conducted for every hazardous materials location designated as having a moderate or high probability for an incident. In addition to risk evaluation, vulnerability—what in the community is susceptible to damage should a release occur—also must be examined.

A hazards analysis program provides the following benefits:

- It lets firefighters know what to expect.
- It provides planning for less frequent incidents.
- It creates an awareness of new hazards.
- It may indicate a need for preventive actions, such as monitoring systems and facility modifications.
- It increases the chances of successful emergency operations.

An evaluation team familiar with the response area can facilitate the hazards analysis process. The team should include fire officers and members from each battalion or district, as well as representatives from prevention, and the hazardous materials section. In addition, personnel from outside of the fire department may sometimes be included, such as emergency management staff, local health or environmental department officials, and other technical specialists. The primary concern here is geographic, as most firefighters are very familiar with their "first-due" area.

The four components of a hazards analysis program are:

1. **Hazards identification** typically provides specific information about situations that have the potential for causing injury to life or damage to property and the environment caused by hazardous materials spills or releases. Hazards identification initially is based on a review of the community's history of incidents, and evaluating those facilities which have submitted chemical lists and reporting forms under SARA, Title III, and related state and local right-to-know legislation. Information should include:

- chemical identification;
- location of facilities that manufacture, store, use or move hazardous materials;
- the types and designs of chemical containers or vessels;
- the quantity of material that could be involved in a release;
- the nature of the hazard associated with the hazardous materials release (e.g., fire, explosion, toxicity, etc.).

2. **Vulnerability analysis** identifies areas in the community that may be affected or exposed, and what facilities, property, or environment may be susceptible to damage should a hazardous materials release occur. A comprehensive vulnerability analysis includes information on:

- The size and extent of vulnerable zones, specifically, what size area may be significantly affected as a result of a spill or release of a known quantity of a specific hazardous material under defined conditions. Computer dispersion models, such as ALOHA and ARCHIE, are extremely helpful tools for this process.
- The population, in terms of numbers, density, and types. For example, facility employees, residents, hospitals, nursing homes, etc.
- Private and public property that may be damaged, including essential support systems (e.g., water supply, power, communications) and transportation corridors and facilities.
- The environment that may be affected, and the impact of a release on sensitive natural areas and wildlife.

3. **Risk analysis** is an assessment of both the probability or likelihood of an accidental release, and the actual consequences that might occur. The risk analysis is a judgment of incident probability and severity based on the previous incident history, local experience, and the best available hazard and technological information.

4. **Evaluate emergency response resources.** Based on potential risks, consider the personnel, equipment, and supplies necessary for firefighting, EMS, protective actions, traffic control, etc. Inventory available equipment and supplies along with their ability to function. For example, are firefighting foam supplies adequate to control and suppress vapors from a gasoline tank truck rollover?

A completed hazards analysis should allow fire service managers to determine what level of response to emphasize, what resources will be required to achieve that response, and what type and quantity of mutual aid and other support services will be required.

The hazards analysis process also is an integral element of the Process Safety Management (PSM) program being implemented at industries that manufacture, store, and use chemicals. Among the hazards analysis methods commonly used by safety professionals within industry include:

1. **What-If Analysis.** This method asks a series of questions, such as, "What if Pump X stops running?" or "What if an operator opens the wrong valve?" to explore possible hazard scenarios and consequences. This method often is used to examine proposed changes to a facility.
2. **HAZOP Study.** This is the most popular method of hazards analysis used by the petroleum and chemical industries. The hazard and operability (HAZOP) study brings together a multidisciplinary team, usu-

ally of five to seven people, to brainstorm and identify the consequences of deviations from design intent for various operations. Specific guide words ("No," "More," "Less," "Reverse," etc.) are applied to parameters such as product flows and pressures in a systematic manner. It requires the involvement of a number of people, working with an experienced team leader.

3. **Failure Modes, Effects, and Criticality Analysis (FMECA).** This method tabulates each system or unit of equipment, along with its failure modes, the effect of each failure on the system or unit, and how critical each failure is to the integrity of the system. Based on this information failure modes can be ranked according to criticality to determine which are the most likely to cause a serious accident.

4. **Fault Tree Analysis.** A formalized deductive technique that works backwards from a defined accident to identify and graphically display the combination of equipment failures and operational errors that led up to the accident. It can be used to estimate the quantitative likelihood of events.

5. **Event Tree Analysis.** A formalized deductive technique that works forward from specific events or sequences of events that could lead to an incident. It graphically displays the events that could result in hazards and can be used to calculate the likelihood of occurrence of an accident sequence. It is the reverse of fault tree analysis.

EMERGENCY OPERATIONS PLANNING

Hazardous materials management is a multidisciplinary issue that goes beyond the resources and capabilities of any single agency or organization. Given the variety of "players" that typically respond to a major hazardous materials emergency, the emergency operations plan and related procedures will establish the framework for how the emergency response effort will operate. Therefore, in order to manage the overall hazardous materials problem effectively within the community, a comprehensive planning process must be initiated. This effort usually is referred to as "contingency planning" or "emergency operations planning."

Of the many federal, state, and local requirements that apply to emergency operations planning, the one that most directly affects the fire service is Title III of the Superfund Amendments and Reauthorization Act of 1986. Title III requires that SERCs and LEPCs be established. Title III also outlines specific requirements covering factors such as Extremely Hazardous Substances (EHS), threshold planning quantities, the makeup of LEPCs, dissemination of the planning, chemical lists, and MSDS information to the community and the general public, facility inventories, and toxic chemical release reporting.

The LEPC is the coordinating point for the development of the emergency operations plan. The fire department, as a member of the LEPC and the initial responder to most hazardous materials emergencies, must play a leadership role in the overall development and implementation of all plans and procedures developed by the committee. However, experience has shown that having plans and procedures alone is not sufficient, as the procedures must reflect the ability to handle not only the major emergency, but also the day-to-day operations. Remember these two points: first, emergency response plans and procedures which are not "user friendly" do not get used; and, second, "compliance-oriented" emergency response plans are not necessarily operationally effective.

Figure 19-1 shows graphically the overview of the hazardous materials emergency planning process, described in these steps:

- Organizing the planning team. Planning requires both fire service and community involvement throughout the process. Experience has shown that plans prepared by only one person or a single agency are doomed to failure. *Remember,* there is no single agency (public or private) that can effectively manage a major hazardous materials emergency alone.
- Defining and implementing the major tasks of the planning team. These include reviewing any existing plans, identifying hazards, and analyzing and assessing current prevention and response capabilities.
- Writing the plan. There are two approaches to this step. The first is to develop or revise a hazardous materials appendix or a section of a multihazard emergency operations plan; the second is to develop or revise a single-hazard plan specifically for hazardous materials. Once the plan is written, it must be approved by the LEPC and all the respective planning groups involved. Again, the fire department must be a major player during this development process.
- Revising, testing, and maintaining the plan. Every emergency plan must be evaluated and kept up to date through the review of actual responses, simulation exercises, and the ongoing collection of new data and information.

While community-level emergency planning is essential, completing a plan does not guarantee that the community is actually prepared for a hazardous materials incident. Planning is only one of the elements of a total hazardous materials management system.

Prevention

The responsibility for preventing hazardous materials releases is an effort shared by both the public and private sectors. Because of their regulatory and enforcement capabilities, however, public sector agencies generally receive the greatest attention and often "carry the biggest stick."

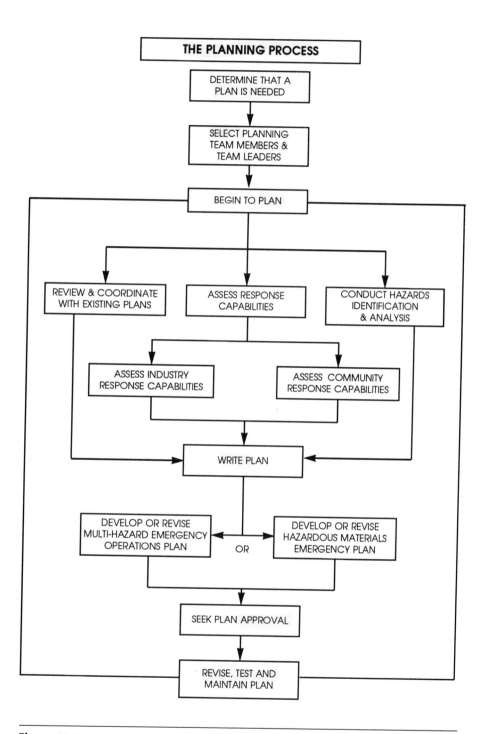

Figure 19-1.

Prevention activities often include the following:

- *Hazardous Materials Process and Container Design and Construction Standards.* Almost all hazardous materials facilities, containers, and processes are designed and constructed to some standard. This standard of care may be based on voluntary consensus standards, such as those developed by the NFPA and the ASTM, or on government regulations. Many major petrochemical, hazardous materials companies, and industry trade associations also have developed their own respective engineering standards and guidelines.

  All containers used for the transportation of hazardous materials are designed and constructed to both specification and performance regulations established by the U.S. Department of Transportation (DOT). These regulations can be referenced in Title 49 of the *Code of Federal Regulations* (CFR). In certain situations, hazardous materials may be shipped in non-DOT specification containers which have received a DOT exemption.

- *Inspection and Enforcement.* Fixed facilities, transportation vehicles, and transportation containers are subject to some form of hazardous materials inspection. Fixed facilities commonly are inspected by state and federal OSHA and EPA inspectors, in addition to state fire marshals and local fire departments. Keep in mind that many of these inspections will focus on fire safety and life safety issues, and may not adequately address either the environmental or process safety issues.

  Transportation vehicle inspections generally are based on criteria established under Title 49 CFR. The enforcing agency is often the state police, but this can vary according to the individual state, the hazardous materials being transported, and the mode of transportation. Some local fire departments, such as Aurora, Colorado, routinely perform inspections of hazardous materials cargo tank trucks.

  The U.S. DOT agencies which have hazardous materials regulatory responsibilities include the following:

  - The Office of Hazardous Materials Transportation (OHMT) of the Research and Special Programs Administration (RSPA) is responsible for all hazardous materials transportation regulations except bulk shipment by ship or barge, including designating and classifying hazardous materials, container safety standards, label and placarding requirements, and handling, stowing, and other in-transit requirements.
  - The Office of Motor Carrier Safety (OMCS) of the Federal Highway Administration (FHA) is responsible for inspection and enforcement activities relating to hazardous materials highway transportation and depot trans-shipment points.

- The Federal Railroad Administration (FRA) is responsible for enforcement of regulations relating to hazardous materials carried by rail or held in depots and freight yards.
- The Federal Aviation Administration (FAA) is responsible for the enforcement of regulations relating to hazardous materials shipments on domestic and foreign carriers operating at U.S. airports and in cargo handling areas.
- The U.S. Coast Guard (USCG) is responsible for the inspection and enforcement of regulations relating to hazardous materials in port areas and on domestic and foreign ships and barges operating in the navigable waters of the United States.

- *Public Education.* Hazardous materials are a concern not only for industry, but for the community as well. The average homeowner contributes to this problem by improperly disposing of substances such as used motor oil, paints, solvents, batteries, and other chemicals used in and around the home. As a result, many communities have initiated full-time household chemical waste awareness, education, and disposal programs. In other instances, communities have established collection stations for used motor oil and chemical cleanup days in an effort to cope with the problem.

- *Handling, Notification, and Reporting Requirements.* These guidelines actually act as a bridge between planning and prevention functions. There are many federal, state, and local regulations which require those who manufacture, store, or transport hazardous materials and hazardous wastes to comply with certain handling, notification and reporting rules. Key federal regulations include CERCLA (Superfund), RCRA and SARA, Title III. There also are many state regulations which are similar in scope and often exceed the federal standard requirements.

Response

When the prevention and enforcement functions fail, response activities begin. Since it is impossible to eliminate all risks associated with the manufacture, storage, and use of hazardous materials, the need for a well-trained, effective emergency response capability will always exist. Response activities should be based on the information and probabilities identified during the planning process as well as on an evaluation of the local hazardous materials problem. While every community should have access to a hazardous materials response capability, that capability does not always have to be provided by either local government or the fire service. Numerous states and regions have established both statewide and regional hazardous materials response team systems which ensure the delivery of a competent and effective capability in a timely manner.

RESPONSE LEVEL	DESCRIPTION	RESOURCES	EXAMPLES
LEVEL I **POTENTIAL EMERGENCY CONDITIONS**	AN INCIDENT OR THREAT OF A RELEASE WHICH CAN BE CONTROLLED BY THE FIRST RESPONDER. IT DOES NOT REQUIRE EVACUATION, BEYOND THE INVOLVED STRUCTURE OR IMMEDIATE OUTSIDE AREA. THE INCIDENT IS CONFINED TO A SMALL AREA AND POSES NO IMMEDIATE THREAT TO LIFE AND PROPERTY.	ESSENTIALLY A LOCAL LEVEL RESPONSE WITH NOTIFICATION OF THE APPROPRIATE LOCAL, STATE AND FEDERAL AGENCIES. REQUIRED RESOURCES MAY INCLUDE: • FIRE DEPARTMENT • EMERGENCY MEDICAL SERVICES (EMS) • LAW ENFORCEMENT • PUBLIC INFORMATION OFFICER (PIO) • CHEMTREC • NATIONAL RESPONSE CENTER	EXAMPLES–500 GALLON FUEL OIL SPILL, INADVERTENT MIXTURE OF CHEMICALS, NATURAL GAS IN A BUILDING, ETC.
LEVEL II **LIMITED EMERGENCY CONDITIONS**	AN INCIDENT INVOLVING A GREATER HAZARD OR LARGER AREA THAN LEVEL I WHICH POSES A POTENTIAL THREAT TO LIFE AND PROPERTY. IT MAY REQUIRE A LIMITED EVACUATION OF THE SURROUNDING AREA.	REQUIRES RESOURCES BEYOND THE CAPABILITIES OF THE INITIAL LOCAL RESPONSE PERSONNEL. MAY REQUIRE A MUTUAL AID RESPONSE AND RESOURCES FROM OTHER LOCAL AND STATE ORGANIZATIONS. MAY INCLUDE: • ALL LEVEL I AGENCIES • HAZMAT RESPONSE TEAMS • PUBLIC WORKS DEPARTMENT • HEALTH DEPARTMENT • RED CROSS • REGIONAL EMERGENCY MANAGEMENT STAFF • STATE POLICE • PUBLIC UTILITIES	EXAMPLES-MINOR CHEMICAL RELEASE IN AN INDUSTRIAL FACILITY, A GASOLINE TANK TRUCK ROLLOVER, A CHLORINE LEAK AT A WATER TREATMENT FACILITY, ETC.
LEVEL III **FULL EMERGENCY CONDITION**	AN INCIDENT INVOLVING A SEVERE HAZARD OR A LARGE AREA WHICH POSES AN EXTREME THREAT TO LIFE AND PROPERTY WHICH MAY REQUIRE A LARGE SCALE EVACUATION.	REQUIRES RESOURCES BEYOND THOSE AVAILABLE IN THE COMMUNITY. MAY REQUIRE THE RESOURCES AND EXPERTISE OF REGIONAL, STATE, FEDERAL AND PRIVATE ORGANIZATIONS. MAY INCLUDE: • LEVEL I AND II AGENCIES • MUTUAL AID FIRE, LAW ENFORCEMENT AND EMS • STATE EMERGENCY MANAGEMENT STAFF • STATE DEPARTMENT OF ENVIRONMENTAL RESOURCES • STATE DEPARTMENT OF HEALTH • ENVIRONMENTAL PROTECTION AGENCY (EPA) • U.S. COAST GUARD • FEDERAL EMERGENCY MANAGEMENT AGENCY (FEMA)	MAJOR TRAIN DERAILMENT WITH FIRE, EXPLOSION OR TOXICITY HAZARD, A MIGRATING VAPOR CLOUD RELEASE FROM A PETROCHEMICAL PROCESSING FACILITY

"Hazardous Materials - Noll. Hildebrand, Yvorra ©1988 Peake Productions

Figure 19-2. *Levels of Hazardous Materials Incidents*

LEVELS OF INCIDENTS

Fortunately, not every incident is a major emergency. Response to a hazardous materials release may range from a single engine company responding to a natural gas leak in the street, to a railroad derailment involving dozens of government and private agencies and their associated personnel.

These incidents can be categorized based on their severity and the resources they require. Figure 19-2 outlines these response levels.

RESPONSE GROUPS

The emergency response community consists of various agencies and individuals that respond to hazardous materials incidents. They can be categorized based on their knowledge, expertise, and resources.

These responders can be compared to the levels of capability found in a typical Emergency Medical Services (EMS) system. In that system, an injury such as a fractured arm can be managed effectively by a First Responder or Emergency Medical Technician—Ambulance (EMT-A), while a cardiac emergency requires the services of an EMT-I (Intermediate) or an EMT-P (Paramedic).

In the same way, a diesel fuel spill usually can be contained by first responders, such as a fire department engine company using dispersants or an absorbent. An accident that involves a poison or reactive chemical will, however, require the on-scene expertise of a hazardous materials technician or hazardous materials response team. Figure 19-3 illustrates this comparison.

HAZARDOUS MATERIALS RESPONSE TEAMS (HMRT)

In order to respond to hazardous materials emergencies in a more effective and efficient manner, many communities and areas have established Hazardous Materials Response Teams (HMRT). NFPA 472 defines an HMRT as an organized group of trained response personnel operating under the Emergency Response Plan and appropriate standard operating procedures, who are expected to perform work to handle and control actual or potential leaks or spills of hazardous materials that require close approach to the material. The HMRT members perform response to releases for the purpose of control or stabilization of the incident.

HMRTs typically function as an Incident Command System (ICS) branch under the direct control of a Hazardous Materials Officer. Based on their assessment of the hazardous materials problem, the HMRT, through the Hazardous Materials Branch Director, provides the Incident Commander with a list of options and a recommendation for mitigation of the hazardous materials problem. However, the final decision is always made by the Incident Commander.

HMRT personnel are trained to a minimum of the OSHA Hazardous Materials Technician level, and must participate in a medical surveillance program that is based on the requirements of 29 CFR 1910.120. Among the specialized equipment carried by an HMRT are reference libraries, computers and communications equipment, personal protective clothing and equipment, direct-reading monitoring and detection equipment, control and mitigation supplies and equipment, and decontamination supplies and equipment.

The need for an HMRT should be one of the outputs of the hazards analysis and planning process. In evaluating this need, however, the chief fire officer should consider the following points:

- No single agency can effectively manage the hazardous materials issue by itself. While the fire department may operate the HMRT, it must do

HAZARDOUS MATERIALS VS EMS
COMPARING RESPONSE GROUPS

KNOWLEDGE LEVEL	EMERGENCY MEDICAL SERVICES 	HAZARDOUS MATERIALS RESPONSE 
BASIC	FIRST RESPONDER	FIRST RESPONDER
INTERMEDIATE	EMERGENCY MEDICAL TECHNICIAN	HAZARDOUS MATERIALS TECHNICIAN
ADVANCED	PARAMEDIC	HAZARDOUS MATERIALS SPECIALIST

"Hazardous Materials - Noll. Hildebrand, Yvorra ©1988 Peake Productions

Figure 19-3.

so by working closely with other local, state, and federal governmental agencies.

- Not every community requires a HMRT; however, every community should have access to this capability through either local, regional, or state resources.
- A HMRT will not necessarily solve the community hazardous materials problem. Remember that the hazardous materials management system consists of planning, prevention, response and recovery.
- There are numerous constraints and requirements associated with the delivery of an effective HMRT capability, including legal, insurance and political issues, both initial and continuing funding sources, resource determination and acquisition, personnel and staffing, and initial and continuing training requirements.

Types of Hazardous Materials Response Teams

Two basic types of HMRTs can be found throughout the fire service:

- *Technical Information HMRT.* This is an HMRT that provides technical assistance and information to the Incident Commander, but has a limited hands-on capability. This type of HMRT would be useful in very rural areas where there is a need for hazardous materials technical expertise, but the volume of incidents and the resource and training requirements do not justify having a "hands-on," offensive-oriented HMRT.
  The technical information team would be capable of accessing technical information and resources (e.g., emergency response guidebooks, computer databases, cellular telephone capability, etc.), and would provide both strategical and tactical control recommendations to the Incident Commander. However, it would have a very limited protective clothing and control equipment inventory, with its capabilities primarily defensive oriented. In this case, key HMRT personnel would be trained to the hazardous materials technician level, while support personnel would be trained to the first responder operations level and be provided with additional training in specific areas (e.g., hazard and risk analysis).
- *Hands-On HMRT.* These are HMRTs that are trained to the Hazardous Materials Technician level, and that are expected to handle and control actual or potential releases of hazardous materials. In some instances, there may be two levels of Hands-On HMRTs, based on the level of personal protective clothing and equipment carried on the hazardous materials unit. A Level II HMRT would be limited to chemical splash protective clothing (EPA Level B), basic monitoring devices, and defensive and limited offensive control equipment and supplies. In contrast, a Level III HMRT would carry chemical vapor protective clothing (EPA Level A),

advanced monitoring equipment, and specialized control equipment to implement offensive control measures. In addition, a Level III HMRT typically would have a greater staffing level than a Level II HMRT.

Consider the following example. Regional and statewide hazardous materials response systems have been developed in some areas of the country, including Virginia, Pennsylvania, and California. A number of these response systems have different levels of HMRTs based on the HMRT's staffing and equipment inventory. For example, the state of Virginia is divided into six regions; each region is staffed by a Level III HMRT which responds to the most serious emergencies. However, the more routine and less significant incidents are handled by several Level II HMRTs which are dispersed throughout each of the six regions.

HMRT EVALUATION CRITERIA

In addition to the potential and actual hazardous materials incident experience identified during the planning process, there are criteria which must be assessed during the HMRT evaluation process. These criteria apply equally for both new and established HMRTs.

LEGAL AND RELATED FACTORS
Legal and related factors should include:

- *Legislative Authority.* Within the local or regional government, is there any legislation that assigns responsibility for hazardous materials response to a specific agency or organization? If so, is the fire department assigned as the lead agency? Is hazardous materials response an element within the fire department's charter or mission statement? If the fire department is not the lead agency, what is and what is its relationship to the fire department?

- *Potential Liabilities.* Although it is impossible to eliminate completely the potential for being the subject of a regulatory citation or liability suit, there are actions a fire service manager can take to minimize the potential of a successful suit or regulatory citation. These include developing and revising the emergency response plan and SOPs, updating mutual aid pacts to ensure that hazardous materials response activities are included, implementing procedures for cost reimbursement for hazardous materials supplies and equipment, and developing "Good Samaritan" or similar legislation to make it easier to use private sector and outside specialists for technical expertise.

- *Insurance Coverage.* Does the present insurance policy cover HMRT activities? If the HMRT consists of personnel from several different fire departments or public organizations, how is the insurance policy structured? What is the HMRT's responsibility after the emergency phase is stabilized?

POLITICAL FACTORS

For better or for worse, chief fire officers must live and operate in a political environment. In the event of a major emergency, political leaders will take "public heat." Likewise, political leaders may use emergency responders and the fire department as scapegoats for emergency response problems and failures.

Major hazardous materials emergencies often are tragedies for fire department personnel and the community, but they also represent opportunities to acquire resources, and for policy and management action. One fire service colleague referred to this as "crisis diplomacy." Take every opportunity to enlighten your leaders about the need for an effective hazardous materials response program, and the inherent problems associated with delivering a timely, professional, well-trained and well-equipped hazardous materials response capability.

ECONOMIC FACTORS

Regardless of the type of HMRT being evaluated or already in place, recognize that an HMRT requires a tremendous financial commitment both to initiate and sustain. While costs can vary greatly, initial costs have ranged from $100,000 to $1,000,000, depending on equipment, supply and vehicle requirements, and the method of HMRT staffing.

A critical economic issue is cost recovery for the expenses associated with delivering the emergency response. In general, recent court cases nationwide have shown that in the absence of state or local legislation authorizing cost recovery for emergency responders, it is somewhat difficult to successfully recoup associated expenses from the responsible party. If you are fortunate to have cost reimbursement legislation in place, it is critical that you document all "billable" expenses. There is a growing trend by responsible parties (i.e., the spiller) to have an independent third party review both fire service and emergency response hazardous materials response invoices to ensure that all expenses were related to the emergency response effort.

When you search for alternative funding sources, consider industry, public or private sector grants, and public interest groups. In some areas, fines assessed for environmental crimes and chemical discharges have been given to the LEPC and local emergency response units to assist in HMRT operations and training. Some recommendations to consider when you approach private sector organizations include:

- Determine your needs and list them.
- Make your requests specific.
- Have several options.
- Procure in-house items that generally are easier to access (e.g., asking a gas company to provide meters, which is an item it already owns).
- Don't forget skills and services as an option.

PERSONNEL AND STAFFING

The staffing and operation of the HMRT will be dependent on the HMRT's scope of operations. Options vary, ranging from career staffing of a dedicated hazardous materials unit, to career staffing on a shared function unit (e.g., engine company/hazardous materials unit). In other instances, staffing may be entirely through volunteer personnel or some combination of career and volunteer.

When you initially select personnel for a fire department HMRT, consider several points. First, just because a person is a good firefighter does not mean that he will automatically be a good hazardous materials responder. This is particularly critical in organizations that may rely on career personnel for dedicated or shared-function HMRTs. Second, technical smarts or "book smarts" do not necessarily equate to "street smarts." A person does not have to be a chemist to be an effective hazardous materials responder; however, that person must have an understanding of chemistry and be able to ask the right questions and interpret the responses. Third, depending on how long the HMRT has been in existence, the selection process can be viewed as the fire department equivalent of the NFL draft. When HMRTs first start out, look for the best players regardless of their specific field of expertise. Emphasis should be on team players with an established reputation. As time progresses, however, you will identify areas or gaps within your HMRT structure and you should select specific types of personnel. Examples would include personnel who have strong technical backgrounds, mechanical skills, and command and control expertise, and EMS support personnel.

Once personnel are selected for the HMRT, they must be enrolled in a medical surveillance program. Components of the medical surveillance program include a baseline examination prior to assignment on the HMRT, and periodic medical examinations. These typically are given at 12-month intervals but not at intervals greater than 24 months based on a physician's recommendations. They also are given at termination of employment or on reassignment from the HMRT, after any exposure to a hazardous material, and at such times as the physician deems necessary.

Finally, an HMRT must be trained properly. The two primary information sources for establishing an HMRT training program are OSHA 1910.120 and NFPA 472. While OSHA 1910.120 outlines the regulatory requirements (what you have to do), NFPA 472 spells out the specific training and educational competencies for the training program (how you can do it).

NFPA 472, Section 4-1, recommends that HMRT personnel be trained to the Hazardous Materials Technician level. According to OSHA 1910.120(q), the Hazardous Materials Technician requires a minimum of 24 hours of initial training at the First Responder Operations level. However, hazardous materials emergency response operations require that personnel have a much broader and comprehensive background; it is extremely unlikely that any person given only 24 hours of hazardous materials technician training could be expected to become a viable and functioning HMRT member. As a point of reference, most fire department HMRT programs require 80 to 200 hours of initial hazardous materials training before someone can be classified as an HMRT member. In addition, there is the need for both annual refresher and continuing education.

TOOLS, RESOURCES, AND EQUIPMENT
Specialized supplies and equipment are needed for personal protection, monitoring and detection, and mitigation and control agents/supplies. In addition, there is the need for a vehicle. All of these items must be selected based on the scope of the HMRT's operations. Many fire service managers falsely believe that they have a HMRT capability, when in reality they lack the necessary supplies and equipment to perform the job both safely and effectively.

While there is no single information source, there are a number of references the fire service manager can consult in this area, including the *NFPA Hazardous Materials Response Handbook* and the *EPA Hazardous Materials Team Planning Guidance*. In addition, several states, including Virginia, Pennsylvania, and California, have established equipment lists for HMRTs which are either certified by the state or receive state funding. To be certified, the teams must carry the equipment on the list.

Cleanup and recovery

Cleanup and recovery operations are designed to restore a facility, community or both to normal as soon as possible. In many instances, chemicals involved in a hazardous materials release will eventually be classified as hazardous wastes. Cleanup and recovery operations fall under the guidelines of both CERCLA and RCRA.

Cleanup and recovery operations can be classified based on whether they are short- or long-term. Short-term activities are actions that immediately follow a hazardous materials release, and are directed primarily toward removing any immediate hazards and restoring vital support services (i.e., reopening transportation systems, drinking water systems, etc.) to minimum operating standards. Short-term activities can last up to several weeks.

In contrast, long-term activities are remedial actions that return vital support systems to normal or improved operating levels. Examples include ground water treatment operations, the mitigation of both aboveground and underground spills, and the monitoring of flammable and toxic contaminants. These activities may not be directly related to a specific hazardous materials incident, but often are the result of abandoned industrial or hazardous waste sites. These operations can extend over months or years.

FIRE SERVICE ROLE DURING CLEANUP OPERATIONS

Fire service personnel usually are not responsible for the cleanup and recovery of hazardous materials releases; however, depending on the nature of the incident, they may continue to be responsible for site safety until the incident is terminated.

At short-term operations immediately following an incident, the Incident Commander should ensure that the work area is controlled closely, that the general public is denied entry, and that the safety of emergency responders and the public is maintained during cleanup and recovery operations. When interfacing with both industry responders and contractors, the Incident Commander should ensure that they are trained to meet the requirements of OSHA 1910.120.

Long-term cleanup and recovery operations normally do not require the continuous presence of the fire service. Depending on the size and scope of the cleanup, a contractor or government official, the Remedial Project Manager (RPM), will be the central contact point. The fire department should be familiar with the cleanup operation, including its organizational structure, the RPM, work plan, time schedule, and site safety plan. Cleanup operations should conform to the general health and safety requirements of both state and federal EPA and OSHA standards.

Although the fire service may not have the regulatory authority to conduct inspections or issue citations at cleanup operations, its personnel can bring specific concerns to the attention of the state or federal regulatory agency that has jurisdiction.

INCIDENT MANAGEMENT OPERATIONS

An effective hazardous materials response system differs little from a computer. With computers, it is the software package that drives or directs the computer's hardware or machinery. Similarly, in hazardous materials response, it is the standard operating procedures that drive and give direction to emergency response personnel and how they use their equipment.

A type of commonly used incident management procedure, and the one that will be used in this section, is the "Eight-Step Process."© Published in *Hazardous Materials: Managing The Incident,* the copyrighted process is a structured system that has one specific goal: to maximize the safety of both emergency responders and the general public. It establishes a management structure that fits any hazardous materials response, large or small, and emphasizes tactical decisionmaking points.

Essentially, there are eight basic functions that must be evaluated at a hazardous materials emergency. These eight functions typically follow an implementation timeline at the incident. They are:

1. Site management and control.
2. Identify the problem.
3. Hazard and risk evaluation.
4. Select personal protective clothing and equipment.
5. Information management and resource coordination.
6. Implement response objectives.
7. Decontamination procedures.
8. Terminate the incident.

Site management and control

Site management refers to managing the physical layout of an incident. It is one of the most critical areas of managing an emergency, as experience has shown that incidents poorly managed in the initial stages become increasingly difficult to control as the emergency progresses both over time and in complexity. The response effort during the first minutes often determines the direction the remainder of the incident will follow.

Some of the specific tasks associated with site management include:

- How to approach the scene and position emergency response units. This focuses on the basic concepts of approaching the emergency scene in such a manner that responders do not become part of the problem (e.g., uphill, upwind, based on nature/location of the incident).
- How to establish command and implement the Incident Command System (ICS). To be effective, the ICS must be implemented when the first emergency response unit arrives on scene.
- How to stage other responding emergency units in order to minimize safety concerns.
- How to isolate and deny entry, and how to establish safety control zones initially. Failure to isolate the area during the initial stages of an incident will lead to increased potential for exposure and injury. At a minimum, a hot zone must be established. (See the information on control zones below.)
- What initial public protective actions will protect the community. These can be either evacuation, protection-in-place, or some combination of the two.

Control zones

Critical to safe operations is establishing and maintaining control zones. Control zones must be established by the Incident Commander at all hazardous materials incidents. The Hazardous Materials Officer normally provides the necessary technical information and recommendations to assist the Incident Commander in determining the control zone size and its boundaries. The shape and dimensions of the control zones depend on such factors as the size and nature of the release (e.g., liquid versus vapor, instantaneous versus continuous release), chemical concentrations present and related health exposure values, wind direction and velocity, surrounding topography, adjacent exposures, etc.

Control zones are broken into three categories: hot zone, warm zone, and cold zone, shown in Figure 19-4.

1. *Hot Zone (Restricted, High-Hazard Area)*

    The immediate hazard area surrounding the problem or release site, it extends far enough to prevent adverse effects from hazardous materials releases to personnel outside of the zone. To be entered only by a minimum of two hazardous materials trained personnel or individuals who possess particular knowledge of the problem or situation, under monitored conditions. During both entry and reconnaissance operations, a backup team (minimum of two personnel) with appropriate protection

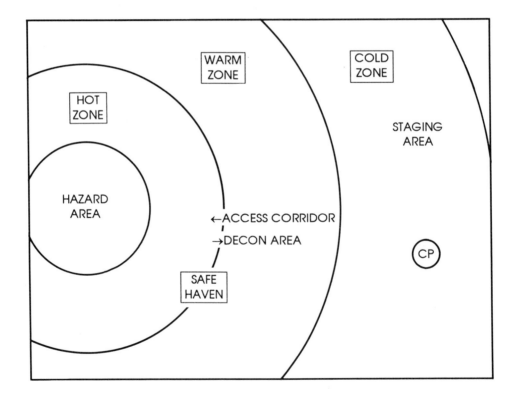

Figure 19-4.

should be stationed at the edge of the hot zone or in a location where they can gain access to the entry team quickly in an emergency situation.

2. *Warm Zone (Limited Access Area, Decontamination Zone)*
   The area surrounding the hot zone and bounded by the cold zone where entry support and decontamination operations take place, it includes a corridor with access control points to assist in reducing the spread of contamination. Entry is restricted to emergency response personnel, as well as those assigned by the Incident Commander. Individuals who enter the warm zone must wear appropriate personal protective clothing.

3. *Cold Zone (Support Area)*
   The area surrounding the warm zone which presents no hazard to emergency response personnel and equipment, it is reserved for emergency services functions only, such as the command post and other support functions deemed necessary to control the incident. Support personnel without the proper level of personal protective clothing should be limited to this zone only.
   Outer boundaries of the hazard control zones normally will be identified by either banner tape, traffic cones, or some other identifiable markings.

Identify the Problem

Once the hazard area is isolated, identifying the problem, including the materials and container involved, becomes the cornerstone of all further decisionmaking. Basic principles of identification in an emergency focus on the following concepts:

- Recognize that hazardous materials are present.
- Identify the hazardous material(s) involved.
- If it is not possible to specifically identify the material(s) involved, then try to determine its hazard classification (e.g., corrosive, poison gas, etc.).
- Upon your arrival on the scene, always verify the information you are initially given. DO NOT ASSUME THAT THE INITIAL INFORMATION YOU HAVE RECEIVED IS ALWAYS CORRECT!

How you recognize and identify hazardous materials typically is based on:

- Occupancy and location;
- Container shapes;
- Markings and colors;

- Placards and labels;
- Shipping papers and facility documents;
- Monitoring and detection instruments; and
- Senses.

Most critical for the fire officer are situations where emergency operations already are underway when it is discovered that hazardous materials are involved. In these instances, direct your efforts toward establishing an effective site management and control policy, and limiting the spread of contaminants. Personnel who have been exposed or contaminated must not carry the hazardous material beyond the immediate control area.

Hazard and risk evaluation

Evaluating hazard information and assessing the relative risks are critical decisionmaking points in successful hazardous materials incident management. The decision to intervene or, more often, **not to** intervene is not easy. While most individuals recognize the immediate need to isolate the area, deny entry, and identify the materials involved, many overlook the need for developing effective analytical skills.

A hazard refers to a danger or peril. In hazardous materials response, it usually refers to the physical properties, chemical properties, or both, of a material, such as flammability properties, exposure values, and chemical protective clothing compatibility. At an emergency, all of these elements are regarded as constant values (i.e., they do not change regardless of the location of the emergency) and can be referenced from emergency response guidebooks and Material Safety Data Sheets (MSDS).

A risk is the probability of suffering a harm or loss. Risks are intangibles; they differ at every hazardous materials incident, can change during the course of an incident, and must be evaluated by knowledgeable emergency response personnel. What factors influence the level of risk?

- *Hazard class and quantity of material(s) involved.* Risks generally are greater when you must deal with bulk quantities of hazardous materials in storage or transportation than when the substances are in limited-quantity, individual containers. However, this must be balanced against the specific materials or class of materials involved, such as toluene (aromatic hydrocarbon, flammable liquid) versus phosphine (flammable and poison gas).
- *Container type, the type of "stress" applied, and the container's ability to adapt to the stressor.* As long as the hazardous materials stays in its container, there are no problems. Therefore, emergency responders must be able to analyze the type of hazardous materials container and

pertinent safety features, and the type of stress being applied to the container (e.g., thermal, mechanical, chemical or a combination).

- *Proximity of exposures.* This includes the size, distance, and rate of dispersion of a chemical release. Exposures would include emergency responders, the community, property, the environment, and systems disruptions (e.g., shutdown of transportation corridors, loss of community water supplies and utilities, etc.).
- *Level of available resources.* This includes responders' training and expertise in dealing with the hazardous materials involved, and associated response times. For example, fire departments have a great deal of experience in handling flammable liquid and gas emergencies, but do not have a commensurate level of training and experience in handling fires and emergencies that involve clandestine drug labs.

Although the risks associated with hazardous materials response can never be eliminated, they can be managed successfully. Hazardous materials responders must see their role as risk evaluators, not risk takers.

Hazard and risk assessment can be viewed in terms of three tasks: gathering hazard data and information; compiling data and information into a useful format; and, evaluating risks.

Sources of hazard data and information

Sources of hazard data and information can be categorized as follows:

EMERGENCY RESPONSE GUIDEBOOKS

Most responders rely on three to five basic guidebooks as their primary sources. Keep these operational considerations in mind when you use guidebooks:

- You must know *how* to use guidebooks in order to use them effectively.
- Many responders evaluate a minimum of three independent information sources and reference guidebooks before they allow personnel to operate in a hostile environment.
- If information among different sources conflicts, always select the most conservative recommendations or values.
- Be realistic in your evaluation of the data contained in guidebooks. For example, most first responders do not carry any air monitoring equipment. However, it should be obvious that a continuous release from a bulk container of a chemical with relatively low TLV-TWA (Threshold Weighted Value—Time-weighted value) and Immediately Dangerous to

Life or Health (IDLH) values can easily exceed safe exposure levels and require the use of personal protective clothing and equipment.

EMERGENCY RESPONSE TELEPHONE CENTERS

There are a number of private and public sector hazardous materials telephone centers whose functions include providing immediate chemical hazard information, accessing secondary forms of expertise for additional action and information, and acting as a clearinghouse for spill notifications.

Among the most widely used chemical information and industry access hotlines are CHEMTREC (800-424-9300) and CANUTEC in Canada (613-996-6666). CHEMTREC's purpose is twofold. First, it provides immediate advice to callers anywhere on how to cope with chemicals involved in a transportation or fixed facility emergency. Second, it can access shippers or other forms of expertise for additional and appropriate followup action and information. CHEMTREC also has the ability to download emergency information to the field via fax and computer modem.

CANUTEC is the Canadian counterpart of CHEMTREC, and provides assistance in identifying and establishing contact with shippers and manufacturers that originate in Canada.

For emergency medical issues, the Agency for Toxic Substances and Disease Registry (ATSDR) provides a 24-hour link with medical professionals who can provide appropriate advice (404-639-0615). Within 10 minutes of a call, ATSDR will link the caller with an emergency response coordinator who can give advice on immediate actions. Within 20 minutes, the agency can provide access to toxicologists, environmental health scientists, chemists, and others.

The National Response Center (NRC) (800-424-8802, 202-426-2675, or 267-2675 in the Washington, DC area) is used for the required reporting of hazardous materials transportation incidents that cause death, serious injury, property damage in excess of $50,000, or a continuing threat to life and property. The NRC must be notified by the responsible party (i.e., the spiller) if hazardous materials releases exceed the reportable quantity provisions of CERCLA. The NRC also can help with identifying materials, technical information, and initial response actions.

ELECTRONIC DATABASES

Portable computers with modems and telephone hookups provide easy access to both public and private-sector databases during an incident. In addition, a number of hazardous materials response teams have acquired computer software packages that contain various databases and reference guidebooks. Examples include CAMEO, Tomes and Tomes Plus, and RTECS (Registry of Toxic Effects of Chemical Substances).

TECHNICAL INFORMATION SPECIALISTS

These are personnel who work with chemicals or with chemical processing or who are knowledgeable in specialized areas, such as container design, toxicology, or environmental sciences.

MSDS/RIGHT-TO-KNOW INFORMATION

Many state and local worker right-to-know laws have been enacted across the country. In addition, OSHA has issued it Hazard Communication Standard for chemical markings and worker exposures to chemicals in the workplace, and EPA has implemented the Emergency Planning and Community Right-to-Know Act of 1986 (SARA, Title III). These laws have given responders substantial access to information, as well as the burden of how to handle it effectively.

Compiling hazard information

In the process of assessing risks, response personnel will need to gather and update information from a variety of sources. To manage this information effectively, many responders rely on printed log sheets and checklists to ensure that all aspects have been addressed. Regardless of its exact design, some logical, functional system must be used.

Risk assessment

The primary objective of risk assessment is to determine whether or not emergency response personnel should intervene, and what strategical objectives and tactical options they should pursue. To determine the answers to these questions, responders must first estimate the likely harm that could occur without intervention. The question of the day becomes, "What will happen if we do nothing?" Using nonintervention as the baseline, responders then can evaluate other available strategical options in terms of their effect on the final outcome of the emergency.

This evaluation and comparison process is built around two interrelated actions. First, the Incident Commander must visualize the likely behavior of the hazardous material and its container (How will the juice behave when it gets out of the can?). Second, he must describe the likely outcome of that behavior (How will it harm me?).

The Incident Commander, as the risk evaluator, should be able to assess the following conditions:

- Previous and current status of the incident.
- Overall condition of the hazardous materials container.
- Environmental conditions, including run-off, wind, precipitation, topography, etc.
- Exposures, including people (facility, emergency responders, and the public), property, environment, and systems disruption.
- Comparison of resources available versus the level required to respond to the problem. Evaluate the risks of personnel intervening directly in the emergency. Consider the limitations of the people involved and their equipment.
- Estimation of likely harm without active emergency response intervention, and development of response objectives.

Based on the answers to these questions, you can develop strategic goals and the associated tactical objectives. Strategic goals are usually very broad in nature and are determined at the Command level. Several strategic goals may be pursued simultaneously during an incident. Examples of common strategic goals include the following:

- Rescue.
- Spill control (confinement).
- Fire control.
- Public protective actions.
- Leak control (containment).
- Recovery.

In contrast, tactical objectives are the specific objectives used to achieve strategic goals. Tactics normally are decided at the Section and Branch levels in the command structure. For example, tactical objectives to achieve the strategic goal of spill control (confinement) would include absorption, diking, damming, and diversion.

If the Incident Commander hopes to have strategic goals understood and implemented, they must be packaged and communicated in simple terms. If strategic goals are unclear, tactical objectives will become equally muddied. Hazardous materials strategic goals and tactical objectives can be implemented from three distinct operational modes:

Offensive Mode. Offensive-mode operations commit resources to aggressive leak, spill, and fire control objectives. An offensive strategic goal/ tactical objective is achieved by implementing specific types of offensive operations which are designed to quickly control or mitigate the problem. Although offensive operations can increase the risk of emergency responders, the risk may be justified if rescue operations can be achieved quickly, if the spill can be confined or contained rapidly, or the fire can be extinguished quickly.

Defensive Mode. Defensive-mode operations commit resources (people, equipment, and supplies) to less aggressive objectives. A defensive strategic goal/tactical objective is achieved by using specific types of defensive tactics, such as diverting or diking the hazardous materials. A defensive plan may require "conceding" certain areas to the emergency, while directing response efforts toward limiting the overall size or spread of the problem (e.g., concentrating all efforts on building dikes in advance of a spill to prevent contamination of a fresh water supply).

Nonintervention Mode. Nonintervention means taking no action. The basic plan calls for responders to wait out the sequence of events underway until the incident has run its course and the risk of intervening has been reduced to an acceptable level, for example, waiting for an LPG container to burn off. This strategy usually produces the best outcome when the Incident Commander determines that implementing offensive or defensive strategic goals/tactical objectives would expose responders to an unacceptable risk. In other words, the potential costs of action far exceed any benefits, e.g., a BLEVE scenario.

Select personal protective clothing and equipment

Based on the assessment of the materials involved, the relative hazards and risks, and the selection of response objectives, the necessary level of personal protective clothing and equipment is selected. Since no one type of protective clothing will satisfy personal protection needs under all circumstances, chief fire officers should be familiar with the types and levels available.

The protective clothing used at hazardous materials emergencies can be categorized several ways. For the purposes of our discussion, it will be broken into three generic levels:

1. STRUCTURAL FIREFIGHTING CLOTHING

Although its hazardous materials applications are limited, structural firefighting gear can still offer sufficient protection to the user who is aware of the hazards encountered and the limitations of the clothing. It is typically worn in conjunction with self-contained breathing apparatus (SCBA). Structural clothing may be used under the following conditions:

- Contact with splashes of extremely hazardous substances is unlikely.
- Total atmospheric concentrations do not contain high levels of chemicals toxic to the skin.

- There are no adverse effects from chemical exposure to small areas of unprotected skin.

However, the bottom line is that structural firefighting clothing is not designed to offer any chemical protection.

2. CHEMICAL PROTECTIVE CLOTHING

Chemical protective clothing (CPC) is designed to protect the skin and eyes from direct contact with the chemical(s) involved. Respiratory protection is worn in conjunction with the clothing. CPC is divided into two groups: chemical splash and chemical vapor protective clothing. However, the EPA also has developed a classification system for the various levels of CPC.

Chemical splash protective clothing (EPA Levels B and C) consists of several pieces of clothing and equipment designed to provide skin and eye protection from chemical splashes. It does not provide total body protection from gases, airborne dusts, and vapors. For hazardous materials operations, SCBA or airline hose units also must be provided for respiratory protection. However, if responders have conducted air monitoring of the site, respiratory protection may be downgraded to air purification respirators (APR's).

Chemical splash protective clothing would be used under the following conditions:

- The vapors or gases present are not suspected of containing high concentrations of chemicals which are harmful to or can be absorbed by the skin.
- It is highly unlikely that the user will be exposed to high concentrations of vapors, gases, particulates, or splashes which will affect any exposed skin areas.
- Operations will not be conducted in a flammable atmosphere. However, in some situations, it is possible to wear chemical splash protective clothing with structural firefighting clothing to combine chemical and thermal protection.

Chemical vapor protective clothing (EPA Level A) offers full-body protection against a hostile chemical environment when used with air-supplied respiratory devices. Unlike chemical splash protective clothing, it provides a sealed, integral system of protection.

Chemical vapor protective clothing would be used under the following conditions:

- Extremely hazardous substances are known or suspected to be present, (i.e., chlorine, cyanide compounds, toxic and infectious substances), and skin contact is possible.

- Potential contact with substances that harm or destroy skin (e.g., corrosives) is anticipated.
- Anticipated operations involve a potential for splash or exposure to vapors, gases, or particulates capable of being absorbed through the skin.
- Anticipated operations involve unknown or unidentified substances and require intervention by emergency response personnel.

3. HIGH-TEMPERATURE PROTECTIVE CLOTHING

High-temperature clothing is designed for protection from short-term exposures to high temperatures. There are two types: proximity and fire entry suits. These ensembles are worn in high-heat environments that would exceed the protection capabilities offered by structural firefighting gear. Flammable liquid and gas firefighting are good examples. This clothing is not designed to provide any chemical protection.

Proximity suits are constructed for short-duration, close proximity to flame and radiant heat. They also will withstand exposures to steam, liquids, and weak chemicals, and commonly are used by airport firefighters.

Fire entry suits offer complete protection for short-duration entries (a maximum of 60 seconds of total suit exposure) into total flame environments. They are found in petroleum facilities where flammable gases, liquids, and other reactive chemicals are processed.

CHEMICAL RESISTANCE

Among the primary concerns when using CPC are chemical resistance and clothing integrity. CPC resistance is described in terms of chemical degradation, penetration, and permeation. **Degradation** is the physical destruction or decomposition of a clothing material because of exposure to chemicals, use, or ambient conditions (e.g., storage in sunlight). It is noted by such visible signs as charring, shrinking, or dissolving, or loss of tensile strength. **Penetration** is the flow of a hazardous liquid chemical through zippers, stitched seams, pinholes, or other imperfections in the material (e.g., suit fasteners, exhalation valves, etc.).

In contrast, **permeation** is the process by which a liquid chemical moves through a given material on a molecular level. Unlike both degradation and penetration, there often are no obvious physical indicators that the chemical has passed through the CPC. Permeation is a significant concern when evaluating protective clothing contamination and decontamination.

Permeation through an impervious barrier is a three-step process consisting of:

1. adsorption of the chemical into the outer surfaces of the material, generally not detectable by the wearer;
2. diffusion of the chemical through the material; and
3. desorption of the chemical from the inner surface of the material; this typically is the first time the user will detect the chemical inside his protective clothing.

When evaluating chemical permeation charts supplied by a CPC manufacturer, the term breakthrough time will be listed. Breakthrough time is defined as the time from the initial chemical attack on the outside of the material until its desorption and detection inside. Knowing the breakthrough time allows responders to estimate the duration of maximum protection under a worst-case scenario of continuous chemical contact.

HEAT STRESS

The issue of heat stress is extremely important for personnel who wear CPC. Both chemical splash and chemical vapor protective suits are designed to protect the user from a hostile environment and prevent the passage of contaminants into the "protective envelope." Unfortunately, they also reduce the body's ability to discard excess heat via natural body ventilation.

A key indicator of body heat levels is the core body temperature. If body heat cannot be eliminated, it will accumulate and elevate the core temperature. Physical reactions include heat rash, heat cramps, heat exhaustion, and heat stroke. Guidelines for reducing heat stress include the following:

- Have responders maintain an optimal level of physical fitness.
- Provide plenty of liquids. To replace body fluids (water and electrolytes), use electrolyte mixes.
- Use body cooling devices (e.g., cooling vests) to aid natural body ventilation. Keep in mind that these devices add weight and their use must be carefully balanced against worker efficiency.
- Install mobile showers and portable hose-down facilities to reduce body temperatures and cool protective clothing.
- Rotate personnel on a shift basis.
- Provide shelter or shaded areas to protect personnel during rest periods. Entry personnel should be placed in cool areas before and after entry operations (e.g., air-conditioned ambulances).

In summary, the evaluation, selection, and use of protective clothing at a hazardous materials emergency should be viewed from a "systems" perspective that considers:

- an evaluation of the hostile environment and the objective of the entry;

- what type of personal protective clothing is required, and what its associated limitations are; and
- what the impact of the PPE is on individual human and physiological factors. Of critical importance are the effects of heat stress.

Information management and resource coordination

This refers to the process of ensuring that all information and resources collected and required during the course of the incident are coordinated. The success of this coordination effort is directly related to the implementation of local Incident Command System (ICS) procedures. If the ICS elements identified in Site Management and Control have not been implemented, it will be extremely difficult for the various agencies and units represented on scene to operate in a safe and effective manner. These ICS elements include the establishment and transfer of command, the establishment of a command post, and the designation of sectors and sector officers.

Coordinating information at a hazardous materials incident can be a complex, time-consuming task. While it is difficult to operate safely when little or no information is available, it can be even more harmful to operate when you are overwhelmed with people and data that cannot be organized effectively for evaluation and decisionmaking.

Information management plays a role after the fact, for documentation. As with any major incident, it is important to establish a paper trail that documents the events before, during, and after the incident.

The most effective way to manage the facts, figures, and observations from different available sources is by using checklists. Checklists eliminate the guesswork and also the likelihood that important data or information may be overlooked during the stress of the emergency.

Implement response objectives

Based on the hazard and risk evaluation, the Incident Commander determines the overall strategic goals, tactical objectives, and action plan for the emergency. Remember that strategic goals are very broad in nature and are determined at the Command level. Several strategic goals may be pursued simultaneously during an incident. Examples of common strategic goals include the following:

- Rescue.
- Spill control (confinement).
- Fire control.
- Public protective actions.

- Leak control (containment).
- Recovery.

Tactical objectives are the specific objectives used to achieve strategic goals. Tactics normally are decided at the Section and Branch levels in the command structure. For example, tactical objectives to achieve the strategic goal of spill control (confinement) would include absorption, diking, damming, and diversion.

If the Incident Commander hopes to have goals understood and implemented, they must be packaged and communicated in simple terms. If strategic goals are unclear, tactical objectives will become equally muddied. Hazardous materials strategic goals and tactical objectives can be implemented from these distinct operational modes:

Defensive Mode—Defensive-mode operations commit resources (people, equipment, and supplies) to less aggressive objectives. As a general rule, defensive operations should be implemented to the fullest extent before you attempt more aggressive offensive operations.

Defense operations often are directed toward keeping the hazardous materials *confined* to a specific area. Defensive operations may require "conceding" certain areas to the emergency, while directing response efforts limiting the overall size or spread of the problem (e.g., concentrating all efforts on building dikes in advance of a spill to prevent contamination of a fresh water supply). Some of the advantages of defensive mode operations are:

- The problem may be controlled without directly exposing emergency responders to the released hazardous materials.
- In some cases operations can be performed without the need for specialized protective clothing or equipment.
- Special hazardous materials leak control equipment may not be required.
- First responders usually can perform most spill control operations with minimal supervision.

Offensive Mode—In situations where defensive options have not produced the desired results or the public is at great risk from exposure, aggressive, well-planned offensive operations may be required. Offensive objectives are directed toward keeping the hazardous materials *contained*. They typically require personnel to operate within the hot zone and at a higher level of potential exposure. Examples would include plugging and patching leaking containers, applying specialized leak control kits, etc.

It is important to recognize that unless specialized training has been provided, firefighters at the First Responder Operations level will be unable to perform most offensive tactical options.

While offensive options subject responders to a potentially higher level of risk, they have several advantages over defensive options:

- Environmental damage is minimized. This is especially true in cases where liquids may be released and enter drainage systems or water supplies, thereby creating major hazards and pollution problems.
- On-scene operating time is usually reduced. Leaks controlled and stopped at the container can limit the spread of the material and eliminate the need for evacuation. This is particularly true when the hazardous materials is a vapor or gas and is toxic.
- Cleanup costs usually are reduced when contaminants are limited to small areas or have not contaminated either ground or surface waters.

Realistically, defensive and offensive tactical options can be used at the same time. For example, first responders can begin downstream spill control operations while HMRT members prepare for entry operations to control the release at the container.

Nonintervention Mode—Nonintervention means taking no action. Operations focus on maintaining a passive position in a safe location and allowing the hazardous materials incident to follow its "natural course" with no direct emergency response intervention. An example would include a potential BLEVE or reactive chemicals scenario, or a situation where emergency responders are awaiting the arrival at the scene of additional responders or resources before initiating control operations.

Before initiating any entry operations, make sure that properly equipped backup personnel wearing the appropriate level of personal protective clothing are in place. Also have the entry teams monitored by emergency medical services (EMS) personnel and brief them before you allow them to enter the hot zone. At a minimum, this briefing should include the following:

- Having personnel remove all watches and jewelry and leave personal valuables behind.
- Explaining the objectives of the entry operation.
- Performing radio communications, SCBA and CPC checks.
- Identifying emergency escape signals.
- Decontamination area location, setup, and procedures.

Finally, while cleanup and recovery operations typically are not performed by emergency responders, they still often have control and overall responsibility of the emergency scene. Experience has shown that many accidents and injuries occur during this phase of the emergency. The incident may have been prolonged, personnel have become tired and want to wrap up the emergency, and a new cast of players arrives on the incident scene (e.g., contractors, industry representatives, government officials, etc.). This combination often sets up a scenario where safety can be compromised if responders do not remain alert.

The Incident Commander should ensure that the work area is closely controlled, that the general public is denied entry, and that the safety of emergency responders and the public is maintained during cleanup and recovery operations. When interfacing with both industry responders and contractors, the Incident Commander should ensure that they are trained to meet the requirements of OSHA 1910.120.

Decontamination procedures

Decontamination is the physical process, chemical process, or a combination of the two, for making personnel, equipment, and supplies safe by eliminating harmful substances, and it is essential to ensure the safety of both personnel and property. The success of decontamination is tied directly to how well the Incident Commander can control on-scene personnel and operations.

BASIC CONCEPTS

Contamination Prevention

If contact can be controlled and minimized, the potential for contamination can be reduced or possibly eliminated. Stress work practices that minimize contact with hazardous substances. Don't walk through areas of obvious contamination; touch potentially hazardous substances as little as is possible and reasonably practical. If contact is made, remove the contaminant as soon as possible.

Types of Contamination

There are two types of contamination: surface and permeation. Surface contaminants have not been absorbed into the surface, and normally are easier to detect and remove than permeated contaminants. Typical examples include dusts, powders, asbestos fibers, etc.

Permeated contaminants have been absorbed into the material, and often are difficult or impossible to detect or remove. If the contaminants which have permeated a material are not removed by decontamination, they may continue to permeate through the fabric and cause an exposure on the inside of a protective clothing material. Permeation is affected by the following factors:

- Contact time. The longer a contaminant is in contact with an object, the greater the probability and extent of permeation.
- Concentration. Molecules flow from areas of high concentration to areas of low concentration. The greater the concentration, the greater the potential for permeation to occur.
- Temperature. Increased temperatures generally increase the rate of permeation.
- Physical state. As a rule, gases, vapors, and low-viscosity liquids tend to permeate more readily than high-viscosity liquids or solids.

Methods of Decontamination

While decontamination is performed to protect health and safety, it also can **create** hazards under certain situations. For example, decon methods may be incompatible with the hazardous materials involved and react violently. Further, they may pose a direct health hazard to personnel who inhale the hazardous vapors.

Information on decon methods, solutions, and techniques is available from shippers, manufacturers, and medical facilities, including poison control centers, and other technical resources, such as CHEMTREC, and other hazardous materials databases.

The physical and chemical compatibility of the decon solutions must be determined before they are used. Any decon method that permeates, degrades, damages, or otherwise impairs the safe function of PPE should not be used unless dictated by unusual circumstances.

⚠ **CAUTION:** Beware of decon methods that can pose a direct health hazard to emergency response personnel. Measures must be taken to protect both decon workers and the personnel being decontaminated.

Methods of decontamination can be divided into physical and chemical:

Physical Methods

—Brushing or scraping.
—Dilution.
—Absorption.
—Heat.
—Use of lower or high air pressure (NOTE: Pressurized air may cause contaminants to become airborne, resulting in an inhalation hazard and

spreading the contaminant. OSHA regulations restrict the use of pressurized air for people.).
—Vacuuming.
—Disposal.

Chemical Methods

—Chemical degradation (use of solvents, surfactants, cleaners, etc.).
—Neutralization.
—Solidification.
—Disinfection and sterilization.

Personal Protection of Decon Workers

Response personnel who serve on the decon crew must be protected properly. In some situations, decon personnel should wear the same level of PPE as personnel who are operating in the hot zone, for instance, in incidents that involve poison liquids and gases. In most situations, however, decon personnel are sufficiently protected by wearing PPE one level below that of the entry crews. In addition, if you are using a multistation decon system, decon personnel who initially come in contact with personnel and equipment leaving the hot zone often will often require more protection than those decon workers assigned to the final station in the decon corridor.

All decon personnel must be decontaminated before they leave the decon area (warm zone). The extent of their decontamination process is based on the types of contaminants involved in the emergency, and the type of work performed in the decon operation.

Testing for Decontamination Effectiveness

Decon methods vary in their effectiveness for removing different substances. The effectiveness of any decon method should be assessed at the beginning of the decon operation and periodically throughout the operation. If contaminated materials are not being removed or are permeating through protective clothing, the decon operation must be revised.

In assessing the effectiveness of decontamination, it is helpful to use visual observation to look for stains, discolorations, corrosive effects, etc. Monitoring devices such as photo-ionization detectors (PIDs) and detector tubes can show that contamination levels are at least below the device's detection limit. Wipe sampling gives you after-the-fact information on the effectiveness of decon. Once a wipe swab is taken, it is analyzed in a laboratory. Protective clothing, equipment, and skin may be tested using wipe samples.

TECHNICAL DECONTAMINATION

Technical decon refers to the decontamination of the equipment and personal protective clothing used by emergency responders or other support personnel. In a field setting, technical decon consists of a three-stage, multistation field decon system, while fixed facilities will often incorporate the use of safety showers. If you use safety showers, locate them close to the emergency scene, and determine whether the waste-water treatment facility will be able to handle the associated contaminants and runoff.

Decontamination Group Supervisor

At working hazardous materials incidents where an HMRT is on scene, the team is responsible for determining decontamination methods, procedures, and implementation. Within the ICS structure, the Hazardous Materials Branch Director designates a Decontamination Group Supervisor to manage and coordinate all decon operations. The Decontamination Group Supervisor shall assume responsibility for establishing a decontamination site and ensuring that all personnel, clothing, and equipment are cleaned prior to their being returned to service.

The specific tasks and duties of the Decon Group Supervisor shall be as follows:

- Assure that the decontamination area is set up and that sufficient materials are available for decon operations.
- Coordinate the selection of decon operations, procedures and protective clothing with the Safety Officer and the Operations Section Chief, as appropriate.

Equipment Decontamination Concerns

All equipment, including vehicles, monitoring instruments, hand tools, etc., should be decontaminated on site before it crosses the hot zone and leaves the site. Fire hose should be cleaned following the manufacturer's recommendations. For most materials, detergents clean adequately. However, certain detergents and cleaning agents may damage fire hose fibers. The fire hose should then be rinsed thoroughly to prevent any fiber weakening, then marked and pressure tested before it is placed back in service.

Hand tools may be cleaned for reuse or disposed of. Cleaning methods include hand cleaning, or, more commonly, pressure washing or steam cleaning. Weigh the cost of the item against the cost of decontamination and the probability that it can be cleaned completely.

For vehicle decon, it may be necessary to construct a decon pad. A decon pad can be a concrete slab or a pool liner covered with gravel. Engines exposed to toxic dusts or vapors should have their air filters replaced. If the engine has been exposed to corrosive atmospheres, the engine should be inspected by a mechanic. Permeable materials, such as seats, floorboards, and steering wheels may have to be removed and disposed of. All such decon activities should be done while the vehicle is on the decon pad.

Postincident Decon Concerns

After incident operations terminate, it may be necessary to collect and contain all disposable clothing, plastic sheeting, and other discarded materials. All containers that held contaminated materials should be sealed, marked and isolated. Also, determine if any equipment needs to be isolated for further analysis or decontamination.

PATIENT DECONTAMINATION

In certain emergencies personnel can be exposed to hazardous materials. If a patient is treated and transported to a hospital before decontamination, it will expose the patient, emergency medical responders, and hospital staff to the chemical threat.

Individuals exposed to hazardous materials should be decontaminated as much as possible before transport to a medical facility. Proper and immediate field decon procedures help to limit patient exposure, and protect both EMS and hospital personnel. The extent of field decon depends on a correct determination of whether the patient was exposed or contaminated, and the possibility of secondary contamination. The medical facility must be advised that a chemically contaminated patient is being transported there.

Terminate the incident

Once the emergency phase has ended, a number of additional procedures must be completed. Termination activities are divided into three phases: debriefing emergency response personnel and the incident staff, postincident analysis, and incident critique.

INCIDENT DEBRIEFING

Incident debriefings can be held during the final phases of terminating the emergency or after emergency responders have been released. A debriefing should meet the following objectives:

- Inform emergency response personnel of possible hazardous materials exposures and associated signs and symptoms.
- Identify equipment damage and unsafe conditions that require immediate attention or isolation for further evaluation.
- Assign information-gathering responsibilities for a postincident analysis and critique.
- Summarize the activities performed by each element within the Incident Command System.
- Reinforce positive aspects of the emergency response.

The debriefing is most effective when one individual is selected to lead it. The Incident Commander may not be the best facilitator, but he should be present to summarize the incident from the perspective of the command staff and to reinforce the performance of the command staff and response personnel. The debriefing session should be concise, cover only the major aspects of the incident, and be limited to no more than approximately 30 minutes.

The following subjects are recommended in their preferred order:

- Health information. Discuss exact materials and potential stresses to which personnel have been exposed, including exposure signs and symptoms. Also discuss need for any followup medical evaluations and the documentation of exposure levels.
- Review equipment and apparatus exposure. Identify equipment and apparatus potentially exposed, and plan for special cleaning or disposal. Identify personnel and procedures to decontaminate or dispose of equipment.
- Identify problems that require immediate action, including equipment or procedural failures, major personnel problems, or legal implications of response and recovery operations.
- Reinforce operations that went correctly.
- Express appreciation to personnel for a job well done.

POSTINCIDENT ANALYSIS

The postincident analysis is a reconstruction of the emergency response to establish a clear picture of the events that occurred. The primary objective of the postincident analysis is to improve future emergency response operations.

An individual or task force is selected to collect information relevant to the emergency response and recovery operations, as well as issues raised at the debriefing session. This will guarantee that sensitive or unverified information is not released improperly. A checklist of key data and documentation should include information on the cause of the incident and contributing factors, chemical hazard information from available resources, and records on levels of exposure and decontamination.

Additional information can be acquired from interviews with ERT person-nel, mutual aid units, and any photographs or videotapes made of the emer-gency response effort. This material also helps to document information for the postincident investigation and for potential cost recovery efforts.

When all data have been assembled and a rough draft report has been pre-pared, the report should be reviewed by the key players at the emergency to verify the contents. Then the analysis can commence. Postincident analysis should focus on five key topics:

- command and control;
- tactical operations;
- resources;
- support services; and
- plans and planning.

Once the postincident analysis is completed, it should be forwarded to management for review and then distributed to those responsible for appropri-ate action. Conclusions and recommendations should be incorporated into the existing Emergency Response Plan and procedures or used as the basis for developing a new or revised ERP.

CRITIQUE

An effective incident critique or self-evaluation supported by senior man-agement is a positive way to outline and discuss lessons learned. A commit-ment to perform a critique of emergency response operations that detects deficiencies will improve performance and planning by increasing efficiency.

The purpose of a critique is to develop recommendations for improving the emergency response system rather than to find fault with the performance of ERT personnel. The crucial player in the critique is the facilitator who leads the process. A facilitator can be any individual who is comfortable and effec-tive working in front of a group, is knowledgeable about the ERP and SOPs, and is experienced in emergency response. This individual does not necessar-ily have to be part of the response effort.

The following is a recommended critique format for large-scale emergency responses:

Begin with a critique by participants. Each individual makes a statement relevant to his performance and what he feels are the major issues. Depending on time available, more detail may be added. There should be no interruptions during this phase.

Go on to a critique of operations. Participants then comment on the strengths and weaknesses of each section's or sector's actions and contri-butions. Through a spokesperson, each section or sector presents problems encountered, unanticipated events, and lessons learned. Each presentation should be kept to five minutes.

Conclude with a critique session. At the end of the critique, participants focus on the problems that should be addressed by each group. The facilitator encourages discussion, reinforces constructive comments, and records important points.

Following the critique, the facilitator forwards written comments to management. The comments should emphasize suggestions for improving emergency response capabilities and for revising or upgrading the emergency response program. A final report then is circulated within the emergency response organization for all personnel to review.

SUMMARY

This chapter has given you an overview of hazardous materials emergency response operations in a field setting by presenting the key legislative, regulatory, and consensus standards that affect fire service hazardous materials planning and emergency response operations, an overview of the Hazardous Materials Management System for managing the community's hazardous materials problem, and an eight-step methodology for the on-scene management of a hazardous materials emergency.

APPENDIX I

Incident Command System Checklist

INCIDENT COMMAND SYSTEM CHECKLIST

ON-SCENE INCIDENT COMMANDER

I. GENERAL INFORMATION

This checklist is designed to be used by the individual who will function as the On-Scene Incident Commander ("COMMAND") upon their arrival at the emergency scene.

COMMAND is directly responsible for managing the following field activities:

- ❑ Formulate and implement the emergency action plan.
- ❑ Establish Section officers, as necessary, and coordinate their activities.
- ❑ Coordinate with the Safety Officer to ensure that field activities are conducted safely.
- ❑ Oversee all field operations and logistics.
- ❑ Advise the Emergency Operations Center (EOC) of the incident status.

The radio designation for the On-Scene Incident Commander will be "COMMAND."

II. INCIDENT INFORMATION

DATE _____   TIME _____

LOCATION _____

NATURE OF THE INCIDENT _____

MATERIALS / PROCESS INVOLVED _____

Page 1

III.   TASKS AND DUTIES: THE EIGHT STEP INCIDENT MANAGEMENT PROCEDURE

STEP-1: Site Management and Control

❑ During approach to the incident scene, avoid committing or positioning personnel or apparatus in a hazardous position or situation. Ensure that there is an escape route out of the area if the situation should deteriorate.

❑ Determine the following information:

___ YES ___ NO	Are all personnel accounted for?
___	Number and location of injured personnel? _____
___ YES ___ NO	Will standard firefighting protective clothing adequate protection for the material(s) involved?

▲ CAUTION: All personnel responding to an incident where hazardous vapor releases may potentially occur shall wear personal protective clothing and self-contained breathing apparatus (SCBA). These shall be used until air monitoring tests confirm that the equipment is not necessary. All entry operations in the area shall be performed using a buddy system, with back-up personnel in-place.

❑ Assume Command and establish a Command Post. The Incident Commander should be identified by use of a command vest. Initial responsibilities should include receiving a briefing from the first-due fire officer on-scene. The briefing should include a status of the incident, initial control and countermeasures presently being used/implemented, names of agencies notified and additional resources requested.

❑ Restrict access to the emergency site to only authorized essential personnel. The location of the controlled access area should be communicated to all personnel operating at the emergency.

❑ Establish command staff and sector officers, as necessary.

❑ Establish a staging area for additional responding mutual aid equipment and personnel.

❑ Initiate employee and public protective actions (evacuation or protection-in-place). If necessary. Ensure that all personnel are accounted.

STEP-2: Identify the Problem

☐ Identify, confirm, and verify the nature of the problem. As necessary, determine the following:

___ What materials are involved?
_____
_____
_____

___ What type of container or area is involved (i.e., structure, tanks, pipeline, etc.)? _____
_____
_____

___ Who is the **Facility Liaison** (specify by name and title)? _____
_____
_____

___ YES ___ NO Was the original release observed by facility personnel?

☐ Determine the Level of Incident according to the community incident classification system.

___ **Level 1 (Incident)** - Low danger to life, property and the environment. An incident or threat of release which can be controlled by the first responders. It does not require evacuation, beyond the involved structure or immediate outside area. The incident is confined to a small area and poses no immediate threat to life and property.

___ **Level 2 (Serious Incident)** - Moderate danger to life, property and the environment. An incident involving a greater hazard and larger area than Level I which poses a potential threat to life and property. It may require a limited evacuation or protection-in-place of the surrounding area.

___ **Level 3 (Crisis Situation)** - Extreme danger to life, property and the environment. An incident involving a severe hazard or a large area which poses an extreme threat to life and property and which may require a large scale evacuation or protection-in-place.

STEP-3: Evaluate the Hazards and Risks

☐ Evaluate the overall incident situation, including:

- *Previous and current status of the incident.*

  ___ YES ___ NO | Were there any abnormal operating conditions immediately before the emergency? Explain.

  _____

  _____

  ___ YES ___ NO | Were there any equipment problems or changes immediately before the emergency . Explain.

  _____

  _____

- *Overall condition of the haz mat containment systems.*

  ___ YES ___ NO | Are relief valves present? Operating?

  ___ YES ___ NO | Is there an emergency shutdown system?

  ___ YES ___ NO | Have power and all other emergency sources been isolated?

- *Environmental conditions, including runoff, wind, precipitation, topography, etc.?*

  ___ YES ___ NO | Is drainage control in-place? What is the capacity?

  ___ YES ___ NO | Are hydrocarbons floating on runoff water?

  ___ YES ___ NO | Is the runoff hazardous to emergency responders?

- *Exposures, including people (both facility, emergency responders and the public), property, environment and systems disruption (i.e., shutdown of highway traffic).*

  ___ YES ___ NO | Are exposures protected?

- *Comparison of resources available vs. the level required to respond to the problem. Evaluate the risks of personnel intervening directly in the emergency. Consider the limitations of the people involved and their equipment.*

  ___ YES ___ NO | Are fixed fire protection and chemical mitigation systems present? Have they been activated?

- *Estimation of likely harm without active emergency response intervention, and the development of response objectives.*

  __ YES __ NO | Has an isolation strategy been developed?

- *Modifications to the suggested size and perimeters of the hazard control zones.*

  __ YES __ NO | Are the hazard control zones adequate?

❑ Monitor the emergency scene to determine the concentration of contaminants present (e.g., toxicity, flammability, oxygen deficiency) and their approximate location(s).

▲ **CAUTION:** Emergency responders taking air samples must use personal protective equipment and SCBA to match the potential hazard.

❑ Based upon the hazard and risk assessment process, determine whether the incident should be handled offensively, defensively, or by non-intervention. Remember that offensive tactics increase the risks to emergency responders.

  __ Offensive Tactics = require responders to control/mitigate the emergency from within the area of high risk.

  __ Defensive Tactics = permits responders to control/mitigate the emergency remote from the area of highest risk.

  __ Non-Intervention Tactics = pursuing a passive attack posture until the arrival of additional personnel or equipment.

❑ Other related considerations. _____

_____
_____
_____
_____

STEP-4: Select the Proper Level of Personal Protective Clothing

❑ Determine the level of personal protective clothing required:

  ___ Structural Firefighting Clothing
  ___ Chemical Vapor Protective Clothing (EPA Level A)
  ___ Chemical Splash Protective Clothing (EPA Level B)
  ___ High Temperature Protective Clothing (proximity and fire entry suits)

❑ Ensure that all emergency response personnel are using the proper protective equipment and clothing equal to the hazards present. Do not place personnel in an unsafe emergency situation.

❏ Order specialized equipment and expertise early in the incident. If you are unsure what your requirements are, always call for the highest level of assistance available. **Do not wait to call for emergency assistance.**

> ▲ **CAUTION**: Structural firefighting clothing is **NOT** designed to offer any chemical protection, and turnout boots will provide only limited protection against liquids in-depth. Personnel should be aware of the potential chemical burn hazards associated with the runoff water and accumulated liquids which exist at facility emergencies, and should avoid kneeling in areas where such hazards exist.

STEP-5: Coordinate Information and Resources

❏ Confirm that the command post is in a safe area. The command post must be physically separated from all personnel and units involved in the tactical operation. **All personnel not directly involved in the overall command and control should be removed from the Command Post.**

❏ Ensure that all appropriate notifications are made, as appropriate. Remember that Federal and State regulations require proper and prompt notification of regulatory authorities.

❏ Expand the Incident Command System and create additional sections and sectors, as necessary.

❏ Confirm orders and follow through to ensure that they are fully understood and correctly implemented. Maintain strict control of the situation.

❏ Make sure that there is continuing progress toward solving the emergency in a timely manner. Do not delay in calling for either additional personnel and equipment or outside/mutual aid assistance if conditions appear to be deteriorating.

❏ Provide regular briefing sessions for all Section Officers on the status of the incident at regular intervals. All Section Officers, in turn, are responsible for briefing their Sector personnel, as necessary.

❏ If activated, provide regular updates to the Emergency Operations Center.

STEP-6: Control of the Hazardous Materials Release

❑ Implement response objectives. Remember that offensive tactics increase the risks to emergency responders.

— Offensive Tactics = require responders to control/mitigate the emergency from within the area of high risk.

— Defensive Tactics = permits responders to control/mitigate the emergency remote from the area of highest risk.

— Non-Intervention Tactics = pursuing a passive attack posture until the arrival of additional personnel or equipment.

❑ Initiate public protective actions (evacuation or protection-in-place), if necessary.

❑ Evaluate the risks of offensive tactics before sending emergency response teams into the hazard area.

❑ Ensure that properly equipped back-up personnel wearing the appropriate level of personal protective clothing are in-place before initiating entry operations.

❑ Ensure that Entry Teams have been briefed before being allowed to enter the hot zone.

STEP-7: Decontamination and Clean-Up Operations

❑ Ensure that Decontamination Sector operations are coordinated with Entry and the Haz Mat Safety Officer. This should include:

__ Decon area is properly located within the warm zone.
__ Decon area is well-marked and identified.
__ The proper decon method and type of personal protective clothing to be used by the Decon Team has been determined and communicated, as appropriate.

❑ Ensure decontamination of emergency response personnel before they leave the scene. For example, H_2S vapors, flammable gases, and some toxic and corrosive gases can saturate firefighter's protective clothing and be carried into "safe" areas.

❑ Establish a plan to cleanup or dispose of contaminated supplies and equipment before cleaning up the site of a release. Federal and state laws require proper disposal of hazardous waste.

STEP-8: Terminate the Emergency

❑ Account for all personnel before leaving the scene of the emergency.

❑ Conduct an incident debriefing session for all personnel. Provide any background information necessary to ensure that health exposure are documented.

❑ Document all operational, regulatory and medical phases of the emergency, as appropriate. In addition, obtain the names and telephone numbers of all key individuals. This should include state, federal and regional government officials, contractors, facility officials, and media contacts.

NOTES

NOTES:

20

Aircraft Crash Rescue and Firefighting

JOHN N. CARR and LESLIE P. OMANS

CHAPTER HIGHLIGHTS

- The air traffic control system and unique fire protection and emergency response conditions encountered at airports.
- The basic types of aircraft accidents that can occur on and off airports, common crash dynamics, and incident scene conditions that will be encountered.
- The basic types of aircraft, their construction, systems, and other important characteristics.
- The hazards and other safety considerations commonly encountered at aircraft incidents.
- The fire department tactical considerations required by the common types of aircraft accidents.
- Procedures used to rescue, triage, treat, and transport survivors of a major aircraft accident.
- Actions necessary for proper management of fatalities and wreckage at aircraft incidents.
- Aircraft scene security requirements and other important law enforcement considerations.
- Fire department involvement in the aircraft accident investigation process.
- Critical incident stress commonly encountered by emergency responders at aircraft incidents and management techniques.

*A*T MOST INCIDENTS to which the fire department responds, such as the wide variety of fire and rescue situations, it is the primary agency on scene and in control of the incident from beginning to end. Other agencies, such as medical and law enforcement professions will be involved, but only in a support function. An aircraft incident can differ greatly and present management, coordination, and communication challenges many fire officers are not accustomed to or prepared for. Almost always, the fire department will function as the Incident Commander during the initial stages of the incident. Once the fires are extinguished, and survivors are rescued and transported to hospitals, the fire department's roles and responsibilities will phase down.

Aircraft incidents are rare events. Many fire officers may go their entire career without responding to one. If they do, it will probably be the most complicated, demanding, and stressful incident they encounter. Statistics show that a high percentage of commercial aircraft accidents are survivable. Of the persons that survive the impact, as many as 75 percent ultimately will die of burns and smoke inhalations. In order to save lives, many tasks have to be accomplished quickly and simultaneously. There will be many hazards and dangers to personnel. Aircraft incidents are almost always multi-agency incidents involving many major organizations, responsibilities, and activities. The management requirements of the incident will vary, change, and evolve through several phases, beginning with the fire and rescue response and ending with the scene cleanup and recovery. The fire service will be involved to some degree throughout the long and involved process.

This chapter will focus on what the trained and experienced fire officer needs to understand in order to function effectively, efficiently, and safely during major aircraft incidents. The objective is to cover information that will be of value to large, small, urban, suburban, rural, military, paid, and volunteer fire departments. The chapter will begin by reviewing the characteristics of the different types of aircraft incidents. Next, the nature of the aviation environment will be discussed with a focus on the unique situations and safety considerations that will be encountered at airports. The different types of aircraft, their features, construction, and systems will be addressed, concentrating on the hazards they present to responding fire personnel. The chapter then will look at the unique fire protection situation, regulations and procedures, and equipment required at airports. Fire department tactical operations will be reviewed for high- and low-impact crashes, fire and fire-free incidents, forcible entry and extrication situations, interior fires, hazardous cargo incidents, and other common aircraft emergencies. Separate sections also will address important information about the rescue and treatment of victims, assistance provided by law enforcement and other key agencies, proper management of fatalities, scene preservation, and the fire service's involvement in the accident investigation process. The chapter will conclude with a discussion of the critical incident stress aspects of a major aircraft incident.

TYPES OF AIRCRAFT INCIDENTS

There are several ways to categorize the many types of aircraft incidents. One way is by the type of aircraft involved. Smaller general aviation aircraft present a firefighting and rescue problem similar to a highway vehicle accident. Where the aircraft comes down, such as at the site of an apartment building, shopping center, school, dry wildland or water area, rugged or inaccessible terrain can further complicate the situation. As the involved aircraft gets larger, from corporate, small commuter, to the largest commuter, or largest of jet transports, more people and more fuel will be involved, making the rescue and firefighting operations much more complicated. Larger aircraft also are built stronger for high-altitude pressurization, making them less accessible and more difficult to deal with in crash situations. Military aircraft may be transporting exotic and dangerous materials, weapons and armament, ejection seats and canopies. Cargo aircraft may carry large quantities of hazardous materials. Although there are commonalities and similarities in all crash situations, the bigger the aircraft, the more complicated, challenging, and demanding the problem will be for emergency responders.

Another way to categorize aircraft incidents is "off-airport" versus "on-airport" incidents. Any time an aircraft contacts the ground on other than a runway, it usually has tragic results. Most **off-airport** incidents involve what is called a "high-impact crash." It often follows a period of little or no pilot control, with the plane barely kept airborne. If members of the flight crew are in control of the aircraft they often can reach an airport. The aircraft usually comes down at a high rate of speed and at an abnormal angle. Fire involvement, total breakup of the aircraft, and the loss of life of everyone on board are common in these types of incidents. These incidents are almost always handled by structural firefighters using traditional fire apparatus and equipment. In the rare situation where there is *no* post-crash fire, there may be many survivors. Firefighters should be prepared for very demanding extrication and rescue operations. Weather, darkness, rugged terrain, watery environments, spectators, displaced persons, news media attention, and many other influences can make the off-airport incident very difficult to control and manage.

Although "high-impact" accidents do occur at airports, most **on-airport** incidents involve what are termed "low-impact" crashes. In low-impact crashes there is usually some degree of pilot control and the aircraft comes down at a reasonably level angle. This is where the fire service can save lives because there are often specialized airport firefighting resources that can respond quickly and begin fire control and rescue operations. Off-airport structural firefighters will still be heavily involved in, and committed to, any major

A high-impact, off-airport crash in rugged terrain.

A low-impact, on-airport crash with some degree of pilot control and the probability of high survivability.

on-airport incident and should be trained accordingly. Other on-airport fire department emergencies may involve interior fires on passenger and cargo aircraft, wheel, brake, and gear emergencies, engine fires, fuel spills, hazardous cargo situations, aircraft collisions, bomb incidents, and military aircraft emergencies.

THE AVIATION ENVIRONMENT

Every major metropolitan area in the country has a congested airspace over it. Some are worse than others. In addition to the air traffic that just flies through these areas, many different types of aircraft may be competing with each other to land or take off at major international and municipal airports, military airfields, and a host of smaller airports. Smaller private, general aviation aircraft operate at the lower altitudes, usually under visual (VFR) conditions. The larger commercial, corporate, and military aircraft operate at the higher altitudes under instrument (IFR) and visual operations. Most rural areas of the country are under or near air traffic routes or corridors. If an aircraft has an in-flight emergency, it may attempt an emergency landing at the nearest airport that can accommodate it. An aircraft incident can occur any time, anyplace, and in any fire department's jurisdiction.

In conjunction with the pilots, it is the air traffic control system's responsibility to coordinate, sequence, and separate the movement of these aircraft. As the larger aircraft travel across the country, they come into contact with, and are guided by, "air traffic control centers." As these aircraft enter their area of destination, they come into contact with an "approach control." When they leave that area they work with "departure control." When they reach a certain distance, altitude, or location they switch over to the air traffic control tower for the airport of their destination. There are radar systems and procedures to control the safe flow of air traffic and prevent midair collisions. Normally aircraft land and take off into the wind. Statistics indicate that 80 percent of the aviation accidents occur during 7 percent of the flight involving the take-off and landing phase. Abnormal weather, wind, and ice conditions also can increase the chance of an aircraft accident.

The airport itself represents a self-contained community with unique inherent situations, problems, and procedures. It is a very dangerous environment. A collision between a fire department vehicle and an aircraft can have expensive and tragic consequences. Even a runway incursion (a term used to describe an unauthorized entry into an airport aircraft operating area) that causes an aircraft to take evasive action can result in an investigation, report, and a nasty letter from the Federal Aviation Administration (FAA). Understanding the operational policies and procedures of the airport is essential for effective and, above all, safe emergency response.

An example of a well marked airport fire access gate.

Airport Access

Airports are high-security areas and access to them may be difficult and complicated for responding fire agencies. Airport access roads and gates should be highlighted on all response maps, and marked well and made highly visible. Adequate rendezvous or staging locations should be predesignated around the airport. There are no standard access gates! They may be staffed with guards, be operated manually or mechanically, have electrical or metal sensors, open with a card or key, be padlocked or banded, or of the breakaway type.

Runways, Taxiways, and Other Airport Movement Areas

Most airports have free travel areas. This means that vehicles can move independent of tower directions. Examples of these free travel areas are access or perimeter roads and service roads. Perimeter roads usually skirt the perimeter of the airport and present little danger with respect to aircraft operations. In contrast, service roads are used by aircraft service and emergency vehicles. Examples of these vehicles would be fuel trucks, baggage trains and tugs, food service trucks, and various utility vehicles. Service roads usually are identified by contrasting striping that differs from all other ground striping. Service roads are usually within close proximity of aircraft operations. Exercising extreme caution and traveling at slow speeds are standard operating policy.

All airports have taxiways. These are low- and high-speed aircraft traffic areas and should be given all safety considerations. They have been designed to enable aircraft to travel between ramps, jetways, parking areas, and runways. Taxiways are striped yellow on each edge, with a yellow center stripe. They normally are referred to as parallel or cross taxiways. Some are numbered numerically, while others are designated alphabetically; still others use both systems. There are no standards for taxiway designation, but indications are that most airports use letters from the beginning of the alphabet for cross taxiways and letters from the end of of the alphabet for parallel taxiways. Taxiways also have a blue lighting system for night operations. Taxiway signs are black and yellow and illuminated at night. Taxiways have hold bars that serve as the airport's stop sign. These duel bars are striped yellow and are similar to highway striping. One bar is solid, the other broken. The solid bar indicates a stop unless directed by the tower, and the broken bar indicates freedom to cross. The broken bar is usually closest to the runway.

Runways are the paved areas for landing and departing aircraft. They have a white stripe on each edge with a white center stripe and are designated

A taxiway hold short bar. The airport stop sign for aircraft and vehicle traffic.

numerically by compass headings. There are numerous configurations for runways. Some cross each other while others are parallel. Parallel runways usually share the same compass heading but are called left or right. For example, parallel runways with a heading of 180 degrees would be designated as 18 right and left. The opposite ends of these runways would be numbered 36 right and left (180 plus 180 = 360 degrees); this is called the reciprocal end of the runway. Runways may have other markings, such as touchdown bars and distance markers.

Runways have white lighting systems for night or poor visibility operations. The ends of most runways also are marked with threshold lights. These two-color lights have a green side that faces the arrival or landing direction, and a red side that faces the actual runway. This light alerts you to the fact that you are on an active runway. Being either on the threshold, showing a green light, or on the usable runway, showing red lights, is a danger zone, and one that should be avoided. Runway identifiers (markers) are usually red and white and illuminated at night.

Aircraft normally take off and land into the wind; however, an aircraft in distress will use the most available runway regardless of wind conditions. Runways may have overrun areas at each end called thresholds. Threshold areas are marked with large yellow chevrons. Although not designed for land-

A view of a typical aviation operational area which includes parallel and cross taxiways and an active runway.

ings or takeoffs, they are paved and will support the weight of an aircraft on the ground. They are unsafe areas for emergency responders during aircraft operations on the corresponding runway.

At controlled airports, vehicle traffic is permitted on runways and taxiways only with permission from the tower. Extreme caution and constant vigilance must be exercised when operating on runways and taxiways. Unless the airport has been closed, any vehicles on the aircraft operating areas must maintain radio and visual contact with the tower or be escorted by someone who does. It is critical for their safety that fire personnel understand that they cannot indiscriminately drive onto active airport areas, even with red lights and sirens.

Fueling Operations

The fueling operation is a highly volatile activity and constant hazard, and represents the number one fire prevention consideration at airports. Fuel is delivered to airports by tank truck, rail cars, or pipelines. It is stored in above- or belowground bulk storage tanks. The fuel is loaded onto aircraft by one of three methods. At the larger and newer airport facilities, the fuel is transferred by underground piping which terminates at an underground fuel hydrant located in each commercial aircraft ramp parking area. A fuel service truck then connects to this underground system and meters the fuel into the aircraft.

The most common method of aircraft fuel delivery is by tank truck. These tankers transport fuel from a storage location and pump their contents into the aircraft. The capacities of these tankers range from 500 to 10,000-gallons. The fueler must hold a "dead man switch" on in order to load the tank truck or transfer fuel into the aircraft. These switches can be blocked open. Fuel trucks are required to have emergency shutdown switches at each end of the truck. With the tremendous quantities of fuel dispensed daily, fuel spills are common aircraft-related emergencies at airports.

The third method uses fueling islands, similar to an automobile gas station, where small aircraft taxi up and get fuel. During any aircraft fueling operation, bonding and grounding cables are used to eliminate static electrical charges. Larger aircraft receive fuel through single-point fueling connections, located under the wing or in the side of the fuselage, where all onboard fuel tanks can be filled from one location. They also have over-the-wing fueling locations. Smaller aircraft predominantly use the over-the-wing method.

Airport Structures

Many types of structures, varying in size and purpose, are present at airports. Hangars present a hazard because of the quantity of fuel on board aircraft parked inside. Often, hazardous aircraft maintenance, repair, and servicing activities are conducted inside airport hangars. Many have very sophisticated fixed fire detection, alarm, and extinguishing systems. Hangars, as is the case with other types of airport structures, can be used during emergencies to provide staging areas for personnel, for medical triage and temporary morgue facilities, for rehabilitation areas, and for incident command posts.

Many airports present a structural fire protection problem similar to that of a small city. Hotels, restaurants, high-rise buildings, air traffic control tower, huge parking garages, and offices could be affected by an aircraft incident. Air cargo buildings are found at most airports. These buildings are not always identified as hazardous materials storage facilities and present obvious hazards. Hazardous materials shipments (dangerous goods) transported by aircraft have increased tremendously. With this growth, the handling and storage of hazardous materials have become a growing concern for airport administrators.

Most airports have terminal areas which represent a tremendous life hazard. Terminal buildings are classified as assembly occupancies. The potential for, and impact of, an emergency evacuation often are overlooked and underestimated. Some airports have passengers walk from the terminal to the aircraft outside on a ramp area, exposing boarding and deplaning passengers to a wide spectrum of dangers, including fueling, baggage loading, and other aircraft servicing operations. Providing jetways or enclosed passageways from the terminal to the aircraft is the most modern approach to passenger loading and off loading. Jetways are ideal for weather and external hazard protection, and provide additional channeled security access points. However, jetways also create their own hazards. Aircraft have caught fire while parked in ramp areas, and a jetway tunnel provides a direct means of communicating fire or smoke from an involved aircraft into the airport terminal.

Terminals contain a diverse array of occupancies such as conference rooms, restaurants, V.I.P. lounges, etc. These can provide excellent areas for distressed and bereaved relatives, emotional stress debriefing teams, key airline administrators, news media, and airline and airport administrators not actively engaged at the emergency scene. Terminals also have an abundance of resources such as communications, food service, rest areas, and creature comfort facilities.

Airport Communications

Airports use a unique system of communication. The air traffic control tower is responsible for all communications and movement on the airfield. Depending on whether the airport is a civilian or military operation, most towers are staffed and operated by FAA or Department of Defense personnel. Specialized aircraft terminology, procedures, and phrases, and the phonetic alphabet are used. For their personal safety, firefighters who protect the airport or respond to it should be familiar with the airport communication system and procedures. The FAA has several excellent pamphlets and video programs available on this subject.

The primary means of communications at airports is by aircraft-type radios. Both vehicles and aircraft moving about the "Aircraft Operating Areas (AOA)" communicate with the tower via the "ground control frequency." This is the channel most used by fire personnel to get information from the tower about the emergency situation and to get clearance to move apparatus to various locations on the airport. Fire department vehicles without ground control radio capability can have fire dispatch or communications personnel call the tower by telephone with requests for information or airport access. Another method is to request the assistance of airport personnel with the proper radios to provide escorts or perform needed ground communications. Some suggested persons to use are airport operations, maintenance, and security personnel, as well as airline and other airport tenants.

Aircraft in the process of approaching, landing, or departing from the airport communicate on a "runway or tower radio frequency." Emergency personnel may use this channel to talk to aircraft pilots or monitor their conversations with the tower during inflight emergencies. Airports without a control tower, or during hours when the tower is closed, use a "Unicom Frequency" or "Common Traffic Advisory Frequency (CTAF)" to control landings, takeoffs, and ground movements. At some airports they may be the same frequency. Pilots or vehicle operators monitor airport activity, communicate with each other, and announce their intended actions on these frequencies. If the airport is uncontrolled or the tower is closed, an incoming pilot may announce an inflight emergency on these channels with the hope that someone on the ground will hear it and notify the local emergency services. The airport also may have "Fixed Based Operators (FBOs)" that provide fuel, aircraft maintenance, car rentals, and other services needed by private pilots. They may have their own radio frequency that pilots could use to declare an emergency. There is also an internationally recognized "Aircraft Emergency Frequency." Any pilot in trouble will get the most attention on this channel, because it is monitored constantly by air traffic control centers, approach/departure control facilities, and other pilots.

Airport control towers also have an alternate communications system, called light signals. Used primarily to signal aircraft that are having radio communication problems, it also can be used to signal vehicles not equipped with aircraft radios. You can get the tower personnel's attention by pointing a vehicle toward the tower, turning on all emergency lights, and flashing the headlights. This is a seldom-used system and may be difficult to access. The following signals are used:

Steady green light—Cleared to cross, proceed, or go.

Steady red light—Stop, do not proceed.

Flashing red light or flashing runway lights—Clear the taxiway or runway immediately.

Flashing white light—Return to starting point.

Alternating green and red light—General warning. Exercise extreme caution.

Always be aware of and constantly looking for the presence of aircraft. Unless otherwise instructed by the control tower, yield the right of way to aircraft. Especially in large aircraft, the pilot's view of the ground areas immediately in front of and adjacent to the sides of the aircraft is limited, and nonexistent for any areas behind the wings of the aircraft. Whenever possible approach the aircraft from a direction that enables the pilot to see you. Be aware also of nonstandard approach paths, particularly for helicopters. Turn on vehicle headlights, beacons, and other flashing lights when on the AOA. Move in an expeditious manner across runways and taxiways, being aware of the air traffic flow whenever possible. Contact the control tower at regular intervals to remind them of your presence when you are in the active areas for extended periods of time.

An air traffic controller using light signals, an alternative means of communications for aircraft and vehicle traffic.

TYPES OF AIRCRAFT

GENERAL AVIATION AIRCRAFT

Single- or twin-engine aircraft, known as general aviation aircraft, are constructed of lighweight metal with reciprocating engines. They typically carry from one to six passengers. Fuel capacities range from 30 to 90 gallons of highly volatile aviation gasoline. A good rule of thumb is to approximate 15 gallons of fuel per seat in the aircraft. Most are not designed for high-altitude pressurization and present an emergency access problem similar to that of an automobile. Doors and hatches are relatively easy to operate or force open. (Pressurized aircraft are much more rigidly constructed, harder to access, and use oxygen systems.) This category also includes lightweights, homebuilts, gliders, hot air balloons, and privately owned, former military aircraft. Statistically, general aviation aircraft account for the majority of aircraft accidents.

Corporate Aircraft

There are many different models and manufacturers of corporate aircraft. They are usually multi-engine aircraft that use turbo-prop or jet engines. A turbo-prop is a jet engine that drives a propeller. Most corporate aircraft use Jet-A, a kerosene-grade fuel. They are also predominantly pressurized aircraft and have "plug" type doors and hatches. This means that the door is larger than the opening. These are custom-built aircraft and feature a wide variety of occupant loads and interior arrangements. Fuel loads can range from several hundred to more than a thousand gallons.

Commuter Aircraft

These aircraft nearly always have twin, reciprocating or turbo-prop engines, and use aviation gasoline to Jet-A. Fuel quantities range from several hundred to more than a thousand gallons. Passenger capacities vary from 12 to 30. Access and cargo doors usually are found on the left side of the aircraft. Almost all are pressurized aircraft. The interiors of corporate and commuter aircraft tend to be cramped and congested, and present a difficult environment in which to move and work under emergency conditions.

COMMERCIAL AIR CARRIER AIRCRAFT

Categorized as narrow or wide-body aircraft, narrow body aircraft make up most of the commercial aircraft that use major airports. Firefighters would be most likely to encounter, and should be familiar with, various models of the

Commuter and commercial narrow body aircraft. These aircraft comprise the majority of the commercial fleet.

Boeing 727, 737, 757, DC-9, MD-80, Airbus A320, and Foker F100. These aircraft have two to three jet engines and fuel capacities from 5,000 to 12,000 gallons of Jet-A. The average passenger capacities range from 85 to 200. They have one aisle and overhead luggage compartments. Plug-type doors swing out and forward when opened and are equipped with escape slides. Only the escape slides on the 757, F100, and A320 can be deactivated from the outside by operating the exterior door handle. Always stand aft of narrow body aircraft doors when opening from the outside and be prepared for a slide to inflate. In addition to the over-wing escape hatches, some of these aircraft also may have rear airstairs or tail cones that can be jettisoned. A typical flight crew on a narrow-body aircraft may consist of a captain, first officer (copilot), a flight engineer on the older aircraft, and up to five flight attendants.

The common wide-body aircraft that serve most major airports include the Boeing 747, 767, and 777, DC-10, MD-11, L1011, Airbus A300 and A310. Passenger capacities can reach 500. Fuel capacities range from 12,000 to more than 40,000 gallons of kerosene Jet-A. The flight crew typically consists of 2 to 3 officers and 8 to 10 flight attendants. Although some swing open (747 and 777), most exit and service doors are operated by aircraft electrical power and rotate up into the overhead area of the fuselage. In an emergency situation, pneumatic or spring tension propels the door upward. Each exit door is equipped with a double-wide evacuation slide which usually can be disarmed from the exterior of the aircraft. Most wide-body aircraft have two aisles running fore and aft, creating a center section of seats.

CARGO AIRCRAFT

Larger cargo aircraft often are called freighters. The common cargo aircraft serving most commercial airports include the Boeing 727, 757, DC-9, DC-8, DC-10, MD-11, and 747. Older large, propeller-driven aircraft also are used in many areas. Smaller single- and twin-engine aircraft, called "feeders," move cargo from smaller to larger airports and may load directly onto the larger freighters. Many of the freighters are former passenger aircraft that have been retrofitted to carry cargo. Some of the original passenger doors and hatches may not be operational. Large, hydraulically operated cargo doors usually are located forward or aft of the wing on the left side. Although most have a manual emergency method, electrical power is needed to open these doors under normal conditions. On a few freighters the nose or tail may swing or lift open. Cargo is usually loaded into containers, called igloos, or secured to metal pallets. Once loaded it is usually impossible to move through the cargo compartment. **Always** treat a cargo aircraft accident as a possible hazardous materials incident.

A narrow body DC-8 freighter aircraft with the main cargo door in the open position.

MILITARY AIRCRAFT

This category covers a wide variety of aircraft, including military versions of the civilian aircraft listed in the previous sections. It includes specialized fighters and bombers, cargo, fueling, reconnaissance aircraft, and helicopters. Hazards presented by military aircraft can include liquid oxygen (LOX), exotic fuels, composite construction materials, weapons, armament, and other explosives, canopy and ejection seat systems, powerful radar systems, and jet-assisted takeoff (JATO) rocket motors. If you must deal with military aircraft, stabilize the situation first, isolate the aircraft, notify personnel at the nearest military base, wait for their arrival, and let them handle the aircraft and incident scene.

ROTARY WING AIRCRAFT (HELICOPTERS)

The aircraft discussed in the previous sections are referred to as "fixed wing" aircraft. Rotary wing aircraft are not as rigidly constructed and tend to break up on impact more readily than do traditional fixed-wing aircraft. They also tend to fall like a rock when they lose power. Fuel tanks most likely will be found in various locations, often under the seats or in the belly of the aircraft. Fuel loads can be upward of several hundred gallons. The newer aircraft use turbine (jet) engines and fuel. There are many uses for helicopters, including air ambulances, construction, law enforcement, firefighting, news media, and general business activities.

MISCELLANEOUS

This category includes other types of aircraft that present unique situations for firefighters and do not fit into the previously discussed categories. They include the space shuttle and blimps, as well as experimental, charter, antique, WWII vintage bomber, agricultural spraying, firefighting air tanker, skydiver transport aircraft, and many other specialized types of aircraft.

AIRCRAFT CONSTRUCTION AND OTHER CHARACTERISTICS

Most aircraft are constructed of lightweight aluminum alloys. Aluminum will not withstand direct fire impingement for more than 90 to 120 seconds without melting. Aluminum is also a nonferrous metal, does not spark, and is relatively easy to cut with a rescue saw. Other construction materials you will encounter include steel, wood, magnesium, titanium, fiberglass, plastics, rubber, and composite materials. Large aircraft

Interior view of typical large-frame aircraft construction. This photograph portrays circumferentials "formers," longerons "stringers," and the rivet-fastened exterior metallic skin.

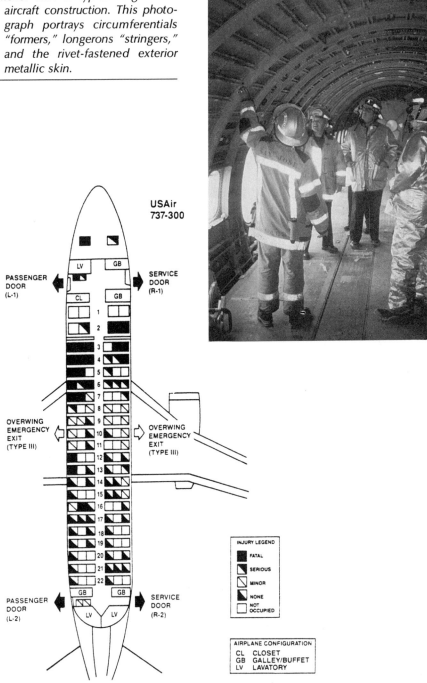

USAir 737-300

PASSENGER DOOR (L-1)

SERVICE DOOR (R-1)

LV | GB | CL | GB

1 2 3 4 5 6 7 8 9 10 11 12 13 14 15 16 17 18 19 20 21 22

OVERWING EMERGENCY EXIT (TYPE III)

OVERWING EMERGENCY EXIT (TYPE III)

PASSENGER DOOR (L-2)

SERVICE DOOR (R-2)

GB | GB | LV | LV

INJURY LEGEND

- FATAL
- SERIOUS
- MINOR
- NONE
- NOT OCCUPIED

AIRPLANE CONFIGURATION

CL CLOSET
GB GALLEY/BUFFET
LV LAVATORY

Narrow body aircraft door numbering. Note that over-the-wing exits are not included in the door numbering sequence.

construction usually consists of vertical formers or circumferentials, connected by horizontal longerons or stringers, and covered with an exterior skin. Most aircraft construction components are fastened by rivets. Between the exterior skin and plastic interior will be some type of insulation. The space between the structural members, overhead ceiling area, and belly of the aircraft provides numerous concealed spaces for vertical and horizontal fire spread. Windows are usually double or triple panes and made of heavy plastic. Aircraft engines are numbered sequentially from left to right, facing forward in the plane. Doors are designated as left or right and numbered sequentially from the nose to the tail. The door used by passengers to board and deplane on most narrow-bodied aircraft is called "Door 1 Left." Commercial aircraft almost always have door opening instructions on the outside of each door.

AIRCRAFT HAZARDS AND SAFETY CONSIDERATIONS

A major aircraft incident is a very dangerous situation for emergency responders. The materials used to construct the aircraft, contained in on-board systems, and carried as cargo or attachments automatically make aircraft emergencies hazardous materials situations. All personnel working in the immediate incident area, hot zone, or hazard reduction area should be in full protective gear, with rubber fire boots, gloves, helmet, eye protection, and, most of the time, breathing apparatus. Standard structural protective turnout or bunker gear is adequate for aviation incidents. Aluminized reflective gear would make firefighters more comfortable near large fuel spill fires, which tend to give off tremendous amounts of radiated heat. With modern fire apparatus and foam agents, spill fires usually are controlled quickly, eliminating the radiated heat problem. Firefighters need to be trained, equipped, and ready to quickly switch from exterior spill control tactics to interior structural firefighting techniques within the fuselage.

Safety officer(s) should be assigned as soon as possible to identify incident scene hazards, protect emergency personnel, monitor response activities, and develop an incident safety plan. Access to the immediate incident area should be limited to personnel who have legitimate tasks to accomplish. Adequate lighting should be provided during nighttime operations. Consider requesting an aircraft mechanic to help stabilize aircraft systems and to provide technical assistance as needed. Emergency charts, available from aircraft manufacturers, provide a tremendous amount of information, e.g., system locations, recommended cut-in areas, door and hatch operation, shut-down procedures, and other important or dangerous features. Many airport fire departments have developed very comprehensive and easy-to-use pre-emergency plans for the aircraft typically found in their response area. Computer-generated aircraft information programs also are being developed.

FUEL

If an aircraft catches fire on impact, the chances of saving its occupants decrease considerably. If there is no post-crash fire, the presence of the fuel complicates the rescue operation significantly and endangers emergency responders. The two types of aircraft fuel are aviation gasolines, often called avgas, and turbine or jet fuels. Most general aviation and older, large-frame piston-engined aircraft use aviation gasoline. Aviation gasolines have very low flash points (−45°F.), rapid flame spread, and are always ready to ignite. Among the many ignition sources present at aircraft incidents are friction, hot engine surfaces, static electricity, fire apparatus and power equipment, cameras, radios, and aircraft electrical and radar systems.

All civilian jet or turboprop aircraft use Jet-A, or JP-5, as it is referred to in the military. This is a highly refined kerosene fuel that has a flashpoint in excess of 100°F. It is considered a flammable liquid but does not ignite as readily as avgas. As an aircraft and its fuel cells break up on impact, the fuel is usually released in the form of a "fuel mist." In a mist form, kerosene is as explosively ignitable as aviation gasoline. A common grade of jet fuel used by the military is called JP-18, or which has a flashpoint a little lower than JP-5. Most aircraft fuels will burn with relatively the same intensity and will present the same conditions when on fire. All are lighter than water and will not mix with it, causing them to float. Their vapors are heavier than air, will flow downwind, and collect in low areas. Besides being extremely flammable, all aircraft fuels are also toxic, skin irritants, and can cause respiratory problems. Consider setting up a decontamination area at aircraft incidents. When any type of aircraft fuel is spilled, always apply a foam blanket, maintain it with regular reapplications of fresh foam, and monitor the scene with combustible vapor detectors.

Aircraft fuel is often referred to in pounds. Fuel is almost always located in the wings. The exterior wing surface is commonly part of the fuel cell and called a "wet wing" or "integral fuel cell." Fuel tanks also may be found in the belly of the fuselage, vertical and horizontal stabilizers, on wing tips, and under aircraft fuel pods (military aircraft) that often can be jettisoned. Jet aircraft, with engines located in their tail sections, have fuel lines running through the interior walls. It is common to find fuel leaking and spilled on the interior of crashed rear-engine aircraft. Fuel lines can be constructed of metal, rubber, or combinations of materials, and have red markings. Most fuel systems can be controlled by plugging and crimping lines, and by shutting down fuel pumps by securing aircraft power and fuel controls in the flight deck.

An aircraft hydraulic accumulator and associated piping. These accumulators and piping store toxic hydraulic fluid under extremely high pressure and are very dangerous if their integrity is compromised.

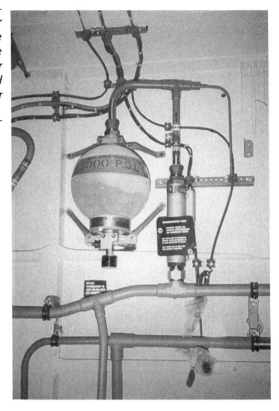

HYDRAULIC SYSTEMS AND FLUIDS

Smaller aircraft use a mineral-oil type of hydraulic fluid. The larger jet aircraft use a phosphate ester type fluid called Skydrol. Skydrol is purple in color. It is corrosive, toxic, and flammable. This fluid can destroy many materials, including turnout gear. Extensive hydraulic systems can be found throughout most modern aircraft and include piping, reservoirs, and pressure accumulators. System pressures can be as high as 3,000 psi parked or in flight. Small leaks may be difficult to detect and can easily lacerate, inject, or irritate exposed skin areas, as well as contaminate the eyes. Hydraulic piping has blue and yellow markings.

OXYGEN SYSTEMS

Most older major aircraft have compressed-oxygen systems on board. In the past, these systems have significantly accelerated aircraft interior fires. Most compressed-oxygen systems can be controlled by closing the valves on each individual cylinder. Cylinders can be found anywhere in the fuselage of the aircraft. Oxygen piping has green identification markings. There also may be portable oxygen cylinders on board. Newer air carrier aircraft use chemi-

Aircraft compressed cylinders have significantly accelerated aircraft fires and will explode when exposed to high heat situations.

cally generated oxygen systems for passenger use. They are usually located in the backs of seats and in the overhead luggage racks. These systems can reach temperatures of 400° to 500°F when operating. Some military aircraft, usually of the fighter, attack, and bomber category, may have liquid oxygen (LOX) systems on board. LOX is a light blue liquid that boils into gaseous oxygen at −297°F. The military recommends spraying liquid oxygen leaks with a water spray. The resulting ice buildup will form a seal, stopping the oxygen flow.

ELECTRICAL SYSTEMS

Aircraft electrical systems range from 12-volt to 220-volt and present both an ignition and shock hazard. Several different types of electrical systems may be encountered on the same aircraft. Responding fire personnel should make every effort to shut down the power in the flight deck and disconnect the battery or batteries. Tape or tag the cockpit power switch to prevent it from being switched back on during post-incident activities. Almost all large aircraft use

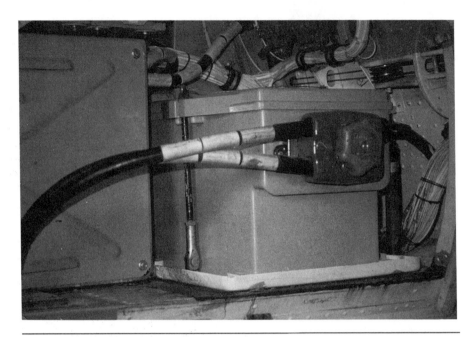

A large aircraft battery. Usually housed in the avionics compartment with its quick disconnect wheel in place.

Nicad batteries, which can undergo thermal run-away and overheating. On large air carrier aircraft, there will usually be one, or sometimes two batteries located in an avionics compartment, in the belly of the aircraft, just aft of the nose gear. This makes them very difficult to reach when the aircraft is crashed and on its belly. Consider cutting into the aircraft to disconnect the battery if it is inaccessible by normal means. On general aviation, corporate, commuter, helicopters, and military aircraft, the battery or batteries could be in any number of locations. Large aircraft batteries have a wheel or tee handle that requires counterclockwise turns to quick disconnect. Battery pliers are rarely needed. Electrical wiring is located throughout the aircraft, but does not present a problem if the power has been secured. Remember, all aircraft controls and instruments changed or affected during the emergency response must be noted, recorded, and reported to the investigating authorities.

ANTI-ICING FLUIDS

These fluids usually are made up of 85 percent alcohol and 15 percent glycerin. Some aircraft engines also may have alcohol/water injection systems. While not as great a hazard as other aircraft fuels, alcohol will burn with an almost invisible flame. Usually only limited amounts of alcohols will be encountered in aviation environments.

PRESSURIZED CYLINDERS

There can be many pressurized cylinders located throughout large aircraft. Some, such as oxygen cylinders, have pressure relief valves; others do not. Pressurized cylinders may be used for hydraulic fluids, fire extinguishing systems, rain repellant, pneumatic systems, and other compressed gases. These types of cylinders have been known to explosively disintegrate during aircraft firefighting operations.

TIRE, RIM, AND WHEEL ASSEMBLIES

Large aircraft tires may have pressures up to and in excess of 200 psi. They are usually filled with nitrogen, an inert gas, because of the tremendous amount of heat generated during takeoffs and landings. Tires can explode with the force of a bomb when overpressurized, overheated, or damaged during crash impacts. People have been dismembered and killed by disintegrating tires. While not a frequent occurrence, it is worthwhile to stay away from tires during aircraft incidents. Rims often are made of magnesium or other cast metals, which can fracture under certain conditions. If the tire is still inflated, the pressure can throw rim fragments and shrapnel several

A large main landing gear assembly. These overpressurized gear assemblies, especially the tires and rims, are subject to explode when overpressurized, overheated, or damaged during hot landings or crash impact.

hundred feet. Most wheels have a fusible plug that releases the air at a certain pressure. Deflating the tires eliminates most of the danger presented by wheel assemblies. Avoid areas opposite the sides of aircraft wheel assemblies. Approach wheels from the front or rear of the aircraft cautiously, and only if absolutely necessary.

HAZARDOUS CARGO

Dangerous cargos can be encountered on any aircraft. Hazardous cargos on aircraft are usually called dangerous goods or restricted articles. Hazardous materials can be shipped on cargo and passenger aircraft. Dangerous items may be carried in personal luggage, in the mail, or shipped as ordinary cargo, making their presence difficult to detect. They can create problems during interior fires significantly and can be scattered in an impact area after a crash.

AIRCRAFT WRECKAGE

The incident scene may be covered with jagged and sharp metal fragments of various sizes that could damage vehicle tires and injure personnel who are not properly protected. Fire apparatus drivers may be blocked by, or have to negotiate around, large pieces of aircraft wreckage. Large intact sections of aircraft fuselage may need to be supported or braced to prevent them from rolling over or collapsing. Working in and around a damaged fuselage presents hazards that can injure unprotected personnel.

UTILITIES AND OTHER INCIDENT SCENE HAZARDS

Whatever the aircraft struck on the ground, such as structures and trees, may add to the debris at the incident scene. Especially in off-airport incidents, downed live electrical wires, broken gas lines, and damaged water systems may be encountered. The incident scene terrain may be steep, rugged, slippery, dense with vegetation, and otherwise very difficult in which to work.

BODIES AND BODY FLUIDS

Air carrier passenger aircraft can carry hundreds of people. Many high-impact aircraft incidents have resulted in a significant loss of life and disintegration of the bodies. Bodies, body parts, and body fluids can be encountered anywhere in the aircraft wreckage and at the incident scene. Personnel working in these areas should be properly protected from skin injuries, mucous membrane (eyes, mouth, nose) contamination, and bloodborne pathogen exposures.

COMPOSITE MATERIALS

There are many different types, configurations, and applications of composite materials on aircraft. Used primarily for their strength and lightness, most are tiny slivers or fibers of a material that are bonded together with an epoxy. When torn apart or involved in fire, these sharp fibers are released into the air or scattered around the impact area. Some of these materials may create a respiratory or skin irritation hazard in crash, fire, or forcible entry situations, similar to those of asbestos fibers. By quickly extinguishing post-crash fires and keeping the incident scene wet with foam or water, most of the composite fibers can be controlled. The most well known are the carbon graphite, boron tungsten, and kevlar composite materials. Composites can be encountered anywhere on an aircraft. Some newer military aircraft fuselages are constructed predominantly of composites. When composite materials are encountered, decontamination should be considered.

COMBUSTIBLE AND DANGEROUS METALS

Magnesium and titanium can be found in landing gear and engine areas, in wheel rims, and various other locations on aircraft. Used for their light weight and strength, they are very difficult to extinguish when burning and give off very toxic products of combustion. Specialized extinguishing agents are available, but none is very effective. The military recommends using water fog in large quantities. One tactic is to protect exposures and let the material burn out. Small quantities can sometimes be moved from the immediate incident site and allowed to burn in a safe location. Very small amounts of radioactive metals may also be found on some aircraft. Consider surveying an aircraft accident scene with radiological monitoring equipment.

ROCKET ENGINES (JATO), HYPERBOLIC, AND OTHER EXOTIC FUELS (MILITARY AIRCRAFT)

In "Jet-Assisted Takeoffs" small rocket engines usually are used in clusters to provide extra thrust during takeoff. If this type of aircraft system is involved in fire, extreme care should be used when approaching the area. No attempt should be made to extinguish the engine if it should ignite. It will burn intensely for a short time. Rocket fuels also can be very toxic and dangerous if broken up by impact forces and in the crash site. Most rocket engines consist of a fuel, typically ammonia, hydrazine, hydrogen, analine, and furfuryl alcohol, and an oxidizing material such as chlorine trifluoride, fluorine, nitric acid, hydrogen peroxide, and nitrogen tetroxide. Toxic hydrazine also is used as emergency power unit (EPU) fuel on some fighter aircraft.

EJECTION SEATS AND CANOPIES (MILITARY AIRCRAFT)

Seats that can be ejected and canopies that can be jettisoned are found on most military fighter, attack, and bomber aircraft. Fire personnel also may encounter privately owned former American and foreign military aircraft with these features. Both ejection seats and canopies usually use an explosive or rocket system to complete the emergency escape process. It is a very dangerous and complicated procedure to safely eject seats and canopies. Untrained civilian fire personnel should **never attempt to stabilize military aircraft ejection seats or canopy.** Let experienced military personnel handle the situation.

ARMAMENT AND WEAPONS (MILITARY AIRCRAFT)

Approach military aircraft with the attitude that they may include such dangerous weaponry as cannons, rockets, bombs, and various pyrotechnics. Fire personnel and equipment should stay out of an area in front of and behind the aircraft, from wing tip to wing tip. Rockets and guns usually fire off toward the front and rocket blasts release to the rear of the aircraft. Tests have shown that when exposed to fire, weapons "cook off" anywhere from immediately to up to eight minutes. They can become very unstable when exposed to heat and activated by the force of a firefighting hose stream. Stay as far away from military aircraft as possible. If approach is absolutely necessary, do so at a 45-degree angle to the fuselage to avoid the weapons and wheel hazards.

OTHER TOXIC, COMBUSTIBLE, OR HAZARDOUS MATERIALS ON AIRCRAFT

The interior finishes, furnishings, and luggage compartments of commercial passenger aircraft are loaded with plastics, foam rubber, and other ordinary combustibles that can produce huge quantities of toxic products of combustion under fire conditions. Other materials used in the operation of the aircraft, such as containers of windshield rain repellant, can be toxic if released or exposed to fire. An agricultural spraying aircraft may have toxic pesticides and herbicides on board.

JET ENGINE BLAST

Jet blast velocities in excess of 30 mph and 44 feet per second are considered undesirable for personnel and equipment. People and vehicles have been blown end over end by jet blasts. This dangerous situation is created at taxiing thrusts and above. Jet blast velocities may cause loose objects on the ground to become potential missiles and be thrown considerable distances. Hot engines may continue to be an ignition hazard for up to 20 to 30 minutes after shutdown.

JET ENGINE INTAKES

People have been sucked into jet intakes with tragic results. Stay at least 25 feet away from jet intakes. A good indication that the engines are running is that the aircraft red rotating beacons will be on.

PROPELLERS AND ROTORS

It is relatively safe to approach a propeller from the rear. Propwash from propellers turning at breakaway or taxiing thrust can pick up and project loose objects. Never approach the front or sides of a propeller at these thrusts. Stay at least 15 feet away from the fronts and sides of propellers at idle speeds. Piston aircraft engines in certain situations may start up with a slight movement of a propeller, so do not touch. Tail rotors on helicopters are very dangerous. Main rotors may drop down as they decelerate. Always approach a helicopter in as low a position as possible and in view of and as directed by the pilot.

ESCAPE SLIDES

Unless deactivated or disarmed, slides inflate within 5 to 10 seconds. They inflate with enough force to knock a firefighter down or off a ladder. Escape slides on most narrow-bodied commercial aircraft cannot be disarmed from the outside. The exceptions are the F100, A320, and 757. The opposite is true for most wide-bodied aircraft. Always stand or place ladders aft of aircraft doors. Most doors swing forward or up into the overhead. Very few corporate and commuter aircraft have escape slides. Escape slides are the fastest method of evacuating an aircraft. Approximately 10 percent of the persons who use the slides suffer minor injuries, including abrasions, contusions, strains, and sprains. If the emergency situation does not warrant an emergency evacuation, attempt to advise the pilots, and remove the occupants with portable air stairs. If slides are deployed, assign emergency responders to hold them down in windy conditions and help evacuees off. Persons may be coming off the aircraft without their shoes.

RADAR

Radar beams, much like microwaves, can present an ignition and health hazard. Most commercial weather, mapping, airborne radar systems are not operated on the ground. Never approach the nose of an aircraft if you suspect that the radar system is on. If the aircraft engines and power have been shut down, so has the radar. Some military aircraft have very powerful radar systems which may be obvious by the presence of radar domes.

AIRPORT FIRE DEPARTMENT RESOURCES

Federal Aviation Administration Requirements

Federal Aviation Administration regulations require a certain number of aircraft rescue and firefighting (ARFF) apparatus and a certain level of extinguishing agent capability at indexed airports. The term ARFF is used now instead of the previous term, Crash Fire Rescue (CFR). An indexed airport is one that serves a certain number of *scheduled air carrier passenger aircraft* (at least five per day). The airport's index number determines the minimum number of ARFF apparatus required and quantities of extinguishing agent they must carry. There are five index categories, A through E. An Index A airport serves smaller air carrier passenger aircraft of less than 90 feet in length. A minimum of one ARFF vehicle that carries a minimum of 500 pounds of dry chemical agent or 450 pounds of dry chemical with 50 gallons of AFFF is required. Other agents may be substituted for the dry chemical, such as halon replacements and carbon dioxide. An Index E airport serves every type of aircraft, including those longer than 200 feet. A minimum of three ARFF vehicles that carry 6,000 gallons or more of water, plus the required quantity of foam concentrate and secondary agent, are required.

FAA indices and fire apparatus requirements are based strictly on scheduled commercial passenger aircraft serving the airport. An airport could have the largest cargo and military aircraft using it. No airport firefighting capability would be required unless the regular, ticket-purchasing passenger element is present. The ARFF apparatus are purchased predominantly with Airport Improvement Program (AIP) funds. This money also is used for security, runway, taxiway, and other airport improvements.

The vehicles are required to carry enough foam concentrate for two loads of water. This means that at an aircraft incident the ARFF units can be refilled with water once, without having to add foam concentrate. Most airport fire departments store enough foam concentrate to replenish their ARFF apparatus several times. It is important that firefighting vehicles are resupplied with water and foam concentrate at the incident scene. Having ARFF units leave the scene early in the firefighting and rescue operations could cause emergency responders to lose control of the fire. Resupply will involve personnel bringing foam out in containers, tank trailer, or a foam tender. Water for the ARFF units will usually be resupplied initially using water tenders or engine water tanks, and later in the incident by laying water supply hoselines out to the scene. The latter is possible only if hydrants are available nearby. Few airports have underground hydrants out on the runway and taxiway areas of the airports. Most are located near airport structures and perimeter roads.

Annually, FAA personnel inspect the airport, as well as the airport fire protection, looking at airport fire department training records, apparatus foam test records, the condition of apparatus and equipment, and the knowledge level of the personnel. An unannounced response test is conducted. The first ARFF vehicle must be able to respond to the middle of the most remote runway and discharge agent within three minutes. The other required ARFF units must arrive and discharge agent within four minutes. Airport fire stations usually are positioned in order to gain access to the active areas of the airport and respond to all locations within the required time. Larger airports must have additional fire stations, with the required apparatus and extinguishing agent, to meet these response criteria. All airport fire personnel also must participate in a minimum of one simulated aircraft live fire training evolution annually. At least one fire department EMT is required to be on duty at indexed airports.

The FAA requires enough on-duty personnel to get the required number of vehicles to an aircraft incident scene and discharge the required flow of extinguishing agent. This usually can be accomplished with one driver operating the top turret nozzle. At least two fire personnel should be assigned to each ARFF apparatus to assist with radio operation (ground control and fire channels), watch for aircraft on the AOA, help guide the vehicle onto the incident scene, operate multiple turrets, as well as get out of the apparatus and do something. The extra person on each apparatus can assist with evacuation, access, rescue, treatment, aircraft stabilization, handline and interior fire attack operations, and setting up the Incident Command System.

Airport Fire Apparatus

ARFF units vary from quick-response "Rapid Intervention Vehicles (RIV)" to rescue vehicles to major vehicles that carry 1,000 gallons or more of foam. ARFF vehicles are very large, fast, sophisticated, and complex pieces of equipment to operate. They can discharge foam while moving. These apparatus also carry a complement of medical equipment, ladders, self-contained breathing apparatus, and extinguishers. Dry powder extinguishers usually are available for magnesium and other combustible metal fires. Among the rescue tools carried may be hydraulic spreaders, cutters, and rams, rescue saws, pneumatic drills, chisels, and a wide assortment of hand tools. Other equipment can include electrical generators, lights, air bags for light aircraft recovery, and ventilation fans.

Aircraft Emergency Alerts

For airport firefighters, there are basically three types of aircraft emergency situations, commonly referred to as Alert I, II, and III. Some airport fire agencies use colors or codes to represent different types of aircraft emergencies and the response of a prearranged number of emergency resources. An *Alert I* occurs when a pilot is reporting a problem that is not confirmed, usually not declaring an emergency, and not requesting the airport fire equipment. This often occurs when the pilot makes a statement about the aircraft that concerns tower personnel, such as ice buildup on the wings, low engine oil pressure, or some type of indicating light or gauge reading. Airport fire personnel will gear up and pull the ARFF vehicles out onto the ramp in front of the station, ready to respond. Fire officers usually can elect to upgrade an Alert I to an Alert II based on the report from the tower.

An *Alert II* usually is activated when a large aircraft is involved, there is an indication of a possible serious problem with the aircraft, or there is a confirmed genuine emergency. It can range from hydraulic system problems, an indication of unsafe gear, or shutdown of an engine, to an actual inflight fire or serious aircraft control problem. Additional off-airport fire resources often will be requested and prestaged at the airport. The ARFF units usually respond to standby locations near the runway designated to receive the involved aircraft. One ARFF unit, often the Rapid Intervention or Chase vehicle, will be positioned near the expected touchdown location and pursue it down the runway. Other available ARFF units will be positioned further down the airport and will converge on the aircraft as it comes to a stop. ARFF equipment should stand by at a safe distance away from the intended runway in case the aircraft, or parts of it, leave the pavement on impact.

Alert I and II involve preparations for emergencies where the aircraft is still airborne. An *Alert III* is the most serious of the alerts and indicates the aircraft is on the ground and an actual emergency situation (aborted takeoff, cabin fire, crash, etc.) is occurring. Airport ARFF units respond directly from the fire station to the scene and immediately begin incident control measures. An Alert II will be upgraded to a III if the aircraft lands with actual complications.

Most aircraft incidents tend to overwhelm the on-airport fire department resources. Agreements with off-airport fire departments are usually established to provide additional equipment and personnel. It is important that these "structural" firefighters, as well as any off-airport emergency responders, be trained in the unique safety considerations, tactical considerations, and aviation environmental concerns presented by aircraft and airport emergencies. Rendezvous locations, access through security gates, and escorts to the incident scene should be preplanned. Off-airport resources should have maps and plans and be familiar with using them.

INCIDENT NOTIFICATION

AIRPORT AIRCRAFT INCIDENTS

The air traffic control tower usually has a direct telephone line to the airport fire department and sometimes to the local fire communications center and airport management. When tower personnel pick up the "Crash Phone," it rings at the other locations and a conference call is conducted. The following information is provided by the FAA air traffic controllers:

- aircraft type, identification, and company name;
- nature of the emergency;
- location of the incident or runway to be used and estimated touchdown time for aircraft that have not yet arrived;
- number of occupants on board;
- amount of fuel on board (in pounds or flying time);
- presence of hazardous cargo; and
- any other pertinent information

Airport fire personnel evaluate the report quickly and may request additional resources and assistance from the local fire communications center. Any incident that involves a large aircraft or smaller one with high occupant load should involve the response of additional resources from off-airport fire stations. If a "catastrophic accident" is indicated, more alarms, resources, and activation of the local multiple-casualty incident plan should be requested. The airport fire department also may request more equipment based on the "size-up" en route and upon arriving on scene.

OFF-AIRPORT AIRCRAFT INCIDENTS

Reporting parties usually notify fire and police directly via the 911 system. Communications or dispatch determines what fire units are first due to the incident location and dispatches them. Additional fire, law enforcement, medical, and emergency resources are requested as needed. In most cases the emergency communications system will be overloaded with callers. The exact location, type of incident, and amount of area involved may be initially difficult to determine by the dispatchers. It is important that the first responders to arrive at the scene give an accurate and complete report on conditions.

FIRE DEPARTMENT OPERATIONS AT AIRCRAFT INCIDENTS

The fire department provides incident command during the initial stages of an aircraft incident, when fire suppression, hazard control, extrication, rescue, triage, and treatment of victim activities are being conducted. This period usually lasts from 1 to 12 hours. Although the fire department may be on the scene assisting as needed (standby during aircraft defueling, assisting with body recovery, dealing with hazardous materials, etc.), depending on the situation and location, either the airport or police department provides incident command during the remainder of the incident. The coroner, during body recovery, and the National Transportation Safety Board, during the investigation, will control the accident scene. A person or persons from the agency with the greatest jurisdiction (municipality or county) over the accident scene still will have to manage the overall needs of the incident. Joint or unified command usually is established that involves representatives from several agencies or jurisdictions.

LARGE-FRAME AIRCRAFT LOW-IMPACT CRASH WITH FIRE

As stated previously, in a low-impact crash there is some degree of pilot control and the aircraft is fairly level prior to impact. These types of incidents occur often at airports. The fuselage may remain substantially intact and many aircraft occupants may survive the impact forces. Post-crash fire is common.

There are different fire department phases during an on-airport, low-impact incident. The first is the *response phase*. ARFF vehicles are extremely large, heavy, and fast. They rarely experience the extreme demands presented by a response to a major aircraft incident. It is critical that fire personnel stay calm and get the equipment to the scene quickly, without disabling it en route. Clearance from the tower to approach the scene will be requested over the ground control frequency. The ARFF commander also will ask the tower and airport operations to close the airport to other air traffic during a major incident. If the airport is not closed, escorts may be needed to get other responding off-airport fire resources to the scene safely across active aircraft areas. Once they reach the scene, ARFF vehicles may have to negotiate around wreckage, victims, and other obstructions. ARFF vehicles may encounter traction problems off paved road surfaces in wet and snowy conditions. The extra person on each vehicle, if available, may have to get out and guide the apparatus through obstacles into the most advantageous positions. Additional resources are requested based on the size-up en route and upon arrival on scene.

Next is the *positioning phase*. The aluminum fuselage skin of the aircraft will begin to fail quickly (90-120 seconds) when exposed to direct flame contact. Once the skin is penetrated, fire will spread quickly to the interior of the aircraft, presenting a much more difficult fire control problem, and severely jeopardize the lives of the persons still on board. The ARFF vehicles should be positioned around the aircraft so that all ground fuel spill fire can be controlled and the entire fuselage can be protected and kept cool. Wreckage, terrain, and wind direction affect how and where apparatus are positioned. Because foam bubbles are used to extinguish and blanket the fire, the least-desirable position for ARFF units is directly downwind.

During the fire attack and control phases, apparatus turrets should be used to apply massive quantities of foam to quickly control the spill fire. Turret operators should make every effort to conserve, and not waste, extinguishing agent. Most ARFF apparatus can exhaust their agent capacity in less than two minutes. After the turrets have knocked down as much of the spill fire as possible, hoselines should be deployed to extinguish the spill fire that turrets were unable to reach, protect aircraft occupant escape paths, and stop any interior fire spread. Driver operators should remain with their ARFF vehicles, using the turrets to prevent a re-ignition of spilled fuel and to protect firefighters working in hazardous areas. Under the incident command organization the incident scene could be divided into geographical divisions. One way is to designate each side of the fuselage or significant aircraft wreckage along the crash path as a separate "division."

Also during the fire attack and control phases, rescue, medical, and resupply phases are started. These functional tactical objectives could be assigned to be accomplished by "groups" of fire personnel and equipment. The rescue, extrication, and medical activities will be discussed later in this chapter. As other off-airport fire companies start arriving, additional hoselines are connected to and deployed from the ARFF vehicles and some of the responding structural apparatus. Every door and hatch on the aircraft should be accessed, usually with ladders, and opened. There may be victims overcome or trapped just inside these locations. Care should be taken during the opening of doors because of the potential of escape slides to inflate. The leading and trailing edges of the wings should be laddered. Extend additional hoselines to these locations and inside the aircraft to protect the evacuation and control interior fire spread. At this point in the emergency, the incident is similar to a building or structure fire. Rescue personnel should enter the aircraft to assist with the removal of persons incapacitated, trapped, or otherwise still on board. Other emergency responders should round up persons that have escaped the aircraft and are milling around the incident scene. Paramedics and firefighters should set up and start the medical triage, treatment, and transportation activities and organization. The airline will provide cargo and passenger information. As soon as possible, an inventory of the survivors and fatalities should be started to assure that everyone is accounted for. Other fire companies may ventilate the interior of the aircraft with fans and holes cut into the top of the fuselage. Cargo compartments should be opened to check for and control fire spread in these areas.

ARFF vehicles attacking an aircraft post-crash fire situation using top turrets for mass application of agent.

Handline operations at an aircraft incident. Handlines protect and maintain rescue areas and are the main attack lines for aircraft interior firefighting.

ARFF apparatus usually do not carry enough extinguishing agent to control a large aircraft fuel spill and interior fire. As the first off-airport engines start arriving, their officers and firefighters should begin additional fire attack and rescue operations. The drivers of each engine could then pump the contents of their water tanks into the ARFF vehicles and begin a water shuttling operation from hydrants along the perimeter of the airport. Larger capacity water tenders can assist with transporting water to the scene. When sufficient resources are controlling fires and rescuing aircraft occupants, the next available engines should lay large-diameter water supply hoses from hydrants to the incident scene. Because of the distances that may be encountered, this can be a very time-consuming operation, one that requires several engine companies, in relay, to accomplish. Additional foam concentrate supplies should be brought to the scene to refill foam tanks.

In all aviation incidents, aircraft stabilization should occur as soon as possible. Electrical, fuel, oxygen, and other hazardous aircraft systems must be controlled. Aircraft batteries should be disconnected. Landing gear should be pinned or somehow secured. Unstable fuselage sections should be braced and shored up using cranes, jacks, heavy timbers and other materials and equipment. Airline and airport personnel may assist with these tasks. Cargo and passenger information can be obtained from the airlines. During the final phase, overhaul, all fire extension is located and extinguished. Baggage and cargo may have to be removed to extinguish deep-seated fires. The aircraft may be defueled. Dangerous cargo must be dealt with properly. All other hazards should be abated prior to body recovery and accident investigation activities.

AIRCRAFT AND STRUCTURE INCIDENTS

An aircraft accident that involves a structure can further complicate an already difficult situation. This is especially true if the structure has a high occupant load and limited access conditions, for example, schools, apartment complexes, office buildings, high-rises, or shopping centers. The fuel on board the aircraft can rapidly involve the structure. Aircraft occupants can be still alive, trapped in a fuselage that is on top of or impaled in the building, as well as buried under debris. The building may be structurally weakened and in danger of collapsing. Every effort should be made to make the aircraft and structure safe to work in and around. The fire department response may require a combination of confined space, building collapse, structural firefighting, and aircraft tactical procedures.

AIRCRAFT FORCIBLE ENTRY AND VICTIM EXTRICATION

Sometimes during aviation accidents, large aircraft will auger in and not catch fire. Fuselage sections may be upside down, collapsed, crushed, and

LEFT: *Forcible entry being initiated on a heavy frame aircraft using hydraulic spreaders, cutters, and rams.*

BELOW: *An unstable aircraft in a less-than-ideal environment. Aircraft structures, wings, fuselage, and vertical and horizontal stabilizers must be stabilized to ensure the safety of survivors and rescue personnel.*

severely compacted. Normal doors and hatches may not operate properly. Seats, overhead luggage racks, galleys, and other interior components may have broken loose, slid forward, and buried aircraft occupants. Survivors may be hopelessly trapped within a jumbled mass of aircraft parts, luggage, and bodies. Fuel may be leaking in and around the aircraft. This type of aircraft incident presents a very complicated, time-consuming, and challenging situation for responding firefighters.

First, the aircraft and surrounding area must be made as safe as possible for fire department operations. In off-airport situations, trees, brush, and other obstructing vegetation must be removed to gain access to the aircraft, to create a safe area in which to work, and a secure location for victims. In hilly terrain, steps and level areas may have to be cut into hillsides around the aircraft to provide safe footing. Unstable fuselage sections will have to be stabilized. Cribbing is used to prevent the aircraft from sliding or rolling, while shoring is used to keep the fuselage from further downward collapse. Heavy timber and large-capacity jacks may be needed. Forcible entry efforts at one area of a large aircraft may cause changes in other areas of the fuselage and these should be anticipated. Forcible entry and extrication operations require a high level of supervision and attention to safety. If the aircraft moves during rescue operations it may further injure trapped survivors, endanger rescue personnel, and possibly liberate more fuel into the immediate impact area.

In addition to stabilizing the aircraft, certain aircraft systems also should be stabilized. Aircraft electrical power should be shut down in the pilot's compartment, and the battery(s) disconnected. Oxygen and hydraulic systems can sometimes be controlled and pressures in system piping relieved by qualified aircraft mechanics only. Fuel leaks should be controlled by shutting down fuel controls and valves, crimping fuel lines, and plugging leaks. Fuel in and around the fuselage should be covered with foam, dirt, or other absorbent material. Protective foam hoselines should be staffed and ready for use throughout the rescue area. Defueling the aircraft may not be possible before rescuing trapped persons. Fire department hazardous materials team personnel can use combustible vapor detectors to search for explosive concentrations of fuel vapors in the rescue area. The location of dangerous aircraft systems, piping, compressed gas cylinders, wheel assemblies, combustible metal, composite materials, and other hazards to rescuers should be identified. Areas to avoid during cutting-in operations can be marked on the outside of the aircraft with markers or spray paint. Airline representatives and aircraft mechanics can be consulted, and aircraft crash charts used to help locate hazards and stabilize the aircraft. A good rule of thumb for most large aircraft is to cut within 20 inches of the windows to avoid systems. The rivet pattern on the exterior skin will indicate the location of the aircraft structural framework. Avoid cutting operations on skin areas congested with rivets because this usually indicates large structural members underneath. Determine the location of the passenger deck and avoid it. It is usually highly reinforced and has most of the aircraft system piping, conduit, and cables located immediately underneath.

Identify access points into the aircraft. All normal egress doors and hatches should be opened if possible. Pressurized aircraft doors and hatches are difficult or impossible to force open. It is often easier to cut the entire door and frame out of the aircraft than to force it open. Use care in opening doors on aircraft (narrow body type) in which escape slides cannot be disarmed from the outside. Slides can inflate in approximately 5 to 10 seconds. Impact-caused openings can also be enlarged. Jagged metal around access points may have to be removed or padded to prevent injuries to victims and rescuers. Attempt to determine the condition and location of debris, fatalities, and survivors on the inside of the aircraft. Well-trained aircraft firefighters are constantly undergoing aircraft familiarization training and can determine the normal interior arrangement of most passenger aircraft. Smaller rescue personnel may be able to enter the interior of the aircraft to begin first aid treatment and give a report on the interior situation.

Forcible entry operations are always a very time-consuming, last-resort activity. Firefighters and officers should be divided into rescue teams and assigned to a section of the aircraft. Backup teams should be standing by and ready. An "Equipment Resource Pool" can be established as close to the aircraft as possible and tarps spread on the ground. Various fire apparatus and rescue units should be brought to the resource pool and stripped of their rescue tools and equipment. Similar types of tools and equipment should be stockpiled in different areas of the resource pool, such as hydraulic tools, rescue saws, air chisels, air bags, axes, hand tools, etc. The resource pool should be adequately staffed with fire personnel. It is their responsibility to provide needed tools to each rescue team and to service tools, i.e., changing saw blades, refueling power tools, and other maintenance functions. Rescue teams should never have to waste time searching for a needed tool or piece of equipment, or servicing equipment. They should be free to concentrate on gaining access to and removing trapped survivors.

Rescue teams should develop entry and extrication plans and begin rescue operations. The success of the operation depends on the skill, creativity, ingenuity, and determination of the rescue personnel. Rescue team personnel must evaluate operations constantly, develop new plans, and try different procedures. There is no set of standard techniques to cut into and disentangle aircraft structures. The most productive tools to use are rescue saws and hydraulic spreaders, cutters, and rams. Any type of tool could be used in an aircraft forcible entry and extrication. Remember, every aircraft and crash situation is different, and fire officers should keep an open mind and be willing to use any tool or equipment and try any technique. However, almost every power tool is also a potential ignition source. It is critical that the scene be rendered safe and monitored constantly for flammable fuel vapors. Rescue saws will cause sparks when cutting ferrous metal aircraft materials. A small command span of control, numerous safety officers, and good communication among the rescue teams are important.

Bodies may have to be moved to reach survivors. Aircraft parts, cargo, and controls may have to be removed or changed. Any changes to original body positions and aircraft structures can affect body identification and the accident investigation. All rescue operations should be well documented with photographs, video and audio recordings, and drawings, if necessary. When removed, seats, bodies, personal items, and aircraft parts should be labeled and stored temporarily in a location adjacent to where they were removed so that the coroner and NTSB personnel can determine their original location. If possible, seats removed from the aircraft should be placed in their original arrangement outside the aircraft and indicate seat occupants.

Firefighters will probably not have the luxury of placing and stabilizing each victim onto a backboard prior to their removal from the aircraft. In order to get to other survivors quickly, victims may have to be lifted and carried from the aircraft as gently and expeditiously as possible, then moved to the nearest safe location, secured to backboards, triaged, and moved to the appropriate treatment unit. This rescue operation should continue uninterrupted until the entire aircraft has been searched and every survivor removed.

HIGH-IMPACT CRASHES

This type of incident frequently occurs off the airport. There is usually little or no pilot control of the aircraft prior to impact. The aircraft often hits the ground at a steep angle, abnormal orientation, and at a high rate of speed. Although there is always the possibility of survivors, most often the entire aircraft and occupants disintegrate on impact. There also may be injuries and fatalities involving persons on the ground. The aircraft will be broken into many, small, unidentifiable parts. Fatality identification will be very difficult because of extensive mutilation. Most of the fuel on the aircraft will be thrown into the air in a mist-like cloud, ignited, and most likely burned off by the time emergency responders start to arrive.

Firefighters may encounter a large fire involving many acres or city blocks of structures, vehicles, vegetation, aircraft wreckage, and other ordinary combustibles in the area. Such a scene is difficult to approach and work in because of damaged electrical wires, jagged metal, hazardous aircraft parts, bodies and body parts, spectators, and traffic congestion. The 911 system will be jammed with callers. The exact location of the incident and amount of area involved may initially be difficult to determine.

Standard structural fire department tactics and strategies can be used to control this type of aircraft incident. The focus is on saving the persons and property that were in the area prior to impact. As multiple-alarm and mutual aid fire resources converge on the scene, they should be assigned from the staging area into the incident. The entire impact area should be surrounded and divided into geographical areas of control called "divisions." Fire officers are tasked with determining tactical objectives for their assigned division and what resources are needed; they then begin operations to accomplish the objectives, and give regular updated condition reports to the Incident Commander or operations section chief. Other firefighting personnel, equipment, and resources may be assigned to groups, and tasked with functional responsibilities such as rescue, hazardous materials, and medical. Many objectives and goals have to be addressed simultaneously.

The first priority is the rescue of endangered persons. Involved structures and aircraft sections should be searched for survivors, as should structures threatened by fire spread. As an adequate water supply is established, the next priority is to protect uninvolved structures and other exposures. The downwind area of the incident should probably get the greatest attention, because of flying firebrands. Structures may have to be identified as losers and written off in order to concentrate on ones that can be saved. Once horizontal fire spread is stabilized, firefighting resources should attack and extinguish the main body of fire. A defensive strategy that incorporates large-flow firefighting appliances and hoselines may be used. Salvage activities need to be conducted in an attempt to save personal items in structures partially involved in fire. After the main body of fire is knocked down, fire crews will enter the impact area to overhaul and extinguish any residual fire. Bodies and body parts should be left as found and covered up as much as possible. As with all aircraft incidents, every effort should be made to protect the aircraft debris, wreckage, and incident scene.

AIRCRAFT INTERIOR FIRES

Major interior fires have started on passenger aircraft in flight and while parked on airport ramp areas. Standard structural firefighting techniques, with some slight modifications, should be used to control these types of fires. Obviously, it is important to apply extinguishing agent to the fire. With aircraft interior fires, ARFF apparatus turrets are useless. There is no need to protect the fuselage and keep it cool when the fire is on the inside. If the aircraft is parked against a jetway, the aircraft or the jetway should be moved or hoselines positioned to prevent the spread of smoke and fire into the terminal. If aircraft occupant evacuation is underway, fire personnel should assist in every way possible. This may involve holding down the bottom of escape slides and helping people off. Initial fire attack hoselines should be deployed to protect the evacuation. A good initial attack position is through the overwing exits. The wing surface provides a platform to work from, and fire spreading from the front or back of the aircraft can be stopped from this location.

Once everyone who can be evacuated has been, an aggressive search, rescue, and fire attack should be made from all available openings in the aircraft. Every door (including cargo areas) and hatch should be opened and hoselines deployed into the aircraft. Primary and secondary searches must be conducted for persons who may have been overcome between seats, in lavatories, in the pilot's compartment, and in other aircraft areas. Many survivors may be suffering from exposure to smoke, and thermal burns. As soon as possible, the number of fatalities and survivors should be compared to the list in the passenger manifest.

The aircraft typically is elevated on its landing gear. Firefighters can use the tops of ARFF apparatus, airline air stairs, and other elevating devices as platforms from which to work. There are many avenues for the fire to spread in the walls, floors, and ceiling areas of the aircraft. These areas have to be opened up and checked for fire involvement. Sometimes, hidden fire can be detected visually by blistered and discolored fuselage surfaces, surfaces that feel hot to the touch, or with special thermal imaging devices. As with any aviation incident, the aircraft and its systems should be stabilized. Landing gear should be pinned. Ground power units, auxiliary power units, and aircraft batteries should be shut down. Any fueling operations should be stopped and exposed fueling equipment moved. With the assistance of airline representatives and aircraft mechanics, other important aircraft systems also may be controlled.

If the fire has not vented itself, the top of the aircraft can be opened up with rescue saws from fire department elevating platforms. Fans also can be set up to ventilate smoke-filled interiors. Cargo compartments should be opened up as soon as possible and endangered mail, baggage, animals, and other cargo protected or removed.

CARGO AIRCRAFT INCIDENTS

Almost anything can be and is transported by aircraft. The air freight business has become a very profitable endeavor. Air freight activity has increased dramatically over the past 10 years. Many former trucking companies, including the U.S. Postal Service, have their own fleets of cargo aircraft. Many are former passenger aircraft retrofitted to accommodate cargo containers (called igloos), pallets, and bulk-loaded packages. Many of these companies transport hazardous materials. Tremendous quantities of cargo are transported. For example, a DC-8 freighter can carry approximately 100,000 pounds of cargo. Most cargo containers can have as much as 10,000 pounds loaded inside. Containers may be constructed of metal, fiberglass, and wood. Pallets look like large, square metal cookie sheets with cargo secured with netting and plastic.

On the narrow-body cargo freighters, the upper cargo deck typically is loaded with containers and the lower areas bulk loaded with individual packages. Wide-body cargo aircraft usually have containers in both upper and lower areas. Containers are loaded and unloaded with special cargo-lifting devices, slid on floor rollers inside the aircraft, and locked in place at their

A stubborn freighter aircraft interior fire.

assigned position. Once the aircraft is loaded, it is usually impossible to move through the interior of the aircraft, over the cargo load. There are only a few inches of clearance between the igloos and the interior walls of the cargo compartment. A fire or hazardous material spill inside the cargo hold would be very difficult to reach without unloading or cutting into the aircraft. Dangerous cargos that would be relatively easy to deal with when spilled in the open on the ramp area are much more concentrated and hazardous in the tight confines inside an aircraft.

There are several different types of cargo carried on aircraft. Some materials are forbidden on any type of aircraft and are specifically listed in the air cargo regulations. Many materials can be transported only on cargo aircraft and are forbidden on passenger aircraft. These are called "Cargo-Aircraft-Only" materials and have an orange label that specifies this affixed to each package. This label should be a warning to fire personnel that especially dangerous materials are involved. In addition, there are the other shipments that can be carried on any type of aircraft. Many passenger aircraft carry limited quantities of cargo. They are limited to 50 pounds of allowable type dangerous goods and 150 pounds of nonflammable compressed gas per "inaccessible" cargo hold. Most passenger aircraft have two inaccessible cargo holds in their belly areas. An exception to this is a part-passenger, part-cargo aircraft called a "Combi." Combi aircraft have an accessible cargo area on the passenger deck and can carry unlimited quantities of passenger-aircraft-allowable dangerous materials. These types of aircraft usually are encountered at airports that serve international air carriers. Many domestic passenger carriers limit the types of hazardous cargo they transport. The last type of dangerous cargo is the unknown type carried in passenger luggage, the mail, or undeclared as ordinary cargo.

On cargo freighter aircraft, "cargo-aircraft-only" shipments are required to be accessible by the crew in flight. This is so the crew can control fires and other emergencies that involve hazardous cargo before they get out of hand. Unfortunately, the crew usually only has some portable fire extinguishers, several small SCBAs, and the orange DOT *Guidebook* to deal with "dangerous goods" on board. Except for radioactives, most cargo carriers put all the dangerous cargo in the front of the aircraft, next to the pilot's compartment. Radioactives usually are stowed in the lower area of the tail section. Cargo containers are loaded into position, and numbered from the front of the aircraft. Expect to find the cargo-aircraft-only materials in the first positions. Dangerous goods that can be carried on passenger aircraft can be carried anywhere on a cargo aircraft.

Somewhere on the flight deck there should be paperwork associated with any dangerous shipments on board. Each carrier gives the form a different name, but it is commonly referred to as the "pilot's notification." It lists each hazardous material's proper shipping name, hazard class, UN number, quantity, location, and type of packaging. The crew also has a load plan that indicates the weights and other important information, such as the presence of hazardous materials, at each cargo position. Much more information is on a form called a "Shipper's Declaration of Dangerous Goods." A copy is attached to the outside of each package or shipment, and retained by the shipper and air carrier at the airport of departure. Crew members may not have copies of these forms in their possession. Most hazardous material paperwork on aircraft has red candy-striped borders. This should be another danger signal to arriving fire personnel. Igloos or containers usually have a card affixed that indicates that hazardous materials are inside. Usually this card lists only the hazard class numbers. One major carrier paints the top of its "Haz Cans" or containers loaded with dangerous goods a red color. Although there are a few segregation requirements, some "scary" combinations of materials can still be encountered in the same container.

Like the shipper's declaration of dangerous goods, the hazardous cargo package has a considerable amount of valuable information on it. It has the address of the shipper and consignee (destination being shipped to) which can be contacted for information and, sometimes, assistance. It has the UN number, proper shipping name, liquid arrows or "this-end-up" marking, and a label for each hazard. It must be in an approved container or package. With liquids there usually is an inner and outer package and, in between, enough inert absorbent to handle all the material if it should leak. Approved package types also have to pass a wide variety of tests. Unless it was damaged during loading, there is rarely a problem with properly packaged dangerous goods. More than half the aircraft hazardous material incidents reported involve undeclared materials shipped as ordinary cargo.

Military transport aircraft have their own dangerous cargo regulations. In peacetime, their procedures are very similar to that of civilian air cargo carriers. In times of international conflict, regulations may be relaxed to expedite the transport of needed military materials. The best person to contact regarding the cargo and associated paperwork on a military transport aircraft is the load master. As with any military aircraft, the best recommendation for civilian fire officers is to stabilize the situation and leave it alone until the proper military authorities arrive on the scene.

It is important that first responders recognize incidents that are hazardous materials emergencies. Recognized and recommended hazardous material incident response and management procedures should be used. The first actions should be to position upwind and isolate all persons from the involved area. Persons down in the spill area should be rescued only when the hazards have been identified and proper protective gear is available for rescue personnel. Decontamination should be provided for victims and emergency responders. Information should be gathered about the cargo, incident situation, and potential methods of control. Manufacturers, shippers, and consignees may be contacted for assistance. The situation should be managed and stabilized by a fire department hazardous material team, possibly assisted by other mutual aid hazardous materials response teams. The most likely scenario is that the material(s) will be recovered and the scene rendered safe by a contractor hired by the air carrier and monitored by fire department.

AIRCRAFT ENGINE FIRES

There are several types of engine emergencies that may be encountered by fire personnel. Unless the aircraft crashes off the airport, most aircraft engine problems will be handled by fire departments that protect or respond to airports. Sometimes, during the startup of a jet engine, excess fuel may build up and ignite in the rear burner section of the engine. Often, the pilots or an aircraft mechanic handle this situation without requesting the response of fire equipment. Usually the turbine fans are turned on in an attempt to blow the excess fuel out the back of the engine. If this method does not work or the fire does not burn out, the fire may have to be extinguished by discharging an agent from a safe distance and location into the tail cone of the engine. There is no universal agreement on what is the best extinguishing agent to use on an engine fire. Fire department standard operating procedures may call for the use of either dry chemical, halon, or foam. A clean extinguishing agent, such as halon or a halon replacement, causes minimal damage to the engine and may not necessitate an engine overhaul.

Aircraft engines are designed to have combustion occur in certain parts of their interiors. Between an engine and the cowling or exterior engine housing are located various electrical equipment, fuel and lubricating pumps or lines. It is this area that the aircraft engine fire extinguishing system is primarily designed to protect. A fire in this area of the engine is called an "accessory fire." If the on-board fire extinguishing system is not used or does not control the fire, then firefighters have to discharge agent through special fire access openings or normal engine entry points. The same procedures are used to control an auxiliary power unit (APU) fire. An APU is a small jet engine used to generate electrical power on a large aircraft.

Sometimes aircraft engines disintegrate or come apart, usually in flight or at takeoff thrusts. Engine parts have penetrated fuselage and wing surfaces, seriously injuring aircraft occupants, starting interior fires, and damaging vital flight systems. In this situation, the engine usually is a total loss and any method or extinguishing agent can be used to control the emergency. In any aircraft engine emergency, the primary tactical objective is to protect the occupants, fuel cells, and the rest of the aircraft.

HOT BRAKES AND WHEEL ASSEMBLY FIRES

Sometimes aircraft brakes overheat during landing. Initial actions should be to stand by in a safe location and let the brakes cool down naturally. In propeller aircraft, the props can be used to flow cooling air past the wheels. Some aircraft firefighting manuals recommend using smoke ejectors or blowers for this. Because of the danger of rims fracturing or the fusible plug releasing, emergency personnel should not approach landing gear and wheels from the sides. Approach and standby locations should be from forward or to the rear of the wheels. If the tires start to catch fire, a dry agent such as a dry chemical should be used from a safe distance. Aqueous or cooling-type extinguishing agents can chill the hot metal of the aircraft rim and increase the chance that it will disintegrate.

AGRICULTURAL SPRAYING AIRCRAFT INCIDENTS

Fixed and rotary wing aircraft are used for aircraft spraying operations, dispersing a wide variety of very toxic liquids and dusts. Different pesticides and herbicides are used depending on the type of pest or time of year. The materials are usually mixed and diluted before being loaded onto the aircraft. Most fixed-wing aircraft are loaded at an airport and flown to the job site. Some spraying companies may have their own landing facilities away from an actual airport. Helicopters often are trailered to the job site and loaded there. Various support vehicles are used with these aircraft. They contain extra quantities of the material being sprayed, fuel for the aircraft, and other necessary supplies and equipment.

Most significant incidents occur at the job location and usually are caused when the aircraft touches trees, utility lines, or the ground during normal operations. Most aircraft can carry several hundred gallons of spraying material. On fixed-wing aircraft, the material tank is located between the aircraft engine and the cockpit. There is a good chance that the pilot, as well as much of the impact area, will be contaminated by the spraying material. As with any hazardous materials incident, work from an upwind direction. Although any fire can be extinguished by firefighters operating from a safe distance and in full protective gear and SCBA, the actual recovery of the pilot and control of the spilled material should be accomplished using the proper level of hazardous material protection. Attempt to contact the owner of the property or aircraft to identify the material being sprayed. The *Farm Chemical Handbook* is a valuable reference resource to have available. Follow proper and recognized hazardous material incident action steps. If necessary, cover spill materials with dirt, absorbents, or covers. Decontaminate any victims before transporting them to the hospital. Thoroughly decontaminate all personnel and equipment used during the emergency response.

AIRCRAFT INCIDENTS IN REMOTE AND DIFFICULT-TO-ACCESS AREAS

Accidents in remote and rural areas could present some very difficult problems for rescue personnel. The exact impact area may be difficult to locate. The scene may not be accessible with normal emergency response apparatus and equipment. All-terrain vehicles, helicopters, and specialized rescue procedures may be necessary. The logistics of getting necessary resources to the scene and removing the injured could require considerable work and creativity. The environment itself may present many obstacles and hazards such as dangerous wildlife, steep elevations, dense vegetation, and rugged terrain.

WATER INCIDENTS

Many airports have areas of water directly off or adjacent to their runways. The FAA requires applicable airports to plan and prepare for aircraft water incidents. If a pilot needs to make an emergency landing off an airport at night, he usually goes for dark areas with few or no lights. Often these are water areas. Obviously boats, helicopters, rafts and flotation devices, divers, special protective gear, and other specialized equipment will be needed. Besides the unique conditions presented by a water environment, this scenario presents many of the same problems listed in the previous paragraph. All fire department personnel should consider the structures, natural features, and other conditions in their jurisdictions, and how they will affect operations during aircraft incidents, and plan and prepare for that potential.

MEDICAL OPERATIONS: VICTIM TRIAGE, TREATMENT, AND TRANSPORTATION

The vast majority of the incidents for which the fire service provides medical assistance involve one to five patients. These situations usually are handled easily by initial responding units. Each patient is given maximum treatment and attention. Fire personnel typically do not have to make many priority decisions. As soon as patients are stabilized and become available for transportation, they are loaded into waiting ambulances and whisked off to a nearby hospital.

The multi-casualty situation created by a large passenger aircraft disaster can easily overwhelm both initial responders and the entire emergency medical system in a given area. This is the classic mass-casualty situation. First responders often do not have enough resources, personnel, or time to deal adequately with each patient. There may not be enough ambulances or emergency room space to handle the number of victims. Fire departments will work with many other organizations, including private ambulance companies (both air and vehicle), hospitals, volunteer groups, health departments, disaster coordinators, military, search and rescue organizations, and the U.S. Coast Guard, among others.

The object is to minimize the suffering and additional handling, start advance treatment as soon as possible, and keep track of and get all injured persons to a hospital as quickly as possible. This is accomplished through a well-trained, prepared, organized, and efficient medical group that may involve many different fire, EMS, and disaster-related agencies and organizations. Standardized caches of medical supplies should be strategically located so they can be quickly and easily transported.

The fire service will be heavily involved in the rescue, triage, treatment, and transportation of persons injured in an aircraft accident. A medical organizational system and structure has been developed for managing multi-casualty incidents. It is designed as a division or group under the operations section in the standard Incident Command System. It can be broken down further into triage, treatment, and transportation. Triage is made up of search and rescue teams and triage teams. Treatment is subdivided into immediate, delayed, and minor treatment units. Transportation is made up of transportation recorder, transportation control, medical communications, medical supply, and ambulance staging. There also may be an air operations unit for fixed- and rotary-wing air ambulances, as well as a morgue unit.

A well-organized medical triage and treatment area for an aircraft incident.

Search, Rescue, and Triage Operations

Search and rescue teams, usually firefighters, will enter the immediate incident area to locate victims. Some victims may have to be extricated or disentangled from the wreckage. Victims can be triaged where they are found if it is safe to do so. Triage is a method of sorting or prioritizing victims according to the severity of their injuries, order of transportation, and need for treatment. If it is not safe to triage victims in the immediate incident area, they must be moved to the closest safe area or to the treatment area where they can be triaged. Survivors may be scattered throughout an extensive crash path. Victims found in nonhazardous areas may be triaged by nonfire medical personnel. Obvious fatalities are left undisturbed, where and how they are found, unless their remains are in danger of further damage or they have to be moved to reach survivors. Human remains should be covered as soon as possible. If a body must be moved, try to document its original location, condition, and personal effects with a drawing, video, or photographs.

"Simple Triage And Rapid Treatment or Transportation" (START), using a recognized triage tag, is the most widely used and recommended method of triaging victims. It is a simple system that allows firefighters to triage a patient in approximately 30 seconds. The victim's condition is assessed and he is assigned to one of four groups. There are distinct colors on the triage tag that correspond with each of the four groups. Black is deceased. Red is Priority I or victims suffering life-threatening injuries that require "Immediate" transportation to, and treatment at, a hospital. Yellow is Priority II or victims with serious injuries whose transportation can be "Delayed" until all Priority I patients have been transported. Green is Priority III, noninjured or persons with minor injuries. After the person is assessed, the lesser priority sections located at the bottom of the triage tag are removed, and the tag is placed around the victim's neck. Triage tags are an excellent method to easily identify the medical status of large numbers of injured at a major incident scene, as well as to document vital signs taken and treatment rendered prior to arrival at a hospital emergency room. It is important that the fire service use the same recognized triage tag used by other fire and medical emergency agencies in its area. Different types of triage procedures and tags have caused problems at past aircraft incidents.

As the first search, rescue, and triage teams enter the incident area, direct all victims and survivors who can move to a collection area. A bullhorn or apparatus PA system can be used. The collection area could be another vehicle, landmark, or other easily identifiable safe area. These victims can be tagged Green or Priority III because they can move on their own and follow simple commands. Emergency personnel then begin to triage the other victims, using three assessments to assign victims to one of the four triage categories. These assessments are respirations, profusion or circulation, and mental status.

Treatment and Transportation

Patients now are moved to a treatment area. Persons on backboards should have a minimum of four, and preferably six, bearers. Moving loaded backboards with fewer persons can injure and fatigue rescue workers. A quick and simple method of securing the patients to backboards should be available, such as velcro straps. Many jurisdictions use disposable fiberboard backboards. During inclement weather, patients may need to be moved by vehicle to a protected treatment area out of the elements.

The treatment area should be as close to the incident as is safe, to minimize the distance patients have to be moved after triage. The treatment area is divided into three units that correspond with the Priority I (Red), II (Yellow), and III (Green) on the triage tag. Colored tarps, barrier tape, cones, barricades, and signs often are used to differentiate the three units. Sometimes apparatus is used to separate the units, and tarps are stretched between the vehicles to provide shade or shelter. Advanced EMTs or paramedics are put in charge of each treatment unit. Hospitals also may send response teams made up of physicians and nurses to the scene. As patients wait for transportation to a hospital they are given a much more thorough evaluation. Injuries are identified. Patients may receive advanced medical treatment, such as IVs, administration of drugs, fracture immobilization, and bandaging. Any additional treatment and information are noted on the triage tag, so that when the patient reaches the hospital there is a record of his immediate medical history. A patient's status may be upgraded to a higher priority in the treatment area. Persons who pass away in the treatment area are moved to a temporary morgue set up at the scene, preferably in a refrigerated truck. The Priority III Unit may be separated or located visually away from the other two units to shield those patients from unpleasant sights and sounds.

Priority III noninjured or persons with minor injuries can be transported in nonambulance transportation, such as buses. The longer these individuals stay at the scene and observe the aircraft wreckage and the more seriously injured victims, the more emotional problems they will have. They all should still be examined by a physician at a hospital. A minimum of an EMT should accompany these patients on the bus in the event a medical emergency arises en route.

From the treatment area injured survivors are moved into the transportation system. Each treatment unit keeps a log of information concerning the patients in its area, as well as their triage tag number. A Transportation Control Officer coordinates patient transportation. A transportation recorder maintains records relating to patient name, sex, approximate age, injuries, priority, time, mode of transportation, triage tag number, and hospital destination. During several past aircraft incidents, victims were rescued and transported, but lost in the recordkeeping process. This can cause unnecessary confusion, unneeded search activities, and embarrassment for the response organization. A medical communication leader should establish a communications link with medical facilities, determine hospital availability and capabilities, and designate patient destinations. The duties of the ambulance staging leader and medical supply officer are self-explanatory.

LAW ENFORCEMENT CONSIDERATIONS

In addition to emergency medical, law enforcement is one of the most important agencies and organizations that firefighters will have to work and communicate with at aircraft incidents. One of the key problems identified in many past aircraft incidents is the failure of police and fire to interact adequately or even collocate at the same command post. It is critical that these two agencies work together. Law enforcement personnel can perform many important functions, provide specialized resources and skills, and make the fire officer's job much easier.

Fire officers assume command during the initial phase of the incident dealing with fire control, victim rescue, treatment, and transportation, abatement of hazardous conditions, and stabilization of the aircraft and incident scene. Although they have equipment and personnel on scene throughout the remainder of the incident in a standby, assistance-as-needed mode, most of the fire department functions will be completed within a few hours to one day. Once these traditional duties have been undertaken, the incident becomes basically similar to a crime scene. In off-airport incidents, the law enforcement jurisdiction with the greatest jurisdictional responsibility assumes command. In on-airport incidents, law enforcement may share or turn over command to airport management.

Fire officers should expect to work with a wide variety of law enforcement agencies and organizations during and after an aircraft incident. These groups could include local police and sheriffs, highway patrol, state police, federal marshals, military police, Federal Bureau of Investigation (FBI), Drug Enforcement Agency (DEA), Bureau of Alcohol, Tobacco and Firearms (ATF), U.S. Customs, the Immigration and Naturalization Service, U.S. Coast Guard, postal inspectors, wildlife protection and animal control officers, harbor patrol, U.S. Environmental Protection Agency, and private security companies. It is important that fire officials immediately interact and collocate with law enforcement personnel when first arriving on scene. Quickly identify areas of responsibility, needs, and an initial action plan. A common problem identified during aircraft incident critiques is the issue of separate command posts, and a lack of communication and coordination between police and fire. Often, police officers are the first emergency responders on the scene, provide the first report on conditions, perform size-up, and identify the exact location, type of aircraft, and many other important bits of information to help fire officers size up the situation en route.

Scene Security

Scene security is the most important initial function of law enforcement. Most of the law enforcement personnel will help to establish security perimeters. How quickly and effectively law enforcement accomplishes this task has an impact on the ability of the fire department to perform its job. This is much more difficult to accomplish in off-airport incidents. While an airport is usually already a highly secured area, it may present additional security problems, such as active aircraft operations and the need to deal with persons waiting for the aircraft involved in the incident.

Any aircraft incident, especially off the airport, draws crowds of spectators, pedestrians, sightseers, souvenir hunters, onlookers, criminals, and, possibly, looters. They will interfere with and inhibit your operations unless you control them immediately at the start of the incident. Have law enforcement agencies set up an inner security perimeter a minimum of 300 feet from the outer limits of the wreckage, debris, crash path, and immediate incident scene. This is to preserve the scene and wreckage, as well as allow for unhampered rescue, medical, and fire operations. This is usually handled by the police agency with primary jurisdiction.

An outer or secondary perimeter should be established at least three blocks out from the inner perimeter. Outside the outer perimeter is where spectators and the press are kept. Between the two perimeters is the location of the staging area, command post, rehabilitation area, victim treatment and transportation, and other incident functions. Both perimeters should be larger than immediately necessary to allow them to be reduced later. Assisting or mutual-aid police agencies usually handle the outer perimeter. With on-airport incidents, this is usually the perimeter fence around the airport. Other airport entry points may have to be guarded or secured. Police also may be tasked with addressing the needs of residents inside the security perimeters or near the crash site.

Consider having the police sweep areas inside the perimeters for unauthorized persons and to evacuate residents. It can be difficult to move persons whose property is threatened by fire, or who are missing family members or pets. When you identify the staging area location, designate a route into the incident for emergency responders. Have law enforcement close this access to all but authorized persons and emergency equipment. Otherwise, spectators and other nonincident-related persons will park and abandon their vehicles, blocking and congesting streets around the incident scene. Police may have to route traffic away from or around the incident and conduct a massive towing operation. Scene preservation usually requires massive numbers of police officers from many agencies for extended time periods.

A designated access point into the incident must be identified and staffed with police officers. A method of passes or other types of identification should be established to allow only authorized persons into the incident scene. This method may have to be changed daily, and is something that should be preplanned.

There are other types of security perimeters that may have to be established. It is not uncommon to have many helicopters from involved agencies and the news media, as well as private aircraft, converge over the incident. They can present a danger to themselves as well as to persons on the ground. If aircraft overhead are a problem, causing noise, rotorwash, and congestion, request an immediate airspace restriction through the nearest FAA air traffic control facility (tower). If it is a water incident, the U.S. Coast Guard, harbor patrol, lifeguards, or other marine law enforcement agencies can establish a safety zone around the incident.

While they are maintaining security perimeters, law enforcement officers may be in a position to observe the scene impartially. Most fire, rescue, and medical personnel will be overwhelmed initially and preoccupied with the tasks at hand. Trained police officers can always be on the lookout for hazardous materials, valuables, mail, money, evidence of criminal activity in the

A guarded inner security perimeter with a designated entry point.

wreckage (guns, drugs), and hazards to emergency personnel, such as compressed gas cylinders, aircraft tire and wheel assemblies, hazardous cargo, and other dangerous aircraft parts, wreckage, or environmental hazards. Police officers can set up barricades and barrier tape around dangerous areas or items that need to be protected, such as the flight data and cockpit voice recorders. They may be able to photograph, videotape, or perform other incident documentation. They can identify and gather information from potential witnesses.

Other Important Law Enforcement Activities

Police officers can be used to gather important information, such as passenger and cargo manifests, dangerous goods paperwork, and other important information from the involved airline. They can be responsible for mail on board or other special property that has to be located and protected. Often, officials, politicians, and other dignitaries may request tours of the incident scene. Other emergency response organizations may send "go teams" to evaluate the incident, operations, and to gather information for training. The FAA and National Transportation Safety Board both need support and assistance during the investigation. Law enforcement can entertain and satisfy the needs of these individuals, freeing key personnel to deal with other incident-related needs. They make excellent liaison officers.

It can take several hours to establish effective media relations and control. The media response will be large and quick. The media typically use every means possible to get into the scene and can cause major problems for perimeter control. Until information officers from all the key organizations arrive and set up a formal media organization and area, police officers have to contain and control the press.

Law enforcement personnel have many skills that are helpful during body recovery, identification, and information collection. Police officers may be used in the incident morgue to photograph and fingerprint victims and do recordkeeping, and other stenographic functions. Officers often are used to visit the residences of the deceased to gather information such as dental records, pictures, descriptions, and other information to help establish identification. Police have access to scientific and crime labs, and staff artists.

Law enforcement personnel may perform criminal investigations and other crime-related functions associated with the incident. The police department usually can handle any bombs or explosives. Its personnel may help collect, manage, and disseminate the thousands of items of victims' personal property and other material items associated with the incident.

Police officers often can provide many specialized resources such as divers, x-ray machines, bomb control equipment, search and rescue teams, helicopters, boats, communication equipment, mobile command posts, computers, and other useful equipment. In some areas and airports, the police provide rescue, extrication, medical, and firefighting equipment. They can provide psychological services for victims and emergency responders.

OTHER KEY ORGANIZATIONS

Airport administrators are an integral part of an emergency response to an aircraft incident at an airport. They manage the airport and can make the necessary decisions regarding its operation under emergency conditions. They also may have jurisdictional power with respect to emergency operations. The airport department can provide or locate many different types of equipment, expertise, and resources needed by the fire department. Airport department personnel can escort fire equipment to the scene and assume responsibility for many of the nontactical functions in the incident command structure. They can make the required notifications for off-airport incidents. Airport managers often have a considerable amount of political power, making the fire officer's job easier or harder depending on the quality of the working relationship.

Airline officials also play an important role in an aviation incident. They own the aircraft as well as the problem. Their help with passenger, crew, and cargo manifests is valuable in determining the situation at the scene. They also are accountable for notification of relatives at the point of departure, as well as caring for those waiting for the arrival of the ill-fated aircraft. Airline personnel also have equipment, such as air stairs, forklifts, tugs, and additional resources that can be used at an aircraft accident scene. They can provide hangars for staging areas and other incident organizational facilities. The airlines also can apply some political pressure if they are unhappy with the fire department's handling of the incident.

Without question, the *news media* will respond, unrequested. News media vans monitor emergency frequencies constantly and usually arrive at the scene quickly. A major aircraft accident immediately becomes a very hot news item. Fire officers should be prepared to accommodate and manage the media. They can make the incident positive on behalf of emergency responders or be extremely critical. Media management should be a joint and unified activity involving the fire department, law enforcement, airport, emergency medical organization, and the airlines. Individual agencies should not be talking to the press independently. All fire personnel also should understand that they are not to talk to the press unless directed to do so by the incident information unit. Media information packets can be prepared before an incident that include media guidelines: what they can and cannot do, airport and aircraft information, and other related items of interest. A media area should be set up where information updates and press releases are provided at regular intervals. Tours of the incident scene that do not interfere with tactical operations also should be provided regularly. The media area should be located where there is access to phones, parking for media vehicles, restrooms, refreshments, and other sup-

An excellent example of news media management at the accident scene.

port items. Treating the press professionally not only promotes good rapport, but may discourage freelancing.

BODY RECOVERY AND FATALITY MANAGEMENT

Fire officers should be aware of and practice proper procedures when dealing with aircraft incident fatalities. How the fire service handles bodies at the incident scene can help or complicate the body recovery and identification process. Fire personnel often assist the proper authorities during the extrication and recovery of bodies and personal property. The subject of body management is very controversial and emotional. The local coroner or medical examiner needs to educate disaster responders and the community about the body recovery process and the need for proper methods. Who is responsible, who is involved, and the sequence of events must be explained clearly in disaster plans and local statutes. The news media must understand that names of suspected victims will not be released until positive identification has been made of as many victims as possible.

Air crashes frequently are of such impact or with accompanying conflagrations that identifying deceased victims can be quite difficult. Exposure to fire and dismemberment of victims is often extreme. Human remains and personal items may be dispersed over a wide area. Frustrated rescuers may have handled bodies and evidence improperly. In large accidents, with many fatalities, recovery and investigation may take many days. Adverse weather conditions, remoteness, and difficult access to the accident site further complicate this phase of the incident.

The coroner or medical examiner is responsible for the extremely time-consuming, detailed, thorough, and important part of an aircraft incident: investigating and determining the cause and manner of all sudden deaths. He directs and coordinates the recovery, collection, identification, storage, security, and processing of the deceased and their personal effects. It is the coroner who releases the names of the deceased to the press and next of kin or relatives. He coordinates the release of the bodies or remains of the accident victims for burial or transport to other communities.

The National Transportation Safety Board also is very involved in the management of the fatalities of an aircraft accident. The board is empowered by the Federal Aviation Act of 1958 to order and follow up on the autopsies of the crew and passengers.

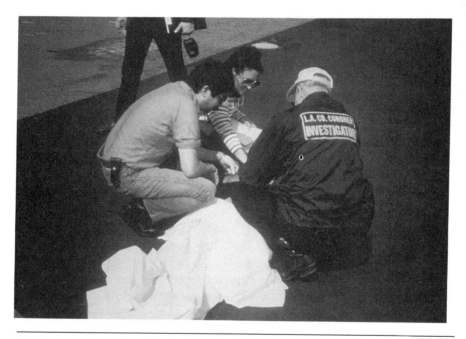

Fatality management and documentation operations.

Importance of Proper Fatality Management

Proper procedures are necessary to avoid legal problems with the next of kin. This is particularly important when aircraft accidents occur in locations other than the victims' permanent places of residence. The coroner's ultimate findings can have many legal implications. The sequence, such as which partner of a married couple died first, can affect inheritances. Final identification permits the issuance of a certificate of death. The amount of pain and suffering a victim experienced will affect the amount of insurance settlements. Whether the person died from the impact of the crash, from fire, or from natural causes affects the amount of money that may be awarded. The determination of injuries caused from the crash versus previous injuries is important. A determination that the victim was under the influence of alcohol may nullify some insurance policies.

There may be a possibility of criminal activity associated with the accident that can be disclosed by the body recovery, investigation, and autopsy process. Evidence of weapons, bombs, and suicide may be indicated during fatality management. Less-than-complete postmortem examinations and investigations have caused more problems and work. Much vital information can be lost. This can be avoided by better advanced planning and preparedness by local authorities.

Proper fatality management can help prevent future accidents and increase air safety. This process can provide medical evidence which is of great value in terms of human engineering and survivability. Examining the bodies of aircraft victims can establish patterns of injuries and survivability that can be used to design seat belts and escape devices, enhance fire protection and emergency response, and improve aircraft construction and crash dynamics.

Thorough examinations of bodies, the documentation of where they were located at the scene, and extensive and comprehensive photographs and videos can greatly help NTSB investigators. Document and determine the location of each crew member at the time of the accident. Typical injuries to hands, forearms, feet, and lower legs indicate who was operating the aircraft controls and their location in the aircraft. False identities are a consideration on air carrier passenger manifests. (Passengers on commercial aircraft do travel under assumed names, while others do not occupy their assigned seats.)

Proper Rescue Procedures by Fire Personnel

Rescuers must be aware of the importance of taking all practical steps to facilitate the identification of aircraft accident victims. They must protect and secure any traces and clues that might assist in the identification of bodies. An undisturbed accident site produces the most reliable evidence for determining cause and corrective actions that will help prevent a similar accident in the future.

The wreckage should remain as undisturbed as possible until the arrival of NTSB and coroner's investigators. The areas immediately surrounding the location of the deceased should be completely secured. Bodies and body parts should be covered as soon as possible with whatever is available on fire apparatus or in structures in the area. Extrication and removal of bodies and personal effects before the arrival of the appropriate authorities should be accomplished only to prevent their destruction, to reach survivors, or for other similar compelling reasons. There are many examples of bodies having been moved, by well-intentioned rescue personnel, shortly after the aircraft fire was controlled and before the arrival of the coroner. The locations of the bodies in the wreckage were not charted or documented. Markers were not used to show the locations of the bodies. No official photographs were taken. It was very difficult to determine the original location of the crew or passengers, or to recover important clues in those areas that would have made final identification much easier. Keep in mind that it is a misdemeanor to willfully touch, remove, or disturb the body, clothing, or any article on or near a body.

If it becomes necessary to move bodies or parts of the wreckage, photographs from a minimum of four views, videos, or both should be taken to show their relative position within the crash scene. A sketch or plot plan also should be completed. Tags should be affixed to each body or part displaced and cor-

A marker which indicates the location of an aviation accident fatality.

responding stakes or tags placed at that location. A journal should be kept of all related activities and tag numbers. Special precautions should be taken to avoid disturbing anything in the cockpit area.

The following information is needed by the coroner:

- Type of incident.
- Approximate number of victims.
- Any known hazards at the scene.
- Exact location of incident.
- Access route to disaster site.
- Command post location.
- Which agencies and key persons are involved in incident.
- Time of occurrence, if known.
- Any other information that may affect fatality activities.

Special Incident Scene Procedures

There is no typical aircraft accident, but there is a typical procedure for preparing for the investigation. It starts with advance planning and preparation. The identification process itself begins at the accident scene. The success of the investigation and identification of the victims depend on the thoroughness of the rescue and recovery workers themselves more than anything else. It is their preliminary work at the scene that can facilitate or jeopardize the subsequent investigation. Because of the potential for critical incident stress reactions, it is not recommended that the same emergency response personnel who were involved in the initial firefighting and rescue be involved in the body recovery. Assigned firefighters and other workers should be thoroughly instructed in their task and its importance. Tasks should be kept short and simple. Work at the scene should always be supervised by an investigator, experienced pathologist, or police officer.

A grid pattern often is established over the entire crash site using plastic tape, wooden stakes, or other similar materials. The size of the grid squares depends on the amount of wreckage and bodies in the area, as well as on the landmarks being used as reference points. The more wreckage and body parts in an area, the smaller the grids. Squares also can be broken into subgrids in congested areas.

It is suggested that grid lines be laid out by compass headings. Lines running north and south can be numbered, while east and west lines can have a letter designation. Grid lines can be quickly laid out using a transit. Public works, local contract surveying teams, or other engineering personnel can perform this function. It is recommended that the investigation of each grid square start from the same corner, such as the northeast corner. The grid pattern enables you to rapidly measure and record the exact location where each item or victim was found. An alphanumeric representation of the recovery location is written on all tags and paperwork associated with that victim, body part, or personal item.

Photographs, videos, and charting should be conducted prior to and during each recovery. This should be done from a minimum of four angles or views. Lots of film, blank videos, batteries, and other supplies will be needed. Identifying numbers should be included in the pictures and videos. Videos also allow you to document verbally. The location of the body or item with respect to the aircraft, wreckage, debris, landmarks, and other bodies is very important. The recovery team should become familiar with the accident scene before removal activities.

Recovery personnel should be suitably dressed for the process. Identifying vests, passes, arm bands, and hats can be used. The double protection offered by disposable plastic gloves layered under sturdy leather gloves should be used. Plastic tears easily on sharp aircraft fragments. Leather absorbs fluids and decreases the sense of touch. Rubber, steel-soled and toed boots are a must. An appropriate apron also may be helpful. Consider tetanus shots for recovery personnel, as well as personnel decontamination, and cleaning of turnout gear, and other bloodborne pathogen procedures.

Body Removal

Bodies are removed from the crash site in a systematic fashion, usually starting at the front of the aircraft. There will be pressure from the NTSB team to remove and evaluate the flight crew first to determine if they were physically or mentally impaired. Each body is assigned a body and removal number. A preselected block of case numbers should be set aside.

The label or tag should be written in indelible ink or crayon and affixed securely to the body or item. Additional tags, with corresponding numbers, should be attached to the body bag, as well as a stake or marker placed at the original body location. Some body bags have a pocket on the outside to hold such tags. A cache of body pouches, identification tags, and survey stakes should be established before an aircraft disaster. Body bags usually are available from major local suppliers of caskets, from funeral directors and their equipment supply firms, and from local military facilities.

During the "bagging process" each body, the clothes removed from it, associated property and effects, attached debris, and adjacent body fragments should be placed in each bag. Different-sized bags or other receptacles should be provided for the separate preservation of such personal belongings as jewelry, dentures, etc. An incorrectly assigned item could cause a great deal of additional work and lead to errors in identification. Effective and rapid identification of remains is contingent on maintaining personal effects, human remains, and debris intact and free from contamination prior to examination.

Portions of bodies found together often are removed together under one removal tag, with each body part tagged with the same number. Unidentified remains, separated limbs, and tissue should be tagged, bagged, documented, weighed, and photographed separately.

The following documentation is needed at the scene:

- body and removal number;
- location where found (grid alphanumerical indicator);
- time and date;
- names of persons handling body;
- approximate weight and height;
- color of hair and eyes;
- scars, tattoos, birthmarks, etc.;
- description of jewelry, clothing, and personal property found; and
- other items of interest.

Each bag recovered often is removed to a refrigerated truck or trailer set up near the recovery operation. This is one of the many resources that should be planned for in advance. These vehicles should have metal interiors and no wooden floors. The average 24-hour ambient temperature should be 35° to 40°F. Be sure to cover the business name on the outside of the vehicle. Vehicles should be returned to the supplier or lender steam cleaned and certified clean by the local health department.

Refrigeration helps to control odors, decomposition, and breakdown of the bodies. Insects usually will not be a problem during the first few days. A study of a major crash in the Everglades area of Florida indicated that bodies remained in the field for more than 50 hours with no insect-related problems. Flies and maggots breed best in moist, high-humidity conditions with very little activity around. All the bodies from most major aviation disasters can be recovered in 24 to 48 hours, depending on the organization and preparedness of the local authorities.

Other specialized equipment may be needed at the scene. For example, in accidents that involve collisions with structures, heavy equipment such as cranes and tractors may be needed to remove debris so that bodies can be recovered. When the first sign of a body is uncovered, work must proceed slowly, with personnel often using hand tools. Crashes in isolated areas, such as mountains, swamps, deserts, and bodies of water, may require boats, helicopters, divers, and four-wheel-drive vehicles.

THE ACCIDENT INVESTIGATION PROCESS

Fire officers should be familiar with the aircraft accident investigation process. The emergency response will be closely scrutinized by the NTSB,

FAA, news media, attorneys representing potential claimants, and other interested parties. The NTSB is starting to comment on the actions taken by, and performance of, fire departments during aircraft incidents. Fire officers can and should participate in certain phases of the investigation. Investigative reports can affect the reputation and liability of a department. As with fatalities, fire department activities involving the incident scene and aircraft wreckage can affect the ability of investigators to determine the cause of the crash.

Accident Notification Procedures

According to the *Aircraft Accident Investigations Manual* published by the NTSB, the definition of an "Aircraft Accident" is an occurrence associated with the operation of an aircraft that takes place between the time any person boards the aircraft with the intention of flight, until such person has disembarked, in which: (1) any person suffers death or serious injury as a result of coming in contact with anything attached thereto, or in which the aircraft receives substantial damage, except when the injuries are from natural causes, are self-inflicted or inflicted by other persons, or when the injuries are to stowaways hiding outside the areas normally available to the passengers and crew; or (2) the aircraft incurs damage or structural failure which adversely affects the structure strength, performance, or flight characteristics of the aircraft and which would normally require major repair or replacement of the affected component.

The nearest NTSB field office must be notified when an aircraft accident or any of the following incidents have occurred. Notification also can be made by contacting the nearest FAA facility, such as an airport air traffic control tower, which can notify the NTSB.

- In-flight fire (The flight starts when the first occupant boards the aircraft and ends when the last one leaves the aircraft. The NTSB is not interested in fires involving aircraft parked and unattended).
- Aircraft collide in flight.
- Damage to property, other than the aircraft, estimated to exceed $25,000.
- Malfunction or failure of certain flight control, engine, electrical, or hydraulic aircraft systems.
- An evacuation of aircraft in which an emergency egress system is used.
- Inability of any required flight crew member to perform his normal flight duties as a result of injury or illness.
- An aircraft is overdue and is believed to have been involved in an accident.

The notification shall contain the following information:

- Type, nationality, and registration marks of the aircraft.
- Name of owner and operator of the aircraft.
- Name of the pilot in command.
- Date and time of accident or incident.
- Last point of departure, and point of intended landing.
- Position of the aircraft with reference to some easily defined geographical point.
- Number of crew and passengers on board killed and seriously injured, as well as others on ground killed or seriously injured.
- Nature of the accident or incident, the weather, and extent of damage to the aircraft.
- Physical characteristics of the accident site.
- A description of any explosive or radioactive materials, or other dangerous articles carried.
- Identification of the originating authority.

Types of Investigations

Accidents are categorized by "Type A," which are catastrophic accidents investigated by a Washington, DC-based team, and "Type B" accidents which are investigated by a field office with possibly some group structure. The following are the different types of investigative responses that fire officers will encounter:

A *full-go team* is made up of 10 specialists on 24-hour call. It responds from Washington DC, and is headed by an Investigator in Charge (IIC). Whether or not a full-go-team is sent depends on the accident type, aircraft type, aircraft loss, ground loss, number of fatalities and injuries, amount of public interest, and likelihood of a formal board report or public hearing. Sometimes a *partial go team* will respond.

A *full field team* is used for less complicated air carrier and certain large business aircraft accidents.

A *partial field team* handles the majority of nonfatal air carrier and fatal large-business-aircraft accidents.

Regular Investigations are handled by a single field office investigator and include nonfatal air taxi and general aviation fatal accidents. The bulk of the NTSB investigations in the field are one-person operations.

Federal Aviation Administration (FAA) Involvement

The FAA has enforcement and regulatory powers. Under the Department of Transportation, the FAA promulgates and enforces the Federal Aviation

Regulations (FARs). It also certifies civil aircraft for worthiness, and airmen and air carriers for competency.

An FAA representative may be the first federal official on the scene. The FAA is responsible for an aircraft accident investigation if there is a violation of the FARs, performance of FAA facilities (air traffic control) or functions, air worthiness of FAA-certified aircraft, or competency of FAA-certified airmen, air agencies, commercial operators, or air carriers. FAA personnel will probably examine airport fire department training and fire apparatus maintenance records after a major accident at an airport.

Military Involvement in Investigations

The NTSB has primary jurisdiction over accidents involving both civil and military aircraft. The applicable branch of the military is invited and allowed to participate in the investigation.

In accidents involving only military aircraft, the applicable military branch has primary jurisdiction. For national security reasons, the military exercises tighter control of scene security, investigative procedures, and information gathered. Military accident sites also are much more hazardous because of the possible involvement of weapons and other exotic aircraft materials and systems. The military provides the NTSB and the FAA with accident information that can contribute to air safety. In the event of a military aircraft accident, the nearest military base should be notified so personnel there can make the other necessary notifications. The following Military Safety Centers investigate military aircraft accidents:

Director
U.S. Army Agency for Aviation Safety
Fort Rucker, Alabama 36360

Commander
U.S. Naval Aviation Safety Center
U.S. Naval Air Station
Norfolk, Virginia 23511

Deputy Inspector General for Inspections and Safety
Office of the Inspector General
U.S. Air Force
Norton Air Force Base, California 92409
(also investigates accidents involving State Air National Guard)

Chief, Aviation Safety Branch (IGS-1)
U.S. Coast Guard Headquarters
400 7th Street S.W.
Washington D.C. 20591

Other Agencies Involved in Aircraft Accident Investigations

The FBI becomes involved in aircraft accidents when known or suspected acts of air piracy or criminal acts (murder, suicides, bombs, illegal drugs) have occurred. The FBI disaster team also assists local jurisdictions with fingerprinting and body identification. FBI field offices around the country can contact and gather information about victims from family, friends, dentists, employers, and other confidential sources. FBI laboratories may be used for special tests and studies.

The U.S. Postal Service is responsible for recovering mail from aircraft wreckages. Postal inspectors also investigate criminal activity associated with the mail and aircraft accidents. They have been involved in aircraft incidents when bombs or undeclared hazardous materials have been shipped in mail on aircraft.

Security of Aircraft Wreckage

One of the first things the first-arriving NTSB representative ascertains is whether the wreckage is undisturbed, protected, and being guarded effectively by appropriate law enforcement officials. He provides local authorities with clear instructions on how security must be maintained. MINIMAL DISTURBANCE OF THE WRECKAGE IS EXTREMELY IMPORTANT.

Part 830 of the "Procedural Regulations of the Safety Board" state clearly that prior to arrival of the board, the aircraft wreckage, mail, or cargo may be disturbed or moved *only* to the extent necessary to remove persons injured or trapped, protect wreckage from further damage, or protect the public from injury. Where it is necessary to disturb or move wreckage, sketches, descriptive notes, photographs, videos, etc., shall be made of the locale, including original position and condition of the wreckage and any significant impact marks.

Arrival of the First NTSB Representative

Before the Washington, DC team arrives, the nearest NTSB field office representative establishes initial liaison with local authorities. This representative reaches the accident scene as soon as possible and remains there. With personal contact and the display of his official badge, the field representative conveys to local authorities and the news media that the NTSB has complete control and authority over the crash site. This does not mean that he replaces the fire or other officer as the Incident Commander. The representative immediately contacts fire, police, and the Incident Commander at the scene. These agencies are briefed on their responsibilities and the needs of the NTSB. A quick check of the scene and situation is made to make sure the wreckage and bodies, especially of the crew, are being protected. Every effort is made by the field representative to garner the good will and active support of local authorities and all others involved in the accident.

Based on an evaluation of the situation, conditions, and circumstances, the initial on-scene representative plans and determines a systematic course of action for the NTSB. As much pertinent information as possible is gathered to brief the Washington go-team when it arrives. Arrangements are made for necessary autopsies, especially of the flight crew. The representative performs preliminary investigative efforts. Witnesses are identified and interviewed. The wreckage is photographed thoroughly as early in the incident as possible. Arrangements are made for a meeting place and hotel accommodations for team members. The flight data and cockpit voice recorders are retrieved and shipped to Washington, DC. Interested parties are briefed on NTSB investigative procedures. The representative also may determine which local authorities are to be named as parties to the investigation. It is important and recommended that representatives from local agencies, such as fire, police, coroner, and the airport participate in the investigation to ensure that local organizations are represented properly.

Investigation Organization

When the "Investigator in Charge (IIC)" arrives, an initial organizational meeting is conducted to explain the investigative procedures. *"Parties of Interest"* are invited to participate in the various working groups. Parties of Interest are persons, government agencies, companies, and associations whose employees, functions, activities, or procedures were involved in the accident or who can provide qualified personnel to actively assist in the investigation. Some examples of parties of interest are fire department officers, the FAA, the involved air carrier, aircraft manufacturer, manufacturers of various aircraft systems, and associations that represent pilots, flight engineers, air traffic controllers, mechanics, and flight attendants.

Various *"Working Groups"* are established. Parties of interest assign their representatives to applicable investigative groups. An appropriate NTSB investigator is put in charge of each working group. Members of groups can be removed for failure to comply with assigned duties, acting in a manner prejudicial to the investigation, or for not remaining with the group until the field phase is completed. Any person who represents claimants or insurers is prohibited from participating. Except for a few prearranged organizations, the NTSB does not seek potential parties. Interested parties must request to participate.

There also may be *"Observers to the Investigation."* Some examples are, again, fire department officers, accredited members of aeronautical organizations, operators of like equipment, designated military personnel, and representatives of foreign governments. Observers can only attend the initial organizational meeting and final "wind-up meeting," not progress meetings. At frequent intervals during the investigation, the Investigator in Charge holds meetings of various groups, usually at the end of each day of field investigation, to review work progress. During progress meetings, each group leader gives a presentation and there is a free exchange of ideas and information. Often the meetings uncover some facts that can help another group or team with its work.

Some or all of the following "Working Groups" may be established during the investigation:

- **Structures Group.** Examines fuselage, wing, and landing gear wreckage. May reconstruct aircraft from wreckage, use mockups, and plot a "Wreckage Distribution Chart."
- **Systems Group.** Responsible for documenting cockpit controls and instruments, as well as all other subsystems such as electrical, hydraulic, de-icing, oxygen, pneumatics, navigation, lights, and communications. Off-site component testing may be done at NTSB and independent testing facilities.
- **Power Plant Group.** Responsible for everything associated with aircraft engines, such as the fuel system, propellers, thrust reversers, and auxiliary power units.
- **Maintenance Records Group.** Reviews all records to ascertain the history of the aircraft involved in the accident.
- **Operations Group.** Determines all facts relating to the history of the flight, such as activities of the crew prior to the accident, employment records, crew training, company procedures, and weight and balance information.
- **Weather Group.** Collects and reviews all available weather data pertinent to the accident.
- **Air Traffic Control Group.** Interviews controllers and reviews pertinent voice recordings. The air traffic control system is extremely complex and difficult to investigate.
- **Witness Investigations Group.** Locates witnesses and obtains factual accounts of everything seen or heard which may have a bearing on the accident.
- **Human Factors Group.** Looks into crash dynamics, survivability aspects and, most important, the ARFF, rescue, and medical response.

Fire department representatives usually have the opportunity to participate on the witness and human factors groups.

Aircraft Recorders

Flight data recorders are required on all large U.S.-registered air carrier aircraft that are certified for operation above 25,000 feet or are turbine-engine powered. These units are installed as far aft in the aircraft as possible. They may be orange, bright yellow, or red, and are marked "Flight Recorder—Do Not Open" in several languages. There are three types of flight data recorders: foil medium, digital, cassette or magazine. Do not damage or remove foil medium and latest calibration data. Do not open and protect them from magnetic fields. Never remove the tape or recording medium. If it is broken, wrap the box in polyethylene plastic. If it has been in water, keep it immersed in fresh water and do not let it dry out.

Cockpit voice recorders have a minimum of 30 minutes of operating time or retention period. They are required to be operating before beginning the "Before Engine Start Checklist" and to run continuously until completion of "Final Checklist" after landing. This device is a 5″ × 8″ × 13″ red or orange box with reflective strips. It is a continuous tape and will bulk erase if its power source is not disconnected or shut down. It may have an underwater locater attached. Do not attempt to play it in the field. As is the case with

Flight data and cockpit recorders. These instruments are analyzed by authorities to determine the cause of the accident. This equipment must be recovered and safeguarded.

the flight data recorder, it should be shipped to the proper authorities in Washington, DC as soon as possible. This almost always is handled by the NTSB.

Other NTSB Investigative Activities

Aircraft wreckage is recovered to the extent necessary to determine probable cause and make appropriate recommendations. The investigation is less involved when the cause of the crash is known, such as in a witnessed midair collision. The wreckage eventually is returned to the owner and the initial on-scene investigation eventually is closed. Scene control is released to local authorities. Items not needed for investigation are released to the aircraft owner, next of kin, or insurance companies.

A "Technical Review Meeting" may be held in Washington, DC. Parties to the investigation are allowed to participate. All investigative information collected to that point is reviewed to make sure it is sufficient, accurate, and complete. Factual reports are presented by each working group. Any disputes are resolved and additional investigation may be proposed. Fire department representatives should attend to protect their interests.

A "Public Hearing" also may be called to inform the public or create a record of facts, conditions, and circumstances. It is purely a fact-finding proceeding with no intended legal issues or adverse parties. Whether a public hearing is conducted depends on the number of fatalities, type and newness of aircraft involved, type of accident and safety issues involved, the repetitiveness of the accident, amount of public interest, and benefits of public exposure to the issues. It typically is held in the city closest to the accident site. It also may be held in Washington, DC or another site if extensive news coverage is expected. A "Board of Inquiry" also may be conducted.

Eventually the NTSB issues a report, which consists of analysis, findings, and probable cause. Recommendations usually are made to improve aviation safety. The NTSB cannot enforce its recommendations. Only the FAA and legislatures can make law. The NTSB also conducts in-depth studies of significant safety problems and makes reports setting forth the facts, findings, and action proposals. The board also issues various alerts, bulletins, and notes.

CRITICAL INCIDENT STRESS

Aircraft accidents are the classic "critical incident stress" emergency situation. Critical Incident Stress (CIS), also called Post-Traumatic Stress Disorder (PTSD), occurs when emergency service personnel experience an event that causes unusually strong emotional reactions. High-impact crashes in the 1970s that involved large passenger aircraft highlighted the fact that emergency workers can themselves become psychological victims. What fire personnel may experience during aircraft or other mass casualty incidents can overwhelm their ability to cope or surpass the normal coping mechanisms. CIS can interfere with a person's ability to function at an incident scene or on the job, for days, weeks, or months after experiencing a critical incident.

Characteristics of Critical Incidents

The critical aspects of an aircraft incident that may trigger a stress reaction can include some or all of the following characteristics:

* Any emotionally profound situation, such as one that involves the death of children.
* Situations that attract extensive news media attention.
* Any loss of life that follows an extraordinary and prolonged expenditure of physical and emotional energy.
* Particularly gruesome or gory incidents or incidents that involve overwhelming carnage and suffering.
* Any incident outside the range of normal human experience.
* Incidents where emergency personnel are rendered helpless and lives are lost.
* An incident in which the circumstances are so unusual, or the sights, smells, and sounds so distressing as to produce a high level of immediate or delayed emotional stress.
* Personal identification with the victims or circumstances.

Other types of job-related stressors can make the situation even worse. Inclement weather, poor footing, smoke, high noise, crowds, inadequate lighting, heavy, restrictive protective equipment, lack of food and beverages, and equipment problems are some common physical stressors. Some organizational stressors that can affect fire officers at aircraft incidents are interdepartmental problems, interagency problems and issues, role conflicts, inadequate training, and limited resources.

Signs and Symptoms of Critical Incident Stress

Critical incident stress can happen to anyone, regardless of prior experiences or years of service. A review of major incidents where numerous injuries or fatalities have occurred indicates that significant numbers of emergency responders experience some sort of stress-related symptoms during and after incidents. Eighty-seven percent were found to experience short-term, transitory reactions, but did not suffer long-term detrimental effects. Three to 10 percent did experience continuous, long-term, detrimental effects. Without professional intervention, these people sometimes may experience problems at work, deteriorating family relationships, and other health problems.

There are many signs and symptoms of psychological reactions to stressful events. Some physical characteristics manifested by fire personnel during or after aircraft incident operations are fatigue, nausea, headaches, profuse sweating, and restlessness. Sometimes chest pain, difficulty breathing, elevated blood pressure, and rapid heart rates may be encountered. Cognitive signs and symptoms may include confusion, disorientation, blaming others, lack of concentration, indecisiveness, heightened or decreased alertness, and forgetfulness. Emotional manifestations can include anxiety, guilt, grief, denial, depression, apprehension, irritability, apathy, and anger. Changes in behavior can include emotional outbursts, a loss of or increase in appetite, withdrawal, communication problems, increased alcohol consumption or smoking, pacing, gallows humor, diminished sex drive, marital or family problems, obsessive interest in the incident, visual flashbacks, or poor job performance, attendance, attitude, or appearance. Basically, any abnormal or extreme change in a person should be investigated. The more signs and symptoms that are present, the greater the likelihood that a person is in need of medical or psychological evaluation and help.

Coping Mechanisms

Cover up bodies, body parts, and other gruesome sights as soon as possible. Rotate personnel out of the incident area on a regular basis. Set up a rehabilitation area with healthy food and liquid refreshment. Avoid sugar, caffeine, and suggestive foods like barbequed chicken or pizza. Provide restroom facilities and a quiet, out-of-the-way area to sit, lie down, and rest. Make sure personnel have clean, dry clothing or gear available. Know and recognize the symptoms of critical incident stress and intervene early. Have an established crisis intervention team, system, and resources.

If you are affected by a critical incident, try to rest more. Spend time with others, especially friends and family. Realize that recurring thoughts, dreams, flashbacks, and other incident-related feelings are normal. They tend to decrease over time and become less painful. Try to maintain as normal a schedule and level of activity as possible. Eat well-balanced and regular meals, even if you are not hungry. Physical exercise and relaxation are very important during the first 24 to 48 hours. Express feelings as they arise. Ignoring them will only make things worse. Realize that others also may be under the same stress.

Types of Intervention Techniques

A CIS training program presented to personnel on a regular basis can prepare them for incident-related stress and help minimize its effects. Having a pre-established crisis intervention program, made up of mental health professionals and peer support emergency personnel, is extremely valuable. Consider providing on-site evaluation and counseling by CIS team members when time and circumstances permit. The mental health professional, chaplain, or peer-support personnel who perform this task should not be involved in scene management. Peer support personnel are fellow fire personnel trained and experienced in CIS procedures, who can provide support and act as a liaison between the mental health professional and the affected personnel. Peers directly involved in the incident should not help with CIS activities.

Debriefings and defusings can be used to provide psychological and emotional support for persons after an occurrence. Defusings usually are conducted shortly after the incident, involve small groups, and usually last approximately an hour. A formal debriefing, if needed, often is conducted 24 to 72 hours after the incident and may last several hours. These processes provide a safe, supportive environment in which personnel can discuss their feelings and reactions. They greatly help to reduce the intensity and duration of stress reactions, as well as long-term syndromes. They are an opportunity to assess the need for follow-up or more involved treatment. The sessions can be used to prepare and educate personnel about the normal reactions to expect, coping mechanisms, available help, and to develop group cohesiveness and support. The process is not meant to be a critique of performance or emergency operations. All participants should agree to keep the results of these sessions in strict confidence. Rank is not important; each participant should be respected as an individual. The location selected for the debriefing should be free of distractions and represent a neutral environment. It is recommended that attendance be mandatory. No one should be forced to talk, just required to listen. Individual consultations and follow-up debriefings may need to be conducted weeks or months after a critical incident. A 24-hour referral phone number can be set up, as can spouse support programs.

SUMMARY

Every aircraft incident is different. They can happen any time, anywhere, and in any fire department's jurisdiction. The environment, the type, size, and occupant load of the aircraft, the degree of impact, and whether there is a post-crash fire or not are some of the many factors that affect the decisions made and actions taken by the fire officer. Most accidents occur at or near an airport.

Airports present fire officers with many specialized physical, operational, communication, safety, and response conditions.

Aircraft can be categorized as general aviation, corporate, commuter, commercial air carrier, cargo, military, and rotary-wing types. Each category has unique crash dynamics, fire control, access, rescue, and hazard characteristics. Responding fire personnel should understand aircraft construction, systems, and other features in order to perform effectively and safely. The aluminum construction, tremendous quantities of fuel carried, high occupant loads, and limited means of escape create a narrow window of time in which to control a fire and save the aircraft's occupants. Many activities must be accomplished simultaneously, efficiently, and quickly. An aircraft incident scene should be treated as a hazardous material incident site would be. Full protective gear, safety officers, and good scene management are critical. Fuel, hydraulic, oxygen, and electrical systems, pressurized cylinders, wheel assemblies, dangerous cargo, jagged and unstable wreckage, downed electrical utilities, body fluids, composite materials, combustible metals, ejection seats, military weapons, aircraft engines, escape slides, and radar are some of the hazards that will threaten, test, and challenge emergency personnel.

An airport presents many unique fire protection situations, conditions, and requirements. There are certain FAA regulations that must be met. Airport fire resources can be overwhelmed quickly by a major aircraft accident. Off-airport fire companies will perform many of the fire control, rescue, and water supply functions. Responding fire companies must not enter the active aircraft areas of the airport without clearance or an escort. It is important that airport and off-airport fire personnel plan and train together. The fire service most likely will assume the incident command role during the initial part of the emergency. Fire officers should understand the roles, responsibilities, and needs of the other key response agencies to avoid conflicts, duplication of effort, and other problems.

During an airport low-impact crash, the initial tactical objective is to extinguish the fuel spill fire and protect the fuselage. Afterwards, the operation changes quickly to an interior, structure-type operation. Airport ARFF apparatus usually do not carry enough agent to fully handle most major aircraft incidents. Off-airport fire companies usually are tasked with resupplying the airport fire apparatus at the incident scene by first shuttling water and then establishing a continuous supply. The aircraft should be stabilized as soon as possible by disconnecting the battery, controlling the fuel system, pinning landing gear, and other control actions. An aircraft mechanic should be requested to provide assistance with the aircraft.

During victim extrication operations, unstable fuselage sections should be supported to prevent rolling, sliding, or collapse which could injure trapped occupants and emergency responders. The incident scene should be rendered safe to work in, especially with respect to spilled fuel and vapors. Forcible entry on aircraft is very time consuming and labor intensive. It should be a last-resort consideration. Normal doors, hatches, and crash-induced openings should be used first. Around the windows is usually the best location to avoid aircraft systems during cutting operations. A rescue tool resource pool should be established during extended extrication operations to stage and service needed rescue equipment.

Aircraft interior fires should be treated in a manner similar to a structure on wheels. Every opening on the aircraft should be opened and accessed with hoselines. Structural ventilation techniques often can be used with positive results. At off-airport high-impact aircraft incidents, standard structural tactics and strategies also are used. Any large incident scene should be divided into manageable geographic divisions and functional groups. Hazardous cargos can be encountered on passenger and cargo aircraft. "Cargo-aircraft-only" shipments usually are loaded near the flight deck where the crew can access them during a flight. The shipping papers will be found somewhere in the flight deck area. A considerable amount of information also can be found on the hazardous material shipment itself. Avoid the sides of wheels, front and rear of military aircraft, propellers, and jet engine intakes during aircraft emergencies.

All emergency responders should use the same recognized triage tag at an aircraft incident and be skilled in its use. Common problems encountered during medical operations are documentation and recordkeeping of the injured through the triage, treatment, and transportation process. The primary function law enforcement agencies perform is incident scene security. They should establish adequate inner and outer security perimeters as soon as possible. Do not move bodies or aircraft wreckage unless absolutely necessary, but if you do, document all movements. Cover bodies and body parts immediately. An aircraft accident is the classic critical stress type incident. The psychological and emotional needs of emergency responders should be addressed during and after the incident.

21

Wildland Firefighting

JAMES L. McFADDEN and
JOHN R. HAWKINS

CHAPTER HIGHLIGHTS

- Our number one priority is firefighter safety.
- Wildland/Interface fires are our challenge for the 21st century.
- We must know our resource capabilities to plan operations.
- Fire behavior: it's not a mystery, but our lack of understanding.

*A*LTHOUGH LARGE-SCALE WILDLAND fires may not occur on a regular basis in some parts of the country, there are few areas that do not have the potential for them. Analyses of wildland fires in the United States during the past several years indicate that these types of fires are occurring more frequently and, in many cases, in places where they seldom have occurred in the past.

The recent increase in the number and severity of large-scale wildland fires can probably be attributed to two factors. The first is changes in national weather patterns that have been creating drought-like conditions and erratic wind movement in many areas, both of which are conducive to the development and spread of fires when wildland fuels are present. A second reason is the expanding development of many communities to the point where there is direct encroachment into wildland areas, thus causing an interface problem.

When interface fires occur they can present unique problems in terms of Incident Command and effective control. The failure to recognize this fact can have a serious negative impact on the ability of fire department officers to deal with them.

The management of a large-scale wildland fire can be very demanding and complex because of the large number of potential problems that can occur.

Conditions that exist where the fire starts, or that develop before it can be extinguished, can rapidly change it from an incipient blaze to a major emergency. Many of the existing conditions, such as the weather, topography, fuel, and exposures can compound and result in fires that are extremely fast moving and totally unpredictable. In these situations, the control capability of even the largest fire departments can be stretched to the limit because of the amount of resources and degree of logistical support required, and the fact that the incident may continue over a prolonged period of time and cover great distances.

Since the possibility of these types of fires exists to some degree in most communities, fire department officers must be prepared to deal with them by understanding the types of problems that can be encountered and identifying possible solutions to these problems prior to the event.

The information that follows focuses on problems associated with wildland fires and offers strategic and tactical considerations that fire officers can use in these fire situations.

WEATHER

Weather is the most important and variable factor that affects wildland fire spread. With this in mind, the importance of the weather and its impact on general chief officers' knowledge and the application of that knowledge at actual emergencies become extremely important.

Anyone acquainted with the behavior of a wildland fire recognizes the vital influence of the weather. Likewise, anyone who has studied weather is impressed with the complexity of the science.

At every level, there are great fundamental laws that are constantly at work making and remaking the weather.

When experienced officers are given a general prediction of the weather, they automatically convert the prediction into anticipated fuel conditions and fire behavior. The long habit of associating brisk, dry winds with severe burning conditions is inclined to make anyone forget that the first is cause and the other effect.

Three master forces govern the making of weather upon earth: heat from the sun, called solar energy; the force of gravity; and, the inclination of all elements to seek a state of balance or equilibrium.

Temperature

Wood ignites between 400 and 700° F. Normally the woody fuels of the wildland will burst into flame at approximately 540° F (assuming sufficient oxygen is present). Of course, the time required to produce fire at this temperature will vary with the amount of moisture in the fuel that first must be driven out by the heat of ignition.

The highest temperature that the sun could be expected to reach on a wind-sheltered surface is 150° or 160° F. This is far below the point of self-ignition of wildland fuels. However, solar heating is significant, aside from the drying effect of such a high temperature, in that the fuel that gains a boost of a 100° or more from the sun is well along toward the ignition temperature before the igniting source is applied.

Of course, the officer may take advantage of the same rule operating in reverse, especially at night or during periods of relatively cool air. Heavy fuel may be separated and turned over to cause it to give up accumulated heat into the air. This leads to temperature reductions and mimics the effects of night-time cooling.

Another variable is that of daily, or diurnal, temperatures. Diurnal temperature variation is dependent on the same factors discussed in seasonal temperatures. Typically, daily temperatures are the coolest at daybreak with warming continuing until mid-afternoon when temperatures are at their highest, followed by evening cooling; again, the angle at which the sun's radiation strikes the earth is important. Topographic features can modify the process, with southern-facing slopes receiving more radiation than northern-facing slopes.

Smoldering fuels along a fire line will begin to support flame production as the sun moves higher in the morning sky. With the arrival of mid-afternoon, the sun will have brought fuel temperatures to their peak and fire will probably be making concerted runs into new, formerly unburned fuels. A general cooling will take place as the sun falls closer to the horizon and flame production eventually may die back as nightfall signals a return to a smoldering fire line. An important departure from this situation occurs when fire burns as fiercely in darkness as it did in the daytime as a result of yet another weather influence, wind.

Stable and unstable air masses

Stability and instability refer to a relationship between the vertical temperature distribution within an air mass and a vertically moving parcel of air. If air mass temperature decreases sharply with altitude (generally, greater than 5° F per 1,000 feet of change in altitude), conditions are favorable for air currents to rise vertically through the air mass. Thus, an unstable condition is said to exist, because vertically rising warmer air can continue to move with little or no restriction. Under this condition, calm fires may suddenly explode violently and with erratic behavior. Unstable air above the ground surface is responsible. A simple example of increased fire activity due to the vertical air mass profile regularly exists in a fireplace. When the damper is opened, the fire increases in intensity. The same phenomenon occurs when the "atmosphere damper" is open because of unstable air.

Hot air rises, with the rising air mass getting cooler with increased altitude. In an unstable condition, an air mass, which is warmer nearer the ground, rises and keeps right on going, higher and higher, faster and faster, creating unstable air aloft. As the hot air ascends, it pushes aside colder, heavier air. Displaced, this heavier air descends toward the ground and flattens out on reaching the earth's surface. Firefighters get a sudden "unexpected" wind. The fire is suddenly intensified and pushed in assorted directions, perhaps across a newly constructed fire line.

In contrast, when the temperature near the ground is more approximate to that aloft, warm air travels slowly upward and, upon reaching cooler air, is cooled itself and stops rising. This is a stable condition: vertical air movement is limited, and a temperature equalization occurs.

Temperature inversions

As discussed earlier, under most conditions warmer air is nearer the earth's surface, with cooler air at higher elevations. However, there also are normal conditions under which quite the opposite is true. Such an "opposite" is called a temperature inversion. In an inversion, cooler air is found nearer the surface, and warmer air at a higher elevation.

Along the coasts, marine inversions develop when cool, moist ocean air flows across the lowlands or through hill and mountain passes, to settle heavily within land depressions. This cooler air has a covering layer of warmer air; thus, a temperature inversion exists. When a mass of air is cooled by nighttime temperatures and becomes sufficiently heavy with moisture, it will flow downslope to collect in land depressions, such as bowl-shaped valleys. A covering layer of warmer air above, sometimes at a point along a canyon wall, creates an inversion of temperatures.

It is well known that wildfire spread slows during cooler nighttime hours. Many large fires are contained during this period.

Certainly, fire burning in the cooler environment of an inversion can be expected to subside, and becomes dormant and sluggish as higher relative humidity and higher fuel moistures become controlling factors. Firefighters working the fire line in a warmer layer above the inversion probably will be faced with fire activities quite different from their counterparts in the cooler area below. While nighttime temperatures generally can be expected to drop at all elevations, they will be less advantageous in the warm upper air lid of the inversion. The area along a slope where fire activity remains active above an inversion is called the thermal zone or thermal belt.

Inversions become most dangerous when a lower-elevation fire suddenly burns through the inversion lid into the warmer air above. Intense burning, accelerated fire spread, and higher flame lengths can place unprepared fire-fighters in immediate jeopardy.

Relative humidity

Water vapor, which is simply water in a gaseous state, is a very important weather factor. When an air mass that is passing over a water surface picks up vapor, the process is called evaporation. The oceans are the primary source of water vapor to the atmosphere. Lakes, rivers, moist soil, snow, and vegetation furnish lesser amounts.

The dew point is the temperature (at any given altitude) at which air becomes completely saturated. If an air temperature of 60° F decreased to a dew point of 40° F, fog or rain will result. The term relative humidity indicates the ratio of the amount of vapor actually present to the maximum amount that the air potentially could hold. If relative humidity is 100 percent, the air is said to be completely saturated; i.e., it can hold no more water vapor.

In contrast, if the relative humidity is measured at 50 percent, then the air is only saturated by half and potentially can hold 50 percent more water vapor. When the relative humidity drops below about 30 percent, the situation becomes favorable for intense wildland fire spread. The dryer air is better able to pick up water vapor from the fuel; consequently, less time is required for heat to bring about combustion. Fuels absorb and give up moisture at different rates; larger fuels, such as logs, are affected by humidity changes very slowly. Grass, a lighter fuel, is affected quite readily and may not burn at all when a relative humidity of 30 percent or higher is present for an hour or so.

Firefighters can take advantage of humidity in many ways. Sometimes it is desirable to use low humidities to burn away undesired fuels more easily. Other times, fire officers must wait for the rising humidities of night to more directly attack a formerly hot burning fire that is subsiding. Failing to recognize the effects of humidity can work against fire officers. Many firing out or backfiring operations have been outright failures because late afternoon or nighttime humidities prevented even grasses from burning cleanly, and fire officers found themselves faced with an incomplete burn which more than likely would roar to life with the heat of the next day.

Wind velocity and direction

Wind is simply the movement of air. The average person thinks of wind as generally horizontal air movement fast enough to be felt. That is only because a person is much less aware of the causes than of the horizontal air movement one can feel and observe as a mover of light objects.

Over the face of the earth several major forces work unceasingly to stimulate air movement. First, there are the vast areas of heated earth surface which produce rising air currents that return to earth in the cooler regions; next is the gravitational effect of the turning earth on these tremendous churning currents. The changing seasons alter the pattern of wind movement because the hot and cold regions of the earth shift about. The wind (and with it all weather behavior) is modified by the effects of bodies of water and land masses, and then by lesser features in local areas.

Wind reacts like a fluid; it can be compressed under pressure, expanded and contracted with heat and cold, and made moist or dry. It may pause unmoving and then spring in any direction with violent gusts.

Wind movement is critically important to the fire officer. It appears that the best approach to becoming a master of such a flexible and untamed natural element is for fire officers to become acquainted with the air movement habits of their own regions.

If fuel and topographic conditions do not adversely influence fire spread, then a strong wind in one prevailing direction will cause a long wedge or elliptically shaped fire. This results not only from the driving force of the wind, but also because intensified combustion will demand an indraft of wind toward the fire from the flanks.

Winds may cause fires to jump prepared fire control lines or natural barriers. Winds can drive a crown fire through tree tops when normally a lack of understory heat would prevent a crown fire from developing.

Large fires make their own local weather, especially with respect to air movements. Large convection updrafts cause air currents along the ground to move toward the fire and sometimes cause downdrafts of importance reaching out beyond the fire perimeter. Smoke clouds may shade the sun and alter the temporary radiation of solar heat toward and away from the earth, resulting in changed winds and fire behavior.

Over broad areas such as plains or long, wide valleys, the prevailing direction of the wind can be predicted quite easily. But in irregular topography, local wind courses may be quite different from the major prevailing conditions and also more changeable from time to time. Irregular topographic objects and vegetation act as a friction source on ground wind movements.

Winds change direction and intensity throughout the day and night. The particular condition in each locality will depend on the temperature changes in and around local topography. Large bodies of water, such as the ocean and lakes, usually cause winds to blow inland (onshore wind) as the sun warms the land area about mid-day. The wind blows seaward (offshore wind) at night when the land cools more rapidly than the water area. Isolated mountains draw air upward as in a chimney when the mountain slopes warm under the sunshine. The local effects of topography on wind are as varied as the shapes of the topographic features. The directions and velocities of the wind, the time of day, the aspect (exposure of the slope) with respect to the moving sun, and many other influencing factors control the way surface winds blow. The gradient (general) winds blowing above the surface are the predominant element much of the time. But whenever these winds weaken in the presence of strong daytime heating and nighttime cooling, convective winds of local origin become important features of weather in areas of broken topography.

The formation of cumulus clouds directly over peaks or ridges can have a marked influence on wind velocities and direction. As the clouds grow, strong indrafts are created that can increase upslope winds on the higher land surfaces. When a thunderstorm cloud (cell) is in its most active form (mature stage), large volumes of cold air may cascade to the ground as a strong downdraft. Although they usually last only a few minutes, these gusty winds can strike suddenly and violently with speeds up to 50 miles per hour and higher. Meteorologists refer to this type of downdraft as a microburst.

The passage of a cold front will invariably affect wind velocity and, more often than not, cause a shift in wind direction. Cold fronts will often give visible evidence of their presence in the form of high clouds. As these fronts pass, there usually will be a marked increase in wind velocity, followed by an abrupt clockwise shift in wind direction of 45 to 180 degrees.

The one general statement that can be made about expected normal wind movement in the mountains is that upslope winds will occur as the result of surface heating in the daytime and downslope winds will occur as the result of surface cooling at night.

Orientation of topography is an important factor governing strength and timing of wind flow. Upflow begins first on the east-facing slopes as the sun rises and slopes heat. Other areas are affected gradually, soon after the sun strikes their slopes. The intensity of upslope wind increases as daytime heating continues. South and southwest slopes heat the most and therefore have the strongest upslope winds. Often velocities are considerably greater than those on opposite north slopes. Morning upslope winds flow straight up slopes and minor draws. The increased velocity of canyon winds later in the day turns the direction of upslope winds diagonally up-canyon. Therefore, first expect upslope winds with initial morning heating, followed by up-canyon winds with maximum afternoon warming.

The change from upslope to downslope wind will usually begin on those areas first shaded from the sun. First, the upslope wind will diminish gradually; there will be period of calm and then a gentle downslope movement will begin. A large drainage can easily have varying degrees of this transition in process at the same time, depending on exposure or decreasing exposure to the heating rays of the sun. When all areas are in the shadows, the downward movement of air strengthens until winds are moving in a 180-degree change of direction from daytime flows.

Strong up-canyon or upslope winds can be quite turbulent and will form large eddies at bends and tributary junctions. Fires burning in these locations will behave very erratically and may spread alternately one way and then another, but generally will move upslope and up-canyon.

Daytime heating often produces rising convective winds that are capable of holding gradient winds aloft. In contrast, strong gradient winds can completely obliterate local wind patterns. The gradient wind effect will vary with the stability of the lower atmosphere. Stable layers, of which inversions are an extreme type, tend to "insulate" the local wind patterns from the gradient wind, thus minimizing its effect. When the lower atmosphere becomes less stable, there is opportunity for more interchange between the gradient level and the surface layer and the gradient wind effects are greater.

A gradient wind blowing toward the sea will reduce the sea breeze and, if strong enough, may block the sea breeze entirely.

Along the coastal ranges of the West Coast mountains, marine air intrusion complicates the fire officer's ability to forecast wind movement. All of the preceding discussion of convective winds would lead one to believe that downslope winds in the heat of summer day are either nonexistent or rare. Such is not the case. They do occur regularly and frequently. Marine air moving inland over the coastal mountains can often spill into **east**-facing canyons or draws and flow beneath the locally created warmer upslope winds. The heavier marine air will flow first through saddles and over low points and follow drainages and slopes closely, thus reversing ground wind direction from upslope to downslope. The change in direction can occur rather quickly. Cases have been recorded where the reversal took place within a few minutes, with the downslope wind velocity considerably greater than the preceding upslope wind. Obviously, this sudden shift in wind direction can adversely affect fire behavior in the areas involved.

Wind of any kind has a marked influence on fire intensity and behavior. But foehn winds have the most devastating and adverse effect on fires.

Foehn winds are known as north winds in Northern California, mono winds in the Central Sierras, and as Santa Ana (also called Santana) winds in Southern California. In the Rockies they are called chinooks. Such winds are capable of reaching extremely high velocities—80 to 90 miles per hour—across ridge tops and peaks. Foehn winds blow from high atmospheric pressure and elevation to low atmospheric pressure and elevation. They are characterized by blowing downhill while hugging the land profile, being warm (at least warmer than they were at the same elevation on the windward side of the mountain), and becoming progressively more desiccating (drying) as they descend. They can blow unabated around the clock for several days.

A fire occurring under extreme foehn wind conditions can spread with such violence that control forces will be temporarily powerless to take control action, except in the rear and on the flanks. Spot fires can occur in dehydrated fuels a mile or more in advance of the main fire and become raging infernos on their own before being joined by the original fire front.

Such fires are capable of crossing both natural and manmade barriers not only through long distance spotting, but by direct contact with new fuels when winds literally flatten flame sheets horizontally. Flame lengths of more than 100 to 200 feet are not uncommon.

Wind direction generally is responsive to the direction from which the greater atmospheric pressure bears, as that dominant pressure is modified by local pressures and topographic wind channels. Wind speed is responsive entirely to the strength of the dominant force that causes a pressure to bear on an air mass from any single direction at any single instant. The rules are rather simple. Wind velocity is disturbed by vertical obstructions and will not return to its velocity previous to the obstruction for a distance of seven times the height of the obstruction. The result can be most complex, especially in the broken topography where so many wildland fires occur.

A knowledge of the change of local climate during the day and night is of vital importance to the fire officer. The long, quiet flank of the fire at dawn may suddenly become the fire's head when the usual afternoon wind shifts direction, and the fire officer may become humiliated. Ignorance then has become responsible for an unnecessary disaster. Wildland fire officers who know and use the "Ten Standard Firefighting Orders," as well as have a working knowledge of the "Eighteen Situations That Shout Watch Out!" will be better able to use information on current and expected weather conditions to advantage.

Wind not only affects fire behavior, but creates related safety problems for fire officers. Perhaps the most common is eye injury from wind-blown material. In addition, specialized equipment such as aircraft will find limited use in high winds. Air tankers and helicopters lose effectiveness when wind speeds reach 20 to 30 mph. Above 30 mph, air tankers will normally be grounded because of their ineffectiveness and for safety reasons.

Fuel moisture

We have considered water vapor in the air (measured as humidity) and the effect of temperature on fire behavior. Both relative humidity and temperature are important, but what really concerns the fire officer is the condition of the fuel that will feed the fire.

Whether that fuel will be available to burn depends on its moisture content. Moisture in the fuel will not burn; it must be converted to steam by heat and driven away before combustion can take place. Air moisture is absorbed into dry fuel or taken away from the fuel by dryer air during nature's eternal quest to reach equilibrium.

While many parts of the country are subject to considerable rainfall, it is almost a forgotten element in most fire behavior discussions. If rain is the fire officer's friend, absent during the dry season, it nevertheless provides quantities of moisture to soak into the fuels during the wet season. By delivering water to the soil reservoir, it sets the length of the growing season for vegetation, thus controlling the moisture content of living fuels, and, often, the severity of the fire season.

As the stored rain moisture is dissipated into the air through growing leaves, or by evaporation from logs and litter, cumulative fuel moisture loss can be measured. This moisture loss can easily be measured as a loss in weight of the fuel particles. Eventually, the lighter dry fuels will lose their stored winter moisture and then reflect only a change in moisture content as air humidity causes water vapor to move into and away from the body of the fuels.

Heavy fuel such as logs will give up and absorb their moisture slowly. Dry leaves and grass will respond quickly to the relative humidity of the air; their moisture level will vary from hour to hour and day to day. Green, living leaves naturally respond in accordance with the complex transpiration habits developed by each species.

The fuel that will not burn in a midnight or early morning backfire will probably be ready to roar when the decreasing air humidity of mid-morning or afternoon arrives.

TOPOGRAPHY

Of the three major factors influencing wildland fires—weather, topography, and fuel—topography is the most static, but quite often the most dramatic in terms of fire behavior. The word topography refers to the earth's surface in relation to the shape of all land forms and waterways. It is the elevation or relief. Simply, topography means the lay of the land.

Elevation

Elevation has an effect on fire behavior both in relation to local changes in elevation in relative terms, and by changes in elevation above sea level in general terms.

On a summer's day, going from a valley bottom of 1,500 feet above sea level to a mountain meadow of 5,000-foot elevation, points out some dramatic weather and fuel changes.

Generally, the temperature drops as elevation increases and the fuel type may change from grass to timber. Changes in elevation cause dramatic fuel changes, and as elevation increases, precipitation increases as well. The snow pack in the mountains also has a distinct influence on burning conditions and fuel types.

Elevation has a strong influence on the length of the fire season. The lower elevations have longer fire seasons than the higher ones. The higher elevations also have a strong influence on the movement of air between the valleys and the mountains.

The elevation at which a fire is burning in relation to the surrounding topography is important. Depending on the fire's location, it may be influenced by strong local effects under stable overall weather conditions. It is important for the fire officer to understand the topographic influences on local weather as it changes by day and night. Under settled, mid-summer atmospheric conditions, a daily interchange of air flow occurs between the mountain tops and the valley bottoms.

The heating of the air which is in contact with the ground during the day and cooling of the air during the night are responsible for this important air movement and, hence, fire movement process. During the day, the air in the canyon and valley bottoms becomes relatively warmer than the air at higher elevations. Warm air rises, causing up-canyon and upslope winds. The time of day that the upslope winds start is usually predictable. If the air warms quickly, the rapid upslope wind may cause eddies and general turbulence.

At night the situation is reversed. When the heating of the lower elevations by the sun stops, the rising air becomes heavier and no longer rises. The sun sets and the slope surfaces automatically start to cool. The air above the now-cool slopes takes on the temperature characteristics of the ground below it. Gravity then comes into play, and the heavier air from the relatively cooler elevations starts its downslope flow. Because the air is cool, the flow is in layers (laminar) and moves smoothly down the slope. As a result of this airflow interchange, temperatures in the valley bottoms normally become cooler than the surrounding ridges and slopes. These changes in air flow and temperature, caused by elevation, can be predicted by the fire officer. Obviously, for tactical and safety reasons, the placement of ground attack forces should be structured to take advantage of these changes. Due to these topographical and meteorological interplays, a basic rule of thumb should be restated: generally, winds blow upcanyon during the day and downcanyon at night.

Some species of vegetation need the amount of sun heating that develops on southern exposures, whereas others cannot survive in it. However, the requirements for moisture are probably more important than heat and sunlight in determining the type of plant species, growth rate, and size of each species. Higher temperatures and generally prevailing southwest winds remove the moisture more rapidly from the southern exposures both from evaporation from the soil and ground litter, and also from transpiration from the plants. The result is that the vegetation that adapts to these southern exposures is dryer, sparser, and more flammable than the vegetation that grows on the northern-facing slopes. Rainfall on both north and south slopes may even be equal, but the deeper soil on the north slope, coupled with less sunlight and heat, will produce a remarkably different micro or highly localized climate. This climate and soil difference will produce a heavier vegetative cover on northern slopes.

Because of the drier, sparser flash fuel types that grow on the southern exposures, the potential for fire ignition and rapid fire spread is greater than on the north slopes. Also, southern exposures are generally more prone to the occurrence of spot fires than northern exposures. Weather and fuel conditions combined with the interactions of people (people tend to be outdoors, e.g., camping in warmer weather) have caused a unique cyclical effect on the southern exposures.

Slope

The degree or steepness of a slope is quite a different factor influencing vegetation, fire behavior, and rate of fire spread, but as in most areas of firefighting, there is a strong interrelationship between slope and the other physical factors affecting fire behavior. Slope is basically the change in elevation divided by the corresponding change in horizontal distance and is expressed as a percentage. A 5 percent slope means a 5-foot rise in elevation for each 100 feet of horizontal distance. To calculate slope, simply divide the horizontal distance by the change in elevation and multiply the figure by 100 percent. For example, if the elevation rose 40 feet in a distance of 200 feet, dividing 40 by 200 and multiplying by 100 percent equals a slope of 20 percent. It is most important to remember that slope is expressed as a percentage and not in degrees of angle.

A 45-degree angle is a slope of 100 percent, because for each elevational foot increase, the horizontal distance increases by one foot.

It is a basic rule in wildland firefighting that if all things remain unchanged, a fire will burn faster uphill and more slowly downhill. For every 20 percent increase in slope, the given rate of spread of a fire will double. Yet why do relatively minor changes in slope have such a strong effect on the rate of spread? Changes in slope have a distinct effect on two methods of heat transfer: convection and radiation, and two of the important elements of combustion: heat and oxygen.

As a fire burns up a steep slope, the angle of the flame is closer to the fuel than it is during a fire burning on a lesser slope or level ground. The radiation of these flames on the increased slope removes the fuel moisture and preheats the unburned fuel.

The convective effects of heat transfer cause the hot air and gases to also rise, thus providing additional heat to the unburned fuel. The convective heat of a fire, as evidenced by the size and shape of the smoke column, also picks up and supports fire brands that, in turn, may fall ahead of the main fire and cause spot fires. These spot fires, like the main fire, require large amounts of oxygen. This oxygen is supplied from the area near the fire and also may be preheated; this too increases the rate of combustion. Because of indraft effect, spot fires and the main fire will tend to draw toward each other at an increased rate. Extreme examples of adverse fire behavior can take place under such conditions.

As previously stated, winds generally blow upslope during the day and downslope during the night. If downslope winds are strong enough, their effect may completely offset the factors governing the upslope spread of fire and may actually cause a fire to burn downhill at an accelerated rate. A knowledge of local winds and micro climates is of the upmost importance to the Incident Commander.

In areas of broken topography or high aerial fuels, a fire of low intensity may cross into an unburned drainage ditch or canyon and slowly burn downhill. As the fire burns downhill, its pattern is usually highly irregular. This irregular pattern is caused by the rolling of burning material downslope and a generally slower rate of spread. This happens quite often at night, and the fire leaves an unburned canopy of dried-out, preheated fuel. Under such conditions a dangerous reburn of the same area can take place. Strong safety precautions, including the clear identification of escape routes, must be taken to ensure firefighter safety.

Distinct topographical features

There are several distinct topographical features that have a strong effect on fire behavior and control methods.

WIDE CANYONS

The prevailing wind direction will not be affected by the general direction of the wide canyon's orientation. The wind will not be deflected by any sharp up- or downwind drafts. With distance, cross-canyon fallout of spot fires is not common, except in high winds. Aspect has a strong effect on fuel and fire behavior conditions.

NARROW CANYONS

Narrow canyons normally have more independent wind currents than wide canyons. The wind usually follows the direction of the canyon. Sharp breaks and forks in the canyon may cause strong eddies and turbulent drafts. Because of relative distance and stronger, more turbulent wind conditions in narrow canyons, spot fires are more common. Aspect has little effect on changes in fuel conditions in the bottom of narrow canyons.

STEEP SLOPES

The steeper the slope, the more likely it is that a fire will drive upward in a wedge shape, forming a narrow head. The rapid movement of the fire may cause strong indrafts on the flanks. The occurrence of spot fires in front of the main fire is likely.

RIDGES

Quite often, as a fire reaches a ridge top, it meets an opposing airflow from the other side of the ridge. Such a condition will slow the spread of the fire, but also may cause adverse fire behavior. The topography and opposing winds will cause eddies and turbulence.

CHIMNEYS

A chimney, as the name implies, depicts topographic features that form narrow draws and gulches that are actually minute box canyons. These chimneys draw the fire as does an actual chimney from a stove. Strong upcanyon winds are drawn into the topographic features of the chimney and confined to the shape of the chimney by its steep side slopes. Firefighters have been trapped at the head of chimneys with resulting loss of life, injuries, and damaged equipment.

Even a shallow chimney of 5 feet deep and less than 100 feet long can cause an increase in the rate of spread and intensity of the fire.

PHYSICAL BARRIERS

Barriers can have a significant influence on the spread of wildfires. Barriers, either natural or manmade, often become aids that help control portions of the fire. Natural barriers include rock slides and other barren areas, lakes, rivers, dry stream and river beds, and the ocean. Areas that contain wet vegetation, such as some agricultural zones and riverbed vegetation, also may slow or stop the spread of a fire. In addition, certain types of fuel may not burn at different times of the year, such as grassland in winter or spring.

Topography has a strong influence both on how a fire burns and on the type of fire attack methods and equipment that are used in wildland firefighting.

Artificial barriers are manmade changes in topography, such as major highways and other road systems, fire breaks, fuel breaks, power line clearances, reservoirs, housing developments and land clearing. Changes of natural vegetation to agricultural use may help or hinder the control of a fire. Each of these barriers may affect the spread of the fire directly, through the absence of fuels, or indirectly, through the modification of relative humidity, local winds, and other fire weather conditions.

FUEL

Fuel is the third major element that affects fire behavior. Fuel is one of the three sides of the fire triangle and is a necessary element for combustion to take place. Fuel is any substance that will ignite and burn. Most fuels are nothing more than different species of vegetation. There are many different biological classifications of such vegetative types. Here, however, we will only generally identify and classify fuels as they relate to wildland firefighting. The fuel types will be discussed in terms of their flammability and burning characteristics.

In wildland firefighting, fuels are not limited strictly to either living or dead vegetative types. In urbanized areas contiguous to or surrounded by wildland fuels, human structural improvements provide fuel for wildland fires, affecting not only firefighting tactics but actual fire behavior.

For purposes of identification, wildland fuels are grouped with respect to whether they are living or dead, their position on the ground or in the air, their size, the relative rate at which they burn, and their compactness, continuity, volume, and moisture content.

One of the first categorizations of fuels must be in terms of whether the fuel is alive or dead. Obviously, dead fuels ignite and burn much more easily, although living fuels are a definite part of the fuel loading after combustion occurs. Dead fuels include dry grass, material that has fallen from the vegetation and remains suspended on live branches, or that rests on the ground, and limbs that have died and remain affixed to the vegetation skeleton structure. Live fuels are still a part of the growing plant and contain some amount of sap or moisture. With the exception of annual grass, which dies out each year, most wildland fuels enjoy a spring growing period when the moisture content often reaches 250 percent of normal. With the advent of the dry season, fuels begin to lose live fuel moisture and reach a dormancy period when the moisture content may bottom out at 50 percent. This concept directly affects fuel quantity and availability.

Fuel quantity and availability

Measurements of fuel quantity often are expressed in tons per acre and refer to the combustible fuel available. Quantities can range from 1 ton per acre for some grass types, to 200 or more tons per acre for heavy slash (forest tree refuse on the ground, often the result of logging) areas. In actual fire situations estimations are usually made by trained observers in order to establish guidelines for the difficulty of control. From time to time actual samples are measured to verify casual observations.

In considerations of fuels in relation to suppression activities, fuels are divided into three main categories: light, medium, and heavy. This broad classification is generally sufficient for wildland firefighting operations. Light fuel usually consists of grass and mixed light brush, usually up to two to three feet in height. Medium fuel consists of brush six feet in height or lower that grows in fairly thick stands. Heavy fuel refers to thick brush taller than six feet, timber slash, and standing conifer and hardwood trees.

The fuel that is actually burning determines the fuel quantity designation to use. A pine needle or grass fire of low intensity, burning on a forest floor, would be considered a fire in light fuel even though it is burning in a timber-covered area. It is generally better to use relative terms rather than numerical designations when dealing with fuel quantities.

Fuel availability refers to the proportion of fuel, usually finer fuel, that will burn in a wildland fire. Fuel availability varies with the time of year. A dry grass fuel that is available to burn in the summer may well be green and unavailable to burn in the winter. In a grass fire it is quite easy to determine fuel availability, since most of the available fuel burns during a fire. In brush and forest fuel types, fuel availability varies widely with fuel moisture conditions and with the thickness of the fuel itself. Fuel availability also varies with the duration and intensity of the fire. Therefore, fuel availability is determined by the time of year and the amount and type of fuel consumed under a specific set of burning conditions.

Ground fuels

Generally ground fuels, whether living or dead, are fuels that are in the ground, e.g., roots and buried logs on the ground as in the case of leaves, twigs and pine needles, or in close proximity to the ground, such as grass and brush.

However, the distinction between ground fuels and aerial fuels is probably more difficult to define because some of the most prominent fuels fit both classifications. Intermediate fuels are given the broad name of brush or chaparral. Brush is a generalized fuel term, whereas chaparral refers to a dry Mediterranean climate type of vegetation. Mature plant species of the brush type range in height from only a few inches to more than 20 feet above the ground. The differences depend on the individual species and growing site. The major value in any definition of fuels is the creation of a general reference term for fuel types that have similar burning tendencies. The compactness of fuel particles and their size regulate the transfer of heat and the availability of oxygen to the fuel itself. These two factors allow for great differences in the burning characteristics of various brush-type fuels.

When low aerial fuels or the ground fuels are such that they often ignite easily, burn rapidly, and have relatively complete combustion, they are called flash fuels. Among the different vegetative types listed as ground fuels are grass, sage, and other perennials. Any low-brush growth that does not allow for the easy movement of air through the foliage would be considered a ground fuel, including small trees growing as reproduction (plantation) timber.

Nonliving ground fuels include downed logs, heavy limbs, and smaller twigs, leaves, needles, bark, duff, and cones. Timber slash is a prime example of a ground fuel. In some areas this slash can be 4 to 8 feet deep and fuel weight can exceed 200 tons per acre. Fires in slash pose unique and very difficult suppression problems.

Some types of ground fuels pose other problems because of their ease of ignition. Punky logs (old, dead, and decaying logs) or any type of pulverized wood material allow for quick ignition when exposed to sufficient radiant heat, sparks, or firebrands. Large logs, particularly if their surface is not punky or splintered, may resist ignition, and, once burning, may not aid the fire's spread. However, if a group of logs at a lumber mill site or at a lumber mill log deck catch fire, the close proximity of the burning logs to each other can cause a tremendous heat buildup and spread fire through radiation, convection, and by spot fires caused from firebrands.

Large limbs burn more easily when dead needles are attached. Pine slash poses this hazard for several years while fir limbs usually drop their needles after the first year.

Several types of needles and leaves become ready firebrands when they are lifted into the fire's convection column. Eucalyptus, because of the oil content in the bark and leaves, and the aerodynamics of each, can cause a major fire-spotting problem. In parts of Australia where burning and fuel conditions resemble those in the United States, eucalyptus firebrands have caused spotting for a distance of several miles ahead of the main fire.

In its cured state, grass is a fast-burning ground fuel. Its density and thickness allow a maximum amount of oxygen to be available for flame production. In other than early-season fires, when certain grasses still maintain some moisture, combustion is usually complete. Grass fires are relatively easy to suppress and, once out, provide a safe area for firefighters to retreat if necessary. Grass is also an easy fuel in which to construct a fire line and a good fuel to use in backfiring operations. Never overlook that a fast-moving grass fire can be extremely dangerous to firefighter safety. A change in wind can cause a rapid change in the fire's direction. Firefighters have been killed and injured while fighting grass fires because they underestimated the potential of this light flashy fuel.

Unlike grass, where changes in seasonal rainfall may affect fuel quantity quite dramatically, the quantity of fine fuels in many mature brush fields and forest-covered areas remains relatively stable. This is true unless temporarily reduced by fire, or increased by such factors as a severe snow (down and dead fuel), insects, windstorms, drought, or logging operations (slash).

The rate at which leaves, bark, twigs, and other fine fuel material are deposited on the ground varies according to the type and density of the parent fuel. The rate of decomposition depends on several variables, most importantly fungi and microfauna. The presence of these two elements depends on climate and the environment of the litter bed itself. A litter bed in the process of breaking down and decomposing is referred to as duff. Fires in duff, although not spectacular, can cause many fire control problems if fire lines are not properly constructed and the fire is not suppressed completely.

A fire in duff and peat can creep along for long periods of time and escape established control lines. Therefore, duff/peat fires must be suppressed completely to prevent "rekindles."

Ground litter is often used by pack rats to form nests. These nests are usually about three feet high and three to six feet in diameter. They are filled with thousands of twigs and small branches and are tinder dry. Spot fires can easily ignite in the nests, and once on fire, are difficult to extinguish and mop up.

Sawdust is a ground fuel that produces a slow-burning, smoldering type of fire with little or no active flame production. Sawdust fires are very difficult to extinguish and very seldom does the extensive use of water suppress this type of fire. The material must be separated and allowed to burn out or be extinguished by extensive handwork and mopup operations. Some sawdust piles have been known to burn for months or longer. The safety hazard in sawdust fire operations is that the fire will burn underneath the surface and cause burned-out areas that are not visible. These burned-out areas produce large caverns and sinkholes that contain hot material; this poses a distinct safety hazard for firefighters.

Aerial fuels

Classifying aerial fuels is considerably less complex than ground fuels. Aerial fuels consist of snags, tree crowns, branches, and the higher-brush canopies. Aerial fuels are physically separated from the ground and from each other. Their placement allows air to reach them freely and circulate around the available fuel.

Living and dead leaves and needles are considered aerial fuels while located above the ground, as are bark, lichens, moss, and vines such as poison oak. The needles of most evergreens and the leaves of some hardwoods are highly flammable because of the availability of air, exposure to higher-level winds, and high oil or sap content.

Dead tree limbs near the ground or in the proximity of hot, burning ground fuels can provide a ladder (called ladder fuels) for a fire to reach the aerial fuel or crowns of certain types of trees. Once the fire is established in the crowns of a few trees, radiation and convection can sustain a crown fire.

Snags are dead, standing trees that cause a multitude of problems for the fire officer. Snags are caused by the natural death of a tree from drought, disease, insets, animals, and, quite often, previous fires. Burning embers can ignite a snag quickly, and once a snag is burning, it can spread fire for some distance. Extinguishing a fire in a snag is difficult, because in most cases the snag must be cut down before the fire can be extinguished. Obviously, felling burning and weakened snags can pose serious safety problems for suppression personnel.

High brush is classified as an aerial fuel when it is distinctly separated from ground fuels. Most brush 10 feet or taller falls into this classification.

Obviously there are several fuel types that fall into both classifications or under certain conditions will be classified as a ground fuel, and under more lush growing conditions be considered an aerial fuel. What is important is to learn the burning characteristics of both ground and aerial fuels under various weather patterns and topographic features.

Structural fuels

Many profound textbooks and training manuals have been written on the burning characteristics and behavior of structural fires. This chapter will deal only with structural fuels as they directly relate to wildland fires. Structural development and encroachment into previously underdeveloped wildland areas are taking place at an ever increasing rate. Wildland fire officers must learn how to protect structures from wildland fires, how to extinguish structure fires once they ignite, and how structural fire fuels interrelate with a wildland fire. Every fire department should accept that its mission includes protecting both structural and wildland fire environments.

Structural fuels are a high-volume fuel and produce large amounts of radiant and convective heat. Once a structure becomes involved, it can spread quickly to other nearby structures and uninvolved wildland fuels. The heat generated in a structural fire tends to remove the moisture from fuels for some distance. Because an involved structure will burn for some time, it provides a long-term source of ignition for other fuels.

The biggest problem with structures is their roof construction. Many homes, cabins, and resorts in wildland areas have roofs constructed of wood or shake shingles. These roofs provide a ready place for spot fires to start and, once ignited, are difficult to extinguish.

Burning shingles are uplifted rapidly into the convection column and can travel great distances before they land on the ground to start new spot fires. During the Paint Fire (Santa Barbara, California, June 1990), which destroyed 450 homes, much of the fire's rapid spread (3.5 miles forward spread distance in 81 minutes) was attributed to shake shingle roofs. Shingles can easily cause spot fires across fire lines, endangering firefighters.

Fuel arrangement

The two major factors that affect fuel arrangement are the continuity of the fuel and its density. These two factors determine the actual burning conditions under other given circumstances.

Continuity refers to the distribution of fuel particles with respect to each other and their relative distances that may or may not allow the transfer of heat from one fuel particle to another. The rate of a fire's spread and the total heat generated over any area are dependent on the continuity of the fuel. Areas that have some distance between fuel particles, such as in deserts or high-alpine areas, are termed patchy fuel areas. Rocks, plowed land, wet drainages, green herbs, and other noncombustible objects also produce areas of patchy fuel. Generally, areas of patchy fuel favor firefighting efforts. However, some areas of patchy fuel can cause problems for the fire officer; sparse fuel may cause backfiring operations to be difficult or totally ineffective. Rocky areas are difficult areas in which to operate mechanized equipment and the construction of fire lines in such areas is slow and tedious.

Areas of uniform fuel consist of fuel stands that evenly and continuously cover a sizable location. This uniformity relates to the continuity of the fuel rather than to the pureness of the stand of a specific species. If other fire behavior variables remain constant, it is fairly easy to determine rates of spread in a uniform fuel cover.

Compactness refers to the proximity of fuel particles to one another with respect to the unobstructed flow of air around the particles. Compactness is an opposite characteristic from continuity in that close continuity produces faster and greater heat spread. Compactness could mean less heat generation and the discouragement of combustion because of lack of sufficient oxygen to sustain an active combustion process.

A grain field fire is a good example of a fire in fuel of uniform continuity. Usually these fires burn hot and produce a relatively rapid rate of spread. In contrast, a fire burning in leaf mold, a fuel of great compactness, tends to burn with little flame production and produces a relatively slow rate of spread.

Both the continuity and compactness of fuels vary from high to low combustion rates as local weather conditions take effect. For instance, an area may be so thinly covered with scattered fuel that, normally, its poor continuity (patchy fuel) will reduce both the chances of a fire starting and the possible spread of a fire once it starts. Desert brush growing in a mountain rain shadow would be a good example of such a fuel, yet a strong, dry foehn wind could produce a hot-burning fire that would increase the rate of combustion and tend to bridge the gaps in the available fuel. The expanding fire would produce more intense flame production and, at the same time, the strong wind would be pushing the convective heat through the available sparse desert fuel in a leeward direction.

Suspended pine needles on timber slash may be loose enough that fire would not move along the clumps on a high-humidity day, but the same fuel is adequately compacted to carry fire with a slight breeze on a dry day. Certain tree needles on the ground will nearly always be less combustible than pine needles or oak leaves at the same place and time. This is because nonpine needles rest together so compactly that not enough oxygen is available for rapid combustion.

Fuel moisture

Fuel moisture is a most important factor in determining the burning capability of different wildland fuels. It is the measured amount of moisture available in various fuels. It is measured by weighing a sample fuel stick with the fuel moisture expressed as a percentage. Fuel moisture readings of below 10 percent indicate that available vegetation is in a combustible state. Remember, a kiln-dried 2'' x 4'' board has a fuel moisture of 12 to 14 percent. During foehn wind conditions, fuel moisture readings have been recorded as low as 2.5 percent. When fuel moisture is low, fires start easily because the ignition source has very little moisture to evaporate from the fuel. The applied heat quickly causes flammable gases to vaporize and the fuel to ignite. When fuel moisture is high, many ignition sources such as sparks, smoking materials such as tobacco, exhaust, carbon, etc., may cool down before the water vapor is removed from the fuel and flame-producing gas starts to vaporize. Generally, as fuel moisture increases, rate of spread decreases and as fuel moisture decreases, rate of spread increases. However, if fuel moisture is already low, a further reduction will cause the rate of spread to increase five to six times.

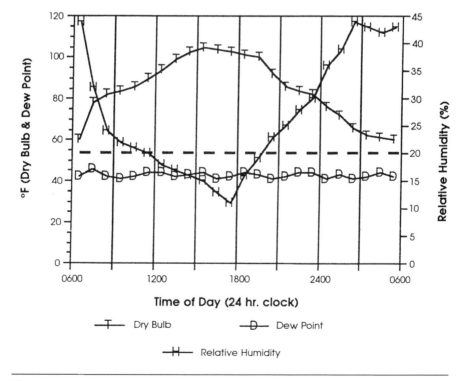

Figure 21-1.

Fuel moisture is controlled by two major factors: weather and the curing stage. Weather considerations that influence fuel moisture are temperature, relative humidity, wind speed, and precipitation. The curing stage factors that affect fuel moisture are the type of vegetation, time of year or season, and days since new growth. These factors, combined with seasonal weather, determine if the fuel is green, curing, or cured.

Fuel temperature

Fuel temperatures influence both the chance of a fire starting and the rate of spread after it starts. Air temperature and direct sunlight are responsible for corresponding fuel temperatures. As fuel temperature rises, less heat is needed from an ignition source to start a fire. Most wildland fuels will ignite in a temperature range of from 400° to 700° F. During the night the temperature of a fuel might drop to 50° or 60° F; this same fuel could rise to a temperature of some 150° F on a hot day. Most of us have experienced this higher-than-air temperature factor; it happens when we touch a steering wheel after a vehicle has been parked in the sun for some length of time.

The rate of spread will increase at a greater rate than a proportioned increase in the fuel temperature. For instance, if a fuel temperature of 61° F causes a rate of spread factor of 1, a rise in fuel temperature to 100° F will result in a spread factor of 2, or twice as fast if all other variables remain constant. The effect of temperature is quite evident when we realize that most wildland fires start and spread the fastest during the heat of the day, usually from 10:00 a.m. to 4:00 p.m.

Since it is impractical to measure fuel temperatures while fighting a fire, keep these general guidelines in mind:

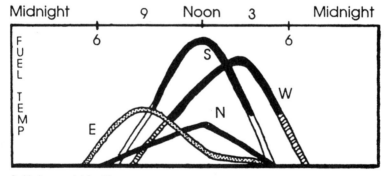

1. Hot or cold fuel?
2. Where are we on the flammability curve?
3. Is fire behavior getting more or less extreme?
4. Set tactics to match 1, 2, and 3 above.

Courtesy of Doug Campbell, Ojui, Ca.

Figure 21-2.

- The rate of spread factor is doubled long before the fuel temperature is doubled.
- Fine fuels are heated more quickly and easily by air temperature and direct sunlight than by heavy and compacted fuels.
- During the hottest part of the day, all fuels on the south-and west-facing exposures will have higher fuel temperatures than those on the north- and east-facing slopes.
- Heavy fuels will usually have a lower fuel temperature than the surrounding fine fuels in the daytime, and the reverse is true at night.
- When fuels are exposed to direct sunlight, ground fuels will usually have a higher temperature than aerial fuels.

The behavior of a wildland fire will vary as it consumes different types and amounts of fuel under varying weather and topographic conditions. The strategy and tactics used to control a wildland fire must be influenced by an understanding of how a fire will react to all fuel types and the other major factors affecting wildland fire behavior.

FIRE BEHAVIOR

General fire behavior

Fuel, topography, and weather are found to have varying influences on fire behavior. Any one of these may be dominant in influencing what any individual fire will do, but it usually is the combined effect of all three that dictates the fire's behavior. The particular topography does not change, of course, but wind movements are influenced by orientation of topography and, hence, the direction that fires will burn. The actual shape of topography will similarly have its effect. For instance, a saddle or low point in a ridge will act as a funnel, tending to draw a fire in its direction.

Severe funneling action often occurs on steeper slopes, as rising air currents are forced upward through narrow, chimney-like ravines or gullies. Even with very sparse vegetative cover, fire is capable of moving long distances in an extremely short time. Fatalities have occurred within chimneys when the superheated air alone, rising from fire downslope, actually seared the lungs and depleted the oxygen supplies of firefighters. It has long been established that it is dangerous to work above wildland fires. This is no different than working on a floor directly above the fire location. The danger factors must be multiplied many times when personnel are at the top of, or within, chimney-like terrain.

Fires will burn very rapidly upslope, but in the absence of other strong influences, will usually burn slowly downslope. Fires burning in the upper portions of steep slopes or backing downhill often spread themselves rather quickly by means of rolling pieces of flaming fuel. Pine cones are noted for this because of their rounded shape. Pine cones that are lying on the ground are loosened as they burn and will then roll downslope into unburned fuel.

Fires spreading upslope or with the wind assume a wedge-like shape. The point of the wedge is the fire head where the most rapid spread occurs. The flanks of the fire will gradually widen with the passage of time. That portion of both flanks immediately behind the head will unquestionably be influenced by an indraft caused by the convection column at the head. A shift in wind will, of course, cause a greater movement of the former leeward flank and probably change the direction of the head.

Should the head of this theoretical fire be stopped suddenly and no action occurs on the remainder of the fire, the rate of spread of the flanks will increase. If the wind is strong, or the slope is steep, the original forward impetus of the fire remains unchanged. It is probable that the fire will now progress with two new heads (on either side of the old) until they join, or until one becomes dominant.

Depending on fuel type and condition, spot fires can occur ahead of both small and large fires. Burning embers are carried with the wind in the convective updrafts with the smoke and are dropped in unburned fuel in advance of the main fire. Embers will nearly always come from the underside of the heaviest smoke concentration. Flying embers also can originate from burning snags or trees with punky pockets on fire, and again the spots will occur downwind. The rapid spread of a fire up a steep slope to a ridge crest often will result in spot fires on the opposite downslope side or even on the upslope of the next ridge in advance. Spotting also can be expected downwind when individual trees "torch out" or when large piles of dead material such as slash are burning at peak intensities.

A small fire is not necessarily safer for firefighters to work with than a larger fire. Small grass fires have overrun many engine companies and personnel have sustained serious burns. Regardless of the size of the fire, fatalities are most likely to occur during docile periods of fire behavior and under what appear to be innocent overall conditions.

When the relative humidity drops below about 30 percent, the situation is favorable for wildfires. For every 20-degree increase in temperature, the relative humidity is reduced by one-half. As the humidity drops, the chances become greater for a smaller fire to grow unless an adequate suppression force is available.

Spotting

One of the characteristics of a small fire that is frequently difficult to handle is spotting. Spotting is an important eventuality on many wildland fires.

Spotting occurs when wind and convection columns broadcast hot "fire-brands" into the unburned (green) fuel ahead of the main fire. The use of look-outs can sometimes expedite quick attacks on spot fires, although, in many instances, the embers evade discovery until a later time, when sufficient smoke begins rising above the foliage canopy. Patrolling officers often are the first to detect hot material outside the line.

Although spotting is often related to such firebrands as wood shakes and ash from burning brush and timber, there are other causes as well. Small animals, such as rabbits, have been observed carrying fire into unburned fuel. Although burning grass seems often to be consumed by fire, spots can and do occur in the green well ahead of the main fire, such as across several lanes of a freeway. Spotting occurs more easily across narrow ravines than wider ones, and given favorable conditions, spots quickly spread to become fire problems themselves.

Small fires

Work should begin on the flank which has the greatest potential, keeping in mind the necessity of protecting important exposures and holding the fire to a small size. Many small fires, and resulting larger ones, originate along roadways from a number of causes. The roadway serves as an excellent anchor point from which to begin work along the chosen flank.

Smaller fires in brush may dictate the use of a "hot-spotting" team, whose job it will be to pass up dormant or slower burning portions of line in order to knock down portions with greater activity. Hot spotting can be carried out by either an engine company or a fire crew as a delaying tactic until additional forces arrive. Hot spotting, if it is successful (and it has been on thousands of smaller fires), can save the day in terms of avoiding a long duration battle with an extended or major fire. This tactic also can be used on large fires.

Smaller fires can be quite damaging to improvements such as fences, out-buildings, and homes because a small fire burns, generally untouched, from the time of its origin until the first-in company arrives. Thus, even a small, one-acre grass fire will have had sufficient time to move into an area of improvements and, lacking attack by locals, do considerable damage. Of course, on many such fires near residential areas, the locals can and do knock down many potentially dangerous fires. Because many fires start near or in populated areas, first-in companies can expect traffic congestion, dense smoke, confusion, and fire ingress problems.

Small, hot, running fires can be knocked down successfully by an alert, well-trained company if access to the fire is known and available. When fence lines and other security measures are present, access can be very restrictive to firefighting efforts.

Small does not mean easy when it comes to firefighting. Because of the intense aggressiveness needed to hold such a fire to a small size, most any nozzle person will tell you that it was hard, very hot work along the fire line and that although the action may have been short-lived, it was nip-and-tuck for a period of time.

Large fires

Historically, statistics have shown that 95 percent of reported wildland fires have been contained within the first burning period. The other five percent could have been reduced by more presuppression efforts, more effort at the proper place, or by less human carelessness at the improper time. Yet many of the large fires have resulted from adverse conditions of weather or topography.

As a wildland fire approaches and enters a populated area, such as a subdivision, fire officers must turn their attention to saving homes and other improvements. The delegation of wildland fire control efforts to the protection of specialized exposures often outdistances the capabilities of available personnel and equipment. Engine companies, fire crews, bulldozers or tractor plows, and even retardant-dropping aircraft, must concern themselves not with a single wildland fire strategy situation, but, rather, a large number of specialized and individualized strategy situations. If personnel reinforcements are inadequate, wildland fire control may be hindered greatly. Therefore, it is critical that initial attack Incident Commanders order reinforcements early to ensure an integrated attack on both the wildland and structural problems.

If weather is to blame for a small fire's growth, then the odds against the fire officer increase as the weather becomes more adverse. It has been stated that a doubled wind speed may quadruple the fire spread when wind is 10 mph and higher. Reducing fuel moisture by half (when it is already low) may cause fire spread to be not twice but five or six times as fast.

Added to whatever adversity may exist because of the shape of topography or the weather, large fires have unique characteristics that mean trouble for the fire officer. They have the tendency to crown and spot ahead because of the buildup of convection currents. Also the effect of upslope radiation is increased as the intensity of the fire increases.

On the other hand, unless unusually heavy and dry winds from one general direction overwhelm the effect of local broken topography, a large fire can be expected to subside considerably when it reaches a ridge top. This will result from the heavy indraft demanded by the large fire running uphill.

The development of strong convection columns over large fires, with smoke rising tens of thousands of feet into the air, is one of the most striking differences between small and large fires. The essential cause of this difference is, quite naturally, found in the difference in the concentrated heat mass.

Consider the several steps of cause and effect with respect to the single matter of spot fires caused by firebrands that originate from the main fire. If the air mass over the fire is stable, that air will resist the development of a strong convection updraft in the form of a heavy smoke column.

Consequently, the fire will burn less intensely than it would under a strong updraft. It does not mean that there will be no spot fires, but that the spot fires that develop under stable air are much more likely to be fewer in number and start less downwind from the fire's head. Unstable air is more conducive to the development of a strong convection column and a more intense fire. The stronger updraft naturally has more carrying capacity for burning embers. But it should be noted that the longer time period in the stronger updraft will allow many of the potential firebrands to lose most of their heat, and, when they reach their height and fall out of the smoke column, they probably are entering an atmosphere cooler than that at the ground level.

Should a force of wind aloft be brought to bear on each of the fire conditions, tilted convection columns will result. The column that occurs in unstable air will be stronger and will carry firebrands higher and higher. On the other hand, the less intense updraft may drop firebrands sooner, closer, and hotter, and in a more concentrated pattern in front of the advancing fire.

Long-distance spotting will more than likely occur on the right flank of an advancing fire because of the tendency of the smoke column under the influence of wind to rotate in a clockwise direction with increased height.

A convection column is not a "chimney" in the sense that all the air must flow into the bottom of the convection coil. Most combustion takes place near the ground where the oxygen requirements are most intense. Nevertheless, some combustion of gases occurs in the rising heat columns. To supply needed oxygen, and undoubtedly because it is entrapped in the rolling updraft, outside air is gathered into and along the vertical exterior wall of the rising convection column.

Normally, a general indraft into the convection column can be expected from all sides. If there is a prevailing wind, wind speeds on the leeward (advancing) side of the column will usually be less than on the windward side of the flanks. But, occasionally, pronounced outdrafts (winds moving away from the column at a greater velocity than the free air movement) have been observed on the leeward side. No guidelines can be given as to their occurrence since there appears to be no correlation to fire size or intensity, or with weather conditions. Several instances have been observed where winds in advance of the fire were double or even quadruple the velocity of winds along the flanks or rear. In any event, fire control personnel should be alert to the occurrence of this phenomenon. The possibility that the wind velocity could increase two- to fourfold in advance of the fire front could drastically change fire suppression strategy.

Another important difference between small and large fires is the relative unimportance of size, distribution, and arrangement of fuel particles in favor of total fuel volume in the high-intensity fires. Under extreme conditions, larger-size fuels will burn faster and hotter, producing temperatures up to 2,650° F. This intense heat results in the rapid consumption of large areas with extreme violence and nearly total consumption of all combustible material.

Area ignition

The logs in the cold fireplace were giving out a desultory smudge when a merry blaze was desired. A crumpled newspaper was then ignited and pushed toward the throat of the fireplace. Suddenly the gaseous smudge around the logs burst into flame and the logs began to crackle with combustion.

What caused the outburst of flame in the fireplace? Two vital sides of the fire triangle had been strengthened where the fuel was situated although the action that caused it occurred elsewhere. No doubt the most important action was the creation of a convective updraft in the chimney, thus pulling in more oxygen for the fuel. More specifically, a sharp indraft against the flank of the fuel facing the open room was created. Second, heat radiation from the burning newspaper raised the temperature of the flammable gas around the smoldering fuel to the extent that it was ready to ignite in the richer air brought in by the convective updraft.

This principle of augmented ignition and combustion from an adjacent source of heat has long been appreciated by experienced fire officers. However, its full significance from the standpoint of potential destruction seems generally to have been overlooked from a scientific perspective, that is, until the occurrence of "fire storms" in large cities created by wartime bombing.

The phenomenon of increased intensity of conflagration as a result of multiple adjacent points of combustion is termed area ignition. The same boost produced by the burning newspaper in the fireplace can be compounded outward in geometric proportion as the individual sources of fire act on one another in an open area.

A large fire tends to beget a larger fire principally because adverse conditions around a fire act to make bad things become even worse. Part of the subsequent trouble may be due to the effect of area ignition as it occurs in a natural manner during the progress of the wildfire. However, this phenomenon is much more likely to occur outside than within the perimeter of a large fire. This would happen when a number of spot fires outside the fire area flare up in unison in fuel that is highly combustible. This, of course, constitutes an added hazard for the fire officer.

Aside from spot fires and concentrated lightning strikes, a great quantity of the vegetation burned as a result of the area ignition process is by human design. The arsonist has made use of it as well as the backfiring specialist and the cattle rancher who used controlled fire to eliminate unwanted vegetation.

When a number of fires are ignited geographically so that the heat of each one affects the other, the following situation develops. Radiant heat prepares large amounts of unburned vegetation for easy ignition at approximately the same time. If we could look down on such a condition of multiple fires at an early stage we might observe perhaps one-tenth of the area in flames. This would leave some nine times the flaming area in a state rapidly approaching a readiness for ignition. While this is developing, the individual convection currents are thrusting hot air upward. Each creates indrafts at its base.

Soon the convection updrafts begin to mingle and multiply the dimensions of the invisible "chimney." A constantly and dynamically increasing supply of air generates numerous fires into one massive flame front. A blowup has been created. Whether it has been created intentionally or otherwise, the blowup can be a fire of such intensity that it is difficult to hold it within prescribed lines.

It is obvious that this condition should not normally be expected from a fire moving outward from a central source, actually flaming for the most part at the perimeter and leaving behind only the ashes of the fuel it has consumed. If quantities of fuel are bypassed, either unburned or smoldering, the powerful forces of multiple ignition may suddenly be unleashed at one critical moment when heat, air, and the crucial spark of ignition are ready.

Area influence

The effects of fire burning large areas in a relatively short period of time can extend for a considerable distance from the actual flames. This may influence fire behavior in other areas, sometimes with adverse effects. It, therefore, is quite important for fire officers to be aware of rapid fire occurrence on any part of the fire and be alert for possible dynamic changes resulting in their own areas.

Dynamic fire spread can adversely affect "firing out" operations. Particular care should be taken when firing is conducted down long ridges where major bends in the control line are unavoidable.

Ideally, firing operations are conducted from the top of a ridge moving downhill into the intended burn with no wind or only a light and favorable wind. With such favorable conditions, firing along the line should proceed rapidly in order to take advantage of the situation before more critical burning conditions develop. Caution and safety must never be compromised.

However, we must never forget that a major run of the main fire or the backfire near the top of the ridge can change the wind flow and adversely affect the backfire. For example, if there is a sharp bend in the line near the newly developed backfire, the combination of topography and wind change at this point could become quite serious. Under no-wind or light-wind conditions, indrafts into a large fire can affect wind flow for a considerable distance downslope from the fire area. More information on backfiring or firing out can be found in the Wildland Strategy and Tactics section.

Two major convection columns burning in close proximity to each other usually will result in a very rapid and violent burnout of the intervening vegetation.

Fire whirls

A fire whirl can be described as a violent, noisy tornado of fire, shaped like an elongated inverted funnel. A fire whirl spins at an extremely high velocity and emits a loud roar that is best compared to the sound of an aircraft engine. Its size can vary from a few feet to several hundred feel in diameter and from a few feet to 4,000 feet in height.

Fire whirls are usually associated with large fires, although they have occurred in small fires. This is probably because some of the conditions (unstable air is one) conducive to whirlwind formation are also factors in the creation of large fires.

The cyclonic action (rapidly whirling fire around the outer perimeter of a center cone of air or gas) can pick up debris, sometimes including small logs, and raise it to great heights. A central "tube" is present whether or not it is always visible.

Topography plays an important part in fire whirl occurrence. Although fire whirls have been known to happen in flat terrain, by far the majority occur in mountainous areas. Some generalities can be made about possible locations and conditions for whirls. At the same time there have been notable exceptions observed that have little or nothing in common with these general rules of behavior.

The majority of whirlwinds observed by fire officers have generally occurred on the leeward sides of ridges, near the top. The shearing action on wind flowing over the abrupt edge of a ridge has been found to be present in the formation of dust devils.

All of the theories on whirlwind formation include air stability as an important factor. Some, however, advance the belief that it is a local thermal instability caused by the fire and not the degree of upper air instability that has the greatest effect. But others point to the extremely unstable upper air conditions known to exist when large, destructive fire whirls have occurred. Unfortunately, in the past too little attention has been paid by fire officers to upper air instability as an indicator of potentially violent fire behavior.

Heat supplied by the fire provides the "trigger" to set the whirl in motion when all of the other factors are present. Sometimes a mass of fire is required; this usually results in a rather large whirl. At other times, relatively small whirls have formed along a moderately burning fire edge with no noticeable increase in fire intensity prior to their formation.

AIR ATTACK

Tactical use of aircraft

Each fire has a different set of circumstances that can only be evaluated effectively by the people at the scene. The Incident Commander and the Air Attack Supervisor (air coordinator) must work as a team to make the most effective and economical use of firefighting aircraft. They must take advantage of favorable weather conditions and information so that unnecessary drops are not made. Air Attack supervisors and Incident Commanders continuously evaluate the need for additional airdrops. Under the most critical fire conditions, the number of air tankers that can be used effectively will provide one drop every five minutes, using whatever size aircraft is available. On fast-moving fires with a broad front the most beneficial use of air tankers will probably be to attack active flanks. This is, without successful ground-holding action, any contribution on a hot front may be wasted, while the same retarding effort on the flank can result in a secured piece of line. If a fast-moving head is narrow enough, several drops may be adequate to stop the forward drive of the fire.

Before air tankers were available, it was a generally accepted axiom that little, except a hazardous position, could result from taking action against the head of a fire moving up a steep slope, even in relatively light fuel.

The most common action was to attempt to hold the fire at the ridge; this sacrificed the broadening flanks. In many cases the most logical strategy with airdrops was to pretreat a ridge or bench where both retardant material and the natural decrease in fire intensity would have the most beneficial result. On the other hand, the possibility of greatly reducing fire intensity, or even eliminating the active fire spread with air tankers used on the upslope offered a new dimension to the strategy of fire control. However, success with this technique should be expected only if the frequency of drops can dominate a rate of fire spread that could cause the fire to outflank the retardant line.

The effectiveness of air tankers increases as the following conditions are approached:

- grass or light brush fuel predominates;
- wind movement decreases;
- topography becomes less steep;
- the time of fire incidence passes mid-afternoon; and
- the distance to the fire from the airport decreases within the 20-minute maximum ideal first-attack striking limit.

Finally, all retardant drops must be followed up by ground action. Fires do burn through drops and, therefore, must never be considered as the final action until fire crews or engine companies have secured the fire.

During critical periods of backfiring operations, an orbiting air tanker may be desirable to provide immediate action on spot fires.

If a series of separate fires starts occurring almost simultaneously in the same general area, air tankers normally can be used most successfully on small and isolated fires.

Aircraft limitations

Certain conditions can seriously limit the use of air tankers. Incident Commanders should recognize that:

- Steep topography seriously reduces air tanker effectiveness. Deep canyons may rule out their use entirely for certain fire targets.
- Winds in excess of 20 mph sharply reduce air tanker effectiveness. Shifting and high-velocity winds (> 30 mph) and turbulent air may restrict or exclude air tanker use.
- Early morning and late afternoon are periods when air tankers may be less effective. Deep shadows cast by the sun over certain aspects of topography make it difficult for pilots to see fire targets or ground obstructions.
- Dense smoke may make air tanker operations both hazardous and ineffective on part or all of the fire area.
- Air tankers cannot be used at night, a period when a fire normally is expected to become less active.
- Tall, dense timber and snags may require air tankers to make drops at higher-than-desirable altitudes and may intercept most of the retardant before it reaches the fire.

Aircraft capabilities

Most air tankers are capable of dropping retardant in three patterns:

1. Salvo: total load at one time and place. All tanks open.
2. Trail: overlapping series of from two to eight tanks in tandem.
2. Split: single drop from one tank at a time at widely spread intervals, or two to eight times on the same place or on separate small fires.

The latest tank configuration on aircraft uses constant flow doors. Based on the fire's intensity, the pilot can select the desired coverage and the doors on the tank will open according to the selection made by the pilot. After the air tanker passes over the drop zone, the doors are closed and another pass can be made. Air tankers with constant flow tanks deliver more consistent drops at a lower cost per gallon of retardant.

Often, airdrops are made on a fire before ground forces arrive. Such a "delaying tactic" pays big dividends when the drops are successful in holding the fire to initial attack size.

Air tankers generally operate under the direction of an Air Attack Supervisor, who works constantly via radio communication with the Incident Commander on the ground. The following is a typical sequence of events one might observe at the fire scene.

The Incident Commander has a need for an airdrop on a portion of the fire that cannot be reached by the fire engines. The Incident Commander calls the Air Attack Supervisor on the radio and describes what it is the air tanker is to accomplish, i.e., "have one air tanker drop on the right flank. Advise the air tanker to be careful of a power line near the head." Air Attack acknowledges, and directs the type of drop to the air tanker by radio.

Air Attack evaluates the effectiveness of the drop and converses with the Incident Commander about additional needs. Fire crews or engine companies will immediately be sent up to the right flank to work on the fire line which, it is hoped, is burning with less intensity following the retardant application.

Aircraft safety

Alertness along the fire line helps personnel to avoid possible serious injuries from the weight and force of the falling retardant payload. While aircraft do fly at sufficient altitudes to permit the falling retardant to disperse in the form of a rain or heavy mist, occasionally the payload does not break up, and personnel have been hurt and equipment damaged. When the retardant hits in a mass, it is capable of tearing brush out of the ground, kicking rocks into the air, or knocking personnel off their feet.

Sometimes fire conditions along the fire line become untenable or pose a potential threat to firefighters. In such cases, it is not uncommon for fire officers to ask for a protective retardant drop. The point to be made about such a request is this: if asked, any air officer would probably say that the very conditions that threaten firefighters also are obscuring the pilot's visibility.

The aircraft may be unable to locate the firefighters in time to help them. Even with the brightly colored fire-resistant clothing worn on the ground, it may be difficult to pinpoint the area of need and to establish a proper drop pattern because of the dense smoke. Therefore, a dependence on aircraft to perform such a function should not take the place of escape routes, communications, lookouts, and other preventive measures. Air tanker movement adjacent to the fire line can fan the fire, setting a dormant section ablaze, or can force a change in spread direction. Both contingencies are detrimental to firefighting efforts and accentuate the relative immobility of ground personnel.

The more heavily loaded the aircraft, and the lower and slower it flies, the stronger the vortex turbulence will be and the more likely to reach the ground. The vortex may strike the ground with velocities up to 25 mph, sufficient to cause sudden and violent changes in fire behavior on calm days in patchy fuels. Wind gustiness and surrounding high vegetation tend to break up or diminish vortex intensity.

Firefighters should be alert for trouble during air tanker drops when:

- the air is still and calm;
- the fire is burning in open brush or scattered timber;
- the air tanker is large or heavily loaded; and
- the air tanker is flying low and slowly.

The air tanker pilot should be aware of the problems the aircraft can cause. The pilot may know the effect of vortex wakes on aircraft, but may not know the effect on a fire. During situations of possible danger from vortex wakes, pilots should:

- avoid flying parallel with the fire line more than necessary;
- remain high, except when making the actual drop; and
- ensure that firefighters are alert to the presence of the air tanker, the pilot's intentions, or both.

Helicopters

One of the principal advantages of a helicopter is its ability to operate from locations near and on the fire line. Its vertical take-off and landing characteristics make it a valuable piece of equipment for close support action for ground-based and other aerial operations. Various accessory attachments are available that permit a helicopter to perform certain jobs that would be difficult, if not impossible, by any other means.

Helibases are main bases of operation serving a fire. They should be located near a good access road. Helispots are temporarily used sites located on or near the fire perimeter for the purpose of delivering or returning personnel and equipment. Depending on terrain and the ease of vegetation removal for safe take-offs and landings, helispots can be constructed in meadows, on mountain peaks, or on ridge tops and saddles. During some fires of longer duration, helispots may be used to stockpile sleeping bags, lunches, drinking water, back pumps, and extra tools. Fire crews are flown to these helispots to work a shift, then, perhaps, return to the site for supplies and to spend the next shift sleeping in a designated area adjacent to the helispot. A miniature "incident base" is thus created that can be advantageous in reducing the number of ferrying trips to and from the fire line. The procedure also allows for a longer period of fire line construction because travel times are not involved, and it eases the logistical requirements of the planning section. Helispots are identified by name or number on maps for easy location by personnel. Pilots approaching helispots are able to confirm identification from the air because the helispot is marked with a large plastic sign or by some other means.

Helicopters also may be used to apply liquids, such as water or foam, over key fire line targets. Because of their ability to hover, they can be directed precisely via radio communication with ground personnel. Some helicopters carry a collapsible water tank which can be strategically placed on the fire line. A portable "floto-pump" is placed in the tank, which can be filled by helicopters using water drops in the tank. Firefighters then are afforded some of the benefits of having a fire engine in undrivable terrain at their disposal. The floto-pump includes a complement of fire hose, adapters, nozzles, and hose clamps.

Helicopters are useful for transporting injured firefighters, including burn victims, who are flown to predesignated hospital burn wards. Helicopters often have served dramatically to evacuate persons stranded or threatened by fire.

Most agencies that supply and coordinate helicopters require certain data on each load of personnel and equipment. Manifests are routinely filled out prior to each assignment. Fire tools are secured in groups and each firefighter's weight is recorded to assure that the weight limitations of the ship are not violated. Logistically, it is desirable, but often most difficult, to keep track of a crew once it has been dropped on the fire line at a helispot. The fire crew that is scheduled to return to the pickup point may end up in quite a different location. There are several reasons for this, including reassignment to another section of fire line, the necessity, for various reasons, to walk the crew out rather than fly, easier access to another helispot, etc. As is the case in so many fire operations, good communications can help prevent misplacement of personnel and equipment even on remote sections of line.

All fire control personnel are subject to assignment with or around helicopters. They should have at least a general familiarity with the type of work that can be accomplished as well as the limitations. Those employees who will be engaged directly in some activity involving the craft must, of course, have a thorough understanding of the part they are to play. All personnel who may possibly be working near, or be transported by, helicopters should be trained in safety practices, and they shall observe such precautions at all times.

TACTICS AND STRATEGY

This section is divided into two major parts: one deals with the concepts of fire command and strategic objectives, and the other with the actual tactical deployment of suppression resources. Strategy deals with the major objectives of managing a fire, i.e., **what** to do, while fire tactics, **how** to do it, involve the actual number and the individual designation of the units that are to accomplish the identified strategies. For example, during the planning stages of a fire suppression operation, the objectives may be to minimize all structural losses and to prevent the fire from crossing a specific highway. These two major objectives are considered part of the fire strategy.

To successfully identify and implement the strategies and resulting tactics necessary to accomplish control and extinguishment of a fire, the Incident Commander must have a working understanding of the four major components of sound fire management. These components are as applicable on a small grass fire that requires only three or four engines as they are on a major fire that requires hundreds of suppression units supported by complex Command and General Staff functions.

Many times firefighters start suppression operations based on what they determine is the immediate requirement of the situation. They augment their resources based on what the fire is doing. Their organization grows with little concern for long-term objectives, and the command and suppression structure becomes chaotic, with overall poor results. Such management, more of a happening than a managed affair, results from a reactive rather than a proactive approach to proper and cognitive fire command.

Fire command consists of the proactive consideration and intelligent use of four basic management elements: planning, organizing, directing, and controlling. The Incident Commander must formulate a plan of action, build an organization to accomplish the objectives and strategies as outlined in the plan, direct the organization by communicating the strategies and tactics to the necessary members of the organization, and, finally, control the identified fire organization with adequate systems so the Incident Command staff can meet the objectives as outlined. Successful fire command must incorporate planning, organizing, directing, and controlling.

Planning

A plan is formulated which is based on considerations of the past, present, and future factors that affect the fire. A plan is an ordered sequence of events over a specified period of time to accomplish a specific objective(s).

The fire suppression planning process consists of three separate elements: an information-gathering system, an information evaluation and prediction system, and a constant re-evaluation system. These elements provide the basis for size-up that will be covered in detail in this chapter.

In wildland fire situations the information-gathering system may consist of facts gathered from prefire plans, observations and radio traffic from the first-in companies, information from the dispatch center, and communicated observations from aircraft, such as air attack and helicopters. Information also is gathered from reconnaissance personnel and the personal observations of the command officers. The information evaluation and predictions system consists of the Incident Commander and various staff members.

The re-evaluation system is a never-ending process. With good firefighters and command officers, effective planning is a dynamic and ongoing process. A good plan is constantly adjusted based on the fire and the proactiveness of the suppression forces.

Ideally, fire command incident action plans should be based on facts alone. Actually, however, beliefs sometimes alter facts. What one sees and hears often is influenced by experience, or the lack of it. Attitudes, sentiments, values, and, therefore, planning conclusions, are not always based on facts alone. Successful firefighters objectively, rather than subjectively, view data in order to develop effective control plans.

Organization

A fire organization, simply stated, is a group of fire officers and firefighters working together to achieve a common objective. To be effective, the organization must include the following elements:

- a system of authority and responsibility;
- a system of direction and communication;
- consolidated action toward identified objectives; and
- a system of maintaining acceptable norms and standards.

The system of authority and responsibility is usually outlined with a legal basis in mind. The fire service functions by the operation and organizational guidelines and orders that are developed by each department. Much of the United States has adopted the Incident Command System (ICS), and, as such, each department has developed specific operational policies and procedures.

ICS is communicated through an organizational chart and supplemental position descriptions.

The organization must maintain a system of direction and communication. This system can consist of face-to-face contacts, written messages, and radio and telephone communications, including electronic mail and facsimile transmissions.

An important key to a successful organization is coordinated action toward specific objectives. This coordinated action is based on how well the forces are organized and how realistically the objectives have been identified.

The important elements to consider in a fire suppression organization are span of control, unity of command, clear definition of authority and responsibility, and unity of objective.

Span of control relates to the number of people or units a manager can effectively direct or supervise. For example, a management unit is an individual (firefighter), or a unit such as a fire crew, that reports directly to one supervisor. Generally, in a fire organization, the span of control number should be no fewer than three nor more than seven; five is the optimum.

Proper unity of command dictates that each firefighter should have only one supervisor. Although almost all fire officers agree with this concept, it is the one principle most violated on the fireground.

A clear definition of authority and responsibility is paramount to fire suppression efforts. Each person should be given clear authority to carry out the responsibilities assigned to him.

The unity of objective must be clearly understood and pragmatically pursued in order to accomplish the overall goal of putting out the fire. All fire officers and firefighters must play a supporting role in achieving a single purpose or objective(s).

Direction

The third element of fire management involves direction. The issuing of directives during the fighting of a moving wildland fire requires a clear understanding of the process of human communications under stressful conditions and the necessary parts of a proper and effective directive.

A directive is simply an act of communicating that involves some specifics as to the accomplishment of a task. In order for a directive to be clear and effective, it should provide the following information:

- WHO is to perform the work;
- WHAT is to be done;
- WHEN it is to be done;
- WHERE it is to be done; and
- WHY it is to be done.

Sometimes the "WHY" is implied or understood and does not have to be fully explained in the directive.

The following is an example of a proper incident directive that meets the requirements of providing "WHO, WHAT, WHEN, WHERE, and WHY."

"Engines 28 and 72, upon arrival at the fire, start a progressive hose lay on the right flank. This hose lay is needed to tie in with the tractor plow line that is progressing on the left flank."

After a directive is issued, it is important to ask, "Do you have any questions?" Good directives involve two-way communication and are best handled on a face-to-face basis.

Controls

Controls are methods or systems designed to inform the Incident Commander of operations progress and breakdowns so the system can be adjusted and corrected to meet the objectives as identified in the incident action plan. To ensure a proper set of controls, a fire organization must contain several important elements.

One of these elements is visual control, that is, actually observing what progress is taking place. Periodic reporting from different suppression units and fire officers can pass along pertinent information. Monitoring radio traffic and holding face-to-face meetings with responsible members of the incident organization can provide timely controls. Also, pilots of aircraft, both fixed and rotor wing, can quickly provide important and timely information to field commanders.

Consideration should be given to establishing strategic control points that evaluate individual objectives that are part of the overall incident action plan. If an incident strategic objective dictates that the wildland fire not cross the Mississippi river, then a strategic control point would be any extension of the fire over the river. From a command standpoint, the use of strategic control points greatly helps an Incident Commander to clearly determine the need to adjust tactical operations or re-evaluate the overall plan and, perhaps, change the incident objectives. The concept of control points also can be extended to tactics through the use of tactical control points.

The chapter thus far has covered the concepts of fire management and the development of strategic objectives. From this point on, the fireground tactics, suppression methods, and the deployment of fire attack resources will be addressed.

WILDLAND SIZE-UP

Size-up is an estimate of the needed actions and resources required to extinguish a fire.

FIRE SIZE-UP IS MADE AT FIVE TIMES:

1. Upon receiving a call.
2. While en route to the fire.
3. At first sight of the fire.
4. Upon arrival at the fire.
5. During the entire life of the fire.

Before any strategic objectives can be identified or any suppression companies put to work, one all-important process must take place.

Fire departments exist to combat fires. This fact should not be forgotten. Although it is true that fire service administrative procedures are important, the fire service does not exist solely for the purpose of being well run. Administrative, financial, and political decisions can be reached after considerable counseling and conjecture and can, and often are, revised if found to be inappropriate or lacking. However, fireground decisions must be made quickly. The fireground situation does not allow the first-in officer the luxury of consultation and calculated deliberation.

The officer's initial decisions are usually irreversible and the consequences of errors can quickly compound and become disastrous. Unlike staff officers in the fire service and executives in industry, the fireground officer must base all important decisions on hastily obtained information gathered under the most stressful conditions.

This process of hastily gathering important information is called size-up. Size-up is the basic foundation for subsequent firefighting decisions and operations. The old saying that a building is no stronger than the foundation it rests on has a direct application to fire size-up. Build a house with square corners and plumb walls and any addition is simple; the same applies to any emergency organization.

Size-up should begin long before the fire actually starts. Fire officers should be familiar with the fuel types, topographical features, exposure problems, and daily weather patterns in their areas of responsibility. Having this basic information can provide a foundation for future observations. When the alarm sounds, each firefighter should know the general fire behavior that can be expected, the location of the fire, and the types of physical factors that are present: fuel, topography, road access, structural exposure, water supplies, natural or technological barriers, and the number and types of suppression resources dispatched.

Once the fire is actually viewed (ideally from several vantage points), the specific size-up, which consists of three general interrelated mental evaluations, may start.

WHAT HAS HAPPENED?

EXAMPLE:
The fire has burned 5 acres of grass and 2 small outbuildings in 10 minutes.

WHAT IS HAPPENING?

EXAMPLE:
The fire is spreading rapidly on the right flank and is moving into five-foot

brush. It is starting to spot. It is within 200 feet of a barn, ranch house, and stock pen.

WHAT WILL HAPPEN?

EXAMPLE:

If no suppression is undertaken, the fire will continue to move into the brush; the spot fires will increase in size; and the ranch house and barn will catch fire, as will other structures in the path of the fire.

SIZE-UP STEPS

These six steps must be considered in all wildland fire situations; however, not all of them may apply in every case.

1. PRE-ARRIVAL CONSIDERATIONS

Prior to your arrival at the fire or even prior to dispatch, there are several facts you should take into consideration:

- **Fuel-Topography.** What effect will the existing fuel and topography have on current and expected fire behavior? How will these factors hinder or aid fire control?

  EXAMPLES:
  - A fire currently burning in grass and extending into brush will increase in intensity but should slow in rate of spread.
  - A fire currently burning on flat ground and moving onto a steeper slope will increase in rate of spread.

- **Weather.** What effect will the key variable to wildland firefighting have on the fire's behavior?

  EXAMPLE:
  - Wind speed and direction will both increase the rate of spread and change the direction of spread.

- **Time.** Are we just starting into a burning period with conditions that will become more adverse to control or is it late in the day when the fire danger is dropping?

  EXAMPLE:
  - Everything being equal, wildland fire spread tends to subside in the late afternoon.

- **Type of Fire.** Is it grass, brush, timber, or exposures? What types of equipment are necessary to effect control?

EXAMPLES:

- For a total wildland fire, resources may include bulldozers or tractor plows, or fire engines for mobile pumping.
- For a wildland fire with structures threatened, resources may include fire engines with large tank capacities and heavy stream appliances in addition to normal wildland firefighting resources.

- **General Location.** What effect does the location have on access, exposures, natural barriers, water supplies, and effectiveness for air attack?

2. WHERE IS THE FIRE?

What is the exact location of the fire? Check maps, talk to locals, obtain information from air units.

3. WHAT IS BURNING?

What is actually burning—grass, brush, timber, or combinations?

4. WHAT WILL BURN?

Consider all previous factors and determine what could quickly become involved in the fire—heavier fuel, structures, recreational areas.

5. LIFE HAZARDS

Always consider life hazard from the time of initial dispatch. It is axiomatic to state that rescue takes precedence over firefighting. However, after going through the previous four steps, you will be better prepared mentally to plan the rescue actions and subsequent attack operations.

6. RESOURCES SITUATION

Consider whether the initial dispatch is sufficient to handle the fire based on the information gathered in the previous five steps. Consider available personnel, apparatus capabilities, water supply, fire defense improvements, logistical support, and resistance to control.

Remember—no fire is static, therefore, your size-up should not be static. Many fires have been lost because despite the fact that the Incident Commander made a good initial size-up, he failed to reappraise the situation. Continue your size-up throughout the confinement, extinguishment, and mopup process. Many firefighters have been killed or injured because sudden changes in weather affected fire behavior.

Wildland fire tactics

Firefighters have a choice of two major methods for combating wildland fires: direct attack and indirect attack. Quite often the method chosen is based on fuel types, exposure problems, fire behavior, and availability of suppression resources. The safety requirements for the personnel involved should be considered first when choosing a method or combination of methods.

Direct attack

The direct attack method involves working directly at the fire's edge. This type of suppression action would involve laying hose and spraying water on the fire's edge, constructing handlines along the direct edge of the fire, making air tanker or helicopter drops to support firefighters working on the perimeter, and having bulldozers or tractor plows construct a line along the edge of the fire. This method has several tactical advantages. The applied suppression resources instantly produce results in the amount of fire controlled.

This method requires a continuous and finished line. The line should be started from an anchor point such as a road, plowed field, or other manmade or natural barrier. The direct attack will limit the fire's ability to build up momentum and eliminates the need for backfiring or firing out. It is generally used on fires in the initial attack phase and can be used on the flanks and head. The main objective is to stop the spread of the fire as soon as possible.

The advantages of the direct method are that it holds the size of the fire to minimum acreage, takes advantage of portions of the line that have gone out because of a lack of fuel or poor burning conditions, eliminates fuels at the fire's edge, provides for direct operational control and higher levels of firefighter safety, and reduces loss of resources caused by backfiring or allowing the fire to run to predetermined control lines.

The disadvantages of the direct attack are that it might not be effective against an intensely hot or fast-moving fire; results in an irregular and thus, long fire line to construct; it exposes firefighters to direct flame and smoke; it normally does not take advantage of natural or manmade barriers in the fire's path, and it requires additional mopup. Direct fire attack requires close coordination of the suppression forces involved.

Indirect attack

The indirect attack method consists of fighting a wildland fire by constructing control lines at a considerable distance ahead of the main fire. It is used when the fire is burning too hot and rapidly to use direct attack methods or when too few suppression forces are available to use direct attack methods. The preconstructed lines put in ahead of the fire are either fired out or held by ground and air forces and become the final control line.

The advantages of the indirect attack method are that the burned area can be determined by a preconstructed line that often can be completed with fewer suppression resources, the amount of total fire line is limited, firefighters can work away from large amounts of heat and smoke, and mopup is limited.

The disadvantages of the indirect method are that no fire can be extinguished while the control lines are being constructed, additional acreage is sacrificed, portions of the fire line that may have gone out aren't used, firefighters are placed in front of an advancing fire, secondary lines may have to be constructed, and a frontal stand by firefighters, a successful expected backfiring operation, or both, is required. In terms of firefighter safety, the indirect attack is the most dangerous.

Application of attack methods

No one method must be followed exclusively throughout fire suppression operations. More often, on any sizable fire, both methods are used. On one flank it may be possible to use dozers or tractor plows and engines on a direct attack, using handline construction and hose lays on the other flank. Line construction that involves burning out might be the selected tactic while dozers or tractor plows and fire crews might be constructing the line well in advance of the fire's head to be backfired and held at a later time.

Backfiring and burning-out actions

There is a distinct difference between backfiring and burning out. These two terms have been used interchangeably with resulting confusion for many years. The term "burning out," sometimes also called "firing out," refers to the removal by fire of residual fuel between a constructed line and the edge of a dead fire. The term also refers to the burning of fuel to protect structures or other improvements. Sometimes burning out is described as a defensive measure when timing is not critical and the action will not be affected by the main fire.

Backfiring is an indirect fire control action typically used against a rapidly spreading fire. The fuel between the preplanned control line and the active fire's edge is intentionally fired to eliminate fuel in advance of the fire. This widens the control line to possibly change the fire's direction and to slow the fire's progress. Backfiring may be described as an offensive measure because of effects of the main fire and the critical timing necessary for success.

Planned backfiring often involves considerable planning, organizing, and physical preparation. The decision to backfire should be made by the command function, communicated through line channels, and executed at the division level by strike teams or individual increments. Under special circumstances or in emergencies, line personnel may be forced to backfire and notify higher command level concurrently.

Safety considerations must be the first priority. No backfiring operation, regardless of the importance of the strategic values involved, is worth risking one human life. The probabilities of both success and failure must be calculated and considered by command personnel because any backfire could result in losing the fire and the subsequent compounded damages.

Knowing when and how to conduct a backfiring operation properly is essential because such operations can control a major fire rapidly with relatively limited suppression resources. Overall fire strategy and resulting tactics must be understood by all personnel involved in the backfiring operation since the fire behavior on other portions of the control line is likely to be affected.

Backfiring should be directly correlated to the behavior of the fire. If the main fire is burning intensely and spreading rapidly, backfire quickly enough to prevent the fire from jumping the prepared or proposed control lines.

When weather, fuel, topography, and sufficient suppression forces are favorable to a backfiring operation it should proceed without delay. Many fires have been lost because of indecision and many backfires have only created additional problems because time was wasted and burning conditions changed to less than favorable, causing the backfire to "lay down" or go out. At times, the same indecision and burning conditions can cause backfires to escape, resulting in additional problems. Fire officers must evaluate the decision carefully. The tactic should be performed only by trained and experienced firefighters.

Backfiring and fire behavior

Active fires (either the main fire or intentionally set backfires) produce conditions that draw other fires. The larger and more intense a fire becomes, the more it affects local weather conditions, thus greatly influencing additional fires at greater and greater distances. Noticeable wind direction and intensity changes have taken place more than a mile away from a fast-moving fire in heavy fuel.

Once a decision to backfire has been made, several important guidelines should be followed:

- Backfiring operations should always be directed by an officer who understands fire behavior and knows how to take advantage of favorable topography, fuel, and weather conditions. The officer must know the overall fire strategy and be kept constantly informed about the progress of the main fire. The officer should have considerable experience based on other firing operations.

- When the fire danger is extreme, backfiring is most hazardous and may fail. Suppression action on the flanks may prove to be more effective.
- A backfire should be started as close as possible to the main fire, balancing the time needed to establish an effective line against the rate of spread of the main fire. Always allow a margin of time.
- Once backfiring has started, it is essential that all fuel between the backfire and the main fire be burned.
- Backfiring should be conducted by a group of highly experienced firefighters under experienced leadership.
- Sufficient forces should be committed to hold the line created by the backfire.
- The main fire and the backfire should meet a safe distance from the control line, because intense and erratic fire behavior is common as the two fires meet.
- Weather conditions, both current and predicted, should be noted at all times.
- Never start more fire than that which can be controlled by personnel assigned to the holding operation. However, once started, the backfire should gain maximum depth in the shortest amount of time.
- Remember, there will always be a calculated risk in backfiring operations!

Tandem action

A tandem action (e.g., two engines attacking a flank of a fire) is a form of direct attack that involves suppression units working together or in tandem. It is often used on a fast-moving fire and is effective for perimeter control. A tandem action can develop rapidly into a pincer action once the movement of the suppression forces becomes faster than the spread of the fire and it is determined that the head of the fire can be pinched off.

The key to a tandem action is to combine units to gain more fire line control than the sum of the units working individually. Also, greater control is established and units in a mutual supporting role provide for a greater margin of safety.

Pincer action

A pincer action may be used on a fire of any size; however, it is used most often on small fires. The objective of a pincer action is to move along both flanks of the fire and eventually have the flanking forces move closer together, finally pinching off the head and encircling the fire.

The forces used in a pincer action may be fire crews, bulldozers or tractor plows, engines, aircraft, or a combination thereof.

Flanking action

A flanking action can be conducted by any type of ground or air suppression resources. The objective of a flanking action is to prevent the fire from spreading on a given flank, thus threatening some exposure such as heavier fuel or an area of structural development. Most forces typically are concentrated on an identified flank.

Envelopment action

An envelopment action consists of taking suppression action on a fire at many points in many directions at the same time. It provides for rapid attack and, if coordinated properly, can be highly effective on smaller fires.

It requires the commitment of a large number of suppression forces and the establishment of close command. Units taking part in this type of action should be experienced and aggressive.

WILDLAND FIRE SAFETY

In the last 10 years, National Fire Protection Association (NFPA) annual reports have shown that firefighter deaths at wildland fires have been rising. In fact, reports for some years show wildland fires to be the number one cause of line-of-duty firefighter deaths. This section will not attempt to analyze the cause of these fatalities, but will provide some standard and tested orders to prevent injuries and deaths to firefighters battling wildland fires. While much of what follows may seem to be common sense, there have been no instances of firefighters being killed when all of the Ten Standard Firefighting Orders have been followed.

Standard firefighting orders:

1. Keep **informed** on **fire weather** conditions and forecasts.
2. **Know** what your **fire** is **doing** at all times; **observe** personally, use scouts.
3. Base all actions on current and expected **fire behavior**.

4. Have **escape routes** for everyone and make them **known**.
5. Post a **lookout** when there is possible danger.
6. Be **alert**, keep **calm, think** clearly, and **act** decisively.
7. Maintain prompt **communications** with your crew, your boss, and adjoining forces.
8. Give clear **instructions** and be sure they are **understood**.
9. Maintain **control** of your **personnel** at all times.
10. **Fight fire aggressively** but provide for **safety first**.

The following "18 Situations that Shout Watch Out!," should be recognized as situations during which there were firefighter deaths. Being aware of these situations and being able to recognize them can prevent future accidents.

"18" situations that shout watch out:

1. The fire is **not scouted** and **sized up**.
2. You are in country **not seen** in **daylight**.
3. **Safety zones** and **escape routes** are **not identified**.
4. **Unfamiliar** with weather and local factors influencing **fire behavior**.
5. You are **uninformed** on **strategy, tactics**, and **hazards**.
6. **Instructions** and **assignments** are **not clear**.
7. You have **no communications link** with crew members and supervisors.
8. You're **constructing** a **line without** a **safe anchor point**.
9. Building **fire line** or laying a **hose downhill** with **fire below**.
10. Attempting a **frontal assault** on the **fire**.
11. Their is **unburned fuel between you** and the **fire**.
12. **Cannot see main fire** and **not in contact** with **anyone** who can.
13. On a hillside where **rolling fuel** can **ignite fuel below** you.
14. The **weather** is getting **hotter** and **drier**.
15. **Wind increases** and/or **changes direction**.
16. You're getting **frequent spot fires across** the **fire line**.
17. Terrain and fuels make **escape** to **safety zones difficult**.
18. You **feel like** taking a **nap** near the fire line.

The 18 situations that shout "Watch Out!"

1. THE FIRE IS NOT SCOUTED AND SIZED UP.

As with any battle, you must know what is facing you to successfully combat the enemy. This is called developing situation status and is a major part of any ICS planning effort. Situation status is as important on small fires as on large fires. You must know the fire's location in relation to the general topography and the fire's direction of spread; developments, communities, and structures that are burning or threatened; and access routes to the fire.

You build your attack plan from situation and resource status inputs. Your plan is only as good as the inputs. Therefore, it is critical that you scout the fire in a timely and effective manner. Scouting the fire will help you develop a good plan. You will learn the best access; where the fire is burning, and its projected direction of travel; whether the fire can be safely fought with ground-based firefighters or whether aircraft will be needed to support the firefighters; and whether the fire will be contained during initial attack actions or the fire will become a major fire.

There are numerous ways to scout and size up a fire. You may be able to drive to the fire and see it in its entirety. Or, you may be able to walk to the fire and do the same. In some cases, you may rely on a distant view from a remote observation point. Aircraft often provide an early and effective size-up of ongoing fires. Using maps to frame your topographical reference will really assist in bringing the fire into focus with the local terrain and developments.

Some fires will be very difficult or impossible to immediately scout and size up. The difficulty will often be related to fire access. Fires at night will be difficult to size up because you cannot easily see the fire and because the fire often will look much larger than it actually is.

Finally, safety must be a major consideration when scouting or sizing up fires. Strict adherence to the 10 Standard Fire Orders, 18 Situations that Shout Watch Out!, Downhill Firefighting Guidelines, and LCES guidelines is a must. You may have to wait for an aircraft to recon the fire before you take action. To do otherwise could lead to a disaster as tragic as that of looking down the barrel of a loaded gun to see if there is a shell in the chamber.

2. YOU ARE IN COUNTRY THAT YOU HAVE NOT SEEN IN DAYLIGHT.

There is something quite different about a fire line at night. The shape of the land, the configuration of the vegetation, even the distances between points can present the firefighter with new and increased safety problems to consider.

It is likely that as a particular fire extends over several days, the personnel who work the night shift will continue to work the night shift, and, likewise, the day shift will always work the day shift. The point is that the night-shift people will start their first shift with little or no opportunity to see the terrain, fuels, and exposures, and even after repeating the night shift, will perhaps not have all the information needed to work with a higher degree of safety. If, perchance, the night shift can glean some information from the day shift, then perhaps the situation will become a bit safer. Fire organizations work best when communication channels are open; sharing experiences and accomplishments among crews who work opposite shifts is probably the best way to find out about the work and fire progress during the preceding 12-hour period.

Topographical maps, when available, are also helpful to the person who has not seen the fire line in daylight. Being able to locate avalanche slides, mine shafts, stream beds, jeep trails, and other features will certainly be useful. Lack of visibility can be negotiated, in part, by artificial lighting, such as by firefighter head lamps. It is simple enough, provided every person is equipped with a light. Yet on countless fires, an entire crew often will walk into a fire by daylight, and find itself in darkness hours later, unable to work. The supervisor must make a last-minute check with the subordinates for items such as head lamps which may well go forgotten when it is still daylight at the start of a shift.

Briefing sessions often can disclose other important bits of information, such as the types of fuel, including dangerous snags, locations of cleared areas which can be used for emergency airlift by helicopters, and the access routes to spot fires which may be located well outside the fire line. While darkness does take away some of the visibility, the supervisor who obtains information through use of maps and through the eyes of others will certainly be able to assign work that can be accomplished with a reasonable degree of efficiency and safety.

3. SAFETY ZONES AND ESCAPE ROUTES ARE NOT IDENTIFIED.

Escape routes and safety zones represent two of the four very important components of LCES (Lookouts, Communications, Escape Routes, and Safety Zones). Once a lookout has communicated a major safety concern, you must know where your escape routes are, where they lead, and how to access them. They should lead to safety zones or away from immediate danger.

Every firefighter should always have at least one, preferably two escape routes. Even if the supervisor does not identify escape routes, individual firefighters must always be thinking about their most immediate escape routes. An escape route must easily lead the firefighters away from the fire. It must not be a difficult trail to traverse because it is a steep slope or there are any other topographical hindrances. A simple escape route may require that the firefighter move a few feet away from a flare-up. Or, the escape route may require that the firefighter move a mile or more to safety. When the distance becomes greater, sufficient lead time must be allowed after notification before the risk becomes so great that the firefighter cannot make the travel distance in time to avoid the fire.

Lack of adequate escape routes and safety zones can be a problem on small as well as large fires. When being briefed after just arriving at a fire, supervisors must ask or ensure that the briefing addresses escape routes and safety zones.

How large is an effective safety zone? The size of the safety zone will depend on its chosen location in relation to surrounding topography and with due regard to the surrounding fuels. It must be large enough for firefighters to take refuge without deploying shelters and not be injured. Topographical location of the zone must be considered. It should be neither in nor at the head of a saddle, a chimney or a chute. A good rule of thumb is to estimate the flame length of the fire if it were to hit the safety zone. Then, make the safety zone diameter at least one and a half times as large as the projected flame length. Firefighters should then take refuge at the lee side of the safety zone.

If supervisors or individual firefighters are not satisfied with escape routes and safety zones, an assignment may be rejected as unsafe. There is no other choice. In the past, had firefighters rejected unsafe assignments where escape routes and safety zones did not exist, they would be alive today.

4. YOU ARE WORKING IN AN AREA WHERE THE LOCAL FACTORS THAT ARE INFLUENCING FIRE BEHAVIOR ARE UNFAMILIAR.

Fuel, weather, and topography are important factors at every fire. To fight a wildfire effectively, an optimal situation would exist if each firefighter were familiar with the specific weather, fuel, and topography factors present at the burning of every fire. Unfortunately, many small fires and most large fires draw personnel from areas some distance from the fire scene; they have not previously spent enough time in the fire scene area to become familiar with the factors. In fact, some may never have been in the area before. A knowledge of local factors probably suggests a knowledge of all three factors, because each is influenced to some degree by the others. For example, a knowledge of local weather conditions goes hand in glove with a knowledge of topography; how else would one explain the effect of an upcanyon wind as it passes through a saddle? Further, the spread of fire through that saddle will be affected by the fuels within it, and even beyond.

It stands to reason then, that when a fire is burning in a particular area, the people who have firsthand local information about that area should be used in the development of strategy for that fire. Such a person is valuable because of his familiarity with roads, natural barriers, types of fuel (including improvements), and wind characteristics.

Firefighters who are not familiar with the local factors, and who are not in communication with anyone who is familiar, must take steps to minimize their disadvantage. Posting lookouts serves to alert crews to existing and predicted fire behavior. Staying together as a crew, united under a specific plan of action, assures that everyone knows what is to be done and what to do if the situation necessitates change. The supervisor who attended the briefing session back at the base or camp and who paid attention to what was said will be a more effective leader on the fire line. Radio communications can be an advantage only if each person knows with whom to talk and on what frequency.

5. YOU ARE UNINFORMED ABOUT STRATEGY, TACTICS, AND HAZARDS.

You must know the plan and the hazards to be able to fight the fire effectively. Communications is the name of the firefighting game. It is critical to safe mitigation of the problem.

Strategy is a command function and represents "WHAT" you must accomplish. Tactics are a function of the Operations Section Chief if activated; otherwise they are a function of the Incident Commander, and represent "HOW" the strategy will be implemented.

Consider an analogy between this situation and professional football. What chance of success would a football team have if it did not scout future opponents, develop a game plan (strategy and tactics), and evaluate the safety risk to its personnel? And what kind of football coaching staff would develop a game plan and fail to communicate it to the team? Firefighting is different based on the safety risk to life (firefighters, public safety officials, and the public) and property.

There is no choice other than to ensure that firefighters are informed on strategy, tactics, and hazards.

6. YOU HAVE BEEN GIVEN AN ASSIGNMENT BUT THE INSTRUCTIONS ARE NOT CLEAR.

To fight a fire effectively, individuals and teams must have a clear understanding of their exact assignment. Certainly personnel with less experience can be expected to run across more tasks with which they are unfamiliar than will their experienced counterparts. Yet the most experienced of personnel often misinterpret instructions or, as supervisors, assign work to others without giving their subordinates all of the pertinent information they need to do the job. Communication, whether written, oral, or otherwise, must be a clear exchange of information. Both parties must come away with the same interpretation of what was said. Face-to-face communication is the most effective. It is critical to understand and acknowledge the directive.

One way to reduce the chance of error is to write down the information or instruction, then repeat it to the person who gave it. A person should not let the opportunity slip by to secure all the information necessary. Once out on the fire line it may be too late to obtain timely clarification. The result could be both unproductive or downright dangerous. If an assignment is not clear, the first, most immediate thing to do is to simply point this out.

This is not always easy given the hustle and bustle of many fire situations, but absolute clarification is mandatory. Let's say, for example, that you are with a strike team of fire engines assigned along a drivable section of fire line. You are to "work your way" to a certain location as quickly as you can before nightfall and tie in with another strike team of engines. How would you interpret this? To merely drive along the fire line as quickly as you can and meet the other engines? Or, did "work your way" mean that the engines are to work the fire's edge, such as by pumping water on burning material, and to continue until tying in with the other engines?

This is an example of a very typical situation. Be sure to clarify the assignment while the person giving it is still available.

Obviously, part of the story is whether or not a person has sufficient experience to know if additional information is, in fact, needed. However, no one should leave for any assignment until he knows exactly what is expected.

7. YOU HAVE NO COMMUNICATIONS LINK WITH CREW MEMBERS AND SUPERVISORS.

Communication is vital to firefighters who must know what is happening at all times. When a crew becomes separated from the supervisor, communications may be become difficult or impossible.

Supervisors must ensure that communication links are maintained. There are many types of links. Radios are the most common. Face-to-face communication is the best because you can read the immediate reaction of the firefighter to whom you are talking. Some fire crews have developed very effective whistle codes. The codes might be one blast for stop, look, and listen; two blasts for look uphill; three blasts for look downhill; and three repeated blasts for an emergency (Swiftwater rescue uses similar whistle codes).

A review of past accidents clearly shows that where communication links failed, accidents immediately often followed. In some cases, firefighters were fortunate to have been the victims of only near misses. Always communicate effectively with your fellow firefighters, your supervisor, and adjoining forces.

8. YOU ARE CONSTRUCTING A LINE WITHOUT A SAFE ANCHOR POINT.

Wildland firefighting is basically perimeter control. Once you start to fight the fire, you must ensure that the fire does not break out behind you. This is done by anchoring the fire where you start your attack.

To anchor a fire means to start your attack on the fire at some point at which you can tie the fire to a manmade or natural barrier. Doing so will help to prevent the fire from "fish hooking" out behind and entrapping you.

An example might be pulling up to a roadside grass fire, immediately pulling a 1½-inch or 1¾-inch preconnect line and starting an initial fire attack at the roadside. You are effectively anchoring the fire so that you can progress around the fire's perimeter, suppressing it. By anchoring the fire, you have ensured that the fire will not come around behind you and trap firefighters.

A much more dangerous situation evolves when you make a downhill attack on a wildland fire where the toe of the fire is not anchored. Without the toe anchored, you risk, as you make your attack down the hillside, having the fire come around below and trap you. This happened on the Loop fire on November 1, 1969, in the Angeles National Forest, where 13 firefighters died in a period of less than one minute. The firefighters were within only a few hundred feet of tying their handline into the bottom of the fire. But the toe of the fire was not anchored, resulting in a fast uphill spread of fire in a chimney where the firefighters were coming downhill.

9. YOU ARE BUILDING A LINE DOWNHILL TOWARD A FIRE.

Fire normally burns faster uphill than it will downhill. Approaching from the uphill side of the fire places firefighters who may be constructing a line or extending hose in a very precarious position. A person cannot outrun an uphill fire. Additionally, convected hot air will be rising through the areas above, making it difficult to breathe or see. A crew working on a slope has poorer footing, no matter which direction the fire line goes. Definite escape routes must be established and each firefighter must be advised of the location of such routes. The crew must remain together and a lookout should be posted to assist in monitoring the fire situation.

The rising hot air currents previously mentioned will be forcing the fuels to give up fuel moisture; the more they give up, the closer they come to their ignition temperatures. Firebrands are likely to start spot fires and firefighters may suddenly find themselves between the fires, or within a cluster of fires. This situation may preclude the use of the originally planned escape routes. The advancing flame front itself, lying parallel to the ground as it most often does on slopes, will extend quickly into new fuels. The advance may be so rapid as to easily cross constructed handlines, hose lays, or dozer or tractor plow lines, as well as retardant-treated areas. On steeper slopes, fire will drive upward in a wedge-shaped burn, but will often seek natural chutes or chimneys. More than one fire head can develop, and, as the fire burns into different elevations or into new slope exposures, it can be driven in new directions and at different rates of spread by the influence of wind.

A lookout should be posted to keep crews advised about the progress of the main fire and to watch for spots. Crews should be in communication with each other.

Although a fire crew approaching the main fire from below is taking the safest route, the existence or possibility of spot fires below the access route has to be seriously considered.

In this situation, the fire is at the bottom of a ravine or chimney. The safest approach will be from point A (below the fire), which will bring the crew in from a flank. In contrast, an approach from point B (above the fire) will expose the crew to superheated air or direct flame in the event the fire moves up the chimney. Approaching a fire from the uphill side is always dangerous; approaching it via a chimney has meant death for many firefighters.

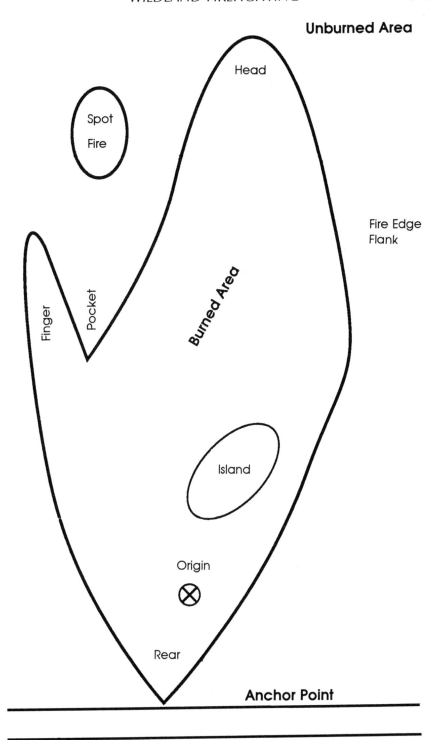

Figure 21-3.

Each of these possibilities can drastically affect the strategy situation. As a fire burns uphill, it carries with it the effects of flame, smoke, heat, spread, speed, and the possibility of entrapment for the firefighter. Knowing who is working above and below, what their assignment is, and what type of equipment they have is critical. All ground attack increments are at a disadvantage given the hazards of being uphill from a fire. Even bulldozers or tractor plows, which the reader might envision as being relatively impervious to fire because of their mass, are slow moving and susceptible to being overrun. In addition, bulldozers or tractor plows are driven by firefighters who have the same limitations as any other person on the fire line.

Safety islands can be constructed by bulldozers, tractor plows, or fire crews when needed, and these can serve as a refuge for any persons near enough to use them. Sometimes, however, safety islands are impossible to construct, which is often the case in very rocky terrain. Of course, time must be available to select the appropriate island location and then to construct it. Good communication within a crew and among crews will be important on all fires, and particularly so when working downhill toward one. Bulldozer swampers also must be kept informed, because their assignment often places them in areas of poor overall visibility.

As a final emphasis, firefighters can and have suffered fatalities from just the superheated air alone that sweeps upslope from a fire below. This is especially so when fires are burning at the bottom of, or within, a chute or chimney such as a natural gully or canyon. The fire itself may be hundreds of yards away, yet the rising convected heat can sear the lungs of any firefighter who may be in its path. Working downhill toward a fire is hazardous enough; it should never be accomplished via a vertical chute or chimney. Whenever possible, fire should be approached from beneath or from the flanks.

At any given time, either flank may become too hot or fast burning to work. This condition may arise suddenly, forcing the choice of an escape route. The safest area generally will be inside the burn at point "A". However, if that route is not possible, firefighters should move toward the flank. Escape routes must be considered before the problem arises.

Flank "B" would be the least threatening because there is less flame activity on the side.

10. YOU ARE ATTEMPTING TO ATTACK THE HEAD OF A FIRE WITH ENGINES.

At times a situation arises that calls for a frontal "stand' against an approaching fire. The decision to use this tactic can stem from several fire situations. A fire may have eluded a flanking attack because of its size or speed of spread. Or, accessibility problems may have precluded approach by personnel but the fire is now approaching an area where it can be attacked. The primary dangers in a frontal attack are apparent in a situation where personnel are "out front" of a wildland fire. The fire may overrun the most elaborate of counterforces, or it may spot well beyond them. Time is needed not only to move in the necessary forces, but to assure a reasonable degree of safety by using safety island construction and briefing personnel on the plan of action and alternate plans of action.

In the past, such stands often have been enacted hastily, yet necessarily, as a last effort to hold the fire at a particular road or other barrier before it moves into an area of habitation, remoteness, or other aspect. This plan of action will no doubt be used many more times in the future; however, it does not allow a plan to be developed as completely as it can be when more time is available.

Newer chief and company officers may not have the breadth of experience to react safely to a fire that is approaching them head on. Sometimes, compared to a military stand, firefighters often must "dig in" and hope to hold a particular road or drainage. Even when sufficient time is available, and a plan of action has been worked out well enough in advance, and when safety zones can be established, several nonproductive and potentially dangerous events can, and have, occurred. For example, while one crew has been initiating backfires, a second crew, or even aircraft, not aware of the situation, has been trying to extinguish it. Or, an engine company may find an easy access to the head, perhaps at a point where the fire may be easily picked up. If that engine gets between the main fire and a backfire, it can spell trouble.

The reader should be able to detect here the importance of communication. Even the most minimal communication is perhaps better than none; the point is that on a frontal attack, there is a definite need for explicit instructions, perhaps more so than what is needed for other firefighting procedures. Flexibility in planning, and planning far enough ahead of time can go a long way toward affording the Incident Commander or line officer enough time to build a plan and notify all the participants. When fire engines are to be placed in stationary positions, they should always be parked for the speediest of departures. Vehicles are best moved in a forward gear rather than in reverse, and they should be parked so that backing out is not necessary. The backing should take place when the fire necessitates. If attack lines are to be used, they should never be smaller than one and a half inches in size and they should be kept in place to provide protection for hose and ignitable equipment. A charged engine fire protection line should be checked for readiness.

When bulldozers or tractor plows are available, safe parking can be established to isolate the other vehicles from the green fuel lying between them and the head. Personnel and equipment should not be located at the top of any draw, ravine, or canyon, or within a saddle, because of the tendency, even the proclivity, of fire to choose these routes. All safety gear, including goggles, should be in place; wet handkerchiefs may provide some relief from the smoke that is liable to blow across the area.

11. YOU ARE IN HEAVY COVER AND THERE IS UNBURNED FUEL BETWEEN YOU AND THE MAIN FIRE.

The indirect method of firefighting dictates that work is accomplished at some distance from, and usually parallel to, the fire's edge. This procedure quite often presents a special safety problem of one sort or another, although it does allow firefighters to work in a somewhat cooler environment away from the approaching flames.

In terms of access to the burn, a most dangerous situation arises because firefighters are actually in the green, and they can easily be overrun by the fire as they attempt to move through the intervening strip between the constructed fire line and the fire itself. Because it is true that in the vast majority of cases the burn is the safest place of refuge for personnel in time of danger, gaining access to that refuge by struggling through the green diminishes the very safety factor that we are seeking. This, of course, is the point because the indirect method does not allow firefighters "one foot in the burn." To make things worse, they must find their way through heavy vegetative cover in the green to the safety of the burn. Such a venture is usually unsafe, if not impossible. The fire officer must plan escape routes that can be used when entry into the burn is not possible.

In addition to the possibility of the main fire overrunning personnel who are working in an area where unburned fuel lies between them and the fire, spot fires can occur behind the crew, leaving members in a situation where the main fire is on one side and the spot fire is on another. Again, there may be no safe way to escape. A lookout always must be posted to keep a close eye on the fire's exact location. Communication between the supervisor and the crew, and others along the line must be effective. Escape routes must be established and the handline construction must be extra clean. Although this scenario refers to working in heavy fuels, never underestimate the flashy characteristics of lighter fuels, such as grass.

12. YOU CANNOT SEE THE MAIN FIRE AND ARE NOT IN COMMUNICATION WITH ANYONE WHO CAN.

Inherent in this situation are two areas of danger: the inability to see what is going on and a lack of communication. Firefighters who cannot see the fire lack the ability to do something about it and to do so in a safe manner. This, coupled with an inability to communicate, spells potential trouble.

To gain access to the fire line, personnel and equipment often must cross expanses of unburned fuel via unimproved or improved roads, or even cross country. Access may be by vehicle or on foot. The dynamics of a moving wildfire demand the utmost attention by the personnel who are attempting to approach it; a lack of visibility calls for accurate assessments gleaned from earlier briefings, plus knowledge of local weather, fuel, and topography. Ground forces are relatively immobile in some situations, such as when on foot, or when traveling in vehicles that are crossing rough or steep terrain.

Many fuels are difficult, if not impossible, to penetrate because of the thicket characteristics of the plants. Remember, in most situations, the safest spot at a fire is right on the fire's edge. Access to the burn is important, and personnel can keep track of the fire's progress. Once on the line, personnel should not venture into the green or otherwise lose the advantage of good fire line visibility and relative mobility of the fire line and burn. When spot fires outside the line require movement through the green, visibility also may become impaired. A separate "Watch Out" situation regarding spot fires is included later in this chapter. Scouting may provide a vantage point to help the crew develop its own lookout and necessary communication. Supervisors must establish escape routes and make them known to others. The use of topographical maps may provide important information about natural barriers, mine shafts, and the destination of jeep trails which transverse the area. In some instances, aircraft can assist in monitoring the progress of the main fire and informing ground personnel.

13. YOU ARE ON A HILLSIDE WHERE HOT, ROLLING MATERIAL CAN IGNITE FUEL BELOW.

This situation can occur at any time that the slope affords the opportunity for pine cones, logs, etc., to travel downhill. In one case, the following happened: a lightning fire had ignited a small fire in rather light fuels on a ridge above a deep ravine through which a river flowed. Fire crews made up of personnel from several engines had all but tied in the line. The remaining fire line dipped down a steep slope which led to the river, and one crew was working this portion of line. Suddenly, a burning log above worked loose, and rolled past the crew into the green below. Immediately, a new fire ran upslope toward the firefighters above. A second crew closer to the ridge top was able to scramble to safety. For those who were working on the lower part of the fire, however, there was no time to reach the safety of the ridge top. All reached the safety of the river and watched, from a wet vantage point, as both sides of the canyon burned off. The fire was finally controlled at several thousands of acres. One single log changed the strategy situation from initial attack to major, and, had the river not been available, it is certainly possible that some serious injuries might have occurred.

Pine cones roll even more easily because of their round shape. During the daytime, these rolling materials normally will ignite fuels which will burn upslope with rising convection currents. Sometimes they will ignite spots that do nothing more than creep through the duff or ground litter. Smoldering, they lie waiting for sufficient oxygen to burst into flame. In gaining access to a smoldering fire when the route is through the green, it is important to construct a cleared line with hand tools. This hand-constructed fire line will permit egress if needed, in addition to serving as a locator for personnel on future work shifts. At night, when air currents normally flow downslope, fires caused by rolling materials may progress downhill and can do so at alarming rates under ideal burning conditions.

All fires on slopes that have undercut lines must be adequately trenched to catch rolling materials and prevent their journey into green fuels below. Such trenches must be properly constructed, with no rounded berm which only provides the material with a roller coaster ride across the line. The bottom lip of the trench should be vertical to catch the material properly. Posting a lookout can provide timely discovery of new fires. Adequate communication to alert the crew is vital. Escape routes must be established before leaving the main fire to work on spot fires, and the whole issue of rolling materials should be discussed before beginning work.

Personnel walking along undercut fire lines must walk in the trench bottom rather than on the berm to prevent damaging the catching ability of the trench.

14. YOU FEEL THE WEATHER GETTING HOTTER AND DRIER.

The fire that was less active during the night can be predicted to become increasingly active as the morning sun begins its heating process. Moisture accumulated by fuels at night was partly responsible for a more dormant fire line. Warmth from the sun will begin the process of extracting the moisture, hence the probable increase in fire activity as the day progresses toward mid-afternoon.

Generally, fire line personnel shift changes occur early in the morning to take advantage of the more favorable weather influences. In the very late afternoon or early evening, as the daytime influences give way, another shift change of personnel generally takes place.

All-out efforts made during the period of high fuel moisture account for the containment and control of many large fires. Day shift personnel should be in place before the sun exerts much influence. The firefighters will note, as temperatures rise, that new smoke will appear within the burn, and that smoldering duff now supports visible flame. Flammable gases which may be lying within a depression in the green may suddenly avail themselves of an ignition source, immediately engulfing an area, sometimes of considerable size, in flame. The five-foot fire line that sufficed the day before may become much too narrow to hold a fire that is now burning under hotter, drier conditions.

Flash fuels burn with extreme fierceness and even heavy, slow-burning fuels become susceptible to ignition. Spotting across the line becomes more pronounced, along with the danger of pursuing small fires starting within the green. Fire runs upslope may be almost simultaneous in nature, arriving at ridge tops quickly and just as quickly jumping across ravines and canyons on opposite slopes. With the arrival of hotter, drier weather, a new strategy situation develops. Firefighters must take into account each of the signals that Mother Nature presents concerning the weather, and perhaps in particular, the signal of a hotter, drier day.

The engine company in this scenario is in position to begin a progressive hose lay up the left flank. Because the fire burned primarily through the lower branches and duff, part of the canopy can initiate a fire run from within the burn itself and can place the company in an unsafe situation with fire moving toward them. Firefighters must be alert to the possibility of fire crowning in the canopy, even during what appears to be a mopup situation.

With hotter, drier weather, the possibility of the fire crowning increases considerably.

15. YOU NOTICE A WIND CHANGE.

Of all the influences on a fire's behavior, wind is probably the most critical in directing and spreading wildfire. Wind flattens out the flames, facilitating ignition of new fuels and enhancing the speed of flame spread. A section of line which previously had favorable wind blowing from the green into the burn may suddenly reverse, blowing hot material or flames into new fuels. A change in the wind may necessitate a change in the attack and firefighters must remain flexible to meet any new situations. Using fire weather forecasting to predict wind changes is an important consideration in developing strategy plans. Expect daytime upslope winds to change to downslope in darkness. The initial abatement of upslope flow can take place as soon as a particular slope becomes shaded from the sun. The shade may result from the setting of the sun, or from shielding of the sun by terrain, such as a mountain top. There are situations where two wind directions or speeds can occur simultaneously and at different elevations. A foehn wind blowing from the north or east may be surfacing gradually along the upper mountain slopes, while at the lower elevations, a westerly marine flow exists. Expect a change to a predominantly easterly flow as the foehn wind descends to the lower elevations. Foehn winds and other influences, such as cloud formations, are discussed elsewhere in depth.

It is important for firefighters to both understand and use predicted wind and wind changes, and to remain alert to both existing and altering forces. Air masses and fronts often dictate the placement of personnel and equipment, attack methods, and other situations that have a direct bearing on the success of fire control and safety considerations.

16. YOU ARE GETTING FREQUENT SPOT FIRES OVER YOUR LINE.

Spot fires are visible indicators of fire behavior which demand attention and evaluation. Strong winds, ground debris, snags, and low fuel moisture are among the mechanisms that cause or encourage spotting. Remember, firebrands such as wooden shake shingles have been responsible not only for spot fires from rooftop to rooftop, but for starting new conflagrations many miles away. Under most circumstances, spot fires are indicative of extreme burning conditions. Spot fires are, in reality, new fires; remember, all fires are small in their incipient stage. Spot fires can themselves become large fires. Spotting can suddenly isolate personnel and equipment between two or more fires, and fire engines, bulldozers or tractor plows, and personnel have been trapped and burned under these conditions. Spot fires that occur across a constructed fire line seriously jeopardize work and are often hazardous or impossible to reach. Spots can never be ignored because left alone, they will continue to grow, perhaps requiring additional personnel and equipment to control. Firefighters on the line, whether engaged in fire control or patrol of a "cold" line, must be on the lookout for telltale smoke rising from the green beyond them.

To reach spot fires, fuel must be cut out along the access path to facilitate ready escape routes if the need should arise. Crawling through the underbrush to reach a spot is asking for trouble; whether located upslope, downslope, or on flat terrain, a spot fire is capable of overrunning a crew. Because of the strong convective influences of the main fire, spot fires can suddenly be drawn toward personnel and equipment on the line, or toward those who are already within the green area en route to work the spot fire.

In this situation, or when conditions are such that the spot runs away from the main fire, it may be advisable to pull out of the area temporarily because rapidly building spot fires do influence the rate of spread of the main fire. The intervening strip between the two can burn out in an almost simultaneous action. When it can be accomplished with a degree of safety, and as soon as possible, spots should be attacked aggressively. This is, in part, to reduce the likelihood of two large fires rather than one. When the wind and other conditions mentioned earlier exist, the time has come to double-check the location and alertness of the lookout, so that he might shorten the discovery time for spots. When aircraft, including helicopters, are used on spot fires, ground personnel will be well advised to remember the vortex turbulence on the fire and the possibility of multi-directional spread.

17. YOU ARE IN AN AREA WHERE TERRAIN OR GROUND COVER MAKES TRAVEL SLOW AND DIFFICULT.

As we know, a crew that is walking or working on level ground must maintain at least 10 feet of clearance between each person. This gives a margin of safety for swinging tools and throwing brush. On a slope, new hazards may be present, such as falling rocks and the potential for slipping. Of course, regardless of slope, all personnel must know exactly what their location is in relationship to the main fire. The rule to "keep one foot in the burn" assures this, although in the indirect attack method, personnel are not immediately adjacent to the burn. Irregular terrain, such as that found in gullies and ravines, can put firefighters out of sight of other personnel; also, many fuels restrict visibility and confuse travel routes. Oftentimes, a scout must be sent ahead, under the watchful eye of a lookout, to determine the best route for the crew to take. However, it may be wiser to walk along the longer route if taking that route will ensure that personnel can exit directly into the burn. When fire slops below a ridge and burns on steep terrain, no easy solution may be available. An under-cut line will probably have to be put in, but personnel will at some point probably be walking or working in an area above the fire, an obviously dangerous situation. Sometimes, access to a fire that is burning on a steep slope can be gained by walking in from below. Or, it may be that rather than gambling on the safety of the personnel, the best decision is to wait until the fire moves into negotiable territory. Even the most valuable timber resources or watershed fuels must be left to burn if the probable tradeoff for suppression subjects fire-fighters to any danger. When personnel walk down slopes, they must be staggered so that at no time will one person be directly above another.

Staggering the positions of personnel helps prevent rocks from being dis-lodged by persons above and inflicting injuries to personnel below. Personnel who traverse slopes above a fire are in a precarious position; even in the case of a chimney which is devoid of all vegetation, superheated air rising from burning fuels far below have been known to sear firefighters' lungs, causing almost instant death.

Crews that are attempting to gain access to spot fires in the green should cut their way into the spot to provide a safe escape route.

Access to fires caused by lightning strikes or to spot fires often necessi-tates travel through hidden terrain or heavy cover. Some vegetation is dense and cannot be traversed without crawling on the hands and knees. This method is dangerous because the firefighter cannot see the fire action. Look for a bet-ter route or cut a hand line to the fire to facilitate speedy withdrawal if it becomes necessary.

This situation calls for cutting away fuel to provide access to the spot fires. The procedure also provides an escape route back to the main burn in case spot fires become too aggressive.

When the fuels restrict visibility of the fire or make travel difficult, special safety considerations must be addressed.

To re-emphasize, access to a spot fire should be gained by cutting a hand-line from the main fire line to the spot. This procedure allows speedy with-drawal if the spot fire becomes too hot to approach or if it makes a run toward the main fire.

18. YOU FEEL LIKE TAKING A NAP ALONG THE FIRE LINE.

Compared to the other situations, readers may think that the issue of whether or not to sleep along the fire line is elementary or just "common sense." Yet certainly there are times when the most alert firefighter reaches the point when he cannot go on and simply must grab a quick wink. What is dangerous about a fire line nap? How does sleep fit into the firefighter's assignment? Every person on the line is a lookout and a sleeping firefighter can't be watching for spot fires. On some fires, a special fire line sleeping area may be needed to rest off-shift crews on the fire itself. Seldom, however, will a regular work shift, night or day, incorporate an individual discretion to sleep on the line. The fire that springs up and makes an effort to cross the line or the flame that burns through the hoseline can overrun a sleeping firefighter.

In summary, sleep, like any other fire line activity, is a function that is part of an overall plan. Supervisors authorize sleep when it is appropriate and, in doing so, assure that fire control efforts do not suffer and that all safety considerations have been met.

Definitely no less important than the previous "Orders" and "Situations" are the "Common Denominators of Fire Behavior on Tragedy and Near-Miss Forest Fires" by Wilson and Sorenson, the Downhill Fire Line Construction Guidelines and LCES.

Common denominators of fire behavior on tragedy fires:

1. **Small fires** or on **isolated parts** of larger fires.
2. **Wind** shifts or changes in velocity.
3. Deceptively **light fuels**.
4. Fire's response to **chimneys,** chutes, and on steep slopes.

Downhill fire line construction guidelines:

A fire line should not be built downhill in steep terrain and fast-burning fuels unless there is no suitable alternative for controlling the fire, and then only when the following safety requirements are adhered to:

1. The decision is made by a competent firefighter after thorough scouting.
2. The toe of the fire is anchored.
3. The fire line does not lie in or adjacent to a chimney or chute that could burn out while the crew is in the vicinity.
4. Communications are established between the crew working downhill and the crew working toward it, which may be at the toe of the fire. When neither crew can adequately observe the fire, communications will be established between the crew and a lookout posted where the fire's behavior can be seen.
5. The crew will be able to rapidly reach a zone of safety from any point along the line if the fire unexpectedly crosses below them.
6. Direct attack will be used whenever possible.

7. If direct attack is not possible, the fire line should be completed between anchor points before being fired out. Firing operations should proceed with assured access to the burned-out part of the fire line or other safety zones.
8. Full compliance with the 10 Standard Orders is assured.
9. Full compliance with the 18 Situations that Shout Watch Out! is assured.

LCES—A key to safety in the wildland environment:

L — Lookout(s)
C — Communication(s)
E — escape routes
S — Safety zone(s)

No writing on wildland firefighting safety would be complete without mentioning protective clothing and fire shelters. Just as a firefighter would not consider entering a burning building without proper turnouts and an SCBA, no firefighter should consider attacking a wildland fire without approved wildland protective clothing and a fire shelter. To expect one set of protective clothing to be suitable for both missions is no more acceptable than asking a firefighter in turnouts to handle a hazardous materials incident.

Fire shelters have and will continue to save firefighters' lives. Every fire officer and firefighter must be trained in the use of, and carry with them, a fire shelter. Information and training are available from most wildland firefighting agencies.

TEN FIREFIGHTING ORDERS

1. Keep informed about fire weather conditions and forecasts.
2. Know what the fire is doing at all times.
3. Base all actions on the current and expected behavior of the fire.
4. Plan escape routes for everyone and make them known.
5. Post a lookout when there is possible danger.
6. Be alert, keep calm, think clearly, and act decisively.
7. Maintain prompt communication with your crew, your supervisor, and adjoining forces.
8. Give clear instructions and be sure they are understood.
9. Maintain control of your personnel at all times.
10. Fight fire aggressively, but provide for safety first.

For purposes of clarity and to emphasize the importance that the ten orders have on the overall wildfire safety plan, they can be broken down as follows:

FIRE BEHAVIOR:

1. Keep informed about fire weather conditions and forecasts.
2. Know what the fire is doing at all times.
3. Base all actions on the current and expected behavior of the fire.

SAFETY:

4. Plan escape routes for everyone and make the routes known.
5. Post a lookout where there is possible danger.
6. Be alert, keep calm, think clearly, and act decisively.

OPERATIONS CONTROL:

7. Maintain prompt communication with your crew, your supervisor, and adjoining forces.
8. Give clear instructions and be sure they are understood.
9. Maintain control of your crew at all times.
10. Ultimate Goal; fight fire aggressively, but provide for safety first.

APPENDIX

*Figure 21-4. Vertical Air Movemenr - An Unstable Condition
(See page 824)*

Figure 21-5. The inversion is broken. (See page 824)

Figure 21-6. Upslope winds in the daytime - downslope at night. (See page 827)

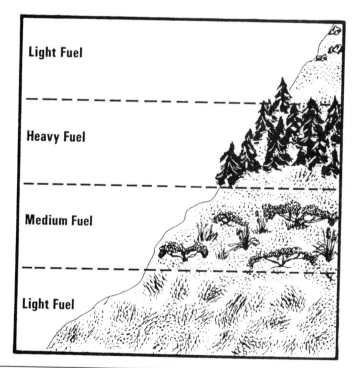

Light Fuel

Heavy Fuel

Medium Fuel

Light Fuel

Figure 21-7. Change in elevation and fuel. (See page 830)

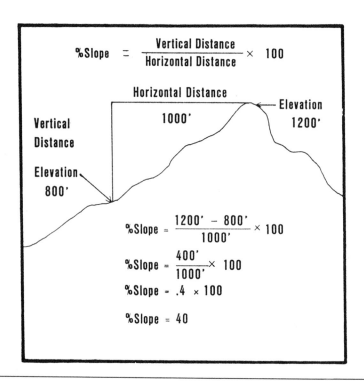

$$\%\text{Slope} = \frac{\text{Vertical Distance}}{\text{Horizontal Distance}} \times 100$$

Horizontal Distance
1000'

Elevation
1200'

Vertical
Distance

Elevation
800'

$$\%\text{Slope} = \frac{1200' - 800'}{1000'} \times 100$$

$$\%\text{Slope} = \frac{400'}{1000'} \times 100$$

$$\%\text{Slope} = .4 \times 100$$

$$\%\text{Slope} = 40$$

Figure 21-8. How to compute slope %. (See page 832)

Aerial Fuels

Ground Fuels

Figure 21-9. Ground and Aerial fuels. (See page 837)

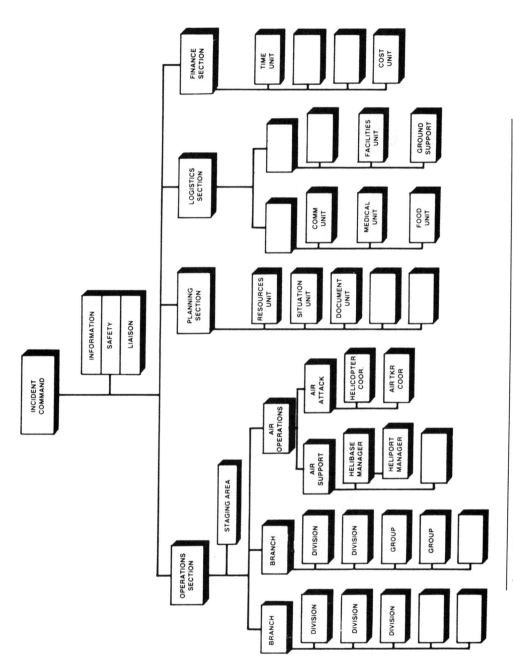

Figure 21-10. ICS Organization Chart. (See page 856)

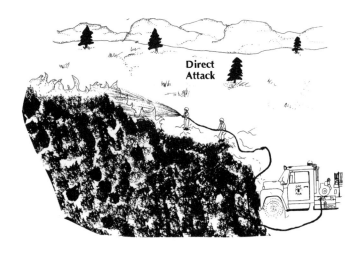

Figure 21-11. Direct Method of Attack. (See page 863)

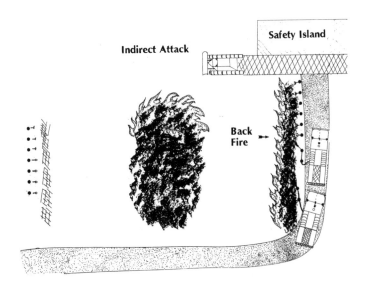

Figure 21-12. Indirect method of Attack. (See page 863)

Parallel Attack

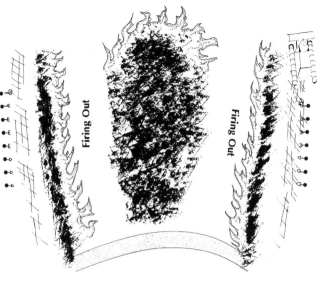

Firing Out

Firing Out

Parallel Method of Attack

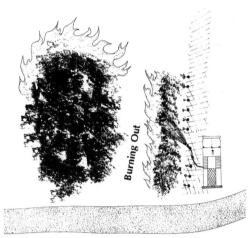

Burning Out

Burning Out (Firing Out)

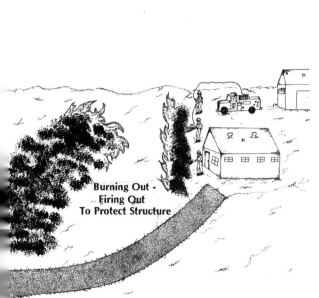

Burning Out -
Firing Out
To Protect Structure

Burning Out Around a Structure

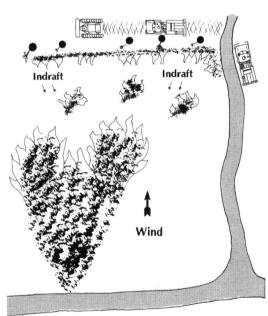

Indraft

Indraft

Wind

Backfiring

Figure 21-13. (See page 864)

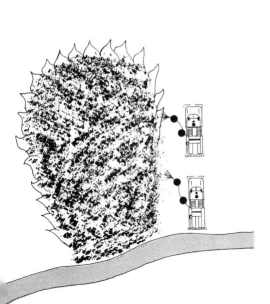

Tandem Action

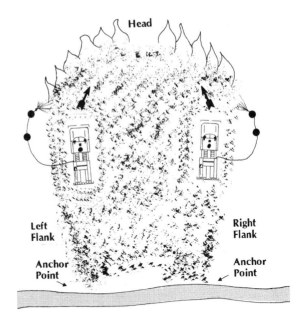

Head

Left Flank

Right Flank

Anchor Point

Anchor Point

Pincer Action

Head

Anchor Point

Anchor Point

Flanking Action

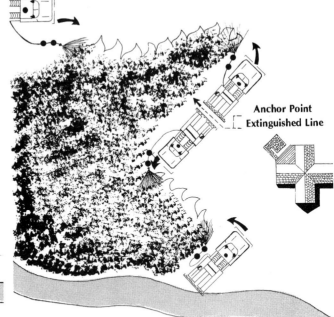

Anchor Point Extinguished Line

Envelopment Action

Figure 21.14. (See page 866)

22

Emergency Medical Services

GORDON M. SACHS

C H A P T E R   H I G H L I G H T S

• The history, background, and development of prehospital emergency medical services.

• The components of an EMS System, and how the definition and components have changed since the Emergency Medical Services Systems Act of 1973.

• The fire department's role in the EMS System.

• Four different EMS training levels, and the difference between basic life support and advanced life support.

• Three important nonclinical aspects of EMS that should receive special attention in a fire department.

• Past, present and future fire service EMS issues.

• EMS Leadership/Management process used to deal with problems or issues.

*A*N EMERGENCY MEDICAL SERVICES (EMS) system is essentially a comprehensive, coordinated arrangement of health and safety resources that serves to provide timely and effective care to victims of sudden illness and injury. As an integral part of this system, prehospital EMS plays a critical role in the effectiveness, efficiency, safety, and quality of the total system. Every fire department is a key component of its EMS system, whether or not it provides ambulance transportation, or is even routinely dispatched on EMS calls.

The American fire service's role in EMS is continually expanding. As a result, many fire departments are expanding their services to meet the needs of the citizens, or customers, they serve. Many departments are even changing their names to "fire and EMS department" or "emergency services"; this is a sign of the future of the American fire service.

HISTORY AND BACKGROUND

In many ways the growth of EMS across the nation is the result of public demand. Before the 1960s, the victim of a medical emergency did not receive much medical assistance other than transportation to the hospital. Often staffed by only a driver, ambulance services until that time offered little in the way of lifesaving care.

The first recorded ambulances date back to the Crusades, and the first prehospital care was provided during the Napoleonic Wars in the late 18th and early 19th centuries. America's first ambulance service was reportedly started by the U. S. Army in 1865. This was followed closely by city ambulance services in many parts of the country, typically established by hospitals. This type of system—hospitals providing a vehicle to transport patients when necessary—continued in urban areas of the country through the 1930s, while rural areas had no prehospital care system other than local doctors making "house calls."

During World War II, the loss of hospital personnel to the war effort caused many hospitals to turn their ambulance services over to volunteer groups and agencies capable of operating a motor vehicle for this type of service. Typically, this was a fire department, police department, or funeral home. In some places local citizens collaborated to provide the service, forming independent ambulance corps or rescue squads. At this time ambulance services were still little more than "horizontal taxi" operations; medical training, if any, was rudimentary.

The evolution of EMS within the fire service is sketchy, and there is no record of the first fire department to provide EMS as a routine service. Most fire departments began providing the service as a reaction to a crisis—absorbing the service during World War II, following a major disaster where EMS was not available in sufficient quantity, or when the quality or timeliness of EMS was in question. Like the hospital, the local fire department operated 24 hours each day for emergency response, and was an obvious candidate as a "first-on-the-scene" EMS provider. Often, the firefighter had to both rescue and administer aid to victims of a fire. It did not take long for many communities to recognize this potential source of assistance during all types of medical emergencies, and add ambulance services to the fire department's functions.

During the 1960s, the medical community focused on the problem of heart attacks. Technical developments led to knowledge about electrical defibrillation and closed-chest pulmonary resuscitation. While these positive steps were reducing the death rate of patients who reached the hospital, any major reduction in overall mortality was still limited because many persons died at the scene or en route to the hospital. Consequently, an emphasis was placed on upgrading ambulance technicians nationwide to Advanced First Aid and Cardiopulmonary Resuscitation (CPR) training.

As a result of increased attention to the medical community's goal of reducing the overall mortality rate through increased preparedness, emergency medical care began to receive added attention throughout the country. The long-range effects of quality emergency medical care on mortality were discussed in a 1966 report by the National Research Council's National Science Foundation, titled "Accidental Death and Disability, the Neglected Disease of Modern Society." The report concluded that of the mobile emergency teams studied, most had an average response time of more than 40 minutes, and had inadequately equipped and trained crews. This study, and others, resulted in the development of prehospital EMS, although it would require nearly a decade for this reformation to take shape.

Primarily as a result of concern over highway safety, the Highway Safety Act of 1966 (Standard 11) addressed EMS issues by developing specifications that covered ambulance attendant training, equipment requirements, and the design of the emergency vehicle itself. A series of national training courses were created, and were implemented in many communities across the country. Many fire departments, while not providing ambulance services, sought to meet these emergency medical training requirements and began responding to medical emergencies to provide "first response" medical care until an ambulance from another agency arrived.

The Emergency Medical Services Systems Act of 1973 designated federal funding for improved EMS across the nation though the development of regional EMS systems. Specific requirements outlined under this act—training and certification, interagency cooperation, equipment development, communications, and public education—are still recognized today as key elements of effective EMS. Fire departments, with regionalized training and certification programs provided a ready model for the development of regional EMS systems, and were set up—using communications technology and strategically located stations—to be able to reach anywhere in a community within minutes.

In the mid-1980s, much of the federal funding for EMS programs was reduced or eliminated, and, as a result, EMS systems became more dependent on state and local funding. Many of the differences in levels of service that persist today—the lack of universal 911 coverage, for example—can be traced to the decline in federal funding.

Since the mid-1960s, and particularly since the mid-1980s, the number of fire departments that provide EMS as a significant part of their service has increased. Many departments that already were providing EMS have expanded their level of service, or have started providing transport services in addition to first response. Greater public demand for increased services may be one reason, and another the decrease in the number of fires as a result of increased fire prevention and protection efforts. Another major reason is because the fire chief of today has come up through the ranks with a knowledge and understanding of what EMS is, and perhaps was even an EMS provider. This "hands-on" perspective can go a long way toward developing the relationships that are necessary for a fire department to be a successful part of an emergency medical services system.

THE EMERGENCY MEDICAL SERVICES SYSTEM

Terminology is always important when dealing with a critical issue like EMS, because confusion or inaccurate perceptions can lead to organizational differences or disputes, and ultimately to ineffective service or harm to patients. One often-misinterpreted term is "EMS system." It is important that fire departments realize that prehospital EMS is only one small, yet important part, of an EMS system.

The Emergency Medical Services Systems Act of 1973 (Public Law 93-154) defined an EMS system and the components that such a system must have. The program regulations for this law referred to this definition of an EMS System:

> [An EMS system] provides for the arrangement of personnel, facilities, and equipment for the effective and coordinated delivery of health care services in an appropriate geographical area under emergency conditions (occurring either as a result of the patient's condition or of natural disasters or similar situations) and which is administered by a public or nonprofit private entity which has the authority and the resources to provide effective administration of the system.

This original definition of an EMS system listed 15 component parts, which included:

- manpower;
- training;
- communications;
- transportation;
- facilities;
- access to specialized care facilities;
- coordination with other emergency services;
- citizen involvement in policy-making;
- provision of services without regard to ability to pay;

- follow-up care and rehabilitation;
- standardized recordkeeping system;
- public information and education;
- review and evaluation;
- a mass casualty and disaster plan; and
- linkages with other agencies.

In January 1993, the National Association of State EMS Directors (NASEMSD) and the National Association of EMS Physicians (NAEMSP) ratified a joint position statement which, in effect, revised the 20-year-old definition of an EMS system to be more applicable to today. This new definition, widely recognized by national fire service and EMS organizations, states that an EMS system is:

A comprehensive, coordinated arrangement of resources and functions which are organized to respond in a timely, staged manner to targeted medical emergencies, regardless of their cause and the patient's ability to pay, and to minimize their physical and emotional impact.

The NASEMSD/NAEMSP position paper lists the resources of an EMS system as currently including (but expanding beyond):

- Professional, occupational, and lay disciplines, such as prehospital EMS providers and other public safety personnel, and includes emergency medical/public safety dispatchers.
- Facilities, agencies, and organizations, including fire departments, rescue squads, ambulance companies, law enforcement agencies, as well as hospitals, government agencies, and EMS professional organizations.
- Equipment, such as ambulances and rescue vehicles, medical equipment and supplies, extrication devices, communications equipment, and personal protective equipment.
- Funding, whether from various government sources, fees and other revenue sources, reimbursement mechanisms, or donations.

Functions of a comprehensive EMS system include:

- System organization and management.
- Medical direction.
- Human resources and education.
- Communications.
- Transportation.
- Definitive care (facilities).
- Quality assurance/improvement, evaluation, and data collection.
- Public information and education.

- Disaster medical services.
- Research.
- Care of special-needs patients.

The resources and functions of an EMS system are coordinated through specific stages of EMS response to medical emergencies, and these stages define the scope of the total system. According to the NASEMSD/NAEMSP position paper, the stages of EMS response are (in order):

1. Prevention (injuries/illnesses that don't happen).
2. Detection (realizing that a situation requiring medical attention has occurred).
3. Notification (calling EMS).
4. Dispatch (trained EMS personnel).
5. Pre-arrival (providing instructions on basic care to the caller while EMS personnel are en route).
6. On scene (care provided by EMS personnel).
7. Transport and facility notification (by EMS personnel).
8. Emergency department/receiving facility (care provided at the emergency facility the patient is taken to).
9. Inter-facility transport (if the patient is taken to another facility after evaluation/stabilization).
10. Critical care (specialized care for seriously injured/ill patients).
11. Inpatient care (care provided after being admitted to the hospital).
12. Rehabilitation (to return the patient to the appropriate "quality of life").
13. Follow-up (as required, based on the type of injury/illness).

These stages are applicable to all types of medical emergencies. Fire departments are typically involved in the first seven stages; many departments also provide inter-facility transportation.

It is clear that prehospital EMS is only part of the EMS system. The fire department, as a part of its regular functions, is involved in the EMS system from public education and prevention activities, through dispatch and on-scene activities, and often through transport. Similarly, hospitals may be involved in prevention, medical control, and receiving, through critical care and rehabilitation. Because an EMS system is pluralistic, no single agency can take credit for managing and operating the entire EMS system.

The NASEMSD/NAEMSP position paper also addresses the concern that fire departments providing EMS often put a greater emphasis on firefighting than on EMS, while the majority of their emergency response activity is EMS related. There are similar concerns about specialty hospitals, health care agencies, and other related services. The position paper states:

When EMS, at any response stage, is provided by an agency or institution that also provides non-EMS services, the role and responsibilities of that agency or institution as a sub-component of the EMS system must not be jeopardized by its non-EMS role(s) and responsibilities. Quality patient care will depend upon total commitment to the development and operation of an integrated and comprehensive EMS system.

If the fire service is to provide efficient, effective prehospital EMS, it must operate as part of the total EMS system. This may be an adjustment to some traditional viewpoints, as the fire service has often looked at itself as an untouchable island or monopoly in the area of providing public safety services. Many fire departments, however, have been successful at being an integral part of the overall "EMS team."

EMS IN THE FIRE SERVICE

Today as many as 85 percent of the approximately 34,000 fire departments in the United States are routinely dispatched on emergency medical calls.

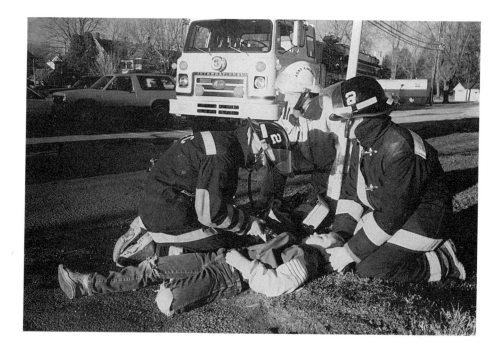

Personnel in these departments are trained to the level of "First Responder," "Emergency Medical Technician (EMT) Basic," "EMT-Intermediate," or Paramedic. Those trained at the First Responder and EMT-Basic levels provide Basic Life Support (BLS) care, while those trained at the EMT-Intermediate and Paramedic level provide Advanced Life Support (ALS) care. Modern technology has led to the availability of semi-automatic defibrillators; personnel at all levels can receive training and become certified to use this piece of life-saving equipment.

While emergency medical care and transportation are provided by many fire departments, many communities use a system in which the fire department responds to EMS calls in an engine or ladder truck as a "first response" unit. Personnel on that unit may be trained at the BLS or ALS level, and provide care until an ambulance arrives. Further care and transportation to a medical facility may be provided by a private, for-profit ambulance company, separate municipal EMS agency, or hospital-based ambulance service. Whether fire service or not, EMS providers may be career or volunteer, and may respond in BLS ambulances, ALS ambulances, or aeromedical ambulances (such as helicopters), in addition to the first response unit.

New designs in apparatus for EMS response include ambulances that also have a small pump, water tank, and one or two 1½-inch hoselines, and full-size pumpers with enclosed cabs that have an ambulance cot and EMS equipment for transporting patients when necessary. First response units in the future may range from specially equipped sedans to sport utility vehicles to other small response units. The future will probably see totally redesigned ambulances with side loading capabilities, where the cot is secured across the width of the ambulance, and the personnel ride facing only forward or backward for safety.

The need for clarity in terminology has not been more evident in EMS than when referring to "first responders." First Responder systems are often confused with the level of EMS training known as "First Responder"; these are often confused with the level of hazardous materials emergency response training.

First responder systems refer to those prehospital EMS systems where the closest emergency response unit with EMS-trained personnel is dispatched, along with a transporting EMS unit. The personnel may be trained at the first responder level; however, more often they are trained at the EMT, EMT-I, or paramedic level. The first-response unit is usually a nontransporting unit—typically an engine company, but often a rescue or squad company or even a ladder company. Some fire departments use ambulances as first-response units, but have arrangements for the transport of noncritical patients with a private ambulance company.

The benefit of a first response system is the rapid arrival of EMS providers, without the financial burden on a department to have ambulance transportation capabilities at every station. Similarly, private EMS companies can increase their efficiency without jeopardizing patient care as well. It is up to the citizens to determine the level of service they want; however, the highest level of care provided at the scene must be continued during transport. Thus, if ALS care is provided by first responders at the scene, an ALS provider must accompany the patient to the hospital. Most fire departments that provide first response at the ALS level also provide ALS transportation or work in a system that uses ALS transportation. Others operate under an agreement that stipulates that the ALS firefighter accompanies the patient to the hospital in the ambulance; in this case, the department must determine whether the fire company has adequate staffing to remain in service, and must have arrangements for the return of the ALS firefighter to his station.

Many fire departments and nonfire EMS departments use "tiered" EMS response systems, which are related to first response systems. There are three primary types of tiered systems: 1) ALS ambulances respond to all calls, but can turn a patient over to a BLS unit for transport; 2) a BLS ambulance is dispatched on all calls, while an ALS ambulance is only dispatched on ALS calls; and 3) a nontransporting ALS unit is dispatched with a transporting BLS unit. These tiered systems work very effectively, whether or not the fire department provides the transport services, because they allow for a given number of ALS units to serve a large population, while maintaining a rapid response time.

Nonclinical Aspects of EMS

There are many aspects of EMS, particularly related to EMS management and leadership, that have little to do with the provision of medical care. These are the somewhat generic aspects of:

- Human resource management.
- The management of nonhuman resources (such as vehicles, equipment, and facilities).
- Customer service.
- Interactions with external agencies (including the medical director who is an integral part of a fire department's EMS activities).
- Training and certification/licensure.
- Information management (because of the medico-legal aspects of recordkeeping that must be addressed, and the need for confidentiality).
- An understanding of current issues affecting EMS (such as health care reform and violence in the workplace).

While all of these are important, special emphasis must be given to three specific areas: public information, education, and relations; risk management; and quality management.

Public information, education, and relations

EMS Public Information, Education, and Relations (PIER) programs provide the means for promoting an EMS system, developing positive public attitudes, and informing citizens about specific EMS issues and techniques. Public information deals with providing facts, typically incident related, to the public. Public education programs teach functional knowledge, skills, or both, as a means of modifying behavior. Public relations programs are designed to create an attitude or general impression, generally positive, rather than to convey specific information.

An EMS PIER is vital to a successful EMS service. Public support, system abuse, public awareness, and education are all areas which a PIER campaign can address. Such a program is very similar to a public fire education program, but addresses specific EMS issues such as injury prevention, calling for medical help appropriately, and citizen CPR. Together, public fire education and public EMS education programs are often referred to as "life safety education."

A good example of a comprehensive EMS PIER campaign is "Make the Right Call—EMS" designed by the United States Fire Administration (USFA) and the National Highway Traffic Safety Administration (NHTSA). "Make the Right Call—EMS" provides information and materials to local fire and EMS departments to teach their citizens:

- what EMS is;
- how to recognize a medical emergency;
- when and when not to call EMS;
- how to call for emergency help; and
- what to do until help arrives.

The campaign includes posters, pamphlets, classroom presentations and workshop guidelines, as well as two videotapes: one for general audiences and one for children. (Campaign materials are available at no cost from the USFA.)

Risk management

Risk management in any health care setting is not just about preventing monetary losses; it is about preventing disability, loss of life, or irreparable business damage as a result of the provision of patient care. Risk management involves direct "hands-on" patient care as well as various indirect aspects of patient care, including the development of effective training programs and the selection of qualified personnel. Regardless of its specific focus, however, the overall goal of risk management is to reduce the frequency and severity of preventable, adverse events that create losses.

Risk management includes the development and application of an occupational safety and health program designed to reduce the risks to EMS personnel in all aspects of their work environment. Measures must be implemented to make the EMS workplace as safe as possible for employees, physically, emotionally, and in terms of mental health. This is done by identifying potential risks; measuring risks to determine their probability; developing strategies to lessen risks; implementing these strategies; and monitoring strategies and activities to ensure their effectiveness. Infection control and hazardous materials response are areas where such risk management measures have been mandated by law.

For risk management efforts to be successful, they require support from personnel at all levels of the organization. Problem identification often requires considerable fact-finding and information-gathering activities; those who perform risk management functions must be seen as trustworthy in order for personnel to be forthcoming about risk management issues. For the risk management process to be successful, it is important that organization members understand it and feel that they are valuable contributors to it, not that the process is being forced on them.

Quality management

Quality management differs from traditional quality assurance programs in that the definition of quality is "meeting the needs and expectations of the customer." In this case, customers include patients and their families, physicians, nurses, taxpayers, visitors to the area, and suppliers. Each customer has different needs and expectations regarding quality; these must be balanced to provide the best result for the ultimate consumer—the patient. In this context, "quality" includes both the clinical quality of medical care (how well the care is provided and how the care affects the patient's outcome), as well as the customer's perception of that care. This extends the concept of quality beyond the traditional focus on clinical proficiency, to include all aspects of care.

The goal of every EMS system should be to continuously evaluate itself and constantly strive for performance improvement. In order to do this, it is first necessary to establish difficult but achievable goals for every behavior inherent in the system. Examples of such goals would include "a response time of six minutes or less to 90 percent of all ALS calls," and "an on-scene time of no more than 10 minutes on 95 percent of all trauma calls." The role of quality management then is to measure the system's actual performance against those goals. If data analysis reveals that an EMS system is meeting performance goals, new goals should be set which encourage higher levels of performance. If, however, it appears that a system is continually falling below the standards set, the system should be analyzed to determine the cause(s) of the problem. Once the cause has been identified, a plan should be developed and implemented to correct the problem.

There are many benefits of adopting a quality management process, including improved patient care, higher employee morale, greater patient satisfaction and outcomes, and decreased cost. For the process to succeed, however, everyone in the EMS organization, particularly those at the top, must be involved and committed to performance improvement.

Fire chiefs often view EMS strictly in terms of providing emergency care, and overlook the other important aspects of EMS. Unfortunately, this can lead to a misrepresentation of the department's needs related to EMS at budget time, in public forums, or during times of crisis. There are many aspects of EMS that are not clinical in nature, and should be fully integrated with other related department activities or programs. These include, but are not limited to, public information, education, and relations; risk management; and quality management.

CHALLENGES AND ISSUES FACING FIRE SERVICE EMS

There have always been challenges to fire service EMS, and the future holds more of these than ever before. To avoid being discouraged, however, it is important to point out that past challenges have been overcome by those with a vision of making EMS an integral part of the fire service.

The biggest EMS challenge to the fire service has been acceptance. Almost a moot point now, there was a time when many firefighters and fire chiefs wanted nothing to do with EMS because it was viewed as a new service and they had joined the fire department "to fight fires." Often, it was a lack of understanding about EMS, an insecurity about learning EMS skills, or a similar attitude that was actually the cause of this negativity. In some areas fire department EMS providers still face a lack of acceptance by medical personnel, such as physicians and nurses. Again, these attitudes may spring from job insecurity or a lack of understanding.

As may be expected, funding for fire service EMS has been, is, and probably always will be a challenge. In the past, EMS had to compete with fire suppression forces, fire prevention, and even equipment maintenance for funding. Now, with EMS making up the majority of a fire department's emergency responses, a more complicated type of competition—from the private sector—is surfacing. Financial concerns—costs, budgeting, and even revenue—are important EMS considerations. Many fire departments find that EMS is "keeping them in business," because the fire problem is decreasing and EMS responses are increasing; on the plus side, fire departments can bill for EMS service.

There are many other issues facing EMS today, and an even longer laundry list of items will confront fire service EMS in the future. Among today's issues are:

- Privatization. Private companies being contracted to provide EMS for municipalities.
- Legislation and standards. Requirements, often in the name of responder safety, which put fiscal and policy requirements on fire and EMS departments.
- Health care reform. Changes in the way health care is administered may affect the fire department's role in the EMS system.
- Expanded roles for EMS providers. Many departments are now offering services beyond emergency response, including vaccinations, home health care, and episodic care.
- The changing workforce. Workplace diversity is a very important management issue in the emergency services.
- Increased educational and training demands, including certification and licensure. These requirements cover personnel, time, and funding.
- Accreditation. All EMS departments may be required to be "accredited" by a national accreditation agency in the future; fire departments must begin preparing now.
- Overcoming tradition. This is the "square wheel" which has kept the fire service from forging ahead in the delivery of services such as EMS.

Additional fire service EMS issues of the future include:

- Improvements in technology that will affect communications, equipment, and vehicles.
- A demand for an increasing scope of practice for EMS providers, including providing primary care and public health services.
- Bidding for services, with the potential for losing EMS transportation services.
- A better educated, more savvy public (due, in part, to television), which will result in higher expectations.
- A changing and aging population, changing public education needs, and increasing responses.
- The need to manage fire service EMS competently, like a business.
- Increased research in EMS, necessitating a close working relationship with medical directors, hospitals, and research institutions.
- Regionalization/consolidation of EMS services.
- The need to market the organization and services provided as a private business would.

FIRE SERVICE EMS LEADERSHIP/MANAGEMENT

Fire chiefs and other fire service EMS managers need to be ready to face the challenges and issues confronting fire service EMS today and in the future. They need the knowledge, skills, and abilities to move forward, to effect change, and to break traditional paradigms that have held the fire service back for so many years. These leaders and managers must ensure an efficient and dynamic EMS system given current EMS requirements and future EMS trends. One way to do this is by following the "EMS Leadership/Management Process" taught by the National Fire Academy.

The EMS Leadership/Management Process involves analyzing a problem or issue, setting appropriate goals, and establishing and maintaining an effective approach to the challenge or opportunity, while focusing on the department's vision for EMS. Ideally, EMS leaders and managers should complete the entire process for virtually every issue/topic they confront. The process uses the following six steps:

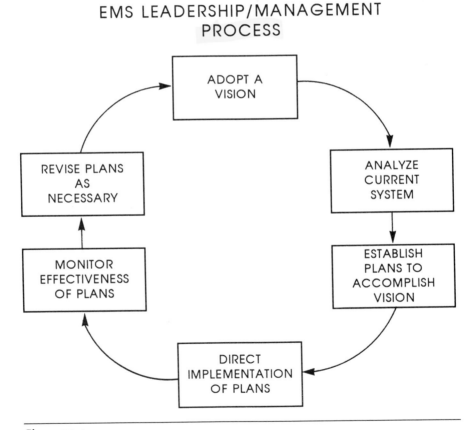

Figure 22-1.

Step 1

Adopt a Vision. Adopt a vision for EMS in order to develop an effective, viable EMS system consistent with that vision. Rationale: Leaders must have a vision of the future of the constantly evolving field of EMS, and must identify their organizational and personnel mission, consistent with that broader vision for EMS. (Note: This step differs from specific goal setting, which is done as part of Step 3.)

Step 2

Analyze System. Analyze performance and characteristics of current EMS system. Rationale: Leaders and managers must understand the current system—its level of performance, functioning, and local needs—as a baseline from which to effectively lead that system toward fulfillment of its mission.

Step 3

Establish Plan. Set/establish the plans and policies necessary to accomplish the vision. Rationale: Once the current system is evaluated and understood, plans and policies which lead that system from its current status toward fulfillment of its mission must be developed.

Step 4

Direct Implementation. Direct/motivate/inspire the implementation of plans and policies required to achieve the vision. Rationale: In order to succeed, leaders and managers must ensure that organizational policies are embraced and plans are followed. Often, they must "sell" or justify policies and programs both inside and outside the organization. They must have the savvy and exercise the interpersonal skills necessary to achieve the vision, and the judgment to delegate the operational and technical aspects of this step, as appropriate.

Step 5

Monitor Effectiveness. Monitor the effectiveness of changes through sound analysis techniques. Rationale: Leaders and managers must understand the effects of their actions by systematically monitoring system performance. Effective documentation systems and procedures must be in place to ensure accurate data analysis and interpretation.

Step 6

Revise Appropriately. Generate solutions to refine and improve the system and continue to monitor. Rationale: The EMS Leadership/ Management Process is cyclical; leaders and managers must constantly develop, implement, and evaluate refinements. Effective leaders must continually modify their vision and develop new, creative strategies and policies in light of future opportunities and challenges.

EMS management resources

There are many local, state, national, and federal resources which can help fire service EMS leaders and managers apply the EMS Leadership/ Management Process and meet the challenges of the future. Rather than trying to reinvent the wheel, fire departments should look to other emergency services (even those outside the fire service) for ideas and advice. Regional EMS councils, public health agencies, health care entities, and hospitals (especially emergency departments) are also available to provide information and, possibly, other resources.

At the state level, many fire departments already have a relationship with the state fire marshal's office, state fire academy, and other fire-related organizations. These groups may have EMS information or EMS management-related courses available. State agencies that do have this type of information, however, are also available to fire departments. These agencies include the state EMS director and state EMS training coordinator. These state EMS offices are often in the state health department, but deal in particular with EMS system issues, including issues related to prehospital EMS.

At the national level, there are many fire- and EMS-related organizations. Most fire departments are familiar with the fire organizations, but often are not aware of the EMS activities of these organizations. For example, the International Association of Fire Chiefs (IAFC) has an EMS Section that deals with fire service EMS issues on a national level, and the National Volunteer Fire Council (NVFC) now represents the voice of both fire service and nonfire service volunteer EMS personnel across the country. While not specifically a fire-related organization, NAEMSP has, as members, many fire department medical directors. Another important national organization is the National EMS Alliance (NEMSA), an "organization of EMS organizations" whose mission is to promote cooperative working relationships between and among EMS organizations. With the support of groups like the American College of Emergency Physicians, the American Ambulance Association, and NAEMSP, NEMSA will be a powerful EMS ally. And the fire service, through the IAFC, International Association of Fire Fighters (IAFF), and National Fire Protection Association (NFPA), is a part of it.

There are several federal agencies that are involved programmatically in EMS. Some agencies conduct research, others compile statistics, and still others develop or provide training materials or information to assist fire and EMS departments and providers across the country. The agencies most likely to have information of use to the fire service EMS include:

- U. S. Department of Agriculture/Rural Development Administration (low-interest loans for rural EMS facilities and equipment);
- U. S. Department of Transportation/National Highway Traffic Safety

Administration/EMS Division (national standard EMS training curricula, EMS PIER information, and some grant programs);
• Federal Emergency Management Agency/United States Fire Administration (EMS publications and information); and
• General Services Administration (specifications for ambulances).

These agencies coordinate their activities through the Federal Interagency Committee on EMS, which is chaired by the USFA.

One federal agency of special note is USFA's National Fire Academy (NFA), which has a comprehensive EMS Management curriculum. EMS courses at NFA include *Management of EMS*; *Advanced Leadership Issues in EMS*; EMS hazardous materials courses; and health and safety courses. There are other EMS-related courses at NFA taught outside the EMS Management Curriculum as well.

SUMMARY

EMS is a primary service provided by the majority of fire departments across the country. Within these departments, EMS typically accounts for 70 to 80 percent of the emergency activity. Life safety education programs are now encompassing both public fire and public EMS education as a part of an overall PIER program. What used to be firefighter safety programs are now department risk management programs, and what used to be EMS quality assurance programs have become department-wide quality management programs. In other words, it is almost impossible to segregate EMS from the other functions of a fire department; in fact, many departments are now called "fire and EMS" or "emergency services."

EMS has changed dramatically since the Emergency Medical Services Systems Act of 1973 was promulgated, and it continues to change at a rapid rate. To keep abreast of these changes and remain a viable EMS agency, fire departments must have a vision for the future of EMS, and must use the EMS Leadership/ Management Process as they confront different issues and challenges. Fire departments also must tap into the many local, state, national, and federal resources that are available to them.

The prehospital component of an EMS system is recognized as "a public safety entity delivering a public health service." As always, the main purpose of EMS is patient care; however, if EMS in the fire service is not managed appropriately, it won't remain in the fire service very long. Another entity will be providing the patient care to the citizens the fire department is sworn to serve, and reaping the revenue and public relations benefits.

23

Volunteer, On-Call, and Combination Departments

RICHARD A. MARINUCCI

CHAPTER HIGHLIGHTS

- Recruitment and selection are closely related and success at both is essential for volunteer, on-call, and combination departments.
- Training must be comprehensive for the services provided, while considering scheduling to meet concerns of the membership.
- Fire prevention services must be considered an important function of all departments.

*A*CCORDING TO THE National Fire Protection Association (NFPA) only an estimated 6 percent of the more than 30,000 fire departments in the United States are fully career. Approximately 94 percent of the fire departments use the services of volunteer members (volunteer shall mean firefighters who are not considered career or full-time employees, regardless of whether or not they receive compensation); 90 percent are mostly or exclusively volunteer.*

Volunteer firefighters provide fire protection and other emergency services in a variety of communities either solely as volunteers or as part of a combination department (departments that use both career and volunteer firefighters, regardless of the percentage of each). Although many communities use volunteers out of necessity, for reasons of cost, political climate, growth of community or the transition of the department, others choose this method of fire protection not only for its cost savings, but because it provides competent professional service that meets the needs of the community.

There are benefits and drawbacks to any type of service system. Using

---

*United States Fire Department Profile Through 1989, Carter, Michael J., December, 1990.

volunteers and on-call firefighters is popular for financial reasons, and also has these advantages: greater community involvement in the fire department; a fostering of creativity, innovation, and dialogue; an adequate personnel pool in a labor-intensive business; and a way to address specific community needs. The negative aspects include longer response times, the fact that member's lack of time may limit the abilities of the department, and conflicts between career and volunteer members that can detract from the fire department's mission. Either way, it is helpful to know both the positive and negative aspects of each type of fire department service.

Good management and administrative practices are as important in volunteer and combination departments as they are in any company. Chiefs of these departments are expected to lead and perform, are held accountable for their actions, and are faced with ever increasing responsibilities. They require knowledge of laws and regulations. Clearly, chiefs of volunteer and combination departments need not only the knowledge and skills essential in all administrators, but also the capability to deal with the unique nature of these organizations. Often the financial constraints of a combination or volunteer department require that the chief seek better or innovative ways to tackle problems by examining and evaluating traditions and investigating alternate methods. As a leader, you must recognize the need to develop new practices and expand current ones.

RECRUITMENT

No fire department can function or survive without adequate staffing. The most important responsibilities of volunteer, on-call, and combination departments are to recruit and retain enough qualified firefighters to provide the required services. There is a direct correlation between recruiting and retention, in that the reasons that current members stay are very often because of the same benefits that attract potential recruits. Members join the fire department for excitement, the opportunity to save lives, for challenge and recognition, a chance to contribute to the community and to learn new skills, and for social involvement and camaraderie. These reasons remain important after an individual joins and continue throughout his "career" with the department. If you can provide for these needs, you can address both recruitment and retention. As fire chief, you must view the firefighters as your "customers"; they provide service to their "customers," the citizens.

Recruitment is the process of attracting and evaluating potential candidates for the department. It includes all steps in the hiring process, beginning with advertising (both formal and informal), application, testing, and selection. Retention is keeping personnel once they have been hired or enlisted. You need to establish a reasonable goal with respect to longevity before you can address the issue of retention. (How many years of service can be expected from each successful recruit?)

While statistics indicate that, overall, the number of active volunteers in the United States is on the decline, there are many departments that are able to meet their personnel needs through successful recruitment and retention. If you select the right people, they will stay. This chapter suggests how to recruit and retain, but don't fail to research the techniques of other successful fire departments. The departments that have active enlistment processes provide many great examples of both how to recruit and how to establish effective programs designed to retain existing members. The networking you do with other fire chiefs, similar departments, and professional organizations, such as the International Association of Fire Chiefs, NFPA, and National Volunteer Fire Council, is a good means of getting information. Also consider the techniques used by other volunteer organizations or agencies that need to recruit and retain, for example, the Red Cross or police auxiliaries. Find out what works for them and whether their ideas can be adapted to your organization. While there are many ways to generate applications and arouse interest in a fire department, failure to consider all aspects of the entire system is simply an exercise in futility.

Don't forget to consider as part of your system the impact of the department on people's families, jobs and social lives—you are asking them to make a major commitment to the department. If the department does not compen-

Professional organizations and associations, and associations like the IAFC, NFPA, and NVFC can offer assistance.

sate for the disruptions it causes or does not meet the needs of the individual, recruitment and especially retention will suffer. The department must be well-organized, professional, and competent, and also must be fun.

Evaluate Your Department

Before you bring any additional members into the department, you need to evaluate your organization. Does your department have a mission with established goals and objectives? If not, the organization will flounder, creating confusion for both existing members and recruits. How do you develop a fire department that is effective and efficient? Remember that ineffective, mismanaged, or incompetent organizations can neither attract members nor hold on to quality firefighters within the organization. Competent individuals do not want to continue to volunteer their time if their needs are not met or the organization is not effective. Try to keep thinking about why people join—to meet specific needs of achievement, recognition, ability to do the job and so on. If you do not meet these needs, you will not attract or keep good people.

How do you develop an effective organization that emphasizes skills in the areas of administration and management?

You begin by establishing a plan. Because recruitment is not just the chief's job, this plan must be developed by and involve the entire department. Every department member has a proprietary interest in recruiting quality people to maintain the organization. This "buy-in" cannot be overemphasized. Consider establishing a recruitment committee to develop the plan, offer suggestions, and get the commitment of the entire department.

Next, determine personnel needs by estimating the number of personnel needed, required skills, and the type of person desired, and base your numbers on services provided, operating activity levels, and the ancillary services offered or required. You will find it helpful to develop job descriptions.

One question seldom asked is, "Exactly how many firefighters are needed to properly discharge the duties of the fire department?" Because this question is rarely asked, the actual roster size of many departments is arbitrary or is a historically significant same number. Establish your rosters based on level of service, response load, services provided, and the operating history of the department. Once you have the appropriate number, you have a better idea of the task before you. If you need to add only a few people, your level of recruiting effort will be less than that of departments that need to add significant numbers of personnel.

To sell, you need to know your product. Develop a list of the benefits of membership. You need to know what you are offering potential members. Recruiting for the fire department really should not be that difficult because the service has a lot to offer: excitement, friendship, respect, the chance to save a life, and a whole host of other positive reasons. You can convince people you have a great product (or opportunity) for them if you know exactly what it is. Discover the actual benefits by talking to those who have them—the existing membership. Ask current members what they like and don't like, what works for them, and for any suggestions they may have. By identifying the privileges of membership, you can respond to people who want to know "what's in it for me."

Next, establish the criteria for the position of firefighter. There should be some physical as well as academic requirements. These standards may vary based on the services your department provides. For example, departments that provide extensive emergency medical services need members who can handle the rigors of intense medical training. At a minimum, such members need a high school diploma as a prerequisite. Require an agility test and physical examination and examine the NFPA's guidelines as well as the sample provided in the technical resources section. Although many people think volunteer fire departments differ from paid departments, most must adhere to a variety of federal and state laws, including the Americans With Disabilities Act, Civil Rights Act, and other antidiscrimination laws. The physical and intellectual requirements must be job related with no bias shown toward any particular group of people or protected class. The laws in this field change rapidly, so you need to consult with an attorney to reduce the risk of violating labor or other laws. Also, assistance is available from a variety of state and federal organizations such as municipal leagues, risk management agencies, and professional associations. Chapter 4 of this Handbook, Management and the Law, covers most of the relevant laws.

Look at how much time the individual volunteer needs to be successful and how much time a person must contribute to be considered an active volunteer. It is only fair that you be able to give this information to potential recruits, so that you don't waste their time or yours. Review any special needs of your department; for example, do you need daytime personnel to fill certain spots on the roster?

What are the skills, knowledge, and abilities needed for the job? List the prerequisites needed to meet these requirements. What are the elements which indicate possible success as a volunteer firefighter? These include time available for the job, stability, physical skills, ability and willingness to train and learn, basic communication skills and other related issues.

Next identify your target group or the audience from which you will seek potential recruits. It may be helpful to develop a list of exactly what kinds of people you are trying to find. Keep this list very broad so you do not eliminate any particular group. While there may be some typical profiles for members, leaving the target group as large as possible enhances your selection field. Eliminate your stereotypes and begin to look outside the traditional volunteers, i.e., white males. Investigate ways to attract females, minorities, or others not typically associated with volunteer fire departments. Get rid of any predetermined mind-sets. Having a variety of members enhances your service to the

ABOVE: *Whether paid, part-time, or volunteer, the job of firefighter requires physical activity. Develop a test to be included as part of your selection process.*

RIGHT: *Encouraging membership of women firefighters increases the talent pool from which to select volunteer firefighters.*

community because they give you a better perspective of the citizens you are trying to serve. Citizens will have a better understanding of the department and a better relationship with it. Volunteerism by the community is for the community and must reflect the community to be truly successful.

Move ahead to developing a strategy for where to look and ways to advertise. There are many avenues for reaching the public and advertising your needs. While you can use the media, information meetings, signs and posters, or newsletters, probably the most effective recruitment tool is personal contact between department members and potential recruits. Current members should ask outsiders to join. This seems to be the most effective and proven method of recruitment. If your members are doing the recruiting, they will be looking for potential successful candidates and thereby become part of the process. This is helpful when the candidate actually joins, because current members can help the recruit succeed and stay with the department. The personal touch also "shows off your product" and, if your quality people are the sales staff, the product sells itself. Proud members are your best salespeople. Outsiders need to be coaxed into joining because they often are unsure of their interests or what the job entails. Show your members how to recruit by suggesting that when they talk to potential recruits, they introduce themselves and discuss their background, history of the department, membership benefits; and how to apply.

Conducting an informal meeting can help explain the work of volunteer firefighters and the needs of the department.

Make clear to your members that recruiting is a continuous process, one that requires diligence and commitment. They should always be scouting prospective members. If you were to check with other departments and chiefs, you would be amazed at the variety of locations where volunteers have been found. In fact, check your own department's membership—you may be surprised at the various backgrounds of your members.

Another good way to get your message out and explain your department is by holding a "recruit night." The recruit night is an opportunity to invite all potential candidates to the fire station for an informational meeting. You can explain department operations, answer questions, and sell your department to interested parties. This also is a good time to discourage candidates who are unable to meet your predetermined requirements. Use slide programs, station tours, and personal contact with firefighters to deliver your message.

After you collect the applications, continue the selection process. (The application is part of the selection process.) This can include a written test, agility test, oral interviews, and background checks. The costs of tests may be a factor in your process and should be considered when you establish the order in which tests are used. Do the least expensive tests first to eliminate unsuccessful candidates, then use the more costly tests. A good selection process helps to weed out unacceptable candidates before you waste a lot of time, energy, and money on training.

RETENTION AND MOTIVATION

Retaining and motivating a volunteer or on-call firefighter is no different than keeping and motivating any other employee. You must understand why the firefighters joined and what makes them stay. These members want recognition for a job well done and a voice in the operations. To show your appreciation, and depending on the background of your department, consider:

- Awards programs to recognize the accomplishments of your members. (A sample is provided in the appendix).
- Recognition banquets.
- Tax incentives. (Some states allow municipalities to offer these. Check your jurisdiction's laws.)
- Length-of-service awards.
- Retirement benefits.
- Health insurance.
- Employee assistance programs.
- Social activities.
- Tuition reimbursement.
- Free use of public facilities.
- Longevity pay or bonuses.

Recognition is part of any successful retention program.

Involve families in department-sponsored activities

- Disability insurance.
- Newsletters.

While all of these programs and benefits can be considered incentives, probably the greatest incentive for people is to be treated fairly and with respect. With this in mind, it is important to train managers, chiefs, and officers. How firefighters are treated will have more impact on retention than any other programs or "gimmicks."

TRAINING

Good training is what ensures the response readiness of all of the members, but training has become more complex as a result of the changing demands on the fire service. Legislation and the time needed to train have become big constraints. Changes in legislation at the state and federal level require specific numbers of hours of training for firefighters to become certified, licensed, or just to meet the law.

Training is essential for firefighting, hazardous material response, EMS, rescue, and special incidents, but the burden of needing to provide so much training can create a barrier to quality training in any and all areas because of the time requirements and the need for special knowledge of equipment. The volume of emergency activity, and competition for leisure time, family life, and work all become factors. These barriers can be overcome if you plan carefully and implement worthwhile training. The following three steps can help you to plan.

1. EVALUATE TRAINING NEEDS

Your initial evaluation should be with respect to the type and amount of training necessary to prepare personnel for their job responsibilities. This is based on legislative mandates, desired service levels for the community, and the desire of individual department members and the chief to commit to training, while working within the above-mentioned time constraints.

2. ESTABLISH THE TRAINING SCHEDULE

Next, establish a schedule based on these needs, keeping in mind the availability of volunteers and on-call firefighters. Remember they can't get all the training at one time; you have to consider the time they spend responding to emergencies as well as the time they need for their personal lives and full-time jobs.

You will need to extend the usual time period scheduled for training. Perhaps it would be better to spread two or three sessions over the period

Live fire training is essential in developing and maintaining firefighting skills.

of a month than it would be to schedule an entire weekend of training. You may wish to take a multi-year approach to offering the necessary training, allowing personnel a few years to obtain the certifications and licenses required by your department. If there is no sense of urgency, allow members to proceed at a reasonable pace, one that does not overwhelm them individually. However you choose to schedule training, prioritize it based on your needs (i.e. types of fires, EMS, rescue, etc.)

3. ESTABLISH THE POSITION OF TRAINING OFFICER

Each department needs a training officer responsible for coordinating all training activities. Depending on the size of the department, additional instructors also may be needed. One of the advantages of volunteers is that they bring to the organization skills from their primary employment. Use as much of this talent as you can by developing their instructional capabilities. Some states have certification requirements for instructors. Check your state's requirements.

A training program must include both the basics for everyone, and some alternatives based on members' levels of experience. Not all members need the same training all of the time. For example, the basic skills in entry-level training are for recruits; senior firefighters need more advanced training. Specialized training should be offered for recruits, firefighters, and officers. There should be officer classes for current officers, as well as courses designed to prepare future officers. These courses should include the Incident Command System, fireground tactics and strategy, personnel management, and leadership.

The department also may require specific training to maintain licenses and certifications. Some state laws, for example, require continuing education credits to maintain emergency medical technician (EMT) status. Also, OSHA and other federal laws require specific training for hazardous materials responders. Training should begin with "need to know" information and expand to "nice to know" information as time allows.

Training is extremely important in preparing personnel to properly discharge their duties as firefighters. Quality training is not only essential but, when conducted properly, enhances the perception the public has of department members. Members tend to feel good if their training is good. Continue training to keep skill levels high. Training can motivate and set or change policy. Consider it an investment in the future.

PROMOTIONS

For immediate and long-term development of any fire department, there must be a fair and equitable promotional system that moves competent, qualified personnel up to appropriate positions in the organization. To establish a promotional system that considers the individuals, the positions needed, and the political realities of the department, there are three steps that should be taken:

1. Establish the officer's position with a corresponding job description.
2. Establish criteria for officers (prerequisites for the positions, i.e., knowledge, skills, and abilities).
3. Establish a selection process.

There are two reasons to have officer positions in volunteer and on-call departments. First, some positions are needed to run the organization efficiently and lend command and control. Second, some positions may be needed as a motivational tool for volunteer firefighters, so you need to create a "career" ladder. Having officer positions available allows a firefighter to establish goals and strive to accomplish something within the organization. Many people seek promotion and are extremely proud when they finally earn their "stripes." Having multiple officer ranks also allows you to develop future leaders for your organization.

Some of the prerequisites you can use for officer positions include experience, previous training, evaluations, and past contributions to the department. By establishing training requirements for promotional opportunities you can motivate members to train as well as improve the status for each position. This also improves public perception of, and public confidence in, the department's ability.

Probably the most difficult decision to make is choosing the appropriate method for selecting officers. Three methods commonly used are:

1. voting by membership;
2. appointment by the chief; and
3. a competitive testing process.

All of these methods have advantages and disadvantages and have met with varying degrees of success in other departments.

Voting can easily make officer selection a popularity contest, restricting officers when tough decisions need to be made. Promotions based on voting also can expose the department to liability problems if qualifications are not used as part of the promotion process. On the positive side, elected officers may receive more support from the membership.

Appointment by the chief may be perceived as favoritism, but does allow the chief to better develop his own team. Since the chief is responsible for the entire organization, proper choices can be made. Still, personalities can cloud the selections.

Competitive testing generally is perceived as being the most fair, but should not be construed as foolproof. There is always the human factor to consider. Competitive testing probably offers the best long-term solution for making promotions.

Department history and culture play important roles in selecting an appropriate promotional process. Regardless of the selection method, the most important part of promotion is to establish prerequisites for the positions to ensure that only qualified people will compete. Training requirements must be part of any promotional procedure.

QUALITY CONTROL

One of the greatest challenges faced by volunteer and on-call departments is how to maintain quality service to the community. There is a general decline in the number of fires, experience, and adequate training facilities to expose members to live burn situations. There is no question that these issues affect the quality of service delivery.

Quality control is a consideration in training and also in the constant evaluation of the physical and mental preparedness of department members. To have able and ready firefighters, there is a need for **training** to promote growth in firefighting skills (and EMS, Haz Mat, etc.); **skills maintenance** for all members; **practice** to ensure efficient, effective delivery; and **testing** to validate that all members are prepared at all times.

Because calls for assistance can occur at any time, all members must be capable of performing their assigned duties. Even with fewer practice fires, members still must be motivated to maintain their skill levels despite the fact that the department is unable to monitor their skill levels on a daily basis. To motivate them to do the best possible job and prepare themselves, the department can monitor by using both random testing and scheduled annual testing. Tactical simulation training with slides, simulators, or both, is an effective alternative to actual command to maintain command skills and expose senior firefighters and junior officers to command training. You must define the skills, knowledge, and abilities required to perform each job and take the necessary steps to ensure that each member is capable.

POLICIES AND PROCEDURES

Every organization needs a set of rules to govern its members, including do's, don'ts, and guidelines for the department's various functions and operations. These rules are a control device as well as a means of communicating the expected behavior and performance requirements to the membership. The whole package includes rules and regulations, special orders, policies and procedures.

- Rules and regulations are the basic internal "laws" that govern the department.
- Special orders are emergency directives needed to address concerns on a short-term basis.
- Policies and procedures offer guidelines on actions.

Drafting rules and policies is one of the most difficult tasks for department managers. It is a time-consuming and not particularly popular job. But help is available! Ask other fire departments and professional organizations, such as the International Association of Fire Chiefs for recommendations. You also can adapt procedures used by nonfire-service organizations (police agencies, private sector groups, etc.). Keep in mind that the committee process lends itself well to the development of rules and regulations, and certain policies and procedures. If you have department members help to draft the rules, group ownership should lead to acceptance and greater compliance. The committee should reflect the make-up of the department, and include firefighters and junior- and senior-level officers. Keep the committee large enough to include adequate representation, but small enough to operate capably.

Prepare a simple document that outlines the do's and don'ts of acceptable behavior. Define the discipline process, including how to file charges and the procedures for grievances and appeals. Include the organization chart, which establishes the vertical and horizontal relationships and responsibilities.

The policies and procedures developed to provide department operating guidelines could include administration; fireground operations; maintenance of apparatus, equipment, and stations; safety; hazardous materials; training; membership benefits; and communication. Before the policies and procedures are adopted, there should be time allowed for review prior to implementation. An attorney and the governing body (fire board, city council, commissioners, etc.) all should participate in the review process.

EMERGENCY SCENE OPERATIONS

Like any other fire department function, the emergency scene needs to be managed and organized. The Incident Command System (ICS) was developed for this purpose, and it provides a good basis for operations. A formal incident command system is required under the federal law SARA Title III, CFR 1910.120 and could be required by your jurisdiction. Also, national standards, which can be used to argue liability cases, also recommend the use of a formal Incident Command System.

The number of firefighters responding and their method of response (on fire trucks or private vehicles) affect the organization, command, and control of the fireground.

While there are actual incident command systems already on paper, the unique circumstances of volunteer, on-call, and combination departments may require adapting the specifics of local systems. Can you answer the following questions for your volunteer or combination department?

- Who will respond on each and every run?
- In what order will they arrive?
- Will they arrive on fire apparatus as part of a team, or individually in privately owned vehicles?
- Given the time of day and day of week, how many people will respond?

Since fires and other emergencies can happen at any time and since there is no guarantee that all members of a volunteer department will always be available, your Incident Command System must be flexible enough to be used in all situations.

Of particular importance in combination departments in the issue of chain of command—who has the ultimate authority at an emergency scene? This must be resolved and made perfectly clear to all members of the department. Some departments have had success both in designating career members as Incident Commander and also in designating volunteers to be in charge. This is certainly a local decision. One approach is to allow for a transition process. When new career personnel are hired, they often do not have the necessary training and experience, but as they put in time and attend classes, this changes. A gradual, well-planned, phase-in program might both address the concerns of the department and allow for *the most competent* command at an emergency scene.

ACCOUNTABILITY

Tracking emergency personnel at the scene is extremely important and complex. The Incident Commander must be able to track the location and identity of each responder. The nature of volunteer fire departments does not guarantee who will respond or even when or if a member might arrive. Personnel may or may not arrive with fire apparatus. Each department needs a personnel tracking system that begins with arrival at the station or on the scene, and continues through scene operations. Existing systems range from using name tags which are delivered to the Incident Commander or are left with appropriate fire apparatus, to actual tracking devices that sound an alarm if a firefighter is "down." Regardless of the system used, all personnel must report to the officer in charge for assignment. This lets the officer know what personnel resources are available.

Volunteer and combination departments have the added challenge of knowing that any department member could be faced with making initial decisions on the fireground and implementing the Incident Command System. Each member must be able to initiate the incident command process and keep it operational until the first-arriving officer can assume command. Therefore, all members must receive ICS training, be given the opportunity to practice, and be familiar with the transfer of command. Training helps to compensate for some members' lack of experience and for the nature of the volunteer and combination services. It is more difficult to use an Incident Command System in a volunteer or combination department than in a traditional paid department.

Develop an incident command procedure for emergency scenes, custom fit it to your department, and train all members in its use and operation.

SUPPORT AND AUXILIARY SERVICES

Fire Prevention

If you want to offer your community a total service package you must include fire prevention programs which may not traditionally be part of a volunteer fire department. Combination departments have a distinct advantage in this area because paid personnel can be used for fire prevention. All volunteer

Public fire safety education can provide added benefits of improving public relations.

departments share the difficult task of finding enough time and enough interested personnel for these services. To be successful, you need to make fire prevention activities a job requirement.

Fire prevention activities include fire safety inspections, public fire safety education, and fire investigations. Whether a volunteer department is able to perform inspections is based on the number of buildings that need to be inspected, and the availability of personnel to receive the proper training. If there are relatively few buildings, personnel can be trained to perform these services on a part-time basis. But do not overlook the level and type of inspections to be performed. They can vary from simple safety inspections (exit lights, extinguishers and smoke detectors checked) to complete code enforcement with legal authority to obtain compliance. Not all departments can perform full inspections and if yours cannot, you must look to other agencies for support. Local building departments, or county or state agencies may be able to provide inspection services. In combination departments, paid personnel are the logical choice to perform these duties. This increases productivity because downtime spent waiting for alarms is used to enhance fire safety.

Public fire safety education is becoming an important tool in reducing the number of fires, fire fatalities, and injuries. Any department can become involved in public fire safety education to different degrees, but there must be both desire and interest on the part of some of the department's members. Typically, one or two "champions" can promote the cause of public fire safety education. If one or more members are interested, and they have the chief's support, the program will succeed. The department benefits because it is educating the public, and public fire safety education has become a tremendous public relations tool. Through public education, departments can gain support for other programs, including suppression operations, station improvements, additional apparatus or replacement apparatus, personnel benefits, uniforms, safety equipment, etc. Like other activities, you must plan for public education by identifying the target audience, the message you want to deliver, and the method you will use to deliver it. Public education can be offered through schools, the media, open houses and presentations, or by involvement in such other community activities as parades, civic activities, and honor guards at festivals. Look for volunteers who have talent or experience in this area.

Prefire Planning

Gathering information before an emergency promotes firefighter safety and gives the fire department the best opportunity to perform properly at the scene of an emergency. Check commercial, industrial, institutional, recreational, and residential (apartments, townhouses, hotels, and motels) properties within the community. Some activities may be required under county, state, or federal law. Whether a legal requirement or not, this information gathering should be mandatory for all departments, paid, combination, or volunteer. Use a simple format. Computers are not necessary because a single sheet of paper can be used to provide basic information on each occupancy. Put these in loose-leaf notebooks and carry on each fire apparatus. If the dispatch center has the resources to provide the information, keep it there, out of the weather. Either way, have the information accessible so that first responders can begin emergency scene operations.

Fire Investigation

Fire departments are responsible for determining the origin and cause of fires to which they respond. Fire investigation takes experience and getting the training is difficult. It is sometimes easier to ask county or state agencies to provide this service. Some mutual aid organizations have pooled their resources to create investigation teams or task groups, an approach that minimizes the demands on any one department. However, larger departments may have personnel interested in performing this service. If so, they need training and the appropriate credentials. If your personnel are willing, your department will benefit.

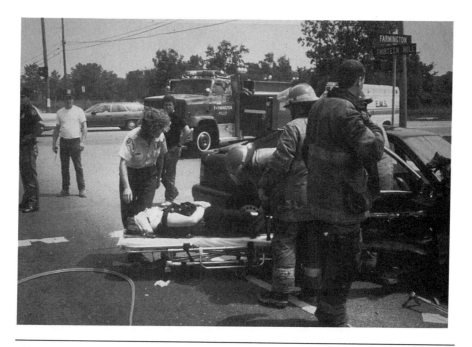

The addition of EMS responsibilities significantly increases the number of emergencies and the training requirements.

EMS

One of the biggest decisions that any fire department must make is whether or not to offer emergency medical service and to what degree. The trend certainly is to become involved—a majority of fire departments in the United States provide EMS service to their communities. Where there are volunteer, on-call, and combination departments, the municipality or community must decide if it wants to become involved. If so, it has to decide the type and level of service to be provided, i.e., basic, advanced, or first responder (or something in between).

Adding to the complex nature of EMS are special rescue situations. Some departments may be involved in these whether they participate directly in EMS or not. Special rescues include underwater, high-angle, extrication, confined space operations, and search and rescue.

The biggest concern for volunteer departments is finding the time necessary to complete the mandatory EMS training, including initial training and the continuing education credits necessary to maintain certification. Typically, medical calls account for anywhere from 50 to 80 percent of a fire department's runs. This added activity, in addition to the time necessary for training, can put a tremendous burden on the fire department and its personnel.

Hazardous Materials

Hazardous material responsibilities have added another burden to volunteer fire departments. Too often the fire department is the only responder available. These departments must try to decide to what extent they want to become involved and what costs they are willing to absorb. Most volunteer departments would be advised to seek other alternatives, such as using mutual aid, regional hazardous materials teams, or private contractors. If a department does want to respond to hazardous materials incidents, it should investigate all applicable state and federal laws.

Fundraising

Many volunteer departments are not supported by tax revenue and must raise money for department operations. The fire service is the only government agency that is forced to raise funds. Some departments choose to do fundraising to limit the extent to which government agencies control them. If you must do fundraising, assess your needs by asking how much money is needed. Involve the entire department and the community. Form a steering committee. Check the laws of your state and municipality. Some successful fundraising events have included carnivals, bake sales, raffles, bingo, dinners and the like. Get creative. If you don't like fundraising, make an appeal for funding through taxes.

CONCLUSION

Volunteer, on-call, and combination departments can be an efficient, effective means to provide emergency service to a community. These departments typically use the innovation and creativity of their members to solve problems. Administrators and managers of these departments must know and understand the advantages as well as the history of the department. Good management and administrative practices are essential.

APPENDIX I
Sample Personnel Procedure

Promotions   No: _____
Rescinds: _____   Effective: _____

I. SCOPE
This procedure shall apply to members seeking promotion to the positions of Sergeant, Lieutenant and Captain.

II. PURPOSE
To outline the policy and procedure, along with minimum requirements to be attained, before being considered for promotion.

III. PROCEDURE
The promotion to the position of Officer within the Fire Department will be accomplished through a consistent, organized, and fair process. When a vacancy in the Officer's Cadre of one of the fire stations occurs and a replacement is desired, the position will be posted at all stations for a period of two weeks. Those members interested shall apply, in writing, to their District Chief within the specified time frame.

Candidates that meet the minimum qualifications for the position as outlined in these procedures will be evaluated based on written and oral examinations, seniority, and a review by the District Chief responsible for the promotion. The written test will consist of questions developed specifically for the vacated position and will address fire suppression knowledge, Department procedures and directives, emergency medical service, hazardous materials, fire prevention practices (i.e., preplans) and station policies. For the oral examination, a panel will be established consisting of Department officers not affiliated with the station requesting the promotions. A single interview board will be used to evaluate candidates seeking a position. The District Chief will provide input into the selection process by reviewing and evaluating each candidate. The final score will be calculated with the following percentages:

Written Examination: 30 percent
Oral Examination: 30 percent
District Chief Evaluation: 35 percent
Seniority: 1 percent per year, up to 5 years
(Seniority points shall accrue from the point a member is eligible for a promotion.)

The candidate with the highest score then will be recommended to the Fire Chief for promotion. Individuals promoted to the rank of Sergeant, Lieutenant, or Captain shall serve a one-year probationary period from the date of appointment.

PREREQUISITES FOR OFFICERS' POSITIONS
In order to be considered for promotion to the position of Sergeant, Lieutenant,

or Captain, Department members must meet the following requirements. Equivalency will be evaluated by the Fire Chief.

  I. **SERGEANT**
- A. Three years on the Department
- B. Fire Fighter II
- C. Fire Officer I
- D. State-licensed E.M.T.
- E. Good history of community service
- F. Satisfactory evaluations and service record
- G. Run Percentage greater than 45 percent during the past 12 months

  II. **LIEUTENANT**
- A. Sergeant's qualifications
- B. One year as a Sergeant
- C. Fire Officer I certification
- D. Fire Officer II
- E. Satisfactory Sergeant evaluation and service record

  III. **CAPTAIN**
- A. Lieutenant's qualifications
- B. Lieutenant for two years
- C. Fire Officer II certification
- D. Fire Officer III
- E. Satisfactory Lieutenant evaluation and service record

APPENDIX II
Sample Personnel Procedure

FIRE DEPARTMENT

Awards and Recognition   No: _____
Rescinds: _____   Effective: _____

During the course of the year members of the _____ Fire Department often do things that deserve special recognition. The Department intends to identify and recognize these individuals because of their various achievements.

These approved awards shall be presented during the annual Fire Department Banquet:

1. MEDAL OF VALOR
2. MEDAL OF BRAVERY
3. FIREFIGHTER OF THE YEAR
4. LIFE-SAVING AWARD
5. CAREER FIREFIGHTER OF THE YEAR
6. STATION FIREFIGHTER OF THE YEAR
7. MERITORIOUS SERVICE AWARD
8. UNIT CITATION
9. RECRUIT OF THE YEAR

Criteria for awards are as follows:

1. **MEDAL OF VALOR**

    This award shall be presented by the Fire Chief to members who have, under especially hazardous conditions, courageously risked their own life to save another. The intention of this is to reward the truly outstanding performances under times of duress and shall be considered for emergencies only. Members receiving this award shall be nominated for the International Association of Fire Chiefs' Benjamin Franklin Fire Service Award.

2. **MEDAL OF BRAVERY**

    This award shall be second only to the Medal of Valor and will be presented to a member for an act which exhibited disregard for personal safety in an effort to save another. This generally will be considered for members acting above and beyond the call of duty and within safe operating policies and procedures of the Fire Department.

3. **FIREFIGHTER OF THE YEAR (DEPARTMENT)**

    This award is intended for the Department member who, over the course of the year, has continually put forth an effort of the highest degree. This may involve fire suppression, emergency medical service, fire prevention, training, or any combination of the above. Further, it may involve an individual event or a collection of exceptional performances. Any current member of the Department may nominate anyone for whatever reasons he or she feels are appropriate. The award will be presented by the Fire Chief at the Annual Awards Banquet, and the recipient also will serve as the official representative at the City Service Awards Program.

4. **LIFE-SAVING AWARD**

   To be awarded to an individual for the saving of a human life. Intended for an individual ***directly*** responsible for the saving of a human life and shall be issued to members of the Department for the saving of a life through various actions such as the application of prehospital emergency medical care or public safety measures.

5. **CAREER FIREFIGHTER OF THE YEAR**

   This award will be presented by the Deputy Fire Chief to the career firefighter who, as nominated by his/her fellow firefighters, is most deserving. Each career member is entitled to submit the name of any career member whom he/she feels is deserving of this award.

6. **STATION FIREFIGHTER OF THE YEAR**

   This award shall be presented by the District Chief at each of the four stations to the member who, as nominated by his/her fellow firefighters at his/her station, is most deserving. All members are entitled to nominate one member from his/her station. District Chiefs are not entitled for nomination.

7. **MERITORIOUS SERVICE AWARD**

   This shall be awarded to members of the Department whose actions have distinguished them from standard performance expected of the position. This award may apply to any phase of the Department.

8. **UNIT CITATION**

   This award may be presented to members of the Department who participated in an action that contributed to the overall professionalism of the _____ Fire Department. This award may apply to any phase of the Department.

9. **RECRUIT OF THE YEAR**

   This award shall be given to the recruit firefighter who best exemplifies the conduct required of a _____ firefighter and continually demonstrates readiness, performance, and excellence in completing the recruit training program. The recruit shall display maturity and leadership potential before fellow recruits and, through dedication and commitment to duty, makes a significant contribution to advancing the goals of the Department.

The following are additional awards that may be presented at any time during the year or during Department or Station functions.

10. CERTIFICATE OF APPRECIATION
11. CERTIFICATE OF TRAINING
12. V.F.W./OPTIMISTS CLUB FIREFIGHTER OF THE YEAR
13. LETTER OF APPRECIATION
14. HIGHEST RESPONSE RECORD

10. **CERTIFICATE OF APPRECIATION**
    Awarded to members who do a good job and merit recognition from the Fire Chief. The award may apply to any phase of the Department. This also may be presented to civilians.

11. **CERTIFICATE OF TRAINING**
    Presented to members who have successfully completed courses approved by the Department.

12. **V.F.W./OPTIMISTS CLUB FIREFIGHTER OF THE YEAR**
    This award is intended for the Department member who, over the course of his/her career, has distinguished him/herself by putting forth an effort of the highest degree. Any current member of the Department may nominate another member. The recipient will be honored at the V.F.W./Optimists Club annual awards ceremonies.

13. **LETTER OF APPRECIATION**
    The letter of appreciation may be sent by any officer of the Department to any member for his/her contributions or support in various events approved by the Department.

14. **HIGHEST RESPONSE RECORD**
    This will be awarded to the member who has responded to the most incidents during a calendar year.

NOMINATIONS

Any member of the Fire Department may nominate another at the time of the incident or occurrence. Submittals should be made within 60 days of the incident. Nominations shall be forwarded to the Station Representative of the Awards Committee, who will submit the nomination to the Awards Committee for review.

For the selection of Department Firefighter of the Year, nominations will be accepted by the Awards Committee. A minimum of three nominations will be forwarded to the Fire Chief for his/her review and selection. The Awards Committee may select an individual to provide a minimum of three nominees.

The Awards Committee will accept nominations for V.F.W./Optimists Club Firefighter of the Year. Nominations will be reviewed and the Awards Committee will recommend the recipient to the Fire Chief for approval.

RIBBON PLACEMENT

Ribbons will be placed in order from highest to lowest as follows.

MEDAL OF VALOR	METAL BOLD BAR
MEDAL OF BRAVERY	METAL BRONZE BAR
FIREFIGHTER OF THE YEAR	SOLID BLUE
LIFE-SAVING AWARD	WHITE/BLUE
V.F.W./OPTIMISTS FIREFIGHTER OF THE YEAR	SOLID RED
CAREER FIREFIGHTER OF THE YEAR	BLUE/WHITE/BLUE
STATION FIREFIGHTER OF THE YEAR	RED/WHITE/RED
MERITORIOUS SERVICE AWARD	RED/WHITE/BLUE
UNIT CITATION	SOLID WHITE
RECRUIT OF THE YEAR	N/A

The ***Medal of Valor*** and the ***Medal of Honor*** always will be placed above and centered on any ribbons displayed on the uniform. The following are examples of ribbon placement:

MEDAL OF VALOR

MEDAL OF VALOR/HONOR

HIGHEST

HIGHEST

APPENDIX III
Sample Fire Prevention Procedure

_____ **FIRE DEPARTMENT**

Pre-emergency Information Sheets   No: _____
Rescinds: _____   Effective: _____

Fire Department personnel shall complete and distribute a pre-emergency information sheet for all addresses in the City with the exception of one- and two-family dwellings. The purpose will be to provide information to responding personnel that will be beneficial during times of emergencies.

The information shall be gathered any time Department personnel completely tour any building. Examples of this would include annual inspections of occupancies, station tours of buildings, or as part of assignments for training programs. Though these can be completed by anyone at any time, the vast majority will be conducted during the duty day in conjunction with the inspection program. Personnel working during the day will be responsible for the completion of the forms in addition to the paperwork associated with the inspection. Indicate on the inspection form who is responsible for submitting the preplan.

If a sheet has been completed for an occupancy, any subsequent contact with the building shall be used to update the existing information sheet. The information shall be recorded on the forms provided and will be distributed to the first-due station, squad, and district chief, Department staff officers, dispatch, and Headquarters for file purposes. This information shall be carried on the squad. If the person completing the information sheet feels that more information is required and it is not offered by the occupant, he/she may use the "Right-to-Know" law to request this information. Members completing the form shall submit it to Headquarters for review and copying for distribution. The member who prepares the preplan shall be indicated on the inspection form submitted by the full-time firefighter.

In order to maximize the benefit of these sheets, time at each station drill shall be set aside for the review of any recently completed forms. Normally, a mention of the pre-emergency information sheets to the personnel will be sufficient, with members reviewing them on their own. But certain occupancies, because of the nature of the hazards present, may require a more in-depth review of the information.

_____ **FIRE DEPARTMENT**

WORKSHEET FOR COMPLETING THE
PRE-EMERGENCY INFORMATION SHEETS

The following is provided as a guide for completing the pre-emergency information sheets for all addresses within the community.

1. Indicate the address of the building. There is no need to indicate subdivisions within a particular address such as suite numbers or apartment numbers. If further delineation is necessary, please include this under special considerations or other information.

2. The name of the building, if applicable, should be used.

3. Include the phone number of the occupancy.

4. *Special considerations:* List any information vital to know prior to the initiation of any Fire Department operations. This space is intended to "flag" any special information necessary, but not to describe it in detail. These items may include unusual construction features, water supply problems, handicapped persons, and the like. If possible, please make any notes on the drawing. Under sprinklers and standpipes, please supply the appropriate information.

5. *Hazardous chemicals:* Indicate if hazardous chemicals are present and how they would affect our operation.

6. Draw a simple site plan of the occupancy. Please include a floor plan by level (one floor plan is sufficient if all floors are similar). Also include fire separation walls, access points noting doors, windows, etc., stairwells and elevators, and the utility shutoff locations. (Please write out electric meter, gas, etc.) Also on the drawing, indicate north with respect to the drawing, and, if at all possible, make your drawing so that north faces the top of the page. Also include on your drawing, fire hydrant locations, fire department connections, any internal fire protection systems, i.e., standpipe locations, etc. and the locations of any hazardous materials or processes. This may be done by placing a number and circling it on the plan and then listing on the back of the form, the number under the hazardous chemical information. The general area of the chemical is sufficient.

7. *Emergency action information:* This is intended to provide any special considerations for Fire Department operations. For example, we may want to evacuate the area immediately, well involved fires may indicate an early collapse, hidden fire areas, concealed spaces, water runoff into sewers, etc.

8. At the bottom of the page please put the station number, the person preparing, and the date. This date will be the date completed.

9. On the back of the sheet please complete all the occupancy information, owner, contact person, alarm company, with the appropriate phone numbers. If possible, obtain two contact persons with phone numbers for emergency contact.

10. *Utilities:* List the location of the gas meter and shutoff, and the electric meter and any electrical panels.

11. *Fire protections:* List the location if it is a limited sprinkler system. Also include any systems, water supply (domestic), pump, tank, etc. For standpipes, list the location of the standpipe connections, i.e., in north and south stairwells, or in hallways of each floor, etc. Valve/control location, indicate where the controls are if applicable. Under other protection systems, list special systems and locations such as Halon systems in computer rooms, CO_2 systems, etc.

12. *Building construction:* Indicate the type of roof construction, wall construction, how many levels above and below grade (a basement is considered a level), whether HVAC is on the interior or on the roof, and if there is roof access via an interior hatch. Also indicate any other information pertinent to the building construction.

13. This space is provided for any other information that you feel would be beneficial but is not found in any other area of this form.

14. *Hazardous Chemical Information:* From what you can note on the inspection and the employer's hazardous chemical list (a requirement for employers under Right-to-know), list any chemicals in excess of five pounds or five gallons. This is a general guide and some chemicals may require listing in any quantity while others may require much more. List the chemicals numerically corresponding to the numbers on the building plan on the front of the sheet. List the common name first (what is it called by the users), followed by the chemical name (this would be the specific chemical make-up). In the next column state the location of the chemicals at the time of the inspection using general terms and the four compass directions. (For example, the northeast corner of the basement.) Use abbreviations as necessary. With the location, also list the maximum quantity of the chemical that may be on the premises at any given time. In the case of an occupancy which does not have any large quantity of chemicals but has numerous small containers, list an average mixture of the chemicals present. (For example, 60 quart containers of oil base paint, 5 one gallon containers of thinners, etc.) Lastly, list the DOT "Hazardous Materials Response Guidebook" guide number for that particular commodity.

Upon completion, please submit the form to Headquarters as soon as possible. It will be reviewed and copied for distribution as called for in the procedures.

Contact Person		Title	Phone
1			
2			
3			

Alarm Company: Phone:

Building Construction	Suppression Systems
Type:	FDC:
Roof:	Riser(s):
Levels:	Valves:
HVAC Location:	Standpipes:
Roof Hatch: Location	Other:

Special Considerations:

HAZARDOUS CHEMICALS				
CHEMICAL NAME	TRADE NAME	LOCATION	QTY	DOT #
1				
2				
3				
4				
5				
6				
7				
8				
9				
10				
11				
12				

PRE-INCIDENT EMERGENCY SHEET

				St. #
Address: Name: Phone:	Drawn By:	Date:	Insp. No.	
	Sprinklers (Full)	Y	N	
Knox Box Y N Location:	Sprinklers (Partial)	Y	N	
	Standpipes	Y	N	
Special Considerations:	Haz. Mat.	Y	N	

N

V. FIRE PREVENTION AND LOSS REDUCTION

24

Planning Community Fire Defenses

JACK A. BENNETT

C H A P T E R　　H I G H L I G H T S

- The concept of master planning and the importance of the "safety element" in the general plan.
- Implementing "planning teams" within the department for the purpose of preparing the fire protection plan.
- The importance of the fire chief's role in the master planning process and in political and legislative activities.
- How to use the methodologies described to produce a fire risk analysis.

THE CONCEPT OF MASTER PLANNING

SINCE THE COLONIAL DAYS in the United States, the fire service has evolved into the first line of defense from unfriendly fires, emergency medical incidents, and a long list of other related emergencies.

How did Benjamin Franklin and the pioneers after him decide where to locate the fire station in the village? How did they evaluate the needs of the "community at risk?" Whatever they did, most of us in this century are still living with their decisions or doing something to change their system to meet today's needs. The heart of master planning for fire protection is found in the following questions, questions which must be asked by all fire chiefs:

- What are the greatest risks in the community?
- What does the community expect from the fire service?
- What level of service does the community get from the fire service?

- Can the level of service be improved?
- If improvements are necessary, what will they cost?
- What can the community afford?

This chapter will discuss master planning concepts, the role of the fire service in the planning and implementation phases, the methodologies used to complete the planning and implementation phases, and the future of planning community fire defenses, with an emphasis on environmental concerns.

THE GENERAL PLAN

The responsibility for master planning normally is delegated to local government. This planning process sets authority for regulating land use through zoning requirements, regulating or restricting the amount of growth, and establishing local controls over all types of new and existing developments. Guiding this process is a document called the "General Plan." In most cases these General Plan documents are legally mandated, and the local governing body usually passes ordinances to put the General Plan in place. This process usually requires public hearings and, sometimes, voter approval before the plans are enacted as statutes by local government. These General Plan documents also contain data and analysis sections where the conclusions are supported and quantified.

The city of Sunnyvale, California, has a Public Safety Department. A resolution was passed to place the Fire Services Section as a subsection in the General Plan of the community. (See sample in Technical Resources Section.)

The state of California and many other states require General Plans to be adopted, and then reviewed periodically. (State of California, Government code, Section 65032.)

The components of a General Plan are shown in Figure 24-1

The safety element of the General Plan will contain information about fire protection in the community. Too often these "safety elements" are incomplete and have not had the input of the local fire department. The information in this chapter will help you to be a "facilitator and motivator" in the preparation of the safety element of the General Plan.

The information on fire protection may include project-specific plans, building construction fire protection ordinances, interior and exterior life safety measures, and special ordinances dealing with the fire problems of the community. The most recent special ordinances deal with the wildland/urban interface and intermix problems throughout the United States. There will be specific references to wildland planning and fire protection later in this chapter.

Along with these special wildland ordinances come maintenance requirements that should be an annual program requirement. This is especially true

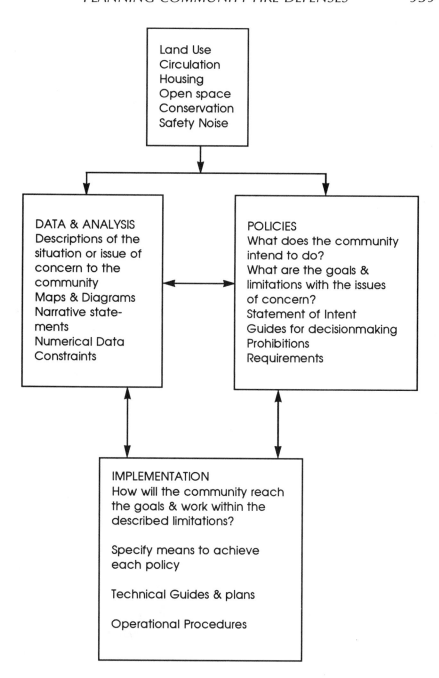

Figure 24-1. Components of a General Plan

in wildland vegetation management. A wildland vegetation program needs annual maintenance because of changes that occur, and growth in vegetation types and amounts.

Fire protection master planning

The 17th edition of the National Fire Protection Association (NFPA) *Handbook,* contains an excellent reference to master planning and fire prevention:

> Master Planning is a participative process which should result in the establishment of a fire prevention and control system which is goal-oriented, long-term, comprehensive, provides known cost/loss performance, and adapts continually to the changing needs of your community.

Fire protection master planning should involve all community governmental agencies, specifically as each affects or in any way supports the fire prevention and control system. There also must be an opportunity to interact with private fire protection systems, appropriate citizen groups, and with national, state, and regional fire service organizations. Master planning involves the participation, cooperation, and commitment of all parties interested in the development of a defined cost-loss relationship for community fire protection. Master planning allows you to systematically analyze fire prevention and control through common-sense procedures. Master planning has three phases:

1. Preplanning. During **the preplanning phase** necessary commitments, committees, estimates and schedules are assembled, and go-ahead approvals are received.
2. Planning. **The planning phase** is a time of gathering and analyzing data, setting goals and objectives, determining an acceptable level of fire protection service, identifying alternatives and constructing the plan.
3. Implementation. **The implementation phase** never ends, because the plan is ongoing and is always being revised and updated. (The *NFPA Handbook,* 17th Edition, Section 10-49.)

The planning process involves the following elements:

- **The mission statement** of the municipality, and especially of the fire department. Mission statements tend to be very broad in concept and are not related to individual objectives, for example:
  "To protect the citizens of the fire district from emergencies and

disasters through fire suppression, emergency medical services, hazard-ous materials mitigation, fire prevention and public education programs."

This mission statement can be amplified through specific objectives, tasks and programs. Consider taking each element of the mission state-ment and establishing a list of objectives for it, for example:

Fire suppression objectives would include the ability to respond to all emergencies with response time of five minutes anywhere in the dis-trict; the capability to maintain all equipment and apparatus in a high state of readiness; and the ability to implement training programs to meet the demands of the public in firefighting and emergency medical services.

- **An environmental evaluation** should be made of the community to identify the factors that influence the welfare of the citizens. These fac-tors can include weather, water, transportation, use of hazardous mate-rials in the workplace, noise and air pollution. A key environmental concern is the impact of the wildland/urban interface-intermix problems of the community.

- **Organizational factors** play an important role in this process. Especially important is the difference between a municipality, a fire dis-trict, and a volunteer fire department district organization. Generally speaking, a city government includes a city council, a mayor (or city manager), and various department heads. In a municipality there are layers of functional organization and resources. The resources are asso-ciated with the various departments. In a municipality, the fire depart-ment uses the resources of the city government to provide public works, personnel, administration, payroll, and other services.

  In a fire district the organization is entirely different. The fire dis-trict must structure its organization to include all of those services and resources internally. The office staff provides personnel, payroll, accounts receivable and payable, employee benefits and coordination of Workmen's Compensation.

  The district's various officers may be assigned to oversee facilities and supplies, communications, training, safety and apparatus and equipment. Because of these differences, the budgets of the municipal fire department and the fire district are very different. The third orga-nization is the volunteer fire department. Here you will usually find "line officers" for the suppression side of the organization, and support personnel or "administrative officers" who are responsible for business and finance. The planning process must have a high degree of account-ability to be effective in these organizations.

- **The objectives of the organization** must be developed internally by the members, and externally with community input from outside of the organization. These objectives must pertain to specific programs that will influence the overall fire protection plan. Examples include automatic sprinkler requirements for businesses and residential occupancies, life safety requirements in places of public assembly, and brush clearance requirements for areas that are in the wildland/urban interface or intermix environment.

- **The implementation** of the objectives has to be accomplished with careful understanding of the impact on the community. This implementation phase is done in concert with the annual budget and the interaction of the community. There must be an "action plan." The action plan spells out what, how, when, where, and by whom tasks will be performed. Time lines are a critical part of any action plan. Time lines spell out specifically when the task is *expected* to be completed and, later, can show also when the task actually *was* completed.

- **The final element** is the *continuous review and evaluation* of the fire protection plan. This becomes perhaps the most important ongoing element. The department must schedule routine discussions of the fire protection plan. It may be necessary to rewrite certain portions of the plan at intervals, depending on the rate of change in the fire protection environment. In the evaluation and review phase, do not overlook community involvement and any external factors which may have changed or been modified.

THE PLANNING METHODOLOGIES

The field of fire protection is already very complex and will continue to be complicated in our technological society. To carry out his responsibilities and duties, the fire chief will expend great effort to cope in this environment. Individual skills can make or break a fire chief's survival.

One of the skills that the fire chief must use is *planning*. In the past, in fact even today, planning skills have not always received enough attention from city managers and directors as they search for the best fire chief. The planning skill may be the most important. This section will introduce planning concepts and ideas to assist both new and experienced chief officers.

The methodologies used to develop the fire protection plan rely on the following factors:

- **Human resources.** These can be from the fire department organization and the community.
- **Planning experience.** Consider outside assistance.
- **Management control.** This can be by a city council, board of supervisors and directors or commissioners of the district or volunteer fire department.
- **Internal and external pressures.** These will be evident and may result

from the affirmative action, valuing differences, and management diversity.

In the book, *Managing Fire Services,* (2nd. Ed. 1988), Robert Burns discusses the "components of the fire protection plan," citing "The departments of fire, building, planning, water, public works, police, education, private industry (fire brigades) and federal, state, county and local agencies."

He also describes three levels of planning: long-range, operational, and tactical.

When a fire department or a fire district needs to evaluate its effectiveness, the "fire risk analysis" system proves its worth.

The demands on the fire service are becoming more complex and diverse. We now spend more of our time responding to emergency medical service and hazardous materials incidents than to fire calls. What level of service does the community expect of the fire department? The department must identify the risk it faces and the probable outcome if certain actions are not implemented.

The community fire protection system includes all public and private services available to protect people and property from fire and to mitigate other emergencies.

The elements that affect this complex system are:

—state government	—county board of supervisors
—federal government	—board of directors-commissioners
—building departments	—media; written, radio and T.V.
—planning departments	—national fire associations
—public works departments	—insurance companies
—utility organizations	—labor organizations
—educational systems	—fire service organizations
—citizen organizations	

Finally, the fire risk system should provide, at a reasonable cost, an acceptable level of fire protection and related services.

There are other planning elements that will be used during the overall process. These include prioritization of subjects, finance considerations, employer/employee relations, and, most importantly, the documentation of the **plan** and approval by the city council or board of directors.

There are some "change factors" that also are important to consider in the planning process:

* **Personal future**—Career opportunities, growth, and upward mobility.
* **Organization future**—Grows out of individual effort and loyalty.
* **Societal future**—Economics, social values, and public perceptions.

(International City Management Association, *Managing Fire Services,* 2nd Ed. 1988.)

The entire planning process is most interesting and challenging. One challenge is the long-range plan which describes the next five years of the department. This is called "visioning" by some managers. In today's world of dynamic changes, a useful and valid five-year plan requires excellent staff work and many difficult and thoughtful decisions. It is, however, a worthwhile and profitable management exercise. To remain current yet still be a five-year plan, it must be updated annually; to do so drop the year just ending and add a new "fifth" year.

A more accurate and currently applicable approach to planning is a two-year plan that is updated every year at a management retreat or general planning session. There are two more important factors in this planning process. One is the input and coordination of the decisionmakers (city council and/or board of directors) during the planning phases. This involves the policy makers in the overall plans of the department. Then, when support for the budget becomes necessary, these people are in a position of having already given their tacit approval for the programs. The other element is the input from the firefighters' representatives (labor union or association). The fire chief's world can become extremely difficult if he does not cooperate and coordinate with the labor element of the department. Remember, while the fire chief does not always have to agree, it is essential to meet and confer with firefighters' representatives.

Several excellent reference books on the general subject of planning are listed in the reference section of this book.

THE "COMMUNITY FINGERPRINT"

Establishing the "community fingerprint" is the next step in planning for fire protection. It is very important to start the planning process with a good understanding of the community and its variables.

These variables include:

- demographics;
- economics;
- environment;
- weather;
- culture; and
- ethnic influence

DEMOGRAPHICS

Demography is the study of a community's characteristics, for example, size, growth, density, distribution, and vital statistics. These data frequently can be found in the nearest public library or city hall. It is important to collect four or five years' worth of data to determine whether there are changes in the demographic information. Perhaps there is a trend which may have a serious impact on future fire protection planning.

For instance, in the past 10 years in the San Fernando Valley area of Los Angeles a trend has been emerging. The Valley once was considered a bedroom community of the city with housing scattered among ranches and agricultural activities. These agricultural areas were replaced with residential developments and shopping centers. Later the housing stock changed from single-family dwellings to multiple-family dwellings, condominiums and town houses.

When these apartment houses and condos were newly constructed, they were well maintained, with few reports of fires. Today, in many areas of the San Fernando Valley, fires occur more frequently and there is a definite change in the living environment.

Similar changes in demographics are occurring in almost every community. The fire protection planner must be aware of and plan to meet the changes.

ECONOMICS

Economics can drive the fire protection planning situation in a positive or a negative direction. The financial condition of federal, state, county and local governments is at risk these days and it clearly is having an impact on the communities. The state of California recently operated for more than 40 days without a budget. In the legislative process to resolve this crisis, many changes were made in the financing of local government. In some cases this meant closing fire stations, reducing company staffing and making overall reductions in normal services. There is a very urgent financial question, "What can the community afford for fire protection?"

The economic situation, good or bad, affects our ability to provide first-class fire service.

ENVIRONMENT

The environment is one of the newest and most important factors to be considered in a community evaluation. The agendas of many environmental groups will affect your planning and ability to provide fire protection. The impact of these groups can be felt as a fire chief plans to build a new fire station.

Have any environmental impact reports been filed? Or negative declarations? (Negative declarations state the reasons for not complying with a full environmental impact report.) Have you considered the existence of the brown beetle or the yellow butterfly in your plans to build the new training facility? Have you considered the environmental impact of flowing large quantities of water during a heavy-stream training exercise? Is it still possible to conduct a live fire training exercise and meet the requirements of the air quality management board? All of these questions will arise in fire protection planning.

High among environmental considerations in many areas of the country is the impact of wildland/urban interface-intermix fires and their threat to the community.

Several fire protection planning models are available for these wildland areas. Of these, one is the Prescott, Arizona, Wildland/Urban Interface Commission, the other, the San Mateo County Fire-Safe Program. Both encourage the participation of many agencies, private citizens, and businesses in the community. The San Mateo County Program began as the "San Mateo Wildland Hazard Task Force." It started within the San Mateo Fire Chiefs Association and grew into a multi-agency group of interested lay people and professionals. Initial funding came from the California Department of Forestry and Fire Protection.

Recently, the organization has been looking at other funding and grants to carry on its goals and objectives. These goals include a three-part attack on the wildland/urban fire problem, code enforcement; public education and vegetation management. The membership now includes water departments, park and recreation departments, the National Park Service, the county, city fire departments and fire districts, and local citizen groups. (The technical resources section includes information about the *four-step system* of education and political alliances within the community, the "public policy summary," and the "memorandum of understanding" used in the Prescott, Arizona program. This information is found in the document "Developing Strategies in the Wildland/Urban Interface," Western Fire Chiefs Association, 1991.)

Other environmental factors which must be considered are:

- **Residential structures**—Types of construction and occupancies.
- **Mobile environment**—Types of transportation in the community.
- **Community**—Public assembly occupancies, offices, hospitals, schools, churches, businesses, and hotels.
- **Industrial environment**—Factories, warehouses, and industrial manufacturing.
- **Outdoors**—wildlands, forest, timber and crops.
- **Other structures**—vacant, under construction, bridges, tunnels, etc.
- **Other**—all other and unclassified properties, museums, historical buildings.

WEATHER

Weather conditions affect all fire departments across the United States in their efforts to control emergency incidents. Western states experience droughts, dry winds, and hot temperatures, while in the Midwest rain, floods, and tornadoes are common. Eastern states suffer cold weather and winds that have an effect on fire department operations.

What are the weather conditions in your community? Are there seasons? How does the wind affect fire conditions? It has been said that fire without wind is a piece of cake, but a fire with high winds can be very dangerous. This holds true for both structure and wildland fires. As the pieces of the fire protection plan fit together, weather will play an important role.

CULTURE

Webster defines culture variously as a particular form of civilization; the beliefs, customs, arts, and institutions of a society at a given time; a refinement in intellectual and artistic taste; and, the art of developing the intellectual faculties through education.

The planner must have a feel for this community "culture." What are the customs? What are the beliefs? What institutions are prevalent in the community? How will these institutions affect the fire department in its quest for an effective fire protection plan? There are tests that can identify a type of culture and belief. These tests are administered to employees and citizens (local service clubs may assist in the testing procedures and involve citizens from the community) and will show the degree of participation you might expect from the community. Will the community support the new plan?

Understanding the community also can be accomplished by attending city council meetings. Listen to the people who speak. Listen also to the elected officials. Are they pro- growth or anti-growth? Are they fiscal conservatives or liberal spenders? Are they more interested in staff reports and surveys than in getting the job done? All of these observations will assist the planner.

ETHNIC INFLUENCE

What is the ethnic makeup of the community? Is there any one group that is particularly affected by the emergency problems in the community? Is this group active in the affairs of the community? Are there social and economic problems associated with any particular group? Is any one ethnic group suffering an unusually high proportion of fire injuries and/or fire deaths within its neighborhoods? Can these problems be mitigated through education or other means? The planner must have this kind of information to be able to prepare the fire protection plan with these factors as a part of the process.

THE FIRE DEPARTMENT ROLE

It is very important for the fire department personnel involved to understand their role in the planning process. This is the time for the fire department to take a leadership position. The following are roles useful in moving the plan forward:

—Facilitator   —Motivator
—Communicator   —Legislator (and/or legislative advocate)
—Politician   —Salesperson

FACILITATOR

The facilitator keeps the group on track. The following checklist can help the fire chief serve in the role of facilitator:

- Keep a focus on the group's process.
- Keep a tempo going with daily objectives.
- Develop a design (an outline to follow).
- Develop a purpose statement and focus on that statement daily.
- Have a relaxed demeanor.
- Be committed to the objectives.
- Be receptive to ideas.
- Care about the project.
- Understand conflict resolution.
- Be flexible.
- Be a good listener.
- Be a participant.
- Show enthusiasm.
- Make every effort to be at each session.
- Pay attention to details.

Being a facilitator can be interesting and demanding. The fire chief shows his interest by facilitating the planning process.

MOTIVATOR

The fire chief's role as motivator is very closely aligned with the "leadership" factor in the process. The motivation factor will be present if the chief expresses ideas, supports other ideas, sets the pace and establishes a "vision" for the group.

Also, a motivator focuses on a better, more positive future, encourages hopes and dreams, appeals to common values and interests, states positive outcomes, emphasizes the strength of the unified group, uses word pictures, images and metaphors, communicates enthusiasm, and kindles excitement.

COMMUNICATOR

The art of communication is not all talking. It also has to do with being a good listener. The key is connecting with the other person or group. There are five basic activities that pertain to good listening:

1. Clarifying.
2. Restating.
3. Maintaining a neutral position.
4. Reflecting.
5. Summarizing.

Although the best form of communication is face to face, the fire department role in the planning process also means that written communications originate in the department and must be followed up with personal contact. This is very important in scheduling meetings and events.

Good communication sets the stage for the leadership role of the fire department. It reinforces the impression that the fire department can and will play an active, intelligent role in the planning process.

LEGISLATOR/LEGISLATIVE ADVOCATE

Over the years the fire service has learned many bitter lessons regarding legislation. We have been the victims of too many pieces of legislation that have interfered with our day-to-day operations, our finances, our ability to deliver our normal level of service, and the safety of the public. Thanks to the efforts of former Congressman Curt Weldon and others, the national fire service is enjoying a higher degree of legislative interaction. The Congressional Fire Service Caucus, one of the largest on Capitol Hill, is a prime example of this effort to be more involved in the rulemaking process. We should pick up that "gauntlet" and continue to run with it, especially locally.

The fire service today is affected by various federal, state, and local laws and ordinances that require operational changes, and changes in education and training that exceed the training levels of yesterday. Hazardous materials and EMS are just two of the areas that require additional effort, funds and programs. Recently, disaster preparedness has become significant for fire departments. Some fire departments, for example, the Los Angeles City Fire Department and others, are taking over the entire city disaster preparedness program.

California's legislature recently passed a new law called the Hansen-Green Fire Safety Act of California (1990), which allows fire departments to enforce more restrictive fire safety laws than the fire marshal or state building department. However, the legislation restricted the fire districts in that they can enforce more restrictive regulations **but** they must have those regulations ratified by each one of the cities and the county before they can become law. This is a negative legislative action that affects basic fire protection operation. There are other state codes that allow local jurisdictions to have more restrictive fire protection laws than those enacted at state level.

The fire service obviously needs more advocates active in federal, state and local legislative programs. This is one of the most important roles the fire department must play in fire protection planning.

POLITICIAN

The fire department must interact within the community in a political sense. The fire chief must interact with the various members of the city council and various boards and commissions. This can be a real learning experience for a new fire chief.

A good starting point is regular attendance at city council meetings and other government functions. Attending local Chamber of Commerce meetings and affairs also is very helpful. The fire chief should consider joining the chamber of commerce and such other community organizations as the **Lions,** and **Rotary** clubs, and other high-profile community service organizations. These political connections certainly help the fire chief locally.

Membership in state-wide organizations such as the state firefighters association, or fire chiefs associations is a must for the department and the chief.

It is with the help of these organizations that good legislation is promoted and bad legislation is defeated.

SALESPERSON

Marketing your fire department is a subject that needs to be high on your priority list. Telling the world how good you are, through the visual or written media, will make a big difference when you are trying to sell a new fire protection plan or accomplish anything that requires communication with and understanding of others. Some fire departments use the medium of television for public education announcements and to communicate to the public stories about recent fires and how the fire department saved property and lives. Broadcasting radio announcements over local stations is another method. Publishing a newsletter periodically about the department and its employees, and including public education announcements is easy to do now with a personal computer and a publication software program. The biggest cost is mailing the newsletter. Cut mailing costs by using the local markets and stores for distribution or by working with the chamber of commerce to get the message out to the citizens. (See the copy of the *Alert* newsletter from the Menlo Park Fire Protection District in the appendix)

FIRE RISK ANALYSIS

Fire Risk Analysis is a Systems Approach that involves the following steps:

1. The community fire protection system.
2. The community at risk.
3. The fire suppression capability.
4. The unprotected risk.
5. The strategies to consider.

The first step is to form a team to conduct the study. Place one person in charge. The team may consist of a chief officer, company officer(s) and members. The project research then can be delegated and divided among the members of the team.

The balance of this section consists of checklists for each of the main steps with explanations for each item on the checklist.

Step 1—The community fire protection system

EVALUATE YOUR COMMUNITY'S FIRE PROTECTION SYSTEM

Begin by developing a description of your community's fire protection resources and systems.

Efficient and effective use of public and private fire protection resources is the anticipated result of good planning. In today's environment, the service demands of the fire department include fire prevention, fire safety education, emergency medical services, and hazardous materials controls. The community fire protection system includes *all* public and private services which are available to protect people and property from fire, explosion and other hazardous situations.

The primary elements of the community fire protection system are the fire department, private fire protection entities, federal, state, and county governments, public utilities, building departments (building inspections, permits), planning departments (zoning regulations), and schools (both public and private).

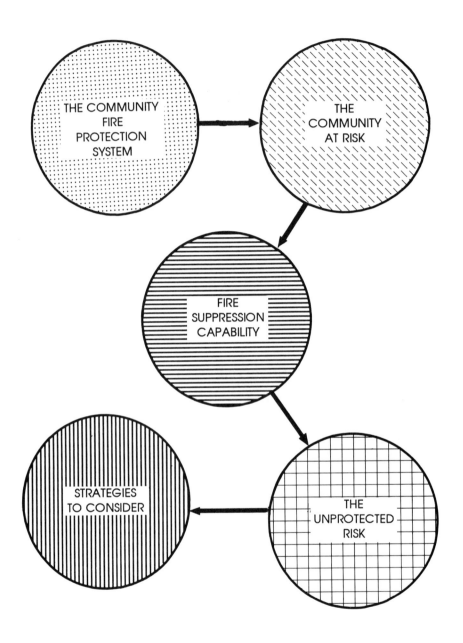

Figure 24-2. Fire Risk Analysis-A Systems Approach

A GENERAL STATEMENT OF BUILT-IN FIRE PROTECTION SYSTEMS

This statement includes the requirements for automatic fire sprinklers in various types of occupancies. Describe these requirements in detail. Is there a certain part of the community that is not affected by these requirements? The ordinances are not always enacted retroactively and, therefore, buildings constructed before a certain date may not require sprinklers.

THE FIRE PREVENTION CODE REQUIREMENTS OTHER THAN SPRINKLERS SYSTEMS

There are many fire prevention code requirements that have an effect on life safety and property damage. These requirements should be described in this section. They may include the requirements for automatic fire doors and windows, fire separations (to separate hazardous areas), occupancy load requirements for public assembly type occupancies, flame spread requirements for decorations, and exit signs and exit door hardware. All of these requirements are a part of the community fire protection system.

Step 2—The community at risk

DESCRIBE COMMUNITY DEMOGRAPHICS

This is where statistical information about the present population and future population growth is described. This information is available from the public library, the Chamber of Commerce, or the county's tax records. Is growth expected in a geographic area of your community? New housing and shopping malls? Industrial parks and new commercial areas?

DESCRIBE WHAT HAS BEEN BURNING IN THE COMMUNITY

Use statistical information that describes the fire activity in the community. What types of occupancies were involved? Has the number of fires been decreasing or increasing? A good way to display this type of information is to compare local statistics with state, county, and national statistics.

DESCRIBE WHAT IS AVAILABLE TO BURN IN THE COMMUNITY

This is the section that describes the target hazards in the community. A target hazard is a building or occupancy that is unusually dangerous in terms of life loss or has a high potential for property damage. It may be that old hotel that houses many senior citizens, or the chemical plant near the river that has little built-in fire protection. It also may be an area of the community that borders a wildland fire hazard area.

Occupancies that have life loss potential are a priority in this analysis. You should ask the following questions when evaluating a life loss target hazard:

- What is the occupancy type? Crowded occupancies present a potential problem.
- Are there sprinklers or other fire protection systems? Is there some type of early warning system, e.g., smoke and heat detectors, or a fire alarm system?
- What is the condition of the building? What is its age? Is the housekeeping good? What is the condition of the structural members? Are there poke-throughs in walls and ceilings? Is there a chronic storage problem in the hallways or fire escapes?
- What is the occupant load? How many occupants are in the building during the day and at night?
- What is the age of the occupants? The very young and the very old are high-risk groups.
- What is the physical condition of occupants? (ambulatory or nonambulatory)
- What is their means of egress from the building? Are there exterior or interior fire escapes? Are there adequate exit signs? Is there adequate lighting in the exit hallways and stairways?
- Have these occupants received any evacuation training? Are they supervised, as in nursing homes and similar institutions?

Identification of target hazards also may be by other hazards associated with the building or occupancy. A large-loss fire in a "one-industry town" will have a big economic impact on the entire community.

The remaining factor in "what is available to burn" and the identification of "target hazards" is the application of the fire flow requirements for the community. Fire flow, which at first seems more appropriately included under Step 3, Fire Suppression Capability, is introduced at this point under "what is available to burn," because structures are evaluated in terms of fire flow requirements. Once the flow requirements have been determined, they can be used to assist in determining manpower and equipment needs.

FIRE FLOW REQUIREMENTS

The fire flow requirement is the amount of water needed to extinguish a fire in a given occupancy. The flow is always stated in gallons per minute (gpm) and may be required for a specific period of time.

The needed fire flow allows planners to study resource needs within the fire department. How many pumping engines will deliver how many gallons per minute? How many firefighters will be needed to handle the hoselines, and nozzles, or to operate large stream appliances? Hand-held lines will flow from 100 gpm to 250 gpm, requiring one to three firefighters. It follows that the higher the required fire flow, the more firefighters will be required. Large stream appliances will deliver 300 gpm and more, usually with fewer personnel.

There should have been a water flow test performed within the previous three years. This often is done during hydrant testing, with flow test information recorded by geographical location. The type of occupancies and what fire flow is required also must be listed. This information shows areas in the community that have good water supplies and those that have inadequate supplies.

It also should be noted that the water flow requirements are based on the occupancy being fully involved with fire and requiring the maximum gpms. It is obvious also that fixed fire protection systems will reduce the required flow.

Another factor in this equation is that if the maximum fire flow is 3,000 gpm for your community, and a certain occupancy exceeds that demand, you will need to plan additional resources for the probable fire. This could mean implementing automatic or mutual aid agreements.

THE IDENTIFICATION OF "FIRE MANAGEMENT AREAS"

One of the last requirements in the Community at Risk section is the identification of "fire management areas" (FMAs). Fire management areas are designated when the community is divided into manageable pieces. These are specifically identified on a community map. It may be advantageous to divide the community into FMAs by using natural geographical separations.

Natural separations include rivers, freeways, main streets, railroad tracks, and open space areas.

Another way to determine FMAs is to place a grid overlay on the map of your community. Be careful not to make too many FMAs by using a grid system that is too small. Some fire departments have made their FMAs consistent with their first-in districts (those districts where an engine company normally should be the first in when responding from the fire station). If you have six fire stations, then you should have six "first-in districts" and six FMAs.

Step 3—The fire suppression capability

EVALUATE YOUR DEPARTMENT AND ITS ORGANIZATION

This is the place to describe the organization of the fire department. An organization chart should show the chain of command and responsibilities for various functional activities in the department. Record the number and location of fire stations, the number of personnel (both uniformed and civilian), and the number, type, and location of apparatus.

Describe your staffing level per company and any special staffing plans that you have adopted. Special staffing plans may include additional firefighters during the busier times of the day or week, or special overtime plans to staff companies during personnel vacancies. Charts would be helpful in describing this type of information.

THE SERVICE TIME FOR EMERGENCY AND NONEMERGENCY RESPONSES SHOULD BE MADE AVAILABLE IN THIS SECTION

Is your average response time under five minutes? What is your total average "time in service" for both emergency and nonemergency incidents?

This information usually can be found in the department's annual statistical report and in the dispatch records.

THE LIFE LOSS AND FIRE INJURY STATISTICS FOR THE LAST FIVE YEARS

This information is available from fire reports, dispatch records, and incident reports previously filed or recorded.

THE FIRE LOSS REPORTS FOR THE LAST FIVE YEARS

This information also is available from incident reports, fire prevention records, or the annual report.

YOUR COMMUNICATION SYSTEM

Describe how your companies are dispatched. Do you have your own dispatch center? Are you contracting with another agency for the dispatch service? What type of emergencies are being received at the dispatch center? Is the 9-1-1 system or enhanced 9-1-1 being used?

What are you using for a radio system? How many frequencies are available? Do you share a frequency with other agencies? Do you have a mutual aid frequency that is used for larger emergencies? You should describe that system and how it is activated.

DESCRIBE YOUR MUTUAL AID AND AUTOMATIC AID RESOURCES

Mutual aid resources are those from other fire departments and agencies not in your own geographic area. Typically a cooperatively established system is designed to activate these mutual aid companies. The dispatch center is charged with this responsibility and implements the mutual aid plan when it is needed. Automatic aid resources are preplanned with adjoining fire departments and agencies.

These may include an engine or truck company that is automatically dispatched to certain areas of your city or to special occupancies that represent a special hazard (Life loss and property damage).

Step 4—The unprotected risk

DETERMINE WHAT IS THE UNPROTECTED RISK

Unprotected risk is the degree of imbalance that exists between risk and suppression capability. If suppression forces available to respond to any location are inadequate to deal with the fire situation, that particular situation must be considered part of the community's unprotected risk.

Unprotected risk can be reduced or eliminated by decreasing the risk or increasing the suppression capability. Risk can be reduced by the classic three "Es":

- **Education**—educating the public, particularly the owners and operators of properties at risk, creating in them an understanding of *why* their property cannot be protected effectively by the public fire forces and *how* they can reduce the imbalance.
- **Engineering**—requiring built-in structural fire protection measures, retrofitted if necessary, and fire protection systems (automatic sprinklers, special hazard systems, alarm systems), through codes and ordinances.
- **Enforcement**—assuring, through frequent and competent inspection,

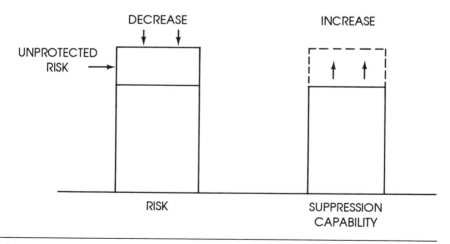

Figure 24-3.

that all statutory fire protection and fire prevention measures are in full compliance.

Suppression capability can be increased by upgrading the water supply system; adding or relocating fire stations, apparatus, and personnel; improving training, strategy and tactics; and improving communications and mutual aid.

While improving suppression capability has been the traditional fire service response to risk imbalance, we have never been able to fully close the gap. We will always need suppression forces and they should be the best we can provide, but the final answer lies in risk reduction through education, engineering, and enforcement. Make sure both are a part of your fire protection plan.

ESTABLISH THE CONCEPT OF ACCEPTABLE RISK

"Acceptable risk" is the level of unprotected risk with which the community is willing to live. Unfortunately, few citizens have any understanding that they have, by default, established a level of acceptable risk. When a fire occurs, they fully expect the fire department to arrive with red lights, sirens, and the equipment and personnel to suppress the situation. Sometimes we win, sometimes we lose.

A significant part of "classic" master planning is to give the community a clear understanding of what the fire department can do and what it cannot do. We should make every effort to explain to the community the purpose and goals of higher taxes for improved fire suppression, or the need for more stringent fire protection and fire prevention codes, or for private investment in improved fire safety. The final decisions will be made in the councils of government and in the marketplace, where dollars drive decisions. It is the responsibility of the fire chief to see that those decisions are made with all the necessary information and the most complete understanding that we can provide. Only then will "acceptable risk" be a meaningful concept.

Step 5—Strategies to consider

The closing stage is the time to evaluate all of the information and establish some final plans or strategies.

One of the final planning actions is examining the location of the existing fire stations. Fire station location be determined based on the factors discussed here.

Fire stations should be located near major streets. Traffic patterns and use must be determined. However, the new fire station should not be located on the busiest street in town. Surrounding land uses must be considered. The environmental impact report will have to address apparatus noise and other station activities. Future land use requiring additional fire suppression efforts also must be examined. A new development with 1,000 homes, a new industrial center with hazardous materials, or a new baseball stadium, are all examples of land use considerations which affect the fire protection system.

The most important factor is apparatus response times. Can you meet the four- to five-minute response time 95 percent of the time? Can maximum coverage of the entire area be accomplished from that location? Consider greater alarms. Consider freeways and railroads that might be impassable.

Station location analysis also requires three basic types of data:

1. The nature of the incidents experienced.
2. The locations of most fires (areas of response concentration).
3. The response times to these locations.

Prime considerations in the "nature of the incident" data category are the number of structure fires and the number of emergency medical incidents.

The response times throughout the community can be measured by actual incidents, the history of those calls, or by driving the district and measuring the times for a specific area. When describing the response times to the city council, consider mentioning the "time-temperature curve" and explaining how important a rapid response is in saving lives and property.

There also are national standards to consider. The NFPA recommends that a first-due engine company be located within two miles of residential areas, within one and a half miles of commercial areas, and within one mile of buildings that require a 5,000-gpm fire flow. These are broad standards. The amount of built-in fire protection (automatic sprinklers) will affect how this national standard is applied.

Comparisons

It may be very helpful to compare your fire department with those of neighboring agencies of similar size. You might be able to profitably incorporate the answers to these questions; comparing your statistics with those of other communities:

- What is the fire protection cost per capita?
- What is the fire loss per capita?
- What were the fire loss trends in the last five years?
- What are the total alarms annually?
- What type of structural fires are occurring?
- What is the total number of emergency medical calls?
- How many hazardous materials responses occur annually?

Insurance ratings

Another area is the impact of the insurance industry on the community. What is the recognized authority for setting insurance rates in your area? Is it the Insurance Services Office (ISO)? Are rates based on ISO's information and individual insurance company analyses?

A hypothetical fire department that has just been rated by the ISO and has received a rating of III should ask what it can do to improve the rating. ISO rating personnel can assist in identifying these factors. It may be that the fire department would have to establish additional fire stations, place additional personnel on all companies, increase the number of dispatchers on duty at all times, and improve the city water supply system. Chapter 5 of this Handbook describes the ISO rating system.

It would be difficult for a fire department to complete all of those recommendations at once, but they should be in the department's long-range plan and methods to fill the needs should be established as resources permit.

Additional considerations

The plan should include a section on additional considerations that addresses recommendations in such areas as:

- Employee preparedness training;
- Citizen training and preparedness;
- Marketing the department's role in the community;
- Consolidation of services within and with other agencies;
- Water supply contingencies during disasters;
- Prefire planning and inspection by all suppression and prevention personnel;
- Employee physical fitness levels. Programs to improve and maintain fitness levels; and
- Employee skill levels and formal education.

Final recommendations

The closing portion of the final risk analysis contains the final recommendations. These are developed with the fire chief, the staff, other employees, the labor union or association, and most importantly, citizens who have an interest in the subject. The question of community fire protection must involve the entire community. When that large fire loss occurs, citizens must understand that the loss was because the "acceptable loss" levels were exceeded. In this way citizens will better understand fire protection in the community. Data analysis information should be displayed in public meetings and other forums to inform the citizens of the concepts of "unprotected risk," "protected risk," and "acceptable risk."

Once the recommendations have been developed, discussed, prioritized and finalized, they should be presented to the decisionmaking authority in the city or fire district for consideration.

Suggested format for final report

1. A well-designed, colorful cover. The title must be highly visible.
2. An inside title page. Include date of report, name of official sender (the fire chief) and the names of those who participated in the preparation of the report.
3. Table of contents. Do this last to incorporate any changes made in the report as it is put together.
4. A chart or graphic symbol that communicates the essence of the report.
5. An executive overview of the report. A summary of the goals and objectives. A purpose statement. Keep this to no more than two pages.
6. The contents of the report divided into sections or divisions. Each section should have a cover page with a short description of that section. It is helpful if the cover pages of each section are of a different color.
7. A glossary of terms and a bibliography or reference section at the end of the report.

Once the final report has been completed, it will need to be "marketed" throughout the community. Because you have involved the community in the planning process, this selling job may not be too difficult. Be ready to share your hard work with other fire departments and government agencies. They may want to use your methods to determine their fire protection plan for the future.

SUMMARY

The concept of master planning involves participation by many players. The state, city, county, and special districts all participate in this process of planning for the future.

This chapter encourages a high level of participation by the fire chief in this process. It requires a high degree of communication between the fire chief and the other city planners and politicians.

The concept of "planning teams" within the fire department, managed by the fire chief, is the suggested method to use. These planning teams are capable of producing significant results with a high degree of initiative and vision.

The planning teams must understand the "fingerprint" of the community, i.e., demographics, economics, environment, culture and ethnic influence. These questions must be answered at the beginning of the planning process.

Fire department personnel and, most importantly, the fire chief, must play an active role in the development of the fire protection plan. The roles of facilitating, motivating, and communicating will all bring results. The fire chief must be active in the legislative process within his own organization and at city, state and federal levels. There have been many occasions when the fire service has not been active in the legislative process and it has been the beneficiary of poor legislation. The political battleground is another area that needs the full attention of the fire chief. The fire chief should develop a good understanding of the political atmosphere in the community.

The five steps of the fire risk analysis system will provide a methodology for the fire chief to follow in developing the fire protection plan.

The Technical Resources section includes material to assist the fire chief both in understanding and implementing fire protection planning in his community.

25

The Fire Prevention Bureau

GLENN P. CORBETT

C H A P T E R   H I G H L I G H T S

• The historical development of fire prevention activities in the United States, the current thrust of fire prevention efforts, and the future influence of fire prevention goals within the fire service.

• Fire prevention bureau organization in different types of departments.

• The members of a fire prevention bureau, their duties, and how they are selected for appointment to the bureau. The positive traits of an effective chief of fire prevention.

• How a well-organized bureau operates efficiently.

• Codes enforced by a fire prevention bureau and fire companies, the types of plans reviewed and inspections performed, and the legal issues involved therein.

• Organizations that promulgate model codes as well as the techniques used to adopt codes at the local level.

*A*S THE FOCAL point of a fire department's efforts to minimize fire losses in a community, the fire prevention bureau plays a key role in improving the safety and quality of life of the citizens it serves. In most department mission statements, fire prevention usually is listed as the fire department's primary goal.

Fire prevention efforts will play an increasingly important part in fire department activities into the 21st century, primarily because of the tremendous fiscal constraints being placed on the fire service. With fewer firefighters and fewer fire stations, a shift to mandated installations of fixed suppression systems and increased public education, both key fire prevention bureau activities, is likely.

The chief of the fire prevention bureau plays a pivotal role in leading a department to meet this newly enhanced role. The position requires technical and legal competency, political awareness, and persistence. Changes in a fire prevention bureau do not occur overnight; long-range planning and goal-setting require a fire prevention chief to persevere.

This chapter will discuss the organization and operation of the fire prevention bureau. It also will discuss a fire prevention bureau's three basic activities: code enforcement, public education, and fire investigation. Code enforcement is reviewed in detail; public education and fire investigation are given an overview treatment since they are the topics of Chapters 27 and 28, respectively.

The fire prevention bureau can be considered symbolic of a fire department's mission—to prevent fires and minimize losses. Over the years, the public has developed certain expectations of fire prevention bureaus, i.e., to identify and abate fire hazards in the community. The public also expects the fire prevention bureau, as well as the fire service as a whole, to be their fire protection experts.

It is important then that chief officers have a working knowledge of how a bureau functions to meet this critical goal of proactively protecting lives and property from fire. With these expectations in mind, this chapter strives to provide a detailed overview of fire prevention bureaus and how they can be used to meet public expectations.

The chapter opens with a historical look at fire prevention activities and concludes with a glimpse into the future. The intervening detailed text describes the organization and management of a fire prevention bureau, the bureau's personnel, as well as the codes and other tools used to carry out its charge of preventing fires.

HISTORICAL PERSPECTIVE

Fire prevention activities actually predate the creation of organized fire departments in the U.S. Fire was a constant threat to early European settlements in America. Major fires struck in Jamestown, Virginia in 1608 and Plymouth, Massachusetts in 1623.[1]

Fire regulations in the early years primarily affected the construction, height, and maintenance of chimneys. The carrying of hot coals from fireplace to fireplace was also a constant source of large blazes. Wooden building construction aggravated the situation.

Boston banned smoking paraphernalia in 1638.[2] Ten years later, Peter Stuyvesant forbade the use of wood or plaster chimneys in New Amsterdam (New York City).[3]

Stuyvesant also appointed four fire wardens who served without pay. They inspected chimneys and patrolled for fire hazards. They also assessed large fines for carelessness. The fines were used to buy firefighting buckets, ladders, and hooks.

Arson was a problem then as now. A rash of arson fires prompted Boston to pass legislation in 1652 that imposed punishments of flogging or death for convicted arsonists.[4]

Besides inspections of chimneys, fire wardens also performed fire watch duties in many cities. Patrolling the streets at night, they would use large "rattles" to summon assistance and notify the city of a fire.

Ben Franklin, the father of the organized volunteer fire service, also was an early supporter of fire prevention. His words, "an ounce of prevention is worth a pound of cure," are famous. In addition to inventing the efficient and safe "Franklin stove," he also was a proponent of chimney cleaning and the proper handling of burning materials.

Even when rudimentary fire apparatus was introduced in major U.S. cities during the first half of the 18th century, fires still were a major threat. Major conflagrations, some larger than even today's biggest fires, continued to plague our cities into the 20th century.

These conflagrations were the impetus for the fire service to begin to take an active role in fire prevention activities. The National Association of Fire Engineers (later to become the International Association of Fire Chiefs) during its first annual meeting in 1873 developed a list of eight fire safety concerns:[5]

Fire wardens were the predecessors of today's fire inspectors. They continued to play an important role through the 19th century, as evidenced by this New York City helmet from c. 1855. In 1850, the fire wardens (appointed from the rank of firefighter) made inspections at construction sites throughout the city looking for deficiencies, inspected other buildings for improper storage, and strived to "inquire and examine into any and every violation of any of the provisions of the acts previously passed for the prevention of fires in the city of New York. . . ."

PHOTO COURTESY GORDON L. CORBETT JR.

& Safety concerns

1. The limitation or disuse of combustible materials in the structures of buildings, the reduction of the excessive height in buildings, and restriction of the dangers of elevators, passages, hatchways, and mansards.
2. The isolation of each apartment in a building from other apartments and of every building from those adjacent by high party walls.
3. The safe construction of heating apparatus.
4. The presence and care of trustworthy watchmen in warehouses, factories, and theaters, especially during the night.
5. The regulation of the storage of inflammable materials and use of same for heating or illumination. Also the exclusion of rubbish liable to spontaneous ignition.
6. The most available method for the repression of incendiarism.
7. A system of minute and impartial inspection after the occurrence of every fire, and rigid inquiry into the causes, with reference to future avoidance.
8. Fire escapes actually serviceable for invalids, women, and children.

It is interesting that many of the recommendations outlined above were the basis for a number of our current fire and building code requirements. The early recognition of the importance of fire investigations is an insight as well. Even the reference to "fire escapes actually serviceable for invalids" only has recently come to the fore in the form of the Americans with Disabilities Act.

A few years later, in 1884, former Chief Damrell of the Boston Fire Department presented a committee report to the National Association of Fire Engineers concerning the formulation of a building code. This pioneering work was important in the development of the first model building code in the United States.[6]

The insurance industry, also seeing the obvious need for a set of standardized building regulations, especially after having to pay the extraordinary claims which resulted from conflagrations, promulgated the "National Building Code" in 1906. This first model code (a uniform set of construction requirements to be adopted by the cities) published by the National Board of Fire Underwriters was patterned after Damrell's report and the New York State Building Code which recently had been published.[7]

Life safety also became a major code concern during the early 20th century, primarily because of the Triangle Shirtwaist factory fire in New York in 1911. The fire killed 146 textile workers. It led the National Fire Protection Association (NFPA) to form the Committee on Safety, which eventually developed what was to become NFPA 101, *Code for Safety to Life from Fire in Buildings and Structures*.

In retrospect it seems likely that this fire also prompted many fire departments to form fire prevention bureaus. New York City, in fact, formed its bureau shortly after the Triangle fire in 1911, although some fire prevention bureaus were in existence before 1911.[8]

Unfortunately, the formulation and actual adoption of fire safety code requirements have, in many cases, come only after the occurrence of tragic fires. For example, consider the following "occupancy-specific" fires. Each of these major fires led to legislative and code changes targeted to their particular occupancy types:

—1903 Iroquois Theater fire, Chicago, IL, 602 dead
—1942 Cocoanut Grove Nightclub fire, Boston, MA, 492 dead
—1944 Ringling Bros. Circus tent fire, Hartford, CT, 162 dead
—1946 Winecoff Hotel fire, Atlanta, GA, 119 dead
—1958 Our Lady of Angels school fire, Chicago IL, 95 dead
—1977 Beverly Hills Supper Club fire, Southgate KY, 165 dead
—1980 MGM (high-rise) Hotel fire, Las Vegas, NV, 85 dead
—1982 K-Mart warehouse fire, Bucks County, PA, 100 million dollar loss

It is likely that the 1993 World Trade Center bombing and fire in New York City (six dead) will be added to this list of historic fires. The fire service, in all likelihood, will study this incident and develop code changes as a result.

Another fire prevention effort—public education—has its roots in the early part of this century. In October of 1922, President Harding initiated the first Fire Prevention Week in remembrance of the Great Chicago fire of October 1871.

The latter half of this century has seen the development of fire codes, codes developed specifically to address hazardous activities in and around buildings, and maintenance of fire safety features of buildings themselves. Although a fire code is not considered a building construction code, current fire codes have blurred this distinction.

There are three national fire codes (with corresponding building codes) in the United States: the National (formerly the Basic) Fire Prevention Code developed in 1969, the Uniform Fire Code developed in 1971, and, the Standard Fire Prevention Code developed in 1974.

These codes tend to be adopted by jurisdictions on a regional basis. The National Fire Prevention Code is used primarily in the Northeast and Midwest, the Uniform Fire Code in the West and Southwest, and the Standard Fire Prevention Code in the Southeast.

The NFPA recently promulgated an enhanced and updated NFPA 1, *Fire Prevention Code*. It has yet to see widespread adoption.

These codes, as well as their building code counterparts, have grown explosively in the last 15 years. The fire codes have expanded to include protection against hazardous materials as well, whether or not the hazard is fire-related.

Although approximately 6,000 people still die annually in fires, the public's fear of fire has diminished somewhat in this century. Today, true conflagrations are rare. Overall, the number of fires per capita since the beginning of this century has decreased. This is the direct result of improved firefighting and fire protection equipment, better training, enhanced public fire prevention education activities, better building and fire codes, and better origin and cause determination and prosecution of fires considered suspicious.

There is still work to be done to lower the number of annual fire fatalities. We remain suppression-oriented—an admission of our failure to prevent fires in the first place.

ORGANIZATIONAL STRUCTURE

Fire prevention bureaus, also known as "fire marshal's offices" or "bureaus of combustibles," range in size from a single individual to more than 100 people. Volunteer departments may have only one or two part-time inspectors, while large paid departments may have a full complement of inspectors, fire protection engineers, plan reviewers, investigators, educators, administrators, and clerical staff.

The number of bureau personnel is a function both of the size of the community served and the number of specific duties carried out by the bureau. For example, some larger departments assign individuals exclusively to high-rise structures and others to institutional occupancies. Some smaller departments neither investigate fires nor have a public education specialist.

Reporting to the chief of department, the head of the bureau may be known as the chief of fire prevention, fire marshal, or fire official. It is the duty of the chief of fire prevention to administer the overall activities of the bureau, assist other fire department division heads, and interact with other city agencies that affect fire prevention.

As the manager of fire prevention activities within the department, the chief of fire prevention is a key individual within the department as a whole. For the most part, this individual is second only to the chief of department in terms of responsibility and exposure.

The following qualities are characteristic of most successful fire prevention chiefs:

- **Level-headed.** The chief must be cool under pressure. Contrary to popular belief, an active bureau can be a pressure cooker. Great demands are placed on the individual in charge.
- **Technically agile.** The fire prevention chief must act quickly when confronted with a technical problem, be able to break down and understand technical issues, and be prepared to convey such information to higher authorities (including the fire chief and city management).

- **In control.** The chief is not a dictator, but a person who exudes an air of authority and leadership.
- **Nonwavering.** When under pressure, the chief must stand by his personal convictions, as well as back those of subordinates (assuming, of course, such convictions are legitimate and legal).
- **Good communicator.** "People" skills and writing skills are important elements of this position. The fire prevention chief's professionalism reflects both on him and the department as a whole.
- **Politically astute.** This is a highly political position. Enforcing regulations does not turn land developers into friends. Fire prevention chiefs must know how to navigate shark-infested waters and still meet their objectives (see discussion below).
- **Energetic.** Directing a bureau is a mentally strenuous job, one that can take its toll eventually.

New fire prevention chiefs often experience culture shock when they come into the bureau after having been in the field. The workload, myriad problems addressed by the bureau, and the public's attitude toward the bureau all contribute to the culture shock.

A fire prevention bureau's progress is measured in years, not months. New fire prevention chiefs must expect to spend time understanding a city's unique fire problems as well as invest time in developing and implementing their own programs, hence the need to "stick it out." For meaningful results, a commitment of at least five years is probably necessary.

Politics plays a critical part in fire prevention bureau activities. Before an individual accepts a fire prevention chief position, he must be assured of a commitment to fire safety from the top city management and the fire chief, a commitment that will be backed up. Without such commitments, an individual should be prepared to spend time spinning his wheels.

This does not mean that city management will not occasionally influence bureau decisions. The fire prevention chief is expected to defend the bureau's position, and to do so with technical accuracy. Compromises sometimes have to be made. A fire prevention chief who feels uncomfortable with a compromise should have no qualms about passing it to the chief of department.

The chief of fire prevention in volunteer departments usually is appointed by the chief of department, municipal governing body, or both, to oversee fire prevention activities. In smaller volunteer departments, this individual typically works part-time and may or may not be compensated on an annual basis. Medium-sized and large volunteer departments may have a full-time fire prevention officer.

In either case, part-time inspectors who work a few hours a week may be used. Since volunteer departments vary widely in size and fire prevention duties, other organizational structures may be encountered.

In paid departments, the chief of fire prevention is most often promoted into the position. In larger paid departments, the chief of fire prevention oversees three distinct sections that correspond to the bureau's primary activities: code enforcement, public education, and investigations. Each of these sections is managed by a support officer.

At the section level, the captains and lieutenants are the "backbone" of the bureau. It is these individuals who carry out the code enforcement program (which is subdivided into inspections and plan review in some larger departments), investigations, and public education activities.

One group of personnel often overlooked in the organizational structure is civilian clerical staff. They play a critical role in keeping the bureau running smoothly, especially since they handle the paperwork that is the lifeblood of the bureau.

Recently, fire departments have begun to introduce specially trained individuals into the bureau from the outside, for example, fire protection engineers whose technical expertise enhances the bureau's capabilities.

Personnel and Basic Training and Performance Requirements

As mentioned above, paid departments traditionally use lieutenants and captains to staff task-oriented positions. It is advantageous to have officers from the firefighting ranks in the bureau since firefighting experience can be useful in code enforcement and fire investigations. Such officers also tend to learn fire prevention techniques and skills more readily than civilians with no fire protection experience. These officers possess a level of fire protection expertise that is necessary for a successful fire prevention effort.

This is especially true with respect to model fire prevention codes, which have become more complex and more voluminous in the last 15 years. For example, more technical and diverse industrial processes have led to greatly expanded code provisions for the use and storage of hazardous materials. These code changes, as well as increasing litigation against fire departments, demand that bureaus be staffed by highly trained and technically competent inspectors. Some departments have hired fire protection engineers to assist them in meeting these technical demands.

More recently, there have been sweeping changes in the field of fire investigation, changes that have made this area of fire prevention more technical. Findings from laboratory research on fire dynamics are being applied in fire investigation and investigations themselves increasingly are being conducted with greater scientific scrutiny. Some of the old fire investigation "principles" and accepted practices have been discarded as fire investigation has become more scientifically based. Many of these changes can be attributed to NFPA 921, *Guide for Fire and Explosion Investigations,* first published by the NFPA in 1992.

From a financial perspective, many fiscally strained departments are looking to the fire prevention bureau to cut back expenditures, sometimes "civilianizing" the bureau by hiring civilians as inspectors and public educators instead of uniformed personnel. In worst-case financial situations, departments have had to eliminate positions.

These staffing changes have underscored the demand for personnel standards, i.e., state-developed standards or national standards of practice, such as those published by the NFPA.

To be certified and recertified under state standards an individual must participate in a set number of hours of training as well as meet specific areas of proficiency. States that enforce their own standards apply them primarily to fire inspectors; some of these states also have standards for fire investigators, including requirements for peace officer status.

Some states adopt the NFPA standards directly as their statewide minimum performance requirement. NFPA 1031, *Standard for Professional Qualifications for Fire Inspector*, NFPA 1033, *Standard for Professional Qualifications for Fire Investigator*, and NFPA 1035, *Standard for Professional Qualifications for Public Fire Educator*, are the three minimum standards applicable to fire prevention bureaus.

Officers of fire prevention bureaus must meet their state's requirements. In the absence of state requirements, a fire prevention chief must, at a minimum, strive to have his staff meet the NFPA standards. An untrained fire prevention staff is dangerous both to the public and to firefighters as well as a waste of a city's financial resources.

Selection of Personnel for the Bureau

Placing the proper individuals in the bureau is an important goal for a fire prevention chief. In the past, fire prevention bureaus were a dumping ground in some fire departments. The lame, lazy, troublemakers, and those who wanted to ride out their last days in the department found their way into the fire prevention bureau. Fortunately, those days are slowly coming to an end.

It is critical that prospective personnel for the fire prevention bureau be selected based on their desire to work in the bureau, make a difference, be willing and able to learn, commit to the job for an extended period of time, and be willing to take on a new set of responsibilities, which are much different than those they had in a fire company.

It is becoming apparent that the practice of forced transfers into a fire prevention bureau, including those of promotional transfers, can be a problem, manifested by high turnover and dissatisfaction among personnel.

Some departments have had success in requiring a tour of duty in the bureau prior to promotion to the senior ranks. This policy can be beneficial, especially if new personnel are exposed to the realities of fire prevention work and can acquire an appreciation for it. On the other hand, requiring these individuals to stay in the bureau for an extended period of time (forced transfers) can have a detrimental effect.

Bureau personnel encounter the public on a different plane than do their firefighting counterparts. Members of the bureau often must respond to citizen complaints. They rarely receive the accolades given to firefighters during emergency situations. Fire prevention is often a thankless job.

One problem in retaining trained fire prevention personnel is that very often individuals must leave the bureau to be promoted. Thus, an experienced person leaves the bureau, increasing turnover and necessitating the training of yet another person.

In today's technically complicated and demanding fire prevention bureau, personnel problems can prove disastrous. A smooth-running and competent fire prevention bureau needs a cadre of experienced, well-trained, and self-motivated individuals to maintain consistency and continuity.

As mentioned earlier, the use of civilians is on the rise in fire prevention bureaus and it is an advantageous practice based on:

- lower salaries and less costly benefits;
- lower overtime costs;
- overall lower turnover rates; and
- the special talents some civilians offer (previous work as a fire protection system installer/designer or firefighter in another jurisdiction, for example).

The disadvantages of using civilian personnel include:

- civilians who lack fire protection experience start much lower on the fire protection "learning curve";
- civilians without fire service experience may find understanding fire code provisions concerning fire department operations more difficult;
- civilians are often considered "outsiders" by uniformed personnel;
- civilians may find few or nonexistent promotional possibilities; and
- the pay and benefits disparity between uniformed inspectors and civilians may lead to animosity among the civilians.

By exploring personnel options, the fire prevention chief can put the "best team on the field." Without the proper personnel, a fire prevention bureau is bound to fail in its objectives.

Since clerical staff often deal with the public, their ability to work well under pressure and to maintain a positive demeanor are important qualities. Because they route numerous phone calls and queries from the public, they often are the first contact the public has with the bureau. Overall, they must understand the bureau operations and objectives.

Today, fire protection engineers and technicians are slowly finding their way into fire departments across the country (as this handbook was going to press, it was estimated that approximately 100 fire protection engineers and technicians were working in fire departments). The fire protection engineers are graduates of the University of Maryland or Worcester Polytechnic Institute. Fire protection engineering technicians very often are graduates of Oklahoma State University.

Fire protection engineers and technicians bring substantial technical expertise to the fire prevention bureau. This is especially helpful in the area of plan review and inspections of complicated projects, where they can use their training to ensure that codes are enforced properly. As fire codes become more performance based (described below), the use of fire protection engineers and technicians in fire departments will increase.

Other fire protection engineering and technician duties include fire investigation, where the engineer's and technician's knowledge of fire dynamics can help investigators to determine the origin and cause of a fire. They also can assist the incident commander at major fires by providing information on fire protection systems, water supplies, etc.

FACILITIES AND EQUIPMENT

The facilities and equipment of the bureau are important. The offices and associated areas must provide a good working environment, an atmosphere of professionalism, and project the seriousness with which the bureau carries out its fire prevention duties. A fire prevention office located at the back of an apparatus bay or in a dormitory area is certainly inappropriate.

The fire prevention chief and other fire prevention administrators such as battalion chiefs responsible for the three "sections" of code enforcement, investigations, and public education as well as a fire protection engineering administrator need individual offices equipped with a desk, chair, bookcase, and small conference table with a few chairs.

Inspectors and public educators need individual desks, chairs, and telephones. Sharing desks, chairs, and telephones is problematic. Space dividers can be used here, because inspectors and educators spend most of their time in the field. They are usually in the office early in the morning and late in the afternoon.

Plan reviewers and fire protection engineers need individual offices. Space dividers provide neither privacy nor a noise-free atmosphere where they can concentrate to review a set of plans. Each should have a desk, chairs, bookcases and a drafting table for plan review.

In addition to individual offices, investigators need an interrogation room, a secure and protected evidence room, a laboratory, and possibly even a holding cell for arson suspects.

Other rooms needed by all bureau personnel include a library, conference room(s), and a training room. A large 12-seat conference room and a small six-seat room may be needed in larger departments). Rooms for dispatch, clerical and permit-writing staff, as well as a reception area, also are important.

Reliable radio equipment is needed to ensure constant contact with fire prevention personnel and to maintain busy schedules. Each investigator, inspector, and educator should have a portable radio with automobile charger. This is important especially for operations that involve more than one bureau person, for example, a stake out by investigators or a fire alarm test of a large building by several inspectors.

Separate radio frequencies must be provided for inspectors and investigators, obviously both of them different from the firefighting frequencies.

Automobiles also are important for inspectors, investigators, and educators. These personnel are highly mobile; they need individually assigned and comfortable (quite a bit of time is spent in the car) automobiles.

The bureau's telephone system is a critical piece of equipment. The heavy volume of calls justifies the use of a quality system, one that minimizes the frustrations of the public and fire prevention personnel alike.

An automated system, with a quick default to a "human," is probably the best type, because people become frustrated quickly when they must deal with a completely automated system. The system must have an adequate number of incoming phone lines—a constant busy signal also generates numerous complaints.

The message-taking capability of an automated system is perhaps its best feature. This eliminates the avalanche of paper messages and avoids missed messages.

Inspector-specific Equipment

Equipment needed for public educators often includes a variety of technical aids, while investigators need specialized detection and laboratory equipment, photography equipment, surveillance equipment, etc.

For fire inspectors, however, a basic list of equipment includes:

—metal clipboard with cover;
—hardhat;
—flashlight;
—street mapbook;
—personal copy of fire code, building code and amendments;
—full complement of inspection forms, traffic, and misdemeanor ticket books;
—tape measure; and
—hydrant wrench.

A relatively new piece of equipment used by some fire prevention bureaus is the hand-held electronic clipboard. These devices record the results of inspections electronically, store the information, and then "download" the stored information into the bureau's record system when desired. Of course, paperwork is minimal when such equipment is used.

Expensive, infrequently used equipment—water flow test kits, binoculars, distance measuring wheel, explosimeters/gas detectors, photo equipment, and a blast monitor to measure particle velocities and frequencies in blasting operations—is stored at the bureau office. Such equipment typically is signed out before it is used.

Recordkeeping

Most paper-intensive organizations, including fire prevention bureaus, have benefitted from computers. A computer's capability to store tremendous amounts of information and to generate data instantly assist fire prevention bureaus tremendously. Such data are especially helpful when a fire prevention chief is studying bureau statistics for a report or checking up on progress made by specific programs that have been implemented.

Each of the two general types of computers—mainframes and personal computers—has its own advantages and disadvantages for a fire prevention bureau. It is up to the fire prevention chief to research what type is best for the particular bureau.

Records typically kept in computer files include inspections, plan reviews (including a tracking system to follow projects through the approval process), licenses and permits issued by the bureau, fee records, violations, court orders, etc. In addition, the computer can be used for its word processing capabilities.

Records that are stored in the computer can be retrieved by address, project name, or myriad other project-specific information. The computer also can perform such calculations as how many fire alarm system permits were issued during a given period of time.

The computer has not eliminated paper files, however. Correspondence, photos, and similar hard copies still must be kept for future reference. Backup hard copies of records entered into the computer also are often kept in paper files for a short time. Such paper files should be organized by project address, for easy retrieval.

You also can create information files for specific topics such as fireworks or blasting operations.

A "tickler" paper file is a good idea. This is a file of documents flagged for specific action at a future date, for example, a manufacturing company commits to providing sprinklers in its building in five years. The tickler file is referred to periodically to review what outstanding actions must be taken by specific parties.

An important related issue is forms. Your bureau needs to use standardized forms so that your personnel can become familiar with them and can scan them quickly for pertinent information.

Code Enforcement

Code enforcement personnel typically comprise the largest contingent within the bureau. It is in this area that fire prevention chiefs expend the greatest resources.

Code enforcement can be broken down into two distinct subsections: plans review and inspections, although not all fire prevention bureaus perform all of these types of inspections and plan reviews.

Personnel may review one or more of the following types of plans:

- Subdivision plats.
- Site plans.
- Water supply plans, both public right-of-way and private water supply plans.
- Building permit plans, including architectural and mechanical, electrical, and plumbing plans.
- Automatic sprinkler system and standpipe system plans.
- Fire alarm system plans.
- Specialized fire protection system plans, including CO_2 systems, dry chemical systems, and halon/"safe agent" systems.

Obviously, not every aspect of these different types of plans is fire-related. The fire department looks only at the relevant parts of the plans for which they have been designated as a review authority. The fire department may, in fact, be only one of several city departments that review these plans. After the plan review, the fire prevention bureau renders comments, and either disapproves or approves the set of plans. After approval a permit is issued by either the fire prevention bureau or another plan review coordinating agency, such as the city's building department.

Plan review personnel sometimes provide such other services as preconstruction meetings, or preliminary plan reviews designed to help architects, contractors, and developers meet fire code requirements. Fees may be assessed for these services.

TYPES OF INSPECTIONS

- **Site** inspections during construction to check fire department access and water supply for firefighting.
- **Building shell** inspections before a building is occupied.
- **Certificate of occupancy** inspections to ensure that an existing or new building is ready for a specific type of occupancy.
- **Licensing** inspections of specific occupancies, such as liquor stores or day care centers, for which a city or state-issued permit requires a fire inspection.
- **Complaint** inspections to follow up on complaints from the public or fire companies about overcrowding in public assemblies or locked exit doors, etc.
- **Nighttime** inspections of such buildings as nightclubs where operating hours preclude their inspection during daytime hours.
- **Reinspections** of buildings that fail initial inspections.
- **Substandard or vacant building** inspections of buildings targeted for demolition by the city.
- **Fire protection system** inspections of systems in new or remodeled buildings to verify repairs to existing systems that were not in compliance.
- **Routine** inspections of all "inspectable" occupancies, essentially all occupancies except one- and two-family dwellings in the jurisdiction on at least an annual basis. A routine inspection is the type carried out by nearly all fire prevention bureaus.

Most medium and large cities assign inspectors to specific districts. This way the workload can be handled more easily and the inspectors within a district can become more familiar with their area. Inspectors can be given routine inspection sheets for their districts which they complete when they have time.

In large cities it is advantageous to assign specific inspectors to particular types of target hazards, for example, handling all institutional occupancies, all educational occupancies, or all high-rise buildings. This makes it possible to turn inspectors into specialists.

Code enforcement inspectors sometimes perform other duties, for instance, fire watches or crowd control details in buildings for sporting events or concerts, or in other places of assembly. In most cases, the promoter or other party that requests the fire watch detail pays the fee for the bureau's services, on an overtime or flat-rate basis. Inspections of outdoor festivals and carnivals can include inspecting cooking appliances and electrical wiring for adequate fire safety. Fire watches are necessary in buildings where fire protection systems are temporarily disabled.

A fire code specialist should be assigned in the bureau to answer telephone questions too technical to be handled by clerical personnel. Designate a specific telephone for code questions and use a machine to record messages for the technical specialist to return quickly. By assigning a specific person who is knowledgeable and has good research skills you can avoid interrupting or tying up other bureau personnel.

Bureaus also issue permits, and, in some cases, license individuals for particular occupations. For example, permits are issued for welding operations and fireworks displays, and tests are given to individuals employed in fire-related jobs, such as blasters who use explosives; obtaining the license is contingent on passing the test.

Legal issues

An important consideration for fire prevention officers is the legal authority with which the bureau performs its duties. Bureau personnel need to understand the breadth of this authority and its limitations.

The legal authority to perform fire code enforcement may come from state laws as well from city or county ordinances, including provisions in an adopted model fire code. State laws usually outline proper due process and warrant procedures, while local ordinances specify what constitutes a fire code violation and the corresponding type of infraction (most fire code violations are misdemeanors).

Since the laws that regulate fire code enforcement vary from jurisdiction to jurisdiction, the following general concerns should be researched to customize a legal program to a particular fire prevention bureau:

- What legislation created your fire prevention bureau? Does the legislation specify the bureau's duties?
- Who is authorized to conduct fire inspections? Are firefighters included?
- What are the proper legal procedures for conducting an inspection? Must the fire inspector demand entry? Is the fire inspector prohibited from inspecting specific occupancies such as one- and two-family dwellings?
- What is the legal recourse for a fire inspector who has been denied entry? Are search warrants required and where can they be obtained?
- What type of paperwork must be completed for a fire code violation and to whom must copies be given? May the fire inspector issue citations for violations? How are the citations processed?
- How is the fire code violator's case decided—by a Board of Appeals or the court system? What are the violator's appeal rights?
- What is the fire inspector's authority in the case of an imminent hazard (an especially hazardous condition that must be abated immediately)?

May the inspector order a building to be vacated in such a situation? May the fire inspector seek a court injunction to abate a hazardous condition?

These questions show that the legal ramifications of fire code enforcement on the fire prevention bureau are significant. It is important that the fire prevention bureau's chief officer meet with the jurisdiction's attorney first, to establish a proper legal process for code enforcement, and then periodically to keep the attorney apprised of bureau activities and to seek legal advice.

Fire Company Inspections

Some paid departments use fire companies to carry out routine inspections. These company inspections can be very useful in reducing a jurisdiction's overall fire hazards and making fire companies more productive.

Fire companies should not undertake facility preplanning activities at the same time they are conducting an inspection. Inspecting and preplanning have different objectives. In addition, permission granted to conduct a preplan does not extend to conducting an inspection—entry for an inspection may have been denied.

Normally, firefighters are trained to conduct basic inspections, looking for the fire hazards typically found in various occupancies. These inspections are usually not as thorough as one conducted by a fire inspector. The International Fire Code Institute (which publishes the Uniform Fire Code) recently established a certification program for fire company officers who supervise company inspections.

One or more members of the fire prevention bureau must be assigned to coordinate the results of these inspections, review the inspection reports, and follow up on noted violations or any difficult problems.

FIRE CODES AND FIRE-RELATED CODES/STANDARDS

At the heart of any code enforcement program is an adopted fire code and related standards. It is this adopted fire code and the adopted standards that the fire prevention bureau derives its authority, its teeth. Codes and standards establish minimum requirements, but should not prevent or discourage someone from exceeding the minimum requirement. (See the discussion on mini-maxi codes.)

Over the years the terms code and standard have come to have specific, different meanings. Basically, a code dictates WHEN a specific requirement must be met, while a standard dictates HOW to meet a specific requirement. This distinction is important, especially when you must decide which regulation to apply to a particular situation.

The text of specific codes and standards may be considered either prescriptive or performance. The difference is very important in determining how much leeway there is to comply with a particular requirement.

Prescriptive codes or standards explicitly spell out requirements, i.e., "the enclosure wall of a stairwell in a five-story building shall be of eight-inch-wide concrete block (cells filled) construction and have a fire-resistive rating of two hours." A performance-type requirement might read "the enclosure wall of a stairwell in a five-story building must be capable of withstanding a five-megawatt fire for the full duration of egress from the building."

A prescriptive example is very specific—it prescribes only one way to meet the requirement, whereas a performance-type requirement allows latitude for compliance. A rice paper wall might comply if it met the egress time requirements!

To date, most fire codes and standards have been exclusively prescriptive in nature, but this is changing—performance-type requirements are slowly finding their way into the codes.

Model fire codes and standards are developed by several different national code-writing organizations. While all of the code-writing organizations have different membership rules, development procedures, and voting rules, they all follow a basic pattern.

Committees of organization members are formed to develop and prepare a particular code or standard. Under the NFPA's structure, committee members are selected based on their interest group, so that the NFPA can balance the committee by appointing representatives from each interest group.

Once a subcommittee has prepared a draft document, it is voted on by the full committee. In some organizations, such as the NFPA, the document is then made available for public comment.

Documents for which public comments are received may be revised to reflect the comments. The revised document is voted on again by the committee.

The document then is presented to the organization's general membership for a vote of acceptance. These voting sessions are held at annual or semi-annual meetings.

The NFPA's membership essentially votes on an entire code or standard at a time, and may vote on 30 different codes or standards at one meeting. This is because the NFPA has nearly 300 fire-related codes and standards.

This is in contrast to organizations that prepare the three regional model fire prevention codes. These organizations vote on their one code, code section by code section. Also, because membership is limited in these organizations, only fire officials (and other code officials in the case of the National Fire Prevention Code) may vote on the fire codes.

Outlined below are the code-writing organizations and the codes and standards they publish.

There are four national fire prevention codes: the *National Code* (used in the Northeast), the *Uniform Code* (used in the West and Southwest), the *Standard Code* (used in the Southeast), and NFPA 1, *Fire Prevention Code*. All reference NFPA standards for various code provisions.

The Building Officials and Code Administrators, International (BOCA) publishes the *National Code*. It is voted on only by BOCA member code officials, including individuals who enforce the fire code.

The International Fire Code Institute, in conjunction with the Western Fire Chiefs and the International Conference of Building Officials (ICBO), prepares the *Uniform Code*. It is voted on by members of the International Fire Code Institute only. The *Uniform Fire Code* is perhaps the most technical and does contain some building construction requirements (it has elements of a building code in certain sections).

The *Standard Code* is prepared by the Southern Building Code Congress, International (SBCCI). It is voted on exclusively by members of the Southwestern and Southeastern Fire Chiefs Associations.

NFPA 1, *Fire Prevention Code* recently was greatly expanded. It is very similar to the other three model fire codes, but benefits from the NFPA's oversight, thereby avoiding conflict with the other NFPA codes and standards. There is no corresponding building code, however.

The *National, Uniform,* and *Standard* codes are published every three years, with interim supplements prepared in intervening years.

These fire prevention codes are considered "maintenance" codes. They are not building codes—except for certain provisions in the Uniform code, as described—but apply to the hazardous processes and activities in and around a building. They do, however, contain requirements for maintaining building fire protection features.

Relevant areas include general fire safety provisions such as water supplies for firefighting and fire department access; requirements for special occupancies such as places of assembly and woodworking shops; requirements for special processes such as spray finishing; requirements for such equipment as mechanical refrigeration systems; and, particular hazards such as flammable/combustible liquids and high-piled stock.

Although the fire codes apply primarily to the building's occupancy, the fire prevention bureau should not wait until a certificate of occupancy is issued by the building department. Many of the fire code's provisions will affect the building itself.

The NFPA publishes a variety of fire protection codes and standards relating to all facets of fire protection. These include installation standards for most fire protection systems, standards that cover various hazardous materials and processes, and personnel standards.

Included in the NFPA documents is NFPA 101, *Code for Safety to Life from Fire in Buildings and Structures,* a quasi-building and fire code that has elements of both a fire and building code.

The *Life Safety Code* has been adopted by some jurisdictions, particularly at the state level. It also is often used by institutional occupancies such as hospitals and nursing homes. Few cities adopt it because it is neither a complete fire nor building code.

BUILDING CODES

Building codes also have a great impact on fire safety. A large majority of the model building code provisions are fire related.

Building codes cover such particulars as building area and height limitations based on building construction type, firewalls, shaft requirements, egress requirements, fire-rated separations, etc. It is imperative that fire inspectors and plan reviewers be well versed in both the building code and the fire code.

Three building codes correspond to the fire prevention codes described above: the *National Building Code,* prepared by BOCA; the *Uniform Building Code,* prepared by ICBO; and the *Standard Building Code,* prepared by SBCCI.

MECHANICAL AND PLUMBING CODES

There are companion mechanical and plumbing codes that complement the three building and fire codes (not including NFPA 1) mentioned above. The *National, Uniform,* and *Standard* codes all generally correlate, with a few exceptions.

The mechanical code has implications for the fire inspector because it is in this code that heating appliance requirements as well as requirements for smoke detectors in air-handling systems are found.

The plumbing code also has implications for the fire inspector and plan reviewer. One example is the regulations that govern combined domestic and fire protection water supplies used in single-family home fire sprinkler systems.

ELECTRICAL CODE

The *National Electrical Code,* used for nearly all electrical installations in the U.S., is published by the NFPA as NFPA 70.

Within its many pages, the fire inspector or plan reviewer can find requirements for fire alarm system wiring and wiring used in hazardous environments.

ZONING AND SUBDIVISION REGULATIONS

These regulations are developed by local municipalities or counties. They can be described as "quality of life" regulations, intended to bring order and minimum infrastructure requirements to the various neighborhoods and sectors of a jurisdiction.

These regulations do have some impact on fire prevention activities. For example, zoning regulations often prohibit dangerous industrial facilities from being constructed in residential areas.

Subdivision regulations usually specify minimum public roadway widths that affect fire apparatus access. They sometimes specify water supply requirements, including fire flow and hydrant placement. These water regulations also may be found in the regulations of the local water purveyor or even the fire code itself.

The jurisdiction's planning department normally has jurisdiction over these documents and may ask the fire prevention bureau for assistance on technical issues involving these documents.

ORGANIZATIONS WITH AN INTEREST IN FIRE PREVENTION

Two organizations, Underwriters Laboratories (UL) and Factory Mutual (FM), prepare documents that influence fire prevention activities. Underwriters Laboratories has been conducting tests and developing standards of safety for nearly 100 years. These standards and tests apply to such diverse products as fire extinguishers, fire doors, foam concentrate, and sprinkler heads.

Equipment that meets UL's standards is listed in one of UL's listing directories. Fire codes often require that equipment used for fire protection service be listed. Listed is not the same as approved, which means acceptable to the Authority Having Jurisdiction, in this case the fire prevention bureau.

Factory Mutual also conducts tests on fire protection equipment, particularly equipment found in industrial facilities and publishes a list of "approved" equipment. In addition, FM publishes a set of Loss Prevention Data Sheets which are particularly useful for determining appropriate fire protection measures for industrial processes.

ADOPTION OF FIRE CODES AND STANDARDS

To be enforced, a fire code or standard must be adopted or referenced within a statute enacted by a city, county, state, or other political subdivision. Otherwise it is not enforceable.

The authority to adopt fire regulations at the local level comes from the state. The state empowers the jurisdictions within the state to enact laws not reserved for the state itself. This distinction is important since states with a state-wide fire code often limit individual cities in the adoption of their own fire codes. Progressive state code statutes do not restrict subdivisions from enacting more stringent provisions, if they so desire.

States with a so-called "mini-maxi" code allow individual cities to adopt their own fire codes; however, the city's adopted code must meet the minimum requirements of the state code and cannot exceed the state code's requirements. Such a situation leaves little room to handle particular problems within an individual city. This is the reason many fire prevention chiefs look unfavorably on state mini-maxi codes.

Once a jurisdiction has selected a particular fire code for adoption, it usually develops a set of amendments to meet local conditions. These amendments serve to address the unique fire hazards of the community.

Since the fire code normally will be adopted along with the jurisdiction's other codes, such as the building code and plumbing code, it is best to meet with representatives of the other city departments that enforce those codes. This is a good way to resolve conflicts among amendments.

Once a working draft of an ordinance has been prepared, the fire prevention chief should meet with any groups affected by the regulations. These groups could include the Chamber of Commerce, architects' and engineering associations, developers, contractors, and other interested parties. Hold working sessions with these groups to determine points of disagreement.

The fire prevention chief should consider all suggestions from these groups and review any found to be unacceptable. Determine how much the fire prevention bureau is giving up. It is better to accept some of the changes to, in effect, lose a few battles but win the war. Regardless, you must be comfortable with the net result.

The Board of Appeals (described below) normally has its say on the code and any amendments. Having the board on your side makes the adoption of codes and amendments easier because board members tend to be appointed by council members or commissioners.

Take the time to explain the code to the adopting body. Highlight its benefits, how it compares with the present code, and the implications of its adoption. Do not hide any significant implications, but do not overemphasize them either. With these efforts and with your information on the table, you have the best chance at adoption.

Application and Interpretation of Fire Codes and Standards

Well-trained inspectors and plan reviewers are expected to enforce the fire codes and standards uniformly. There is no room for selective enforcement.

They are expected to prepare complete inspection and plan review reports, documenting all deficiencies noted during inspections or plan reviews. In the case of inspections, reasonable compliance dates should be set and followup inspections conducted.

An advantage to standardized basic and advanced training for fire prevention personnel is that all of them will handle similar situations in the same manner. This avoids multiple interpretations.

While it is desirable to have perfectly clear codes and standards, the reality is that most fire codes and standards are not written with perfect clarity. This means that different people render different interpretations. In some cases, what a fire inspector or plan reviewer stipulates may be construed by a citizen as a misinterpretation or nonrequirement of the code or standard.

Two safety nets help rectify this situation. The fire prevention code organizations and the NFPA all have staff to assist in interpretations. Keep in mind, however, that these interpretations are the opinion of the individual staff member.

The NFPA has a special formal interpretation process. Written inquiries that pose specific questions on a particular code or standard section are reviewed by the committee that prepared the document and a formal interpretation is issued.

Neither an informal interpretation by a code-writing organization staff member nor a formal interpretation from the NFPA have the effect of law within a given jurisdiction where the code in question has been legally adopted. They merely attempt to resolve a problem before it is taken before the Board of Appeals, the legal means of conflict resolution.

The Board of Appeals is a board appointed by the governing body of the jurisdiction, such as the city council. The composition of the board varies from jurisdiction to jurisdiction, but often includes members who represent various interest groups in the city, i.e., developers, architects, engineers, and contractors, as well as citizens at large. Many board charters require that some of the members have specific fire protection experience.

The board can vote on interpretations of the code as well as the acceptability of alternative means of code compliance. Its duties tend to be narrowly defined; unless specifically stated, the board cannot waive code requirements for an appellant.

THE FUTURE OF FIRE PREVENTION

Fire prevention activities will begin to accelerate as we enter the next century. Departments still will be expected to do more with less, necessitating creative approaches to reducing fire losses through fire prevention.

Fire prevention bureau personnel will be expected to have greater technical capabilities. Only constant training will keep them proficient in technological advances.

As more and more fire protection systems are installed, the demands on fire prevention bureaus to oversee proper maintenance of the systems surely will increase. In addition, since more reliance will be placed on these systems because of diminishing firefighting resources, there is little room for error.

New firefighters will be trained differently when it comes to fire prevention. Their in-depth training will include instruction on effective fire prevention techniques. They will be made increasingly aware of their fire prevention responsibilities and why fire prevention must be the department's—and their—top priority.

Will fire prevention bureau personnel ever outnumber the number of firefighters in a department? If the fire service does not start making fire prevention a priority, who will?

NOTES

1. Cannon, Donald J., *Heritage of Flames*, Pound Ridge, NY: Artisan Books, 1977, p. 356.

2. Ditzel, Paul C., *Fire Engines, Firefighters*, New York, NY: Crown Publishers, 1976, p. 18.

3. Costello, Augustine E., *Our Firemen, A History of the New York Fire Department, Volunteer and Paid*, New York, NY: Augustine E. Costello, 1887, p. 6.

4. Brayley, Arthur W., *A Complete History of the Boston Fire Department, Including the Fire Alarm Service and the Protective Department, from 1630 to 1888*, Boston, Mass. John P. Dale and Company, 1889, pp. 6–7.

5. O'Brien, Donald M., *A Century of Progress Through Service: The Centennial History of the International Association of Fire Chiefs, 1873–1973*, Washington, DC: IAFC, 1972, p. 94.

6. Ibid, p. 94.

7. Ibid, pp. 94–95.

8. Ditzel, Paul C., *Fire Engines, Firefighters*, New York, NY, Crown Publishers, 1976, p. 187.

26

Fire Protection Systems

GLENN P. CORBETT

CHAPTER HIGHLIGHTS

- The historical development of fire protection systems, how they have changed over time, and their future.
- The role the fire prevention bureau plays in ensuring the proper design, installation, and inspection of fire protection systems.
- General preplanning criteria for all system types.
- How each specific type of system operates, possible system problems, and how to properly support and manage the system.
- How to develop detailed preplans for specific systems in the jurisdiction.

THE ROLE OF "fixed" fire protection systems in the protection of lives and property has continued to change and expand over the past 100 years. The fire service has played an important part in the installation and use of these systems in the home and in the workplace.

Fixed fire protection systems include all active equipment that:

- detect and annunciate a fire or other threatening condition (fire alarm system);
- automatically suppress or extinguish a fire (automatic sprinkler system);
- communicate to and aid occupants who are evacuating a building (public address system); or
- aid firefighters in the suppression of a fire (standpipe system).

In this chapter we will not consider the passive ("structural") fire protection features of buildings such as fire walls or fire-rated floor and door assemblies.

As we leap into the 21st century, it is apparent that these "private" fire protection systems will play an even more important role in solving America's fire problem, a problem evidenced by the fire death rates in the United States and Canada, which are among the highest of any developed nations. Ever-increasing reliance must be placed on these systems, and the extent to which the fire service participates in this accelerating shift to fixed protection will ultimately define the fire service itself.

It is interesting to note that these systems are no longer referred to as "auxiliary" equipment, implying the "backseat" position the systems held in relation to manual firefighting in the past. Today these systems are recognized as an important, front-line segment of the effort to minimize life and property losses from fire.

As a chief officer, it is essential that you have a working knowledge of how these systems operate and how they can or do interface with your fireground operations. It is equally important that you recognize the critical role the fire service plays or must play in encouraging their installation as well as monitoring their design and maintenance.

Overall, the goal of this chapter is to provide the chief officer with a working knowledge of fire protection system design and operation, as well as an understanding of the interface between these systems and a fire department at the scene of a fire. Such technical skills are becoming an increasingly necessary expectation of the public at large.

This chapter will take a detailed look at the fire protection systems a chief officer will encounter during his career. The chapter opens with a historical perspective of fire protection systems. An explanation of the crucial role the fire department's fire prevention bureau plays in ensuring proper system installation and operational readiness then is offered.

General preplanning considerations common to all systems are provided for chief officers. Four general system categories—water-based fire suppression systems, special agent fire suppression systems, fire alarm and communication systems, and smoke management systems—then are established in order to better understand common characteristics among systems.

Finally, a detailed view is given of each system type. This critical information is coupled with specific preplanning criteria for each type of system. The chapter concludes with a look at the future of fire protection systems.

HISTORICAL PERSPECTIVE

Although simple fire protection equipment was in use in the United States during the 18th century, it wasn't until the Industrial Revolution of the 19th century that reliable fire protection systems found their place in the American landscape.

In 1852, William Channing installed the first municipal fire alarm system in Boston. Previously, cities had relied on fire watches by individuals stationed in towers overlooking the city. Channing's system consisted of 45 telegraph boxes, each of which contained a coded wheel that electrically transmitted the box number when turned manually.[1] In principle, Channing's telegraph boxes are essentially the same type of municipal fire alarm box still found today in some older cities.

Sprinkler systems, originally developed to protect the mills and warehouses of the Northeast, first appeared as networks of perforated pipes. The pipes, drilled with small holes, applied water over the entire area below and adjacent to the pipes. Valves, connected to a water supply, were opened manually to allow water to enter the system. A riser and valve typically were provided for each floor of the building, allowing the operator to apply water to an entire floor at a time.

The first perforated pipe system was installed in 1852.[2] Very often, the water supplies were inadequate for these systems. In addition, the insurance industry tended to look unfavorably on these systems because they created extensive water damage and, on some occasions, the wrong valve was opened.

The first truly successful sprinkler system, one that used sprinkler heads, a tank, and alarm, was developed in 1864 by an English inventor named Stewart Harrison.[3] It was not until 1874, however, that the first "commercial" sprinkler head, manufactured and sold for property protection, was developed by Henry Parmalee in New Haven, Connecticut.

In appearance, Parmalee's sprinkler system was similar today's sprinkler systems. Sprinkler heads, or "fire extinguishers" as they were known, were laid out on a 10-foot by 10-foot spacing, arranged on a typical "tree" piping network, and designed to open individually by melting of the metallic fusible element. A lever on the riser's alarm valve operated a steam whistle under water flow conditions. In addition, one-inch hoselines were attached about every 80 feet to the piping for manual fire attack by fire brigades.

Parmalee also alluded to the availability of a dry pipe sprinkler system in his sales brochure. He stated that for one particular system design "the pipes are kept free from water by a pressure of air," for use in freezing environments.[4]

Soon after the introduction of Parmalee's automatic sprinkler head, the Providence Steam and Gas Pipe Company acquired the production and sales rights for this sprinkler head in the late 1870s.

It is interesting to note that the Providence Steam and Gas Pipe Company's early sales literature discussed the capability of attaching automatic sprinkler piping to existing standpipes, to specifically protect "lofty stores and warehouses." Water supplied from a fire department's steam fire engine to the fire department connection allowed a fire department to apply water to the fire area, and only the fire area. For the fire service, this accentuated the benefits of providing automatic sprinklers in tall buildings, where it was "practically impossible to get water in the upper stories from our steamers."[5]

Effective operation of dry pipe sprinkler systems in the late 19th century was problematic. Some systems used unreliable "electric circuits, systems of wires with fusible links, or systems of small pipes provided with fusible openings." Baltimore even banned the use of dry-pipe sprinkler systems that depended on electricity to operate.[6]

In 1873, the concern over increasingly tall buildings prompted the National Association of Fire Engineers (later to become the International Association of Fire Chiefs) during its first meeting to call for a ". . . reduction in the excessive height of buildings . . ." The first issue of the *National Firemen's Journal*, which later became *Fire Engineering*, made mention on November 17, 1877, of buildings ". . . run up into the air at a height of six and eight stories."

It appears that the use of standpipes dates back at least to the early 1870s, probably in response to the first "high-rise" buildings. The Providence Steam and Gas Pipe Company in 1879 mentions the prevalence of these systems by stating ". . . standpipes now so generally introduced in such buildings, [lofty stores and warehouses] in the principal cities . . ."

Automatic detection systems also came into use during the 1870s. These early systems used thermostats with bimetallic components (two metals which have different thermal expansion rates) that expand and complete an electric circuit when heated by a fire. These systems evidently were used exclusively for property protection.

Unfortunately, these early systems tended to create numerous false alarms because of their extreme sensitivity to slight building movements (when heavy machinery was moved) and frequent wire breaks, among other reasons. Many municipalities would not allow these systems to be tied to their municipal box alarm systems.[7]

During the latter half of the 19th century, the insurance industry's role in fire protection system design and installation began to accelerate. In 1883, an organization called the Associated Fire Mutual Insurance Companies (composed of several mutual insurance companies) began to hold joint meetings. In 1888 this organization renamed itself the Associated Factory Mutual Fire Insurance Companies, finally becoming the Factory Mutual System in 1967. Factory Mutual has made major contributions to both the research and the actual application of fire protection systems.

In 1893, the then new electric light became a topic of concern for the insurance industry, including the Western Underwriters Association. It hired an electrical engineer, William Merrill, and created a laboratory for him in a firehouse at 22nd and Wentworth Streets in Chicago.[8] This laboratory became Underwriters Laboratory in 1896. Underwriters Laboratories has been a leader in national fire safety through its tests of fire protection equipment, components, and their system compatibility.

In 1896, a meeting of several insurance companies was convened to address the problem of the many and varied sprinkler design standards that were beginning to proliferate. The group agreed to one design standard and published it. This group took the name of the National Fire Protection Association (NFPA) and has been creating and publishing a variety of fire protection standards ever since.

The 1920s saw the introduction of the use of carbon dioxide as an extinguishing agent. Between 1928 and 1931, the National Foam Company developed its first chemical foam powders and foam chambers which were used to protect flammable liquid storage tanks.[9]

Dry chemical extinguishing systems came into existence during the late 1930s. The first dry chemical system was listed by Underwriters Laboratories on October 25, 1954.[10]

Immediately following World War II, the first halogenated agent extinguishing system was installed to protect aircraft engines.

Carbon tetrachloride (a member of the halogenated agent family) was used for many years as an extinguishing agent in portable pump extinguishers and hanging or throwable "grenades." These were banned from use during the 1960s because of the toxic effects of phosgene gas (generated during the extinguishment process) and corrosive problems.

In early 1970 the first residential smoke detector was developed and marketed. Economical designs and fire service support led to their installation in the majority of American homes. This development has been one of the most important life safety advances to date.

On the heels of the immensely successful smoke detector program came the development of the residential sprinkler head and residential sprinkler systems during the late 1970s and early 1980s. Again, an economical design combined with the backing of the fire service led to the installation of these systems in many parts of the country.

As we near the end of the 20th century, environmental concerns are having an impact on fire protection systems. Concerns over the depletion of the earth's ozone layer are causing the cessation of production of many halogenated fire protection agents. New "environment-friendly" agents are being developed as replacements.

Concerns about the contamination of water supplies caused by runoff during fires are being voiced. Requirements to contain water from sprinkler systems used to protect hazardous materials are found in various fire codes. Backflow-prevention devices also are being required on many water-based suppression systems. It is likely that foam discharges will be targeted and will require impoundment.

Dwindling natural resources, costs to the construction industry, and scarce public tax dollars may drive many communities to mandate fixed suppression systems (most likely sprinkler systems) in many occupancies, thereby allowing smaller water supplies for new or expanding communities to be built. It also is likely that fewer fire stations will have to be built to serve these same communities.

While no one can predict the future, economics will, in all probability, drive the installation of fixed fire protection systems during the 21st century.

SYSTEM DESIGN REVIEW AND INSPECTION

For a fire protection system to operate properly, it must first be designed correctly, then installed properly and maintained regularly. Consequently, a fire department's fire prevention bureau plays an important role in ensuring a fire protection system's reliability through proper plan review and inspection techniques. Technical competency on the part of plan review and inspection personnel is one of the keys to ensuring that a fire protection system will function properly when it is activated.

In most jurisdictions, the authority to review and inspect new fire protection systems rests with the fire department. In some cities, however, the building inspection department is responsible for overseeing the installation of fire protection systems. Maintenance inspections of existing systems almost always are conducted by the fire department.

In jurisdictions in which the building inspection department (or agency other than the fire department) is charged with overseeing fire protection system installations, the fire department should keep "close tabs" on such activities and results. Unfortunately, building inspectors often do not receive the necessary level of training to inspect these systems properly. In addition, they frequently are kept busy verifying code compliance with the myriad other requirements found in the building code.

The local ordinance(s) that requires the installation of the fire protection systems must clearly identify the agency responsible for system reviews and inspections. This delineation normally is established in the adopted fire and building codes. A memorandum of understanding among departments helps to clarify any unresolved issues.

As part of a fire and building codes adoption process, specific fire protection system design standards (such as the NFPA fire protection system standards) also should be adopted. These design standards may be referenced within the fire and building code or may be specified as part of the overall adopting ordinance. In either case, the specific edition and year of the referenced design standard must be included.

In addition to the adopted design standards, technical reference information for the fire prevention bureau's library is needed to carry out review and inspection duties. Equipment testing organization publications such as the Underwriters Laboratories' *Fire Protection Equipment Directory* are essential to ensure that the equipment proposed for use in a system is listed, that the equipment is being used within the limits of its listing criteria, and that it is compatible with other components. Equipment incompatibility is a source of system failures, particularly with alarm systems.

Factory Mutual's Loss Prevention Data Sheet Series (a 12-volume set) is especially helpful when dealing with complex industrial fire protection system design and inspection problems. In some cases, these data sheets provide additional and more detailed information than the NFPA documents.

PLAN REVIEW AND INSPECTION PERSONNEL

Fire department personnel who review and inspect fire protection systems must be thoroughly trained and receive constant in-service training to keep informed of the latest trends.

In large departments, it is often advantageous to use "specialists" for each type of system. Having certified plan reviewers and inspectors in the different types of systems is both a desirable goal and a source of pride.

For example, it is beneficial to have fire inspectors certified by the National Institute for Certification in Engineering Technologies. Certification is offered for automatic sprinkler systems, fire alarm systems, and special hazards systems. While these certifications are intended for system designers, fire department inspectors should have a level of expertise at least equivalent to that of a system designer.

Many fire department and county and state fire marshals' offices now employ civilian fire protection engineers or fire protection technicians (who have previous design experience) to perform reviews and inspections of fire protection systems. These individuals often bring a high level of expertise to the position. Some of these civilian specialists also have operational fire service experience.

Trained fire protection engineers and technicians can "hit the ground running." An added benefit typically is an overall lower turnover rate for individuals in these positions.

Uniformed personnel have the advantage of having seen and used different fire protection systems during actual fires. This field experience is especially useful to them when they review equipment—a standpipe system or fire alarm control panel layouts, for example. It also is helpful to have a fire officer train the department's fire companies, since he understands how a system will interface with their operations.

In the selection of a uniformed member, it is important to choose an individual who will remain in the position for at least four or five years, because of the need for continuity in review inspection duties and investment in him of a large amount of technical training.

Smaller career departments and volunteer departments may find it advantageous to hire a fire protection engineer to review and inspect large projects. The local chapter of the Society of Fire Protection Engineers can assist in locating a qualified individual.

Recordkeeping and Permits

A very important fire prevention bureau duty is to create and retain installation and related fire protection system inspection records. These records include the original fire-department-approved "shop drawings" prepared for the system installation, acceptance tests and inspections, and the periodic inspections made of the system after installation.

These records should be filed by street address, including suite number where appropriate, and include the project and building name. It usually is beneficial to rely on the same filing system used for other inspections so that a complete "picture" of the building is available from one file.

Computerized recordkeeping greatly expands the information database available to the officer in charge of the fire prevention bureau. Besides having information about a particular building at your fingertips, the computer can generate statistical information on the number of inspections conducted, number of plans reviewed, or total fees collected. This information can be used for annual reports, cost recovery analyses, or to justify increases in personnel levels.

It is expensive to conduct plan reviews and inspections. To offset these costs, fire prevention bureaus often collect permit fees. Permit fees are based on the cost of the service, i.e., plan review, inspections, and administrative work. While the amount of salary money expended should be recovered through the fees, fee schedules should not be perceived as a penalty or a tax on a system or its components.

Some departments' sprinkler and fire alarm system fees are based on the number of devices, with minimum and maximum fees set. For example, a charge of $.50 per device (sprinkler head or detection device) is assessed for new system installations, with a minimum fee of $100.00.

Plan Review

Before a fire protection system is installed, its design should be reviewed by the fire prevention bureau. In many states and jurisdictions, these plan reviews must be prepared by a licensed professional engineer or licensed technician. Installation contractors should be licensed and bonded.

Plan reviews should be conducted in a room dedicated for that purpose, where distractions can be minimized. The proper tools and research documents, including a drafting table, architect's and engineer's scales, calculator, and a full set of the adopted codes and standards of the jurisdiction, and other reference materials, must be provided.

It is the duty of plan review personnel to study the plans thoroughly and identify both real and potential problems in system design. This review involves:

- establishing the goal of the system;
- ensuring that the type of fire protection system selected is appropriate for the hazard;
- verifying that the system to be used is within the scope of its capabilities; and
- assuring that coverage is complete and adequate.

Predesign conferences devoted to discussing large and complicated systems should be conducted with the system designer to avoid mistakes and misunderstandings.

During system review, the plan reviewer must verify that all details necessary for the system's installation are shown on the plans. Nothing should be left to chance; promises made to perform or install, or provisional approvals granted resulting in mistakes are costly to correct retroactively. Mistakes ultimately can result in lawsuits because incomplete or faulty installations can cause unnecessary damage. Many design standards have checklists of the details that should be shown on the plans; plan reviewers may even wish to add to these lists as local needs, standards, codes, or statutes dictate.

A full set of equipment specifications and a full set of calculations, where appropriate, also are needed. Specifications are especially useful in verifying the compatibility of different pieces of equipment and for equipment listings by organizations such as Underwriters Laboratories. It is necessary to review calculations to verify that pipe of the proper size has been selected (in the case of most sprinkler and standpipe systems, for example) or wiring of the proper size has been used (in the case of an alarm system, for example).

After a set of plans has been reviewed and approved, the appropriate approval stamps are affixed to them. If the plans are rejected, a review comment sheet must be provided. This sheet identifies the problems and specifically identifies the numerical citation in the design standard that applies to the design deficiency. Systems should not be installed until the plans have been approved and the permit issued.

INSPECTIONS, TESTS, AND SYSTEM MAINTENANCE

After system installation, acceptance inspections and tests are performed to verify that the system was installed as shown on the approved set of plans and that it works properly. The installing contractor notifies the fire prevention bureau in advance to schedule the inspection or test, and he is required to provide all the necessary equipment, adequate personnel, and the approved set of plans to the inspector at the site. In most cases, the inspector merely witnesses tests, but does not participate in them; this is a local decision which should be based on legal considerations. Participating in a test can expose a fire inspector to potential injury, and the fire department to liability.

The fire inspector should take advantage of the opportunity to invite nearby fire companies and the responding first-alarm chief when he witnesses the testing of large or complicated systems. This is a chance for firefighters to gain valuable information and assistance for their preplanning efforts. In volunteer departments, it is advantageous to have the inspections or tests conducted at night or on Saturdays. Many building owners are willing to pay for the contractor's overtime costs, if necessary.

Inspections of fire protection systems ensure that the installed systems meet the appropriate installation standard and follow the approved set of plans. To conduct a proper inspection the inspector must "walk" the entire system, approved plans in hand.

A variety of tests are performed on the different types of fire protection systems. The design standards previously discussed typically contain a list of acceptance tests and, in some cases, periodic post-acceptance tests.

Listed below are examples of fire protection systems acceptance tests.

Water supply networks

- Hydrostatic test to verify piping integrity under pressure.
- Flow test of all appurtenances (hydrants, monitors, etc.) for proper flow/operation.
- Test of all electric supervisory alarm devices for proper operation.

Automatic sprinkler systems

- Hydrostatic test to verify piping integrity under pressure.
- "Main drain" test to check both water supply adequacy and that all supply valves are open.
- Test of the water motor gong.
- Test of all electric waterflow and supervisory alarm devices for proper operation.
- "Trip" test of dry pipe system's dry valve.
- Test of all initiation devices (smoke detectors, heat detectors, etc.) for preaction and deluge system.
- Discharge test of deluge system.

Standpipe systems

- Hydrostatic test to verify piping integrity under pressure.
- Flow test of system to verify flow and pressure.

- Test of all electric waterflow and supervisory alarm devices for proper operation.
- Test of hose valves to ensure proper operation.

Fire pumps

- Flow test of pump using flow meter or test header (to 150 percent of rated capacity) to verify discharge and water supply.
- Test of automatic/manual start/stop pump.
- Test of transfer to emergency power, where applicable.

Water spray systems

- Hydrostatic test to verify piping integrity under pressure.
- "Main drain" test to check both water supply adequacy and that all supply valves are open.
- Test of the water motor gong.
- Test of all electric waterflow and supervisory alarm devices for proper operation.
- Test of all initiation devices (smoke detectors, heat detectors, etc.) for water spray system.
- Discharge test of water spray system to verify coverage.

Foam extinguishing system

- Hydrostatic test to verify piping integrity under pressure.
- Test of all electric waterflow and supervisory alarm devices for proper operation.
- Test of all initiation devices (flame detectors, etc.) for foam system as appropriate.
- Discharge test of foam system to verify foam concentration and distribution.

Carbon dioxide system

- Discharge test to verify proper operation, proper concentration, and proper operation of related equipment shutdown (air-handling system) or door closure.

Dry/wet chemical system

- Discharge test (if possible) to verify distribution and performance.
- Test of proper operation of mechanical/electrical release components and related equipment shutdown (fuel gas supply, etc.)

Halogenated/clean agent systems

- Test of proper operation of electrical release components and related equipment closure/shutdown (door closure, air-handling unit shutdown, etc.).
- "Puff test" which uses nitrogen to verify that piping is unobstructed.
- Enclosure integrity test that uses a "door fan" to verify the "tightness" of the enclosure.

Fire alarm and communication systems

- Operational tests of entire system(s) and every component to verify proper operation, including audibility/visibility of signaling devices, response of initiating devices, interfaces between systems (elevators, smoke control, etc.), and proper device supervision.
- Test of adequacy of secondary power supply under both detection and alarm load conditions.

Smoke management systems

- Operational tests of system to measure pressure differentials, smoke movement patterns, air velocity across openings, exhaust rates, etc., depending on system design.
- Test of interface between smoke management system and detection system and test of smoke management system under secondary power supply.
- Test of system manual controls for use of fire department.

Refer to the appropriate NFPA standard for a complete list of all acceptance and periodic tests/inspections for fire protection systems.

It is essential to record and retain all system inspections and tests. Besides the typical project name, address, and date, the records should include the quantitative and qualitative results of the inspection or test, the name of the inspector who conducts the inspection or test, and the portion of the system inspected or tested (if not the complete system).

Probably the most challenging task for the chief of the fire prevention bureau is to ensure that fire protection systems are maintained in a state of complete operational readiness. This challenge will increase as many more fire protection systems continue to be installed each year.

It is essential that the fire prevention bureau require periodic inspections of all systems in the jurisdiction. These inspections and any necessary repairs or upgrades must be conducted by competent contractors, licensed where required, who are thoroughly familiar with the systems they inspect.

As mentioned earlier, some of the design standards include periodic maintenance inspections and tests that must be conducted. Additionally, National Fire Protection Association Standard 25, *Standard for the Inspection, Testing, and Maintenance of Water-Based Fire Protection Systems,* is available.

NFPA 25 provides a list of tests as well as their frequency for water-based suppression systems such as automatic sprinkler and standpipe systems. Adoption and enforcement of this document by a jurisdiction will assure that a water-based suppression system will function properly when called on.

The fire prevention bureau should receive copies of all contractor inspections and tests, as well as any repairs or upgrades. If a system has failed or not been inspected at all, an inspection by a fire department inspector is necessary to rectify the situation.

In addition, fire prevention bureau personnel must conduct their own inspections of fire protection systems; these inspections can be conducted during routine building inspections.

Fire companies also play an important role in maintaining system readiness. In-service company inspections should include basic checks of installed fire protection systems. This typically includes such tasks as ensuring that water supply valves are open and that alarm system panels are free of trouble conditions. Any deficiencies noted are given to the building owner and copies are forwarded to the fire prevention bureau for follow-up. Simple checklists for fire companies, with code or standard section citations, which can assist them in their inspections, as well as increase their level of knowledge, can be developed from books such as the NFPA's *Fire Protection Systems Inspection Test and Maintenance Manual.*

GENERAL PREPLANNING CONSIDERATIONS FOR FIRE COMPANIES

Before discussing the specific types of fire protection systems, a generic preplanning overview common to all system types is presented. Additional specific preplan concerns are identified for each type of fire protection system in the section that follows.

When developing a preplan, it is important to identify all fire protection systems within the building or facility under consideration. Since these systems will have a direct impact on the outcome of the fire, the chief officer must have complete details about the system(s).

Preplan notes should include the following general system details:

* specific system type;
* system capacity or capability;
* extent of coverage of the system;
* specific details of system operation (especially for complicated systems) and interfaces with other systems;

- specific details of system activation and shutdown; and
- the name and telephone number of a service contractor available at all times to assist the fire department in the use or repair of complicated or large systems during an extended fire incident.

All drawings prepared for preplans should use a common set of symbols to identify equipment, such as those found in NFPA 170, *Firesafety Symbols.* The drawings should show the extent of protection of the fire protection system(s), including delineation lines to show coverage, as well as all critical equipment, e.g., control panels, control valves, and fire department connections.

Fire protection engineers can provide technical assistance when fire companies are preparing preplans and also by providing training on the design and use of fire protection systems. If your department is fortunate to have a fire protection engineer on staff, he should be recalled to all multiple-alarm fires. He can assist the chief officer at major fires by answering questions on the use of a particular fire protection system or water supply concerns.

If your department does not have a fire protection engineer, the local chapter of the Society of Fire Protection Engineers can locate a person for your department.

Preplanning Industrial Facilities

When it prepares preplans for industrial facilities that have a fire brigade, the municipal fire department should initiate a meeting to discuss joint preplanning. Such preplans should include details about the command structure and identify the fire attack and support teams that will be used at the fire scene. These details affect the amount and type of training that the municipal firefighters and officers will receive concerning fixed fire protection systems installed at the facility.

At complex industrial facilities, it is essential to have a competent identified representative to meet the responding municipal fire units to take them directly to the incident location.

On-site visits to the industrial facility should be made for joint training exercises for fire brigade and fire department personnel that include actually using the fixed fire protection equipment.

One issue not to overlook is the compatibility of fire brigade and fire department equipment. Obviously, the threads on hose, fire department connections, hydrants, and hose valves must match or adapters must be provided. Foam concentrate and foam equipment also must be checked for capability, proper operation, and compatibility; mixing different types of foam concentrate or using the wrong type of foam on a particular fire can spell disaster on the fireground. Certain dry chemical extinguishing agents can deteriorate or destroy foam blankets.

TYPES OF FIRE PROTECTION SYSTEMS

Chief officers may encounter several different types of fire protection systems installed in buildings or other structures. These systems can be grouped into four major categories:

- Water-based fire suppression systems—the water supply network, automatic sprinkler systems, standpipe systems, water spray systems, and water mist systems.
- Special agent fire suppression systems—foam extinguishing systems, carbon dioxide extinguishing systems, halogenated and clean agent extinguishing systems, and dry or wet chemical extinguishing systems.
- Fire alarm and communication systems.
- Smoke management systems.

While most fire protection systems are "stand-alone" systems, many interface with other types of systems to some extent. An example of this interface scenario is a covered mall's sprinkler system with a waterflow switch connected to an alarm system to alert building occupants of a fire condition and activate smoke removal fans. Another very common example of an interface is a high-rise building's fire alarm system which is used to initiate a recall of elevators, start the stairwell pressurization system, and initiate a smoke management system.

In some cases, different fire protection systems are combined, with the intended result that they work together as a single system; for example, a preaction sprinkler system that relies on smoke detection devices to activate a deluge valve and allow water to enter the sprinkler piping and air to escape.

Chief officers must keep system interfaces and system combinations in mind when they analyze individual fire protection systems. They also must pay attention to the unique characteristics of each system that they study, such as the extent of protection and specific startup and shutdown instructions.

What follows is a discussion of the details of each type of fire protection system. The different types of systems are placed into the four categories identified above. Descriptions of the systems, preplanning concerns, and firefighting considerations are offered for each system type.

Water-Based Suppression Systems

All water-based suppression systems, including automatic sprinkler systems, standpipe systems, and water spray systems, have a water supply network that supplies them. A discussion of water-based suppression systems begins with an overview of this water supply network.

Water Supply Network

The water supply network of a water-based fire protection system can vary in size from a small pipe supplying a Class II standpipe in a single building to a large piping network that supplies dozens of fire hydrants and several sprinkler systems in a large industrial plant. The size and extent of the water supply network depend on the magnitude of hazards, number of hazards present, and the desired level of protection.

The major components of a "private" water supply network include the water source, fire pump, piping (fire main), valves, fire department connections, fire hydrants, and hose houses.

WATER SOURCE

The water source for many water-based suppression systems is simply a connection to a public utility's water mains, whereas in large industrial and commercial facilities, it may be a gravity tank or reservoir. Pressure tanks may also be found in some tall high-rise buildings, and some older sprinkler systems where a water supply is very limited, or nonexistent.

The connection made directly to a public utility main is probably the most common. These connections typically are made by the public utility that owns the main, or a contractor approved by the utility's management.

Connecting to a public utility usually means there will be good maintenance of the public mains. Unfortunately, the water supply available in the public mains can be inconsistent or deteriorate over time, especially in rapidly developing areas. Water supply tests should be conducted regularly to detect any changes or drops in available pressure or flow.

On-site gravity tanks are elevated wood or steel tanks often found on older water supply networks. New gravity tank installations are somewhat rare and usually found only in very large industrial and commercial plants as well as in taller high-rise buildings. Standard wood tank sizes range from 5,000 gallons to 100,000 gallons, while steel tanks range in size from 5,000 to 500,000 gallons. Size is based on the demands of the systems it supplies and the size of the physical plant. The tanks are usually monitored for water level and low water temperature.

Gravity tanks use elevation to create "head" pressure in the system. In many cases, this pressure head eliminates the need for pressure-boosting pumps. Gravity tanks are, however, subject to freezing and leaks (heaters can be installed), and their size requires significant maintenance.

Reservoirs often are found in large industrial facilities located in remote areas. In some cases, the reservoirs are actually "natural" sources, for example ponds or lakes, while in other cases they are manmade. Fabric reservoirs, whose walls are made of a rubberized material, are an example of the manmade type.

Fire pumps suction water from reservoirs and deliver it to the fire protection systems. Concerns about using reservoirs include the fact that debris may be drawn out of natural reservoirs, clogging the pump intake or the small piping found in the fire protection systems themselves; the possible failure of pumps to start or prime; and temperature effects on the reservoir.

Pressure tanks often are used to supply water-based suppression systems in remote areas, some tall high-rise buildings, and some older systems. Most often they are steel tanks which normally range in size from 3,000 gallons to 9,000 gallons. The tanks are filled to two-thirds of capacity with water and then pressurized with air (to at least 75 psi) for the remaining tank capacity.

This large gravity tank supplied the water-based fire protection systems at the Dole Cannery in Honolulu from many years. While such tanks are infrequently installed today, firefighters should establish the quantity and pressure of firefighting water they can provide for industrial facilities.   PHOTO COURTESY OF AUTHOR

These tanks are sized based on the demand, including duration, of the system or section of system it supplies. Pressure tanks are provided with air pressure gauges and water level gauges.

Where no water is available, pressure tanks are often the only economical alternative. The system design standards anticipate that the fire will be extinguished before the pressure tank's water supply is exhausted.

FIRE PUMPS

Fire pumps are provided for one of two reasons: to provide a sole supply of water or to "boost" the pressure available to a fire protection system from a public water supply. Pumps can range in size from 25 gpm to 5,000 gpm, although the majority of pumps are in the 500-gpm to 2,500-gpm range, and are designed to deliver a variety of pressures.

Fire pumps may be driven by an electric motor (powered by the public electric utility) or by a diesel engine (which can drive the pump at varying speeds). While they are extremely rare, steam-driven pumps may be found in old industrial facilities. LPG, natural gas, and gasoline drivers have not been permitted on new installations since 1971.

The fire pump controller is the "brains" of a fire pump installation. Preplans must note the procedures to start and stop the pump as well as any associated power transfer switches.   PHOTO COURTESY OF AUTHOR

While most pumps installed today are automatic starting, there are many existing manual-start pumps. Most of the manual-start pumps that do exist supply standpipe systems.

The important components of a fire pump installation are the controller, which starts and stops the pump, pressure gauges installed on the intake and discharge sides of the pump, and bypass piping that goes "around" the pump in order to allow the pump to be taken out of service and still provide unimpeded flow (albeit at a lower pressure) to the systems. Relief valves for variable speed drivers also are provided.

"Jockey" pumps are small-capacity pressure maintenance pumps (usually a capacity of a few gpm) used to maintain the required suppression system pressure which may gradually fail due to normal leakage. A significant drop in system pressure (due to actual operation of the system) will activate the main fire pump since the jockey pump will be unable to maintain the system pressure.

Piping

Private underground fire main piping brings water from the source to the fire protection system. The pipes vary in size from 6 inches to as large as 20 inches (smaller pipes are permitted in certain limited situations). Today, the size of the pipe most often is based on the hydraulic calculation of the largest system or hydrant demand to be met. In the past, pipe sizes often were based on engineering judgment or flow or capacity tables.

The pipes are made of ductile iron, asbestos cement, or polyvinyl chloride, although other types are permitted. Cast iron pipes can be found in older installations.

Restraint, in the form of thrust blocks or "rods," prevents pipe movement at locations where the pipe changes direction. New piping is tested to a working pressure of 200 psi, or 50 psi over the maximum static pressure when the static pressure is over 150 psi.

Valves and Other Water Control Equipment

Among the different types of valves installed in the underground piping network are control valves, drain valves, check valves (including alarm valves), pressure-regulating valves, detector check valves, and backflow preventors.

Control valves shut off a source of water, for example, the valve at the connection to the city main, or isolate a particular section of large water supply networks to keep one area charged while shutting down an adjacent area.

A control valve can be a post indicator valve, wall post indicator valve, post indicator valve assembly, outside stem and yoke valve, or a nonindicating underground gate valve with roadway box.

You can see whether an indicating control valve is open or closed just by looking at it. Post indicator valves and wall post indicator valves have windows with lettered "target" plates that show you instantly whether the valve is "open" or "shut." Post indicator valves are freestanding posts in the yard outside the building and often are found in large commercial facilities. Wall post indicator valves are found on the exterior walls of buildings and control system risers are located right behind the valves on the inside of the building.

Post indicator valve assemblies also are freestanding posts in the yard. They have a set of holes; when a person can see "through" the holes, the valve is in the open position.

Outside stem and yoke (OS&Y) valves sometimes are used as control valves in the water supply network outside the building in some installations, and often inside the building. The stem moves in and out of the valve as the valve (gate) is opened or closed; a fully extended stem that projects out of the valve wheel indicates that the valve/gate is fully open. If they are placed in the water supply network outside of a building they usually are located in covered pits, in conjunction with a detector check valve or above ground in conjunction with a reduced pressure principle backflow preventor.

Underground nonindicating gate valves with a roadway box are found in some installations. They must be operated with a T-wrench (key) to open or close them. There is no visual indication of whether they are open or closed; the valve must be test-turned with the T-wrench to determine if it is open or closed.

Water purveyors are increasingly require the installation of backflow preventors such as this well-insulated one (but missing the required "indicating" valve stems). Recognize that such devices create friction loss, reducing the pressure available to the water-based suppression system. PHOTO COURTESY OF AUTHOR

Check valves are installed at strategic locations to permit water flow only in one direction. A typical location for a check valve is in the piping between a fire department connection and the fire main being supplied; this way water cannot come out of the fire department connection.

Pressure-regulating devices tend to be used where excessive pressures may be supplied from the public utility. These pressure-regulating devices reduce the pressure supplied to the private fire main, thereby avoiding damage.

Finally, double-check detector check valves and reduced pressure (RP) principle backflow preventors are being used with more regularity today because of concerns about water theft and water quality. Double-check detector check values measure the amount of water used by the building owner (even small amounts) and also provide a certain degree of backflow prevention. RP backflow prevention valves provide a high degree of protection against the flow of water from a fire protection system back into the public water supply. A reduced pressure gap between the two check valves in the device will discharge any backflow into the ground rather than let it get into the public main.

Fire Department Connections

Fire department connections are used to allow the fire department to pump into a water-based suppression system and boost its water supply. They usually are considered auxiliary devices; water-based suppression systems must have an automatic water supply. One notable exception is the dry Class I standpipe system for which the fire department connection is the sole source of water. Fire department connections also may be found on ammonia diffusion systems.

The fire department connection is provided with at least two 2½-inch hose connections. Large-demand systems may have multiple inlets (each inlet should be provided with a "clapper," similar to a swing check valve, in the hose connection piping), while buildings with large street frontages may have more than one fire department connection. Some cities even use 5-inch "sexless" (storz) couplings in lieu of the 2½-inch inlets to connect large-diameter hose.

Fire department connections are located either in the yard or on the building itself. When located in the yard, the fire department connection often supplies multiple systems, and even multiple buildings. When located on a building, the fire department connection may supply a single system or a group of systems (risers) on a "manifold" just inside the building.

Unfortunately, some fire department connections only supply a portion of a building, especially in large structures. In the case of a high-rise, one fire department connection may supply the lower floors and another the upper floors. In these cases, identification signs should be provided.

Fire Hydrants

Private fire hydrants may be one of two types: a "yard" hydrant or a municipal-type hydrant. Yard hydrants came into existence when many industrial plants had fire brigades and "hose" houses. These hydrants have only two 2½-inch outlets with no steamer or pumper connection. Handlines were attached directly to the hydrant to fight the fire; pumpers did not take suction from the yard hydrant. In some especially misleading situations, municipal-type hydrants (two 2½-inch outlets and pumper connection) are placed on a yard system intended for handline use only.

Yard hydrant installations often have hydrants placed in the fields around the plant buildings. The supply main to these hydrants usually has a single fire department connection located at or near the main entrance to the plant and close to a public fire hydrant.

The major problem associated with this yard hydrant arrangement is that the fire department pumper that pumps into the single fire department connection at the plant entrance is not only supplying water to the sprinkler systems in the plant, but also to the yard hydrants. Any engine companies in the plant that are taking suction from the yard hydrants for handlines, etc., are stealing water from the same main that is supplying the sprinkler system. This depletes the water supply to the sprinkler system, which can have disastrous results.

Most municipalities that have yard hydrants have standard operating procedures that prohibit their use.

This is an old yard hydrant at a dye plant—note the two - 2½" outlets. Such hydrants are intended for supplying handlines directly—they are not intended to supply pumpers!   PHOTO COURTESY OF PAUL DANSUCH

Hose Houses and Monitor Nozzles

Hose houses are wooden or metal structures located over or adjacent to a yard hydrant. They contain several hundred feet of 2½-inch handline hose, a nozzle, and a hydrant wrench. The hose house serves as a "station" where industrial fire brigade members can get the handline to fight a fire directly "off" of the yard hydrant.

New hose houses are fairly rare, and some existing ones are being removed. Only very large industrial facilities still use them.

Unfortunately, even though hose houses have disappeared from many industrial plants, the yard hydrants have not. Many insurance companies still insist that they be installed, even though no one will be using handlines directly off of them to fight fires.

Monitor nozzles also may be located on a water supply network. They are found in industrial facilities, protecting bulk storage of lumber, coal, or similar combustibles, or as exposure protection for tanks that contain flammable or hazardous materials. Monitor nozzles also are used to mitigate accidental releases of hydrofluoric acid vapors in refineries.

Water supply network—Preplanning Considerations

The first step in preplanning a water supply network is to get accurate, up-to-date installation drawings from the owner, and use information to prepare a preplan sketch. Include the following:

- location, size (including duration), and type of water source;
- location, size, and type of fire pump(s);
- piping arrangement, size, and connections;
- location and type of all water supply control valves and equipment, including notations concerning the direction of opening for all nonindicating valves;
- location of the fire department connection and the number of inlets and thread type (note where it is different from thread normally used by the department). Where the fire department connection is "in the yard," determine the connecting point of the fire department connection to the underground piping, noting what it does and does not supply. If the fire department connection piping is located on the building, note if the piping connection to the riser is made above or below the system(s) control valve(s), and determine whether supplying the fire department connection with a pumper "bypasses" all potentially closed valves;
- location, thread, type (yard hydrant versus municipal type) of all private fire hydrants, paying attention to the number and size of nozzle outlets;
- location of public hydrants in streets surrounding the property that may be used to supply the fire department connection; and

This building has a multitude of fire department connections. Preplans must establish the areas each fire department connection (f.d.c.) serves. Signage for each f.d.c. indicating such information should be provided. PHOTO COURTESY OF PAUL DANSUCH

This set of sprinkler risers is supplied by a manifold. It is important to ensure that a firefighter has been assigned to verify all riser valves are open especially because pumping into the fire department connections (and through the manifold) will bypass closed valves. PHOTO COURTESY OF AUTHOR

- location, type, and size of all hose houses and monitors. Note capacity/ demand of monitor nozzles.

Once prepared, this sketch can be used as a basis for writing fire company preplanning instructions which identify specific tasks to perform; then individual company assignments can be established.

In your review of the water source, determine the amount of water available and at what pressure; flow tests may have to be conducted. Correlate the demand of the water-based suppression system with the available water supply and see how much is "left over" for attack lines and master streams.

If the water source is "limited," for example, in a pressure tank or gravity tank, determine the duration.

Fire pump preplan notes must include the method used to start and stop the pump. Where manual-start pumps are used, the various pressure settings and speeds for the anticipated demands must be established. In the case of multiple pumps, determine whether they are to be used together or if one is a backup to the other. A small sketch that shows the piping surrounding the pump, with all valves and pressure gauges identified, should be included.

In your review of water control valves, it is important to identify which valves will be closed after a fire is extinguished; the valve selected may be a riser control valve inside the building.

Additionally, identify "isolation" control valves that may be closed in the event of a piping break so that a portion of the system may be maintained in service. This may be the result of an underground main break or an explosion inside the building that destroys the suppression system.

Probably the most important preplanning consideration is the fire department connection. The preplan notes must indicate the fire department connection supply priorities. It should be the first- or second-arriving engine company on the first-alarm assignment. Note the direction of water flow for check valves and backflow preventors. Where will water be directed if the fire department connection is supplied?

What systems are supplied by each fire department connection and what is the coverage area of each fire department connection? The fire prevention bureau can assist in requiring appropriate signs when there are multiple fire department connections.

The pressure and flow requirements to be supplied to the fire department connection must be established. For sprinkler systems, this information sometimes is available on hydraulic design information signs on the system riser, but only if the signs are present. These signs specify the minimum flow and pressure at which the system was hydraulically designed to operate.

In the absence of such signs, NFPA 13E, *Recommendations for Fire Department Operations in Properties Protected by Sprinkler and Standpipe Systems,* recommends that the supply line(s) to sprinkler systems be pressurized to a minimum of 150 psi. Keep in mind that many systems have a maximum working pressure of 175 psi.

Many sources specify that at least two lines be stretched to the fire department connection: stretch and supply with one line and augment with the second. If additional fire department connection inlets are provided, they should be supplied as fire conditions dictate. For example, a large fire in a high-piled stock warehouse would need a large supply of water into the sprinkler system.

Determinations of pressure requirements for a standpipe system must be based on the size and type of hoseline used and the location (floor) of the fire. NFPA 13E recommends that for buildings up to 100 feet in height, 100 psi should be provided at the fire department connection for attack lines using solid stream nozzles and 150 psi at the fire department connection for attack lines using "spray" nozzles. For buildings of 100 feet or more, 5 psi should be added for each successive floor to the fire floor.

It appears that the pressures specified above in NFPA 13E assume little or no friction loss in the standpipe system and large handlines (2½-inch); it is advisable to increase the pressure when it is supplying "high" flows to 1½-inch or 1¾-inch handlines which use combination or automatic nozzles.

For example, for a flow of 200 gpm through 150 feet of 1¾-inch hose with an automatic nozzle operating at a fire on the tenth floor of a building, the pressure required at the fire department connection would be:

Nozzle pressure	100 psi
Friction loss through 150' 1¾-inch handline	75 psi
Pressure to overcome elevation loss to tenth floor	45 psi
Friction loss in riser and fittings	25 psi
total	245 psi

In all cases, the preplan must note the pressure capabilities of the system. Keep in mind that many sprinkler systems and standpipe systems are hydrostatically tested to only 200 psi, so you need to determine the maximum pressure you can pump into the system without damaging it.

Fire department connections to water spray systems often require a significant amount of water to be supplied to the system (the nozzles on many systems are normally open). Since these systems typically are hydraulically calculated, the preplan should make note of the pressure and flow demand of the system that must be supplied through the fire department connection.

Another extremely important consideration in planning is the role of fire hydrants. The specific hydrants that will be used **must** be identified, keeping in mind that suppression systems must not be "robbed" of water. The fire hydrant that will supply the fire department connection (through a pumper) must be identified. Normally, it is beneficial to use public hydrants to supply the pumpers supplying the fire department connection.

Two-way yard hydrants (2-½-inch nozzle outlets) must never be used to supply pumpers. Three-way municipal-type private hydrants (2½-inch, 1-4¼-inch nozzle outlets) should only be used when it is certain that water will not be taken from the suppression systems.

For example, if municipal-type private hydrants are located on the piping "downstream" of a fire department connection that supplies a suppression system (the hydrants are pressurized by the fire department connection), they must not be used to supply pumpers.

AUTOMATIC SPRINKLER SYSTEMS

Automatic sprinkler systems provide a high degree of life safety and property protection. Their capabilities in fire control are unparalleled.

NFPA 13, *Standard for the Installation of Sprinkler Systems,* defines the system as:

> an integrated system of underground and overhead piping designed in accordance with fire protection engineering standards. The installation includes one or more automatic water supplies. The portion of the sprinkler system aboveground is a network of specially sized or hydraulically designed piping installed in a building, structure, or area, generally overhead, and to which sprinkler heads are attached in a systematic pattern. The valve controlling each system riser is located in the system riser or its supply piping. Each sprinkler system riser includes a device for actuating an alarm when the system is in operation. The system is usually activated by heat from a fire and discharges water over the fire area.

Two methods are used for sprinkler system design: hydraulic and pipe schedule. Today most sprinkler systems are "hydraulically" designed. Essentially, calculations are performed to select the pipe sizes, taking into account the pressure loss of the water flowing through the pipes. The goal is to provide a specific uniform water "density" (expressed in $gpm/ft.^2$) over a specified area (a specific number of heads in a "demand area"). In some cases, the pipes may be selected based on the need to provide a specific flow or pressure from a certain number of sprinklers.

A "pipe schedule" design involves selecting pipe sizes from a chart (schedule) that permit a maximum number of sprinklers on a specific size pipe. As of 1991, NFPA 13 limits the use of pipe schedule designs to additions and modifications of existing pipe schedule systems, small installations, or certain larger systems where the residual pressure is at least 50 psi. Pipe schedule designs typically are not as economical as hydraulic designs.

With the exception of deluge and exposure protection systems, sprinkler system designs do not anticipate that every head on the system would open. In most cases, the number of heads anticipated to open ranges from a few heads up to about 50, depending on the compartmentation in the building and the type of occupancy.

Sprinkler system designs take into account the hazard level of the occupancy. Five hazard levels are specified: light hazard; ordinary hazard-group 1; ordinary hazard-group 2; extra hazard-group 1; and extra hazard-group 2. Ordinary hazard-group 3 was eliminated in the 1991 edition of NFPA 13.

Light-hazard occupancies include hospitals and schools, ordinary hazard-group 1 occupancies include parking garages and laundromats, while ordinary hazard-group 2 occupancies include dry cleaning and wood machining operations. Extra hazard-group 1 occupancies include die-casting and saw mills, while extra hazard-group 2 occupancies include flammable liquid spraying and plastics processing.

Sprinkler spacing typically is based on **hazard level, construction type** of the building, and **type of head.** In some cases, specific spacing criteria required by testing laboratories, such as Underwriters Laboratories, will have an effect on sprinkler head layout.

There are six types of sprinkler systems: wet pipe, dry pipe, preaction, deluge, combined dry pipe-preaction, and exposure protection. A description of each follows.

Wet pipe

In a wet pipe sprinkler system pipes normally are filled with water. When a sprinkler head operates, water is discharged immediately from the head. This is the least complicated and most common of all system types.

The wet pipe system has a main riser, the location for a variety of equipment: riser control valve (in most cases), alarm valve (or, alternatively, a water flow switch and check valve) and "trim." Trim includes pressure gauge(s), alarm piping, and test line, a main drain located above the alarm check valve, and a retard chamber.

The alarm valve performs two functions. As a check valve, it keeps water in the system from flowing back into the water supply. Additionally, when a sprinkler head activates and water starts to flow into the system, a small amount of water is sent through ¾-inch piping to a water-driven motor gong (water motor gong), giving an alarm that the system has activated. A test pipe is provided on the riser to test the water motor gong.

In areas where there are frequent fluctuations in water main pressure, a retard chamber may be installed, particularly if the system is equipped with an electric alarm pressure switch. When the alarm valve operates, the flow of water to the motor gong or pressure switch first goes to the retard chamber. The retard chamber (capacity of 1½ to 2½ gallons) has a drain line on the bottom and the continuation of the alarm line on the top. The retard chamber must be filled in order for water to be sent to the pressure switch or the motor gong.

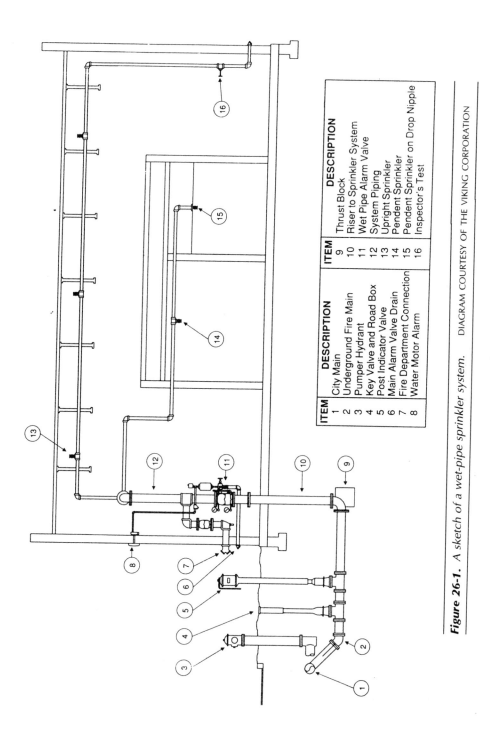

ITEM	DESCRIPTION	ITEM	DESCRIPTION
1	City Main	9	Thrust Block
2	Underground Fire Main	10	Riser to Sprinkler System
3	Pumper Hydrant	11	Wet Pipe Alarm Valve
4	Key Valve and Road Box	12	System Piping
5	Post Indicator Valve	13	Upright Sprinkler
6	Main Alarm Valve Drain	14	Pendent Sprinkler
7	Fire Department Connection	15	Pendent Sprinkler on Drop Nipple
8	Water Motor Alarm	16	Inspector's Test

Figure 26-1. A sketch of a wet-pipe sprinkler system.   DIAGRAM COURTESY OF THE VIKING CORPORATION

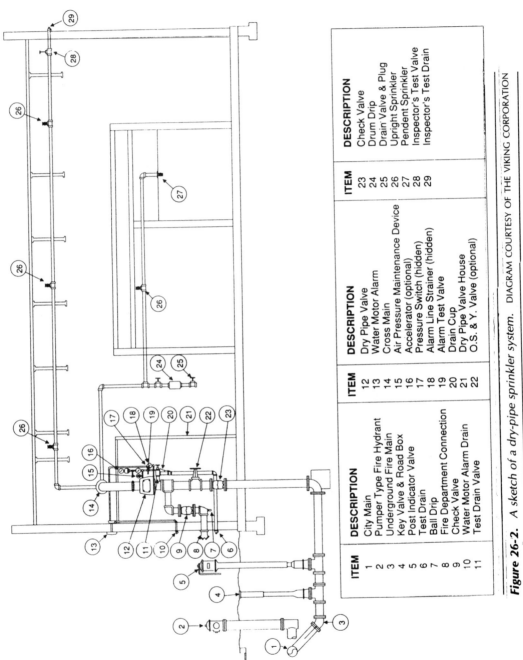

ITEM	DESCRIPTION
1	City Main
2	Pumper Type Fire Hydrant
3	Underground Fire Main
4	Key Valve & Road Box
5	Post Indicator Valve
6	Test Drain
7	Ball Drip
8	Fire Department Connection
9	Check Valve
10	Water Motor Alarm Drain
11	Test Drain Valve

ITEM	DESCRIPTION
12	Dry Pipe Valve
13	Water Motor Alarm
14	Cross Main
15	Air Pressure Maintenance Device
16	Accelerator (optional)
17	Pressure Switch (hidden)
18	Alarm Line Strainer (hidden)
19	Alarm Test Valve
20	Drain Cup
21	Dry Pipe Valve House
22	O.S. & Y. Valve (optional)

ITEM	DESCRIPTION
23	Check Valve
24	Drum Drip
25	Drain Valve & Plug
26	Upright Sprinkler
27	Pendent Sprinkler
28	Inspector's Test Valve
29	Inspector's Test Drain

Figure 26-2. *A sketch of a dry-pipe sprinkler system.*   DIAGRAM COURTESY OF THE VIKING CORPORATION

Momentary pressure surges will only partially fill the retard chamber and drain out of the bottom.

In some cases, the alarm valve is replaced with a check valve and an electric water flow switch. When water flows through the system because of a head activation, the water flow switch is activated. The flow switch's paddle in the pipe is moved by the flowing water and sends an electrical signal to an electric bell.

A pressure gauge is provided on both sides of the alarm check valve; the bottom gauge indicates city pressure and the top gauge indicates system pressure.

A main drain valve also is provided on the riser. Usually two inches in size (smaller on some small risers), the main drain allows for water to drain from the system fairly quickly.

When a fire department connection (FDC) is located on a building, the FDC piping usually is connected above the riser's alarm valve or check valve. In this manner, an engine company can "bypass" a closed control valve. An exception is where a "manifold" of risers (a group of system risers with a common supply pipe) is installed; then the FDC piping may be connected to the manifold's common supply pipe, below the riser control valves.

An inspector's test valve is provided on the system, typically in the highest and most remote area away from the riser, in order to simulate the operation of a single sprinkler, testing the system alarm devices.

Some wet pipe systems have antifreeze systems connected to them that protect small, unheated areas such as loading docks. Filled with a nonfreezing solution such as propylene glycol or glycerine, these systems are limited in size, normally a maximum of 40 heads.

A relatively new type of wet pipe system is the residential sprinkler system, a life safety system developed in the early 1980s to save lives. Two installation standards were developed to cover these systems: NFPA 13D, *Standard for the Installation of Sprinkler Systems in One- and Two-Family Dwellings and Mobile Homes*, and NFPA 13R, the *Standard for the Installation of Sprinkler Systems in Residential Occupancies Up to & Including Four Stories in Height*. Systems installed in buildings of more than four stories follow NFPA 13.

Residential sprinkler systems provide sprinkler protection in areas of the structure where fires statistically start: kitchens, bedrooms, and living rooms. Sprinklers are omitted from such areas as unused attics, floor voids, and certain small closets and bathrooms. This makes the systems more economical and more likely to be installed.

Residential sprinkler systems use special residential sprinkler heads which were developed specifically to respond quickly to a growing fire, before hazardous conditions develop, and provide spray patterns that cover combustibles located at the perimeter of a room, such as a couch against a wall.

Dry pipe

Dry pipe systems are systems in which the pipes are filled with pressurized air. When a sprinkler head is activated, the air is released through the open sprinkler head, allowing the dry pipe valve to open and discharge water through the system to the head(s).

Dry pipe systems are used in areas subject to freezing, i.e., buildings or areas that cannot be maintained at a temperature of 40°F or more.

Dry pipe systems use a dry pipe valve, essentially a "differential" check valve, that contains either one clapper or two interconnected clappers. The single, and simpler, clapper dry pipe valve has pressurized air on top of the clapper and the pressurized water supply on the bottom side off the clapper.

In the case of two interconnected clappers, one serves as the "air" clapper and the other the "water" clapper inside the dry pipe valve. The top "air" clapper's seat is larger than the bottom "water" clapper's seat. Because of these size differences, often enhanced by mechanical linkage, between the top and bottom seats, the clappers can "hold back" five to six psi of water for every one psi of air. Most dry valves are pressurized to no more than 30 to 40 psi of air pressure. Air compressors are used to maintain the required air pressure.

A small amount of "priming" water is provided above the air clapper in order to maintain the integrity of the rubber or neoprene seals on the air clapper and to ensure a proper seal of the water and air clappers.

Besides the dry pipe valve, a dry pipe system's riser also consists of a control valve and trim, including two pressure gauges—one to measure water pressure below the dry pipe valve, the other to measure air pressure above the dry pipe valve.

A ¾-inch pipe from the dry pipe valve to the water-driven motor gong (water motor gong) is provided, as well as a test pipe for the gong. The water motor gong line usually includes a pressure switch. The electric pressure switch, sensing water pressure in the normally dry water motor gong piping, is used to send a signal that water is flowing in the system.

A main drain valve also is provided on the riser. Usually two inches in size (smaller on some small risers), the main drain is located below the dry pipe valve and allows for a fairly quick draining of water from the system.

The riser control valve is usually an OS&Y valve. In some cases, an exterior wall post indicator valve or post indicator valve will be used in lieu of an OS&Y valve.

When a fire department connection is installed on the building (as opposed to being installed in the yard), the FDC piping usually is connected to the riser between the dry pipe valve and the control valve. In this manner, an engine company can bypass a closed control valve. An exception to this situation is where a "manifold" of risers (a group of system risers with a common supply pipe) is installed; in this case, the FDC piping probably would be connected to the manifold's common supply pipe.

Dry pipe valves also may include an <u>accelerator,</u> a device that speeds up the opening of the dry pipe valve itself. After a sprinkler head is activated, air is expelled rapidly through the accelerator. This air is diverted under the air clapper, forcing it to open more quickly.

Some systems have an exhauster installed on the dry pipe system riser. While exhausters are increasingly rare, these devices expel air quickly from the system when a sprinkler head operates, through a two-inch exhauster outlet.

Within the dry pipe system itself, special drains are provided on "low points" on the system. Water vapor in the dry pipe's air collects at the points and must be drained; otherwise a collection of water would freeze and crack the pipes.

An inspector's test valve is provided on the system, typically in the most remote area away from the riser, in order to simulate the operation of a single sprinkler, testing the system alarm devices.

Preaction

A preaction system uses detection devices in conjunction with a sprinkler system in which the sprinkler piping is kept empty. A preaction valve (in many cases actually a deluge valve) on the riser allows water to enter the sprinkler piping when sprinklers, detection devices, or both (such as smoke detectors) are activated.

Preaction systems are categorized into three types: non-interlock systems, single interlock systems, and double interlock systems. In a non-interlock system, water enters the piping if either a sprinkler head or a detection device operates. In order for a single interlock system to operate, a detection device must operate before water will enter the sprinkler piping. A double interlock system needs both a sprinkler head and a detection device to operate before water will enter the piping.

Preaction systems are used in areas where water damage is a concern, e.g., computer rooms, electrical control rooms, etc. They also are used in cold storage rooms where an accidental pipe break would have disastrous results.

In systems of more than 20 sprinklers, a supervisory air or nitrogen pressure must be maintained in the sprinkler piping. A loss of this pressure in the piping, caused by a head opening or a pipe break, is a signal of trouble. In addition, the detection devices themselves must be supervised in systems of more than 20 sprinklers.

The detection devices used to activate the system—smoke detectors in computer rooms, spot heat detectors in electrical rooms, and line type heat detectors for cold storage rooms—depend on the environment. Other detection devices include rate-of-rise detectors, combination rate-of-rise/fixed temperature, and flame detectors. Extra detection devices, connected to the detection system, are provided at an accessible location (floor level) so that the system can be tested.

"Pilot-line" sprinkler heads (essentially a set of supplementary sprinkler heads on a small-diameter, air-filled pipe adjacent to the "normal" sprinkler piping) also are used for detection purposes. These heads are used as detection devices only; they do not apply water.

As with the detection devices, the preaction valve itself may be operated by one of three methods: hydraulically, pneumatically, or electrically. A manual release is provided for the system.

The riser of the preaction system includes the preaction (deluge) valve with trim, check valve, and, typically, a control valve. The trim includes pressure gauges above and below the preaction valve, a pressure-operated relief valve, and the piping to a water motor gong.

The control valve is normally an OS&Y valve that is found on the riser of the system. In some cases, an exterior wall post indicator valve or post indicator valve is used in lieu of an OS&Y valve.

A rubber seat check valve is installed above the preaction valve to maintain the supervisory air pressure. A small amount of priming water is used above the check valve to maintain the air seal. A main system drain, typically two inches on most systems, is provided above the check valve.

Deluge

Aircraft hangars and flammable liquid facilities are two examples of buildings protected by deluge sprinkler systems. Deluge systems are sprinkler systems that have open sprinklers—no operating element—and empty piping, maintained at atmospheric pressure. A detection system is used to activate the system; it opens a deluge valve, allowing water to flow from every head on the system.

Since all heads are open on the system, a large amount of water must be supplied. Pumps typically are used to meet the heavy demand and, to hold the large quantities of water, storage tanks are common.

The deluge valve itself may be operated electrically, pneumatically, or hydraulically. A manual release is provided for the system.

Electrically operated deluge valves often use rate-of-rise/fixed temperature or fixed temperature-only detectors to operate the system. Flame detectors sometimes are used, especially where very rapid response is necessary. If there are 20 detectors or more, electrical supervision of the circuit is required. Upon activation of the electrical detection device, a solenoid-actuation valve is activated, allowing the deluge valve to open and flood the system.

Heat-actuated detectors, essentially rate-of-rise detection devices, often are used to activate pneumatically operated deluge valves. These detection devices are located on one eighth-inch copper tubing. If it serves more than 20 detectors, the copper tubing is pressurized to 1.5 inches psi with air or nitrogen and supervised to ensure integrity.

When heated quickly by a developing fire, a pressure buildup in the heat detector is transmitted through the copper tubing to a control panel. A diaphragm-operated release is activated, allowing a weight to drop and open the latch of the deluge valve. Water then enters the system.

Hydraulically operated deluge valves can use water-filled or air-filled one half-inch pilot lines containing closed sprinklers for activation. Electrical detectors with a solenoid valve also are used.

Extra detection devices connected to the detection system are provided at an accessible location (floor level) so that the system can be tested.

The riser of the deluge system includes the deluge valve with trim, check valve, and, typically, a control valve. The trim includes a pressure gauge below the deluge valve, a pressure-operated relief valve, two-inch main drain, and the piping to a water motor gong.

The control valve is typically an OS&Y valve that is located on the system's riser. In some cases, an exterior wall post indicator valve or post indicator valve is used in lieu of an OS&Y valve.

Combined dry pipe/preaction

The installation of combined dry pipe/preaction systems is fairly rare today. In the past they were used in large, long, unheated structures such as shipping piers. Essentially a large dry pipe system with a corresponding detection system, they eliminated the need for multiple dry pipe system risers. Combined dry pipe/preaction systems are usually larger (more heads) than a "normal" dry pipe sprinkler system.

The combined dry pipe/preaction system riser is essentially a pair of parallel-piped dry pipe alarm valves with a corresponding detection system. The detection system, either pneumatically operated rate-of-rise heat detectors or electrically operated heat detectors, opens the dry pipe valve before the system's sprinkler heads operate. An accelerator is provided at the riser and an exhauster is installed at the end of the system's feed main in order to more quickly fill the piping with water.

The combined dry pipe/preaction system riser is similar to the riser on both dry pipe and preaction systems. Typically each dry pipe valve has its own control valve. Check valves are installed above each dry pipe valve. A manual means of activating the system also is provided.

Exposure protection

Exposure protection sprinkler systems are installed on the exteriors of buildings to protect them from fires in adjacent structures. Protection for openings is especially important. Water must be applied directly to the walls and openings to cool exposed surfaces.

Special nozzles often are used for cornice and window protection. Sprinklers used may be open or fusible link, depending on system design.

Lines of sprinklers are used at various floor levels of the building, taking into account the cumulative effects of the water curtain as it cascades down the exterior of the building.

The system itself may be automatic or manually operated. If automatic, it may be a wet pipe system, dry pipe system, or a system that uses weather-protected detection devices located on the exterior of the building.

If manually operated, personnel must be available at all times to activate the system.

The risers of these systems correspond to the type of system (wet pipe, dry pipe, etc.). Each system has a riser control valve, drain, and a pressure gauge directly below the control valve. Piping on the system is usually galvanized so that it is corrosion resistant.

System piping and types of sprinklers

Sprinkler system piping is typically steel pipe with cast iron or malleable fittings, or rubber-gasketed couplings. Copper tubing is used on some systems. Piping exposed to the elements is usually galvanized to inhibit the development of rust, especially scale, inside the pipe.

Residential sprinkler systems may use chlorinated polyvinyl chloride pipe (cpvc) and occasionally polybutylene pipe. Cpvc pipe also has been used to retrofit sprinkler systems in existing commercial buildings.

Sprinkler pipe must be adequately supported, with pipe hangers spaced a maximum of 12 feet to 15 feet for steel pipe. Other types of piping and tubing have smaller spacings between hangers. Risers also require special piping support.

There are many types of sprinkler heads in use.

Upright and pendent sprinklers

Probably the most common heads in use, these protect many types of occupancies from warehouses to office buildings. They are typically automatic, responding to the heat of a fire when a fusible element melts or a glass bulb breaks and water is applied to the fire.

The discharge orifice size typically used for these heads is ½-inch, while $^{17}/_{32}$-inch heads are used to protect warehouses and other industrial concerns. The larger orifice sizes allow for increased discharge of water and often are used to protect against the effects of higher challenge fires found in high-rack storage.

A wide range of temperature ratings is found for these heads. The specific temperature selected is predicated on the ambient temperature conditions "seen" by the head or the hazard level of the occupancy as in some warehouse situations where it is desirable to limit the number of heads opening in order to conserve the overall water supply.

In some cases, the fusible element or glass bulb has been removed from the sprinkler, making it an "open" sprinkler. These heads are used on deluge-type systems.

The pendent and upright designations refer to the direction of the water toward the sprinkler's deflector; the water is directed downward against the deflector (pendent) or the water is directed upward against the deflector (upright). The deflector "shapes" the stream of water leaving the sprinkler orifice, giving it the traditional "umbrella" pattern.

Sidewall sprinklers

These heads are used in settings where it is preferable or cost-effective to avoid having a sprinkler head in the center of a room, for example, in bedrooms or small offices. The heads are installed on a side wall of the room near the ceiling. These heads can "throw" water a considerable distance; in some cases extended coverage sidewall sprinklers throw water more than 20 feet.

Concealed, flush, and recessed sprinklers

These essentially pendent sprinklers are designed to be aesthetically pleasing when used with a lay-in ceiling tile system. Their deflectors are hidden behind cover plates (in the case of concealed sprinklers) or protrude only slightly below the ceiling tile (recessed or flush sprinklers).

Dry sprinklers

Dry sprinklers (pendent, upright, or sidewall) are used to protect the unheated areas of a building. The heads are provided with air-filled pipe extension nipples with a seal to prevent water from getting into the nipple and freezing. These heads (with nipple extension) extend off wet pipe sprinkler systems to protect areas such as walk-in coolers.

Large-drop sprinklers

These heads were developed to address the high-challenge fires that involve such commodities as high-piled plastics. They produce large water drops which can penetrate the fire plume's significant thermal updraft.

Early Suppression—Fast Response Automatic Sprinklers

Developed relatively recently, these heads are designed for certain high-piled protection needs. They work by combining a quicker response to a developing fire compared to other sprinkler heads, with the application of large amounts of water. The result is fire suppression rather than just fire control.

These heads have the added advantage of eliminating the need for rack storage ("in-rack") sprinklers in high-rack storage. These heads do have significant water supply needs, however.

Rack Storage Automatic Sprinklers

These heads are used in the racks of high-piled combustible storage when solid shelves are present in the racks, when the amount of water capable of being applied solely by the sprinklers at ceiling level is deficient, or when excessive pile heights and hazard level necessitate their use.

Corrosion-Resistant Automatic Sprinklers

These sprinklers are used under conditions of ambient corrosive atmospheres. Factory-applied coatings to protect the sprinkler include wax and lead.

Special Application Sprinklers and Nozzles

A wide variety of sprinklers are available to protect specific concerns or hazards. For example, special window sprinklers are used on the exterior of buildings to protect the windows against an exposing fire across an alley.

Special application sprinklers and nozzles are selected based on their flow characteristics, specific spray patterns, or both.

Automatic Sprinkler System—Preplanning Considerations

Once a preplan for the water supply network is prepared, a preplan must be developed for the automatic sprinkler system itself. These two preplans can then be integrated into one comprehensive preplan.

The automatic sprinkler system preplan should begin with a sketch of the protected building's interior that shows the:

- interior building layout, identifying the location of fire-rated partitions (including rating) and openings (including the type of opening protection), stairwells, openings to the exterior, and other important features;
- type of automatic sprinkler system and extent of protection showing lines of demarcation where partial protection is present or where there are multiple systems;
- location of "main" riser(s) with alarm valve and trim, as well as any other risers "downstream" of the main riser;

- location of control valves, including the "main" control valve, riser isolation valves, floor control valves, as when the sprinkler system and a standpipe system share a common riser, and any other control valves. Any valves hidden above ceilings or in other "out-of-the-way" places must be noted;
- location of manual release in the case of deluge, preaction, and combined dry-pipe/preaction systems;
- location and piping arrangement of a fire pump as well as starting, stopping, and running procedures (see the previous section on water supply network);
- fire department connection location, thread type, number of inlets, and point of connection to system, above or below the system control valve (see the previous section on water supply network);
- connection to other systems such as fire alarm systems, as well as the response of these other systems under water flow conditions (activation of smoke removal fans, activation of audiovisual alarm devices, etc.); and
- name and telephone number of the system's service contractor, if known.

Once the information noted above has been detailed on the sketch, preplanning instructions can be prepared. This is the time to identify specific tasks to be performed, including the need to dispatch a firefighter(s) with radio to the main control valve and fire pump.

When you review the extent of a "partial" system's protection, pay particular attention to what it is protecting; normally this is a particular hazard such as a paint spray booth or a stage. Know where to expect fire extension, outside the area of protection, and note locations where "protected" hoselines might be placed, such as at fire door openings.

Consider residential sprinkler systems as partial systems. In most cases they do not protect attic areas or floors in lightweight truss construction. Fires in these areas obviously would not be affected by the sprinkler system and could grow to large proportions.

With the locations of the main riser(s) and all control valves identified, specify the actual procedures to be used and actions to be performed in case of a fire incident.

In some cases, isolation or floor control valves may need to be closed after a fire to allow a portion of the system to remain charged. For example, an officer who is directing a high-rise fire may order the sprinkler system's floor control valve to be shut down, leaving the standpipe hose valve operational for final knockdown.

In all cases, know what all control valves control and what will happen when individual control valves are shut down. Establish proper procedures for fire pumps and fire department connections.

Automatic Sprinkler Systems—Firefighting Considerations

In some cases, a fire in a sprinklered building will be extinguished before your arrival. This is especially true of occupancies such as offices and retail stores.

However, it is best to assume that the fire is still burning in the building. Make sure that a fire company is supplying the fire department connection, a firefighter has been assigned to verify that the main control valve is open and is awaiting your instructions for shutdown, and that any fire pumps are operating properly.

With a working fire in progress, the firefighter at the main riser control valve or fire pump should determine if the system is flowing water. Besides the obvious ringing of the water motor gong (or outside electric bell), the riser may appear to be "cold and sweaty." A tool or ear placed against the riser may detect water flow vibrations. Gauges that show equal pressure, above and below the sprinkler valve vibrating gauge needles, or both, also indicate water flow.

The assigned firefighter should report any of the following adverse or questionable conditions to the incident commander:

- The main control valve (or other normally open valve) is closed.
- The pressure gauges show no pressure in the system (a valve has been shut down outside the building).
- A dry pipe system's dry pipe valve air pressure gauge shows 40 psi or less and no water has been flowing, i.e., the system has not "tripped" (clapper has not opened). A tripped system will "pin" the air gauge needle as far as it will go, corresponding to the water pressure in the system.
- Order manual activation of the preaction, deluge, or combined dry pipe/preaction manual release.
- A preaction, deluge, or combined dry pipe/preaction system has not activated.
- Fire pump problems, including the failure of the fire pump to start, pump cavitation (may sound like rocks are running through the pump), or the pump gauges show low supply, or low discharge pressure

When these problems arise at the main riser or fire pump, the incident commander can take the following corresponding actions:

- Order a closed main control valve opened immediately, recognizing that the fire may have built up enough headway to overwhelm the system (too many heads have operated).
- Attempt to find and open any closed exterior control valves, realizing

that by the time they are opened the system may be overwhelmed (too many heads have opened).

- Realize that with a working fire and dry pipe valve that has failed to operate (0 psi air pressure), the dry pipe valve clapper may be "welded" (rusted) closed inside from a lack of trip testing or maintenance and nothing can be done in a timely manner. The building is effectively unsprinklered.

- The dry pipe valve also can fail to trip because of water "columning." Over time water leaks past the top of the clapper and fills up the pipe above the dry pipe valve. When a fire occurs and opens sprinkler heads, the dry pipe valve cannot trip. Pumping into the fire department connection should open the clapper in such a situation.

- Attempt to start the pump manually at the controller if it has failed to start. If the pump still cannot be started, open the two bypass control valves if present. Cavitating pumps should probably be shut down and the bypass opened to avoid danger to personnel. Unusual pressure gauge readings are a clue to look for closed valves.

The Incident Commander must constantly assess the fire conditions, asking such questions as whether the fire is darkening down, or if it has been extinguished. If not, why not? Fire control should be expected, especially when fire department pumpers have been supplying the fire department connection. Do more lines need to be connected to the fire department connection?

Pay close attention to the water that is being used on the fireground. Is the sprinkler system receiving adequate water? The pump operator who is supplying the fire department connection must tell the Incident Commander about such problems as whether the pumper's suction pressure is too low or water is not flowing into the system.

Once the fire has been extinguished, the system can be shut down. The determination that the fire is in fact extinguished is sometimes a difficult one to make, especially in warehouse occupancies. Sprinkler spray cools smoke and drives it to the floor, making visibility nearly impossible.

Handlines must be in place before the system is shut down and the firefighter at the main control valve must remain ready to open it at a moment's notice. Closing valves prematurely often has meant losing control of fires and subsequent loss of buildings.

The firefighter at the sprinkler control valve can help to drain the system by opening the main drain. This minimizes water damage by draining water through the heads.

Whether to put the system back into service is a local decision; some departments replace sprinkler heads, place "chocks" in open heads, etc. Some departments even reset dry pipe valves, but this is a complex operation that should be performed only by thoroughly trained individuals.

If it is your department's policy to replace heads, make sure that you do so with replacements of exactly the same type and temperature rating. Make sure that the replacement head is the same style, temperature rating, orifice size, and thread; to do otherwise can threaten the integrity of the system, from a hydraulic or a coverage standpoint.

Pay particular attention at warehouse fires, where fire protection engineers install $^{17}/_{32}$-inch orifice heads with ½-inch N.P.T. (National Pipe Thread) in existing systems in order to increase the amount of water applied by the system. To replace these larger orifice heads with ½-inch orifice heads and ½-inch N.P.T. may prevent the system from protecting the hazard properly, as well as negating the efforts of the fire protection engineer. When large orifice heads are used in new sprinkler systems, heads with $^{17}/_{32}''$ orifice must be used with $^{17}/_{32}''$ N.P.T.

Today many departments leave system restoration to the building owner for liability reasons. A fire watch sometimes is kept until the system is put back in order.

In all cases, the fire prevention bureau should be notified to conduct a followup inspection of the system.

STANDPIPE SYSTEMS

A standpipe system is a fixed network of piping and hose valves, and, in some cases, hose for occupant use, installed throughout a building to supply water for firefighting purposes. With standpipe systems fire departments can attack fires rapidly without having to stretch numerous lengths of hose into and through a building. Standpipe systems for firefighters usually are installed in buildings that are relatively high or have very large floor areas.

In some installations, standpipe systems are provided for building occupants so that they can attack a fire with a sustained and more powerful piece of firefighting equipment than a fire extinguisher.

Building and fire codes typically specify when a standpipe system is required. For instance, some codes require that standpipe systems for firefighters be provided in buildings of four stories or greater in height and in covered mall buildings. Standpipe systems for occupants are provided in buildings of fewer than four stories in height but which have more than 20,000 square feet per floor, in rooms used for exhibition, in large places of assembly, and on stages. When there are automatic sprinkler systems, the requirements for standpipes sometimes are modified.

Standpipe systems are designed and installed under one of two standards—NFPA 14 or the Uniform Building Code's (UBC) Standard 38-2. While these standards are similar in many respects, there are distinct differences.

There are three classes of standpipe systems: Class I, Class II, and Class

III. Class I standpipe systems are for firefighter use, Class II standpipe systems for building occupants, and Class III standpipe systems for both firefighters and building occupants. There are also "combined" systems in which sprinkler systems are combined with standpipe systems and both share a common water supply.

Class I systems have 2½-inch valves (usually without hose). Class II systems have 1½-inch hose valves with 100 feet of hose (125 feet in New York City) and a nozzle. Class III systems have both 2½-inch and 1½-inch hose valves with 100 feet of 1½-inch hose and a nozzle. Some Class III systems may have only 2½-inch hose valves with 1½-inch reducers on the valve and no hose, especially in sprinklered buildings.

The 2½-inch hose valves (Class I and III systems) are found in the following locations: in fire-rated stair enclosures; at horizontal exits; on the "floor" itself, when the travel distance to an exit exceeds certain limitations, usually located in protected areas such as a rated corridor; and at specific locations in covered mall buildings.

One and one-half inch hose valves (Class II and III systems) are spaced to provide a hose valve within 130 feet (100 feet of hose and a 30-foot stream) of all portions of the building.

Standpipe systems may be further classified according to whether or not the piping is always filled with water. These types (as described in NFPA 14) include:

- **Automatic-wet** is a wet standpipe system that has a water supply that is capable of supplying the system demand automatically. This is the most common type.
- **Manual-wet** is a wet standpipe system that is connected to a small water supply to maintain water in the system, but which does not have a water supply capable of delivering the system demand attached to the system. Manual wet pipe systems require water from a fire department pumper (or the like) to be pumped into the system to supply the system demand. These are used in some covered mall buildings.
- **Automatic-dry** is a dry standpipe system, normally filled with pressurized air, that is arranged through the use of devices, such as a dry pipe valve, to automatically admit water into the system piping when the hose valve is opened. The water supply for an automatic-dry pipe standpipe system is capable of meeting the system demand.
- **Semiautomatic-dry** is a dry standpipe system that is arranged through the use of a device, such as a deluge valve, to admit water into the system piping upon activation of a remote device located at a hose connection. A remote control activation device is provided at each hose connection. The water supply for a semiautomatic-dry standpipe system is capable of supplying the system demand.
- **Manual-dry** is a dry standpipe system that does not have a permanent

water supply attached to the system. Manual-dry systems require water from a fire department pumper to be pumped into the system through the fire department connection to supply the system demand.

System components

Standpipe risers are the supply pipes that serve hose valves in a building. Most Class I and III standpipe system risers are located in stairwells, especially since the 2½-inch hose valves must be located in these rated enclosures. Each stairwell normally will have its own riser.

Class II risers often are located in nonfire-rated pipe chases with other domestic piping that serves the building. In some cases, the Class II standpipe riser may actually be the same pipe supplying domestic water needs in the building.

Class I and III systems often use 4-inch and 6-inch risers, while 8-inch risers frequently are used in very tall buildings. The risers are usually steel, with cast or malleable iron fittings, although copper tubing is sometimes found. Stairwell risers are supported on the floor of the stairwell using riser clamps.

The type of piping materials used in Class II systems is the same as is used in Class I and III systems. Riser sizes are on the order of 2½ inches or 3 inches, although smaller risers may be found in small Class II systems.

This roof manifold is useful for exposure fires as well as for testing the standpipe system. PHOTO COURTESY OF AUTHOR

The risers in Class I and III systems are interconnected at the bottom. In addition, an "isolation" OS&Y valve is placed at the base of each system riser so that if one riser is damaged, the valve can be closed and still leave any other risers in operation.

Additional isolation valves also are provided at the riser on each floor level on Class II and III systems which have 1½-inch hose stations. These are provided so that the hose station can be removed from service, leaving the riser in an operational state.

Pressure gauges are provided at the top of each riser; this is useful in system testing. Class I and III systems also are provided with a single hose valve on the roof or a "roof manifold" which consists of multiple hose valves.

Roof hose valves are especially useful for exposure protection for fires in adjacent buildings as well as for testing the system. A control valve at the top of the riser is used to control the water to the hose valve by keeping the piping dry to prevent freezing. An OS&Y valve in the stairwell or a post indicator valve (PIV valve) on the roof may be used.

Fire department connections are provided for Class I and III systems. Many Class II systems do not have a fire department connection.

As described above, the size of the hose valve used on a system depends on the system class. All hose valves have a handwheel to open the valve as well as a threaded outlet onto which hose is attached. The threads used may be National Standard, Western Standard, New York Corporation, iron pipe thread (primarily on Class II 1½-inch hose valves), or a variety of other hose threads used across the country. Obviously, the hose thread used on the system must match the thread used by the local fire department. Unfortunately, this may not be true if an installer fails to determine the appropriate thread, and installs a valve with the wrong thread.

The hose valves differ in operating principle, primarily because of the desired water flow and outlet pressure specified by the system designer. These operating differences are described in detail below.

When pressures at a hose valve are excessive, as determined in the various installation standards, a pressure-regulating device is used. This device can take the form of a pressure-restricting device, pressure-reducing valve, or a pressure-control valve.

It is very important to recognize the difference between the terms pressure-regulating device, pressure-restricting device, pressure-reducing valves, and pressure-control valve. Each term has a different meaning. Here, according to NFPA 14, are the definitions:

- **Pressure-regulating device.** A device designed for the purpose of reducing, regulating, controlling or restricting water pressure. Examples include pressure-reducing valves, pressure-control valves, and pressure-restricting devices.
- **Pressure-restricting device.** A valve or device designed for the pur-

pose of reducing the downstream water pressure under flowing (residual) conditions only.

- **Pressure-reducing valve.** A valve designed for the purpose of reducing the downstream pressure under both flowing (residual) and nonflowing (static) conditions.
- **Pressure-control valve.** A pilot-operated valve designed for the purpose of reducing the downstream water pressure to a specific value under both flowing (residual) and nonflowing (static) conditions.

The type of pressure-regulating device is based on the type (1½ inch or 2½ inch) hose valve and the pressure conditions.

The 1993 edition of NFPA 14 specifies that the 1½-inch hose valves of Class II and III systems be provided with pressure restriction devices when "flowing" (residual) pressures that exceed 100 psi. A 1½-inch pressure-regulating hose valve is required to bring the pressure down to 100 psi where the static and residual pressures exceed 175 psi.

The 1993 edition of NFPA 14 also requires that the 2½-inch hose valves of Class I and III systems be pressure-reducing valves when the static pressure exceeds 175 psi, reducing the pressure to 175 psi. Older standpipe system design requirements, however, actually limited the outlet pressure to 100 psi.

Pressure-restriction devices for 1½-inch hose valves may be one of three types: the pressure-restricting disc, the adjustable-pressure restricter, and the pressure-restricting hose valve. Essentially, these devices work on the same principle, i.e., they restrict the flow of water and create turbulence, which in turn induces friction loss and a resulting loss of pressure under flowing conditions.

The pressure-restricting disc is a circular disc with a hole in the center that is placed in the hose valve discharge. It can be removed easily from the discharge of the hose valve, allowing full flow through the valve.

The adjustable pressure restricter is essentially a coupling attached to a hose valve in which a series of adjustable fan-shaped openings restrict the flow of water. This device can be removed from the hose valve, allowing full flow through the valve.

The pressure-restricting hose valve is the last type of pressure restricter. In this case, the hose valve itself is fitted with an external pin which allows the valve to be opened only a certain number of turns corresponding to a desired outlet pressure. In this case, by removing the pin the hose valve may be opened fully, allowing full flow.

Pressure-reducing hose valves (either 1½-inch or 2½-inch) have created some controversy recently, especially since the "One Meridian Plaza" fire in Philadelphia, Pennsylvania, in February 1991. This controversy arises because some pressure-reducing valves (also described as "direct-acting") are field adjustable, i.e., the pressures can be changed while the hose valve is on the riser, while some are not (the pressures are set at the factory and cannot be changed). In addition, the field-adjustable valves used in some installations require special tools and special knowledge to calibrate them.

While not true of all manufacturers' pressure-reducing hose valves, many are larger in size than "normal," nonpressure-reducing hose valves. It is imperative that firefighters preplan all standpipe systems, including determining the specific type of hose valve, how it works, and possible adjustments.

System Pressures and Flows

Standpipe systems are designed with a specific pressure and flow in mind. The pressure supplied is based on the size of the hose valve (1½-inch or 2½-inch). The flow of water provided depends on the class of system and, in the case of Class I and III systems, the number of risers.

Until recently, the pressures and flows provided by Class I and III standpipe systems remained constant for many years. These flows and pressures were based on the use of the 2½-inch handline, the "standard" of the fire service. This 2½-inch handline with smooth bore nozzle flowed 250 gpm at 50 psi nozzle pressure.

Things began to change around World War II, however. One hundred-psi combination nozzles (followed by automatic nozzles) and 1½-inch hose (followed by 1¾-inch hose) began to replace the "cumbersome" 2½-inch handline with smooth bore nozzle in the majority of engine company standpipe packs.

While these hoseline changes were taking place, the standpipe system itself remained virtually unchanged. Standpipes continued to be designed, as they had been for many years, to provide 250 gpm at 65 psi at the topmost hose valve outlet on each riser (500 gpm from the hydraulically most remote riser in some cases) at a pressure of 65 psi.

A recent survey by the NFPA indicates that nearly all fire departments use 1½-inch or 1¾-inch hose in their standpipe packs. Therein lies the problem—most standpipe installations were designed with 2½-inch handlines in mind but are actually being used with smaller diameter "friction-loss-intensive" hose and nozzles with higher operating pressures.

What all this means is that many standpipe systems will provide only 65 psi residual pressure at the top of the riser. Obviously, when you use 1½-inch or 1¾-inch hose and nozzles with 100 psi operating pressures, the fire department connection becomes a critical piece of equipment and must be supplied adequately to provide the necessary pressure at the nozzle.

Another pressure incompatibility problem is found in the pressure-reducing hose valves used on some existing Class I and III systems. As mentioned above, until recently many systems used pressure-reducing hose valves that allowed a maximum of 100 psi residual pressure from the hose valves on the riser. A fire department that is using 100-psi nozzles and encounters a system of this type has to change something; it must either replace the hose valves on the system or use lower operating pressure nozzles and, in some cases, larger diameter handlines.

It is important that chief officers address these "pressure problems," first through preplanning, and then on the fireground.

psi

Today, the 1993 edition of NFPA 14 has "upped" the minimum pressure for 2½-inch hose valves of Class I and III systems to 100 psi. UBC Standard 38-2 also currently requires 100 psi for the 2½-inch hose valves of Class I and III systems.

The 1½-inch hose valves of Class II and III systems are still required to be provided with a minimum of 65 psi outlet pressure from the topmost outlet under NFPA 14 and UBC Standard 38-2.

Obviously, if a fire department is using nozzles that require 100 psi, the 100 psi supplied from the outlet of the topmost 2½-inch hose valve will be inadequate if friction loss is taken into account. As you move down the riser towards the water supply, the outlet pressure increases from each succeeding hose valve, up to 175 psi, when pressure-reducing hose valves come into play.

Therefore, the pressure supplied to the fire department connection becomes critical. To obtain the proper pressures, especially on the upper portions of a standpipe riser, the engine company pump operator must boost the pressure.

The standpipe design standards have based the required flow on the system class as well as the number of risers, in the case of Class I and III systems.

For a Class II system, the requirement is simply 100 gpm from the hydraulically most remote hose valve outlet, irrespective of the number of hose stations.

gpm

In the case of Class I and III systems, the flow is based on the number of risers. Until recently, the required flow under NFPA 14 and UBC Standard 38-2 was 500 gpm from the two topmost hose outlets on the hydraulically most remote riser, plus 250 gpm from the topmost outlet of each additional riser, for a total not to exceed 2,500 gpm. If the building was provided with automatic sprinklers throughout, the total standpipe flow demand did not have to exceed 1,500 gpm for light-hazard occupancies, 2,000 gpm for ordinary-hazard occupancies or the sprinkler demand, including hose stream allowance, whichever is greater.

The 1991 UBC Standard 38-2 and 1993 NFPA 14 have reduced the water supply requirements. They require a maximum of 1,250 gpm for unsprinklered buildings, and for fully sprinklered buildings, 1,000 gpm or the sprinkler demand, including hose stream allowance, whichever is greater.

It is important to establish the dates of standpipe system installations in your jurisdiction and hence the standard under which they were built. Besides the "evidence" found in the building itself, record checking can help establish the water supply the standpipe system was intended to provide.

Standpipe Systems—Preplanning Considerations

Once a preplan for the water supply network has been prepared, a preplan for the standpipe system itself must be developed. These two preplans can then be integrated into one comprehensive preplan.

The standpipe system preplan should begin with a sketch of the building's interior that shows:

- interior building layout, including the location of fire-resistive partitions (including rating) and openings (including the type of opening protection), stairwells, openings to the exterior, and other important features.
- class of standpipe system and type (e.g., automatic-wet, manual-wet, etc.).
- the total maximum flow from the system as well as the minimum flow and pressure from any individual hose valve.
- location of "main" riser as well as other risers in stairwells, etc.
- location of control valves, including the "main" control valve, riser isolation valves, and "lateral" isolation valves (particularly for the 1½-inch hose stations of Class II and III standpipes). Specifically note where valves are hidden above ceilings or in other "out-of-the-way" places.
- the type of hose valves, including the use of pressure-regulating devices. Specifically note the field adjustability (and how to adjust them) or nonfield adjustability of pressure-regulating devices.
- the pressure rating of piping and fittings (usually the "weakest link").
- location and piping arrangement of a fire pump as well as starting, stopping, and running procedures (see the previous section on the water supply network).
- fire department connection location(s), thread type, number of inlets, and point of connection to the system, above or below the system control valve (see the previous section on the water supply network).
- connection to other systems, such as fire alarm systems.
- name and telephone number of the system's service contractor, if known.

Once the information noted above has been detailed on the sketch, prepare preplanning instructions that identify the specific tasks to be performed, including the need to dispatch a firefighter(s) with radio to the main control valve and fire pump.

In all cases, know what all control valves control and what will happen when individual isolation control valves are shut down. Establish proper procedures for fire pumps and fire department connections as described in the previous section concerning the water supply network.

Establish the minimum pressure needed at the fire department connection to supply the topmost hose valves in the system. With this fire department connection pressure information in hand and pressure ratings of piping and fittings, compare the two. Does the pressure to supply the topmost hose outlets exceed the pressure ratings of the pipe and fittings? If so, you are facing major problems and changes will have to be made!

Standard operating procedures should establish how hose is stretched from the standpipe. Normally the hose is connected to the standpipe on the floor below the fire.

The flaking of hose depends on fire conditions and physical conditions at the scene. It is ideal to flake hose up the stairs one floor past the fire floor if conditions permit. Sometimes it is easier to flake out on the landing below the fire; other times you may be forced to flake one floor below the hookup floor.

Standpipe System Firefighting Considerations

In a standpipe-equipped building with a working fire, the initial decision must be whether or not to use the standpipe. Normally, fires at or below the fourth floor dictate that the hose be stretched from the pumper directly to the fire. You can, of course, modify this when large building setbacks or other problems would necessitate very long hose stretches from the pumper to the fire.

A Class II system should be only used by firefighters when the fire may be easily controlled and a backup hoseline is being stretched from a fire department pumper. Firefighters should not use the often unlined and unmaintained "house lines"; use your own hose. Remember, many Class II standpipes do not have fire department connections and the pressure supplied to the outlet may be only 65 psi (remove any pressure-restricting devices).

Ensure that a fire company is supplying the fire department connection and pressure governors have been set, a firefighter has been assigned to verify that the main control valve is open (or to open the valve in the case of a manual-dry system), and fire pumps are operating properly (or start the fire pump in the case of a semiautomatic wet system).

The firefighter with radio at the main riser control valve or fire pump should report any of the following adverse or questionable conditions to the Incident Commander:

- the main control valve or other normally open valve is closed.
- any pressure gauges show no pressure in the system, meaning that a valve has been shut down outside the building.
- there are fire pump problems, including the failure of the fire pump to start, pump cavitation (may sound like rocks are running through the pump), or the pumps show low supply, or low discharge pressure.

When any of these problems arise at the main riser or fire pump, the Incident Commander can take the following actions:

- notify the hoseline crew(s) that there is a problem and try to describe it;
- order the immediate opening of a main closed control valve.
- attempt to start the fire pump if it has failed to start by trying manually at the controller. If the pump still cannot be started, open the two bypass valves, if present, to gain some, albeit low, pressure in the system. Cavitating pumps should probably be shut down and the bypass opened to avoid danger to personnel. Unusual pressure gauge readings are a sign to look for closed valves.

To bypass a closed valve, or a fire department connection into which you cannot connect, you may be able to pump into the outlet of a hose valve with a double female coupling and some rope for support to get water into a riser. This can be done only on "normal" hose valves; pressure-reducing hose valves will not allow water to be pumped into the valve from the outlet side of the hose valve.

Firefighters who hook up to a standpipe must look for damage and vandalism problems, especially in manual-dry systems. Keep an eye out for debris jammed into hose valves, missing parts (usually brass), and open hose valves. Incident Commanders must be prepared to order additional firefighters to shut down hose valves not in use to stop a cascade of water in the stairwell, as well as to shut down adjacent risers when one is damaged, or to relocate an attack line when the desirable riser is damaged.

In addition, attack crews must relay any flow or pressure problems to the Incident Commander.

Once the fire has been extinguished, the system should be drained and put back into service. Firefighters can speed up drainage by opening the main drain on the system.

The fire prevention bureau should be notified so it can conduct a follow-up inspection.

WATER SPRAY SYSTEMS

Water spray systems are very similar to deluge automatic sprinkler systems, except that instead of open sprinkler heads, open nozzles (there is no fusible element) are used. The piping, fitting, valves, etc., are essentially the same as those used in an automatic deluge sprinkler system.

Water spray systems are used to protect specific pieces of equipment or storage vessels. Electrical transformers, propane storage tanks, and tanks used to store flammable or combustible liquids are all examples of types of hazards protected by water spray systems. NFPA 15, *Standard for Water-Spray Fixed Systems for Fire Protection,* stipulates the requirements for the design and installation of these systems.

Water spray systems usually are installed for one of four reasons: to provide fire extinguishment through surface cooling, smothering through steam, emulsification, or dilution; to control burning, to provide exposure protection by applying cooling water on the surface of an exposed vessel; or to provide a method of preventing a fire from starting through the use of water to cool, dilute, dissolve, or disperse flammable vapor concentrations before they reach the lower explosive limit. In addition, water spray systems sometimes are used in buildings to prevent fire spread through openings where fire doors cannot be installed.

Through the use of actuation systems and a deluge valve, these systems operate automatically. In addition, a manual release is provided to operate the deluge valve, allowing water to enter the system and flow from the nozzles. Some manual-only systems do exist, but require constant attention to assure that the valves will be open. It should be noted that all manual fire protection systems are prime targets for "Murphy's Law."

These automatic systems are actuated electrically through the use of detection devices, hydraulically, or pneumatically. When the automatic actuation system operates, the deluge valve opens.

These systems are designed hydraulically with hydraulic calculations, similar to those of an automatic deluge sprinkler system, a design which anticipates all nozzles are open. Spray systems have significant water supply demands depending on the number of nozzles.

System components

Water spray systems use essentially the same components as deluge automatic sprinkler systems. Since many of these systems are installed outdoors, galvanized pipe and fittings often are used.

Detection devices for electrically actuated deluge valves include flammable gas detectors and thermostats.

Of particular note are the spray nozzles used in water spray systems. These nozzles create specific spray patterns—conical, umbrella, or fan-shaped—and are selected and arranged to provide optimal coverage, while ensuring that the proper density of water is being applied over the surface of the protected equipment. Wind effects are considered.

Proper drainage is necessary for the area surrounding the protected equipment. Draining can be provided by using grading, diking, trenching, or enclosed drains, depending on the hazardous nature of the equipment protected.

Water Spray System Preplanning Considerations

Once the plan for the water supply network has been prepared, a preplan for the water spray system itself must be developed. These two preplans can then be integrated into one comprehensive preplan.

The water spray system preplan should begin with a sketch of the equipment protected and water spray system, including:

- layout and description of equipment protected;
- type of water spray system (i.e., extinguishment system, burning control system, exposure protection system, fire prevention system);
- location of main riser, control valve(s), and manual release;
- type of operation of deluge (electrical, pneumatic, or hydraulic);
- location and piping arrangement of a fire pump as well as starting, stopping, and running procedures;
- fire department connection location, thread type, and number of inlets;
- connection to other systems such as fire alarm systems;
- location and type of drainage provided; and
- name and telephone number of the system's service contractor, if known.

Once the information noted above has been detailed on the sketch, prepare preplanning instructions, identifying the specific tasks to be performed, and establishing specific company assignments.

With the location of the main riser and control valve at hand, specify the actual procedures to be used and the actions to take in case of a fire incident. Detail the need to dispatch a firefighter(s) with radio to the main control valve and fire pump.

Establish proper procedures for fire pumps and fire department connections as described in the section on water supply network.

Establish the minimum pressure needed at the fire department connection to supply the system and determine the quantity of water needed to supply the system (is the water available from a municipal hydrant?).

Water Spray System Firefighting Considerations

Verify that a fire company is supplying the fire department connection, a firefighter has been assigned to verify that the main control valve is open (or assign one to open the valve in the case of a manual system), and fire pumps are operating properly.

The firefighter at the main riser control valve or fire pump should report any of the following adverse or questionable conditions to the Incident Commander:

- the main control valve (or other normally open valve) is closed.
- pressure gauges show no pressure in the system (a valve has been shut down).
- the deluge valve has failed to trip.
- fire pump problems, including the failure of the fire pump to start, pump cavitation (may sound like rocks are running through the pump), or pumps show low supply or low discharge pressure.

When confronted with these problems at the main riser/fire pump, the Incident Commander can take the following actions:

- order immediate opening of a closed main control valve.
- order the manual release to be activated to put the system in operation.
- start the fire pump if it has failed to start, manually at the controller. If the pump still cannot be started, open the two bypass valves (if present). Cavitating pumps should probably be shut down (and bypass opened) to avoid danger to personnel. Unusual pressure gauge readings are a sign to look for closed valves.

Once the fire has been extinguished, the system should be drained. Firefighters can speed drainage by opening the main drain on the system. To place the system back into service it is necessary to call the service company to reset the deluge valve, among other things.

The fire prevention bureau should be notified so it can conduct a follow-up inspection.

WATER MIST SYSTEMS

A relatively new system appearing on the American fire protection landscape is the water mist system. These systems have been used abroad for some time; one type of installation has been cruise ships.

Water mist systems using small water droplets, with their size measured in terms of microns, have distinct advantages over other water-based suppression systems. They use a smaller amount of water to achieve fire control, and they are seen as a replacement extinguishing system for some halogenated agent systems.

The very fine drops of a water mist system have exceptional cooling capabilities. In addition, the water drops tend to exclude oxygen in the combustion zone of a fire's flame.

As these systems are being developed, three system nozzle pressure ranges are being identified. High-pressure nozzles operate at 500 to 4,000 psi, intermediate-pressure nozzles operate at between 250 and 500 psi, and low-pressure nozzles at less than 250 psi.

Additionally, three types of nozzles will be used by these systems: impingement nozzles, air-atomizing nozzles, and pressure jet nozzles.

Water mist systems also may be described in terms of overall design pressure and operation. One type of system is pressurized with a gaseous agent such as air (stored air pressurized to 1,500 psi) used in conjunction with water (pressurized to a maximum of 175 psi); this system is known as a "twin fluid/air atomizing system." Two other systems use water pressure only: "high-pressure hydraulic systems" operate at 500 psi and higher, while "low/intermediate pressure systems" operate at a maximum water pressure of 175 psi.

Water mist systems probably will be used in a variety of applications, including electric power generating systems, telecommunications, and even in some residential settings. An NFPA committee was established in 1993 to consider the design and installation requirements for NFPA 750, a standard to be written in the next two to three years.

SPECIAL-AGENT FIRE EXTINGUISHING SYSTEMS

Special hazards require special protection. Very often, the use of water is incompatible, inefficient, or undesirable for various types of materials. Other extinguishing agents are called for.

For example, water is inefficient for extinguishing fires that involve many flammable and combustible liquids. Applying water to molten metals can lead to explosions. Rare paper documents or some computer equipment can be damaged by water.

Different types of extinguishing agents have been developed to protect special hazards. It is important to understand how different special-agent extinguishing systems work and how the agents themselves act to extinguish a fire.

Special-agent systems include foam extinguishing systems, carbon dioxide extinguishing systems, halogenated/clean agent extinguishing systems, and dry/wet chemical extinguishing systems.

FOAM EXTINGUISHING SYSTEMS

Foam extinguishing systems use the cooling, blanketing, and vapor suppression effects of foam to extinguish a fire. Foam systems often are found in areas where flammable and combustible liquids are used or stored, such as tank farms, bulk terminals, and flammable liquid storage warehouses. Class

A combustibles and some Class B fires also may be protected using high-expansion foam.

A variety of types of foam systems exist, each of which has a standard or recommended practice for system design and installation. These systems fall into one of two groups.

One group is covered by the NFPA "11" series; these concerns use special application devices. The other group, the NFPA "16" series, consists of systems that are similar to sprinkler systems and use sprinkler heads to apply foam.

The system types and standards or recommended practices include

- NFPA 11, *Standard for Low Expansion Foam and Combined Agent Systems*
- NFPA 11A, *Standard for Medium- and High-Expansion Foam Systems*
- NFPA 16, *Standard on Deluge Foam-Water Sprinkler- and Foam-Water Spray Systems*
- NFPA 16A, *Recommended Practice for the Installation of Closed-Head Foam-Water Sprinkler Systems.*

Types of foams include chemical foams which are no longer used, and mechanical foams. Mechanical foams can be classified as low-, medium-, or high-expansion.

Low-expansion foams, the most popular, include:

- protein—has become outdated in most respects;
- fluoroprotein—can be used for subsurface injection;
- aqueous film-forming foam (AFFF);
- multipurpose synthetic—can be used on hydrocarbons as well as polar solvents and can be used subsurface on hydrocarbons only; and
- film-forming fluoroprotein (FFFP).

Low-expansion systems covered under the NFPA 11 series are used primarily on flammable liquid storage tanks. Essentially, foam is applied either through foam applicators on the top of the tank or through subsurface injection.

Tank farms may have several tanks that need to be protected, but will have one "foam house" that serves all the tanks. It is in this foam house that the mixing of water and foam concentrate takes place. Individual valves for each tank normally are provided in close proximity to the foam house, allowing a firefighter to send foam through piping to foam applicator(s) on specific tanks.

Several different methods are used to proportion foam in the foam house:

- balanced pressure proportioning, using a foam concentrate pump. Foam is delivered from a storage tank, via a foam concentrate pump, to a "ratio controller," where it is injected into the water stream;

- balanced pressure proportioning, bladder type. Foam is expelled from tank through water pressure applied to a foam bladder inside a tank and then to a "ratio controller" where it is injected into the water stream;
- balanced pressure proportioning, pressure-tank type. Concentrate tank is pressurized, forcing foam concentrate into proportioner; and
- line type proportioning using the venturi principle.

Besides containing the proportioning system, foam houses also contain the foam storage tank. This tank, very often made of polyethylene to prevent corrosion, may store up to several thousand gallons of foam concentrate, depending on the size and number of flammable liquid tanks. The building also may contain a fire pump to boost water pressure to the system.

Application devices for flammable liquid storage tanks are categorized as Type I or Type II discharge outlets. Type I, including "Moeller tubes" and foam troughs or chutes, are rarely used today.

A foam chamber can be seen atop the vertical pipe running up the side of this flammable liquid storage tank.   PHOTO COURTESY OF AUTHOR

Today, Type II discharge outlets, including foam chambers, are used on the rim of a tank to protect the seal area, even though they can apply foam across the burning surface of a tank. Depending on the size of the tank, more than one foam chamber may be installed.

Subsurface injection of foam solution usually takes place on a "product" pipeline. Foam is pumped through this product line into the tank.

Most foam systems at tank farms are operated manually, so it is necessary to open valves and start the pumps. In rare instances, some foam systems actually require the use of fire department pumpers to supply water, proportion foam, or both. It is important to know how all foam systems in your jurisdiction operate.

High-expansion foam systems, while rarely installed today, are sometimes found in hangars and warehouses. They use large-capacity foam generators to "pour" foam over the area being protected, subsequently filling the space with foam, often in less than 10 minutes. Since this system fills the space completely, evacuation alarms are used to direct people out of the building. The location of make-up air for these systems is critical—the air must be cool and devoid of any contaminants (smoke).

The NFPA 16 group of foam systems is very similar to sprinkler systems. In fact, the only difference is that a foam proportioning system is located at the main riser. The system typically uses either a foam concentrate pump or bladder-balanced pressure proportioning system. Enough concentrate for 10 to 20 minutes of operation usually is provided.

These systems are used to protect flammable liquid storage warehouses, flammable liquid processing buildings, and loading racks. In fact, some flammable liquid storage warehouses with wet pipe sprinkler systems are being retrofitted with foam equipment to improve the protection.

In appearance, the foam deluge or foam spray system looks just like a deluge or wet pipe sprinkler system, respectively. For the fire service, these foam systems can be treated as sprinkler systems, with a few important modifications.

While a fire department connection is provided, engine companies must not overpressurize these systems beyond the system design pressure; this can cause the proportioning system to fail. The system should be provided with the pressure required by the system design, and no more. The hydraulic design reference sign on the riser specifies the system operating pressure.

Also, water should not be discharged onto the foam blanket once it has been established; use compatible foam handlines for any mop-up operations.

Foam Extinguishing System Preplanning Considerations

The preplan should begin with a sketch of the tank/building protected and the foam system. This sketch should include

- layout and description of the tank building to be protected, e.g., type of flammable liquids, including flash point, size of tank or barrels and building size in square feet;
- type of system, manual or automatic, and type of proportioning system;
- start, stop and run procedures for foam concentrate pump, as applicable;
- type of foam—what types of liquid fires can it be used to control and can it be used for subsurface injection?;
- size of concentrate tank;
- design flow and pressure of system;
- location of all control valves and what they cover. In the case of tanks, what valve covers what tank?;
- location and piping arrangement of a fire pump as well as start, stop, and run procedures;
- fire department connection location, thread type, number of inlets;
- name and telephone number of the facility's liaison person; and
- name and telephone number of the system's service contractor, if known.

Once the information noted above has been detailed on the sketch, prepare preplanning instructions.

In the case of a foam house operation, the means of placing the foam system in operation, with a detailed, step-by-step set of procedures, must be written down. With a limited supply of foam concentrate, you may get only one chance to get it right. Outline the need to dispatch a firefighter(s) with radio to oversee operations in the foam house, including opening the proper valves.

Establish the proper operating procedures for any fire pumps as applicable.

Establish the need for use of the fire department connection. Is it merely to boost water pressure or supply all the water needed by the system? What pressures and flows must be supplied, based on the hydraulic reference sign on the riser?

Foam Extinguishing System Firefighting Considerations

In the case of a fire at a tank farm, ensure that a firefighter has been assigned to the foam house. He should make sure that the proper valve(s) are operated to direct foam to the correct tank, as well as to verify operating procedures for the foam concentrate pump and fire pump. He also should verify that all other equipment is in proper operating order.

It is necessary to inspect the tank involved in the fire before any attack is launched. Verify that the foam chambers and subsurface injection equipment are still intact. They may have been blown off or destroyed. Can foam be applied through the application device and delivered to the burning surface of the liquid?

Fire department pumpers must be connected to the fire department connection, ready to supply it.

On orders from the Incident Commander, the foam attack should begin. Do not initiate it until all requisite tasks have been completed and are ready.

Foam attacks on tanks should be continued for several minutes after the last signs of fire are gone in order to effect cooldown and secure the foam blanket.

High-expansion foam systems must be allowed to "soak" the fire, especially deep-seated fires. Make sure you account for all building occupants. Also check that hot embers, smoke, etc., are not getting into the air system's make-up; it will destroy the blanket.

Before "opening up" a building in which high-expansion foam has been used, have handlines in place in case of flare-ups. Incident Commanders must not allow firefighters into the building for final mop-up until it is clear that they will not get lost in the foam blanket and are wearing SCBA.

Firefighting operations in buildings protected with foam water sprinkler systems should follow the same procedures used in "normal" water-sprinklered buildings, with the two important modifications mentioned below.

Do not overpressurize the system through the fire department connection; supply the pressure indicated on the hydraulic reference sign on the riser. Use compatible (same type of foam—AFFF, multipurpose, etc.) foam mop-up lines from the fire department pumper, not water handlines.

CARBON DIOXIDE EXTINGUISHING SYSTEMS

Carbon dioxide is an extinguishing agent used for a variety of hazards: gas turbine generators, printing presses, aluminum rolling mills, oil quench tanks, cargo ships, and tankers, to name a few. Carbon dioxide's smothering effects and dilution of oxygen in the discharge area and to a very minor degree, cooling effects in some cases, allow it to extinguish fires readily. This fire extinguishing benefit is harmful to human life; however, the design concentrations used to extinguish a fire will not support life, suffocating people in the total flooding discharge areas.

Carbon dioxide does not damage equipment, is nonconductive, odorless, and leaves no residue. It has a vapor density that is about one and a half times greater than air.

Carbon dioxide systems can be used in a local application, e.g., to protect a piece of equipment like a cooking range hood, or for total flooding in an enclosure, such as in a flammable liquid storage room.

Carbon dioxide systems use two types of storage arrangements: high pressure and low pressure. The type of storage system depends on the quantity of carbon dioxide to be stored. In either case, carbon dioxide is stored as a liquid in the container. High-pressure storage systems are used when the amount of carbon dioxide is relatively small, especially when used with local application systems. The carbon dioxide is stored in high-pressure cylinders at 850 psi.

When the amount of carbon dioxide needed exceeds approximately 4,000 pounds (2,000 pounds for main discharge and 2,000 pounds for reserve), low-pressure storage systems become more economical. Carbon dioxide in these systems is refrigerated to 0°F at 300 psi in insulated tanks.

Carbon dioxide design concentrations are at least 34 percent, but may be greater depending on the flammable materials involved. Some design concentrations approach 75 percent for areas where the potential for deep-seated fires is high.

Calculations are performed to determine the proper amount of carbon dioxide needed and the distribution of pipe sizes. These calculations are based on the design concentration and the desired discharge from each of the nozzles used to apply the carbon dioxide.

System components

The storage cylinders of high-pressure systems must meet specific Department of Transportation design standards. This is especially important because of the high pressures encountered.

Low-pressure storage containers range in size from one ton to several hun-

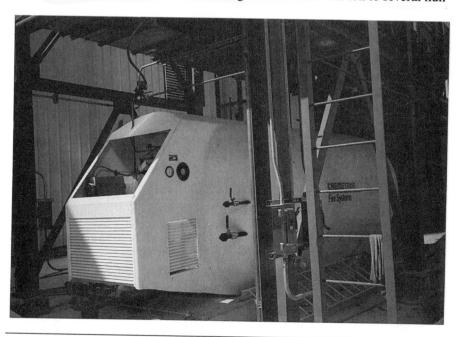

This refrigerated low pressure carbon dioxide storage tank is used to protect an aluminum rolling mill.
PHOTO COURTESY OF RICHARD MAZUCA

dred tons. The container must be refrigerated to keep the temperature at 0°F. A relief valve is provided to relieve pressure in case of a failure of the refrigeration system. Liquid level and pressure gauges are provided.

The piping is normally steel pipe, but may be copper or brass. Piping and fittings must have good low-temperature characteristics.

Special application nozzles, with varying discharge patterns, are used to apply the carbon dioxide. They also are numbered with a code to indicate the diameter in 1/32-inch increments of a single-orifice standard nozzle that has the same flow rate (a number 4 nozzle has the same flow rate as a 4/32-inch diameter standard orifice). A " + " sign indicates a 1/64-inch larger size.

Detection systems to activate the carbon dioxide system include flammable gas detectors to discharge the carbon dioxide before an explosion, heat detectors, flame detectors, and, in some cases, smoke detectors. Manual releases also are provided.

Predischarge alarms to alert personnel in the discharge area to get out are provided. Signs and discharge warning signals provided around the enclosure warn people to leave and not to enter. These signs must be multi-lingual when appropriate.

Door closers and air-handling system shutdown relays are provided to seal the area and contain the carbon dioxide.

In some installations, supplementary carbon dioxide hoselines are installed for use by occupants on small, localized fires.

Carbon Dioxide System Preplanning Considerations

The preplan should begin with a sketch of the building and equipment protected and the carbon dioxide system. This sketch should include:

- system type notation (local application or total flooding);
- layout and description of the areas and equipment protected and type of flammable materials involved;
- building exits and entry points;
- design concentration and amount of soaking time, if any;
- location of containers;
- type of system (low-pressure, high-pressure), quantity of carbon dioxide, and whether "reserve" capacity is provided;
- location and type of discharge alarms;
- type of detection system and manual release locations;
- location of all "sealing" equipment such as door closers, dampers, etc.; and
- name and telephone number of the system's service contractor, if known.

Once the information noted above has been detailed on the sketch, prepare preplanning instructions, identifying specific tasks to be performed, and establishing specific company assignments.

The use of self-contained breathing apparatus is essential during emergency operations where carbon dioxide systems are involved! Preplans must note this critical element.

Establish that fire company(s) will stand ready for fire attack after the system has been given a chance to extinguish the fire. Determine what hoselines will be used and where.

Determine the location(s) where carbon dioxide will be expelled from the area and make sure that these release points will not endanger personnel. Determine how many fans will be needed and where.

Make arrangements for a fire company, using handheld gas detectors to determine that the atmosphere in the building is suitable for human habitation.

Carbon Dioxide System Firefighting Considerations

Fires that involve carbon dioxide systems must be handled very carefully, especially in terms of personnel control. This is the only type of system that uses an extinguishing agent that is inherently dangerous to firefighters.

Determine on arrival whether all people have been evacuated from the building. If there are any missing persons start a search and rescue operation, controlled strictly by the Incident Commander.

Before anyone enters a space charged with carbon dioxide to rescue trapped occupants, try to identify their specific locations. Review the sketch of the area from preplans with entry and exit points. Consider using life rope to keep personnel from becoming lost. Protective handlines should be in place in case the fire reignites after the enclosure has been opened.

All personnel who enter the building must be in full protective gear, including SCBA! Keep track of the time spent in the space and the amount of air used, and leave enough time to get out.

Visibility will be very difficult because of the condensed water vapor from the system discharge. Be careful not to fall into pits, stairwells, or other floor openings, or trip over equipment.

Carbon dioxide settles in low areas such as basements and pits (where several industrial workers have been found dead after a system discharge).

Clear all areas of carbon dioxide after the fire with precautionary handlines in place to knock down any flare-up. Use fans to exhaust carbon dioxide.

Use handheld gas detectors in all areas to make sure no dangerous level of carbon dioxide is present before personnel remove their SCBA or allow building occupants back into the building.

HALOGENATED/CLEAN AGENT EXTINGUISHING SYSTEMS

Halogenated agent extinguishing systems that use Halon 1301 or Halon 1211 are being phased out. While they are relatively new extinguishing agents, Halon 1301 (bromotrifluoromethane) and Halon 1211 (bromochlorodifluoromethane) have been determined to potentially deplete the earth's ozone layer.

There are, however, still many existing Halon 1301 systems that were installed under NFPA 12A, *Standard on Halon 1301 Fire Extinguishing Agent Systems*. There are even fewer existing Halon 1211 systems which were installed under NFPA 12B, *Standard on Halon 1211 Fire Extinguishing Systems*.

Although existing Halon 1301 supplies may be used in existing halon systems, the search has begun for new "clean" agents. A new standard, NFPA 2001, has been developed for these new agents. The common names as opposed to the chemical names of these agents include FM 100 and FM 200, PFC-410, FE 25 and FE 13, Inergen, and NAP S-III.

It may be possible that existing halon systems can be reused with a few of the new agents, perhaps with system modifications. The next few years will determine what these agents "look like" and what modifications will have to be made to existing systems.

Since many of these Halon 1301 systems still exist, a brief description is in order.

Halogenated agents such as Halon 1301 and 1211 work to extinguish fires by inhibiting the chemical chain reaction of the combustion process. The halogen gases such as bromine, and chlorine are the important actors in this inhibiting process. Halon 1301 is a colorless, odorless gas under normal conditions.

The halon agents can be used in a variety of applications such as for electrical equipment (computer rooms were the most popular application of the Halon 1301 system), flammable liquids and gases, thermoplastics, and high-value items because it leaves no residue. It cannot be used on materials that have their own oxidizing agent: reactive metals (such as sodium, magnesium, etc.), metal hydrides, and materials subject to autothermal decomposition.

Most systems are of the total flooding type, although some local application systems exist. For the agent to work properly, a design concentration of five percent usually is required; it may be higher for some materials, such as those subject to deep-seated fires.

Even though people can be exposed to low concentrations of Halon 1301 for short periods of time, self-contained breathing apparatus should always be worn in any area that contains the agent. Under the thermal decomposition of a fire, the halons will break down into free bromine, and chlorine as well as other dangerous materials. Always stipulate that SCBA be worn!

System components

Basically, a halon system is composed of storage containers of halon, a piping network with nozzles to deliver and distribute the halon, and a detection system with control panel to initiate the system. Additional equipment includes predischarge alarms to evacuate people before the system is "dumped," and a manual release for the system, with door closers and dampers to seal the enclosure.

Calculations are prepared to determine pipe sizes and amount of halon needed.

Halon is stored as a liquefied gas under pressure in cylinders or spheres. These containers are superpressurized with nitrogen to 360 psig or 600 psig, enough to make sure that the halon is expelled from the container. Containers must meet Department of Transportation specifications.

Very often steel piping is used. Special corrosion-resistant nozzles, designed to deliver a specific amount of halon and, in a specific pattern, are used.

Detection devices are normally ionization and photoelectric smoke detectors, often "cross-zoned." A detector from each of two zones must both activate to avoid false discharges.

Halogenated agent extinguishing systems are being phased out, due the halon's contribution to the depletion of the earth's ozone layer. Hopefully, an alternative agent will be developed which can reuse a set of halon storage containers such as these.

Halogenated/Clean Agent Extinguishing System Preplanning Considerations

The preplan should begin with a sketch of the protected area/equipment and the halon system, including:

- system type notation (local application or total flooding);
- layout and description of the area and equipment protected and type of flammable materials;
- building exits and entry points;
- type of system (Halon 1301 or 1211), quantity of halon, and whether "reserve" capacity is provided;
- design concentration and amount of "soaking time," if any;
- container location;
- type of detection system and manual release locations;
- location and types of discharge alarms;
- location of all "sealing" equipment such as door closers and dampers, etc.; and
- name and telephone number of the system's service contractor, if known.

Once the information noted above has been detailed on the sketch, prepare preplanning instructions.

The use of self-contained breathing apparatus is essential for operations that involve halon systems. Preplans must note this important element.

Establish that fire company(s) will stand ready for fire attack after the system has been given a chance to extinguish the fire. Determine what hoselines will be used and where.

Determine the location(s) where halon will be expelled from the area and make sure these release points will not endanger personnel. Determine how many fans will be used and where.

Determine what fire company will use handheld gas detectors to determine that the atmosphere in the building is suitable for human habitation.

Halogenated/Clean Agent Extinguishing System Firefighting Considerations

Fires where halon systems (especially those of high concentration) are present must be handled carefully, especially in terms of area personnel control. A halon system that has discharged can be potentially hazardous to firefighters if they inhale the gases.

Arriving personnel must determine whether all people have been evacuated from the building, specifically the halon-protected area. If there are any missing persons, search and rescue operations will be needed.

Try to establish the specific locations of any trapped persons before anyone enters the halon-charged area(s). Review the sketch of the area from preplans with entry and exit points. Protective handlines should be in place in case the fire reignites after the space is opened.

All personnel who enter the building must be in full protective gear, including SCBA. Keep track of the amount of time spent in the space and make sure personnel have enough air to get out.

Since Halon 1301 has a density five times that of air, it settles in low areas such as pits and under computer room floors.

Clear all areas of halon after the fire has been extinguished; keep precautionary handlines in place to knock down any flare-ups. Use fans to exhaust the halon.

Use handheld gas detectors in all areas to make sure no halon is present before personnel remove SCBA and before allowing building occupants to re-enter the building.

DRY/WET CHEMICAL EXTINGUISHING SYSTEMS

Dry and wet chemical extinguishing systems are very common. Most restaurant cooking hoods and factory paint spray booths have them. Most dry/wet chemical systems are "pre-engineered," i.e., the manufacturer already has calculated the pipe sizes and amount of agent needed to protect a specific size and type of hazard. Engineered systems are larger and usually protect more extensive hazards such as flammable liquid storage rooms.

These systems are installed under NFPA 17, *Standard for Dry Chemical Extinguishing Systems,* or NFPA 17A, *Standard on Wet Chemical Extinguishing Systems.* The dry chemicals used include sodium bicarbonate, potassium bicarbonate, potassium chloride, and monoammonium phosphate. The wet chemical is a mixture of water and a potassium carbonate-based chemical or a potassium acetate-based chemical, or a mixture of water and both chemicals. Wet chemicals often are used in cooking hood systems because of their ease of cleanup.

There has been considerable discussion about the extinguishment mechanism used by dry chemicals to extinguish a fire. It is generally agreed that dry chemicals inhibit the combustion chain reaction of a fire. Additionally, others believe that the physical blanketing oxygen dilution as a result of carbon dioxide and water vapor produced by the fine solid particles, and the reflection of heat by the dry chemical particles, in some way help to extinguish a fire.

A dry chemical system consists of a storage container(s), release and detection system, and a piping and nozzle network. The system may be local application or total flooding.

System components

There are two types of dry chemical system storage and discharge arrangements. The first is a system that uses a container, usually a cartridge, of expellent gas and another container of dry chemical. When the expellent gas is released, it pressurizes the other container of dry chemical, forcing the dry chemical into the piping network.

The other type of storage and discharge arrangement is simply a container of dry chemical pressurized with nitrogen. The dry chemical is expelled by the nitrogen in the container upon system activation.

In either case, a control head, activated electrically, pneumatically, or mechanically, allows the expellent gas to expel the dry chemical when the detection system is activated.

Probably the most common detection device used on these systems is the fusible link, hence, the mechanically operated control head. Heat detectors are used to activate electrically operated control heads.

Piping is usually schedule 40 galvanized steel pipe with galvanized steel or malleable iron fittings. Special dry chemical nozzles are used with specific discharge patterns. When the piping is laid out (pre-engineered or engineered), the designer must make sure that the system is "balanced" so that there is proper flow from each nozzle.

A manual release is provided for the system. Supplementary equipment shutdown (fans, doors, natural gas or electrical supplies) may be incorporated in the design. Alarms and dry chemical hoselines also may be provided.

Dry/Wet Chemical Extinguishing Systems Preplanning Considerations

The preplan should begin with a sketch of the protected area/equipment and the dry/wet chemical system which includes:

- system type notation (local application or total flooding);
- layout and description of the area or equipment protected and type of flammable materials;
- type of system (wet or dry chemical), quantity of agent, and whether "reserve" capacity is provided;
- container location;
- type of detection system and manual release locations;

- location and types of discharge alarms;
- location of all "sealing" equipment such as door closers, dampers, etc.; and
- name and telephone number of the system's service contractor, if known.

Once the information noted above has been detailed on the sketch, prepare preplanning instructions.

It is important that self-contained breathing apparatus be used for operations in areas of total flooding dry chemical systems. Preplans must note this important element. For total flooding systems, a fire company(s) must stand ready to attack any flare-ups once the protected space is "opened up." Determine what hoselines will be used and where.

Dry/Wet Chemical Extinguishing System Firefighting Considerations

In most cases, a dry/wet chemical system will have discharged before responders arrive; it is hoped that the system will have extinguished the fire. Unfortunately, especially with respect to fires in restaurant cooking hoods, these systems do fail to extinguish the fire. Sometimes they knock down the main body of fire but cannot "catch" fire that has extended.

If it has not discharged, consider using the manual release if you think the system can be of any material value.

All personnel who enter areas with total flooding dry chemical systems must be in full protective gear, including SCBA. Firefighters should avoid breathing the dry chemical.

FIRE ALARM AND COMMUNICATION SYSTEMS

Fire alarm and communication systems play an important role in both life safety and property protection. Detection devices sense a fire condition that is annunciated by alarm and communications equipment. Detection devices also may initiate activation of extinguishing systems and notify the fire department, resulting in property saved from fire.

Among the many design advances taking place is that detection devices are constantly being updated to minimize false alarm problems. Alarm devices also are being modified to better serve the hearing and visually impaired.

Communication systems include both public address-voice alarm and firefighter communication systems. They are especially important in high-rises and other large structures because of the significant distance between a lobby command post and the outer reaches of the building where occupants and fire-fighters may be located. These systems also help responders to conduct more orderly evacuations since most exit systems cannot sustain the load of total structure evacuation at one time.

Fire Alarm Systems

Fire alarm system is a general term used to describe a variety of specific types of systems. Each of these systems uses a combination of alarm and detection devices, but the systems have various methods of transmitting and monitoring the alarm condition.

NFPA 72, *Installation, Maintenance and Use of Protective Signaling Systems,* was revised a few years ago to include all protective signaling systems that previously had been covered by separate standards (NFPA 72A, 72B, 72C, and 72D). The standards for central station signaling systems (formerly NFPA 71), automatic fire detection devices (formerly NFPA 72E), household (residential) fire warning appliances (formerly NFPA 74), notification appliances (formerly NFPA 72G) and the guide used for testing systems (formerly NFPA 72H) are also now all covered under the 1993 edition of NFPA 72.

What follows are simplified descriptions of the five different types of protective signaling systems.

- **A local system** is one in which alarm conditions are transmitted only within the building in which the alarm originates. No monitoring is conducted outside the building.
- **An auxiliary system** essentially is a building alarm system that is connected to a municipal alarm system, usually through the use of a telegraph "master box" at a protected building; alarms are transmitted directly to the fire department.
- **A remote station system** is used where multiple buildings, under the same or different ownership, usually at different sites, transmit alarm conditions via a digital alarm communicator or supervised dedicated circuits, to a remote location such as a fire station.
- **A proprietary system** has alarm conditions from various buildings, often all on the same site and under the same ownership, transmitted to a monitoring station on the same site.
- **A central station system** has alarm conditions at various buildings in a city (or larger area), all under different ownership, monitored by a third party at a central location.

While these alarm system descriptions are broad and somewhat simplistic, they show the distinctions between each type. Such distinctions are important so that fire officers can understand what a particular alarm system will and will not do.

Found in theaters, hospitals, and apartment buildings, local systems are probably the most common, and usually the most economical.

Central station systems are the next most common system because many sprinklered buildings must be monitored constantly.

The remote station is gaining in popularity. In the past, alarms were transmitted off site to a fire station or police station. Today, however, these systems are used by property owners who own many buildings, all at different sites. The property owner transmits alarms from all his buildings to a monitoring station under his ownership.

Proprietary systems are used at large industrial complexes. Several buildings can be monitored at one location in the industrial plant.

Finally, the auxiliary system has disappeared from many cities because most cities have removed the telegraph alarm systems to which the auxiliary systems were connected.

Generally, an alarm system has three basic components:

- initiating devices—automatic or manual devices whose operation results in the transmitting of a fire alarm, and include such devices as manual pull stations and smoke detectors;
- indicating devices, such as horns, sirens, and strobe lights which warn of a fire condition; and
- a control panel (the brain of the system), which receives, processes, and annunciates an alarm condition.

Protective Signaling System Components

A multitude of different types of initiating devices are available for use in alarm systems. The largest group, automatic detection devices, use the fire's "signature"—heat, luminosity, and smoke—for operation.

Initiating Devices

- Manual pull stations include single- or double-action type, coded or noncoded types, breakglass or nonbreakglass types, and presignal or general alarm through a key switch or pull station type.
- "Spot" smoke detectors include ionization smoke detectors and photo-electric smoke detectors.
- "Line type" smoke detectors include cloud chamber smoke detectors and projected beam smoke detectors.
- Duct smoke detectors.

- "Spot" heat detectors include fixed-temperature heat detectors, nonrestorable fusible element heat detectors, combination rate-of-rise/ fixed temperature heat detectors, restorable bimetallic strip and disc heat detectors, rate compensation heat detectors, and thermoelectric effect heat detectors.
- "Line type" heat detectors include wire pair with thermally sensitive insulation, stainless steel capillary tube, and tubular rate-of-rise heat detectors.
- Gas-sensing detectors using semiconductor or catalytic element principle.
- Flame detectors; ultraviolet-single wavelength type, infrared-single wavelength type, ultraviolet/infrared type, multiple-wavelength infrared type, and multiband type.
- Water flow switch used on wet-pipe sprinkler system.
- Water pressure switch used on wet and dry-pipe sprinkler system.
- Supervisory switches to monitor sprinkler system control valves, low and high air pressure, temperature, tank water level.

Indicating Devices

Indicating devices include a variety of visual and audible equipment:

- horn;
- bell;
- chimes, buzzers, sirens;
- speakers;
- strobes; and
- lamps.

Fire alarm control panel

This is the "brain" or nerve center of a fire alarm system. Initiating and indicating devices are wired into the panel. It is through this wiring that electrical signals are sent to and from the alarm panel receiving and initiating an alarm.

As such, the alarm panel is usually the focus of the Incident Commander's attention when responders fight a fire in a building protected with a fire alarm system.

Of prominence on the alarm panel is the array of lamps, usually light-emitting diodes or LED, used to annunciate an alarm (red lamp) or trouble condition (yellow lamp). The lamps are organized by "zone." A zone represents a group of initiating or indicating devices.

For example, a high-rise alarm panel may have its detection devices zoned by type and by floor. The 15th floor may have 3 initiating device zones: one for smoke detectors, one for heat detectors, and one manual pull station.

Zones may be organized in many ways: by device, by floor, by wing of the building, etc. The key to remember is that the alarm panel exists not only to "process" alarm signals but also to annunciate the alarm location and alarm type. This annunciation is the critical type of information an Incident Commander needs. Zone labeling on the panel must be complete, sufficiently detailed, and immediately understandable!

The alarm panel also contains other features: alarm and supervisory signal silence switches, small horns to indicate a trouble condition, lamp test switches, and city disconnect switches. Relays may be provided in the panel to activate smoke control systems or to recall elevators.

A battery to act as a secondary power supply sometimes is included on the panel. Some systems use on-site emergency generators for their secondary power supply.

Remote annunciator panels may be provided at the main building entrance. These panels only annunciate alarm or trouble conditions by zone; they often do not have the "control" features of a regular fire alarm control panel.

A new type of fire alarm control panel is now found in many buildings.

This set of fire alarms and other fire protection panels is located in a high-rise fire control room. It is important that chief officers be able to interact with, and understand, these systems in an emergency—preplanning and training is critical.

PHOTO COURTESY OF AUTHOR

It features textual messages on a screen in lieu of the lamps previously discussed. These systems have the capability to alert the Incident Commander to
the specific device which has alarmed and when it alarmed (the device is
addressable). A printer also may be provided to give a "hard copy" of the control panel's status at specific times.

Signaling methods also are changing. The "multiplex" signaling method
is a simultaneous or sequential transmission, or both, and reception of multiple
signals in a communication channel.

Another relatively new type of signaling system uses no wiring between
the fire alarm panel and initiating/indicating devices; it is a "wireless" system.
Batteries in the initiating/indicating devices allow them to send and receive
alarm signals via radio waves.

Fire Alarm System Preplanning Considerations

Preplanning responses to facilities that have a fire alarm system is relatively easy. The preplan should note:

- location of the fire alarm control panel and any remote annunciators;
- type of alarm system, i.e., local, auxiliary, remote, proprietary, or central station;

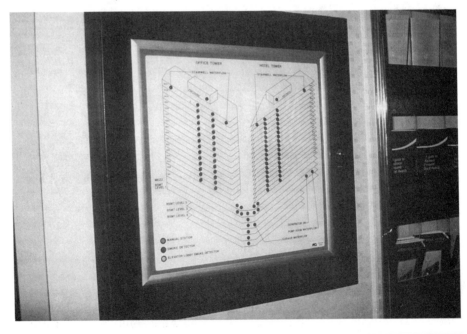

A remote annunciator such as this can enable the chief officer to quickly establish the
alarm location when entering the building.   PHOTO COURTESY OF AUTHOR

- area protected by system, whether complete or partial coverage;
- type of initiating devices and general layout (a sketch of typical floor is helpful);
- zoning provided what is on each zone and what area it covers for "lamp annunciation" systems;
- means of annunciation, i.e., LED/lamp or textual readout;
- any special features; and
- name and telephone of the system's service contractor, if possible.

With this information in hand, the Incident Commander can have a good idea of what to expect from the system.

The preplan should specify whether an individual, chief's aide, or other designated member is to be assigned to the fire alarm control panel for large buildings. In the case of a high-rise, the Incident Commander may monitor the fire alarm panel since he normally will be positioned in the high-rise central fire control room where the panel should be located.

Fire Alarm System Firefighting Considerations

The use of a fire alarm system during a fire can be of great assistance. At a glance, the location and type of devices activated can be seen.

The information gained from the panel must be evaluated carefully, however. For example, be careful when you evaluate smoke detector signals. While the smoke detectors can indicate the movement of smoke in the building, they can be activated at a location remote from the seat of the fire because of smoke migration. Be aware of the fact that manual pull stations may have been activated at a location remote from the fire because the pull station was the first one encountered by a fleeing individual.

Water flow switches at sprinkler system stairwell floor control valves are probably the best device to indicate that a fire is burning and where. They rarely "lie," since water flowing is a good indication of a real fire and not a false alarm.

COMMUNICATION SYSTEMS

Public address and voice alarm and firefighter communications systems are important pieces of equipment for the fire service. In the case of a public address system, it gives the Incident Commander the ability to give instructions to building occupants on a selective (a few floors) or an all-call (all areas of the building) basis. He may instruct occupants on some floors to evacuate and have others remain in place as well as give reassuring messages. A voice alarm is preceded by a tone alert and then a prerecorded set of instructions is given to building occupants.

Firefighter communication systems give the chief officer the ability to talk to firefighting crews in a building without using a department radio. Such communications can reduce traffic on the department radio.

Firefighter communication systems are two-way telephone systems which may take the form of permanently wired telephone handset stations mounted on walls at strategic locations. More often, telephone jacks, into which portable handsets can be plugged, are provided.

At a minimum, one jack or telephone station per floor and one per stairwell must be provided. The model building codes also require that they be provided at elevator lobbies and in elevator cabs.

NFPA 72 is the standard used to design public address and voice alarm systems and for "building" firefighter communication systems.

System Components

Both types of communication systems are similar in appearance. In fact, some systems may combine both communication functions.

The public address or voice alarm panel may have the following features: a means to initiate the evacuation tone, the tone alert, and voice directions on an all-call or selective basis. A microphone is provided to give the voice directions to building occupants.

The firefighters' communication system panel has a telephone handset on the panel. In addition, a signal is provided to indicate a "call-in," e.g., a firefighter who is trying to contact the central fire control station. The system is often capable of communicating simultaneously with five interconnected telephone stations.

Communication System Preplanning Considerations

Communication system preplans can be prepared with the following information:

- location of the public address or voice alarm and firefighters' communications panel(s);
- area protected by system(s), whether complete or partial coverage;
- text of prerecorded messages;
- type of firefighters' telephones, i.e., permanent handset or portable telephone handsets, including number and storage location of portable units;
- location of firefighter telephone jacks as applicable;

- any special features; and
- name and telephone of the system's service contractor, if possible.

With this information, the Incident Commander can have a good idea of what to expect from the system.

The preplan should specify whether an individual, e.g., chief's aide, or other designated member, is to be assigned to the firefighters' or public address-voice alarm control panel(s). The Incident Commander may take control of the systems since he normally will be positioned in the central fire control room.

Communication System Firefighting Considerations

The use of a public address system during a fire can be extremely helpful. It allows the Incident Commander to gain the occupants' attention during a fire, and direct them to a specific stairwell, freeing other stairwell(s) for firefighting operations. Used early in the incident, this can potentially prevent unnecessary and uncoordinated evacuations, which could substantially complicate an incident.

Since often only five firefighter telephone handsets can be used simultaneously, and a system using phone jacks may have only five portable handsets, it is important to use them judiciously. Give priority use to sector officers who are overseeing critical operations, e.g., fire extinguishment, search operations above the fire floor, etc.

SMOKE MANAGEMENT SYSTEMS

The newest type of fire protection system used in buildings, smoke management systems are being installed at an increasing rate. The Uniform Building Code has a specific chapter that deals with smoke management systems, and some model fire codes require their use in certain occupancies.

Smoke management systems are used in a variety of places, including high-rise buildings, high-piled stock warehouses, hospitals, covered mall buildings, and atria.

Unfortunately, the code requirements for smoke management systems (dating to the late 1970s) have outpaced the engineering design criteria for them. These engineering design criteria did not begin in earnest until the mid-1980s.

The result is that there are many different, nonstandard systems in existing buildings. While a lack of standardization may not necessarily be a bad thing in a general design sense, it is a problem for firefighters. They have to be trained on the operating details of every system and cannot expect the same smoke management "results" from different systems.

Today, most systems are designed under the guidance of NFPA 92A, *Recommended Practices on Smoke Control Systems,* and NFPA 92B, *Guide for Smoke Management Systems in Malls, Atria, and Large Areas.*

Smoke management systems may use a building's "normal" air-handling system or may use dedicated equipment. The systems may be complicated or simple.

Automatic sprinkler systems are critical to the majority of smoke management systems because they limit the amount of smoke generated and allow the smoke management system to do its job. A fire in an unsprinklered structure usually generates more smoke than a smoke management system can handle.

To manage smoke is to "handle" smoke, to make it "behave" by using pressure differentials, air flow, dilution, or purging. Most smoke management systems use one, some, or all of these to achieve smoke management.

Generally, for the purposes of the fire service, smoke management systems can be grouped into four categories: smoke control (pressurization), smoke purging (venting), zoned smoke control (a combination of pressurization and venting), and air flow. Most systems fit into one of these categories.

Smoke control systems include stairwell pressurization systems found in high-rise buildings. For buildings equipped with automatic sprinklers, high-rise stairwells are pressurized to .15 inches water column (all doors closed) to prevent smoke migration into the stairwell.

A barometric relief at the top of the stairwell is usually provided to relieve excess pressure. Air, supplied by a fan, is "injected" into the stair shaft approximately every five floors to create the pressure.

An "upgraded" version of the stairwell pressurization system is the smoke-proof enclosure. Besides the pressurization of the stair shaft, a vestibule maintained under negative pressure is added between the stair shaft and the building corridor. A minimum pressure of .05 inches water column is maintained in the stair shaft (all doors closed) as well as .10 inches water column between the stair shaft and vestibule.

Smoke purging is merely the process of venting the smoke out of the space under consideration. A good example of this system is one that uses exhaust fans (on the order of 30,000 cfm each) placed on the roofs of high-piled stock warehouses as required by the Uniform and Standard Fire Codes. These systems allow firefighters to gain some visibility during a warehouse fire.

Atrium smoke management systems are a good example of purging with a fair amount of dilution. Smoke is usually exhausted out the top of the atrium.

Zoned smoke control is used in high-rise buildings and covered mall buildings. Detection systems play an important role in activating these systems.

The high-rise zone smoke control technique has been termed the "pressure sandwich." Simply, the fire floor is exhausted and the floors above and below are pressurized to keep smoke on the fire floor.

A similar approach is used in covered mall buildings. They are zoned by tenant area or mall (pedestrian walkway) area. With a fire in a tenant zone, the tenant zone is exhausted and the mall pressurized. With a fire in the mall area, the reverse is true.

Air flow smoke management systems use the movement of air across an opening to "push back" smoke. An example is a shaft opening which cannot be enclosed; air flow is provided to keep smoke from moving up the shaft.

The key point to be made about smoke management systems is that you must know each one intimately. Preplanning is essential.

System components

A smoke management system consists of a combination of any or all of the following: fans, ductwork, relays tied to detection and other systems, control panels, dampers, wiring, pressure relief devices, and louvers.

Of special note is the temperature rating of the components. Since most smoke management systems are used in conjunction with sprinkler systems, you can anticipate the generation of "cold" smoke. Many smoke management systems cannot handle "hot" smoke for extended periods of time. One notable exception is in high-piled stock warehouses where fans are required to withstand temperatures of 1,000°F for 15 minutes.

Smoke Management System Preplanning Considerations

Preplanning is critical for these systems! As a minimum, the preplan should include:

- a general description of system type (smoke control, purge, zoned smoke control, or air flow);
- location and extent of the system;
- the system's design goal, i.e., what will it do? (in quantifiable terms);
- whether the system is manual, automatic or both;
- equipment used to activate the system (smoke detector, sprinkler water flow switch, etc.);
- a **detailed** description of the operational sequence of the system, step by step, i.e., when it is activated, what turns on, what turns off;
- location and type of manual control panel. Give **DETAILS** on how to use the panel and what each switch controls;
- name and telephone number of the system's service contractor, if possible.

Once this information has been assembled, procedures to be used by the fire department during an incident can be established. Make sure that a fire company or individual is to be assigned to operate the smoke management system. Set up a "walk-through" training session of the system by responding personnel before an incident occurs. Determine what actions will and will not be taken.

It is important to work with building maintenance personnel because they usually are the most knowledgeable about the system, and they are immediately available.

Smoke Management System Firefighting Operations

On arrival, the Incident Commander should assess the smoke conditions. Is the automatic smoke management system working properly? If not, can he determine why?

Keep in mind that many automatic zoned smoke control systems in high-

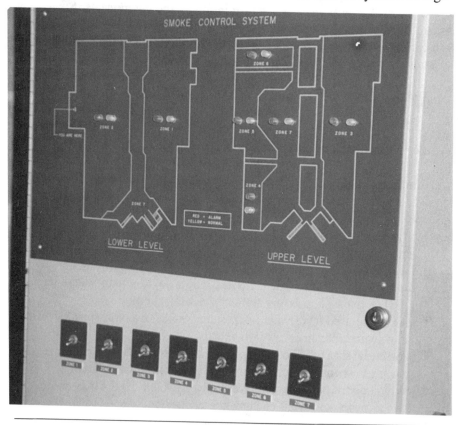

This covered mall's smoke management system panel shows the status of the equipment in each area as well as provide switches to activate/shut down the system in each area.

PHOTO COURTESY OF AUTHOR

rise buildings are activated by smoke detectors. And if a detector activates that is not on the fire floor, it can cause problems. Be prepared to order a shutdown if such problems are encountered.

On arrival, make sure that a fire company or individual is in radio contact at the control panel, awaiting your instructions.

The fire company or individual assigned to the panel must be knowledgeable about it and trained in its use. Randomly throwing switches is dangerous for both fellow firefighters and the system alike. Throwing the wrong switch can intensify the fire. With a fan running, closing a damper can overpressurize ductwork and bring it crashing to the floor.

If orders are given to activate or shut down a smoke management system, the orders must be very specific and very clear. The orders must indicate which specific area of the building should be activated or shut down. NOTHING must be left to guesswork.

Before activating a system, it is advisable to keep firefighters out of the fire area in case something goes wrong.

If the system is not performing properly, it is usually best to shut it down in an orderly manner.

THE FUTURE OF FIRE PROTECTION SYSTEMS

The role of fire protection systems will continue to expand in the future. It is likely that these systems will be found in most new construction during the next century.

The new types of systems will be more precise in their detection and extinguishment of fires. Fire extinguishing systems will use their agents more conservatively, to save money and reduce cleanup costs.

Fires will be detected earlier, resulting in fewer losses. The systems will discriminate more effectively between the products of combustion from unwanted fires and "friendly fires."

As these systems become more sophisticated, their complexity also will increase, leading to more complex design and installation standards as well as more extensive maintenance procedures.

It is essential that the fire service be prepared to meet this challenge. This will require a commitment of more extensive and enhanced training. More importantly, a commitment to stand behind the installation of fire protection systems as a "new way of doing business" must be made.

NOTES

1. Channing, William F., "The America Fire-Alarm Telegraph, Ninth Annual Report of the Board of Regents, Smithsonian Institution," Washington, D.C., Smithsonian Institution, 1855

2. "The 1983 Fire Almanac," Quincy, Massachusetts, National Fire Protection Association, 1983, pg. 709

3. Woodbury, C.H., "Modern Development and Early History of Automatic Sprinklers," New York, New York, reproduced from Casser's Magazine, 1892, pg. 3

4. Parmalee, Henry S., "Parmalee's Patent Automatic Fire Extinguisher and Alarm," New Haven, Connecticut, Stafford Printing, circa 1874–1878, pg. 8

5. Providence Steam and Gas Company, "Henry Parmalee's Automatic Sprinkler and Fire Alarm," Brett Lithography, 1879, pg. 14

6. Goldstein, Albert, "A Standard System of Automated Fire Alarm Protection," published as a treatise before the Franklin Institute, Philadelphia September 18, 1894, pg. 11

7. Ibid, pgs. 4–5

8. Jensen, Rolf, "Automated Sprinkler Systems Handbook, Chapter 1, The Historic Development of the Sprinkler Standard," Quincy, Massachusetts, 1991, pg. 652

9. "National Foam Engineering Manual," Lionville, Pennsylvania, 1987, pg. 2

10. Bryan, John L., "Fire Suppression and Detection Systems," New York, New York, Macmillan Publishing Co., 1993, pg. 205

27

Public Education

MARY NACHBAR

CHAPTER HIGHLIGHTS

- The difference between public education and public information.
- The process and techniques of reviewing educational materials.
- Developing coalitions to support public education efforts.
- The qualifications of a public educator based on NFPA 1035.
- How to implement a school-based safety curriculum to work toward a fire-safe generation.
- Methodologies for reaching high-risk, hard-to-reach populations.
- The myth about fire prevention week.
- How to secure funding and budgetary resources for successful public education.
- Past lessons and solutions for the future.

THIS CHAPTER OUTLINES how to set up a public education initiative in your community. Some of the ideas offered may initially seem non-traditional, but they are based on substantial experience in firefighting, prevention, investigation, hazardous materials and data analysis.

Historically, prevention efforts have addressed only fire-related education, but the role of public education no longer can be viewed exclusively in terms of fire. The fire service has a primary mission in every community to protect life, property, and the environment.

An analysis of national statistics reported to the National Fire Incident Reporting System (NFIRS) clearly shows that fewer than 20 percent of today's fire department responses are to actual working fires; the rest involve calls for emergency medical services, natural and man-made disasters, etc. We are the first to be called when people power is needed immediately. Nowhere else in the community is there a number to call to achieve the miracle the fire service can provide in minutes: trained, caring, available people.

As the attitudes and myths about fires and accidents are explored here, it may cause you to examine your own perspective on the issues. You will be introduced to the new direction in public education—injury prevention and control—and analyze an accident sequence model that will help you to understand and focus on specific strategies to determine and solve your problems relating to public education and its objectives. You also will examine data as a means to assist you not only with developing a public education program but to use as a management tool to measure and control the problem.

It would be fair to inform you at this point what will not be in this chapter. You will not see pictures of clowns, or puppets, or references to videos or other such resources or materials. Although these are valuable tools for public educators, they are not the focus of this chapter. Also the how-to's of presenting programs or training will not be addressed here because this type of training is available at most local colleges or through public education conferences offered around the country. This chapter will address the process of setting up a public education initiative and the sequential steps that must be taken.

Remember as you read through this chapter, that as a fire chief or chief officer you have a responsibility to ensure that your community is safe from fire. Public education is only one of your department's functions, and you will know how well you are accomplishing your mission by the number of runs, deaths, and injuries that occur in your jurisdiction. Good public education initiatives do not occur without your support or without resources to accomplish the goal of protecting life and property.

With carefully developed controls, the success of your Public Education program efforts can be measured partially through loss reduction, but more reliably through application of knowledge gained, and the community support for continued funding for the program. If yours is a high-visibility fire department, it will survive because the community will know exactly what it is you do for them and how well you do it.

It has been said that "Life must be lived forward, but can only be understood backwards." The information in this chapter is designed to assist you and ultimately, the people you serve to live a safe life forward, without having to look back on needless tragedies that could have been avoided.

ATTITUDES AND MYTHS ABOUT FIRE

A look at some common myths and attitudes that often interfere with the successful implementation of public education programs is useful before discussing how to initiate one. Many of the myths about fire are held by members of the fire service as well as the public.

MYTH—THEY (THE PUBLIC) WILL LISTEN TO EVERYTHING WE TELL THEM!

Taking this brief true/false test may help to make the point that not everyone heeds safety messages.

1. I always use a seat belt while riding in or driving a vehicle, including emergency vehicles. T_____ F_____
2. I never drive if I have had a couple of beers or drinks. T_____ F_____
3. I never salt my food. T_____ F_____
4. I do not smoke or use tobacco products. T_____ F_____
5. I never exceed the speed limit. T_____ F_____
6. I exercise aerobically for 30 minutes every day. T_____ F_____

If your answers were true to all of these statements you are a saint and represent a very small part of the population! The point is, we receive a tremendous number of messages that compete for our attention, and are related to health and well being, yet we do not always change our behavior.

Given our own failure to heed messages, why do we think that because we hand people a brochure, or give children a coloring book, they will take our messages to heart? For a message to translate into positive behavior, to become instinctual, and to be practiced, people must feel the message is valuable enough to move them to do something about the problem addressed. This does not happen overnight and it doesn't result from simply reading a brochure or hearing a lecture one time. Think, for instance, how long it has taken to get people to wear seat belts; even now compliance is far short of what it should be.

MYTH—FIRE HAPPENS TO OTHER PEOPLE!

According to NFPA and NFIRS data, one in five people will have a fire in his lifetime that will necessitate calling the fire department. This is extremely discouraging news given that only 15 percent of fires are ever reported to the fire service. We have all heard stories told by people who have had significant fires that were potentially threatening to both life and property, but never reported them to the fire service. The potential is frightening.

MYTH—THE FIRE DEPARTMENT WILL SAVE ME!

This myth has been popular with the public for years. The fact is, people have died in home fires while living immediately adjacent to or across the street from a fire station. There are no guarantees in a fire; once it begins it can grow rapidly, generating deadly smoke that kills long before visible flames are present. The best protection a person can have is knowing how to prevent a fire and how to survive should a fire occur.

MYTH—THE INSURANCE COMPANY WILL PAY!

Insurance covers only tangible items lost in a fire. The reality is that insurance companies can never replace family heirlooms, photos collected for years, journals written to document a life, memories hidden in a scrapbook, or most important, the loss of a life. It is after this realization that the tragedy of a fire becomes real.

Additionally, the International Association of Arson Investigators (IAAI) reports that $.25 of every dollar spent for insurance coverage goes to pay off arson claims. It is not the insurance company that pays, it is the people who buy the insurance. When a fire loss occurs, intentional or unintentional, we all pay; therefore, we all lose. Fire losses go far beyond the victim, yet few understand the effect on the entire community.

MYTH—HOLLYWOOD FIRES ARE REAL!

The fact is, Hollywood movies and television have given people a false sense of security about fire. How often have you seen the Hollywood hero fight the bad guys amidst flames and explosions, only to walk away unscathed. Hollywood has now taken it one step further. The sound stage where much of the movie *Backdraft* was filmed has now been turned into an attraction where 35,000 people per day can stand on a platform overlooking the area where Hollywood heroes Kurt Russell and Scott Glen "duked it out" while flames licked at their heels. The following description comes from Northwest Airlines' in-flight-magazine.

Upon entering a 500,000-cubic-foot sound stage, guests witness a backdraft flame spinning wildly about the building. Massive explosions of flammable fuel drums are triggered, causing overhead pipes to burst and spew venomous contents toward onlookers below. The fire storm surrounds guests in a pulsating holocaust of heat and thunder. The flames consume precious air as temperatures reach in excess of 2,000 degrees. Protecting guests is a unique ceiling-to-floor invisible "air curtain." The imposing fire ball consumes the roof and platform supporting the audience. The resultant red-hot tangle of melted metal collapses, leaving thrilled guests poised precariously amongst the unabated flames.

MYTH—THE FIRE WAS AN ACCIDENT!

This is the "Accident Attitude Theory" mentioned in the introduction. In reality, it might be said that there is no such thing as an accident when it comes to most fires, injuries, or deaths. *There are only caused occurrences.* If you disagree with this conclusion, consider this premise: in Webster's dictionary we find the word "accident" to mean "an event occurring by chance." Winning the lottery is an accident. Having a fire is not. When the words "accident" or "accidental" are included in fire incident reports, or told to the media, we perpetuate the myth that the fire was an unavoidable event. Nearly every fire is the result of carelessness, heedlessness, thoughtlessness, or ignorance on the part of someone. It is not a cigarette that falls asleep while someone is smoking it. The events we commonly refer to as accidental are really controllable and avoidable. This is a harsh reality, yet true.

The founders of the Mothers Against Drunk Drivers (MADD) campaign, begun 10 years ago, were dealing with the same issues and perceptions about drinking and driving. They began to break the accident theory myth by insisting that fatal collisions that involved alcohol were the fault of the intoxicated drivers, the persons who served them the alcohol, or both. They began forming coalitions to solve the problem. Designated driver programs cropped up and lawsuits targeting intoxicated drivers and those who served them until they were too drunk to legally drive were initiated. Cities, counties, and states began massive efforts to get intoxicated drivers off the streets.

The program evolved and after many years, attitudes *have* changed. While it now is considered socially unacceptable to drink and drive, consider this observation from a fire specialist, "If a drunk on the road kills someone while under the influence, that person is charged and faces penalties, fines, and a possible prison sentence. However, if that same person comes home drunk, lights a cigarette, falls asleep and a fire ensues, killing others in the structure, a collection is taken up, new housing is found for them, clothing is replaced and they are considered the victims of an accident."

Change takes place slowly. However, if we want change, no matter how uncomfortable it may feel, we must begin the long journey toward making fire as socially unacceptable as drinking and driving. People are both the victims and the perpetrators of fire. The idea is not to prosecute the victims; it is to put the responsibility for the fire where it belongs, on the person who started it. If we begin to teach the public that fires are acts of carelessness, ignorance, or thoughtlessness, we can slowly begin to reinforce the message that fire tragedies are preventable events, caused by people, and they need not occur.

If you were to review fire incident reports in your community you would discover that the human element is predominant in most fires. Removing the word "accidental" from our incident reports would help. Fires then could be identified as "intentional," "unintentional," "act of nature," (e.g., lightning) or "undetermined after investigation." While this would be a shift from traditional thinking in the U.S., countries that have adopted this philosophy do not seem to have our fire problems.

One last thought on this issue is the notion that if fire prevention and public education prevent all the fires we will lose our jobs in the fire service. Dr. William Hayden, an injury control specialist who developed the "injury control sequence model" addressed later in this chapter, has this to say,

"Prevention will not cut funds/resources; it will generate the need for better equipment, people, etc., because of the injury control necessary after an incident occurs." Prevention is an ongoing effort. If we truly want to accomplish our mission of saving lives and property, we have to look at reallocating many more fire department resources into prevention activities in the future.

Public education is a lifelong event; it must be repeated from birth to the grave. If we do not undertake prevention initiatives, others will take the lead. Fire prevention and life safety are being taught by many organizations such as visiting nurses' programs (fire safety for older citizens), hospitals, social service agencies, the Red Cross, injury control organizations, and private individuals.

FIRE PROTECTION

We offer the public three basic types of fire protection:

1. *Active protection*—the response services we provide to the community.
2. *Passive Protection*—programs of code enforcement and prevention services that require such built-in protection as rated walls, fire separations, sprinklers, smoke detectors, and alarm systems, that many people do not even notice in a structure.
3. *Personal Protection*—the safety and survival information we offer to the community to help citizens protect themselves and to prevent incidents from occurring.

Let us consider a new twist on the fire triangle:

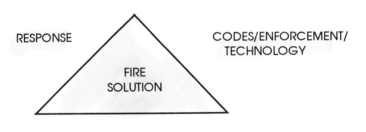

If you take any one of these three elements away from fire service operations, you will *never* stop fires, deaths, or injuries in your community.

ESTABLISHING A PUBLIC EDUCATION INITIATIVE

It is important to understand the difference between education and information. Chances are, many fire departments perform public *information* programs rather than public *education* programs. While both have a place in your efforts, *public information* means, in essence, that information is relayed to the public by various means, i.e., brochures, billboards, coloring books, public service announcements, and large group speeches, none of which has a feedback mechanism. The advantage of public information programs is that large numbers of people can be reached quickly.

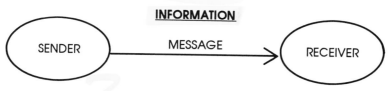

The disadvantage of a public information program is that once the information is given, there is no way to measure whether the intended audience received and understood the message.

On the other hand, *public education* programs have specific, measurable goals, identified objectives and a built-in evaluation tool, such as a pre-test and post-test, demonstration, or some type of closure activity that has the learner repeat back the information. The instructor then evaluates the knowledge gain.

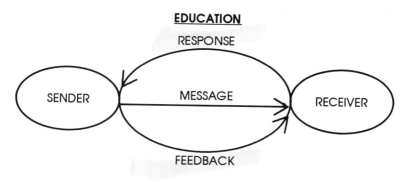

The disadvantage of public education is that you typically can reach only smaller numbers of people at one time. The advantage is that there is a high message transfer and retention rate when you test all participants for knowledge gained or skills learned.

A good public education campaign may include both the information and education components; information alone is not enough to solve the fire problem. Remember, "If teaching were the same as telling, think how smart we would all be."

In some fire departments, public education is a year-round effort, with Fire Prevention Week (FPW) considered only the springboard to kick off their efforts or a high visibility time to reinforce messages. However, many other fire departments engage in an all-out effort during FPW, putting all their eggs into one basket. Before your department does this, stop and consider what causes fires in our communities. Across the nation the major fire causes (people-related) are heating, cooking, arson, and improper use of electrical appliances, and flammable liquids—not necessarily in that order. Nonetheless, when you consider the magnitude of time and resources it would take to educate everyone in your community about these causes, and taking into consideration the various age levels of the audiences you must reach, one week a year is not enough. What we need to do is to establish networks or coalitions with many people and organizations such as school systems, mental health communities, seniors, business communities, and any other groups that can help us to reach the target audience in our efforts to fight the fire and burn problem.

Simply stated, a coalition is an alliance of interested parties merged to solve a problem, in this case, the fire or injury problems of the community. A little known fact is that for each person who loses a job because of a fire, nine other people in the community are affected. In other words, if a fire destroys a business and 100 people lose their jobs, 900 other people will be affected. Fire must be treated as an injury to the community and the community must help the fire service to reduce the fire incident rate.

A training program, "Partnerships Against Fire," was developed in the early 1980s by the U.S. Fire Administration (USFA) in conjunction with the National Criminal Justice Association under a grant titled the National Community Volunteer Fire Prevention Program. The premise was to develop coalitions in states and communities to combat the fire problem. A community coalition can be as simple as enlisting the support and resources of a few community members or as complex as a large-scale effort in a metropolitan area that would consist of several levels and perhaps use an ad-hoc committee structure to accomplish its mission. Partnerships Against Fire materials are available at no charge from the U.S. Fire Administration.

THE PLANNING PROCESS

Successful Prevention Program Initiatives

The three basic elements of a successful prevention initiative are the campaign/program, resources, and community support.

The **Campaign/Program** must be skill based, engaging, sound in concept, and age and audience appropriate.

SKILL-BASED/CHANGE

This means that the people who attend your program will leave with one or more skills. This approach equips people with workable skills that are easily learned and readily usable. Prevention campaigns/programs also must incorporate some kind of change, i.e., changes to the environment or to products, or changes by humans.

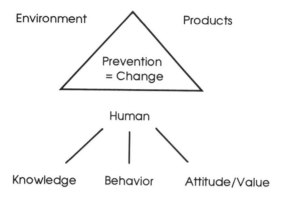

Environmental changes include passive types of protection, such as sprinkler systems required by codes, that can be used to reduce the risks if a fire should occur. While passive protection may alter the outcome of a fire, it doesn't prevent a fire from starting. In the article, "Sprinklers: Who Has Them? How Well Do They Work?" in the November/December 1993 issue of *Fire Journal,* John R. Hall, Ph.D., wrote,

Minnetonka, MN Mayor Larry Donlin braved the USFA sprinkler trailer demonstration and became an avid supporter of sprinklers.

Sprinklers usually prevent large loss of life. For the past decade, the NFPA's statistics have consistently shown that properly installed and maintained sprinklers prevent deaths outside the area of fire origin in all but a few unusual situations. The NFPA has no record of a fire killing more than two people in a completely sprinklered building where the system was operating properly, except in the case of explosions and flash fires in which industrial fire brigade members or employees were killed during fire suppression operations.

In other words there are no guarantees that once a fire occurs people will be safe, however, the outcome may be significantly different in an environment where built-in fire protection features are present.

Chief Jim Estepp of the Prince George's County (Maryland) Fire Department initiated a campaign for sprinkler requirements for all new residential facilities being constructed, because of growing demands placed on the fire service and projected fire department budget cuts. When the higher cost of suppression activities in the future was added to the equation, it was decided to change the environment by requiring sprinklers. Public educators played a major role in selling the concept to the community.

Product change is another way to effect behavior change. Consider child-resistant cigarette lighters, fire-safe cigarettes, and flame retardant clothing for the young and the elderly. Another good example is kerosene heaters. Because of fire and burn problems associated with these heaters, safety features that included automatic shut-off of tipped-over units, guards over the heating elements, and more easily accessible fill features gradually were added by the manufacturers. In addition, a long list of safety precautions was printed in the manufacturers' instructions. Product changes can help to reduce the fire risk, but, as is the case with cigarette lighters, adults must take responsibility for keeping them out of the reach of children. Nothing is foolproof.

Human change can occur at one or more of the following three levels: knowledge, behavior, or attitude/value. People who have learned positive, behaviorally oriented skills and knowledge will value the skill-based message, return home and do what you want them to do. They also will use the knowledge and skills in a fire situation. In a study of victim behavior in fires, it was learned that people acted appropriately to escape a fire if they had been given the proper steps to take prior to the event. It was determined that "panic" was *usually not* a factor in a fire; people acted according to the limited knowledge they had at the time, which might be interpreted by the fire service as panic. The author of the study stressed that if we want people to survive, we must tell them everything they need to *know* and *do* to make appropriate decisions in the event of a fire.

Further evidence of how people behave in fire emergencies was presented to public educators at the November 1993 meeting of the National Fire Protection Association (NFPA). In a paper titled "Human Factors: Lessons for

Public Fire Educators: Lessons from Major Fires," Mark Chubb of the Southern Building Code Congress International, Inc., described a fire at a health care facility in June of 1992:

> This fire illustrated the value of prior experience and the need for training, in order to ensure that occupants respond in a timely and effective fashion to situations in which the threat is not overwhelming, but sufficient clues are present to indicate action is required. The interviews with survivors also highlighted the fact that none of the occupants considered the situation ambiguous and that each proceeded to act in a sequential fashion without considering a broad range of alternative courses of action. As the situation progressed, those who approached the fire moved away from it and took actions consistent with the level of danger they perceived. Eventually each of the survivors reached a point where they surmised that *immediate* action to evacuate the building was required to achieve the overriding goal of survival.

This is evidence that public educators must be very clear about the specific actions people should take and the need for occupants to *practice* to improve their decisionmaking capabilities, thereby improving their ability to deal with dangerous situations in a timely and effective fashion.

A skill-based campaign and program development are essential because of the competition for messages, time, and money. A recent study showed that in the 1950s most people were confronted with more than 1,500 messages a day. By the 1980s that increased to more then 3,000 inputs daily, with an average of about 15 seconds spent on each message. Obviously, we need to be able to get the attention of our audience quickly, while still giving them a skill to perform.

What are some of the messages that have been developed recently that are great attention getters, but do not instruct the audience? MADD's billboard campaign showed a vehicle collision, with fire, and the words "Have you toasted a friend lately?" There was no other message. While it had a theme and got people's attention it did offer information about behavior change. The implied message was that drinking and driving don't mix, but this was not stated on the billboard. Beware of being so clever with your theme that your safety message—what you want the public to do—is lost.

The average person today looks at a picture, poster or visual for three to five seconds. Jan Gratton, a fire safety representative and NFPA board member, conducted a study of posters and what messages people got from them. Of the ones that lacked a skill-based message, after 90 seconds people still could not identify what action the poster wanted them to take. The U.S. Forest Service's "Smokey The Bear" posters of the past had the message "Only you can prevent forest fires." While this was the attitude they wanted to convey, it did not provide the viewer with a skill to perform to stop the problem. A recent

Smokey poster shows simply an empty black space, with the words "This used to be a Forest." Again, no action is stated. With only three to five seconds to get our message to the public we can ill afford to waste time or money presenting this type of information to the public. Skill-based, positive behavior messages are essential to any program or campaign.

Cognitive research says that people need to see or do something 25 to 30 times to make it a habit. Reaching the public, therefore, takes more than a single-shot approach. Teaching skills needs to be based on repetition. Additionally, public education efforts must be used when the enemy—fire—strikes. Associated with every incident is a window of opportunity when the public and media are receptive to a fire safety message. If you are not ready with a "Pearl Harbor chest," ammunition for times when the enemy "fire" strikes, full of prepared messages to respond to the media and public instantaneously, you will have missed the most valuable opportunity you have to alter people's attitudes and to change behavior.

Once a fire has occurred, it is time to get into the prevention mode. If you are not ready with information to be disseminated immediately, you will have lost the fire prevention fight just as surely as you would lose a structure had the fire trucks and firefighters not shown up at all. Being prepared on the prevention line is just as important as being prepared on the fire line. It is doubly sad to lose both a life and the opportunity to save another.

ENGAGING

The program and related materials must enable you to get and keep the audience's attention. Show people what you want them to do and get them to picture themselves doing what you want them to do. If you can engage the audience you can hold people's attention from beginning to end.

SOUND IN CONCEPT

Your program must show a sound rationale for the activities you want the audience to do. Don't teach Stop, Drop and Roll to people who are frail or mobility impaired. They will take the attitude, "If I can't do it, why are you teaching it to me?" You will lose your credibility and your opportunity.

AGE AND AUDIENCE APPROPRIATE

Programs have to be geared to a specific audience with materials that are appropriate for the age group targeted. For example, simply determining that the target audience will be the elderly is too broad. You must identify a specific population within the elderly community, e.g., frail elderly seniors who live independently, or mobility-impaired seniors.

Direct the message's content toward identified hazards and keep all messages behaviorally specific and positive in nature. All of the aforementioned strategies are not new; NFPA's "Learn Not to Burn" program applied these basic principles:

- Appeal to existing motives that people have for being safe. Do not threaten.
- Be explicit about proper behavior and specific in directing messages to a particular group.
- Show people what you want them to do and tell them exactly how to do it.

Numerous success stories have been documented in which people remembered the simple, clear messages they heard or saw on television, and then responded correctly in an emergency situation. Think carefully when you plan your program and messages, and use strategies that have proved effective.

For every program that you develop you will need to go through an identification process to define exactly your local fire problem. If you work for a small department without a lot of runs, then you will base your identification process on *potential* fire problems in your community. Where there are people there are fires.

IDENTIFY YOUR LOCAL FIRE PROBLEM

First identify the specific fire problems in your community, county, or state. Do not use a shotgun approach; it will not work. You need to take aim and focus on a specific target. One way to identify these specific targets is to participate in a system to collect incident data. The National Fire Incident Reporting System (NFIRS), operated jointly by the National Fire Information Council (NFIC) and the USFA, is one of the best tools a fire department can use. It not only helps you to identify your specific public education goals and objectives, it also can assist you in managing your department. It provides you with information on fire causes, response times, staffing and equipment used, and death and injury data, all of which can be used to identify training and education objectives.

The NFIRS system is used by 13,000 fire departments nationwide. The reports can be produced manually or by computer. The information is generated locally and then sent to the state where it is linked with data from other fire departments to determine statewide problems. Each of the 42 states that uses the system generates a report of its statewide fire problem; data then are submitted to NFIC where they are combined with data from other states to identify the magnitude of the total U.S. fire problem.

Data are one of the most important elements you need to set up your public education program. If you don't know where you are, how will you know how

Data constitute one of the most important elements of defining a public education program.

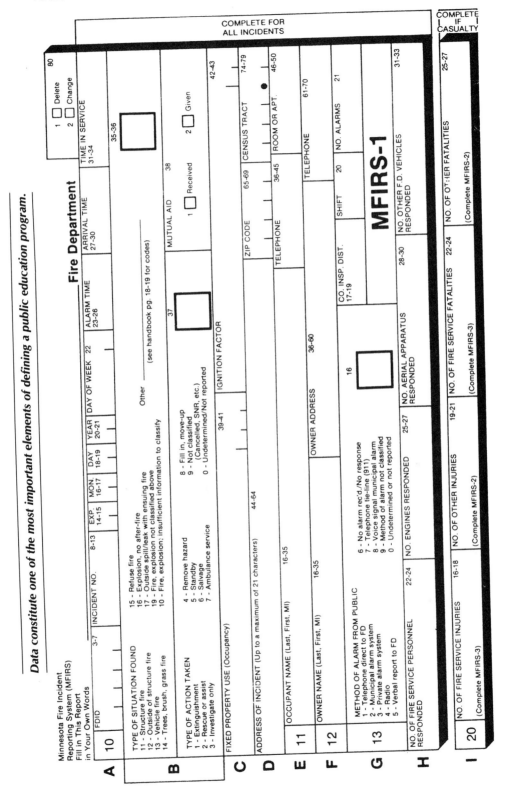

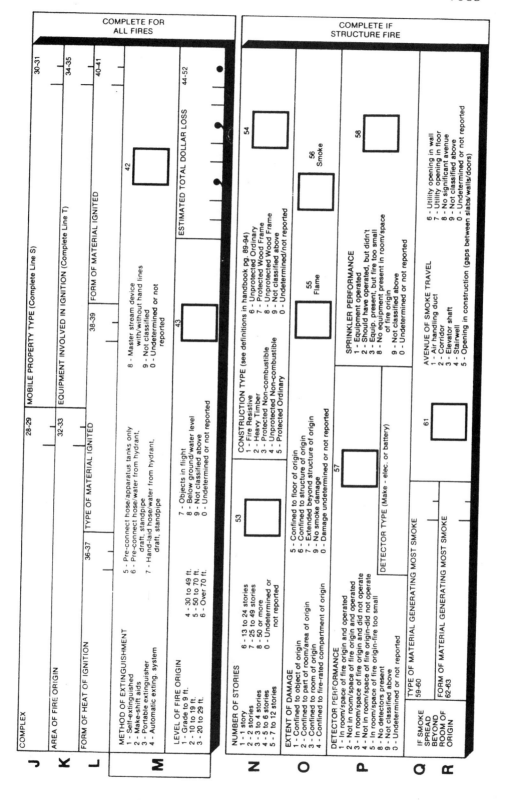

		YEAR 16-17	MAKE	18-32 MODEL	33-47 SERIAL NO.	48-67 LICENSE	68-77
S 30	IF MOBILE PROPERTY						
T 40	IF EQUIP. INVOLVED IN IGNITION	YEAR 16-17	MAKE	18-32 MODEL	33-47 SERIAL NO.	48-67	

	MILES TO & FROM FIRE
OFFICER IN CHARGE (Name, Position, Assignment) DATE	FIRE CHIEF PAID MORE THAN $50 ANNUALLY? ☐ Yes ☐ No
U MEMBER MAKING REPORT (If Different From Above) DATE	NAME OF FIRE CHIEF

REMARKS:

Entries contained in this report are intended for the sole use of the State Fire Marshal. Estimations and evaluations made herein represent "most likely" and "most probable" cause and effect. Therefore, any representation as to validity or accuracy of reported conditions outside the State Fire Marshal's Office is neither intended nor implied.

ORIGINAL — State Fire Marshal
DUPLICATE — Local Fire Department

Department of Public Safety
State Fire Marshal Division
285 Bigelow Building
450 North Syndicate Street
St. Paul, Minnesota 55104

MFIRS-1 (7-84)
PS06015

or when you get to where you want to go? Other sources of data include local hospitals, clinics, insurance company records, ambulance services, and law enforcement agencies. Remember that only 15 percent of the fires and injuries that occur are ever reported to the fire department. By linking fire data with other data sources you get a truer picture of the total problem in your community.

A review of the fire data in your community will give you information on fire cause, the use or activation of on-site fire protection equipment, information for demographic research on high-risk victims, time of day and time of week of fire events, and behaviors that need to be addressed in your public education efforts. Over a period of time you also will identify fire incident trends developing in your community as well as fire and/or injury reduction trends that occur over time. With incident data and reviews of investigative reports you will be ready to begin the process of systematically solving the fire problem. You may think this is too much work, but, remember, so is firefighting. No one said this was the easy part of our job. In fact, if your public education program is done well it can be one of the most difficult, yet rewarding programs in the fire department. Remember, our mission is to save lives and property; we cannot always accomplish this on the end of a hoseline.

Once you have identified the local fire, burn, death or injury problems you must establish priorities—specific causes on which to focus. This information then can be tied into census tract data to determine the demographics of the area. The next step is to develop the "Sequence of Events" to determine how incidents occur. In every scenario there is a chain of events that occurs before the incident. This process is similar to performing a task analysis of the event and aids you in determining what skills are most important for people to learn. One way to do this is by developing a simple form. It is helpful to list column headings on a piece of paper. For example:

Type of Incident: Children Playing With Lighter

(#3) P, E or H	(#1) Sequence leading to incident	(#2) Interventions	
H	Parent brings lighter into house	Leave in Car	Determine every conceivable intervention you can think of.
H & P	Parent is a smoker	Fire-Safe Cig. Stop smoking	
H	Parent leaves lighter on table	Have lock box handy	
H	Child finds lighter and takes it into bedroom	Put out of reach	
P & E	Child spins wheel; lighter ignites bed clothes	Fire-safe Lighter/ flame-retard bedding	
P, H & E	Fire Department responds to put out fire	Install fire sprinkler child firesetter intervention	

(P = Product   E = Environment   H = Human behavior)

In STEP ONE you develop the **sequence of events** that leads up to the incident. Start with the precondition phase that leads to the incident and continue on through the first aid and suppression phases (not shown on this chart). Oftentimes people do not perceive the suppression and first aid phases as part of the incident; however, it is very much a part of what has occurred. Sequencing is the first critical step in identifying intervention strategies. The process helps us to understand the events that lead up to an incident.

In STEP TWO **list the interventions** for each identified sequence of events leading to the incident. There may be several for each. Consider all the possibilities. This is where most people stop, when in actuality this is the beginning of the planning process. Interventions in the example sequence could include: stop smoking; work in partnerships with other smoking programs; make lighter inaccessible (high, out of sight, locked); introduce education intervention for child; incorporate Learn Not to Burn Curriculum in school (teach children what to do when they find matches or lighters and how to understand the role fire plays in their lives); redesign product (safe lighter, flame-retardant bedclothes, sprinkler systems, smoke detectors); teach a child to call 911; train 911 operators in how to respond to a child in a fire emergency; improve fire response (staffing, equipment, etc.). The list could go on

Identifying all possible interventions in the "sequence of events" is essential to choosing the right strategy for your efforts and will provide your coalition with multiple ways to attack the problem.

and on and should include setting up a child fire-setting program. In this step it is better to be specific rather than general.

In STEP THREE determine if the intervention is a **product**-related issue, **environment** or **human issue** and mark it accordingly on your worksheet. The reason for this is that for these three issues, different interventions need to take place. Some could require a legislative solution, such as changing the environment by requiring sprinkler installation. Another may require contacting the manufacturer or consumer-advocate groups, while the human interventions could be handled through public education programs.

In STEP FOUR **determine the behavior message.** It is in this step that you design a program that will tell your audience what to do; this step is key to the success of your program. The skill-based message must be action oriented and portray a positive behavior message. For example, always begin with an action word:

Stop smoking
Put lighter out of sight
Report a fire to an adult
Buy flame-retardant bedding
Install residential fire sprinklers
    and smoke detectors

Remove lighters from child's reach
Give a lighter to a grown-up
Call the fire department
Buy child-proof lighters

RESOURCES AND OBJECTIVES

Select the resources and objectives of the program depending on what is available in the community. In this phase the fire service and coalition must become critical consumers to make sure that all materials and program objectives meet the criteria listed previously; this will be key in the evaluation process of the program. Brainstorm this element with all members of your coalition or network. Remember, many of your coalition members are not content experts; they are user experts and will add what-ifs that will assist you in determining your resources. This also will indicate to you that they have "bought into" the program.

Depending on the community's resources, strategies may vary from using the mass media, to in-school programs, or community-wide programs, or may include all three. In Phoenix, Arizona, for example, the fire department was responding to an inordinate number of drownings. With no other resources to address this issue the fire department realized that it needed to develop a school-based curriculum that addressed other injury prevention aspects. The department called it "Urban Survival," with messages taught by classroom teachers and enhanced by visits from fire department personnel and other injury specialists. The department also developed a mass media campaign and a community-based program to teach pool safety. The program is held in April each year and is called "April Pool's Day." Whether you purchase materials or create your own, remember that your materials must be skill-based, engaging, sound in concept, and be age and audience appropriate.

When determining program **objectives,** you must agree on specific, measurable and attainable objectives that are compatible with your resources, time limits, money, and material and people resources. The objectives should focus on a clear, specific solution to the problem you have identified. Using the baseline data developed in the identification process will help you to determine your objectives and will become an important part of the statistical review in the evaluation phase of your program. Changes indicated in the baseline data will be a good indicator that your program is working, or, in some instances, that a change is necessary.

TARGETING THE APPROPRIATE AUDIENCE

Determine the audience to whom you will target the message. Consider audiences as having three levels: primary, secondary, and tertiary. The primary

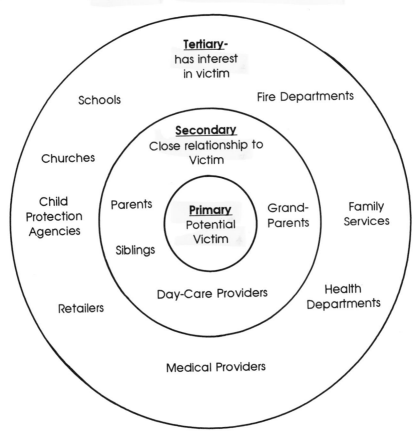

audience is the potential victim or the most likely victim. The secondary audience is closely associated with or in a personal relationship with the primary audience. The tertiary audience consists of persons or organizations with an interest in the primary or secondary audience. Messages may be for primary audiences through secondary audiences. The tertiary audience may provide the resources or medium to get the message to both. Your targeted message may transcend all three levels with specific programs geared toward each.

When you determine your target audience, remember—the message must be age and audience appropriate for the particular group.

MATERIALS REVIEW

During this phase you will review options for program materials:

- Use available materials as is (this may be the least effective in getting coalition buy-in).
- Modify existing materials (better buy-in).
- Create your own materials (this gets more "fingerprints" on the program).

Look for skills, age, and audience appropriateness, make sure materials are attention getting, and don't confuse theme with behavior. The 1991 Fire Prevention week theme was "Fire won't wait, Plan your escape." The theme was "Fire won't wait"; the behavior was "Plan your escape."

Whether you are reviewing materials or creating them, keep the following points in mind:

- The largest print on the document should always be used for the behavior.
- When you create or review a poster or a visual the behavior message should be below the photo. The eye naturally falls below the art.
- The message should start with an action word.
- Messages should be verbally and visually consistent.
- When you review materials, review lots of materials. A good method to use is one that lets you see at a glance which materials you rated best.

Number and list the materials. As you review each one, put the number in the appropriate box. When you are finished you will see readily which are the best materials for your specific program.

There are many materials on the market and a lot of competition for your safety and prevention dollars. As a consumer with limited funds, you must be choosy about what you buy. Before you buy, ask

	Low					High
	1	2	3	4	5	6
Skill based						
Age/Audience Appropriate						
Engaging						
Sound in concept						

- Does the material match or enhance my program objectives?
- Does it contain positive behavioral messages? Does it tell someone what to do?
- Is the material age- and audience-appropriate for my intended audience?
- Is the material culturally sensitive to my target audience?
- Is the reading level appropriate for my intended audience?
- Does the cost of the material justify its expense toward meeting my objectives?
- Is it within my budget?

By asking yourself these simple questions you will be able to determine the most cost-effective, educationally sound materials for your program. You also may wish to evaluate materials you currently have on hand against these questions. Each message should *instruct*. We can no longer afford to waste dollars and people resources on messages that do not offer positive behavioral messages. Such messages as "smoke detectors save lives," be "fire wise," and "don't smoke in bed," do not give people results-oriented skills.

When you design the campaign or program and choose materials and resources, try to develop multiple messages using multiple paths and multiple audiences to address a single problem. As often as possible, identify materials that have multiple uses also. Don't end up with "buyer's remorse" by spending lots of money for something that will not address the fire problem.

PROGRAM EVALUATION

The **evaluation** process takes place throughout the course of a public education campaign or program. Evaluation gives planners, presenters, and public educators information on staffing, scheduling, materials acquisition, audiences, etc., while the program is in progress.

During the evaluation process you may compare new data to baseline data, or to determine the impact of your efforts, you simply might compare pre- and post-test data to provide a reliable measurement of the effectiveness or impact of the program. Another method is to compare death, injury, incident, or property loss data before, during, and after the program. For example, in Minnesota, fire deaths declined by 20 percent from the 1970s to the 1980s. After a two-year smoke detector campaign in 1990 and 1991 fire deaths declined another 36 percent. The NFIC/USFA NFIRS reporting system is useful for making these types of comparisons.

Other tools include post-program questionnaires sent to participants, phone or door-to-door surveys to determine behavior changes, such as installing smoke detectors, completion of an inspection checklist, storage of flammable liquids, etc. Changes in fire risk are also a good measurement tool; determine the number of hazards in each home, before and after. This also can serve as future baseline data.

The secret to developing a campaign or program is to ask:

- What are the issues and problems?
- What materials and methods would I use?
- Who is the target audience?
- Will I use a public information program format or an educational program format?
- How will I evaluate the program?

Support

As a chief officer of the department you have an important role to play in establishing successful intervention strategies; your expressions of support for the program to community officials and community leaders will lend credibility to program needs. Your participation, along with the participation of community leaders, the coalition, and your public education officer, will ensure the program's successful implementation.

As chief, you may want to make a commitment to get the fire safety education goals and mission incorporated into the policies of other agencies in your community. This would ensure that the necessary resources will be available to solve the fire problem of the community by the community.

Programs versus programs

Public education programs can be defined on two levels. The "big P" program is the fire department's overall program effort. The "little p" program is the program aimed at a specific problem. After the little p program data have been collected, the results should be summarized and analyzed. If the stated p program goals were achieved, it is time to return to the P Program and determine the identification and selection process for the next p program. This process will help fire department leadership to determine staffing and funding levels and planning and implementation strategies for future p programs and for the P Program.

This planning process was developed by the National Fire Academy and is taught at many state and local fire schools. It is simple to use, yet helps you to strategically and sequentially attack your local or potential fire problem. If a small community does not have an identified fire problem it must still look at potential fire problems. Repeated all too often across the country is the scenario of a small town with a population of 200 to 1,000 that experiences a tragic fire that pulls the community together, after the fact. In the small town of Remer, Minnesota, on January 1, 1989, ten members of three families, (two adults and eight children) perished in a house fire. There were no smoke detectors present. Because the tragedy affected three families in a small community, there were significant disruptions to schools, businesses and individuals' personal lives. We cannot always rely solely on run numbers to determine the fire problem in our communities. If there are people living there, there is potential for fire every day. It is better for a community to work together before a tragic event than to deal with the pain, tragedy, and emotions after the fact.

DESIGNING THE PROGRAM

In the design phase you simply take all the information you gathered in the identification process and determine which issues you must address, your target audience, and where you will tackle the problem using the "sequence of injury" model. Establish measurable program objectives and choose program materials or make the decision to create your own. You will make your decision on program format, that is, information versus education, or a combination of both. A well-balanced program will include both formats. Remember also that evaluation is a significant part of all public education initiatives, and is an integral part of the program design process.

Thinking long term, we need to begin shifting our educational efforts from strictly reactionary behavior messages (what to do if a fire occurs), to prevention messages that give people knowledge, skills, or both to prevent fires. Both reaction and prevention skills are essential skills; it is through prevention strategies that we will begin to systematically achieve our mission of saving lives and property by preventing fires before they occur.

Most of the determinations prescribed in the design phase will be part of the decision process made by your coalition. In order for all of this to work, the coalition needs a strong leader. This will be an important role of the fire public educator you choose to manage your program initiative.

QUALIFICATIONS OF A PUBLIC EDUCATOR

The qualifications for a public educator can be found in NFPA 1035, *Standard for Professional Qualifications for Public Fire Educator.* NFPA 1035 is a job performance standard and identifies the essential duties and responsibilities of a public educator. The standard is generic and covers what a public educator must **do** as opposed to everything he must **know.** The standard can be used by the fire service or by injury prevention specialists. Specific content is not addressed in the standard.

The standard is written for three levels of educator. A Level I Educator is an individual who has demonstrated the ability to coordinate and deliver existing education programs and information as specified in the standard. Level II individuals have demonstrated the ability to prepare educational programs and information to meet the identified needs as specified in the standard. Level III individuals have demonstrated the ability to create, administer, and evaluate educational programs and information as specified in the standard.

Each level identifies three major job duties: *administrative* duties that deal with recordkeeping, scheduling, budgets, creating educational goals and evaluating subordinates; *planning and development* duties that deal with establishing program priorities through data analysis and local needs, implementing program evaluation, developing funding proposals, planning resources, including staff, materials, and equipment, and evaluations of current and future trends; and, *education* duties that deal with selecting and presenting programs and materials, methodology, materials development, development or adaptation of lesson plans to fit local needs and audiences, creating original resource materials, and creating training programs for other public educators.

In many departments the individual assigned to the public education functions will operate at all levels. It is important for this individual to be able to interact with fire department and community leaders, and to have good verbal, written, and organizational skills. Such individuals also must have solid educational and classroom skills beyond content knowledge. The public educator is, in many cases, your link with the public, someone who represents you and the department's goals and objectives. This person must be credible as well as have specialized training skills in curriculum development and presentation.

The qualifications should not be taken lightly and individuals for this position should be chosen with these skills in mind.

FUNDING

Funding is another critical factor in the success of your public education efforts. Fire department budgets do not always include funding for a comprehensive public education effort, therefore, fundraising is essential. Again, this is where your coalition of community leaders and volunteers can be an integral part of the funding process.

Success in your efforts depends on several key elements. Credibility, believability, and visibility are the leading factors in "success."

Donors must believe:

- That a problem or potential problem exists;
- That the problem will have a *personal* effect on them or on the community;
- That there is a solution to the problem;
- That the organization you represent has the solution, a track record and a network to influence the solution; and
- That the organization has the accountability to manage the process.

Visibility must be established beyond the response efforts of the fire department. The department and its programs must be visible within the community and to community leaders. Find out who the prospects are and get leaders in the fire department and the coalition to open their doors. Or, you could simply invite the mayor, police chief, community leaders, business leaders, or volunteer leaders to an informal breakfast or lunch meeting to explain that they have been identified as potential investors in the "wellness of the community" by providing funding or in-kind support to solve the fire or injury problem.

You must have a specific plan and have done your homework, i.e., identified the specific goals and scope of your program. The scope of your project should include the fundraising goals and objectives based on the problem(s). List the types of services that will be provided to solve the problem. Identify sites, occasions, or both, for program presentation or participation. You also must define the length of the program; no project is forever. Each one should have a beginning and an end. Also identify agencies, groups, or individuals that have tie-ins with the program.

Fundraising is, in part, resource raising. To identify your needs, use the following process. From your goals and objectives and proposed program design determine your material or resource needs. Define the elements of your materials. For example, if you identified a brochure as your resource piece you need to establish: quantity needed; format (single-page, two-sided, trifold, etc.); type of paper (glossy, dull); size; single or multi-color; and artwork or layout work needed. After these decisions have been made, develop a matrix like the one below to help you determine needs based on the above criteria.

Product: Brochure

Need: 15,000, tri-fold, glossy 8.5 × 14, four-color, with photo and artwork

NEED	HAVE	ACQUIRE
Paper/glossy Heavy wt. 70 lb. 8.5″ x 14″ Qty 15,000 $300.00	7,000 sheets in basement $140.00	8,000 sheets $160.00
Printer four-color fold $500.00		$500.00
Graphic artwork 10 hours @ $40 each = $400.00	Committee member donated 5 hours $200.00	5 hours $200.00
Photographer 16 hrs @ $20 = $800.00	Use FD Photographer $800.00	
Typesetter 4 hours @ $25 = $100.00		4 hours $100.00
		This total represents investment opportunities
Total $2,100.00	$1,140.00	$960.00

This process should be used through the distribution and delivery of the material. It will give you a worksheet for funding and planning a budget for the entire program. Use this on all phases of the program and always assign a dollar value to everything, including donated work, to demonstrate the total value of the program.

When you do fundraising, use the product worksheet to show potential donors the specific needs, whether services or dollars. Additionally, most companies would rather be a partner in a project than fund it solely. The product form also can be adapted to your entire program need and would include staff costs and salaries, and teacher costs and salaries. Include all costs and needs of the program. After going through this process you also may discover that the scope of your program may be too large and you will have to re-evaluate your scope, goals, and objectives. There is nothing wrong with solving a problem using the smaller bite process. After all, the only way to eat a chocolate elephant is one bite at a time.

Another aspect to consider in fundraising is "donor" benefits. People give for many reasons: out of a sense of compassion or altruism, for tax deductions, to build up self-esteem, and to get visibility. Your job is to give them a multitude of reasons to give, and adapt your approach to people based on why they would give. Find out who knows whom, and what resources they can provide. Ask for in-kind contributions first, then cash. If you are going to pursue fund-raising events, evaluate giving in your community. Learn how the community views itself and select events that are appropriate for the community.

If you develop a major program that requires lots of resources you may wish to consider other sources, for example, government grants, or private corporate or independent foundations. These resources generally fund projects over $100,000. If you use this route for funds, follow the directions and guidelines for the grant procedure "to the letter" to ensure that you are not eliminated for a minor technicality; always include an executive summary whether it is requested or not.

Remember, community involvement usually generates more resources and investment in your project. After all, the fire and burn problem belongs to the entire community.

OTHER CONSIDERATIONS IN PUBLIC EDUCATION EFFORTS

Solving the fire problem in the U.S. will require every resource available. One of the most underused yet effective resources is the school system. Yes, we go there with our apparatus and visit the kindergarten and perhaps the third or fifth graders, but we miss the real benefits of using the schools. There have been 22 key fire safety behaviors identified as the minimum knowledge level a person needs in order to be fire safe. When we spend our 30 minutes to an hour in the schools once or twice a year, we cannot possibly address all the safety messages needed to prevent or survive a fire.

By establishing a school curriculum, which teachers who have a captive audience for seven hours a day and are experts on the developmental stages and learning characteristics of children can use, we can ensure that the children are receiving the safety skills for life. Remember, cognitive research says that you need to see or do something 25 to 30 times to make it a habit. Teachers in a school setting can repeat the messages to ensure that the information is retained and is sequential with other messages the children must know.

If you are familiar with Bloom's Taxonomy, you will recall that there are six levels of cognitive learning:

1. Knowledge.
2. Comprehension.
3. Application.
4. Analysis.
5. Synthesis.
6. Evaluation.

For the most part the fire service has a limited amount of time to spend with students. After presenting the Stop, Drop, and Roll message to students, have you ever come back and asked children what they should do if the smoke detector sounds an alarm? Most of the time you'll get the answer Stop, Drop and Roll. The child is only at the **knowledge** level of repeating information word for word.

For a message to reach students at the **application** level, they must learn the *knowledge*, i.e., be able to repeat it back, *comprehend* the knowledge, i.e., understand its meaning, and *apply* the knowledge or skill, i.e., behave properly when a smoke detector operates or their clothing catches fire.

The significance of a teacher-based curriculum is that the teacher teaches the students the content and fire personnel reinforce the message when they visit the classroom. It is easy for teachers to learn fire safety content, after all, they often are called on to teach new subjects; therefore, they can use their teaching skills to teach the safety messages.

There are several excellent curriculums that have been tested and found to be educationally sound and age-group specific. NFPA's Learn Not To Burn Curriculum (LNTB), activity resource books, and preschool programs are being used in approximately 49,000 schools nationwide. As great as that may sound, it only represents approximately five percent of the schools in America. The curriculum consists of three levels: level I is for kindergarten through second grade, level II is for the third through fifth grades, and level III is sixth to eighth graders. The behaviors are the same throughout the curriculum, but reach higher levels of sophistication as the level increases.

The LNTB Resource Activity books are for kindergarteners through third graders and provide a multitude of worksheets and activities for school and home; they copy well and are very inexpensive and easy to use. Likewise, the preschool program for three- to five-year-olds deals with eight specific behaviors and incorporates songs and activities to teach the messages.

Another educationally sound curriculum was developed by the Pan Education Institute of Independence, Missouri. Project Life, as it is called, uses two furry creatures called fire ferrets to teach the messages. Included in the kit are a teacher's manual, student manuals, videos, puppets, and children's fire stories.

Both curriculums come with evaluation instruments and content information for teachers. The specific behavioral messages have listed outcomes. Additionally, the behaviors can be integrated into other subject areas such as math, science, language arts, physical education, music, art, etc. The subject may be language arts, but the message is fire.

There are two other specialty curriculums of interest. One is the "Smoke Detectives" curriculum developed by State Farm Insurance. The curriculum, which comes with lesson guides and a video, has message content on smoke detectors and exiting procedures for homes.

The second is the Fireproof Children© curriculum. It was developed by

National Fire Services Support Services, Inc. which is a group that includes two mental health professionals and two fire investigators. The curriculum, which addresses the issues of children and fire play, is an intervention program that includes activities, songs, and plays. The curriculum is an excellent tool as a resource and an educational program for teachers and students. (FIREPROOF CHILDREN also includes a manual and videocassette program for fire departments, enabling the departments to institute and implement the intervention program.)

When you have the schools involved in the teaching process you double, maybe even triple your efforts. Children represent only about 16 percent of the population we must reach, and we have many other people in the community to educate. Remember fire safety education is a lifelong process. By getting the schools involved in teaching the content and behaviors we can focus on addressing other identified high-risk issues and populations such as the elderly, the economically disadvantaged, or ethnic groups that need special attention. There is so much to do, yet so little time to do it all.

The significance of enlisting as many people as possible in the community, from the high-risk groups, to the elderly, parents and the business community, cannot be stressed enough. If you are serious about solving the problem, you

Chippewa Native American children learn about smoke detectors at a safety program designed for families moving into new homes on the reservation. The event lasted all day and each member of the family attended before moving into their new home.

must step back and take a serious look at what you are doing and what needs to be done. A fire department that only fights fires is not serving the community to the fullest. To save lives and property we must protect people through code enforcement and public education efforts as well. The day of the one-service fire department no longer exists. We must compete for money, visibility and our place in the community. We are the leaders, the protectors, and the safety providers for our community.

CONCLUSION

Public education is a function that takes time and thought. Data must be used to focus your efforts on the real or potential problems that exist in your community. Messages must be both skill specific to educate people on what to do to survive a fire, or how to prevent a fire from occurring, and age and audience appropriate.

There is a tremendous amount of existing material, some good, some not so good. Take the time to evaluate your resource materials and become a wise consumer. Remember, people spend three to five seconds looking at a visual, so make your point and make it the focus of the resource.

While public education should be part of every fire department's functions, not everyone is a public educator. Finding the right person to lead your public education efforts is a major consideration. A strong leader, with skills in educational methodology and knowledge of fire, is the most likely candidate. Don't assume that this rules out firefighters, quite the contrary; they can be and often are excellent at presenting information to the public. The point is that firefighters need to be trained to teach fire safety messages just as they are trained to fight fires. This training is a function of the public educator.

The public educator may not always be a full-time staff member; he might in fact be a volunteer in your department or from the community. There are "spark plugs" in every department and in every community willing to work on safety education efforts. It is your job to seek them out, nurture them, and to support them in your public education efforts.

Evaluation is a key element in every little p and big P program. You need to be able to measure the effectiveness of your efforts and document the outcomes. Do this by establishing measurable program objectives. Documentation is essential for future funding and support for your programs.

The methods of the past are not necessarily the best methods for the future. As you begin to focus on specific issues, high-risk behaviors and high-risk populations, you must evaluate your methodologies and seek help from the experts who work with these people on a daily basis. To reach high-risk populations such as low-income families, the elderly, and minority populations today requires a completely different approach from what was used to reach middle-class suburban Americans yesterday. As your fire problems change so should your strategies. Stay as current on the needs of the community as you do with the needs of technology and training of your firefighters.

The best way to start any program or effort is to start—today. Do not delay because the potential for a tragic fire loss in your community could be right around the corner. Each step you take puts you one step closer to a fire-safe community and one step farther from a tragedy. Bring your community together to *solve* the problem, not to *mourn* the tragedy.

28

Arson Detection & Investigation

CHARLES G. KING

*A*LTHOUGH THE FIRE CHIEF's primary responsibilities are to suppress fires and save lives and property, it has become increasingly apparent that fire officers who have been trained to recognize a suspicious fire are able to provide invaluable assistance to the arson investigator. The more the fire officer knows about identifying and preserving evidence, protecting and maintaining a fire scene, and courtroom demeanor, the better equipped he is to objectively provide the facts necessary for the arrest, prosecution, and conviction of an arsonist.

In addition to criminal cases that result from the commission of the crime of arson, the fire officer today also has to be aware of the dramatic increase in civil litigation. Because accidental fires are often said to have been caused by products alleged to have been poorly designed or defective, fire personnel are called upon to testify in civil cases as well.

The purpose of this chapter is to explain to fire chiefs and Incident Commanders how to correctly identify a suspicious fire, and how to initiate a proper chain of events that will support the work of the fire investigator. This means not only widening your body of knowledge to include evidence that an arson may have occurred, but also increasing your awareness of the limitations of your knowledge so that unnecessary criminal or civil litigation does not result from a "wrong call."

In dealing with arson investigators, whether they are city or state fire marshals, state police, or from the private sector, the fire officer steps outside the area of fire suppression and prevention and into the realm of fire investigation. This is an exciting and challenging field, one that demands great responsibility and which requires trained and experienced personnel. Because of the very specific nature of the training required to perform the tasks of the fire investigator, it should be stated clearly that in no way, shape, or form should the suppression officer be involved in fire investigation per se.

Regardless of his private thoughts about where or how a fire may have started, carelessly written or spoken words from a firefighter about the "cause" of a fire can result in the loss of a criminal case that otherwise might have been prosecuted successfully, or in the arrest of an individual innocent of any crime, or, in the instance of civil litigation, the involvement of non-culpable individuals or organizations in multimillion-dollar lawsuits.

Before getting into the specifics of how to determine whether a fire is suspicious, it is necessary to stress the importance of that little slot on your fire incident report that says "Cause of Fire."

It is commonly known that the words "arson" or "suspicious" usually will result in a criminal investigation by fire marshals or authorized investigators. It is imperative, though, that firefighting personnel realize that a non-suspicious fire with a carelessly attributed "Cause" entered on the incident report can have ramifications that involve dozens of people and millions of dollars. It is equally important to understand that a suspicious fire called "accidental" can have disastrous results.

In a recent product liability case, a young man and woman were found dead in the front and back seats, respectively, of an American-built automobile. The car had been burned. The bodies had been burned, and there were obvious indications of foul play (drug use by the victims, presence of an accelerant, unidentified male in the vehicle prior to the fire). However, investigators at the fire scene, who had scant knowledge of fire analysis, decided that the cause of the fire was a mechanical defect in the engine compartment. As a result of this "call," the criminal investigation was called off; a lawsuit was initiated against the car company for many millions of dollars; enormous court costs, attorney and expert-witness fees were incurred; and the manufacturer was falsely accused of having produced a defective product. Years later, the company that produced the car was exonerated in a jury trial.

But because of that hastily made determination by an unqualified investigator, not only was there a tremendous waste of time, money, and resources, there is also a murderer who has never been apprehended, for a crime that was never called a crime.

Rule of thumb: Stick to your area of expertise.

Because of the recent explosion in fire-related civil litigation which can involve anything from product liability lawsuits to personal injury lawsuits, it is imperative that we recognize how a fire incident report can be used, justly or unjustly, in the long term.

Phrases such as "the product malfunctioned" or "the product was defective" should be eliminated from your vocabularies when you prepare incident reports. Fire chiefs and fire officers are not product designers, engineers, metallurgists, etc.

When, as fire suppression officers, we say that the fire started in the engine compartment of a car, we have the experience, and we can provide the facts, to support this opinion. But when we state that the carburetor or the throttle body injector was defective, and thus caused the fire, then we're out of our league. Similarly, if we say that the area of origin is the kitchen at a point where the refrigerator was located, we're on safe ground. But if we expand our opinion to designate the refrigerator's compressor as the cause of the fire, we are once again in an area where we don't belong.

Incident commanders have a compulsive need to fill in the box labeled "Cause of Fire" *with* a cause, even if they don't know one. Many times, however, it is appropriate to check "Undetermined" as the cause. Or, to rephrase that, If you don't know, don't say.

Before an arson investigator arrives at a fire scene, the Incident Commander (IC) is the officer in charge, and it is the IC who alerts the investigator to "come and look at this one"; who initiates an investigation; and who, in most cases, fills in the box labeled "Cause and Origin."

What does "cause and origin" mean? Why has it become a catch phrase to signify "everything you have always wanted to know about fire investigation"? If we know the cause of the fire, does that imply that the origin is obvious? Or is the reverse closer to the truth?

Although the investigation of fires has conventionally been referred to as "cause and origin," it is more appropriate to refer to it as "origin and cause." Why? Because we have to know *where* a fire started before we can determine *how* it started.

As ICs and fire officers, you already have a working knowledge of many of the variables that are important to the fire investigator. In origin and cause investigations this knowledge will be of inestimable value because the more familiar you are with the "normal" course of a fire, the easier it is for you to recognize the indicators of a fire that is burning, or has burned, in a manner contrary to what falls within the normal range.

We know, for example, that the way fire usually burns is "up and out." Toss a lighted match into a kitchen wastebasket. After the resulting fire has

Figure 28-1.

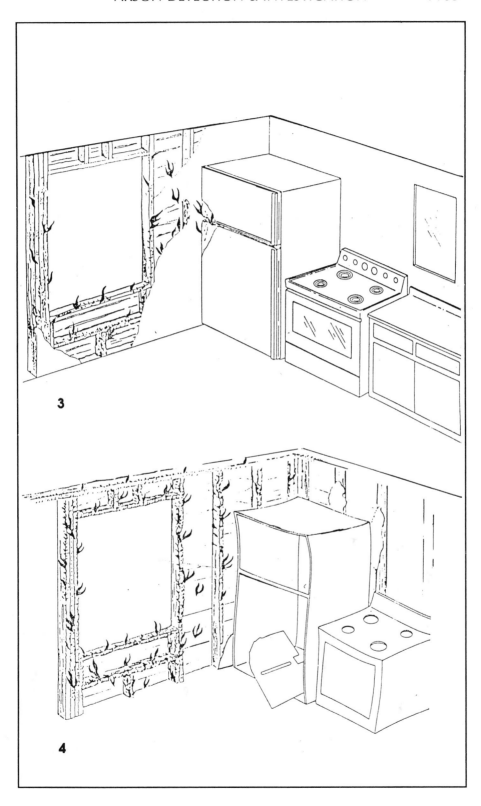

3

4

been extinguished, there will be an unmistakable "V" pattern burned into the paneling that clearly and simply illustrates the natural path and pattern of fire. The lowest point of burning and the lowest point of the "V" will be the bottom of the wastebasket. In fact, the wastebasket itself may be gone. Whatever combustibles were in it will have been partially or totally consumed. From the bottom of the wastebasket, the fire will have burned "up and out." (Figures 28-1 to 28-4).

No matter what has burned—a grease-filled frying pan left on an open flame, a frayed extension cord trampled once too often by foot traffic, an unattended iron left on a silk blouse, or a cigarette smoldering between the cushions of a favorite chair—what we expect to see when we respond to the fire is that it consumed combustibles *above* the point at which it originated.

Therefore, when a fire doesn't burn in the "normal" manner, our antennas go up. Why is there a big, charred hole in the middle of the floor? Why does the fire appear to have burned downward, toward the basement? Why is there an odor of accelerants at the fire scene? What is this burn pattern in the shape of a puddle at the bottom of the stairs? Why did the room (or house or building) become fully involved so rapidly even though the response time to the fire alarm was immediate? Why is such an inordinate quantity of combustibles laid out in an apparent "trail" from place to place?

As fire officers, your professional life is fire. Although thinking in terms of suppression and prevention is as basic to you as breathing, considering the needs of the fire investigator is not a part of your job description, but preserving the scene so that the fire investigator can *do* the fire investigation **should** be part of your job description.

Before a fire can be recognized as suspicious, we first must know what to look for at a fire scene. As an Incident Commander, you exercise control of your firefighting forces while they operate at the fire scene. Radio communications are good, and you know where everyone is and what they are doing.

After extinguishment and during overhaul, you should exercise the same control and command that you did during the fire, in a hands-on operation that directs your fire personnel to what should be thrown out, what should be preserved, and how.

PRESERVING THE FIRE SCENE AND TAKING SAMPLES

At the point in time when you decide that there is something suspicious about the fire you are fighting, you will request the response of a fire investigation team. Most fire departments have arson units which can respond to the scene immediately. In rural areas, this responsibility can be split or shared between the State Police, and county fire coordinators, or among individual firefighters who have attended special courses in how to assist with arson investigation. In this age of budget cuts, the arson investigation unit is often the last to be created and the first to be cut. Since the need to investigate fires is constant, it is often wise to send interested and motivated members of your department to as many fire investigation seminars or courses as possible. This investment in time and money pays off in the long run in terms of deterrence: arsonists are identified and prosecuted. It is your responsibility to find out who is in charge of fire investigation in your area.

Whether a fire investigator responds immediately to your call or at a later time, the fire scene must be controlled continuously by either the fire department or the police department. From a legal standpoint, it is extremely important to preserve evidence and to ensure the security of the fire scene. This means denying access to *everyone,* including the owner of the building. In many jurisdictions, this requirement is satisfied simply by leaving fire or police personnel on the premises, to secure the scene. If the fire department relinquishes control of the fire scene, the arson investigators are not permitted back on the premises without written permission from the owner or a search warrant from the court.

To assist the arson investigators with their investigation, try, as much as possible, to preserve the area of origin in its original condition. If the furnishings of a room absolutely must be discarded, keep this debris in a separate area. It often can be put back into the room if the arson investigator needs to reconstruct the scene.

The accelerant most often used to commit arson is gasoline. Your nose is the best hydrocarbon detector in the world. If you smell gasoline, you can be sure it's there.

Something to keep in mind about scene preservation is that the fire investigator may have to take samples of materials to send to a laboratory for analysis. Despite the efficiency of the nose, its "findings" aren't admissible in court.

Consider the fire investigator's needs in your selection and use of overhauling streams. Your job, of course, is extinguishment. But whenever preservation of the scene doesn't interfere with that job, be as careful as you can not to wash away the evidence.

If the fire investigator suspects that a flammable liquid may have been poured on the flooring in a room, he will want to look in low areas where an accelerant could have collected for samples to send to the lab. This would include floor drains or traps. If he thinks the accelerant may have been sprayed or tossed around the area, he also will check nearby absorbent materials for flammable liquid residue. He will try to get both samples that contain the accelerant, and ones that do *not,* the first as evidence of arson, the second as control samples. When he collects samples of burned flooring or beams, the fire investigator will take samples of the less-burned areas rather than the more heavily charred ones, because the less-burned areas are more likely to have retained traces of the accelerant.

Despite everyone's best efforts, test results often come back negative, even when we are certain that an accelerant was used. There are many reasons for this: the accelerant was consumed in the fire; the water used in firefighting operations washed the accelerant away; or the laboratory which tested the sample had inadequate facilities or personnel.

WHERE TO LOOK FOR EVIDENCE OF ARSON

As discussed earlier, before we can determine *how* a fire started, we have to know *where* it started. Origin first. Then cause. And it is after the fire has been suppressed that we usually begin our origin and cause investigation.

This brings us to the main differences in operational concerns of the firefighter and the fire investigator. For one thing, their perspectives are as far apart as the ceiling is from the floor. We know fire burns up, so firefighters usually pull down ceilings and look for fire extension *above* the fire.

Fire investigators, on the other hand, look downward for the *lowest* point of burning. Debris from ceilings and walls often covers and shields evidence on the floor, but after the debris is carefully removed, indications of low burning often will appear. Cleaning out an area of origin to look for evidence of the fire's real cause is a tough job, but discovering a clear and distinct burn pattern is one of the rewards for the fire investigator.

Burn Patterns

Although burn patterns are what remain in the debris at a fire scene, it is possible to get useful information about a fire that is still in progress. If it is burning in an unusual manner (too hot, too fast, or with uncharacteristic flames) and your experience tells you that "something is wrong," call in the fire investigator while the fire is still in progress; this enables him to get even more information for his investigation.

Burn patterns are unique. The trained fire investigator can often "read" in the debris the difference between an accidental fire and one that was set deliberately. The more time you spend with a fire investigator who explains these differences to you, the easier it will be for you to know *when* a burn pattern is unusual, and when to call in the expert.

Multiple points of origin should be at the top of your "list of things to look for" at a fire scene. If you find two fires in the same room that aren't connected, or fires in separate rooms or areas with no path or pattern of fire between them, these are very clear signs that you may seriously suspect arson.

Since fire burns "up and out," if you have a lateral burn pattern along a significant horizontal expanse of wall or baseboard, this, too, is an indication that a flammable liquid may have been used.

Pour or spill patterns usually "pool" at the lowest point of the surface on which they've been poured (Figure 28-5). If this is on the floor or along a baseboard, the burning may be on the underside of the floorboards or beams, and visible from the basement or the floor below (Figure 28-6). Often, too, you may find indications of "weeping" on the floor joists (Figure 28-7). This "weeping" takes the form of a burn pattern on the wood which replicates the dripping liquid (Figure 28-8).

If you locate a burn pattern that indicates that fire seems to have adhered to a vertical surface, what you may be looking at is the result of an incendiary device such as a Molotov cocktail. Such a device combines an accelerant with fuel oil or soap flakes; after ignition, the flaming mix sticks to almost anything on which it lands.

Should you come upon any of the burn patterns mentioned above, or any flame, char, or early collapse of the structure not easily explained by your experience and knowledge of how fires burn, call for an expert investigation. If the fire doesn't "feel" right, it probably isn't. As the Incident Commander, it's your job to recognize **when** to ask. It's the fire investigator's job to **find** the answers.

General Overview of Fire Premises

Although most of the principles discussed so far refer to fires that occur in all types of premises, there are certain characteristics of fires in commercial buildings which, once you are aware of them, can be of particular interest to the fire investigator.

Questions you can ask to assist fire investigators with commercial building fires include:

* Is there a sprinkler system?
* Did it work? If not, why not?
* Were the system supply valves tampered with?
* Was there any water in the sprinkler pipes in the first place? (While we're on the subject of sprinkler systems, when is the last time you looked to make sure that sprinkler heads were indeed in place overhead after a fire? An accelerated fire can overcome a sprinkler system.)
* If the sprinkler sends a signal to a central station, was it transmitted or bypassed?
* Does the building have a burglar alarm system? Was it operating on arrival? Did your forcible entry activities cause it to operate?
* Were there obvious items missing from the buildings. Stock? Pictures on desks? Trophies? Calculators or computers? Books on shelves?
* Was there forced entry?

Questioning the owners of a building is best left to trained investigators,

Accelerant seeped into wood surface of table, and flames burned downward, leaving unmistakable flammable liquid burn pattern.

Horizontal burning along baseboards, and hole burned through floor where flammable liquid had been poured.

Heavy attack of flames on flooring at location where flammable liquid was poured. Note charring under floor, where the accelerant has seeped through floorboards and burned downward into cross beam.

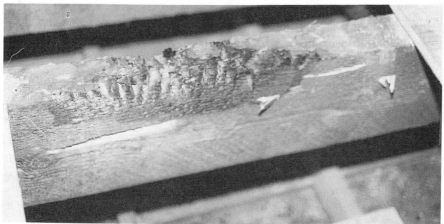

"Weeping" burn patterns on cross beams where flammable liquid has seeped under floor boards, and flames consumed the accelerant in a downward paths.

but many of your observations can and should be passed on. For example, was the owner already present when the fire apparatus arrived? Had he been on the premises prior to the fire? Did he arrive during firefighting operations? Did he seem nervous? Was he argumentative? Did he in any way appear to be interfering with (inhibiting) fire operations? Was he reluctant or unwilling to answer questions? Was his insurance agent at the fire before *you* got there?

Get the name, address and phone number of the person who turned in the alarm, and any person who discovered the fire. Often, they are the same individual, and are usually eager to talk to the firefighters about what they saw. This is particularly important when an incendiary fire is started by a "vanity firesetter," a type of arsonist who not only "discovers" the fire and calls in the alarm, but usually is "courageously" attempting to extinguish the fire when the apparatus arrives.

Also, whenever possible, have one of your fire personnel get the license plate numbers of vehicles on the street. The owners of these vehicles are potential witnesses or suspects, and when the fire investigators get there the vehicles could be gone.

Locating the Point of Origin

In doing your sizeup, you notice that most of the fire is coming from the rear bedroom. After the fire has been extinguished, you enter the house and see little damage as you go down the hall. As you continue you observe smoke damage and, perhaps, a mid-line, horizontal heat pattern that leaves the lower wall relatively clean, but covers the upper wall with a film of dark soot. You note a high char pattern on the door frame leading into the rear bedroom, and that the bedroom itself is gutted. This is most likely the area of origin of the fire, where you first saw the flames during your sizeup.

Now that you are at the area of origin, look for the lowest point of burning. Many times, there is a "V" pattern emanating from the point of origin, sometimes not. "Vs" come in many shapes and sizes, depending on what burned and what was in its path, but generally speaking, the lowest point of burning is where the cause is or was. We have all seen heavy drapes fall onto the floor, giving the appearance of two separate fires under the windows. But drapes in the *middle* of the floor! Or clothing *in* the bathtub!

Multiple fires, accelerants, trailers, incendiary devices and objects burning in an atypical way are all obvious reasons to call in a fire investigator.

ACCIDENTAL FIRES

What about accidental fires? If an occupant is careless and causes a fire, he or she may be under the impression that the insurance company will not pay for the damage, and will be quite adamant that the refrigerator, stove, or air conditioner blew up. If the same carelessness resulted in the injury or death of a loved one, the occupant's feelings of guilt at having caused the fire may make the protestations even more vehement.

If you take these witness statements at face value and put them down as the cause of the fire, the end result may well be a lawsuit against the manufacturer of the refrigerator stove, microwave, or whatever, claiming that the fire was caused by a product defect. Thousands of dollars could be spent proving or defending an allegation that lacked substance and should never have been brought to court in the first place.

No matter where the area of origin is, and no matter what the occupant tells you, the fire investigator must determine the cause of the fire based on burn patterns alone. When there are not enough burn patterns to allow the investigator to reach a conclusion about origin and cause, then regardless of what the witnesses have said, "Undetermined" has to be what the investigator lists as his "cause." If, on the other hand, the burn patterns are consistent with witness statements, but the investigator doesn't feel he has enough to determine a cause for the fire, he may feel he can legitimately attribute a "Probable Cause" for the fire.

Burn patterns, however, are not probabilities. They are facts. How the facts are interpreted depends on the experience, ability, knowledge, talent, and integrity of the fire investigator. In an instance where an appliance really did cause a fire, what kinds of evidence would the fire investigator look for in the debris that might lead to that conclusion?

- He sees beading on the electrical cord leading from the toaster. Fact.
- He sees charred wood on the counter in the protected area underneath the toaster. Fact.
- He sees that the bottom shelf of the cabinet over the toaster has burned through completely. Fact.
- He notes that the worst burning in the house is in the kitchen, and that the worst burning in the kitchen is on the counter where the toaster was located. Fact.
- He discovers that the lever of the toaster is in the ON position, where it has been "frozen" by the fire. Fact.

It is after the fire investigator has finished his inspection of the scene that the statements of the occupants become relevant. For example, Mrs. Smith reveals that at 4:00 a.m., she got up to make herself an English muffin, depressed the lever on the toaster, but then became so sleepy that she went back to bed without taking the muffin out of the toaster and without unplugging it. At *that* point, after the fire investigator has already analyzed the burn patterns and come to a preliminary conclusion, your witness statement *then* becomes corroborative evidence.

When you have to check the box attributing the "Cause" of the fire, remember to limit your "call" to what you know, not to what you have been told or to conjecture. Speculation leads to frivolous lawsuits.

When you have good reason to believe that an appliance is involved, stay within your area of expertise. It's perfectly reasonable to say that the area of origin was the kitchen, and that the point of origin was *where* a toaster or refrigerator or coffee pot was located. But once you attribute a specific cause, such as a defect or malfunction in the heater coil or defrost timer or compressor, you're in over your head, and you may be questioned technically in a court of law about an opinion that you cannot substantiate.

FIRE SCENE FATALITIES

With respect to fire investigation, there are few things more important than knowing how to handle a fatality at a fire scene. If the fire was set intentionally the crime is arson homicide. In addition to overseeing and directing firefighting activities, you now have to deal with police personnel and fire investigators, as well as insurance companies and, perhaps, private consultants.

Fire department personnel are not trained in crime scene investigation. If someone had been shot and was lying in the middle of the floor and there were no fire, your people probably wouldn't touch anything, and you'd know enough to have them rope off the area until the forensic team arrived. That's easy. But if there's a fire, the body often is discovered during overhaul operations. When this happens, everything should stop, like a freeze frame on a movie. From that point on, only the most minimal activities should take place.

As a general rule, we can state that at an ordinary house fire without massive destruction or collapse, where a body is found is the location at which the person died. Since a person's natural inclination is to flee fire, you want to determine if that's what the victim was trying to do. If a victim is not found in a position that suggests an attempt to escape, you must ask yourself why. Were there building code violations, such as barred windows or blocked exits? Was it an illegal occupancy? Did it lack a secondary means of egress, or smoke alarms, sprinkler systems, etc.? If you find a wheelchair, crutches, or a walker, consider that the person may have had a condition that prevented an escape.

Did you notice medication by the bedside? Could the cause of death have been suicide? Did you look for a note? The presence of beer cans or liquor bottles also could be a factor. Was it careless handling of smoking materials and was alcohol involved? Remember, careless handling of smoking materials involves two things—a match and a cigarette—that represents two separate ignition sources. What about previous fires at the same location? Did you have someone check your fire department's records?

A fatality at a fire leaves all fire personnel with a sense of loss, and in some ways, of failure, no matter how impossible the odds. There is always an uneasy silence at the scene of a fire death and an urgency to put the body in a body bag and take it away. These feelings of urgency can hamper the thoroughness of the investigation.

The victim should be left exactly where found. A cover can be placed carefully over the body to prevent water and debris from falling on it. Minimize the use of water. If a body has been exposed to fire, it is usually found in a pugilistic position. Coagulation of the muscles due to heat causes contraction of the muscle fibres with resultant flexion of the limbs. Thus, the upper extremities assume a position suggestive of a boxer holding his hands up in front of him. Assumption of the pugilistic attitude is unrelated to whether the individual was alive or dead prior to the fire.

It is also not uncommon to find that the body has been charred and singed. Most often charring of a body occurs after death. Blistering of the skin does not indicate that the deceased was alive at the time the burns were suffered. The skin may have split; there may be long-bone fractures; the skull may have exploded. You may observe a protruding tongue, loss of tissue, small steam blisters, and singed blisters filled with fluid. Soot in the mouth and nostrils generally means that the victim was alive at the time of the fire and inhaled the products of combustion; a cherry-red appearance is synonymous with carbon monoxide poisoning.

At a catastrophe where there are multiple fatalities, all victims and body parts should be left in the same position where they were found. Where possible, the body parts should be numbered consecutively to help the medical examiners to relate the parts to each other and to interpret and identify them during autopsies.

In most large cities, there are teams of homicide investigators, crime scene units, and medical examiners whose efforts make thorough investigation easier. Handling the body itself or the area where a crime was possibly committed, should be left to these experts. As a chief officer, you must protect, record, and recall the fire scene as much as possible to contribute to the effectiveness of the subsequent fire investigation.

No one likes this kind of work, but your efforts could make the difference in whether a homicide is detected or goes unnoticed and unsolved.

Conclusion

As you can see, origin and cause investigation has many faces. Using your knowledge, training, and professional skills both during and after the fire can be the factor that makes what initially is treated as an accidental fire be treated as an arson instead. It was after *you* noticed the inexplicable low burning where there were no apparent combustibles; after *you* noticed the two separate and distinct areas of origin of the fire, with no connecting burn pattern in between; after *you* smelled gasoline on arrival; after *you* noticed that there had been forced entry prior to the arrival of the apparatus; and, after *you*, suspicious that there was more there than met the eye, called in the trained fire experts to do a comprehensive investigation of the fire.

One way to keep your observations or those of your personnel objective is to put them in the form of a report. Reports are less necessary in areas where arson investigation units can respond rapidly, and more necessary where arson investigators are few and far between. As fire chief, it is your job to designate responsibility for filling out this report, or, possibly, to fill it out yourself, depending on the size of your department.

ARSON IDENTIFICATION REPORT

The responsibility for the preparation and submission of a fire report should belong to the officer in charge of the first hoseline in the initial attack on the fire, usually the first-due engine company officer. (See the sample report form located at the end of this chapter).

The logic behind assigning responsibility to this officer is that he is the first link in the chain of fire suppression, and therefore also in fire detection. This doesn't mean that all observations at the fire scene are exclusively this officer's responsibility, but that all input should be channeled to and through this individual.

In most firefighting units, it is the responsibility of the ladder company to gain entry, vent the fire, and examine the structure. Therefore, the ladder company officer should be required to report all pertinent facts to the first-due engine company officer. This would include whether or not the firefighters had to force entry into the building, how entry was made, and by whom, any unusual fire behavior, odors, floor conditions, abnormal fire extensions to internal exposures, etc.

Additional companies and special units that respond to the scene also would be responsible for reporting anything and everything that they think might indicate that they are fighting a suspicious fire.

There are six major elements of early and successful detection of arson:

1. Observation of the nature and extent of the fire.
2. Observation of weather conditions.
3. Observation of people and vehicles.
4. written record of how entry was made and by whom.
5. observation of the building interior.
6. preservation of evidence.

Familiarizing yourself with all of these elements, and making your personnel aware of them will translate to information that the fire investigator will ask for and use.

1. Observation of the nature and extent of the fire

After arriving at the fire scene, it is the engine company officer's job to assess the location and extent of the fire in order to select and position the first hoseline. He should be looking at *this* area, where the first handline was stretched when conducting an investigation after the fire is under control. It could be the area of origin.

While positioning the first hoseline, the engine company officer's total concentration is on reaching and extinguishing the fire. However, at the same time, the officer should be trained to take a "mental photograph" of how the scene looked on arrival, so that he can refer to it later when filling out the arson detection report. While filling out this report, the company officer also can check his own fire scene observations against those of the other company personnel. Among the questions that should be asked are:

- What is burning, and where?
- What color are the flames?
- Do you detect any significant combustion byproducts?
- How is the fire spreading, at what speed, and in what direction?
- Does the fire seem to be coming from two or more separate and distinct locations?
- Are there any perceptible odors such as ozone, kerosene, rubber, gasoline, wood, etc.?

It isn't essential that firefighters routinely record the color of smoke, because smoke color has less informational value today than it did years ago, before the invention and use of synthetic products. Most household items now are made of petroleum-based products and polyvinyl chloride, which produce the same color smoke as hydrocarbon-based accelerants.

2. Observation of weather conditions

Rapid fire spread does not necessarily indicate the use of an accelerant, because very strong wind can spread a fire quickly. On the other hand, since exposure to heavy rain will normally cause a fire to "bank down," if you see a fire that does not "bank down" when subjected to rainy weather, this uncharacteristic behavior might indicate the presence of an accelerant. Therefore, knowledge of weather conditions and how they affect burning enhances our understanding and interpretation of how fire burns.

The engine company officer should record all relevant data about the weather, wind direction, visibility, and related factors. If possible, a sketch that indicates north, south, east, and west should be made of the fire premises.

This information will not only help the arson investigator to determine the cause of the fire, it also will be invaluable to the firefighter or officer who might have to testify in court—possibly years later—about firefighting conditions that he might otherwise have long since forgotten.

3. Observations of people and vehicles.

Although it is rare to see an automobile speeding away from the scene of an arson, it's not unreasonable to ask a firefighter to record the license plate numbers of vehicles parked near the scene of a *suspicious* fire. This will be extremely helpful to the arson investigator in locating potential witnesses. One person who may be able to do this is the pump operator of the first engine company on the scene. This member is in the best location, and, *after the fire scene has been stabilized,* should have enough time to record this information.

4. Written record of how entry was made and by whom.

From the standpoint of arson investigators and prosecutors, how and where the firefighters gained entry to the burning building can make or break a case. This is because when a crime has been committed, one of the elements that proves arson is "exclusive opportunity."

Therefore, if an incendiary fire occurred at the "Milltown Restaurant" at midnight, and the restaurant was locked when the fire department arrived, then the firefighters who forced entry, whether by front door, rear door, windows, or through the roof, are the prosecution's witnesses that the owner or anyone who had access via a set of keys had "exclusive opportunity" to enter the premises, and therefore, exclusive opportunity to have set the fire.

The names, assignments, addresses, telephone numbers, and descriptions of the actions taken by each firefighter who forced entry must be documented in the arson detection report.

At this point in the report, the firefighters also should note whether or not they heard or activated any security alarm or smoke and heat detection system, sprinkler system, etc.

5. Observations of the building's interior

A firefighter's primary objective after gaining entry to a burning building is to "knock the fire down." Therefore, this would be a good time for him to make mental notes of the size, type, direction, location, and spread of the flames. This should include whether:

- The fire appeared in two or more separate locations, with no apparent connection, i.e., two separate and distinct areas of burning with no path of fire in between.

- The fire moved in an irregular manner or in an unusual direction, i.e., horizontally along the baseboard, down a staircase instead of up, or "walking" across the floor.
- The flames reacted abnormally to the water from the hoseline? *Straight streams* ordinarily "darken down" the fire immediately, but if a flammable liquid is present, the flames will tend to spread in different directions, as if being pushed by the water. If a *fog stream* is used, the fire tends to reflash upon application of water, wherever flammable liquid is present.
- More water than normal was required to put out this fire.
- The fire reacted more violently when more water was applied.
- Any extinguishing agents, other than water, were needed to put out the fire.

After the fire is under control and there is more time to notice things, firefighters should look at the interior of the building they have entered, using as a frame of reference either their own home or a business with which they are familiar. This helps them to establish a "norm" or benchmark against which they can compare the fire scene. For example, houses normally contain television sets, furniture, clothing, books, and framed pictures of loved ones, and businesses typically contain office equipment and furnishings, stock and machinery.

If a home or business lacks any of these items, this fact should be brought to the attention of fire investigators immediately, if possible, and also recorded on the arson detection report.

Instead of removing furniture and equipment, an arsonist might have piled them into a pyre and ignited it, or arranged towels, toilet paper, and newspapers as trailers to spread a set fire. Observations of this nature obviously belong in the report.

Remind firefighters that in their observations of the presence or absence of normal household or office furnishings, there may be perfectly legitimate reasons for a lack of clothing or missing furniture. In one case, an innocent man was accused of arson because there were no clothes in his closet, and his sofa and recliner had been removed from the living room.

The subsequent origin and cause investigation proved that the fire started in an electrical wire in the wall. Once arson was eliminated as a cause, the local sheriff found out that the clothes were at the laundry, and the sofa and chair were being stored in the garage temporarily until the owner's dog had been trained not to gnaw the furniture.

Indicators of arson are just that. They are facts that should be brought to the attention of the fire investigators; their relevance becomes apparent after the origin and cause investigation has been completed, and in combination with all other facts.

6. Preservation of evidence

Although it would be nice if firefighters could put out a fire and preserve evidence at the same time, it is more logical to assume that firefighters will concentrate on fighting the fire first, and will wait to begin the process of preserving evidence until after the fire has been brought under control, when things no longer are quite as urgent.

Here are some tips for fire personnel on the scene:

- To prevent scattering of evidence, use a fog nozzle; if you have an adjustable nozzle, "crack" the bail or shutoff to break up the solid stream.
- Limit traffic or other activity at the location where a suspicious fire is believed to have originated.
- If a flammable burn pattern is discovered, treat this area as if it were extremely delicate, i.e., as if it were made of glass. Cover it, cordon it off, or use any means available to keep it intact, shielded, and undamaged. And, of course, record this finding later on the arson detection form.
- If any suspicious objects are found at the fire scene, for example, gasoline cans, timing devices, chemicals, candles, or trailers, do not disturb or remove them. Proceed as noted above to cordon off, preserve, and record the scene.
- If a camera is available, take pictures and submit them later with the report; if possible, hold off on overhaul and salvage operations until the entire fire scene has been photographed.

Many an arson conviction is lost because a well-meaning firefighter took a can of gasoline, placed it in the chief's car, and drove the car to the station to protect the evidence until the arson investigator arrived.

A chief officer who brings a camera to a fire scene (which is strongly recommended) is doubtless doing "more than the job requires." When dealing with arson, though, that's sometimes what's necessary to get the job done. One principle to follow at the scene of a suspicious fire is to "shoot first and ask questions later." Often, justice has been served only because some dedicated fire chief cared enough to document the incident scene with photographs.

Preparation, Continuity, and Submission of the Report

Ideally, if a fire is perceived to be suspicious, *arson investigators should be called to the fire scene during firefighting operations.* If this proves to be impossible, a first draft of the arson detection report should be filled out at the fire scene by the engine company officer with the firefighters' assistance. Given the realities of exhaustion, frozen fingers, hospitalizations of some firefighters, and lack of light, the more practical approach is to complete the form back in quarters. In that case, the completed report will be an after-the-fact aid to the investigation, but no less important as a result of its delayed submission.

Filling out the arson detection report also can be used as an "arson awareness" drill, and a means of training personnel.

COURTROOM DEMEANOR

The purpose of this chapter is to enable you, as fire officers, to assist the fire investigator in preserving and gathering evidence that can be used to arrest, prosecute, and convict the arsonist.

This brings us to the very real possibility that at some point, a firefighter or fire officer might be expected to testify about actions taken or observations made during firefighting operations.

During the trial of a suspected arsonist, the prosecution may fail to get a conviction unless the fire officer on the witness stand makes a proper appearance and presents his testimony fully, clearly, and understandably.

The pressure can be great, because the fire officer (or firefighter) may be the state's principal witness. To help prepare fire personnel for court appearances, suggest they address the following:

Suitable Attire. Make sure witnesses are dressed appropriately, neat and conservative civilian suit and tie, or a clean, pressed uniform.

Official Documents. Have them check all their official reports, notes, records, documents, etc. These records can and should be referred to on the witness stand. Witnesses are not expected to have memorized everything.

Early Arrival. Have witnesses appear in court ahead of time for any last-minute conferences with the state's attorney, and check in with the court clerk to let him know they have arrived.

Review Material. Have witnesses look over their materials before trial and make sure they've either brought any physical evidence or that it is available.

First Impression. When witnesses are sworn in, they should face the court clerk with hand raised, and answer "I do," firmly. They should give name, rank, and assignment to the stenographer in a clear, audible voice.

Behavior on the Witness Stand

These instructions are applicable for anyone in your department who must testify.

Sit upright.

Keep your feet flat on the floor.

Keep your hands in a natural position.

Be matter-of-fact in your responses. Avoid nervous mannerisms or gestures.

Avoid fiddling with keys, pencils or papers. It is important for you, as a witness, to exercise dignity, courtesy, and courage.

Refer to the defendant as "the defendant," or by using "Mr., Mrs., or Miss," and the defendant's name.

Be courteous. Courtesy often calls for patience. Defense counsels often ask and repeat questions to upset you or annoy you. Do not get perturbed. *You* are not on trial.

Avoid arguing with defense counsel. It's not your job to win the case for the prosecution. It is only your job to present the facts with dignity. The defense counsel will try to get you to lose your temper. That's a fight you can't win.

Testify with confidence. This is possible only if you have complete and full knowledge of the facts. If you are asked a question to which you do not know the answer, don't try to "fudge" it. Simply state, "I don't know." Similarly, if you don't remember something say, "I don't remember."

Do not hesitate or avoid answering questions. However, give yourself time to understand the question.

If you do not understand a question or have not heard it, ask to have it repeated or rephrased.

Remain impartial. Testimony should relate to the exact facts in the case. There should never be any demonstration of bias toward or against the defendant.

Stay alert at all times.

Listen attentively to all questions, remarks, and statements made by counsel and members of the court.

Give accurate statements of facts. No guesswork or speculation is acceptable. In response to questions that deal with measurements, such as distances, temperatures, times, etc., where it is difficult to be exact, qualify your answer with the words "about" or "approximately."

Always tell the truth.

Avoid the use of slang or improper language on the witness stand unless it is absolutely necessary to the evidence, for example, when you are quoting a statement that was taken or overheard.

Remember that the jury is composed of lay people. If you use technical language, follow it up by explaining in simpler terms what you have just said. The fire service has its own jargon; sometimes fire personnel assume everyone understands what is being said.

Speak clearly and loudly enough to be heard during your entire testimony.

Do not hesitate to correct mistakes or errors that you made.

Remember, you are only presenting the facts, i.e., what you did and observed during the course of fire suppression operations. Do not give the impression that you, personally, are seeking a conviction. You are neither the judge nor the jury.

Don't volunteer information.

Use your notes to refresh your memory, but ask the court's permission before doing so.

Remember that the defense counsel has the right to cross-examine. The object of cross-examination is to test the credibility, knowledge, recollection, bias, prejudice, or intent of a witness relative to his testimony on direct examination.

Keep in mind that prior convictions of the defendant are not admissible and should not be introduced by you, even if you are aware of any.

Leave after you finish testifying and have been dismissed. If the district attorney has no further need for your services, leave the courtroom and the immediate area.

Although the preceding advice applies primarily to the criminal cases for which you or your personnel will be called to testify, more and more often firefighters are being asked to testify in civil litigation. Everything discussed above is equally applicable in a civil case. Your testimony as a fire officer is given considerable weight, because you are in court to state the facts: what you did; what you observed; and what you heard, not necessarily to argue for either the plaintiff or the defendant.

CONFIDENTIALITY

A common saying with regard to arson is that "the building was sold to the insurance company." This may be a light-hearted tension breaker among firefighters at the scene, but if it's said loudly enough and heard by the wrong person, the statement can come back to haunt whoever makes it.

Any comments about the suspicious nature of a fire, including the odor of gasoline, the reputation of the owner of the fire premises, the amount of insurance coverage, and all other comments that cast aspersion should be kept among fire personnel. If a member wants to discuss questionable circumstances with colleagues or superiors, it should be done discreetly and quietly. No one wants a prejudicial statement to be overheard by a journalist, the building's owner, an attorney, an adjuster, or anyone else for that matter. Nor, after the fire is over, does anyone want to broadcast suspicions to the world at large. Doing this can hamper an investigation and possibly jeopardize the entire case.

Another type of prejudicial statement to avoid making is a declaration by the Incident Commander to a member of the press or the owner or someone else, that the cause of the fire is not suspicious, but electrical in nature or accidental, or an act of God. If the arson investigators subsequently determine that the fire was actually incendiary, such a premature statement by any fire department member about the cause can create enormous problems in the later prosecution of the suspect. As a worst-case scenario, a firefighter or fire officer could later be pitted in court against an arson investigator as to the cause of the fire.

SUMMARY

The purpose of this chapter is to foster teamwork by helping fire officers understand how they can use their knowledge, skills, and experience, in concert with the expertise of fire investigators, *against* the arsonist. No slip-ups or mistakes should ever get in the way of this team effort or hamper its performance. We want to cooperate so well that evidence which formerly fell through the cracks is now signed, sealed, and delivered to the prosecutor.

TECHNICAL ASSISTANCE AND OTHER RESOURCES

Many colleges and the National Fire Academy offer arson detection and investigation courses. Insurance companies periodically hold seminars for their claims adjusters, and often welcome fire personnel. Municipal and state agencies are another source of training. The International Association of Arson Investigators (IAAI) is an organization that offers many programs, and publications to which you can subscribe. The National Fire Protection Association (NFPA) is another organization that publishes reference materials and standards, including videotapes, books, pamphlets and telephone assistance.

For further information, contact:

International Association of Arson Investigators
P.O. Box 600
Marlboro, Massachusetts 01752

National Fire Protection Association
1 Batterymarch Park
Quincy, Massachusetts 02269-9101

References

Carroll, John R., *Physical And Technical Aspects of Fire And Arson Investigation,* Springfield, IL: Charles C. Thomas, 1978.

DiMaio, Dominick J. and Vincent J. M. DiMaio, *Forensic Pathology,* New York, NY: Elsevier Science Publishing Co., Inc., 1989.

De Hahn, John, *Kirk's Fire Investigation.* 3rd Ed. New York: Prentice-Hall, 1990

Publications

Fire Engineering
Park 80 West, Plaza II
Saddle Brook, New Jersey 07662
(201) 845-0800

SAMPLE ARSON DETECTION REPORT

Date of Alarm: _____ Day of Alarm: _____ Time: _____

Location of Alarm: _____

_____

Who Turned in Alarm (Name & Address): _____

_____

Nature & Extent of Fire: (Speed and Direction of fire: Two separate fires? Unusual odors?, etc.)

_____

_____

_____

_____

Exact Area of Most Intense Burning: _____

_____

_____

Was Entry Forced: _____ Yes _____ NO

Entry: *Name*   *Unit*   *Where Entered*

Alarm and Sprinklers. Describe Condition Upon Arrival: _____

_____

_____

Reaction of Flames to Suppression Activity. Describe: _____

_____

_____

Any Special Problems in Fighting the Fire?_____

_____

_____

_____

Anything Unusual About Building Contents?_____

_____

_____

Were any Fire Enhancers Discovered (Trailers? Gasoline cans? Ignition devices, etc.)?_____

_____

_____

Where Found _____

_____

Were Photographs Taken and By Whom?_____

_____

_____

Was Anything Removed from the Fire Scene?_____

_____

By Whom?_____

_____

Deaths: _____   Injuries: _____

     _____   _____

     _____   _____

     _____   _____

Where were Injured Taken?_____

_____

Weather Conditions: Temperature: _____ Wind: _____

Suspicious Persons at Scene: _____

_____

License Plate Numbers of Vehicles at Scene: _____

_____

_____

Report Prepared By: _____   Rank: _____

Unit Assignment: _____   Phone No.: _____

Additional Information: _____

_____

_____

_____

_____

_____

_____

_____

_____

_____

_____

VI. THE FUTURE

29

THE NEXT GENERATION

JOHN GRANITO

C H A P T E R H I G H L I G H T S

- Distinguish between changes internal to the "fire service" and change in the broader field of "fire protection."
- Types of change possible for organizations.
- Major external pressures for fire service change.
- Logical extensions of fire department service.
- The important role of fire service leaders in designing the future.

*T*HE FUTURE OF THE fire service has become a topic of great interest in recent years, probably because its future obviously is going to be quite different from its past. Much of our thinking about the future centers on the changes that advanced technology will bring—such advances as enhanced computer programs, lighter and more effective protective clothing, personal and vehicle sensing and tracking devices, more versatile vehicles, on-off sprinklers, improved extinguishing agents, interactive video training programs, and virtual reality instruments. These are fascinating topics.

PRESSURES FOR FIRE SERVICE CHANGE

It appears, however, that the driving forces behind fire service change have more to do with finances and the general direction of society than with the tools of our trade. Our equipment and technology will continue to be very important, but their change value will relate quite directly to their ability to move us along in the directions set by a tighter economy and a dynamic culture. Our society now emphasizes a broad spectrum of needs, ranging from more effective crime control to vastly improved schools. In the minds of many these supersede fire protection. Simply put, the fire service will be changed more by external forces—the way our world is moving, and less for instance, by an ever increasing ability to reach higher floors with aerial ladders, or work harder and longer inside burning buildings.

To gain increased public support, some departments work hard to demonstrate that there are additional tasks related to the safety and well-being of the public that are most logically performed by fire departments. Their message thus becomes, "We are doing the old things such as fire suppression more effectively, and there are some new jobs such as public education that we can do quite well."

Keeping the public and our municipal officials aware of the presence and the high value of the local fire department is an important reason to market it. Advertising the service aspects of the department by increasing public appearances, stimulating positive media coverage, and making presentations at gatherings are all necessary.

These and other marketing efforts certainly are useful activities, and the fire service should engage in more of them. But, unfortunately, they probably are not enough to bring the fire service sufficient needed resources. Part of the reason for this is that the devastating municipal conflagrations, which in earlier times took out block after block, are fewer and farther between, and most citizens still consider suppression to be a fire department's key service. When devastating fires do occur, such as the 1992 and 1993 California fires, or the Los Angeles civil disturbance fires of 1992, neither the general public nor municipal officials propose massive strengthening of fire suppression forces. To use a related example from 1992, Hurricane Andrew was the costliest natural disaster ever to occur in the United States, but even the fire service did not recommend that its own forces be enlarged enough to deal with the rescue and recovery phases of any such future occurrences. Rather, it was the military that was suggested for the lead agency role. There is a growing tendency for people to assume community-wide fire risks rather than increase funding costs.

By 1993 it appeared that the number of fires in the United States was decreasing, even though some large-scale fires continued to occur. Until at least the mid-1990s, departments with increased, or even stable response run numbers often maintained their statistics by using emergency medical and other nonfire runs to justify continued financial support and garner ongoing and positive community interest.

It seems then that whatever form the fire service takes in the future, that form will be shaped not only by what the fire service demonstrates it can do, but even more so by what society deems desirable and affordable. A crucial issue for the future is whether the fire service can influence public perception so that fire departments are viewed as exceedingly important agencies that deserve continuing strong support. Very likely this ultimately will need to be a key goal of chiefs in most communities.

Change and the Future

Predicting the future of the fire service is not easy because it is both a complex system and a unique culture which is propelled forcefully by its history and tradition. In fact, except for certain military services, there probably is no other organization with such a striking and influential history. Most of the internal operating procedures and much of the service delivery levels of fire departments went almost unchanged for decades. Had it not been for strong external pressures, including the necessity for more effective prevention measures, coupled with a tight economy, it is unlikely that we would have seen such additions to fire department programs as widespread comprehensive prevention projects, EMS, or the pronounced movement into technical rescue services, for example. All of these tend to maintain workload as they broaden and expand service delivery.

For an organization to change, pressure must build either internally, externally, or both. Most change in the corporate world is brought about by shifts in the external market plus changes in internal capabilities, such as advances in technology. When competition is intense and technological advancement is rapid—as in the computer industry—products change often. When competition is intense and technological advancement is not as rapid—as in the automotive industry—then change is more evolutionary and tends to focus on cosmetic variables. If external pressures for change are more than the organization can bear, or more than it wants to deal with—such as what happened to full service gasoline stations—then the organization disappears completely or becomes transformed into something very different, such as convenience stores.

There are many variations in organizational change, of course, including product changes and marketing techniques, but not in the inner workings of the occupation, as might be the case in the medical profession. Conversely there is the organization that changes everything from its name to its logo, but continues to market the same product. This type of change is sometimes referred to as "old wine in new bottles" and might be typified by bank mergers which proclaim, "A new name, but the same service you've always known." With some organizations, change, whether structural or product-oriented, is viewed as a negative. Thus, relatively little is different in the legal profession today, except for mass marketing brought on by increased competition.

For fire departments to receive sufficient public support they will need to change in ways that make a positive difference to those who control resources. If the assumption is made that we do not wish to see public fire and rescue departments slowly disappear from our communities, replaced by other types of organizations, fire service leaders will need to understand fully what types of changes will guarantee a viable future. It appears that "old wine in new bottles" will not suffice. External pressures for organizational change will need to be matched by internally sponsored change.

Changes in fire suppression departments have not kept pace with the volume and speed of change in the broad and complex field of fire protection. While fire suppression departments have changed somewhat, and will continue to change, they are only one component of the larger field of fire protection. In fire protection, however, advances are made in a number of different specialties, such as detection, code design, architecture, engineering, construction materials, building techniques, arson investigation, and public safety education. Of course, as suppression departments adopt technological advancements in related fields and become strong advocates for safer environments, by advocating residential sprinkler protection, for example, they will hasten their own change rate by taking advantage of improvements created elsewhere, thereby helping themselves to maintain a prominent position in the more global fire protection arena. If a modern high-rise fire protection package requires that the fire department provide only mop-up and salvage work, then the department's future is diminished, unless it can assume additional important roles.

It is becoming increasingly important for fire departments to stay current in all technological advancements which conceivably could contribute to fire safety and more effective, efficient, and safe operations. The increasing use of continuous automatic vehicle locator instruments as part of computer-aided dispatch systems is an example. In addition to the obvious life and property safety considerations, it is better for the "official" fire safety organization to manage the entry of new participants and new technology to the field, than for new entrants to simply announce to the public that they now have the solution for sale. By doing more to create and manage future changes, the fire service can help to design its own future and provide a safer environment for the nation's communities as well. The central issue is whether society, in general, and specific communities in particular, believe that fire departments are important.

Whenever fire departments become more intrinsically involved in the many disciplines that influence public safety, then the helping power of "fire protection" grows, and so too does the perception that fire departments are an essential and key element in the community protection package. Fire protection includes not just what we call fire departments, but other specialized professions and occupations. For example, architects who create safe designs for large shopping malls are partners in fire protection, as are fire apparatus designers, even though neither is an employee of the local department. More and more, the safety of communities will be shaped by nondepartment influences such as television cable companies and telephone companies, each of which has the technical capability to monitor the interior environment of buildings, including heat and air sampling, and to report problems immediately to occupants and a response agency.

In terms of technology, fire departments need to not only participate, but lead. Suppose, for example, that a local communications company announced that for a small monthly fee it could attach a device to residential telephones that could sense any smoke in the house. Then, a device would ring the phones with a double loud bell continuously to alert any occupants, and summon the local fire department immediately with an automatic dial, in effect, a combination smoke detector and automatic alarm. Undoubtedly, this service would sell. Now, imagine this announcement being made without any prior discussion with the fire department personnel in that area. What do you think would happen? The local departments would be forced immediately to react to two possible scenarios. In one scenario the new device leads to foul-ups, and the local department is viewed as part of the problem; in the other, the device is a success, and the local department gets none of the credit.

Influencing the Future

To exercise more expert influence over the future of fire protection, and more control over the future status of the fire service, departments need, as their primary change methodology, to become more proactive and less reactive. For example, fire departments could shift the responsibility for vast problems caused them by unnecessary automatic alarms to the designers, manufacturers, and installers of those troublesome systems. In another area, the fire service could become more active in trying to change certain construction practices which endanger responders.

A second way to expand the future of the North American fire service is to expand the number and variety of services it provides. This change methodology is called "related diversification" in the business world, and it is a topic of much discussion and disagreement in the fire service.

What might related diversification look like in the fire service? Setting aside fire department emergency medical services—which are fairly widespread—the list includes comprehensive inspection services, hazard preplanning, building plans review, public education, automatic alarm monitoring, disaster planning and response, hazardous materials incident response, vehicle extrication, whitewater rescue, water search and recovery, ice rescue, mountain search and rescue, trench and structure collapse search and rescue, high-angle rescue, salvage and property conservation work, fire cause investigation, arson casework, juvenile fire-setting counseling, Explorer Scout work, and others. While few departments, if any, offer all of these services, the majority offer one or more of them, and most would agree that these are appropriate services for a modern fire and rescue department.

There are four other major categories of activities possible, in addition to those which come rather naturally to organized fire protection and emergency response groups. The first category relates directly to public and environmental safety and property conservation. It includes such activities as regularly scheduled smoke detector checks; hazardous waste collection; vehicle and heating system exhaust leak checks; radon gas checks; wood stove checks; loan of chimney cleaning tools; swimming pool safety classes; babysitter training; wildland/urban interface property checks; industrial fire brigade training; health care facility safety training; volunteer disaster response team training; "stay alive 'til we arrive" training; scald and burn prevention education; urban survival education (programs that teach parents and children about topics ranging from swimming pool safety to precautions for latchkey children), sprinkler retrofit and new residential sprinkler classes; hydrant flushing, painting, and clearing, and, fire lane parking checks, etc. Even building inspection programs can contribute to municipal anti-crime efforts by identifying "crack houses," and areas of homeless persons and vacant commercial properties that could be targeted by arsonists. These services are offered by some departments, but are the exception. Look for more and more departments to offer them, not just for the sake of diversification, but to ensure themselves a viable future. Most of these services are not being offered on a regular basis by community organizations, and many belong, appropriately, with fire departments.

The second category consists of activities that some believe are applicable to career departments, which are staffed continuously. While these activities contribute to municipal operations, they are not related to fire, medical, or rescue programs, but tend to be suggested because of the notion that full-time, paid fire personnel might conceivably be idle, and that fire stations are typically distributed throughout a city. These sometimes unpopular activities range from establishing tourist information services, runaway child help points, and bicycle inspection programs at stations, to administering gun surrendering programs, running city printing and binding operations, and conducting parking meter repairs by in-quarters fire department personnel. The concept of combining the duties of police officers and fire personnel to create "public safety officers," while neither very workable nor very popular, is an example of a fairly old concept in this category.

A third category of activities, sometimes discussed when local officials and local firefighters are not in accord, features tasks which can easily be construed as punishment, including cutting grass and shoveling snow at city-owned buildings or taking residential meter readings for a municipally owned utility.

The last, and a separate set of activities in which some departments are engaging, consists of repairing, rebuilding, or constructing new apparatus, equipment, or minor facilities; installing radios and warning lights on fire vehicles (and sometimes on the vehicles of other city departments); and, related tasks such as working on power equipment and breathing apparatus. Many departments do this type of work on a regular basis.

As more departments take on new and additional tasks, and do so successfully, the composite picture of the future becomes more clearly defined. In reality, the future of the fire service reaches some departments before it reaches others. Why? Some departments sense what society needs and can afford, and what they logically can offer and they begin to deliver these services without waiting for the rest of the fire service to catch up. As the percentage of related safety-service delivery items increases, the delivery organizations become less suppression oriented and more oriented toward general safety services.

The concept of the future is complex, since it can be viewed best more as a trip along time than a snapshot of any given point on the time line. Because most of us want a better future, we tend to be interested in shaping our future. To shape the future of the fire service most effectively, what happens in our microcosm should make sense with respect to society in general. Our shapes for the future should be congruent. Therefore, volunteer firefighters who continually tell the community that the time demands on them are overwhelming, and who then are disappointed because they have recruiting problems, are not operating in congruent ways. Career firefighters who work and live in communities with high unemployment and who park trucks advertising their "moonlighting" businesses alongside the fire station also are sending a confusing message.

The past 20 years are filled with examples of established business practices which have either changed considerably (such as the telephone company), are nearly extinct (such as home visits by doctors), or have disappeared (such as the repair of tube type television sets). The old-style diner is giving way to the drive-through window, milk is not delivered but purchased at a convenience store, the grocery checkout person "optically scans" rather than punches keys, and there are fewer office assistants and more networked PCs. There is no reason to suspect that the fire service, even in its new, slightly reshaped format, will not undergo considerably more change in the coming years.

MAJOR CONCERNS OF FIRE PERSONNEL FOR THE FUTURE

Twenty-five experienced **volunteer** fire service representatives from across the country recently recorded their seven major concerns for the 1990s: financial support, recruitment and retention, safety and health, training, certification, codes and standards, and liability.

Twenty **urban** fire chiefs also listed their major concerns for career departments: financial support; expanding service delivery items; health and safety; crew size and other response variables, including types of apparatus and station location; development of comprehensive fire protection measures and programs; marketing and public image; training and other legitimate demands on time and budget; and personnel management and labor relations.

To these extensive lists can be added the following issues which relate to community fire protection and are crucial to the future:

- The growing belief on the part of city managers, finance directors, elected officials, and some citizens that the cost of fire protection, both career and volunteer, is much too high.
- The debates among various fire service and municipal management organizations about the size of response crews, and how crew size can be determined.
- The need for more research and development which might lead to substantial improvements in suppression work, and in other aspects of fire protection.
- The power struggles and battle campaigns among the various fire service organizations.
- The animosity between volunteer and career personnel which exists in many places.
- The general unwillingness of both organized labor and department leadership to adopt significant change, and their inclination to fight delaying actions.
- The lack of accurate information and knowledge about fire department operations on the part of elected officials and municipal administrators.
- The serious questioning by some municipal administrators of their career fire departments, usually brought on by what they view as high costs for little productivity.
- The lack of a scientifically gathered and credible, database which could serve as a reference and as a basis of agreement on budget and other issues.
- The continuing fracturing of the fire service caused by the emergence of speciality service groups.
- The willingness, and sometimes the eagerness, of outsiders, including agencies and organizations, to deal directly with, fund, and empower splinter groups, to the detriment of fire departments.
- Crew sizes in career departments which are reduced by reductions in force, hiring freezes, injuries, sickness, and days off, plus personnel on disability who are never replaced with new hires and sometimes not even replaced by call-backs, leading to closed stations and companies out of service.
- Moratoria on vehicle replacement, and equipment purchases.
- Demands to increase productivity, sometimes by adding assignments not at all related to community safety.
- Debilitating battles among city officials, fire chiefs, and organized labor.
- The resurgence of arguments for private EMS providers, commercial fire suppression companies, the merging of fire and police services,

part-time paid firefighters, and the consolidations of departments without knowledge of what might be gained or lost.
• Communities which are having extreme difficulty in recruiting and retaining volunteers.
• The difficulty we have in viewing ourselves in nontraditional roles and as having something other than a "macho" image.

On the positive side, there has been a growing acceptance of the need for increased health and safety measures; a willingness here and there to try new approaches to persistent problems and challenges; a shift toward comprehensive fire prevention, public education, and built-in alarm and extinguishing systems; and an expansion of the service delivery package. A very important gain has been made in the widespread movement toward professionalism, toward continuing education, and toward the use of certain technological advancements, such as computers. On the whole, however, the prognosis is for continuing challenges and the need for improved change management within departments.

The Next Generation

What might lie ahead for the fire service? In the more densely populated urban and suburban areas, larger city departments plus county-wide departments or regionalized approaches to cost effectiveness are to be expected. Consolidation in those areas without large city or county departments is already happening, and will be more common during the late 1990s.

Many consolidations will follow the existing pattern of merging suburban and rural departments, but not city or town-wide departments; these retain their autonomy. Annexation of rural areas to cities, however, will become more popular, as more rural areas seek municipal services.

Regionalization most often will consist of arrangements among a number of autonomous departments to conduct joint purchasing, dispatching, training, computer services, hazardous materials response, vehicle maintenance, and other such collaborative cost-effective moves. The most common and time-honored example, of course, is mutual aid for suppression. These are examples of what might be termed "functional consolidation."

Given a choice, most departments would much prefer to go it alone, but in many regions that luxury is disappearing fast. Sufficient budget support—often from federal revenue sharing—is now passé. The concept of widespread consolidation and regionalization is already beginning to apply to volunteer as well as career departments, even given the exceedingly strong tradition of home rule in the United States and Canada.

The use of combination departments, including those which employ both full-time and part-time personnel, and the use of two-way pagers for selecting predetermined call-back groups of off-duty career firefighters, should remain popular. With cost-free volunteer service quickly disappearing in some parts of the country, firefighter labor organizations might want to consider enrolling part-time personnel as dues-paying adjunct members, just as some school teachers' organizations enroll teacher-aides. With changes in state legislation, labor organizations of full-time personnel could recruit as adjunct members what are now termed "call-firefighters" or "reimbursed volunteers."

Over the next 20 years, our national budget will be affected by the growing prosperity of the European Common Market, the emerging economic dominance of the Pacific Rim countries, the price of national health care, larger criminal justice systems, improved schools, and the emergence of small, nuclear-equipped countries. These interests will prompt continuing defense and other expenditures that probably will not allow us the level of national prosperity we have had in the past. Most communities will lack the funds to maintain the existing style of fire protection. Some states already are gathering the statistics to demonstrate "average reasonable costs" of fire protection and other municipal services to various sized communities. Therefore, it appears possible that some public service organizations, such as fire, police, and libraries, will be pressured to become less labor intensive and thus less costly.

Some communities will transfer cost payment from the municipal tax bill to user fees. In some fire districts, property owners pay a "benefit charge" which varies depending on exactly what services are provided and how much local fire insurance costs. But, obviously, if a service costs more than residents can afford, no matter what the fee is called, there will be loud taxpayer complaints.

Because fire suppression budgets will remain very tight, there will be continued use of call-back and part-time personnel, as well as fewer stations and longer running times. It seems likely that many small to mid-sized communities with career departments will staff task force groups for initial attack with full-time, on-duty personnel at fewer stations, and will use paged call-backs on reserve apparatus to handle sustained attack and simultaneous runs. Unless area departments enter into formal, regionalized agreements, mutual aid as we have known it will become weakened. Downsized departments will be less able or reluctant to send much assistance out of town, a problem when many areas already depend heavily on automatic mutual aid response for initial attacks on key targets.

While it is possible that organized labor will grow in numbers, negotiating ultimately may take place at regional or state levels, resulting in more standardized contracts. Final and formal agreements concerning crew size will be reached, simply because the interested groups will work through all sides of the problem and arrive at either a joint policy statement, a recommended practice, or a national standard that specifies how many people should constitute the minimum initial attack team for various types of incidents, and in what timeframe they should arrive.

It is interesting to speculate on possible long-term approaches to fire protection that take into account continuing concerns over both costs and safety. Four such possible directions are:

- Continuing improvements in fixed extinguishing systems and the laws that mandate their use;
- Lower combustibility and toxic release rates of building and furnishing materials;
- The perfection of devices to apply extinguishing agents from a safe distance by guided projectiles, or large PPV airstreams, or in close proximity by robots; and
- The perfection of devices to generate controllable laser beams, wave emissions, or electromagnetic fields, which will extinguish flames from safe distances without the use of water.

Before these approaches are refined, we can expect fewer fires, but much larger ones with higher losses. This is because fire prevention will be more effective, but our suppression capability will have been weakened. Robotic devices may hold promise, but they must be used in conjunction with improved fixed extinguishing systems and automatic sensing and alarm devices. Interior attacks by personnel may take place less often than they do now, but they will continue to be essential. Unfortunately, we already have seen the beginning of more frequent "surround and drown" or concede orders because of reduced suppression staffing forces or the nature and size of today's fires. Many departments which almost always held fires to "room and contents" now aim to contain the fire to the building of origin. Longer runs and reduced initial attack forces create this situation and fire service leaders will need to develop more powerful arguments to correct it than we have been able to mount in the past.

Suppression vehicles will become smaller and more specialized. In other countries, for example, aerial apparatus carry nothing but the aerial device itself, and smaller equipment trucks carry the balance of the equipment. In the U.S. we already are seeing equipment trucks called ladder tenders. They are smaller, faster, and less expensive, and they may alter our pattern of aerial deployment. After all, how often are 45- or 50-foot banger ladders thrown? How many people are needed to use even half of the ground ladders carried on a fully equipped aerial? How do we fill eight- and ten-seat crew cab pumpers when so few departments—career or volunteer—ride with more than three, four, or five members, including the driver?

With respect to some response vehicles, however, we are beginning to see generalization rather than specialization. We now are seeing true rapid intervention vehicles in their infancy: rescue-pumpers; flying squads with capacity pumps; ambulance-pumpers that carry extrication and technical rescue equipment as well as a gurney compartment; combination hazardous materials and command post vehicles; combination lighting and air trucks; and modern tanker-pumpers. Many departments will have two or more specialized vehicles available for instant selection by responders, depending on the type of call. Now, in some departments, pumper crews can select either the pumper or an aide car, for example, depending on whether the call is for a suppression job or an emergency medical run.

THE STRUCTURE OF FIRE DEPARTMENTS IN THE NEXT GENERATION

As we move into the 21st century we may see four basic types of departments providing fire protection and other safety services to communities. Indeed, we are seeing the beginning of these in the mid-1990s. The transition will be from generic types of fire departments, where the essential difference among departments is the salaried status of the firefighters, to organizations that will specialize in providing different service packages. The type of service provided will be determined by local needs, and the format for delivery—the type, size, and status of the department, plus its operating procedures—will be determined by available resources, both financial and human.

Rural Protection

Rural areas, the first to be considered here, are typified by smaller and more scattered populations, with fire hazards that include hamlets and small villages, isolated industrial buildings, waste collection and transfer sites, wildland-structural interfaces, both small and large consolidated school buildings, transportation routes, long response runs, and isolated homes, churches, and other structures.

Unless a large industrial package is part of the tax base, financial resources for protection will continue to be limited. The fire protection organization typically will be volunteer, and runs will be long because of the necessity of drawing volunteers from the small centers where they may live and work. The basic protection services provided by what undoubtedly will be called a fire-rescue department will consist of fire suppression, rescue and EMS, disaster response, and modest fire prevention and public education programs, all run by volunteers. Increasing pressures for lower costs and increased resources will bring about regional cooperation, expanded beyond what is now available in rural mutual aid agreements to include shared dispatching, training programs, computerized record-keeping, and specialty vehicles.

In most instances, financial support will come from the local tax base, special sales taxes or similar allocations, plus some subscription charges for special services such as EMS, or for suppression service outside of the basic area of coverage. With time for volunteer involvement limited, the now common fundraising activities of volunteer departments also will become more limited. In some states, the financial burden of meeting imposed equipment and training mandates will be helped by a state-wide tax base. There also may be formalized equipment recycling programs that will benefit rural departments.

In addition to the many volunteer recruitment and retention programs now used, the problems of recruiting and retaining volunteers will be eased in several other ways. First, more nonfirefighting volunteers will be used for a variety of jobs, from clerical work and public education to equipment maintenance, inspections, and training. "They also serve who don't haul hose." Second, legal, legislative, and OSHA provisions might be instituted to allow some rural township employees to train for and participate in firefighting activities as part of their regular job assignment, rather than as volunteer department members. This might lead to some highway department pick-up trucks, for example, carrying firefighting gear, and some county vehicles carrying state-purchased skid load water tanks and pumps. This method of providing additional personnel, however, is extremely problematical because significant changes in federal and state legislation are necessary for implementation, in most, if not all instances. Third, low-cost housing will be provided in or near some rural stations as an inducement to membership. Fourth, volunteers will be encouraged, rather than discouraged, to use the volunteer station to fix their personal vehicles, to work on personal hobbies, for some family and social events, and for such other activities as physical fitness training, where individuals are not likely to own the required equipment. This method of keeping at least a few volunteer firefighters at the station for longer periods of time provides, at those times, a quicker response. Retirement provisions, insurance coverage, and other economic enhancements are proving to be quite effective in attracting and retaining volunteers, and in some regions may well prove to be the most effective retention magnet for volunteers who have other strong demands on their time.

Suburban and Ring-City Areas

Areas which are more densely populated than rural districts and which are somewhat urbanized typically have a mixture of hazards. These include commercial and industrial sites such as office and high-tech parks, shopping malls, country clubs, factories, warehouse facilities, hospitals, schools, high-rise structures, older retail strips, new and old apartment buildings, and single-family residences. In some communities these may be in isolated, hard-to-reach locations. Transportation routes and hazardous materials locations are common.

The departments in these areas are, in many sections of North America, entirely volunteer, but increasingly will become either combination volunteer and paid, or fully paid organizations. Where rural volunteer departments are able to deliver suppression services and, perhaps, EMS and disaster assistance, the suburban departments will be called upon to provide from a dozen to possibly 20 or more functions. The number of services provided to a community will be a function of whether there are staffed stations, how much funding is available, expressed or determined community needs, local inventiveness, the use of specialized citizen volunteers, and the cooperation of organized labor in expanding the service program.

In suburban and ring-city locations there are various community needs which can be met very well by fully paid or a combination of full-time and part-time department members. These needs include specialized suppression and rescue situations, automatic fire and medic alarm monitoring, environmental testing, code enforcement, and health screening. It is likely that this type of department will offer the most flexibility, the greatest number of services, and have the highest per capita resources. It is possible that more interesting community safety action will be found here than anywhere else, except in the most progressive larger cities.

Urban and Inner City Areas

Just how large and diverse the service delivery package in urbanized areas will be is a function of the financial status of cities, the suppression-EMS-inspection workload of the local department, and the agreements which may be reached between labor and management relative to staffing. In the most fiscally constrained areas and situations, programs might be limited to suppression, preplanning, and perhaps first-responder EMS services. In other places, the number of services might be as high as 12 or 15. These additional services will tend to be the most crucial ones found in the suburban-ring city departments, and could include emergency-related tasks such as water rescue and confined space operations, plus nonemergency tasks such as building inspections and community affairs.

Where station crews have frequent runs, services will tend to exclude in-house activities such as CPR classes or walk-in health screening. Where EMS continues to be provided from another organization, and where specialty vehicles and crews run from selected stations, other stations may be able to offer some in-station special services. With labor agreements flexible enough to allow for differentiated work assignments, urban and inner city departments may vary the service package from station to station, with a total spectrum of services that is very broad. A very important element is emergency run workload, which determines available time.

In congested urban areas especially, careful choices will have to be made about which response capabilities are desired. Response capabilities, which take into consideration such variables as desired response time, number of initial attack crew members, and number and types of vehicles most needed at the scene, must be established in fairly precise terms and should govern station location and crew size. Such additional variables as simultaneous alarms, multiple alarms, and target hazards in the district also must be calculated. Newer techniques, including advanced computerized mapping, are especially helpful in dealing with these questions.

The very important issues of firefighter health and safety will continue to exert strong pressures on all constituencies in the fire protection field, including architects, equipment designers, city officials, educators, fire department personnel, organized labor, and those who prepare standards and legislation. Ultimately the answers to questions about the relationship of crew size to firefighter safety and other such issues will be settled, very likely by either interorganizational agreements or national standards. Other issues, for example, the health and physical condition of individual suppression personnel, also will be addressed. Improving health and safety conditions throughout the fire service, and not just in the more progressive departments, will be a continuing effort. Once the global issues are settled, attention will turn to the condition of individual department members. We might, for example, see a push for more aerobic exercise equipment in stations and more emphasis on healthy life styles and eating habits, since heart disease is such a problem. This focus should apply not just to urban paid departments, but to all departments.

Special-Purpose Organizations

The fourth type of department will continue to consist of special-purpose organizations, some of which are public and some of which are not. These are departments that protect wildland areas, airports, marine terminals, certain industries, nuclear facilities, and other relatively specialized or unique settings. These special-purpose organizations typically offer only inspection, rescue, and suppression services, plus some prevention education.

Not only will specialized departments continue to exist, but more of them will be created in special districts.

THE CRUCIAL ROLE OF CHIEF OFFICERS AND OTHER FIRE SERVICE LEADERS

There is an old saying, "There is so much handwriting on the wall that the wall is falling down." If fire service leaders ignore the handwriting on the wall—that says to keep up with a changing environment!—it's possible, even probable, that what we know as the municipal fire service could weaken considerably. Essential parts of our wall could crumble.

Can you imagine a community with the following provisions? First, all prehospital medical service, from neighborhood health screening to ALS transport, is conducted by either a private provider or an EMS city agency. Second, the EMS organization runs several light rescue-extrication vehicles, enough to cover the city, working in conjunction with its ambulances. Third, the county's emergency management office, aided in large disasters by the National Guard, provides disaster response services plus heavy rescue response, in conjunction with the local department of public works. Or, multi-purpose emergency services could be provided by the police department. Fourth, all inspection services are performed by the building department. Fifth, all fire prevention and public education is presented by education specialists employed by the school board. Sixth, hazardous materials incident response and recovery are the responsibility of private providers. Seventh, selected police patrol units are light trucks equipped with a water tank, a booster pump, protective gear, and small tools. Last, a much reduced number of quint firefighting vehicles, manned by a small core of firefighters and augmented by an auxiliary, respond to working fires.

It is possible that each of these modes of operation is being practiced now, someplace in the United States. Happily, all of them are not in simultaneous use in any given municipality. There is a great deal wrong with this scenario, and the fire service needs to work against its ever being implemented. However, its attractiveness to money managers is obvious. A scenario that reduces the fire department to a small suppression force, with other services farmed out to existing organizations, is an attractive option for citizens concerned about taxes and escalating costs. The fire service, however, realizes that this fragmented approach to public safety is not only inadequate, but dangerous for our communities.

The fire service must do more than hold the line. It must become more proactive, guiding communities toward sound public safety decisions. Our society, always in flux, now has a vastly increased rate of change and the number of people affected by the changes (and thus reacting to them) is so much greater. Generally, the more people affected by change, the more pronounced the reaction. To complicate matters, significant change is occurring in all of our basic institutions, ranging from the family and religion to our economic, social, and environmental structures.

The societal changes and modified concepts that have emerged during the last 10 or 15 years already have affected many individual fire departments as well as the fire service generally. In some instances the impact has been direct, at other times indirect. The results have shaped the trends fire officials already are having to deal with, trends toward increased calculated risk, broad-based planning groups, increased accountability, the demand for cost effectiveness, interest in nontraditional solution paths, a focus on the rights of consumers, increased litigation, and more publicity for a variety of detection, alarm, and fixed extinguishing systems and comprehensive prevention measures.

The problems and issues associated with these trends can be viewed as helpful to fire officials as hurdles to be crossed. If fire department personnel are to play the major role in shaping the future of fire departments (or whatever those departments may be called), they will need to guide communities to the best fire protection possible.

As expected, the role of the chief of department will continue to be crucial to success. More and more, chiefs will need to function as top-level executives and members of the larger teams of executives who will deal with community-wide challenges. Departments will become "mission driven" and the strengths and talents of all members will need to be channeled by chiefs and other officers to meet the future head on.

Glossary

CHAPTER 2. OFFICE MANAGEMENT AND WORK FLOW

Cross-functional (jobs). Jobs requiring multiple skills, tasks, and reporting procedures.

Cumulative Trauma Disorder (CTD). Physical disorders developing from, or aggravated by, the cumulative application of biomechanical stress to tissues and joints.

Ergonomics. The study of the physical relationship of people and the way they use equipment for their operation.

Information Technology. The information, equipment, techniques, and processes that are converted to outputs for the organization.

Line Position. A position delivering service or goods to a "customer."

Networking. People exchanging ideas and other resources via face-to-face meetings or through information technologies.

(Organization) Complexity. The number of tasks required, span of control, and geographic layout of an organization.

Organization Development. An evolving collection of philosophies, concepts, and techniques which aims to improve an organization's performance through diagnosis, feedback, planning, and intervention.

(Organization) Structure. The arrangement of the formal organization and its parts.

Open Systems Model. A concept borrowed from the biological sciences referring to the functions that take place between a system and its environment.

Paradigm. A model or example.

Private Sector. A private, "for profit" organization.

Processes. The way people, groups, or organizations relate and interact.

Public Sector. A government or public institution.

Staff Position. A position supporting those in the organization delivering service or goods to "customers."

Standardization. The more routine the work, the more it is considered to be structured. Standardization is accomplished through goals, rules, policies, procedures, job specifications, and formalized training.

CHAPTER 5. INSURANCE GRADING OF FIRE DEPARTMENTS

Basic Fire Flow. The quantity of water, expressed in gpms, which is one of the three elements examined in determining the number of "needed engine companies," required by an ISO survey. It is represented by the fifth highest of the needed fire flows in the city, excluding any buildings that are graded by CRS as a sprinklered building.

Commercial Risk Services (CRS). A nonprofit subsidiary of the ISO which performs the functions of specific property surveys and public protection surveys that were previously conducted by the ISO and its predecessors.

Creditable Rate Flow. The maximum amount of water that will be credited as being available to suppress a fire at a test location selected for an ISO grading. It is determined by taking the lesser of the supply works capacity, main capacity, hydrant distribution and needed fire flow.

Divergence. In the computation of the public protection classification developed during an ISO survey, a factor equal to the difference between fire department credit and water supply credit, which may be subtracted from a city's grade. It represents the difference between the capability of a city's fire department and the capability of its water system.

Existing Engine (Ladder-Service) Company. The actual number of engine, ladder, and/or service companies which are staffed and respond to first alarms in a city. (As opposed to "needed engine companies.")

Fire Suppression Rating Schedule (FSRS). The grading schedule adopted by the ISO in 1980 and which is currently used to develop protection classifications for both the city as a whole, as well as for individual properties within the city which have a needed fire flow greater than 3,500 gpm.

Hydrant Distribution. The assignment of a gpm equivalent to hydrants located within 1,000 feet of a test location for an ISO survey, based on the distance of the hydrant to the test building. The nearer the hydrant, the more gpms credited. One of the four elements examined to determine the creditable rate of flow at a test location.

Insurance Services Office (ISO). A nonprofit organization created by the merger of a number of different insurance-related organizations which provides a wide variety of consulting, rate setting, and actuarial services to all property and liability insuring companies.

Main Capacity. The ability of a water system to deliver water at a test location for an ISO survey. One of the four elements examined to determine the creditable rate of flow at a test location.

Maximum Daily Consumption. The average rate of water consumption during the 24-hour period in which the highest consumption total is recorded during the last three-year period, excluding occurrences caused by system changes or unusual occurrences.

Needed Engine (Ladder-Service) Companies. The number of engine ladder, and/or service companies which are required by either basic fire flow, distribution, or operations pursuant to an ISO survey. In contrast to the number of existing engine companies, etc., which already exist within the city.

Needed Fire Flow (NFF). A quantity of water, expressed in gpms, that is theoretically necessary to suppress a fire in a given building. Factors such as construction, occupancy, and fire exposure fire/communication are taken into account when determining the needed fire flow. One of the four elements examined in determining the creditable rate of flow at an ISO survey test location.

Public Protection Classification. The number which represents the classification assigned to a city pursuant to an ISO survey, with 1 being the best and 10 representing less than minimum recognized fire protection and which measures a city's ability to suppress fires in buildings of average size. In determining the public protection classification, the handling and receiving of fire alarms, the city's water supply, and the fire department are all reviewed.

Supply Works Capacity. The normally available amount of water from all water sources which can be used to suppress a fire in a city which includes the use and/or effect of storage, pumps, filters, emergency supplies, suction (static) supplies, and fire department supply (i.e., tanker shuttles). One of the four elements used to determine the creditable rate of flow at an ISO test location.

CHAPTER 6. LEADERSHIP FOR TODAY AND TOMORROW

Comfort Work Zone. That area of production between the minimum and maximum level of performance where people will do just enough work to get along.

Committee. Sometimes called a task force, it is an effective method of facilitating coordination.

Communications. The conveying and receiving of ideas, attitudes, and objectives through written, verbal and nonverbal means of intercourse.

Content Theory of Motivation. Assumes that the answer to motivation problems lies within the complete understanding of the people involved.

Contingency Approach to Leadership. A leader's ability to lead is based on the task situation and the degree to which the leader's style, approach, and personality fit the group.

Controlling. A process established by a leader which ensures that a task is being carried out, completed, or both.

Coordinating. The orderly synchronization of the efforts of a group to assure that those efforts are properly timed and are correct as to quantity and quality of work expected.

Courage. The state or quality of mind or spirit that enables one to face danger with self-possession, confidence, and resolution. It is not the absence of fear, but rather the ability to act in spite of our fears.

Delegation of Responsibilities and Authority. The assigning of a task to a subordinate and the authority to carry out the task to fruition.

Directing. The facilitating and coaching of those people whom the supervisor is directly responsible to supervise.

Excellence. A commitment to be the best.

Evaluation and Appraisal. Determination of how well employees are doing as far as their work is concerned and how they can improve their progress or lack of progress.

Goal. A level of competence or rank, or a task we wish to complete.

Herzberg's Two-Factor Theory of Needs. Maintenance needs and Motivational needs.

Horizontal Coordination. Deals with activities that occur within a level of an organization.

Informal Organization. A group of employees who share the same general goals, likes and dislikes, and interests.

Innovation. A commitment to continuous improvement.

Integrity. The ability to walk our talk, deal with issues straight out, and do what we say in our mission statement.

Line Functions. Those functions which are directly related to accomplishing the department's goals.

Logical Assignment. Giving the right task to the right person.

Management. Management is a process of structuring the activities of an organization in such a way that it achieves the maximum efficiency and effectiveness in the use of human and physical resources.

Maslow's Hierarchy of Needs. Physical, Security, Affiliation, Esteem, and Self-Actualization.

Mission Statement. A mission statement puts into words what is in your vision.

Motivation. The desire to accomplish tasks, move other people to accomplish tasks, or both.

Objective. An individual task that needs to be completed in order to reach a goal.

Organizing. That phase of management which occurs when the manager takes all the aspects of the plan, brings them all together, and organizes them into a smooth working unit.

Path Goal Approach to Leadership. The most effective leaders are those who assist their subordinates in achieving both their personal goals and the goals of the organization.

Planning. Looking ahead and creating a scheme or method in order to attain a particular goal or objective.

Process Theory of Motivation. It is the situation and the leadership climate that effect changes in people.

Self-actualization. The realization of a person's hopes and expectations.

Situational Approach to Leadership. Theorizes that leaders can be products of a particular situation.

Span of control. The number of people a supervisor can supervise effectively.

Specialization of Labor. Work is divided into like units and delegated to the appropriate bureau or division.

Staff Functions. Those functions which are not directly related to accomplishing the department's goals.

Team Building. The developing of team spirit, which is the drive that keeps the team bubbling with enthusiasm, cohesiveness, and producing good results.

Unity of Command. One worker, one boss.

Vertical Coordination. Coordination of the various levels within an organization.

Vision. Your vision is what you are all about, it is your purpose, it is in what direction you are headed.

Vroom's Expectancy Theory. A worker will be motivated if that worker expects that his action will lead to the preferred outcome.

CHAPTER 9. THE NATIONAL PROFESSIONAL QUALIFICATIONS SYSTEM

Accredit. To give official authorization to or approve a process or procedure, to recognize as conforming to a standard, and to recognize an entity (e.g., an educational institution) as maintaining standards that qualify its graduates for admission to higher or more specialized institutions or for professional practice. (NFPA 1000)

Certification. Attests authoritatively; specifically, the issuance of a document that states that one has demonstrated the knowledge and skills necessary to function in a field. (NFPA 1000)

Evaluate. The process of testing, examining, and finding the individual competent.

National Certification. That certification issued by a national organization or body.

Performance Competency Standards. Those statements that describe job task, list the items necessary to complete the task, and define measurable or observable outcomes and evaluation areas for the specific task. (NFPA 1000—Job Performance Requirement)

Performance Objective. That statement to which the individual must be evaluated.

Prerequisite Knowledge. Fundamental knowledge one must have in order to perform a specific task.

Prerequisite Skills. The essential skills one must have in order to perform a specific task. (NFPA)

CHAPTER 10. TRAINING AND EDUCATION

Certification. Attests authoritatively; specifically, the issuance of a document that states that one has demonstrated the knowledge and skills necessary to function in a field. (NFPA 1000)

Accredit. To give official authorization to or approve a process or procedure, to recognize as conforming to a standard, and to recognize an entity (e.g., an educational institution) as maintaining standards that qualify its graduates for admission to higher or more specialized institutions or for professional practice. (NFPA 1000)

National Certification. Certification issued by a national organization or body.

Performance Competency Standards. Those statements that describe job tasks, list the items necessary to complete the task, and define measurable or observable outcomes and evaluation areas for the specific task. (NFPA 1000—Job Performance Requirement)

Evaluate. The process of testing, examining, and finding an individual competent.

Performance Objective. That statement against which an individual is evaluated.

Prerequisite Skills. The essential skills one must have to perform a specific task. (NFPA)

Prerequisite Knowledge. Fundamental knowledge one must have to perform a specific task.

CHAPTER 11. FIRE DEPARTMENT APPARATUS

Box Pan Construction. A construction method that uses an external flat panel with a hollow pan attached to the inside. The compartment locking mechanism is contained inside the hollow portion of the door.

Class D Extinguisher. A portable extinguisher used on combustible metal fires.

Driveline. The connection from the transmission to the driving axles, including driveshafts, slip joints, universal joints, and differential.

GAWR. Gross Axle Weight Rating, the load-carrying rating of a single axle.

GVWR. Gross Vehicle Weight Rating, the value specified as the loaded weight rating of a single vehicle.

Halon. A liquefied compressed gas that will not support combustion, used as an extinguishing agent.

Impeller. A revolving hollow disc with vanes, driven by the pump shaft, that transmits motion to the water, using centrifugal force.

Inertia. The tendency of matter to remain at rest or in motion, such as water inside a closed tank.

Interlock. A device or arrangement by means of which the functioning of one part is controlled by the functioning of another.

P.O.D. Platform On Demand, a container-like box that is transported by truck and rolled off at the scene of an emergency.

Polar Solvent Foams. Used for extinguishing fires on water soluble materials that are destructive to regular or AFFF foams.

Rated Tip Load. The rated capacity of an aerial ladder, carried at the tip off the fly, with the ladder horizontal and at maximum extension. The aerial must operate in any position while carrying the rated load.

Service Brakes. Brakes that are used to stop the vehicle under normal operating conditions.

Special Purpose Vehicles. Rescue, Hazardous Materials, and Breathing Air Apparatus (NFPA 1905).

Swash Partitions. Baffles installed inside the tank to impede the motion of the water and to prevent the buildup of inertia.

Tandem Axles. Two rear drive axle units coupled by a power divider.

Tillerman. The operator of a steerable rear axle of a tractor-type aerial truck.

Torsional Stress. A twisting or torquing motion.

Venturi Effect. When water under pressure passes through a restriction, a low-pressure area is created at the restriction. This action allows a liquid, at atmospheric pressure, to be introduced into the stream through a pick-up tube.

CHAPTER 15. FIRE DEPARTMENT COMMUNICATIONS

Ad Valorem Tax. See Tax.

Administration. That section of an agency with the responsibility to make policy decisions regarding the direction of the agency.

CAD. In the public safety communications business means *Computer-Aided Dispatch*. However, in other professions, the acronym CAD can stand for *Computer-Aided Design*.

Call Taker. A communications center worker whose job is to simply answer the calls for service and determine first, whether there is an emergency, and second, pass the call onto an agency equipped to respond. The call taker allows the dispatcher to concentrate on assisting the field equipment to arrive at the scene of the call for service in a timely fashion.

CEM. An agency of a political jurisdiction relating to management of disasters and catastrophes. CEM is an acronym for Civil Emergency Management. It developed as a result of the restructuring of antiquated Civil Defense agencies.

Central Station. A fire or security alarm monitoring point connected to premises that do not belong to or have any business or ownership relationship to the monitoring point. Similar to Proprietary Station.

Code of Conduct. A collection of policies which, adopted by an organization or an individual, clearly state the way an employee or individual relates to himself and others in the organization, or to the public, during the conduct of business or profession.

Commercial Building. That classification of building generally accepted to be other than one- or two-family dwellings. The term *commercial* is principally a zoning term, not a building code term.

CPU. Central Processing Unit. The principal or main part of a computer where all the calculating and data handling functions are carried out.

Data. Facts and figures regarding an event or series of events. Data usually stand on their own and have no apparent relationship to other data collections until that relationship is intentionally drawn. At this point data collections and their relationships turn into information.

Disaster. An incident that either at the outset, or by expansion, has progressed to the point where the resources of the primary agency are outstripped. The word is used in the context of *emergency, disaster,* and *catastrophe.* Catastrophe implies the incident has outstripped the resources available in the region.

Emergency. A routine incident attended by a public safety agency. In this context, the term "emergency" implies that the incident resource needs easily fall within the resources available to the attending agency.

EMS. Emergency Medical Services.

Enhanced 911. Enhanced 911 adds the ability of the emergency services dispatcher or call taker answering a call for service to view on a cathode ray tube (CRT) the address and phone number of the telephone line from which the call is made.

FAX. An electronic means of transmitting images from one point to another via telephone or radio communications media. The word FAX is derived from the word *facsimilie.*

Fee. Method of realizing revenues used by political jurisdictions. The amount of money paid to the jurisdiction must be related in some way to the cost of delivering the service. This relationship is called the *rational nexus,* or rational connection.

First Responders. Private-sector technicians who come to the scene of a fire alarm system's activities and receive control of the building from the responding fire company.

FM. Frequency Modulation. A method of placing voice or data information on a radio signal wherein the frequency of the signal changes very slightly from the no-data condition to the data condition.

Hardware. Electronic or mechanical components of a system of any kind, for example, the computer's central processing unit is a piece of hardware in the context of a data processing system.

Hertz. An electrical term representing the frequency or rate at which the electrons in an alternating circuit change direction in a conductor. The term is used out of respect to a famous inventor in the field of electricity named Hertz.

Joint Response Agreement. An agreement between two political jurisdictions under which both jurisdictions determine the closest emergency facilities of either jurisdiction to respond to an address without regard to the address or political boundaries.

Keypad. A configuration of push buttons similar to the conventional telephone push button dial. Numbers 1 through 9 plus # and * signs are common.

Manual. As used, relating to the handling of records, i.e., hand sorting, picking, filing, and similar operations. It is referred to in contrast to automatic electronic or automatic mechanical methods of handling data and information.

MHz. Megahertz. 1,000,000 Hertz.

Microwave. Relates to a radio frequency spectrum wherein data and voice information are typically transmitted on one channel. The term *microwave* refers to the relatively short length of the radio wavelengths in the portion of the radio spectrum wherein these transmissions take place.

Model Building Codes. Building codes which are regionally, nationally, or internationally accepted by construction professionals as containing procedures and practices conducive to reasonable and prudent building construction. Contrasts to local building codes arrived at by political motivations or special interest urgings.

Modem. An electronic device used to connect data communications equipment to telephone or radio communications equipment. The modem translates the electronic signals into a form suitable for transmission over the telephone or radio. The term is formed from the two words, *modulator* and *demodulator.*

MSAG. Refers to the Master Street Address Guide. The accuracy of this database determines the precision to which emergency units can be quickly dispatched to an event.

Mutual Aid. A result of a written interlocal/intergovernment agreement that provides for assistance from an emergency agency to another emergency agency upon request without the need for high level approval in each instance before the second agency can respond. In most states, mutual aid results from a call from the requesting agency only after the first responding agency arrives on the incident scene and requests help from a secondary agency. See Joint Response.

911. A modern telephone service wherein a user who dials the numbers 9, 1, and 1 on the telephone keypad, or rotary dial, is automatically connected with the emergency services serving the area wherein the call is made. This service eliminates the need for a stranger in a geographic area to know details about the various emergency service agencies serving the address from which the call is made.

Nonuniformed. In many agencies those employees who are not required by state or local law to obtain special certifications in firefighting principles and methods are called "nonuniformed" personnel. The term "civilian" in the fire service traditionally refers to employees or other members of the community who are not skilled in firefighting principles and methods.

Operations. That section of an agency that delivers services directly to the client, customer, or public.

Physical Plant. Structures, piping, roads, and similar capital investments necessary to support an agency such as a fire department.

Potable Water. Water of such quality it can be used as drinking water.

Prefire Planning. A planning process used by fire departments to determine the actual layout, features, functions, and hazards in an occupancy or structure during normal working hours. Findings are documented and reduced to a plan usable during an emergency incident.

Private Sector. An organization owned or operated by an individual or corporate entity not supported by public funds such as taxes, or operated by public political jurisdictions.

Privatization. The process of turning operations or services provided by political jurisdictions over to agencies operated as members of the private sector.

Proprietary Station. A fire or security alarm monitoring point connected to premises having a business or ownership relationship to the monitoring point. Similar to Central Station.

PSAP. Public Safety Answering Point. The public safety end of a 911 call for service. The PSAP determines what kind of service is sent to the incident.

Radio Shack. A building or enclosure exclusively used for the housekeeping and protection of radio communications receivers and transmitters.

RF. Radio frequency.

Semiconductor. Electronic device based on what is called *silicon* technology, e.g. transistor, diode.

Solid State Electronic Equipment. Electronic equipment using semiconductor technology rather than vacuum tube technology in the circuitry.

SOP. Standard Operating Procedures. In some organizations called Standing Operating Procedures.

Support. That section of an agency that delivers services to other sections within an agency, but not to the client, customer, or public.

Taxes. Revenue-gathering method used by political jurisdictions. Taxes reflect a method using the value of some purchase possession, such as real estate, to levy a responsibility on the owner to pay funds to the political jurisdiction. Examples are sales taxes, and property taxes.

Trunking Radio System. A radio system which serves more than one agency on a fewer number of channels. A radio system wherein there is no specific frequency on which any agency operates.

UPS. Uninterruptable Power Supply. A type of electrical power supply frequently used in computer systems. The distinguishing characteristic of a properly designed UPS is the ability to supply a source of power to a user during a commercial power failure in such a fashion that the user does not detect there has been a commercial power failure.

CHAPTER 16. FIRE DEPARTMENT WATER SUPPLY

Adequacy. The water system's ability to deliver maximum daily domestic consumption plus the Needed Fire Flow at a location.

Basic Fire Flow. The fifth highest Needed Fire Flow which is considered a representative flow for the community.

Dual Pumping. Two pumps connected to the same hydrant, usually pump intake to intake.

Needed Fire Flow. The rate of flow expressed in gallons per minute at 20 psi residual pressure necessary to control a fire within a specific nature.

Reliability. The ability to continuously supply water even if a part of the system is out of service.

Required Fire Flow. The amount of water necessary to control a fire in a building based on area, height, construction, occupancy, and exposures.

Supplemental Pumping. A pumper at a secondary source providing additional water for effective streams to apparatus at the scene working from a primary water source.

Tandem Pumping. A short relay between two pumpers connected pump discharge to pump intake.

CHAPTER 17. FIRE COMPANY OPERATIONS

Engine Company. A group of firefighters whose primary function is to apply water to the fire.

Truck Company (also "Ladder" or "Hook and Ladder Company"). A group of firefighters organized to perform the various fireground tasks other than the application of water.

Company Officer. An officer, most usually a Captain or Lieutenant, assigned to lead and supervise a company.

Fireground. The fire and the surrounding area where operations are conducted. The scene of the fire.

Incident Command System (ICS). A structured model plan designed to make sure essential functions are carried out in a systematic manner at a fire or other emergency.

Incident Commander (IC). The officer in charge of operations at an emergency incident.

CHAPTER 19. HAZARDOUS MATERIALS OPERATIONS

Absorbent Material. A material designed to pick up and hold liquid hazardous material to prevent contamination spread. Materials include sawdust, clays, charcoal and polyolefin-type fibers.

Absorption. 1) The process of absorbing or "picking up" a liquid hazardous material to prevent enlargement of the contaminated area. 2) Movement of a toxicant into the circulatory system by oral, dermal, or inhalation exposure.

Adsorption. Process of adhering to a surface.

Air Monitoring. To measure, record, and/or detect pollutants in ambient air.

Air Purifying Respirators (APR). Personal Protective Equipment; a breathing mask with specific chemical cartridges designed to either filter particulates or absorb contaminants before they enter the worker's breathing zone. They are intended to be used only in atmospheres where the chemical hazards and concentrations are known.

American National Standards Institute (ANSI). A clearinghouse for nationally coordinated voluntary safety, engineering, and industrial consensus standards developed by trade associations, industrial firms, technical societies, consumer organizations, and government agencies.

Boiling Liquid Expanding Vapor Explosion (BLEVE). A container failure with a release of energy, often rapid and violent, which is accompanied by a release of gas to the atmosphere and propulsion of the container or container pieces due to an overpressure rupture.

Boom. A floating physical barrier serving as a continuous obstruction to the spread of a contaminant.

Breakthrough Time. The elapsed time between initial contact of the hazardous chemical with the outside surface of a barrier, such as protective clothing material, and the time at which the chemical can be detected at the inside surface of the material.

Buddy System. A system of organizing employees into work groups in such a manner that each employee of the work group is designated to be observed by at least one other employee in the work group (per OSHA 1910.120(a)(3)).

Canadian Transport Emergency Center (CANUTEC). A 24-hour, government-sponsored hot line for chemical emergencies. (The Canadian version of CHEMTREC).

Centers for Disease Control and Prevention (CDC). The federally funded research organization tasked with disease control and research.

Chemical Manufacturers Association. The parent organization that operates CHEMTREC.

Chemical Protective Clothing Material. Any material or combination of materials used in an item of clothing for the purpose of isolating parts of the wearer's body from contact with a hazardous chemical.

Chemical Protective Suit. Single or multi-piece garment constructed of chemical protective clothing materials designed and configured to protect the wearer's torso, head, arms, legs, hands, and feet.

Chemical Resistance. The ability to resist chemical attack. The attack is dependent on the method of test and its severity is measured by determining the changes in physical properties. Time, temperature, stress, and reagent all may be factors that affect the chemical resistance of a material.

Chemical-Resistant Materials. Materials that are specifically designed to inhibit or resist the passage of chemicals into and through the material by the processes of penetration, permeation, or degradation.

Chemical Transportation Emergency Center (CHEMTREC). The Chemical Transportation Emergency Center, operated by the Chemical Manufacturers Association (CMA), can provide information and technical assistance to emergency responders. (Phone number: 1-800-424-9300)

Chemnet. A mutual aid network of chemical shippers and contractors. It is activated when a member shipper cannot respond promptly to an incident involving chemicals. (Contact is made through CHEMTREC.)

Clandestine Laboratory. An operation consisting of a sufficient combination of apparatus and chemicals that either have been or could be used in the illegal manufacture/synthesis of controlled substances.

Clean Air Act (CAA). National legislation which resulted in EPA regulations and standards governing airborne emissions and ambient air quality.

Cleanup. Incident scene activities directed toward removing hazardous materials, contamination, debris, damaged containers, tools, dirt, water, and road surfaces in accordance with proper and legal standards, and returning the site to as near a normal state as existed prior to the incident.

Code of Federal Regulations **(CFR).** A collection of regulations established by federal law. Contact with the agency that issues the regulation is recommended for both details and interpretation.

Cold Zone. The area outside of the Warm Zone. Equipment and personnel are not expected to become contaminated in this area. This is the area where resources are assembled to support the hazardous materials operation.

Colorimetric Tubes. Glass tubes containing a chemically treated substrate that reacts with specific airborne chemicals to produce a distinctive color. The tubes are calibrated to indicate approximate concentrations in air.

Command Post. The location from which all incident operations are directed and planning functions are performed. The communications center is often incorporated into the command post. (NIIMS)

Community Awareness and Emergency Response (CAER). A program developed by the Chemical Manufacturers Association (CMA) to provide guidance for chemical plant managers to assist them in developing integrated hazardous materials emergency response plans between the plant and the community.

Compatibility. The matching of protective chemical clothing to the hazardous material involved to provide the best protection for the worker.

Compatibility Charts. Permeation and penetration data supplied by manufacturers of chemical protective clothing to indicate chemical resistance and breakthrough time of various garment materials as tested against a battery of chemicals. These test data should be in accordance with ASTM and NFPA standards.

Comprehensive Environmental Response, Compensation and Liability Act (CERCLA). Known as CERCLA or SUPERFUND, it addresses hazardous substance releases into the environment and the cleanup of inactive hazardous waste sites. It also requires those who release hazardous substances, as defined by the Environmental Protection Agency (EPA), above certain levels (known as "reportable quantities") to notify the National Response Center.

Computer-Aided Management of Emergency Operations (CAMEO). A computer database storage-retrieval system of preplanning and emergency data for on-scene use at hazardous materials incidents.

Confinement. Procedures taken to keep a material in a defined or localized area.

Contact. Being exposed to an undesirable or unknown substance that may pose a threat to health and safety.

Container. Any device in which a hazardous material is stored, transported, disposed of, or otherwise handled.

Containment. All activities necessary to bring the incident to a point of stabilization and to establish a degree of safety for emergency personnel greater than existed upon arrival.

Contamination. An uncontained substance or process that poses a threat to life, health, or the environment. (NFPA 472, sections 1-3)

Control. The procedures, techniques, and methods used in the mitigation of a hazardous materials incident, including containment, extinguishment, and confinement.

Control Zones. The designation of areas as a hazardous materials incident based on safety and the degree of hazard.

Damming. A procedure consisting of constructing a dike or embankment to totally immobilize a flowing waterway contaminated with a liquid or solid hazardous substance. (PA, 600/2-77-277)

Decon. Popular abbreviation referring to the process of decontamination.

Decontamination. The physical and/or chemical process of reducing and preventing the spread of contamination from persons and equipment used at a hazardous materials incident. (Also referred to as "contamination reduction.") (NFPA 472, 1-3)

Decontamination Corridor. A distinct area within the "Warm Zone" that functions as a protective buffer and bridge between the "Hot Zone" and the "Cold Zone," where decontamination stations and personnel are located to conduct decontamination procedures.

Decontamination Officer. A position within the Hazardous Materials Sector which has responsibility for identifying the location of the decontamination corridor, assigning stations, managing all decontamination procedures, and identifying the types of decontamination necessary.

Decontamination Team (Decon-Team). A group of personnel and resources operating within a decontamination corridor.

Degradation. The loss in physical properties of an item of protective clothing due to exposure to chemicals, use, or ambient conditions.

Detectors.

Combustible Gas Indicator (CGI) detector: Measures the presence of a combustible gas or vapor in air.

Corrosivity (pH) detector: A meter or paper that indicates the relative acidity or alkalinity of a substance, generally using an international scale of 0 (acid) through 14 (alkalicaustic). (See pH.)

Flame Ionization Detector (FID): A device used to determine the presence of hydrocarbons in air.

Gas Chromatograph/Mass Spectrometer detector: An instrument used for identifying and analyzing organics.

Heat detector: An instrument used to detect heat by sensing infrared waves.

Photo-ionization Detector (PID): A device used to determine the presence of gases/vapors in low concentrations in air.

Radiation Beta Survey detector: An instrument used to detect beta radiation.

Radiation Dosimeter detector: An instrument which measures the amount of radiation to which a person has been exposed.

Radiation Gamma Survey detector: An instrument used for the detection of ionizing radiation, principally gamma radiation, by means of a gas-filled tube.

Temperature detector: An instrument, either mechanical or electronic, used to determine the temperature of ambient air, liquids, or surfaces.

Dike. An embankment or ridge, natural or manmade, used to control the movement of liquids, sludges, solids, or other materials.

Dike Overflow. A dike constructed in a manner that allows uncontaminated water to flow unobstructed over the dike while keeping the contaminant behind the dike.

Dike Underflow. A dike constructed in a manner that allows uncontaminated water to flow unobstructed under the dike while keeping the contaminant behind the dike.

Dispersion. To spread, scatter, or diffuse through air, soil, surface, or ground water.

Disposal Drum. A reference to a specially constructed drum used to overpack damaged or leaking containers of hazardous materials for shipment.

Diversion. The intentional, controlled movement of a hazardous material to relocate it into an area where it will pose less harm to the community and the environment.

Double gloving. A set of gloves worn over those already in place for enhanced protection.

Emergency Medical Services (EMS). Functions as required to provide emergency medical care for ill or injured persons by trained providers.

Emergency Operations Center (EOC). The secured site where government officials exercise centralized direction and control in an emergency. The EOC serves as a resource center and coordination point for additional field assistance. It also provides executive directives to and liaison for state and federal government representatives, and considers and mandates protective actions.

Emergency Response. Response to any occurrence which has or could result in a release of a hazardous substance.

Emergency Response Organization. An organization that uses personnel trained in emergency response.

Emergency Response Personnel. Personnel assigned to organizations that have the responsibility for responding to different types of emergency situations.

Environmental Protection Agency (EPA). The purpose of the Environmental Protection Agency (EPA) is to protect and enhance our environment today and for future generations to the fullest extent possible under the laws enacted by the U.S. Congress. The Agency's mission is to control and abate pollution in the areas of water, air, solid waste, pesticides, noise, and radiation. EPA's mandate is to mount an integrated, coordinated attack on environmental pollution in cooperation with state and local governments.

EPA. See Environmental Protection Agency.

Evacuation. The removal of potentially endangered, but not yet exposed, persons from an area threatened by a hazardous materials incident.

Exposure. The subjecting of a person to a toxic substance or harmful physical agent through any route of entry.

First Responder. The first trained person(s) to arrive at the scene of a hazardous materials incident. May be from the public or private sector of emergency services.

First Responder Awareness Level. Individuals who are likely to witness or discover a hazardous substance release who have been trained to initiate an emergency response sequence by notifying the proper authorities of the release. They would take no further action beyond notifying the authorities of the release.

First Responder Operations Level. Individuals who respond to releases or potential releases of hazardous substances as part of the initial response to the site for the purpose of protecting nearby persons, property, or the environment from the effects of the release. They are trained to respond in a defensive fashion without actually trying to stop the release. Their function is to contain the release from a safe distance, keep it from spreading, and prevent exposures.

Full Protective Clothing. Protective clothing worn primarily by firefighters which includes helmet, coat, pants, boots, gloves, and self-contained breathing apparatus designed for structural firefighting. It does not provide specialized chemical protection.

Hazard Class. The eight classes of hazardous materials as categorized and defined by the Department of Transportation in 49 CFR.

Hazardous Material. A substance (solid, liquid, or gas) capable of posing an unreasonable risk to health, safety, the environment, or property.

Hazardous Materials Response Team (HMRT). An organized group of employees, designated by the employer, who are expected to perform work to handle and control actual or potential leaks or spills of hazardous substances requiring possible close approach to the substance. A Hazardous Materials Team may be a separate component of a fire brigade or a fire department or other appropriately trained and equipped units from public or private agencies.

Hazmat. Acronym used for Hazardous Materials.

HMRT. (See Hazardous Materials Response Team)

Hot Zone. An area immediately surrounding a hazardous materials incident, which extends far enough to prevent adverse effects from hazardous materials releases to personnel outside the zone. This zone is also referred to as the "exclusion zone," the "red zone," and the "restricted zone" in other documents.

Immediately Dangerous to Life or Health (IDLH). An atmospheric concentration of any toxic, corrosive or asphyxiant substance that poses an immediate threat to life or would cause irreversible or delayed adverse health effects or would interfere with an individual's ability to escape from a dangerous atmosphere.

Incident. An event involving a hazardous material or a release or potential release of a hazardous material.

Incident Command. A disciplined method of management established for the specific purpose of control and direction of resources and personnel.

Incident Commander. The person responsible for all decisions relating to the management of the incident.

Incident Command System (ICS). An organized system of roles, responsibilities, and standard operating procedures used to manage and direct emergency operations.

Isolating the Scene. Preventing persons and equipment from becoming exposed to a release or threatened release of a hazardous material by the establishment of site control zones.

Leak. The uncontrolled release of a hazardous material which could pose a threat to health, safety, and/or the environment.

Leak Control Compounds. Substances used for the plugging and patching of leaks in non-pressurized containers.

Leak Control Devices. Tools and equipment used for the plugging and patching of leaks in non-pressurized and some low-pressure containers, pipes, and tanks.

Level of Protection. In addition to appropriate respiratory protection, designations of types of personal protective equipment to be worn based on NFPA standards and EPA classifications.

Level A: Vapor protective suit for hazardous chemical emergencies.

Level B: Liquid splash protective suit for hazardous chemical emergencies.

Level C: Limited use protective suit for hazardous chemical emergencies.

Local Emergency Planning Committee (LEPC). A committee appointed by a state emergency response commission, as required by SARA Title III, to formulate a comprehensive emergency plan for its corresponding local government or mutual aid region.

Material Safety Data Sheet (MSDS). A document which contains information about the specific identity of hazardous chemicals, including information on health effects, first aid, chemical and physical properties, and emergency phone numbers.

Monitoring. The act of systematically checking to determine contaminant levels and atmospheric conditions.

Monitoring Equipment. Instruments and devices used to identify, qualify, and/or quantify contaminants.

MSDS. See Material Safety Data Sheet.

National Fire Protection Association (NFPA). An international voluntary membership organization which promotes improved fire protection and prevention, establishes safeguards against loss of life and property by fire, and writes and publishes the National Fire Standards.

National Interagency Incident Management System (NIIMS). A standardized systems approach to incident management that consists of five major subdivisions collectively providing a total systems approach to all-risk incident management.

National Institute for Occupational Safety and Health (NIOSH). A federal agency which, among other activities, tests and certifies respiratory protective devices, and air sampling detector tubes, and recommends occupational exposure limits for various substances.

National Response Center (NRC). Communications center operated by the U.S. Coast Guard in Washington, DC. It provides information on suggested technical emergency actions, and is the federal spill notification point. The NRC must be notified within 24 hours of any spill of a reportable quantity of a hazardous substance by the spiller.

Occupational Safety and Health Administration (OSHA). Branch of the United States Department of Labor. An agency with safety and health regulatory and enforcement authorities for most United States industries, businesses and states.

Oxygen-Deficient Atmosphere. An atmosphere which contains an oxygen content less than 19.5% by volume at sea level.

Penetration. The movement of liquid molecules through a chemical protective clothing item, suit, garment or material.

Permeation. The movement of vapor or gas molecules through a chemical protective garment material.

Personal Protective Equipment (PPE). Equipment provided to shield or isolate a person from the chemical, physical, and thermal hazards that may be encountered at a hazardous materials incident. Adequate personal protective equipment should protect the respiratory system, skin, eyes, face, hands, feet, head, body, and hearing. Personal protective equipment includes personal protective clothing, self-contained positive pressure breathing apparatus, and air purifying respirators.

Postincident Analysis. The termination phase of an incident that includes completion of the required forms and documentation for conducting a critique.

Risk Analysis. A process to analyze the probability that harm may occur to life, property, and the environment and to note the risks to be taken to identify the incident objectives.

Safety Officer. Selected by the Incident Commander, a person at an emergency incident responsible for assuring that all overall operations performed at the incident by all agencies present are done so with respect to the highest levels of safety and health. The Safety Officer shall report directly to the Incident Commander.

SARA. See Superfund Amendments and Reauthorization Act.

SCBA. See Self-Contained Breathing Apparatus.

Scene. The location affected or potentially affected by a hazard.

Self-Contained Breathing Apparatus (SCBA). A positive pressure, self-contained breathing apparatus (SCBA) or combination SCBA/supplied air breathing apparatus certified by the National Institute for Occupational Safety and Health (NIOSH) and the Mine Safety and Health Administration (MSHA), or the appropriate approval agency for use in atmospheres that are immediately dangerous to life or health (IDLH).

Sheltering In Place/In-Place Protection. To direct people to quickly go inside a building and remain inside until the danger passes.

Shipping Papers. Generic term used to refer to documents that must accompany all shipments of goods for transportation. These include Hazardous Waste Manifest, Bill of Lading, and Consists, etc. Shipping papers are intended to describe what hazardous materials are contained within the shipment, if any.

Spill. The release of a liquid, powder, or solid hazardous material in a manner that poses a threat to air, water, ground, and to the environment.

Staging Area. The safe area established for temporary location of available resources closer to the incident site to reduce response time.

Superfund Amendments and Reauthorization Act (SARA). Created for the purpose of establishing federal statutes for right-to-know standards, and emergency response to hazardous materials incidents, it reauthorized the federal Superfund, and mandated states to implement equivalent regulations/requirements.

Termination. That portion of incident management during which personnel are involved in documenting safety procedures, site operations, hazards faced, and lessons learned from the incident. Termination is divided into three phases: Debriefing, Postincident Analysis, and Critique.

Transportation Community Awareness and Emergency Response (TRANSCAER). A program developed by the Chemical Manufacturers Association (CMA) to provide guidance for chemical shippers and transporters to assist them in developing integrated hazardous materials emergency response plans between their organizations and the community.

Warm Zone. The area where personnel and equipment decontamination and hot zone support take place. It includes control points for the access corridor and thus assists in reducing the spread of contamination. This is also referred to as the "decontamination," "contamination reduction," "yellow zone," "support zone," or "limited access zone" in other documents.

CHAPTER 20. AIRCRAFT CRASH RESCUE AND FIREFIGHTING

Aircraft Classes:

Heavy: Maximum certificated take-off weight of 300,000 lbs. or more.

Large: More than 12,500 lbs. up to 300,000 lbs. maximum certificated take-off weight.

Small: 12,500 lbs. or less maximum certificated take-off weight.

Abort. An aircraft terminates a planned maneuver, e.g., an aborted take-off.

Air Traffic Control. The agency which has jurisdiction over air traffic, which is the Federal Aviation Administration (FAA), and which operates control towers at major airports. This includes individual airport towers, departure control, centers, and approach control facilities.

Aircraft Accident. An occurrence associated with the operation of an aircraft that takes place between the time any person boards the aircraft with the intention of flight, until such person has disembarked, in which: (1) any person suffers death or serious injury as a result of coming in contact with anything attached thereto, or in which the aircraft receives substantial damage, except when the injuries are from natural causes, are self-inflicted or inflicted by other persons, or when the injuries are to stowaways hiding outside the areas normally available to the passengers and crew; or (2) the aircraft incurs damage or structural failure which adversely affects the structure strength, performance, or flight characteristics of the aircraft and which normally would require major repair or replacement of the affected component.

Aircraft Rescue & Firefighting (ARFF). The firefighting action taken to prevent, control, or extinguish fire involving, or adjacent to an aircraft, for the purpose of providing maximum fuselage integrity and escape area for its occupants. Rescue and firefighting personnel, to the extent possible, will assist in evacuation of the aircraft using normal and/or emergency means of egress. Additionally, rescue and firefighting personnel, by whatever means necessary, and to the extent possible, enter the aircraft and provide all possible assistance in the evacuation of the occupants and control of any interior fire spread.

Airfield Operations Area. Area confined within the security boundaries of the airport, usually referred to as the "AOA."

Airframe. Generally, the parts of the airplane having to do with flight, such as fuselage, nacelles, cowlings, fairings, empennage, flight surfaces, landing gears, etc., other than the engines or propellers.

Airport Access Road. Those roads which are provided and maintained on airport property for the purpose of providing emergency vehicles and other required airport vehicular traffic access to operational areas, taxiways, runways and remote areas of the airport.

Airside. The movement area of an airport, adjacent terrain, and buildings or portions thereof, access to which is controlled, usually by an FAA Air Traffic Control Facility (Tower). Also called the "Active Area" of the airport.

Approach Zone. Designated clear area just before aircraft reaches runway.

Apron. Wide paved (sometimes unpaved) parking and tiedown areas off of, and away from, runways.

APU. Auxiliary Power Unit.

Air Traffic Control (ATC). The radio control center for aircraft at an airport staffed by FAA personnel.

Base Leg. Position of an aircraft which is on a 90° landing approach to the active runway.

Belly. Underside of fuselage.

Cabin. The area of the fuselage where passengers ride.

Canopy. Transparent enclosure over a cockpit on some models of aircraft.

Crash Fire Rescue (CFR). Older term for airport aircraft rescue and firefighting (ARFF) resources.

Circumferentials. The frames which form the cross-sections of the fuselage. Also called Formers or Ribs.

Closed Runway. A runway unusable for aircraft operations and closed by airport management. Usually marked with a large painted or lighted X.

Cockpit. Fuselage compartment where the pilot and/or flight crew sit to fly the aircraft. Also referred to as the "Flight Deck" or "Pilot's Compartment."

Cockpit Voice Recorder (CVR). The cockpit voice recorder monitors crew communication through a pickup on the flight deck to a recorder, usually mounted in the tail area of the aircraft and designed to withstand certain impact forces and a degree of fire. The CVR recorder is a continuous 30-minute tape that requires the power to be removed by pulling the CVR circuit breaker in the flight deck to preserve communication recordings that may be vital to the accident investigation.

Cowling. Removable covering around engine sections.

Critical Rescue and Firefighting Access Area. This is the rectangular area surrounding any given runway. Its width extends 150 m (500 ft.) outward from each side of the runway centerline, and its length is 1,000 m (3,300 ft.) beyond each threshold.

Dangerous Cargo. Hazardous materials classification for aircraft transportation.

Delayed Treatment. Second priority in patient treatment. These people require aid, but injuries are less severe.

Departure Control. A function of an approach control facility providing air traffic control service for departing aircraft.

Downwind Leg. That portion of the aircraft traffic pattern in which the aircraft is traveling with the wind parallel to the runway.

Empennage. The tail assembly of the aircraft which includes the horizontal and vertical stabilizers, the rudder, and the elevators mounted on them.

Engine Numbers. Engines of a multi-engine airplane are numbered from left to right—1,2,3— relative to left and right of the pilot seated in the cockpit.

Engines. The motive powers of aircraft. The engine of a single-engine plane may be located in front of the pilot's cockpit, or, as in military types, may be located aft of the cockpit. In multi-engine craft, they may be located on the wings, in streamlined housings known as nacelles, or in nacelles aft of the wings, just forward of the tail, or in the tail section, as in the Boeing 727. Piston-driven engines are usually housed in the forward section of the nacelle, and are enclosed by a removable cowling forming the front part of the nacelle skin surface. Behind the engine, a bulkhead (firewall) separates the engine from the rest of the nacelle and the wing structure. This space to the rear of the engine may contain lubricating oil or hydraulic fluid tanks. It also may house a retractable landing gear, or other equipment, such as batteries. The jet engine and its accessories occupy the entire nacelle.

Evacuation Time. The time between the accident/incident and the removal of all surviving occupants. A Federal Aviation Administration requirement prior to certification of civil air transport aircraft stipulates that the complete evacuation of all occupants using one-half of the required exits must be demonstrated in 90 seconds or less. Accident records indicate that this time is usually exceeded under conditions of actual emergency.

Federal Aviation Administration (FAA). The FAA is an independent agency of the U.S. federal government charged with the primary responsibility of regulating the safety of both military and civil aviation.

Final Approach. That portion of the landing pattern in which the aircraft is lined up with the runway heading straight in to land. The aircraft is designated as being "on final."

Flameout. Unintended loss of combustion in turbine engines resulting in loss of engine power.

Flaps. An adjustable airfoil attached to the leading edge on smaller airplane wings, which improves the aerodynamic performance of the airplane during take-offs and landings. The amount of flap setting desired is selected by the pilot prior to take-off or landing.

Flight Data Recorder (FDR). The flight data recorder is an instrument that monitors performance characteristics of aircraft in flight. It is mounted in the tail area of the aircraft and designed to withstand certain impact forces and a degree of fire. Its purpose is to provide investigators with flight performance data that may be relevant in determining the cause of an accident.

Flight Deck. The pilot's compartment of large aircraft.

Fuel Hydrant. Underground fueling hydrants located around terminal satellites for the purpose of refueling aircraft.

Fuselage. The fuselage is the main body of the airplane, to which the wings and tail are attached. In most commercial aircraft, the fuselage is constructed with two decks. If it were possible to view a modern passenger plane during construction, one would see a network of angle frames and bulkheads which make up the compartmentation of an aircraft and add the needed strength to the fuselage. The arrangement of the compartments in the lower deck of a large aircraft generally follows a standard pattern. Up forward is the nose wheel well containing batteries and the aircraft's installed firefighting system. Directly aft of the nose wheel well are the forward cargo compartments, then the center section where the wings of the plane extend right and left from the fuselage. From the center section back to the tail of the aircraft lies the rear cargo compartment. In the upper deck and starting at the nose of the plane is the cockpit of the flight deck, which houses all controls and instruments used in flying. (Scores of fluid lines and electrical wiring terminate at these controls and instruments.) The cockpit is separated by a bulkhead or partition which includes a door for entrance and exit. From the cockpit aft are compartments, including the main cabin, the galley, and toilets.

Galley. Food preparation area on commercial jet aircraft.

Gates. Numerically designated areas of an airport terminal used for the purpose of passenger boarding and off-loading.

Hydrant Cart. A motorized vehicle with metering and pressure reducing capabilities, used in fueling operations when fuel hydrants are used for fueling of aircraft.

ICAO. International Civil Aviation Organization.

Immediate Treatment. A patient who requires rapid assessment and medical intervention for survival.

In-Flight Emergency. Emergencies that affect the operation integrity of an aircraft while in flight.

Inboard or Outboard. Terminology used to give reference points to certain sections of the airplane. For example, the engine closest to the fuselage would be referred to as the "inboard engine," and the engine furthest from the fuselage would be the "outboard engine." Also used in referring to flaps, ailerons, fuel tank locations, and other similar items.

Inner Perimeter. That area which is secured to allow effective command, communication and coordination control, and to allow for safe operations to deal with an emergency, including the immense ingress and egress needs of emergency response personnel and vehicles.

Instrument Flight Rules (IFR). Apply when visibility is *less* than 3 miles and ceiling is *below* 1,000 feet.

Investigation. A process conducted for the purpose of accident prevention that includes the gathering and analysis of information, the drawing of conclusions, including the determination of cause(s) and, when appropriate, the making of safety recommendations.

Itinerant. Privately owned aircraft with no regularly scheduled destination.

Jetways. Enclosed telescoping ramp for passenger loading and unloading from aircraft to satellite.

Landing Gear. System of struts, or other shock-absorbing devices, and tires, wheel, and brakes which the airplane lands on and which absorb and reduce the shock of the landing. Also called the "undercarriage." Types of landing gear are fixed, retractable, and tricycle.

Landing Roll. The distance from the point of touchdown to the point where the aircraft can be brought to a stop or exit the runway.

Leading or Trailing Edges. The forward or rearward edges of an airfoil. Forward being leading edge, and rearward being the trailing edge. The applies to tail surfaces, wings, props, rotor blades, and other items.

Longerons. The principal longitudinal structural members of the fuselage.

Main Cabin. Where passengers or cargo are carried.

Medical Group Organizational Structure. This is designed to provide the Incident Commander with a basic expandable system for handling patients in a multi-casualty incident.

Medical Supply Cache. A cache consists of standardized medical supplies and equipment stored in a predetermined location for dispatch to incidents.

Medical Team. Combinations of medically trained personnel who are responsible for on-scene patient treatment.

Medical Transportation Area. That portion of the triage area where injured persons are staged for transportation to medical facilities under the direct supervision of a medical transportation officer.

Minor Treatment. These patients' injuries require simple and rudimentary first-aid.

Movement Area. Areas of the airport that are used for taxiing/hovering, air taxiing, take-off and landing of aircraft, exclusive of loading ramps and parking areas.

Notice to Airmen/Notam. A notice containing information concerning the establishment, condition, and change in any component (facility, service, or procedure), the timely knowledge of which is essential to personnel concerned with flight operations.

Outboard. Section of a wing or its contents and attachments farther from the fuselage, or center lines.

Outer Perimeter. Area outside of the inner perimeter that is secured for immediate support operational requirements, free from unauthorized or uncontrolled interference.

Parallel Runways. Two or more runways at the same airport whose centerlines are parallel. In addition to the runway number, parallel runways are designed as "L" (left) and "R" (right).

Patient Transportation Recorder. Supervised by the Patient Transportation Supervisor. Responsible for recording pertinent information regarding off-incident transportation of patients.

Phonetic Alphabet:

A	ALPHA	J	JULIET	S	SIERRA
B	BRAVO	K	KILO	T	TANCO
C	CHARLIE	L	LIMA	U	UNIFORM
D	DELTA	M	MIKE	V	VICTOR
E	ECHO	N	NOVEMBER	W	WISKEY
F	FOXTROT	O	OSCAR	X	X-RAY
G	GOLF	P	PAPA	Y	YANKEE
H	HOTEL	Q	QUEBEC	Z	ZULU
I	INDIA	R	ROMEO		

Pod. The enclosed streamline housing around the jet engine.

Potential Fire Zones—Jet Engines. While the construction of the jet engine is arranged to minimize hazards by separating the engine into several compartments, the head, high-pressure fuel lines and a fresh air supply, as combined in a turbo-prop aircraft, invite fire. Typical compartments include: (1) accessory compartment (starter, generator, fuel pump); (2) compressor compartment; (3) tail pipe section (area immediately adjacent to the engine burner); and (4) aft fuselage.

Prop Wash. Wind driven astern by an operating propeller.

Propellers. System of airfoils (blades) attached to a hub which, when rotated, will propel air. It usually has three or four blades on commercial aircraft. It can be revolved by piston or turboprop-type engines.

Pylon, Nacelle Strut. The structure that attaches a jet engine to the wing.

Ramp. (1) Paved loading or parking for aircraft, and/or (2) passenger stairway from ground to aircraft door.

Rapid Intervention Vehicle (RIV). A complementary vehicle to the major firefighting vehicles. The design and purpose of the RIV is to provide a means of bringing extinguishing agent to the aircraft crash scene significantly faster (up to 60 seconds) than can be achieved by major firefighting vehicles. The RIV brings to the crash scene the quantity and discharge capacity of extinguishing agent necessary to: extinguish an incipient fire; hold a fire from enlarging until larger crash vehicles arrive; and/or maintain at least *one* fire-free, clear escape path for the rescue of passengers and crew. At smaller airports where existing fire station locations and CFR vehicles provide acceptable rapid response, use of an RIV may not be necessary if it cannot provide a significant improvement in response time.

Rendezvous Point. A prearranged reference point, i.e., road junction, crossroad, or other specified place, to which personnel/vehicles responding to an emergency situation initially proceed to receive directions to staging areas and/or the accident/incident site.

Root. The area where the wing attaches to the fuselage of the aircraft.

Rotor. A rotating airfoil assembly, either "main" or "tail" found on helicopters.

Rudder. The upright movable part of a tail assembly which controls the direction of the airplane.

Runway. A defined rectangular area on a land airport for the landing and take-off of aircraft. Runways are normally numbered in relation to their magnetic direction rounded off to the nearest 10°.

S.T.A.R.T. Acronym for *Simple Triage And Rapid Treatment/Transport.* This is the initial triage system that has been adopted for use by the Fire Chiefs Association.

Slides or Chutes. Inflatable slides for emergency evacuation of aircraft.

Slipstream (or Prowash). Wind or air displaced, or pushed rearward, when the propeller is rotated; or when the aircraft moves through the air.

Souls on Board. Term used by air traffic controllers to refer to the number of living people on the aircraft.

Spars. Chief structural member of the wing, which is a beam-like structure that runs from the wing root out through the wing to the tip. The ribs attach to this structure.

Stabilizer. Any airfoil, the primary function of which is to increase the stability of the aircraft. The term stabilizer is most commonly used in reference to the fixed horizontal tail surface of the aircraft.

Stiffeners. Secondary structural members of fuselage and wings.

Stringer. Long, heavy horizontal timber used for any of several connective or supportive purposes.

Strut. Shock-absorbing device used on landing gear which uses the principle of air over hydraulic fluid. The air being compressed to cushion the shock of landing and the bumps of taxiing.

Tagging. Method used to identify casualties as requiring immediate care (Priority 1), delayed care (Priority II), or minor care (Priority III), or as deceased.

Taxiways. Designated aircraft taxiing routes. May have number or letter designations. Will soon be all lettered.

Threshold. The beginning of a runway.

Thrust. Forward reaction produced by forcing air to the rear either by propeller, a turbojet, or a ram jet-type powerplant. On turbojet aircraft the power produced is measured in pounds of thrust.

Touchdown Zone. The first 3,000 feet of the runway beginning at the landing threshold.

Torching. The burning of fuel at the end of an exhaust pipe or stack of a reciprocating aircraft engine, the result of excessive richness in the fuel air mixture.

Tower/Airport Traffic Control Tower (ATCT). A terminal facility that uses air/ground communications, visual sighting, and other devices to provide air traffic control services to aircraft operating in the vicinity of the airport or in the movement area.

Trailing Edge. Rearmost edge of a wing of propeller blade, as distinguished from the leading or forward edge.

Triage. The screening and classification of sick, wounded, or injured persons to determine priority needs in order to ensure the efficient use of medical manpower, equipment and facilities.

Triage Tag. A tag used by triage personnel to identify and document the patient's medical condition.

Turbo Prop Aircraft. An aircraft having a jet engine in which the energy of the jet drives the propeller.

Turboprop Engine. A gas turbine power plant for a propeller plane. To the basic turbojet components—compressor, combustor, and turbine—is added a power turbine driving the propeller. In a helicopter, the free-turbine turboprop engine, without mechanical connection with the main engine rotor, drives the rotor.

Turbojet Engine. A thermal-air-jet engine in which the incoming air is compressed, heated by burning fuel at compressor pressure, released through a turbine, and then ejected at high velocity. This provides thrust by rapid exhaust rearward from the tail pipe (jet nozzle). The turbine is used only to drive the compressor and engine-driven accessories.

Visual Flight Rules (VFR). Applicable when visibility is *greater* than three (3) miles and the flight path may be controlled by visual reference to the ground.

Wet Wing. Terminology used to denote wing fuel tanks.

Wind Sock. Cone-shaped cloth sock which hangs in an open area of the airport to serve as a weather vane, indicating wind direction.

Wing. Main lifting and supporting surface of the aircraft in flight.

Wing Flaps. Hinged flaps attached to the trailing edges of the airplane wings, used to lower the landing speed and to control flight characteristics.

Wing Root. The area where the wing attaches the fuselage of the airplane. Also where electrical wiring bundles, fuel lines, and flight control cables are routed from the wing to the cockpit.

Wing Tanks. The portion of the wings used to store gasoline. Wing tanks are built in, or are a self-contained bladder type.

CHAPTER 21. WILDLAND FIREFIGHTING

Aerial Torch. An ignition device suspended under a helicopter, capable of dispensing ignited fuel to the ground for assistance in burnout or backfiring.

Agency. Generally used to denote a unit of government such as a federal agency, state department, or fire district which has legal authority to organize and direct a firefighting service or which has responsibility and authority for contracting for fire protection. (Should not be confused with the fire department proper.)

Responsible agency. That fire protection agency having actual responsibility for taking fire attack action at the location under consideration; may often be a contractor.

Receiving, requesting, sending, (agency or unit). When a fire agency, service, unit, or fire department requests physical assistance, or receives or sends such physical assistance to another, confusion may result with respect to which agency or unit was involved in the receiving and which was involved in the sending. This distinction is important not only during the dispatching of such aid, but also in the consideration of reimbursements and the fire records. Those terms were developed to eliminate such possible confusion.

Air Cargo. All goods and material items transported and delivered entirely by aircraft.

Air-Ground Detection. A fire detection system combining fixed coverage of key areas by ground detectors with aerial patrol.

Air Tanker. Fixed wing aircraft certified by the FAA and used by control agencies to drop water or fire retardant chemicals on fires.

Alidade. A straightedge equipped with sights; an essential part of a directional device for locating fires.

Allowable Burned Area. The maximum average loss in acreage burned for a given period of years that is considered acceptable under organized fire control for a given area.

Anchor Point. An advantageous location, usually a barrier to fire spread, from which to start constructing a fire line. Used to minimize the chance of being flanked by the fire while the line is being constructed. Also may refer to a safe point for a constructed line.

Area Ignition. The ignition of a number of individual fires throughout an area, either simultaneously or in quick succession, and so spaced that they soon influence and support each other to produce fast, hot spread of fire throughout the area. See simultaneous ignition.

Area of Influence. A delineated area surrounding an air base which can be reached first by aircraft from the particular base.

Aspect. The direction in which the slope of a hill or mountain faces (Also known as exposure).

Attack a Fire. Attempt to limit the spread of a fire by cooling, smothering, or removing or otherwise treating the fuel around its perimeter. See direct method, indirect method, parallel method.

Azimuth. Direction from a point, measured in degrees clockwise from true north.

Azimuth Circle. A circle graduated in degrees of angle in clockwise direction.

Back Azimuth. Azimuth plus 180°; direction opposite to azimuth.

Backfire. (1) A fire set along the inner edge of a fire control line (i.e., toward a going fire) with the expectation that it will be influenced by the advance of the main fire and thus burn out the intervening flammable vegetation. (2) A tactic usually used only when other fire control methods are judged impractical. (3) Not the same as burning out.

Banking Snags. The act of throwing mineral soil about the base of an unlighted snag to prevent it taking fire.

Base. A logistical location for a large fire operation.

Base, Home Base. Place of regular assignment of a crew, fire engine, aircraft or employee.

Berm. Ridge of dirt or debris slightly above the normal ground surface resulting from line construction. Sometimes created on a slope to stop rolling material.

Blind Areas. An area behind some sight barrier in which neither the ground nor its vegetation can be seen from a given observation point under favorable light and atmospheric conditions.

Blowup. Sudden increase in fire intensity or rate of spread sufficient to preclude direct control or to upset existing control plans. Often accompanied by violent conviction; may have other characteristics of a firestorm.

Branch. That organizational level having functional/geographic responsibility for major segments of incident operations. The branch level is organizationally between section and division/group.

Broadcast Burning. Intentional burning in which fire is intended to spread over all of a specific ground area.

Brush. Shrubs and stands of short scrubby tree species that do not reach merchantable size. (Not a synonym for slash or reproduction.)

Buildup. An increasing condition as may be applied to specific situations, e.g., weather, fire hazard, organization, etc.

Burning Block. In control or prescribed burning, an area having sufficiently uniform vegetation stand and fuel conditions to be treated uniformly under a given burning prescription. The size ranges from the smallest that allows an economically acceptable cost per acre up to the largest that can conveniently be treated (physically and safely) in one burning period.

Burning Conditions. The state of the combined factors of environment that affect fire in a given fuel association.

Burning Index. A number in an arithmetic scale determined from fuel moisture content, wind speed, and other selected factors that affect burning conditions, and from which the ease of ignition of fires and their probable behavior may be determined. (See danger index.)

Burning Index Class. A segment of a burning index scale identified by such qualitative terms as low, medium, high, very high, or extreme, or by numerals 1, 2, 3, . . . 10.

Burning Index Matter. A device used to determine burning index for different combinations of burning index factors.

Burning Out. That part of the indirect or parallel method of fire control consisting of removing by fire the unburned fuels inside the fire line.

Burning Patterns of Large Fires:

Time pattern. A fast-moving fire with regular or irregular, but well-defined perimeter. Possibly some spotting within close proximity to main fire.

Spotty pattern. Considerable spotting well ahead of main fire creates a perimeter that is very irregular and difficult to determine. Unusual fire behavior may be expected.

Area ignition pattern. Caused by an extremely violent fire caused by many spot fires interacting on each other. Slowed up conditions usually result.

Burning Period. A period of time beginning when the fire starts and ending at 10:00 a.m. on the day following.

Calculated Probabilities. Evaluation of all existing factors pertinent to probable future behavior of a going fire and of the potential ability of available forces to carry out control operations on a given time schedule.

Camp. A geographical site, within the general incident area, separate from incident base, equipped and staffed to provide food, water, and sanitary services to incident personnel.

Catface. A defect on the surface of a tree resulting from a wound in which healing has not re-established the normal cross section. See fire scar.

Center Firing. A technique of broadcast burning in which fires are set in the center of the area to create a strong draft. Additional fires are then set progressively nearer the outer control lines as in-draft builds up to draw them in toward the center. See simultaneous ignition and area ignition.

Check-in. Locations where assigned resources check in at an incident. The locations are incident command post, incident base, camps, staging areas, helibases, and division/group supervisors.

Class of Fire (as to kind of fire). Fire in solid fuels, including forest fires.

Class A: Fire in solid fuels, including forest fires.

Class B: Fire in flammable liquids.

Class C: Fire in electrical equipment.

Class D: Fire in flammable metals.

Class of Fire (as to size of forest fire)

Class A: .25 acre or less

Class B: .26 acre through 10 acres

Class C: 10.1 through 100 acres

Class D: 100.1 through 300 acres

Class E: 300.1 through 1,000 acres

Class F: 1,000.1 through 5,000 acres

Class G: More than 5,000 acres

Clean Burning. Same as burning out.

Clear Text: The use of plain English in radio communications transmissions. No ten codes or agency-specific codes are used when using clear text.

Closed Area. An area in which specified activities or entry are temporarily restricted to reduce risk of human-caused fires.

Closure. Legal restriction (but not necessarily complete elimination) of specific activities such as smoking, camping, or entry in order to prevent fires in a given area.

Cold Front. The leading edge of a relatively cold air mass which displaces warmer air.

Cold Trailing. A method of controlling a partly dead fire edge by carefully inspecting and feeling with the hand to detect any fire by digging out every live spot, and trenching any live edge.

Command. The act of directing, ordering, and/or controlling resources by virtue of explicit legal, agency, or delegated authority. The Command Function is responsible for developing fire strategy and managing the fire organization.

Command Staff. The command staff consists of the information officer, safety officer, and liaison officer, who report directly to the Incident Commander.

Condition of Vegetation. Stage of growth, or degree of flammability of vegetation that forms part of a fuel complex. "Herbaceous stage" is at times used when referring to herbaceous vegetation alone. In grass areas minimum qualitative distinctions for stages of annual growth are usually termed green or curing, and dry or cured.

Conduction. Transfer of heat energy from particle to particle of matter by contact and through a conducting medium.

Conflagration. A raging, destructive fire. Fast-moving fire fronts over large areas.

Contained Fire. There is a line completely around the fire and any spot fires therefrom, and there is a good chance that these lines can be held through the next burning period.

Controlled Fire. A fire in which the perimeter spread of a wildfire has been halted by natural or manmade barriers and has remained under control throughout the first succeeding burning period.

Control Force. Organization of personnel and equipment used to control the fire.

Control Line. An inclusive term for all constructed or natural fire barriers and treated fire edge used to control a fire's spread. See fire line.

Control Time. See Elapsed Time.

Convection. Refers to the thermally induced, vertical motion of air.

Convection Column. The ascending column of gases, smoke, and debris produced by the combustion process of a fire.

Contour Line. A continuing line on a topographic map connecting points of equal elevation, generally indicating vertical distance above sea level.

Control Line. See Fire Line.

Cooperating Agency. An agency supplying assistance other than direct suppression, rescue, support, or service functions, to the incident control effort (e.g., Red Cross, law enforcement agency, telephone company, etc.).

Coordination. The process of systematically analyzing a situation, developing relevant information, and informing appropriate command authority (for its decision) of viable alternatives for selection of the most effective combination of available resources to meet specific objectives.

Cover Type. The dominant form of vegetation growing on a given land area; generally given some common group name as dominant genera, such as grass, sage, chaparral, woodland, coniferous, or may be more specific, such as chamise-manzanita, pine-fir, etc.

Cross Shot. Intersecting lines of sight from two points to the same object. Frequently used to determine the location of a fire from lookouts.

Crown Fire. A fire that advances from top to top of trees or shrubs more or less independently of the surface fire. Sometimes crown fires are classed as either running or dependent, to distinguish the degree of independence from the surface fire.

Crowning. Fire advancing from crown to crown of trees or shrubs.

Cumulus Buildup. Cumulus clouds which are in the process of developing to great heights but have not yet reached the thunderstorm stage. Tops still have a rounded, cauliflower-like appearance and have not spread out into an anvil shape. (See thunderhead.)

Danger Index. A relative number indicating the severity of forest fire danger as determined from burning conditions and other variable factors of fire danger. (See burning index.)

Debris Burning fire. A fire spreading from any fire originally set for the purpose of clearing land or for rubbish, garbage, range, stubble, or meadow burning and by burning out animals, insects, or reptiles, and for fires caused by hot ashes, dumps, or incinerators. Includes range improvement escapes.

Detection. The act or system of discovering and locating fires.

Direct Method. A method of suppression that treats the fire as a whole, or all of its burning edge, by wetting, cooling, smothering, or chemically quenching the fire or by mechanically separating the fire from unburned fuel.

Direct Protection (action or responsibility). A term which indicates the particular fire protection organization that has primary responsibility for attacking an uncontrolled fire and for directing the suppression action. Such responsibility may develop through law, contract, or personal interest of the firefighting agent (e.g., a lumber operator). Several agencies or entities may have some basic responsibility (e.g., private owner) without being known as the fire organization having direct protection responsibility.

Discovery. Determination that a fire exists. In contrast to detection, location of a fire is not required.

Discovery Time. See Elapsed Time.

Diurnal. Weather changes due to day and night conditions.

Division. A division is a designated area or distance of fire perimeter, usually determined by a combination of topographical features and fire control problems, whereon the work can be generally supervised on the ground by a Division Supervisor.

Dozer. A mechanical piece of heavy equipment with tracks that can clear a fire line.

Dozer Line. Fire line constructed by a bulldozer.

Drift Smoke. Smoke that has drifted from its point of origin and has lost any original billow form.

Drop. Water, foam, or chemical retardant dropped on the fire by air tankers or copters.

Dry Lightning Storm. A lightning storm with negligible precipitation reaching the ground.

Duff. The partly decomposed organic material of the forest floor beneath the litter of freshly fallen twigs, needles and leaves. (See litter.)

Eddy. A large or small whirl of air situated in the main current. Quite often caused by a natural or manmade obstruction.

Edge Firing. A technique of firing in which fires are set along the inside edges of a fire line.

Elapsed Time. Term indicating total time used to complete any given step or steps in fire suppression. The basic steps are listed chronologically below:

Discovery Time. Elapsed time from start of a fire (known or estimated) until the time of the first discovery that results directly in suppression action.

Report Time. Elapsed time from discovery of a fire until the first person who does effective work on the fire is notified of its existence and location.

Getaway Time. Elapsed time from report of a fire to the persons who do first effective work on it until they respond to it.

Travel Time. Elapsed time from beginning of actual travel by the first persons doing effective work on a fire until they begin work on the fire.

Control Time. Elapsed time from first work on a fire until holding the control line is assured.

Mop-up Time. Elapsed time from time of control until the end of organized mop-up.

Patrol Time. Elapsed time from completion of organized mop-up until a fire is declared out.

Envelopment Action. See Tactics.

ETA. Estimated time of arrival.

Extended Attack Fire. A fire on which the first attack forces must be substantially augmented by additional numbers of personnel and equipment, but involves two divisions of fire line perimeter.

Extra Burning Period. For any particular fire which is neither contained nor controlled, any 24-hour period following the termination of the first burning period.

Extra Period Fire. A fire not contained by 10:00 a.m. of the day following discovery of the fire.

Exposure. See Aspect.

Facilitating Agents. The working persons and groups, away from the fire area, who aid the fire control effort by providing some special services within their own authority. Included would be civil officials, police, lookout observers, dispatchers, etc.

False Alarm. A reported smoke or fire requiring no suppression action, e.g., permit burning under control, mill smoke, false smoke (dust, fog, etc.).

Feeling for Fire. Examining burned material after fire is apparently out, using bare hands to find any live coals.

Fingers of a Fire. The long narrow tongues of a fire projecting from the main body.

Fire Agency. An agency compelled and authorized under statutes of law, the responsibility for control of fire within a designated area or upon certain designated lands.

Fire Behavior. The manner in which fuel ignites, flame develops, and fire spreads and exhibits other phenomena.

Firebreak. A strip of land on which the vegetation is removed each season, down to mineral soil, for fire control purposes.

Fire Control. Embraces all efforts taken to abate an existing fire nuisance, beginning at the time of discovery of the fire and ending with its complete extinguishment (including patrol of a "contained" fire area).

Fire Control Action Plan. A plan of action based on the fire danger for the area. A plan for prompt dispatch of fire control forces judged necessary to cope with a fire strategy-situation predicted for the particular area.

Fire Control Equipment. All tools, machinery, special devices and vehicles used in fire suppression operations.

Fire Control Organization. Includes those established crews, fire suppression leaders, fire engines, lookout stations and other facilities which are obtained before or after the start of a fire, essentially for the purpose of detecting, attacking and fighting fires.

Fire Control Planning. The systematic technological and administrative management process of designing the organization, facilities, and procedures to protect wildland from unwanted fire.

Fire Cooperator. A local person or agency who has agreed in advance to perform specified fire control services and who has received advanced training or instructions in giving such service. Also called "cooperator" or "planned cooperator."

Fire Crew. Predetermined individuals who are supervised, organized, and trained principally for clearing brush as a fire suppression measure. Fire line cut by fire crew averages 3 feet in width in grass to more than 15 feet in heavy fuels. Also called "hand crew."

Fire Damage. The loss, expressed in money or other units, caused by fire. Includes all indirect losses such as reduction in future values produced by the forest area, as well as direct losses of cover, improvement, wildland, etc., killed or consumed by fire.

Fire Danger. Resultant of both constant and variable fire danger factors, which affect the inception, spread, and difficulty of control of fires and the damage they cause.

Fire Danger Rating. A fire control management system that integrates the effects of selected fire danger factors into one or more qualitative or numerical indices of current protection needs.

Fire Devil. See Whirlwind.

Fire Edge. The exterior boundary of a fire at any given moment.

Fire Effects. Any consequence—neutral, detrimental, or beneficial—resulting from fire.

Fire Front. That part of the edge of the fire on which the rate of spread is usually most pronounced.

Fire Line. The part of a control line that is scraped or dug to mineral soil. Sometimes called fire trail. Also called control line, dozer line, tractor plow line, or handline.

Fire Perimeter. The active burning edge of a fire or its exterior burned limits.

Fire Protection. Embraces the two major phases of work involved with the prevention and the reduction of damage caused by uncontrolled fire; fire prevention and fire control.

Fire Prevention. Involves all manner of effort to prevent the ignition and initial spread of an unwanted fire, including the escape of a useful or controlled fire into an uncontrolled and hazardous state which then requires the abatement action. Law enforcement, including investigation of fire causes and the apprehension and prosecution of violators, is considered to be a fire prevention activity.

Fire Retardant. Any substance that by chemical or physical action reduces flammability of combustibles.

Fire Scar. (1) A healing or healed injury or wound, caused or accentuated by fire, on a woody plant. (See catface.) (2) The scar made on a landscape by fire.

Fire Season. The period or periods of the year during which fires are likely to occur, spread, and do sufficient damage to warrant organized fire control.

Fire Service. A term used to denote all types of fire control organizations which take direct action to extinguish fires. (See agency. See fire control organization.)

Fire Status Map. A map maintained on a fire to show, at given times, the location of the fire, deployment of suppression forces, and progress of suppression.

Fire Storm. Violent convection caused by a large, continuous area of intense fire. Often characterized by destructively violent surface in-drafts near and beyond the perimeter, and sometimes by tornado-like whirls.

Fire Strategy Situation. The total fire problem together with the action required to control it. The three Fire Strategy-Situations are Initial Attack, Extended Attack, and Major.

Fire Weather Forecast. A weather prediction specifically prepared for use in forest fire control.

Fire Whirl. See Whirlwind.

Firing Out. See Burning Out.

First Attack. The first organized suppression work on a fire.

First Attack Team. The first fire control forces dispatched to a fire (supported by Lookout and Dispatcher).

First Work Period. The time between discovery of a fire and 10:00 a.m. of the following calendar day. Also called initial shift. Succeeding work periods are 24 hours beginning at 10:00 a.m.

Flammability. The relative ease or difficulty with which fuels ignite and burn regardless of the quantity of the fuels. (Preferred to "inflammability.")

Flanking Action. See Tactics.

Flanks of a Fire. The parts of a fire's perimeter that are roughly parallel to the main direction of spread.

Flare-up. Any sudden acceleration of fire spread or intensification of the fire. Unlike blowup, a flare-up is of relatively short duration and does not radically change existing control plans.

Flash Fuels. Fuels such as grass, leaves, draped pine needles, fern, tree moss, and some kinds of slash which ignite readily and are consumed rapidly when dry. Also called fine fuels.

Foehn (German word pronounced "phone"). A dry wind with strong downward component. Locally called Santana, North, Mono, Chinook.

Follow-up. The action of reinforcing the first persons who go to a fire by sending additional personnel or equipment to facilitate suppression. Sometimes called reinforcement.

Forest Fire. A fire burning uncontrolled on lands covered wholly or in part by timber, brush, grass, grain, or other inflammable vegetation.

Forest Fire. (statistical definition). Any fire which meets the legal definition for a forest fire (see above) and which is also reportable as a forest fire under existing instructions.

Fuel Moisture Content. The quantity of moisture in fuel expressed as a percentage of the weight when thoroughly dried at 212°F.

Fuel Type. An identifiable association of fuel elements of distinctive species, form, size, arrangement, or other characteristics that will cause a predictable rate of fire spread or difficulty of control under specified weather conditions.

Fuel Break. A wide strip or block of land on which the vegetation has been permanently modified to a low-volume fuel type so that fires burning into it can be controlled more readily.

General Staff. The group of incident command personnel who function as chiefs under ICS, including the Incident Commander, Operations Section Chief, Planning Section Chief, Logistics Section Chief, and Finance Section Chief.

Getaway Time. See elapsed time.

Going Fire. A current fire during the period between time of start and its being declared out.

GPM. Gallons (of water) per minute.

Gradient Wind. A free-flowing prevailing wind moving at an elevation (2,000 feet and more above the surface) where it is not influenced by topography.

Ground Fire. Fire that consumes the organic material beneath the surface litter of the forest floor, e.g., a peat fire.

Group. A functional division (e.g., dozer line construction group, structure protection group, environmental resource rehab group, etc.).

Hand Crew. See "Fire Crew."

Hand Line. Fire line cut by a fire crew. See fire line.

Hazard. A fuel complex defined by kind, arrangement, volume, condition, and location that forms a special threat of ignition or of suppression difficulty.

Hazard Reduction. Any treatment of a hazard that reduces the threat of ignition and spread of fire.

Head of a Fire. The most rapidly spreading portion of a fire's perimeter, usually to the leeward or upslope. See also parts of a fire.

Heat Transfer. The process by which heat is imparted from one body to another. (See conduction, convection, radiation.)

Heavy Fuels. Fuels of large diameter such as snags, logs, and large limb wood, which ignite and are consumed more slowly than flash fuels. Also called coarse fuels.

Held Line. All worked control line that still contains the fire when mop-up is completed. Excludes lost line, natural barriers not backfired, and unused secondary lines.

Helibase. A location within the general incident area for parking, fueling, maintenance, and loading of helicopters.

Helispot. A temporary landing spot for helicopters normally constructed on or near fire line for access of personnel and supplies.

Helitack Crew. A crew of specialists trained to work with helicopters in fire control who are familiar with helicopter fire control accessories and fire control helitack methods.

Helitank. The tank attached to the helicopter containing water or fire retardant chemicals for dropping on fires.

Helitanker. Helicopter with tanks attached for dropping water or fire retardant chemicals on fires.

Holdover Fire. A fire that remains dormant for a considerable time. Also called hangover or sleeper fire.

Hose Lay. The arrangement of connected lengths of fire hose and accessories on the ground beginning at the first pumping unit and ending at the point of water delivery. (See progressive hose lay, simple hose lay.)

Hot Spot. A particularly active part of a fire.

Hot Spotting. Checking the spread of a fire at points of more rapid spread or special threat. It is usually the initial step in prompt control with emphasis on first priorities.

Incendiary Fire. A fire willfully set by anyone to burn vegetation or property not owned or controlled by them and without consent of the owner or their agent.

Incident Action Plan (IAP). The incident action plan, which is initially prepared by the initial attack Incident Commander and may be expanded for a major incident to a multi-page comprehensive document that contains general control objectives reflecting the overall incident strategy and specific action plans (tactics) for the subsequent operational periods.

Incident Base. That location at which the primary logistics functions are coordinated and administered. (The incident name or other designator will be added to the term "Base.") The incident command post may be collocated with the base. There is only one base per incident.

Incident Command Post (ICP or CP). The location at which the primary command functions are executed and usually collocated with the incident base.

Incident Command System (ICS). The combination of facilities, equipment, personnel, procedures, and communications operating within a common organizational structure with responsibility for the management of assigned resources to effectively accomplish stated objectives pertaining to an incident.

Independent Action. suppression action by other than the regular fire control organization or cooperators.

Indirect Attack. See Indirect Method and Parallel Method.

Indirect Method. A method of suppression in which the control line is located along natural firebreaks, favorable breaks in topography, or at considerable distance from the fire and the intervening fuel is burned out. (See burning out.) The strip of fuel to be burned out is wider than in the parallel method and usually allows a choice of the time when the burning out will be done.

Initial Attack Incident Commander. The Incident Commander at the time that the first attack forces commence suppression work on the fire.

Initial Attack Fire. A fire that is controlled by the first dispatched forces without need for major reinforcements and within the first burning period. Involves one division of fire line perimeter.

Initial Shift. See First Work Period.

Instability. A condition of the atmosphere in which the lapse rate is such that a parcel of air given an initial vertical impulse will tend to move from its original level with increasing speed.

Inversion. A layer of comparatively warm air overlaying cool air. This is a stable atmospheric condition. The atmosphere in an inversion will resist vertical motion.

Jurisdictional Agency. The agency having jurisdiction and responsibility for a specific geographical area.

Knock Down. To reduce flame or heat on the more vigorously burning parts of a fire edge.

Lapse Rate. The rate of change of temperature in the atmosphere because of changes in elevation.

Liaison. (from the French "to tie together"; has several accepted pronunciations, generally "lee-ayzon" or "lay-ee-son") To maintain intercommunication and mutual understanding.

Light Burning. Periodic broadcast burning intended to prevent accumulation of fuels in quantities that would cause excessive damage or difficult suppression in the event of accidental fire.

Lightning Fire. A fire caused directly or indirectly by lightning.

Litter. The top layer of the forest floor, composed of loose debris of dead sticks, branches, twigs, and recently fallen leaves or needles, little altered in structure by decomposition. (See duff.)

Local Winds. Winds peculiar to a particular place.

Logistics Section. The Logistics Section provides all of the supplies, service, and facilities to personnel and machines of the Command and Operations function.

Lookout. (1) A person designated to detect and report fires from a vantage point. (2) A lookout station. (3) An observer used to warn firefighters of safety problems.

Lookout Tower. A structure to enable a person to be above nearby obstructions to sight. It is usually capped by either a lookout house or observatory.

Major Fire. A fire that burns into the second burning period or requires extensive control forces. A base is established.

Marine Air. Air which has high moisture content and the temperature characteristics of a water surface due to extensive exposure to that surface.

Mop up. The act of making a fire safe after it is controlled, such as extinguishing or removing burning material along or near the control line, felling snags, trenching logs to prevent rolling, etc.

Mop-up Time. See Elapsed Time.

Motorized Firebreak. A low-quality roadway along ridges.

Move Up. A prearranged system of moving personnel and equipment in order to have such forces more strategically available for dispatch throughout an area which has been weakened by the earlier dispatch of regular assigned forces.

Mutual Aid. Some form of direct assistance from one fire service to another during a time of fire emergency. In order to be "mutual," such assistance should follow as a result of an arrangement prior to the need between the agencies involved in which it has been agreed that firefighting assistance will be rendered from each to the other, generally at the request of the receiving agency.

National Interagency Incident Management System (NIIMS). Consists of five major subdivisions which collectively provide a total systems approach to all-risk incident management. The subsystems are the incident command system, training, qualifications and certification, supporting technologies, and publications management.

Net Fire Effects. The sum of all effects, both detrimental and beneficial, resulting from burning.

Normal Fire Season. (1) A season in which weather, fire danger, and number and distribution of fires are about average. (2) Period of the year that normally comprises fire season.

One-lick Method. See Progressive Method.

Operational Period. The period of time scheduled for execution of a given set of operation actions as specified in the incident action plan.

Operations Section. The Operations section includes all activities of personnel and equipment directly engaged in controlling the fire.

Overhead. Supervisory or specialist personnel working in some capacity related to the control of a going fire (or fires) but not including leaders of regularly organized crews and equipment drivers or operators while engaged in their regularly assigned duties.

Para Cargo. Anything intentionally dropped or intended for dropping from any aircraft by parachute, other retarding devices, or free fall.

Parallel Method. A method of suppression in which a fire line is constructed approximately parallel to and just far enough from the fire edge to enable personnel and equipment to work effectively, though the line may be shortened by cutting across unburned fingers. The intervening strip of unburned fuel is normally burned out as the control line proceeds but may be allowed to burn out unassisted where this occurs without undue delay or threat to the line.

Parts of a Fire. On typical free-burning fires the spread is uneven, with the main spread moving with the wind or upslope. The most rapidly moving portion is designated as the head of the fire, the adjoining portions of the perimeter at right angles to the head are known as the flanks, and the slowest-moving portions are known as the rear.

Patrol. Effort directed toward permanently assuring that there will be no escape of a controlled fire; includes activity after the fire is declared to be controlled in mopping up around the fire line and such close visual watch of the line as is deemed necessary.

Patrol Line. See Elapsed Time.

Planned Initial Attack Zone. An area surrounding an aircraft base of a 15-minute flight radius from the base, estimated for the average speed of the particular types of aircraft from the time of takeoff.

Planning Meeting. Under ICS, a meeting, held as needed, throughout the duration of the incident, to select strategies and tactics for incident control operations and for service and support planning.

Point of Attack. That part of the fire on which work is started when suppression forces arrive.

Preparedness. (1) Condition or degree of being completely ready to cope with a potential fire situation. (2) Mental readiness to recognize changes in fire danger and act promptly when action is appropriate.

Progressive Hose Lay. A hose lay in which double shutoff wyes or tees are inserted in the main line at intervals and lateral lines are run along the fire edge, thus permitting continuous application of water during extension of the lay.

Progressive Method of Line Construction. A system of organizing personnel to build fire lines in which they advance without changing relative positions in line. There are two principal methods of applying the system: (1) Work is begun with a suitable space, such as 15 feet, between personnel. Whenever one person overtakes another, all of those ahead move one space forward and resume work on the uncompleted part of the line. The last person does not move ahead until the work is completed in his/her space. Forward progress of the crew is coordinated by a crew leader. This method of organization is termed move-up. (2) Each person does one to several licks or strokes of work and moves forward a specified distance. The distance is determined by the number of crew members equipped with a given tool and the number of licks needed per unit of line to complete the work for that tool. This method is termed one-lick.

Protection Boundary. The exterior boundary of an area within which a given agency has assumed primary fire attack responsibility. (Any variation from this definition should be based on a written understanding among the parties directly involved in the protection of the particular land area).

Psychrometer. An instrument contained in a field weather kit used to measure relative humidity.

Radiation. The transfer of energy (heat) through space.

Rate of Speed. The relative activity of a fire in extending its horizontal dimensions. It is expressed as rate of increase of the total perimeter of the fire, as rate of forward spread of the fire front, or as rate of increase in area, depending on the intended use of the information. Usually it is expressed in feet per minute or acres per hour for a specific period of the fire's history.

Rear of a Fire. The portion of the edge of a fire opposite the head.

Reburn. (1) Subsequent burning of an area in which fire has previously burned but has left flammable fuel that ignites when burning conditions are more favorable. (2) An area that has reburned.

Regular Forces. All of the personnel on a department payroll other than paid pick-up labor, and all of the equipment, materials, or supplies under custody of the department. The term distinguishes and sets apart other forces that may be acquired temporarily to assist in fire control work, such as prisoners, wards, volunteers, rented equipment and mutual aid assistance. The latter segregation may be referred to as temporary or extra forces.

Reinforced Attack. Those resources requested in addition to the initial attack.

Relative Humidity. The ratio of the amount of moisture in a given volume of space to the amount that volume would contain if it were saturated. The ratio of the actual vapor pressure in the saturated vapor pressure.

Report Time. See Elapsed Time.

Resistance to Control. The relative difficulty of constructing and holding a control line as affected by resistance to line construction and by fire behavior. Also called difficulty of control. (See resistance to line construction.)

Resistance to Line Construction. The relative difficulty of constructing a control line as determined by the fuel, topography, and soil. (See resistance to control.)

Resources. All personnel and major items of equipment available, or potentially available, for assignment to incident tasks on which status is maintained.

RESTAT. Under ICS, an acronym for the resources unit, under the planning section which keeps all resource status.

Responsibile Fire Agency. The agency assuming attack responsibility for the control of fires upon any particular land area.

Risk. (1) The chance of a fire starting as determined by the presence and activity of causative agents. (2) Causative agents. (3) To expose to loss or injury, a calculated risk.

Running. Behavior of a fire spreading rapidly with a well-defined head. (See smoldering, spotting.)

Safety Island. An area used for escape in the event the line is outflanked or in case a spot fire caused fuels outside the control line to render the line unsafe. In firing operations crews progress so as to maintain a safety island close at hand by allowing the fuels inside the control line to be consumed before going ahead.

Scratch Lines. An unfinished preliminary control line hastily established or constructed as an emergency measure to check the spread of a fire.

Set. (noun) (1) An individual incendiary fire. (2) The point or points of origin of an incendiary fire. (3) Material left to ignite an incendiary fire at a later time. (verb) To ignite a fire.

Severity Index. A number that indicates the relative net cumulative effects of daily fire danger on the fire load for an area during a selected period, such as a fire season.

Simple Hose Lay. A hose lay consisting of consecutively coupled lengths of hose without laterals. (See progressive hose lay.)

Simultaneous Ignition. A technique of broadcast burning or backfiring by which the fuel on an area to be burned is ignited at many points simultaneously and the acts are so spaced that each received timely stimulation by radiation from the adjoining sets. By such techniques, all burn together quickly and a hot, clean burn is possible under unfavorable burning conditions where single sets would not spread. (See area ignition.)

SITSTAT. Under ICS, an acronym for the situation unit, under the planning section, which keeps all situation status.

Size-up. The observation and evaluation of existing factors which, as affected by assumed future conditions, will affect all or any of the problems involved in the control of a fire. To estimate the needed actions and facilities required to extinguish a fire.

Slash. Debris left after logging, pruning, thinning, or brush cutting. It includes logs, chunks, bark, branches, stumps, and broken understory trees or brush.

Sleeper Fire. A fire that remains dormant for a considerable time. Also called hangover or hold-over fire.

Slopover. The extension of a fire on the ground over a crest and generally downslope beyond a line where it was intended or expected the fire would cease. Such a movement of continuous burning over a barrier in a generally upslope direction would be more properly considered an "escape."

Smoldering. Behavior of a fire burning without flame and barely spreading.

Snag. A standing dead tree or part of a dead tree from which at least the leaves and smaller branches have fallen. Often called stub, if less than 20 feet tall.

Span of Control. The maximum number of subordinates who can be directly supervised by one person without loss of efficiency. In fire suppression the number varies by activity.

Speed of Attack. The sum total of lapse time off, report time, getaway time, and travel time. (See also elapsed time.)

Spot Fire. A fire which is caused by the transfer of burning material through the air into flammable material beyond the perimeter of the fire of origin.

Spotting. Behavior of a fire producing sparks or embers that are carried by the wind and start new fires beyond the zone of direct ignition by the main fire.

Spread Index. A number related to the relative rate of forward movement of surface fires.

Stable Air. Air in which vertical currents are resisted due to buoyancy characteristics.

Standby Crew. A group of personnel specially organized, trained, and placed for quick suppression work on fires.

Staging Area. That location where incident personnel and equipment are assigned on a three-minute available status.

Strength of Attack. The number of personnel and equipment with which a fire is attacked. Normally based on the predicted fire strategy-situation.

Strike Team. Under ICS, specified combinations of the same kind and types of resources, with common communications and a leader.

Suppress a Fire. Extinguish a fire or confine the area it burns within fixed boundaries.

Suppressant. Water or chemical solution which is applied directly to burning fuel. Intended to extinguish rather than retard.

Surface Fire. Fire that burns surface litter, other loose debris of the forest floor, and small vegetation.

Suppression Crew. Two or more personnel assigned primarily to work as a unit and located at some strategic place so that they (the crew) may be dispatched to perform work of early attack and abatement of fires.

Strip Burning. (1) Setting fire to a narrow strip of fuel adjacent to a control line and then burning successively wider inside as the preceding strip burns out. (2) Burning only a narrow strip or strips of slash through a cutting unit and leaving the remainder.

Tactics of Attack. The details of action (strategy embraces the broad application of plans and action to a problem). Several tactics of attack are listed below.

Pincer action. Direct attack around a fire in opposite directions by two or more work units.

Tandem action. Direct attack along a part of the fire perimeter by fire engines, bulldozers, and crews, one following another.

Envelopment action. Striking key or critical segments around the entire perimeter at approximately the same time.

Protective action. Concentration on protection of separate flammable property within a broad fire area.

Confining action. A concentrated attack on a key or critical portion of the fire for the purpose of confining the spread in that area.

Flanking action. An attack made along the flanks of a fire when an attack on the head of the fire is not feasible.

Area control action. An indirect attack in which fire intensity and difficult topography make it necessary to establish control lines that encompass a natural area well in advance of the fire perimeter.

Task Force. A group of resources with common communications and a leader temporarily assigned for a specific mission.

Thunderhead. A popular term for the anvil of a cumulonimbus cloud, but frequently applied to the entire cumulus cloud which has developed an anvil top or the crystal stage. Lightning and precipitation are usually occurring at this stage.

Tie in. Connecting a control line to another line or an intended fire control barrier.

Topography. The land surface configuration, including manmade and natural features.

Tractor Plow. Any tracked vehicle with a plow for exposing mineral soil, with transportation and personnel for its operation.

Tractor Plow Line. Fire line cut by a tractor plow. See fire line.

Trench. A ditch dug on a slope below a fire, designed to catch rolling burning material.

Truck-trail. A substantial transportation route for fire type motor vehicles, built prior to a fire.

Turbulence. Irregular air motion, for example, that produced when air flows over the uneven surface of the earth. It gives rise to gusts and lulls in the wind. (See eddy.)

Uncontrolled. The condition of a fire or part of a fire that has not been checked by natural barriers or by control measures.

Undercut Line. A fire line below a fire on a slope. Normally requires trenching. (See trench.) Also called underslung line.

Unified Command. A method for all agencies or individuals who have jurisdictional responsibility, and in some cases those who have functional responsibility, to contribute to: (1) determining overall objectives for the incident, and (2) selecting a strategy to achieve the objectives.

Unstable Air. Air in which vertical currents, when started, will continue and become intensified. (See stable air.) Evidenced by cumulus clouds, gusty winds, dust devils, and fire whirlwinds.

Vortex Turbulence. Whirlwinds that project downward from the wings or rotors of low-flying aircraft. Vortex turbulence can adversely affect fire behavior.

Watershed. The soil, topography, and vegetation of an area which contributes to the retention and flow of water received as precipitation.

Water Supply Map. A map showing location of supplies of water readily available for pumps, tanks, engines, camp use, etc.

Water Tender. Any ground vehicle capable of transporting specific quantities of water.

Wet Water. Water with added chemicals, called wetting agents, that increase its spreading and penetrating properties.

Wildland. (1) Uncultivated land, except fallow lands. (2) Chiefly timber, range watershed, and brush lands not under cultivation.

Wildfire. An uncontrolled fire burning on wildland or in other continuous vegetation.

Whirlwind. A spinning, moving column of ascending air rising from a vortex. Over a fire area may carry aloft smoke, debris, and flames. These range from a foot or two in diameter to small tornadoes in size and intensity. (Also called fire whirl or fire devil.)

CHAPTER 22. EMERGENCY MEDICAL SERVICES

Advanced Life Support (ALS). All basic life support measures, plus invasive medical procedures, including: intravenous therapy; administration of antiarrhythmic medications and other specified drugs, medications, and solutions; use of adjunctive ventilation which may be authorized by state law and performed under medical control.

Basic Life Support (BLS). Generally limited to airway maintenance, ventilatory (breathing) support, CPR, hemorrhage control, splinting of suspected fractures, management of spinal injury, protection and transportation of the patient in accordance with accepted procedures. BLS providers with special training can use automatic or semi-automatic defibrillators for cardiac defibrillation as well.

Clinical. Procedures that relate specifically to the treatment of injured or ill persons.

Customers. Anyone who may use, support, or participate in the delivery of services, including patients and their families, firefighters and EMS providers, physicians, nurses, taxpayers, visitors to the area, and suppliers.

Emergency Medical Services. The provision of service to patients with medical emergencies, particularly the prehospital delivery of these services.

Emergency Medical Services System. A comprehensive, coordinated arrangement of resources and functions which are organized to respond in a timely, staged manner to targeted medical emergencies, regardless of their cause and the patient's ability to pay, and to minimize their physical and emotional impact.

Emergency Services. Agencies which provide the essential public safety services of fire suppression, emergency medical services, rescue, and hazardous materials response.

EMS. Emergency medical services.

First Responder. 1. The basic level of medical training for emergency response personnel. 2. Personnel on a first response unit (may be trained at any level of EMS).

First Responder System. A tiered EMS system in which the closest emergency response unit with trained EMS providers responds to medical emergencies.

First Response Unit. An emergency response unit with personnel trained at any EMS level, dispatched to provide medical care prior to the arrival of an EMS transport unit.

Life Safety Education. Public education programs which are designed to teach citizens about fire safety, injury prevention, traffic safety, and other aspects of rural and urban survival.

Medical Director. A physician who advises the fire chief on EMS issues, and who approves the training and protocol development related to EMS for a department. In many departments, prehospital EMS providers actually operate under the medical director's license.

PIER. Public Information, Education, and Relations. EMS PIER programs provide the means for promoting an EMS system, developing positive public attitudes, and informing citizens on specific EMS issues and techniques.

Prehospital. The aspect of the EMS system that occurs prior to the delivery of an injured or ill patient to a medical facility.

Quality Management. Actions taken to meet the needs and expectations of the customer, including both the clinical quality of medical care and the customer's perception of that care. This extends the concept of quality beyond the traditional focus on clinical proficiency, to include all aspects of care.

Risk Management. Actions taken to prevent disability, loss of life, or irreparable business damage as a result of the provision of emergency medical services.

Tiered Response System. An EMS delivery system designed to ensure that the appropriate level of EMS care and transportation is provided to all patients, while ensuring the response of the closest EMS unit. The three primary types of tiered systems are 1) ALS ambulances respond to all calls, but can turn a patient over to a BLS unit for transport; 2) a BLS ambulance is dispatched on all calls, while an ALS ambulance is only dispatched on ALS calls; and 3) a nontransporting ALS unit is dispatched with a transporting BLS unit.

CHAPTER 24. PLANNING COMMUNITY FIRE DEFENSES

Automatic Aid. Assistance from surrounding fire agencies, automatically dispatched to specific occupancies, usually by formal agreement.

Facilitator. The leader, coordinator, and controller of the group or team.

Fire Flow. The amount of water needed to extinguish a fire.

Fire Management Areas (FMAs). The areas in a community divided into manageable sections geographically.

Fire Protection. Includes fire suppression, and built-in fire protection systems like automatic fire sprinklers.

Initial Attack. First-arriving fire units' tactical action at a fire incident.

Level of Service. Available fire stations, companies, and related services.

Mutual Aid. Assistance from surrounding fire agencies. May be a formal agreement or a state plan.

Sustained Attack. First and subsequent fire units' attack on the fire.

Target Hazards. Those occupancies that present the greatest risk of life and property damage.

Vegetation. The grass, brush and forest bio mass.

Wildland. The geographical area of a community that is grass, brush, or forest covered.

Wildland/Interface. The geographical portion of the community where homes are adjacent to wildland areas.

Bibliography and Technical Resources

CHAPTER 2. OFFICE MANAGEMENT AND WORK FLOW

Arndt, R., Ph.D., *Working Posture and Muskulo-skeletal Problems of Video Display Terminal Operators—Review and Appraisal,* University of Wisconsin: Department of Preventative Medicine.

Burke, W.W., *Organization Development—Principles and Practices,* Harper Collins Publishers, 1982.

Cummings, T.G., and C.G. Worley. *Organization Development and Change,* West Publishing Company, 1993.

Fletcher, Bretschneider, Marchand, Rosenbaum, Betot and Richter. "Managing Information Technology: Transforming County Governments in the 1990's." *Governing,* August 1992.

Handy, C., *The Age of Unreason,* Boston, MA: Harvard Business School Press, 1990.

Robbins, S., *Organization Theory—Structure, Design, and Applications,* Englewood Cliffs, NJ: Prentice-Hall 1990.

Sauter, S., L.J. Chapman, and S.J. Knutson. *Improving VDT Work,* University of Wisconsin: Department of Preventative Medicine.

Sproul, L. and S. Kiesler, *Connections,* MIT Press, Cambridge, Massachusetts: MIT Press, 1993.

Tubbs, S.L., *A Systems Approach to Small Group Interaction,* McGraw-Hill, 1992.

Working Safely with Video Display Terminals, U.S. Department of Labor, Occupational Safety and Health Administration, 1988.

CHAPTER 3. FINANCIAL MANAGEMENT

Books

Arens, Alvin A. and James K. Loebbecke. *Auditing: An Integrated Approach.* Englewood Cliffs, NJ: Prentice Hall, Inc., 1984.

Beams, Floyd A., *Advanced Accounting,* Englewood Cliffs, NJ: Prentice Hall, Inc., 1982.

Below, Patrick J., George L. Morrisey, and Betty L. Acomb. *The Executive Guide to Strategic Planning,* San Francisco: Jossey Bass, 1987.

Frank, James E., *Community Experience with Fire Impact Fees: A National Study.* Florida State University, 1985.

Getz, Malcolm, *Economics of the Urban Fire Department,* Baltimore, MD.: Johns Hopkins University Press, 1979.

Griesemer, James R., *Accountants' and Administrators' Guide: Budgeting for Results in Government.*

Hay & Engstrom, *Accounting for Government and Nonprofit Entities,* 6th Ed. Homewood, IL: Dow Jones-Irwin, 1981.

Hickey, Harry E., *Public Fire Safety Organization: A Systems Approach.* Boston MA: NFPA, 1973.

Luther, William M., *The Marketing Plan: How to Prepare and Implement It.* New York, NY: Amacom, 1982.

Miller, Girard, *Executive Budgetary Presentations: The Cutting Edge,* Chicago: Municipal Finance Officers Association, 1982.

Municipal Finance Officers Association, *Government Accounting, Auditing, and Financial Reporting,* Chicago, IL: 1980.

Smalley, James C., *Funding Sources for Fire Departments.* Quincy, MA: NFPA 1983.

Spiro, Herbert T., *Finance for the Nonfinancial Manager;* 2nd Ed. New York, NY: John Wiley and Sons.

Periodicals

Gaeber, Ted, and David Osborne. "Reinventing Government: An Agenda for the 1990s." *Public Management,* March 1982, pp 4–8.

Carter, Ph.D., Harry R., "Fire Finances: A Historical Perspective." *The Voice,* ISFSI, October 1991, pp 22–25.

Carter, Ph.D., Harry R., "Managing Fire Resources: Financial Management Systems." *The Voice,* February 1992, pp 27–28.

Coleman, Ronny J., "Budgeting for the 90s." *Fire Chief,* January 1990, pp 47–51.

Hughs, George M., "Spending Fire Department Money." *Fire Command,* August 1986 pp 28–30.

Glen Hahn Cope, "Municipal Budgeting and Productivity," *Baseline Data Report,* 21.2 (1989) Washington, DC: International City Management Association.

Craley, Michael, "Legal Insights." *Chief Fire Executive,* January/February 1987, pp 59–62.

Craley, Michael, "Legal Insights: Recover for the Costs of Providing Fire Protection Services." *Chief Fire Executive,* January/February/ March 1989, p 7.

"Can/Should a City Charge for Fire Calls?" *The Minnesota Fire Chief,* March/April 1989, pp 8–9.

Kelley, Joseph T., "Using Graphs to Present Financial Information." *MIS Report,* February 1989, pp 1–15.

Nestor, Roy, "How to Advance by Retreating." *Chief Fire Executive,* September/October 1987, pp 20–40.

Pierson, Joy, Craig Bagemihl, and Janice Tevanian. "Analyzing Services to Balance the Budget." *MIS Report,* August 1991, pp 1–17.

Rosenhan, A.K., "Managing the Purchase of New Apparatus," *Chief Fire Executive,* September 1990, pp 40–41.

Shouldis, William, "Productivity: The Total Cost Approach." *Fire Engineering,* August 1985, pp 25–28.

Smalley, James, "Community Facilities Loan Program." *Fire Command,* December 1985, pp 24–26.

Smalley, James, "Spending Resources in the Right Places." *Fire Command,* December 1985, p 46.

Research Paper

Lippe, III, Henry, "Strategic Planning for the Fire Service Executive: A Look at Corporate Management, Leadership, and Vision." Applied Research Project, NFA, Executive Fire Officer Program, January 1991.

CHAPTER 5. INSURANCE GRADING OF FIRE DEPARTMENTS

Standards

American Water Works Association (AWWA) Manual M-17.

National Fire Protection Association (NFPA) 1221—*Standard for the Installation, Maintenance and Use of Public Fire Service Communication Systems,* 1991 edition.

NFPA 1901—*Standard for Pumper Fire Apparatus,* 1991 edition.

NFPA 1904—*Standard for Aerial Ladder & Elevating Platform Fire Apparatus,* 1991 edition.

NFPA 1911—*Standard for Service Tests of Pumps on Fire Department Apparatus,* 1991 edition.

NFPA 1962—*Standard for the Care, Use & Service Testing of Fire Hose Including Couplings & Nozzles,* 1988 edition.

Publications

Fire Suppression Rating Schedule, ISO Commercial Risk Services, 1980 edition.

Books

Coleman, Ronny J. & Granito, John A., eds., *Managing Fire Services,* Washington, DC: International City Management Association, 1988

Chief Officer, Stillwater OK: International Fire Service Training Association, 1984.

Laughlin, Jerry W., ed., *Water Supplies for Fire Protection,* Stillwater OK: The International Fire Service Training Association, 1978.

Pressman, Jerrold S. & Thompson, B.J., *Managing a Fire Safe Environment: A Cost Effective Approach,* California: Fire Management Publications, 1989.

Carter, Harry R. & Rausch, Edwin, *Management in the Fire Service,* Quincy, MA. National Fire Protection Association (NFPA), 1989.

Cote, Arthur E., ed., *Fire Protection Handbook* 17th Ed., Quincy MA: NFPA, 1991.

Periodicals

Polson, James A. "ISO Takes a New Approach . . ." *The International Fire Chief,* July 1980, pp. 20–21.

Grill, Mike, "How One Community Improved its ISO Rating," *Fire Chief,* March 1991, pp. 32–35, 105–106.

Gage, Dennis N. "ISO Rates Alternative Water Supply," *NFPA Journal,* September/October 1991, pp. 83 & 106.

CHAPTER 6. LEADERSHIP FOR TODAY AND TOMORROW

Books

Bullock, Robert P. *Social Factors Related to Job Satisfaction.* Columbus, OH: Ohio State University, 1952.

Campbell, Donald T. *Leadership and its Effect on the Group.* Columbus, OH: Ohio State University, 1956.

Coons, Ralph M., and Ralph M. Stogdill. *Leader Behavior: Its Description and Measurement.* Columbus, OH: Ohio State University, 1957.

Dale, Ernest. *Management—Theory and Practice.* New York: McGraw-Hill.

Dessler, Gary. *Management Fundamentals, A Framework.* Reston, VA: Reston Publishing Company.

Drucker, Peter. *The Practice of Management.* New York: Harper Brothers.

Fulmer, Robert M. *The New Management.* New York: Macmillan Publishing Company, Inc., 1978.

Gratz, David B. *Fire Department Management: Scope and Method.* Beverly Hills, CA: Glencoe Press, 1972.

Hamm, Robert F. *Leadership in the Fire Service.* Stillwater, OK: Oklahoma State University, 1967.

Hamphill, John K. *Situational Factors in Leadership.* Columbus, OH: Ohio State University, 1949.

Herzberg, Frederick. *Work and the Nature of Man.* New York: World Publishing Company, 1966.

International City Management Association. *Municipal Fire Administration.* Washington, DC: International City Management Association, 1979.

Jaynes, William E., Ellis L. Scott, and Ralph M. Stogdill. *Leadership and Role Expectations.* Columbus, OH: Ohio State University, 1956.

Johnson Foundation. *Wingspread Conference on Fire Service Administration, Education and Research.* Racine, WI: Johnson Foundation.

Koontz, Harold, and Cyril O'Donnell. *Principles of Management.* New York: McGraw-Hill.

Koontz, Harold, Cyril O'Donnell, and Heinz Weilrich. *Essentials of Management.* New York: McGraw-Hill, 1982.

Likert, Rensis. *New Patterns of Management.* New York: McGraw-Hill 1961.

Limon, Herbert. *Administrative Behavior.* New York: Macmillan Company, 1957.

Maslow, Abraham. *Motivation and Personality.* New York: Harper and Brothers.

McGregor, Douglas. *The Human Side of Enterprise.* New York: McGraw-Hill.

McCall, Morgan W., and Michael M. Lombardo. *Leadership: Where Else Can We Go?* Durham, NC: Duke University Press, 1978.

National Fire Protection Association. *Management of a Fire Department.* Quincy, MA: National Fire Protection Association.

National Fire Protection Association. *Organization of the Fire Department.* Quincy, MA: National Fire Protection Association.

Patterson, Walter, and Arthur Pell. *Fire Officer's Guide to Leadership.* Garrison on Hudson, New York: 1963.

Stogdill, Ralph M. *Leadership and Structures of Personal Interaction.* Columbus, OH: Ohio State University, 1957.

Strauss and Sayles. *The Human Problems of Management.* New Jersey: Prentice Hall, 1967.

Periodicals

Frost, Dean E., Fred E. Fiedler, and Jeff W. Anderson. "The Role of Personal Risk Taking in Effective Leadership." *Human Relations,* 32.2, February 1983, pp 185–202.

Frost Dean E. "Role Perceptions and Behavior of the Immediate Superior: Moderating Effects on the Prediction of Leadership Effectiveness." *Organizational Behavior and Human Performance,* 31.1, February 1983, pp 123–142.

Ghiselli, Edwin. "The Validity of Management Traits Related to Occupational Level." *Personal Psychology,* 16 (1963). pp 109–113.

House, Robert. "A Path Goal Theory of Leadership Effectiveness," *Administrative Science Quarterly,* 16.3, September 1971, pp 321–338.

Maslow, Abraham H. "The Theory of Human Motivation," *Psychology Review,* July 1943, pp 370–396.

Rees, R.T., and J.G. O'Karma. "Perception of Supervisor Leadership Style in a Formal Organization. *Group and Organizational Studies,* 5.1, March 1980, pp 65–69.

Tannenbaum, Robert, and Warren Schmidt. "How to Choose a Leadership Pattern." *Harvard Business Review,* 5.3, May-June 1973, pp 162–180.

Wood, Stuart, "Motivation and Leadership." *Management Accounting,* (British) 62.2, February 1984, pp 32–33.

Yukl, Gary A., and David D. Van Fleet. "Cross Situational Multimethod Research on Military Leader Effectiveness." *Organizational Behavior and Human Performance,* 30.1 August 1982, pp 87–108.

Manual

Jackson, Douglas N. *Jackson Personality Inventory.* Goshen NY: Research Psychologists Press Inc., 1976.

CHAPTER 7. PERSONNEL ADMINISTRATION

Public Law (PL) 102–345
United States Code 42 USC-100
U.S. *Code of Federal Regulations* 29 CFR 100
Federal Register FR 1/1/9
Presidential Executive Orders:
   No. 11141 (Age Discrimination)
   No. 11246 (Civil Rights)
   No. 11625 (Minority Business)
   No. 11914 (Handicapped and Rehabilitation)
Affirmative Action
   Office of Federal Contract Compliance Program
   U.S. Department of Labor
   135 High Street, Room 311
   Hartford, Connecticut 06103
Equal Employment Opportunity
   U.S. Equal Employment Opportunity Commission
   1801 L Street NW
   Washington, DC 20507
ERISA/Pensions
   Division of Technical Assistance and Inquiries
   Pension and Welfare Benefits Administration
   U.S. Department of Labor
   200 Constitution Avenue NW
   Washington, DC 20210-0999
Safety and Health
   Occupational Safety and Health Administration
   U.S. Department of Labor, Region I
   133 Portland Street, 15th floor
   Boston, MA 02114
Unemployment Compensation
   U.S. Employment Service
   Employment and Training Administration
   U.S. Department of Labor
   200 Constitution Avenue NW
   Washington, DC 20210
Workers' Compensation
   U.S. Department of Labor, Region I
   1 Congress Street, 11th floor
   Boston, MA 02114

CHAPTER 8. SAFETY AND OCCUPATIONAL HEALTH

Brunacini, Alan V. Fireground Command. Phoenix, AZ: Phoenix Fire Department.

California State Board of Fire Services, *Incident Command System*, Stillwater, OK: Fire Protection Publications, 1st Ed. 1983.

Cote, Arthur E., ed. *Fire Protection Handbook*. 17th ed. Quincy, MA: National Fire Protection Association, 1992.

Himmelstein, Jay S. and Glenn S. Pransky, *Worker Fitness and Risk Evaluations*, Philadelphia, PA: Hanley & Belfus, 1988.

Fire Department Occupational Safety, Stillwater OK: Fire Protection Publications, 2nd Ed. 1991.

NFPA 471, *Recommend Practice for Responding to Hazardous Materials Incidents*
472, *Standard for Professional Competence of Responders to Hazardous Materials Incidents*

NFPA 1001, *Standard for Fire Fighter Professional Qualifications*
1002, *Standard for Fire Apparatus Driver/Operator Professional Qualifications*
1021, *Standard for Fire Officer Professional Qualifications*
1403, *Standard on Live Fire Training Evolutions in Structures*
1404, *Standard for Fire Department Self-Contained Breathing Apparatus Program*
1500, *Standard on Fire Department Occupational Safety and Health Program*
1521, *Standard for Fire Department Safety Officer*
1561, *Standard for Fire Department Incident Management Systems*
1581, *Standard on Fire Department Infection Control Programs*
1582, *Standard on Medical Requirements for Fire Fighters*
1901, *Standard for Pumper Fire Apparatus*
1904, *Standard for Aerial Ladder and Elevating Platforms Fire Apparatus*
1971, *Standard on Protective Clothing for Structural Fire Fighting* (also 1972, 1973, 1974, 1975)
1981, *Standard on Open-Circuit Self-Contained Breathing Apparatus for Fire Fighters*

Roche, Kevin M. and Bruce W. Teele. *The NFPA 1500 Handbook*, 1st Ed. Quincy, MA: National Fire Protection Association. 1993.

CHAPTER 9. THE NATIONAL PROFESSIONAL QUALIFICATIONS SYSTEM

Suggested Readings

Amabili, Louis J. "Fire Officer Development—An Historical Overview, As I See It." *VOICE*, June 1992.

Becknell, John. "Air-Medical Accreditation Update." *JEMS*, October 1992.

Clark, Burton A. "Higher Education and Fire Service Professionalism." *Fire Chief*, September 1993.

Davis, Larry. "The Instructor and Standards." *The VOICE*, June 1993.

The Emergency Management Accreditation and Certification System Board. "Emergency Management Accreditation and Certification System Operational Procedures." International Society of Fire Service Instructors, Board of Directors: Draft December 6, 1991.

The Emergency Management Accreditation and Certification System. *The Emergency Management Accreditation and Certification System 1993 General Information Booklet*. Ashland, MA: The Emergency Management Accreditation and Certification System, 1993.

The Emergency Vehicle Mechanics Certification Commission, Apparatus Maintenance Section. "Emergency Vehicle Technician Certification Program." International Association of Fire Chiefs, February 1991.

Estepp, M.H. "In Search of Fire Service Professionalism." *IAFC On Scene*, June 1, 1992.

Estepp, M.H. and Joellen L. Kelly. "National Fire Service Certification." *Firehouse*, November 1993.

The Fire Problem. Boston, MA: National Fire Protection Association, 1972: 54.

The Fire Chief's Handbook. 4th Ed. Saddle Brook, NJ: Fire Engineering Books & Videos. 1978. Chapter 21.

Gratz, David B. "History—Organization—Status of the National Professional Qualifications System for the Fire Service 1972–1988."

National Professional Qualifications Board, December 31, 1988.

International Fire Service Accreditation Congress. "International Fire Service Accreditation Congressional Procedures." Oklahoma State University: June 1992.

International Fire Service Training Association. *Fire Department Company Officer.* 2nd Ed. Stillwater, OK: Oklahoma State University, 1989: 144–147.

JEMS. "Air Medical Accreditation Is Off and Flying." *JEMS,* April 1993.

JEMS. "CAAS Accredits 21 EMS Services." *JEMS,* April 1993.

The Johnson Foundation. A Wingspread Conference on *Fire Service Administration, Education and Research.* Racine WI: The Johnson Foundation, February, 1966.

The Johnson Foundation. A Wingspread Conference Report on Wingspread II Statements of National Significance to *The Fire Problem in the United States.* Racine WI: The Johnson Foundation, 1976.

Kerns, Donald. "Ambulance Service Accreditation—Setting the Standard." *Rescue-EMS Magazine,* October 1992.

Kirchner, Albert G. Jr. "Where Is The 'Road Map To The Future' In Fire Service Training?" *Fire-Rescue News,* 1993.

Managing Fire Services. 2nd Ed. Washington, DC: International City Management Association, 1988: 18.

Melson, Randall J. and Bruce J. Walz. "Mastering EMS Management, Are Graduate Degrees Necessary?" *The Journal of Emergency Medical Services,* September 1992.

Monigold, Gerald E. *Administrative Study for State Fire Training Programs.* Champaign, IL: The Board of Trustees of the University of Illinois, 1989: Section 6: Fire Service Personnel Certification: 22–25.

Morse, H. Newcomb. *Legal Insight: Court Decisions Affecting Paid and Volunteer Fire Officers and Fire Fighters.* Boston, MA: National Fire Protection Association, 1973: 65–65.

Murray, Jim. "Confessions of a CAAS Reviewer." *JEMS,* June 1993.

National Association of State Directors of Fire Training and Education. *Review and Discussion of Fire Service Certification and Accreditation Issues: Report on the Fire Training and Certification Program Accreditation Conference.* Columbia, MO: National Association of State Directors of Fire Training and Education, 1990.

National Board on Fire Service Professional Qualifications. "Operational Procedures for the National Board on Fire Service Professional Qualifications Accreditation Process." September 30, 1991.

ANSI/NFPA 472, *Standard for Professional Competence of Responders to Hazardous Materials Incidents.* 1992.

NFPA 1000, *Standard on Fire Service Professional Qualifications Accreditation and Certification Systems.* Draft 1994.

NFPA 1001, *Standard for Fire Fighter Professional Qualifications.* 1992.

NFPA 1002, *Standard for Fire Apparatus Driver/Operator Professional Qualifications.* 1993.

NFPA 1003, *Standard for Professional Qualifications for Airport Professional Fire Fighters.* 1987.

NFPA 1021, *Standard for Fire Officer Professional Qualifications.* 1992.

NFPA 1031, *Standard for Professional Qualifications for Fire Inspector.* 1993.

NFPA 1033, *Standard for Professional Qualifications for Fire Investigator.* 1993.

NFPA 1035, *Standard for Professional Qualifications for Public Fire Educator.* 1993.

NFPA 1041, *Standard for Professional Qualifications for Fire Service Instructor.* 1992.

NFPA 1201, *Recommendations for Developing Fire Protection Services for the Public.* 1989.

NFPA 1403, *Standard on Live Fire Training Evolutions in Structures.* 1992.

NFPA 1404, *Standard for a Fire Department Self-Contained Breathing Apparatus Program.* 1989.

NFPA 1521, *Standard for Fire Department Safety Officer.* 1992.

Randelman, William. "In Praise of NPQB." *Fire Chief,* February 1989.

Schumacher, Joe. "Training Academy . . ."Colorado's Firefighter Certification Academy." *Firehouse,* September 1992.

Stewart, Rob. *The Volunteer Firefighters' Management Book.* New York, NY: The Bobbs-Merrill Company, Incorporated, 1982: 186–187.

Organizational Contact List

National Board on Fire Service Professional
Qualifications
Office of the Secretary-Treasurer
P.O. Box 492
Quincy, MA 02269

International Fire Service Accreditation
Congress
Manager
Oklahoma State University
Fire Publications Building
Stillwater, OK 74078-0118

Emergency Management Accreditation and
Certification System
Administrative Office
c/o The Alliance for Fire and Emergency
Management
30 Main Street
Ashland, MA 01721

National Coordinating Council on Emergency Management
7297 Lee Highway, Unit N
Falls Church, VA 22042

World Safety Organization
World Management Center
305 East Market Street
P.O. Box 518
Warrensburg, MO 64093 USA

Emergency Vehicles Technician (EVT)
P.O. Box 894
Dundee, IL 60118
(708) 426-4075

CHAPTER 11. FIRE DEPARTMENT APPARATUS

Aircraft Fire Protection and Rescue Procedures.
International Fire Service Training Association, Stillwater, OK: Oklahoma State University. 1978.

Carr, J. and L. Omans. "Writing Specifications for
ARFF Vehicles." *Fire Engineering,* Vol 145,
No. 6 (June 1992) pp 85–90.

Carter H., and E. Rausch, *Management in the Fire
Service,* 2nd Ed., Quincy, MA: National Fire
Protection Association.

Ditzel, P., *Fire Engines, Firefighters,* New York:
Crown Publishers, 1976.

Downey, R., *The Rescue Company,* Saddle Brook,
NJ: Fire Engineering Books & Videos, 1992.

Fire Department Aerial Apparatus. International
Fire Service Training Association, Stillwater,
OK: Oklahoma State University, 1991.

Fire Department Pumping Apparatus. International Fire Service Training Association,
Stillwater, OK: Oklahoma State University,
1989.

Fornell, D., *Fire Stream Management Handbook,*
Saddle Brook, NJ: Fire Engineering Books &
Videos, 1991.

*Guide for Preparing Fire Pumper Apparatus Spec-
ifications.* Washington, DC: U.S. Fire
Administration, National Fire Data Center.
October 1980.

Isman, W., *Fire Service Pump Operator's Handbook,* Saddle Brook, NJ: Fire Engineering
Books & Videos. 1984.

Mahoney, G., *Introduction to Fire Apparatus and
Equipment,* 2nd Ed., Saddle Brook, NJ: Fire
Engineering Books & Videos, 1986.

Fire Protection Handbook, 17th Ed. Quincy, MA:
National Fire Protection Association. 1991.

NFPA 414, *Standard for Aircraft Rescue and Fire
Fighting Vehicles.*

NFPA 1901, *Standard for Pumper Fire Apparatus.*

NFPA 1902, *Standard for Initial Attack Fire
Apparatus.*

NFPA 1903, *Standard for Mobile Water Supplies.*

NFPA 1904, *Standard for Aerial Ladder and Elevating Platform Fire Apparatus.*

NFPA 1911, *Standard on Service Tests of Pumps
on Fire Department Apparatus.*

NFPA 1914, *Standard for Testing Fire Department
Aerial Devices.*

CHAPTER 12. APPARATUS SPECIFICATION & PURCHASING

*A Guide to Funding Alternatives for Fire and
Emergency Medical Services Departments*
(FA141), Washington, DC: Federal Emer-
gency Management Agency, 1993.

Dolezal, F., *Repowering, Rehabilitating and
Reconditioning,* Fairfax, VA: International
Association of Fire Chiefs Foundation.

Eisner, H., "Show and Tell." *Firehouse* Dec. 1993:
pp. 72–73

Fire Protection Handbook, 17th Ed., Quincy, MA:
National Fire Protection Association, 1991.

Peters, W., "Apparatus Bid Evaluation: Simplifying a Difficult Process." *Fire Engineering,* Oct. 1993: pp. 31–39.

Fire Apparatus Purchasing Handbook, Saddle Brook, NJ: Fire Engineering Books & Videos, 1994.

"Inspection Trips, Your Vacation or Vacation?" *Fire Engineering,* May 1991: pp. 16–23

"Is Refurbishing Right for You?" *Fire Engineering,* Oct. 1992: pp. 47–54

CHAPTER 14. FIRE STATION AND FACILITY DESIGN

Technical Resources

American Institute of Architects
P.O. Box 57454
Washington, DC 20037
  #6N802 *You and Your Architect*
  #A101 *Standard Form of Agreement Between Owner and Contractor*
  #A201 *General Conditions of the Contract for Construction*
  #B141 *Standard Form of Agreement Between Owner and Architect*

Architectural and Transportation Barriers Compliance Board
1331 K Street, NW
Suite 1000
Washington, DC 20004
800-USA-ABLE
  ADA Accessibility Guidelines for Buildings and Facilities

Circul-Air Corporation
29230 Ryan Road
Warren, MI 48092
313-574-1150
  Fire Station Design (a collection of fire station plans)

Federal Emergency Management Agency
P.O. Box 70274
Washington, DC 20024
Att: Publications
  FEMA-15 *Design Guidelines for Flood Damage Reduction*
  FEMA-102 *Floodproofing Non-Residential Structures*

National Fire Protection Association
1 Batterymarch Park
P.O. Box 9101
Quincy, MA 02269-9904
1-800-344-3555
  NFPA 101, *Code for Safety to Life from Fire in Buildings and Structures*
  NFPA 1201, *Recommendations for Developing Fire Protection Services for the Public*
  NFPA 1402, *Standard on Building Fire Service Training Centers*
  NFPA 1500, *Standard on Fire Department Occupational Safety and Health Program*

RS Means Company Inc.
P.O. Box 800
Kingston, MA 02364-0800
  Means Building Construction Cost Data (Published Annually)

CHAPTER 16. FIRE DEPARTMENT WATER SUPPLY

American Water Works Association, *Distribution System Requirements for Fire Protection,* AWWA M3I, Denver, CO: AWWA, 1989.

Brock, Pat D., *Fire Protection Hydraulics and Water Supply Analysis,* Fire Protection Publications, Stillwater, OK, 1990.

Eckman, William, *The Fire Department Water Supply Handbook,* Saddle Brook, NJ: Fire Engineering Books & Videos, 1994.

Fornell, David P., *Fire Stream Management Handbook,* Saddle Brook, NJ: Fire Engineering Books & Videos, 1991.

Fire Suppression Rating Schedule, New York, NY: 1980.

International Fire Service Training Association (IFSTA). *Water Supplies for Fire Protection,* 4th Ed, Stillwater, OK: Fire Protection Publications, 1993.

Linder, Kenneth W., "Water Supply Requirements for Fire Protection" in A. E. Cote, ed., *Fire Protection Handbook,* Quincy, MA: National Fire Protection Association, 1991.

NFPA 1231, *Standard on Water Supplies for Suburban and Rural Fire Fighting,* Quincy, MA: National Fire Protection Association, 1993.

NFPA 1901, *Standard for Pumper Fire Apparatus,* Quincy, MA: National Fire Protection Association, 1991.

NFPA 1903, *Standard for Mobile Water Supply*

Fire Apparatus, Quincy, MA: National Fire Protection Association, 1991.

Planning for Water Supply and Distribution in the Wildland/Urban Interface, Quincy, MA: National Fire Protection Association, 1993.

Wisconsin Department of Natural Resources, *A Guide to Planning and Installing Dry Fire Hydrants.* Ladysmith, WI.

CHAPTER 17. COMPANY OPERATIONS, STRATEGIES AND TACTICS

Brannigan, Francis. *Building Construction for the Fire Service.* 3rd Ed. Quincy, MA: National Fire Protection Association, 1992.

Brunacini, Alan. *The Fireground Commander,* Quincy, MA: National Fire Protection Association, 1985.

Clark, William. *Firefighting Principles and Practices,* 2nd Ed. Saddle Brook, NJ: Fire Engineering Books & Videos, 1991.

Davis, Larry. *Rural Firefighting Operations,* Ashland, MA: International Society of Fire Service Instructors, 1986.

Fornell, David. *Fire Stream Management,* Saddle Brook, NJ: Fire Engineering Books & Videos, 1991.

Gardiner, Daniel B.C. *Managing Operations,* Ashland, MA: International Society of Fire Service Instructors, 1991.

Gratz, David. *Fire Service Management, Scope and Method,* Beverly Hills, CA: Glencoe Press, 1972.

International Fire Service Training Association, *Fire Department Company Officer,* Stillwater, OK: Fire Protection Publications, 1981.

Norman, John. *Fire Officer's Handbook of Tactics,* Saddle Brook, NJ: Fire Engineering Books & Videos, 1991

Richman, Hal. *Engine Company Fireground Operations,* 2nd Ed. Quincy, MA: National Fire Protection Association, 1991.

————*Truck Company Fireground Operations,* 2nd Ed. Quincy, MA: National Fire Protection Association, 1991.

CHAPTER 18. RESCUE OPERATIONS

Borden, Frank W., *Managing Urban Search and Rescue Using the Incident Command System.* April 1991.

————*Initial Response Strategies for Heavy Rescue Operations.* June 1992.

Downey, Ray, "The Rescue Company." *Fire Engineering,* 1992.

Federal Emergency Management Agency, *Urban Search and Rescue Response System Operational System Description.* 1992.

Los Angeles City Fire Department, *Collapsed Trench and Confined Space Rescue.* US&R Module 7, 1992.

Los Angeles City Fire Department, Training Bulletins on Vehicular Accidents, Metrorail, and Swift Water Rescue.

McGroarty, Mike, "The Stages of Structural Collapse." 1990.

Moede, John, "Medical Aspects of Urban Heavy Rescue" *Pre-Hospital Disaster Medicine,* 6.3, July–September 1991.

National Fire Protection Association, Urban Search and Rescue, 1470 Standards Committee, "Draft Standards." 1992.

CHAPTER 19. HAZARDOUS MATERIALS OPERATIONS

Agency for Toxic Substances and Disease Registry (ATSDR), *Managing Hazardous Materials Incidents: A Planning Guide for the Management of Contaminated Patients* (Volumes I and II), Atlanta, GA: ATSDR, 1992.

Borak, Jonathan, M.D., Michael Callan and William Abbott, *Hazardous Materials Exposure: Emergency Response and Patient Care,* Brady/Prentice Hall, Inc., 1991.

Bronstein, Alvin C. and Phillip L. Currance, *Emergency Care for Hazardous Materials Exposure,* St. Louis, MO: The C. V. Mosby Company, 1988.

Brunacini, Alan V., *Fire Command,* Boston, MA: National Fire Protection Association, 1985.

Federal Emergency Management Agency, et. al. *Liability Issues in Emergency Management.* Emmitsburg, MD: National Emergency Training Center, 1992.

Fire, Frank L., *The Common Sense Approach to*

Hazardous Materials, New York, NY: Fire Engineering, 1986.

Fire, Frank L., Nancy K. Grant and David H. Hoover, *SARA TITLE III—Intent and Implementation of Hazardous Materials Regulations.* New York, NY: Fire Engineering Books and Videos.

International Fire Service Training Association (IFSTA), *Hazardous Materials for the First Responder,* 2nd Ed., Stillwater, OK: IFSTA, Oklahoma State University, 1995.

Isman, Warren E. and Gene P. Carlson, *Hazardous Materials,* Encino, CA: Glencoe Publishing Company, 1980.

National Fire Protection Association, *Hazardous Materials Response Handbook,* 2nd Ed., Boston, MA: National Fire Protection Association, 1992.

National Fire Protection Association, NFPA 1561, *Technical Standard on Fire Department Incident Management Systems,* Boston, MA: National Fire Protection Association, 1990.

National Fire Service Incident Management Consortium, *Model Procedures for Structural Firefighting,* Stillwater, OK: Oklahoma State University, Fire Protection Publications, 1993.

National Institute for Occupational Safety and Health (NIOSH), *Occupational Safety and Health Guidance Manual for Hazardous Waste Site Activities,* Washington, DC: NIOSH, OSHA, USCG, EPA, 1985.

National Response Team, *Haz Mat Emergency Planning Guide* (NRT-1), Washington, DC: National Response Team, 1987.

Noll, Gregory G. and Michael S. Hildebrand, *Gasoline Tank Truck Emergencies: Guidelines and Procedures,* Stillwater, OK: Fire Protection Publications, Oklahoma State University, 1992.

Noll, Gregory G. Michael S. Hildebrand and James G. Yvorra, *Hazardous Materials: Managing the Incident,* 2nd Ed., Stillwater, OK: Fire Protection Publications, Oklahoma State University, 1995.

National Inter-Agency Incident Management System (NIIMS), *Incident Command System,* Stillwater, OK: Fire Protection Publications, Oklahoma State University, 1983.

Stringfield, William H., *A Fire Department's Guide to Implementing SARA, TITLE III and the OSHA Hazardous Materials Standard,* Ashland, MA: International Society of Fire Service Instructors, 1987.

Stutz, Douglas R. and Stanley J. Janusz, *Hazardous Materials Injuries: A Handbook for Pre-Hospital Care,* 2nd Ed., Beltsville, MD: Bradford Communications Corp., 1988.

U.S. Environmental Protection Agency, *Haz Mat Team Planning Guidance,* Washington, DC: EPA, 1990.

U.S. Environmental Protection Agency, et. al., *Technical Guidance for Hazards Analysis—Emergency Planning for Extremely Hazardous Substances,* Washington, DC: EPA, FEMA, DOT, 1987.

U.S. Environmental Safety and Health Administration, *HAZWOPER Quips,* Washington, DC: OSHA Office of Health Compliance Assistance, March 1993.

York, Kenneth J. and Gerald L. Grey, *Haz Mat/ Waste Handling for the Emergency Responder,* New York, NY: Fire Engineering, 1989.

Technical Resources

Trade and business associations

American Petroleum Institute
1220 L Street, NW
Washington, DC 20005
202/682-8000

Chemical Manufacturers Association
2501 M Street, NW
Washington, DC 20037
202/887-1100

Chemical Producers and Distributors Association
Suite 202
1220 19th Street, NW
Washington, DC 20006
202/872-8110

Chlorine Institute
2001 L Street, NW
Washington, DC 20036
202/775-2790

Institute of Makers of Explosives
Suite 310
1120 19th Street, NW
Washington, DC 20036
202/429-9280

National Association of Chemical Distributors
1200 17th Street, NW
Washington, DC 20036
202/296-9200

Synthetic Organic Chemical Manufacturers Association
Suite 300
1330 Connecticut Avenue, NW
Washington, DC 20036
202/659-0060

Professional organizations

American Institute of Chemical Engineers' Center for Chemical Process
Safety
345 East 47th Street
New York, NY 10017
212/705-7319

International Association of Fire Chiefs—Hazardous Materials Committee
4025 Fair Ridge Drive
Fairfax, VA 22033-2868
703/273-0911

National Fire Protection Association
Hazardous Materials Committee Staff Liaison
1 Batterymarch Park
Quincy, MA 02269
617/770-3000

The Alliance for Fire and Emergency Management
Hazardous Materials Training and Education Association
30 Main Street
Ashland, MA 01721
508/881-8114

International Association of Fire Fighters
Hazardous Materials Training Office
1750 New York Avenue, NW—3rd Floor
Washington, DC 20006

Federal government agencies

Agency for Toxic Substances and Disease Registry
Emergency Response and Consultation Branch
Division of Health Assessment and Consultation
1600 Clifton Road, NE
Atlanta, GA 30333
404/639-6360
404/639-0615—24-hour Emergency Response Assistance Number

Environmental Protection Agency
Chemical Emergency Preparedness and Prevention Office

OS-120
401 M Street, SW
Washington, DC 20460
202/260-8600

EPA Emergency Planning and Community Right-to-Know Hotline
800/535-0202
NOTE: Answers questions concerning chemical accident prevention, accidental release provisions of the Clean Air Amendments of 1990, SARA, Title III, emergency preparedness, and other related issues. In addition, EPA has a number of various handouts and publications pertaining to hazardous materials emergency planning and response.

Occupational Safety and Health Administration
Office of Information and Consumer Affairs
U.S. Department of Labor
Room N3647
200 Constitution Ave. NW
Washington, DC 20210
202/523-8151

Listing of OSHA and non-OSHA states

States and territories currently having a delegated OSHA enforcement program and where state and local government employers are covered by OSHA 1910.120:

Alaska	Arizona	California
Connecticut	Hawaii	Indiana
Iowa	Kentucky	Maryland
Michigan	Minnesota	Nevada
New Mexico	New York	North
Oregon	Puerto Rico	Carolina
Tennessee	Utah	South
Virginia	Virgin Islands	Carolina
Wyoming		Vermont
		Washington

States currently NOT having a delegated OSHA enforcement program and where state and local government employers are covered by the EPA Section 311 regulations:

Alabama	Arkansas	Colorado
District of	Delaware	Florida
Columbia	Idaho	Illinois
Georgia	Louisiana	Maine
Kansas	Mississippi	Missouri
Massachusetts	Nebraska	New
Montana	North Dakota	Hampshire
New Jersey	Pennsylvania	Ohio
Oklahoma	Texas	Rhode Island
South Dakota		West Virginia
Wisconsin		

CHAPTER 20. AIRCRAFT CRASH RESCUE AND FIREFIGHTING

Aircraft Identification Books

A Field Guide to Airplanes, 2nd Ed., M.R. Montgomery and Gerald Foster, Houghton Mifflin Company, ISBN 0-395-62888-1.

Aircraft Ground Service Guide, 1992, Jerry L. Clausing, Sandpiper Publications, 1197 West 500 South, Woods Cross, Utah 84807, 801-292-6511, Library of Congress #TX 2 744 535.

Airlifes General Aviation, A Guide to Postwar General Aviation Manufacturers and Their Aircraft, First Edition, R.W. Simpson, ISBN 1-85310-194-X.

Airline Seating Guide, Carlson Publishing Company, P.O. Box 888, Los Alamitos, CA 90702.

Airport Airplanes, An Illustrated Handbook Allowing Rapid Identification by Amateur Observers of Airplanes Flown by Major Airlines, William and Frank Berk, Plymouth Press, Ltd., 42500 Five Mile Road, Plymouth, MI 48170-2544, ISBN 1-882663-00-4.

Civil Aircraft of the World, Gordon Swanborough, Charles Scribner & Sons, ISBN 0-684-16616-X.

Concise Guide to Commercial Aircraft of the World, David Mondey, Temple Press, ISBN 0-600-34950-0.

Encyclopedia of The World's Commercial and Private Aircraft, David Mondey, Crescent Books, ISBN 0-517-362856.

Jane's World Aircraft Recognition Handbook, Derek Wood, Jane's Publishing Company, ISBN 0-7106-0343-6.

Observers Aircraft, William Green, Penguin Books, ISBN-0-7232-3697-6.

Aircraft Rescue & Firefighting Information

A.R.F.F. Directory, William J. Joiner, 105 Newman Avenue, Centreville, Maryland 21610, 410-758-0119.

Aircraft Rescue and Fire Fighting, 3rd Ed., Fire Protection Publications, Oklahoma State University, Stillwater, Oklahoma 74078, 1-800-654-4055, ISBN 0-87939-099-9.

Crash, Fire, and Rescue Handbook. Charles Bellomo and John Lynch, Aviation Maintenance Publishers, P.O. Box 890, Basin, Wyoming 82410, 307-568-2413.

ICAO Publications, International Civil Aviation Organization, 1000 Sherbrooke Street West, Montreal, Quebec, Canada H3A 2R2.

International Standards and Recommended Practices, Aerodromes (Annex 14), 8th Edition, 1983.

Airport Services Manual, Part 1, Rescue and Fire Fighting, 2nd Ed., 1984.

Emergency Response Guidance for Aircraft Incidents Involving Dangerous Goods, 1st Ed., 1987.

Military Publications

Air Force Technical Manual, 00-105E-9, *Aircraft Emergency Fire Protection Information*, available from HQ WR-ALC (MMEOTD), Robbins AFB, GA 31093.

Navy and Marine, NAVAIR 00-80R-14, *Aircraft Fire Fighting and Rescue Manual for U.S. Naval and Marine Air Stations and Facilities*, available from Naval Air Technical Service Facility, 700 Robbins Avenue, Philadelphia, PA 19111.

Army Technical Manual 5-315, available from the Superintendent of Documents, U.S. Government Printing Office, Washington DC 20402.

National Fire Protection Association Publications, 1 Batterymarch Park, P.O. Box 9101, Quincy, MA 02269-9101, 800-735-0100.

NFPA 402M, *Manual for Aircraft Rescue and Fire Fighting Operational Procedures*, 1991.

NFPA 403, *Standard for Aircraft Rescue and Fire Fighting Services at Airports*, 1993.

NFPA 407, *Standard for Aircraft Fuel Servicing*, 1990.

NFPA 412, *Standard for Evaluating Aircraft Rescue and Fire Fighting Foam Equipment*, 1993.

NFPA 414, *Standard for Aircraft Rescue and Fire Fighting Vehicles*, 1990.

NFPA 1003, *Standard for Airport Fire Fighter Professional Qualifications*, 1987.

Federal Aviation Administration Publications

Available from the Department of Transportation, Distribution Unit, M-494.3, Washington, DC 20590.

Advisory Circular Checklist and Status of Other FAA Publications

150/5200-12A, *Fire Department Responsibility in Protecting Evidence at the Scene of an Aircraft Accident* (4-8-85) (AAS-100).

150/5210-6C, *Aircraft Fire and Rescue Facilities and Extinguishing Agents* (1-28-85) (AAS-100).

150/5210-78, *Aircraft Fire and Rescue Communications* (4-30-84) (AAS-120).

150/5210-13, *Water Rescue Plans, Facilities, and Equipment* (5-4-72) (AAS-300).

150/5210-14, *Airport Fire and Rescue Personnel Protective Clothing* (3-12-86) (AAS-100).

150/5220-10, *Guide Specifications for Water/Foam Type Aircraft Fire and Rescue Trucks* (5-26-72) (AAS-300).

150/5220-14A, *Airport Fire and Rescue Vehicle Specification Guide* (2-25-85) (AAS-100).

150/5230-4, *Aircraft Fuel Storage, Handling, and Dispensing on Airports* (8-27-82) (AAS-300), Change #1 (2-20-86), Change #2 (7-1-87).

150/5280-1, *Airport Operations Manual* (6-16-72) (AAS-310) and Change #1 (3-24-81).

150/5340-IE, *Marking of Paved Areas on Airports*, (11-4-80) (AAS-200).

150/5340-18B, *Standards for Airport Sign Systems* (8-21-84) (AAS-200).

National Transportation Safety Board Documents

National Transportation Safety Board, Public Inquiries Section, Room 805F, 800 Independence Avenue, S.W., Washington D.C. 20594, 202-382-6735.

Accident Briefs (Non-major Accident Reports)

Accident Reports (Major Accidents)

Annual Report to Congress

Annual Review of Aircraft Accident Data—U.S. Air Carrier Operations

Annual Review of Aircraft Accident Data—U.S. General Aviation

Computer Tapes of Aviation Accident Data

News Digest

NTSB Directives

Regulations of the NTSB

Safety Studies

Safety Recommendations

Special Investigations

Investigation Manual—Aircraft Accidents and Incidents, National Transportation Safety Board, Order NTSB 6200.1A.

National Technical Information Service, 5285 Port Royal Road, Springfield, Virginia 22162, 703-487-4650 (Copies of reports no longer available from NTSB).

Miscellaneous Aircraft-Related Information/Books

Air Crash Investigation of General Aviation Aircraft, Glenn Ellis, A Glendale Book, ISBN 0-914-565-00-1.

Air Crashes, What Went Wrong, Why, and What Can Be Done About It, Richard L. Collins, Thompson-Grant Aviation Library, ISBN 1-56566-066-4.

Air Disasters, Stanley Stewart, Hippocrene Books, Inc., ISBN 0-87052-385-6.

Airport Planning and Management, Alexander T. Wells, TAB Books, Inc., ISBN 0-8306-2189-X.

Air Traffic Control Book, Walter S. Luffsey, Air Traffic Control Association, ISBN 0-679-73050-8.

Blind Trust, John J. Nance, ISBN 0-688-06967-3.

Collision Course, The Truth About Airline Safety, Ralph Nader and Wesley J. Smith, TAB Books, ISBN 0-8306-4271-4.

Commercial Aviation Safety, Alexander Wells, TAB Books, ISBN 0-8306-2194-6.

Emergency! Crisis in the Cockpit, Stanley Stewart, TAB Books, ISBN 0-8306-6499-8.

Emergency Response to Crisis, A Crisis Intervention Guidebook for Emergency Services Personnel, Jeffrey T. Mitchell, Ph.D., Robert J. Brady Company, ISBN 0-87619-828-0.

Emergency Services Stress, Guidelines for Preserving the Health and Careers of Emergency Services Personnel, Jeffrey T. Mitchell, Ph.D., Prentice-Hall, Inc., ISBN 0-89303-687-0.

Fire and Rain, A Tragedy in American Aviation, Jerome Greer Chandler, Texas Monthly Press, ISBN 0-87719-048-8.

IATA Dangerous Goods Publications, International Air Transport Association Headquarters, IATA Building, 2000 Peel Street, Montreal, Canada H3A 2R4.

Terror in the Skies, The Inside Story of the World's Worst Air Crashes, David Grayson, Citadel Press, ISBN 0-8065-1091-9.

The Pilot's Air Traffic Control Handbook, Paul E. Illman, TAB Books, ISBN 0-8006-0435-9

The Pilot's Reference to ATC Procedures and Phraseology, Thomas S. Mills and Janet S. Archibald, Fourth Edition, REAVCO Publishing, P.O. Box 7902, Van Nuys, CA 91409, ISBN 0-9325695-05-2.

Periodicals

Aviation Safety, The Twice Monthly Journal of Accident Prevention, P.O. Box 420234, Palm Coast, FL 32142, 800-829-9162.

NTSB Reporter, Peter Katz Productions, Inc., P.O. Box 831, White Plains, NY 10602-0831, 914-949-7443.

CHAPTER 22. EMERGENCY MEDICAL SERVICES

Advanced Leadership Issues in Emergency Medical Services (Student Manual). Emmitsburg, MD: United States Fire Administration/ National Fire Academy, 1994.

Braun, O., R. McCallion, and Fazackerley, J. "Characteristics of Midsized Urban EMS Systems." *Annals of Emergency Medicine,* May 1990, pp 536–546.

Brown, Doug. "Future of EMS in the Fire Service." *Responder,* September 1994, pp 27–29.

Emergency Medical Services: 1990 and Beyond. Washington, DC: National Highway Traffic Safety Administration, 1990.

Emergency Medical Services Management Resource Directory. Washington, DC: United States Fire Administration, 1992.

Fire Service EMS Planning Guide. Washington, DC: United States Fire Administration, 1982.

Fire Service EMS Program Management Guide. Washington, DC: United States Fire Administration, 1981.

Fitch, J., R. Keller, D. Raynor, and C. Zalar. *EMS Management: Beyond the Street.* 2nd Ed. Carlsbad, California: JEMS Communications, 1993.

Joint Position Statement on Emergency Medical Services and Emergency Medical Services Systems. National Association of State EMS Directors and National Association of EMS Physicians, 1993.

"Make the Right Call—EMS" Public EMS education campaign. Washington, DC: United States Fire Administration, 1994.

Management of Emergency Medical Services (Student Manual). Emmitsburg, MD: United States Fire Administration/National Fire Academy, 1994.

Managing Fire Services. Washington, DC: International City Management Association, 1988.

Page, James O. *Emergency Medical Services for Fire Departments.* Boston: National Fire Protection Association, 1975.

Report on the National Forum on Emergency Medical Services Management. Washington, DC: United States Fire Administration, 1992.

Sachs, Gordon M. "Don't Overlook the Obvious." *Fire Engineering,* February 1994, pp 61–63.

Sachs, Gordon M. "What Does EMS Mean to the Fire Service?" *Fire Engineering,* July 1993, pp 22–25.

CHAPTER 25. FIRE PROTECTION CODES AND ORDINANCES

Building Officials and Code Administrators International, *The National Fire Prevention Code,* Country Club Hills, IL.: BOCA, 1993.

Clet, Vince H. *Fire-Related Codes, Laws, and Ordinances,* Encino, CA.: Glencoe Publishing Co., 1978.

Factory Mutual Engineering Corporation, *Loss Prevention Data Books,* Norwood, MA.: Factory Mutual Engineering and Research, 1994.

International Fire Code Institute, *Uniform Fire Code,* Whittier, CA.: International Conference of Building Officials and Western Fire Chiefs Association, 1994.

International Fire Service Training Association, *Fire Inspection and Code Enforcement,* 5th Ed. Stillwater, OK.: Fire Protection Publications, Oklahoma State University, 1987.

National Fire Protection Association, Quincy, MA.: *Fire Protection Handbook,* 17th Ed. 1991

——*Inspection Manual,* 7th Ed. 1991

——*NFPA 1031, Standard for Professional Qualifications for Fire Inspector,* 1993

——*NFPA 1033, Standard for Professional Qualifications for Fire Investigator,* 1993

——*NFPA 1035, Standard for Professional Qualifications for Public Fire Educator,* 1993

Robertson, James C. *Introduction to Fire Prevention,* New York, N.Y.: Macmillan Publishing Company, 1989.

The Southern Building Code Congress International, *Standard Fire Prevention Code,* Birmingham, AL: SBCCI, 1994.

Southern Building Code Congress International, *Fire Protection Principles and Code Applications Manual,* Birmingham, AL: SBCCI, 1992.

Underwriters Laboratories Directories, Northbrook, IL: 1994:

——*Building Materials*

——*Fire Protection Equipment*

——*Fire Resistance*

——*Hazardous Location Equipment*

CHAPTER 26. FIRE PROTECTION SYSTEMS

Bryan, John L., *Automatic Sprinkler and Standpipe Systems.* Quincy, MA: National Fire Protection Association, 1990.

Bryan, John L., *Fire Suppression and Detection Systems.* New York, NY: Macmillan Publishing Co., 1993.

Bukowski, Richard and O'Laughlin, Robert. *Fire Alarm Signaling Systems.* Quincy, MA: National Fire Protection Association, 1994.

Coleman, Ronny. *Residential Sprinkler Systems.* Quincy, MA: National Fire Protection Association, 1991.

Duncan, Justin. *Fire Protection Systems.* Troy, MI: Business News Publishing Company, 1994.

Factory Mutual Engineering and Research. "Fighting Fires in Sprinklered Buildings," booklet and seminar, Norwood, MA.

International Fire Service Training Association. "Fire Inspection and Code Enforcement," 5th Ed. Stillwater, OK, Fire Protection Publication, Oklahoma State Univ., 1987

National Fire Protection Association, Quincy, MA.

Automatic Sprinkler Systems Handbook, 6th Ed., 1994.

Fire Protection Handbook, 17th Ed., 1991.

Fire Protection Systems—Inspection, Tests and Maintenance Manual, 2nd Ed., 1993.

Inspection Manual, 7th Ed., 1994.

National Fire Alarm Code Handbook, 1993.

National Fire Codes, including:

NFPA 11, *Standard for Low Expansion Foam,* 1994.

NFPA 11A, *Standard for Medium and High Expansion Foam Systems,* 1994.

NFPA 12, *Standard on Carbon Dioxide Extinguishing Systems,* 1993.

NFPA 12A, *Standard on Halon 1301 Fire Extinguishing Systems,* 1992.

NFPA 12B, *Standard on Halon 1211 Fire Extinguishing Systems,* 1990.

NFPA 13, *Standard for Installation of Sprinkler Systems,* 1994.

NFPA 13D, *Standard for Sprinkler Systems in One and Two family Dwellings and Manufactured Homes,* 1994.

NFPA 13E, *Recommendations for Fire Department Operations in Properties Protected by Sprinkler and Standpipe Systems,* 1989.

NFPA 13R, *Standard for the Installation of Sprinkler systems in Residential Occupancies up to and Including Four Stories in Height,* 1994.

NFPA 14, *Standard for Standpipe and Hose Systems,* 1993.

NFPA 15, *Standard for Water Spray Fixed Systems,* 1990.

NFPA 16, *Standard on Deluge Foam-Water Sprinkler and Foam-Water Spray Systems,* 1991.

NFPA 16A, *Recommended Practice for the Installation of Closed-Head Foam-Water Sprinkler Systems*, 1994.

NFPA 17, *Standard for Dry Chemical Extinguishing Systems*, 1994.

NFPA 17A, *Standard on Wet Chemical Extinguishing Systems*, 1994.

NFPA 20, *Standard for the Installation of Centrifugal Fire Pumps*, 1993.

NFPA 22, *Standard for Water Tanks for Private Fire Protection*, 1993.

NFPA 24, *Standard for the Installation of Private Fire Service Mains*, 1992.

NFPA 25, *Standard on Inspection, Testing, and Maintenance of Water Based Fire Protection Systems*, 1992.

NFPA 72, *Installation, Maintenance, and Use of Protective Signaling Systems*, 1993.

NFPA 92A, *Recommended Practices on Smoke Control Systems*, 1993.

NFPA 92B, *Guide for Smoke Management Systems in Malls, Atria, and Large Areas*, 1991.

NFPA 170, *Firesafety Symbols*, 1994.

NFPA 204M, *Guide for Smoke and Heat Venting*, 1991.

NFPA 291, *Recommended Practice for Fire Flow Testing and Marking of Hydrants*, 1988.

NFPA 2001, *Standard on Clean Agent Fire Extinguishing Systems*, 1994.

Underwriters Laboratories Directory—Fire Protection Equipment, Northbrook, IL., 1994.

Index